THE ANCIENT GREEK HERO

in 24 Hours

THE

ANCIENT
GREEK
HERO

in 24 Hours

GREGORY NAGY

THE BELKNAP PRESS OF HARVARD UNIVERSITY PRESS

CAMBRIDGE, MASSACHUSETTS   LONDON, ENGLAND   2013

Library of Congress Cataloging-in-Publication Data

Nagy, Gregory.
The ancient Greek hero in 24 hours / Gregory Nagy.
pages cm
Includes bibliographical references and index.
ISBN 978-0-674-07340-1 (alk. paper)
1. Greek literature—History and criticism.   2. Heroes in literature.   I. Title.
PA3015.H43N338 2013
880.9'352—dc23   2012047971

Contents

Acknowledgments

I am deeply grateful to all those who helped me produce *The Ancient Greek Hero in 24 Hours,* and I offer special thanks to the following: Erika Bainbridge, Natasha Bershadsky, Patrick Coleman, Maša Ćulumović, Jeffrey Emanuel, Claudia Filos, Alexander Forte, Douglas Frame, Richard Im, Rob Jenson, Kevin McGrath, Leonard Muellner, Anita Nikkanen, Jill Robbins, Sharmila Sen, William P. Sisler, Noel Spencer, Thomas Temple Wright, Christine Thorsteinsson, Valerie Woelfel. This book, stemming from a course that I have taught almost every year since the late 1970s at Harvard University (in two versions: one for the Faculty of Arts and Sciences and the other, with Kevin McGrath, for the Division of Continuing Education), is dedicated to all the students and teaching assistants who have helped me shape the course over all these years.

THE ANCIENT GREEK HERO

in 24 Hours

Introduction

00§1. *The Ancient Greek Hero in 24 Hours* is based on a course that I have taught at Harvard University since the late 1970s. This course, "Concepts of the Hero in Greek Civilization," now renamed "The Ancient Greek Hero," centers on selected readings of texts, all translated from the original Greek into English. The texts include the Homeric *Iliad* and *Odyssey;* the Hesiodic *Theogony* and *Works and Days;* selected songs of Sappho and Pindar; selections from the *Histories* of Herodotus; the *Agamemnon, Libation Bearers,* and *Eumenides* of Aeschylus; the *Oedipus Tyrannus* and *Oedipus at Colonus* of Sophocles; the *Hippolytus* and *Bacchae* of Euripides; and the *Apology* and *Phaedo* of Plato. Also included are selections from Pausanias and Philostratus. These texts are supplemented by illustrations, mostly images of Athenian vase paintings, which can be found in Hour 7.

00§2. All the texts I have just listed are available free of charge in an online *Sourcebook of Original Greek Texts Translated into English* (chs.harvard.edu), which I have edited with the help of fellow teachers and researchers. The editing of this *Sourcebook* is an ongoing project that I hope will outlast my own lifetime. All the translations in this online *Sourcebook* are free from copyright restrictions, because they belong either to me, to other authors who have waived copyright, or to authors who died in a time that precedes any further application of copyright. The texts of these translations are periodically reviewed and modified, and the modifications are indicated by way of special formatting designed to show the differences between the original translator's version and the modified version.

00§3. *The Ancient Greek Hero in 24 Hours* is divided into five parts. The number of hours dedicated to each part is tightened up as the argumentation intensifies, and the hours themselves get shorter. Part I, consisting of Hours 1 through 12, is primarily about heroes as reflected in the oldest surviving forms of ancient Greek epic and lyric poetry. Part II, Hours 13 through 15, is about heroes in a variety of prose media. Part III, Hours 16 through 21, is about heroes in ancient Greek tragedy. Part IV, Hours 22–23, is about heroes in two dialogues of Plato. And Part V, confined to Hour 24, is about the hero as a transcendent concept. In two of the hours, there are additional sections. Hour 7, for example, is followed by sections numbered Hour 7a, Hour 7b, Hour 7c, and so on; sections will add more reading time, so readers may wish to return to them later.

Dating of the Texts

00§4. The timespan for most of these texts extends from the eighth through the fourth centuries BCE ('Before the Common Era'). Some of the texts, however, date from later periods; for example, Pausanias is dated to the second century CE ('Common Era'). When I say 'ancient Greek history', the term *ancient* includes three periods:

> *archaic:* from the eighth century down to roughly the middle of the fifth century
> *classical:* roughly, the second half of the fifth century
> *post-classical:* fourth century and beyond

A convenient point for dividing classical and post-classical is the death of Socrates in 399 BCE.

'Ancient Greece'

> There is no place where one really feels at home anymore. So the thing that one longs to get back to, before anything else, is whatever place there may be where one could feel at home, and that is because it is in that place—and in that place alone—where one would really like to feel at home. That place is the world of the Greeks.
>
> Friedrich Nietzsche, "The Will to Power: Attempt at a
> Revaluation of All Values" (1885)*

00§5. In the ancient world of the classical period, 'Greece' was not really a 'country' or a 'nation' as we ordinarily think of these terms. Rather, it was a cultural

---

* "Man ist nirgends mehr heimisch, man verlangt zunächst nach Dem zurück, wo man irgendwie heimisch sein kann, weil man dort allein heimisch sein möchte: und das ist die griechische Welt!" F. Nietzsche, *Der Wille zur Macht: Versuch einer Umwertung aller Werte* (written in 1885, first published in 1901, Book 2 Section 419). In the References, I give a more complete citation.

constellation of competing city-states that had a single language in common, Greek. In the classical period, speakers of the Greek language called themselves *Hellēnes* or 'Hellenes'.

oo§6. Among the most prominent of the ancient Greek city-states were Athens, Sparta, Corinth, Argos, and Thebes, all of them located in the part of the Mediterranean region that we know today as 'modern Greece'. There were also other prominent ancient Greek city-states in other parts of the Mediterranean region. To the east, on the coast of Asia Minor, which is now part of the modern state of Turkey, were Greek cities like Miletus and Smyrna (now Izmir); facing the coast of Asia Minor were Greek island states like Samos and Chios. Further to the north was a federation of Greek cities located both on the island of Lesbos and on the facing mainland of Asia Minor. Still further north, guarding the entrance to the Black Sea, was the Greek city of Byzantium, later to be called Constantinople (now Istanbul). Far to the south, in African Libya, was the Greek city of Cyrene. Further to the east in Northern Africa, in Egypt, was arguably the greatest of all Greek cities in the ancient world, Alexandria, founded by Alexander the Great in the fourth century BCE. To the west were other great Greek cities like Syracuse on the island of Sicily as well as Tarentum and Neapolis (now Napoli or Naples) in what is now the modern state of Italy. Still further west, in what is now the modern state of France, was the Greek (formerly Phoenician) city of Massalia (now Marseille).

oo§7. The ancient Greeks would agree that they shared the same language, despite the staggering variety of local dialects. They would even agree that they shared a civilization, though they would be intensely contentious about what exactly that shared civilization looked like. Each city-state had its own institutions, that is, its own government, constitution, laws, calendars, religious practices, and so on. Both the sharing and the contentiousness lie at the root of the very essence of the city-state. What I am translating here as 'city-state' is the Greek word *polis*. This is the word from which the English words *political* and *politics* are derived.

oo§8. In the fourth century BCE, the Greek philosopher Aristotle made a basic observation about the ancient Greek *polis* in a treatise known today as the *Politics*. The original Greek wording, *ho anthrōpos phusei politikon zōion* (Aristotle *Politics* I 1253a2–3), can be translated literally this way: 'A human [*anthrōpos*] is by nature an organism of the *polis* [*politikon zōion*]'.* We see in

---

* ὁ ἄνθρωπος φύσει πολιτικὸν ζῷον.

this wording the basis for a distinctly Greek concept of civilization. What Aristotle is really saying here is that humans achieve their ultimate potential within a society that is the *polis*. From this point of view, the ultimate human potential is achieved politically. The original Greek wording of this observation by Aristotle is frequently rendered this way into English: 'Man is a political animal'. Such a rendering does not do justice to the original formulation, since current uses of the word *political* do not convey accurately the historical realities of the ancient Greek *polis*.

00§9. There are some basic aspects of Greek civilization about which most ancient Greeks in the classical period could agree:

1. *Interpolitical festivals.* Two primary examples are the Olympic festival (the 'Olympics') at Olympia and the Pythian festival at Delphi.
2. *Interpolitical repositories of shared knowledge.* A primary example is Delphi.
3. *Interpolitical poetry.* Two primary examples are a set of monumental poems known as the *Iliad* and the *Odyssey*, attributed to a prehistoric figure named Homer, and another set of poems known as the *Theogony* and *Works and Days*, attributed to a prehistoric figure named Hesiod.

00§10. I have used the term *interpolitical* here instead of *international* because I do not want to imply that each *polis* was a nation. In most of my published work, however, I use the term *Panhellenic* instead of *interpolitical*. The term *Panhellenic*, or *pan-Hellenic*, is derived from the ancient Greek compound noun *pan-Hellēnes*, 'all Greeks', which is attested in the Hesiodic *Works and Days* (528)* in the sense of referring to 'all Greeks under the sun'† (526–528).‡ This use of the compound noun *pan-Hellēnes* in the absolutizing sense of 'all Greeks' helps explain the later use of the non-compound noun *Hellēnes* ('Hellenes') to mean 'Greeks' in the classical period; earlier, *Hellēnes* had been used to designate a subset of Greeks dwelling in a region known as Thessaly rather than any full complement of Greeks. As the linguistic evidence shows, the non-compound noun *Hellēnes* acquired the meaning of 'Greeks' from the built-in politics of the compound noun *pan-Hellēnes*, the basic meaning of which can be

---

* πανελλήνεσσι.

† ἠέλιος . . . πανελλήνεσσι φαείνει.

‡ Nagy 2009a:274–275. Secondary sources such as Nagy 2009a are all listed in the References at the end of this book. In most cases, I will use abbreviations that can be found right before the References. An example of such abbreviations is *HQ* in the note that follows.

paraphrased this way: Hellenes (as a subset of Greeks) and all other Greeks (as a notionally complete set of Greeks).*

00§11. I understand the concept of *Panhellenic* or *Panhellenism* as a cultural as well as a political impulse that became the least common denominator of ancient Greek civilization in the classical period. And the impulse of Panhellenism was already at work in Homeric and Hesiodic poetry. In the Homeric *Iliad,* for example, the names Achaeans and Danaans and Argives are used synonymously in the universalizing sense of Panhellenes or 'all Hellenes' or 'all Greeks'.

00§12. In the classical period, an authoritative source goes on record to say that Homer and Hesiod are the foundation for all civilization. That source is the historian Herodotus, who lived in the fifth century BCE. According to Herodotus (2.53.1–3), Homer and Hesiod are the repository of knowledge that provides the basics of education for all Hellenes.† And such basics, as we will see in this book, are conceived primarily in terms of religion, which requires an overall knowledge of the forms and the functions of the gods.

00§13. Here I make two points about the historical realities of ancient Greek religion:

1. When we apply the term *religion* to such traditional practices as the worship of gods in the classical period of Greek civilization as also in earlier periods, we need to think of such practices in terms of an interaction between *myth* and *ritual.* Here is a quick working definition of *myth* and *ritual* together: Ritual is doing things and saying things in a way that is considered sacred. Myth is saying things in a way that is also considered sacred. So ritual frames myth.

2. Not only were the gods worshipped in ancient Greek religion; heroes, too, were worshipped. Besides the word *worship,* we may use the word *cult,* as in the term *hero cult.* Other relevant concepts are *cultivate* and *culture.* The concepts of (1) a *hero cult* and (2) the *cult hero* who is worshipped in hero cult will figure prominently in the readings ahead.

00§14. Our readings will start with Homer. This prehistoric figure, who is credited with the composition of the *Iliad* and the *Odyssey,* represents an inter-

---

* *HQ* 39n40. From the start, I alert the reader to the fact that *notionally* is one of my favorite words. I use it to indicate that the statement I am making reflects not my own thinking but rather the thought patterns of others.
† Commentary in *PH* 215–216 = 8§2.

political or Panhellenic perspective on the Greeks. Homeric poetry is not tied down to any one *polis*. It presents the least common denominator in the cultural education of the elite of all city-states.

00§15. But how can a narrative or 'story' like the *Iliad* become an instrument of education? This book offers answers to that question.

PART ONE

HEROES IN EPIC AND LYRIC POETRY

Introduction to Homeric Poetry

0§1. Before I delve into the 24 hours of this book, I would like to familiarize the reader with Homeric poetry, which is the primary medium that I will be analyzing in the first 11 hours.

0§2. Homeric poetry is a cover term for two epics, the *Iliad* and the *Odyssey*. The major part of this introduction will deal with the *Iliad*.* This epic is in and of itself the best introduction to its companion piece, the *Odyssey*.

0§3. Admired through the ages as the ultimate epic, the *Iliad,* along with the *Odyssey,* was venerated by the ancient Greeks as the cornerstone of their civilization. By force of its prestige, the *Iliad* sets the standard for the definition of the word *epic:* an expansive poem of enormous scope, composed in an old-fashioned and superbly elevated style of language, concerning the wondrous deeds of heroes. That these deeds were meant to arouse a sense of wonder or marvel is difficult for the modern mind to comprehend, especially in a time when even such words as *wonderful* or *marvelous* have lost much of their evocative power. Nor is it any easier to grasp the ancient Greek concept of *hero* (the English word is descended from the Greek), going beyond the word's ordinary levels of meaning in casual contemporary usage.

0§4. Who, then, were these heroes? In ancient Greek traditions, heroes were humans, male or female, of the remote past, endowed with superhuman abilities and descended from the immortal gods themselves. A prime example is Achilles. The greatest hero of the *Iliad,* Achilles was the son of Thetis, a sea-goddess known for her far-reaching cosmic powers.

0§5. It is clear in the epic, however, that the father of Achilles is mortal, and that this greatest of heroes must therefore be mortal as well. So, too, with all the ancient Greek heroes: even though they are all descended in some way or another from the gods, however many generations removed, heroes are mortals,

---

* This introduction to Homeric poetry is based on an essay I wrote (Nagy 1992) to introduce the "Everyman's Library" edition of Robert Fitzgerald's translation of the Homeric *Iliad.*

subject to death. No matter how many immortals you find in a family tree, the intrusion of even a single mortal will make all successive descendants mortal. Mortality, not immortality, is the dominant gene.

0§6. True, in some stories the gods themselves can miraculously restore the hero to life after death—a life of immortality. The story of Hēraklēs, who had been sired by Zeus, the chief of all the gods, is perhaps the most celebrated instance. In Hour 1 of this book, we will examine the broad outlines of the story. But even in the case of Hēraklēs, as we will see, the hero has to die before achieving immortality. Only after the most excruciating pain, culminating in his death on a funeral pyre on the peak of Mount Oeta, is Hēraklēs at long last admitted to the company of immortals. In short, the hero can be *immortalized,* but the fundamental painful fact remains: the hero is not by nature *immortal.*

0§7. As I will argue in Hours 10 and 11, the *Odyssey* is an extended narrative about heroic immortalization. But this immortalization happens only on a symbolic level. As the *Odyssey* makes clear, if only in a prophecy beyond the framework of the epic, Odysseus will have to die.

0§8. By contrast with heroes, the gods themselves are exempt from the ultimate pain of death. An exception that proves the rule is the god Arēs, who goes through the motions of death after he is taken off guard and wounded by the mortal Diomedes in Scroll V of the *Iliad.** As we will see in Hour 5, there is a touch of humor in the Homeric treatment of this death scene, because "death" as experienced here by the Olympian god Arēs is only a mock death. In the world of epic, the dead seriousness of death can be experienced only by humans.

0§9. Mortality is the dominant theme in the stories of ancient Greek heroes, and the *Iliad* and the *Odyssey* are no exceptions. Mortality is the burning question for the heroes of these epics, and for Achilles and Odysseus in particular. The human condition of mortality, with all its ordeals, defines heroic life itself. The certainty that one day you will die makes you human, distinct from animals who are unaware of their future death, and from the immortal gods. All the ordeals of the human condition culminate in the ultimate ordeal of a warrior hero's violent death in battle, detailed in all its ghastly varieties by the poetry of the *Iliad.*

---

*I deliberately said 'Scroll V' of the *Iliad*, not 'Book V.' My intent is to drive home the reality of the 'scrolls' or 'rolls' of papyrus, on which the 'books' of the Homeric *Iliad* and *Odyssey* were written in the ancient world. Here and everywhere, I number the 'books' of the *Iliad* in upper-case roman numerals and the corresponding 'books' of the *Odyssey* in lower-case roman numerals.

0§10. This deep preoccupation with the primal experience of violent death in war has several possible explanations. Some argue that the answer has to be sought in the simple fact that ancient Greek society accepted war as a necessary and even important part of life. Others seek a deeper answer by pointing to the poet's awestruck sense of uncontrollable forces at work in the universe, even of a personified concept of Force itself, which then becomes, through the poet's own artistic powers, some kind of eerie aesthetic thing.

0§11. But there are other answers as well, owing to approaches that delve deeply into the role of religion and, more specifically, into the religious practices of hero worship and animal sacrifice in ancient Greece. Of particular interest is the well-attested Greek custom of worshipping a hero precisely by way of slaughtering a sacrificial animal, ordinarily a ram. A striking example is the seasonally recurring sacrifice of a black ram at the precinct of the cult hero Pelops at the site of the Olympics (Pausanias 5.13.1–2).*

0§12. There is broad cultural evidence suggesting that hero worship in ancient Greece was not created out of stories like that of the *Iliad* and the *Odyssey* but was in fact independent of them. The stories, for their part, were based on religious practices, though not always directly. Some myths even draw into an explicit parallel the violent death of a hero and the sacrificial slaughter of an animal. For example, the description of the death of the hero Patroklos in *Iliad* XVI parallels in striking detail the stylized description, documented elsewhere in Homeric poetry (*Odyssey* iii), of the slaughter of a sacrificial heifer: in both cases, the victim is first stunned and disoriented by a fatal blow from behind, then struck frontally by another fatal blow, and then finally administered the coup de grâce. For another example, we may consider an ancient Greek vase painting that represents the same heroic warrior Patroklos in the shape of a sacrificial ram lying supine with its legs in the air and its throat slit open (lettering next to the painted figure indicates Patroklos).†

0§13. Evidence also places these practices of hero worship and animal sacrifice precisely during the era when the stories of the *Iliad* and the *Odyssey* took shape. Yet curiously, we find virtually no direct mention in either epic of hero worship and very little detailed description of animal sacrifice.‡ Homeric poetry, as a medium that achieved its general appeal to the Greeks by virtue of

---

* *PH* 123 = 4§10, with further references and commentary.

† This painting, along with another, related painting, is analyzed by Tarenzi 2005, who makes major improvements on the earlier interpretations of Griffiths 1985 and 1989.

‡ There are, however, a number of indirect references to hero cult: Nagy 2012b.

circumventing the parochial concerns of specific locales or regions, tended to avoid realistic descriptions of any ritual, not just ritual sacrifice. This pattern of avoidance is to be expected, given that in ancient Greece any ritual tends to be a localized phenomenon.

0§14. The sacrificial scenes we do find in the epics are markedly stylized, devoid of the kind of details that characterize real sacrifices as documented in archaeological and historical evidence. In real sacrifice the parts of the animal victim's body correspond to the members of the body politic. The ritual dismemberment of the animal's body in sacrifice sets a mental pattern for the idea of the reassembly of the hero's body in myths of immortalization. Given, then, that Homeric poetry avoids delving into the details of dismemberment as it applies to animals, in that it avoids the details of sacrificial practice, we may expect a parallel avoidance of the topic of immortalization for the hero. The local practices of hero worship, contemporaneous with the evolution of Homeric poetry as we know it, are clearly founded on religious notions of heroic immortalization.*

0§15. While personal immortalization is thus too localized in orientation for epics, the hero's death in battle, in all its stunning varieties, is universally acceptable. The *Iliad* seems to make up for its avoidance of details concerning the sacrifices of animals by dwelling on details about the martial deaths of heroes. In this way Homeric poetry, with its staggering volume of minutely detailed descriptions of the deaths of warriors, can serve as a compensation for sacrifice itself.†

0§16. Such deep concerns about the human condition are organized by Homeric poetry in a framework of heroic portraits, with those of Achilles and Odysseus serving as the centerpieces of the *Iliad* and the *Odyssey* respectively.

0§17. I concentrate here on Achilles. Here is a monolithic and fiercely uncompromising man who actively chooses violent death over life in order to win the glory of being remembered forever in epic poetry (*Iliad* IX 413). Here is a man of unbending principle who cannot allow his values to be compromised—not even by the desperate needs of his near and dear friends, who are begging him to bend his will, bend it just enough to save his own people. Here is a man of constant sorrow, who can never forgive himself for having unwittingly allowed his nearest and dearest friend, Patroklos, to take his place in battle and be

---

* More in Nagy 2012b.
† *PH* 143 = 5§13n40.

killed in his stead, slaughtered like a sacrificial animal—all on account of Achilles' own refusal to bend his will by coming to the aid of his fellow warriors. Here is a man, finally, of unspeakable anger, an anger so intense that the poetry of the *Iliad* words it the same way that it words the anger of the gods, even of Zeus himself.

o§18. The gods of the *Iliad* express their anger actively, as in descriptions of the destructive fire unleashed by the thunderbolt of Zeus. The central hero of the *Iliad* at first expresses his anger passively, by withdrawing his vital presence from his own people. The hero's anger is directed away from the enemy and toward his own people, whose king, Agamemnon, has insulted Achilles' honor and demeaned his sense of self. This passive anger of Achilles translates into the active success of the Trojan enemy in the hero's absence, and for now the most successful Trojan of them all is Hector, the hero who becomes the most hated opponent of Achilles. Hector's temporary success is compared, ironically, to the destructive fire unleashed by the thunderbolt of Zeus. In this way, the passive anger of the hero translates symbolically into the active anger of the god.* Then, in response to the killing of Patroklos by Hector, Achilles' anger modulates into an active phase—active no longer in a symbolic but in a real sense. The hero's anger is redirected, away from his own people and back toward his enemy, especially toward Hector.

o§19. This new phase of Achilles' anger consumes the hero in a paroxysm of self-destructiveness. His fiery rage plummets him into the depths of brutality, as he begins to view the enemy as the ultimate Other, to be hated with such an intensity that Achilles can even bring himself, in a moment of ultimate fury, to express that most ghastly of desires, to eat the flesh of Hector, the man he is about to kill. The *Iliad* is the story of a hero's pain, culminating in an anger that degrades him to the level of a savage animal, to the depths of bestiality. This same pain, however, this same intense feeling of loss, will ultimately make the savage anger subside in a moment of heroic self-recognition that elevates Achilles to the highest realms of humanity, of humanism. At the end of the *Iliad*, as he begins to recognize the pain of his deadliest enemy, of the Other, he begins to achieve a true recognition of the Self. The anger is at an end. And the story can end as well.

o§20. We find the clearest statement about the subject of the *Iliad* in the original Greek poem's very first word: *Anger.* The Greek word here is *mēnis*

---

* *BA* 321–338 = 20§§5–19.

($\mu\hat{\eta}\nu\iota\nu$ . . . in *Iliad* I 1), which is no ordinary anger; rather, it is "a feeling not separate from the actions it entails, of a *cosmic sanction*, of a social force whose activation brings drastic consequences on the whole community."* The song of the *Iliad*—for at the time, poets were singers, performers, and their poems were sung—is about this anger, the doomed and ruinous anger, of the hero Achilles:

HOUR 0 TEXT A

|₁ Anger [*mēnis*], goddess, sing it, of Achilles son of Peleus—|₂ disastrous [*oulomenē*] anger that made countless pains [*algea*] for the Achaeans, |₃ and many steadfast lives [*psūkhai*] it drove down to Hādēs, |₄ heroes' lives, but their bodies† it made prizes for dogs |₅ and for all birds, and the Will of Zeus was reaching its fulfillment [*telos*]—|₆ sing starting from the point where the two—I now see it—first had a falling out, engaging in strife [*eris*], |₇ I mean, [Agamemnon] the son of Atreus, lord of men, and radiant Achilles. |₈ So, which one of the gods was it who impelled the two to fight with each other in strife [*eris*]? |₉ It was [Apollo] the son of Leto and of Zeus. For he [= Apollo], infuriated at the king [= Agamemnon], |₁₀ caused an evil disease to arise throughout the mass of warriors, and the people were getting destroyed.

Iliad I 1–10‡

The singer was following the rules of his craft in summing up the whole song, all 100,000 or so words, in one single word, the first word of the song.§

0§21. So also in the *Odyssey*, the first word, *Man*, tells the subject of the song.** There the singer calls upon the Muse, goddess of the special Memory that makes him a singer, to tell him the story of the Man, the versatile man, the

---

* Muellner 1996:8. The word *mēnis* has been thoroughly and perceptively analyzed in Muellner's book. Another important book on anger in Homeric poetry is Walsh 2005.

† The word for 'body' here is *autos*, which means literally 'self'. So the bodies of the heroes who were killed in the Trojan War are the heroes 'themselves'. By contrast, the *psūkhai*, or 'lives', of the heroes that are driven down to Hādēs are not the heroes 'themselves'. After death, *psūkhē*, or 'life', is no longer the 'self'.

‡ |₁ Μῆνιν ἄειδε θεὰ Πηληϊάδεω Ἀχιλῆος |₂ οὐλομένην, ἣ μυρί' Ἀχαιοῖς ἄλγε' ἔθηκε |₃ πολλὰς δ' ἰφθίμους ψυχὰς Ἄϊδι προΐαψεν |₄ ἡρώων, αὐτοὺς δὲ ἑλώρια τεῦχε κύνεσσιν |₅ οἰωνοῖσί τε πᾶσι, Διὸς δ' ἐτελείετο βουλή, |₆ ἐξ οὗ δὴ τὰ πρῶτα διαστήτην ἐρίσαντε |₇ Ἀτρεΐδης τε ἄναξ ἀνδρῶν καὶ δῖος Ἀχιλεύς. |₈ Τίς τάρ σφωε θεῶν ἔριδι ξυνέηκε μάχεσθαι; |₉ Λητοῦς καὶ Διὸς υἱός· ὁ γὰρ βασιλῆϊ χολωθεὶς |₁₀ νοῦσον ἀνὰ στρατὸν ὄρσε κακήν, ὀλέκοντο δὲ λαοί.

§ Muellner 1996:9. Albert Lord (1960) used the words *singer* and *song* in his definitive study of oral poetics.

** The Greek word here is *anēr* (ἄνδρα . . . in *Odyssey* i 1).

hero Odysseus, who wandered so many countless ways in his voyages at sea after his heroic exploit of masterminding the capture and destruction of Troy. The Muse is imagined as telling the singer his song, and the singer can then sing this song to others:

Hour 0 Text B

|₁ That man, tell me O Muse the song of that man, that versatile [*polutropos*] man, who in very many ways |₂ veered from his path and wandered off far and wide, after he had destroyed the sacred citadel of Troy. |₃ Many different cities of many different people did he see, getting to know different ways of thinking [*noos*]. |₄ Many were the pains [*algea*] he suffered in his heart [*thūmos*] while crossing the sea |₅ struggling to merit [*arnusthai*] the saving of his own life [*psūkhē*] and his own homecoming [*nostos*] as well as the homecoming of his comrades [*hetairoi*]. |₆ But do what he might he could not save his comrades [*hetairoi*], even though he very much wanted to. |₇ For they perished through their own deeds of sheer recklessness, |₈ disconnected [*nēpioi*]* as they were, because of what they did to the cattle of the sun-god Hēlios. |₉ They ate them. So the god [Hēlios] deprived them of their day of homecoming [*nostimon*]. |₁₀ Starting from any single point of departure, O goddess, daughter of Zeus, tell me, as you have told those who came before me.

Odyssey i 1–10†

0§22. In the same way in the *Iliad*, the singer calls upon the Muse to tell the story of the Anger, the disastrous anger, of the hero Achilles, which caused countless losses and woes for Greeks and Trojans alike in the war that culminated in the destruction of Troy.

0§23. We see from the beginnings of both the *Iliad* and the *Odyssey* that the rules of the singer's craft extend beyond the naming of the main subject with the first word. In the original Greek of both the *Iliad* and the *Odyssey*, the first word announcing the subject—*Anger, Man*—is followed by a specially chosen adjective setting the mood: disastrous anger, versatile man. This, in turn, is

---

* On the meaning of *nēpios* as 'disconnected', see the Core Vocabulary.

† |₁ ἄνδρα μοι ἔννεπε, Μοῦσα, πολύτροπον, ὃς μάλα πολλὰ |₂ πλάγχθη, ἐπεὶ Τροίης ἱερὸν πτολίεθρον ἔπερσε· |₃ πολλῶν δ᾿ ἀνθρώπων ἴδεν ἄστεα καὶ νόον ἔγνω, |₄ πολλὰ δ᾿ ὅ γ᾿ ἐν πόντῳ πάθεν ἄλγεα ὃν κατὰ θυμόν, |₅ ἀρνύμενος ἥν τε ψυχὴν καὶ νόστον ἑταίρων. |₆ ἀλλ᾿ οὐδ᾿ ὣς ἑτάρους ἐρρύσατο, ἱέμενός περ· |₇ αὐτῶν γὰρ σφετέρῃσιν ἀτασθαλίῃσιν ὄλοντο, |₈ νήπιοι, οἳ κατὰ βοῦς Ὑπερίονος Ἠελίοιο |₉ ἤσθιον· αὐτὰρ ὁ τοῖσιν ἀφείλετο νόστιμον ἦμαρ. |₁₀ τῶν ἁμόθεν γε, θεά, θύγατερ Διός, εἰπὲ καὶ ἡμῖν.

followed by a relative clause that frames the story by outlining the plot—the disastrous anger that caused countless pains, the versatile man who wandered countless ways.

0§24. The symmetry of these two monumental compositions, the *Iliad* and the *Odyssey*, goes beyond their strict adherence to the rules of introducing an ancient Greek song. For they counterbalance each other throughout their vast stretches of narrative, in a steady, rhythmic flow of verses known as dactylic hexameters (the *Iliad* contains over 15,000 of these verses and the *Odyssey* over 12,000). The counterbalancing focuses on the central plot and the characterization of the principal hero in each. Achilles' monolithic personality, that of the mightiest warrior of his era who was monumentally proud of his martial exploits and his physical prowess, is matched against the many-sidedness of Odysseus, famed for his crafty stratagems and cunning intelligence.

0§25. The symmetry of the *Iliad* and the *Odyssey* goes even further: between them, these two songs give the impression of incorporating most of whatever was worth retelling about the heroic age—at least from the standpoint of the Greeks in the classical period of the fifth century BCE and thereafter. The staggering comprehensiveness of these two songs is apparent even from a cursory glance. For example, the *Iliad* not only tells the story that it says it will tell, about Achilles' anger and how it led to countless pains as the Greeks went on fighting it out with the Trojans and striving to ward off the fiery onslaught of Hector. It also manages to retell or even relive, though with varying degrees of directness or fullness of narrative, the entire Tale of Troy, including from the earlier points of the storyline such memorable moments as the Judgment of Paris, the Abduction of Helen, and the Assembly of Ships. More than that: the *Iliad* foreshadows the Death of Achilles, which does not occur within the bounds of its own plot. In short, although the story of the *Iliad* directly covers only a brief stretch of the whole story of Troy, thereby resembling the compressed time frame of classical Greek tragedy (Aristotle makes this observation in his *Poetics*), it still manages to mention something about virtually everything that happened at Troy, otherwise known as Ilion. Hence the epic's title—the Tale of Ilion, the *Iliad*. The *Odyssey* adds much more, especially about the so-called epic Cycle. It even features the story of the Trojan Horse in Scroll viii.

0§26. For the Greeks of the fifth century BCE and thereafter, the *Iliad* and the *Odyssey*, these two seemingly all-inclusive and symmetrical songs, were the creation of the Master Singer called Homer, reputed to have lived centuries earlier. Homer was presumed to be contemporaneous or near-contemporaneous with another Master Singer called Hesiod, who was credited with two other definitive symmetrical songs, the *Theogony* and the *Works and Days*. About the real Homer, we can recover next to nothing from the ancient world. Nor do we have much better luck with Hesiod, except perhaps for whatever the singer says about himself in his own two songs. In the case of Homer, we do not even have this much to start with, at least not in the *Iliad* or the *Odyssey:* in neither song does the singer say anything about himself that could be construed as historical information.* It can even be said that there is no evidence for the existence of a Homer—and hardly that much more for the existence of a Hesiod.

0§27. What we do know for sure, however, is that the Greeks of the classical period thought of Homer and Hesiod as their first authors, their primary authors. So it is not only for the modern reader that Homer and Hesiod represent the earliest phase of Greek literature. It is, moreover, a historical fact that Homer and Hesiod were eventually credited by the ancient Greeks with the founding of Greek literature. As I noted earlier, our primary authority for this fact is none other than the so-called Father of History himself, Herodotus, who observes in Scroll 2 (53.1–3) of his *Histories* that Homer and Hesiod, by way of their songs, had given the Greeks their first definitive statement about the gods. In a traditional society like that of the ancient Greeks, where the very idea of defining the gods is the equivalent of defining the society itself, this observation by Herodotus amounts to a claim that the songs of Homer and Hesiod are the basis of Greek civilization.

0§28. Who, then, was Homer? It is no exaggeration to answer that, along with Hesiod, he had become the prime culture hero of Greek civilization in the classical period of the fifth century and thereafter. It was a common practice of the ancient Greeks to attribute any major achievement of society, even if this achievement may have taken place through a lengthy period of social evolution, to the personal breakthrough of a culture hero, who was pictured as having made his monumental contribution in the earliest imaginable era of the culture. Greek myths about lawgivers, for example, tended to reconstruct these figures, whether or not they ever really existed, as the originators of the sum total of customary law as it evolved through time.† The same sort of evolutionary model may well apply to the figure of Homer as an originator of heroic song.‡

---

* In the *Homeric Hymn to Apollo*, however, the speaker who presents himself as Homer has much to say that is parallel to what the speaker of the Hesiodic *Theogony* says about himself. See Nagy 2009a.

† Nagy 1985:32 = §13.

‡ HQ 29–63.

0§29. The model can even be extended from Homer to Homeric song. There is evidence that a type of story, represented in a wide variety of cultures where the evolution of a song tradition moves slowly ahead in time until it reaches a relatively static phase, reinterprets itself as if it resulted from a single event. There were many such stories about Homer in ancient Greece, and what matters most is not so much the stories themselves as what they reveal about society's need to account for the evolution of Homeric song. The internal evidence of the Homeric verses, both in their linguistic development and in their datable references, points to an ongoing evolution of Homeric song embracing a vast stretch of time that lasted perhaps as long as a thousand years, extending from the second millennium BCE. This period culminated in a static phase that lasted about two centuries, framed by a formative stage in the later part of the eighth century BCE, when the epic was taking on its present shape, and a definitive stage, in the middle of the sixth, when the epic reached its final form.*

0§30. The basic historical fact remains, in any case, that the figure of Homer had become, by the classical period of the fifth century BCE, a primary culture hero credited with the creation of the *Iliad* and the *Odyssey*. Little wonder, then, that so many Greek cities—Athens included—claimed to be his birthplace. Such rivalry for the possession of Homer points to the increasingly widespread refinement of his identity through the cultural significance of Homeric song.

0§31. The subject of the *Iliad* bears witness to the cultural primacy of Homer in Greek civilization. This epic is not just about the anger of Achilles in particular and the age of heroes in general. The *Iliad* purports to say everything that is worth saying about the Greeks—the Hellenes, as they called themselves in the classical period. Not that the *Iliad* calls them Greeks. The Greeks in this song are a larger-than-life cultural construct of what they imagined themselves to have been in the distant age of heroes. These Greeks are retrojected Greeks, given such alternative Homeric names as Achaeans, Argives, Danaans, all three of which are used interchangeably to refer to these heroic ancestors whose very existence in song is for the Greeks the basis for their own self-definition as a people. It is as if the *Iliad,* in mirroring for the Greeks of the present an archetypal image of themselves in the past, served as an autobiography of a people.

0§32. On the surface these ancestral Greeks of the *Iliad* are on the offensive, attacking Troy. Beneath the surface, they are on the defensive, trying desperately to ward off the fiery onslaught of Hector, the leading Trojan hero. Here is

* *HQ* 41–43.

how the words of Hector foretell the climactic moment when his fire will reach the ships of the Achaeans:

Hour 0 Text C

$|_{180}$ But when I get to the hollow ships $|_{181}$ let there be some memory [*mnēmosunē*], in the future, of the burning fire, $|_{182}$ how I will set the ships on fire and kill $|_{183}$ the Argives [= Achaeans] right by their ships, confounded as they will be by the smoke.*

Iliad VIII 180–183†

0§33. With all their ships beached on the shores of the Hellespont, marked for destruction by the threatening fire of Hector, the ancestral Greeks are vulnerable to nothing short of extinction. The *Iliad* makes it quite clear: if their ships burn, the Greeks will never return home, to become the seafaring people who are the present audience of the *Iliad*. In the *Iliad,* the very survival of this seafaring nation is at stake.

0§34. But what exactly is this Greek nation? The very idea of nationhood is an incongruity if we apply it to the era when the *Iliad* and the *Odyssey* took shape. From the eighth through the fifth centuries BCE, as I have already noted, the geographical area that we now recognize as ancient Greece was an agglomerate of territories controlled by scores of independent and competing city-states. The most important and prestigious of these were Athens, Sparta, Argos, Thebes, and Corinth. Each city-state, or *polis,* was a social entity unto itself, with its own government, customary laws, religious practices, and dialect. The topic of the city-state will take us, in Hours 9, 10, and 11, to the hidden agenda of the *Odyssey.*

0§35. The fragmentation of Greece in this era was so pronounced that, looking back, it is hard to find genuine instances of cultural cohesion. One early example is the Olympics; another is the Oracle of Apollo at Delphi; still another, and the most obvious, is the poetic legacy of Homer and Hesiod. The Homeric *Iliad* and *Odyssey* together can be viewed as a marvel of cultural synthesis, integrating the diverse institutional heritage of this plurality of city-states, this kaleidoscopic Greek-speaking world, into a unified statement of cultural identity, of civilization.

0§36. The cultural universalism of the *Iliad* and the *Odyssey* can best be ap-

---

* Commentary in *BA* 335 = 20§16.

† $|_{180}$ ἀλλ' ὅτε κεν δὴ νηυσὶν ἔπι γλαφυρῇσι γένωμαι, $|_{181}$ μνημοσύνη τις ἔπειτα πυρὸς δηΐοιο γενέσθω, $|_{182}$ ὡς πυρὶ νῆας ἐνιπρήσω, κτείνω δὲ καὶ αὐτοὺς $|_{183}$ Ἀργείους παρὰ νηυσὶν ἀτυζομένους ὑπὸ καπνοῦ.

preciated when we consider the extent of the diversity that separated the Greek
city-states from one another. Nowhere is this diversity more apparent than in
the realm of religious practices. How people worshipped any given god, as we
know from the historical evidence of the classical era and thereafter, differed
dramatically from one city-state to another. Yet the *Iliad* and the *Odyssey* spoke
of the gods in a way that united the varied cultural perceptions and sensitivities
of a vast variety of city-states, large and small. The religious dimensions of these
gods, with Zeus, Hērā, Athena, Poseidon, and Apollo in the forefront, were destined to be shaded over by this Homeric process of synthesis, but their divine
reality became highlighted as a cultural permanence in the same process. The
modern reader may be struck by what seems on the surface to be a distinctly
irreligious attitude of Homeric song toward the gods, but the universal cultural edifice of these gods' lofty abode on Mount Olympus was in fact built up
from a diversity of unspoken religious foundations. When Herodotus is saying that Homer and Hesiod, by way of their songs, had given the Greeks their
first definitive statement about the gods, he is in effect acknowledging the
Olympian synthesis that had been bestowed on civilization by Homeric and
Hesiodic song. It is the history of Greek civilization, then, that the Homeric *Iliad* and *Odyssey* define.

o§37. To say that an epic like the *Iliad* is about the Greeks and what it is to be
a Greek is not far from saying that the *Iliad* is about Achilles. We have already
seen how this hero, as the very first words of the song make clear, is the focal point of the *Iliad*. Given the importance of this epic to the Greeks, we may
interpret this single fact to mean that Achilles is also a focal point of Greek civilization. Just how important he is, however, can be illustrated beyond the testimony of Homeric song. Let us take, for example, an inherited custom connected with the premier social event for all Greeks, the festival of the Olympics.
We know from ancient sources that the traditional ceremony inaugurating this
seasonally recurring Panhellenic festival centers on Achilles: on an appointed
day when the Games are to begin, the local women of Elis, the site where the
Olympics were held, fix their gaze on the sun as it sets into the Western hori-
zon—and begin ceremonially to weep for the hero (Pausanias 6.23.3).*

o§38. The prestige that ancient Greek civilization accorded to the figure of
Achilles, and the strong emotional attachment that goes with it, are worthy of
our attention especially because modern readers, both men and women, young

---

* *BA* 9 = Introduction §17; also *BA* 114 = 6§26.

and old, often find themselves relatively unresponsive to this sullen and darkly brooding hero. Few today feel empathy for his sorrow, which the hero of the *Iliad* himself describes as an everlasting one. The modern reader finds it much easier to feel empathy for Hector, the champion hero of the Trojans. In *Iliad* VI, Hector's heart-wrenching farewell to his wife and small son, soon to become his widow and orphan, is often singled out by modern readers as the most memorable scene of the entire epic. For the ancient Greeks as well, we may be sure, the figure of Hector evoked empathy. The difference, however, is that for them, the pathos of Hector resembles most closely the pathos of Achilles himself. Just as Hector's death evokes the sorrow of unfulfilled promise, even more so does the death of Achilles.

0§39. While Hector is the idealized husband and father cut down in his prime, Achilles is the idealized bridegroom, sensual in his heroic beauty and likewise doomed to an untimely death. In the songs of Sappho, as we will see in Hour 5, it is Achilles who figures as the ultimate bridegroom. The very mention of him in song conjures up the picture of a beautiful plant that is cut down at the peak of its growth. This is how his own mother sings of Achilles in Scroll XVIII of the *Iliad,* in a beautiful song of lament that prefigures the hero's untimely death:

HOUR 0 TEXT D

|$_{54}$ Ah me, the pitiful one! Ah me, the mother, so sad it is, of the very best. |$_{55}$ I gave birth to a faultless and strong son, |$_{56}$ the very best of heroes. And he shot up [*anedramen*] equal [*īsos*] to a seedling [*ernos*]. |$_{57}$ I nurtured him like a shoot in the choicest spot of the orchard, |$_{58}$ only to send him off on curved ships to Troy, to fight Trojan men. |$_{59}$ And I will never be welcoming him |$_{60}$ back home as returning warrior, back to the House of Peleus. |$_{61}$ And as long as he lives and sees the light of the sun, |$_{62}$ he will have sorrow [*akh-nutai*], and though I go to him I cannot help him.

Iliad XVIII 54–62*

* |$_{54}$ ὤ μοι ἐγὼ δειλή, ὤ μοι δυσαριστοτόκεια, |$_{55}$ ἥ τ' ἐπεὶ ἂρ τέκον υἱὸν ἀμύμονά τε κρατερόν τε |$_{56}$ ἔξοχον ἡρώων· ὁ δ' ἀνέδραμεν ἔρνεϊ ἶσος· |$_{57}$ τὸν μὲν ἐγὼ θρέψασα φυτὸν ὣς γουνῷ ἀλωῆς |$_{58}$ νηυσὶν ἐπιπροέηκα κορωνίσιν Ἴλιον εἴσω |$_{59}$ Τρωσὶ μαχησόμενον· τὸν δ' οὐχ ὑποδέξομαι αὖτις |$_{60}$ οἴκαδε νοστήσαντα δόμον Πηλήιον εἴσω. |$_{61}$ ὄφρα δέ μοι ζώει καὶ ὁρᾷ φάος ἠελίοιο |$_{62}$ ἄχνυται, οὐδέ τί οἱ δύναμαι χραισμῆσαι ἰοῦσα.

0§40. All the wistful beauty of sorrow for a life cut short comes alive in song, and that song of the hero's mother extends into a song that becomes the *Iliad* itself, as we will see in Hours 3 and 4. For the culture of the Greeks was, and still is, a *song culture*.* For them, to weep is to sing a lament, and the sorrow, in all its natural reality of physically crying and sobbing, is not at all incompatible with the art of the song: it flows into it.

0§41. If we consider the evocative power that we can sometimes find in even the simplest contemporary popular tunes about the sorrows of war and death, we will have at least something to compare with the emotional and aesthetic response to Achilles in the song culture of the ancient Greek world. Thinking of Achilles leads to beautiful sad songs. As we recall the detail about the institutionalized weeping of the local women at the commencement of the Olympics, we may note that this act of weeping was considered an act of singing—or keening. In the words of the fifth-century poet Pindar, the keening of the Muses, the 'Maidens of Helicon', over the dead Achilles extends into the song of the present. I preview here the words of Pindar, which I will analyze in some detail when we reach Hour 4:

HOUR 0 TEXT E

|$_{56}$ Even when he [= Achilles] died, the songs did not leave him, |$_{57}$ but the Maidens of Helicon [= the Muses] stood by his pyre and his funeral mound, |$_{58}$ and, as they stood there, they poured forth a song of lamentation [*thrēnos*] that is famed far and wide. |$_{59}$ And so it was that the immortal gods decided |$_{60}$ to hand over the man, genuine [*esthlos*] as he was even after he had perished [*phthi-n-ein*]† in death, to the songs of the goddesses [= the Muses].

Pindar *Isthmian* 8 lines 56–60‡

0§42. The sadness of Achilles' song is of course a necessity of tradition, just as the hero's death, his mortality, is necessary. The hero, the story of the hero, cannot be complete if he lives on. For in death the hero wins the ultimate prize

---

* On the term *song culture*, I offer a critical analysis in *PH* 19 = 1§5n7.

† In Hour 4, I will elaborate on the word *phthi-n-ein* in the sense of 'perish' and even 'wilt'.

‡ |$_{56}$ τὸν μὲν οὐδὲ θανόντ' ἀοιδαὶ <ἐπ>έλιπον, |$_{57}$ ἀλλά οἱ παρά τε πυρὰν τάφον θ' Ἑλικώνιαι παρθένοι |$_{58}$ στάν, ἐπὶ θρῆνόν τε πολύφαμον ἔχεαν. |$_{59}$ ἔδοξ' ἦρα καὶ ἀθανάτοις, |$_{60}$ ἐσλόν γε φῶτα καὶ φθίμενον ὕμνοις θεᾶν διδόμεν.

of life eternal in song. As Achilles himself declares, his heroic death will transcend the fleeting beauty of earthbound life:

Hour 0 Text F

|₄₁₀ My mother Thetis, goddess with silver steps, tells me that |₄₁₁ I carry the burden of two different fated ways [*kēres*] leading to the final moment [*telos*] of death. |₄₁₂ If I stay here and fight at the walls of the city of the Trojans, |₄₁₃ then my safe homecoming [*nostos*] will be destroyed for me, but I will have a glory [*kleos*] that is imperishable [*aphthiton*]*. |₄₁₄ Whereas if I go back home, returning to the dear land of my forefathers, |₄₁₅ then it is my glory [*kleos*], genuine [*esthlon*] as it is, that will be destroyed for me, but my life force [*aiōn*] will then |₄₁₆ last me a long time, and the final moment [*telos*] of death will not be swift in catching up with me.

Iliad IX 410–416†

0§43. The Greek word *kleos,* which translates here as 'glory', conventionally refers to the glory of song, while *aphthiton,* or 'imperishable', evokes the idea of a vitality that animates the universe.‡ The hero's glory in song, then, unlike the hero, will never die. For Achilles, as we will see in Hour 4, the song of *kleos* will remain forever alive in the civilization that sings his glorious epic.

0§44. For Odysseus, as we will see in Hour 9, no such choice needs to be made. The song of his homecoming, his *nostos,* will be the same as his *kleos.* Like the *kleos* of Achilles, the *kleos* of Odysseus—and of Penelope—will be sung for all time, as we hear it proclaimed at the end of the *Odyssey.*

0§45. But how was Homeric poetry transmitted, supposedly for all time? A crucial aspect of Homeric transmission (and we will see more about this later, in Hour 7e) was the tradition of performing the *Iliad* and the *Odyssey* at a seasonally recurring festival in Athens. The festival was the Great Panathenaia, celebrated every four years in mid-August, and the performers of Homeric poetry at this festival were professional reciters known as *rhapsōidoi,* or 'rhapsodes'.

---

*In Hour 4, I will elaborate on the meaning of *aphthiton* as 'imperishable' and, in some specialized contexts, as 'unwilting'.

† |₄₁₀ μήτηρ γάρ τέ μέ φησι θεὰ Θέτις ἀργυρόπεζα |₄₁₁ διχθαδίας κῆρας φερέμεν θανάτοιο τέλος δέ. |₄₁₂ εἰ μέν κ᾽ αὖθι μένων Τρώων πόλιν ἀμφιμάχωμαι, |₄₁₃ ὤλετο μέν μοι νόστος, ἀτὰρ κλέος ἄφθιτον ἔσται· |₄₁₄ εἰ δέ κεν οἴκαδ᾽ ἵκωμι φίλην ἐς πατρίδα γαῖαν, |₄₁₅ ὤλετό μοι κλέος ἐσθλόν, ἐπὶ δηρὸν δέ μοι αἰὼν |₄₁₆ ἔσσεται, οὐδέ κέ μ᾽ ὦκα τέλος θανάτοιο κιχείη.

‡ More in Hour 4 about such an evocation.

An important source of information about the classical phase of this Homeric tradition is Plato's *Ion,* a dialogue named after a virtuoso rhapsode who was active in the late fifth century BCE and who specialized in performing the Homeric *Iliad* and *Odyssey.* In Plato's *Ion* (535d), we see a vivid description of the rhapsode Ion in the act of performing Homeric poetry before an audience of more than 20,000 at the Great Panathenaia. What I find especially remarkable about this description is the highlighting of moments when the audience, supposedly all 20,000 of them, reacts to climactic moments in the narration of the *Iliad* and the *Odyssey.* At these moments, they all break down and weep as they visualize the saddest things they are hearing—or feel their hair stand on end as they visualize the most terrifying things. I say *visualize* here because the word for 'audience' in the original wording of Plato's *Ion* is *theōmenoi,* which literally means 'spectators' or, better, 'visualizers':

HOUR 0 TEXT G

{Socrates is speaking}: Hold it right there. Tell me this, Ion—respond to what I ask without concealment. When you say well the epic verses and induce a feeling of bedazzlement [*ekplēxis*] for the *spectators* [*theōmenoi*]—as you sing of Odysseus leaping onto the threshold and revealing himself to the suitors and pouring out the arrows at his feet, or of Achilles rushing at Hector, or something connected to the pitiful things about Andromache or Hecuba or Priam—are you then in your right mind, or outside yourself? Does your mind [*psūkhē*], possessed by the god [*enthousiazein*], suppose that you are in the midst of the actions you describe in Ithaca or Troy, or wherever the epic verses have it?*

Plato *Ion* 535b–c†

0§46. From the standpoint of Aristotle's *Poetics* (1449b24–28), the audience at such climactic moments of Homeric narration is experiencing the primal emotions of *phobos,* 'fear', and *eleos,* 'pity'. And, as we see from the words of

---

*Commentary in *HC* 417–418, 447–449 = 3§§143–144, 199–200.

†ΣΩ. Ἔχε δή μοι τόδε εἰπέ, ὦ Ἴων, καὶ μὴ ἀποκρύψῃ ὅτι ἄν σε ἔρωμαι· ὅταν εὖ εἴπῃς ἔπη καὶ ἐκπλήξῃς μάλιστα τοὺς θεωμένους, ἢ τὸν Ὀδυσσέα ὅταν ἐπὶ τὸν οὐδὸν ἐφαλλόμενον ᾄδῃς, ἐκφανῆ γιγνόμενον τοῖς μνηστῆρσι καὶ ἐκχέοντα τοὺς ὀιστοὺς πρὸ τῶν ποδῶν, ἢ Ἀχιλλέα ἐπὶ τὸν Ἕκτορα ὁρμῶντα, ἢ καὶ τῶν περὶ Ἀνδρομάχην ἐλεινῶν τι ἢ περὶ Ἑκάβην ἢ περὶ Πρίαμον, τότε πότερον ἔμφρων εἶ ἢ ἔξω {c} σαυτοῦ γίγνῃ καὶ παρὰ τοῖς πράγμασιν οἴεταί σου εἶναι ἡ ψυχὴ οἷς λέγεις ἐνθουσιάζουσα, ἢ ἐν Ἰθάκῃ οὖσιν ἢ ἐν Τροίᾳ ἢ ὅπως ἂν καὶ τὰ ἔπη ἔχῃ;

Plato's *Ion,* the performer of Homeric poetry brings to life these climactic moments of fear and pity as he retells the story. There he is, standing on an elevated platform and gazing down upon a sea of faces in the audience. His eyes seek out and find contact with their eyes, and now the audience can all react simultaneously to the rhapsode's Homeric performance. Teary eyes alternate with looks of terror or even sheer wonder as the story of Homeric song oscillates from one emotion to another. Here is the way the rhapsode describes his audience:

HOUR 0 TEXT H

As I look down at them from the platform on high, I see them, each and every time, crying or looking terrified, filled with a sense of wonder at what is being retold.

Plato *Ion* 535e*

0§47. Yes, the songs of Achilles and Odysseus were ever being retold, nurtured by the song culture that had generated them. But beyond the song culture, beyond Greek civilization, the epic lives on even in our time, and the wonder of it all is that one of its heroes himself foretold it.

---

* καθορῶ γὰρ ἑκάστοτε αὐτοὺς ἄνωθεν ἀπὸ τοῦ βήματος κλάοντάς τε καὶ δεινὸν ἐμβλέποντας καὶ συνθαμβοῦντας τοῖς λεγομένοις.

HOUR 1

The Homeric Iliad *and the Glory of the Unseasonal Hero*

The Meaning of Kleos

1§1. There are two key words for this hour. The first of the two is *kleos*: 'glory, fame, that which is heard'; or, 'the poem or song that conveys glory, fame, that which is heard'. We will turn to the second of the two words when we reach the paragraphs starting at §26.

1§2. But I begin with *kleos*, 'glory'. This word was used in ancient Greek poetry or song to refer to the poetry or the song that glorifies the heroes of the distant heroic past. Since the references to *kleos* in ancient Greek poetry and song make no distinction between poetry and song, I will simply use the word *song* whenever I refer to the basic meaning of *kleos*.

1§3. A specific form of poetry is *epic*, which is the medium of the Homeric *Iliad* and *Odyssey*, and a general form of song is what we know today as *lyric*. I will have more to say later about epic and lyric. For now I simply repeat my working definition of epic, as I formulated it in the Introduction to Homeric Poetry: an expansive poem of enormous scope, composed in an old-fashioned and superbly elevated style of language, concerning the wondrous deeds of heroes.

1§4. The song of *kleos* glorifies not only the heroes of the distant past, which is a heroic age. It glorifies also the gods—as they existed in the heroic age and as they continued to exist for their worshippers at any given moment in historical time.

1§5. Why did the ancient Greeks glorify heroes? Partly because they worshipped not only gods but also heroes. As I noted in the Introduction, we see here a fundamental fact of ancient Greek history: the ancient Greeks practiced *hero worship*, to which I refer more specifically as *hero cult*.

1§6. Let us return to the main topic of this hour, as signaled by the key word *kleos*. This word was used in Homeric poetry to refer to both the *medium* and the *message* of the glory of heroes. The dictum of Marshall McLuhan (1964) applies here: the medium is the message.

The Kleos *of Achilles as Epic 'Glory'*

1§7. I begin by concentrating on the medium of song as marked by the word *kleos*. In ancient Greek song culture, *kleos* was the primary medium for communicating the concept of the hero, which is the primary topic (or 'message') of these 24 hours.

1§8. In the *Iliad*, the main hero, Achilles, is quoted as saying:

HOUR 1 TEXT A = HOUR 0 TEXT F

|410 My mother Thetis, goddess with silver steps, tells me that |411 I carry the burden of two different fated ways [*kēres*] leading to the final moment [*telos*] of death. |412 If I stay here and fight at the walls of the city of the Trojans, |413 then my safe homecoming [*nostos*] will be destroyed for me, but I will have a glory [*kleos*]* that is imperishable [*aphthiton*].† |414 Whereas if I go back home, returning to the dear land of my forefathers, |415 then it is my glory [*kleos*],‡ genuine [*esthlon*] as it is, that will be destroyed for me, but my life force [*aiōn*] will then |416 last me a long time, and the final moment [*telos*] of death will not be swift in catching up with me.

Iliad IX 410–416§

1§9. This translation, which is my own, is different from what we read in Samuel Butler's translation of the *Iliad* (London 1898), which is available online for free by way of the Perseus Project (and also by way of other media, such as Project Gutenberg). The original wording of Butler (1898) is as follows:

My mother Thetis tells me that there are two ways in which I may meet my end. If I stay here and fight, *I will not return alive but my name will*

---

* Here, then, is the key word: *kleos*, 'glory'.
† In Hour 4, I will elaborate on the word *aphthiton* in the sense of 'imperishable'.
‡ So *kleos*, 'glory', is evidently being contrasted with *nostos*, 'homecoming'.
§ |410 μήτηρ γάρ τέ μέ φησι θεὰ Θέτις ἀργυρόπεζα |411 διχθαδίας κῆρας φερέμεν θανάτοιο τέλος δέ. |412 εἰ μέν κ᾽ αὖθι μένων Τρώων πόλιν ἀμφιμάχωμαι, |413 ὤλετο μέν μοι νόστος, ἀτὰρ κλέος ἄφθιτον ἔσται· |414 εἰ δέ κεν οἴκαδ᾽ ἵκωμι φίλην ἐς πατρίδα γαῖαν, |415 ὤλετό μοι κλέος ἐσθλόν, ἐπὶ δηρὸν δέ μοι αἰὼν |416 ἔσσεται, οὐδέ κέ μ᾽ ὦκα τέλος θανάτοιο κιχείη.

live for ever: whereas if I go home my name will die, but it will be long ere death shall take me.

1§10. In the *Sourcebook of Original Greek Texts (in English Translation) about the Ancient Greek Hero* (chs.harvard.edu), which as I already said is available online for free, the reader will see that I use my own translation for the verses we have just been considering, *Iliad* IX 410–416. In general, however, the translated text of the Homeric *Iliad* and *Odyssey* in this online *Sourcebook* is based on Butler's original translation (*Iliad* 1898 and *Odyssey* 1900). In editing this *Sourcebook* with the help of fellow teachers and researchers, my practice has been to modify the original translation wherever I see a need to substitute a more accurate translation, as in the case of *Iliad* IX 410–416.

1§11. That said, I return to Samuel Butler's translation of *Iliad* IX 410–416, as I quoted it in §9. It is a literary translation, not a literal one. In general, Butler's translation of the *Iliad* and the *Odyssey* is meant to be pleasing to the ear when read out loud. In the case of *Iliad* IX 410–416, his translation successfully captures the general idea of what is being said by Achilles. I focus our attention on the part that I highlighted earlier: "I will not return alive but my name will live for ever." In place of this literary version, the *Sourcebook* shows my more literal translation of the original Greek, which is contained in one single verse:

then my safe homecoming [*nostos*] will be destroyed for me, but I will have a glory [*kleos*] that is imperishable [*aphthiton*].

Iliad IX 413

1§12. In what follows, I will make a set of arguments encapsulated here in one thesis sentence:

In *Iliad* IX 413, the main hero of the *Iliad* leaves as his signature the *kleos* of his own epic, which turns out to be the *Iliad.*

1§13. To make the arguments I hope to make, I start by offering my working interpretation of this verse. From here on, I call this kind of interpretation *exegesis,* which is an ancient Greek term referring to a close reading of a given text. Here, then, is my exegesis:

Achilles has started to understand the consequences of his decision to reject the option of a safe *nostos* or 'homecoming'. He is in the process of deciding to choose the other option: he will stay at Troy and continue to fight in the Trojan War. Choosing this option will result in his death, and he is starting to understand that. In the fullness of time, he will be ready to give up his life in exchange for getting a *kleos,* which is a poetic 'glory' described as lasting forever. This *kleos* is the tale of Troy, the *Iliad* (the name of the poem, *Iliad,* means 'tale of Ilion'; Ilion is the other name for 'Troy'). Achilles the hero gets included in the *Iliad* by dying a warrior's death. The consolation prize for his death *is* the *kleos* of the *Iliad.*

A Much Shorter Version of Epic 'Glory'

1§14. Having considered the *kleos,* or epic 'glory', of Achilles, I turn to the *kleos* of another hero:

HOUR 1 TEXT B

$|_{218}$ Tell me now you Muses dwelling on Olympus, $|_{219}$ who was the first to come up and face Agamemnon, $|_{220}$ either among the Trojans or among their famous allies? $|_{221}$ It was Iphidamas son of Antenor, a man both good and great, $|_{222}$ who was raised in fertile Thrace the mother of sheep. $|_{223}$ Kissēs in his own house raised him when he was little. $|_{224}$ Kissēs was his mother's father, father to Theano, the one with the fair cheeks. $|_{225}$ When he [= Iphidamas] reached the stage of adolescence, which brings luminous glory, $|_{226}$ he [= Kissēs] wanted to keep him at home and to give him his own daughter in marriage, $|_{227}$ but as soon as he [= Iphidamas] had married, he left the bride chamber and *went off seeking the kleos of the Achaeans* $|_{228}$ along with twelve curved ships that followed him.

Iliad XI 218–228*

1§15. This passage, Text B, resembles Text A in the way it highlights a hero's obsession with the goal of dying the right way in order to be remembered for-

---

* $|_{218}$ Ἔσπετε νῦν μοι Μοῦσαι Ὀλύμπια δώματ' ἔχουσαι $|_{219}$ ὅς τις δὴ πρῶτος Ἀγαμέμνονος ἀντίον ἦλθεν $|_{220}$ ἢ αὐτῶν Τρώων ἠὲ κλειτῶν ἐπικούρων. $|_{221}$ Ἰφιδάμας Ἀντηνορίδης ἠΰς τε μέγας τε $|_{222}$ ὃς τράφη ἐν Θρῄκῃ ἐριβώλακι μητέρι μήλων· $|_{223}$ Κισσῆς τόν γ' ἔθρεψε δόμοις ἔνι τυτθὸν ἐόντα $|_{224}$ μητροπάτωρ, ὃς τίκτε Θεανὼ καλλιπάρῃον· $|_{225}$ αὐτὰρ ἐπεί ῥ' ἥβης ἐρικυδέος ἵκετο μέτρον, $|_{226}$ αὐτοῦ μιν κατέρυκε, δίδου δ' ὅ γε θυγατέρα ἥν· $|_{227}$ γήμας δ' ἐκ θαλάμοιο μετὰ κλέος ἵκετ' Ἀχαιῶν $|_{228}$ σὺν δυοκαίδεκα νηυσὶ κορωνίσιν, αἵ οἱ ἕποντο.

ever in the *kleos,* or 'glory', of song. In this case, however, the hero is not a major figure of the *Iliad,* like Achilles. Rather, the hero here in Text B is mentioned only this one time in the *Iliad,* in what amounts to a short story embedded inside the overall story of the *Iliad.*

1§16. To distinguish the story of the *Iliad* from such short stories that exist *inside* the story of the *Iliad,* I will as a rule refer to the *Iliad* as the 'Narrative', with an upper-case *N,* and to the stories *inside* the *Iliad* as 'narratives', with lower-case *n.* Such narratives are 'micro-narratives' in comparison to the 'macro-Narrative' that is the *Iliad.* Also, I will as a rule use the word 'Narrator' in referring to 'Homer', whom I have already described as a culture hero venerated by the ancient Greeks as the ultimate 'singer' of the *Iliad* and the *Odyssey.*

1§17. To appreciate the poetic artistry that produced the micro-narrative that we have just read in Text B, we must consider the artistic device of *compression* in the traditional media of ancient Greek songmaking. This device of compression is to be contrasted with the device of *expansion.* Whereas expansion produces macro-Narratives, such as the monumental composition of the *Iliad* itself, compression produces micro-narratives, such as the story-within-a-story that we are now considering.* In many ways, a "trailer" in today's culture of film-making is produced by techniques of compression that resemble the techniques used in producing such micro-narratives in ancient Greek songmaking.

1§18. I concentrate on the next-to-last verse of this micro-narrative:

> but as soon as he had married, he left the bride chamber and *went off*
> *seeking the kleos of the Achaeans*
>
> *Iliad* XI 227

1§19. This micro-narrative is about a hero who decides to interrupt his honeymoon to go to Troy to fight on the side of the Trojans against the Achaeans. These Achaeans, as we saw in the Introduction, are the Greeks of the heroic age. So now, this hero has just been killed in battle. Why did he give up his life, a life of newlywed bliss, just to fight and die at Troy? The Narrator of the macro-Narrative gives the answer to this question: this hero did it to get included in the *kleos,* or epic 'glory' of the Greek song culture. He was 'seeking the *kleos* of the Achaeans'. This *kleos* is the macro-Narrative of the *Iliad.*

1§20. We see here a hero gaining inclusion in the *Iliad* by dying a warrior's

---

* More on expansion and compression in *HQ* 76–77.

death. To that extent, he is like the major hero Achilles, whose death is the core theme of the *Iliad.* But this minor hero, Iphidamas, dies for just a "bit part." By contrast, Achilles will die for the lead part.

The Immortalizing Power of Kleos *as Epic 'Glory'*

1§21. So why is the *kleos* of the Achaeans so important that one is ready to die for it—not only an Achilles, the best of the Achaeans, but even a non-Achaean, as in the case of our "bit player" Iphidamas? The answer has to do with the immortalizing power of *kleos* as epic 'glory', which as we have seen is described as *aphthiton,* 'imperishable', in *Iliad* IX 413. Achilles will choose the glory of epic song, which is a thing of art, over his own life, which is a thing of nature. The thing of art is destined to last forever, while his own life, as a thing of nature, is destined for death.

1§22. In the culture represented by the heroes of the *Iliad,* the distinction between art and nature, between the artificial and the natural, is not the same as in our modern cultures. Their culture was a song culture, as I have described it earlier. In our modern cultures, artificial implies 'unreal' while natural implies 'real.' In a song culture, by contrast, the artificial can be just as real as the natural, since the words of an 'artificial' song can be just as real as the words of 'natural' speech in a real-life experience. In a song culture, the song can be just as real as life itself.

1§23. In ancient Greek song culture, the tale or story of the *Iliad* was felt to be not only real but also true. As we will see in later hours, the Homeric *Iliad* was felt to convey the ultimate truth-values of the ancient Greek song culture.

1§24. Because we as users of the English language have a different cultural perspective on the words *tale* and *story,* which for us imply fiction and are therefore not expected to be 'true', I have also been using the more neutral word *narrative* in referring to the tale or story of the *Iliad* and other such tales or stories.*

1§25. For Achilles, the major hero of the *Iliad,* the song of *kleos* is just as real as is his very own life. The infinite time of the artificial song, the *kleos aphthiton,* or 'imperishable glory' (at *Iliad* IX 413), is just as real to him as the finite time of his natural life.

---

* A modern attempt to capture a sense of the 'trueness' of song is a poem by Wallace Stevens, "Peter Quince at the Clavier" (1915).

The Meaning of Hōrā

1§26. The very idea of such a coexistence between infinite time and finite time brings me to the second key word for this hour. It is *hōrā* (plural *hōrai*), 'season, seasonality, the right time, the perfect time'. This word *hōrā* stood for natural time in a natural life, in a natural life-cycle. The English word *hour* is derived from ancient Greek *hōrā*, as in the expression 'The hour is near'.

1§27. The goddess of *hōrā* was *Hērā* (the two forms *hōrā* and *Hērā* are linguistically related to each other). She was the goddess of seasons, in charge of making everything happen on time, happen in season, and happen in a timely way.

1§28. Related to these two words *hōrā* and *Hērā* is *hērōs* (singular) / *hērōes* (plural), meaning 'hero'. As we will see, the precise moment when everything comes together for the hero is the moment of death. The hero is 'on time' at the *hōrā* or 'time' of death. Before death and in fact during their whole lifetime, however, heroes are *not on time*: as we will see, they are *unseasonal*.

1§29. In Text A, we have seen Achilles thinking about his future death as glorified by the medium of *kleos*. In a sense, we see him 'scripting' his death. And this 'scripting' is all about *timing*. The timing of heroic death is all-important for the hero.

The Need for Heroes to 'Script' Their Own Death

1§30. Here I return to a point I made earlier: in a song culture, the song can be just as real as life itself. To experience song in a song culture is to experience real life. But there is a paradox here, as we will see: for the Greek hero, the ultimate real-life experience is not life but death. In some situations, death can even become an alternative to sex. So death must be a defining moment of reality for the hero, and it must be not feared but welcomed, since the hero must ultimately achieve the perfect moment of a perfect death. And such a perfect moment must be recorded in song, which brings *kleos,* or 'glory'. Thus heroes feel a need to 'script' their own death with their dying words.

1§31. We find an example in Aeschylus' *Agamemnon* 1444–1445, a passage we will encounter in Hour 16.* In that passage, we will read the words of the last

---

* An English-language translation of Aeschylus' *Agamemnon* is available in the online *Sourcebook* (chs. harvard.edu).

song of sorrow sung by Cassandra, one of the most engaging female heroes in the ancient texts we read.

1§32. In ancient Greek traditions, a hero's dying words can be pictured as a *swan song.* According to such traditions, the swan sings its most beautiful song at the moment of its death. We will consider this myth in more detail toward the end of this book, when we read Plato's *Phaedo:* in that work, Socrates talks about the concept of the swan song at the moment of his own death by hemlock. What Socrates is quoted as saying in the *Phaedo,* as we will see, turns out to be his own swan song.

1§33. I see a point of comparison in modern popular culture. The example I have in mind comes from the film *Bladerunner,* directed by Ridley Scott (1982), based on the science fiction novel *Do Androids Dream of Electric Sheep?* by Philip K. Dick (1968). In particular, I have in mind the moment when Roy Blatty, an artificial human, 'scripts' his own death, which is meant to be natural.

1§34. We now turn to a model for Achilles in the 'scripting' of his own death. This model is a hero from an earlier age, who exemplifies the perfect timing of his own death. That hero is Hēraklēs, otherwise known by the Romanized version of his name, Hercules.

Hēraklēs as a Model Hero

1§35. Hēraklēs is more than a model for Achilles. He is a model for all heroes. As we will see, his story brings to life the meaning of the ancient Greek word for hero, *hērōs,* and the meanings of the related word for seasonality, *hōrā,* and for the goddess of seasonality herself, *Hērā.* As we will also see, even his name tells the story: *Hēraklēs* means 'he who has the *kleos* of *Hērā*'.

1§36. In the *Iliad,* we find an embedded micro-narrative that tells the story of Hēraklēs as it relates to the story of Achilles in the macro-Narrative that is the *Iliad.* I quote the entire micro-narrative:

HOUR 1 TEXT C

$|_{76}$ Then Agamemnon, the king of men, spoke up at their meeting, $|_{77}$ right there from the place where he was sitting, not even standing up in the middle of the assembly. $|_{78}$ "Near and dear ones," said he, "Danaan [= Achaean] heroes, attendants [*therapontes*] of Arēs! $|_{79}$ It is a good thing to listen when a man stands up to speak, and it is not seemly $|_{80}$

to speak in relay after him.* It would be hard for someone to do that, even if he is a practiced speaker. |₈₁ For how could any man in an assembly either hear anything when there is an uproar |₈₂ or say anything? Even a public speaker who speaks clearly will be disconcerted by it. |₈₃ What I will do is to make a declaration addressed to [Achilles] the son of Peleus. As for the rest of you |₈₄ Argives [= Achaeans], you should understand and know well, each one of you, the words [*mūthos*] that I say for the record. |₈₅ By now the Achaeans have been saying these words [*mūthos*] to me many times, |₈₆ and they have been blaming me. But I am not responsible [*aitios*]. |₈₇ No, those who are really responsible are Zeus and Fate [Moira] and the Fury [Erinys] who roams in the mist. |₈₈ They are the ones who, at the public assembly, had put savage derangement [*atē*] into my thinking [*phrenes*] |₈₉ on that day when I myself deprived Achilles of his honorific portion [*geras*]. |₉₀ But what could I do? The god is the one who brings everything to its fulfillment [*teleutân*]. |₉₁ That goddess Atē, senior daughter of Zeus—she makes everyone veer off-course [*aâsthai*], |₉₂ that disastrous one [*oulomenē*], the one who has delicate steps. She never makes contact with the ground of the threshold, |₉₃ never even going near it, but instead she hovers over the heads of men, bringing harm to mortals. |₉₄ In her harmfulness, she has incapacitated others as well [besides me], and I have in mind one person in particular. |₉₅ Yes, once upon a time even Zeus veered off-course [*aâsthai*], who is said to be the best |₉₆ among men and gods. Even he |₉₇ was deceived; Hērā did it, with her devious ways of thinking, female that she is. |₉₈ It happened on the day when the mighty Hēraklēs |₉₉ was about to be born of Alkmene in Thebes, the city garlanded by good walls. |₁₀₀ He [= Zeus], making a formal declaration [*eukhesthai*], spoke up at a meeting of all the gods and said: |₁₀₁ 'hear me, all gods and all goddesses, |₁₀₂ and let me say to you what the heart [*thūmos*] in my chest tells me to say. |₁₀₃ Today the goddess who presides over the pains of childbirth, Eileithuia, will help bring forth a man into the light, |₁₀₄ revealing him, and he will be king over all the people who live around him. |₁₀₅ He comes from an ancestral line of men who are descended from blood that comes from me.' |₁₀₆ Thinking devious thoughts, the goddess Hērā ad-

---

* The previous speaker was Achilles.

dressed him [= Zeus]: |₁₀₇ 'You will be mistaken, and you will not be able to make a fulfillment [*telos*] of the words [*mūthos*] that you have spoken for the record. |₁₀₈ But come, Olympian god, swear for me a binding oath: |₁₀₉ swear that he will really be king over all the people who live around him, |₁₁₀ I mean, the one who on this day shall fall to the ground between the legs of a woman |₁₁₁ who is descended from men who come from your line of ancestry, from blood that comes from you.' |₁₁₂ So she spoke. And Zeus did not at all notice [*noeîn*] her devious thinking, |₁₁₃ but he swore a great oath. And right then and there, he veered off-course [*aâsthai*] in a big way. |₁₁₄ Meanwhile, Hērā sped off, leaving the ridges of Olympus behind, |₁₁₅ and swiftly she reached Achaean Argos. She knew that she would find there |₁₁₆ the strong wife of Sthenelos son of Perseus. |₁₁₇ She was pregnant with a dear son, and she was in her sixth* month. |₁₁₈ And she brought him forth into the light, even though he was still premature in his months. |₁₁₉ Meanwhile she put a pause on the time of delivery for Alkmene, holding back the divine powers of labor, the Eileithuiai. |₁₂₀ And then she herself went to tell the news to Zeus the son of Kronos, saying: |₁₂₁ 'Zeus the father, you with the gleaming thunderbolt, I will put a word into your thoughts: |₁₂₂ there has just been born a man, a noble one, who will be king over the Argives. |₁₂₃ He is Eurystheus son of Sthenelos son of Perseus. |₁₂₄ He is from your line of ancestry, and it is not unseemly for him to be king over the Argives.' |₁₂₅ So she spoke, and he was struck in his mind [*phrēn*] with a sharp sorrow [*akhos*]. |₁₂₆ And right away he grabbed the goddess Atē by the head—that head covered with luxuriant curls— |₁₂₇ since he was angry in his thinking [*phrenes*], and he swore a binding oath |₁₂₈ that never will she come to Olympus and to the starry sky |₁₂₉ never again will she come back, that goddess Atē, who makes everyone veer off-course [*aâsthai*]. |₁₃₀ And so saying he threw her down from the starry sky, |₁₃₁ having whirled her around in his hand. And then she [= Atē] came to the fields where mortals live and work. |₁₃₂ He [= Zeus] always mourned the fact that she ever existed, every time he saw how his own dear son |₁₃₃ was having one of his degrading Labors [*āthloi*] to work on. |₁₃₄ So also I [= Agamemnon], while the great

---

*In the original Greek, with its inclusive counting system (which has no concept of zero), the numbering is 'seventh'.

Hector, the one with the gleaming helmet, |₁₃₅ was destroying the Argives [= Achaeans] at the sterns of the beached ships, |₁₃₆ was not able to keep out of my mind the veering [atē] I experienced once I veered off-course [aâsthai]. |₁₃₇ But since I did veer off-course [aâsthai] and since Zeus took away from me my thinking, |₁₃₈ I now want to make amends, and to give untold amounts of compensation."

Iliad XIX 76–138*

Before I proceed, let me pause to comment on details in the text that will not be obvious to someone who has just read the *Iliad* for the first time.

COMMENTARY ON HOUR 1 TEXT C

Verses 76–82. Agamemnon, who is the high king among all the kings of the Achaean warriors participating in the war at Troy, is speaking here in a public

---

* |₇₆ τοῖσι δὲ καὶ μετέειπεν ἄναξ ἀνδρῶν Ἀγαμέμνων |₇₇ αὐτόθεν ἐξ ἕδρης, οὐδ᾽ ἐν μέσσοισιν ἀναστάς· |₇₈ ὦ φίλοι ἥρωες Δαναοὶ θεράποντες Ἄρηος |₇₉ ἑσταότος μὲν καλὸν ἀκούειν, οὐδὲ ἔοικεν |₈₀ ὑββάλλειν· χαλεπὸν γὰρ ἐπισταμένῳ περ ἐόντι. |₈₁ ἀνδρῶν δ᾽ ἐν πολλῷ ὁμάδῳ πῶς κέν τις ἀκούσαι |₈₂ ἢ εἴποι; βλάβεται δὲ λιγύς περ ἐὼν ἀγορητής. |₈₃ Πηλείδη μὲν ἐγὼν ἐνδείξομαι· αὐτὰρ οἱ ἄλλοι |₈₄ σύνθεσθ᾽ Ἀργεῖοι, μῦθόν τ᾽ εὖ γνῶτε ἕκαστος. |₈₅ πολλάκι δή μοι τοῦτον Ἀχαιοὶ μῦθον ἔειπον |₈₆ καί τέ με νεικείεσκον· ἐγὼ δ᾽ οὐκ αἴτιός εἰμι, |₈₇ ἀλλὰ Ζεὺς καὶ Μοῖρα καὶ ἠεροφοῖτις Ἐρινύς, |₈₈ οἵ τέ μοι εἰν ἀγορῇ φρεσὶν ἔμβαλον ἄγριον ἄτην, |₈₉ ἤματι τῷ ὅτ᾽ Ἀχιλλῆος γέρας αὐτὸς ἀπηύρων. |₉₀ ἀλλὰ τί κεν ῥέξαιμι; θεὸς διὰ πάντα τελευτᾷ. |₉₁ πρέσβα Διὸς θυγάτηρ Ἄτη, ἣ πάντας ἀᾶται, |₉₂ οὐλομένη· τῇ μέν θ᾽ ἁπαλοὶ πόδες· οὐ γὰρ ἐπ᾽ οὔδει |₉₃ πίλναται, ἀλλ᾽ ἄρα ἥ γε κατ᾽ ἀνδρῶν κράατα βαίνει |₉₄ —βλάπτουσ᾽ ἀνθρώπους· κατὰ δ᾽ οὖν ἕτερόν γε πέδησε. |₉₅ καὶ γὰρ δή νύ ποτε Ζεὺς ἄσατο, τόν περ ἄριστον |₉₆ ἀνδρῶν ἠδὲ θεῶν φασ᾽ ἔμμεναι· ἀλλ᾽ ἄρα καὶ τὸν |₉₇ Ἥρη θῆλυς ἐοῦσα δολοφροσύνης ἀπάτησεν, |₉₈ ἤματι τῷ ὅτ᾽ ἔμελλε βίην Ἡρακληείην |₉₉ Ἀλκμήνη τέξεσθαι ἐϋστεφάνῳ ἐνὶ Θήβῃ. |₁₀₀ ἤτοι ὅ γ᾽ εὐχόμενος μετέφη πάντεσσι θεοῖσι· |₁₀₁ κέκλυτέ μευ πάντες τε θεοὶ πᾶσαί τε θέαιναι, |₁₀₂ ὄφρ᾽ εἴπω τά με θυμὸς ἐνὶ στήθεσσιν ἀνώγει. |₁₀₃ σήμερον ἄνδρα φόως δὲ μογοστόκος Εἰλείθυια |₁₀₄ ἐκφανεῖ, ὃς πάντεσσι περικτιόνεσσιν ἀνάξει |₁₀₅ τῶν ἀνδρῶν γενεῆς οἵ θ᾽ αἵματος ἐξ ἐμεῦ εἰσί. |₁₀₆ τὸν δὲ δολοφρονέουσα προσηύδα πότνια Ἥρη· |₁₀₇ ψευστήσεις, οὐδ᾽ αὖτε τέλος μύθῳ ἐπιθήσεις. |₁₀₈ εἰ δ᾽ ἄγε νῦν μοι ὄμοσσον Ὀλύμπιε καρτερὸν ὅρκον, |₁₀₉ ἦ μὲν τὸν πάντεσσι περικτιόνεσσιν ἀνάξειν |₁₁₀ ὅς κεν ἐπ᾽ ἤματι τῷδε πέσῃ μετὰ ποσσὶ γυναικὸς |₁₁₁ τῶν ἀνδρῶν οἳ σῆς ἐξ αἵματός εἰσι γενέθλης. |₁₁₂ ὣς ἔφατο· Ζεὺς δ᾽ οὔ τι δολοφροσύνην ἐνόησεν, |₁₁₃ ἀλλ᾽ ὄμοσεν μέγαν ὅρκον, ἔπειτα δὲ πολλὸν ἀάσθη. |₁₁₄ Ἥρη δ᾽ ἀΐξασα λίπεν ῥίον Οὐλύμποιο, |₁₁₅ καρπαλίμως δ᾽ ἵκετ᾽ Ἄργος Ἀχαιικόν, ἔνθ᾽ ἄρα ᾔδη |₁₁₆ ἰφθίμην ἄλοχον Σθενέλου Περσηϊάδαο. |₁₁₇ ἣ δ᾽ ἐκύει φίλον υἱόν, ὁ δ᾽ ἕβδομος ἑστήκει μείς· |₁₁₈ ἐκ δ᾽ ἄγαγε πρὸ φόως δὲ καὶ ἠλιτόμηνον ἐόντα, |₁₁₉ Ἀλκμήνης δ᾽ ἀπέπαυσε τόκον, σχέθε δ᾽ Εἰλειθυίας. |₁₂₀ αὐτὴ δ᾽ ἀγγελέουσα Δία Κρονίωνα προσηύδα· |₁₂₁ Ζεῦ πάτερ ἀργικέραυνε ἔπος τί τοι ἐν φρεσὶ θήσω· |₁₂₂ ἤδη ἀνὴρ γέγον᾽ ἐσθλὸς ὃς Ἀργείοισιν ἀνάξει |₁₂₃ Εὐρυσθεὺς Σθενέλοιο πάϊς Περσηϊάδαο |₁₂₄ σὸν γένος· οὔ οἱ ἀεικὲς ἀνασσέμεν Ἀργείοισιν. |₁₂₅ ὣς φάτο, τὸν δ᾽ ἄχος ὀξὺ κατὰ φρένα τύψε βαθεῖαν. |₁₂₆ αὐτίκα δ᾽ εἷλ᾽ Ἄτην κεφαλῆς λιπαροπλοκάμοιο |₁₂₇ χωόμενος φρεσὶν ᾗσι, καὶ ὤμοσε καρτερὸν ὅρκον |₁₂₈ μή ποτ᾽ ἐς Οὔλυμπόν τε καὶ οὐρανὸν ἀστερόεντα |₁₂₉ αὖτις ἐλεύσεσθαι Ἄτην, ἣ πάντας ἀᾶται. |₁₃₀ ὣς εἰπὼν ἔρριψεν ἀπ᾽ οὐρανοῦ ἀστερόεντος |₁₃₁ χειρὶ περιστρέψας· τάχα δ᾽ ἵκετο ἔργ᾽ ἀνθρώπων. |₁₃₂ τὴν αἰεὶ στενάχεσχ᾽ ὅθ᾽ ἑὸν φίλον υἱὸν ὁρῷτο |₁₃₃ ἔργον ἀεικὲς ἔχοντα ὑπ᾽ Εὐρυσθῆος ἀέθλων. |₁₃₄ ὣς καὶ ἐγών, ὅτε δ᾽ αὖτε μέγας κορυθαίολος Ἕκτωρ |₁₃₅ Ἀργείους ὀλέκεσκεν ἐπὶ πρυμνῇσι νέεσσιν, |₁₃₆ οὐ δυνάμην λελαθέσθ᾽ Ἄτης ᾗ πρῶτον ἀάσθην. |₁₃₇ ἀλλ᾽ ἐπεὶ ἀασάμην καί μευ φρένας ἐξέλετο Ζεύς, |₁₃₈ ἂψ ἐθέλω ἀρέσαι, δόμεναί τ᾽ ἀπερείσι᾽ ἄποινα.

assembly of the Achaeans. Strangely, he speaks to his fellow warriors while remaining in a seated position (77), saying that it is a good thing to listen to a man who speaks in a standing position and that it is hard for even a good speaker to *hupoballein** him (80). So what does this mean? Achilles had just spoken to the assembly at verses 56–73, and verse 55 makes it explicit that *he* was standing.† In the Greek-English dictionary of Liddell, Scott, and Jones (abbreviated LSJ), *hupoballein* is interpreted as 'interrupt' in the context of verse 80 here. A related context is the adverb *hupoblēdēn*‡ at *Iliad* I 292, where Achilles is responding to Agamemnon in the course of their famous quarrel. Some translate that adverb as 'interruptingly'.§ Instead, I interpret *hupoballein* and *hupoblēdēn* as 'speak in relay [after someone]' and 'speaking in relay' respectively, and I argue that the concept of relay speaking is a characteristic of competitive speech-making.** As Richard Martin has shown, the *Iliad* can dramatize Agamemnon and Achilles in the act of competing with each other as speakers, not only as warriors and leaders, and Achilles is consistently portrayed as the better speaker by far.†† At *Iliad* I 292, where I interpret *hupoblēdēn* as 'speaking in relay', Achilles engages in verbal combat with Agamemnon not so much by way of 'interrupting' as by picking up the train of thought exactly where his opponent left off—and out-performing him in the process. So, here at *Iliad* XIX 80, Agamemnon backs off from verbal combat with Achilles, using as an excuse the fact that he is wounded: I can't stand up, and therefore I can't compete by picking up the train of thought where Achilles left off—and therefore I can't out-perform him (and perhaps I don't anymore have the stomach even to try to do so). The successful performer remains standing, and the unsuccessful performer fails to stand up and compete by taking his turn, choosing instead to sit it out. He will still speak to Achilles, but he will speak without offering any more competition.‡‡

Verse 83. Instead of competing with Achilles as a public speaker, Agamemnon says that all he wants to do now is to make Achilles an offer.

Verses 83–84. Agamemnon says that he will say a *mūthos* (84, 85). As Richard Martin has shown, this word as used in Homeric poetry means 'something

---

* ὑββάλλειν.
† For more on this contrast between the seated Agamemnon and the standing Achilles, see Elmer 2013:127.
‡ ὑποβλήδην.
§ Details in *PR* 20.
** *PR* 21–22.
†† Martin 1989:117; also 63, 69–70, 98, 113, 117, 119, 133, 202, 219, 223, 228.
‡‡ *PR* 21.

said for the record'; *mūthos* "is a speech-act indicating authority, performed at length, *usually in public,* with a focus on full attention to every detail."* Another example of *mūthos* occurs at verse 107, where it is Zeus who says something for the record. Among the subcategories of the kinds of things that are 'said for the record' are stories that we call myths. In Homeric terms, any story that is called a *mūthos* is genuine and true, because it is said for the record; the modern derivative *myth* has obviously veered from this meaning.†

Verses 85–86. According to Agamemnon, the myth about Hēraklēs has been used against him by the Achaeans. But he will now use the same myth to excuse himself.

Verses 86–87. The kind of excuse that Agamemnon uses—that he is not personally *aitios,* 'responsible', because the gods caused him to experience *atē,* 'derangement'—is explored at length in Greek tragedy. We will see it most clearly in a tragedy of Aeschylus, the *Agamemnon,* as analyzed in Hour 16.

Verse 88. The word *atē,* 'derangement', is both a passive experience, as described here by Agamemnon, and an active force that is personified as the goddess Atē, as we see later at verse 91 and following.

Verse 91. In Homeric poetry, the word *atē,* 'derangement', is perceived as a noun derived from the verb *aâsthai,* 'veer off-course'.‡

Verse 95. Once again, *aâsthai,* 'veer off-course', is used as the verb of *atē,* 'derangement'.

Verse 105. The wording of Zeus hides the fact that Hēraklēs was fathered directly by him.

Verse 111. The wording of Hērā hides the fact that she is speaking about the mother-to-be of Eurystheus, and that this woman is the wife of the hero Sthenelos, who is the son of the hero Perseus, who in turn was fathered directly by Zeus. Later, at verses 116 and 123, the identity of this woman is revealed. For now, however, Zeus is being deceived into thinking that Hērā is speaking about the mother-to-be of Hēraklēs.

Verse 113. Once again, *aâsthai,* 'veer off-course', is used as the verb of *atē,* 'derangement'.

Verse 117. The mother-to-be of Eurystheus is said to be in her sixth month of pregnancy, and so she has three more months to go before her due date. In the

---

* Martin 1989:12.

† *HQ* 119–125, 127–133, 152.

‡ Extensive commentary on the meaning of *atē* can be found in *PH* 242–243 = 8§§41–42.

original Greek, with its inclusive counting system, the actual numbering is 'seventh', but I translate it as 'sixth'.

Verses 136–137. Once again, *aâsthai,* 'veer off-course', is used as the verb of *atē,* 'derangement'.

Now that this commentary is in place, I can return to my line of argumentation.

1§37. In the passage we have just read, Text C, the high king Agamemnon is telling the story about Hēraklēs and his inferior cousin Eurystheus. The goddess Hērā accelerated the birth of Eurystheus and retarded the birth of Hēraklēs, so that Eurystheus the inferior hero became king, entitled to give commands to the superior hero Hēraklēs. As we see in the *Herakles* of Euripides, Hēraklēs qualifies as the supreme hero of them all, the *aristos,* or 'best', of all humans (verse 150; see also verses 183, 208, 1306).* Still, the heroic superiority of Hēraklēs is trumped by the social superiority of Eurystheus, who is entitled by seniority in birth to become the high king and to give orders to Hēraklēs. Similarly, the heroic superiority of Achilles is trumped by the social superiority of Agamemnon at the beginning of the *Iliad.*

1§38. The twist in this story told by Agamemnon, in micro-narrative form, is made clear by the macro-Narrative of the story that is the *Iliad.* In terms of Agamemnon's micro-narrative, the point of his story is that Atē, the goddess of 'derangement', made it possible for Zeus himself to make a mistake in the story about Hēraklēs, just as this same goddess Atē made it possible for Agamemnon to make a mistake in the story of the *Iliad.* In terms of the macro-Narrative of the *Iliad,* however, the parallel extends much further: the mistake in the story about Hēraklēs and Eurystheus is that the hero who was superior as a hero became socially inferior, and that is also the mistake in the story about Achilles and Agamemnon as narrated in the overall *Iliad:* Achilles is superior to Agamemnon as a hero, but he is socially inferior to him, and that is why Agamemnon seemed to get away with the mistake of asserting his social superiority at the expense of Achilles. Like Hēraklēs, who is constrained by the social superiority of Eurystheus and follows his commands in performing *āthloi,* 'labors' (XIX 133), so also Achilles is constrained by the social superiority of Agamemnon in offering no physical resistance to the taking of the young woman Briseis, his war prize, by the inferior hero.

---

* An English-language translation of Euripides' *Herakles* is available in the online *Sourcebook* (chs.harvard.edu).

1§39. The performance of *āthloi*, 'labors', by Hēraklēs is mentioned in passing by this micro-narrative in the *Iliad* (XIX 133). As we are about to see from other sources, the Labors of Hēraklēs lead to the *kleos*, 'glory', that Hēraklēs earns as a hero, and these Labors would never have been performed if Hērā, the goddess of seasons, had not made Hēraklēs the hero unseasonal by being born after rather than before his inferior cousin. So Hēraklēs owes the *kleos* that he earns from his Labors to Hērā.

The Labors of Hēraklēs

1§40. There are many different kinds of Labors performed by Hēraklēs, as we see from an extensive retelling by Diodorus of Sicily (4.8–4.39). The work of this author, who lived in the first century BCE, is not part of our reading list of ancient texts, as contained in the *Sourcebook,* and so I will summarize his narrative here to highlight some essential features of the overall story of Hēraklēs.

1§41. One of the Labors of Hēraklēs, as we see from Diodorus, was the foundation of the athletic festival of the Olympics. The story as retold by Diodorus (4.14.1–2) says that Hēraklēs not only founded this major festival but also competed in every athletic event on the prototypical occasion of the first Olympics. At that time, he won first prize in every Olympic event. This tradition about Hēraklēs is the perfect illustration of a fundamental connection between the labor of a hero and the competition of an athlete at athletic events like the Olympics. As we can see when we read Hour 8b, the hero's labor and the athlete's competition are the "same thing," from the standpoint of ancient Greek concepts of the hero. The Greek word for the hero's labor and for the athlete's competition is the same: *āthlos*. Our English word *athlete* is a borrowing from the Greek word *āthlētēs*, which is derived from *āthlos*.

1§42. Before we consider further Labors performed by Hēraklēs, I would like to paraphrase the beginning of the story of these Labors as narrated by Diodorus (4.9.2–4.9.5):

> The supreme god and king of gods, Zeus, impregnates Alkmene, a mortal woman (4.9.2). The wife of Zeus, the goddess Hērā, is jealous; she decides to intervene in the life of the hero who is about to be born, Hēraklēs (4.9.4). If this hero had been born on schedule, *on time, in time,* he would have been the supreme king of his time; but Hērā makes sure that Hēraklēs is born not on schedule, *not on time, not in time.*

Hēraklēs' inferior cousin, Eurystheus, is born ahead of him and thus is fated to become king instead of Hēraklēs (4.9.4–5). During all of Hēraklēs' lifetime, Eurystheus persecutes him directly; Hērā persecutes him indirectly. The superior hero has to spend his entire lifespan obeying the orders of the inferior king (4.9.5). Hēraklēs follows up on each one of the orders, and his accomplishments in the process add up to the Labors of Hēraklēs.

1§43. In the classical period, the Labors of Hēraklēs were represented most famously in a set of relief sculptures that decorated the Temple of Zeus in Olympia, built in the fifth century BCE. These relief sculptures, the technical term for which is *metopes,* focused on a canonical number of twelve Labors performed by Hēraklēs. Diodorus narrates all twelve (4.11.3–4.26.4):

1. Hēraklēs kills the Nemean Lion (4.11.3–4).
2. Hēraklēs kills the Lernaean Hydra (4.11.5–6).
3. Hēraklēs kills the Erymanthian Boar (4.12.1–2).
4. Hēraklēs hunts down the Hind with the Golden Horn (4.13.1).
5. Hēraklēs clears the Stymphalian Marsh of the noxious birds that infested it (4.13.2).
6. Hēraklēs clears the manure from the Augean Stables (4.13.3).
7. Hēraklēs captures the Cretan Bull alive and brings it to the Peloponnesus (4.13.4).
8. Hēraklēs corrals the Horses of Diomedes, eaters of human flesh (4.15.3–4).
9. Hēraklēs captures the waistband or 'girdle' of the Amazon Hippolyte (4.16.1–4).
10. Hēraklēs rustles the Cattle of Geryon (4.17.1–2).
11. Hēraklēs descends to Hādēs and brings up Cerberus the Hound of Hādēs from the zone of darkness to the zone of light and life (4.26.1).
12. Hēraklēs gathers the Golden Apples of the Hesperides (4.26.2–4).

1§44. In the catalogue of the Labors of Hēraklēs as sung and danced in praise of the hero by the chorus in the tragedy by Euripides entitled the *Herakles* (lines 348–440), the last of these Labors to be mentioned is the descent of Hēraklēs to Hādēs (425–435); in the imagery of Euripides, and elsewhere in Greek poetry and song, as we will see, the experience of going into Hādēs is explicitly the experience of dying, and the experience of coming back out of Hādēs is implicitly the experience of resurrection (lines 143–146).

Hēraklēs and the Meaning of Kleos

1§45. Hēraklēs' heroic deeds in performing these Labors and many others are the raw material for the heroic song, *kleos*, that is sung about him. The connection of the name of Hēraklēs with these deeds and with the medium of *kleos* that glorifies them is made explicit in the *Herakles* of Euripides (lines 271, 1335, 1370). This connection of the hero's name with these deeds of *kleos* is also made explicit by Diodorus (1.24.4 and 4.10.1).* And, as I have already noted, Hēraklēs owes the *kleos* that he earns from his Labors to Hērā. That is how he gets his name *Hēraklēs*, which means 'he who has the *kleos* of Hērā'.† The goddess of *being on time* makes sure that the hero should start off his lifespan by *not being on time* and that he should go through life by trying to catch up—and never quite managing to do so until the very end. Hēraklēs gets all caught up only at the final moment of his life, at the moment of death.

1§46. I continue here my paraphrase of Diodorus (4.38.1–4.39.3):

> At the final moment of Hēraklēs' heroic lifespan, he experiences the most painful death imaginable, climaxed by burning to death. This form of death is an ultimate test of the nervous system, by ancient Greek heroic standards. Here is how it happens. Hēraklēs is fatally poisoned when his skin makes contact with the semen of a dying Centaur. The estranged wife of Hēraklēs, Deianeira, had preserved this poisonous substance in a vial, and she smears it on an undergarment called a khiton that she sends to Hēraklēs in a vain attempt to regain his affections; the hero had asked for a cloak and a khiton to be sent to him so that he could perform a sacrifice to Zeus after capturing Iole, a younger woman whom he now intends to marry (4.38.1–2). Hēraklēs gets dressed for the sacrifice and puts on the khiton. The consequences

---

* Diodorus 1.24.4 attributes this information to Matris of Thebes, *FGH* 39 F 2; in 4.10.1, Diodorus actually retells the version attributed to Matris.

† On the linguistic validity of the etymology of his name, see *HQ* 48n79. The problem of the short *a* in the middle of the form *Hēraklēs* can best be addressed by comparing the short *a* in the middle of the form *Alkăthoos*, the name of a hero of Megara (as in Theognis 774) who is closely related thematically to Hēraklēs. I owe this solution to Alexander Nikolaev.

are fatal. Once the skin of Hēraklēs makes contact with the poison smeared on the undergarment, he starts burning up on the inside as the poison rapidly pervades his body from the outside. The pain is excruciating, and Hēraklēs knows he is doomed. He arranges with the people of Trachis to have them build for him a funeral pyre on the peak of Mount Oeta, and then he climbs up on top of the funeral pyre (4.38.3–4). He yearns to be put out of his misery, ready to die and be consumed by the fires of the funeral pyre; he calls on his friend Philoktetes to light his pyre (4.38.4). At that precise moment of agonizing death, a flaming thunderbolt from his father Zeus strikes him. He goes up in flames, in a spectacular explosion of fire (4.38.4–5). In the aftermath, those who attended the primal scene find no physical trace of Hēraklēs, not even bones (4.38.5). They go home to Trachis, but Menoitios, the father of Patroklos, will later establish a hero cult for Hēraklēs at Opous, and the Thebans have a similar hero cult for him (4.38.1). Others, however, especially the Athenians, worship Hēraklēs not as a hero but as a god (4.39.1). The rationale for this alternative custom is given by the continuation of the myth as retold by Diodorus: at the moment of his death, Hēraklēs regains consciousness and finds himself on the top of Mount Olympus, in the company of the gods (4.39.2–3). He has awakened to find himself immortalized. He is then adopted by the *theoi*, 'gods', on Mount Olympus as one of their own (the technical Greek term is *apotheosis*). Hērā now changes identities —from Hēraklēs' stepmother to Hēraklēs' mother (4.39.2). The procedure is specified by Diodorus, and I translate literally (4.39.2): 'Hērā got into her bed and drew Hēraklēs close to her body; then she ejected him through her clothes to the ground, re-enacting [= making *mīmēsis* of] genuine birth' *(tēn de teknōsin genesthai phasi toiautēn: tēn Hēran anabasan epi klinēn kai ton Hēraklea proslabomenēn pros to sōma dia tōn endumatōn apheinai pros tēn gēn, mimoumenēn tēn alēthinēn genesin).**

1§47. Birth by Hērā is the hero's rebirth, a birth into immortality.† Death by lightning is the key to this rebirth: the thunderbolt of Zeus, so prominently fea-

---

* In Hour 8e, I will analyze the meaning of *mīmēsis* as 're-enactment'.

† This formulation comes from the analysis in EH §75, and the rest of my paragraph here draws further on that analysis.

tured in the poetry of cosmogony and anthropogony, simultaneously destroys and regenerates. Elysium, one of many different names given to an imagined paradisiacal place of immortalization for heroes after death, is related to the word *en-ēlusion*, which designates a place struck by lightning—a place made sacred by contact with the thunderbolt of Zeus.* As I said in the Introduction to Homeric Poetry (0§6), the hero can be *immortalized*, but the fundamental painful fact remains: the hero is not by nature *immortal*.

1§48. By now we can see that the name *Hēraklēs*, 'he who has the glory [*kleos*] of Hērā', marks both the medium and the message of the hero. But when we first consider the meaning of the name of Hēraklēs, our first impression is that this name is illogical: it seems to us strange that Hēraklēs should be named after Hērā—that his poetic glory, or *kleos*, should depend on Hērā. After all, Hēraklēs is persecuted by Hērā throughout his heroic lifespan. And yet, without this unseasonality, without the disequilibrium brought about by the persecution of Hērā, Hēraklēs would never have achieved the equilibrium of immortality and the *kleos*, or 'glory', that makes his achievements live forever in song.

Hēraklēs and the Idea of the Hero

1§49. At the core of the narratives about Hēraklēs is the meaning of *hērōs*, 'hero', as a cognate of *Hērā*, the goddess of seasonality and equilibrium, and of *hōrā*, a noun that actually means 'seasonality' in the context of designating hero cult, as in the *Homeric Hymn to Demeter* 265.† The decisive verse that I cite here from *Homeric Hymn to Demeter* will be quoted in Hour 8 Text C and analyzed in Hour 8§§20–21. The unseasonality of the *hērōs* in mortal life leads to the *telos*, or 'fulfillment', of *hōrā*, 'seasonality', in immortal life, which is achieved in the setting of hero cult, as we will see in Hour 13§§11–22. Such a concept of *telos* as 'fulfillment' is also expressed by an adjectival derivative of *telos*, which is *teleia*, used as a cult epithet that conventionally describes the goddess *Hērā*.‡ That is, *Hērā* is the goddess of *telos* in the sense of 'fulfillment', as we will see in Hour 13§18.

1§50. Overall, the narratives about Hēraklēs fit neatly into a model of the hero as I outline it in a general article on the topic of the epic hero.§ I offer here

---

* *GM* 140–142.
† *PH* 140n27 = 5§7; *GM* 136. See also Davidson 1980 and 2013a:89–90.
‡ This cult epithet for Hērā, *teleia*, is attested, for example, in Aristophanes *Women at the Thesmophoria* 973.
§ *EH* §§105–110.

a shortened version of the outline that I develop there. In terms of that outline, there are three characteristics of the hero:

1. The hero is unseasonal.
2. The hero is extreme—positively (for example, 'best' in whatever category) or negatively (the negative aspect can be a function of the hero's unseasonality).
3. The hero is antagonistic toward the god who seems to be most like the hero; antagonism does not rule out an element of attraction—often a 'fatal attraction'—which is played out in a variety of ways.

1§51. All three characteristics converge in the figure of the hero Hēraklēs:

1. He is made unseasonal by Hērā.
2. His unseasonality makes it possible for him to perform his extraordinary Labors. He also commits some deeds that are morally questionable: for example, he destroys the city of Iole and kills the brothers of this princess in order to capture her as his bride—even though he is already married to Deianeira (Diodorus of Sicily 4.37.5).
3. He is antagonistic with Hērā throughout his lifespan, but he becomes reconciled with her through death: as we have seen, the hero becomes the virtual son of Hērā by being reborn from her. As the hero's name makes clear, he owes his heroic identity to his *kleos* and, ultimately, to Hērā. A parallel is the antagonism of Juno, the Roman equivalent of Hērā, toward the hero Aeneas in Virgil's *Aeneid.*

1§52. Before we go on, I must highlight the fact that the story of Hēraklēs includes the committing of deeds that are morally questionable. *It is essential to keep in mind that whenever heroes commit deeds that violate moral codes, such deeds are not condoned by the heroic narrative.* As we will see later, in Hours 6, 7, 8, and 18, the pollution of a hero in myth is relevant to the worship of that hero in ritual.

1§53. That said, I now proceed with paraphrases of two further details about the life of Hēraklēs:

Hērā finds an abandoned baby, who happens to be Hēraklēs. She takes a fancy to the baby and breast-feeds it, but the baby bites her. This part of the narrative is reported by Diodorus of Sicily (4.9.6). Another part of the narrative is reported elsewhere: the breast-feeding of Hēraklēs by Hērā goes awry and results in a cosmic spilling of milk, a galaxy (Greek *galakt-* means 'milk')—that is, the Milky Way ([Eratosthenes] *Katasterismoi* 3.44; Hyginus *Astronomica* 2.43; "Achilles" *Astronomica* 24).

Hēraklēs' mortal mother, Alkmene, conceives another son by her mortal husband, Amphitryon, on the same night she conceives her son Hēraklēs by her immortal paramour, Zeus (Apollodorus *Library* 2.4.8). This twin, Iphikles, is mortal. The other twin, Hēraklēs, is mortal only on his mother's side. I do not say *half-mortal* or *half-divine* in this case, and I will give my reasons when we reach Hour 6.

Achilles and the Idea of the Hero

1§54. Now that I have outlined the basics of the narratives about Hēraklēs, I turn to the basics about Achilles. We find in the figure of Achilles the same three heroic characteristics that we found in Hēraklēs:

1. He is unseasonal: in *Iliad* XXIV 540, Achilles is explicitly described as *pan-a-(h)ōr-ios*, 'the most unseasonal of them all'.* His unseasonality is a major cause of his grief, which makes him *a man of constant sorrow*. In using this phrase, I have in mind here the title of a traditional American folk song, first recorded by Dick Burnett, a partially blind fiddler from Kentucky. The grief over the unseasonality of Achilles is best expressed by the hero's mother, Thetis, in *Iliad* XVIII 54–62, a passage that will figure prominently in Hour 4§23.

2. He is extreme, mostly in a positive sense, since he is 'best' in many categories, and 'best of the Achaeans' in the Homeric *Iliad*; occasionally, however, he is extreme in a negative sense, as in his moments of martial fury. In Hour 6, I will have more to say about such martial fury, otherwise known as *warp spasm*.

3. He is antagonistic to the god Apollo, to whom he bears an uncanny resemblance. Again in Hour 6, I will have more to say about the antagonism of Apollo with the hero Achilles.

* *HQ* 48.

Achilles and the Meaning of Kleos

1§55. There is another important parallel between Hēraklēs and Achilles: the use of the word *kleos*, 'glory', in identifying Hēraklēs as a hero is relevant to the fact that the same word is used in identifying Achilles as an epic hero in the Homeric *Iliad*. In the *Iliad*, *kleos* designates not only 'glory' but also, more specifically, *the glory of the hero as conferred by epic*. As we have seen in Hour 1 Text A, *Iliad* IX 413, Achilles chooses *kleos* over life itself, and he owes his heroic identity to this *kleos*.*

1§56. So we end up where we started, with the hero Achilles. He chooses *kleos* over life itself, and he owes his heroic identity to this *kleos*. He achieves the major goal of the hero: to have his identity put permanently *on record* through *kleos*. For us, a common way to express this goal is to say: 'You'll go down in history.' For the earliest periods of ancient Greece, the equivalent of this kind of 'history' is *kleos*.

1§57. In J. D. Salinger's *Catcher in the Rye* (1951), Holden Caulfield is given this lesson by the teacher: "The mark of the immature man is that he wants to die nobly for a cause, while the mark of a mature man is that he wants to live humbly for one."

1§58. My guess is that Achilles would respond negatively to such a teaching: *in that case, I would rather be immature than mature*. Still, as we will see, Achilles will achieve a maturity, a seasonality, at the moment in the *Iliad* when he comes to terms with his own impending heroic death.

1§59. I close for now by quoting what the teacher goes on to say in Salinger's narrative: "Many, many men have been just as troubled morally and spiritually as you are right now. Happily, some of them *kept records* of their troubles. You'll learn from them . . . if you want to. It's a beautiful reciprocal arrangement. And it isn't education. It's history. It's poetry."†

---

* *HR* 39–48.
† Emphasis is mine.

Achilles as Epic Hero and the Idea of Total Recall in Song

The Meaning of Memnēmai

2§1. The key word for this hour is *memnēmai*, which means 'I have total recall' in special contexts and 'I remember' in ordinary contexts. The special contexts involve *memory by way of song*. I will get to the specifics later.

HOUR 2 TEXT A

|₅₂₇ *I totally recall [me-mnē-mai] how this was done—it happened a long time ago, it is not something new—*|₅₂₈ recalling exactly how it was. I will tell it in your company—since you are all near and dear [*philoi*].

Iliad IX 527–528*

2§2. In the paragraphs that follow, I offer an exegesis of this passage (in the previous hour, I defined *exegesis* as an ancient Greek term referring to *a close reading of a given text*).

2§3. So now I proceed to analyze the verb *memnēmai*, containing the root *mnē-*, which means 'I remember'. When this verb takes an object in the genitive case, it means 'I remember' in a general sense: 'I have memories of . . .' But when this verb takes an object in the accusative case, as here, it means 'I remember' in a special sense: 'I remember totally . . .'

Phoenix and His Total Recall

2§4. The hero Phoenix, an old man, is about to tell a tale that he says he remembers totally. This tale is a micro-narrative embedded in the macro-Narrative

---

* |₅₂₇ μέμνημαι τόδε ἔργον ἐγὼ πάλαι οὔ τι νέον γε |₅₂₈ ὡς ἦν· ἐν δ' ὑμῖν ἐρέω πάντεσσι φίλοισι.

that is the *Iliad*. Before Phoenix tells his tale, he speaks to those who are listening to him, telling them that they are *philoi*, 'near and dear' to him. Who are these 'near and dear' listeners?

2§5. From the standpoint of Phoenix, there are six listeners. These are (1) the hero Achilles; (2) the hero Patroklos, who is the best friend of Achilles; (3 and 4) the heroes Ajax and Odysseus; and (5 and 6) two professional announcers, or 'heralds'. From the standpoint of those who are listening to a performance of the Homeric *Iliad*, however, they too are listeners. So the question is, are they also 'near and dear'? My answer, as we will see in what follows, is that the audience of Homeric poetry is *presumed* to be near and dear.

2§6. The word *philoi*, which I translate here as 'near and dear', can also be translated simply as 'friends' in this same context. This word *philos* (plural *philoi*) means 'friend' as a noun and 'near and dear' as an adjective. It is a term of endearment, an emotional term. As we will see later, this emotional term is most important for understanding the story of Phoenix.

2§7. Phoenix says that he has a total recall of the tale he is about to tell his 'near and dear' listeners. Whereas in the original Greek, the word for such total recall is *memnēmai,* the term I use here, *total recall,* is borrowed from popular culture. I have in mind a film entitled *Total Recall* (1990), directed by Paul Verhoeven, featuring Arnold Schwarzenegger and Sharon Stone, which was based on a science fiction "novelette" by Philip K. Dick, "We Can Remember It for You Wholesale," first published in *The Magazine of Fantasy & Science Fiction* (April 1966).

2§8. I find it relevant here to recall something we just read in the previous hour. It was a quotation from J. D. Salinger's *Catcher in the Rye,* where Holden Caulfield is being given a lesson by his teacher: "The mark of the immature man is that he wants to die nobly for a cause, while the mark of a mature man is that he wants to live humbly for one." The teacher goes on to say: "Many, many men have been just as troubled morally and spiritually as you are right now. Happily, some of them *kept records* of their troubles. You'll learn from them . . . if you want to. It's a beautiful reciprocal arrangement. And it isn't education. It's history. It's poetry."*

2§9. The word *history* here refers simply to *keeping a record.* For the moment, I highlight the idea of *keeping a record.* We have an interesting way of using the word *record* these days—in an era when new technologies have replaced the old vinyl "records." Some of us still speak of "records" even though vinyl imprints

---

* Emphasis is mine.

hardly exist anymore. I suspect we speak this way because the idea of *memory* is embedded in the word *records*.

2§10. Let us pursue further the concept of *keeping a record, recording, putting on record*. In the earliest phases of ancient Greek song culture, the process of keeping a record of things that must be remembered, of putting things on the record, was not ordinarily done by way of writing. Writing did not become a widespread technology in the ancient Greek world until around the fifth century BCE, and even then it was confined to the uppermost strata of society. In the archaic period of Greek history (that is, the era extending from the eighth century to the middle of the fifth century), the idea of recording was mostly a matter of memory and of techniques of memory, mnemonics. It is in this connection that we confront the mentality of *total recall*.

2§11. The wording *total recall* is meant to convey a special mentality of remembering, of putting things on record, common in traditional societies. In terms of this mentality, *to remember is to re-live an experience*, including someone else's experience, including even the experiences of heroes in the remote past of the heroic age.

The Idea of Kleos *as a Medium of Total Recall*

2§12. The process of *remembering* in ancient Greek song culture requires a special medium, *song*. When I say *song* here, I include *poetry*, even though the word *poetry* in modern usage is understood to be different from *song*. In the ancient Greek song culture, however, both poetry and song are understood to be a medium of *singing*. And such singing is an *oral tradition*. The epic poetry of the Homeric *Iliad* and *Odyssey* derives from such an oral tradition of singing, which is a process of *composition-in-performance*. That is, composition is an aspect of performance and vice versa.* In this kind of oral tradition, there is no script, since the technology of writing is not required for composition-in-performance. In Homeric poetry, the basic medium of remembering is heroic song, or *kleos*.

2§13. This word *kleos*, 'glory', which we considered in Hour 1, will figure prominently here in Hour 2 as well. I started the present hour by referring to a tale told by the old hero Phoenix. When he introduces his tale, Phoenix uses this word *kleos* in the context of referring to his total recall:

* *HQ* 17.

HOUR 2 TEXT B (WHICH INCLUDES TEXT A)

|₅₂₄ This is how [houtōs] we [= I, Phoenix] learned it, the glories [klea] of men [andrōn] of an earlier time [prosthen], |₅₂₅ who were heroes [hērōes], whenever one of them was overcome by tempestuous anger. |₅₂₆ They could be persuaded by way of gifts and could be swayed by words. |₅₂₇ I totally recall [me-mnē-mai] how this was done—it happened a long time ago, it is not something new— |₅₂₈ recalling exactly how it was. I will tell it in your company—since you are all near and dear [philoi].

Iliad IX 524–528*

2§14. The word *klea*, 'glories', the abbreviated plural form of *kleos*, 'glory', is combined here in verses 524 and 525 with *tōn prosthen . . . andrōn*, 'of men of an earlier time', and *hērōōn*, 'of heroes [hērōes]'. This expression *tōn prosthen . . . klea andrōn* | *hērōōn*, 'the glories of men of an earlier time, who were heroes', or a shorter form of the expression, *klea andrōn*, 'the glories of men', is used in Homeric poetry to refer to *epic narrative*. When Phoenix uses this expression here, he is referring to an epic tale that he is about to tell about the hero Meleagros. As we will see, this same expression *klea andrōn (hērōōn)*, 'the glories of men (who were heroes)', applies not only to the epic narrative about Meleagros but also to the epic narrative about Achilles, which is the *Iliad*.

The Idea of Kleos as Epic Narrative

2§15. In general, the word *kleos* applies to epic narrative as performed by the master Narrator of Homeric poetry. Etymologically, *kleos* is a noun derived from the verb *kluein*, 'hear', and it means 'that which is heard'. In the *Iliad*, the master Narrator declares that *the epic he narrates is something he 'hears' from goddesses of poetic memory called the Muses, who know everything because they were present when everything was done and when everything was said.* Here is the passage in which the master Narrator makes his declaration:

---

* |₅₂₄ οὕτω καὶ τῶν πρόσθεν ἐπευθόμεθα κλέα ἀνδρῶν |₅₂₅ ἡρώων, ὅτε κέν τιν' ἐπιζάφελος χόλος ἵκοι. |₅₂₆ δωρητοί τε πέλοντο παράρρητοί τ' ἐπέεσσι. |₅₂₇ μέμνημαι τόδε ἔργον ἐγὼ πάλαι οὔ τι νέον γε |₅₂₈ ὡς ἦν· ἐν δ' ὑμῖν ἐρέω πάντεσσι φίλοισι.

HOUR 2 TEXT C

|₄₈₄ And now, tell me, O Muses, you who live in your Olympian abodes,
|₄₈₅ since *you* are goddesses and you were *there* and you know every-
thing, |₄₈₆ but we [= the Narrator] only hear the *kleos* and we know
nothing |₄₈₇—who were the chiefs and princes of the Danaans [= the
Achaeans]?

Iliad II 484–487*

2§16. When we read this passage initially, our first impression may be that
the Narrator of epic is making a modest statement about the limitations of his
own knowledge. In fact, however, what we are seeing here is just the opposite.
The Narrator is making a most proud and boastful statement. He is boasting
that his mind is directly connected to what the Muses as goddesses of memory
actually saw and heard. The Muses 'tell' him what they saw and heard. What he
narrates about heroes and even about gods is exactly what the Muses *saw*. What
he quotes from the spoken words of heroes and even of gods is exactly what the
Muses *heard*. The Narrator's mind is supposed to see and hear what the Muses
saw and heard. *His mind has the power of total recall.*

2§17. The Narrator here is calling on the Muses as goddesses of memory to
tell him a part of the epic narrative about the Trojan War. This part of the tale of
Troy is generally known as the Catalogue of Ships, and it tells about which warriors came to Troy and in how many ships and so on. The Muses are expected to
tell the tale exactly to the Narrator, and the Narrator will tell the tale exactly
to his listeners. Modern readers can easily get distracted and even bored when
they read through the Catalogue, but it was of the greatest cultural interest and
importance to the listeners of the *Iliad* in ancient times. So important was the
Catalogue that the Narrator needed special powers of memory to get it right.
That is why the Narrator here prays to the Muses, as if he had just started his
overall narration. In fact, however, he has already prayed to 'the Muse' at the
start of the *Iliad*.

2§18. The Muses, as we have just seen, are supposed to know absolutely everything. They are *all-knowing*, that is, *omniscient*. So *the omniscient Muses are*

---

* |₄₈₄ Ἔσπετε νῦν μοι Μοῦσαι Ὀλύμπια δώματ' ἔχουσαι· |₄₈₅ ὑμεῖς γὰρ θεαί ἐστε πάρεστέ τε ἴστέ τε
πάντα, |₄₈₆ ἡμεῖς δὲ κλέος οἶον ἀκούομεν οὐδέ τι ἴδμεν· |₄₈₇ οἵ τινες ἡγεμόνες Δαναῶν καὶ κοίρανοι
ἦσαν.

goddesses of total recall, and their absolute power of recall is expressed by an active form of the verb *mnē-* in the sense of 'remind' (at *Iliad* II 492).* The master Narrator of the *Iliad* receives from these goddesses their absolute power of total recall when he prays to them to tell him everything about the Achaean forces that sailed to Troy (II 484, 491–492). Inspired by the omniscient Muses, the master Narrator becomes an omniscient Narrator. Although he says he will not exercise the option of telling everything in full, deciding instead to tell only the salient details by concentrating on the names of the leaders of the warriors who sailed to Troy and on the precise number of each leader's ships (II 493), the master Narrator insists on his power of total recall.† The very idea of such mental power is basic to Homeric poetry.

2§19. The Narrator is saying here that he does not have to know anything: all he has to do is to 'hear the *kleos*'. Since the goddesses of memory were there when the heroic actions happened, and since they saw and heard everything, they know everything. The Narrator needs to know nothing; he needs to experience nothing. To repeat, all he has to do is to 'hear the *kleos*' from the goddesses of memory and then to narrate what he is hearing to those who are listening to him.

2§20. What the omniscient Muses *see* and what they *hear* is a *total recall*: they recall everything that has ever happened, whereas the Narrator only *hears* 'that which is heard', which is the *kleos* from the Muses.‡ The Narrator of epic depends on these goddesses to tell him exactly what they *saw* and to quote for him exactly what they *heard*.

2§21. But what about a story-within-a-story, that is, when a narrator narrates a micro-narrative within the macro-Narrative of the *Iliad*? In such a situation, the narrator of that micro-narrative has to reassure *his* listeners that he has total recall matching the total recall of the Narrator of the macro-Narrative, which is the *Iliad*. This is what happens when the old hero Phoenix, in *Iliad* IX, begins to narrate to the hero Achilles and to the other listeners the story of the earlier hero Meleagros. Phoenix is telling this story about Meleagros because he wants

---

* *BA* 17 = 1§3n2; see also West 2007:34. The noun *Mousa*, 'Muse', derives from the Indo-European root **men-*, the basic meaning of which is 'put in mind' in verb formations with transitive function and 'have in mind' in those with intransitive function. This etymology is reflected in the mythological relationship of the divine Muses with *mnēmosunē* in the sense of 'poetic recall', personified as their divine mother, Mnemosyne.

† *HTL* 175n78; also 80n75.

‡ *BA* 15–18 = 1§§2–4.

to persuade Achilles to accept the offer of Agamemnon. That is the purpose of this narrator. As we will see, however, the purpose of the master Narrator of the *Iliad* is different: it goes far beyond the purpose of Phoenix.

2§22. When Phoenix says that he has total recall, totally recalling the epic action he narrates, his power of memory depends on the power of the omniscient Narrator who tells the framing story of the *Iliad,* and that power in turn depends on the power of the omniscient Muses themselves, who are given credit for controlling the master Narrative. Phoenix has total recall because he uses the medium of epic poetry and because his mind is connected to the power source of that poetry.

An Epic Tale Told by Phoenix

2§23. In Text B, as we have seen, Phoenix refers to his tale as *tōn prosthen . . . klea andrōn | hērōōn,* 'the glories [*kleos* plural] of men of an earlier time, who were heroes' (IX 524–525). It is an epic tale about the hero Meleagros and his anger against his people, parallel to the framing epic tale about the hero Achilles and his anger against his own people, the Achaeans (as I noted in the Introduction to this book, these people are also known as the Argives or the Danaans). The telling of the tale by Phoenix is an activation of epic within epic.

2§24. Phoenix is a hero in the epic of the Homeric *Iliad,* and this epic is a narrative about the distant heroic past—from the standpoint of listeners who live in a present tense devoid of contemporary heroes. But Phoenix here is narrating to listeners who live in that distant heroic past tense. And his narrative-within-a-narrative is about heroes who lived in an even more distant heroic past tense.

2§25. There are close parallels between the framing epic about the anger of Achilles and the framed epic about the anger of Meleagros. Just as the framed epic about Meleagros is a poetic recollection of the *klea,* 'glories', of heroes of the past, so too is the framing epic about Achilles. That framing epic, which is the *Iliad,* is a poetic recollection by the Muse whom the master Narrator invokes to sing the story of the anger of Achilles (I 1). As the narrator of a framed epic, Phoenix does not have to invoke the Muses as goddesses of memory, since the Narrator of the framing epic has already invoked them for him.

2§26. In performing *tōn prosthen . . . klea andrōn | hērōōn,* 'the glories [*kleos* plural] of men of an earlier time, who were heroes' (at *Iliad* IX 524–525, as quoted in Text B), Phoenix expresses himself in the medium of poetry because he is speaking inside a medium that *is* poetry. He is speaking in the language of epic poetry just as the master Narrator, who is quoting him, also speaks in that same language. When Phoenix says *memnēmai*, he is in effect saying: *I have total recall by way of speaking in the medium of epic poetry.*

The Form of Epic Poetry

2§27. The form of this medium of epic poetry, which calls itself *kleos* or *klea andrōn*, is called the *dactylic hexameter.* Over 15,000 of these dactylic hexameter lines make up the *Iliad.* Here is the basic rhythm of this form:

—u u—u u—u u—u u—u u——

("—" = long syllable, "u" = short syllable).

   2§28. When the master Narrator speaks the *kleos* or *klea andrōn,* he is speaking in dactylic hexameters. When the master Narrator quotes characters speaking, whether these characters are heroes or gods, they too are speaking the *kleos* or *klea andrōn,* and so they, too, are imagined as speaking in dactylic hexameters. That is how the Muses, who saw everything and heard everything, speak the *kleos* or *klea andrōn.* Notionally, the Muses heard the heroes and gods speaking in dactylic hexameters, and then the Muses spoke these dactylic hexameters for the master Narrator to hear, so that he might speak them to his listeners.

To Sing the Klea Andrōn, 'Glories of Men'

2§29. In Text B, *Iliad* IX 524–525, we have seen the expression *tōn prosthen . . . klea andrōn | hērōōn,* 'the glories of men of an earlier time, who were heroes', at the beginning of the epic tale told by Phoenix. I will now contrast this context of *klea andrōn* with the context of another example of this same expression, *klea andrōn,* 'glories of men (heroes)'. This other example occurs at a slightly earlier point in the master Narrative, in *Iliad* IX 189, when Achilles himself is pictured as literally 'singing' *(aeidein)* the *klea andrōn* in his shelter.* The master Narrator does not say what the subject of this song sung by Achilles may have been. All we are told is that Achilles was 'singing' *(aeidein)* the *klea andrōn,* and that

---

* Here and elsewhere, I refer to the *klisiē* of Achilles as a 'shelter', not a 'tent'. I explain why in *HPC* 152–153 = II§§56–59.

he was accompanying himself on a lyre. Here is the passage that shows the key wording:

HOUR 2 TEXT D

|₁₈₅ The two of them* reached the shelters and the ships of the Myrmidons, |₁₈₆ and they found Achilles diverting his heart [*phrēn*] as he was playing on a clear-sounding lyre [*phorminx*], |₁₈₇ a beautiful one, of exquisite workmanship, and its cross-bar was of silver. |₁₈₈ It was part of the spoils that he had taken when he destroyed the city of Eëtion, |₁₈₉ and he was now diverting his heart [*thūmos*] with it as he was singing [*aeidein*] the glories of men [*klea andrōn*]. |₁₉₀ Patroklos was the only other person there. He [= Patroklos] sat in silence, facing him [= Achilles], |₁₉₁ and waiting for the Aeacid [= Achilles] to leave off singing [*aeidein*]. |₁₉₂ Meanwhile the two of them† came in—radiant Odysseus‡ leading the way—|₁₉₃ and stood before him. Achilles sprang up from his seat |₁₉₄ with the lyre [*phorminx*] still in his hand, |₁₉₅ and Patroklos, when he saw the guests, rose also.§

Iliad IX 185–195**

2§30. The medium of *klea andrōn*, 'glories of heroes', is represented here as an act of *singing*, even though the medium of epic as performed by rhapsodes in the classical period was *recited* rather than *sung*.†† By *recited* I mean (1) performed without singing and (2) performed without instrumental accompaniment.‡‡ Still, the medium of epic refers to itself as an act of singing, as we see even in the first verse of the *Iliad* (I 1), when the Narrator prays to the Muse to

---

* In the original Greek, it is not clear whether the wording for 'the two of them' refers to Ajax and Phoenix or to Ajax and Odysseus, or to a combination of all three, who are being accompanied by the two heralds Odios and Eurybates (on whom see *Iliad* IX 170). For a survey of different interpretations, see *HQ* 138–145.

† See the previous note.

‡ In the original Greek, it is not clear whether Odysseus is named here in addition to the two others or as one of the two others. In my view, the unclearness in this context is intentional: see *HQ* 141–144.

§ As the context makes clear (*Iliad* IX 200–204 and thereafter), the scene is taking place inside the shelter of Achilles, not outside it.

** |₁₈₅ Μυρμιδόνων δ' ἐπί τε κλισίας καὶ νῆας ἱκέσθην, |₁₈₆ τὸν δ' εὗρον φρένα τερπόμενον φόρμιγγι λιγείῃ |₁₈₇ καλῇ δαιδαλέῃ, ἐπὶ δ' ἀργύρεον ζυγὸν ἦεν, |₁₈₈ τὴν ἄρετ' ἐξ ἐνάρων πόλιν Ἠετίωνος ὀλέσσας· |₁₈₉ τῇ ὅ γε θυμὸν ἔτερπεν, ἄειδε δ' ἄρα κλέα ἀνδρῶν. |₁₉₀ Πάτροκλος δέ οἱ οἶος ἐναντίος ἧστο σιωπῇ, |₁₉₁ δέγμενος Αἰακίδην ὁπότε λήξειεν ἀείδων, |₁₉₂ τὼ δὲ βάτην προτέρω, ἡγεῖτο δὲ δῖος Ὀδυσσεύς, |₁₉₃ στὰν δὲ πρόσθ' αὐτοῖο· ταφὼν δ' ἀνόρουσεν Ἀχιλλεὺς |₁₉₄ αὐτῇ σὺν φόρμιγγι λιπὼν ἕδος ἔνθα θάασσεν. |₁₉₅ ὣς δ' αὔτως Πάτροκλος, ἐπεὶ ἴδε φῶτας, ἀνέστη.

†† *HC* 362–363, 370–371 = 3§§29, 41.

‡‡ *PR* 36, 41–42.

'sing' *(aeidein)* to him the anger of Achilles. Similarly in the *Odyssey* (viii 83), the epic performer Demodokos is described as 'singing' *(aeidein)* the *klea andrōn*, 'glory of heroes', and he sings while accompanying himself on the lyre (viii 67).

2§31. What we see in Text D, the passage I just quoted from *Iliad* IX 185–195, is a clue about Achilles himself as a virtuoso performer of song. He is not only the subject of songs sung by the master Narrator of epic—songs that would qualify as *klea andrōn*, 'glories of men (heroes)'. Achilles is also the performer of such songs. And the same goes for Patroklos or *Patrokleēs*, the meaning of whose name encapsulates, as we will see, the very idea of *klea andrōn*. And, as we will also see, Patroklos in this passage is waiting for his turn to sing the *klea andrōn*.

The Klea Andrōn, *'Glories of Men', as Heroic Song*

2§32. In a lecture delivered at Skidmore College in 1990, Albert B. Lord spoke about a medium that he described as *heroic song*. According to Lord, the Homeric expression *klea andrōn*, 'glories of men (heroes)', refers to such a medium.

2§33. Lord was comparing here the ancient Homeric medium of epic with media of 'heroic song' that survived into the twentieth century. Among these survivals is a tradition of epic singing in the South Slavic areas of the Balkans, specifically in the former Yugoslavia. Lord (who died in 1991) and his teacher Milman Parry (who died in 1935) pioneered the systematic study of oral traditions of such heroic song in the former Yugoslavia, especially in Bosnia and in parts of Serbia. Both Parry and Lord were professors at Harvard University (Parry died a violent death at age thirty-three, when he was still only an assistant professor; as for Lord, he eventually became one of the most accomplished and respected senior professors in the history of the university). Both Parry and Lord were classicists as well as ethnographers, and their knowledge of Homeric poetry turned out to be a valuable source of comparative insights in their study of the living oral traditions of the South Slavic peoples. For an introduction to the path-finding research of Parry and Lord, I recommend the well-known book of Albert Lord, *The Singer of Tales.**

---

* Lord 1960; in 2000, Stephen Mitchell and I edited a second edition in which we included a new introduction on the impact of Lord's work since 1960.

2§34. In Lord's 1990 lecture mentioning the *klea andrōn*, 'glories of men (heroes)', he refers to one of the greatest singers whose songs were studied by Parry and Lord, Avdo Međedović. One of Avdo's songs, recorded by Milman Parry, contained as many as 12,000 lines.

2§35. What is a "line" in the case of South Slavic heroic songs? The basic rhythmical unit is the heroic decasyllable, and the basic rhythm of this unit is

—u—u—u—u—u.

This was the rhythmical framework for the wording used by singers like Avdo in composing their heroic songs.

2§36. In this light, let us consider again the tale told by Phoenix. As we saw in Text A, *Iliad* IX 527–528, the key word that introduces this old hero's narrative is *memnēmai* (527), which I translate as 'I have total recall, I totally recall'.

2§37. Phoenix has total recall because he uses the medium of epic song and because his mind is connected to the power source of such singing; in fact, he *has* to use song, because he is inside the medium of song. To repeat, he is *speaking in dactylic hexameters,* just like the Narrator who quotes him. When Phoenix says *memnēmai,* he is in effect saying: *'I have total recall by means of using the medium of epic song'.*

2§38. Similarly, as we have already seen in Hour 1, *kleos* means not just *glory* but *glory achieved by way of using the medium of song. This medium is a way of speaking in a special way, of using special speech.* On this subject, I cite an essential work by Richard Martin: he shows that narratives within the master Narrative of the *Iliad* contain markers for and about the listeners of the master Narrative.*

2§39. So a special way of speaking, a special speech, marks what is being *performed,* not just said. Here I repeat the essential wording in Text B, *Iliad* IX 524–525, where Phoenix says:

|₅₂₄ This is how [*houtōs*] we [= I, Phoenix] learned it, the glories [*klea*] of men [*andrōn*] of an earlier time [*prosthen*], |₅₂₅ who were heroes [*hērōes*], whenever one of them was overcome by tempestuous anger.

---

* Martin 1989.

The epic poetry of *kleos* is a *performance*. And, as we have seen, this performance is figured as a kind of *singing*.

2§40. We moderns need to keep in mind that some of the things we tend to do in everyday ways, like remembering something, can be done differently in premodern societies. We have already seen an example in ancient Greek song culture, where the total recall of something can be accomplished by singing it. More generally, singing something can be the same thing as doing something in the world of some song cultures.

The Concept of a Speech Act

2§41. Relevant here is the concept of a *speech act,* as originally formulated by J. L. Austin in his influential book *How to Do Things with Words* (Oxford 1962), based on the William James Lectures that Austin delivered at Harvard University in 1955. In terms of Austin's theory, in some situations we actually do things by way of saying things. But we have to say these things *in the right context.* For example, "You're fired!" is a speech act, but only in certain contexts, as when an employer says these words to an employee. Another example is "I do," which is a speech act only in the context of answering the question: "Do you take this woman/man to be your lawfully wedded wife/husband?" Still another example is "All hands on deck," which is a speech act only in the context of sailing a ship, when the commanding officer says these words.

2§42. Something that Austin did not consider in the book I just cited is the idea that poetry or song can also be a speech act *when poetry or song is performed in oral traditions.** This idea is very much at work in the Homeric *Iliad* and *Odyssey.* As I have shown in my research, Homeric poetry can be considered a speech act in its own right because *it is a medium that is performed.* This kind of poetry comes to life only in *performance,* in *live performance.* And such performance could take place within the framework of an *oral tradition,* which as I already said is *a specialized language of composition-in-performance.*† And a culture that uses poetry or song as a speech act is what I have been calling a *song culture.*

2§43. All through this hour, starting with *Iliad* IX 527 in Text A, I have been

---

* *HQ* 132–133.
† Again, *HQ* 132–133.

concentrating on a most striking example of such a speech act: it is the total re-call, by the old hero Phoenix, of the epic tale of Meleagros and Kleopatra.

Back to the Epic Tale Told by Phoenix

2§44. This tale that Phoenix tells is a beautiful example of *compression*. (I have already explained the principle of compression in Hour 1.) As we are about to see, *the climax of the compressed narrative told by Phoenix will be signaled at a moment in the tale when the wording describes a woman who is crying.* The name of this woman, as we will also see, is *Kleopatra.* I now turn to this climactic moment, as narrated by Phoenix:

HOUR 2 TEXT E

|₅₅₀ So long as Meleagros, dear [*philos*] to Arēs, was fighting in the war, |₅₅₁ things went badly for the Kouretes [of the city of Pleuron], and they could not |₅₅₂ put up a resistance [against the Aetolians] outside the city walls [of Pleuron, the city of the Kouretes], even though they [= the Kouretes] had a multitude of fighters. |₅₅₃ But as soon as anger [*kho-los*] entered Meleagros—the kind of anger that affects also others, |₅₅₄ making their thinking [*noos*] swell to the point of bursting inside their chest even if at other times they have sound thoughts [*phroneîn*], |₅₅₅ [then things changed:] he [= Meleagros] was angry [*khōomenos*] in his heart at his dear mother, Althaea, |₅₅₆ and he was lying around, next to his wife, whom he had courted and married in the proper way. She was the beautiful Kleopatra, |₅₅₇ whose mother was Marpessa, the one with the beautiful ankles, daughter of Euenos, |₅₅₈ and whose father was Idēs, a man most powerful among those earthbound men |₅₅₉ who lived in those times. It was he [= Idēs] who had grabbed his bow and had stood up against the lord |₅₆₀ Phoebus Apollo, and he [= Idēs] had done it for the sake of his bride [*numphē*], the one with the beautiful ankles [= Marpessa]. |₅₆₁ She [= Kleopatra] had been given a special name by the father and by the queen mother back then [when she was growing up] in the palace. |₅₆₂ They called her *Alcyone,* making that a second name for her, because her |₅₆₃ mother [= Marpessa] was feeling the same pain [*oitos*] felt by the *halcyon* bird, known for her many sor-rows [*penthos*]. |₅₆₄ She [= Marpessa] was crying because she had been seized and carried away by the one who has far-reaching power, Phoe-

bus Apollo. |$_{565}$ So, right next to her [= Kleopatra], he [= Meleagros] lay down, nursing his anger [*kholos*]—an anger that brings pains [*algea*] to the heart [*thūmos*]. |$_{566}$ He was angry [*kholoûsthai*] about the curses [*ārai*] that had been made by his own mother. She [= Meleagros's mother Althaea] had been praying to the gods, |$_{567}$ making many curses [*ārâsthai*] in her sorrow [*akhos*] over the killing of her brother [by her son Meleagros]. |$_{568}$ Many times did she beat the earth, nourisher of many, with her hands, |$_{569}$ calling upon Hādēs and on terrifying Persephone. |$_{570}$ She had gone down on her knees and was sitting there; her chest and her lap were wet with tears |$_{571}$ as she prayed that they [= the gods] should consign her son to death. And she was heard by a Fury [Erinys] that roams in the mist, |$_{572}$ a Fury heard her, from down below in Erebos—with a heart that cannot be assuaged. |$_{573}$ And then it was that the din of battle rose up all around the gates [of the people of Calydon], and also the dull thump |$_{574}$ of the battering against their walls. Now he [= Meleagros] was sought out by the *elders* |$_{575}$ of the Aetolians [= the people of Calydon]; they were supplicating [*lissesthai*] him, and they came along with the best *priests* of the gods. |$_{576}$ They were supplicating him [= Meleagros] to come out [from where he was lying down with his wife] and rescue them from harm, promising him a big gift. |$_{577}$ They told him that, wherever the most fertile plain in the whole region of lovely Calydon may be, |$_{578}$ at that place he could choose a most beautiful precinct [*temenos*] of land, |$_{579}$ fifty acres, half of which would be a vineyard |$_{580}$ while the other half would be a field open for plowing. |$_{581}$ He was also supplicated many times by the old charioteer *Oineus*, |$_{582}$ who was standing at the threshold of the chamber with the high ceiling |$_{583}$ and beating at the locked double door, hoping to supplicate him by touching his knees. |$_{584}$ Many times did his *sisters* and his *mother* the queen |$_{585}$ supplicate [*lissesthai*] him. But all the more did he say "no!" Many times did his *comrades* [*hetairoi*] supplicate him, |$_{586}$ those who were most cherished by him and were the most near and dear [*philoi*] of them all, |$_{587}$ but, try as they might, they could not persuade the heart [*thūmos*] in his chest |$_{588}$ not until the moment when his chamber got a direct hit, and the walls of the high fortifications |$_{589}$ were getting scaled by the Kouretes, who were starting to set fire to the great city [of Calydon]. |$_{590}$ Then at long last Meleagros was addressed by his *wife,* who wears her waistband so beautifully around her waist. |₅₉₁ She was crying as she supplicated [*lissesthai*] him, telling everything in detail |₅₉₂—all the sorrowful things [*kēdea*] that happen to those mortals whose city is captured. |₅₉₃ They kill the men. Fire turns the city to ashes. |₅₉₄ They take away the children and the wives, who wear their waistbands so beautifully around their waists. |₅₉₅ His heart was stirred when he heard what bad things will happen. |₅₉₆ He got up and went off. Then he covered his body with shining armor. |₅₉₇ And this is how [*houtōs*] he rescued the Aetolians from the evil day [of destruction].|₅₉₈ He yielded to his heart [*thūmos*]. But they [= the Aetolians] no longer carried out the fulfillment [*teleîn*] of their offers of gifts |₅₉₉—those many pleasing [*kharienta*] things that they had offered. But, in any case, he protected them from the evil event. |₆₀₀ As for you [= Achilles], don't go on thinking [*noeîn*] in your mind [*phrenes*] the way you are thinking now. Don't let a superhuman force [*daimōn*] do something to you |₆₀₁ right here, turning you away, my near and dear one [*philos*]. It would be a worse prospect |₆₀₂ to try to rescue the ships [of the Achaeans] if they are set on fire. So, since the gifts are waiting for you, |₆₀₃ get going! For if you do that, the Achaeans will honor [*tīnein*] you—same as a god. |₆₀₄ But if you have no gifts when you do go into the war, that destroyer of men, |₆₀₅ you will no longer have honor [*tīmē*] the same way, even if you have succeeded in blocking the [enemy's] forces of war.

Iliad IX 550–605*

---

* |₅₅₀ ὄφρα μὲν οὖν Μελέαγρος ἄρηι φίλος πολέμιζε, |₅₅₁ τόφρα δὲ Κουρήτεσσι κακῶς ἦν, οὐδὲ δύναντο |₅₅₂ τείχεος ἔκτοσθεν μίμνειν πολέες περ ἐόντες· |₅₅₃ ἀλλ' ὅτε δὴ Μελέαγρον ἔδυ χόλος, ὅς τε καὶ ἄλλων |₅₅₄ οἰδάνει ἐν στήθεσσι νόον πύκα περ φρονεόντων, |₅₅₅ ἤτοι ὃ μητρὶ φίλῃ Ἀλθαίῃ χωόμενος κῆρ |₅₅₆ κεῖτο παρὰ μνηστῇ ἀλόχῳ καλῇ Κλεοπάτρῃ |₅₅₇ κούρῃ Μαρπήσσης καλλισφύρου Εὐηνίνης |₅₅₈ Ἴδεώ θ', ὃς κάρτιστος ἐπιχθονίων γένετ' ἀνδρῶν |₅₅₉ τῶν τότε· καί ῥα ἄνακτος ἐναντίον εἵλετο τόξον |₅₆₀ Φοίβου Ἀπόλλωνος καλλισφύρου εἵνεκα νύμφης, |₅₆₁ τὴν δὲ τότ' ἐν μεγάροισι πατὴρ καὶ πότνια μήτηρ |₅₆₂ Ἀλκυόνην καλέεσκον ἐπώνυμον, οὕνεκ' ἄρ' αὐτῆς |₅₆₃ μήτηρ ἀλκυόνος πολυπενθέος οἶτον ἔχουσα |₅₆₄ κλαῖεν ὅ μιν ἑκάεργος ἀνήρπασε Φοῖβος Ἀπόλλων· |₅₆₅ τῇ ὅ γε παρκατέλεκτο χόλον θυμαλγέα πέσσων |₅₆₆ ἐξ ἀρέων μητρὸς κεχολωμένος, ἥ ῥα θεοῖσι |₅₆₇ πόλλ' ἀχέουσ' ἠρᾶτο κασιγνήτοιο φόνοιο, |₅₆₈ πολλὰ δὲ καὶ γαῖαν πολυφόρβην χερσὶν ἀλοία |₅₆₉ κικλήσκουσ' Ἀΐδην καὶ ἐπαινὴν Περσεφόνειαν |₅₇₀ πρόχνυ καθεζομένη, δεύοντο δὲ δάκρυσι κόλποι, |₅₇₁ παιδὶ δόμεν θάνατον· τῆς δ' ἠεροφοῖτις Ἐρινὺς |₅₇₂ ἔκλυεν ἐξ Ἐρέβεσφιν ἀμείλιχον ἦτορ ἔχουσα. |₅₇₃ τῶν δὲ τάχ' ἀμφὶ πύλας ὅμαδος καὶ δοῦπος ὀρώρει |₅₇₄ πύργων βαλλομένων· τὸν δὲ λίσσοντο γέροντες |₅₇₅ Αἰτωλῶν, πέμπον δὲ θεῶν ἱερῆας ἀρίστους, |₅₇₆ ἐξελθεῖν καὶ ἀμῦναι ὑποσχόμενοι μέγα δῶρον· |₅₇₇ ὁππόθι πιότατον πεδίον Καλυδῶνος ἐραννῆς, |₅₇₈ ἔνθά μιν ἤνωγον τέμενος περικαλλὲς ἑλέσθαι |₅₇₉ πεντηκοντόγυον, τὸ μὲν ἥμισυ οἰνοπέδοιο, |₅₈₀ ἥμισυ δὲ ψιλὴν ἄροσιν πεδίοιο ταμέσθαι. |₅₈₁ πολλὰ δέ μιν λιτάνευε γέρων ἱππηλάτα Οἰνεὺς |₅₈₂ οὐδοῦ ἐπεμβεβαὼς ὑψηρεφέος θαλάμοιο, |₅₈₃ σείων κολλητὰς σανίδας γουνούμενος υἱόν· |₅₈₄ πολλὰ δὲ τόν γε κασίγνηται καὶ πότνια μήτηρ |₅₈₅ ἐλλίσσονθ'· ὃ δὲ μᾶλλον ἀναίνετο· πολλὰ δ' ἑταῖροι,

2§45. I draw special attention to verse 556 here, where we see the name of *Kleopatra*, who is the wife of Meleagros. (This figure is not to be confused with the historical figure Kleopatra, also spelled in the Romanized form *Cleopatra*.) I also draw attention to verse 562, where we see the second name of the wife of Meleagros, which is *Alcyone*. In ancient Greek lore, the *alcyon* / *halcyon* is a bird that sings songs of lament over the destruction of cities. In Hour 3, I will follow up on the lament of Kleopatra and the general idea of lament in ancient Greek song culture.

2§46. The story of Meleagros and his lamenting wife, Kleopatra, is a micro-narrative meant for Achilles and for the *Iliad*, which is the macro-Narrative about Achilles; in its *compressed* form, the Meleagros narrative "replays" or "repeats" some of the major themes of the *expanded* form that is the *Iliad*.

2§47. An essential word in the micro-narrative is the adjective *philos*, 'near and dear', at verse 601. The superlative form of this adjective is *philtatos*, 'most near and dear', or *philtatoi* in the plural. The plural form *philtatoi*, 'most near and dear [*philoi*]', is applied to the comrades of Meleagros at verse 586. As we are about to see, this adjective *philos* measures the hero's *ascending scale of affection**: elders, priests, father, sisters, mother, comrades [*hetairoi*], and, finally, *wife*.

2§48. I will now explain why I highlight the word *wife* at the very end of this list of words. The sequence in which these words are presented in the narration corresponds to a principle that I have just described as the hero's *ascending scale of affection*. As we are about to see, the placement of the *wife* in the final position of this sequence is dictated by the logic of the micro-narrative itself, not by the logic of its narrator Phoenix. And the logic of this micro-narrative is shaped by the emotions of Meleagros.

2§49. The emotions of Achilles, which shape the macro-Narrative of the *Il-*

|₅₈₆ οἳ οἱ κεδνότατοι καὶ φίλτατοι ἦσαν ἁπάντων· |₅₈₇ ἀλλ’ οὐδ’ ὣς τοῦ θυμὸν ἐνὶ στήθεσσιν ἔπειθον, |₅₈₈ πρίν γ’ ὅτε δὴ θάλαμος πύκ’ ἐβάλλετο, τοὶ δ’ ἐπὶ πύργων |₅₈₉ βαῖνον Κουρῆτες καὶ ἐνέπρηθον μέγα ἄστυ. |₅₉₀ καὶ τότε δὴ Μελέαγρον ἐΰζωνος παράκοιτις |₅₉₁ λίσσετ’ ὀδυρομένη, καί οἱ κατέλεξεν ἅπαντα |₅₉₂ κήδε’, ὅσ’ ἀνθρώποισι πέλει τῶν ἄστυ ἁλώῃ· |₅₉₃ ἄνδρας μὲν κτείνουσι, πόλιν δέ τε πῦρ ἀμαθύνει, |₅₉₄ τέκνα δέ τ’ ἄλλοι ἄγουσι βαθυζώνους τε γυναῖκας. |₅₉₅ τοῦ δ’ ὠρίνετο θυμὸς ἀκούοντος κακὰ ἔργα, |₅₉₆ βῆ δ’ ἰέναι, χροῒ δ’ ἔντε’ ἐδύσετο παμφανόωντα. |₅₉₇ ὣς ὃ μὲν Αἰτωλοῖσιν ἀπήμυνεν κακὸν ἦμαρ |₅₉₈ εἴξας Ⅎ θυμῷ· τῷ δ’ οὐκέτι δῶρα τέλεσσαν |₅₉₉ πολλά τε καὶ χαρίεντα, κακὸν δ’ ἤμυνε καὶ αὔτως. |₆₀₀ ἀλλὰ σὺ μή μοι ταῦτα νόει φρεσί, μὴ δέ σε δαίμων |₆₀₁ ἐνταῦθα τρέψειε φίλος· κάκιον δέ κεν εἴη |₆₀₂ νηυσὶν καιομένῃσιν ἀμυνέμεν· ἀλλ’ ἐπὶ δώρων |₆₀₃ ἔρχεο· ἶσον γάρ σε θεῷ τίσουσιν Ἀχαιοί. |₆₀₄ εἰ δέ κ’ ἄτερ δώρων πόλεμον φθισήνορα δύῃς |₆₀₅ οὐκέθ’ ὁμῶς τιμῆς ἔσεαι πόλεμόν περ ἀλαλκών.

* The term *ascending scale of affections* is explained in *BA* 104–105 = 6§15, including references to the history of the term.

iad, can be understood by thinking through these emotions of Meleagros, which shape the micro-narrative told by Phoenix in *Iliad* IX. A key to these emotions is the principle of an *ascending scale of affection.* As we are about to see, this principle is on full display in the Meleagros narrative, which calls itself *klea andrōn,* 'glories of men' (IX 524), told in the midst of *philoi,* 'friends, near and dear ones' (IX 528), as we saw in Text B.

2§50. As we analyze the emotions that are activated in this micro-narrative, it is important to consider again the meaning of *philoi,* 'friends, near and dear ones', and this word's links with the emotion of *love.* The lament of Kleopatra highlights the emotion of *love* as well as the emotion of *sadness* or *sorrow* or *grief* as well as the emotions of *anger* and *fear.* The story of Meleagros and Kleopatra explores the combinations and permutations of all these emotions.

2§51. The song culture of "classical" opera likewise explores such combinations and permutations of emotions. In the Renaissance, opera was thought to be a "reinvention" of ancient drama and, by extension, of epic themes transmitted by drama, especially by tragedy.

2§52. In opera, confusion of emotions is an emotion in its own right, since it is meant to be a mixture of more than one emotion. That is, confusion results from a fusion of grief and anger, anger and hate, hate and love, and so on. Such fusion, as we will see later, is evident in Greek epic and tragedy as well.

2§53. In the story of Meleagros and Kleopatra, two emotions that we see foregrounded are *fear* and *pity.*

The Emotions of Fear and Pity

2§54. Aristotle thought that the emotions of *phobos,* 'fear', and *eleos,* 'pity', are essential for understanding tragedy (*Poetics* 1449b24–28). The same can be said for understanding the epic of the *Iliad,* which Aristotle saw as a prototype of tragedy.* Here I offer some background on these and other emotions as expressed in ancient Greek song culture.

2§55. The English translations 'fear' and 'pity' do not quite capture the range of meanings embedded in the original Greek words. It is easier if we start thinking of the contrast of fear and pity in different terms:

fear: a feeling of repulsion when you see or hear someone else suffering
    (that is, you feel like getting as far away as possible from that person)

---

* HC 78 = 1§10.

> *pity*: a feeling of attraction when you see or hear someone else suffering
>   (that is, you feel like getting closer to that person).

When you yourself are suffering, you feel grief. When you feel fear or pity, you are repelled by or attracted to the grief.

2§56. Of course, the emotion of fear goes beyond what you feel about the grief of others: you can more basically fear *for yourself*. But the same basic feeling is at work when you experience fear in reaction to someone else's suffering: you are afraid that something might happen to *you* that will make *you* suffer the same way. Another word that I will use from here on to express the idea of fear is *terror*.

2§57. This background will help us analyze the micro-narrative about Meleagros and his wife, Kleopatra.

2§58. In the case of the emotions that we know as *sadness* and *love,* I can offer some analogies in contemporary popular media:

In the film *Bladerunner,* which I cited already in Hour 1§33, there are two scenes that illustrate the idea that the musical recalling of a memory is the "same thing" as the reliving of an experience, with all its emotions. If you "recall" someone else's experience by way of song or music, then that experience and all its emotions become your own, even if they had not been originally yours.

The Story of Meleagros and Kleopatra

2§59. The total recall of Phoenix in telling the story of Meleagros focuses on the wife of Meleagros, named Kleopatra, and on the meaning of her name, Kleopatra. This name Kleopatra in the micro-narrative will be relevant to the name of Patroklos, the best friend of Achilles, in the macro-Narrative.*

2§60. As Achilles contemplates the decisions he has to make in the course of a narrative that centers on his own epic actions, he is invited by Phoenix to contemplate the decisions made by an earlier hero in the course of an earlier epic. As we saw, that hero is Meleagros, who figures in an earlier epic called the *klea andrōn | hērōōn,* 'the glories of men who were heroes', in *Iliad* IX 524–525, Text B. The framed epic about Meleagros, quoted as a direct speech by the framing epic, is introduced by way of a special word *houtōs,* 'this is how', at IX 524, Text B, signaling the activation of a special form of speech known as the *ainos.*† Here

---

* In what follows, I give an epitomized version of an argument I presented in Nagy 2007b.
† *PH* 200 = 7§1n4.

is my working definition of *ainos: a performance of ambivalent wording that becomes clarified once it is correctly understood and then applied in moments of making moral decisions affecting those who are near and dear.**

2§61. The *ainos* that Phoenix tells in the *Iliad,* drawing on narratives concerning the hero Meleagros, is intended to persuade Achilles to accept an offer made by Agamemnon. That is the short-range intention of Phoenix as a narrator narrating within the master Narration that is the *Iliad.* But the long-range intention of the master Narrator is quite different from the short-range intention of Phoenix. The master Narrative shows that the embedded narrative of Phoenix was misguided—that is, misguided by hindsight. If Achilles had accepted the offer of Agamemnon, as Phoenix had intended, this acceptance would have undermined the epic reputation of Achilles.†

2§62. So the reaction of Achilles to the *ainos* performed by Phoenix needs to be viewed within the framework of the master Narrative performed by the master Narrator. From the standpoint of Achilles as a character who takes shape within the plot of the overall epic that is the *Iliad,* the consequences of his decisions in reacting to the subplot of the epic about Meleagros are still unclear at the moment when he makes these decisions. From the standpoint of the master Narrator who narrates the plot of the *Iliad,* by contrast, the consequences are quite clear, since the master Narration takes shape by way of an interaction between the framed micro-narrative about the anger of Meleagros and the framing macro-Narrative about the anger of Achilles. The short-range agenda of Phoenix and Achilles will be transformed into the long-range agenda of the master Narrative, which will ultimately correspond to what actually happens to Achilles in his own heroic life. *In the world of epic, heroes live out their lives by living the narratives that are their lives.*

2§63. The point of the story as told by Phoenix is that Achilles must identify with those who are *philoi,* 'near and dear'—and must therefore rejoin his comrades in war. Phoenix himself, along with Odysseus and Ajax, is a representative of these comrades by virtue of being sent as a delegate to Achilles.

2§64. More must be said here about the word *philos* (in the singular) or *philoi* (in the plural), which as we have seen means 'friend' as a noun and 'near and dear' as an adjective. The translation 'dear' conveys the fact that this word has an important *emotional* component. As we will see, the meaning of the framed micro-narrative of Phoenix emerges from the framing macro-Narrative of the

---

* *PH* 199–202 = 7§§1–4.
† *HQ* 142–143.

Iliad. As we will also see, the central theme has to do with the power of emotions, and the central character turns out to be someone who is not mentioned a single time in the framed micro-narrative: that someone is Achilles' best friend, the hero Patroklos.

2§65. From the standpoint of Phoenix as narrator, the word *philoi* applies primarily to Achilles at the moment when he begins to tell his story (IX 528). But this word applies also to the whole group of epic characters who are listening to the telling of this story. This group, as we have seen, is composed of (1) Odysseus and Ajax, who are the other two delegates besides Phoenix; (2) the two heralds who accompany the three delegates; (3) Achilles himself; and (4) Patroklos. Inside the story told by Phoenix, the comrades who approach Meleagros as delegates are the *philtatoi,* that is, those persons who are 'nearest and dearest' to the hero (IX 585–587). So, from the short-range perspective of Phoenix as the narrator of the *ainos* about Meleagros, the three comrades who approach Achilles as delegates must be the persons who are nearest and dearest to him. From the long-range perspective of the master Narrator, however, it is not Phoenix and the two other delegates but Patroklos who must be nearest and dearest to Achilles. Later on in the *Iliad,* after Patroklos is killed in battle, Achilles recognizes this hero as the one who was all along the *philtatos,* the 'nearest and dearest' of them all (XVII 411, 655).*

2§66. The story about Meleagros as narrated by Phoenix is already anticipating such a long-range recognition. The micro-narrative indicates, by way of the sequence of delegates who are sent to Meleagros, that hero's *ascending scale of affection.* The order in which the delegates are mentioned corresponds to the order in which they are placed in the hero's emotional world of affections. Delegates who are mentioned earlier are placed relatively lower in the hero's ascending scale of affection, while delegates who are mentioned later are placed relatively higher. The scale of lower to higher goes from the elders [verse 574] to the priests [verse 575] to the father [verse 581] to the sisters [verse 584] to the mother [verse 584] to the comrades [verse 585]. At first it seems as if the comrades are at the top of this hero's ascending scale of affection, since they seem to be the last and the latest delegates to be mentioned; and, on top of that, they are actually described by Phoenix as *philtatoi,* the 'nearest and dearest' (IX 585–587). But there is someone who is even nearer and dearer to Meleagros than the comrades. In the logic of the story, that someone turns out to be the wife of Meleagros (IX 588–596). In this hero's ascending scale of affection, his wife ulti-

---

*BA 104–105 = 6§15.

mately outranks even his comrades approaching him as delegates. Likewise in Achilles' ascending scale of affection, there is someone who ultimately outranks the comrades approaching him as delegates. For Achilles that someone is Patroklos, who was all along the *philtatos,* the 'nearest and dearest' of them all (XVII 411, 655). The name of this hero in its full form, *Patrokleēs,* matches in meaning the name given to the wife of Meleagros in the *ainos* narrated by Phoenix: she is *Kleopatra* (IX 556). These two names, *Patrokleēs* / *Kleopatra,* both mean 'the one who has the glory [*kleos*] of the ancestors [*pateres*]'.* Both these names amount to a periphrasis of the expression *tōn prosthen . . . klea andrōn* | *hērōōn,* 'the glories [*kleos* plural] of men of an earlier time, who were heroes' (IX 524–525), which refers to the *ainos* narrated by Phoenix to a group of listeners including not only the delegates approaching Achilles but also Achilles and Patroklos themselves (IX 527–528). Phoenix is presuming that all his listeners are *philoi,* 'near and dear' to him (IX 528). I already quoted all this wording in Text B.

2§67. Even before the arrival of the delegates, Achilles himself is pictured as singing the glories of heroes, the *klea andrōn* (IX 189). At this moment, he is alone except for one person. With him is Patroklos, who is intently listening to him and waiting for his own turn to sing, ready to start at whatever point Achilles leaves off singing (IX 190–191). As Patroklos gets ready to continue the song sung by Achilles, the song of Achilles is getting ready to become the song of Patroklos. So the hero whose name conveys the very idea of *klea andrōn,* 'glories of men (who are heroes)', is figured here as the personal embodiment of the *klea andrōn.*† I already quoted all this wording in Text D.

2§68. As we will see in hours to come, Achilles himself is a virtuoso in expressing emotions by way of song, that is, by way of *klea andrōn.* Especially the emotions of sorrow, anger, hatred, and even love.

2§69. The *ainos* told by Phoenix, to which he refers as *klea andrōn* (at *Iliad* IX 524, as quoted in Text B), connects with the song of Achilles, to which the master Narrator refers likewise as *klea andrōn* (at IX 189, as quoted in Text D). The *ainos* also connects with Patroklos as the one person who is nearest and dearest to Achilles. Patroklos is at the very top of that hero's ascending scale of affection.

2§70. What must mean more than anything else to Achilles is not only Patroklos himself but also the actual meaning of the name *Patrokleēs,* which con-

---

* *BA* 104–105, 106–109 = 6§§15, 17–19.
† *PP* 72–73, *PR* 17.

veys the idea of the *klea andrōn*. For Achilles, the words *klea andrōn* represent the master Narrative in the actual process of being narrated in the epic of the *Iliad*. For Achilles, it is a narrative of his own making. And it is the speech act of narration in the making.

2§71. Just as the song of Achilles is identified with the master Narrative of the *Iliad*, so also the style of this hero's language is identified with the overall style of the master Narrator. In other words, the language of Achilles mirrors the language of the master Narrator. Empirical studies of the language of Homeric diction have shown that the language of Achilles is made distinct from the language of other heroes quoted in the *Iliad*, and this distinctness carries over into the language of the master Narrator, which is thus made distinct from the language of other narrators of epic.* It is as if the *klea andrōn* as sung by Achilles— and as heard by Patroklos—were the model for the overall *klea andrōn* as sung by Homer.

2§72. The *ainos* as told by Phoenix, to which he refers as *klea andrōn* (at *Iliad* IX 524, as quoted in Text B), connects with the overall *klea andrōn* as told by the master Narrator. The connection is made by way of poetic conventions distinguishing the *ainos* from epic. One of these conventions is a set of three features characterizing the rhetoric of the *ainos*. Unlike epic, the *ainos* requires three qualifications of its listeners in order to be understood:

1. The listeners must be *sophoi*, 'skilled', in understanding the message encoded in the poetry. That is, they must be mentally qualified.
2. They must be *agathoi*, 'noble'. That is, they must be morally qualified.
3. They must be *philoi*, 'near and dear', to each other and to the one who is telling them the *ainos*. That is, they must be emotionally qualified. Communication is achieved through a special sense of community, that is, through recognizing "the ties that bind."†

2§73. Each of these three features of the *ainos* is made explicit in the songmaking medium of Pindar, whose songs date back to the first half of the fifth century BCE. The medium of Pindar actually refers to itself as *ainos*.‡

---

* Martin 1989:225, 227, 233, 237.

† *PH* 148 = 6§5. See also Nagy 2011c §131, citing Schwartz 2003:383, who has shown that the three requirements for understanding the ancient Greek *ainos*, as I have just summarized them here, are related to a cognate set of three requirements for understanding the phraseology that he analyzes in the Zoroastrian texts of the ancient Iranian *Gāthās*, especially with reference to the *Yasnas* 30, 31, and 46 (pp. 383–384). Schwartz has thus found comparative evidence indicating that the poetics of the *ainos* stem from Indo-European prototypes.

‡ *PH* 148–150 = 6§§5–8.

2§74. One of these three features of the *ainos* is also made explicit in the *ainos* narrated by Phoenix, that is, in the *tōn prosthen . . . klea andrōn | hērōōn,* 'the glories [*kleos* plural] of men of an earlier time, who were heroes' (at *Iliad* IX 524–525, as quoted in Text B). When it comes to the emotional qualifications required for understanding the *ainos* spoken by Phoenix, we have already seen that the speaker refers to his listeners as *philoi,* 'near and dear' to him (IX 528). So the emotional requirements of the *ainos* are made quite explicit. By contrast, when it comes to the moral requirements for understanding the *ainos,* they are merely implicit in the word *philoi.* The moral message as encoded in his *ainos* becomes explicit only at a later point, once the outcome of the master Narrative is clarified. That point is reached when Patroklos is killed while fighting for his comrades. It is only then that Achilles, for whom the story about the anger of Meleagros was intended, ultimately recognizes the moral message of that story.

2§75. This kind of recognition, to borrow from the wording used in the lyric poetry of Pindar, shows that the listener has become *sophos,* 'skilled', in understanding the message encoded in the *ainos.* In the story told by Phoenix, that message is conveyed by the figure of Kleopatra, who is nearest and dearest to Meleagros in that hero's ascending scale of affection. In the logic of the embedded narrative, that figure promotes the moral principle of fighting for one's comrades, just as the figure of Patroklos, who is nearest and dearest to Achilles, promotes the same principle in the logic of the master Narrative.

2§76. Patroklos not only promotes that principle: he exemplifies it through his own epic actions, thereby forfeiting his life. Then, responding to the lesson learned from the death of Patroklos, Achilles will express his willingness to forfeit his own life in order to avenge the death of Patroklos (*Iliad* XVIII 90–126). Thus Achilles will be justifying the principle for which Patroklos had died, this principle of *klea andrōn.*

Plato's Reading of the Iliad

2§77. Plato, who lived in the fourth century BCE, shows his understanding of this moral principle as developed in the master Narrative of the *Iliad:* in Plato's *Apology of Socrates* (28c–d), we see a paraphrase of the relevant verses of the *Iliad* (XVIII 90–104), along with some quotations of the original wording. Likewise in Plato's *Symposium* (179e–180a), we see a second paraphrase of the same verses. In the case of that second paraphrase, however, the choice made by Achilles to forfeit his life in order to avenge the death of Patroklos appears to be conflated with another choice that faces the hero. At an earlier point in the *Iliad,* in the context of the so-called Embassy Scene where Achilles is speaking to Phoenix and the other delegates (IX 410–416), he says that he must decide between two *kēres* or 'fated ways' (IX 411): either he dies at a ripe old age after a safe *nostos,* 'homecoming', to his homeland Phthia or he dies young on the battlefield in Troy—and thereby wins for himself a *kleos,* 'glory', that will last forever (IX 413). This is the passage I first quoted in Hour 0 Text F and in Hour 1 Text A.

2§78. Plato's apparent conflation of two choices facing Achilles turns out to be justified: the two choices are in fact one choice. In the Embassy Scene of the *Iliad,* when Achilles says he must choose between two *kēres* or 'fated ways' (IX 411), either a *nostos,* 'homecoming', or a *kleos,* 'glory', that will last forever (IX 413), he is actually not yet ready to make his choice: the two alternative fates have simply been foretold for him by his mother, the goddess Thetis (IX 410–411). Later on, after Patroklos has been killed, Achilles is facing the same choice, but by now he has made his decision. He says that there cannot be a homecoming for him (*nosteîn* XVIII 90) because he must kill Hector in order to avenge the death of Patroklos, and, once he kills Hector, his own death in battle will become a certainty (XVIII 90–93), just as his mother had foretold—and as she now foretells again (XVIII 96–97). By choosing to kill Hector, Achilles chooses to die young on the battlefield, and he refers to this death as his inevitable *kēr,* or 'fated way' (XVIII 115). As his compensation, however, he will now win *kleos,* 'glory', for himself (XVIII 121).

The Epic Choice of Achilles

2§79. So, ultimately, Achilles decides to choose *kleos* over life itself. Earlier on, however, when the choice is first formulated in the Embassy Scene, it is not yet clear which of the two *kēres* or 'fated ways' (IX 411), will be chosen by the hero— whether it will be a *nostos,* 'homecoming', or the *kleos,* 'glory', that will last forever (IX 413). The hero is saying that he loves life more than any property he can win for himself by fighting in Troy, and such property is defined in terms of raiding cattle in particular and acquiring wealth in general (IX 401–408). Still earlier, in the so-called Quarrel Scene at the very start of the epic, in *Iliad* I, such property is defined in terms of the women as well as the cattle and the general wealth that the hero has already acquired in the course of raiding the territories of Aeolic-speaking Greeks in the vicinity of Troy.

2§80. I add here that the word *Aeolic* refers to the Greek dialect spoken on the island of Lesbos and the facing mainland of Asia Minor, as well as the dialect spoken in Thessaly, the homeland of Achilles. Thessaly is on the European side of the Aegean Sea. As we will see, the European provenance of Aeolic Achilles is politicized in the poetic traditions about this hero.

2§81. At the start of the *Iliad*, the hero's sense of *tīmē*, 'honor', is simply a function of all the property he has acquired. The prime example is Briseis, a woman whom Achilles captured in one of his raiding expeditions in the territories of the Aeolic-speaking Greeks of Asia Minor. (In using this geographical term, I include the offshore island of Lesbos.) In the Quarrel Scene at the beginning of the *Iliad*, when Briseis is forcibly taken from Achilles by Agamemnon, she is treated merely as a war-prize, a trophy, and the hero's loss is seen as a loss of property. And yet, though the hero's honor is expressed exclusively in terms of property in the Quarrel Scene of *Iliad* I, things have changed by the time Achilles speaks to Phoenix in the Embassy Scene of *Iliad* IX. By then, Achilles has rethought the loss of Briseis. By now this loss has become the loss of a personal relationship, and Achilles even says he loves Briseis as he would love a wife (IX 340–343). I will have more to say about this in Hour 8.

2§82. Here I must return to the story told by the old man Phoenix to the young man Achilles about the hero Meleagros and his wife, Kleopatra (*Iliad* IX 527–599). I highlight again the fact that the old man refers to his story as *tōn prosthen . . . klea andrōn | hērōōn*, the 'glories of men of an earlier time, who were heroes' (IX 524–525). This story about Meleagros, a hero who seems at first to love his wife more than he loves his own comrades, will now take on a special meaning for the hero of the master Narrative that is the *Iliad*.

2§83. But vital questions remain: does Achilles love his would-be wife more than he loves his comrades—or even more than life itself? Here is where the name of the wife of Meleagros, *Kleopatra*, becomes essential. As we have seen, the meaning of *Kleopatra* is parallel to the meaning of *Patrokleēs*, the name of the one person who means more to Achilles than anyone else in the whole world. After Patroklos is killed, this hero is recognized as the one single person who was nearest and dearest to Achilles. After the death of Patroklos, Achilles can now say that all along he has valued Patroklos as much as he has valued his own life (XVIII 80–82).

2§84. So the hero Ajax misses the point when he accuses Achilles of loving Briseis more than he loves his comrades (IX 622–638). Achilles loves his would-be wife the same way that Meleagros loves Kleopatra, but there is a deeper meaning to be found in that hero's love for Kleopatra, and that deeper meaning has to do with the relevance of the name of Kleopatra to Achilles. What Achilles loves more than anything else in the whole world is what the name of Kleopatra means to Meleagros—and what the name of his own nearest and dearest comrade, Patroklos, means to him. That is because these two names *Patrokleēs* / *Kleopatra* both mean 'the one who has the glory [*kleos*] of the ancestors [*pateres*]', and, as I have argued, both these names amount to a periphrasis of the expression *tōn prosthen . . . klea andrōn* | *hērōōn,* 'the glories [*kleos* plural] of men of an earlier time who were heroes' (IX 524–525).

2§85. Just as Patroklos made the epic choice of loving his comrades more than life itself, actually giving up his life for them, so also Achilles will now make the epic choice of giving up his own life for his comrade Patroklos—and for the meaning of Patroklos. The meaning of the name of Patroklos, 'the one who has the glory [*kleos*] of the ancestors [*pateres*]', recapitulates the epic choice of Achilles, who ultimately opts for *kleos* over life itself. That is why, as we will see in Hour 4, the epic *kleos* chosen by Achilles must be *aphthiton,* 'imperishable', forever (IX 413): the *kleos* of Achilles must not ever lose its divine vitality.

Achilles and the Poetics of Lament

The Meaning of Akhos *and* Penthos

3§1. There are two key words for this hour, *akhos* and *penthos,* and the meaning of both words is 'grief, sorrow; public expression of grief, sorrow, by way of lamentation or keening'.

A Man of Constant Sorrow

3§2. The word *akhos* is connected with the name of Achilles in the *Iliad.* And the meaning of the word *akhos,* which conveys intense grief, sorrow, and pain, is connected with a central theme that is linked with Achilles in the Homeric *Iliad*: Achilles is *a man of constant sorrow.* I have used this phrase once before, in Hour 1, in relation to the title of a traditional American folk song. I am thinking now also of an expression in Isaiah 53:3 as translated in the King James Bible: "a man of sorrows, and acquainted with grief." One of my major research projects over the years has been the study of this central theme of grief and sorrow as experienced by Achilles and by his people, the Achaeans. Essential for such a study are the principal words that express all that grief and sorrow, namely, *akhos* and its synonym *penthos.* We can see this theme of grief and sorrow already at the very beginning of the *Iliad*:

HOUR 3 TEXT A

|188 Thus he [= Agamemnon] spoke. And the son of Peleus [= Achilles] felt grief [*akhos*], and the heart |189 within his shaggy chest was divided |190 whether to draw the sharp sword at his thigh |191 and make the others get up and scatter while he kills the son of Atreus [= Ag-

amemnon], |₁₉₂ or whether to check his anger [*kholos*] and restrain his heart [*thūmos*].

Iliad I 188–192*

3§3. So Achilles experiences *akhos* right away, and the grief, sorrow, and pain of this *akhos* modulates right away into *kholos,* anger.

Achilles and Penthesileia the Amazon

3§4. Just as the word *akhos* is connected with the name of Achilles, its synonym *penthos* is connected with the name of an Amazon called Penthesileia. The story of Penthesileia the Amazon is preserved in an ancient plot summary by Proclus of a lost epic, the *Aithiopis*, or 'Song of the Ethiopians', attributed to Arctinus of Miletus, which belonged to a body of epic poetry known in the ancient world as the epic Cycle:

HOUR 3 TEXT B

|₂₂ The Amazon *Penthesileia* arrives, |₂₃ as an ally of the Trojans. She is the daughter of Arēs and Thracian |₂₄ by birth. In the middle of her *aristeia* [= greatest epic moments], Achilles kills her and the Trojans |₂₅ arrange for her funeral. And Achilles kills Thersites, who reviled |₂₅ him with abusive words for conceiving a passionate love for Penthesileia, |₂₇ so he said.

Plot summary by Proclus of the *Aithiopis* by Arctinus of Miletus p. 105 lines 22–26†

What we read here in this ancient plot summary is all that we have left, unfortunately, about Penthesileia the Amazon.‡

3§5. We must ponder a basic question about the plot of this lost epic, the

---

* |₁₈₈ Ὣς φάτο· Πηλεΐωνι δ' ἄχος γένετ', ἐν δέ οἱ ἦτορ |₁₈₉ στήθεσσιν λασίοισι διάνδιχα μερμήριξεν, |₁₉₀ ἢ ὅ γε φάσγανον ὀξὺ ἐρυσσάμενος παρὰ μηροῦ |₁₉₁ τοὺς μὲν ἀναστήσειεν, ὁ δ' Ἀτρεΐδην ἐναρίζοι, |₁₉₂ ἦε χόλον παύσειεν ἐρητύσειέ τε θυμόν.

† |₂₂ Ἀμαζὼν Πενθεσίλεια παραγίνεται |₂₃ Τρωσὶ συμμαχήσουσα, Ἄρεως μὲν θυγάτηρ, Θρᾷσσα δὲ τὸ |₂₄ γένος· καὶ κτείνει αὐτὴν ἀριστεύουσαν Ἀχιλλεύς, οἱ δὲ Τρῶες |₂₄ αὐτὴν θάπτουσι. καὶ Ἀχιλλεὺς Θερσίτην ἀναιρεῖ λοιδορηθεὶς |₂₅ πρὸς αὐτοῦ καὶ ὀνειδισθεὶς τὸν ἐπὶ τῇ Πενθεσιλείᾳ |₂₆ λεγόμενον ἔρωτα.

‡ An English-language translation of the entire ancient plot summary of the *Aithiopis* in available in the on-line *Sourcebook* (chs.harvard.edu).

Aithiopis, as retold by Proclus in his plot summary. The question is this: when Thersites says that Achilles is in love with the Amazon Penthesileia, why is Achilles angry enough to kill him? My answer is this: it would seem that Achilles is in a state of denial about having fallen in love with the beautiful and powerful Amazon whom he has just killed.

3§6. As we know from the narrative about Thersites in *Iliad* II, we are dealing here with a character who understands the truth about heroes, even though he retells that truth in a distorted and offensive way that makes the offended heroes want to kill him. A close reading of the Thersites narrative in *Iliad* II shows that there is a kernel of truth in what he says about Agamemnon and Achilles when he speaks in public about the big quarrel between those two heroes.*
Thersites is lucky to escape with his life for what he says here in the *Iliad,* but his luck finally runs out in the *Aithiopis.*

3§7. We know that Thersites was on to something when he mocked Achilles for falling in love with Penthesileia. We know this from the evidence of ancient vase paintings, dating from the sixth and fifth centuries, where we see depictions of the actual moment when Achilles kills the beautiful Amazon. I cite two vase paintings, showing the killing of the Amazon Penthesileia by Achilles: http://www.britishmuseum.org/explore/highlights/highlight_objects/gr/ b/black-figured_wine_jar.aspx (late sixth century); and http://commons. wikimedia.org/wiki/File:Akhilleus_Penthesileia_Staaliche_Antikensammlungen _2688.jpg (mid-fifth century).

3§8. These evocative paintings, which show the eye contact between Achilles and Penthesileia at the precise moment when he plunges his weapon into her beautiful body, convey a remarkable convergence of themes linked with death and sex—and we will observe many other examples of such convergence as we proceed in our readings from ancient Greek song culture. Coming up, in Hour 5, is an example from the lyric songs of Sappho, Song 31.

3§9. A big question remains: why would Achilles fall in love with the Amazon Penthesileia in particular? A key to the answer is the name of this Amazon, *Penthesileia,* which means 'she who has *penthos* for the people [*lāos*]'. This name is a perfect parallel to the name of *Achilles,* the full form of which can be reconstructed linguistically as **Akhi-lāos* and which is understood in the specialized language of Homeric poetry to mean 'he who has *akhos* for the people [*lāos*]'.†
Not only the names of these epic characters but even the characters themselves are beautifully matched. When Achilles and Penthesileia are engaged in mortal

---

* *BA* 259–264 = 14§§10–14.

† This reconstruction is explained in *BA* 94–117 = 6§§1–30 and in *HTL* 131–137.

combat, as they are represented in the vase paintings, their eyes meet at the precise moment when he kills her. *And what Achilles sees in Penthesileia is a female reflection of his male self.* All along, Penthesileia has been his other self in the feminine gender, as even her name shows, and now he has killed her. The death of Penthesileia thus becomes a source of grief, sorrow, and overwhelming sadness for Achilles, this man of constant sorrow. Both these epic names—and the epic characters that are tied to them—have to do with themes of lament, as signaled by the words *akhos* and *penthos*. Both these words point to the 'grief' or 'sorrow' or 'sadness' of lament.

The Essentials of Singing Laments

3§10. How, then, is 'grief' or 'sorrow' or 'sadness' expressed by *lament*? It is by *crying* and *singing* at the same time. When people like you and me cry, we just cry. When people in a song culture cry, they *lament*. That is, they sing while they cry, they cry while they sing, and this kind of singing *is* crying; this kind of crying *is* singing. The physical aspects of crying are all integrated into the singing: the flow of tears, the choking of the voice, the convulsions of the body, and so on, are all part of the singing.

3§11. Anthropologists have collected many examples of laments that are sung and cried by persons in the depths of real grief. I could illustrate here by way of citing performances in Modern Greek contexts. There has been a great deal of ethnographic research on laments in Modern Greek song culture. A particularly useful work that surveys the vast evidence is the book of Margaret Alexiou, *The Ritual Lament in Greek Tradition.** But I choose here instead to focus on a lament in the context of a historically unrelated song culture. In doing so, I am engaging in typological comparison, which is a kind of comparative method that has to do with the study of parallelisms between structures as structures pure and simple, without any presuppositions. Such a mode of comparison is especially useful in fields like linguistics: comparing parallel structures in languages—even if the given languages are unrelated to each other—is a proven way of enhancing one's overall understanding of the linguistic structures being compared.†

3§12. The lament I have in mind is a northern Hungarian lament, sung—and cried—by an old woman who was mourning two adult sons, both of whom

---

* Alexiou 1974; the second edition (2002) features an important new introduction by Yatromanolakis and Roilos.

† On the concept of typological parallels, see EH §4, with bibliography.

were evidently killed in war. The recording of the lament was initiated many years ago by Zoltán Kodály, himself a Hungarian. Kodály was not only a celebrated composer (my late father, a pianist, was one of his pupils) but also a respected ethnographer and ethnomusicologist who studied the song cultures of Eastern Europe and elsewhere. He arranged for the "live" recordings of a wide variety of folk performances (between 1934 and 1940), including laments. What I transcribe here is a part of the lament I have chosen:*

01. jaj jaj énnekem bánatos anyának!	jaj jaj for me, sorrowful mother!
02. jaj jaj jaj jaj, jaj jaj jaj, Gézikám!	jaj jaj jaj jaj, jaj jaj jaj, my little Géza!
03. Elrabolták a fiam tőlem	They robbed my son from me.
04. Gézikám, Gézikám!	my little Géza! my little Géza!
05. Hun vagy édes fiam?	where are you, my sweet son?
06. Drága gyerekem!	my dear child
07. jaj jaj jaj jaj jaj jaj!	jaj jaj jaj jaj jaj jaj
08. jaj minden szentek napja	jaj, every saint's day,
09. úgy járkálok a sírok közt,	how I wander among the graves
10. hogy nem tanálom a sírodat	—but I can't find your grave.
11. Gézikám édes fiam	my little Géza, my sweet son
12. Gézikám Dezsőkém	my little Géza, my little Dezső
13. Dezsőkém édes fiam	my little Dezső, my sweet son
14. drága gyerekeim!	my dear children
15. Hun vagytok, merre vagytok?	where are you, where are you headed?
16. jaj de szerencsétlen anya vagyok!	jaj, how luckless a mother I am
17. A gyerekeim elsodródtak tőlem messze a vihar.	My children have been swept away, far away, by the storm.
18. Nem tanálom, nem tanálom,	I can't find them, I can't find them.
19. jaj nekem, jaj nekem!	jaj for me, jaj for me
20. Itthon vagyok evvel a bánatos szívű apátokval,	I'm here at home with this father of yours with the sad heart.
21. akinek minden héten kiszedik a vérit.	Every week they rip out his veins

---

* The wording I have quoted is on Side 1 Section 12 of the vinyl record distributed by Qualiton Production in 1964. It is transcribed by Henry Bayerle. For general information about the collecting of Hungarian laments, see http://www.zti.hu/folkmusic/folk_music_research_workshop.htm#cata.

22. Jaj jaj jaj, olyan kínosan néz szegény!	jaj jaj jaj, he looks so tortured
23. Jaj jaj jaj jaj jaj jaj nekem	Jaj jaj jaj jaj jaj jaj for me
24. Hova legyek, mit csináljak?	where am I headed, what am I to do?
25. Kihö forduljak panaszra?	where shall I turn for consolation?
26. Ki segít rajtam, ki vigasztal engem?	who will help me, who will comfort me?
27. Ki ad nekem egy darabka kenyeret	who will give to me a little piece of bread,
28. édes fiaim énnekem?	my sweet sons, to me?
29. jaj . . .	Jaj . . .
30. jaj, hova legyek, mit csináljak?	jaj, where am I headed, what am I to do?
31. jaj, kihö menjek?	jaj, where am I to go?
32. Kihö menjek panaszra, édes fiaim, drága gyerekeim?	where shall I turn for consolation, my sweet sons, my dear children?
33. Nincs aki azt mondaná nekem,	There is nobody who would say to me,
34. hogy édesanyám de szeretlek!	My sweet mother, how I love you!
35. Gézikám drága gyerekem,	My little Géza, my dear child,
36. aki ölelt-csókolt minden pillanatban engem.	who hugged and kissed me every moment.
37. Anyukám, nem tehetek róla,	My dear little mother [= "mommy"], I can't help it,
38. de nagyon-nagyon szeretlek!	but I love you very very much.

Pondering the words of this lament, I note here especially the many ways in which the lamenting woman expresses her feelings of losing control and order. A sense of disorientation sets in, especially at lines 18 and following, and this disorientation leads to a time warp: at lines 32 and following, the lamenting woman's memories modulate from the present to the distant past; she returns to a time when she is still a young mother taking care of her loving child. Her lamenting words picture the child as he is kissing her, trying to comfort her, and the child's words are quoted directly: I am so sorry, 'Mommy', I can't help it, I didn't mean to hurt you. The incapacitation caused by death is all-pervasive here. Earlier, at lines 20–21, the father, too, is pictured as incapacitated by grief, as if all his blood had been forcibly drained from his body.

3§13. It is a well-known fact, learned from ethnographic research on laments, that such sad songs centering on the death of loved ones can modulate into love songs.* The converse also happens: love songs can modulate into laments, especially in the case of love songs that center not only on lovers who are lost or dead but also on the loss or death of love itself. Just as laments express sorrow and love together in the course of mourning the death of a loved one, so also love songs can readily express the same two emotions of sorrow and love together. And why should a traditional love song be sad? The reason is that most traditional love songs are preoccupied with the theme of *unrequited love*. And, in most song cultures, love songs about unrequited love are felt to be deeply erotic.

3§14. Below is an example of such a song. It is a Hungarian love song, from the region of Transylvania, and the name of the love song is *Szerelem*, which means 'love'. This song was used by the director of the film *The English Patient* (1996), both at the beginning of the film and also in the course of the action in the film, as for example in an intensely erotic love scene when the Hungarian character plays on an old "phonograph" machine a vinyl record of this love song. Here are the words of the first two stanzas:

Szerelem, szerelem,	O, love love
átkozott gyötrelem,	accursed torture
mért nem virágoztál	why did you not blossom
minden fatetején?	on every treetop?
Minden fa tetején,	On the top of every tree,
diófa levelén.	on the leaf of a walnut tree,
úgy szakisztott volna	so it would have been plucked by
minden leány s legény.	every maiden and unmarried young man.

When we listen to this song, we hear an example of stylized crying. That is to say, the singer is not really crying, since the crying is stylized.

3§15. In most traditional song cultures, including Greek song culture, laments and love songs are performed primarily by women, and many of the formal gestures of lament are specific to women. The performance of songs by women is a most important matter in ancient Greek song culture. And it is a most important matter to consider right now, as we study the Homeric *Iliad*, since the traditions of such performances pervade the *Iliad*. And I argue that

* Nagy 2010b:34.

Homeric poetry needs to be rethought in the light of the women's song traditions that pervade it.

A Conventional Gesture in Women's Laments

3§16. A moment ago, I mentioned formal gestures of lament that are specific to women. Now I point to an example of such a gesture in the singing of ancient Greek laments: women conventionally let down their hair while lamenting. This spontaneous but traditional gesture is an expression of *loss of control and order* in one's personal life. There are also other spontaneous but traditional ways of expressing loss of control and order, such as *tearing one's hair, scratching one's cheeks, ripping one's fine clothing.*

3§17. In the case of letting down the hair, this ritual gesture is normally preceded by the equally spontaneous but traditional ritual gesture of ripping off the veil that holds the hair together and keeps it composed.

3§18. Here I repeat, from the Introduction to the book, my working definition of ritual and myth. Ritual is doing things and saying things in a way that is considered sacred. Myth is saying things in a way that is also considered sacred. So ritual frames myth.

3§19. Once the veil is torn off, the hair gets let down and becomes completely undone. A spectacular example is the scene in *Iliad* XXII when the wife of Hector, Andromache, rips off her veil, which is the most elaborate headdress to be found in Homeric poetry, before she starts to sing a lament over the death of her husband. By ripping off this veil, Andromache is letting down her beautiful curly hair, violently undoing it. In effect, the Homeric narration here presents to the mind's eye the complete undoing of a woman's composure. Andromache will perform her lament, crying and singing, with her hair completely undone:

Hour 3 Text C

$|_{460}$ She [= Andromache] rushed out of the palace, same as a maenad [*mainas*],* $|_{461}$ with heart throbbing. And her attending women went with her. $|_{462}$ But when she reached the tower and the crowd of warriors, $|_{463}$ she stood on the wall, looking around, and then she noticed him. $|_{464}$ There he was, being dragged right in front of the city. The

---

* I will have more to say about maenads in what follows.

swift chariot team of horses was $|_{465}$ dragging him, far from her caring thoughts, back toward the hollow ships of the Achaeans. $|_{466}$ Over her eyes a dark night spread its cover, $|_{467}$ and she fell backward, gasping out her life's breath [psūkhē]. $|_{468}$ She threw far from her head the splendid adornments that bound her hair $|_{469}$—her frontlet [ampux], her snood [kekruphalos], her plaited headband [anadesmē], $|_{470}$ and, to top it all, the veil [krēdemnon] that had been given to her by golden Aphrodite $|_{471}$ on that day when Hector, the one with the waving plume on his helmet, took her by the hand and led her $|_{472}$ out from the palace of Eëtion, and he gave countless courtship presents. $|_{473}$ Crowding around her stood her husband's sisters and his brothers' wives, $|_{474}$ and they were holding her up. She was barely breathing, to the point of dying. $|_{475}$ But when she recovered her breathing and her life's breath gathered in her heart, $|_{476}$ she started to sing a lament in the midst of the Trojan women.

Iliad XXII 460–476*

3§20. In the verses that follow, the beautiful song of lament sung by Andromache is quoted in full by the master Narrator (XXII 477–514). To appreciate this lament in context, we need to understand the scene of dishevelment that leads up to it, which I have studied at length in an article. Here is an abridged version of what I say about it there:†

> When Andromache suddenly sees the corpse of Hector, dragged behind the chariot of Achilles, she falls into a swoon (XXII 466–467) while at the same time tearing off her elaborate *krēdemnon*, 'veil' (XXII 468–470). In this passionate moment, as her eyes are just about to behold the dreaded sight of her husband's corpse, she is described as looking 'just like a maenad' (*mainadi īsē* XXII 460). Earlier in the *Iliad*,

* $|_{460}$ (Ὣς φαμένη) μεγάροιο διέσσυτο μαινάδι ἴση $|_{461}$ παλλομένη κραδίην· ἅμα δ' ἀμφίπολοι κίον αὐτῇ $|_{462}$ αὐτὰρ ἐπεὶ πύργόν τε καὶ ἀνδρῶν ἷξεν ὅμιλον $|_{463}$ ἔστη παπτήνασ' ἐπὶ τείχεϊ, τὸν δὲ νόησεν $|_{464}$ ἑλκόμενον πρόσθεν πόλιος· ταχέες δέ μιν ἵπποι $|_{465}$ ἕλκον ἀκηδέστως κοίλας ἐπὶ νῆας Ἀχαιῶν. $|_{466}$ τὴν δὲ κατ' ὀφθαλμῶν ἐρεβεννὴ νὺξ ἐκάλυψεν, $|_{467}$ ἤριπε δ' ἐξοπίσω, ἀπὸ δὲ ψυχὴν ἐκάπυσσε. $|_{468}$ τῆλε δ' ἀπὸ κρατὸς βάλε δέσματα σιγαλόεντα, $|_{469}$ ἄμπυκα κεκρύφαλόν τε ἰδὲ πλεκτὴν ἀναδέσμην $|_{470}$ κρήδεμνόν θ', ὅ ῥά οἱ δῶκε χρυσῆ Ἀφροδίτη $|_{471}$ ἤματι τῷ ὅτε μιν κορυθαίολος ἠγάγεθ' Ἕκτωρ $|_{472}$ ἐκ δόμου Ἠετίωνος, ἐπεὶ πόρε μυρία ἕδνα. $|_{473}$ ἀμφὶ δέ μιν γαλόω τε καὶ εἰνατέρες ἅλις ἔσταν, $|_{474}$ αἵ ἑ μετὰ σφίσιν εἶχον ἀτυζομένην ἀπολέσθαι. $|_{475}$ ἣ δ' ἐπεὶ οὖν ἔμπνυτο καὶ ἐς φρένα θυμὸς ἀγέρθη $|_{476}$ ἀμβλήδην γοόωσα μετὰ Τρῳῆσιν ἔειπεν·

† Nagy 2007c:249–250.

in an analogous context, Andromache is pictured as 'looking like a woman possessed' (*mainomenēi eïkuia* VI 389) as she rushes toward the walls of Troy to see for herself the fate of the Trojans on the battlefield.

In this dramatic context, I draw attention to the evocative word *krēdemnon*, 'veil' (XXII 470). It refers to the overall ornamental hair-binding that holds together three separate kinds of ornamental hair-binding that serve to keep Andromache's hair in place, under control (XXII 469).* When Andromache violently tears off from her head this most elaborate veil, causing her hair to come completely undone, she is ritually miming her complete loss of control over her own fate as linked with the fate of her husband: we see here a ritually eroticized gesture that expresses her extreme sexual vulnerability as linked with the violent death and disfiguration of her husband. For Andromache to do violence to her own *krēdemnon* is to express the anticipated violence of her future sexual humiliation at the hands of the enemy. Pointedly, the goddess Aphrodite herself had given this *krēdemnon* to Andromache on her wedding day (XXII 470–471).

Such explicit association of the *krēdemnon* with Aphrodite reveals its erotic properties. The undoing of a woman's hair, caused by the undoing of her *krēdemnon*, produces what I will call an *Aphrodisiac effect*. So long as a woman's *krēdemnon* is in place, her sexuality is under control just as her hair is under control. When the *krēdemnon* is out of place, however, her sexuality threatens to get out of control.

3§21. The lament that is sung by Andromache when she sees the corpse of Hector dragged behind the speeding chariot of Achilles is arguably the most artistic and elaborate of all the laments quoted in the *Iliad* (XXII 477–514). It is also the most lengthy of all Homeric laments. Later, toward the end of the *Iliad*, Andromache sings a lament at the funeral of Hector in Troy, and this lament too is quoted in full by the master Narrator (XXIV 725–745). And earlier, when Andromache speaks to her husband for the last time in a tearful farewell scene,

---

* The three separate terms for ornamental hair-bindings here are *ampux*, 'frontlet', *kekruphalos*, 'snood', and *anadesmē*, 'headband' (*Iliad* XXII 469); the overall hair-binding or 'headdress' that keeps it all in place is the *krēdemnon* (XXII 470). Similarly, Varro (*On the Latin Language* 5.130) speaks of three separate terms for ornamental hair-bindings traditionally used by Roman matrons: *lanea*, 'woolen ribbon', *reticulum*, 'net-cap' or 'snood', and *capital*, 'headband'. To these three words Varro (7.44) adds a fourth, *tutulus* (derived from the adjective *tutus*, 'providing safety'), which seems to be an overall term for the generic veil worn by brides and Vestal Virgins as well as matrons.

her words correspond formally to the words of a lament that could have been sung, with adjustments, at the funeral of Hector, and these words too are quoted in full by the master Narrator (VI 407–439).

3§22. I need to say one more thing right now about the first of the three laments performed by Andromache: in this first lament, Andromache is singing and crying over the death of her husband, Hector, even before he dies. In this case, *her lament is an act of premonition.*

A Typological Comparison of Laments

3§23. I offer here a typological parallel to Andromache's first lament as *an act of premonition.** It comes from the Korean film *Ch'unhyang* (2000), which is based on a traditional Korean *p'ansori* narrative about a righteous young woman named Ch'unhyang, who is of low social status but high moral principles.

3§24. In one scene from this narrative, the young woman breaks out in lament when she absorbs the sad news of a terrible fate that awaits her. In this scene, the secret, high-ranking husband of Ch'unhyang announces that he will abandon her, though only for a while, he claims. The reaction of Ch'unhyang is instantaneous grief. Her sorrow is mixed with feelings of love for her husband, and with feelings of fear and anger that she will lose him forever. She bursts into a lament, accompanied by ritual gestures, such as the violent tearing of her clothes, which is a ritual premonition of the violence she will endure because of her low social rank, now that her secret husband is leaving her. This violent tearing of clothes dramatizes her sexual vulnerability in the uncertain future that now awaits her. In the plot of the Ch'unhyang narrative, that vulnerability will turn out to be a grim reality for this abandoned woman, whose low social status makes her the tragic victim of predatory men of high social status. Her lament is a premonition that anticipates this reality, as she keeps on crying and singing. And the master Narrator quotes the lament of Ch'unhyang as she cries and sings. This way, by quoting the lament of Ch'unhyang, the Narrator performs his own stylized crying and singing, which is more artistic than the lament of Ch'unhyang. When Ch'unhyang is lamenting, her crying and singing are more natural, not as musical as the stylized crying and singing of the master Narrator, and her lament echoes in a kind of delayed reaction the singing of her

---

* On the concept of typological parallels, see again EH §4, with bibliography.

lament as performed by the master Narrator. In the middle of her lament, the macro-Narrative of the film shows flashbacks to happy moments in the past when Ch'unhyang is seen making love to her secret husband. These erotic flashbacks have the effect of intensifying the sorrow of Ch'unhyang as she thinks back to those happy moments in the past that preceded her excruciating pain and suffering in the present. And, conversely, her sorrow intensifies the eroticism of these flashbacks.

3§25. The macro-Narrative of the film *Ch'unhyang* actually shows the master Narrator in action. The camera shows him performing before a large audience representing a broad cross-section of ages and social status. The master Narrator is telling about the excruciating pain and suffering inflicted on Ch'unhyang by her high-ranking tormentor, a magistrate who seeks to alienate her affections from her absent husband. The earlier lament of premonition sung by Ch'unhyang, accompanied by acts of ritual self-degradation like the ripping of her fine clothing, now becomes a lament of actuality, where she cries and sings over the excruciating pain that is being inflicted on her. And the lament that she sings while she is being tortured is quoted by the master Narrator himself, whose stylized crying and singing is foregrounded against the background of the natural crying and singing of Ch'unhyang as she endures the pain inflicted on her. Her crying and singing are echoing the stylized crying and singing of the master Narrator who is quoting her sad song. We see here a typological parallel to the laments of Andromache in the Homeric *Iliad*.

The First Lament of Andromache

3§26. With this comparison in place, I will now analyze the first of the three laments of Andromache in the *Iliad*. I quote only a part of this lament, when we see Andromache singing and crying over the death of her husband, Hector, even before he dies. As I said before, her lament is an act of premonition:

HOUR 3 TEXT D

|$_{407}$ What's gotten into you [Hector]—some kind of superhuman force [*daimōn*]? Your own power [*menos*] is going to make you perish [*phthin-ein*]. You are not showing pity, |$_{408}$ not thinking of your disconnected [*nēpiakhos*] son, and not thinking of me, deprived as I am of good fortune. I will soon become a widow, |$_{409}$ your widow, since you will soon

be killed by the Achaeans. |₄₁₀ They will all rush at you. It would be better for me, |₄₁₁ if I should lose you, to lie dead and be covered over by the earth, since there will no longer |₄₁₂ be anything left to comfort me when you have met your fate. |₄₁₃ I will have nothing but sorrows [*akhos* plural]. I have neither a father nor a queen mother now. |₄₁₄ My father was killed by radiant Achilles |₄₁₅ when that one destroyed the beautifully flourishing city of the Cilicians, |₄₁₆ Thebe, with its lofty gates. So he [= Achilles] killed Eëtion, |₄₁₇ but he did not strip him of his armor—at least he had that much decency in his heart [*thūmos*]—|₄₁₈ and he honored him with the ritual of cremation, burning him together with his armor. |₄₁₉ Then he heaped up a tomb [*sēma*] for him, and elm trees were generated [*phuteuein*] around it |₄₂₀ by forest nymphs who are daughters of Zeus, holder of the aegis. |₄₂₁ I had seven brothers in my father's house, |₄₂₂ but on the same day they all went down into the house of Hādēs. |₄₂₃ For they were all killed by Achilles, swift of foot, the radiant one, |₄₂₄ while they were guarding their ranging cattle and their bright-fleeced sheep. |₄₂₅ My mother— her who had been queen of all the land under the wooded mountain Plakos—|₄₂₆ he [= Achilles] brought here along with the captured treasures, |₄₂₇ and freed her for the price of an untold amount of property, |₄₂₈ but then, in the house of your father [= Priam], she was shot down by Artemis, shooter of arrows. |₄₂₉ Oh, Hector, you who are to me a father, a queen mother, |₄₃₀ a brother, and a husband in his prime—|₄₃₁ please, have pity on me; stay here at the fortifications; |₄₃₂ don't make your child an orphan, and your wife a widow.

Iliad VI 407–432*

* |₄₀₇ δαιμόνιε φθίσει σε τὸ σὸν μένος, οὐδ' ἐλεαίρεις |₄₀₈ παῖδά τε νηπίαχον καὶ ἔμ' ἄμμορον, ἣ τάχα χήρη |₄₀₉ σεῦ ἔσομαι· τάχα γάρ σε κατακτανέουσιν Ἀχαιοὶ |₄₁₀ πάντες ἐφορμηθέντες· ἐμοὶ δέ κε κέρδιον εἴη |₄₁₁ σεῦ ἀφαμαρτούσῃ χθόνα δύμεναι· οὐ γὰρ ἔτ' ἄλλη |₄₁₂ ἔσται θαλπωρὴ ἐπεὶ ἂν σύ γε πότμον ἐπίσπῃς |₄₁₃ ἀλλ' ἄχε'· οὐδέ μοι ἔστι πατὴρ καὶ πότνια μήτηρ. |₄₁₄ ἤτοι γὰρ πατέρ' ἀμὸν ἀπέκτανε δῖος Ἀχιλλεύς, |₄₁₅ ἐκ δὲ πόλιν πέρσεν Κιλίκων εὖ ναιετάουσαν |₄₁₆ Θήβην ὑψίπυλον· κατὰ δ' ἔκτανεν Ἠετίωνα, |₄₁₇ οὐδέ μιν ἐξενάριξε, σεβάσσατο γὰρ τό γε θυμῷ, |₄₁₈ ἀλλ' ἄρα μιν κατέκηε σὺν ἔντεσι δαιδαλέοισιν |₄₁₉ ἠδ' ἐπὶ σῆμ' ἔχεεν· περὶ δὲ πτελέας ἐφύτευσαν |₄₂₀ νύμφαι ὀρεστιάδες κοῦραι Διὸς αἰγιόχοιο. |₄₂₁ οἳ δέ μοι ἑπτὰ κασίγνητοι ἔσαν ἐν μεγάροισιν |₄₂₂ οἳ μὲν πάντες ἰῷ κίον ἤματι Ἄϊδος εἴσω· |₄₂₃ πάντας γὰρ κατέπεφνε ποδάρκης δῖος Ἀχιλλεὺς |₄₂₄ βουσὶν ἐπ' εἰλιπόδεσσι καὶ ἀργεννῇς ὄιεσσι. |₄₂₅ μητέρα δ', ἣ βασίλευεν ὑπὸ Πλάκῳ ὑληέσσῃ, |₄₂₆ τὴν ἐπεὶ ἂρ δεῦρ' ἤγαγ' ἅμ' ἄλλοισι κτεάτεσσιν, |₄₂₇ ἂψ ὅ γε τὴν ἀπέλυσε λαβὼν ἀπερείσι' ἄποινα, |₄₂₈ πατρὸς δ' ἐν μεγάροισι βάλ' Ἄρτεμις ἰοχέαιρα. |₄₂₉ Ἕκτορ ἀτὰρ σύ μοί ἐσσι πατὴρ καὶ πότνια μήτηρ |₄₃₀ ἠδὲ κασίγνητος, σὺ δέ μοι θαλερὸς παρακοίτης· |₄₃₁ ἀλλ' ἄγε νῦν ἐλέαιρε καὶ αὐτοῦ μίμν' ἐπὶ πύργῳ, |₄₃₂ μὴ παῖδ' ὀρφανικὸν θήῃς χήρην τε γυναῖκα.

3§27. As we see in these words of Andromache's lament, the word *akhos*, 'grief, sorrow', at verse 413 is used to express the performance, the singing, of lament.

3§28. In the course of lamenting her sorrows, Andromache makes special mention of the death of her father, whose name is Eëtion—as we know from another context that we will consider shortly. From what Andromache says, it is clear that her father would rank highest in her ascending scale of affection—*if he were alive*. But her father is dead, and so too are her seven brothers and her mother. All Andromache has left is her husband, Hector, who is now the entirety of her ascending scale of affections. Hector has become for Andromache her father, brothers, and mother, as well as her husband. In effect, Andromache is telling Hector: *you're my everything*.

What Achilles Sang

3§29. The death of Eëtion, Andromache's father, who would have ranked highest in Andromache's ascending scale of affection, deepens the irony in a passage we saw earlier. Here I repeat only the relevant verses of that passage:

HOUR 3 TEXT E = HOUR 2 TEXT D

|$_{185}$ The two of them reached the shelters and the ships of the Myrmidons, |$_{186}$ and they found Achilles diverting his heart [*phrēn*] as he was playing on a clear-sounding lyre [*phorminx*], |$_{187}$ a beautiful one, of exquisite workmanship, and its cross-bar was of silver. |$_{188}$ It was part of the spoils that he had taken when he destroyed the city of Eëtion, |$_{189}$ and he was now diverting his heart [*thūmos*] with it as he was singing [*aeidein*] the glories of men [*klea andrōn*]. |$_{190}$ Patroklos was the only other person there. He [= Patroklos] sat in silence, facing him [= Achilles], |$_{191}$ and waiting for the Aeacid [= Achilles] to leave off singing [*aeidein*]. |$_{192}$ Meanwhile the two of them came in—Odysseus leading the way—|$_{193}$ and stood before him. Achilles sprang up from his seat |$_{194}$ with the lyre [*phorminx*] still in his hand, |$_{195}$ and Patroklos, when he saw the guests, rose also.

Iliad IX 185–195

3§30. We see Achilles here singing the *klea andrōn*, the 'glories of heroes of the past' (*Iliad* IX 189)—while accompanying himself on a lyre. And the lyre that he is playing had once belonged to Eëtion, the father of Andromache. As we have just seen from the words of Andromache, Achilles had killed her father, Eëtion. And, evidently, Achilles took away as his prize the lyre of Eëtion, and now he is playing on that lyre as he sings the *klea andrōn*, the 'glories of men'. Achilles is strumming the pain of Andromache. I am reminded of the words of the song *Killing Me Softly* (1973), originally sung by Roberta Flack: "Strumming my pain with his fingers, singing my life with his words, . . ."

3§31. You have to ask yourself: what was Achilles singing about when he sang the *klea andrōn*, the 'glories of heroes of the past' (*Iliad* IX 189)? The master Narrator of the macro-Narrative does not say. There is no quoting or even paraphrasing of the subject of the song sung by Achilles here. But there is a hint about that subject, and that hint is embedded in another vitally important nearby mention of *klea andrōn* in the *Iliad*. We have already seen it. It happens in Text B of Hour 2, when Phoenix is telling the story of the hero Meleagros and his wife Kleopatra, and the old man refers to his micro-narrative as *tōn prosthen . . . klea andrōn | hērōōn*, 'the glories [*kleos* plural] of men of an earlier time who were heroes' (IX 524–525). And what is the subject of that micro-narrative? From the standpoint of Phoenix as the narrator, the subject is the love that a hero owes to his comrades. From the standpoint of the master Narrator of the macro-Narrative that is the *Iliad*, however, the subject is nothing less than the meaning of Kleopatra herself, of her name, which signals the 'glories of the ancestors', the 'glories of heroes of the past'.

The Song of Kleopatra

3§32. The meaning of Kleopatra, as well as the meaning of the song about Kleopatra as told by Phoenix, is relevant to the very idea of lamentation. Inside the song about Kleopatra, that is, inside the *klea andrōn* as performed by Phoenix, Kleopatra is actually shown performing a lament, singing it to her husband, Meleagros, and her song of lament is actually paraphrased in this song of and about Kleopatra (*Iliad* IX 590–594). In this song, that is, in the *klea andrōn* as performed by Phoenix (IX 524), we see that Kleopatra has a second name besides Kleopatra, and that second name is a clear signal of lamentation. That second name is *Alcyone*, and the meaning of that name is transparent. In ancient Greek traditions, as I noted in Hour 2, the *alcyon / halcyon* is a bird that is linked with singing songs of lament, and the *Iliad* makes this link explicit in referring to the name *Alcyone*, given to the lamenting Kleopatra by her lamenting mother and father:

HOUR 3 TEXT F (PART OF HOUR 2 TEXT E)

|₅₆₁ She [= Kleopatra] had been given a special name by the father and by the queen mother back then [when she was growing up] in the palace. |₅₆₂ They called her *Alcyone*, making that a second name for her, because her |₅₆₃ mother [= Marpessa] was feeling the same pain [*oitos*] felt by the *halcyon* bird, known for her many sorrows [*penthos*]. |₅₆₄ She [= Marpessa] was crying because she had been seized and carried away by the one who has far-reaching power, Phoebus Apollo.

Iliad IX 561–564*

3§33. Can we say, then, that the *klea andrōn* sung by Achilles himself is the song of Kleopatra? Yes and no. It is the song of Kleopatra, but it is not only her song. It is also the song of Patroklos. As we have seen in Hour 2, the meaning of the name of Kleopatra is also the meaning of the name of Patroklos, 'the one who has the glory [*kleos*] of the ancestors [*pateres*]', and this meaning recapitulates the epic choice of Achilles, who ultimately opts for *kleos* over life itself. The name of *Kleopatra* contains the same elements as the name of *Patroklos*, only in reverse: 'the one who has the glory [*kleos*] of the ancestors [*pateres*]'.

* |₅₆₁ τὴν δὲ τότ' ἐν μεγάροισι πατὴρ καὶ πότνια μήτηρ |₅₆₂ Ἀλκυόνην καλέεσκον ἐπώνυμον, οὕνεκ' ἄρ' αὐτῆς |₅₆₃ μήτηρ ἀλκυόνος πολυπενθέος οἶτον ἔχουσα |₅₆₄ κλαῖεν ὅ μιν ἑκάεργος ἀνήρπασε Φοῖβος Ἀπόλλων.

Achilles as Lyric Hero in the Songs of Sappho and Pindar

The Meaning of Aphthito-

4§1. The key word for this hour is *aphthito-* in the sense of 'imperishable'. By the time we reach the end of this hour, we will see that *aphthito-* can also be interpreted as 'unwilting' in some specialized contexts. We already saw this word when we read Text A in Hour 1, when the hero Achilles tells about a prophecy made by his divine mother, Thetis:

> |₄₁₂ If I stay here and fight at the walls of the city of the Trojans, then my safe homecoming [*nostos*] will be destroyed for me, but I will have a glory [*kleos*] that is imperishable [*aphthiton*].
>
> *Iliad* IX 412–413*

4§2. Such an idea of a *kleos,* or poetic 'glory' that is *aphthiton* or 'imperishable' forever, can be found not only in epic poetry but also in lyric poetry. For example, as we will soon see, the identical expression *kleos aphthiton,* 'imperishable glory', is used in a song of Sappho, who flourished in the late seventh and early sixth century BCE. And the same idea of 'imperishable glory' is found in a song of Pindar, who flourished in the first half of the fifth century BCE. Although the era of Pindar is more than a century later than the era of Sappho, I will start in Text A with the relevant passage from Pindar (*Isthmian* 8 lines 56–62). Then I will move to text B, which is the relevant passage from Sappho (Song 44, with special reference to *kleos aphthiton,* 'imperishable glory', at line 4).†

---

* |₄₁₂ εἰ μέν κ' αὖθι μένων Τρώων πόλιν ἀμφιμάχωμαι, |₄₁₃ ὤλετο μέν μοι νόστος, ἀτὰρ κλέος ἄφθιτον ἔσται.

† The expression *kleos aphthiton,* 'imperishable glory', is also used in a lyric composition of Ibycus (*PMG* S151.47–48), who flourished in the second half of the sixth century BCE.

The Imperishable Glory of Achilles in a Song of Pindar

4§3. That said, I am ready to focus on a passage that expresses the idea of *kleos aphthiton*, 'imperishable glory'—but without directly using the words *kleos* and *aphthiton*. The passage I will quote, Text A, is taken from a choral lyric song of Pindar. This song is honoring the athletic victory of an aristocrat from the island state of Aegina. The athlete's name is Kleandros. Besides Kleandros, the song also honors his cousin, named Nikokles. And, ultimately, the song honors the hero Achilles, whom the aristocrats of Aegina claimed as one of their ancestors.* Here is what the lyric wording says about Achilles:

Hour 4 Text A (See Also Hour 0 Text E)

|₅₆ Even when he [= Achilles] died, the songs did not leave him, |₅₇ but the Maidens of Helicon [= the Muses] stood by his pyre and his funeral mound, |₅₈ and, as they stood there, they poured forth a song of lamentation [*thrēnos*] that is famed far and wide. |₅₉ And so it was that the immortal gods decided |₆₀ to hand over the man, genuine [*esthlos*] as he was even after he had perished [*phthi-n-ein*] in death, to the songs of the goddesses [= the Muses]. |₆₁ And this, even now, wins as a prize the words of song, as the chariot-team of the Muses starts moving on its way |₆₂ to glorify the memory of Nikokles the boxer.

Pindar *Isthmian* 8.56–62†

4§4. So the lyric song is saying that Achilles will die in war and will thus stop flourishing, that is, he will 'perish', *phthi-n-ein*, but the medium that conveys the message of death will never perish. This medium is pictured as a choral lyric song eternally sung by the Muses as they lament Achilles after he is cut down.‡ The lyric song is pictured as a lament that will be transformed by the Muses into a song of glory. Although Achilles will personally 'perish', *phthi-n-ein*, the song about him is destined to have a poetic glory that will never perish. The lyric wording here corresponds to the epic wording that we have noted in *Iliad* IX

---

* On the *Aiakidai*, 'Aeacids' = 'descendants of Aiakos' (among whom are Achilles and Ajax), as notional ancestors of the aristocratic lineages of the island state of Aegina, see Nagy 2011a.

† |₅₆ τὸν μὲν οὐδὲ θανόντ' ἀοιδαὶ <ἐπ>έλιπον, |₅₇ ἀλλά οἱ παρά τε πυρὰν τάφον θ' Ἑλικώνιαι παρθένοι |₅₈ στάν, ἐπὶ θρῆνόν τε πολύφαμον ἔχεαν. |₅₉ ἔδοξ' ἦρα καὶ ἀθανάτοις, |₆₀ ἐσλόν γε φῶτα καὶ φθίμενον ὕμνοις θεᾶν διδόμεν. |₆₁ τὸ καὶ νῦν φέρει λόγον, ἔσσυταί τε Μοισαῖον ἅρμα Νικοκλέος |₆₂ μνᾶμα πυγμάχου κελαδῆσαι.

‡ *PH* 204–206 = 7§6.

413, quoted in Hour 1 Text A, where it is foretold that the poetic *kleos*, 'glory', of Achilles will be *a-phthi-ton*, 'imperishable', forever.* The Homeric usage of *kleos* in such contexts is parallel to the usage of this same word in the songmaking of Pindar, whose words proudly proclaim his mastery of the prestige conferred by *kleos*, or poetic 'glory' (as in *Nemean* 7.61–63).†

4§5. I follow up here with a brief exegesis of Text A, the Pindaric passage that I quoted just now (*Isthmian* 8 lines 56–62).‡

4§5A, According to Pindar's song, the death of the athlete Nikokles (we do not know for sure how he died, but he may have been killed in the Persian War of 480 BCE) will not impede the glory that he merited as a victorious boxer: rather, the death of this athlete is said to be the key to the continuation of his glory, just as the death of Achilles was the key to the extension of the glory of heroes into the historical present.

4§5B. Pindar's song says that the death of Nikokles, by virtue of his deeds in the historical present, will be honored by the same tradition of song that honored the death of Achilles by virtue of that hero's deeds in the heroic past. Thus the name of Nikokles, *Nīkoklēs*, 'he who has the glory [*kleos*] of victory [*nīkē*]', has a meaning that is relevant to the themes of Pindar's lyric song.

4§5C. But there is another name in this song that is even more relevant. The cousin of Nikokles, whose victory in an athletic event of boxing is highlighted in the song, was a young man named Kleandros, who won the athletic event of the *pankration* at the festival of the Isthmia (celebrated at the Isthmus of Corinth) and who was the primary recipient of honor in this lyric song of Pindar. The name of Kleandros, *Kleandros,* 'he who has the glories of men [*klea andrōn*]', is proclaimed as the first word of this whole song of Pindar's (*Isthmian* 8.1). This placement of his name at the very beginning of the song composed in his honor is remarkable. In no other victory song of Pindar do we find the name of a victor placed in absolute initial position. And the meaning of this name fits perfectly the meaning of the expression *klea andrōn*, 'the glories of men', as we have seen it being used in epic:

---

* A fuller version of the argument is made in *BA* 176–177 = 10§§3–4; also in *PH* 204–206 = 7§6. I disagree with what is said by Rodin 2009:296 about the relevant wording of Pindar *Isthmian* 8.56–60. I especially disagree with his argument that the *kleos* of Achilles is restricted to epic. As we will now see, the *kleos* of Achilles is pictured as extending into lyric, including such forms as the victory odes of Pindar. See also Nagy 2007a ("Lyric and Greek Myth") 36.

† *PH* 147 = 6§3.

‡ There is a fuller version of this exegesis in *PH* 204–206 = 7§§6–7.

HOUR 4 TEXT B (PART OF HOUR 2 TEXT B)

|₅₂₄ This is how [*houtōs*] we [= I, Phoenix] learned it, the glories [*klea*] of men [*andrōn*] of an earlier time [*prosthen*], |₅₂₅ who were heroes [*hērōes*], whenever one of them was overcome by tempestuous anger.

Iliad IX 524–525

HOUR 4 TEXT C = HOUR 2 TEXT D

|₁₈₅ The two of them reached the shelters and the ships of the Myrmidons, |₁₈₆ and they found Achilles diverting his heart [*phrēn*] as he was playing on a clear-sounding lyre [*phorminx*], |₁₈₇ a beautiful one, of exquisite workmanship, and its cross-bar was of silver. |₁₈₈ It was part of the spoils that he had taken when he destroyed the city of Eëtion, |₁₈₉ and he was now diverting his heart [*thūmos*] with it as he was singing [*aeidein*] the glories of men [*klea andrōn*]. |₁₉₀ Patroklos was the only other person there. He [= Patroklos] sat in silence, facing him [= Achilles], |₁₉₁ and waiting for the Aeacid [= Achilles] to leave off singing [*aeidein*]. |₁₉₂ Meanwhile the two of them came in—radiant Odysseus leading the way—|₁₉₃ and stood before him. Achilles sprang up from his seat |₁₉₄ with the lyre [*phorminx*] still in his hand, |₁₉₅ and Patroklos, when he saw the guests, rose also.

Iliad IX 185–195

In these two passages from *Iliad* IX, as we have already seen in Hour 2, the term *klea andrōn*, 'glories of men', refers in the first case to an allusive tale told by Phoenix to Achilles about Meleagros and Kleopatra (524) and, in the second case, to a song sung by Achilles in his shelter (189).

The Lyric Glory of Achilles

4§6. The word *kleos*, when it is used in epic, is not limited to the 'glory' of epic. As I will now argue, the epic *kleos* chosen by Achilles in *Iliad* IX (413) is also a lyric *kleos*. And Achilles himself is not only an epic hero; he is also a lyric hero. The epic wording of the Homeric *Iliad* clearly recognizes that the *kleos* of Achilles is lyric as well as epic.

4§7. I begin with a telling detail. As we can see in the epic of the *Iliad,* Achilles is pictured as singing the *klea andrōn,* 'glories of men' (IX 189), while accompanying himself on a *phorminx* (IX 186, 195), which is a kind of lyre, by which I mean simply a stringed instrument. So it is pertinent to note already at this stage that *the lyre typifies 'lyric' poetry in ancient Greek song culture.* Granted, the mention of a lyre in this passage of the *Iliad* is not decisive, since we can find Homeric contexts that show a singer accompanying himself on a *phorminx* while performing either epic tales (as in *Odyssey* viii 67, 99, 105, 537) or songs that are both sung and danced (as in viii 254, 257, 261).* Still, the fact remains that Achilles is accompanying himself on a lyre (IX 186, 195) when he sings the *klea andrōn,* 'glories of men', in his shelter (IX 189). And all I am saying at this point is that such singing could be lyric as well as epic.

4§8. Pursuing this argument further, I now return to a passage that came up in the previous hour. It is Text D of Hour 3, *Iliad* VI 407–416, 421–432, when Andromache laments the death of her father, whose name is Eëtion. In the light of that passage I quoted earlier, we have seen the deep irony of the reference to the lyre of Achilles in the passage I quoted just a minute ago, Text C, from *Iliad* IX 185–195. Here we see Achilles playing on the lyre that once belonged to Eëtion, the father of Andromache. He is singing and accompanying himself on the lyre. And such self-accompanied singing to the lyre, as I just noted, is the basic principle of what we call *lyric poetry.* And the lyric poem—or, better, lyric song—that Achilles is performing here in *Iliad* IX 189 is the *klea andrōn,* the 'glories of men'.

4§9. A fuller way of referring to such glories, as we saw in Text B, *Iliad* IX 524–525, is *tōn prosthen . . . klea andrōn | hērōōn,* 'the glories [*kleos* plural] of men of an earlier time, who were heroes'. In this Text B, as we have seen, the narrator is Phoenix, who is performing a compressed epic narrative about the hero Meleagros and his wife, Kleopatra. As we have also seen, the name *Kleo-patra* means 'she who has the *kleos* of the ancestors'. In this case, I have described the narrative of Phoenix as an epic within the epic that is the Homeric *Iliad.* So the *klea andrōn,* 'glories of men', can be either epic or lyric.

4§10. When Achilles sings the *klea andrōn,* 'glories of men', in *Iliad* IX (189), his only audience is his best friend, Patroklos, who is waiting for his own turn to sing (190–191). As we have already seen, the one-man audience of the song is

---

* Of the three performances of Demodokos in the narration of *Odyssey* viii, the first and the third are epic while the second is "lyric," in the sense that the second performance includes singing and athletic dancing to the rhythm and melody of the words being sung. See *HPC* 79–93 = I§§188–223.

also the hidden subject of the allusive tale here. And that is because, as we have also seen, the name *Patro-kleēs* means 'he who has the *kleos* of the ancestors'.

4§11. In *Iliad* IX (189), we see the word *kleos*, 'glory', being used explicitly, but the reference to the glory of Patroklos is only implicit; and this *kleos*, given by the medium of epic, describes itself elsewhere as *aphthiton*, 'imperishable' (413). In Pindar's *Isthmian* 8 (56–60), by contrast, the word *kleos* is not being used in reference to glory given by the medium of lyric, though we have already seen it used that way in other lyric contexts, as in *Nemean* 7 (61–63). Nevertheless, the actual reference to the glory of Achilles is explicit here in *Isthmian* 8. And, although *Isthmian* 8 does not show the form *aphthito-*, 'imperishable', with reference to the glory of Achilles, it does show the word *phthimenos*, 'perished', with reference to Achilles himself as the hero who has personally perished while his glory remains imperishable. And this glory extends all the way into the glory of the victorious athlete in the historical present.

4§12. In Pindar's lyric song, as in the epic of the *Iliad*, the *kleos* of the ancestors plays a role. In the lyric song, however, the *kleos* of the ancestors is realized not in the idea built into the name of Patroklos, the *kleos* of the ancestors, but rather in the actual *kleos* of the victor's own ancestors. In this particular song, moreover, the *kleos* of the victor's ancestors is realized in the victor's own name, *Kleandros*. The victor Kleandros is living proof that the *kleos*, or poetic 'glory', of his family is predicated on the achievements of its members. The victor who is being celebrated here in Pindar's lyric song was expected to be celebrated from the start, from the very time that he was named after he was born. He was expected to become what he became through his athletic victory. And he was fortunate enough to live up to his name. A person's name, which he is given at birth on the basis of his ancestry, commits him to his identity. In the case of Kleandros, we see that a historical person can fit the themes of Pindar's songmaking tradition. Even the identity of a historical person, as defined by his name, can fit such themes. This can happen because the family's prestige and their very identity depend on the traditional institution of glorification by way of song.

4§13. Here I return to my argument that the epic *kleos* to be chosen by Achilles in *Iliad* IX 413, quoted in Hour 1 Text A, is also a lyric *kleos*, as we can see from the fact that Achilles is pictured as singing the *klea andrōn*, 'glories of heroes', in *Iliad* IX 189, quoted in Text C, while he accompanies himself on a lyre, which as we have just seen is the stringed instrument that typifies 'lyric' poetry in ancient Greek song culture. And, I must now emphasize, the lyric song that

Achilles sings is relevant to the themes of lament. As we have already noticed, this precious musical instrument had been plundered by Achilles when he captured the native city of Andromache (IX 186–189). The link here with Andromache is essential, in view of the fact that this woman is featured as singing three of the greatest laments in the *Iliad*. As I have already noted in Hour 3, Andromache is performing a formal lament for Hector in *Iliad* XXIV (725–745); also in *Iliad* XXII (477–514), much of what she says corresponds morphologically to the words of a formal lament. Already in her first appearance, in *Iliad* VI (407–439), the language of lament is evident in her words as she and Hector part forever, she going back to her weaving at the loom while he goes off to his death.*

4§14. The song of *klea andrōn*, 'glories of heroes', sung by Achilles inside the epic of the Homeric *Iliad* (IX 189) is like an echo of songs of lament about love and bittersweet sorrow as heard in the lyric tradition.† In that tradition, such songs of lament are typically linked not only with Achilles but also with that most celebrated pair of doomed lovers in ancient Greek song culture, namely, Andromache and the man who earns the ultimate hatred and fury of Achilles in the *Iliad*, Hector.‡ The *kleos* of Achilles is a form of song that dwells on the hatred and the fury, the love and the sorrow—and on the power of song in expressing all these intensely lyrical feelings.

The Imperishable Glory of Hector and Andromache in a Song of Sappho

4§15. The *kleos*, or 'glory', of Achilles in epic is interchangeable with the *kleos*, or 'glory', of Hector and Andromache in lyric, as we learn from Song 44 of Sappho, which is about the wedding of this doomed couple.§ Song 44 is fragmentary, and I quote here only some salient lines:

HOUR 4 TEXT D

|₄ . . . and the rest of Asia . . . imperishable glory [*kleos aphthiton*]. |₅ Hector and his comrades [*sun-(h)etairoi*] led her, the one with the

---

*HC 579–580 = 4§262.

† Nagy 2007a ("Lyric and Greek Myth") 36–38.

‡ HPC 239–240 = II§297.

§ There is much debate about the occasion for singing such a song: there is a quick survey of differing opinions in Dale 2011, especially pp. 58 and 61. I agree with Dale and others when they say that there is no reason to insist that the occasion must be a wedding. But I must add that there is no reason to assume that sad songs cannot be sung at weddings.

glancing looks, |₆ from holy Thebe and . . . Plakia, they led her, the lovely Andromache |₇ in ships over the salty |₈ sea. Many golden bracelets and purple |₉ robes . . . , intricately worked ornaments, |₁₀ countless silver cups and ivory. |₁₁ Thus he spoke. And the dear father quickly stood up. |₁₂ And the news reached the dear ones throughout the broad city. |₁₃ And the Trojans yoked to smooth-running carriages |₁₄ the mules. And the whole ensemble climbed on, |₁₅ all the women and maidens | . . . |₂₁ looking just like the gods [*ikeloi theois*] |₂₂ . . . holy |₂₃ set forth into Troy . . . |₂₄ And the sweet song of the pipe mixed . . . |₂₅ And the sound of the cymbals, and then the maidens |₂₆ sang a sacred song, and all the way to the sky |₂₇ traveled the wondrous echo . . . |₂₈ And everywhere through the streets . . . |₂₉ Mixing bowls and cups . . . |₃₀ And myrrh and cassia and frankincense were mingled. |₃₁ And the older women cried out *elelu.* |₃₂ Meanwhile all the men sang out a lovely high-pitched song, |₃₃ calling on Apollo Pāōn, the far-shooter, master of playing beautifully on the lyre. |₃₄ And they sang the song of Hector and Andromache, both looking just like the gods [*theoeikeloi*].

from Song 44 of Sappho ("The Wedding of Hector and Andromache")*

4§16. There is an all-important comparison to be made here: the happy bride and bridegroom, in the wording of line 4 of Song 44 of Sappho, are destined to have *kleos aphthiton,* 'imperishable glory', and the phrase that we see used here in Sappho's song is identical with the *kleos aphthiton,* 'imperishable glory', of Achilles in line 413 of *Iliad* IX, as quoted in Hour 1 Text A.

4§17. We saw in *Iliad* IX 413 that the main hero of the *Iliad* leaves as his signature the *kleos* of his own epic, which turns out to be the *Iliad.* Now we see that the *kleos aphthiton,* 'imperishable glory', of Achilles in *Iliad* IX is matched by the

* |₄ τάς τ' ἄλλας Ἀσίας .[.]δε.αν κλέος ἄφθιτον· |₅ Ἕκτωρ καὶ συνέταιρ[ο]ι ἄγοισ' ἐλικώπιδα |₆ Θήβας ἐξ ἱέρας Πλακίας τ' ἀ.[..]νάω |₇ ἄβραν Ἀνδρομάχαν ἐνὶ ναῦσιν ἐπ' ἄλμυρον |₈ πόντον· πόλλα δ' [ἐλί]γματα χρύσια κάμματα |₉ πορφύρ[α] καταύτ[. . .]να, ποίκιλ' ἀθύρματα, |₁₀ ἀργύρα τ' ἀνάρ[ι]θμα [ποτή]ρ[ια] καλέφαις. |₁₁ ὢς εἶπ'· ὀτραλέως δ' ἀνόρουσε πάτ[η]ρ φίλος· |₁₂ φάμα δ' ἦλθε κατὰ πτόλιν εὐρύχορον φίλοις. |₁₃ αὖτικ' Ἰλιάδαι σατίναι[ς] ὑπ' εὐτρόχοις |₁₄ ἆγον αἰμιόνοις, ἐπ[έ]βαινε δὲ παῖς ὄχλος |₁₅ γυναίκων τ' ἄμα παρθενίκα[ν] τ . . . [. . .].σφύρων, |₂₁ [. . . ἴ]κελοι θέοι[ς] |₂₂ [. . .] ἄγνον ἀολ[λε]| |₂₃ ὄρμαται[. . .]νον ἐς Ἴλιο[ν] |₂₄ αὖλος δ' ἀδυ[μ]έλησ[. . .] τ' ὀνεμίγνυ[το] |₂₅ ιψ[ό]φο[ς κ]ροτάλ[ων...]ως δ' ἄρα πάρ[θ]ενοι |₂₆ ἄειδον μέλος ἄγν[ον ὔκα] νε δ' ἐς αὔθ[ερα] |₂₇ ἄχω θεσπεσία γελ[. . .] |₂₈ [πάνται δ' ἦς κατ ὄδο[. . .] |₂₉ κράτηρες φίαλαί τ' ὀ[. . .]νεδε[. . .] . . . εακ[.].[. . .] |₃₀ μύρρα καὶ κασία λίβανός τ' ὀνεμείχνυτο |₃₁ γύναικες δ' ἐλέλυσδον ὄσαι προγενέστερα[ι] |₃₂ [πάντες δ' ἄνδρες ἐπήρατον ἰαχον ὄρθιον₃₃ Πάον' ὀνκαλέοντες ἐκάβολον εὐλύραν, |₃₄ ὔμνην δ' Ἕκτορα κ'Α]νδρομάχαν θεοεικέλο[ις]. (In this transcription, the sign "[. . .]" is not meant to indicate the number of letters that are missing; it is merely a short-hand indication of lacunae.)

kleos aphthiton, 'imperishable glory', of Hector and Andromache in Song 44 of Sappho. In the first case, the context of winning such glory is war. In the second case, the context is a wedding.

4§18. Since Song 44 of Sappho is about a wedding, it is important to note right away the traditional wording that applies to brides at weddings. That word is *numphē,* which means both 'bride' (as in *Iliad* XVIII 492) and 'goddess', that is, 'nymph' (as in *Iliad* XXIV 616). By implication, the ritual occasion of a wedding, as formalized in a bridal song, collapses the distinction between 'bride' and 'goddess'. The same can be said, as we will see in Hour 5, about the distinction between 'bridegroom' and 'god'.

4§19. At the climax of the wedding of Hector and Andromache as narrated in Song 44 of Sappho, *the bride and groom are transformed into gods*—at the actual moment of that climax. I will make that argument in Hour 5, along with a related argument. In Hour 5, we will see how something comparable happens at the climactic moment of war: at the actual moment of that climax, *the warrior is transformed into a god.*

4§20. Here I highlight the epithet *theoeikeloi,* 'looking just like the gods', applied to Hector and Andromache as the bridegroom and the bride in line 34 of Song 44 of Sappho; also relevant is *ikeloi theois,* 'looking just like the gods', applied to the couple in line 11. This same epithet *theoeikelos,* 'looking just like the gods', is used in the *Iliad,* but there it is reserved for Achilles (I 131, XIX 155). No other hero receives this epithet in that epic. So the doomed couple and the doomed Achilles are all part of one song, one *kleos.* Such is the *kleos* that Sappho's Song 44 is recreating. In the songmaking traditions of women, this song is morphologically related to but distinct from the epic songs that derive primarily from the songmaking traditions of men. To put it another way, Song 44 of Sappho is an example of *epic as refracted in women's songmaking traditions.**

Achilles as a Bridegroom

4§21. As we have seen so far in Hour 4, Achilles can cross over from the world of epic into the world of lyric. In terms of this crossover, as we will see in Hour 5, Achilles is pictured not only as a warrior but also as a bridegroom. And, like

---

*HQ 57.

Hector, Achilles too is pictured as a bridegroom who is 'equal to the gods'. Unlike Hector, however, Achilles will never get married, and that is why he is lamented in a special way. As we will see in Hour 5, Achilles is lamented as an eternal bridegroom because his fulfillment as a married adult is eternally deferred. For the moment, I will simply preview this idea of Achilles as a bridegroom by highlighting an important piece of information about the poetic tradition of Sappho:

HOUR 4 TEXT E

Himerius (*Orations* 1.16) says: 'Sappho compared the girl to an apple [. . .] she compared the bridegroom to Achilles, and likened the young man's deeds to the hero's'.*

Sappho Fragment 105b

Achilles as a Focus of Lament

4§22. This idea of Achilles as a bridegroom is relevant to the fact that Achilles is a focus of lament in lyric as well as in epic traditions. In lyric, as we will see in Hour 5, the idea of Achilles as a bridegroom is connected with his sorrowful fate of dying young, cut down in the bloom of his youth like a tender seedling that is thus doomed to wilt. This connection is implied in the wording of a fragment from one of the songs of Sappho:

HOUR 4 TEXT F

To what shall I liken you, dear bridegroom, to make the likeness beautiful? | To a tender seedling, I liken you to that most of all.

Sappho Song 115†

4§23. As I will argue in Hour 5, the words of this lyric song are implicitly comparing the bridegroom to Achilles. Leading up to that argument, I will show here in Hour 4 that Achilles himself is compared to a tender seedling in his own right, and that this comparison is a fundamental theme in the lyric traditions of lament. A prime example can be found in the lament of Thetis in *Iliad* XVIII,

---

* More on the testimony of Himerius in Dale 2011, especially pp. 54, 62–64, and 67.

† τίωι σ', ὦ φίλε γάμβρε, κάλως ἐικάσδω; | ὄρπακι βραδίνωι σε μάλιστ' ἐικάσδω.

where the goddess makes such a comparison while expressing her sorrow over the sad fate of her son Achilles:

HOUR 4 TEXT G = HOUR 0 TEXT D

|$_{54}$ Ah me, the pitiful one! Ah me, the mother, so sad it is, of the very best. |$_{55}$ I gave birth to a faultless and strong son, |$_{56}$ the very best of heroes. And he shot up [*anedramen*] equal [*īsos*] to a seedling [*ernos*]. |$_{57}$ I nurtured him like a shoot in the choicest spot of the orchard, |$_{58}$ only to send him off on curved ships to Troy to fight Trojan men. |$_{59}$ And I will never be welcoming him |$_{60}$ back home as returning warrior, back to the House of Peleus. |$_{61}$ And as long as he lives and sees the light of the sun, |$_{62}$ he will have sorrow [*akh-nutai*], and though I go to him I cannot help him. |$_{63}$ Nevertheless I will go, that I may see my dear son and learn |$_{64}$ what sorrow [*penthos*] has befallen him though he is still holding aloof from battle.

Iliad XVIII 54–64*

4§24. The goddess Thetis, in performing her lament, sings to her son Achilles as if he were already dead. She feels the sorrow that he feels over the death of Patroklos, and that sorrow translates into the sorrow that she feels by foreseeing, goddess that she is, the death of Achilles himself. We see here a perfect expression of the theme of *the man of constant sorrow,* and the two most telling words that are used in this passage are (1) the noun *penthos,* 'sorrow', at verse 64 and (2) the verb *akh-nutai,* 'he will have sorrow', at verse 62 corresponding to the noun *akhos,* meaning 'sorrow', which, as I have argued in Hour 3, is the central theme connected with Achilles in the *Iliad.* And, as we will see in Hour 5, the idea of Achilles as an ideal bridegroom is a central theme in traditions of singing songs of lament for this hero.

4§25. In the *Odyssey,* we find a retrospective description of the lament sung by Thetis and her fellow Nereids at the actual funeral of Achilles, followed and augmented by the lament of the Muses themselves:

---

* |$_{54}$ ὤ μοι ἐγὼ δειλή, ὤ μοι δυσαριστοτόκεια, |$_{55}$ ἥ τ' ἐπεὶ ἂρ τέκον υἱὸν ἀμύμονά τε κρατερόν τε |$_{56}$ ἔξοχον ἡρώων· ὁ δ' ἀνέδραμεν ἔρνεϊ ἶσος· |$_{57}$ τὸν μὲν ἐγὼ θρέψασα φυτὸν ὣς γουνῷ ἀλωῆς |$_{58}$ νηυσὶν ἐπιπροέηκα κορωνίσιν Ἴλιον εἴσω |$_{59}$ Τρωσὶ μαχησόμενον· τὸν δ' οὐχ ὑποδέξομαι αὖτις |$_{60}$ οἴκαδε νοστήσαντα δόμον Πηλήϊον εἴσω. |$_{61}$ ὄφρα δέ μοι ζώει καὶ ὁρᾷ φάος ἠελίοιο |$_{62}$ ἄχνυται, οὐδέ τί οἱ δύναμαι χραισμῆσαι ἰοῦσα. |$_{63}$ ἀλλ' εἶμ', ὄφρα ἴδωμι φίλον τέκος, ἠδ' ἐπακούσω |$_{64}$ ὅττί μιν ἵκετο πένθος ἀπὸ πτολέμοιο μένοντα.

HOUR 4 TEXT H

|₅₈ Standing around you were the daughters of the Old One of the sea [= Nereus], |₅₉ weeping piteously, and they [= the Nereids] clothed you [= the corpse of Achilles] in immortalizing [*ambrota*] clothes. |₆₀ The nine Muses also came, all of them, and sang antiphonally with a beautiful voice, |₆₁ singing their song of lament [*thrēnein*]; you could not spot a single person who was not shedding tears, |₆₂ of all the Argives [= Achaeans], so loudly did the piercing sound of lament rise up. |₆₃ Days and nights seven and ten |₆₄ we mourned you, mortals and immortals alike.

Odyssey xxiv 58–64*

4§26. This picturing of Achilles as the focus of lament sung by Thetis and her sister Nereids and then by the Muses is attested in the epic Cycle as well, as we see from a most compressed retelling in the plot summary:

HOUR 4 TEXT I

|₁₂ . . . Thetis |₁₃ comes with the Muses and her sisters and makes a lament [*thrēnos*] for her son. |₁₄ After that, Thetis snatches him off the funeral pyre and carries her |₁₅ son over to the White Island [Leukē]. Meanwhile the Achaeans |₁₆ make [for Achilles] a tomb [*taphos*] and hold funeral games.

Plot summary by Proclus of the *Aithiopis* by Arctinus of Miletus p. 106 lines 12–16†

4§27. As we have seen in Text A, taken from a song of Pindar (*Isthmian* 8.56–62), the lamentation of Achilles by the Muses is what propels the imperishable glory of Achilles, as sung in both epic and lyric. In the words of Pindar, this hero who is glorified by song will die and will thus stop flourishing, that is, he will 'perish', *phthi-n-ein*, but he will have as his eternal consolation the prospect that at least his song will never perish: rather, the song of Achilles will be

---

* |₅₈ ἀμφὶ δέ σ' ἔστησαν κοῦραι ἁλίοιο γέροντος |₅₉ οἴκτρ' ὀλοφυρόμεναι, περὶ δ' ἄμβροτα εἵματα ἕσσαν. |₆₀ Μοῦσαι δ' ἐννέα πᾶσαι ἀμειβόμεναι ὀπὶ καλῇ |₆₁ θρήνεον· ἔνθα κεν οὔ τιν' ἀδάκρυτόν γ' ἐνόησας |₆₂ Ἀργείων· τοῖον γὰρ ὑπώρορε Μοῦσα λίγεια. |₆₃ ἑπτὰ δὲ καὶ δέκα μέν σε ὁμῶς νύκτας τε καὶ ἦμαρ |₆₄ κλαίομεν ἀθάνατοί τε θεοὶ θνητοί τ' ἄνθρωποι.

† |₁₂ . . . καὶ Θέτις |₁₃ ἀφικομένη σὺν Μούσαις καὶ ταῖς ἀδελφαῖς θρηνεῖ τὸν παῖδα· |₁₄ καὶ μετὰ ταῦτα ἐκ τῆς πυρᾶς ἡ Θέτις ἀναρπάσασα τὸν |₁₅ παῖδα εἰς τὴν Λευκὴν νῆσον διακομίζει. οἱ δὲ Ἀχαιοὶ τὸν |₁₆ τάφον χώσαντες ἀγῶνα τιθέασι.

eternally sung by the Muses as they lament the death of the hero. And that eternal song of the Muses translates into an eternity of ongoing epic and lyric singing by mortals inspired by the Muses.

The Unfailing Glory of Achilles

4§28. As we have seen from the wording of the lament of Thetis in *Iliad* XVIII 54–64, Text G, Achilles in death is pictured as a beautiful plant that has been cut down in its prime. That is how Achilles himself can be lamented forever. Here I find it relevant to return to the word used to describe this dead Achilles as the Muses start to sing their own song of lament for him. In Pindar's *Isthmian* 8.56–62, Text A, Achilles is described as *phthi-menos* (60), which I have so far translated simply as 'perished in death'. But the verb *phthi-n-ein* has a deeper meaning than 'perish', and we see that deeper meaning in the contexts of the derivative adjective *a-phthi-to-*, which describes the *kleos*, 'glory', of Achilles in *Iliad* IX 413—and which I have been translating so far simply as 'imperishable'. As we will now see, a more accurate translation of *kleos aphthiton* would be 'unfailing glory'.

4§29. The expression *kleos aphthiton* is of great antiquity. There is a related expression in the oldest attested body of Indic poetry: in the *Rig-Veda* (1.9.7), we see an attestation of the words *śráva(s) ákṣitam*, 'imperishable glory'. The Indic word *śrávas*, 'glory', is cognate with Greek *kleos*, 'glory', while the Indic word *ákṣitam*, 'imperishable', is cognate with Greek *aphthiton*, 'imperishable'. Further, the Greek expression *kleos aphthiton* and the Indic expression *śráva(s) ákṣitam* are attested in cognate syntactical and metrical contexts.

4§30. When I say *cognate* here, I mean that the Indic combination *śrávas + ákṣitam* and the Greek combination *kleos + aphthiton* can be traced back to *a common linguistic origin,* as we can see if we apply methods of analysis developed within the discipline of Indo-European linguistics.* My ongoing work in analyzing such an origin has been summarized in detail elsewhere, and I will be drawing on that summary in the argumentation that follows.†

4§31. On the basis of the Indic comparative evidence, the meaning of *aph-*

---

* *GM* 122–127, *PH* 244–245 = 8§46n126.
† *PH* 3 = 0§5n10, 147 = 6§3n9; 204 = 9§6n23; 223 = 8§11n42; 278 = 10§9n21. Also, in *PH* 244–245 = 8§46n126, I counter various objections to my interpretation of the expression *kleos aphthiton*. Such objections, as readers will (I hope) see if they read through the arguments as I develop them in *PH*, can be refuted on the basis of a thorough examination of all the metrical and syntactical contexts of the expression *kleos aphthiton* in its lyric as well as epic attestations.

thito- / *ákṣita-* can be interpreted not only as 'imperishable' but even as 'unfailing', since other attestations in Indic traditions evoke the metaphor of an *unfailing flow of vitality.**

4§32. For the first time in this book, I have used here the term *metaphor*. It comes from the Greek word *metaphorā*, which means literally a 'transferring' of a meaning. I offer right away a working definition: *metaphor* is an expression of meaning by way of *substituting* something for something else—as distinct from *metonymy,* which is an expression of meaning by way of *connecting* something to something else that is next to it or at least near to it, thereby establishing contact.† If we were to reformulate these working definitions in terms of Prague School linguistics, we would say that the mental process of referring to anything involves, simultaneously, a *horizontal axis of combination* and a *vertical axis of selection.*‡

4§33. The basic idea behind the application of the metaphorical world of *kleos aphthiton* to a hero like Achilles is this: like anything that is natural, Achilles will 'perish' because he will lose the flow of vitality when he is killed, but his *kleos,* 'glory', will never perish because it will never lose its own flow of vitality. And that is because this *kleos,* 'glory', is not a thing of nature: it is a thing of art, a song.

Contrasting the Artificial and the Natural

4§34. In ancient Greek song culture, as I noted in Hour 1, the distinction between *art* and *nature,* between the *artificial* and the *natural,* is not the same as in our modern cultures. When we say that something is *artificial,* we imply that this something is "unreal," while *natural* means "real." In a song culture, by contrast, the artificial can be just as real as the natural, since the words of an "artificial" song can be just as real as the words of "natural" speech in a real-life experience. In a song culture, the song can be just as real as life itself.

4§35. For Achilles, as I also noted in Hour 1, the song of *kleos* is just as real as his very own life is real to him. The infinite time of the artificial song, the *kleos aphthiton,* or 'imperishable glory' (IX 413), is just as real to him as the finite time of his natural life.

4§36. Similarly, the infinite time of the immortal gods is just as real to Ho-

---

* *PH* 147 = 6§3n9, 278 = 10§9n21.
† *HTL* xi.
‡ Ducrot and Todorov 1979:111, with further references.

meric heroes as is the finite time they have as mortals. And the gods, too, are "artificial" but real, just as *kleos*, 'glory', is "artificial" but real. In the Homeric view of the world, even the sky can be seen as artificial, since it belongs to the realm of the immortal gods. By contrast, the earth is natural, since it belongs to the realm of mortal humans. But the point remains that the immortal and the artificial are just as real as the mortal and the natural. And the contrast between the *mortal* and the *immortal* is parallel to a contrast between the *natural* and the *artificial*.*

4§37. The idea that immortality is artificial is conveyed by a metaphor that we see at work in the Greek expression *kleos aphthiton* and in the cognate Indic expression *śráva(s) ákṣitam*. This metaphor refers to a poetic 'glory' that is 'imperishable' or even 'unfailing' in the sense that its vitality, which is imagined as something that flows, will never stop flowing.†

The Unwilting Glory of Achilles

4§38. In the case of Achilles, as we have seen from the lament of Thetis in *Iliad* XVIII 54–64, Text G, this hero's death is conventionally imagined as the cutting down of a tender young plant that is animated by the flow of vitality. Naturally, the cutting down of the plant will stop the flow. But the *kleos*, or poetic 'glory', of Achilles will prolong forever its own flow of vitality, and this immunity from death is conveyed by describing the *kleos* as *aphthiton*. In such contexts, the adjective *aphthito-* can be interpreted not only as 'imperishable' or 'unfailing' but even as 'unwilting'.

4§39. Verbs and nouns derived from the verb *phthi-n-ein*, which I have translated so far as 'perish', convey the idea of *wilting* in contexts referring to the vitality of plants.‡ Unlike natural plants, which go through a cycle of flourishing and then wilting, the *kleos* of Achilles can be imagined as an *unnatural* or *artifi-*

---

* I offer further observations about patterns of contrast between the *natural* and the *artificial* in my article "As the World Runs Out of Breath: Metaphorical Perspectives on the Heavens and the Atmosphere in the Ancient World" (Nagy 1999b), published in a book that has a specially evocative title: *Earth, Air, Fire, Water: Humanistic Studies of the Environment.*

† For an overall survey of the range of meanings inherited by this adjective *aphthito-*, see *BA* 174–189 = 10§§1–19.

‡ For example, in Pindar *Paean* 9.14, the expression καρποῦ φθίσιν refers to 'the wilting of the crops'; see *BA* 174 = 10§3. In Theophrastus *Research about plants* 7.13.6, the expression αὐτὸ τὸ ἄνθος ἅμα τῷ καυλῷ καταφθίνει means 'the blossom [*anthos*] itself wilts [kata-phthinei], along with the stem' (with reference to the narcissus). See also *BA* 178, 179–180, 180 = 10§6; 8; 9, with reference respectively to *Iliad* VI 145–149; I 233–237; *Odyssey* ix 133.

cial plant that will never wilt, never losing its vitality and beauty, its color and aroma.* This plant has become an immortal mutant. So the *kleos aphthiton* of Achilles at *Iliad* IX 413 is a 'glory' that is not only 'imperishable', not only 'unfailing', but even 'unwilting'. And this *kleos aphthiton*, 'unwilting glory', results from a choice that Achilles himself ultimately makes, which is never to return to his homeland of Phthia or *Phthíē*. That form, *Phthíē*, as we see in *Iliad* XIX 328–330 and elsewhere, is directly connected in Homeric poetry with the idea of *phthin-ein*, 'wilting'.†

4§40. By now we have seen that the *kleos aphthiton*, or 'unwilting glory', of Achilles stems from a metaphorical world of lament for a hero who wilts like a beautiful plant in the prime of his youth—and whose death is compensated by a song of glory that will never wilt.

Achilles as a Model for Singing Lyric Songs of Glory

4§41. Achilles himself becomes a model for singing such songs of glory in the Homeric *Iliad*. It happens at the moment when he is pictured as singing to the tune of a lyre that he is playing, as we saw in Text D of Hour 2 (*Iliad* IX 186–189). This lyre, I repeat, once belonged to Eëtion, king of the Aeolic city of Thebe, whom Achilles killed when he captured that city (IX 186–189)—and who was the father of that greatest singer of lamentations in the *Iliad*, Andromache (VI 414–416). What Achilles in the *Iliad* sings to the tune of this Aeolic lyre evokes feelings of love and bittersweet sorrow as heard in lyric song and poetry.‡

4§42. An example of such lyric in historical times is Song 44 of Sappho, about the wedding of Hector and Andromache. The lyric *kleos aphthiton*, 'unwilting glory', of this Aeolic song (line 4) converges with the epic *kleos aphthiton*, 'unwilting glory', that Achilles is promised in the *Iliad* (IX 413), and this convergence of lyric and epic is signaled by the *klea andrōn*, 'glories of men', that Achilles is singing on the Aeolic lyre (IX 189).

Models of Lament

4§43. The lyric virtuosity of Achilles qualifies him as a specialist in the singing of lament. In *Iliad* XIX 315–337, Achilles himself sings a song of lament for

---

* This formulation is backed up by detailed argumentation in *BA* 174–189 = 10§§1–19.
† The details are presented in *BA* 184–185 = 10§14.
‡ *HPC* 239–240 = II§297.

Patroklos, who as we have seen is the single person who means more to Achilles than anyone else in that hero's world. This lament is a model for the laments that will be sung for Achilles himself when he is dead.

4§44. And there are other models as well. As I come to the end of Hour 4, I close with a preview of the lament that Achilles himself will sing in the *Iliad*. I have in mind the lament performed by Briseis, the young woman whom Achilles in *Iliad* IX (342–343) professes to love as if she were his own wife. This lament, which I will analyze in detail when we reach Hour 5, is an expression of sorrow over the death of Patroklos. And the lament of Briseis for Patroklos will become the model for the lament of Achilles himself for his best friend. Here, then, is the lament of Briseis for Patroklos:

HOUR 4 TEXT J

|$_{282}$ Then Briseis, looking like golden Aphrodite, |$_{283}$ saw Patroklos all cut apart by the sharp bronze, and, when she saw him, |$_{284}$ she poured herself all over him in tears and wailed with a voice most clear, and with her hands she tore at |$_{285}$ her breasts and her tender neck and her beautiful face. |$_{286}$ And then she spoke, weeping, this woman who looked like the goddesses: |$_{287}$ "O Patroklos, you have been most gracious to me in my terrible state and most gratifying to my heart. |$_{288}$ You were alive when I last saw you on my way out from the shelter |$_{289}$—and now I come back to find you dead, you, the protector of your people |$_{290}$—that is what I come back to find. Oh, how I have one misfortune after the next to welcome me. |$_{291}$ The man to whom I was given away by my father and by my mother the queen |$_{292}$—I saw that man lying there in front of the city, all cut apart by the sharp bronze, |$_{293}$ and lying near him were my three brothers—all of us were born of one mother—|$_{294}$ they are all a cause for my sorrow, since they have all met up with their time of destruction. |$_{295}$ No, you [= Patroklos] did not let me—back when my husband was killed by swift-footed Achilles, |$_{296}$ killed by him, and when the city of my godlike Mynes [= my husband] was destroyed by him |$_{297}$—you did not let me weep, back then, but you told me that godlike Achilles |$_{298}$ would have me as a properly courted wife, that you would make that happen, and that you would take me on board the ships, |$_{299}$ taking me all the way to Phthia, and that you would arrange for a wedding feast among the Myrmidons. |$_{300}$ So now I cannot stop crying for you, now that you are dead, you who

were always so sweet and gentle." |₃₀₁ So she [= Briseis] spoke, weeping, and the women kept on mourning in response. |₃₀₂ They mourned for Patroklos, that was their pretext, but they were all mourning, each and every one of them, for what they really cared for in their sorrow.

Iliad XIX 282–302*

4§45. In the logic of the epic narrative here, Briseis is not just weeping, not just speaking words of sorrow: she is represented as singing a lament.† And the words of her lament are quoted inside the epic narrative. Following this quotation in *Iliad* XIX (287–300) is the quotation of another lament for Patroklos, this one performed by the hero Achilles himself (315–337); Achilles here is represented as actually singing a lament, just as Briseis actually sings a lament.‡

4§46. We see in this passage that quotes the lament of Briseis a most remarkable feature of Homeric poetry: if a performer of epic quotes a woman who is singing a lament or love song, then *he* is singing a lament or love song. The word "quote" here and elsewhere in such contexts is of course anachronistic. From the standpoint of song culture, it would be better for us to say *perform*.

4§47. When a character like Briseis—or like Achilles himself—is quoted, that character's words become a "super-star" performance. Conversely, when a "super-star" performer like the master Narrator of the *Iliad* quotes the words of a hero like Achilles, the performer himself becomes the hero in the moment of performance. Hero and performer develop a reciprocal relationship. The hero becomes a super-star performer in his own right, while the performer becomes heroic, larger-than-life, even godlike in sacred moments (just as the hero becomes godlike in sacred moments). Achilles is pictured as a super-star performer in his own right when he sings the *klea andrōn* at *Iliad* IX 189, as we saw in Hour 2 Text D.

---

* |₂₈₂ Βρισηὶς δ' ἄρ' ἔπειτ' ἰκέλη χρυσέῃ Ἀφροδίτῃ |₂₈₃ ὡς ἴδε Πάτροκλον δεδαϊγμένον ὀξέϊ χαλκῷ, |₂₈₄ ἀμφ' αὐτῷ χυμένη λίγ' ἐκώκυε, χερσὶ δ' ἄμυσσε |₂₈₅ στήθεά τ' ἠδ' ἁπαλὴν δειρὴν ἰδὲ καλὰ πρόσωπα. |₂₈₆ εἶπε δ' ἄρα κλαίουσα γυνὴ εἰκυῖα θεῇσι· |₂₈₇ Πάτροκλέ μοι δειλῇ πλεῖστον κεχαρισμένε θυμῷ |₂₈₈ ζωὸν μέν σε ἔλειπον ἐγὼ κλισίηθεν ἰοῦσα, |₂₈₉ νῦν δέ σε τεθνηῶτα κιχάνομαι ὄρχαμε λαῶν |₂₉₀ ἂψ ἀνιοῦσ'· ὡς μοι δέχεται κακὸν ἐκ κακοῦ αἰεί. |₂₉₁ ἄνδρα μὲν ᾧ ἔδοσάν με πατὴρ καὶ πότνια μήτηρ |₂₉₂ εἶδον πρὸ πτόλιος δεδαϊγμένον ὀξέϊ χαλκῷ, |₂₉₃ τρεῖς τε κασιγνήτους, τούς μοι μία γείνατο μήτηρ, |₂₉₄ κηδείους, οἳ πάντες ὀλέθριον ἦμαρ ἐπέσπον. |₂₉₅ οὐδὲ μὲν οὐδέ μ' ἔασκες, ὅτ' ἄνδρ' ἐμὸν ὠκὺς Ἀχιλλεὺς |₂₉₆ ἔκτεινεν, πέρσεν δὲ πόλιν θείοιο Μύνητος, |₂₉₇ κλαίειν, ἀλλά μ' ἔφασκες Ἀχιλλῆος θείοιο |₂₉₈ κουριδίην ἄλοχον θήσειν, ἄξειν τ' ἐνὶ νηυσὶν |₂₉₉ ἐς Φθίην, δαίσειν δὲ γάμον μετὰ Μυρμιδόνεσσι. |₃₀₀ τώ σ' ἄμοτον κλαίω τεθνηότα μείλιχον αἰεί. |₃₀₁ Ὣς ἔφατο κλαίουσ', ἐπὶ δὲ στενάχοντο γυναῖκες |₃₀₂ Πάτροκλον πρόφασιν, σφῶν δ' αὐτῶν κήδε' ἑκάστη.

† Nagy 2010b23. See also Dué 2002:70–71, 81; 2006:43–44.

‡ Tsagalis 2004:86, 139–140.

4§48. I bring this analysis to a close by pondering further the implications of the lament of Briseis as quoted in *Iliad* XIX. In her lament, Briseis sings her bittersweet sorrow not only over the death of Patroklos but also over the death of her own fondest hope: when he was alive, Patroklos had promised to arrange for her a marriage to Achilles, but now that Patroklos is dead, the hope of that promise is gone forever (XIX 295–300). As we will see further in Hour 5, the *Iliad* pictures Patroklos as a stand-in for Achilles, his other self, in courtship as well as in war.*

* Nagy 2010b: 23.

When Mortals Become 'Equal' to Immortals: Death of a Hero, Death of a Bridegroom

The Meaning of Daimōn

5§1. The key word for this hour is *daimōn* (plural *daimones*), which I translate for the moment simply as 'superhuman force'. This word is used to refer to an unspecified god or hero intervening in human life. The word *daimōn* is to be contrasted with *theos*, 'god', which is used to refer to a *specified* god.

5§2. In this connection, we may compare the words *polytheism* and *monotheism*. Also *henotheism*. The term *henotheism* refers to the worshipping of one divinity at a time. I think of the one-at-a-time mentality of *henotheism* as *serial monotheism*.

5§3. On the ritual occasion of a wedding in ancient Greek society, at the climactic moment of the wedding mortal humans are equated with the immortal gods. That is what we saw in Hour 4 when we were reading Song 44 of Sappho, about the Wedding of Hector and Andromache. In that song, the bridegroom and the bride are said to be *theoeikeloi*, 'looking just like the gods [*theoi*]' (line 34). Now, as we will see here in Hour 5, the climactic moment of the ritual occasion of fighting in war is likewise signaled by the equating of mortal humans with immortal gods.

The Expression 'Equal to a Daimōn'

5§4. The ritual of war collapses the distinction between human and divine—but only at the precise moment when the warrior comes face-to-face with his own martial death. I should add that the warrior may not necessarily die when he faces death. Still, the warrior's identity is defined by the ritual need for him to face death in war. As we will also see, the medium of epic records the actual moment when the hero faces death in war by applying to the hero the epithet *daimoni īsos,* 'equal [*īsos*] to a superhuman force [*daimōn*]'.

5§5. I concentrate here on the expression *daimoni īsos,* 'equal [*īsos*] to a superhuman force [*daimōn*]'. In the *Iliad,* such wording focuses on the climax of god-hero antagonism. At the moment of such a climax, the hero can be equated with a *daimōn.*

5§6. In the first passage we will examine, the hero Patroklos comes face-to-face with death as he confronts the god Apollo. At this climactic moment of god-hero antagonism, Patroklos is described as 'equal [*īsos*] to a superhuman force [*daimōn*]':

HOUR 5 TEXT A

|₆₉₈ The sons of the Achaeans could now have taken Troy |₆₉₉ by the hands of Patroklos, for he was raging in all directions with his spear, |₇₀₀ if Phoebus Apollo had not made his stand at the well-built wall, |₇₀₁ standing there and thinking destructive thoughts against him [= Patroklos], since he [= Apollo] was supporting the Trojans. |₇₀₂ Three times did he [= Patroklos] reach the base of the high wall, |₇₀₃ that is what Patroklos did, and three times was he beaten back by Apollo, |₇₀₄ who struck with his own immortal hands the luminous shield [of Patroklos]. |₇₀₅ But when he [= Patroklos] rushed ahead for yet a fourth time, *equal [īsos] to a superhuman force [daimōn],* |₇₀₆ he [= Apollo] shouted to him with a terrifying voice and spoke winged words: |₇₀₇ "Draw back, Patroklos, you who are descended from the gods in the sky. It is not your destiny [*aisa*] |₇₀₈ to destroy with your spear the city of the proud Trojans, |₇₀₉ nor will it be the destiny of Achilles, who is a far better man than you are." |₇₁₀ That is what he [= Apollo] said. On hearing this, Patroklos drew quite a way back, |₇₁₁ thus avoiding the *anger [mēnis] of Apollo who shoots from afar.*

Iliad XVI 698–711*

* |₆₉₈ Ἔνθά κεν ὑψίπυλον Τροίην ἕλον υἷες Ἀχαιῶν |₆₉₉ Πατρόκλου ὑπὸ χερσί, περὶ πρὸ γὰρ ἔγχεϊ θῦεν, |₇₀₀ εἰ μὴ Ἀπόλλων Φοῖβος ἐϋδμήτου ἐπὶ πύργου |₇₀₁ ἔστη τῷ ὀλοὰ φρονέων, Τρώεσσι δ' ἀρήγων. |₇₀₂ τρὶς μὲν ἐπ' ἀγκῶνος βῆ τείχεος ὑψηλοῖο |₇₀₃ Πάτροκλος, τρὶς δ' αὐτὸν ἀπεστυφέλιξεν Ἀπόλλων |₇₀₄ χείρεσσ' ἀθανάτῃσι φαεινὴν ἀσπίδα νύσσων. |₇₀₅ ἀλλ' ὅτε δὴ τὸ τέταρτον ἐπέσσυτο δαίμονι ἶσος, |₇₀₆ δεινὰ δ' ὁμοκλήσας ἔπεα πτερόεντα προσηύδα· |₇₀₇ χάζεο διογενὲς Πατρόκλεες· οὐ νύ τοι αἶσα |₇₀₈ σῷ ὑπὸ δουρὶ πόλιν πέρθαι Τρώων ἀγερώχων, |₇₀₉ οὐδ' ὑπ' Ἀχιλλῆος, ὅς περ σέο πολλὸν ἀμείνων. |₇₁₀ Ὣς φάτο, Πάτροκλος δ' ἀνεχάζετο πολλὸν ὀπίσσω |₇₁₁ μῆνιν ἀλευάμενος ἑκατηβόλου Ἀπόλλωνος.

5§7. Here, then, is a moment of "fatal attraction," signaled by the expression *daimoni īsos*, 'equal [*īsos*] to a superhuman force [*daimōn*]'. But who is the *daimōn* in this expression? It must be a god. And, although the word *daimōn* itself partially conceals the identity of the god, the context here gives the answer away: the *daimōn* with whom Patroklos is equated here is the god Apollo himself. And this god is about to kill Patroklos.

5§8. But so far we have seen only a "dress rehearsal." The real moment of identification between hero and god comes the next time, when Patroklos does not back away from Apollo after three attempts but faces him at the fourth attempt. The previous time Patroklos had avoided the *mēnis*, 'anger,' of Apollo (*Iliad* XVI 711). The next time, he fails to avoid it. And I will now quote the passage that tells about this next time.* In this next passage, we finally see that climactic moment of god-hero antagonism, "the *real thing*":

HOUR 5 TEXT B

|₇₈₃ Then Patroklos rushed ahead toward the Trojans, with the worst intentions. |₇₈₄ Three times he rushed at them, and he was *equal [atalantos] to swift Arēs*. |₇₈₅ He [= Patroklos] was making a terrifying shout, and he killed three times nine men. |₇₈₆ But when he [= Patroklos] rushed ahead for yet a fourth time, *equal [īsos] to a superhuman force [daimōn]*, |₇₈₇ then, O Patroklos, the end of your life made its appearance to you. |₇₈₈ Facing you now was Phoebus [Apollo], ready to fight you in grim battle. |₇₈₉ He [= Apollo] was terrifying. But he [= Patroklos] did not notice him as he [= Apollo] was coming at him in the heat of battle. |₇₉₀ For he [= Apollo] was covered in a great cloud of mist as he made contact with him. |₇₉₁ He [= Apollo] stood behind him and he struck him on his back and his broad shoulders |₇₉₂ with the downturned flat of his hand, making his eyes spin. |₇₉₃ His helmet was knocked off his head by Phoebus Apollo, |₇₉₄ and it rolled rattling off under the horses' hooves. |₇₉₅ That is what happened to this helmet, and its horse-tail plumes were all begrimed |₇₉₆ with blood and dust. Before this time, it was not sanctioned |₇₉₇ that this horse-hair helmet should ever get begrimed in the dust, |₇₉₈ while it was protecting the head and comely forehead of that godlike man, |₇₉₉ protecting the head of Achilles. But now Zeus gave it to Hector |₈₀₀ for him to wear on his

---

* This next passage, and the previous passage, are most incisively analyzed by Muellner 1996:10–18.

head. And his [= Hector's] destruction was near. |₈₀₁ Broken completely in his [= Patroklos'] hands was that spear of his that casts a long shadow, |₈₀₂ a huge and heavy and massive piece of weaponry, and from his shoulders |₈₀₃ his shield, strap and all, fell to the ground, with its beautiful edgework. |₈₀₄ Taken away from him was his breastplate, removed by Lord Apollo son of Zeus. |₈₀₅ And his [= Patroklos'] mind was seized by derangement [atē]; his limbs failed him, |₈₀₆ and he just stood there in a daze.

Iliad XVI 783–806*

5§9. At this climactic moment of god-hero antagonism, when Patroklos becomes *equal [īsos] to a superhuman force [daimōn]*, we can see that the partially concealed superhuman force or *daimōn* here is the god Apollo himself. And, at this moment, Patroklos is struck down by the divine hand of Apollo, who is the direct cause of the hero's death. After this blow is delivered by the god himself, Patroklos finds himself dazed and without armor, and now he receives a second blow from the spear of the hero Euphorbos (XVI 806–815); then comes the third and final blow, from the spear of the hero Hector (XVI 816–854). After these three blows, Patroklos finally dies (XVI 855–857).

5§10. The narrative of the *Iliad* makes it clear that Hector succeeded in killing Patroklos only because that hero had first been struck down by the divine hand of the god Apollo himself and had thus been deprived of the protective armor of Achilles. So, if any Achaean now wants to rescue the corpse of Patroklos from the field of battle, he will be fighting not only Hector but also the god Apollo himself. Just as Patroklos was killed because he fought Apollo, so also any other Achaean hero will surely be killed if he now stands up to Hector, since the Achaean will first have to face the god Apollo himself. Such is the thinking of the Achaean hero Menelaos, who says to himself that he would not dare to stand up alone to Hector by attempting to rescue the corpse of Patroklos:

* |₇₈₃ Πάτροκλος δὲ Τρωσὶ κακὰ φρονέων ἐνόρουσε. |₇₈₄ τρὶς μὲν ἔπειτ' ἐπόρουσε θοῷ ἀτάλαντος Ἄρηϊ |₇₈₅ σμερδαλέα ἰάχων, τρὶς δ' ἐννέα φῶτας ἔπεφνεν. |₇₈₆ ἀλλ' ὅτε δὴ τὸ τέταρτον ἐπέσσυτο δαίμονι ἶσος, |₇₈₇ ἔνθ' ἄρα τοι Πάτροκλε φάνη βιότοιο τελευτή· |₇₈₈ ἤντετο γάρ τοι Φοῖβος ἐνὶ κρατερῇ ὑσμίνῃ |₇₈₉ δεινός· ὁ μὲν τὸν ἰόντα κατὰ κλόνον οὐκ ἐνόησεν, |₇₉₀ ἠέρι γὰρ πολλῇ κεκαλυμμένος ἀντεβόλησε· |₇₉₁ στῆ δ' ὄπιθεν, πλῆξεν δὲ μετάφρενον εὐρέε τ' ὤμω |₇₉₂ χειρὶ καταπρηνεῖ, στρεφεδίνηθεν δέ οἱ ὄσσε. |₇₉₃ τοῦ δ' ἀπὸ μὲν κρατὸς κυνέην βάλε Φοῖβος Ἀπόλλων· |₇₉₄ ἡ δὲ κυλινδομένη καναχὴν ἔχε ποσσὶν ὑφ' ἵππων |₇₉₅ αὐλῶπις τρυφάλεια, μιάνθησαν δὲ ἔθειραι |₇₉₆ αἵματι καὶ κονίῃσι· πάρος γε μὲν οὐ θέμις ἦεν |₇₉₇ ἱππόκομον πήληκα μιαίνεσθαι κονίῃσιν, |₇₉₈ ἀλλ' ἀνδρὸς θείοιο κάρη χαρίεν τε μέτωπον |₇₉₉ ῥύετ' Ἀχιλλῆος· τότε δὲ Ζεὺς Ἕκτορι δῶκε |₈₀₀ ᾗ κεφαλῇ φορέειν, σχεδόθεν δέ οἱ ἦεν ὄλεθρος. |₈₀₁ πᾶν δέ οἱ ἐν χείρεσσιν ἄγη δολιχόσκιον ἔγχος |₈₀₂ βριθὺ μέγα στιβαρὸν κεκορυθμένον· αὐτὰρ ἀπ' ὤμων |₈₀₃ ἀσπὶς σὺν τελαμῶνι χαμαὶ πέσε τερμιόεσσα. |₈₀₄ λῦσε δέ οἱ θώρηκα ἄναξ Διὸς υἱὸς Ἀπόλλων. |₈₀₅ τὸν δ' ἄτη φρένας εἷλε, λύθεν δ' ὑπὸ φαίδιμα γυῖα, |₈₀₆ στῆ δὲ ταφών.

Hour 5 Text C

|₉₈ When a man is willing, face-to-face with a *daimōn,* to fight another man |₉₉ whom the god honors, then it becomes a sure thing that a big pain [*pēma*] will roll down [*kulindesthai*] upon him.*

Iliad XVII 98–99†

5§11. The expression *pros daimona,* 'face-to-face with a *daimōn*', here at verse 98 of *Iliad* XVII recurs at verse 104, where Menelaos is thinking further, asking himself whether he would dare to make the attempt even if he is backed up by Ajax, arguably the greatest of all Achaean warriors next to Achilles.‡

5§12. In this context, the use of the word *daimōn* is mystical in not naming the god—but it is ostentatiously mystical. By that I mean that the identity of the *daimōn* is obvious. That *daimōn* is Apollo.

5§13. We see another "dress-rehearsal" at an earlier point in the *Iliad:* the Achaean hero Diomedes is described as *daimoni īsos,* 'equal [*īsos*] to a superhuman force [*daimōn*]', at *Iliad* V 438 and 459 when he makes his own four-stage attempt at facing Apollo in battle. In fact, Diomedes makes two successive four-stage attempts, but he ultimately backs down both times.§

5§14. So the god Apollo causes the death of the hero Patroklos in the *Iliad,* and the death is signaled by the marking of Patroklos as *daimoni īsos,* 'equal [*īsos*] to a superhuman force [*daimōn*]'. By way of this marking, the killer *daimōn* is identified as the god Apollo himself. In fact, Patroklos is the only hero in the *Iliad* who gets struck down directly by the hand of Apollo—or by the hand of any other god.

5§15. Why Patroklos? It is because Patroklos is a stand-in for Achilles. As we will see later, in Hour 6, Patroklos at the moment of his death becomes the ritual substitute of Achilles.

---

* The metaphor here evokes the menacing image of a boulder that breaks off from a cliff overhead and starts rolling downward from the heights above, ever increasing in speed as it nears ground zero. In *Iliad* XIII 136–142, Hector himself is compared to such a breakaway boulder as he rushes toward his enemies. In *Iliad* XVII 685–690, when the death of Patroklos is formally announced, the fact of his death is described at verse 688 as a 'pain' (*pēma*) inflicted by 'a god' (*theos*) who literally 'rolled it down' (*kulindein*) upon the Achaeans.

† |₉₈ ὁππότ᾽ ἀνὴρ ἐθέλῃ πρὸς δαίμονα φωτὶ μάχεσθαι |₉₉ ὅν κε θεὸς τιμᾷ, τάχα οἱ μέγα πῆμα κυλίσθη. Commentary in *BA* 63 = 4§6n1.

‡ On Ajax as a rival of Achilles for the status of 'best of the Achaeans', see *BA* 31–32 = 2§6.

§ On Diomedes as a rival of Achilles for the status of 'best of the Achaeans', see *BA* 30–31 = 2§5.

Apollo as Divine Antagonist of Achilles

5§16. The god Apollo causes the death of not only Patroklos but also Achilles. *Just as Apollo initiates the killing of Patroklos, which is completed by Hector, so also the same god initiates the killing of Achilles himself, which is completed by Paris.* But this greatest of all killings happens not in the *Iliad*. It happens instead in the epic Cycle, specifically, in the *Aithiopis* or 'Song of the Ethiopians':

HOUR 5 TEXT D

|₇ Achilles, while routing the Trojans and |₈ rushing into the citadel, is killed by Paris and Apollo. |₉ When a heated battle starts over the corpse, |₁₀ Ajax picks it up and carries it off to the ships while |₁₁ Odysseus fights off the Trojans.

Plot summary by Proclus of the *Aithiopis* by Arctinus of Miletus p. 106 lines 7–11*

So the death of Achilles happens not in the *Iliad* but beyond the *Iliad*. In the *Iliad*, however, the best friend of Achilles, Patroklos, will stand in for Achilles as the victim of Apollo.

5§17. In the *Iliad*, after Patroklos is killed in battle, Achilles himself takes the place of his best friend in challenging Apollo by rushing at Hector four times, and Achilles, too, is given the epithet *daimoni īsos*, 'equal [*īsos*] to a superhuman force [*daimōn*]', at the precise moment of his fourth try (XX 447), just as Patroklos had been given that same epithet at the moment of his own fourth try, which as we have seen happens not once but twice in two separate four-try sequences (XVI 705, 786). As we have also seen, the fourth try of Patroklos in the second of these two sequences proves to be fatal. By contrast, the fourth try of Achilles is not fatal here in the *Iliad*, because the god Apollo intervenes and hides Hector in a huge cloud of mist (XX 443–444). There are three further moments when Achilles will be given the epithet *daimoni īsos*, 'equal [*īsos*] to a superhuman force [*daimōn*]', in the *Iliad* (XX 493; XXI 18, 227), but in each one of these three moments, the epithet fails to activate the death of Achilles. That death is postponed for a moment that will take place outside the *Iliad* as we know it.

---

* |₇ τρεψάμενος δ' Ἀχιλλεὺς τοὺς Τρῶας καὶ |₈ εἰς τὴν πόλιν συνεισπεσὼν ὑπὸ Πάριδος ἀναιρεῖται καὶ |₉ Ἀπόλλωνος· καὶ περὶ τοῦ πτώματος γενομένης ἰσχυρᾶς |₁₀ μάχης Αἴας ἀνελόμενος ἐπὶ τὰς ναῦς κομίζει, Ὀδυσσέως |₁₁ ἀπομαχομένου τοῖς Τρωσίν.

Arēs as Divine Antagonist of Achilles

5§18. The death of Achilles, prefigured by the death of Patroklos, is an epic theme so all-encompassing that it transcends even the divine antagonism of the god Apollo toward these two heroes. As we will now see, Achilles has not only one divine antagonist but two. His other divine antagonist is Arēs.

5§19. Here we need to confront a major complication. In the second of the two passages centering on the death scene of Patroklos in the *Iliad*, Text B (XVI 783–806), we notice that the hero is being compared not only to an unnamed god, a *daimōn* 'superhuman force' (XVI 786), who turns out to be Apollo, but also to a named god, Arēs (XVI 784). As a warrior, Patroklos is 'equal' (*īsos* 786) not only to the god Apollo in his climactic moment of god-hero antagonism. He is 'equal' (*atalantos* 784) also to the god Arēs.* As we will see in more detail in Hour 6, Arēs is *the god of war* or, more specifically, *the god of martial fury.*

Achilles as Ideal Warrior and Ideal Bridegroom

5§20. We have just seen that Patroklos has as his divine antagonist not only Apollo but also Arēs. And we will now see that Patroklos is a stand-in for Achilles in his antagonism with both these gods. But why is Achilles himself linked to both Arēs and Apollo as divine antagonists? The answer to this question divides into two halves. The first half has to do with Achilles as a warrior and the second with Achilles as a bridegroom.

5§21. We have already seen that Patroklos in the *Iliad* is a stand-in for Achilles as a warrior. So when Patroklos at the moment of his death is 'equal' to both Arēs and Apollo, it is because Achilles in his own right is 'equal' to these two gods as *an ideal warrior*. But now we will see that Achilles is also 'equal' to these same two gods as *an ideal bridegroom*.†

5§22. We have already started to explore in Hour 4 the ritualized equation of bridegrooms with gods: as we saw in Song 44 of Sappho, for example, *the generic bridegroom is equated to a god at the moment when he gets married.* Now we will see that the identity of the god who is being compared to the bridegroom is manifested in the ritual convention of imagining the bridegroom not only as a god but also as a hero, especially as Achilles. And *there are two divine*

* *BA* 293 = 17§5.
† What follows is an epitomized version of parts of Nagy 2007a and 2007b.

models for Achilles as an ideal bridegroom: Arēs and Apollo. As we now proceed through the rest of Hour 5, we will see the active presence of both Arēs and Apollo in the songs of Sappho. Before we turn to studying the relevant songs, however, I will give an overview of the historical background.*

The Historical Background of Sappho's Songs

5§23. Sappho was a woman credited with the composition of some of the most beautiful songs in world literature. This formulation is relevant to what I already noted in Hour 3, that the performance of songs by women is a most important matter in ancient Greek song culture. And it is a most important matter for us to consider the songs of women as we study the Homeric *Iliad,* since the traditions of such songs pervade the epic.

5§24. It makes sense, therefore, to take the time to read in the online *Sourcebook* all the fragments of surviving poetry and song attributed to Sappho and Alcman. Reading these fragments will take less than half an hour. Especially important are the fragments of Sappho. The earlier you acquaint yourself with the traditions of song represented by Sappho, the better you will understand the entirety of ancient Greek song culture.

5§25. Sappho was a Lesbian, by which I mean simply that she originated from an island named Lesbos, situated off the northern coast of Asia Minor. The people of Lesbos spoke a local version of the Greek dialect known as Aeolic, and they were considered to be Asiatic Greeks, as distinct from the European Greeks of, say, Thessaly, who spoke their own local version of Aeolic. I have already mentioned these Aeolic-speaking Greeks in Hours 2 and 4, where we saw that Achilles has a special affinity with these Aeolians. As we will see in more detail later, Achilles himself hails from Aeolic Thessaly.

5§26. In the song culture of the island of Lesbos, the woman Sappho was considered the primary representative of women's songs, while a man called Alcaeus was considered the primary representative of men's songs. According to the traditions of Lesbos, both Sappho and Alcaeus lived in the late seventh and early sixth centuries BCE. That rough date matches a reference in a song of Alcaeus (Fragment 49.12) to a contemporary event that can be dated independently, namely, the destruction of Ascalon by Nebuchadnezzar, king of Babylon, in 604 BCE (Alcaeus *Source* 1).

---

*The eleven paragraphs that follow are based on a longer survey of the historical background of Sappho's songs in Nagy 2007a.

5§27. The songs of Sappho and Alcaeus, taken together, represent the repertoire of the myths and the rituals of the people of Lesbos as expressed in lyric song.

5§28. I insert here a quick working definition of *myth* and *ritual* together, repeated from the Introduction. Ritual is doing things and saying things in a way that is considered *sacred*. Myth is saying things in a way that is also considered *sacred. So ritual frames myth.*

5§29. The songs of Sappho and Alcaeus date back to a period when the city-states of the island of Lesbos were confederated into a single state. This federal state, the political term for which was *sunoikisis* (Thucydides 3.3.1), was dominated by the city of Mytilene, known as the home of Sappho and Alcaeus. There was a single communal place reserved for the festivals of this island federation, and that place was named Messon, the 'middle space'.

5§30. In the words of Alcaeus, this federal space was called the *temenos theōn,* 'sacred precinct of the gods' (Fragment 130b.13). It was the designated place for celebrating a seasonally recurring festival, described in the words of Alcaeus as assemblies or 'comings together' of the people of Lesbos (Fragment 130b). This festival featured as its main spectacle the singing and dancing of choruses of *Lesbiades,* 'women of Lesbos', described as 'exceptional in their beauty' (*krinnomenai phuan* 130b.17). When I say *choruses,* I mean *singing and dancing ensembles.* The Greek word *khoros* refers to *dancing* as well as *singing.*

5§31. The reality of such a festival in Lesbos featuring the choral performances of women is independently verified by a scholion (this word is a technical term referring to a learned note found in a manuscript) attached to a passage in the Homeric *Iliad* (IX 130): from this scholion we learn that the name of the festival was the *Kallisteia,* which can be translated as 'pageant of beauty'. In the relevant Iliadic passage as well as elsewhere in the *Iliad,* there are references to women from Lesbos, described as exceptional in their beauty, who were captured by Achilles in the years that preceded the final destruction of Troy (IX 128–131, 270–273). These direct references in the *Iliad* can be analyzed as indirect references to the festival of the *Kallisteia* in Lesbos.* Another reference to the *Kallisteia* is attested in a poem from the *Greek Anthology* (9.189), which says that this festival takes place within the *temenos,* 'sacred precinct', of the goddess Hērā: this festival, as we learn from the same poem, was the occasion for choral singing and dancing by the women of Lesbos, with Sappho herself pictured as

*HPC 236, 242 = II§§289–290, 302.

the leader of their *khoros,* 'chorus'. As I already said, an ancient Greek chorus was an ensemble of singing *and dancing* performers.

5§32. Sappho in her songs is conventionally pictured as the lead singer of a chorus that consisted of the women of Lesbos, and she speaks as their main choral personality.* As we see in the *Greek Anthology,* she is figured as the lead singer of this chorus of women who sing and dance in the federal space of the people of Lesbos. Sappho's songs are pictured as taking place within this sacred place, marked by the deictic adverb *tuide,* 'here' (as in Sappho Song 17 line 7).

5§33. Elsewhere, too, this same federal space of the people of Lesbos is marked by the deictic adverb *tuide,* 'here' (Sappho Song 96 line 2) as the sacred place of choral performance, and the noun *molpa* (line 5) makes it explicit that the performance takes the form of choral singing and dancing. In archaic poetry, the verb for 'sing and dance in a chorus' is *melpein melpesthai.*†

Transition to Sappho's Songs

5§34. With this overview in place, I am ready to show some of Sappho's most celebrated songs. Two of them in particular, Songs 1 and 31, will have much to tell us about the central question of this hour: how are mortals compared to immortals? I will start with Song 31, which will be a key to understanding how and why the gods Arēs and Apollo are figured as divine models for Achilles as an ideal bridegroom.

5§35. And I will start with Arēs. One thing I need to highlight right away, even before we start reading Song 31 of Sappho, is that we cannot consider this god without considering also the symmetrical goddess Aphrodite.

Arēs and Aphrodite as Models for the Bridegroom and the Bride

5§36. In the wedding songs of Sappho, the god Arēs is a model for the generic *gambros,* 'bridegroom', who is explicitly described as *īsos Areui,* 'equal [*īsos*] to Arēs', in Sappho Song 111.5. Correspondingly, there are many instances of implicit equations of the generic bride with the goddess Aphrodite: in Sappho Song 112, for example, the bridegroom is said to be infused with the divine charisma of Aphrodite, evidently by way of his direct contact with the bride.

5§37. At a wedding, which is a ritual of initiation in terms of ancient Greek

---

PH 370 = 12§60.
† *PH* 350–351 =12§29n62 and n64.

song culture, the likening of the bridegroom and the bride to a god and a goddess leads to death. But this death is only figurative. And that is because *death in rituals of initiation is not physical but psychic.* From cross-cultural surveys of rituals of initiation as practiced in traditional societies around the world, it becomes evident that initiands who are identified with divinities at the moment of initiation are imagined as dying to their old selves as members of a given age-class and being reborn into their new selves as members of the next age-class.* A prime example of such psychic death at a wedding is Song 31 of Sappho, to which I now turn.

Song 31 of Sappho

HOUR 5 TEXT E

|₁ He appears [*phainetai*] to me, that one, equal to the gods [*īsos theoisin*], |₂ that man who, facing you |₃ is seated and, up close, that sweet voice of yours |₄ he listens to, |₅ and how you laugh a laugh that brings desire. Why, it just |₆ makes my heart flutter within my breast. |₇ You see, the moment I look at you, right then, for me |₈ to make any sound at all won't work any more. |₉ My tongue has a breakdown and a delicate |₁₀—all of a sudden—fire rushes under my skin. |₁₁ With my eyes I see not a thing, and there is a roar |₁₂ my ears make. |₁₃ Sweat pours down me and a trembling |₁₄ seizes all of me; paler than grass |₁₅ am I, and a little short of death |₁₆ do I appear [*phainomai*] to myself.

Song 31 of Sappho†

5§38. The form *phainetai*, 'he appears', at line 1 of this song and the form *phainomai*, 'I appear', at line 16 are the third and the first persons of a verb related to the noun *phantasia*, a derivative form that means 'fantasy' in later Greek prose. Or, to put it more accurately, *phantasia* means 'imagined vision' or 'imagination'. The English word *fantasy*, derived from *phantasia*, is actually misleading as a translation, since this word implies a vision that is unreal. In ancient Greek song culture, however, there is no 'fantasy' about the kind of vision that is

---

* PP 101–103.

† |₁ φαίνεταί μοι κῆνος ἴσος θέοισιν |₂ ἔμμεν' ὤνηρ, ὄττις ἐνάντιός τοι |₃ ἰσδάνει καὶ πλάσιον ἆδυ φωνεί-|₄σας ὐπακούει |₅ καὶ γελαίσας ἰμέροεν, τό μ' ἦ μὰν |₆ καρδίαν ἐν στήθεσιν ἐπτόαισεν, |₇ ὠς γὰρ ἔς σ' ἴδω βρόχε' ὤς με φώναι-|₈σ' οὐδ' ἒν ἔτ' εἴκει, |₉ ἀλλὰ κὰμ μὲν γλῶσσα ἔαγε λέπτον |₁₀ δ' αὔτικα χρῶι πῦρ ὐπαδεδρόμηκεν, |₁₁ ὀππάτεσσι δ' οὐδ' ἒν ὄρημμ', ἐπιρρόμ-|₁₂βεισι δ' ἄκουαι, |₁₃ κὰδ δέ μ' ἴδρως ψῦχρος κακχέεται τρόμος δὲ |₁₄ παῖσαν ἄγρει, χλωροτέρα δὲ ποίας |₁₅ ἔμμι, τεθνάκην δ' ὀλίγω 'πιδεύης |₁₆ φαίνομ' ἔμ' αὔται.

seen here in Song 31 of Sappho. This kind of vision is an *epiphany,* and I am now using here another word that actually derives from the same verb *phainetai,* 'he appears' / *phainomai,* 'I appear', as we have just seen it at lines 1 / 16. An epiphany is a vision that is felt to be real, not unreal. It is the appearance of something divine, something that is understood to be absolutely real.

5§39. The 'he' in line 1 of this song refers to a bridegroom, and he is figured as a god at the moment of singing this song. It is as if a god has appeared at a wedding. In the words of line 1 of the song, the bridegroom *phainetai,* 'appears', to be *īsos theoisin,* 'equal [*īsos*] to the gods'. Appearances become realities here. I say this because *phainetai* means not only 'appears' but also 'is manifested in an epiphany', and this epiphany is felt as real.* Literally, the bridegroom 'appears in an epiphany', *phainetai,* in line 1. In ritual terms, the word *phainetai,* 'he appears', here signals a real epiphany. And the word *kēnos (ekeinos),* 'that one', as we will see in Hour 15§45 when we read Philostratus, also signals the epiphany.

5§40. As for the 'you' who is being addressed by the speaker, this 'you' is a she. She is the bride. And just as the bridegroom *phainetai,* 'appears', to be *īsos theoisin* 'equal [*īsos*] to the gods', at line 1 of the song, the bride is figured as a goddess at the same moment in the song. The ritual occasion of a wedding, as formalized in a wedding song, collapses the distinction between 'bride' and 'goddess'. Here I recall what I noted already in Hour 4, where we saw that the word *numphē* means both 'bride' (as in *Iliad* XVIII 492) and 'goddess', that is, 'nymph' (as in *Iliad* XXIV 616).

5§41. And the 'I' who is speaking is also a she. She is the lead singer who sings the song, and she is 'Sappho'. This woman who speaks in the first person here is vicariously speaking for the whole group that is notionally participating in the ritual of the wedding. Such a female lead singer is a *prima donna,* to borrow an Italian term used in the world of opera. And this lead singer, this female speaker, experiences an attraction to both the bridegroom and the bride. Or, we might say, she experiences an attraction to the attraction between the two. The attraction is both aesthetic and erotic. It is a totalizing attraction, creating feelings of total connectedness. And this totalizing connectedness activates all the senses of the speaker, who experiences an "erotic meltdown."

5§42. The feelings come to a climax described as just one moment away from death. Here is the way it is expressed in line 16 of the song: *tethnakēn d'oligō 'pideuēs | phainom' emautāi,* 'and a little short of death | do I appear [*phaino-*

---

* *PH* 201 = 7§2n10.

mai] to myself'. The wording here matches what is expressed in line 1 of the song: *phainetai moi kēnos īsos theoisin* 'that man *appears* [*phainetai*] to me (to be) equal to the gods'. In both line 1 and line 16, what is 'appearing' or 'seeming' on one level is an epiphany on a deeper level. To translate *phainom' emautāi* at line 16 on such a deeper level proves to be difficult: 'I am manifested to myself in an epiphany'.

5§43. The wording in line 16 of Song 31 of Sappho, however we translate it, expresses the idea that the speaker is personally experiencing an epiphany. She undergoes a fusion with divinity, and this fusion is not only aesthetic but also erotic. But I think it would be too simple to say that such an experience is auto-erotic. Rather, as I will argue, it is an experiencing of auto-epiphany. And such an experience is not only erotic; it is also mortally dangerous.

5§44. The epiphany in line 16 of Song 31 induces a near-death experience for the speaker: *tethnakēn d'oligō 'pideuēs | phainom' emautāi*, 'and a little short of death | do *I appear* [*phainomai*] to myself'. We will now see that this figurative personal death, in the ritualized context of a wedding, is modeled on a realized mythical death. As I will argue, death in myth is a prototype for the vicarious experience of the first-person speaker in her interaction with the second-person bride and with the third-person bridegroom. And such an experience of death can be described as an initiation. As I explained a few minutes ago, the likening of a bridegroom and a bride to a god and a goddess leads to a figurative death in rituals of initiation such as weddings.

5§45. Here I return to Text A and Text B, two passages I showed at the beginning of this hour. Both passages were taken from *Iliad* XVI, where we saw the logic of myth at work in the words that tell about the death of Patroklos. In Text A, Patroklos is likened indirectly to Apollo (XVI 705); in Text B, he is likened directly to Arēs (XVI 784) and again indirectly to Apollo (XVI 786). This logic is relevant to Text E, Song 31 of Sappho, where the bridegroom and the bride are likened indirectly to Arēs and Aphrodite. In the logic of myth, as we saw in the *Iliad*, a hero's identity at the moment of death merges with a god's identity, and, at that moment, the hero can be likened to a god. In the logic of ritual, as we have just seen in Song 31 of Sappho, such a merger of identity leads only to a figurative death, a near-death, as expressed in the words that tell about the near-death experience of the woman who is speaking in the first person.*

5§46. Such a moment, when the bridegroom is the god and the bride is the

* PP 87–97.

goddess, is signaled by the epithet *īsos theoisin*, 'equal [*īsos*] to the gods', which is applied to the bridegroom in line 1 of Song 31.

5§47. We have already seen a similar epithet in Hour 4 when we were reading Song 44 of Sappho. There we saw Andromache and Hector as bride and bridegroom, and the two of them were described as *theoeikeloi*, 'looking just like the gods' (line 34). As we saw from the context, the two of them were looking like gods *at their wedding*, that is, at the ritual moment when they got married to each other.

5§48. In the songs of Sappho, we see also other variations in the merging of human and divine identities. In Song 165, for example, we find the wording *phainetai woi kēnos īsos theoisin*, 'he appears [*phainetai*] to her, that one, equal [*īsos*] to the gods'. In that song, the third-person *woi*, 'to her', seems to be referring to the bride, in contrast with the wording we find in line 1 of Song 31, *phainetai moi kēnos īsos theoisin*, 'he appears [*phainetai*] to me, that one, (to be) equal [*īsos*] to the gods', where the first-person *moi*, 'to me', refers to the speaker, who is 'Sappho'. In Song 31, the subjectivity is linked to the first-person speaker, who is the vicarious participant; in Song 165, by contrast, the subjectivity is linked to the third person, who is the immediate participant. There is a shifting of referents that accompanies the shifting of pronouns from 'I' to 'she'.

Song 1 of Sappho

5§49. We are now about to see another shifting of referents, in Song 1 of Sappho. Here the shift is from 'you' to 'I'. In this case, the shift in the ownership of pronouns involves the second-person 'you' of the goddess Aphrodite herself and the first-person 'I' of Sappho. During an epiphany of Aphrodite, Sappho exchanges identities with the goddess. It is a moment of personal fusion with Aphrodite:

HOUR 5 TEXT F

|₁ You with pattern-woven flowers, immortal Aphrodite, |₂ child of Zeus, weaver of wiles, I implore you,|₃ do not devastate with *aches* and *sorrows*,|₄ Mistress, my heart! |₅ But come here [*tuide*], if ever at any other time |₆ hearing my voice from afar, |₇ you heeded me, and leaving the palace of your father, |₈ golden, you came, |₉ having harnessed the chariot; and you were carried along by beautiful |₁₀ swift sparrows over the dark earth |₁₁ swirling with their dense plumage from the sky

through the |₁₂ midst of the aether, |₁₃ and straightaway they arrived.
But you, O holy one, |₁₄ smiling with your immortal looks, |₁₅ kept ask-
ing *what is it once again this time [dēute]* that has happened to me and
for *what* reason |₁₆ *once again this time [dēute]* do I invoke you, |₁₇ and
what is it that I want more than anything to happen |₁₈ to my frenzied
[*mainolās*] heart [*thūmos*]? "Whom am I once again *this* time [*dēute*]
to persuade, |₁₉ setting out to bring her to your love? Who is doing you,
|₂₀ Sappho, wrong? |₂₁ For if she is fleeing now, soon she will give chase.
|₂₂ If she is not taking gifts, soon she will be giving them. |₂₃ If she does
not love, soon she will love |₂₄ even against her will." |₂₅ Come to me
even now, and free me from harsh |₂₆ anxieties, and however many
things |₂₇ my heart [*thūmos*] yearns to get done, *you* do for me. You |₂₈
become my ally in war.

Song 1 of Sappho = Prayer to Aphrodite*

5§50. As the female speaker of Song 1, the 'I' of Sappho is being pictured here
as the lead singer of a choral lyric performance. *She leads off by praying to Aphrodite to be present, that is, to manifest herself in an epiphany.* The goddess is invoked from far away in the sky, which is separated from the earth by the immeasurably vast space of 'aether'. Aphrodite is implored to fill the aching need
caused by the sorrows of love. And, now that she is invoked, despite the overwhelming sense of separation between the divine and the human, Aphrodite
makes her presence felt in a sudden flash, in one single divine moment. So the
goddess appears, that is, she is now present in the sacred space of performance,
and her presence becomes an epiphany for all those who are present. Then, once
Aphrodite is present, she exchanges roles with the prima donna who figures as
the leader of choral performance. In the part of Song 1 that we see enclosed
within quotation marks in the visual formatting of modern editions (lines 18–
24), the first-person 'I' of Sappho is now replaced by Aphrodite herself, who has

---

* |₁ ποικιλόθρον᾽ ἀθανάτ᾽Ἀφρόδιτα, |₂ παῖ Δίος δολόπλοκε, λίσσομαί σε, |₃ μή μ᾽ ἄσαισι μηδ᾽
ὀνίαισι δάμνα, |₄ πότν]ια, θῦμον, |₅ ἀλλὰ τυίδ᾽ ἔλθ᾽, αἴ ποτα κἀτέρωτα |₆ τὰς ἔμας αὔδας ἀίοισα πήλοι
|₇ ἔκλυες, πάτρος δὲ δόμον λίποισα |₈ χρύσιον ἦλθες |₉ ἄρμ᾽ ὑπασδεύξαισα· κάλοι δέ σ᾽ ἆγον |₁₀
ὤκεες στροῦθοι περὶ γᾶς μελαίνας |₁₁ πύκνα δίννεντες πτέρ᾽ ἀπ᾽ ὠράνωἴθε |₁₂ ρος διὰ μέσσω· |₁₃ αἶψα
δ᾽ ἐξίκοντο· σὺ δ᾽, ὦ μάκαιρα, |₁₄ μειδιαί[σαισ᾽ ἀθανάτωι προσώπωι |₁₅ ἤρε᾽ ὄττι δηὖτε πέπονθα κὤττι
|₁₆ δηὖτε κάλημμι |₁₇ κὤττι μοι μάλιστα θέλω γένεσθαι |₁₈ μαινόλαι θύμωι· τίνα δηὖτε πείθω |₁₉ βαῖσ᾽
ἄγην ἐς σὰν φιλότατα; τίς σ᾽, ὦ |₂₀ Ψάπφ᾽, ἀδικήει; |₂₁ καὶ γὰρ αἰ φεύγει, ταχέως διώξει, |₂₂ αἰ δὲ δῶρα
μὴ δέκετ᾽, ἀλλὰ δώσει, |₂₃ αἰ δὲ μὴ φίλει, ταχέως φιλήσει |₂₄ κωὐκ ἐθέλοισα. |₂₅ ἔλθε μοι καὶ νῦν,
χαλέπαν δὲ λῦσον |₂₆ ἐκ μερίμναν, ὄσσα δέ μοι τέλεσσαι |₂₇ θῦμος ἰμέρρει, τέλεσον, σὺ δ᾽ αὔτα |₂₈
σύμμαχος ἔσσο. On the reading βαῖσ᾽ ἄγην at line 19 see PP 98n34.

been a second-person 'you' up to this point. We see here an exchange of roles between the first-person 'I' and the second-person 'you'. The first-person 'I' now becomes Aphrodite, who proceeds to speak in the performing voice of Sappho to Sappho herself, who has now become the second-person 'you'. During Aphrodite's epiphany inside the sacred space of the people of Lesbos, a fusion of identities takes place between the goddess and the prima donna who leads the choral performance *tuide*, 'here' (line 5), that is, in this sacred space.*

5§51. The exchange between the 'I' and the 'you' of Sappho and Aphrodite in Song 1 of Sappho is reflected also in the wording of Song 159 of Sappho, where Aphrodite is imagined once again as speaking to Sappho and addressing her by name. Moreover, in Song 134 of Sappho, the speaker says she is dreaming that she has a dialogue *(dialegesthai)* with Aphrodite.

5§52. Back in Song 1, Sappho prayed to Aphrodite to give her the power that the goddess has, the power to make love happen. She prayed that she may 'get done' whatever it is that Aphrodite 'gets done' in the active voice of the verb meaning 'to get something done', *telessai* (line 26), which is to be contrasted with the passive voice *telesthēn* applying to a passive lover who simply lets love happen (as in Sappho Song 5 line 4, not cited here). To be granted that power is to be the lead singer of the song that has the power to make love happen. Such is the power of song in the songs of Sappho. Such is the power of the prayer that is powered by Song 1 of Sappho.

5§53. Earlier in this hour, I took time out to study the historical context of the myths and rituals of the people of Lesbos in the era of Sappho. I concentrated on the sacred space of their federal precinct, where the festival of the *Kallisteia* was celebrated in choral performances by the women of Lesbos. In Song 1 of Sappho, we can now see a reference to this sacred space, which had been called Messon to indicate a political 'middle ground'. The reference is indicated simply by the deictic adverb *tuide*, 'here' (line 5).

5§54. Song 1 of Sappho can be seen as a *prayer* in the sense of *a totalizing formula* for authorizing choral performances of women at the festival of the *Kallisteia*. The seasonal recurrences of the festival are signaled by the triple deployment of the adverb *dēute*, 'once again this time', in Sappho's prayer (lines 15, 16, 18). Every time in the past that Sappho has invoked Aphrodite by offering to her this prayer that we now hear, the goddess has heeded the prayer and has manifested herself in an ever-new epiphany. And now, once again this time, the god-

---

*PP 97–103.

dess appears to Sappho, who will once again this time speak for the whole chorus as she speaks first for herself and then for Aphrodite and then once again this time for herself.

5§55. In the postclassical era of literary critics like Menander the Rhetorician (3.333–334; Sappho *Source 47*), the description of compositions like Song 1 of Sappho as *prayers* fails to capture the meaning of *an act of prayer in the context of a choral performance.* The modern mind, seizing on current understandings of the word *prayer,* is quick to infer that the "prayers" of Sappho must be mere literary conceits. This is to ignore the dimension of performance, which complements the dimension of composition in the lyric singing that we see in this early period of ancient Greek song culture. It is also to ignore the ritual background of such performance, which complements the mythological background of the composition.*

5§56. What appears to be a private "prayer" uttered by Sappho is at the same time a public act of worship that is notionally sung and danced by the people of Lesbos as represented by a chorus of their women, legendary as they are for their beauty, and as led by the figure of Sappho as their prima donna. What appears to be the most deeply personal experience of Sappho is at the same time the most widely shared communal experience of the people of Lesbos.

The Ritual Background of Song 1 of Sappho

5§57. I now propose to go into more detail about the identification of the speaker with the goddess Aphrodite in Song 1 of Sappho. This identification happens, as we saw, within a lapse of time that we moderns indicate by way of quotation marks, starting with 'Whom am I once again *this* time . . .' and ending with '. . . soon she will love | even against her will'. Within this lapse of time, the 'I' of Sappho becomes the 'I' of Aphrodite, while the 'you' of Aphrodite becomes the 'you' of Sappho. So the lead singer of Song 1, who is the prima donna of the song, becomes a goddess during this lapse of time. And the lead singer here is not only a *prima donna.* She is a *diva,* to borrow another Italian term used in the world of opera. To say it in English, the lead singer is now a *goddess.*

5§58. And what exactly is the moment when the lead singer becomes a goddess? This moment *recurs* every time the song is sung once again, as at a ritual that marks either a girl's coming of age or her wedding. Essential for under-

* See Yatromanolakis 2003.

standing this concept of *recurrence* in Song 1 of Sappho is the concept of *repetition* in ritual, as expressed by the adverb *dēute*, 'once again' (lines 15, 16, 18). I signal here the formulation of Kierkegaard (*Repetition*, 1843): "The dialectic of repetition is easy, for that which is repeated has been—otherwise it could not be repeated—but the very fact that it has been makes the repetition into something new."* Similarly for us modern readers, every time we look back at this passage, there will be something new for us to see.

The Maiden Song of Alcman

5§59. Here is another ancient Greek example of a song performed at a seasonally recurring festival. Once more we will see the ritual practice of equating the prima donna—or we can also say prima ballerina—with a goddess. This time, the equation happens at a "coming out" ritual that marks a coming of age from girlhood to womanhood:

HOUR 5 TEXT G

$|_{39}$ And I sing $|_{40}$ the radiance of Agido, seeing $|_{41}$ her as the sun, which for us $|_{42}$ is shown by Agido—she is the eyewitness—$|_{43}$ to shine [*phainein*] with its sunlight. But for me to praise [*ep-ainein*] her $|_{44}$ or to blame [*mōmēsthai*] her is not allowed by the glorious [*kleenna*] leader of the chorus [*khorēgos* = Hagesikhora]. $|_{45}$ No, she does not at all allow me. For that one [Hagesikhora] appears radiantly to be $|_{46}$ outstanding, as when someone $|_{47}$ sets among grazing cattle a horse, $|_{48}$ well-built, a prize-winner, with thundering hooves, $|_{49}$ something from out of those dreams that happen underneath a rock.†

From the *Partheneion* 'Maiden Song' of Alcman, lines 39–49‡

5§60. Here is a thesis paragraph that is meant to encapsulate the argumentation in the exegesis that follows:

The words in this passage indicate a ritual of female initiation in the

---

* Kierkegaard 1983 [1843]:149. See PP 101–103; also 52.

† On this mystical reference to dreams that are dreamed while sleeping at the foot of a rock formation that looms over the sleeper, I have much more to say in GM 223–262.

‡ $|_{39}$ ἐγὼν δ᾽ ἀείδω $|_{40}$ Ἀγιδῶς τὸ φῶς· ὁρῶ $|_{41}$ ϝ᾽ ὥτ᾽ ἄλιον, ὅνπερ ἇμιν $|_{42}$ Ἀγιδὼ μαρτύρεται $|_{43}$ φαίνην· ἐμὲ δ᾽ οὔτ᾽ ἐπαινῆν $|_{44}$ οὔτε μωμήσθαι νιν ἁ κλεννὰ χοραγὸς $|_{45}$ οὐδ᾽ ἁμῶς ἐῆι· δοκεῖ γὰρ ἤμεν αὔτα $|_{46}$ ἐκπρεπὴς τὼς ὥπερ αἴτις $|_{47}$ ἐν βοτοῖς στάσειεν ἵππον $|_{48}$ παγὸν ἀεθλοφόρον καναχάποδα $|_{49}$ τῶν ὑποπετριδίων ὀνείρων.

public space of Sparta, where the entire male and female population is experiencing contact with the divine. The climactic moment in this ritual is marked by an epiphany, as marked here by the words that I translate 'shine with sunlight'.

Now I proceed to the exegesis.

5§61. This song, conventionally known as the *Partheneion*, the 'Maiden Song', was reputedly composed by a legendary poet named Alcman for performance at a seasonally recurring grand public festival in Sparta.* Year after year, local maidens were specially selected for the occasion of singing and dancing this song in the public space of Sparta, and we have already seen that the word for such singing and dancing was *khoros*, 'chorus, song-and-dance ensemble'. As the girls sang and danced the song, they took on the roles of the names featured in the song. Two names stand out, referring to the two premier roles in the singing and dancing. These names are Hagesikhora and Agido, referring in the song to two competing chorus leaders of what I infer must be two competing choruses.†

5§62. I note the use of the word *khorēgos*, 'chorus-leader', in the song, referring to the girl called Hagesikhora, one of the two chorus leaders. The name Hagesikhora means the same thing as *khorēgos*. As for the other girl, called Agido, the words of the song identify her with the sun itself, but then, right after this declaration, the girl called Hagesikhora is said to match Agido in her own solar radiance. In modern terms, such descriptions as prima donna or prima ballerina surely apply to both girls.

5§63. So the girls who figure as the center of attention in the choral performance of this Song of Maidens by Alcman are being identified with the divine force of the sun itself, just as the girl who is getting married in Song 31 of Sappho is identified with the divinity of love and sexuality, Aphrodite.

5§64. So far, as I have been talking about Song 31 of Sappho, I have not yet said that the goddess who is identified with the bride must be Aphrodite herself. But now, on the basis of the comparisons we can make with the Maiden Song of Alcman, the identification of the bride with the goddess Aphrodite in Song 31 of Sappho has become evident. And it follows that the bridegroom in this same song is identified with the god Ares.

PP 53–54.

† *PP* 57, 89, 92. I also infer that these two competing choruses are representatives of the two royal houses of Sparta.

A Typological Comparison of Initiation Rituals

5§65. Such identification with divinities, as I noted earlier, is well attested in the initiation rituals of a wide variety of societies around the world. In my research, I have studied as a point of typological comparison the Navajo and Apache rituals of girls' initiation into puberty.* Such initiation rituals are customarily performed by and in honor of a young female member of the community when she begins to menstruate. The medium for performance is singing as well as dancing.

5§66. The focal point of these Navajo and Apache rituals of female initiation is the goddess "Changing Woman." More literally, her name means "the woman who is transformed time and again." In the here and now of the Changing Woman ritual, the songs are thought to have the power of re-enacting the prototypical event.

5§67. In the case of the Navajo rituals, the localization of the family building known as the *hogan* becomes sacred space, where the distinctions between the details of myth and the details of ritual can merge in the minds of those who participate in the ritual.† Within the sacred space, the young girl to be initiated becomes *identified* with the goddess Changing Woman. We may also say: *the girl identifies with the goddess.*

5§68. After a pronouncement of blessings in the Navajo ritual, the girl initiand goes out of the *hogan* and runs a race with other young people who are participants in her initiation, and it is ritually prescribed that she must take the lead in the race. We can find a comparable detail in the ancient Greek ritual as enacted in the Maiden Song of Alcman. In this ritual as well, there was some sort of race, as we see from the words of the song referring to the running of the two girls Hagesikhora and Agido in competition with the other girls and with each other (lines 58–59).

5§69. In the Navajo ritual, the prescribed course of the race to be run by the girl initiand is symbolic of the course of the sun. It has been observed that "the race is, in effect, her pursuit of the sun."‡ In the myth of Changing Woman, which is correlated with the ritualized race of the girl initiand, the goddess actually mates with the sun, which is envisioned as a male divinity; at the moment of intercourse, the sun takes on the form of a handsome young man.§ As we will

---

* *PP* ch. 4. In Hour 2, I gave a working definition of the term *typological comparison.*
† *PP* 88.
‡ The sources are documented in *PP* 89–90.
§ *PP* 90.

see later, there is a comparable theme in Song 58 of Sappho (lines 25–26), when the female speaker declares her powerful attraction to the divine power of the shining sun.

5§70. In the Talking God type of *hogan* songs in Navajo ritual, the goddess is conventionally described as moving toward the ritually decorated family *hogan* and then signaling her arrival. As she arrives, the references that are made to the goddess in the song shift from the third to the first person, so that the goddess herself, represented in the words of the singer, now speaks as an "I." It seems that the "I" stands for a composite of the girl initiand and of Changing Woman herself, *though the actual performer is the chief singer,* not the girl. A phrase continually repeated in *Talking God Hogan Song 25* goes like this: "With my sacred power, I am traveling."

5§71. This ritual picturing of a traveling goddess whose climactic epiphany in the here and now signals a shift from speaking about her in the third person to speaking for her in the first person is comparable to the ritual picturing of the goddess Aphrodite as she travels from her celestial realm on high all the way down to the sacred space where Song 1 of Sappho is being performed. In this ancient Greek song we see a shift that is comparable to the shift we just saw in the Navajo ritual: in the Greek song, the main performer or prima donna shifts from speaking to Aphrodite in the second person to speaking for her in the first person, so that Sappho as Aphrodite may now speak directly to Sappho as Sappho herself (starting at line 18 and lasting through line 24).

5§72. Here I conclude my comparative analysis of the ritual practice of equating a prima donna or prima ballerina with the divine in the Maiden Song of Alcman, where a beautiful girl named Agido, who is a prima donna of the choral performance, 'summons' the sun to shine. By now we can see what is meant: the girl literally makes the sun shine. The song identifies the girl Agido with the sun.

Song 16 of Sappho

5§73. In this song as well, we see an identification of the prima donna or prima ballerina with the sun:

HOUR 5 TEXT H

|₁ Some say a massing of chariots and their drivers, some say of foot-soldiers, |₂ some say of ships, if you think of everything that exists on the surface of this black earth, |3 is the most beautiful thing of them

all. But I say it is that one thing |₄ that anyone passionately loves [erâtai].* |₅ It's really quite easy to make this understandable |₆ to everyone, this thing. You see, that woman who was by far supreme |₇ in beauty among all mortals, Helen, |₈ she [. . .] left her best of all husbands, |₉ him she left behind and sailed to Troy, |₁₀ caring not about her daughter and her dear parents, |₁₁ not caring at all. She was swept along [. . .] |₁₅ [All this] reminds me right now of Anaktoria. |₁₆ She is [not] here.† |₁₇ Oh, how I would far rather wish to see her taking a dancing step that arouses passionate love [= eraton], |₁₈ and to see the luminous radiance from the look of her face |₁₉ than to see those chariots of the Lydians and the footsoldiers in their armor |₂₀ as they fight in battle [. . .].

Song 16 of Sappho‡

5§74. This song captures what could be described as Sappho's own personal ascending scale of affection. In the first stanza, consisting of four lines, there are three things to compare with 'that most beautiful thing' that anyone 'passionately loves', erâtai. But each one of these three things pales in comparison to whatever 'that one most beautiful thing' may be. And what is 'that thing'? It is elusive. From the start, the speaker has been speaking about 'that thing'. But then, the next thing you know, she starts saying 'this thing' instead of 'that thing', and, as she goes on to say, it is quite easy, really, to explain 'this thing'.

5§75. The three things that pale in comparison to that one thing that is so passionately desired are three radiant visions of beauty. The first of these visions is the dazzling sight of magnificent chariot fighters in their luminous war chariots as they are massing for frontal assault against their terrified enemy; the second vision is an army of footsoldiers fighting on the battlefield; and the third vision is a fleet of battleships proudly sailing at sea. But none of these three radiant visions of beauty can match that ultimate brightness radiating from the speaker's love object, that unique thing of passionate love, who is a beautiful

---

* Here is a transliteration of the first stanza: oi men ippéōn stroton oi de pesdōn | oi de nāōn phais' epi gān melainan | emmenai kalliston egō de kēn' ot|tō tis erâtai.

† In the papyrus fragment, the negative 'not' is not visible, but its restoration is supported by editors.

‡ |₁ [o]ἰ μὲν ἱππήων στρότον οἱ δὲ πέσδων |₂ οἱ δὲ νάων φαῖσ' ἐπ[ὶ] γᾶν μέλαι[ν]αν |₃ [ἔ]μμεναι κάλλιστον, ἔγω δὲ κῆν' ὅτ-|₄-τω τις ἔραται· |₅ πά]γχυ δ' εὔμαρες σύνετον πόησαι |₆ [π]άντι τ[ο]ῦτ', ἀ γὰρ πόλυ περσκέθοισα |₇ κάλλος [ἀνθ]ρώπων Ἐλένα [τὸ]ν ἄνδρα |₈ τὸν [πανάρ]ιστον |₉ καλλ[ίποι]σ' ἔβα 'ς Τροΐαν πλέοι[σα |₁₀ κωὐδ[ὲ πα]ῖδος οὐδὲ φίλων το[κ]ήων |₁₁ πά[μπαν] ἐμνάσθη, ἀλλὰ παράγαγ' αὔταν |₁₂ [. . .]σαν [. . .] |₁₅ [. . .]με νῦν Ἀνακτορί[ας ὀ]νέμναι-|₁₆ [-σ' οὐ] παρεοίσας, |₁₇ [τᾶ]ς <κ>ε βολλοίμαν ἐρατόν τε βᾶμα |₁₈ κἀμάρυχμα λάμπρον ἴδην προσώπω |₁₉ ἢ τὰ Λύδων ἄρματα †κανοπλοισι |₂₀ [πεσδομ]άχεντας.

diva called Anaktoria. The song now shows Anaktoria in an exquisite moment of singing and dancing in a chorus, and the words of the song point to her lovely step as she dances, a step that is *eraton*, or 'arousing passionate love'.

5§76. And then there is 'the luminous radiance from the look of her face' (*k̇amarukhma lampron idēn prosōpō*). This luminous vision of Anaktoria, the song is saying, cannot be surpassed by anything in the whole wide world. And the radiance of Anaktoria is now directly compared with the radiance of the luminous chariots and the two other luminous foils in the first stanza (lines 1–2).

5§77. The first stanza of this song is a striking example of a priamel, which is a rhetorical device where "A" is highlighted by saying that "B" and "C" and "D" and so on cannot match it. The sequence has to be . . . D C B and finally A.

Another Song of Sappho

5§78. In an article I published about another song of Sappho (I refer to the relevant fragment as Π²), I offer this translation of the last line of the song:*

HOUR 5 TEXT I

Passionate love [*erōs*] for the sun has won for me its radiance and beauty.

Sappho Π² 26

In terms of an alternative interpretation, the translation could be . . .

Passionate love [*erōs*] has won for me the radiance and beauty of the sun.

I prefer the first of these two interpretations, which makes the sun the objective genitive of *erōs*, 'passionate love'. †

Back to Song 16 of Sappho

5§79. Such a genitive construction, if my interpretation holds, is parallel to the phrase *ot | tō tis erātai*, 'whatever one loves passionately', in the first stanza of

---

* Nagy 2010a:189. See also *GM* 261–262; *PH* 285 = 10§18; *PP* 90, 102–203.

† In terms of the first interpretation, the original Greek wording would be τὸ λά[μπρον ἔρως ἀελίω καὶ τὸ κά]λον λέ[λ]ογχε. In terms of the second interpretation, it would be τὸ λά[μπρον ἔρος τὠελίω καὶ τὸ κά]λον λέ[λ]ογχε.

Song 16 of Sappho. This 'whatever' (lines 3–4) is described as *kalliston*, 'the most beautiful thing' in the whole wide world (line 3).

5§80. In Song 16, no vision of beauty can match that ultimate brightness radiating from the speaker's love-object, who is a beautiful diva called Anaktoria. The song focuses on the divine moment when Anaktoria sings and dances in the chorus, and the wording creates a sublime vision of her beauty. In this vision, the beautiful Anaktoria who is imagined in the wording can now come to life, and I have already highlighted the wording that shows 'her dancing step that arouses passionate love and the luminous radiance from the look of her face' (*eraton te bāma | kamarukhma lampron idēn prosōpō*, lines 17–18). This vision cannot be surpassed by anything else in the whole wide world.

5§81. In the logic of Sappho's poetic cosmos, nothing can surpass the radiance of the sun. So the all-surpassing radiance of 'whatever' it is that the speaker says she loves more than anything else on this earth—which is the vision of the singing and dancing Anaktoria—must be the same thing as the sun.

Back to Song 31 of Sappho

5§82. By now we have surveyed a wide variety of songs that feature divine models in ritual contexts like weddings. Applying what we have learned from these songs about the phenomenon that I have been calling *epiphany*, I will now re-examine Song 31 of Sappho. But first, to summarize what I have already argued:

> In Song 31, the erotic experience shared by the 'he' who is the bridegroom and by the 'you' who is the bride is communalized in the reaction of the 'I' who figures as the vicarious participant in the experience. And this reaction is an epiphany in and of itself.
>
> The subjective feelings in this moment of epiphany are linked to the first-person speaker who is Sappho. When we hear *phainetai moi kēnos īsos theoisin*, 'he appears [*phainetai*] to me, that one, (to be) equal [*īsos*] to the gods', at line 1, it is the first-person speaker who is feeling the erotic sensations experienced by the bride in the second person and by the bridegroom in the third person. At the climax of the erotic experience as spoken by the first-person speaker, she says about her feelings: *tethnakēn d'oligō 'pideuēs | phainom' emautāi*, 'and a little short of death | do I appear [*phainomai*] to myself', at line 16. The verb *phainomai*, 'I

appear', here signals again an epiphany—an epiphany that manifests itself to the self, to the speaking 'I'.

5§83. This appearance of the self to the self, as an epiphany, signals the divine
presence of Aphrodite. I waited until now to say this about Song 31, after having
compared other songs that signal the presence of Aphrodite.

5§84. In one sense, what is shown in Song 31 is the epiphany of Aphrodite,
since she is a most appropriate goddess for the occasion of a wedding. In another sense, however, what is shown in Song 31 is the epiphany of the bride,
whose identity fuses with that of Aphrodite at the moment of her wedding. And,
in still another sense, what is shown in Song 31 is the epiphany of the speaking
'I', who identifies with Aphrodite by virtue of vicariously identifying with the
'you' of the bride, who is Aphrodite at this very moment. For Sappho, then, as I
have been arguing, what is seen is an auto-epiphany.

5§85. Just as the vicariousness of Sappho in Song 31 fuses the 'I' who is the
singer with the 'you' who is the bride, so also the 'I' of Sappho in Song 1 fuses
the 'I' who is the singer with the 'you' who is Aphrodite.

5§86. In Song 31 of Sappho, the projection of identity that we see makes it
possible for the singer of the song to become the bride herself and even Aphrodite herself, at least for a moment, just as the singer of Song 1 of Sappho becomes Aphrodite herself for the brief moment when Aphrodite is being quoted
by the singer. In the logic of Song 31, seeing Sappho as Aphrodite for a moment
is just as real as seeing the bride as Aphrodite and just as real as seeing the bridegroom as Arēs.

5§87. Then, when the song comes to an end, everyone can revert to their
human selves—though they may have been upgraded in human status because
they had been part of the song. I find it relevant to compare the words of T. S.
Eliot (*The Dry Salvages*, 1941), "you are the music | While the music lasts."*

Epiphany and Death

5§88. As we have seen, the epiphany in Song 31 of Sappho induces a near-death
experience for the first-person speaker: *tethnakēn d'oligō 'pideuēs | phainom'
emautāi*, 'and a little short of death | do I appear [*phainomai*] to myself', at
line 16. And such a figurative personal death is modeled on a realized mythical

*Eliot 1941 [1963]:199.

death. As I have argued, death in myth is a prototype for the vicarious ritual experience of the first-person speaker in her interaction with the second-person bride and with the third-person bridegroom, who are respectively the vision of Aphrodite and the corresponding vision of Arēs.*

5§89. Here I note again the fact that the generic bridegroom is visualized as *īsos Areui*, 'equal to Arēs', in another song of Sappho (Song 111 line 5). And the bridegroom who gets married in lyric is comparable to the warrior who gets killed in epic. As we have seen from the climactic passage I quoted in Text B from *Iliad* XVI, when the warrior hero Patroklos is killed in battle, that hero is visualized at that moment as *atalantos Arēi*, 'equal to Arēs' (line 784). And Patroklos in such a context is a stand-in for Achilles. So just as Patroklos as a stand-in for Achilles qualifies as 'equal to Arēs', we can expect Achilles himself to qualify for epithets meaning 'equal to Arēs'. What is vital here for my argument is the fact that a bridegroom can be visualized not only as *īsos Arēi*, 'equal to Arēs', but even as Achilles himself in the songs of Sappho.

5§90. The figure of Patroklos as a ritual stand-in for Achilles in the *Iliad* helps us understand what has been up to now a missing link in the picturing of the bridegroom in Song 31 of Sappho. Patroklos as the stand-in for Achilles in epic prefigures Achilles at the moment of his own death in epic, when he, too, like the model bridegroom in lyric, is destined to be 'equal to Arēs'.

5§91. As we saw in Hour 4 Text E, the generic bridegroom was conventionally visualized as Achilles himself in the songs of Sappho (Himerius *Orations* 1.16). Such a lyric convention in the songs of Sappho can be explained as an organic correlation of myth and ritual. In the logic of myth, Achilles never becomes a model husband because War personified, Arēs, cuts him down like a beautiful plant in full bloom. In the logic of ritual, by contrast, Achilles is the perfect model for a bridegroom precisely because he is cut down in war and thus cannot ever became a husband. For love to find its self-expression in the ritual of a wedding, *it needs someone to die for love.*†

5§92. Such a ritual need is expressed in the relationship of Erōs, personified as the god of erotic love, with Aphrodite, the goddess of erotic love. In another song of Sappho, we find an imagined dialogue between Sappho and Aphrodite where the goddess says in her own words that Erōs is her *therapōn* (Sappho Song 159). As we will see in Hour 6, this word means not only 'attendant' but also 'ritual substitute', that is, someone who ritually dies for the sake of the one

---

* A longer version of what I argue here is presented in Nagy 2007a:31–36.
† Nagy 2007a:31–32.

he attends. Pictured as a pubescent (not prepubescent) boy, Erōs is doomed to die for the sake of Aphrodite. In the poetics of Sappho, as later ancient sources tell us (Sappho Fragment 172), *the death of erotic Love personified is a most persistent theme.* That is only natural, since Erōs is a non-Olympian god. Whereas Olympian gods are exempt from death, death comes naturally for divine non-Olympians. The consolation, at least, for the death of Erōs is that he is easily resurrected. It could be said that the resurrection of Erōs is as easy as the revival of lust.

Erōs and Arēs

5§93. The death of Erōs could be pictured as a martial death resulting from the warfare of love. We see clearly the language of love as war in Song 1 of Sappho, where the goddess Aphrodite is invoked in prayer to become a *summakhos,* 'ally in war' (line 28), for Sappho in speaking the words of lyric love song. Conversely, Sappho as the speaker of a lyric love song is offering herself as an 'ally in war' for Aphrodite, thus crossing over into the themes of epic. So we see here that love and war can be aestheticized and eroticized together. Similarly in the *Iliad,* Aphrodite crosses over into the themes of epic by intervening in the epic action—and she gets wounded in doing so, as if she were a mortal (V 327–354).†
Such a pairing of love and war, as we will now see, is reflected in the parallels we find between Aphrodite and Arēs. So we next turn to Arēs, god of war and lover of Aphrodite.

5§94. Parallel to the wounding of the goddess Aphrodite are the two woundings of the god Arēs in the *Iliad:* he too gets wounded as if he were a mortal (V 855–863, XXI 401–408). More than that, the woundings of Arēs are in both cases described as mortal woundings, and the *Iliad* actually shows Arēs in the act of going through the motions of a figurative martial death. Such an epic experience is for Arēs a mock death.*It must be a mock death and not a real death, because Arēs is an Olympian god, and Olympian gods do not die. Such ritualized mockery is typical of "divine burlesque," which represents one of the oldest features of Greek myth. There are striking parallels to be found in Near Eastern sources dating back to the second millennium BCE. ‡

---

* Nagy 2007a:32. The paragraphs that follow are taken from this same essay.
† EH §76.
‡ Burkert 1960:132.

Arēs as a Model for Achilles

5§95. The figurative death of the god Arēs in the *Iliad* is an extreme case of divine mirroring: the immortal god of war gets involved not only in the martial actions of heroes but even in their martial deaths. And he gets so involved because god and hero mirror each other at the moment of a hero's death, which is the climax of the inherent antagonism between them.*At the moment when he dies a warrior's death in place of Achilles, Patroklos is vicariously experiencing such a moment of mirroring between Achilles as warrior and Arēs as god of warriors: that is why Patroklos looks just like Arēs at that moment (*Iliad* XVI 784). †

5§96. As mutual antagonists, the hero Achilles and the god Arēs match each other in life as well as in death. In the case of Achilles, as we see from surviving traces in the epic Cycle, this hero was pictured as an irresistible lover in the imaginations of lovelorn girls hoping to make him their husband‡ In the case of Arēs, as we see when we read the second song of Demodokos in the Homeric *Odyssey,* this god is imagined as an irresistible lover for the goddess of love and sexuality herself, Aphrodite (viii 266–366).

5§97. Among other related characteristics shared by the hero Achilles and the god Arēs is their superhuman speed, as expressed by words like *theein,* 'run'.§ Also, in the case of Achilles, his success in war is closely connected with the use of epithets like *podas ōkus,* 'swift of foot', as at *Iliad* I 58. In the case of Arēs, his own swiftness of foot is pictured as ideal for success in courtship as well as in warfare: in the second of three songs that the singer Demodokos sings in *Odyssey* viii, which is about the love affair of Arēs and Aphrodite, we find that one of the war god's most irresistible attributes is his nimbleness of foot in choral lyric dancing.** And yet, despite his irresistible attractiveness in courting Aphrodite, the dashing young Arēs will never marry. Like the dashing young Achilles, Arēs is eternally the bridegroom and never the husband.

Achilles the Eternal Bridegroom

5§98. I return once again to Hour 4 Text E, where we learned that the generic bridegroom is visualized as Achilles himself in the songmaking of Sappho

---

* EH §§105, 108, 110, 115.

† *BA* 32–34, 292–294 = 2§8, 17§5.

‡ EH §56.

§ I have collected some striking examples in *BA* 326–328 = 20§§9–10.

** *HPC* 90 = I§214.

(Fragment 105b, as reported by Himerius *Orations* 1.16). This visualization is relevant to what we saw in Hour 4 Text F, where the generic bridegroom is pictured as a tender seedling in a song of Sappho (Song 115). And it is relevant also to Hour 4 Text G, where the goddess Thetis in lamenting her son Achilles pictures him as a tender seedling that is doomed to be cut down in war (*Iliad* XVIII 56–59).*

5§99. Just as the generic bridegroom in the songs of Sappho can be visualized as the hero Achilles, so also the generic bride can be visualized as a heroine.† In Aeolic traditions, such heroines figured in myths about the conquests of Achilles—not only martial but also amorous conquests—in the years that preceded the destruction of Troy. These myths told of beautiful Aeolic girls of Asia Minor and the outlying island of Lesbos who had once been immune to love and thus unreachable to their frustrated suitors. But then they fall helplessly in love with Achilles—that dashing young Aeolic hero who had sailed across the sea from his home in European Thessaly to attack the Aeolic people of Asia Minor and Lesbos.‡

5§100. Comparable to these once-unreachable Aeolic girls is a prize apple, unreachable to the apple-pickers, which 'blushes' enticingly from the heights of a "shooter-branch" in a song of Sappho:

HOUR 5 TEXT J

Just like the sweet apple that blushes on top of a branch, | the topmost apple on the topmost branch. It has eluded the notice of the apple pickers. | Oh, but no. It's not that they haven't noticed it. They just couldn't reach it.§

Sappho Fragment 105a

5§101. And the brides of Sappho's songs are conventionally compared to apples:

HOUR 5 TEXT K = HOUR 4 TEXT E

Himerius (*Orations* 1.16) reports: "Sappho compared the girl to an apple [. . .] she compared the bridegroom to Achilles, and likened the young man's deeds to the hero's."

Sappho Fragment 105b

---

* I disagree with the formulation of Dale 2011:53n22: "She is hardly comparing the best of the Achaeans to a twig."

† In what follows, I recapitulate what I argue in Nagy 2007a.

‡ *HPC* = 149, 250–251 = II§§49, 321.

§ On the ancient textual source where we find the quotation of this fragment, see Dale 2011:64.

5§102. Like Sappho's prize apple, these contemporary brides are imagined as unreachable. But they are unreachable only up to the moment when they take the place of Aeolic heroines who had once upon a time fallen in love with Achilles, that model bridegroom. These Aeolic girls of the heroic past are imagined as throwing themselves at Achilles. That is, they throw a metonymic extension of themselves at Achilles by throwing an apple at him: such a theme is attested in the bittersweet story of a lovelorn girl from the Aeolic city of Pedasos (Hesiod Fragment 214).* In the logic of myth, the love felt by such heroines is doomed from the start, and, in the end, they die for their love. In the logic of ritual, however, that same love promises to be requited. Such is the love expressed by girls pictured in the act of throwing apples at their prospective lovers in the songs of Sappho (Song 214A). A moment ago, I described such a ritual throwing of apples as a metonymic extension of the female self, using the term *metonymic* in line with the working definition I offered in Hour 4§32: *metonymy* is an expression of meaning by way of *connecting* something to something else that is next to that something or at least near to it, thereby establishing contact.

Briseis as a Stand-in for Aphrodite

5§103. As I have argued, Achilles in his role as the model bridegroom was imagined as a stand-in for the god Arēs in the songs of Sappho.† And, just as the Aeolic hero Achilles can stand in for the god Arēs at moments that center on the ritual of a wedding, so too can various Aeolic heroines stand in for a goddess, who is none other than Aphrodite, goddess of love and sexuality. A case in point is the captive woman Briseis in the *Iliad*. As I noted already in Hour 4, Briseis is overtly associated with the Aeolic women of Lesbos whom Achilles captured as beauty-prizes in the years that preceded the destruction of Troy (*Iliad* IX 128–131, 270–273; XIX 245–246). And the point is, Briseis is likened to Aphrodite in a most telling context:

HOUR 5 TEXT L = HOUR 4 TEXT J

$|_{282}$ Then Briseis, looking like golden Aphrodite, $|_{283}$ saw Patroklos all cut apart by the sharp bronze, and, when she saw him, $|_{284}$ she poured herself all over him in tears and wailed with a voice most clear, and

* *BA* 141 = 7§29n6.
† More detailed argumentation is in Nagy 2007a:28–37.

with her hands she tore at |₂₈₅ her breasts and her tender neck and her beautiful face. |₂₈₆ And then she spoke, weeping, this woman who looked like the goddesses: |₂₈₇ "O Patroklos, you have been most gracious to me in my terrible state and most gratifying to my heart. |₂₈₈ You were alive when I last saw you on my way out from the shelter |₂₈₉—and now I come back to find you dead, you, the protector of your people |₂₉₀—that is what I come back to find. Oh, how I have one bad thing after the next to welcome me again and again. |₂₉₁ The man to whom I was given away by my father and by my mother the queen |₂₉₂—I saw that man lying there in front of the city, all cut apart by the sharp bronze, |₂₉₃ and lying near him were my three brothers—all of us were born of one mother—|₂₉₄ they are all a cause for my sorrow, since they have all met up with their time of destruction. |₂₉₅ No, you did not let me—back when my husband was killed by swift-footed Achilles, |₂₉₆ killed by him, and when the city of my godlike Mynes [= my husband] was destroyed by him |₂₉₇—you did not let me weep, back then, but you told me that godlike Achilles |₂₉₈ would have me as a properly courted wife, that you would make that happen, and that you would take me on board the ships, |₂₉₉ taking me all the way to Phthia, and that you would arrange for a wedding feast among the Myrmidons. |₃₀₀ So now I cannot stop crying for you, now that you are dead, you who were always so sweet and gentle." |₃₀₁ So she [= Briseis] spoke, weeping, and the women kept on mourning in response. |₃₀₂ They mourned for Patroklos, that was their pretext, but they were all mourning, each and every one of them, for what they really cared for in their sorrow.

Iliad XIX 282–302

5§104. Most remarkably, Briseis is likened to the goddess Aphrodite here in *Iliad* XIX 282 in the context of her beginning to lament for Patroklos, who had been likened to the god Arēs at the moment of his death in *Iliad* XVI 784.

5§105. The epic has quoted, as it were, Briseis in the act of singing a choral lyric song of lament for the death of Patroklos (XIX 287–300), and this quotation of Briseis, along with the framing narrative concerning the antiphonal response of the women attending Briseis (XIX 301–302), re-enacts most accurately the morphology of a genuine choral lyric lament.*

5§106. In her lament, Briseis sings her bittersweet sorrow not only over the

---

* Dué 2002:70–71; HPC 242–350 = II§§303–320.

death of Patroklos but also over the death of her own fondest hope: when he was alive, Patroklos had promised to arrange for her a marriage to Achilles, but now that Patroklos is dead, the hope of that promise is gone forever (XIX 295–300). So the *Iliad* pictures Patroklos as a stand-in for Achilles in courtship as well as in war.* Just as Achilles is featured as an eternal bridegroom who never gets married, so also Patroklos himself becomes such an eternal bridegroom by virtue of being a stand-in for Achilles. I will have much more to say in Hour 6 about Patroklos as a ritual stand-in for Achilles.

The Merging of Identity in Myth and Ritual

5§107. In the ritual of a wedding as celebrated by the songs of Sappho, there is the prospect of a happy ending as the identity of the bride shifts from girl to goddess to woman. In the process of becoming a goddess for a moment, the bride dies to her old self as a girl and is reborn to her new self as a woman. In the corresponding myth, by contrast, there is the prospect of a sad but compellingly erotic ending to the story. The bride-to-be will never get married to the ideal bridegroom, imagined as Achilles. And that is because this most eligible bridegroom will die in war and will never be married.

5§108. The death of Achilles in war is the climax of his erotic charisma. In general, the martial death of heroes is eroticized as the beautiful death, *la belle mort*. Even the body of the dead hero is eroticized—as the beautiful corpse, *le beau mort* (a most striking example is Poem 10 of Tyrtaeus).† Achilles himself is pictured as such a *beau mort* in Homeric poetry. A case in point is the moment when the goddess Thetis and her fellow Nereids lament the future death of her beloved son in war: at that moment, as we have seen in *Iliad* XVIII 54–60, quoted in Hour 4 Text G, the hero Achilles is compared to a beautiful seedling that dies prematurely while it is still in full bloom. ‡ And in Song 105c of Sappho, as we have already noted, we can see a comparable image of a beautiful plant at the moment of death; also comparable is the image of a bridegroom as a beautiful plant in Sappho's Song 115.

5§109. Such themes of eroticized death are relevant to the near-death experience of the speaking 'I' in Song 31 of Sappho. The woman who speaks in the first person here is vicariously speaking for the whole group that attends the wed-

---

* Nagy 2007a:32–34.
† *HC* 578–587 = 4§§259–270; *HPC* 296 = II§425.
‡ *BA* 182–184 = 10§11.

ding. The whole group is notionally participating in the stylized deaths of the male and the female initiands—in this case, of the bridegroom and the bride.

Distinctions between Real Death and Figurative Death in Lyric

5§110. The stylized death of the bridegroom in a wedding as described by Sappho matches the realized death of Achilles in war. Premarital death in ritual marks the transition from bridegroom to husband, while martial death in myth marks an eternal deferral of such a transition. By dying in war, Achilles becomes the very picture of the ultimate bridegroom in eternally suspended animation, forever on the verge of marrying. In the logic of ritual, what is needed for female initiands, especially for brides, is such an eternal bridegroom.*

5§111. As we will see in Hour 20 Text I, a comparable model of unfulfilled desire and unrequited love is the hero Hippolytus in the *Hippolytus* of Euripides: at the end of that drama (1423–1430), we will read an anthropologically accurate description of a ritual of female initiation featuring a chorus of girls performing a lament for the death of Hippolytus as their local cult hero.† As the drama of Euripides will illustrate, the identity of the female initiand depends on the program, as it were, of the ritual of initiation. The nuptial goddess Aphrodite and the prenuptial as well as postnuptial goddess Artemis reveal, as a pair, different phases of erotic engagement in the life cycle of a woman, determining when she is attainable—and when she is unattainable. ‡

5§112. So far, then, we have seen this symmetry:

(1) figurative death in the ritual of a wedding;
(2) real death in the ritual of warfare.

And this symmetry is parallel to the symmetry of *kleos aphthiton*, 'unwilting glory', in epic and lyric, since this expression applies not only to the epic theme of a hero's death in war, as in the case of Achilles in *Iliad* IX 413, quoted in Hour 1 Text A, but also to the lyric theme of a wedding, as in the case of Hector as bridegroom and Andromache as bride in Song 44 of Sappho (line 4). The expression *kleos aphthiton* links the doomed warrior in epic with the wedded couple in lyric.

* Dué 2006:82–83.
† PP 94–96.
‡ Nagy 2007a:34–36.

5§113. Parallel to the linking effected by this expression *kleos aphthiton* is the linking effected by the god Apollo himself: he too links Achilles in epic with Hector and Andromache in lyric. The celebrants at the wedding in Song 44 of Sappho sing Apollo as the subject of their song by invoking the god's epithet *Paean*—who is *Pāōn* in the local dialect of Lesbos—when they celebrate Hector and Andromache as bridegroom and bride (line 33). Apollo as *Paean* is the embodiment of a song called the *paean* (*paiēōn* in Homeric Greek, *paiān* in the dialect of Athens). To sing a paean is to sing a song from Lesbos, as we see from the wording of Archilochus (Poem 121). To sing a paean in the *Iliad* is to sing Apollo as Paean, though Paean is a god in his own right in more archaizing contexts of the *Iliad* (as at V 401 and V 899–901). Elsewhere in the *Iliad*, Achilles calls on the Achaeans to sing a paean, that is, to sing Apollo as Paean when they celebrate the death of Hector in war (XXII 391).*

5§114. As we have already seen, there are also other linkings of the doomed warrior in epic with the wedded couple in lyric. Achilles is *theoeikelos*, 'looking just like the gods', as a warrior in the *Iliad* (I 131, XXIII 155), and so too Hector and Andromache as bridegroom and bride are *theoeikeloi*, 'looking just like the gods', at the moment of their wedding in Song 44 of Sappho (at line 34; also [*i*] *keloi theoi*[*s*], 'looking just like the gods', at line 21). And Achilles is in fact the only recipient of the epithet *theoeikelos*, 'looking just like the gods', in the Homeric *Iliad*. So the warrior who kills Hector attracts the same epithet in epic that Hector attracts in lyric.

Apollo as Model for Achilles

5§115. It remains to ask about the god with whom Achilles is identified in epic and with whom Hector and Andromache are identified in lyric. For this god, epic and lyric are undifferentiated, just as the *kleos aphthiton* of Achilles as warrior in epic is undifferentiated from the *kleos aphthiton* of Hector and Andromache as bridegroom and bride in lyric. This god is Apollo.

5§116. So now, at long last, we turn from Arēs to Apollo as the other divine antagonist of Achilles—and as his other divine model.

5§117. *At the moment of his death, the hero Achilles is destined to confront not only the god Arēs as the generic divine antagonist of warriors but also the god Apollo as his own personal divine antagonist.* This personalized destiny of Achil-

* Nagy 2007a:36–37.

les, as the victim of Apollo, is made explicit in the epic Cycle (plot summary by Proclus of the *Aithiopis* by Arctinus of Miletus p. 106 lines 7–11), but it is only implicit in the *Iliad,* where Patroklos substitutes for Achilles in his antagonism with Apollo just as he substitutes for him in his antagonism with Arēs.

5§118. What makes this destiny of Achilles so personalized is his special connection with song, a medium signaled as *kleos aphthiton*, 'unwilting glory'. The god of this medium is Apollo, who is the god of poetry and song. And such poetry and song are conceived as lyric. To put it another way, such poetry and song can be conceived as a form of epic that is not yet differentiated from lyric.* *Apollo is the god of an older form of epic that is still sung to the accompaniment of the lyre, unlike the newer form of epic, which is unaccompanied by the lyre.* Typical of the newer form of epic is Homeric poetry as we know it.

5§119. Correspondingly, Achilles is the hero of such an older form of epic. In this role, he is imagined as looking exactly like Apollo—beardless and wearing long hair. Like Apollo, Achilles is the essence of a beautiful promise in the making, of a *telos* or 'fulfillment' realized only in performance, only when the song is fully performed.†

5§120. And there is a visual signature of this shared role of god and hero in the *Iliad*. I start with the fact that Achilles is pictured in this epic as singing to the tune of a lyre that he himself is playing (IX 186–189). As we have seen in Hour 4, Achilles had plundered this lyre from the Aeolic city of Thebe, ruled by the king Eëtion (IX 186–189), whom he killed when he captured that city—and who was the father of that greatest singer of lamentations in the *Iliad*, Andromache (VI 414–416). As I argued in Hour 4, Achilles sings to the tune of this Aeolic lyre an echo of the loves and bittersweet sorrows heard in lyric song.‡

5§121. Such a lyrical image of Achilles evokes a correspondingly lyrical image of Apollo. Even in epic, this god is conventionally pictured as a lyric personality. In fact, Apollo controls the medium of lyric, of choral lyric. A prime example is the conventional description of Apollo as the *Mous(h)ēgétēs*, that is, as the choral leader of the Muses.§ Such a description is attested in lyric (an example is Song 208 of Sappho) and even in epic (*Iliad* I 603–604). Apollo accompanies himself on the lyre as he sings and dances, while the Muses are the chorus who also sing and dance (*Homeric Hymn to Hermes* 475–476).

* *PH* 360–361 = 12§§44–45.
† *HTL* 138–143.
‡ *HPC* 239–240 = II§297.
§ *PH* 350–351 = 12§29.

5§122. The god Apollo controls not only lyric but all song and poetry, and he is ultimately in control of all occasions for the performance of song and poetry. In this overarching role, he embodies the authority of poets, that is, of craftsmen who compose song and poetry. This authority transcends such categories as epic and lyric. And it transcends the genres that figure as subcategories of epic and lyric, as well as the occasions that shape those genres. This authority is linked to the authorship of song and poetry.

5§123. It could even be said that the fatal attraction of Achilles for Apollo in the context of their ritual antagonism centers on the fact that the god controls the medium that gives *kleos aphthiton*, 'unwilting glory'.

5§124. I find it relevant to evoke again the words of T. S. Eliot: (*The Dry Salvages*, 1941): "you are the music / While the music lasts." And, now that I have evoked these words, I take the opportunity to go even further: in the long run, these words apply as well to *the premier hero of ancient Greek song culture, Achilles*. He too is the music, while the music lasts—but this music is destined to last forever. That is the message of the *kleos aphthiton*, 'unwilting glory', of Achilles in *Iliad* IX 413, quoted in Hour 1 Text A.

Fatal Attraction

5§125. A question remains: what is it, then, that attracts the hero to the god who will cause his death? I find no direct answer to this question in the passages that we have been reading during this hour, but I will attempt at least to offer this distillation of an indirect answer: *whatever it is in us that makes us human makes us irresistibly attracted to the divine, even at the risk of mortal danger.*

5§126. I find it relevant to quote here a formulation devised by Dio of Prusa ("Dio Chrysostom"), a Greek thinker who lived in a period straddling the first and the second centuries CE. In what I am about to quote, taken from his *Olympic Discourse* (Oration 12), Dio is representing a hypothetical speech delivered by none other than the great sculptor Pheidias of Athens, who is speaking about his masterpiece, the colossal statue of Zeus that he sculpted for the temple of Zeus at Olympia in Elis. In the passage I will be quoting, Pheidias explains his idealizing of the human form in creating the spectacular statue of Olympian Zeus. To justify the idealized human form that he creates for Zeus, the sculptor speaks about a universal need felt by humans not only to imagine gods as existing in the sky or in the cosmos in general but also to have a feeling of divine immediacy by being physically near them, close to them—a feeling achieved by way of mental or even physical contact with statues and with paintings and with other images of the gods:

HOUR 5 TEXT M

Because of their attraction to the divine unknown [*daimonion*],* all humans have a powerful erotic desire [*erōs*] to worship [*timân*] and to take care of [*therapeuein*]† the divinity [*theion*]‡ that they do know, by being up close to it and near to it, as they approach it and try to touch it in an act of persuasion, and they sacrifice to it and offer it garlands. Quite simply, they are like disconnected [*nēpioi*]§ children who have been torn away from their father or mother and who, feeling a terrific urge [*himeros*] and longing [*pothos*], often reach out their hands while they are dreaming, in the direction of their parents who are not there, so also are humans in their relationship with the gods, loving them as they do, and justifiably so, because the gods do good things for them and have an affinity with them. And, in their love for the gods, humans strive in all possible ways to be with them and in their company.

Dio of Prusa 12.60–61**

5§127. In the epic narrative of the *Iliad*, we find a sinister twist to this kind of attraction: whatever it is that attracts a hero like Patroklos to a god like Apollo on the battlefield makes that hero want to kill the god. In trying to kill the god, of course, the hero only brings about his own death. In other words, the fatal attraction experienced by the hero is not even recognized as fatal until it is too late.

---

* This word *daimonion* is derived from *daimōn*, which refers to an unspecified god, whereas *theos* refers to a specific god: see Hour 5§1. That is why I interpret *daimonion* here as the 'divine unknown'.

† For the meaning of this word, see Hour 6§54.

‡ This word *theion* is derived from *theos*, which refers to a specific god. That is why I interpret *theion* here as 'divinity that is known'.

§ On the meaning of *nēpios* as 'disconnected', see the Core Vocabulary.

** διὰ δὲ τὴν πρὸς τὸ δαιμόνιον ὁρμὴν ἰσχυρὸς ἔρως πᾶσιν ἀνθρώποις ἐγγύθεν τιμᾶν καὶ θεραπεύειν τὸ θεῖον, προσιόντας καὶ ἁπτομένους μετὰ πειθοῦς, θύοντας καὶ στεφανοῦντας. ἀτεχνῶς γὰρ ὥσπερ νήπιοι παῖδες πατρὸς ἢ μητρὸς ἀπεσπασμένοι δεινὸν ἵμερον ἔχοντες καὶ πόθον ὀρέγουσι χεῖρας οὐ παροῦσι πολλάκις ὀνειρώττοντες, οὕτω καὶ θεοῖς ἄνθρωποι ἀγαπῶντες δικαίως διά τε εὐεργεσίαν καὶ συγγένειαν, προθυμούμενοι πάντα τρόπον συνεῖναί τε καὶ ὁμιλεῖν.

Patroklos as the Other
Self of Achilles

The Meaning of Therapōn

6§1. The key word for this hour is *therapōn*, 'attendant; ritual substitute'. And the key passage comes from a climactic moment in the *Iliad* when Achilles, while praying that Zeus should preserve Patroklos from harm, uses the word *therapōn* in referring to his nearest and dearest friend:

HOUR 6 TEXT A

|$_{233}$ "King Zeus," he [= Achilles] cried out, "lord of Dodona, god of the Pelasgoi, who dwells afar, |$_{234}$ you who hold stormy Dodona in your sway, where the Selloi, |$_{235}$ your seers, dwell around you with their feet unwashed and their beds made upon the ground—|$_{236}$ just as you heard what I was saying when I prayed to you before, |$_{237}$ and did me honor by sending disaster on the Achaean people, |$_{238}$ so also now grant me the fulfillment of yet a further prayer, and it is this: |$_{239}$ I shall stay here at my assembly [*agōn*] of ships, |$_{240}$ but I shall send my comrade [*hetairos*] into battle at the head of many Myrmidons, |$_{241}$ sending him to fight. Send forth, O all-seeing Zeus, a radiance [*kudos*] to go before him; |$_{242}$ make bold the heart inside his chest so that Hector |$_{243}$ may find out whether he [Patroklos] knows how to fight alone, |$_{244}$ [Patroklos,] my *attendant* [*therapōn*], or whether his hands can only then be so invincible |$_{245}$ with their fury when I myself enter the war struggle of Arēs. |$_{246}$ Afterwards when he [= Patroklos] has chased away from the ships the attack and the cry of battle, |$_{247}$ grant that he may return unharmed to the swift ships, |$_{248}$ with his armor and his comrades [*hetairoi*], fighters in close combat." |$_{249}$ Thus did he [Achilles] pray, and Zeus the Planner heard his prayer. |$_{250}$ Part of it he did indeed grant

him—but the other part he refused. |₂₅₁ He granted that Patroklos should thrust back war and battle from the ships, |₂₅₂ yes, he granted that. But he refused to let him come safely [*ex-apo-ne-e-sthai*] out of the fight.

Iliad XVI 233–252*

Patroklos as Therapōn

6§2. As we read here at verse 244 of *Iliad* XVI, Achilles refers to Patroklos as his own personal *therapōn*. I will argue that we see in this context the oldest recoverable meaning of the word *therapōn*, and that the future events of the narrative will prove this meaning to be true.

6§3. As the master Narrator affirms in this context, the wording of Achilles is mistaken when he expresses his own fond hopes for Patroklos. The future events of the epic will show that Patroklos cannot fight alone, cannot defeat Hector alone, and can succeed only if he fights together with Achilles. Once Patroklos fights alone, he will die. And it is in this telling context, at *Iliad* XVI 244, that the wording of Achilles refers to Patroklos as his personal *therapōn*. So what does it mean, for Patroklos to be the personal *therapōn* of Achilles? As we will now see, it means that *Patroklos is doomed to die as the other self of Achilles*.

6§4. As we notice in other contexts as well, Patroklos is the personal *therapōn* of Achilles (for example, at *Iliad* XVI 165, 653; XVII 164, 388; XVIII 152). And, in each one of these contexts, *therapōn* is conventionally translated as 'attendant'. So what does it mean in particular that the hero Patroklos serves as the 'attendant' of the hero Achilles? As we have seen already from a variety of additional contexts in which the relationship of these two heroes is described, Patroklos is the nearest and dearest comrade of Achilles. Also, Patroklos is subservient to Achilles and to no one else. For example, Achilles orders Patroklos to mix and to pour wine (IX 202–204), and Patroklos complies (IX 205 ἐπεπείθετο);

---

* |₂₃₃ Ζεῦ ἄνα Δωδωναῖε Πελασγικὲ τηλόθι ναίων |₂₃₄ Δωδώνης μεδέων δυσχειμέρου, ἀμφὶ δὲ Σελλοὶ |₂₃₅ σοὶ ναίουσ' ὑποφῆται ἀνιπτόποδες χαμαιεῦναι, |₂₃₆ ἠμὲν δή ποτ' ἐμὸν ἔπος ἔκλυες εὐξαμένοιο, |₂₃₇ τίμησας μὲν ἐμέ, μέγα δ' ἴψαο λαὸν Ἀχαιῶν, |₂₃₈ ἠδ' ἔτι καὶ νῦν μοι τόδ' ἐπικρήηνον ἐέλδωρ· |₂₃₉ αὐτὸς μὲν γὰρ ἐγὼ μενέω νηῶν ἐν ἀγῶνι, |₂₄₀ ἀλλ' ἕταρον πέμπω πολέσιν μετὰ Μυρμιδόνεσσι |₂₄₁ μάρνασθαι· τῷ κῦδος ἅμα πρόες εὐρύοπα Ζεῦ, |₂₄₂ θάρσυνον δέ οἱ ἦτορ ἐνὶ φρεσίν, ὄφρα καὶ Ἕκτωρ |₂₄₃ εἴσεται ἤ ῥα καὶ οἶος ἐπίστηται πολεμίζειν |₂₄₄ ἡμέτερος θεράπων, ἦ οἱ τότε χεῖρες ἄαπτοι |₂₄₅ μαίνονθ', ὁππότ' ἐγώ περ ἴω μετὰ μῶλον Ἄρηος. |₂₄₆ αὐτὰρ ἐπεί κ' ἀπὸ ναῦφι μάχην ἐνοπήν τε δίηται, |₂₄₇ ἀσκηθής μοι ἔπειτα θοὰς ἐπὶ νῆας ἵκοιτο |₂₄₈ τεύχεσί τε ξὺν πᾶσι καὶ ἀγχεμάχοις ἑτάροισιν. |₂₄₉ Ὣς ἔφατ' εὐχόμενος, τοῦ δ' ἔκλυε μητίετα Ζεύς. |₂₅₀ τῷ δ' ἕτερον μὲν ἔδωκε πατήρ, ἕτερον δ' ἀνένευσε· |₂₅₁ νηῶν μέν οἱ ἀπώσασθαι πόλεμόν τε μάχην τε |₂₅₂ δῶκε, σόον δ' ἀνένευσε μάχης ἐξαπονέεσθαι.

also, Patroklos serves the hero Achilles by preparing a meal for the hero and his guests, performing most of the tasks required for the preparation, especially the task of cooking the meat that will be served (IX 206–215). Helping Patroklos perform these tasks is another comrade of Achilles, named Automedon (IX 209). This Automedon, as we will see, is an understudy of Patroklos: at a later point in the narrative, after Patroklos is already dead, Automedon will be described as a *therapōn* of Achilles (XXIV 573).

6§5. More needs to be said about the occasion when Patroklos helps prepare a meal for Achilles and his guests. As the host on this occasion, Achilles assumes a primary role by actually slicing the meat before it is cooked (*Iliad* IX 209) and then distributing for his guests the sliced portions after they are cooked (IX 217). Patroklos is left with the secondary role of distributing portions of bread that he places into baskets (IX 216–217). After Patroklos is dead, Automedon takes his place in the secondary role of distributing bread in baskets on another occasion when Achilles acts as host (XXIV 625–626), while Achilles retains his primary role of distributing the meat (XXIV 626). As we will see later, this role of Automedon is relevant to his service as a *therapōn* of Achilles (XXIV 573).

6§6. From what we have seen so far, then, Patroklos as *therapōn* of Achilles is the nearest and dearest comrade of that primary hero in the *Iliad*. As the personal *therapōn* of Achilles, Patroklos is a secondary hero, and he attends Achilles just as other *therapontes* who are secondary heroes will attend Achilles after Patroklos dies. A simpler way of saying it, as we will soon see, is that *Patroklos cares for Achilles*. For the moment, though, I continue to use the conventional translation for *therapōn* as 'attendant'. But there is more to it, much more.

6§7. The main question comes down to this: how does the conventional definition of *therapōn* as 'attendant' square with that other definition that I gave at the start, 'ritual substitute'? (Both these definitions of *therapōn* are given in the Core Vocabulary.) My answer is that both meanings apply. Patroklos is the 'attendant' of Achilles on the surface, but he is his 'ritual substitute' in the deeper meaning of the master Narrative.

Anatolian Origins of the Word Therapōn

6§8. I now turn to the prehistory of the word *therapōn*, seeking to show that it had once meant 'ritual substitute' and that it had been borrowed into the Greek language from Anatolian languages of Indo-European origin. The borrowing must have happened sometime in the later part of the second millennium BCE, when the two major Indo-European languages of Anatolia were Hittite and Luvian. The major political power in Anatolia at that time was the Hittite Empire. Accordingly, I will use the term "Hittite" as a shorthand way of referring to the relevant linguistic evidence.

6§9. In Hittite ritual texts dating from roughly 1350 to 1250 BCE, we find these two relevant words: *tarpanalli-* (or *tarpalli-*) and *tarpasšša-*.* As Nadia van Brock has shown, these words were used as synonyms, and both meant 'ritual substitute'.†

6§10. Such a meaning, 'ritual substitute', must be understood in the context of an Anatolian ritual of purification that expels pollution from the person to be purified and transfers it into a person or an animal or an object that serves as a ritual substitute; the act of transferring pollution into the victim serving as ritual substitute may be accomplished either by destroying or by banishing the victim, who or which is identified as another self, *un autre soi-même*.‡ According to the logic of this Hittite ritual of substitution, the identification of the self with the victim serving as the other self can take on a wide variety of forms: the victims range from humans to animals to figurines to ceramic vessels.§

6§11. The mentality of identifying with one's victim operates on homological principles. In the case of animal victims designated by the word *tarpalli-*, for example, one ritual text specifies that bulls are to be killed as ritual substitutes for men, while cows are to be killed as substitutes for women.** There are other examples of homologies based primarily on gender. In another ritual text involving the word *tarpalli-*, for instance, bulls and rams and other male animals are killed as ritual substitutes for the king, while corresponding female animals are killed for the queen.†† And there are cases of tighter homologies. In yet another ritual text involving the word *tarpalli-*, for example, it is specified that the

---

* For more on the dating of these Hittite ritual texts, see Kümmel 1967:188. For a survey of attestations, see Tischler 1993:207–212.

† Van Brock 1959:117, with special reference to the Hittite ritual text *Keilschrifttexte aus Boghazköi* IV 6 (*tarpasšša-* at recto line 11, *tarpalli-* at recto line 28; see also verso line 14); Nagy 2008a:55.

‡ Van Brock 1959:119; Nagy 2008a:55. In the myth of Ullikummi, this megalithic monster is described as a *tarpanalli-* of the weather god Teshub, who ultimately destroys him: *Keilschrifturkunden aus Boghazköi* XXXIII 96 + I 8 (also XXXIII 95 + IV 14; also XXXIII 106 + III 35). In such contexts, the word is conventionally translated as 'rival': see Tischler 1993:209–210.

§ Kümmel 1967:131, 150.

** Van Brock 1959:121, with reference to *Keilschrifttexte aus Boghazköi* IX 129 I lines 5–9. For the principle of analogical substitution in general, see Kümmel 1967:22.

†† Van Brock 1959:120–121, with reference to *Keilschrifturkunden aus Boghazköi* VII 10.

victims who are designated as ritual substitutes for the king include men as well as bulls and rams.* In other cases, too, humans are being designated as ritual substitutes.†

6§12. The range of victims that are designated as ritual substitutes, extending all the way to humans, indicates that the victim of the ritual substitution, as the other self, can be identified as closely as possible with the human self—even if the ritual substitute and the human self may not be all that close to each other when they are viewed from outside the world of ritual.‡ What makes the substitute in ritual seem so intimately close to you is that he or she or it must die for you. Here I find it relevant to quote, from a Hittite text about royal ritual substitution, a most explicit formulation expressed in dialogic format:

HOUR 6 TEXT B, FROM A HITTITE TABLET

And for you [= the divinity], here are these ritual substitutes [*tarpalliuš*] | ... And may they die, but I will not die.

Keilschrifturkunden aus Boghazköi XXIV 5 I lines 15–16§

6§13. I draw special attention to these and other cases of ritual substitution in which the person to be purified is a king. In such cases, as van Brock argues, the ritual of substitution is "périodique," ideally annual; and it is a common idea, as we can see from a survey of myths and rituals around the world, that the king is an incarnation of the body politic, of society itself, which needs to be renewed periodically by being purified of pollution.**

6§14. One well-known model of periodic renewal is the festival of the Babylonian New Year, centering on the sacrificial killing of a goat, and it is nowadays

---

* Van Brock 1959:123–125, with reference to *Keilschrifturkunden aus Boghazköi* XXIV 5 + IX 13.

† Van Brock 1959:123; see also especially Kümmel 1967:20 and 121–122, with reference to the mention of a female *tarpašša-* in *Keilschrifttexte aus Boghazköi* IV 6 I line 11.

‡ For a variety of further examples taken from Hittite ritual texts, see Lowenstam 1981:127–130.

§ *nu-wa-at-ta ku-u-uš [tar-pa]-al-li-uš [|] . . . nu-wa ku-u-uš ak-kán-du am-mu-uk-ma-w[a le]-e ak-mi.* Commentary by van Brock 1959:123; also Kümmel 1967:25. At lines 10–16 of this same ritual text, *Keilschrifturkunden aus Boghazköi* XXIV 5 I, we see that a bull is to be driven to a place where it is killed and its body is burned, while the moon god is invoked to witness with his own divine eyes the smoke that rises up to the heavens from the burning body; see also Kümmel 1967:37.

** Van Brock 1959:125. Kümmel 1967:194–195 cautions against anachronistic formulations, but there is no doubt that the ritual purification of the Hittite king extends to a homologous purification of his royal subjects. In the ritual text *Keilschrifttexte aus Boghazköi* XV 1 I lines 19–20 and 39, for example, it is made clear that the removal of pollution extends from the king to the whole army and to the whole land of Ḫatti; commentary by Kümmel 1967:120.

generally agreed that the Hittite rituals of substitution derive at least in part from the Babylonian rituals that marked this festival.* A related practice, attested in texts stemming from the neo-Assyrian empire of the first millennium BCE, is the periodic appointing and subsequent killing of substitute kings. Especially relevant are the correspondences of the kings Asarhaddon (680–669 BCE) and Assurbanipal (668–627 BCE).† Still another related practice is the ritual of the scapegoat described in the Hebrew Bible, *Leviticus* 16:8, whereby a designated goat (which is the *tragos pempomenos* of the Greek Septuagint and the *caper emissarius* of the Latin Vulgate) is not killed but expelled into the wasteland—hence the word *scapegoat*. This periodic expulsion, as is well known, figures as a climactic moment in the rituals and sacred narratives of the Jewish Day of Atonement.

6§15. Since Hittite is an Indo-European language, no matter how deeply it is influenced by Near Eastern civilizations, we may also compare the relevant evidence of Hittite ritual formulations that are cognate with wording found in other Indo-European languages. A case in point is the Latin adjective *sōns / sontis*, meaning 'guilty', which is cognate with

(1) the Greek participle *ōn / ontos* (ὤν / ὄντος) of the verb meaning 'to be', as in *esti* (ἐστι), 'is';

and with

(2) the corresponding Hittite participle *ašān* that likewise means 'to be', as in *ešzi*, 'is'.

6§16. In the Plague Prayers of King Muršilis II, dating from the second half of the fourteenth century BCE, it is prescribed that the king is to utter a "confessional" formula, *ašān-at, iyanun-at*, 'it is true, I did it' (*Keilschrifturkunden aus Boghazköi* XIV 8, in the second prayer); this formula is cognate with the formula implicit in Latin *sōns*, where the meaning 'guilty' is to be understood in

---

* Kümmel 1967:189, 193–194, 196–197.

† Kümmel 1967:169–187. He emphasizes how little textual evidence has been preserved, considering the pervasiveness of the custom of ritual substitution in Near Eastern civilizations (p. 191). The period of the substitute king's tenure can be measured in units of time, such as one hundred days (pp. 176–177, 179). See also Parpola 1983, Excursus pp. xxii–xxxii.

the legal sense of 'declared guilty' or, to say it even more legalistically, 'found guilty'.* So also in the "confessional" formula of the Hittite king, the guilty party must declare that he really 'is' the guilty one, that he really is 'it'.† Similarly in the children's game of tag, the formula 'you're it' indicates by way of the verb 'to be' the identity of who will be 'it'.

6§17. A moment ago, I said that the ritual substitute can seem intimately close to you because he or she or it must die for you, and I gave the example of the formula used by the Hittite king for saying that the *tarpalli-* or ritual substitute will die for him so that he may live. But there are two sides to this formula. The intimate closeness is matched by an alienating distance, marked by pollution, separating the king from his substitute. I draw attention here to a most telling example. In one particular ritual text (*Keilschrifturkunden aus Boghazköi* XXIV 5 + IX 13 I lines 19–26), where the word *tarpalli-*, 'ritual substitute', applies to a prisoner, this ritual substitute is anointed with royal oil, crowned with a diadem, and dressed in the regalia of the king; then this *tarpalli-* is expelled from the king's territory and sent back home to his own territory, so that he takes home with him the pollution that had been intimately associated with the king.‡ I stress here the intimacy of the actual transfer of pollution, even if the pollution itself is alienating. In another ritual text (*Keilschrifttexte aus Boghazköi* XVI 1 I line 10), it is specified that the king is to take off the royal clothing that he wears so that the prisoner who serves as his ritual substitute may now put on this same clothing.§

6§18. In the two examples we have just seen, the ritual substitute is expelled and does not die for the king, but the basic fact remains: the king and the body politic get rid of the pollution by getting rid of the ritual substitute. Let me restate the fact by using the English word *eliminate,* derived from a most telling Latin word, *ē-līmin-āre,* 'take outside the boundary [*līmen*]'. So the king and the body politic *eliminate* the pollution by *eliminating* the ritual substitute. A remarkable parallel is the case of the goat that gets expelled into the wasteland on the Jewish Day of Atonement, instead of getting killed like the sacrificial goat of the Babylonian New Year.

6§19. Rituals of elimination, that is, of expelling a polluted person or animal or thing, are in fact homologous with rituals of killing. For example, when an

* Watkins 1995:167–168.
† Watkins 1967.
‡ Text and commentary by van Brock 1959:123; see also Kümmel 1967:27–32.
§ Commentary by Kümmel 1967:118.

animal is designated as a ritual substitute for the king in Hittite texts, we may expect two alternative outcomes: in some rituals, the animal victim is killed and its body is burned,* but in other rituals the victim is instead expelled.† And I think that there existed a parallel set of two alternative outcomes when a human was designated as a ritual substitute. That is, I think we may expect that human substitutes could be not only expelled but also killed in rituals dating from the Hittite era, just as substitute kings could be killed in rituals dating from a later era represented by neo-Assyrian texts. Granted, the testimony of the existing Hittite ritual texts is opaque concerning the actual killing of humans in contexts of ritual substitution, but the fact remains that there are clear examples of killings of humans in other Hittite ritual contexts.‡

6§20. Throughout this analysis I have refrained from using the term "human sacrifice," since some readers will view the word "sacrifice" too narrowly by thinking only of the killing and subsequent dismembering and cooking and eating of animal victims. If we allowed, however, for a broadening of this word "sacrifice" to include the killing and subsequent burning of animal victims, which as we have seen is an option in the case of animal victims of ritual substitution, then the term "human sacrifice" could still apply in the case of human victims of ritual substitution.

6§21. That said, I bring to a close my analysis of the relevant Hittite evidence by offering this summary, following the earlier formulation by van Brock: *the mentality of substitution rituals requires someone who is notionally close to the king to die or be in some other way eliminated so as to preserve the king.*§

Early Greek Uses of the Words Therapōn, Theraps, Therapeuein

6§22. I now turn to the corresponding evidence in Greek. The Hittite words *tarpanalli- / tarpalli-* and *tarpasšša-*, as van Brock has argued, were borrowed by the Greek language sometime in the second millennium BCE, and the corresponding Greek words were *therapōn* (θεράπων) and *theraps* (θέραψ), both of which can be translated as 'attendant'.** Like the two Hittite words *tarpanalli- /*

---

* *Keilschrifturkunden aus Boghazköi* VII 10 II; see Kümmel 1967:131.

† *Keilschrifttexte aus Boghazköi* XV 1 I; see Kümmel 1967:115.

‡ Kümmel 1967:150–168; at p. 147 he leaves the door ajar for the possibility that a human *tarpanalli-* could in fact be ritually killed.

§ Van Brock 1959:125–126.

** Van Brock 1959:125–126.

tarpalli- and *tarpassša-*, the two Greek words *therapōn* and *theraps* were once synonyms, as is evident from the fact that the verb *therapeuein* is attested as a functional derivative of the noun *therapōn* in Homeric diction. We can see this functional derivation at work when we look at the context of *Odyssey* xiii 265, where this verb *therapeuein* means 'be a *therapōn*', even though it is formally derived not from the noun *therapōn* but from the noun *theraps*, which is absent from Homeric diction.* We find attestations of *theraps* only rarely, as in Ion of Chios F 27 ed. West; Euripides *Ion* 94, *Suppliants* 762. In the fragment from Ion of Chios, the plural form *therapes* refers to attendants who serve wine at a symposium; in the *Ion* of Euripides, the same plural form refers to the priests of Apollo at Delphi who serve as attendants of the god as they approach the streams of the spring Kastalia; and, in the *Suppliants* of Euripides, *therapes* again refers to attendants—in this case, the hero Adrastos is asking the Messenger whether *therapes* have removed the corpses of the fallen dead.

6§23. So how do we explain the meaning of the Hittite words *tarpanalli-* and *tarpassša-* as 'ritual substitute' when we compare the meaning of the borrowed Greek words *therapōn* (θεράπων) and *theraps* (θέραψ) as 'attendant'? Here I return to my formulation summarizing the role of Patroklos as the personal attendant of Achilles:

> Patroklos as *therapōn* of Achilles is the nearest and dearest comrade of that primary hero in the *Iliad*. As the personal *therapōn* of Achilles, Patroklos is a secondary hero, and he attends Achilles just as other *therapontes* who are secondary heroes will attend Achilles after Patroklos dies.

The Therapōn *as Charioteer*

6§24. Building on this formulation, I will now explore another aspect of the service of Patroklos as the personal *therapōn* of Achilles in the *Iliad*: Patroklos serves as the personal charioteer, or *hēniokhos*, of Achilles (ἡνίοχος XXIII 280). The role of Patroklos as the charioteer of Achilles is specially highlighted in *Il-*

---

* Van Brock 1961:118n1, 120n3. We would have expected the denominative verb of *therapōn* to be **therapoheuein*, just as the denominative verb of, say, *hēgemōn*, is *hēgemoneuein*. So the fact that *therapeuein* in the sense of 'be a *therapōn*' functions as the denominative verb of *therapōn* proves that this noun *therapōn* was once a synonym of *theraps*. Tischler 1993:210 explains *theraps* as a back-formation from *therapeuein*, but I find such an explanation counterintuitive.

iad XVII (475–478), where Automedon describes Patroklos as the best of all charioteers by virtue of driving the chariot of Achilles. Automedon, as we have already noted, is described as the *therapōn* of Achilles (XXIV 573; also XVI 865). And, as we will now see, Automedon is also a charioteer, just as Patroklos is a charioteer.

6§25. The wording used by Automedon in *Iliad* XVII (475–478) in describing Patroklos as the best of all charioteers is most relevant to his own role as a charioteer. At the moment of this description in *Iliad* XVII, Patroklos is of course already dead. He died in *Iliad* XVI, getting killed in place of Achilles. And, back then in *Iliad* XVI, it was Automedon who had served as the charioteer of Patroklos. To appreciate this role of Automedon as charioteer of Patroklos, I now review what happened in *Iliad* XVI when Patroklos died fighting Hector.

6§26. The setting for the death of Patroklos in *Iliad* XVI is a classic chariot fight. The fight starts when Patroklos leaps out of his chariot:

HOUR 6 TEXT C

Then Patroklos, from one side, leapt from his chariot, hitting the ground.

Iliad XVI 733*

In a moment, Hector will leap from his own chariot. Before that happens, however, Patroklos picks up a rock and throws it at Kebriones, the charioteer of Hector, hitting Kebriones on the forehead and smashing his skull (*Iliad* XVI 734–754). Then, just as Patroklos had leapt out of his chariot, Hector too leaps out of his own chariot:

HOUR 6 TEXT D

Then Hector, from the other side, leapt from his chariot, hitting the ground.

Iliad XVI 755†

Patroklos and Hector proceed to fight one-on-one in mortal combat on the ground—a combat that is ultimately won by Hector (XVI 756–863).

---

* Πάτροκλος δ' ἑτέρωθεν ἀφ' ἵππων ἆλτο χαμᾶζε.
† Ἕκτωρ δ' αὖθ' ἑτέρωθεν ἀφ' ἵππων ἆλτο χαμᾶζε.

6§27. In this chariot fight that happened back in *Iliad* XVI, I highlight the fact that it is Automedon who serves as chariot driver for Patroklos. And, at this moment, it is Patroklos and not Achilles who is the chariot fighter, since it is Automedon and not Patroklos who is the chariot driver. In preparation for this chariot fight between Patroklos and Hector, it is Automedon, serving as chariot driver for Patroklos, who yokes the horses of Achilles to the chariot (XVI 145–154).

6§28. Like Patroklos, as we have already noted, Automedon is described in the *Iliad* as a *therapōn* of Achilles (XVI 865, XXIV 573). Also, in another Iliadic passage, Automedon and a comrade named Alkimos are described as *therapontes* of Achilles (XXIV 573). That passage goes on to say that Achilles honors these two comrades, Automedon and Alkimos, more than anyone else—now that Patroklos is dead (XXIV 575). And, in still further Iliadic passages, we see that one of the functions of these two honored *therapontes* of Achilles is the unyoking of horses or mules (at XXIV 576) as well as the yoking of horses (at XIX 392–393, where Automedon and Alkimos are yoking Achilles' horses for him). So also, as we have just seen, Automedon yokes the horses of Achilles for Patroklos (at XVI 145–154).

6§29. After the death of Patroklos, when Achilles finally rejoins the Achaeans in battle, his chariot is now driven by Automedon (XIX 395–399). As we have seen, however, Automedon had at an earlier point served as chariot driver for the hero Patroklos when that hero took the place of Achilles in war (XVI 145–154). And here I note a most telling detail about that earlier point in the narrative of the *Iliad*: after Patroklos is killed by Hector, the chariot driver Automedon says that he now wants to become a chariot fighter, but he cannot fight the Trojans while he is still driving the chariot (XVII 463–465). So he asks another comrade, Alkimedon, to take his place as a chariot driver so that he, Automedon, may now become a chariot fighter:

HOUR 6 TEXT E

But you [= Alkimedon], take this whip and these splendid reins, | take them, while I [= Automedon] step off [*apobainein*] from the chariot, so that I may fight.

Iliad XVII 479–480*

And, sure enough, Alkimedon quickly leaps into the chariot, landing on the

---

* ἀλλὰ σὺ μὲν μάστιγα καὶ ἡνία σιγαλόεντα | δέξαι, ἐγὼ δ' ἵππων ἀποβήσομαι, ὄφρα μάχωμαι.

chariot platform (XVII 481 ἐπορούσας) and taking hold of the whip and the reins (XVII 482), while Automedon leaps out of the chariot, that is, he leaps off the chariot platform (XVII 483 ἀπόρουσε) and lands on the ground, where he can then start fighting.* So we see here a functioning dyadic relationship between Automedon as a chariot fighter and Alkimedon as a chariot driver, both of whom are secondary substitutes for the primary substitute Patroklos, the premier chariot driver who became a chariot fighter for Achilles and who thus died for him as his *therapōn*, as his personal ritual substitute.†

6§30. I conclude, then, that the relationship of the chariot fighter to the chariot driver who substitutes for him is parallel to the relationship of a hero like Achilles to a hero like Patroklos, who is his *therapōn*. So now we see, on the basis of evidence from the narrative traditions of Homeric poetry, that Patroklos as the *therapōn* of Achilles does in fact serve as his substitute. In the end, the chariot driver in this case dies in place of the chariot fighter: that is, the chariot driver takes the hit, as it were, for the chariot fighter. But now that we see how Patroklos is a substitute of Achilles, the question remains: how is he not only a substitute but a ritual substitute? We must now examine more closely how the actual concept of a *ritual substitute,* as attested in Anatolian ritual texts, was translated into the ancient Greek song culture.

The Therapōn *as a Ritual Substitute*

6§31. For analyzing the concept of *ritual substitute* as attested in the Greek evidence, an ideal starting point is a climactic passage I already quoted as Text B in Hour 5. This passage, taken from *Iliad* XVI, marks the moment when the warrior hero Patroklos is killed in battle: at this moment, the hero is visualized as *atalantos Arēi*, 'equal [*atalantos*] to Arēs' (verse 784). Here in Hour 6 we will see how and why this description marks Patroklos as a *ritual substitute* for Achilles as the main hero of the *Iliad*.

6§32. To begin, I find it most relevant to consider some basic facts about

---

*The wording that expresses here the complementarity of the chariot fighter and the chariot driver can be found elsewhere as well in the *Iliad*, as at V 218–238. Here we see Aeneas urging Pandaros to leap into the chariot of Aeneas (V 221) so that Pandaros may act as the chariot driver while Aeneas acts as the chariot fighter by leaping out of his chariot and fighting on the ground (226–227). Pandaros refuses, saying that he prefers to fight on the ground (V 238) and telling Aeneas to continue driving his own horses, since they would not get used to a new charioteer (V 230–237). As the narrative proceeds, it becomes clear that the choice made by Pandaros proves to be fatal.

† For more on the multiformity of the figures Alkimedon (/Alkimos) and Automedon as *therapontes*, see Sinos 1980:38n6.

the use of the word *therapōn* in the plural. The plural form is *therapontes*. In the *Iliad*, warriors are conventionally called the *therapontes* of Arēs as the god of war (II 110, VI 67, XV 733, XIX 78).* The first example we saw was in Hour 1 Text C (*Iliad* XIX 78). With this fact in mind, I will now make an argument that I epitomize in the following formulation:

> When a warrior is killed in war, he becomes a *therapōn* or 'ritual substitute' who dies for Arēs by becoming identical to the war god at the moment of death; then, after death, the warrior is eligible to become a cult hero who serves as a sacralized 'attendant' of the war god.†

6§33. We may expect that Achilles, as an epic warrior, is a *therapōn* or 'ritual substitute' of Arēs by virtue of becoming identical to the war god at the moment of death. But there is a complication: in the *Iliad,* such a relationship between Achilles and Arēs is expressed only by way of an intermediary, who is Patroklos. But there is a further complication: Patroklos as an epic warrior is described not as the *therapōn* of Arēs but rather as the *therapōn* of Achilles, and, as such, Patroklos is not only that hero's 'attendant' but also his 'ritual substitute', since he actually dies for Achilles. In view of these two complications, I will argue that Achilles in the *Iliad* dies only indirectly as the *therapōn* of Arēs through the intermediacy of Patroklos, who dies in this epic as the *therapōn* of Achilles.

6§34. Here I come back to *Iliad* XVI 233–248, which was Text A in this hour: there we saw that Patroklos qualifies as *therapōn* of Achilles only so long as he stays within his limits as the recessive equivalent of the dominant hero. Now I will take this formulation one step further: once Patroklos is on his own, he becomes a *therapōn* of Arēs and dies in place of Achilles.‡

6§35. We may expect that Achilles, as an epic warrior, qualifies as *īsos Arēi,* 'equal [*īsos*] to Arēs', just like Patroklos. This description suits Achilles in the *Iliad*—but it applies to him only vicariously by way of Patroklos, who takes upon himself the role of a ritual substitute for Achilles. As we saw in Text B of Hour 5, *Iliad* XVI 784, Patroklos is called *atalantos Arēi,* 'equal to Arēs', at the moment

---

* *BA* 295 = 17§5.

† A longer version of this formulation is presented in *BA* 293–295 = 17§§5–6. I have already noted that the charioteer Alkimos is described as a *therapōn* of Achilles (*Iliad* XXIV 573); now I add that Alkimos is also described as an *ozos Arēos,* 'attendant of Arēs' (XXIV 474 ὄζος Ἄρηος); see *BA* 295 = 17§5n8 on *ozos* as a synonym of *therapōn.*

‡ Sinos 1980:46–54; *BA* 292–293 = 17§4.

when he is killed in war. And, as we will now see, Patroklos is actually called *īsos Arēi*, 'equal to Ares', at the moment when the story of his fatal impersonation of Achilles begins:

HOUR 6 TEXT F

|₅₉₉ He [Nestor] was seen and noted by swift-footed radiant Achilles, |₆₀₀ who was standing on the spacious stern of his ship, |₆₀₁ watching the sheer pain [*ponos*] and tearful struggle of the fight. |₆₀₂ Then, all of a sudden, he called to his comrade [*hetairos*] Patroklos, |₆₀₃ calling from the ship, and he [Patroklos] from inside the tent heard him [Achilles], |₆₀₄ and he [Patroklos] came out, *equal* [*īsos*] *to Ares, and here, I see it, was the beginning of his doom.* |₆₀₅ He [Patroklos], mighty son of Menoitios, was the first to speak, and he said [to Achilles]: |₆₀₆ "Why, Achilles, do you call me? what need do you have for me?"

Iliad XI 599–606*

Here Homeric poetry declares explicitly that the application of the epithet 'equal [*īsos*] to Ares' will doom Patroklos to death.†

6§36. Besides being equated with Ares, however, we saw that Patroklos is also being equated with Apollo. It happens in both Texts A and B of Hour 5, when Patroklos is called *daimoni īsos,* 'equal to a *daimōn*' (XVI 705 and 786). As we saw from the contexts of those passages, the *daimōn*, or 'superhuman force', there is the god Apollo himself.‡ So in those contexts, Patroklos is 'equal' to Apollo, though his identification with that god is not fully spelled out, since the word *daimōn* partly masks the identity of the god.

6§37. As one who is equal to Apollo at the moment of his death, Patroklos participates in a specialized god-hero relationship. By being equal to Ares at the moment of his death, by contrast, Patroklos participates in a generic god-hero relationship that is typical of heroes who are warriors.§ In identifying with both Ares and Apollo, Patroklos is experiencing something that will later be experi-

---

* |₅₉₉ τὸν δὲ ἰδὼν ἐνόησε ποδάρκης δῖος Ἀχιλλεύς· |₆₀₀ ἑστήκει γὰρ ἐπὶ πρυμνῇ μεγακήτεϊ νηΐ |₆₀₁ εἰσορόων πόνον αἰπὺν ἰῶκά τε δακρυόεσσαν. |₆₀₂ αἶψα δ' ἑταῖρον ἐὸν Πατροκλῆα προσέειπε |₆₀₃ φθεγξάμενος παρὰ νηός· ὁ δὲ κλισίηθεν ἀκούσας |₆₀₄ ἔκμολεν ἶσος Ἄρηϊ, κακοῦ δ' ἄρα οἱ πέλεν ἀρχή. |₆₀₅ τὸν πρότερος προσέειπε Μενοιτίου ἄλκιμος υἱός· |₆₀₆ τίπτέ με κικλήσκεις Ἀχιλεῦ; τί δέ σε χρεὼ ἐμεῖο.

† *BA* 32–34 = 2§8; 293–295 = 17§5.
‡ *BA* 293 = 17§5.
§ *BA* 307 = 18§9.

enced by Achilles himself, who will also be identifying with both Arēs and Apollo at the moment of his own heroic death, though his death scene is not directly pictured in the *Iliad*. Rather, the death scene of Achilles is pictured directly in the epic Cycle. In Hour 5 Text D, I already quoted a plot summary of this death scene, and I now quote it here again:

HOUR 6 TEXT G = HOUR 5 TEXT D

|₇ Achilles, while routing the Trojans and |₈ rushing into the citadel, is killed by Paris and Apollo. |₉ When a heated battle starts over the corpse, |₁₀ Ajax picks it up and carries it off to the ships while |₁₁ Odysseus fights off the Trojans.

Plot summary by Proclus of the *Aithiopis* by Arctinus of Miletus p. 106 lines 7–11

6§38. This plot summary does not indicate whether Arēs is understood to be the generalized ritual antagonist of Achilles. All it indicates is that Apollo is the specialized ritual antagonist of that hero. But there is no reason for us to expect an explicit role of Arēs in the death scene of Achilles. After all, there is no explicit role of this war god in the death scene of Patroklos as narrated in the *Iliad*.

6§39. A generic warrior, as we have noted, is called a *therapōn* of Arēs. Generically, then, heroes as warriors die for Arēs. More specifically, however, a special hero will die for his special divine antagonist.

6§40. Generically, Achilles would qualify as a *therapōn* of Arēs; specifically, however, he is a *therapōn* of Apollo, because it is Apollo who will kill him by way of Paris, just as Apollo kills Patroklos by way of Hector. And, while the *therapōn* of Apollo must be Achilles, the *therapōn* of Achilles must be, as we have seen, Patroklos.

6§41. Patroklos must die for Achilles, who must die for Apollo. The death of Patroklos is caused by Arēs generically but it is brought to fulfillment by Apollo personally.

6§42. I return here to the moment when Patroklos dies. At that moment, as we saw in Texts A and B of Hour 5, he is called *daimoni īsos*, 'equal to a *daimōn*' (XVI 705 and 786). In this context, it is clear that the *daimōn* is Apollo, as we can see from the related context of Text C, featuring the expression *pros daimona*, 'face-to-face with the *daimōn*' (XVII 98, also 104).*

---

* *BA* 63 = 4§6n1.

Arēs as Divine Antagonist of Patroklos and Achilles

6§43. So there is no doubt about it, the god Apollo is the direct and specific cause of the deaths of both Patroklos and Achilles. Nevertheless, it is essential to keep in mind that the god Arēs is the indirect and generic cause of these deaths. And we see a trace of this indirect and generic causality when we read that Patroklos is *atalantos Arēi*, 'equal to Ares', at the moment of his death in the *Iliad* (XVI 784). So also Achilles himself, in his climactic moments of rage, is described as *īsos Arēi*, 'equal to Arēs', in the *Iliad* (XX 46). Thus Achilles as well as Patroklos is programmed, as it were, to die a martial death that is caused at least generically by Arēs.

6§44. In this light, we need to consider more closely the identity of the god Arēs. Yes, he is the god of *war*, but he is also, more specifically, the god of *martial fury*.* In war, a warrior who is possessed by the god Arēs experiences this kind of martial fury, which is typically bestial. The Greek word for martial fury is *lussa*, meaning 'wolfish rage'.† Comparable is the Old Norse concept *berserkr* and the Old Irish concept *ríastrad*, 'warp spasm' or 'distortion'.‡ To experience such a martial rage or warp spasm or distortion is to be beside oneself, and to be beside oneself is to be possessed—possessed by Arēs.

6§45. In the *Iliad*, as we will now see, such a state of possession is expressed by way of the word *lussa*, 'wolfish rage'. From here on, I will transliterate this word in its latinized form *lyssa*, since some readers will be more familiar with the spelling *lykos* for the Greek word meaning 'wolf' (the more consistent spelling would be *lukos*).§ In the *Iliad*, a prime example of *lyssa* is the description of Hector, when he gets into a state of martial fury, as a 'rabid dog', a *lyssētēr kuōn* (κύνα λυσσητῆρα VIII 299).** When Hector experiences such a state, *lyssa* literally enters his body and pervades it completely (IX 239). After Hector kills Patroklos and puts on the armor of Achilles that Patroklos had been wearing, Zeus seals Hector into the armor and then Arēs himself literally enters him (δῦ

---

* EH §110.

† Lincoln 1975.

‡ For a comparison of the Old Norse and Old Irish concepts, see Sjoestedt 1940:86. See also Henry 1982. For the translation of Old Irish *ríastrad* as 'warp spasm', see Kinsella 1969. For a lively description of 'warp spasm', see Rees and Rees 1961:248–249.

§ Starting at line 815 of the drama *Herakles* by Euripides, the personification of madness, Lyssa, enters the dramatic space, now that the evil hero Lykos has been killed by Hēraklēs. Now Lyssa will possess Hēraklēs and bring about his madness. At line 865 Lyssa refers to her own wolfish rage, *lyssa* (see also lines 879, 888, 1024).

** At line 934 in the *Herakles* of Euripides, Hēraklēs is rabidly *foaming at the mouth* while he is possessed by the 'wolfish rage', *lyssa*, of Lyssa.

δέ μιν Ἄρης XVII 210), thus possessing him completely. So when Achilles finally kills Hector in *Iliad* XXII, he is in effect killing the embodiment of Ares the war god. Conversely, Achilles himself is possessed by *lyssa* in his most intense moments of martial rage in the *Iliad* (XXI 542). Hector in his own right is described as both *atalantos Arēi*, 'equal to Arēs' (VIII 215, XVII 72), and as *īsos Arēi*, 'equal to Arēs' (XI 295, XIII 802).

6§46. In the case of Achilles, these examples of martial fury are relevant to the second of the three characteristics of the hero that we considered in Hour 1, namely, that the hero is "extreme" both positively and, on special occasions, negatively. Achilles is extreme mostly in a positive sense, since he is 'best' in many categories and since he is even the 'best of the Achaeans' in the Homeric *Iliad*. Occasionally, however, he is extreme in a negative sense, as in his moments of martial fury.*

The Therapeutic Function of the Therapōn

6§47. I return here to the ritual background of the word *therapōn*. So far, we have seen that it was borrowed into the Greek language from Anatolian languages, sometime in the second millennium BCE. The corresponding word in those Anatolian languages meant 'ritual substitute'. Someone who is notionally close to the king, as we have also seen, may have to die in place of the king. But there is more to it than that. Such a death, I argue, has the effect of healing society by way of healing the king, who is viewed as the embodiment of society, of the body politic. (On the king as the embodiment of the body politic, I refer back to §13 in this hour.)

6§48. What I describe here for the first time as a *healing* is an act of purifying the king and his people from impurities, from pollution. If the king is polluted, then society is polluted. That is why the pollution of the king has to be transferred to a ritual substitute who will be eliminated in place of the king and will thus remove the royal pollution while also removing the pollution of society. This principle of purification has been described by van Brock as *the transfer of evil*, "le transfert du mal."† Evil must be passed on, to a sacrificial victim.

* *BA* 321 = 20§5.
† Van Brock 1959:129.

6§49. In Greek visual art, I must now add, the dead hero Patroklos can be represented as a sacrificial ram, who is shown with his throat slit open and with blood streaming from the gaping wound: such a picture is painted on an Attic vase executed by the "Triptolemos Painter," dated around 480 BCE.* Similarly in Hittite rituals of substitution, as we have seen, rams can be sacrificed in place of kings.

6§50. The meaning of the Greek word *therapōn* as *ritual substitute* and the function of such a *therapōn* as a *healer* help explain why the related Greek word *therapeuein* means not only 'be a *therapōn*', as we have seen at *Odyssey* xiii 265, but also 'heal, cure'; we still see such a meaning embedded in the English-language borrowings *therapy* and *therapeutic*. But before I cite some contexts in which the ancient Greek word *therapeuein* means 'heal, cure', I must return once again to that passage at *Odyssey* xiii 265 where *therapeuein* means 'be a *therapōn*', since I have yet to explain the context.

6§51. There are three passages in which the word *therapeuein* seems at first sight to have nothing to do with a meaning such as 'heal, cure'. I start with *Odyssey* xiii 265, the passage we are considering right now. Here the first-person narrator of a "Cretan tale" says that he was unwilling to 'be a *therapōn*', *therapeuein*, for the over-king of Crete, Idomeneus, preferring instead to be the leader of his own comrades. The next passage is at *Homeric Hymn to Apollo* 390, where the god Apollo selects a group of Cretans to serve as his attendants, *therapeuein*, at his shrine in Delphi. Finally, the third passage is at Hesiod *Works and Days* 135, where the prototypical humans who represent the second generation of humankind are said to be unwilling to serve as attendants, *therapeuein*, to the gods; and, as we read in the next verse, these sacrilegious early humans are likewise unwilling to perform sacrifices to the gods at their altars (*Works and Days* 136).†

6§52. As we consider these three passages showing early attestations of the word *therapeuein*, the first one of the three is not decisive in establishing the overall meaning of this word, since the story of the upstart Cretan who refused to serve as *therapōn* to the over-king of Crete has no attested parallels. Still, it is safe to say that the social position of the *therapōn* in this story cannot be too different from the social position of Patroklos himself, who is subservient to

---

* This painting, along with another related painting, is analyzed by Tarenzi 2005.

† Commentary in *BA* 151–152 = 9§§2–3.

Achilles by virtue of serving as that hero's *therapōn*.* But the second and the third attestations are in fact decisive: in these two cases, *therapeuein* refers to the service that needs to be rendered to gods by humans who are designated as the gods' attendants. As we are about to see, the contexts of *therapeuein* in these two cases can help explain later attestations of the verb *therapeuein* in the sense of 'heal, cure'.

6§53. In speaking of later attestations, I have in mind evidence dating from the fifth century and thereafter. In this later era, *therapeuein* in the sense of 'heal, cure' can refer specifically to the procedure of healing a body by removing some form of sickness or, more basically, to the procedure of maintaining the well-being of the body. To maintain the well-being of the body is to keep it healthy— that is, keeping it sound and immune from any sickness.† More generally, *therapeuein* can refer simply to 'taking care of' or 'caring for' another person (an example is Lysias 24.6, with reference to a situation in which the elderly are being cared for by their children). Such a general meaning 'take care of, care for' helps explain the specific meaning of 'heal, cure': we may compare the use in English of the expressions 'take care of' or 'care for' with reference to the care that patients receive from their physicians. It is also relevant here to mention the derivation of the English word *cure* from the Latin *cūra*, meaning 'care'.

6§54. So how are such contexts relevant to the sacral meaning of *therapōn* as a ritual substitute? Here I turn to the sacral contexts of *therapeuein* in the sense of 'take care of, care for'. In these contexts, I argue, the body that is being cared for and kept sound by those who are attending it is either (1) the notional body of a god or (2) the actual body of a cult hero. This sacred body, I further argue, can lend its sacredness to anything that makes contact with it, such as a temple or shrine or any other kind of sacred enclosure. In the case of gods, the sacred power of the sacred body can extend to a sacred simulacrum of the body, such as a sacred statue or picture or any other object that stands for the body of the god. There are many different attestations of *therapeuein* where the object of the verb is whatever sacred thing or place is attended by the attendants who care for it. Here are three shining examples:

---

* Lowenstam 1981:136–140 has argued persuasively that the upstart Cretan in the story told by the disguised Odysseus in *Odyssey* xiii is a narrative stand-in for the Cretan hero Meriones, who refuses to "take the hit," as it were, for the over-king of the Cretans, Idomeneus. On the comparative evidence of Celtic narratives concerning the idea of a "recessive" chariot driver who "takes the hit" for a "dominant" chariot fighter, see J. F. Nagy 1997:199–232.

† Van Brock 1961:123–127 collects examples.

(1) An Attic inscription dating from the fifth century BCE (*Inscriptiones Grae-cae* I³ 1–2 138.17) speaks of the need for *therapeuein*, 'taking care of', the *teme-nos*, 'sacred precinct', of the god Apollo 'in the most beautiful way possi-ble' ([τὸ τε]μένος τὸ Ἀπόλλōνο[ς ἐπιμελέσθōν, ὅπος ἂν κάλλισ]τα θεραπεύεται).

(2) A Cretan inscription dating from the second century BCE (*Inscriptiones Cre-ticae* III:2 1.5) speaks of the need for *therapeuein*, 'taking care of', archaic stat-ues of divinities (τὰ ἀρχαῖα [ἀ]γάλματα θαραπεύσαντες).*

(3) In the *Ion* of Euripides (110–111), dating from the late fifth century BCE, the young hero Ion speaks of his service of *therapeuein*, 'taking care of', the tem-ple of Apollo at Delphi (τοὺς θρέψαντας | Φοίβου ναοὺς θεραπεύω).

6§55. In the light of such attestations of the verb *therapeuein* we can under-stand the earlier attestations of the noun *therapōn* in combination with the gen-itive case of names of gods like Apollo, the Muses, Arēs, and so on.†

6§56. By now we can see that *therapeuein* in the sense of 'maintain the well-being of, take care of, care for' and in the special sense of 'heal, cure' is in fact related to the idea of a ritual substitute who maintains the well-being of some-one superior whom he serves by standing ready to die for that special someone. That is the therapeutic function, as it were, of the *therapōn*. Earlier on, I noted the English-language borrowings *therapy* and *therapeutic*. Now I note a seman-tic parallel in the use of the Greek word *pharmakon*, which means 'drug used for healing' or, more generally, 'drug used for medication or for poisoning', and we see the more specific meaning 'drug used for healing' embedded in the En-glish-language borrowings *pharmacy* and *pharmaceutical*. The meaning of this word *pharmakon* as 'drug used for healing' helps explain the related meaning of a related Greek word. That word is *pharmakos* (as attested in Hipponax F 9.1 and F 10.2 ed. West), which can be translated as 'scapegoat', that is, someone who takes the blame for a pollution that afflicts a whole society.‡ Here again we see at work the principle of a *transfer of evil,* comparable to what we saw in the case of the Hittite ritual substitutes.

---

* This example and the previous one are cited by van Brock 1961:122–123.

† *BA* 295 = 17§6; van Brock 1961:115–117 surveys the various attested combinations of *therapōn* with the name of a god in the genitive case. I note with interest the attestation of the dual form *theraponte* with reference to the twin sons of Poseidon, who are Pelias and Neleus, described as attendants of the god Zeus himself (θεράποντε *Odyssey* xi 255).

‡ I refer here again to the analysis of Kümmel 1967:193.

Patroklos as the Other Self of Achilles

6§57. Having said this much about the word *therapōn*, I turn to another word that is closely linked to the idea of Patroklos as the ritual substitute of Achilles. This other word is *philos*, meaning 'friend' as a noun and 'near and dear' or 'belonging to the self' as an adjective. By contrast with my lengthy investigation of the relevance of the word *therapōn* to Patroklos, I can confine myself here to the shortest of formulations about the parallel relevance of the word *philos*, since I have already analyzed this word at some length in Hour 2.* Here, then, is my formulation, compressed into a single nested paragraph:

> Patroklos as the personal *therapōn* of Achilles is thereby also the nearest and dearest of all the comrades of Achilles. This closeness is measured in terms of the word *philos* in the sense of being 'near and dear' to someone. Achilles considers Patroklos to be the most *philos*, 'near and dear', of them all. Or, if we were to express this idea in terms of the noun *philos*, meaning 'friend', instead of using the adjective *philos*, meaning 'near and dear', we would say that Patroklos is the very best friend of Achilles. This word *philos* defines identity by way of measuring how much you can identify with someone else: the more you love someone, the more you identify with this special someone—and the closer you get to your own self.

6§58. This is why Patroklos is truly the other self or *alter ego* of Achilles. In the *Life of Pythagoras* tradition, the wise man is asked the question 'what is a friend [*philos*]?' and answers that a *philos* is *allos egō*, 'another I' (scholia for *Iliad* XVIII 82). This terminology helps explain the use of the pseudo-scientific Latin term *alter ego* in translations of the works of Freud into English.

Ramifications of the Idea of Another Self

6§59. Such an idea of Patroklos as the other self of Achilles is parallel to the idea of twinning. As I show in a separate essay, this parallelism helps explain other

---

* I repeat here the references to my earlier work: *BA* 82–83 = 5§27; 102–111 = 6§§12–22; see also the work of Sinos 1980.

features that Achilles and Patroklos share, such as the power to heal.* The therapeutic powers of Achilles and Patroklos can be analyzed in this light.†

6§60. The therapeutic function of *caring for* someone as a patient in mythical contexts of healing can be linked with the emotional function of *caring for* someone who is *philos* in these same contexts. That is because *therapeuein* in the emotional sense of 'care for' is linked with *philos* in the sense of 'near and dear';‡ and, further, *therapōn* in the sense of 'ritual substitute' is linked with *philos* in the sense of 'belonging to the self'.§

6§61. As the other self who is ready to die for the self that is Achilles, Patroklos achieves an unsurpassed level of intimacy with the greatest hero of the Homeric *Iliad*. This intimacy is sacral, thus transcending even sexual intimacy. But this sacred intimacy has an uncanny other side to it, which is a kind of sacred alienation. As we saw in the case of the Hittite prisoner, about to be expelled into an alien realm, he must wear the clothing of the king, thus becoming ritually intimate with the body of the king. So too Patroklos wears the armor of Achilles when he dies, and he wears something else that is even more intimately connected with his best friend. Patroklos wears also the epic identity of Achilles, as expressed by the epithets they share. These heroic epithets, such as the ones that make them both 'equal to Arēs', will predestine both of them to live the same way and to die the same way.**

Simone Weil on Sacrificial Substitution

6§62. Simone Weil (1909–1943) thought that evil happens when the suffering of one person is passed on to another person. The mentality is this: *I want you to suffer exactly the way I have suffered*. The problem is, everyone suffers differently. So the transfer of suffering does not make things better. It makes things worse. And that is evil. So evil itself is the transfer of suffering. In French, it is

---

* Here I refer to a forthcoming essay of mine on twins, which will appear in a book edited by Kimberley Patton. I argue there that Achilles and Patroklos are figured as a dyadic pair that resembles in some ways the dyadic pair represented by the "Divine Twins," the Dioskouroi. For important comparative evidence in Celtic traditions, see J. F. Nagy 1997:199–232.

† In the essay I just mentioned in the previous note, I connect my arguments with those of Douglas Frame in an essay that is forthcoming in the same book edited by Kimberley Patton.

‡ On the meaning of *philos* as 'near and dear', derived from *phi* in the sense of 'near', see *GM* 203n7, with further references.

§ *BA* 103–106 = 6§§13–16.

** These last words of Hour 6 are taken from my essay on twins, to which I referred earlier. In that essay, I added one more sentence: *And the sameness of their shared life and death can be seen as an uncanny mix of intimacy and alienation that only twins will ever truly understand.*

"le transfert du mal," as we saw at §48 in this hour. To stop this chain of evil, an existential hero must refuse to transfer the suffering to the next person. And so the hero must absorb the suffering. For that to happen, however, the hero will have to die for the next person in line and for everyone else who is in line. Such a death can be described as an act of sacrificial substitution.

6§63. In her essay "Human Personality" (1943), Weil says: "When harm is done to a man, real evil enters into him; not merely pain and suffering, but the actual horror of evil. Just as men have the power of transmitting good to one another, so they have the power to transmit evil." In "Void and Compensation" (published 1947), Weil says: "The wish to see others suffer exactly what we are suffering. It is because of this that, except in periods of social instability, the spite of those in misfortune is directed against their fellows. That is a factor making for social stability." We read in the same work: "The tendency to spread the suffering beyond ourselves. If through excessive weakness we can neither call forth pity nor do harm to others, we attack *what the universe itself represents for us.* Then every good or beautiful thing is like an insult."

6§64. If we apply here the thinking of Weil, we may think of Patroklos as a hero who refuses to pass on the suffering to the next person. He absorbs the suffering and dies in the act of doing so. He short-circuits evil.

6§65. Such a way of thinking about Patroklos may lead us to a rethinking of this hero's status as the one person who is highest in the ascending scale of affection felt by the hero Achilles.

The Sign of the Hero in Visual and Verbal Art

The Meaning of Sēma

7§1. The key word for this hour is *sēma* (plural *sēmata*), meaning 'sign, signal, symbol; tomb, tomb of a hero'. An important word that derives from this noun *sēma* is the verb *sēmainein*, 'mean [something], indicate [something] by way of a *sēma*'. Modern words that derive from *sēma* include *semantic* and *semiotic*.

7§2. As we saw in Hour 6, Achilles and Patroklos live and die the same way. As we will see in Hour 7, this pattern of identification is not terminated by death. Once these two heroes are both dead, those who are still living will remember them the same way. That is, both Achilles and Patroklos will be remembered as cult heroes. And that remembrance is indicated by the word *sēma*, which is the ultimate sign of the hero.

The Sign of the Hero at a Chariot Race

7§3. I concentrate here on the use of this word *sēma* in two verses, *Iliad* XXIII 326 and 331, concerning the *sēma* or 'sign' given by the hero Nestor to his son, the hero Antilokhos, about the *sēma* or 'tomb' of an unnamed hero. The two verses come from a passage in which Nestor gives instructions to Antilokhos about the driving skills required for a charioteer to make a left turn around a landmark. As we will now learn from the context, this landmark is meant to be used as a turning point in the course of a chariot race that is being planned as the culminating athletic event of the Funeral Games for Patroklos in *Iliad* XXIII. In the words of Nestor, this landmark is either a *sēma*, 'tomb', of an unnamed hero of the distant past (XXIII 331) or it was once upon a time a turning point, a *nussa* (332), used for chariot races that must have taken place in such a distant past. As I will argue, the master Narrative of the *Iliad* shows that this *sēma* or 'tomb' is to be understood as the tomb of Patroklos himself, which he will share with Achilles once Achilles too is dead. To understand this is to understand the *sēma* or 'sign' given by the hero Nestor:

HOUR 7 TEXT A

|$_{326}$ I [= Nestor] will tell you [= Antilokhos] a sign [*sēma*], a very clear one, which will not get lost in your thinking. |$_{327}$ Standing over there is a stump of deadwood, a good reach above ground level. |$_{328}$ It had been either an oak or a pine. And it hasn't rotted away from the rains. |$_{329}$ There are two white rocks propped against either side of it. |$_{330}$ There it is, standing at a point where two roadways meet, and it has a smooth track on both sides of it for driving a chariot. |$_{331}$ It is either the tomb [*sēma*] of some mortal who died a long time ago |$_{332}$ or was a turning point [*nussa*] in the times of earlier men. |$_{333}$ Now swift-footed radiant Achilles has set it up as a turning point [*terma* plural]. |$_{334}$ Get as close to it as you can when you drive your chariot horses toward it, |$_{335}$ and keep leaning toward one side as you stand on the platform of your well-built chariot, |$_{336}$ leaning to the left as you drive your horses. Your right-side horse |$_{337}$ you must goad, calling out to it, and give that horse some slack as you hold its reins, |$_{338}$ while you make your left-side horse get as close as possible [to the turning point], |$_{339}$ so that the hub will seem to be almost grazing the post |$_{340}$—the hub of your well-made chariot wheel. But be careful not to touch the stone [of the turning point], |$_{341}$ or else you will get your horses hurt badly and break your chariot in pieces. |$_{342}$ That would make other people happy, but for you it would be a shame, |$_{343}$ yes it would. So, near and dear [*philos*] as you are to me, you must be sound in your thinking and be careful.

Iliad XXIII 326–343*

---

* |$_{326}$ σῆμα δέ τοι ἐρέω μάλ' ἀριφραδές, οὐδέ σε λήσει. |$_{327}$ ἕστηκε ξύλον αὖον ὅσον τ' ὄργυι' ὑπὲρ αἴης |$_{328}$ ἢ δρυὸς ἢ πεύκης· τὸ μὲν οὐ καταπύθεται ὄμβρῳ, |$_{329}$ λᾶε δὲ τοῦ ἑκάτερθεν ἐρηρέδαται δύο λευκὼ |$_{330}$ ἐν ξυνοχῇσιν ὁδοῦ, λεῖος δ' ἱππόδρομος ἀμφὶς |$_{331}$ ἤ τευ σῆμα βροτοῖο πάλαι κατατεθνηῶτος, |$_{332}$ ἢ τό γε νύσσα τέτυκτο ἐπὶ προτέρων ἀνθρώπων, |$_{333}$ καὶ νῦν τέρματ' ἔθηκε ποδάρκης δῖος Ἀχιλλεύς. |$_{334}$ τῷ σὺ μάλ' ἐγχρίμψας ἐλάαν σχεδὸν ἄρμα καὶ ἵππους, |$_{335}$ αὐτὸς δὲ κλινθῆναι ἐϋπλέκτῳ ἐνὶ δίφρῳ |$_{336}$ ἧκ' ἐπ' ἀριστερὰ τοῖιν· ἀτὰρ τὸν δεξιὸν ἵππον |$_{337}$ κένσαι ὁμοκλήσας, εἶξαί τέ οἱ ἡνία χερσίν. |$_{338}$ ἐν νύσσῃ δέ τοι ἵππος ἀριστερὸς ἐγχριμφθήτω. |$_{339}$ ὡς ἄν τοι πλήμνη γε δοάσσεται ἄκρον ἱκέσθαι |$_{340}$ κύκλου ποιητοῖο· λίθου δ' ἀλέασθαι ἐπαυρεῖν, |$_{341}$ μή πως ἵππους τε τρώσῃς κατά θ' ἄρματα ἄξῃς· |$_{342}$ χάρμα δὲ τοῖς ἄλλοισιν, ἐλεγχείη δὲ σοὶ αὐτῷ |$_{343}$ ἔσσεται· ἀλλὰ φίλος φρονέων πεφυλαγμένος εἶναι.

7§4. The *sēma* that is the 'tomb' of the unnamed hero at verse 331 here is also a 'sign' of that hero's cult, as signaled by the *sēma* or 'sign' that is conveyed at verse 326 by the speaker. That is what I once argued in an essay entitled "*Sēma* and *Noēsis:* The Hero's Tomb and the 'Reading' of Symbols in Homer and Hesiod."* As I pointed out in that essay, we know from evidence external to Homeric poetry that the tomb of a cult hero could be used as the actual turning point of a chariot race: in the historical period, starting with the adoption of chariot racing in the athletic program of the Olympics (this adoption has been dated at around 680 BCE), the turning point of chariot races could be conceptualized as the tomb of a hero, whose restless spirit was capable of "spooking" the horses at the most dangerous moment of the chariot race, the left turn around the turning point.†

7§5. According to the wording of Nestor in the passage I just quoted, however, there seem at first to be two different interpretations of the landmark that he is showing to Antilokhos: what is being visualized is either a tomb of a cult hero from the distant past or a turning point for chariot races that must have taken place in such a distant past. The landmark is an ambivalent sign. At least it seems ambivalent, short range, on the basis of Nestor's wording in this passage. Long range, however, on the basis of the overall plot of the *Iliad,* this wording will lead to a fusion of interpretations. And the sign that seemed at first to be ambivalent will become clear. Long range, the tomb of the unnamed hero from the distant past becomes the same landmark as the turning point of a chariot race from the distant past.‡ That is because the unnamed hero from the distant past becomes a named hero from the immediate present of the *Iliad.* That hero is Patroklos, and he died just now, as it were, in *Iliad* XVI.

7§6. But Patroklos dies not only in the present time of the *Iliad;* he also died a long time ago, from the standpoint of later generations who are listening to the story of the *Iliad.* So the storytelling of the *Iliad* makes it possible for the athletic event of a chariot race from the distant past to become the same thing as the athletic event of a chariot race that is being held right now, in the same

---

*Nagy 1983a, as recast in *GM* 202–222.

† *GM* 215–216, with reference to Pausanias 6.20.15–19 and with further comments. See also Sinos 1980:48–49. For still further comments, see now also Frame 2009:134 (with n31) and 163 (with n54). Race car drivers who participate in the Indianapolis 500 have a saying about how to win: "turn left and drive like hell." Also, we may in general compare the metaphor of "sudden death" in modern athletic events.

‡ *GM* 215–222; *PH* 208–212 = 7§§11–16.

immediate present time of the story, in *Iliad* XXIII. And, as we will see, this race is intended to honor Patroklos as a once and future cult hero.

7§7. The ambivalent wording of Nestor that leads to such a fusion of interpretations qualifies as an *ainos*. In Hour 2, I offered this working definition of the word *ainos*: a performance of ambivalent wording that becomes clarified once it is correctly understood and then applied in moments of making moral decisions affecting those who are near and dear. That definition, which I first applied to the words of Phoenix as spoken primarily to Achilles, applies also here to the words of Nestor as spoken to his son Antilokhos. We can see this application more clearly by reviewing the three qualifications that the *ainos* requires of its listeners:

1. The listeners must be *sophoi*, 'skilled' in understanding the message encoded in the poetry. That is, they must be mentally qualified.
2. They must be *agathoi*, 'noble'. That is, they must be morally qualified.
3. They must be *philoi*, 'near and dear' to each other and to the one who is telling them the *ainos*. That is, they must be emotionally qualified. Communication is achieved through a special sense of community, that is, through recognizing "the ties that bind."

7§8. As we will now see, the hero Antilokhos proves by way of his epic actions that he fits all three qualifications:

1. The mental qualification of Antilokhos is shown by his understanding of the sign given by his father. When Nestor says to his son, 'I will give you this certain sign [*sēma*] which will not get lost in your thinking' (XXIII 326), the idea that this sign 'will not get lost in your thinking' (οὐδέ σε λήσει) is expressed by way of the verb-root *lēth-*, which means 'mentally disconnect'.* The idea that you must not be mentally disconnected from the *sēma*, 'sign', shows that this word *sēma* has to do with a state of mind, a mentality. Antilokhos is visually cued by his father about a landmark that may have been a *nussa*, 'turning point' (XXIII 332), in chariot races of the past. And it will definitely be the *terma*, 'turning point' (plural τέρματ', XXIII 333), in the

---

* This root is found in the mythological name *Lethe*, which is the river of forgetfulness. More precisely, *Lethe* is the name of a river in the underworld that separates the living from the dead, those awake from those asleep, those conscious from those unconscious.

present, during the chariot race in honor of Patroklos.* According to Nestor, when Antilokhos takes a left turn around this *nussa*, 'turning point' (XXIII 338), during the counterclockwise chariot race in which he is about to compete, he will need to be more impulsive on his right side and more restrained on his left side by goading or whipping the horse on the right with his right hand while reining in the horse on the left with his left hand. This way, he will be making the most successful left turn possible. On the elaborate poetics of describing the left turn around a turning point in chariot racing, which requires a perfect combination of impulse and restraint for the successful execution of such a left turn, I am guided by the detailed analysis of Douglas Frame.† But there is a twist here in *Iliad* XXIII, as Frame points out: after the chariot race is under way and the time finally comes for Antilokhos to make his move, he does not interpret literally the visual cue or *sēma*, 'sign', that had been given him by his father. Antilokhos makes his move not at the turning point but at a narrow pass, where he impulsively decides to overtake the chariot of Menelaos that is racing ahead of him: at this point, seeing the visual cue of the narrow pass, Antilokhos even says to himself that his cue 'will not get lost in my thinking' (οὐδέ με λήσει XXIII 416), as expressed by way of the verb-root *lēth-*, which as we saw means 'mentally disconnect'. And now he impulsively drives past the chariot of Menelaos, nearly "fishtailing" it and thus almost causing both chariots to collide and crash—if Menelaos had not slowed down to avoid a collision (XXIII 417–437).‡ Antilokhos here is more impulsive than he is restrained. His action is a balancing of impulsiveness and restraint that favors in this case the impulsive side, which is the right, more than the restraining side, which is the left. That same kind of balancing would have been needed to make a left turn as well, but Antilokhos had redirected his strategy.

2. The moral qualification of Antilokhos is shown by his understanding of the same sign after the chariot race is over. This time, he shows his understanding by way of his behavior toward Menelaos. The impulsiveness of Antilokhos during the chariot race is now counterbalanced by his restraint in the

---

* The plural *termata* of *terma*, 'turning point', here in *Iliad* XXIII 333 expresses the idea that the charioteers of the chariot race held in honor of Patroklos will make their turns around the turning point more than once in the counterclockwise course of the chariot race.

† Frame 2009:133, 144–149, 153–156, 162–166, 331.

‡ Frame 2009:166–168 gives a detailed analysis of the action.

way he speaks and acts after his prize is challenged by an angry Menelaos (XXIII 586–597). And this restraint of Antilokhos gets rewarded: in response, Menelaos is flattered into voluntarily ceding the prize to Antilokhos (XXIII 598–613).* This behavior of Antilokhos may be interpreted as a show of mental agility,† but it is also in keeping with moral proprieties.‡ Although the original *sēma*, 'sign' (XXIII 326), given by Nestor to Antilokhos was specific to the chariot race to be held in honor of Patroklos, the actual interpretation of this sign about the best way to make a left turn around a turning point was not specific but general, even metaphorical. (For my usage of the term *metaphorical* here, I refer back to Hour 4§32.) For Antilokhos, as the narrative of the actual chariot race in *Iliad* XXIII elaborates in detail, the sign of Nestor was not only a lesson in chariot driving. It was also a lesson in sound thinking about the management of any crisis in life and about the moral need to balance impulse and restraint.§ And, at this particular moment in the life of Antilokhos, the balance of impulsiveness and restraint now favors restraint. In terms of this balance, the restraint is now dominant and the impulsiveness is recessive.

3. The emotional qualification of Antilokhos is shown by his ultimate understanding of the original *sēma*, 'sign' (XXIII 326), given to him by Nestor as an indicator of a 'tomb' belonging to a hero from the distant past: as we have seen, the word for this 'tomb' is likewise *sēma* (XXIII 331). And, as I have argued, the hero from the distant past to whom the tomb belongs can be seen as Patroklos, since this hero did in fact die a long time ago, from the standpoint of later generations who are listening to the story of the *Iliad*. But the ultimate meaning of the original *sēma*, 'sign' (XXIII 326), given by Nestor to Antilokhos can go even deeper here: this sign can refer not only to the tomb of an unnamed hero who turns out to be Patroklos but also to the tomb of another unnamed hero who will at a later point turn out to be Antilokhos himself. The cue for this extended identification can be seen in the wording used by Nestor in instructing Antilokhos how to be sound in his thinking and how to be careful in his actions: in this context, Nestor addresses his son as 'near and dear', *philos* (XXIII 343). There is a lesson to be learned here

about being *philos,* and the traditional poetics of this lesson will reach far beyond the narrative of the *Iliad* itself.

I say what I just said because the *sēma,* 'sign', given by Nestor to Antilokhos (XXIII 326) points not only to the immediate epic narrative about the chariot race in honor of Patroklos but also to an ulterior epic narrative mentioned in the epic Cycle (plot summary by Proclus of the *Aithiopis* by Arctinus of Miletus p. 106 lines 4–6; there is also a mention in *Odyssey* iv 186–188): in this narrative, best attested in a retelling by Pindar (*Pythian* 6.28–42), Antilokhos himself dies in a chariot fight, giving up his own life while saving the life of his father, Nestor, whose chariot had been immobilized.* Once again we see the mentality of choosing to die for someone else: *I will die for you.* For Antilokhos, then, the highest point in his ascending scale of affection proves to be his immediate ancestor, that is, his father. And, in the master Narrative of the *Iliad,* such a ranking is relevant to Patroklos himself, since, as we have seen, the name *Patrokleēs* means 'the one who has the glory [*kleos*] of the ancestors [*pateres*]'.

7§9. By now we have seen that there is a visual cue, as expressed by the word *sēma,* for each one of the three qualifications that Antilokhos must have in order to understand the meaning of the *ainos* addressed to him by Nestor:

1. When Antilokhos sees the turning point of the chariot race to be held in honor of Patroklos, what he sees will become the same thing as the *sēma* or 'sign' that he hears spoken to him by Nestor, which is the code that will enable him to win a prize in the race. That is how Antilokhos will become mentally qualified.

2. This *sēma* or 'sign' that Antilokhos sees is not only a code for driving his chariot successfully. It is also a moral code that teaches him to balance his impulsiveness with a sense of restraint. That is how Antilokhos will become morally qualified.

3. This *sēma* or 'sign' that Antilokhos sees by looking at the turning point will become the same thing as the 'tomb' of a hero. By understanding this equation, Antilokhos will live up to the instructions embedded in the *ainos* that he hears from his father, Nestor, who addresses his son as *philos,* 'near and

---

* *PH* 207–214 = 7§§10–18.

dear', in instructing Antilokhos how to be sound in his thinking and how to be careful in his actions. That is how Antilokhos will become emotionally qualified.

7§10. So, unlike the other example of *ainos* that we considered in Hour 2, when Phoenix was speaking to Achilles, our new example of *ainos* conveys its meaning not only verbally but also visually. That is to say, the *ainos* spoken by Nestor to Antilokhos conveys its meaning not only by way of its wording but also by way of a visual cue that we find embedded in that wording, and the word for this visual cue is *sēma*.

The Sign in the Visual Arts

7§11. As we have seen so far, then, *sēma* can mean *picturing by way of words*. Poetry can do that kind of picturing, as in the words spoken by Nestor to Antilokhos in *Iliad* XXIII. And I invoke here a relevant saying attributed to the poet Simonides (whose life overlaps the sixth and fifth centuries BCE), as mediated by Plutarch (*On the Glory of the Athenians* 346f): as the saying goes, *painting is silent poetry, but poetry is talking pictures.** Of course the concept of "talking pictures" is most familiar to us from that moment in the history of filmmaking when the "audio" of recorded speech gets to be finally integrated with the "video" of film. So we may say that Simonides anticipated such a concept, even though the required technology was invented only two and a half millennia later.

7§12. But the *sēma* in ancient Greek song culture works not only as *video* embedded in *audio* but also as *video* pure and simple, in the form of images produced by way of visual arts. I am about to analyze copies of nineteen such images, all of which were originally produced as paintings on vases (the one exception is a bronze plaque featuring in relief a scene that is parallel to a scene in one of the vase paintings). The copies that I show here are line drawings of the original images. Every one of these nineteen images, as we will see, qualifies as a *sēma* in the sense of a 'sign'. Further, any picture that is embedded inside a painted picture may qualify as a *sēma*, once again in the sense of a 'sign'. In Image D of the inventory, for example, we will see a picture of a lion that is painted as a *device* on a shield, and we know from the evidence of poetry that any device

---

* *HC* 129 = 1§127. Nagy 1974:21. See also Lessing 1766 [1984] 4.

displayed on the surface of a warrior's shield is known as a *sēma;* a celebrated example is the array of devices displayed on the shields of the Seven against Thebes in the drama by Aeschylus that is named after these seven heroes.* So when we see a picture of such a *sēma* or device that is painted on the picture of a shield that we see painted on a vase, what we are seeing is a *sēma* inside a *sēma.*

Selected Examples of Signs in the Visual Arts

7§13. In the images that we are about to see, we will find one particular figure that qualifies as a *sēma* in a double sense, both as a 'tomb' and as a special 'sign' in its own right. Already in Image A1, to which I now turn, we will see this figure. By way of this figure, we will see that the *video* of the image corresponds to the *audio* of the *ainos* told in *Iliad* XXIII by Nestor, the father to Antilokhos, the son.

7§14. As we have seen, Antilokhos succeeds in understanding that the 'tomb' of a hero is being signaled for him by a 'sign' that is made, verbally, by his father. So also in Image A1 and in other images that we are about to see, the 'tomb' of a hero is being signaled for the viewer by a 'sign' that is made, visually, by the painter. This visual 'sign', as we will see, is not only the tomb of a hero but also the turning point of a chariot race. And the meaning of this visual 'sign' is to be understood, as we will also see, as an ultimate form of meaning, in and of itself.

7§15. We will start with a line drawing of a picture painted on a kind of vase known as a hydria.† This hydria was produced in Athens at some point during the last few decades of the sixth century BCE and is now housed in the museum of the university in Münster.‡ From here on, I will refer to this vase as the Münster Hydria.

7§16. The original painting of the Münster Hydria was done in a style and technique that art historians describe as Black Figure. In fact, all the paintings we are about to see are Black Figure. The pictures painted on the Münster Hydria have been analyzed in a monograph by Klaus Stähler, whose perceptive observations have strongly influenced my own analysis.§

7§17. The two-dimensional limitations of the line drawing here create the

---

* Nagy 2000.

† Note the spelling: *hydria,* not to be confused with "hydra." The second of these two words, "hydra," comes from a Greek word for a venomous dragon.

‡ At the end of Hour 7, I will attempt a more precise dating of this vase.

§ Stähler 1967.

A1. Münster Hydria, painting on the body of the vase (Wilhelms-Universität, 565)

optical effect of flattening the curvature of the round surface on which the vase painter has painted his picture. But we can see some things more clearly from such a flattened perspective. In particular, I draw attention to the fact that the left and the right edges of the painting have suffered considerable fragmentation. Whereas the dark gray background of the line drawing represents the burnished red color of the fired clay that serves as the background for the black and white colors of the figures that are painted on the red surface of the vase, the light gray background at the left and at the right edges of the line drawing represents the areas of the burnished red background where the paint used for painting the black and white figures is eroded. As for the body of the other half of the vase, it has broken off for the most part.

7§18. The picture is framed by vertical margins painted on both the left and the right, corresponding roughly to the vertical margins that frame the line drawing that we see. The vertical margins are coordinated with the horizontal margins at the bottom and at the top of the picture. The line drawing as we see it shows the horizontal margin at the bottom, under which it shows decorative patterns of leaves repeated in a series; as for the margin at the top, it corresponds to a horizontal zone where we can see the body of the vase modulating into the shoulder; later in my analysis, I will show a line drawing of the picture painted on the shoulder of this vase, Image A2.

7§19. So the vertical and the horizontal margins framing the picture we see in Image A1 create a *window effect*. It is as if the viewer were viewing a scene by looking through a window. In a short while, I will show another clear example of such a window effect.

7§20. Although the paint at both the left and the right edges of the picture we see in Image A1 has chipped off, we can still make out the essentials of what is missing:

> At the left edge of the picture, in the area next to the margin, a missing part is the figure of a charioteer standing on the platform of a chariot. Because most of the paint has eroded in this area, all we see of the chariot is a trace of a chariot wheel. The chariot is being drawn by four horses, fully visible, running at full speed.
>
> Another missing part at the left edge is the head of a figure who is shown running on the ground at full speed alongside the speeding chariot; also missing is the left side of his body (here and elsewhere, in referring to the left and the right sides of human figures, I follow the left-right orientation of the viewer who is facing the picture). It is a male figure, as we can see from his coloring. In Black Figure painting, male skin is ordinarily painted black, while female skin is painted white.
>
> As for the area at the right edge of the picture where the paint has eroded, the missing parts are the head and most of the body of a female figure who is standing in the way of the speeding horses. We know that the figure is female because we see a trace of one of her hands, painted white, near the snout of the horse that is farthest from the viewer.

7§21. The horses driven by the charioteer are shown making a left turn around a tomb, which is pictured as a shining white egg-shaped mass rising out of the earth. We can see that the heads of the horses on the right side of the yoke are positioned further downward while the heads of the horses on the left side are positioned further upward. These positions correspond to what we can visualize in Nestor's words of advice in *Iliad* XXIII about the most successful left turn in a chariot race: driving two horses yoked to the chariot, the competing charioteer has to impel the horse on the right side of the yoke, forcing it to go faster by whipping or goading it, while he has to restrain the horse on the left side, forcing it to go slower by reining it in (XXIII 334–338). Unlike what we see in the chariot race depicted in *Iliad* XXIII, however, there are four rather than two horses that draw the racing chariot here in Image A1. I will return at a later point to this discrepancy.

7§22. The tomb is being guarded by the figure of a fierce lion, the black color of which is foregrounded by the shining white background of the tomb. The appearance of this tomb corresponds to what archaeologists describe as *a tumulus covered with white stucco.** In Black Figure vase paintings, the tumulus of the generic cult hero is conventionally painted shining white, foregrounded against the burnished red background of the fired clay.† As we will see, this shining white tumulus as pictured here in the visual art of the Münster Hydria corresponds to the turning point for the athletic event of a chariot race as described by Nestor in the verbal art of the *Iliad* (XXIII 331–332).

7§23. Levitating over the shining white tumulus in the dead center of this picture is the miniature figure of a fully armed warrior who is shown running at full speed in thin air. The movement of this miniature male figure—from now on I will refer to him as a *homunculus*—mirrors the movement of the male figure who is shown running at full speed on the ground, alongside the speeding chariot.

7§24. Even the appearance of the homunculus running in thin air mirrors the appearance of the male figure running at ground zero. The homunculus is fully armed, equipped with helmet, shield, spear, sword, breastplate, and shinguards.‡ So also the male figure running alongside the chariot is fully armed: although the image of this runner is fragmentary, we can see clearly his shield and the hilt of his sword. We can also see clearly one of his legs; and the wide space separating this leg from the other leg, occluded by the legs of the horses, shows that this runner too is running at full speed, mirroring the momentum of the running homunculus.§ As Stähler demonstrates, and as we will see for ourselves in what follows, this figure who is running at ground zero is Achilles himself.**

7§25. As we will see, the image of the homunculus represents the spirit of

---

* *HPC* 170 = II§90.

† Stähler 1967:19, with citations.

‡ Close examination by Stähler 1967:13 verifies that the painting actually shows the shin guards, even though this aspect of the armor is not clearly visible.

§ Stähler 1967:12.

** Stähler 1967:15, 32–33, 44.

B1. Boston Hydria, painting on the body of the vase (Museum of Fine Arts, Boston, 63.473)

a cult hero whose tomb is marked by the shining white tumulus. Positioned directly above the tumulus and to the right of the homunculus is a painted sequence of five consecutive letters, ΦΣΥΧΕ, running from left to right and signaling the identity of the cult hero: these letters spell out the word *psūkhē*, which I will translate for the moment simply as 'spirit'. As Stähler argues, here this word refers to the spirit of a cult hero, and the cult hero here turns out to be none other than the dead Patroklos.*

7§26. In making his argument, Stähler compares the picture we have just seen, as painted on the Münster Hydria, with other pictures featuring remarkable parallels. Foremost among these other pictures is one that is painted on the body of another hydria, housed in the Museum of Fine Arts in Boston; from here on, I will refer to this other vase as the Boston Hydria. This vase was produced in Athens around the same time as the Münster Hydria, that is, at some point during the last few decades of the sixth century BCE.†

7§27. The picture we see in the line drawing, Image B1 on the Boston Hydria, has been analyzed by Emily Vermeule, whose observations I will follow closely

---

* Stähler 1967:13–14.

† At the end of Hour 7, I will have more to say about the dating of this vase.

in my analysis.* Here too in Image B1, as in Image A1 on the Münster Hydria, we see a tomb in the form of a shining white tumulus highlighted against the burnished red background of the fired clay. As in the case of Image A1, the appearance of this tomb in Image B1 corresponds to what archaeologists describe as *a tumulus covered with white stucco*. I note here in passing an interesting variation on a theme: whereas the tomb in Image A1 was being guarded by a fierce lion, the guardian of the tomb in Image B1 is a snake, and its black color is foregrounded by the shining white background of the tumulus.

7§28. Variations aside, an essential fact remains: in Image B1, as in Image A1, we see the figure of a homunculus hovering over a tomb shaped like a tumulus. And the homunculus of Image B1 is wearing a full set of armor, just like the homunculus of Image A1. Unlike that other homunculus, who levitates above his tomb in Image A1, however, this levitating homunculus in Image B1 is endowed with a pair of wings. So with the addition of these wings, the theme of levitation in thin air above a tomb can be made even more explicit. And, unlike that other homunculus in Image A1, who is labeled as ΦΣΥΧΕ, that is, as a *psūkhē* or 'spirit', this homunculus in Image B1 is actually identified by way of the lettering painted on the picture of the tomb: we see here a sequence of eight consecutive letters, ΠΑΤΡΟΚΛΩ. These letters, running from left to right, spell out *Patroklō*, signaling the name *Patroklos* (in the dative case: so, 'for Patroklos').

7§29. As Stähler argues, the homunculus labeled as *psūkhē* or 'spirit' on the Münster Hydria (Image A1) has the same identity as the corresponding homunculus labeled as *Patroklos* on the Boston Hydria (Image B1).† That is, both of these homunculi represent the spirit of Patroklos as a cult hero who is hovering over the tomb that contains his corpse. It is this same tomb, as Stähler argues further, that will in a future time contain the corpse of Achilles as well; the argument here is based on the fact that Homeric poetry makes explicit references to a tomb that contains the corpses of Patroklos and Achilles together (*Iliad* XXIII 83–84, 91–92, 125–126, 245–248; *Odyssey* xxiv 80–84).‡

7§30. By contrast with such a future time when Achilles, once he is dead, will share the tomb of Patroklos, Achilles is not dead but still very much alive in the present time of the narrative encapsulated in the picture painted on the Boston Hydria. Image B1 shows Achilles near the center of the left side of the painting, at a moment when he is either stepping on or stepping off the platform of a

* Vermeule 1965.
† Stähler 1967:14.
‡ Stähler 1967:14n7.

speeding chariot that is taking a left turn around the tomb that contains the corpse of Patroklos. At this point in my argumentation, I cannot yet say for sure whether the figure of Achilles is stepping into or out of the chariot.

7§31. I focus here on a most telling detail we see in the picture: it is the naked corpse of Hector being dragged behind the speeding chariot. We know it is Hector because the consecutive letters painted over the corpse spell out ΕΚΤΡΩΡ, that is, *Hektōr* (the superfluous "P" in the sequence is simply a mistake in the spelling of the name). We know from two passages in the Homeric *Iliad* (XXII 395–405, XXIV 14–22) that Achilles, infuriated over the killing of his dearest friend, Patroklos, by Hector, tries to avenge this death by fastening the ankles of his slain enemy behind the wheels of his chariot and then dragging Hector's corpse behind his speeding vehicle; in both Iliadic passages, Achilles himself is shown driving the chariot. In Image B1, by contrast, the chariot is driven by a driver wearing the generic full-length gown of a charioteer.

7§32. In the second of the two passages in the *Iliad* where Achilles is pictured in the act of dragging the corpse of Hector behind his speeding chariot, we see that he drives this chariot three times around the tomb of Patroklos (XXIV 14–18), and the word referring to the tomb here is *sēma* (XXIV 16). At an earlier point in the narrative of the *Iliad,* this tomb is described as incomplete: it will not be complete until Achilles himself is buried there together with his best friend, Patroklos (XXIII 245–248).*

7§33. Keeping in mind this Iliadic detail showing Achilles in the act of driving around the tomb of Patroklos three times, I turn to corresponding details in Images A1 and B1: in both images, the four horses driven by the charioteer are shown making a left turn around the tomb of Patroklos. Applying the verbal narrative of the *Iliad* to the visual narrative of Image B1, Vermeule has made this observation about the technique used in the visual narrative: "The technique gives the impression that the myth is circling around in another world, outside the window frame through which the spectator views it, in endless motion which is somehow always arrested at the same place whenever we return to the window."† I already noted the same kind of visual technique when I was analyzing the painted scene we saw in Image A1: there too, as in Image B1, the vertical and the horizontal margins framing the picture create a *window effect*. It is as if the viewer were viewing a scene by looking through a window. Every

---

* *HPC* 173 = II§93.
† Vermeule 1965:45.

time we look through the painted window that frames the painted scene that we see, we return to precisely this same moment.

7§34. Such a moment interrupts a circular motion that could otherwise go on forever. As we have just seen from Vermeule's description of the scene in Image B1 of the Boston Hydria, the chariot of Achilles seems to be circling the tomb of Patroklos endlessly, but its circular motion is arrested at whatever moment the viewer returns to the picture by looking through the window.

7§35. This arresting of motion by way of a stop-motion picture can be compared to what happens in the epic narrative about the dragging of the corpse of Hector behind the speeding chariot of Achilles. As we know from the narrative of the *Iliad,* the speeding chariot of Achilles will ultimately stop, since it is a moral imperative in this epic that the dragging of the corpse of Hector simply must stop. Such a moral imperative is in fact signaled in the *Iliad* immediately after the description of the dragging of the corpse of Hector three times around the tomb of Patroklos (XXIV 14–18). While the god Apollo uses his healing power to keep on preserving the corpse of Hector from the disfigurement intended by Achilles (XXIV 18–21), the other gods, too, are feeling pity for Hector (XXIV 23), and a proposal is made that Hermes the divine messenger should hide Hector's body (XXIV 24), thus preventing for good the attempt of Achilles to disfigure it by dragging it behind his chariot (XXIV 22). All the gods are in favor of this proposal (XXIV 25) except for Hērā, Athena, and Poseidon, who are opposed (XXIV 25–30), and their opposition leads to further deliberation in what is clearly understood to be a council of the gods (XXIV 31–76).

7§36. At this final council of the gods in the *Iliad,* the decision is made to send the goddess Iris, messenger of the Olympians, on a double mission: first she goes off to summon Thetis (74–75), who will be asked by Zeus to persuade her son to return the corpse of Hector to Priam (75–76); then Iris is sent off to Priam, who will receive from the goddess a divine plan designed to make it possible for him to persuade Achilles to return the corpse of his son (143–158). The ultimate outcome of this double mission is that Achilles will finally take pity on Priam and release to him the body of Hector; the elaborate narrative that culminates in this outcome takes up over 500 verses (XXIV 189–694).* Once the double mission of Iris is accomplished, Achilles will never again drag the body of Hector.

7§37. By contrast with the *Iliad,* however, where we see an elaborate and

---

* Friis Johansen 1967:143.

lengthy narrative about the double mission of Iris, the corresponding narrative in Image B1 of the Boston Hydria is simple and brief, virtually instantaneous, and this narrative is about a single mission accomplished by Iris. This goddess, the female counterpart of Hermes as divine messenger of the Olympians, can be seen here in Image B1 at the precise moment when she descends from the Olympian heights and signals, even before her delicate feet have touched the ground, that the dragging of the corpse of Hector must stop. And so the chariot, which is still speeding ahead, must ultimately stop.

7§38. In Image B1 of the Boston Hydria, the signal for ultimately stopping the chariot is a gesture of lament: the goddess Iris is shown raising her arms, indicating the need for pity. And, as we remember from the narrative in the *Iliad*, the emotion of pity was in fact the first reaction of the Olympian gods as they contemplated the dragging of the corpse of Hector by Achilles (XXIV 23). It was this emotion that led to the decision, at the final council of the gods in the *Iliad*, to stop the dragging of the corpse of Hector by Achilles. And it is now this same emotion of pity that Iris is signaling in Image B1 of the Boston Hydria. Further, this signal of pity is picked up by the parents of Hector, Priam and Hecuba, who are seen standing in a portico at the far left of the picture of Image B1: they too make gestures of lament, corresponding to the gesture of Iris.* And this signal of pity emanating from Priam and Hecuba is then finally picked up by Achilles himself, who now turns his head toward Priam and Hecuba as he proceeds to step off the chariot.†

7§39. In terms of my interpretation, then, Achilles here in Image B1 of the Boston Hydria is stepping off his speeding chariot. According to an alternative interpretation, however, Achilles is at this very moment stepping into the chariot, not out of it.‡ In what follows, I will defend my interpretation by surveying other pictures that show details comparable to what we see here in Image B1 of the Boston Hydria. And, as we will see from these pictures, the turning of the head of Achilles in Image B1 is not directly related to the act of stepping on or stepping off a racing chariot.

7§40. I offer now a hint of things to come. The fact is, the turned head of Achilles is a detail that relates directly to the perspective of the narration in Image B1 of the Boston Hydria. I highlight here an unrealistic detail there: it looks

---

* The scene is described by Friis Johansen 1967:150, who points out that Priam, shown with a white beard, is "leaning on a stick and raising his right hand," while Hecuba is "beating her forehead in lamentation."
† *HPC* 172–173 = II§91.
‡ Vermeule 1965:44; Friis Johansen 1967:150.

as if Achilles were holding his shield with his right hand. But in "real life" a warrior holds his shield consistently with his left hand. To represent that, however, the painter would need to show the outside of the shield pointing away from the viewer. So, instead, the painter paints the upper part of Achilles' body, not only his turned head, as pointing toward the left, shield and all, while the lower part of his body, visible below the shield, is pointing to the right.

7§41. But I start with the picture painted on the shoulder of the Münster Hydria. The scene that we see here is a council of the gods, parallel to the final council of the gods in the *Iliad*, where we saw that the Olympians took pity on Hector as they were contemplating from on high the dragging of his corpse by Achilles (XXIV 23). Attending the council of the gods in Image A2 of the Münster Hydria are Zeus and Hermes at center left and center right; the chief of the gods is shown wielding his thunderbolt, while the messenger of the gods holds his heraldic staff, or kerykeion. Further to the right of Hermes is the goddess Athena, armed with shield and aegis. As for the divine figure situated to the right of Athena, we cannot see who it is because of a break in the painting. At the extreme left is Dionysus, wearing a garland of ivy and holding a grapevine.*

7§42. Between Dionysus and Zeus is a goddess, and she is making a gesture: one hand is uplifted, while she holds a rod with the other hand. I conjecture that this goddess is the goddess Iris, female messenger of the Olympians and counterpart of the god Hermes as their male messenger; and I conjecture also that the rod she holds is a kerykeion corresponding to the one held by Hermes. In the case of Iris, however, the kerykeion is turned downward, and we cannot see the tip because of a break in the painting. In another picture that we will see later, however, the downturned kerykeion of Iris is clearly visible in a comparable context.

7§43. These details in Image A2, as painted on the shoulder of the Münster Hydria, are compatible with the details we already saw in Image B1 as painted on the body of the Boston Hydria. In Image B1, the goddess Iris is at the point of accomplishing a mission that was ordained at a council of the gods as pictured in Image A2. The mission of Iris, as we see it pictured in Image B1, is to stop the dragging of the corpse of Hector by Achilles.

7§44. Here I must stop for a moment to make a clarification. It has to do with a remarkable omission in the picture painted on the body of the Münster Hy-

---

* Stähler 1967:16.

A2. Münster Hydria, painting on the shoulder of the vase (Wilhelms-Universität, 565)

dria. As we can see in Image A1 of this vase, the corpse of Hector is not pictured. So the council of the gods, pictured in Image A2 as painted on the shoulder of the Münster Hydria, is less well understood if we connect it with the picture of the speeding chariot team in Image A1 and better understood if we connect it with the corresponding picture of the speeding chariot team in Image B1 of the Boston Hydria, where we can actually see the dragging of the corpse of Hector behind the chariot of Achilles.

7§45. This kind of omission will be more understandable when we view the evidence of other relevant pictures. As we will see, vase paintings of such scenes from Greek myths are selective in what they include and exclude. And here I offer a general observation: there is no such thing as a complete picture of any single myth in any single vase painting.

7§46. That said, I am ready to move on to the next picture, which is painted on the shoulder of the Boston Hydria. This picture, Image B2, is relevant to the picture painted on the body of the same vase, Image B1. Here in Image B2, we see on our right the figure of a chariot driver wearing the generic full-length white gown of a charioteer and driving a four-horse chariot at full speed, while a figure in full armor is running toward the center of the picture, brandishing his spear. On our left in this same picture, racing after the chariot we see on our right, we see another speeding four-horse chariot, and this one is driven by none other than the goddess Athena herself; meanwhile, another figure in full armor is running toward the center of the picture, and he too is brandishing a

B2. Boston Hydria, painting on the shoulder of the vase (Museum of Fine Arts, Boston, 63.473)

spear. This fully armed running figure on our left, as we can tell from the lion-skin he wears, is none other than the hero Hēraklēs, son of the god Zeus; as for the fully armed running figure on our right, he is the hero Kyknos, son of the god Arēs. The story of the mortal combat in chariot fighting between Hēraklēs and Kyknos is recounted in the Hesiodic *Shield of Herakles,* where we see that both Hēraklēs and Kyknos leap to the ground from their chariots and then run at full speed toward each other (verses 370–371). I highlight here a detail: both combatants leap from their speeding chariots (verse 370 θόρον, from the verb *thrōiskein,* 'leap, jump'). Meanwhile, the charioteers driving the chariots of the combatants drive on, keeping as close as possible to the combatants running on the ground (verse 372 ἔμπλην, 'closely').

7§47. Similarly in Image B2 of the Boston Hydria, the drivers are keeping their speeding chariots close to the running combatants. Though it seems at first as if Kyknos were running in the opposite direction of his chariot team, this optical effect is deceptive, since the charioteer of Kyknos is making a left turn here, thus starting to circle back along the curvature of the vase's round sur-face—and thus resuming the direction in which Kyknos is running. In fact, both charioteers here are making left turns and circling back counterclockwise toward their runners. We will soon see comparable pictures of speeding chari-ots making left turns in the course of their counterclockwise trajectories. Mean-while, at the center of the picture here in Image B2, we see a figure who seems to be intervening exactly at the point where the two running warriors will come to blows, that is, at the dead center of the painting; on the basis of other paintings that picture the mortal combat of Hēraklēs and Kyknos, we may infer that the figure in the center here is the god Zeus himself.* And while this intervention is taking place in the picture painted on the shoulder of the Boston Hydria, Image B2, the figure of Iris is intervening at the center of the action in the corresponding picture painted below on the body of this same vase, Image B1.†

7§48. The picturing of fully armed figures running at full speed alongside their speeding chariots in Image B2 of the Boston Hydria brings us back to what we saw earlier in Image A1 of the Münster Hydria: there too, a fully armed figure is running at full speed alongside his speeding chariot, which is making a left turn around a shining white tumulus. As Stähler has demonstrated, this fully armed running figure is Achilles himself, who is mirrored by the fully armed running figure of a wingless homunculus levitating over the tumulus, who in turn is the spirit of Patroklos; and the tumulus over which this spirit of Patroklos levitates is the tomb that he will one day share with Achilles himself.‡

7§49. This same tomb, as we have seen, is pictured in Image B1 of the Boston Hydria, and the winged homunculus who levitates above the shining white tumulus in that picture is actually labeled as Patroklos. And, there too, the speeding four-horse chariot team of Achilles is making a left turn around the tumulus.

7§50. But the focal points are different in Images A1 and B1. Whereas the shining white tumulus is the center of attention in Image A1, it is off-center in Image B1; similarly, whereas the wingless homunculus and the team of speeding horses are situated at the center of Image A1, the winged homunculus and the speeding team of horses are off-center in Image B1. In the case of the horses, they are not only off to the side: we can only see their hind-quarters as they make their left turn around the tomb of Patroklos. Conversely, occupying the center of attention in Image B1 is the figure of Iris, who commands the attention of Achilles indirectly by making a gesture of lament directed at Priam and Hecuba, who in turn make corresponding gestures of lament directed at Achilles. So Achilles now turns his head around and looks back toward the lamenting parents of Hector, thus looking away from the tomb of Patroklos and away from the spirit of Patroklos, who levitates over that tomb. And I have already argued

---

* Shapiro 1984:525 surveys the evidence of comparable vase paintings.

† The parallelism that we see here between two scenes of divine intervention, one in the picture painted on the shoulder of the Boston Hydria and the other on the body of this vase, was noticed by Aliya Williams, who was working on a research project at the Center for Hellenic Studies in spring 2012.

‡ Stähler 1967:14–15.

that the entire upper half of Achilles' body, shield and all, is pointed to the left, toward the lamenting parents of Hector, while the lower half of his body is pointed to the right.

7§51. In Image A1, by contrast, the head of Achilles is unturned: although the head itself is missing, Stähler has noticed traces of the hero's beard in this badly fragmented part of the painting, and the beard is pointing to the right.* So Achilles in Image A1 is looking straight ahead, in the direction of three details in the picture: (1) the shining white tumulus, (2) the spirit of Patroklos, who levitates above the tumulus, and (3) a female figure who is situated at the extreme right of the picture. As I have pointed out already, the fragmentary picture of this female figure in Image A1 shows traces of one of her hands. I now add that this hand is lifted in a gesture that parallels the uplifted hands of the goddess Iris in Image B1. Here, too, in Image A1, I argue, the female figure who is making such a gesture of lament must be Iris.

7§52. As we will now see, comparable pictures show a wide variety of focal points that preoccupy the attention of the viewer. And these focal points will even preoccupy the attention of Achilles himself. In other words, the visual art of vase painting can represent Achilles as a viewer from inside the picture; this way, Achilles can become a participant in the outside viewer's act of viewing the picture. And, in most cases, the head of Achilles is turned in the direction of the focal point that most attracts him.

7§53. We see such an example in Image C, in which a fully armed Achilles runs alongside a speeding chariot. The hero is bearded, equipped with helmet, breastplate, shinguards, two spears, and a shield featuring the picture of a tripod as its device. The speeding chariot, driven by a figure wearing the full-length white gown of a charioteer, is making a left turn around the shining white tumulus of Patroklos, which is guarded in this case by a snake, not by a lion as in the case of the tumulus pictured in Image A1 of the Münster Hydria.

7§54. In the logic of the left turn that is being made by the charioteer here in Image C, the speeding chariot will be circling counterclockwise around the tumulus. And the fully armed Achilles who is running alongside the chariot is likewise circling counterclockwise around this same tumulus. Such a circular trajectory is reflected here in the visual effect of showing the extended leg of Achilles running in the foreground while the tumulus is in the background, but the upper part of his body is in the background while the tumulus is in the fore-

---

* Stähler 1967:12.

C. Neck-amphora (British Museum, London, B239)

ground, as if he were already on the other side of the tumulus, having run half-way around it. While Achilles is running on the viewer's side of the tumulus, he is heading toward our right; while he is running on the other side, however, he is heading toward our left. And in fact the head of Achilles is facing toward our left.

7§55. From what we have seen so far, the shining white tumulus is clearly the center of attention for the outside viewer. But what about the viewpoint of Achilles as an inside viewer? For an answer, we need to look at the sum total of the details we can see here in Image C.

7§56. In Image C as elsewhere, the picturing of the myth is not the complete picture. Parts of the myth are excluded. For example, the spirit of Patroklos is not pictured here. And we can see no Iris. Very much a presence, however, is the corpse of Hector, which is being dragged behind the speeding chariot. Remarkably, the painting of Hector's corpse extends outward to our left, well beyond the left margin of the picture, so that this gruesome sight is actually painted outside the frame of the picture. This exclusion from the frame is comparable to what we saw in Image A1 of the Münster Hydria, where the dragging of Hector's corpse behind the chariot was excluded altogether from the picture, not only from the frame of the picture. The significant absence from the frame of Image C corresponds to the significant absence from the entire painting of Image A1. Either way, then, the dragging of the corpse of Hector by Achilles is evidently an absent signifier in these paintings. And, in the case of Image C,

D. Neck-amphora (Staatliche Museen, Berlin, F 1867)

the exclusion of Hector's corpse from the frame has the effect of ostentatiously drawing attention to the act of dragging the corpse. In making this argument, I highlight the fact that the head of the running Achilles in Image C is turned toward the excluded picture of the dragging of the corpse of Hector.

7§57. The details that we have found in Image C are most readily comparable with what we see in Image D.

In Image D we see once again the fully armed figure of Achilles in the act of running alongside a racing chariot team that is making a left turn around the tumulus of Patroklos. In the logic of the left turn that is being made by the charioteer here in Image D, the speeding chariot is once again circling counterclockwise around the tumulus, as in Image C. And the fully armed Achilles who is running alongside the chariot is likewise circling counterclockwise around this same tumulus. But Image D shows this circular trajectory in a way that differs from what we saw in Image C. This time, the figure of Achilles is running from our right toward our left, as if he had already made the left turn that the speeding chariot is only now about to make. Also, the extended leg of Achilles is in the foreground while the running horses and the tumulus are the background, but his extended arm is in the background while the running horses are in the foreground, as if he were already on the other side of the tumulus. And Achilles is running in the same direction as the winged homunculus who levitates over the tumulus. This homunculus, fully armed, is once again the spirit of Patroklos in his role as a miniature body-double of the fully armed Achilles who is running on the ground.

7§58. Besides the points of comparison with details we have seen in Image C, I must also compare further details that we saw earlier in Image A1 of the Münster Hydria, where the spirit of Patroklos is a fully armed but wingless homunculus who is pictured as a miniature body-double of the fully armed Achilles who is running on the ground alongside his speeding chariot. In Image A1, the levitating figure of Patroklos is running in thin air, heading from our right toward our left, whereas the figure of Achilles is running on the ground, heading from our left toward our right, since he has not yet made the left turn that the speeding chariot is about to make.

7§59. So as I analyze further the picture we saw in Image A1, I am now ready to say that the fully armed figure of Patroklos running in the air is a model for the fully armed figure of Achilles running on the ground, since the running Patroklos would already have run half-way around the tumulus if he had been running on the ground. In the case of Image C, by contrast, Achilles himself has already run half-way around the tumulus. As for Image D, as I have been arguing, Achilles has at least already made the left turn, even if he has not yet circled half-way around the tumulus.*

7§60. Finally, in Image D as well as in Image C, the tumulus is guarded by a snake, not a lion. We do still see a lion in Image D, but only as a picture within the picture. That is, we see a lion featured as the device on the shield of Achilles. Later, when we consider Image K, we will see that snakes, too, can be featured as devices painted on shields.

7§61. Here I must recall what I noted earlier about the embedding of a picture inside a painted picture: such an embedded picture may qualify as a *sēma* in the sense of a 'sign'. And, as I also noted, we know from the evidence of poetry that any device displayed on the surface of a warrior's shield is known as a *sēma*; so, when we see a picture of such a *sēma* or device that is painted on the picture of a shield that we see painted on a vase, what we are seeing is a *sēma* inside a *sēma*. And what we are also seeing is the interchangeability of *sēmata*,

---

* Friis Johansen 1967:147 is unhappy with the fact that the runner in Image D is running "in the opposite direction of the chariot," and he thinks that the painter's representation of the scene in this image is "totally degenerate." In making this assessment, however, he does not take into account the circular trajectory of the chariots as they make their left turns. It should be noted, moreover, that Friis Johansen at the time of his writing did not know about the Münster Hydria or about the book of Stähler 1967. My analysis of Image D differs, however, from that of Stähler 1967:50, 63.

or 'signs' in these pictures. Just as a lion or a snake can be the guardian of a *sēma* in the sense of a 'tomb' that signals a dead hero in a given picture, so also the picture of a lion or of a snake can be a *sēma* in the sense of a 'sign' that serves as a device for signaling the identity of that hero, who can be either Patroklos or Achilles in the set of pictures we are now considering.

7§62. Similarly, the device of a running leg painted on the shield of the winged spirit of Patroklos here in Image D is a *sēma* or 'sign' for identifying Achilles, not Patroklos, as the hero who is best known for his swiftness in running (a distinctive epithet of Achilles in the verbal art of epic is *podas ōkus*, 'swift of foot', as at *Iliad* I 58). In Image B1 of the Boston Hydria, there is a corresponding picture painted on the shield of Achilles himself: we see there a device that features three running legs stemming from a center and seemingly spinning clockwise around that center. This triple-leg device conveys a semantic intensification of the quality of swift-footedness already conveyed by the single-leg device.

7§63. The next example consists of a set of six pictures in a row, each one of which is painted on the smaller surface of a smaller kind of vase, the lekythos.

7§64. In Image E we see once again the corpse of Hector being dragged behind the speeding chariot team, which is once again making a left turn around the tumulus of Patroklos, whose winged spirit levitates above it. Once again the fully armed Achilles is running alongside the chariot. And I note here a detail that we have not seen in the other pictures: a fully armed warrior is being trampled by the galloping horses that draw the onrushing chariot. This detail will be relevant to Image H. Another detail to be noted here in Image E is the picturing of grapes growing on vines to our right; in Image A2, as we saw earlier, the figure of Dionysus is holding a grapevine.*

7§65. In Image F, we see another heretofore unseen detail: a second fully armed warrior who is running alongside the speeding chariot. The first warrior, whose head is turned back, corresponds to the figure of Achilles in the other pictures being compared here.

7§66. In Image G, I note a detail that we have by now seen several times already: the fully armed figure who is running alongside the speeding chariot is shown with his head turned backward, to our left. So the runner is facing the act of dragging the corpse of Hector behind the chariot—an act that we already saw being excluded from the frame of another picture, Image C—and excluded

---

* Stähler 1967:16.

E. Lekythos (Borden Wood, now at the Fitzwilliam Museum, University of Cambridge)

F. Lekythos (The Louvre, Paris, CA 601)

G. Lekythos (Metropolitan Museum of Art, New York, 25.70.2)

H. Lekythos (Bibliothèque Nationale, Paris, 11078)

I. Lekythos (Museo Nazionale, Naples, H 2746)

J. Lekythos (Czartoryski Museum, Krakow, 1245)

altogether from the picture in Images A1 and D. The vision of this act of dragging is fully included, by contrast, in Images B1, E, F, as also here in Image G.

7§67. In Image H, the action is moving clockwise, not counterclockwise as in
the other pictures being compared here. The speeding chariot team is taking a
right turn rather than a left turn around the tumulus of Patroklos, which is situated to our right in this picture. The fully armed figure who is running alongside the speeding chariot has already completed his right turn, but the galloping
horses that draw the chariot are only now starting to make the right turn. The
fully armed figure standing to our left seems on the verge of being trampled by
the onrushing horses. In Image E, we have already seen a moment when a fully
armed figure is being trampled by the galloping horses that draw the onrushing
chariot team.

7§68. In Image I, the action is moving from left to right again. In this picture,
the painter has included no tumulus. So in this picture the chariot team is making a left turn not around a tumulus but only around the round surface of the
vase itself. The fully armed figure of Achilles is running at full speed from left to
right alongside the speeding chariot, but his head is turned around and facing
toward our left. And, at the extreme left, we as viewers from the outside can see
three details that are also to be seen by Achilles as the viewer of the picture from
the inside. These three details are arranged along a vertical axis of vision. At the
upper third of this vertical axis is the figure of Patroklos as a homunculus running in full armor and levitating in thin air. At the middle third, where we might
have expected the placement of a tumulus, we find instead the figure of a snake
that seems to be levitating in thin air. In other pictures we have seen, this snake
would have been positioned as a guardian in front of the tumulus of Patroklos;
in this picture, however, as we have already noted, the painter has painted no
tumulus. Finally, at the lower third of this vertical axis of vision, we see the naked body of Hector dragged behind the speeding chariot. So the view of Achilles is directed at three vertically interchangeable visions in this picture. (Relevant is the term *vertical axis of selection*, as I use it in Hour 4§32.)

7§69. Image J is like Image I in omitting an important detail, the tumulus of
Patroklos. Otherwise, Image J is most rich in details.* And some of these details
are most relevant to what we saw in Image B1 on the Boston Hydria. As in Image B1, we see once again here in Image J the figure of the winged goddess Iris
descending from on high and about to make a landing amid the action, thus

---

* One detail of no importance is the nonce lettering that is painted on this vase: see Friis Johansen 1967: 147.

blocking the momentum of the onrushing four-horse team drawing the chariot that is dragging behind it the corpse of Hector. A fully armed Achilles is running at full speed alongside the speeding chariot. He is looking straight ahead, with Iris in full view. The goddess here has been described as "hastening towards Achilles with the kerykeion [or 'heraldic staff'] in her left hand and her right hand raised, admonishing him, as it were."*

7§70. But now I need to ask: does Achilles comply or not comply with the admonition of the goddess Iris? This question can be linked with another question: is Achilles stepping out of or into the speeding chariot? We can see that his one foot is virtually on the platform of the chariot while his other foot is running on the ground. Either way, whether he is stepping off or stepping on, Achilles is doing so at a run. If he is stepping off the speeding chariot, he has to "hit the ground running"; if he is stepping on, he has to be running at full speed after the speeding chariot in order to leap into it.

7§71. The same two questions apply to the moment that is captured at the center of Image B1 of the Boston Hydria. Here too we see that one foot of Achilles is on the platform of his speeding chariot while the other foot is running on the ground. So once again, I need to ask this question: is Achilles stepping out of or into the speeding chariot? And I ask once again the other question as well: does Achilles comply or not comply with the admonition of the goddess Iris?

7§72. Before I can answer these two questions concerning this most critical moment in the visual narratives of Images J and B1, I first have to adjust the formulation I quoted about the "admonishing" of Achilles by the goddess Iris. As I have shown already, the gesture of raising the hand is a signal for pity. So Iris, following the instructions she received at the council of the gods, is admonishing Achilles to show pity by stopping the mistreatment of his enemy's corpse. In Image J, we see a detail that enhances the sense of pity elicited by the gesture of Iris: in a moment of pathos, the painting shows the long hair of Hector trailing behind him as his corpse is being dragged behind the speeding chariot of Achilles. There is a comparable moment of pathos in the verbal art of the *Iliad,* where we see once again a highlighting of the long hair of Hector as it gets disheveled during the dragging of his corpse behind the speeding chariot of Achilles (XXII 401–402).† That said, I am ready to answer the two questions.

7§73. My answer to the first question is that Achilles will in fact comply with

---

* Friis Johansen 1967:150.

† This detail is noticed by Friis Johansen 1967:150n228. I disagree, however, with his assumption that the painter was directly inspired by the text of the *Iliad* as we have it.

the admonition of Iris: he will show pity by stopping his cruel mistreatment of Hector's corpse. And my answer to the second question is an extension of my answer to the first: such compliance, as I will argue, can come about only if Achilles is stepping out of his speeding chariot instead of stepping into it.

7§74. To make this argument I will use the evidence of four images, K, L, M, and N. In each one of these images, we see moments when the chariot of Achilles has stopped and his horses are standing still.

7§75. Image K shows the goddess Iris, raising her hand in a lamenting gesture of pity. She has stopped the chariot of Achilles. That is my interpretation, which as we will see can be reconciled with the overall myth. When I say *overall myth* here, I include all the variations of the myth as represented in the visual narratives of the four pictures I am showing.

7§76. On the shoulder of the vase featuring Image K, I should add, we see a picture of a chariot in motion, and the charioteer is shown in the act of either stepping on or stepping off the platform of this chariot.

7§77. I note here two other details about Image K:

- There is nonce lettering painted between the figures.*
- We see here Achilles, fully armed and wearing a helmet, as he leans over the naked corpse of Hector. He is holding a shield over the corpse. Over on the side, to our left, we see a helmet and a shield, without anyone to wear it. My conjecture is that this levitating helmet and this levitating shield stand for the armor that had been stripped from the corpse of Hector when Achilles killed him. And the levitating shield features as its device two pictures of snakes, one at the top and one at the bottom. Meanwhile, Achilles is shown looking downward, directly at Hector. My further conjecture is that Achilles here, in an act of pity, is now covering with his own shield the naked body of Hector.

7§78. In Image L, we see again that the goddess Iris, shown here with wings, has stopped the chariot with her lamenting gesture; and again it looks as if Achilles is now attending to the corpse of Hector. There is nonce lettering painted over the corpse. Achilles here is facing not only the corpse of Hector but also the tumulus of Patroklos. Levitating over the tumulus is a winged homunculus who stands for the spirit of Patroklos. There are in fact two winged homunculi painted here at two opposite sides of the vase, who are levitating to

* Friis Johansen 1967:143.

K. Hydria (Hermitage, St. Petersburg, ST165)

L. Lekythos (Delos, B 6137.546)

the left and to the right of the tumulus. Conforming to the curvature of the picture painted on the round surface of the vase, the two winged homunculi provide a single vision of the spirit of Patroklos as seen from the two opposite sides of this vase.

7§79. In Image M, as well, we see that the winged goddess Iris has stopped the chariot, though the fragmentary condition of this part of the picture prevents our seeing her actual gesture of lament; and once again it looks as if Achilles is now attending to the corpse of Hector. He is looking directly at him. The figures here in Image M are identified by the lettering painted next to them. As we start looking from our right, near the top, the painted letters identify the fig-

M. Amphora (British Museum, London, 1899.7–21.3)

N. Hydria, painting on the shoulder of the vase (Museum antiker Kleinkunst, Munich, 1719)

ure of Patroklos (Π<A>ΤΡΟΚΛΟΣ) as the wingless but fully armed homunculus levitating over the tumulus, which features the picture of a guardian snake
on its surface, as if this picture were a device on a shield. Further below, painted
letters identify Achilles (ΑΧΙΛ[Ε]Υ[Σ]) and then Hector (ΗΕΚΤΟΡ); further to our left, the charioteer is identified as Konisalos (ΚΟΝΙ[ΣΑΛ]ΟΣ).
Secondary figures are also identified: the hero standing in front of the horses
is Odysseus (ΟΛΥΤΤΕΥ[Σ]), and there is even a hunting dog named Phaidros
(ΦΑ[ΙΔ]ΡΟΣ). Only Iris is not identified here by way of painted letters: evidently, she needs no identification.

7§80. Finally, in Image N, we see once again the winged goddess Iris; here she is holding the heraldic staff or kerykeion, which is shown pointing downward. Iris is standing in front of the chariot team, which is at a dead stop. Once again, Iris has stopped the chariot. Behind the chariot stands the fully armed Achilles; he has turned away from the chariot and has turned toward the tumulus of Patroklos, which shows again the picture of a snake on its surface, as if this picture were a device on a shield. Levitating over the tumulus of Patroklos is the running figure of a fully armed homunculus representing the spirit of Patroklos. Achilles is facing three visions. They are, from top to bottom: (1) the homunculus, (2) the tumulus showing the picture of the snake, and (3) the corpse of Hector. In Image I, we have seen Achilles facing the same set of visions in the same order, except that the tumulus was not pictured in that image; still, the snake was positioned in exactly the same space where it would be protecting the tumulus—if the tumulus had been painted in that space.

7§81. Having offered my interpretation of Images K, L, M, and N, I need to mention an alternative interpretation, according to which the chariot shown in all four of these images has not yet started to move.* In terms of this interpretation, we would have to say that Achilles has not yet mounted the chariot in order to drag the corpse of Hector behind it.†

7§82. In terms of this alternative interpretation, the four pictures we see in Images K, L, M, and N are based on "departure scenes," in which a warrior is about to mount a chariot with one foot still on the ground while the other foot is already planted on the platform of the vehicle.‡ In Images O and P, I show two beautiful examples of such "departure scenes."

7§83. In Image O, we see the hero Amphiaraos leaving his family to fight in the war of the Seven against Thebes. The family left behind by Amphiaraos (labeled ΑΦΙΑΡΕΟΣ) includes, from left to right: the wife, Eriphyle (ΕΡΙΦΤΛΑ), who is shown holding a tell-tale necklace given to her as a bribe by Polyneikes in return for her persuading her husband to go to war; a nurse (ΑΙΝΙΠΠΑ) carrying an infant (Amphilokhos); two daughters (labeled ΔΑΜΟΦΑΝΑΣΑ and ΕΤΡΤΔΙΚΑ), and a son (Alkmaion). The charioteer (labeled as ΒΑΤΟΝ)

---

* Friis Johansen 1967:139–144. His interpretation is based on a presupposition: that the painters of what I am calling Images K, L, M, and N are modeling their work on the text of *Iliad* XXIV 14–18.

† Friis Johansen 1967:141: "Achilles is just about to begin his daily, macabre drive round the grave of Patroklos, dragging the body of Hector behind his chariot."

‡ Friis Johansen 1967:143.

is about to start driving the chariot; standing in his way on the ground and facing him is a figure (labeled ΛΕΟΝΤΙΣ) who is gesturing toward the departing driver and rider. Standing in front of the chariot team is a male figure (labeled ΗΙΠΠΟΤΙΟΝ), and seated on the ground behind him is another male figure (ΗΑΛΙΜΕΔΕΣ). The scene also features various animals signaling various omens: from left to right, we see two lizards, a hedgehog, a hare, an owl, a scorpion, a snake, and a bird flying from right to left.*

7§84. In Image P as well, a hero is leaving his family to fight in war. In this case, we cannot be certain about the identity of the departing hero, but he may well be Hector, making gestures of farewell to his wife, Andromache, and to their infant son, Astyanax.

7§85. Although Images O and P are parallel in some details to Images K, L, M, and N, the parallelism breaks down when we consider one essential detail. Whereas the hero is mounting his chariot in Images O and P, there is no indication of any such action in Images K, L, M, and N. Here I return to my interpretation of Images K, L, M, and N, each of which shows the chariot of Achilles at a dead stop. In terms of my interpretation, Achilles is not about to mount the chariot in any one of these four pictures. In three of the pictures, Images L, M, and N, he is in fact turned away from the chariot, and he is evidently preoccupied in one way or another with the corpse of Hector. Likewise in the fourth picture, Image K, Achilles is preoccupied with the corpse of Hector.

7§86. And what about Images B1 and J? Are they parallel to Images O and P? In one detail, they are. In Images B1 and J, as we have seen, Achilles is shown with one foot on the platform of the chariot and one foot on the ground. To that extent, Images B1 and J are parallel to Images O and P. But once again the parallelism breaks down when we consider another essential detail. The chariot in

---

*The overall scene is strikingly similar to a scene represented on the Chest of Kypselos, no longer extant but seen and described by Pausanias 5.17.7–8: 'The next thing produced [in the representation] is the house of Amphiaraos, and the infant Amphilokhos is being carried by some old woman or other. In front of the house stands Eriphyle holding the necklace, and near her are her daughters Eurydike and Demonassa, and the boy Alkmaion, naked. [5.17.8] . . . Baton is driving the chariot of Amphiaraos, holding the reins in one hand and a spear in the other. Amphiaraos already has one foot on the chariot, and his sword is unsheathed; he is turned towards Eriphyle and is so carried away in his passion that he can scarcely refrain from her' (ἑξῆς δὲ Ἀμφιαράου τε ἡ οἰκία πεποίηται καὶ Ἀμφίλοχον φέρει νήπιον πρεσβῦτις ἥτις δή· πρὸ δὲ τῆς οἰκίας Ἐριφύλη τὸν ὅρμον ἔχουσα ἕστηκε, παρὰ δὲ αὐτὴν αἱ θυγατέρες Εὐρυδίκη καὶ Δημώνασσα, καὶ Ἀλκμαίων παῖς γυμνός. {5.17.8} . . . Βάτων δέ, ὃς ἡνιοχεῖ τῷ Ἀμφιαράῳ, τάς τε ἡνίας τῶν ἵππων καὶ τῇ χειρὶ ἔχει τῇ ἑτέρᾳ λόγχην. Ἀμφιαράῳ δὲ ὁ μὲν τῶν ποδῶν ἐπιβέβηκεν ἤδη τοῦ ἅρματος, τὸ ξίφος δὲ ἔχει γυμνὸν καὶ ἐς τὴν Ἐριφύλην ἐστὶν ἐπεστραμμένος ἐξαγόμενός τε ὑπὸ τοῦ θυμοῦ, <ὡς μόλις> ἐκείνης ἂν ἀποσχέσθαι).

O. Scene from the "Amphiaraos Vase," found at Cerveteri (once Berlin F 1655, now lost)

P. Bronze sheet no. M78 (Olympia Archaeological Museum)

Images B1 and J is speeding ahead, whereas the chariot in Images O and P is standing still. And it makes good sense that the chariot in Images O and P is not moving. We would expect a departing hero to mount his chariot while it is still standing and before it speeds off. By contrast, the chariot is speeding ahead in Images B1 and J. And why would Achilles be stepping into a speeding chariot at the same moment when Iris makes her appearance in order to stop the dragging of the corpse of Hector? If Achilles were only now stepping into the speeding chariot, he would not yet have started to drag the corpse of Hector.

7§87. So in terms of the narrative about the dragging of Hector's corpse, it makes sense for Achilles to be stepping out of his speeding chariot, not stepping into it, at the moment of reacting to the arrival of the goddess Iris. By contrast, in terms of narratives about departing heroes, it makes sense for the hero to be stepping into a chariot that is still standing and not yet rushing ahead at full speed. So the same pose that shows one foot on the chariot platform and one foot on the ground means two different things in two different narratives: in narratives about the dragging of Hector's corpse, Achilles at the moment of this pose is stepping out of his chariot, while in narratives about the departures, the departing hero is stepping into his chariot.

7§88. The use of the same pose for freezing a moment in two or more different narratives is a common occurrence in the visual art of vase painting. My favorite example is another vase painting that shows a scene that is by now becoming quite familiar for us. In this painting, we are about to see once again the frozen motion picture of a homunculus running in full armor while he is levitating over a shining white tumulus, which is his tomb. In Images A1, B1, D, E, F, G, H, I, L, M, and N we had seen the spirit of Patroklos pictured in such a pose. But that same pose, used in the narrative about the dragging of Hector's corpse by Achilles, can be used in an altogether different narrative. I have in mind the scene that is narrated in Image Q.

7§89. On the shoulder of this hydria, we see the image of two racing chariot teams taking a left turn. But I focus here on the image painted on the body of this vase, where we see a picture highlighting a famous scene in myth: it is the moment when the Trojan princess Polyxena is about to be slaughtered after the capture of Troy by the Achaeans. An epic version of this myth, in which the human sacrifice of Polyxena takes place at the tomb of Achilles, is attested in the epic Cycle (plot summary by Proclus of the *Iliou Persis* by Arctinus of Miletus p. 108 lines 5–8).* We find a comparable version of this myth here in Image Q, where we see the figure of Polyxena being led by her executioners toward the tomb of Achilles; also, we see here the figure of a homunculus in full armor run-

---

* An English-language translation of the entire ancient plot summary of the *Iliou Persis* in available in the online Sourcebook (chs.harvard.edu).

Q. Hydria, painting on the body of the vase (Antikensammlung Berlin, F1902)

ning at full speed in thin air while levitating over this tomb, which is pictured as a shining white tumulus. The homunculus is the angry spirit of the dead hero. And the dead hero here is not Patroklos. He is Achilles himself.

7§90. So the pose of such a running homunculus as it levitates in full armor over a shining white tumulus can signal different narratives in different pictures. In Image Q, this pose signals a narrative about the slaughtering of Polyxena as an act meant to assuage the angry spirit of Achilles, who is already dead but still very angry about his own death. In Images A1, B1, D, E, F, G, H, I, L, M, and N, by contrast, this same pose signals the dragging of Hector's corpse by Achilles, who is still very much alive here and already very angry about the death of his other self, Patroklos. In Image Q, the pose of the homunculus signals a story that has a negative outcome, since the cruel act of executing the princess will not be stopped: in the end, the executioners of Polyxena will not obey the moral imperative of showing pity. In Images A1, B1, D, E, F, G, H, I, L, M, and N, by contrast, the same pose signals a story that does have a positive outcome, since the cruel act of dragging Hector's corpse will in fact be stopped: in the end, Achilles will obey the moral imperative of showing pity.

7§91. Similarly, the pose of a hero with one foot on the platform of a chariot and one foot on the ground can signal different narratives in different pictures. When we see the chariot standing still, as in Image Q, the hero is stepping into his vehicle as he departs for war while he bids farewell to those who are near and dear to him. When the chariot is speeding along, however, as in Images B1 and J, I argue that the hero is stepping out of his vehicle.

7§92. In terms of my argument, what happens after Achilles steps out of his speeding chariot in Images B1 and J is obvious: he runs alongside his vehicle. That is what we see happening in Images A1, C, E, F, G, H, and I. And Achilles keeps on running until his momentum is spent and he finally stops. That is what we see has happened in Images K, L, M, and N. By this time, now that his momentum is spent, Achilles can finally bring himself to show pity for the hero whose corpse he has been dragging around the tumulus of Patroklos.

7§93. We can conclude, then, that the pictures we have seen in Images A1, B1, C, D, E, F, G, H, I, J, K, L, M, and N are telling a consistent story about the furious retaliation of the hero Achilles in response to the killing of Patroklos by Hector. And this story is comparable with the corresponding story about the retaliation as told in the *Iliad*. What is most similar about these two stories is the ultimate outcome: the fury of Achilles will be assuaged, and he will ultimately show pity. But there are significant differences in detail, and I have focused on one difference in particular:

> When Achilles is dragging the corpse of Hector in the *Iliad,* he is driving his own chariot. In the pictures we have seen, by contrast, Achilles leaps out of his speeding chariot and then runs alongside it while his charioteer drives on, continuing to drag the corpse.

The question remains, why is Achilles doing this, and how does his action lead to his ultimate change of heart?

Hour 7a. Myth and Ritual in Pictures of Chariot Scenes Involving Achilles

7A§1. According to an alternative interpretation of Images B1 and J, as I already noted, Achilles is stepping into his speeding chariot, not stepping out of it. But how, then, could we imagine the dragging of Hector's corpse? We would be forced to say that Achilles, after getting into his chariot, will be riding along with his charioteer as the dragging of the corpse gets under way. But the images we have seen show that Achilles is never left standing on the platform of his chariot during the dragging of Hector's corpse. Rather, as we have seen in Images A1, C, E, F, G, H, and I, Achilles is consistently running alongside the speeding chariot. And, as I will show, the act of dragging the corpse and the act of running alongside the speeding chariot are two details that are integrally related to each other in the visual narrative. As we are about to see, one detail belongs to the world of myth, while the other detail belongs to the world of ritual.

7A§2. Only in the *Iliad* is Achilles seen standing on the platform of his chariot during the dragging of Hector's corpse. And that is because this epic pictures Achilles himself as the chariot driver, not as a chariot rider. It happens in *Iliad* XXIV (14–18), where we see Achilles in the act of dragging the corpse of Hector behind his speeding chariot: he is said to be driving his chariot three times around the tomb of Patroklos, and the word referring to the tomb here is *sēma* (XXIV 16).

7A§3. As we have already noted, the dragging of the corpse of Hector is treated as an act of utter cruelty in the narrative of the Homeric *Iliad,* and this cruelty will lead to a call for pity from the Olympian gods themselves as they deliberate in the course of their divine council at the beginning of *Iliad* XXIV. What we have not yet noted, however, is that the actual driving of the chariot around the *sēma* of Patroklos is a vital aspect of a recognizable athletic event. That athletic event is chariot racing.

7A§4. I have already noted a climactic moment in such an athletic event: it is the making of a left turn around a turning point. We have seen this moment described in the narrative about the Funeral Games for Patroklos in *Iliad* XXIII. And we have also seen that the turning point in this narrative becomes equated ultimately with the tomb of Patroklos: the key to this ultimate equation is the *sēma* or 'sign' given by Nestor (XXIII 326) about a turning point that may or may not be the same thing as the *sēma* or 'tomb' of an unknown hero (XXIII 331). At the time of Nestor's speaking, the equation of the turning point with the tomb is still an uncertainty—and the identity of the hero is still an unknown. By the time the chariot race is over, however, this equation has become a reality. That is why, by the time Achilles himself is driving his chariot around the *sēma* of Patroklos (XXIV 16), the equation of this word *sēma* with the tomb of Patroklos is already taken for granted.

7A§5. In Images A1, B1, C, D, E, F, G, and H as well, we see an equation of the tomb of Patroklos with a turning point for the speeding chariot of Achilles. As we have seen in most of these images, the horses drawing the chariot of Achilles are just now at the point of making a left turn around the tomb of Patroklos; and this tomb, painted shining white, is shown as a turning point for the counterclockwise course of the speeding chariot team (only in Image H is there is a clockwise right turn instead of a counterclockwise left turn).

7A§6. To be contrasted is the implicit equation we see in the two verses of *Iliad* XXIII (326 and 331) concerning the *sēma* or 'sign' (XXIII 326) given by the hero Nestor to his son, the hero Antilokhos, about a landmark that may or may not have been the *sēma* or 'tomb' (XXIII 326) of an unnamed cult hero. This landmark was to be used as a turning point in the course of the chariot race that became the culminating athletic event of the Funeral Games for Patroklos in *Iliad* XXIII. But this landmark was ambivalent. In the words of Nestor, it was either a *sēma*, 'tomb', (XXIII 331) of an unnamed hero of the ancestral past or it was once upon a time a turning point, a *nussa* (XXIII 332), used for chariot races that must have taken place in that ancestral past. So the equation of a hero's tomb with a turning point for a chariot was only implicit here in Homeric poetry, whereas it is explicit in Images A1, B1, C, D, E, F, G, and H.

7A§7. The implicitness of such an equation in Homeric poetry extends even further. In the actual narrative about the chariot race held in honor of Patroklos in *Iliad* XXIII, the moment when the competitors in the race have to make their turns around the turning point is never even shown. After the initial mention of the turning point by Nestor in his words of instruction to his son, there is no further mention of it ever again in *Iliad* XXIII. And there is no need for any further mention, since, as we have already seen, Antilokhos will not interpret literally the visual cue or *sēma*, 'sign' (XXIII 326), that had been given to him by his father about the most successful way to turn left around a turning point. As we also saw, Antilokhos will make his move not at the turning point but at a narrow pass, where he impulsively decides to overtake the chariot of Menelaos that he sees racing ahead of him (XXIII 417–437).

7A§8. That said, I can now highlight a major difference between the narrative about the dragging of Hector's corpse in the verbal art of the Homeric *Iliad* and the corresponding narratives in the visual art of Images A1, B1, C, E, F, G, H, I, J, K, L, M, and N. The difference is this: whereas the chariot that is dragging Hector's corpse is driven by Achilles himself in the verbal narrative of the *Iliad* (XXII 395–405, XXIV 14–22), the corresponding chariot in the visual narratives of Images A1, B1, C, E, F, G, H, I, J, K, L, M, and N is being driven by a figure wearing the generic full-length gown of a charioteer.

7A§9. On the François Vase, produced by the painter Kleitias and the potter

Ergotimos around 570 BCE (*ABV* 76 no. 1), we see a picture of the chariot race held at the Funeral Games for Patroklos. The narrative in this picture shows significant differences from the corresponding narrative in *Iliad* XXIII:

- The five competing heroes in the visual narrative of the François Vase are driving four-horse chariots, while the five competing heroes in the verbal narrative of *Iliad* XXIII are driving two-horse chariots.
- The lettering painted over the competing chariot teams in the visual narrative of the François Vase labels the chariot drivers as the heroes Hippothoon, Damasippos, Diomedes, Automedon, and Odysseus (spelled ΟΛΤΤΕΤΣ). The ascending order in which I list these heroes here corresponds to the order in which their chariot teams are pictured from left to right as they race toward the finish line that is situated at the extreme right, which is where Achilles in his capacity as the marshal presiding over the race is waiting for the finish.* As for the chariot race in the verbal narrative of *Iliad* XXIII, the competing heroes are Eumelos, Meriones, Menelaos, Antilokhos, and Diomedes. Again, the ascending order in which I list these heroes here corresponds to the order in which their chariot teams cross the finish line, with Meriones in last place and with Diomedes in first place.†

7A§10. What the two different narratives of the François Vase and of *Iliad* XXIII have in common, however, is more important for now: in both the visual and the verbal narratives of the chariot race held in honor of Patroklos, the heroes are driving their own chariots. Moreover, the picture of the chariot race as painted on the François Vase shows clearly that the competing heroes are wearing the generic full-length gown of a charioteer, not the armor of a warrior.

7A§11. So the full-length gown of the charioteer in the visual narrative of the François Vase is a clear sign that the event being narrated, the chariot race in honor of Patroklos, is an athletic event. So also in the visual narratives of the pictures we have just surveyed, we see the charioteer wearing the same kind of full-length gown, most prominently in Images C, D, G, I, J, K, L, M, and N; in Image B2 as well, the two drivers of the speeding chariots are wearing the generic full-length gown of a charioteer. So though it is true that in other pictures,

---

* On the significance of the order in which the competing chariot teams in the picture painted on the François Vase are reaching the finish line, see Lowenstam 2008:24.

† On the significance of the order in which the competing chariot teams in *Iliad* XXIII reach the finish line, see the in-depth analysis of Frame 2009:131–172.

including B1, the charioteer simply wears the armor of a warrior, the fact remains that the charioteers we see in pictures that tell about the dragging of the corpse of Hector do not necessarily wear the armor of a warrior. This fact squares with what I am arguing, that the event we see being represented in all the pictures showing the dragging of the corpse of Hector is really an athletic event.

7A§12. In pursuing this argument, I now highlight an essential detail that we see in Images B1, C, E, F, G, H, I, and J showing the dragging of the corpse of Hector: the speeding chariot that drags the corpse is circling around the tomb of Patroklos in these images, just as the chariot of Achilles is circling around the same tomb in *Iliad* XXIV (13–18). This detail, as we find it in the visual narratives and also in the verbal narrative, indicates that an athletic event is being represented.

7A§13. Granted, in the case of the verbal narrative in *Iliad* XXIV (13–18), our first impression is that there is nothing athletic about the cruel act of dragging the corpse of Hector behind the speeding chariot that circles around the tomb of Patroklos. But, as I have just argued, the circling of this tomb by the speeding chariot is in fact a primary characteristic of a chariot race. When Nestor gives his advice in *Iliad* XXIII (326–343) about the best way to circle around a turning point in a chariot race, we have seen that this turning point is ultimately to be understood as the tomb of the hero Patroklos. Also, as I noted earlier, we know from historical evidence that the tomb of a hero could in fact be used as the turning point of a chariot race: in the athletic program of the Olympics, for example, the point where the racing chariot teams took their left turns in chariot races could be conceptualized as the tomb of a hero.*

7A§14. In the course of arguing that the act of driving a chariot team around the tomb of Patroklos in *Iliad* XXIV (13–18) as also in Images B1, C, E, F, G, H, I, and J is an athletic event, I have to emphasize that such an event is in both cases being polluted by the cruel behavior of Achilles, who drags behind his racing chariot the corpse of Hector. Such a pollution, as caused here by the hero Achilles, is typical of aetiologies linked with athletic events.

7A§15. When I say aetiology here, I mean *a myth that motivates an institutional reality, especially a ritual.*† In the logic of aetiologies, a ritual practice can be polluted by a hero in myth, and then this pollution will need to be eternally

---

* See again *GM* 215–216, with reference to Pausanias 6.20.15–19 and with further comments.
† *BA* 279 = 16§22.

purified by succeeding generations of ordinary humans who participate in that same seasonally recurring ritual practice.* Typical of such ritual practices are athletic events held at seasonally recurring festivals such as the Olympics. I cite as my prime example a myth about the victory of the hero Pelops in a four-horse chariot race held at the prototypical site of the Olympics. This myth is an aetiology for the athletic event of four-horse chariot racing at the Olympics, as we see from the artful retelling in Pindar's *Olympian* 1.†

7A§16. From another retelling of this aetiological myth, we learn that the basic motivation for the athletic event of the four-horse chariot race at the Olympics was the need to purify the pollution caused by the death of the hero Oinomaos while he was competing in his prototypical four-horse chariot race with the hero Pelops (Phlegon of Tralles *FGH* 257 F 1 lines 8–9).

7A§17. In this case, the myth shows that the athletic event of four-horse chariot racing, viewed as a seasonally recurring ritual practice that was destined to last forever, was needed as an eternal compensation in order to purify a prototypical pollution: as we learn from yet another retelling of the myth, the hero Pelops himself had caused, wittingly or unwittingly, the death of Oinomaos in the course of their chariot race with each other (Apollodorus *Epitome* 2.7).‡

7A§18. So far, I have argued that the circling of the tomb of Patroklos by the chariot team in Images A1, C, E, F, G, H, and I is an athletic event, just as the circling of this tomb by Achilles driving his chariot in *Iliad* XXIV (13–18) is an athletic event. And I have also argued that both of these athletic events are polluted by the cruel behavior of Achilles in dragging the corpse of Hector behind his chariot. But now I must emphasize that these two athletic events are not the same: whereas Achilles himself is driving his chariot in the verbal narrative of *Iliad* XXIV, he is definitely not driving it in the visual narrative of Images A1, C, E, F, G, H, and I. As we have seen in these images, Achilles here is running alongside his chariot, having stepped out of his speeding vehicle, and it is a charioteer who is driving it.

Hour 7b. Apobatic Chariot Racing

7B§1. I have reached the point where I can now describe a different kind of chariot race, featuring not one but two athletes. Just as chariot drivers competed

---

* *PH* 117–135 = 4§§2–26.
† *PH* 127–128 = 4§§15–16.
‡ *PH* 199 = 4§6n15.

with each other in the kind of chariot race that is narrated in *Iliad* XXIII, so also chariot riders competed with each other in a different kind of chariot race, aspects of which are pictured in Images A1, C, E, F, G, H, and I. As we know from ancient sources, the climactic event in this different kind of chariot race is the critical moment when the chariot rider, wearing a helmet and carrying a shield, suddenly leaps out of his speeding chariot and "hits the ground running" in competition with other chariot riders. Such competing chariot riders were known in the ancient world as *apobatai,* meaning 'those who step off'.* In Athens, the word *apobatai* referred to athletes who competed in this special kind of chariot race, and the competition of these *apobatai* was an integral part of the ritualized athletic program of a seasonally recurring Athenian festival known as the Panathenaia, celebrated every year in the late summer.† After 566 BCE, a large-scale version of this festival started operating in the late summer of every fourth year, matching the four-year cycle of the older festival of the Olympics, but the smaller-scale version of the Panathenaia continued to be celebrated in the late summer of the other three years. Whereas the large-scale version of the Panathenaia is known as the Great Panathenaia, which became a rival of the Olympics in the sixth century BCE, the smaller-scale and far older version of the festival is known as the Lesser Panathenaia. As we will see later, the competition of the *apobatai* took place at both the Great and the Lesser Panathenaia. From here on, I will refer to the athletic event of the *apobatai* at the Panathenaia simply in terms of *apobatic chariot racing.*

7B§2. As we know from evidence that I will now examine, the act of 'stepping off' in apobatic chariot racing at the Panathenaia was a spectacular sudden-death feat of athletic bravura, and here is the way I once described it:

> We can imagine all eyes focused on the action that leads up to that moment when the competing athlete, riding on the platform of a four-horse chariot driven at full gallop by his charioteer, suddenly leaps to the ground from the speeding chariot.‡

---

* Photius *Lexicon* α 2449, 2450; *Suda* α 3250; Harpocration s.v. ἀποβάτης, with reference to Theophrastus *Laws* F 15 (ed. Szegedy-Maszák 1981); [Eratosthenes] *Katasterismoi* 1.13; Dionysius of Halicarnassus *Roman Antiquities* 7.73.2–3. For an inventory of inscriptions commemorating the victories of *apobatai* in competitions at the Panathenaia, see Shear 2001:305n341.

† Stähler 1967:15. Also *GM* 94n50 and 220n54; further details in Nagy 2009b; still further details in *HPC* 170–177 = II§§90–111.

‡ *HPC* 172 = II§91.

Another aspect of this chariot racing, I should add, is that the *apobatai* could leap into as well as out of their speeding chariots.* The timing of a leap back into the chariot is not made clear by the ancient sources.

7B§3. Highlights of apobatic chariot racing are depicted in the relief sculptures of the Panathenaic Frieze of the Parthenon, created in the 440s BCE, where we see twenty-one apobatic chariot teams on display, with eleven chariots featured on the north side (North XI–XXIX) and ten on the south side (South XXV–XXXV); in each case, the chariot is shown with four horses, a driver, and an *apobatēs*, who is wearing a helmet and a shield.† The *apobatai* are shown in a variety of poses: *stepping into the chariot, riding in the chariot, stepping out of the chariot, and running alongside the chariot*; in two cases, the *apobatai* are evidently wearing a full set of armor.‡

7B§4. What makes the feat of leaping into or out of a speeding chariot so commandingly distinctive is that the *apobatēs* executes his leap in the mode of an epic warrior. While the fellow athlete who drives the chariot is standing on the right side of the vehicle and wearing the full-length gown of a charioteer, the *apobatēs* standing on the left side wears a helmet and carries a shield. I focus here on the critical moment when the apobatic athlete, holding on to the shield with his left hand, starts loosening the grip of his right hand on the rail of the speeding chariot and then suddenly leaps to the ground:

> Weighted down by all this armor, the *apobatēs* must hit the ground running as he lands on his feet in his high-speed leap from the platform of his chariot. If his run is not broken in a fall, he continues to run down the length of the racecourse in competition with the other running *apobatai*, who have made their own leaps from their own chariots.§

7B§5. I have already noted the fact that the *apobatai* could leap on as well as off the platform of their speeding chariots. Given this fact, I must now ask again

---

* *Etymologicum magnum* p. 124 lines 31–34, and Photius *Lexicon* α 2450.

† Shear 2001:304–305. In another project, I will analyze further the apobatic scenes represented on the Panathenaic Frieze. There I will criticize the conventional use of the term "Panathenaic Procession" with reference to the sum total of events being represented on the Panathenaic Frieze. In the case of the sections that show apobatic chariot teams, I will argue that the stop-motion pictures capture not only moments when these teams are participating in the Panathenaic Procession but also moments of actual engagement in apobatic chariot racing.

‡ Shear 2001:746.

§ *HPC* 172 = II§91. On images showing the *apobatēs* holding on to the chariot rail with his right hand: Shear 2001:303, 305.

the question I had asked earlier about Images B1 and J: is Achilles leaping into or out of the speeding chariot in these two pictures? On the basis of further evidence that I am now about to present, I can reaffirm the answer I gave then: Achilles is leaping out of his chariot.

7B§6. I start this part of my argumentation by returning to Images C, E, F, G, H, and I, where we saw what happens after Achilles leaps out of his speeding chariot: now he runs alongside this vehicle, drawn by a team of four galloping horses driven by the charioteer around the tomb of Patroklos (counterclockwise in Images C, E, F, G, and I, clockwise in Image H). And while Achilles is running alongside the speeding chariot, the corpse of Hector is being dragged behind it. Achilles here is running like an athlete in the athletic event of the *apobatai*. And, except for the fact that he is polluting this athletic event by dragging the corpse of Hector, the hero is going through the motions of performing the athletic feat of an *apobatēs*. Similarly, except for the fact that Achilles is dragging the corpse of Hector in *Iliad* XXIV (13–18), he is going through the motions of performing the athletic feat of a charioteer.

7B§7. Such a pollution, as I argued in Hour 7a, is in both these cases an aspect of an aetiological myth that is linked with the rituals of athletics. In the logic of aetiologies concerning athletics, as I also argued in Hour 7a, the ritual practice of a given athletic event can be polluted by a hero in myth, and then this pollution will need to be eternally purified by succeeding generations of ordinary humans who participate in that same seasonally recurring athletic event.

7B§8. Next I focus on the sheer spectacle of seeing an *apobatēs* step off and then run alongside his speeding chariot at the seasonally recurring festival of the Panathenaia in Athens. We find an eyewitness description of this spectacle in a work that may or may not have been composed by Demosthenes; in any case, the work is contemporaneous with Demosthenes, dated to the fourth century BCE ("pseudo-" Demosthenes 61.22–29). The speaker in this passage refers to the athletic event of the *apobatai* as an *agōn*, 'competition', that is highlighted by the act of *apobainein*, 'stepping down' (τοῦ δ' ἀποβαίνειν . . . ἐπὶ τοῦτον τὸν ἀγῶν[α] 61.23). This athletic event of 'stepping down' from a speeding chariot is singled out as the most similar, among all *agōnismata*, 'forms of competition', to the experiences of warriors in the life-and-death struggles of combat warfare (61.24). As a spectacle, the event of the *apobatai* is described as matching most closely the grandeur of the gods themselves (61.24–25), and thus it is deserving of the greatest of all *āthla*, 'prizes won in contests' (μεγίστων δ' ἄθλων ἠξιωμένον 61.25). The speaker views this kind of competition as the closest thing not only to combat warfare in general but also, in particular, to the scenes of heroic combat as narrated in Homeric poetry: as the speaker says explicitly, 'one could adduce, as the greatest proof, the poetry of Homer' (τεκμήριον δὲ μέγιστον ἄν τις ποιήσαιτο τὴν Ὁμήρου ποίησιν 61.25). That is why, the speaker goes on to say, only the greatest cities of the Hellenic world, such as Athens, preserve the tradition of such *agōnes*, 'competitions' (61.25–26).

7B§9. The speaker then goes on to tell about a spectacular feat once performed by the athlete he is praising ("pseudo-" Demosthenes 61.27–29). Though it is difficult to reconstruct the details of this compressed narration, it appears that our athlete, having leapt from his speeding chariot and running with all his might, was almost run over from behind and trampled to death by horses drawing the chariot of a rival team that was heading full speed toward him. We are reminded of the scene in Image E where an armed figure is getting trampled; and Image H shows a similar scene in the making.

7B§10. I now highlight the critical moment in the narration of the speaker when he in turn highlights the critical moment in the apobatic competition that he is narrating. Instead of losing his nerve, our athlete somehow managed to surpass the momentum of the oncoming chariot team that almost ran over him. That is what we are about to read at the critical moment of the speaker's narration about the apobatic chariot race held at the festival of the Panathenaia in Athens. I now quote the original Greek text of that climactic moment. In this quotation, we hear the speaker directly addressing as 'you' the young athlete whose glorious athletic feat is now being brought back to life in the present time of the narration:

HOUR 7B TEXT B

When the [chariot] teams had started and some had rushed ahead while some were being reined in, you, prevailing over both [the faster and the slower chariot teams], first one and then the other, [surpassing each chariot team] in a way that was most suited [for each situation], seized the victory, winning that envied garland in such a way that, even though it was glorious enough to win, it seemed even more glorious and dazzling that you came out of it safely. For when the chariot of your opponents was speeding toward [*enantion*] you and everyone thought that the momentum of their horses could not be resisted, you, aware that some [runners], even when no danger threatens, become overanxious for their own safety, not only did not lose your head or

your nerve, but by your courage overcame the impetus of their [char-
iot] team and by your speed [as a runner] passed even those contend-
ers [= the other runners] whose luck had not yet had any setbacks.*

"pseudo-" Demosthenes 61.28†

7B§11. This athletic event of the *apobatai* as held at the festival of the Panathenaia in Athens was in one way more conservative than the athletic event of the
chariot race as held at the Funeral Games for Patroklos in *Iliad* XXIII. In that
chariot race, there were only chariot drivers, without chariot riders accompanying them. By contrast, as we have seen, there was a chariot rider standing to the
left of each chariot driver on the platform of the speeding four-horse chariot in
the Panathenaic chariot race of the *apobatai,* and this chariot rider or *apobatēs*
would then leap out of the speeding chariot and back into it in death-defying
maneuvers. As we will now see, such maneuvers re-enacted the leaps executed
by chariot fighters who were fighting in chariot warfare.

Hour 7c. Apobatic Chariot Fighting

7C§1. The ritualized moments of apobatic leaps executed by athletes riding on
speeding chariots in chariot races held at the festival of the Panathenaia in Athens correspond to the mythologized moment of a similar leap executed by
Athena herself as goddess of Athens. As we read in ancient sources reporting on
the relevant local Athenian myth, Athena was the patroness and founder of the
Panathenaia along with her prototypical male protégé, the hero Erikhthonios.‡
These sources indicate that the goddess and the hero were not only the founders of the Panathenaia: they were also the founders of the seasonally recurring apobatic chariot races that took place at this festival of the Panathenaia.
Moreover, the goddess and the hero were even the first participants in the first

---

* As my translation shows, I disagree with those like Crowther 1991 who think that the athlete is the driver, not
the runner.

† τῶν γὰρ ζευγῶν ἀφεθέντων, καὶ τῶν μὲν προορμησάντων, τῶν δ' ὑφηνιοχουμένων, ἀμφοτέρων
περιγενόμενος ὡς ἑκατέρων προσῆκε, τὴν νίκην ἔλαβες, τοιούτου στεφάνου τυχὼν ἐφ' ᾧ, καίπερ καλοῦ
τοῦ νικᾶν ὄντος, κάλλιον ἐδόκει καὶ παραλογώτερον εἶναι τὸ σωθῆναι. φερομένου γὰρ ἐναντίου μέν σοι
τοῦ τῶν ἀντιπάλων ἅρματος, ἁπάντων δ' ἀνυπόστατον οἰομένων εἶναι τὴν τῶν ἵππων δύναμιν, ὁρῶν
αὐτῶν ἐνίους καὶ μηδενὸς δεινοῦ παρόντος ὑπερηγωνιακότας, οὐχ ὅπως ἐξεπλάγης ἢ κατεδειλίασας,
ἀλλὰ τῇ μὲν ἀνδρείᾳ καὶ τῆς τοῦ ζεύγους ὁρμῆς κρείττων ἐγένου, τῷ δὲ τάχει καὶ τοὺς διηυτυχηκότας
τῶν ἀνταγωνιστῶν παρῆλθες.

‡ See especially lines 1–3 of the Parian Marble (inscribed 264/3 BCE), *IG* XII 5 444 = *FGH* 239A, where the
foundation of the Panathenaia is dated at 1505/4 BCE. See also Harpocration s.v. Παναθήναια, drawing on Hel-
lanicus *FGH* 323a F 2 and Androtion *FGH* 324 F 2; scholia for Aelius Aristides 1.362; [Eratosthenes] *Katasterismoi* 1.13; Apollodorus *Library* 3.14.6; scholia for Plato *Parmenides* 127a.

apobatic chariot race ever held at the Panathenaia. At that chariot race, Erikhthonios drove the chariot while Athena made the first apobatic leap ever
made.*

7c§2. And this first leap of Athena was not only the leap of an apobatic athlete; it was also the leap of an apobatic fighter. According to local Athenian
mythmaking, the goddess Athena was the prototypical apobatic fighter: it happened on the day of her birth, when she emerged fully formed and fully armed
from the head of Zeus and immediately joined the other Olympians in their
primordial battle with the Giants.† This battle, envisioned as a primal scene of
apobatic chariot warfare, was spearheaded by the goddess herself as the ultimate apobatic chariot fighter.‡ In terms of Athenian mythmaking, the apobatic
leap of the goddess in the Battle of the Olympians and Giants was the same leap
that she made as the founder of the apobatic chariot race at the Panathenaia.
Her action as a prototypical apobatic fighter thus became a model for all apobatic athletes.

7c§3. The Athenian myth about Athena as an apobatic model brings into
sharper focus the wording of the speaker in the speech I analyzed a moment
ago concerning the athlete who won first prize in an apobatic race held at the
Panathenaia ("pseudo-" Demosthenes 61). The speaker, as we saw, described
the athletic competition of the *apobatai* as an event that matched most closely
the grandeur of the gods themselves (61.24–25); and he went on to say that victory at this event was deserving of the greatest of all *āthla,* 'prizes won in contests' (μεγίστων δ' ἄθλων ἠξιωμένον 61.25). In that same speech, moreover,
the speaker described the athletic competition of *apobatai* as the closest thing
not only to combat warfare in general but also, in particular, to the scenes
of heroic combat as narrated in Homeric poetry. I repeat here his wording:

---

* Of particular interest is a picture painted on a vase produced in Athens around 510 BCE (oinokhoe: Painter
of Oxford 224; National Museum, Copenhagen; Chr. VIII, 340; *ABV* 435, no. 1): it shows Athena as an apobatic
athlete riding on a chariot driven by a male figure who is evidently Erikhthonios. See Shear 2001:305, 529; at
pp. 46–48 she analyzes [Eratosthenes] *Katasterismoi* 1.13 lines 19–22, showing that the apobatic figure described
as wearing a helmet with three plumes must be Athena.

† The basic narrative about the "Gigantomachy" and the centralized role of Athena in this cosmic battle can
be found in the Hesiodic *Theogony* (verses 886–900, 924–926) and in the *Homeric Hymn* (28) *to Athena* (verses
4–6). More on Athena and the Gigantomachy in *HC* 559 = 4§217.

‡ Shear 2001:50–52 analyzes vase paintings that show a conflation of [1] scenes featuring Athena as an apobatic fighter in the Gigantomachy and [2] scenes featuring her as an apobatic athlete. In one painting (British
Museum, London, B676, = *ABV* 555 no. 425), a turning post for chariot racing is positioned in the middle of the
cosmic battle scene.

'one could adduce, as the greatest proof, the poetry of Homer' (τεκμήριον δὲ μέγιστον ἄν τις ποιήσαιτο τὴν Ὁμήρου ποίησιν 61.25).

7c§4. I have already noted how the ritualized moments of such apobatic leaps executed by athletes riding on speeding chariots in chariot races held at the festival of the Panathenaia in Athens correspond to the mythologized moment of a prototypical apobatic leap made by the goddess Athena. But these ritualized moments correspond also to mythologized moments of apobatic leaps made by heroes fighting in chariot warfare as narrated in Homeric poetry. As we will see from the passages I am about to quote from this poetry, such heroic leaps happen at climactic moments in the epic narrative.

7c§5. Before I show the relevant Homeric examples, I start with two other examples I found in forms of poetry that are not Homeric and not even epic. The first of these two examples is a particularly revealing passage I found in the songs of the fifth-century lyric poet Pindar. In this passage, we are about to see the hero Achilles himself in the act of leaping out of his chariot and running furiously toward his mortal enemy, the hero Memnon:

HOUR 7 TEXT C

And it [= the name of the lineage of the Aiakidai, especially the name of Achilles] leapt at the Ethiopians, now that Memnon would not be coming back safely [to his troops]. Heavy combat fell upon them [= the Ethiopians] in the person of Achilles hitting the ground as he stepped down [kata-bainein] from his chariot. That was when he killed [Memnon] the son of the luminous dawn-goddess, with the tip of his raging spear.

Pindar Nemean 6.48–53*

7c§6. The second example comes from a passage we have already considered in another context in this hour. This passage is about the mortal combat in chariot fighting between the heroes Hēraklēs and Kyknos as recounted in the Hesiodic *Shield of Herakles,* where we see that both these heroes leap to the ground from their chariots and then run at full speed toward each other (verses 370–371). I highlight again a detail: both combatants leap from their speeding chariots (θόρον, from the verb thrōiskein, 'leap, jump', verse 370). Meanwhile, the

---

*καὶ ἐς Αἰθίοπας | Μέμνονος οὐκ ἂν ἀπονοστή|σαντος ἔπαλτο· βαρὺ δέ σφιν | νεῖκος Ἀχιλεύς | ἔμπεσε χαμαὶ καταβαὶς ἀφ' ἁρμάτων, | φαεννᾶς υἱὸν εὖτ' ἐνάριξεν Ἀόος ἀκμᾷ | ἔγχεος ζακότοιο.

charioteers driving the chariots of the combatants drive on, keeping as close as possible to the combatants running on the ground (ἔμπλην, 'closely', verse 372).

7c§7. Now I proceed to the Homeric examples. I start with this climatic moment of chariot warfare:

HOUR 7 TEXT D

Hector leapt out of his chariot, armor and all, hitting the ground.

Iliad XI 211*

In other climactic moments as well, Hector is described as leaping out of his chariot:

HOUR 7 TEXT E

Straightaway he [= Hector] leapt out of his chariot, armor and all, hitting the ground.

Iliad V 494, VI 103, XII 81, XIII 749†

7c§8. In comparable wording, Homeric narrative describes four other warriors at moments when they too leap out of their chariots: Menelaos (*Iliad* III 29), Diomedes (IV 419), Sarpedon (XVI 426), and Patroklos (XVI 427). In the case of Menelaos (III 29), he leaps out of his chariot and hits the ground running as he rushes toward Paris to fight him in mortal combat on foot. Paris does not meet him head on but keeps backing up until he melts into a crowd of foot-soldiers who are massed behind him (III 30–37). In the case of Diomedes (IV 419), he leaps off his chariot as he hits the ground running, while his bronze breastplate makes a huge clanging sound upon impact as he rushes toward his enemies, who all shrink back to avoid encountering him in mortal combat on foot (IV 420–421). Similarly, in a scene I cited a moment ago (XII 81), Hector leaps out of his chariot and hits the ground running as he rushes to fight the enemy on foot, and, in this case, his fellow chariot fighters follow his lead and dismount from their chariots, since they too are now ready to fight on foot (XII 82–87). In the case of Sarpedon and Patroklos, we see these two heroes simultaneously leaping out of their chariots and hitting the ground running as they

---

* Ἕκτωρ δ' ἐξ ὀχέων σὺν τεύχεσιν ἆλτο χαμᾶζε.
† αὐτίκα δ' ἐξ ὀχέων σὺν τεύχεσιν ἆλτο χαμᾶζε.

rush toward each other to fight one-on-one in mortal combat on foot—a combat that is won here by Patroklos (XVI 428–507). Later on, when Patroklos is about to engage in mortal combat with Hector, he once again leaps out of his chariot:

Hour 7 Text F = Hour 6 Text C

Then Patroklos, from one side, leapt from his chariot, hitting the ground.

Iliad XVI 733*

What happens next, as we saw already in Hour 6, is that Patroklos picks up a rock and throws it at Kebriones, the charioteer of Hector, hitting Kebriones on the forehead and smashing his skull (*Iliad* XVI 734–754). And then, just as Patroklos had leapt out of his chariot, Hector too leaps out of his own chariot:

Hour 7 Text G = Hour 6 Text D

Then Hector, from the other side, leapt from his chariot, hitting the ground.

Iliad XVI 755†

Patroklos and Hector proceed to fight one-on-one in mortal combat on foot —a combat that is won here by Hector (XVI 756–863).

7C§9. Having reached the end of this collection of apobatic scenes in the *Iliad*, I highlight the fact that Hector is featured far more often than any other Homeric hero in the act of leaping out of his chariot to fight in mortal combat on foot.

Hour 7d. Distinctions between Chariot Fighting and Chariot Racing

7D§1. The moments of apobatic chariot fighting that we have just surveyed in the Homeric *Iliad* differ in one significant detail from corresponding moments of apobatic chariot racing at the festival of the Panathenaia in Athens. Whereas the chariots are drawn by two horses in epic scenes of apobatic chariot fighting,

---

* Πάτροκλος δ' ἑτέρωθεν ἀφ' ἵππων ἆλτο χαμᾶζε.
† Ἕκτωρ δ' αὖθ' ἑτέρωθεν ἀφ' ἵππων ἆλτο χαμᾶζε.

we know for a fact that the athletic event of apobatic chariot racing at the Pana-thenaia involved four-horse chariot teams.* I have already noted the evidence of the Panathenaic Frieze of the Parthenon, where we see twenty-one apobatic chariot teams on display, with eleven chariots featured on the north side (North XI–XXIX) and ten on the south side (South XXV–XXXV); in each case, the chariot is shown with four horses, a driver, and an *apobatēs*.†

7D§2. A two-horse chariot team, known in Latin as the *biga*, was more suit-able for chariot fighting in warfare than a four-horse chariot team, known as the *quadriga*, which was more suitable for chariot racing. There is evidence for the active use of the *biga* in warfare already in the second millennium BCE.‡ As for the *quadriga*, visual representations of its use in racing are poorly attested be-fore the seventh century BCE, but there are clear traces in the seventh; by the time we reach the early sixth century, the visual evidence is ample.§ According to Pausanias (5.8.7), the athletic event of racing in the *quadriga* at the festival of the Olympics was introduced already in the 25th Olympiad, that is, in the year 680 BCE.**

7D§3. In the text of Homeric poetry as we have it, there are two references to the concept of a racing chariot drawn by a team of four horses. The first such reference is in *Odyssey* xiii 81–83, where the speeding ship of the Phaeacians is being compared to a chariot team of four galloping horses. The second refer-ence is in *Iliad* XI 699–672: this passage is about the disputed possession of a chariot team of four prize-winning horses. Since the action in this second pas-sage takes place in the region of Elis, I subscribe to the argument that the Ho-meric narrative here is making a veiled reference to the competition in chariot racing at the seasonally recurring festival of the Olympics in Elis.††

7D§4. In sum, even though the older model of two-horse chariot racing is the dominant pattern in the narrative about the chariot race in *Iliad* XXIII, we have now seen that Homeric poetry also contains two direct references to the newer model of four-horse chariot racing.

7D§5. Moreover, Homeric poetry contains an indirect reference to four-horse apobatic chariot racing. This reference occurs in *Iliad* VIII 185, where it is said

---

* Shear 2001:48, 55, 301, 303, 309.
† Shear 2001:304–305.
‡ Scanlon 2004:67.
§ Scanlon 2004:67–69.
** Scanlon 2004:67 finds this dating plausible.
†† Scanlon 2004:63–89.

that Hector has a four-horse chariot team. This detail can be linked with a fact I have already noted, that Hector is prominently featured as an apobatic chariot fighter in the *Iliad*. So I am ready to argue that the narrative in *Iliad* VIII 185 is making a veiled reference to the competition in apobatic chariot racing at the festival of the Panathenaia in Athens, just as the narrative in *Iliad* XI 699–672 makes a veiled reference to the competition in non-apobatic chariot racing at the festival of the Olympics in Elis.

Hour 7e. Homeric Poetry at the Festival of the Panathenaia in Athens

7E§1. In arguing that Homeric poetry can refer, however indirectly, to apobatic chariot racing at the festival of the Panathenaia in Athens, I find it essential to keep in mind a basic fact: this same festival was the primary setting for the performance of Homeric poetry itself in the sixth century BCE and thereafter. Just as there were seasonally recurring competitions in apobatic chariot racing at the Panathenaia, there were also seasonally recurring competitions in performing the poetry of the Homeric *Iliad* and *Odyssey* at that same festival. By contrast with the yearly apobatic competition at the Panathenaia, however, the grand Homeric competition was held only at the Great Panathenaia, which was celebrated every four years.

7E§2. After its founding in 566 BCE, the quadrennial festival of the Great Panathenaia in Athens rivaled in scale even the Olympics, the official founding date of which was 776 BCE. A centerpiece of the Great Panathenaia was a grand *agōn*, 'competition', in *mousikē tekhnē*, 'the art of the Muses', the importance of which is signaled by Aristotle in the *Constitution of the Athenians* (60.1). Within the overall framework of this grand competition at the Great Panathenaia, there were separate categories of competitions in performing separate categories of *mousikē*. These categories included

(1) singing lyric songs to the accompaniment of a *kithara*, 'lyre';
(2) singing lyric songs to the accompaniment of an *aulos*, 'reed';
(3) playing the *kithara* in the format of an instrumental solo;
(4) playing the *aulos* in the format of an instrumental solo; and
(5) reciting epic poetry without instrumental accompaniment.

At the Great Panathenaia, the performers who competed with each other in reciting epic poetry were called *rhapsōidoi*, 'rhapsodes', and, as we read in ancient sources concerning Athens in the fifth and the fourth centuries BCE, the epic repertoire of these rhapsodes featured the Homeric *Iliad* and *Odyssey* (Plato *Ion* 530a–b, 533b–c; Isocrates *Panegyricus* 159; and Plutarch *Life of Pericles* 13.9–11).

7E§3. This rhapsodic tradition of performing Homeric poetry at the festival of the Great Panathenaia in Athens stemmed ultimately from an earlier Homeric tradition. As Douglas Frame has shown, this Homeric tradition evolved at the festival of the Panionia as celebrated in the eighth and seventh centuries BCE at a centralized sacred space called the Panionion, which was shared by twelve states belonging to a federation known as the Ionian Dodecapolis.*

7E§4. The Homeric tradition became the dominant epic repertoire of the festival of the Great Panathenaia in Athens during the last few decades of the sixth century BCE. The critical moment arrived when the government of Athens, at the initiative of Hipparkhos, son of Peisistratos, instituted a major reform of the performance traditions of epic poetry. This reform, known as the *Panathenaic Regulation,* resulted in the privileging of the Homeric *Iliad* and *Odyssey* over all other epics that had ever been performed before at the Panathenaia. On the basis of references in ancient sources (especially in "Plato" *Hipparkhos* 228b-c), it has been argued, plausibly, that the Panathenaic Regulation was started in the year 522 BCE, when Hipparkhos arranged for the first complete performance of the Homeric *Iliad* and *Odyssey* by *rhapsōidoi,* 'rhapsodes', competing at the festival of the Great Panathenaia in Athens.†

7E§5. But here we run into a problem. Given the fact that the performance of Homeric poetry became a main event at the quadrennial festival of the Great Panathenaia, and given the parallel fact that apobatic chariot racing was another main event at both the quadrennial Great Panathenaia and the annual Lesser Panathenaia, we might have expected to see direct references to apobatic chariot racing in Homeric poetry. But instead, we have seen in *Iliad* XXIII the narration of a non-apobatic chariot race that resembles most closely the chariot race held at the seasonally recurring festival of the Olympics. So why was this non-apobatic kind of chariot racing highlighted in Homeric poetry, and why was apobatic chariot racing correspondingly shaded over?

7E§6. Here is my explanation. The fact is, *apobatic chariot racing at the festival of the Panathenaia in Athens was a competition restricted to Athenian citi-*

---

* *HPC* 22 = I§38, following Frame 2009:551–620. The twelve states of the Ionian Dodecapolis, located on the mainland of Asia Minor and on outlying islands, were Miletus, Myous, Priene, Ephesus, Colophon, Lebedos, Teos, Klazomenai, Phocaea, Samos, Chios, and Erythrai (Herodotus 1.142.3).

† West 1999:382.

zens. This fact is indicated not only by ancient sources* but also by a mass of circumstantial evidence concerning the competition of the *apobatai*.† By contrast, non-apobatic chariot racing at the festival of the Olympics in Elis was a decidedly interpolitical athletic competition. By *interpolitical* I mean that the competitions at the Olympics were open to citizens of all Hellenic city-states, or *poleis*. Accordingly, the prestige of the non-apobatic chariot race at the Olympics was likewise *interpolitical,* whereas the prestige of the apobatic chariot race at the Panathenaia was *political,* by which I mean simply that the prestige of this athletic event was the function of a single city-state or *polis,* Athens.

7E§7. As we saw in Hour 7c above, the ritual of apobatic competition was linked with a charter myth about the genesis of the city of Athens itself at the moment when Athena as the goddess of the city took the first apobatic leap ever taken, in the primal battle of the Olympians and Giants. Here I must add what is said in another part of the charter myth: after leaping in full armor from her war chariot, Athena performed a weapon dance, likewise in full armor: this dance was known as the *purrhikhē*.‡ The meaning of this dance in full armor is something like 'act of fire': in the case of the myth that links this weapon dance with Athena specifically, this meaning conveys the cosmic energy released by the goddess in performing her primordial weapon dance, which literally ignites the field of battle.§ I highlight here this additional part of the relevant charter myth because there was a competition of dancing the weapon dance of the *purrhikhē* at the Panathenaia, and, like the event of the apobatic chariot race, *this competition was restricted to native Athenians.*** So both these events— not only the apobatic chariot race but also the competitive dancing of the *purrhikhē*—were markedly *political* and even *politicized* expressions of local pride at the festival of the Panathenaia in Athens.††

7E§8. Another sign of the distinctly civic nature of the apobatic chariot race

---

* Harpocration s.v. ἀποβάτης reporting the testimony of Theophrastus *Laws* F 15 (ed. Szegedy-Maszák 1981).

† Shear 2001:49, 53, 63, 67, 69, 231–232, 298, 300, 318, 323, 349, 515, 526, 562, 758.

‡ Plato *Laws* 7.796bc, *Cratylus* 406d–407a.

§ Among the ancient sources that refer to the moment of ignition is Aeschylus *Eumenides* 292–296.

** Shear 2001:42, 49, 67, 69, 231–232, 235, 515; like the apobatic chariot race, the *purrhikhē* was a yearly event at the Panathenaia: that is, the competitions were held at both the Great and the Lesser Panathenaia: see Shear p. 40.

†† Shear 2001:49 remarks: "to be an Athenian citizen meant not only dancing in the [*purrhikhē*] but also racing in the apobatic contest, while individuals from other cities watched them compete." Shear p. 515 suggests that competitions of apobatic chariot racing and dancing the *purrhikhē* were integrated into the Panathenaia as early as 566/5 BCE.

is the place where it was held: unlike the competition in non-apobatic chariot racing, which was held at the hippodrome,* the apobatic competition was held along the Panathenaic Way extending from the Dipylon Gate at the Kerameikos to the Eleusinion at the foot of the acropolis.†

7E§9. Standing in sharp contrast with the *political* (in the sense of *politicized*) orientation of the apobatic chariot race at the Panathenaia was the *interpolitical* or *Panhellenic* orientation of the non-apobatic chariot race at the Olympics. Even the elites of Athens recognized the Panhellenic prestige of chariot racing at the festival of the Olympics. As I noted earlier, the traditional founding date for that festival was 776 BCE, in comparison to the festival of the Great Panathenaia, the traditional founding date for which was 566 BCE. During most of the sixth century, which was the same era that marked the foundation of the Great Panathenaia, elite Athenian men were preoccupied with entering and winning the seasonally recurring competition in four-horse chariot racing at the Olympics. As we see from the formulation that I am about to quote, this athletic event outshone in prestige all other athletic events at all other festivals, including the apobatic chariot races at the Panathenaia. Here, then, is the formulation:

> [T]he Athenian elite had [. . .] enjoyed great success in the four-horse chariot event at Olympia, extending to a run of nine known quadriga victories in the twenty-six Olympiads between 592 and 492. Among these were the victory of the tyrant Peisistrat[o]s in 532, and Miltiades' victory in 560 with his dedication, the first by a chariot victor at Olympia [. . .]. Athens' achievement is exceptional, amounting to about 53% of the total of seventeen known quadriga victors, or about 35% of the absolute total of twenty-six at Olympia in a period spanning virtually the entire sixth century.‡

7E§10. Even if the athletic event of the chariot race held at the Olympics in Elis was more prestigious during the sixth century BCE than the corresponding athletic event of the apobatic chariot race held at the Panathenaia in Athens, there was another event at the Panathenaia that eventually outshone in Panhel-

---

* Shear 2001:289, 314, 315–322, 612, 614. On the location of the hippodrome in the deme Xypete, see Shear p. 671.

† Shear 2001:670, 679; also pp. 313, 314, 319, 610.

‡ Scanlon 2004:83.

lenic prestige even the chariot race at the Olympics. I highlight here once again the non-athletic event of rhapsodic competitions in the performance of the Homeric *Iliad* and *Odyssey* at the Great Panathenaia. In the last few decades of the sixth century, especially after 522 BCE, these two epics became the dominant poetic repertoire of rhapsodes competing at the Great Panathenaia, and, in the course of time, they eventually crowded out the other epics. Such other epics were more *epichoric*, that is, they were more *localized*, more Athenian, in their orientation. And, as I will now argue, the vase paintings that we were studying reflect the more localized traditions of such other epics. Conversely, the Homeric *Iliad* and *Odyssey* reflect epic traditions that were more *Panhellenic* and less likely to match the localized traditions of Athens.

Hour 7f. Signs of Alternative Epic Traditions as Reflected in Athenian Vase Paintings

7F§1. I start by reviewing the pictures we see painted on vases like the Münster Hydria (A1) and the Boston Hydria (B1). As I will argue, these pictures interact with localized epic traditions that were current in Athens during the sixth century BCE. Some of the details we find in these localized epic traditions tend to be excluded from the less localized and more "Panionian" epic traditions of Homeric poetry, which as I have been arguing became dominant in Athens only during the era that followed 522 BCE. For example, we will see that details having to do with the athletic tradition of apobatic chariot racing are excluded in Homeric poetry, even though other details having to do with the heroic tradition of apobatic chariot fighting remain included.

7F§2. In the main pictures painted on the Münster Hydria and the Boston Hydria, the representations of apobatic chariot racing feature Achilles himself as the prime apobatic athlete. In Image A1 he is shown in the act of running in full armor alongside his speeding chariot, while in Image B1 we see him in the act of leaping off his speeding chariot and "hitting the ground running."

7F§3. In these pictures we see also another apobatic figure: the homunculus in full armor who is running at full speed in thin air and levitating over a shining white tumulus, which is his tomb. He is Patroklos, and the frozen motion pictures that show him running in the air match the pictures of the apobatic figure of Achilles running on the ground.

7F§4. Finally, we see yet another apobatic figure in Image B1: this third figure is Hector himself, who as we have seen is prominently featured as an apobatic chariot fighter in the *Iliad*. The irony is that this hero's glory days of performing apobatic feats have already been terminated by Achilles, who can now take over as the ultimate apobatic model in this picture.

7F§5. Though we have seen several pictures showing Achilles as an *apobatēs,* I have all along been concentrating on only two of them, Image A1 of the Münster Hydria and Image B1 of the Boston Hydria. Until now, however, I have not yet specified the dating of these two vases—beyond saying that both of them were produced in Athens within the last few decades of the sixth century BCE. In keeping the dating so unspecific, I have been following the lead of art historians. About the Münster Hydria, Stähler says that it must have been produced toward the end of the sixth century BCE;* about the Boston Hydria, Vermeule estimates that the date of production was around 510 BCE.† This dating may be valid from a technical point of view, but the details that we find in the narratives of these paintings must stem from an earlier date. In terms of my argument, *the pictures that we see painted on these vases are interacting with an epic tradition that predates the establishment of the Panathenaic Regulation, which as we have seen can be dated at 522 BCE.*

7F§6. Such an epic tradition that predates the Panathenaic Regulation cannot be described as older than the Homeric tradition that became dominant after the establishment of the Regulation in 522 BCE. It is simply more local, more in tune with local Athenian traditions. Conversely, the Homeric tradition of epic that became dominant after 522 BCE cannot be described as newer than the more localized Athenian tradition. It is simply less localized and more "Panionian." As I said before, I agree with Frame that the Homeric tradition as we have it stems from Panionian epic traditions that evolved in the Ionian Dodecapolis during the eighth and seventh centuries BCE.‡

7F§7. In pursuing my argument, I return to a basic fact about the vase paintings we have studied: in Images A1 and B1 as also in Images C, E, F, G, H, I, and J, the narrative about the dragging of Hector's corpse behind the speeding chariot of Achilles is evidently different from the corresponding narrative of the Homeric *Iliad* in the version that has come down to us. But the dating for this version of the *Iliad,* as we have just seen, cannot be pushed forward in time any later than 522 BCE. That is why I think that the narratives of the pictures painted

* Stähler 1967:8.
† Vermeule 1965:35.
‡ *HPC* 22 = I§38, following Frame 2009:551–620.

on the Münster Hydria and the Boston Hydria date back to a time that is at least slightly earlier than 522 BCE.

7F§8. And here I must express my disagreement with those art historians who assume that the narratives we see pictured on these vases were simply derived from the text of Homeric poetry, and that whatever divergences we find between pictures and text can be explained as haphazard improvisations made by the painters.* I argue, by contrast, that the narratives of the pictures are just as systematic as the narratives of Homeric poetry. Where the narratives converge, the convergences are due, not to some kind of direct borrowing from the verbal medium of Homeric poetry into the visual medium of the paintings, but to an interaction between the visual medium of painting with the verbal medium of epic poetry in general. Each one of these two media is drawing on its own system of expression. Also, where the narratives diverge, the diverging patterns in the two media turn out to be just as systematic as the converging patterns. In terms of my approach, then, the patterns that we see in the visual art of the pictures need to be analyzed as *related to* rather than simply *derived from* the patterns we see at work in the verbal art of Homeric poetry.

7F§9. That said, I now proceed to reassess the main convergences and divergences between the narratives of the vase paintings we have studied and the corresponding narratives in the Homeric *Iliad*:

1a. The narratives of the vase paintings visualize athletic moments that could actually be seen in apobatic four-horse chariot races as organized in historical times at the festival of the Panathenaia in Athens. The hero Achilles himself is shown participating in these moments as a would-be athlete in his own right: just like an *apobatēs* competing in an apobatic chariot race at the Panathenaia, *he leaps out of his speeding chariot and runs alongside it while his charioteer drives the vehicle around a turning point,* which in this case is the tomb of Patroklos. At the same time, however, *this athletic moment is polluted by the dragging of the corpse of Hector behind the speeding chariot.* Some of the vase paintings, such as Image B2, show this polluting act explicitly, while others, such as Image A1, refer to it only implicitly by showing only the council of the gods, an epic event that leads to the termination of the cruelty be-

* An example of this point of view is the discussion by Friis Johansen 1967:138–153.

ing committed by Achilles; another vase painting, Image C, ostentatiously marginalizes this cruelty by situating the polluting act outside the margins that frame its narrative.

1b. The narrative of *Iliad* XXIII visualizes athletic moments in the non-apobatic two-horse chariot race as organized in heroic times by Achilles at the Funeral Games for Patroklos, and such athletic moments could actually be seen in non-apobatic four-horse chariot races as organized in historical times at non-Athenian festivals like the Olympics. The hero Achilles himself participates in the moments narrated in *Iliad* XXIII not as an athlete but as a marshal who presides over all the athletic events at the Funeral Games for Patroklos. Then, in the narration of *Iliad* XXIV, after the Funeral Games are already over, Achilles goes on to participate in an athletic moment as a would-be athlete in his own right: just like a charioteer in a non-apobatic chariot race, *he drives his speeding chariot around a turning point,* which in this case is once again the tomb of Patroklos, and he circles around the tomb three times. At the same time, however, *this athletic moment is polluted by the dragging of the corpse of Hector behind the speeding chariot.*

2a. The narratives of the vase paintings visualize the consequences of a decision ordained by a council of the gods (the council is actually shown in Image A2): the divine messenger Iris is being sent off on a single mission, to confront Achilles directly and to persuade him to stop the pollution by releasing the corpse of Hector to Priam.

2b. The narrative of *Iliad* XXIV likewise visualizes the consequences of a decision ordained by a council of the gods (the proceedings of the council are indicated in verses 31–76): Iris is sent on a double mission, first to Thetis and then to Priam, so that (1) Thetis may follow the Will of Zeus and persuade Achilles to stop the pollution by releasing the corpse of Hector to Priam (verses 75–76, 116) and (2) Priam may then successfully engage in a direct meeting with Achilles in order to bring about the release (verses 117–119).

7F§10. As I have argued in previous work, the divergent narratives that we see in the visual art of the paintings we find on vases like the Münster Hydria and the Boston Hydria are not at all incompatible with the verbal art of epic: they are incompatible only with the version of epic that we see in the Homeric

Iliad as it has come down to us; and I argue that a different and even non-Homeric version of the *Iliad* was interacting with the art of the painters who painted the relevant scenes that we have been studying.* This different version, in terms of my argument, would have matched more closely the narratives we see in the vase paintings.†

Hour 7g. *The Apobatic Moment*

7G§1. In the painting on the Boston Hydria, as I have already argued, we see Achilles at the precise moment when he cuts himself off from the act of dragging the corpse of Hector. This cut-off is synchronized with the precise moment when he leaps off, in the mode of an *apobatēs,* from the platform of the chariot that is dragging the corpse. The leap of Achilles here is the leap of the *apobatēs.* This leap, captured in the painting we see on the Boston Hydria, is what I call *the apobatic moment.*‡ As I will now argue, this moment can be understood only in the context of the poetic as well as the athletic program of the Panathenaia.

7G§2. A preliminary version of this argument has already been presented in my book *Homer the Preclassic.* I will now epitomize the relevant paragraphs, inviting the reader to review at the same time Images A1 and B1 as painted on the two vases that I have been calling the Münster Hydria and the Boston Hydria. This time, we will see these pictures in an inverted sequence of Image B1 followed by Image A1.

7G§3. As we are about to view these two pictures once again, this time back-to-back, I recall the formulation of Emily Vermeule concerning the "window effect" created by the picture frame in both pictures. She had made her original formulation with reference to Image B1 only, but it applies to Image A1 as well. I repeat here how she said it: "The technique gives the impression that the myth is circling around in another world, outside the window frame through which the spectator views it, in endless motion which is somehow always arrested at the same place whenever we return to the window."§

7G§4. I have this question to ask the viewer before the viewing begins again: as you are looking through the window, are you *looking in from the outside* or are you *looking out from the inside?* My own answer is that the viewer is on the

---

* *HPC* 170–177 = II§§90–111.
† *HPC* 176 = II§107.
‡ *HPC* 173 = II§91.
§ Vermeule 1965:45.

inside looking out and seeing a panorama of a heroic world out there, which is a world so immense that it will never ever be fully visible in the interiority of one's own small world of everyday experience. That heroic world is signaled, in both these pictures, by a *sēma*, which is not only a tomb for a hero but also a marker for the meaning of the hero. It is a point of concentration that directs the viewer into the world of heroes. We may take to heart what Nestor had told Antilokhos in *Iliad* XXIII: concentrate on the *sēma*. The medium of the tomb or *sēma* of the hero *is* the message of the sign or *sēma* of the hero.

7G§5. That said, I invite the reader to begin now the viewing of the back-to-back pictures at the end here. This viewing can be coordinated with the following five paragraphs:

1. By contrast with the narration of the *Iliad*, the divine course of action narrated by the painting on the Boston Hydria (Image B1) is explicitly direct: the goddess sent from on high will personally stop the dragging of the corpse of Hector by Achilles. The painting shows the goddess in flight, just as she reaches the moment of her landing on earth: her feet, gracefully poised as if in a dance, are about to touch ground at the center of the picture, and her delicate hands make a gesture of lament evoking pity as she looks toward the lamenting Priam and Hecuba, whose own hands make a parallel gesture of lament evoking pity as they look toward Achilles. The fierce gaze of the furious hero is at this precise moment redirected at Priam and Hecuba, who take their cue, as it were, from the gesture of lament shown by the goddess. The gaze of Achilles is thus directed away from the figure of Patroklos, who is shown hovering over a tomb that for now belongs only to him but will soon belong to Achilles as well. The charioteer of Achilles, seemingly oblivious to the intervention of the goddess, continues to drive the speeding chariot around the tomb, but, at the very same time, we find Achilles in the act of stepping off the platform. And he steps off at the precise moment when he redirects his fierce gaze from his own past and future agony to the present agony of Hector's lamenting father and mother. Here is the hero's *apobatic moment.**

2. The pity of Achilles for the parents of Hector in the painting of the Boston Hydria is achieved by way of a direct divine intervention that

* *HPC* 174 = II§97.

B1. Boston Hydria, painting on the body of the vase (Museum of Fine Arts, Boston, 63.473)

A1. Münster Hydria, painting on the body of the vase (Wilhelms-Universität, 565)

takes place while the dragging of the corpse is in progress. I had written in my earlier work: "Once Achilles steps off his furiously speeding chariot, the fury that fueled that speed must be left behind as he hits the ground running and keeps on running until that fury is spent."*

3. In the case of the main picture we see painted on the Boston Hydria (Image B1), the medium of the painting is evidently referring to a specific context, that is, to the festival of the Panathenaia in Athens, featuring the athletic event of the apobatic contest. The same can be said about the main picture we see painted on the Münster Hydria (Image A1). Here, too, Achilles is represented as an apobatic athlete. He is seen running alongside the speeding chariot, having already leapt off its platform.† By contrast with what we see in these paintings on the Münster Hydria (Image A1) and on the Boston Hydria (Image B1), the Homeric *Iliad* never shows Achilles as an apobatic athlete.

4. In the painting on the Münster Hydria, as also in the painting on the Boston Hydria, a goddess directly intervenes. Though the figure of this goddess is just barely visible on the fragmentary right side of the picture painted on the Münster Hydria, we can see that she is standing in the way of the onrushing chariot.‡ As for the picture painted on the Boston Hydria, it shows that the goddess has just descended from the heights above in order to make her intervention.

5. It has been argued that the main picture on the Münster Hydria represents the notional beginnings of a hero cult for Patroklos.§ I will reformulate this argument in Hour 8, arguing further that this hero cult was shared by Patroklos with Achilles, and that these two heroes presided as cult heroes over the athletic event of the *apobatai* at the festival of the Panathenaia.

---

* *HPC* 174 = II§98.
† *HPC* 175 = II§103.
‡ *HPC* 175 = II§104.
§ Stähler 1967, especially p. 32.

The Psychology of the Hero's Sign in the Homeric Iliad

The Meaning of Psūkhē

8§1. The key word for this hour is *psūkhē,* as used in the context of the key word for the previous hour, *sēma.* This word *psūkhē* can refer either to *the life of someone who is alive* or to *the disembodied conveyor of someone's identity after that someone dies.**

8§2. As we saw in Hour 7, the word *psūkhē* is written out as ΦΣΥΧΕ in a picture painted on an art object that I have been calling the Münster Hydria. I now add that the word *hydria* comes from the Greek word *hudriā,* which designates a vessel designed for holding and pouring hudōr or 'water'. This kind of vessel could be used for the pouring of water in rituals honoring ancestors or cult heroes, and the general term for such ritual pourings—of any liquid—is *libation.* When we reach Hour 17, we will consider in some detail the meaning of libations preformed in honor of ancestors and cult heroes. For now, however, it suffices for me to note that the performing of libations is relevant to the meaning of the word *psūkhē.* Also relevant is the fact that the hydria was a vessel used not only for pouring water but also for storing the bones of the dead: there is a particularly revealing mythological reference to this custom in "Dictys" FGH 49 F 7a (Tebtunis Papyrus 268): at lines 89–91, it is said that the bones of Achilles, together with those of Patroklos, were placed into a hydria and taken away for burial at Sigeion, a city situated on the Hellespont. This city was reputed to be the authentic site of the tomb of Achilles.†

8§3. The lettering that spells out *psūkhē,* as we saw in the picture painted on the Münster Hydria, is situated next to the figure of Patroklos hovering over the

---

* This formulation is based on my work in GM 85–121, where I offer an extensive analysis of the Homeric contexts of the word *psūkhē.*

† In HPC 142–211 = II §§32–213, I analyze in detail the historical background of the conflicting claims made by rival cities, especially Athens and Mytilene, concerning Sigeion as the tomb of Achilles.

sēma, or 'tomb', that is destined to be occupied not only by the body of Patroklos but also by the body of Achilles after he, too, is killed by Apollo. In Hour 7, I indicated the relevant passages where Homeric poetry makes explicit references to a single tomb that is destined to contain the two bodies together: *Iliad* XXIII 83–84, 91–92, 125–126, 245–248; *Odyssey* xxiv 80–84.

8§4. In Hour 7, I used the word 'spirit' in translating the word *psūkhē* as painted next to the figure of Patroklos in the picture of the Münster Hydria. But there is a deeper meaning of *psūkhē* in the context of this picture as a whole. After all, this picture could be called in Greek a *sēma,* just as the tomb of a hero could be called a *sēma.* And the same word *sēma* could refer not only to the tomb of a hero or to a picture of the hero but also to any sign of the hero, such as the lettering that identifies the picture painted on the Münster Hydria. That is what I mean when I say "a psychology of signs." The word *psūkhē* is a marker of such psychology.

8§5. There is "a psychology of signs" not only in the picture we see painted on the body of the Münster Hydria but also in the overall narrative of the Homeric *Iliad.* The use of the word *psūkhē* in the painting, with specific reference to the 'spirit' of the dead Patroklos, is comparable to the use of this same word in the epic.

The Psūkhē *of Patroklos in the* Iliad

8§6. I start with a scene in which the *psūkhē* of Patroklos appears to Achilles in his sleep:

HOUR 8 TEXT A

| $|_{58}$ The others went to their rest each to his own tent, $|_{59}$ but only the son of Peleus, by the shore of the resounding sea, $|_{60}$ only he amidst all his many Myrmidons lay grieving with deep groans $|_{61}$ in an open place on the beach where the waves came surging in, one after another. $|_{62}$ Here sleep took hold of him, releasing him from the cares in his heart. $|_{63}$ It was a sweet sleep that poured all over him, since his shining limbs had been worn down $|_{64}$ with chasing Hector round windy Ilion. $|_{65}$ Then came to him the spirit [*psūkhē*] of unhappy Patroklos, $|_{66}$ resembling in every way the man himself in size and good looks $|_{67}$ and voice. It [= the *psūkhē*] even wore the same clothes he used to wear over his skin. $|_{68}$ It [= the *psūkhē*] stood over his head and addressed to him

these words: |₆₉ "You sleep, Achilles. As for me, you have forgotten all about me |₇₀ you used to be not at all uncaring about me when I was alive, but now that I am dead you care for me no further. |₇₁ Bury me with all speed that I may pass through the gates of Hādēs. |₇₂ Keeping me away from there are the spirits [*psūkhai*], who are images [*eidōla*] of men who have ended their struggles; |₇₃ they [= the spirits] are not yet permitting me to join them beyond the river. |₇₄ So that is how it is, and that is how I am, directionless, at the entrance to the wide gates of the house of Hādēs. |₇₅ Give me now your hand while I weep, and I do weep because never again |₇₆ will I return from the house of Hādēs once you all do what you have to do, which is, to let me have the ritual of fire. |₇₇ And never again will you [= Achilles] and I be alive together as we sit around only in each other's company, separating ourselves from our dear comrades [*hetairoi*], while we keep on sharing, just the two of us, |₇₈ our thoughts with each other. My fate [*kēr*] has its hold on me, |₇₉ that hateful thing. Now it has opened its gaping jaws and swallowed me. It really always had its hold on me, ever since I was born. |₈₀ But you, Achilles, you who look just like the gods [*theoeike-los*], you too have a fate [*moira*] that has its hold on you. |₈₁ You too are fated to die beneath the walls of the noble Trojans. |₈₂ I will tell you one more thing, and I call on you to comply. |₈₃ Do not let my bones be laid to rest apart from your bones, Achilles, |₈₄ but together with them— the same way we were brought up together in your own home, |₈₅ back when I, still a boy, was brought from Opous by [my father] Menoitios. |₈₆ He brought me to your place because of a disastrous [*lugrē*] homi- cide. |₈₇ It happened on the day when I killed the son of Amphidamas. |₈₈ It was involuntary. I was feeling disconnected [*nēpios*].* I got angry during a game of dice. |₈₉ But then [your father] the charioteer Peleus received me in his home, |₉₀ and he raised me in a ritually correct way, naming me to be your attendant [*therapōn*]. |₉₁ So now let the same container enclose our bones for both of us. |₉₂ I mean, the two-handled golden amphora given to you by that lady, your mother."

Iliad XXIII 58–92†

* On the meaning of *nēpios* as 'disconnected', see the Core Vocabulary.

† |₅₈ οἱ μὲν κακκείοντες ἔβαν κλισίην δὲ ἕκαστος, |₅₉ Πηλεΐδης δ' ἐπὶ θινὶ πολυφλοίσβοιο θαλάσσης |₆₀ κεῖτο βαρὺ στενάχων πολέσιν μετὰ Μυρμιδόνεσσιν |₆₁ ἐν καθαρῷ, ὅθι κύματ' ἐπ' ἠιόνος κλύζεσκον· |₆₂ εὖτε τὸν ὕπνος ἔμαρπτε λύων μελεδήματα θυμοῦ |₆₃ νήδυμος ἀμφιχυθείς· μάλα γὰρ κάμε φαίδιμα

8§7. Here in Text A the sharing of one single tomb by Patroklos and Achilles in death is explicitly connected with something that they had shared in life: and that something is the experience of life itself. Here I highlight two of the verses spoken by Patroklos: 'Do not let my bones be laid to rest apart from your bones, Achilles, | but together with them—the same way we were brought up together in your own home' (XXIII 83–84). In these two verses that I have just quoted again from Text A, *the shared upbringing of these two heroes is being equated with a shared life that becomes a model for their shared death.* This shared life makes Patroklos the body-double of Achilles, that is, his other self, and such an identity is indicated here by the word *therapōn* (XXIII 90). As we saw in Hour 6, this word is the key to understanding the very idea of the body-double in Homeric poetry.

8§8. But Patroklos is not only the body-double of Achilles: as we will now see, he is also his spirit-double or "soulmate." Patroklos and Achilles share not only the same *sēma* but also the same *psūkhē*. That is, they share not only the same meaning but even the same psychic energy that leads to the same meaning. That is what is said by the *psūkhē* of Patroklos himself when he tells Achilles that the two of them must share the same tomb in death (XXIII 83–84), precisely because the two of them had been nurtured to go through life together on their own (XXIII 84), separating themselves from the rest of their comrades (XXIII 77) and sharing their thoughts only with each other (XXIII 77–78).

8§9. The idea of *sharing the same thoughts* is expressed here in Text A by the idiom *boulas bouleuein*, 'to plan plans' (βουλὰς ἑζόμενοι βουλεύσομεν XXIII 78). This idiom is appropriate for expressing the communication of thoughts between cult heroes and their worshippers, as we see in an Iliadic passage in which Hector and his advisors consult the thinking of Ilos, who is cult hero of

---

γυῖα |₆₄ Ἕκτορ' ἐπαΐσσων προτὶ Ἴλιον ἠνεμόεσσαν· |₆₅ ἦλθε δ' ἐπὶ ψυχὴ Πατροκλῆος δειλοῖο |₆₆ πάντ' αὐτῷ μέγεθός τε καὶ ὄμματα κάλ' εἴκυῖα |₆₇ καὶ φωνήν, καὶ τοῖα περὶ χροῒ εἵματα ἔστο· |₆₈ στῆ δ' ἄρ' ὑπὲρ κεφαλῆς καί μιν πρὸς μῦθον ἔειπεν· |₆₉ εὕδεις, αὐτὰρ ἐμεῖο λελασμένος ἔπλευ Ἀχιλλεῦ. |₇₀ οὐ μέν μευ ζώοντος ἀκήδεις, ἀλλὰ θανόντος· |₇₁ θάπτέ με ὅττι τάχιστα πύλας Ἀΐδαο περήσω. |₇₂ τῆλέ με εἴργουσι ψυχαὶ εἴδωλα καμόντων, |₇₃ οὐδέ μέ πω μίσγεσθαι ὑπὲρ ποταμοῖο ἐῶσιν, |₇₄ ἀλλ' αὕτως ἀλάλημαι ἀν' εὐρυπυλὲς Ἄϊδος δῶ. |₇₅ καί μοι δὸς τὴν χεῖρ'· ὀλοφύρομαι, οὐ γὰρ ἔτ' αὖτις |₇₆ νίσομαι ἐξ Ἀΐδαο, ἐπήν με πυρὸς λελάχητε. |₇₇ οὐ μὲν γὰρ ζωοί γε φίλων ἀπάνευθεν ἑταίρων |₇₈ βουλὰς ἑζόμενοι βουλεύσομεν, ἀλλ' ἐμὲ μὲν κὴρ |₇₉ ἀμφέχανε στυγερή, ἥ περ λάχε γιγνόμενόν περ· |₈₀ καὶ δὲ σοὶ αὐτῷ μοῖρα, θεοῖς ἐπιείκελ' Ἀχιλλεῦ, |₈₁ τείχει ὕπο Τρώων εὐηφενέων ἀπολέσθαι. |₈₂ ἄλλο δέ τοι ἐρέω καὶ ἐφήσομαι αἴ κε πίθηαι· |₈₃ μὴ ἐμὰ σῶν ἀπάνευθε τιθήμεναι ὀστέ' Ἀχιλλεῦ, |₈₄ ἀλλ' ὁμοῦ ὡς ἐτράφημεν ἐν ὑμετέροισι δόμοισιν, |₈₅ εὖτέ με τυτθὸν ἐόντα Μενοίτιος ἐξ Ὀπόεντος |₈₆ ἤγαγεν ὑμέτερον δ' ἀνδροκτασίης ὕπο λυγρῆς, |₈₇ ἤματι τῷ ὅτε παῖδα κατέκτανον Ἀμφιδάμαντος |₈₈ νήπιος οὐκ ἐθέλων ἀμφ' ἀστραγάλοισι χολωθείς· |₈₉ ἔνθά με δεξάμενος ἐν δώμασιν ἱππότα Πηλεὺς |₉₀ ἔτραφέ τ' ἐνδυκέως καὶ σὸν θεράποντ' ὀνόμηνεν· |₉₁ ὡς δὲ καὶ ὀστέα νῶϊν ὁμὴ σορὸς ἀμφικαλύπτοι |₉₂—χρύσεος ἀμφιφορεύς, τόν τοι πόρε πότνια μήτηρ.

the city of Ilion, that is, of Troy. The consultation happens at the *sēma,* or tomb, of this cult hero:

HOUR 8 TEXT B

Hector, accompanied by all his advisors, | is planning plans [*boulas bouleuei*] at the tomb [*sēma*] of godlike Ilos.*

Iliad X 414–415†

8§10. The use of the word *sēma* here is most suggestive: as we have seen in Hour 7, with reference to the instructions given by Nestor to Antilokhos, this word *sēma* in Homeric diction signals not only the *tomb* of a cult hero (as in XXIII 331) but also a *sign* (as in XXIII 326) that signals the transcendent meaning of that tomb to those who are qualified to understand the mystical language of hero cult. I will have more to say about this mystical language in Hour 15§10.

8§11. I argue, then, that the reference made in Text A to the psychic powers of Patroklos and Achilles as they share each other's thoughts in life (XXIII 77–78) extends to their psychic powers in death: once they are dead, they become cult heroes who will now share their thoughts not only with each other but also with those in the here and now who seek to make mental contact with these two heroes by concentrating on the *sēma* that is shared by them. This shared tomb, as a *sēma,* is the primary visual marker that communicates the shared meaning of Patroklos and Achilles as cult heroes.

The Psūkhē *of Patroklos in the Picture Painted on the Münster Hydria*

8§12. So far, I have been arguing that Patroklos and Achilles share not only the same *sēma* but also the same *psūkhē* in the verbal art of Homeric poetry. Now I extend the argument further: these two heroes share the same *sēma* and the same *psūkhē* also in the visual art of the Münster Hydria. On this vase, the painting of the letters ΦΣΥΧΕ that spell *psūkhē* next to the miniature figure of Patroklos as he levitates over the *sēma* he will share with Achilles applies not only to Patroklos but also to Achilles, whose pose of running at ground zero alongside his speeding chariot mirrors the pose of Patroklos running in thin air above the *sēma* that he will share with his "soulmate."

---

* Commentary in *BA* 145 = 8§8n2 and *PH* 293 = 10§22.

† Ἕκτωρ μὲν μετὰ τοῖσιν, ὅσοι βουληφόροι εἰσί, | βουλὰς βουλεύει θείου παρὰ σήματι Ἴλου.

Achilles and Patroklos as Cult Heroes of Apobatic Chariot Racing

8§13. As I argued in Hour 7, the picture painted on the Münster Hydria represents the heroes Achilles and Patroklos in the act of engaging in the ritual athletic event of the *apobatai*, 'those who step off', as it took place at the Athenian festival of the Panathenaia in the latter part of the sixth century BCE. And here I return to the relevant argument made by Klaus Stähler concerning the apobatic poses of both Achilles and Patroklos as depicted on the Münster Hydria: according to Stähler, *what is being pictured here is the beginning of the hero cult of Patroklos.** Now, in the light of evidence I have assembled from the verbal art of the *Iliad*, I propose to modify his argument: *what is being pictured is the beginning of the joint hero cult of Patroklos and Achilles.* And the ritualized actions of Achilles, as we see from the painting on the Münster Hydria and from other comparable paintings, show the way for the future observance of rituals of hero cult in honor not only of Patroklos but also of Achilles himself.†

8§14. So how are we to imagine these rituals of hero cult as shared by Achilles and Patroklos? I will now argue that these rituals can actually be equated with the athletic event of the *apobatai* as celebrated at the festival of the Panathenaia in Athens. In terms of my argument, the two heroes Achilles and Patroklos presided as cult heroes over this athletic event, which is a ritual of hero cult. And the death of Patroklos, which is the prototype for the death of Achilles himself, is part of the *aetiology* of this athletic event, of this ritual of hero cult. I repeat here my working definition of aetiology as I formulated it in Hour 7A§15 above: *an aetiology is a myth that motivates an institutional reality, especially a ritual.*‡

8§15. So the death of Patroklos is one part of the myth that becomes the aetiology for the apobatic chariot race at the Panathenaia. But there is another part of this myth that we need to keep in mind. This is the dragging of the corpse of Hector behind the speeding chariot of Achilles. In the logic of aetiologies, as I argued in Hour 7A§15 a ritual practice can be polluted by a hero in myth, and then this pollution will need to be eternally purified by succeeding generations of ordinary humans who participate in that same seasonally recurring ritual practice.§ Here, in the case of the apobatic chariot race at the festival of the

---

* Stähler 1967:32.
† *GM* 94n50 and 220n54, building on the argumentation of Stähler as cited in the previous note.
‡ *BA* 279 = 16§22.
§ *PH* 117–135 = 4§§2–26.

Panathenaia, the pollution in myth was the dragging of the corpse of Hector behind the speeding chariot of Achilles. A comparable example is the case of the non-apobatic chariot race at the festival of the Olympics, where the pollution in myth was the killing of Oinomaos in the course of his fatal chariot race with Pelops, who was the cause of this death (Apollodorus *Epitome* 2.7).*

8§16. I must stress once again, however, that Achilles is performing as an athlete even while he is polluting the prototypical athletic event in which he is participating. We saw this most clearly in the vase paintings where he is shown running furiously alongside a speeding chariot that is dragging the corpse of Hector. In these pictures, Achilles is polluting the athletic event of apobatic chariot racing, but he is still performing as an apobatic athlete. So when an athlete is making his own run alongside his own speeding chariot at the apobatic event of the Panathenaia, he is re-enacting the prototypical run of Achilles. That prototypical run in myth is an expression of the hero's fury, which can now translate into the competitive "killer instinct" of the athlete when he makes his own apobatic run.

8§17. I had said in my earlier work: "Once Achilles steps off his furiously speeding chariot, the fury that fueled that speed must be left behind as he hits the ground running and keeps on running until that fury is spent." † Just as the fury of Achilles fuels his run until that fury is spent, so also the athletic energy or "killer instinct" of the *apobatēs* keeps him running and running until his energy is finally spent just as he crosses the finish line.

An Athletic Event at Eleusis

8§18. In earlier work, I have studied other comparable examples of aetiologies for athletic events.‡ In Hour 8a below, I survey many of those aetiologies. For the moment, however, I focus on just one example, which is an aetiology for a seasonally recurring athletic event celebrated at Eleusis.

8§19. This event, known as the *Ballētus,* was a mock battle that was evidently the ritual kernel of a whole complex of events known as the Eleusinian Games.§ Here is how the athletic event is defined in an ancient dictionary attributed to Hesychius (this name is a figurehead for a vast lexicographical tradition stem-

---

* *PH* 199 = 4§6n15.
† *HPC* 174 = II§98.
‡ *PH* chapters 4 and 5.
§ *PH* 121 = 4§7n26. See also Nilsson 1906:414n4 and Pache 2004:76–77.

ming from the Library of Alexandria): '*Ballētus* is a festival in Athens, celebrated in honor of Dēmophōn son of Keleos'.* I have translated the preposition *epi* (ἐπί) here in combination with the name of Dēmophōn in the dative case as 'in honor of Dēmophōn'. But this translation is inadequate and needs to be revised. As I will show later in Hour 8a, it would be more accurate to word it this way: 'in compensation for [the death of] Dēmophōn'. As we will now see, this revised wording is compatible with the myth that serves as the aetiology for the athletic event of the *Ballētus*.

8§20. In the *Homeric Hymn to Demeter*, the athletic competition of the *Ballētus* is overtly described as an act of compensation, recurring at the right season into all eternity, and this competition is understood to be an eternal compensation for a primal pollution caused by human error. That pollution was the unintended death of an infant hero named Dēmophōn. The queen of Eleusis, mother of this infant hero, had unintentionally ruined the plan of the goddess Demeter to make Dēmophōn exempt from death. That moment happens when the queen interrupts Demeter in the sacred act of dipping the infant Dēmophōn into the fire of the household fireplace in order to galvanize this infant into a state of immortality (*Homeric Hymn to Demeter* 239–250). Here I quote the passage that tells about the immediate aftermath, when the goddess angrily condemns the error of the queen and announces that the infant hero Dēmophōn will now be subject to death, like all other mortals. As we are about to see, however, the dooming of the infant to death comes with a compensation:

Hour 8 Text C

|₂₅₉ I [= Demeter] swear by the implacable water of the Styx, the witness of oaths that gods make, as I say this: |₂₆₀ immortal and ageless for all days |₂₆₁ would I have made your dear [*philos*] little boy, and I would have given him honor [*tīmē*] that is unwilting [*a-phthi-tos*]. |₂₆₂ But now there is no way for him to avoid death and doom. |₂₆₃ Still, he will have an honor [*tīmē*] that is unwilting [*a-phthi-tos*], for all time, because on my knees |₂₆₄ he had once sat and slept in my arms. |₂₆₅ At the right season [*hōrā*], every year, |₂₆₆ the sons of the Eleusinians will have a war, a terrible battle among each other. |₂₆₇ They will do so for all days to come.

Homeric Hymn to Demeter 259–267†

---

* Βαλλητύς· ἑορτὴ Ἀθήνησιν, ἐπὶ Δημοφῶντι τῷ Κελεοῦ ἀγομένη.

† |₂₅₉ ἴστω γὰρ θεῶν ὅρκος ἀμείλικτον Στυγὸς ὕδωρ |₂₆₀ ἀθάνατόν κέν τοι καὶ ἀγήραον ἤματα πάντα

I highlight here at verse 265 the noun *hōrā* (plural *hōrai*), 'season, seasonality, the right time, the perfect time', as I defined it in Hour 1§§26–29 and analyzed it in Hour 1§49. As we see from the context that I just quoted here in the *Homeric Hymn to Demeter*, this noun *hōrā* marks *the seasonal recurrence of rituals honoring cult heroes*.

8§21. The death of the infant hero, as we learn from the text I just quoted, will be compensated by seasonally recurring rituals of athletic re-enactment, as expressed by the word *tīmē*, 'honor' (verse 263), which refers here to the honor conferred upon cult heroes in the rituals of hero cult. In this case, the rituals take the form of an athletic competition that overtly simulates warfare. And these rituals will have to recur seasonally, year after year, for a notional eternity. Such a seasonal recurrence is indicated, as we have just seen, by the word *hōrā* at verse 265 of the *Homeric Hymn to Demeter*. And now we see why the *tīmē*, 'honor', that the prototypical hero receives in compensation for his death is described as *a-phthi-tos*, 'unwilting' (verse 263), that is, lasting forever. Another example of such a seasonally recurring ritual is a mock battle of boys competing within a sacralized space known as the *Platanistās*, 'Grove of the Plane Trees', in Sparta: this ritual is described by Pausanias (3.11.2, 3.14.8–9), who notes that the boys made sacrifice to the hero Achilles before they started their mock battle (3.20.8).

Achilles and Dēmophōn as Cult Heroes of Festivals

8§22. As we have just seen in Text C taken from the *Homeric Hymn to Demeter*, the goddess Demeter foretells the *tīmē aphthitos*, 'unwilting honor' (verses 261, 263), of a seasonally recurring athletic event that the hero Dēmophōn will receive as a compensation for his death (verses 265–267). Similarly in the *Iliad*, the goddess Thetis foretells the *kleos aphthiton*, 'unwilting glory' (IX 413), that the hero Achilles will receive as a compensation for his own death:

HOUR 8 TEXT D = HOUR 1 TEXT A = HOUR 0 TEXT F

|$_{410}$ My mother Thetis, goddess with silver steps, tells me that |$_{411}$ I carry the burden of two different fated ways [*kēres*] leading to the final moment [*telos*] of death. |$_{412}$ If I stay here and fight at the walls of the

---

|$_{261}$ παῖδα φίλον ποίησα καὶ ἄφθιτον ὤπασα τιμήν· |$_{262}$ νῦν δ' οὐκ ἔσθ' ὥς κεν θάνατον καὶ κῆρας ἀλύξαι. |$_{263}$ τιμὴ δ' ἄφθιτος αἰὲν ἐπέσσεται οὕνεκα γούνων |$_{264}$ ἡμετέρων ἐπέβη καὶ ἐν ἀγκοίνῃσιν ἴαυσεν. |$_{265}$ ὥρῃσιν δ' ἄρα τῷ γε περιπλομένων ἐνιαυτῶν |$_{266}$ παῖδες Ἐλευσινίων πόλεμον καὶ φύλοπιν αἰνὴν |$_{267}$ αἰὲν ἐν ἀλλήλοισι συνάξουσ' ἤματα πάντα.

city of the Trojans, $|_{413}$ then my safe homecoming [*nostos*] will be destroyed for me, but I will have a glory [*kleos*] that is unwilting [*aphthiton*]. $|_{414}$ Whereas if I go back home, returning to the dear land of my forefathers, $|_{415}$ then it is my glory [*kleos*], genuine [*esthlon*] as it is, that will be destroyed for me, but my life force [*aiōn*] will then $|_{416}$ last me a long time, and the final moment [*telos*] of death will not be swift in catching up with me.

Iliad IX 410–416

8§23. The parallelisms in the wording that we see in these two passages highlight the parallelisms between Dēmophōn and Achilles as heroes who are linked with festivals. Just as the *tīmē*, 'honor', of the hero Dēmophōn takes the form of a seasonally recurring athletic event that is *aphthitos*, 'unwilting' (*Hymn to Demeter* 261, 263), because it will last forever, eternally recycled at the festival of the Eleusinian Games, so also the *kleos*, 'glory', of the hero Achilles takes the form of a seasonally recurring poetic event that is *aphthiton*, 'unwilting' (*Iliad* IX 413), because it too will last forever, eternally recycled in the context of a festival like the Panathenaia.

8§24. In the case of Dēmophōn, his link to the festival of the Eleusinian Games is expressed directly in the *Homeric Hymn to Demeter*. In the case of Achilles, however, his link to the festival of the Panathenaia is expressed only indirectly in the Homeric *Iliad* as we know it. Only in the visual medium of the vase paintings we saw in Hour 7 is the linking of Achilles with the Panathenaia expressed directly, but even in those vase paintings he is linked not with the poetic events that took place at this festival but with the athletic event of the *apobatai* as it took shape at the Panathenaia.

Achilles as a Model of Rhapsodic Performance

8§25. I have found, however, an indirect linking of the *kleos* or epic 'glory' of Achilles with the festival of the Panathenaia: it happens at the moment when the ambassadors sent by Agamemnon to Achilles find him in his shelter, where he is singing the *klea andrōn*, 'glories of men (heroes)':

HOUR 8 TEXT E = HOUR 2 TEXT D

$|_{185}$ The two of them reached the shelters and the ships of the Myrmidons, $|_{186}$ and they found Achilles diverting his heart [*phrēn*] as he was playing on a clear-sounding lyre [*phorminx*], $|_{187}$ a beautiful one, of exquisite workmanship, and its cross-bar was of silver. |₁₈₈ It was part of the spoils that he had taken when he destroyed the city of Eëtion, |₁₈₉ and he was now diverting his heart [*thūmos*] with it as he was *singing* [*aeidein*] the *glories of men* [*klea andrōn*]. |₁₉₀ Patroklos was the only other person there. He [= Patroklos] sat in silence, facing him [= Achilles], |₁₉₁ and waiting for the Aeacid [= Achilles] to leave off *singing* [*aeidein*]. |₁₉₂ Meanwhile the two of them came in—radiant Odysseus leading the way—|₁₉₃ and stood before him. Achilles sprang up from his seat |₁₉₄ with the lyre [*phorminx*] still in his hand, |₁₉₅ and Patroklos, when he saw the guests, rose also.

Iliad IX 185–195

8§26. As I indicated in Hour 2, Achilles is shown here as a model of epic performance. We may compare the evidence of the vase paintings we saw in Hour 7, where Achilles is shown as a model of athletic performance.

8§27. Here in the *Iliad*, Achilles is not only the model subject of songs that are the *klea andrōn*, 'glories of men (heroes)'; he is also the model performer of such songs. And the same goes for Patroklos, or *Patrokleēs*. As we have seen, the meaning of his name, 'he who has the *kleos* of the ancestors', encapsulates the very idea of *klea andrōn*. In the Iliadic passage I have just quoted, Patroklos is not just waiting for Achilles to stop performing the song. Rather, he is waiting for his own turn to perform the song, which must continue:

So long as Achilles alone sings the *klea andrōn*, 'glories of men', these heroic glories cannot be heard by anyone but Patroklos alone. Once Achilles leaves off and Patroklos starts singing, however, the continuum that is the *klea andrōn*—the Homeric tradition itself—can at long last become activated. This is the moment awaited by *Patrokleēs*, 'he who has the *klea* [glories] of the ancestors'. In this Homeric image of Patroklos waiting for his turn to sing, then, we have in capsule form the esthetics of rhapsodic sequencing.*

8§28. As I outlined in Hour 7e above, Homeric poetry was performed at the Panathenaia by *rhapsōidoi*, 'rhapsodes' (Plato *Ion* 530a-b, 533b-c; Isocrates *Panegyricus* 159; and Plutarch *Life of Pericles* 13.9–11). The rhapsodes narrated the *Iliad* and the *Odyssey in relay*, following traditions of *rhapsodic sequencing*: each

---

* *PP* 72–73; see also *HC* 366 = 3§33.

rhapsode waited for his turn to pick up the narrative where the previous rhapsode left off ("Plato" *Hipparkhos* 228b–c; Dieuchidas of Megara *FGH* 485 F 6 via Diogenes Laertius 1.57; Lycurgus *Against Leokrates* 102). And the competition of rhapsodes in performing by relay and in sequence the *Iliad* and the *Odyssey* of Homer at the festival of the Panathenaia was a ritual in and of itself.* Moreover, the principle of equity that was built into this ritual event of rhapsodic competition at the Panathenaia corresponded to the need for equity in ritual events of athletic competition. As Richard Martin observes, "The superb management of athletic games to assure equity could easily have been extended by the promoters of the Panathenaic games in this way."†

8§29. In Hour 7e, I used the term *Panathenaic Regulation* in referring to this tradition of *rhapsodic sequencing* as adopted in Athens. In the sources I have just cited ("Plato" *Hipparkhos* 228b–c; Dieuchidas of Megara *FGH* 485 F 6 via Diogenes Laertius 1.57; Lycurgus *Against Leokrates* 102), we see different versions of stories about initiatives undertaken in the sixth century BCE by the Athenian state to institute such rhapsodic *performance in relay* at the Panathenaia.‡

8§30. This is not to make a specific argument about the dating of Text E, the Iliadic passage showing Achilles and Patroklos performing in relay: it would be a mistake, I think, to date the wording of this passage to such a relatively late era, the sixth century BCE. After all, the tradition of *rhapsodic relay* was already at work in the Homeric tradition as it was evolving in the eighth and seventh centuries BCE at the festival of the Panionia.§ My general argument, rather, is that this tradition of rhapsodic relay, where rhapsodes collaborate as well as compete in the process of performing successive parts of integral compositions like the Homeric *Iliad* and *Odyssey*, can be used to explain the unity of these epics as they evolved over time.**

8§31. So the passage in Text E where we see Achilles and Patroklos performing in relay the *klea andrōn*, 'glories of men (heroes)', is most likely to reflect a relatively early feature of the Homeric tradition. Still, the point remains that the Iliadic reference to such a relay performance of the *klea andrōn*, 'glories of men (heroes)', can be seen as an indirect link to the recycled performances of epic at festivals, including the festival of the Panathenaia.

---

* *HPC* 22 = I§38, with reference to *PR* 42–47. For a comparative perspective on the concept of competition-in-collaboration, see *PP* 18.

† Martin 2000:422.

‡ *PR* 36–69.

§ *HPC* 22 = I§38, following Frame 2009:551–620.

** *PR* 42–47; *HC* 325, 327, 335 = 2§§297, 304, 325; also 354–355, 366–367 = 3§§4, 6, 33.

8§32. So I maintain that the *kleos* of Homeric poetry is in its own right a seasonally recurring ritual event, since both the *Iliad* and the *Odyssey* were performed at the festival of the Panathenaia in Athens. And, as we have seen, the poetic event of a competition in performing the *Iliad* and the *Odyssey* at the Panathenaia was parallel to the athletic event of a competition of *apobatai* at the same festival. This athletic event, as we have also seen, is comparable to the mock battle of the *Ballētus,* which was the primary athletic event of the Eleusinian Games and which qualifies as *tīmē aphthitos,* 'unwilting honor', in the *Homeric Hymn to Demeter* (261, 263), while the primary poetic event of performing epic at the Panathenaia qualifies as *kleos aphthiton,* 'unwilting glory', in the Homeric *Iliad* (IX 413).

Achilles and Patroklos as Cult Heroes of a Poetic Event

8§33. I have argued so far that Dēmophōn as cult hero of the athletic event of the *Ballētus* at the festival of the Eleusinian Games can be seen as a parallel to Achilles and Patroklos as joint cult heroes of the athletic event of the *apobatai* at the festival of the Panathenaia. But now I will argue that the status of Dēmophōn as cult hero of an athletic event can also be seen as a parallel to the status of Achilles and Patroklos as joint cult heroes of the poetic event of performing Homeric poetry at festivals. The parallelism is evident in the words of the goddess Thetis, when she describes Achilles as an infant hero:

HOUR 8 TEXT F = PART OF HOUR 4 TEXT G = HOUR 0 TEXT D

$|_{54}$ Ah me, the pitiful one! Ah me, the mother, so sad it is, of the very best. $|_{55}$ I gave birth to a faultless and strong son, $|_{56}$ the very best of heroes. And he shot up [*anedramen*] equal [*īsos*] to a seedling [*ernos*]. $|_{57}$ I nurtured him like a shoot in the choicest spot of the orchard, $|_{58}$ only to send him off on curved ships to Troy, to fight Trojan men. $|_{59}$ And I will never be welcoming him $|_{60}$ back home as returning warrior, back to the House of Peleus. $|_{61}$ And as long as he lives and sees the light of the sun, $|_{62}$ he will have sorrow [*akh-nutai*], and though I go to him I cannot help him.

Iliad XVIII 54–62

8§34. Similarly in the *Homeric Hymn to Demeter,* we see this description of Dēmophōn as an infant hero:

Hour 8 Text G

|₂₃₃ And so it came to pass that the splendid son of bright-minded Keleos, |₂₃₄ Dēmophōn, who was born to the one with the beautiful waist, Metaneira, |₂₃₅ was nourished in the palace, and he shot up [*aexeto*] equal [*īsos*] to a superhuman force [*daimōn*], |₂₃₆ not eating grain, not sucking from the breast. But Demeter* |₂₃₇ used to anoint him with ambrosia, as if he had been born of the goddess, |₂₃₈ and she would breathe down her sweet breath on him as she held him to her bosom. |₂₃₉ At nights she would conceal him within the power source [*menos*] of fire, as if he were a smoldering log, |₂₄₀ and his dear [*philoi*] parents were kept unaware. But they marveled |₂₄₁ at how full in bloom he came to be, and to look at him was like looking at the gods.

Homeric Hymn to Demeter 233–241†

8§35. I highlight the wording that describes the hero Dēmophōn as he is being nurtured by the goddess Demeter in Text G: 'he shot up [*an-e-drame*] equal [*īsos*] to a superhuman force [*daimōn*]' (verse 235); and I highlight the parallel wording that describes the hero Achilles as he in turn is being nurtured by the goddess Thetis in Text F: 'he shot up [*an-e-dramen*] equal [*īsos*] to a seedling [*ernos*]' (verse 56).‡ These descriptions, replete with vivid imagery centering on the wilting of plants, are typical of cult heroes who are destined to die and then receive as compensation some form of immortalization after death.§

8§36. I will have more to say about such descriptions in Hour 14, where I study further parallels in Hesiodic poetry, but for now I need to concentrate on the actual form of immortalization that Dēmophōn and Achilles will be granted by the divine order. In the case of Dēmophōn, as we saw in Text C (*Homeric Hymn to Demeter* 261, 263), he will be granted *tīmē aphthitos*, 'unwilting honor', by virtue of becoming the cult hero who presides over the prime athletic event of the Eleusinian Games; and, in the case of Achilles in Text D (*Iliad* IX 413), he

---

* At this point there may be a lacuna in the textual transmission.

† |₂₃₃ ὡς ἡ μὲν Κελεοῖο δαΐφρονος ἀγλαὸν υἱὸν |₂₃₄ Δημοφόωνθ, ὃν ἔτικτεν ἐΰζωνος Μετάνειρα, |₂₃₅ ἔτρεφεν ἐν μεγάροις· ὁ δ' ἀέξετο δαίμονι ἶσος |₂₃₆ οὔτ' οὖν σῖτον ἔδων, οὐ θησάμενος. Δημήτηρ |₂₃₇ χρίεσκ' ἀμβροσίῃ ὡς εἰ θεοῦ ἐκγεγαῶτα, |₂₃₈ ἡδὺ καταπνείουσα καὶ ἐν κόλποισιν ἔχουσα· |₂₃₉ νύκτας δὲ κρύπτεσκε πυρὸς μένει ἠΰτε δαλὸν |₂₄₀ λάθρα φίλων γονέων· τοῖς δὲ μέγα θαῦμ' ἐτέτυκτο |₂₄₁ ὡς προθαλὴς τελέθεσκε, θεοῖσι δὲ ἄντα ἐῴκει.

‡ Sinos 1980:28–36.

§ Full argumentation in *BA* 181–192 = 10§§10–22.

will be granted *kleos aphthiton*, 'unwilting glory', by virtue of becoming the cult hero who presides over the prime poetic event of the Panathenaia.

8§37. But this glory of Achilles will be shared in death by Patroklos, who as we have seen in both Texts A and B of Hour 5 receives the epithet 'equal [*īsos*] to a superhuman force [*daimōn*]' when he dies in place of Achilles in the *Iliad* (XVI 705 and 786). So it is more accurate to say that Patroklos as well as Achilles becomes the cult hero of the primary poetic event of the Panathenaia.

8§38. A most revealing reference in the Homeric *Iliad* to the general idea of Achilles and Patroklos as joint cult heroes can be found in *Iliad* XXIII 91–92, two verses that we have already read at the end of Text A as I quoted it earlier in its entirety. In these two verses, the *psūkhē* of Patroklos speaks about a golden amphora that will contain his own bones mixed together with the bones of Achilles. The reference here to this golden amphora, to be placed inside the *sēma* that will be shared by the two heroes, is an implicit sign of the immortalization that awaits Achilles after his bones are regenerated into a living body by the power of the god Dionysus, who had originally given the amphora to Thetis, the mother of Achilles (there is a reference to this myth in Stesichorus *PMG* 234).*

8§39. This reference in *Iliad* XXIII 91–92 to the prospect of heroic immortalization after death is an indication, as we will now see, that the ideology of hero cult is actively in play here in Homeric poetry. It can be said in general that localized myths about the immortalization of heroes after death are linked with localized rituals as practiced in cults of heroes.†

8§40. In the case of the hero Achilles, a myth about his immortalization after death is made explicit in the epic Cycle, where Achilles is immortalized after death (plot summary by Proclus of the *Aithiopis* by Arctinus of Miletus p. 106 lines 11–15). In the Homeric *Iliad* and *Odyssey*, by contrast, the theme of heroic immortalization is nowhere made explicit for Achilles.‡ But we do see in the *Iliad* at least two implicit references to the future immortalization of Achilles, and the passage we have just considered is one of them. There is another implicit reference in *Iliad* XIX 418, where Xanthos the immortal horse of Achilles is about to foretell the hero's immortalization, but the prophecy is silenced by an Erinys or 'Fury'.§

* Nagy 2012b:50–51, following *BA* 209 = 10§50; see also Dué 2001.
† EH §§98–99, 107, 113.
‡ EH §57.
§ Commentary in *BA* 209–210 = 10§50n2.

The Prefiguring of Achilles by Patroklos

8§41. In Homeric poetry, Patroklos as cult hero is more clearly defined than even Achilles himself. That is because Patroklos is not only a body-double but even a story-double of Achilles in the *Iliad*, where things happen to Patroklos that could otherwise have happened only to Achilles.* The most central of these happenings is the ritual death of Patroklos at the hands of the god Apollo in the *Iliad*: as we saw when we were reading Text A (XVI 698–711) and Text B (XVI 783–806) in Hour 5, this happening in the *Iliad* prefigures the death of Achilles beyond the *Iliad*.† And there are also other such happenings in the *Iliad* when the role of Patroklos as a cult hero functions as a substitute for the corresponding role of Achilles. A case in point is the story we see in *Iliad* XVII about the fighting between the Achaeans and the Trojans over the possession of the corpse of Patroklos after he is killed in *Iliad* XVI. Directly comparable is the fighting over the corpse of Achilles as we see it described in *Odyssey* xxiv (37–39). As we will see in Hour 11(§9), the possession of the corpse of a cult hero is essential for the fertility and prosperity of the community that worships that hero.

8§42. In view of this centrality of Patroklos as the surrogate cult hero of the Homeric *Iliad*, it is vital to highlight again here in Hour 8 the centrality of this same figure in the picture of Patroklos as painted on the Münster Hydria. The hero, imagined there as a miniature body-double of Achilles, hovers mid-air over the tomb that he will share with Achilles. And, in this painting, Patroklos is labeled as *psūkhē* (ΦΣΥΧΕ). In Hour 7, I used a neutral translation of this word's meaning, as 'spirit', but the more basic meaning of *psūkhē* is 'breath of life', which in the context of hero cults signals the vital force that departs from the body of the hero at the moment of death—only to be reunited with that body after a transition, through Hādēs, into a paradisiacal setting that transcends the temporal and the spatial constraints of mortality.‡ Such a mystical reunion of the body with the *psūkhē* is the vision that drives the idea of heroic immortalization, which is a basic feature of hero cult.§ In terms of this idea, as I

---

* For a general overview of the role of Patroklos as the narrative surrogate as well as the ritual substitute of Achilles in the *Iliad*, see Nagy 2007b ("Homer and Greek Myth") 64–69.

† On the death of Patroklos as a prefiguration of the death of Achilles, I find the book of Lowenstam 1981 to be of lasting value.

‡ *GM* 88–93, 115–116.

§ *GM* 126n30, 142.

noted a moment ago, there is transition of the *psūkhē* through Hādēs: so this realm of Hādēs is *transitional*, not *eschatological*.

8§43. Eschatology has to do with thinking about afterlife—where one will "end up." From the standpoint of basic Christian eschatology, for example, the stark alternatives are heaven and hell. Homeric eschatology is different. For example, the realm of Hādēs is not "hell."

8§44. Here I offer an overall formulation of the contrast between Hādēs and heroic immortalization in the context of hero cults:

> The cult hero was considered *dead*—from the standpoint of the place where the hero's *sōma*, or 'body', was situated; at the same time, the hero was considered simultaneously *immortalized*—from the standpoint of the paradisiacal place that awaited all heroes after death. Such a paradisiacal place, which was considered *eschatological*, must be contrasted with Hādēs, which was considered *transitional*. The name and even the visualization of this otherworldly place varied from hero cult to hero cult. Some of these names are: Elysium *(Ēlusion)*, the Islands of the Blessed *(Nēsoi Makarōn)*, the White Island *(Leukē)*, and, exceptionally, even Mount Olympus in the case of Hēraklēs. Many of these names were applied also to the actual site or sacred precinct of the hero cult.*

8§45. I will return in Hour 11 to the distinction between *transitional* and *eschatological* phases in an afterlife.

Heroic Immortalization and the Psūkhē

8§46. The theme of heroic immortalization is implicit in the overall use of the word *psūkhē* in Homeric poetry. I emphasize that this theme is implicit, not explicit, and that the formulaic system of Homeric diction shows the implicitness by actually avoiding the use of *psūkhē* in certain situations while substituting alternative words like *thūmos* and *menos* in these situations.†

8§47. One such situation is a set of Homeric scenes where a hero swoons, that is, where he loses consciousness but does not die: in such scenes, it can be said that a hero loses his *psūkhē* when he swoons (as in the case of Sarpedon when he swoons in *Iliad* V 696), but it cannot be said that he wins back his

---

* This formulation is derived from EH §98. For an extended discussion, see *BA* ch. 10 ("Poetic Visions of Immortality for the Hero"). See also Bershadsky 2011:17.

† *GM* 87–88, with references.

psūkhē when he comes to.* If the hero were dead, then he would not come to. But if he is not dead, then he will come to, that is, he will revive. The point is, in Homeric scenes where we see a hero reviving after swooning, that is, where the hero regains consciousness after having passed out temporarily, the 'breath of life' that he regains cannot be expressed by way of the word *psūkhē*, which can be used to express only the loss of consciousness at the moment of swooning or dying but not the regaining of consciousness at the moment of reviving. From the standpoint of Homeric diction, to say that the *psūkhē* as the 'breath of life' is regained after reviving from swooning is evidently too close to saying that the hero will revive not only after swooning but even after dying.†

8§48. This pattern of consistently avoiding references to the return of the *psūkhē* to the body shows a pervasive recognition of the theme of immortalization within the entire system of Homeric poetry. The operation of this system in Homeric poetry, I have argued, indicates that this poetry recognizes and even accepts the idea of heroic immortalization, though this idea is expressed only implicitly.‡

8§49. Just as the idea of heroic immortalization is expressed only implicitly in Homeric poetry, it is implicit also in the picture painted on the Münster Hydria. As I have argued in Hour 7, the painting on this vase signals such a theme not only by picturing the *psūkhē* of Patroklos as it hovers over the tomb that he will be sharing with Achilles but also by even labeling the picture, that is, by painting the consecutive letters ΦΣΥΧΕ to spell *psūkhē*, where the act of painting these letters that spell out *psūkhē* becomes a *sēma*, or 'sign', in its own right.§ And, in the timelessness of the narrative created in this picture, as I have argued here in Hour 8, Patroklos and Achilles share not only the same *sēma* or 'tomb' but even the same *psūkhē*, as indicated by the *sēma* or 'sign' for the word *psūkhē*.

The Psūkhē *as Both Messenger and Message*

8§50. This shared meaning of Patroklos and Achilles as cult heroes is signaled in the *Iliad* not only by the tomb that they share but also by the *psūkhē* or 'spirit' of Patroklos himself, who is sending a message to Achilles. As we have seen in

---

* *GM* 90, with references.
† *GM* 89–92.
‡ Nagy 2012b.
§ See also *GM* 220.

Iliad XXIII (83–84, 91–92), the *psūkhē* of Patroklos directly communicates his message to Achilles, telling him to undertake the construction of their shared tomb. And as I noted, there is a further reference to this tomb in *Iliad* XXIII (125–126). Then, even further on in XXIII (245–248), it is indicated that the tomb to be shared by Achilles and Patroklos will be incomplete so long as only Patroklos occupies it, and that the final act of making the tomb complete must wait till the death of Achilles. That final act is what we see described in *Odyssey* xxiv (80–84). The reference there in the *Odyssey* to the shared tomb of Achilles and Patroklos also complements a set of stylized references to what is understood to be the same tomb in the *Iliad* (especially XIX 368–379).* In Hour 11, I will have more to say about this tomb and about its physical setting.

8§51. Just as the word *psūkhē* signals the message of one tomb to be shared by Achilles and Patroklos as cult heroes in the *Iliad,* the same word signals the same message in the picture painted on the Münster Hydria. In the logic of that picture, the self of Patroklos as a *psūkhē* will become the self of Achilles, whose corpse will be placed inside the same tomb that is already occupied by the corpse of his other self, Patroklos. So the *psūkhē* is both the messenger and the message of the messenger. And the visual cue for this *psūkhē* is the tomb over which the miniature vision of Patroklos levitates, which is not only a *sēma* in the sense of a 'tomb' but also a *sēma* in the sense of a 'sign' of a meaning—or even a 'sign' of meaning itself.

8§52. It is essential for my overall argument to repeat here the simple fact that *sēma* is a Homeric word that means not only 'sign' but also 'tomb'. That is what we saw in Hour 7 when I first showed the verse in *Iliad* XXIII 331, where *sēma* refers to the 'tomb' of the unnamed cult hero. And we saw the same word five verses earlier in *Iliad* XXIII 326, where it refers to the 'sign' given by Nestor to Antilokhos. *When Nestor says the word for 'sign', he is already saying the word for 'tomb'.* Just as the act of painting an image that shows the tomb shared by Patroklos and Achilles becomes a *sēma* or 'sign' of the tomb, so also the act of saying the word *sēma* as a 'sign' becomes a 'sign' of the tomb in the verbal art of the *Iliad*. And the unspecified tomb of the unnamed hero turns out to be the specific tomb of the hero named Patroklos, who will be sharing this tomb with the hero named Achilles. Thus the sign given by Nestor is not just an unspecified sign that tells a chariot driver how to drive his chariot around a turning point that turns out to be tomb of Patroklos. It is also a specific sign that tells the

---

* Detailed analysis in *HPC* 149–170 = II§§50–89.

chariot driver that he is participating in an athletic ritual performed in honor of Patroklos and Achilles as cult heroes.

A Fusion of Heroic Myth and Athletic Ritual

8§53. I must stress once again that the idea of using the tomb of a hero as the turning point in a chariot race stems from the fact that the activity of athletics, like the activity of warfare, was considered to be a ritual. Moreover, the ritual activities of athletics and warfare were conceived as parallel to the mythical deeds of heroes. As I noted already in Hour 1, and as I will elaborate in Hour 8b, *the same wording was used to refer to the ordeals of athletes and warriors in the rituals of athletics and war as was used to refer to the ordeals of heroes in myth.* In the ritual ordeals of athletics and warfare, real people re-enacted the mythical ordeals of heroes. Already in Hour 1, when I looked at the Labors of Hēraklēs, I highlighted the fusion of heroic and athletic actions.

8§54. We are seeing, then, a fusion of heroic myth and athletic ritual in the story about the chariot race in *Iliad* XXIII and about all the other athletic events that are narrated there. The athletic events in which the heroes participate are a matter of ritual, but they are also a matter of myth, because it is the heroes of the heroic age who participate in the athletic events of *Iliad* XXIII, not the real people in the post-heroic age who re-enact the mythical ordeals of heroes.

8§55. What makes the athletic events of *Iliad* XXIII appear to be different from the "real" athletic events of the historical period is this: whatever is happening in *Iliad* XXIII appears to happen only once, whereas "real" athletic events are seasonally recurrent. We can see most clearly this concept of seasonally recurring re-enactment when we read the relevant passage in Text C above, taken from the *Homeric Hymn to Demeter* (259–267).

8§56. But appearances are deceiving. Even the athletic events narrated in the *Iliad* are not really one-time events, since they were narrated again and again at the seasonally recurring festival of the Panathenaia in Athens. In Hour 7e above, I have already given a brief overview of some relevant historical facts that we can piece together about the use of this festival as a venue for the seasonally recurring performances of Homeric poetry during the sixth century BCE and later. On the basis of these facts, I maintain that the athletic events of *Iliad* XXIII are understood to be performed again and again in the recycled performances of Homeric poetry at the festival of the Panathenaia.

8§57. There is a comparable recycling of athletic performance in the picture we see painted on the Münster Hydria. In this picture, Achilles is represented as engaging in *a personalized apobatic race with himself.** He is seen running alongside the speeding chariot, having already leapt off its platform. Meanwhile, the *psūkhē* of Patroklos—which can double for the *psūkhē* of Achilles—is shown hovering over the hero's tomb or *sēma* occupying the dead center of the picture. This *psūkhē* of Patroklos, labeled as ΦΣΥΧΕ in the painting, is running in the air—a miniature version of the running Achilles, who is racing at ground zero in a re-enactment of the race being run by the other self, who is running in the air.

8§58. In the narrative of the Homeric *Iliad* as we have it, by contrast, Achilles is never shown as an apobatic athlete—or as any other kind of athlete. Even at the Funeral Games for Patroklos as retold in the *Iliad,* Achilles delegates the role of the athlete to his fellow heroes. Instead of engaging in any athletic event, Achilles in the Funeral Games reserves for himself the role of the one who presides over all the athletic events. And, in this role of presider, he is substituting for the one hero in *Iliad* XXIII whose death must be compensated by way of athletic competitions. That one hero is Patroklos. Thus Achilles becomes the ritual representative of Patroklos, his other self, by presiding over the athletic competitions at the Funeral Games for his dead friend. His chosen role as presider here is a substitute for the role that he chooses in the vase painting of the Münster Hydria and in other such paintings, in which he engages directly in the athletic competition of the *apobatai.*†

8§59. No matter which hero is shown engaging in athletic events, whether it be Achilles or only his fellow heroes, the fact remains that heroes who engage in these events become models for athletes who compete in these same kinds of events. And they are models because they are shown as competing in athletic ordeals that are instituted explicitly in compensation for the death of one of their own kind, a hero.

8§60. This is not to say that the modeling is consistently positive. We have already seen that the actions of heroes may be negative models—even when they serve as aetiologies for existing institutions like athletic festivals, as in the case of the brutal dragging of Hector's corpse behind the speeding chariot of Achilles. Moreover, the models for heroes who compete in athletics may be their very own selves in other phases of their own lives as narrated in epic. For

---

* *HPC* 175 = II§103.
† *HPC* 175–176 = II§106.

example, the heroes who compete in athletic events at the Funeral Games for Patroklos in the *Iliad* can unwittingly re-enact corresponding heroic events, either positive or negative, that they will experience at some point in their actual lives as characters in the heroic narration.*

8§61. I conclude, then, that the painting on the Münster Hydria shows Achilles as a prototypical participant in his own hero cult by way of participating in the athletic event of the *apobatai*. Through his prototypical participation, Achilles shows the way for future athletes to participate in this athletic event of the *apobatai* at the seasonally recurring festival of the Panathenaia for all time to come.†

8§62. And I offer a parallel conclusion about the Funeral Games for Patroklos in *Iliad* XXIII.‡ Here, too, Achilles is shown as a prototypical participant in his own hero cult by way of participating in the hero cult of his other self, Patroklos. Here, too, he shows the way for future athletes to participate in his own hero cult by way of participating in the kinds of athletic events we see described in *Iliad* XXIII, especially in the chariot race. In this case, however, Achilles does not himself participate in the athletic events of the Funeral Games for Patroklos: rather, it is the other surviving Achaean heroes of the *Iliad* who serve as prototypical participants in the athletic events, while Achilles himself simply presides over these events as if he were already dead, having already achieved the status of the cult hero who will be buried in the tumulus to be shared with his other self, Patroklos.

Back to the Glory of the Ancestors

8§63. In the visual art of the picture painted on the Münster Hydria, we saw a complex sign that combines the painting of the word *psūkhē* with the painting of a shining white tomb, and this complex sign signals the hero Patroklos himself, whose *psūkhē* will become one with the *psūkhē* of Achilles when the two heroes are joined in death, inside the tomb they will share forever. Similarly in the verbal art of Homeric poetry, we see a complex sign that combines two meanings of the word *sēma* as used by Nestor in *Iliad* XXIII before the commencement of the chariot race in honor of Patroklos: it is a 'sign' (XXIII 326) that signals a hero's 'tomb' (XXIII 331), but it signals not only the tomb that Pa-

---

* Whitman 1958:169, Nagy 1990:193, Frame 2009:170–172, 205–216.
† *HPC* 175–176 = II§105.
‡ *HPC* 176 = II§106. See also *GM* 88, 94, 217, 220 and *PH* pp. 207–214 = 7§§10–19.

troklos will share with Achilles but also the very meaning of the hero Patroklos himself. That meaning, as I showed in Hour 2, is recapitulated in the meaning of his name, *Patrokleēs*, 'the one who has the glory [*kleos*] of the ancestors [*pateres*]'.

8§64. This name *Patrokleēs* has a special meaning for Antilokhos, the hero to whom Nestor addresses his *sēma* or 'sign' (XXIII 326) by speaking as an immediate ancestor, that is, as a father. For the hero Antilokhos, as I showed in Hour 7, the highest point in his ascending scale of affection proves to be his immediate ancestor, that is, his father. As we know indirectly from a plot summary of the epic Cycle (plot summary by Proclus of the *Aithiopis* by Arctinus of Miletus p. 106 lines 4–6) and directly from the words of the lyric master Pindar (*Pythian* 6.28–42), Antilokhos himself dies in a chariot fight, giving up his own life while saving the life of his father, Nestor, whose chariot had been immobilized.* Once again we see the mentality of choosing to die for someone else: *I will die for you.*

8§65. This same name *Patrokleēs*, 'the one who has the glory [*kleos*] of the ancestors [*pateres*]', also has a special meaning for Achilles himself. Patroklos is not just the one person who is 'nearest and dearest' to Achilles (*philtatos* XVII 411, 655). Even the meaning of the name of Patroklos, as 'the one who has the glory [*kleos*] of the ancestors [*pateres*]', ranks highest in the ascending scale of affection that defines the hero Achilles. As I showed in Hour 2, the name *Patrokleēs* amounts to a periphrasis of the expression *tōn prosthen . . . klea andrōn | hērōōn*, 'the glories [*kleos* plural] of men of an earlier time who were heroes' (IX 524–525), which is used in Homeric poetry to refer to epic narrative. And what must mean more than anything else to Achilles is not only Patroklos himself but also the actual meaning of his name, *Patrokleēs,* which conveys the idea of 'the glories [*kleos* plural] of men of an earlier time, who were heroes'. For Achilles, as I argued in Hour 2, the meaning of the name of Patroklos represents the epic of the *Iliad* itself. And Achilles will ultimately die for that epic as conveyed by the name of Patroklos, just as Patroklos had died for Achilles.

8§66. The significance of the name of *Patrokleēs* as a sign of the 'fathers' or 'ancestors' in general is relevant to the scene near the end of the *Iliad* in which Priam, as a father, appeals to Achilles to take pity and accept ransom for the body of Hector:

---

* *PH* 207–214 = 7§§10–18.

HOUR 8 TEXT H

|₄₈₆ "Remember your father, O Achilles, you who look just like the gods. |₄₈₇ He [= Peleus, the father of Achilles] is just like me, on the destructive threshold of old age. |₄₈₈ It may be that those who dwell near him |₄₈₉ are wearing him down, and there is no one to keep damage and devastation away from him. |₄₉₀ Yet when he hears of you being still alive, |₄₉₁ he takes pleasure in his heart [thūmos], and every day he is full of hope |₄₉₂ that he will see his dear [philos] son come home to him from Troy; |₄₉₃ but I am the most luckless of all men, since I fathered the best sons |₄₉₄ in the city of Troy, which has power far and wide, and I can now say that there is not one of them left. |₄₉₅ I had fifty sons when the sons of the Achaeans came here; |₄₉₆ nineteen of them were from a single womb, |₄₉₇ and the others were born to me by the women of my halls. |₄₉₈ Many of them have been hamstrung by swift Arēs, |₄₉₉ but he who was the only one left, who was the guardian of the city and ourselves, |₅₀₀ he has been killed by you just now, while he was protecting his fatherland. |₅₀₁ I mean Hector. And it is because of him that I now come to the ships of the Achaeans |₅₀₂ intending to ransom his body from you. And I bring with me great ransom beyond telling. |₅₀₃ Show respect [aideîsthai], O Achilles, to the gods; and have pity on me. |₅₀₄ Remember your own father. But I am far more pitiable, |₅₀₅ for I have steeled myself as no one yet among earthbound mortals has ever steeled himself before me. |₅₀₆ I have raised to my lips the hand of the one who killed my son." |₅₀₇ Thus he [= Priam] spoke, and he stirred up in him [= Achilles] a longing to cry in lament [goos] for his own father. |₅₀₈ He touched the old man's hand and moved him gently away. |₅₀₉ And they both remembered. One of them remembered Hector the man-killer |₅₁₀ and cried for him, shedding tears thick and fast as he lay near the feet of Achilles. |₅₁₁ As for Achilles, he was crying for his own father at one moment, and then, at the very next moment, |₅₁₂ he would be crying for Patroklos. And the sounds of lament rose up all over the dwelling.

Iliad XXIV 486–512*

---

* |₄₈₆ μνῆσαι πατρὸς σοῖο θεοῖς ἐπιείκελ' Ἀχιλλεῦ, |₄₈₇ τηλίκου ὥς περ ἐγών, ὀλοῷ ἐπὶ γήραος οὐδῷ· |₄₈₈ καὶ μέν που κεῖνον περιναιέται ἀμφὶς ἐόντες |₄₈₉ τείρουσ', οὐδέ τίς ἐστιν ἀρὴν καὶ λοιγὸν ἀμῦναι. |₄₉₀ ἀλλ' ἤτοι κεῖνός γε σέθεν ζώοντος ἀκούων |₄₉₁ χαίρει τ' ἐν θυμῷ, ἐπί τ' ἔλπεται ἤματα πάντα

8§67. We see here Achilles weeping alternately for his own father Peleus and for Patroklos, whose name reflects the glory of the 'fathers' or 'ancestors'. The prompt that activates the hero's emotion of sorrow here is the very act of thinking about fathers or ancestors. Achilles thinks of his own father when he sees the sorrow of another father, Priam, over the death of another son, Hector.

8§68. Here at the end of the Homeric *Iliad,* Achilles will now finally emerge from the depths of brutality and ascend to new heights of humanity by way of identifying with his deadliest enemy. A father's tears are what finally move him. He thinks of his own father and, that way, he can think more clearly about the meaning of Patroklos. He will now finally give back to Priam the body of Hector.

Back to the Meaning of Patroklos

8§69. Here I return to the ascending scale of affection in the compressed story about Meleagros and Kleopatra, a story described as *tōn prosthen . . . klea andrōn | hērōōn,* 'the glories of men of an earlier time, who were heroes', in the *Iliad* (IX 524–525). This story, as told by Phoenix to Achilles and Patroklos and the other heroes assembled in the shelter of Achilles, was a story that was meant to be understood by 'friends', *philoi* (IX 528). Or, to put it more accurately, it was a story that was meant for an audience *presumed* to be friends, *philoi*:

HOUR 8 TEXT I = HOUR 2 TEXT B

|₅₂₄ This is how [*houtōs*] we [= I, Phoenix] learned it, the glories [*klea*] of men [*andrōn*] of an earlier time [*prosthen*], |₅₂₅ who were heroes [*hērōes*], whenever one of them was overcome by tempestuous anger. |₅₂₆ They could be persuaded by way of gifts and could be swayed by words. |₅₂₇ I totally recall [*me-mnē-mai*] how this was done—it hap-

---

|₄₉₂ ὄψεσθαι φίλον υἱὸν ἀπὸ Τροίηθεν ἰόντα· |₄₉₃ αὐτὰρ ἐγὼ πανάποτμος, ἐπεὶ τέκον υἷας ἀρίστους |₄₉₄ Τροίῃ ἐν εὐρείῃ, τῶν δ' οὔ τινά φημι λελεῖφθαι. |₄₉₅ πεντήκοντά μοι ἦσαν ὅτ' ἤλυθον υἷες Ἀχαιῶν· |₄₉₆ ἐννεακαίδεκα μέν μοι ἰῆς ἐκ νηδύος ἦσαν, |₄₉₇ τοὺς δ' ἄλλους μοι ἔτικτον ἐνὶ μεγάροισι γυναῖκες. |₄₉₈ τῶν μὲν πολλῶν θοῦρος Ἄρης ὑπὸ γούνατ' ἔλυσεν· |₄₉₉ ὃς δέ μοι οἶος ἔην, εἴρυτο δὲ ἄστυ καὶ αὐτούς, |₅₀₀ τὸν σὺ πρῴην κτεῖνας ἀμυνόμενον περὶ πάτρης |₅₀₁ Ἕκτορα· τοῦ νῦν εἵνεχ' ἱκάνω νῆας Ἀχαιῶν |₅₀₂ λυσόμενος παρὰ σεῖο, φέρω δ' ἀπερείσι' ἄποινα. |₅₀₃ ἀλλ' αἰδεῖο θεοὺς Ἀχιλεῦ, αὐτόν τ' ἐλέησον |₅₀₄ μνησάμενος σοῦ πατρός· ἐγὼ δ' ἐλεεινότερός περ, |₅₀₅ ἔτλην δ' οἶ' οὔ πώ τις ἐπιχθόνιος βροτὸς ἄλλος, |₅₀₆ ἀνδρὸς παιδοφόνοιο ποτὶ στόμα χεῖρ' ὀρέγεσθαι. |₅₀₇ Ὣς φάτο, τῷ δ' ἄρα πατρὸς ὑφ' ἵμερον ὦρσε γόοιο· |₅₀₈ ἁψάμενος δ' ἄρα χειρὸς ἀπώσατο ἦκα γέροντα. |₅₀₉ τὼ δὲ μνησαμένω ὁ μὲν Ἕκτορος ἀνδροφόνοιο |₅₁₀ κλαῖ' ἁδινὰ προπάροιθε ποδῶν Ἀχιλῆος ἐλυσθείς, |₅₁₁ αὐτὰρ Ἀχιλλεὺς κλαῖεν ἑὸν πατέρ', ἄλλοτε δ' αὖτε |₅₁₂ Πάτροκλον· τῶν δὲ στοναχὴ κατὰ δώματ' ὀρώρει.

pened a long time ago, it is not something new— |₅₂₈ recalling exactly how it was. I will tell it in your company—since you are all near and dear [*philoi*].

Iliad IX 524–528*

8§70. As we saw in Hour 2, the Greek word *houtōs*, 'this is how', that introduces this story about the meaning of friendship is a marker of a form of speech known as the *ainos*. And the "moral of the story" as encoded inside this *ainos*, as we also saw in Hour 2, is that Kleopatra as the wife of Meleagros is highest on her husband's ascending scale of affection just as Patroklos as *philos* or 'friend' is correspondingly the highest for Achilles. And these characters in the epic are highest in the ascending scales of Meleagros and Achilles not only because they are wife and friend respectively but also because their names, *Kleopatra* and *Patroklees*, mean the same thing as *tōn prosthen . . . klea andrōn* | *hērōōn*, 'the glories of men of an earlier time, who were heroes', in the *Iliad* (IX 524–525). That is, the name of this wife and the name of this friend mean the same thing as the medium of the epic we know as the Homeric *Iliad*.

8§71. So the question is, who or what is really highest for Achilles in his ascending scale of affection? The answer is, it must be the epic itself, to which Achilles refers as his own *kleos aphthiton*, his 'unwilting glory' (IX 413), quoting the prophecy of his divine mother, Thetis. But Achilles does not yet know the answer to the question I just asked, about the highest of all values, at the moment when he quotes his mother's prophecy about his *kleos aphthiton*. Full knowledge of what he must love more than anything else in the world can be achieved only when the epic is fully told.

8§72. As the plot of the *Iliad* evolves, we can see along the way some indications of the hero's incomplete knowledge of his own epic glory or *kleos*. By the time we reach *Iliad* IX, we can already see at least two other possible priorities for Achilles.

8§73. In terms of the first of these two other priorities, what matters most for Achilles is his love for a woman, Briseis. He says so in the form of a sarcastic question that sets up a contrast between his relationship with Briseis and the

---

* |₅₂₄ οὕτω καὶ τῶν πρόσθεν ἐπευθόμεθα κλέα ἀνδρῶν |₅₂₅ ἡρώων, ὅτε κέν τιν' ἐπιζάφελος χόλος ἵκοι. |₅₂₆ δωρητοί τε πέλοντο παράρρητοί τ' ἐπέεσσι. |₅₂₇ μέμνημαι τόδε ἔργον ἐγὼ πάλαι οὔ τι νέον γε |₅₂₈ ὡς ἦν· ἐν δ' ὑμῖν ἐρέω πάντεσσι φίλοισι.

relationship of the suns of Atreus, that is, of Agamemnon and Menelaos, with their wives:

HOUR 8 TEXT J

|₃₄₀ Are the only mortal men in the world who love their wives |₃₄₁ the sons of Atreus? I ask this question because any man who is noble and sensible |₃₄₂ loves [*philein*] and cherishes her who is his own, just as I, with regard to her [= Briseis] |₃₄₃ with my whole heart did I love [*philein*] her, though she was only the prize of my spear.

Iliad IX 340–343*

8§74. Here in *Iliad* IX, we have already come a long way from *Iliad* I, where Briseis was simply the property of Achilles and thus a mere extension of his honor. Now Briseis is to be a wife for him, just as Kleopatra is a wife for Meleagros.

8§75. In terms of the second of the two other priorities we are now considering, what about the love of Achilles for his comrades? The words of Ajax, who is one of these comrades, show that this rival hero misunderstands the priorities of Achilles:

HOUR 8 TEXT K

|₆₂₂ ... And then Ajax stood up among them, |₆₂₃ the godlike son of Telamon, and he said:|₆₂₄ "Odysseus, descended from the gods, noble son of Laertes, |₆₂₅ let's just go, for I see that there is no fulfillment [*teleutē*] that will come from what we say [= the *mūthos*]. |₆₂₆ No, on this expedition, there will be no action resulting from words. We must go and tell the news as soon as possible |₆₂₇ to the Danaans, even though what we say [= the *mūthos*] will not be good for those |₆₂₈ who are waiting to receive it. As for Achilles, |₆₂₉ a savage feeling [*thūmos*] does he have embedded in his chest, which holds within it that great heart of his. |₆₃₀ What a wretched man he is! He cares nothing for the love [*philotēs*] of his comrades [*hetairoi*]. |₆₃₁ With that love we honored him more than all the others over there by the ships. |₆₃₂ He is pitiless. If a man's brother or son has been killed, |₆₃₃ that man will ac-

---

* |₃₄₀ ἦ μοῦνοι φιλέουσ' ἀλόχους μερόπων ἀνθρώπων |₃₄₁ Ἀτρεῖδαι; ἐπεὶ ὅς τις ἀνὴρ ἀγαθὸς καὶ ἐχέφρων |₃₄₂ τὴν αὑτοῦ φιλέει καὶ κήδεται, ὡς καὶ ἐγὼ τὴν |₃₄₃ ἐκ θυμοῦ φίλεον δουρικτητήν περ ἐοῦσαν.

cept a blood-price [*poinē*] as compensation for the one who was killed, |₆₃₄ and the one who caused the death, having paid a vast sum, can remain in the locale [*dēmos*], |₆₃₅ while the other one's heart and manly feeling [*thūmos*] are checked, |₆₃₆ now that he has accepted the blood-price [*poinē*]. But for you, [Achilles,] a bad and relentless |₆₃₇ feeling [*thūmos*] have the gods put into your chest, and this, all because of just one girl, |₆₃₈ just one."

Iliad IX 622–638*

8§76. Ajax here is thinking that the main hero of the *Iliad* has already made up his mind, preferring Briseis over his comrades. In the long run, however, Achilles will have as his main priority neither Briseis nor his comrades as represented by Ajax. No, his priority will be a concept as encapsulated in the expression *tōn prosthen ... klea andrōn* | *hērōōn,* 'the glories of men of an earlier time, who were heroes'. And this concept will be represented by Patroklos, who is even more than a comrade, more than a wife. For Achilles, Patroklos is his other self. And the life that Achilles shares with this other self is to be valued above everything else. Even more than that, the value of that life is beyond measure. So it becomes impossible to put a price on the value of that life, and this impossibility is summed up in a timeless scene pictured on the Shield of Achilles:

HOUR 8 TEXT L

|₄₉₇ Meanwhile the people were gathered in assembly, and there a quarrel [*neikos*] |₄₉₈ had arisen, and two men were quarreling [*neikeîn*] about the blood-price [*poinē*] |₄₉₉ for a man who had died. One of the two claimed that he had the right to pay off the damages in full, |₅₀₀ declaring this publicly to the population of the district [*dēmos*], and the other of the two was refusing to accept anything.

Iliad XVIII 497–500†

---

* |₆₂₂ ... τοῖσι δ' ἄρ' Αἴας |₆₂₃ ἀντίθεος Τελαμωνιάδης μετὰ μῦθον ἔειπε· |₆₂₄ διογενὲς Λαερτιάδη πολυμήχαν' Ὀδυσσεῦ |₆₂₅ ἴομεν· οὐ γάρ μοι δοκέει μύθοιο τελευτὴ |₆₂₆ τῇδέ γ' ὁδῷ κρανέεσθαι· ἀπαγγεῖλαι δὲ τάχιστα |₆₂₇ χρὴ μῦθον Δαναοῖσι καὶ οὐκ ἀγαθόν περ ἐόντα |₆₂₈ οἵ που νῦν ἔαται ποτιδέγμενοι. αὐτὰρ Ἀχιλλεὺς |₆₂₉ ἄγριον ἐν στήθεσσι θέτο μεγαλήτορα θυμὸν |₆₃₀ σχέτλιος, οὐδὲ μετατρέπεται φιλότητος ἑταίρων |₆₃₁ τῆς ᾗ μιν παρὰ νηυσὶν ἐτίομεν ἔξοχον ἄλλων |₆₃₂ νηλής· καὶ μέν τίς τε κασιγνήτοιο φονῆος |₆₃₃ ποινὴν ἢ οὗ παιδὸς ἐδέξατο τεθνηῶτος· |₆₃₄ καί ῥ' ὃ μὲν ἐν δήμῳ μένει αὐτοῦ πόλλ' ἀποτίσας, |₆₃₅ τοῦ δέ τ' ἐρητύεται κραδίη καὶ θυμὸς ἀγήνωρ· |₆₃₆ ποινὴν δεξαμένῳ· σοὶ δ' ἄλληκτόν τε κακόν τε |₆₃₇ θυμὸν ἐνὶ στήθεσσι θεοὶ θέσαν εἵνεκα κούρης |₆₃₈ οἴης·

† |₄₉₇ λαοὶ δ' εἰν ἀγορῇ ἔσαν ἀθρόοι· ἔνθα δὲ νεῖκος |₄₉₈ ὠρώρει, δύο δ' ἄνδρες ἐνείκεον εἵνεκα ποινῆς |₄₉₉ ἀνδρὸς ἀποφθιμένου· ὃ μὲν εὔχετο πάντ' ἀποδοῦναι |₅₀₀ δήμῳ πιφαύσκων, ὃ δ' ἀναίνετο μηδὲν ἑλέσθαι.

8§77. Here the narrative has zoomed in on a litigation between an anonymous plaintiff and an anonymous defendant. The litigation is all about the need to find the right blood-price to be paid for the loss of a life. The victim whose life has been lost is also anonymous. The anonymous plaintiff, who can be seen as a stand-in for Achilles, refuses to accept compensation offered by the anonymous defendant, who can be seen as a stand-in for Agamemnon. The defendant seeks to compensate for the loss of a human life, but whose life is it? If the defendant stands for Agamemnon, and if the plaintiff stands for Achilles, then maybe the life that cannot be paid for is the life of Achilles. After all, what matters more to Achilles than all the wealth he could possibly imagine is his own life. All the riches of Troy and Delphi put together would be inadequate as payment for this life. Here is how Achilles expresses his love for his own life:

HOUR 8 TEXT M

|₄₀₁ My life [*psūkhē*] is worth more to me than all the wealth |₄₀₂ that was once possessed, so they say, by that well-situated citadel of Ilion, |₄₀₃ back when it was still at peace, before the coming of the Achaeans, |₄₀₄ or than all the treasure that is stored inside when you enter the stone threshold of the one who shoots, |₄₀₅ Phoebus Apollo, at rocky Pytho [= Delphi]. |₄₀₆ Cattle and sheep can be rustled in a raid, |₄₀₇ and one can acquire both tripods and horses with their golden manes if he wants them, |₄₀₈ but a man's life [*psūkhē*] can never come back—it cannot be rustled in a raid |₄₀₉ and thus taken back—once it has passed through the barriers of his teeth.

Iliad IX 401–409*

8§78. But this one life, this one *psūkhē*, belongs not only to Achilles. As we have seen here in Hour 8, this life belongs to Patroklos and Achilles together. The two heroes share one *psūkhē*. That is the psychology of the sign that signals their shared *sēma,* which is not only their shared tomb but also their shared meaning as cult heroes.

8§79. From the standpoint of this timeless picture on the Shield of Achilles, we can now reconsider the three alternative priorities we have been considering

---

* |₄₀₁ οὐ γὰρ ἐμοὶ ψυχῆς ἀντάξιον οὐδ' ὅσα φασὶν |₄₀₂ Ἴλιον ἐκτῆσθαι εὖ ναιόμενον πτολίεθρον |₄₀₃ τὸ πρὶν ἐπ' εἰρήνης, πρὶν ἐλθεῖν υἷας Ἀχαιῶν, |₄₀₄ οὐδ' ὅσα λάϊνος οὐδὸς ἀφήτορος ἐντὸς ἐέργει |₄₀₅ Φοίβου Ἀπόλλωνος Πυθοῖ ἔνι πετρηέσσῃ. |₄₀₆ ληϊστοὶ μὲν γάρ τε βόες καὶ ἴφια μῆλα, |₄₀₇ κτητοὶ δὲ τρίποδές τε καὶ ἵππων ξανθὰ κάρηνα, |₄₀₈ ἀνδρὸς δὲ ψυχὴ πάλιν ἐλθεῖν οὔτε λεϊστὴ |₄₀₉ οὔθ' ἑλετή, ἐπεὶ ἄρ κεν ἀμείψεται ἕρκος ὀδόντων.

264 HEROES IN EPIC AND LYRIC POETRY

for Achilles as the main hero of the *Iliad:* (1) love for a would-be wife or (2) love for his comrades or (3) love for his own life. All three of these alternative priorities are merely foils for the ultimate priority for this hero, which is his love for *tōn prosthen . . . klea andrōn* | *hērōōn*, 'the glories of men of an earlier time, who were heroes', which includes and transcends all the other priorities. And this love is embodied in the figure of Patroklos, ritual substitute of Achilles in the *Iliad*. That is the meaning of Patroklos.

Hour 8a. About the Ritual Origins of Athletics

8A§1. The athletic event of the mock battle or *Ballētus*, as featured in the Eleusinian Games, was understood to be a form of eternal compensation for the primal death of the cult hero Dēmophōn, as we saw from the wording I quoted from the *Homeric Hymn to Demeter* (259–267) in Hour 8 Text C. And there are historical parallels, including the Nemean and the Isthmian Games, which were seasonally recurring festivals featuring athletic competitions intended as eternal compensation for the prototypical deaths of two other infant heroes, Arkhemoros and Melikertes respectively.* I will have more to say presently about those two heroes.

8A§2. Here I invoke, as I have invoked in my earlier research on the ritual origins of Greek athletics,† the relevant evidence assembled by Walter Burkert in his handbook on Greek religion.‡ This evidence indicates that the traditions of ancient Greek athletics evolved out of practices originating from (1) rituals of initiation into adulthood and (2) rituals of compensation for death.

8A§3. These two kinds of rituals are actually related, since the ritual process of initiation, in and of itself, can be seen as a compensation for death. From an anthropological point of view, a common characteristic of initiation rituals is the figuring of death as a prerequisite for a rebirth from one given age class to another, as in the case of initiations from pre-adult into adult status; according to the mentality underlying rituals of initiation, as I have already noted, you must die to your old self in order to be reborn to your new self.§

8A§4. Here is a salient example: in the case of athletic competitions held at the festival of the Lykaia in Arcadia, these competitions were organically connected with rituals that re-enacted the separations of pre-adult and adult-age

---

* Pache 2004:95–180.
† *PH* 118 = 4§4.
‡ Burkert 1985:105–107.
§ *PH* 118–119, 121–122 = 4§§5, 8, with examples and references.

classes, and these rituals were in turn organically connected with a myth that tells about the death and regeneration of an infant hero named Arkas.*

8A§5. A comparable myth tells about the death and regeneration of the infant hero Pelops, which was an aetiology for an athletic competition held at the festival of the Olympics in Olympia. This competition was a single-lap footrace known as the *stadion*.† The myth about the death and regeneration of Pelops is retold in Pindar's *Olympian* 1, where it is artfully juxtaposed with other myths about the origins of the Olympics.‡

8A§6. Such myths can be understood in terms of initiation from boyhood into manhood, for the purpose of preparing men for warfare. Such a ritualized purpose is evident also in such institutions as the seasonally recurring mock battle known as the *Ballētus* at the Eleusinian Games, which we considered in Hour 8 Text C (*Homeric Hymn to Demeter* 259–267). We have also considered in passing a more famous example, and that is the mock battle of Spartan boys in a sacralized space known as the *Platanistās*, 'Grove of the Plane Trees' (Pausanias 3.11.2, 3.14.8–9, at 3.20.8). On the basis of such rituals, we may infer that the institutionalized practices of athletics and warfare were originally viewed as parts of one single ritual continuum.

8A§7. Such an inference, I must emphasize, is not an attempt to essentialize warfare. Given the exponentially increasing horrors of war in modern times, most observers today (including myself) would be repelled by any such attempt. Still, there is no denying that warfare was a fact of life in premodern times—and that it was ritualized in different ways in different societies.

8A§8. Besides the narrative about the death and regeneration of the infant hero Pelops, there is also another narrative that serves as another aetiological myth for yet another athletic event at the Olympics. In this case, the narrative is about the victory of Pelops as an adolescent hero in a four-horse chariot race. In fact, this narrative serves as the aetiological myth for the athletic event of four-horse chariot racing at the Olympics, as we see from the artful retelling in Pindar's *Olympian* 1.§

8A§9. From other retellings of this aetiological myth, we learn that the basic

---

* *PH* 126 = 4§13, following Burkert 1983:86–87.

† Burkert 1983:100; *PH* 125 = 4§12. In terms of myth and ritual, the single-lap and the double-lap footraces known respectively as the *stadion* and the *diaulos* at the Olympics were viewed together as an organic unity (Philostratus *On athletics* 5 and 6 respectively).

‡ *PH* 121–135 = 4§§8–26; Pache 2004:84–94.

§ *PH* 199–200 = 7§1.

motivation for the athletic event of the four-horse chariot race at the Olympics was the death of the hero Oinomaos while he was competing in a prototypical four-horse chariot race with Pelops. We learn what the Delphic Oracle is reputed to have said about the consequences of this prototypical death when we read the reportage of the antiquarian Phlegon of Tralles (*FGH* 257 F 1 lines 8–9): θῆκε δ' ἔπειτα ἔροτιν καὶ ἔπαθλα θανόντι | Οἰνομάῳ, 'then he [Pelops] established a festival and contests for prizes [*ep-āthla*] in honor of the dead Oinomaos'. In terms of this extended narrative, not only the chariot race but the entire festival of the Olympics was founded by Pelops. Moreover, in the words of the Delphic Oracle as reported by Phlegon (lines 6–7), Pelops was in fact only the second founder of the Olympics: the Oracle says that the first founder was Pisos, the eponymous hero of Pisa, a place closely associated with the Olympics. As for the third founder, it was Hēraklēs, as we read further in the words of the Oracle as quoted by Phlegon (lines 9–11): τρίτατος δ' ἐπὶ τοῖς πάϊς Ἀμφιτρύωνος | Ἡρακλέης ἐτέλεσσ' ἔροτιν καὶ ἀγῶνα ἐπὶ μήτρῳ | Τανταλίδῃ Πέλοπι φθιμένῳ, 'after them [= the first two founders of the Olympics] the third was Hēraklēs son of Amphitryon: he established the festival and the competition [*agōn*] in honor of [*epi*] his maternal relative, the dead Pelops, son of Tantalos'.

8A§10. Here we see the same syntactical construction that we saw in the compressed retelling of the aetiological myth that motivated the foundation of the athletic competition 'in honor of' the infant hero Dēmophōn. I repeat here the wording as we found it in Hesychius: Βαλλητύς· ἑορτὴ Ἀθήνησιν, ἐπὶ Δημοφῶντι τῷ Κελεοῦ ἀγομένη, '*Ballētus* is a festival in Athens, celebrated in honor of [*epi*] Dēmophōn son of Keleos'. Once again, I have translated the preposition *epi* (ἐπί) here in combination with the name of Dēmophōn in the dative case as 'in honor of Dēmophōn'. But this translation, as I have already noted, is inadequate, and it would be more accurate to word it this way: 'in compensation for [the death of] Dēmophōn'. After all, as we saw in earlier in Text C taken from the *Homeric Hymn to Demeter* (259–267), the athletic competition of the *Ballētus* is overtly described as an act of compensation, recurring at the right season into all eternity, and this competition is understood to be an eternal compensation for one single all-important fact: that the hero Dēmophōn must die.

8A§11. The necessity of this death, of this primal ordeal of the hero in myth, is what motivates in aetiological terms the corresponding necessity of the seasonally recurring ordeals of participants in the ritual athletic competition of the

Ballētus. And we have just seen a corresponding expression in the words of the Delphic Oracle as quoted by Phlegon (lines 10–11): Ἡρακλέης ἐτέλεσσ' ἔροτιν καὶ ἀγῶνα ἐπὶ μήτρῳ | Τανταλίδῃ Πέλοπι φθιμένῳ, 'Hēraklēs established the festival and the competition [*agōn*] in honor of [*epi*] his maternal relative, the dead Pelops, son of Tantalos'. Again, it would be more accurate to reword the translation: 'in compensation for the death of his maternal relative, Pelops, son of Tantalos'. A parallel translation is needed for the wording attributed to the Delphic Oracle's description of the competitions in honor of Oinomaos as instituted by Pelops. I repeat here the wording as quoted by Phlegon (lines 8–9): θῆκε δ' ἔπειτα ἔροτιν καὶ ἔπαθλα θανόντι | Οἰνομάῳ, 'then he [Pelops] established a festival and contests for prizes [*ep-āthla*] in honor of the dead Oinomaos'. I now retranslate this way: 'then he [Pelops] established a festival and contests for prizes [*-āthla*] in compensation for the death of [*ep-*] Oinomaos'. In this case, as I noted earlier, the myth makes it clear that the compensation was needed because Pelops himself had caused, wittingly or unwittingly, the death of Oinomaos in the course of their chariot race with each other (Apollodorus *Epitome* 2.7).

8A§12. This kind of aetiology is typical of athletic contests. Another example is the *Tlēpolemeia*, a seasonally recurring festival of athletic contests held on the island of Rhodes and named after Tlepolemos, son of Hēraklēs and founder of Rhodes.* In the words of Pindar, this athletic festival was founded by the hero Tlepolemos as a *lutron*, 'compensation', for a 'pitiful misfortune' (λύτρον συμφορᾶς οἰκτρᾶς *Olympian* 7.77). The 'misfortune' or catastrophe to which Pindar's wording refers is the hero's deranged slaying of a maternal relative (7.27–32).†

8A§13. It can be said in general that athletic festivals were aetiologically motivated by myths that told of the pollution resulting from a hero's disastrous death.‡ In the case of the three other most prestigious athletic festivals besides the Olympic Games in the Peloponnesus, which was the region recognized by all Hellenes as the cradle of their ancient Hellenic civilization, the relevant foundation myths are as follows:§

---

* Nilsson 1906:462–463.

† Commentary on Pindar *Olympian* 7.27–32, 77 in *PH* 140 = 5§§6–7.

‡ Roller 1981a:107n4; an extensive set of examples is collected by Pfister 1912:496–497; see also Brelich 1958:94–95.

§ *PH* 120 = 4§6; Roller 1981a:107n5.

- Pythian Games, founded by the Amphiktyones in compensation for the killing of the Python by Apollo: ἐπὶ τῷ Πύθωνος φόνῳ, 'in compensation for the killing of the Python [by Apollo]' (Aristotle F 637.16).
- Isthmian Games, founded by the hero Sisyphus in compensation for the death of the infant hero Melikertes, who was also known as Palaimon: τὸν ἀγῶνα ἐπ' αὐτῷ, 'the competition [agōn] in compensation for [epi] him' (Pausanias 2.1.3).
- Nemean Games, founded by the heroes known as the Seven against Thebes in compensation for the death, by snakebite, of the infant hero Arkhemoros, who was also known as Opheltes: ἄθλησαν ἐπ' Ἀρχεμόρῳ, 'they [= the Seven] endured ordeals [āthloi] in compensation for Arkhemoros' (Bacchylides 9.12). In poetic terms, the antidote for the prototypical snakebite is the singing of ep-aoidai, 'incantations' (Pindar Nemean 8.49), and such songs (aoidai means 'songs') counteract the deadly venom by celebrating athletic victories that are won at the Nemean Games in compensation for the prototypical death (Nemean 49–53).

8A§14. As we have seen, then, the idea of athletics as a ritual activity that compensates for the pollution caused by the death of a hero in myth can be expressed by combining the prefix / preposition / preverb epi- (ἐπι-) with the dative case referring to that hero. And we have seen this usage in the context of athletic competitions that are aetiologically motivated by the pollution caused by the death of a hero in myth, as in the case of the Eleusinian Games as well as the Olympic, Pythian, Isthmian, and Nemean Games.

Hour 8b. The Meaning of Āthlos / Aethlos

8B§1. In the aetiologies we have been examining so far, the Greek word referring to the ritual ordeal of the athlete in the post-heroic age who re-enacts the mythical ordeal of the hero in the heroic age is āthlos, or aethlos in epic diction. As we saw already in Hour 1, Text C, Homeric poetry refers to the Labors of Hēraklēs himself as aethloi (Iliad XIX 133). Someone who participates in such an ordeal is an āthlētēs. As we also saw in Hour 1, this word is borrowed into English as athlete.

8B§2. The rituals of athletic ordeals, as I just noted in Hour 8a, were understood to be a compensation for the myths of heroic ordeals. I recall here the observation of Simone Weil, as we considered it in Hour 6, about the way humans feel about suffering. She observed that suffering needs compensation: *I want you to suffer exactly the way I suffered.* The hero, whose sufferings were imagined to be immeasurably larger-than-life, would thus have a boundless need for compensation. But how can you suffer exactly the way a hero suffered?

8B§3. To endure such suffering, as an athlete, is to re-enact a prototypical ordeal of a hero. A more accurate way of understanding athletic contests in their archaic Greek historical contexts is to keep in mind the meanings of the ancient Greek words *āthlos* (epic *aethlos*), 'ordeal, contest', and *āthlon* (epic *aethlon*), 'prize won in the course of participating in an *āthlos*'; and *āthlētēs*, 'athlete, one who participates in an *āthlos*'. To restate the concept of athletics in ancient Greek terms: an *āthlos* was the ritual 'ordeal' or 'contest' of an athlete engaging in athletic contests that were taking place in the historical present, but it was also the mythological 'ordeal' or 'contest' of a hero engaging in life-and-death contests that took place once upon a time in the heroic past; moreover, the ritual 'ordeals' or 'contests' of the historical present were viewed as *re-enactments* of the mythical 'ordeals' or 'contests' of the heroic past.* As we have seen, the myths about the life-and-death 'ordeals' of heroes functioned as *aetiologies* for the rituals of athletic competition. Here I repeat my working definition of *aetiology* as *a myth that motivates an institutional reality, especially a ritual.*

8B§4. Besides *āthlos* and its derivatives, another ancient Greek word that proves to be essential for understanding the nature of athletic contests in archaic contexts is *agōn*, derived from the root *ag-* of the verb *agō* as it is used in the compound formation *sun-agein,* which means 'bring together, assemble, gather'. Basically, an *agōn* is a 'bringing together' of people; and the occasion of such a 'bringing together' is a 'competition'. This meaning, 'competition', is still evident in the English borrowing of a compound formation involving the word *agōn*, that is, *antagonism.* We can see a comparable idea embedded in the meaning of the Latin word that gives us the English borrowing *competition*: basically, the meaning of Latin *com-petere* is 'to come together', and to *come together* is to *compete.*† In the case of the Greek word *agōn*, the activity of *competition* to which it refers was understood to be a ritual ordeal, just as the Greek word *āthlos* meant 'ordeal' as well as 'contest', that is, *competition*. The concept of 'ordeal' as embedded in the Greek word *agōn* is still evident in the English borrowing *agony*.

---

*   *PH* 137 = 5§3.
†   *PH* 136–137 = 5§2.

8в§5. These words *āthlos* and *agōn* refer to the experience of a ritual ordeal not only in athletics but also in warfare. For example, the expression *arēios agōn*, 'the *agōn* of Arēs', as used by Herodotus (9.33.3) refers to the ritual experience of combat in war. Similarly in the case of *āthlos* (epic *aethlos*), this word refers to the experience of warriors (Herodotus 1.67.1) as well as athletes (Herodotus 5.22.2). In epic, we find *aethlos* applying to the martial efforts, all considered together, of Achaeans and Trojans alike in the Trojan War (*Iliad* III 126) or, considered separately, to the efforts of the Achaeans in general (*Odyssey* iii 262) or of Odysseus in particular (iv 170).

8в§6. When it comes to re-enacting the primal ordeals of heroes, there is a seemingly limitless variety of individual experiences to be matched with the individual experiences of heroes. Every individual has his or her own way of going through an ordeal, as we see in the staggering varieties of violent death in the *Iliad*.

8в§7. Still, as we have just seen by observing the uses of the words *āthlos* and *agōn*, the ritual ordeals of humans fighting in war and the mythical ordeals of heroes fighting in war were not distinguished from each other. In our own terms of thinking, by contrast, when someone undergoes the real experience of war in the historical context of his own life and times, this experience is seen as distinct from the mythical experiences of heroes who fought in wars in mythical times. But the thinking is different in terms of ritual and myth, reflecting the mentality of the ancient Greeks in their own historical context: from their standpoint, a human who fights in war is undergoing a ritual ordeal that *re-enacts* the mythical ordeals of heroes. This way, the distinction between that human's ritual ordeal and the heroes' mythical ordeals is neutralized. And such a mentality of not distinguishing between human experience and heroic experience in the context of ritual and myth applies not only to the ordeals of war but also to the ordeals of athletics.

8в§8. It can be said in general that different aspects of athletics re-enact different aspects of warfare as experienced by heroes. Besides such obvious examples as the throwing of spears or javelins, however, there are other examples in which it is not at all obvious how a given kind of athletic event is related to a given kind of event in warfare, even if these two kinds of events are defined by the same instrument of war. One such example is the athletic event of chariot racing. The question here is this: how exactly is chariot racing as an athletic event related to chariot fighting as an event in warfare? In Hours 7a, 7b, 7c, and 7d, I tried to answer this question by examining two different kinds of chariot racing as attested at two different festivals: the apobatic races at the Panathenaia and the non-apobatic races at the Olympics. In the case of non-apobatic chariot racing, the relatedness of such racing with chariot fighting is not obvious. But it is in fact quite obvious, as we have seen, in the case of apobatic chariot racing.

8B§9. I conclude by summarizing what we have observed about the uses of words like *āthlos* and *agōn*: just as the ritual ordeal of a human who fights in a real war and the mythical ordeals of heroes fighting in mythical wars are not distinguished from each other in the thinking we see reflected in the ancient Greek texts, so also the ritual ordeal of a human who competes in a real athletic contest is not distinguished from the corresponding mythical ordeals of heroes.

Hour 8c. Back to the Panathenaia

8C§1. I return to the Panathenaic Games held at the festival of the Panathenaia in Athens. In this case, I have argued that the athletic event of the *apobatai* as celebrated at this seasonally recurring festival is understood as a ritual that is aetiologically motivated to compensate for a primal event of pollution in myth. That pollution, as I have also argued, is the death of the hero Patroklos, which leads to the revenge taken by Achilles in the form of dragging the corpse of Hector behind his speeding chariot.

8C§2. The athletic event of the *apobatai* at the Panathenaia shows the ritual dimension of the cult hero as a complement to the mythical dimension that we see played out in narratives conveyed by painting as well as by poetry. As we saw earlier, the main painting on the Münster Hydria shows Achilles himself competing in this athletic event, thus becoming a prototypical participant in the hero cult that he shares with his other self, Patroklos. Through his proto-typical competition, Achilles shows the way for future athletes to compete in this athletic event of the *apobatai* at the seasonally recurring festival of the Pana-thenaia for all time to come.*

8C§3. The vase paintings that we saw in Hour 7 consistently show both Achil-les and Patroklos in apobatic poses, which fits their aetiological status as cult heroes presiding over the athletic event of the *apobatai* as held at the festival of the Panathenaia. By contrast with the vase paintings, however, as I showed in Hour 7e, the Homeric *Iliad* as we know it tends to shade over any details that are typical of apobatic chariot racing and to highlight only those details that are typical of non-apobatic chariot racing as we see it attested primarily at the festi-

---

* *HPC* 175–176 = II§105.

val of the Olympics. As I showed in Hour 7f, this tendency as we find it in the Homeric *Iliad* indicates a less Athenian and more "Panionian" version of epic poetry concerning Achilles, Patroklos, and the Trojan War.

8c§4. Even though the text of the Homeric *Iliad* as we have it has shaded over the specific idea of Achilles and Patroklos as cult heroes connected with the aetiology of apobatic chariot racing at the Panathenia in Athens, it still highlights the general idea of Achilles and Patroklos as cult heroes. Even after these two Homeric figures got disconnected from any aetiology concerning any specific event of athletic ritual, they still remained connected, as cult heroes, with non-apobatic chariot racing as a general event of athletic ritual. In Hour 7, I examined the relevant passages in *Iliad* XXIII where the focus for such chariot racing is a turning point that proves to be the tomb of Patroklos. Then, in this hour, I examined other relevant passages in the *Iliad* showing that this tomb of Patroklos turns out to be the same *sēma* as the tomb of Achilles himself.

Hour 8d. Patroklos as a Model for Achilles

8D§1. In the painting of the Münster Hydria, as I argued in Hour 7, Patroklos shows the way for Achilles to undertake the ritualized actions of the *apobatēs*. The homunculus is running the run of the *apobatēs*. He is the model. His message is this: do as I do. So the apobatic run of Achilles at ground zero mirrors the apobatic run of Patroklos in thin air. By way of this mirroring, Achilles himself can in his own turn become a model. And the ritualized actions of Achilles as *apobatēs* will show the way for the future observance of rituals of hero cult not only for Patroklos but even for Achilles himself.* That is why, as we saw in Hour 7, the self of Patroklos as a *psūkhē* will become the self of Achilles, whose corpse will be placed inside the same tomb that is already occupied by the corpse of his other self, Patroklos.

8D§2. The painting on the Münster Hydria signals such a meaning not only by picturing the *psūkhē* of Patroklos as it levitates over the tomb that he will be sharing with Achilles but also by even labeling the picture, that is, by painting the consecutive letters ΦΣΥΧΕ to spell *psūkhē* or 'spirit', where the act of painting these letters that spell out *psūkhē* becomes a *sēma* or 'sign' in its own right.† In the timelessness of the narrative created in this picture, Patroklos and Achil-

---

* *GM* 94n50 and 220n54.
† *GM* 220.

les share not only the same *sēma* or 'tomb' but even the same *psūkhē*, as indicated by the *sēma* or 'sign' for the word *psūkhē*.

Hour 8e. The Mentality of Re-Enactment at Festivals

8e§1. We have seen that the paintings on both the Münster Hydria and the Boston Hydria depict an athletic event that was part of the ritual program of the greatest festival of the Athenians, the Panathenaia. Both depictions show that the *ritual* of an athlete's ordeal re-enacts the *myth* of a hero's ordeal. Here I will explore further the mentality of such re-enactment.

8e§2. I start with a review of my working definitions of *ritual* and *myth*:

> Ritual is doing things and saying things in a way that is considered sacred. Myth is saying things in a way that is also considered sacred. So ritual frames myth.

And now I add this to the working definition:

> The epic of Homeric poetry is a kind of myth. Like all myths, epic is framed by ritual—the ritual of performance. And performance is re-enactment. You can re-enact not just by acting out a ritual but even by telling or retelling a myth that is framed by ritual.

And what I just said about the verbal art of epic applies also to the visual art of painting, as we saw in action when we viewed the pictures painted on the Münster Hydria and the Boston Hydria. These pictures show *ritual* and *myth* together, just as poetry shows ritual and myth together in the chariot race described at *Iliad* XXIII.

8e§3. A Greek word for the re-enactment of myth in ritual is *mīmēsis*. And the ritual process of *mīmēsis* as the re-enacting of an ordeal leads to a ritual process of purification or *katharsis* of emotions. Here I turn to a celebrated formulation of Aristotle, who links *mīmēsis* and *katharsis*, conventionally latinized as *catharsis* in his definition of tragedy. Here is how he says it:

HOUR 8 TEXT N

> Tragedy, then, is the re-enactment [*mīmēsis*] of a serious and complete action. It has magnitude, with language embellished individually for

each of its forms and in each of its parts. It is done by performers [*drôntes*] and not by way of narrative, bringing about through pity [*eleos*] and fear [*phobos*] the purification [*katharsis*] of such emotions [*pathēmata*].

Aristotle *Poetics* 1449b24–28*

8E§4. I sum up, then, what we have learned so far about *mīmēsis*: it is the process of re-enactment in sacred space. What you re-enact is myth, and how you re-enact it is ritual, which brings about a purification of emotions, especially the emotions of pity and fear.

8E§5. This formulation is relevant to the following two points I have already made:

· Aristotle thought that the *Iliad* was a prototype of tragedy (Hour 2§54).
· In tragedy, the emotion of pity is a force of attraction while the emotion of fear is a force of repulsion (Hour 2§55).

8E§6. And the same formulation is also relevant to the following two points:

· The witnessing of brutality activates the emotions of fear and pity.
· The hero's occasional moments of brutality must have been as shocking to the ancients as they are to us.

---

*ἔστιν οὖν τραγῳδία μίμησις πράξεως σπουδαίας καὶ τελείας μέγεθος ἐχούσης, ἡδυσμένῳ λόγῳ χωρὶς ἑκάστῳ τῶν εἰδῶν ἐν τοῖς μορίοις, δρώντων καὶ οὐ δι᾽ ἀπαγγελίας, δι᾽ ἐλέου καὶ φόβου περαίνουσα τὴν τῶν τοιούτων παθημάτων κάθαρσιν.

The Return of Odysseus in the Homeric Odyssey

The Meaning of Nostos

9§1. The key word for this hour is *nostos*, 'return, homecoming; song about homecoming; return to light and life'. The last of these meanings is mystical, having to do with ideas about immortalization after death. Our first impression is that such ideas are foreign to Homeric poetry. When we take a second look, however, we will see that immortalization is a subtext, as it were, even in Homeric poetry. Immortalization is a matter of *eschatology*.

9§2. As I argued already in Hour 8, Hādēs is *transitional* rather than *eschatological*: only paradisiacal places like Elysium *(Ēlusion)*, the Islands of the Blessed *(Nēsoi Makarōn)*, the White Island *(Leukē)*, and, exceptionally, even Mount Olympus in the case of Hēraklēs are eschatological. I will have more to say in Hour 11 about such paradisiacal places.

9§3. For now, however, I concentrate on the concept of *nostos* and how it can express the idea of immortalization after death. As we will see, this idea is embedded in the plot of the *Odyssey,* but only indirectly, as a *metaphor.* (For my usage of the term *metaphor* here, I refer back to Hour 4§32.)

9§4. Let us begin with the very first occurrences of the word *nostos* in the *Odyssey,* in verses 5 and 9 and 13 at the very beginning of the epic:

HOUR 9 TEXT A (SEE ALSO HOUR 0 TEXT B)

|₁ That man, tell me O Muse the song of that man, that versatile [*polutropos*] man, who in very many ways |₂ veered from his path and wandered off far and wide, after he had destroyed the sacred citadel of Troy. |₃ Many different cities of many different people did he see, getting to know different ways of thinking [*noos*]. |₄ Many were the pains [*algea*]

he suffered in his heart [thūmos] while crossing the sea |₅ struggling to merit [arnusthai] the saving of his own life [psūkhē] and his own home-coming [nostos] as well as the homecoming of his comrades [hetairoi]. |₆ But do what he might he could not save his comrades [hetairoi], even though he very much wanted to. |₇ For they perished through their own deeds of sheer recklessness, |₈ disconnected [nēpioi]* as they were, because of what they did to the cattle of the sun-god Hēlios. |₉ They ate them. So the god [Hēlios] deprived them of their day of homecoming [nostimon]. |₁₀ Starting from any single point of departure, O goddess, daughter of Zeus, tell me, as you have told those who came before me. |₁₁ So now all those who escaped precipitous death |₁₂ were safely home, having survived the war and the sea voyage. |₁₃ But he [= Odysseus], apart from the others, though he was longing for his homecoming [nos-tos] and for his wife, |₁₄ was detained by the queenly nymph [numphē] Calypso, who has her own luminous place among all the goddesses . . .

Odyssey i 1–14†

9§5. As we see from this commencement of the story, the *nostos*, 'return', of the epic hero from Troy to his home in Ithaca is still in progress, and the return is stalled from the start. The story will have to recommence, and such a recom-mencement is about to happen. But even before the recommencement, the story already refers to the many different adventures of the hero in the course of his upcoming story. The plot of this story and its main character, once the *Odyssey* is fully told, will be a fusion of many different subplots and even of many differ-ent subcharacters. Of course there is only one Odysseus in the macro-Narrative of the Homeric *Odyssey*, but there are many different kinds of Odysseus and many different kinds of odyssey in the micro-narratives that add up to the macro-Narrative. These different kinds of character and plot fit perfectly the hero who is called *polu-tropos* in the first verse of the *Odyssey*. Initially, I trans-

---

* On the meaning of *nēpios* as 'disconnected', see the Core Vocabulary.

† |₁ ἄνδρα μοι ἔννεπε, Μοῦσα, πολύτροπον, ὃς μάλα πολλὰ |₂ πλάγχθη, ἐπεὶ Τροίης ἱερὸν πτολίεθρον ἔπερσε· |₃ πολλῶν δ' ἀνθρώπων ἴδεν ἄστεα καὶ νόον ἔγνω, |₄ πολλὰ δ' ὅ γ' ἐν πόντῳ πάθεν ἄλγεα ὃν κατὰ θυμόν, |₅ ἀρνύμενος ἥν τε ψυχὴν καὶ νόστον ἑταίρων. |₆ ἀλλ' οὐδ' ὣς ἑτάρους ἐρρύσατο, ἱέμενός περ· |₇ αὐτῶν γὰρ σφετέρῃσιν ἀτασθαλίῃσιν ὄλοντο, |₈ νήπιοι, οἳ κατὰ βοῦς Ὑπερίονος Ἠελίοιο |₉ ἤσθιον· αὐτὰρ ὁ τοῖσιν ἀφείλετο νόστιμον ἦμαρ. |₁₀ τῶν ἁμόθεν γε, θεά, θύγατερ Διός, εἰπὲ καὶ ἡμῖν. |₁₁ ἔνθ' ἄλλοι μὲν πάντες, ὅσοι φύγον αἰπὺν ὄλεθρον, |₁₂ οἴκοι ἔσαν, πόλεμόν τε πεφευγότες ἠδὲ θάλασσαν· |₁₃ τὸν δ' οἶον, νόστου κεχρημένον ἠδὲ γυναικός, |₁₄ νύμφη πότνι' ἔρυκε Καλυψώ, δῖα θεάων.

lated this word as 'versatile', but its more literal meaning is this: 'one who could change in many different ways who he was'.

The Roles of Odysseus

9§6. There are many different roles that fit the versatile character of Odysseus in the Homeric *Odyssey*, and here I list these roles in the format of five headlines:*

1. The soldier of fortune comes back home to Ithaca after the adventures he experiences both during the Trojan War and afterward during his many travels, and then he reclaims his wife, whose faithfulness in his absence determines his true identity.
2. The returning king reclaims his kingdom by becoming reintegrated with his society. The king, as king, is the embodiment of this society, of this body politic; thus the society, as re-embodied by the king, is correspondingly reintegrated. (On the king as the embodiment of the body politic, see Hour 6§13 and §47.)
3. The pilot lost at sea finally finds his bearings and reaches home. The pilot, or *kubernētēs,* a Greek word that was eventually borrowed into Latin as *gubernātor,* is the steersman who directs the metaphorical 'ship of state'. The metaphor is latent in English words derived from Latin *gubernātor,* such as 'govern', 'governor', and 'government'.
4. The seer or shaman returns home from his vision quest.
5. The trickster retraces his misleading steps, returning all the way back home, back where he had started, and thus showing the correct steps that need to be taken in order to live one's own life successfully.

9§7. The five roles of Odysseus as I list them in these five headlines are extrapolated from Albert Lord's far-ranging survey of world-wide parallels to the theme of the epic hero's return in the Homeric *Odyssey.*† As we can see from Lord's survey, the idea of *nostos* is deeply ritualistic. In fact, as I noted at the beginning of this hour, the *nostos* of Odysseus in the *Odyssey* means not only a

---

* These headlines are based on an earlier formulation in EH §52.
† Lord 1960:158–185.

'return' or a 'song about a return' but even a 'return to light and life'.* This ritual-istic meaning, as we will see in Hour 10, has to do with the epic "hidden agenda" of *returning from Hādēs* and the heroic theme of *immortalization after death.*

The Complementarity of the Iliad *and the* Odyssey

9§8. The polytropic character of Odysseus, central epic hero of the *Odyssey*, stands in sharp contrast to the monolithic character of Achilles, the commen-surately central epic hero of the *Iliad*. Whereas Achilles achieves his epic cen-trality by way of his role as a warrior, Odysseus achieves his own kind of epic centrality in an alternative way—as a master of crafty stratagems and cunning intelligence.†

9§9. There are of course many other heroes in Homeric poetry, but Achilles and Odysseus have become the two central points of reference. Just as the cen-tral heroes of the *Iliad* and the *Odyssey* are complementary, so too are the epics that centralize them. The complementarity extends even further: between the two of them, these two epics give the impression of incorporating most of what-ever was worth retelling about the world of heroes.

9§10. In the case of the *Iliad*, as I already noted at the beginning of the book, this epic not only tells the story that it says it will tell, about Achilles' anger and how it led to countless woes as the Greeks went on fighting it out with the Tro-jans and striving to ward off the fiery onslaught of Hector. It also manages to retell the entire Tale of Troy.

9§11. The Homeric *Odyssey* is equally comprehensive by way of telling the story of the hero's *nostos*, 'return, homecoming'. This word, as I noted at the beginning of this hour, means not only 'homecoming' but also 'song about homecoming'.‡ As such, the *Odyssey* is not only a *nostos*: it is a *nostos* to end all other *nostoi*.§ In other words, the *Odyssey* is the final and definitive statement about the theme of a heroic homecoming: in the process of retelling the return of the epic hero Odysseus, the narrative of the *Odyssey* achieves a sense of clo-sure in the retelling of all feats stemming from the heroic age.** The *Odyssey*, as

---

* *GM* 218–219, following Frame 1978.
† This paragraph and the paragraphs that follow are based on the argumentation in EH §§47–50.
‡ *BA* (1999) xii = Preface §16, with reference to *BA* 97 = 6§6n2.
§ *BA* (1999) xii–xiii = Preface §§16–18.
** On the narrative of the *Odyssey* as an act of closure, closing the doors on the heroic age, see Martin 1993.

we will see, provides a retrospective even on those epic moments that are missing in the *Iliad,* such as the story of the Wooden Horse (viii 487–520).

9§12. A central theme unites the Homeric *Iliad* and *Odyssey:* as we see from the pervasive use of the title *aristos Akhaiōn,* 'best of the Achaeans', in both epics, Achilles emerges as the rightful owner of this title in the *Iliad* while Odysseus earns the same title in the *Odyssey.** But the poetry of epic awards this title not by way of measuring the successes achieved by these heroes by virtue of their predominant heroic qualities, namely, strength in the case of Achilles and intelligence in the case of Odysseus. After all, Achilles failed to capture Troy with his heroic strength. As for Odysseus, although he used his heroic intelligence in inventing the Wooden Horse, which was the key to the capture of Troy by the Achaeans, this success did not win for him the title of the 'best of the Achaeans' in the *Iliad.* Rather, Odysseus earned that title by becoming the main hero of the *Odyssey,* just as Achilles earned the same title by becoming the main hero of the *Iliad.*†

9§13. Underlying the complementarity of the *Iliad* and the *Odyssey* and of the main heroes of these two epics is an element of competition. The *kleos* or epic glory of Achilles in the *Iliad* is competitively contrasted with the *kleos* of Odysseus in the *Odyssey.*‡ As we are about to see, the key to understanding such a competition is the Homeric use of the word *nostos* in the sense of a 'song about a homecoming', not just a 'homecoming'. Ironically, as I argue, Odysseus achieves the *kleos* or epic glory of the *Odyssey* not because he destroyed Troy, a feat heralded at the very start of his epic, at verse 2 of the *Odyssey* (as we saw in Text A of this hour), but because he also achieves a *nostos* in both senses of the word: he comes home and thereby becomes the premier hero of a song about homecoming.

9§14. There are further related ironies. As we saw in Text A of Hour 1, Achilles has to choose between *kleos* and *nostos,* forfeiting *nostos* in order to achieve his *kleos* as the central hero of the *Iliad* (IX 413). But Odysseus must have both *kleos* and *nostos* in order to merit his own heroic status in the *Odyssey.*§ The narrative of the *kleos* that Odysseus earns in the *Odyssey* cannot be the *Iliad,*

---

* *BA* ch 2.

† *BA* 35–41 = 2§§10–18.

‡ In the rest of this paragraph and in the next two paragraphs I recapitulate the formulation in *BA* (1999) xii–xiii = Preface §§16–18.

§ *BA* 36–40 = 2§§12–16.

which means 'tale of Troy' (Ilion is the other name for Troy).* The *Iliad* establishes Achilles as the central hero of the story of Troy, even though he failed to destroy the city. Because of the *Iliad* tradition, "the *kleos* of Odysseus at Troy was preempted by the *kleos* of Achilles."† So the *kleos* that Odysseus should get for his success in destroying Troy is elusive, by contrast with the *kleos* that Achilles gets in the *Iliad,* which is permanent. So Odysseus cannot afford to dwell on his success at Troy, because the *kleos* he may get for that success will become permanent only if it extends into the *kleos* that he gets for achieving a successful homecoming. As we see from the wording of the Song of the Sirens in the *Odyssey* (xii 189–191), which I will quote in Hour 10, the sheer pleasure of listening to a song about the destruction of Troy will be in vain if there is no *nostos,* no safe return home from the faraway world of epic heroes; and, by extension, the *Iliad* itself will become a Song of the Sirens without a successful narration of the *Odyssey.*‡

9§15. There is a final irony, developed in the narrative of the *Odyssey* (xi 489–491): Achilles in Hādēs seems tempted to trade epics with Odysseus.§ This he will never do, of course, in his own epic. As Achilles himself predicts in the *Iliad* (IX 413), the *kleos* of his own song will be *aphthiton,* 'unwilting'.

The Heroic Mentality of Achieving Nostos

9§16. As the plot of the *Odyssey* gets under way, the *nostos* of Odysseus is defined by the quest of the hero's son Telemachus to learn the identity of his father—and thus to learn his own identity. I will explain in a minute why I say 'learn' and not 'learn about'. The quest of Telemachus is initiated by the goddess Athena, who specializes in mental power. She is in fact the goddess of intelligence, daughter of the god Zeus and of a goddess named Mētis (Hesiod *Theogony* 886–900); this name Mētis comes from the noun *mētis,* which means 'intelligence', and Athena herself declares that her *kleos,* 'glory', is due to her own *mētis,* 'intelligence' (*Odyssey* xiii 299).** As we can see from a primary epithet of Odysseus, *polumētis,* 'intelligent in many ways' (*Iliad* I 311, etc.; *Odyssey* ii 173, etc.), the goddess Athena must have a special relationship with this hero; in fact,

---

* EH §49.
† *BA* 41 = 2§17.
‡ *BA* (1999) xii = Preface §17n; EH §50; Nagy 2007b:70.
§ *BA* §35 = 2§11; see also Dova 2000.
** *BA* 145 = 8§8.

this same epithet applies to Athena herself (*Homeric Hymn to Athena* 2). We will return in Hour 10, to the word *mētis*. For now, however, the point is simply this: the status of Athena as the goddess of intelligence is relevant to Athena's initial role in the *Odyssey*, where she activates the mental power of Telemachus, son of Odysseus. At a council of the gods, the goddess declares her intention to go to Ithaca to become a mentor to the young epic hero:

HOUR 9 TEXT B

|88 As for me, I will go travel to Ithaca, going to his [= Odysseus'] son |89 in order to give him [= Telemachus] more encouragement and to put power [*menos*] into his heart [*phrenes*].* |90 He is to summon the long-haired Achaeans for a meeting in assembly, |91 and he is to speak out to all the suitors [of his mother Penelope], who persist in |92 slaughtering again and again any number of his sheep and oxen. |93 And I will conduct him to Sparta and to sandy Pylos, |94 and thus he will learn the return [*nostos*] of his dear [*philos*] father, if by chance he [= Telemachus] hears it, |95 and thus may genuine glory [*kleos*] possess him throughout humankind.

Odyssey i 88–95†

9§17. In assuming the role of mentor to Telemachus, the goddess Athena will change her divine shape and take on the human shape of the fatherly epic hero *Mentēs* in *Odyssey* i and then, in *Odyssey* ii and thereafter, of another fatherly epic hero, *Mentōr*. These two names are both related to the noun *menos*. This word, as we can see in the first verse of Text B here, i 88, refers to the heroic 'power' that the goddess Athena says she will put into the heart of Telemachus. The noun *menos*, usually translated as 'power' or 'strength', is derived from the verb-root *mnē-*, meaning 'mentally connect'.‡ Likewise derived from this verb-root are the agent nouns *Men-tēs* and *Men-tōr*, which both mean 'he who connects mentally'. When a divinity connects a hero to his heroic mentality, the

---

* The word *phrenes*, which I translate here as 'heart', expresses in Homeric diction the human capacity to feel and to think, taken together.

† |88 αὐτὰρ ἐγὼν Ἰθάκηνδε ἐλεύσομαι, ὄφρα οἱ υἱὸν |89 μᾶλλον ἐποτρύνω καί οἱ μένος ἐν φρεσὶ θείω, |90 εἰς ἀγορὴν καλέσαντα κάρη κομόωντας Ἀχαιοὺς |91 πᾶσι μνηστήρεσσιν ἀπειπέμεν, οἵ τέ οἱ αἰεὶ |92 μῆλ' ἀδινὰ σφάζουσι καὶ εἰλίποδας ἕλικας βοῦς. |93 πέμψω δ' ἐς Σπάρτην τε καὶ ἐς Πύλον ἠμαθόεντα |94 νόστον πευσόμενον πατρὸς φίλου, ἤν που ἀκούσῃ, |95 ἠδ' ἵνα μιν κλέος ἐσθλὸν ἐν ἀνθρώποισιν ἔχῃσιν.

‡ GM 113.

hero will have *menos,* that is, 'power' or 'strength'. To have heroic power or strength, you have to have a heroic mentality.

9§18. This idea of *heroic mentality* is elegantly recapitulated in the *Odyssey* at the dramatic moment when the goddess Athena has just finished the first phase of her role as mentor to Telemachus, during which phase she had assumed the human shape of the fatherly Mentēs. Having finished with the role of Mentēs, which as we have seen is a name that means literally 'he who connects mentally', the goddess now transforms herself into a bird and flies out of the palace through a lightwell on the roof. Here is the wording that describes what she had accomplished so far in connecting the mind of Telemachus with the mind of his father:

HOUR 9 TEXT C

|₃₂₀ . . . Into his heart [*thūmos*]* |₃₂₁ she [= Athena] had placed power [*menos*] and daring, and she had mentally connected [*hupo-mnē-*] him with his father |₃₂₂ even more than before.

Odyssey i 320–322†

9§19. So in her role as *Mentēs,* which means literally 'he who mentally connects', the goddess has given to the hero Telemachus the *menos* or mental 'power' of connecting with the heroic identity of his father. That act is expressed here by a verb *hupo-mnē-,* which means literally 'mentally connect'.‡

9§20. And what results from such a mental connection? We find an answer in Text B, as I quoted it a few minutes ago. The goddess says in the next-to-last verse, in *Odyssey* i 94, not that Telemachus will learn *about* the *nostos* of Odysseus if he is fortunate enough to hear *about* it. In the original Greek text, the noun *nostos* is the direct object of the verb *punthanesthai,* 'to learn', in verse 94 of Text B here, and that is why I chose to translate the verse this way: 'and thus he will learn [*punthanesthai*] the return [*nostos*] of his dear [*philos*] father, if by

---

* The word *thūmos,* which I translate here as 'heart', expresses in Homeric diction the human capacity to feel and to think, taken together. In some Homeric contexts, *thūmos* is used as a synonym of *phrenes,* which can also be translated as 'heart', as in *Odyssey* i 89, which was the first verse in Text B above. In other Homeric contexts, by contrast, *thūmos* is pictured as the vital force that is contained by the *phrenes:* see GM 113n111. Even in such contexts, both words can be approximated as 'heart'.

† |₃₂₀ . . . τῷ δ' ἐνὶ θυμῷ |₃₂₁ θῆκε μένος καὶ θάρσος, ὑπέμνησέν τέ ἑ πατρὸς |₃₂₂ μᾶλλον ἔτ' ἢ τὸ πάροιθεν.

‡ *GM* 113.

chance he [= Telemachus] hears it.* It is not a question of learning *about* a homecoming, of hearing *about* a homecoming. Rather, Telemachus will learn the actual song of the homecoming, the song of *nostos*. He will actually hear the song from the hero Nestor in *Odyssey* iii and from the hero Menelaos along with his divine consort Helen in *Odyssey* iv.

9§21. As I have been arguing from the start, the *nostos* of Odysseus is not only a 'homecoming' but also a 'song about homecoming'. And now we will see that this song is equivalent to the *kleos* of Odysseus, to his 'glory'.

9§22. This equivalence of *nostos* and *kleos* for Odysseus is evident throughout the story of Telemachus. As we track further the wording used for telling this story, we see that the quest of the son for his father is described as a quest for either the father's *nostos* (as at *Odyssey* ii 360) or the father's *kleos* (as at iii 83).† So these two goals in the son's quest are treated as equivalent. This equivalence extends further. Odysseus must achieve his *kleos,* or epic 'glory', by way of successfully achieving the *nostos* or 'song about homecoming' that is the *Odyssey*. Whereas Achilles has to choose between *nostos,* 'homecoming', and the *kleos,* 'glory', that he gets from his own epic tradition (*Iliad* IX 413), Odysseus must have both *kleos* and *nostos,* because for him his *nostos* in the *Odyssey* is the same thing as his *kleos*.‡ If Odysseus fails to achieve a successful *nostos* in the *Odyssey,* he will also fail to achieve *kleos*. But Odysseus ultimately prevails, and a key to his successful *nostos* is the steadfast faithfulness of his wife, Penelope, who in her own right ultimately shares with Odysseus the *kleos* that marks the hero by the time we reach the end of the *Odyssey* (xxiv 196).§

9§23. In this connection, I find it pertinent to come back to the wording of the goddess Athena in the last verse of Text B, *Odyssey* i 95: it is made explicit there that *kleos* or epic 'glory' will result from the *nostos* of Odysseus. And I now highlight a striking fact about the use of the word *kleos* in that verse. The wording there does not say that the hero will possess *kleos*: rather, it says that *kleos*

---

*Elsewhere, too, in the *Odyssey,* we see *nostos* as the direct object of *punthanesthai,* 'learn' (ii 215, 264, 360; iv 714)—as also of *akouein,* 'hear' (i 287, ii 218). In *BA* 40 = 2§16, I had translated *punthanesthai* (at ii 360) as 'find out about', but my point remains that *nostos* is the direct object of this verb. That is why I now prefer the translation 'learn' to 'learn about'.

† *BA* 40 = 2§16.

‡ *BA* (1999) xii = Preface §§15–16.

§ More needs to be said about this verse at *Odyssey* xxiv 196, where the *kleos* of Odysseus is shared by Penelope. Some interpreters believe that the *kleos* mentioned in this verse belongs to Penelope only, not to Odysseus, whereas I argue that it belongs primarily to Odysseus; for more on these two different interpretations, see *BA* (1999) xii = Preface §16n2.

will possess the hero. Although it is not spelled out in that verse whether the hero is Telemachus or Odysseus himself, the point of reference is obvious: as we can see from reading the *Odyssey* in its entirety, the ultimate subject of *kleos* must be Odysseus himself—when *kleos* possesses this hero, the *kleos* will include all those who have a share in his glory.*

9§24. So far, then, we have seen that Athena is preparing Telemachus to connect mentally with the *nostos* of his father, which is an epic in the making, and that this epic of Odysseus, this *Odyssey,* is a fusion of *nostos* and *kleos.*

A Nostos *in the Making*

9§25. The meaning of *nostos* as a 'song about homecoming' is most evident in the following description of an epic performance where the performer, Phemios by name, is said to be performing a *nostos:*

HOUR 9 TEXT D

$|_{325}$ The famed singer was singing for them [= the suitors], and they in silence $|_{326}$ sat and listened. He [= Phemios the singer] was singing the homecoming [*nostos*] of the Achaeans, $|_{327}$ a disastrous [*lugros*]† homecoming from Troy, and Pallas Athena was the one who brought it all to fulfillment [*epi-tellesthai*]. $|_{328}$ From her room upstairs, this divinely inspired song of his was understood in her mind by $|_{329}$ the daughter of Ikarios, the exceptionally intelligent Penelope, $|_{330}$ and she came down the lofty staircase of her palace. $|_{331}$ She came not alone, but attended by two of her handmaidens. $|_{332}$ When she reached the suitors, this most radiant of women, $|_{333}$ she stood by one of the posts that supported the roof of the halls, $|_{334}$ holding in front of her cheeks a luxuriant veil, $|_{335}$ and a trusted handmaiden stood on either side of her. $|_{336}$ Then, shedding tears, she addressed the godlike singer: $|_{337}$ "Phemios, you know many another thing that charms mortals, $|_{338}$ all about the deeds of men and gods, to which singers give glory [*kleein*]. $|_{339}$ Sing for them [= the suitors] some one of those songs of glory, and

---

* In *Odyssey* xix 108, as I analyze it in Hour 12§4, the disguised Odysseus says to Penelope that she possesses the kind of *kleos,* or 'glory', that a righteous king possesses; the image of the unnamed king here is a placeholder for Odysseus.

† This epithet *lugros,* 'disastrous', is carried over from one verse to the next. The technical term for such carrying over is *enjambment,* and we will see the significance of this device in the analysis that follows.

let them in silence |₃₄₀ drink their wine. But you stop this sad song, |₃₄₁ this disastrous [*lugrē*]* song, which again and again affects my very own [*philon*] heart in my breast, |₃₄₂ wearing it down, since an unforgettable grief [*penthos alaston*] comes over me, more than ever. |₃₄₃ I feel this way because that is the kind of person I long for, recalling his memory again and again, |₃₄₄ the memory of a man whose glory [*kleos*] extends far and wide throughout Hellas and midmost Argos.

Odyssey i 325–344†

9§26. We see here once again that the word *nostos* as a 'song about homecoming' is connected to the *kleos* of Odysseus, which is the 'glory' of his epic. But in this case we see also that *kleos* can make the listener feel *penthos* or 'grief' —such as the *penthos alaston,* 'unforgettable grief' (i 342), felt by Penelope in hearing the epic performed by Phemios.

9§27. At this point in the *Odyssey,* Telemachus does not yet understand the grief experienced by his mother, Penelope, when she hears the *nostos* sung by Phemios, and so the son makes excuses for the singer by claiming that audiences of epic will 'give glory' (*epi-kleein* i 251) most readily to the kind of song that is *neōtatē,* the 'newest' (i 252). Of course such a claim about the attractions of a new song cannot be denied, but the newness of the song in this situation has a deeper meaning. The word *neo-,* 'new', here refers to the appropriateness of the story to the situation in the here and now of performing the story: in this case Odysseus is not yet a character in the story of the *nostos* of the Achaeans as Phemios is singing it, since this story is still in progress, and the audience has not yet heard the end of it, but Odysseus is soon to become the primary character of the story of the *nostos* in the here and now that is being narrated by the epic of the *Odyssey.*‡ And that is because his own *nostos* is literally in the mak-

---

* Here again, the epithet *lugrē,* 'disastrous', is enjambed from one verse to the next.

† |₃₂₅ τοῖσι δ' ἀοιδὸς ἄειδε περικλυτός, οἱ δὲ σιωπῇ |₃₂₆ εἵατ' ἀκούοντες· ὁ δ' Ἀχαιῶν νόστον ἄειδε |₃₂₇ λυγρόν, ὃν ἐκ Τροίης ἐπετείλατο Παλλὰς Ἀθήνη. |₃₂₈ τοῦ δ' ὑπερωϊόθεν φρεσὶ σύνθετο θέσπιν ἀοιδὴν |₃₂₉ κούρη Ἰκαρίοιο, περίφρων Πηνελόπεια· |₃₃₀ κλίμακα δ' ὑψηλὴν κατεβήσετο οἷο δόμοιο, |₃₃₁ οὐκ οἴη, ἅμα τῇ γε καὶ ἀμφίπολοι δύ' ἕποντο. |₃₃₂ ἡ δ' ὅτε δὴ μνηστῆρας ἀφίκετο δῖα γυναικῶν, |₃₃₃ στῆ ῥα παρὰ σταθμὸν τέγεος πύκα ποιητοῖο, |₃₃₄ ἄντα παρειάων σχομένη λιπαρὰ κρήδεμνα· |₃₃₅ ἀμφίπολος δ' ἄρα οἱ κεδνὴ ἑκάτερθε παρέστη. |₃₃₆ δακρύσασα δ' ἔπειτα προσηύδα θεῖον ἀοιδόν· |₃₃₇ "Φήμιε, πολλὰ γὰρ ἄλλα βροτῶν θελκτήρια οἶδας |₃₃₈ ἔργ' ἀνδρῶν τε θεῶν τε, τά τε κλείουσιν ἀοιδοί· |₃₃₉ τῶν ἕν γέ σφιν ἄειδε παρήμενος, οἱ δὲ σιωπῇ |₃₄₀ οἶνον πινόντων· ταύτης δ' ἀποπαύε' ἀοιδῆς |₃₄₁ λυγρῆς, ἥ τέ μοι αἰεὶ ἐνὶ στήθεσσι φίλον κῆρ |₃₄₂ τείρει, ἐπεί με μάλιστα καθίκετο πένθος ἄλαστον. |₃₄₃ τοίην γὰρ κεφαλὴν ποθέω μεμνημένη αἰεὶ |₃₄₄ ἀνδρός, τοῦ κλέος εὐρὺ καθ' Ἑλλάδα καὶ μέσον Ἄργος.

‡ *PH* 69 = 2§33.

ing, since *nostos* means not only 'homecoming' but also 'song about a home-coming'.

Echoes of Lament in a Song about Homecoming

9§28. We saw just a minute ago that *kleos* can make the listener feel *penthos* or 'grief'—such as the grief felt by Penelope in hearing the epic of Phemios. And, as we saw in Hour 3, this word *penthos* means not only 'grief' but also a 'song of grief' as performed in lamentation. Now we will see that there are many things to lament in the song about the homecoming of the Achaeans as reported in the *Odyssey*. In the next paragraph, I offer a summary of the lamentable subtexts, as it were, of the *nostos* song by Phemios.

9§29. The *nostos* or 'song of homecoming' that Phemios sings in *Odyssey* i 326 is described as *lugros*, 'disastrous', at the beginning of the next verse, i 327, just as the *mēnis*, or 'anger', of Achilles that 'Homer' sings in *Iliad* I 1 is described as *oulomenē*, 'disastrous', at the beginning of the next verse, I 2.* The disastrous anger of Achilles had led to immeasurable suffering, caused by Zeus, and the causation is expressed in terms of *telos*, 'fulfillment': 'and the Will of Zeus was being brought to fulfillment [*teleîsthai*]'† (I 5). And so also the goddess Athena made the Achaeans suffer, since she 'brought to fulfillment' a *nostos* that was disastrous for them: 'he [= Phemios] sang the homecoming [*nostos*] of the Achaeans, | a disastrous [*lugros*] homecoming from Troy, and Pallas Athena was the one who brought it all to fulfillment [*epi-tellesthai*]'‡ (i 326–327).§

9§30. From the retrospective standpoint of the *Odyssey*, the suffering of the Achaeans in the course of their homecoming from Troy was caused by Athena because she was angry at them for their immoral behavior in the course of their destroying the city of Troy. The story of Athena's disastrous anger, in its most basic form, is told by Nestor to Telemachus:

HOUR 9 TEXT E

|130 But after we [= the Achaeans] had destroyed the lofty city of Priam
|131 and we went into our ships, the god dispersed us. |132 And then

---

* The parallelism here is accentuated by the fact that the enjambment of the epithet *oulomenē*, 'disastrous', in *Iliad* I 2 is matched by the enjambment of the epithet *lugros*, 'disastrous', in *Odyssey* i 327.

† Διὸς δ' ἐτελείετο βουλή.

‡ ὁ δ' Ἀχαιῶν νόστον ἄειδε | λυγρὸν ὃν ἐκ Τροίης ἐπετείλατο Παλλὰς Ἀθήνη.

§ *BA* 97 = 6§6n2.

it was that Zeus devised in his thinking a plan to make a disastrous [*lugros*] homecoming [*nostos*]* |$_{133}$ for the Argives [= Achaeans]; for they had not at all been either mindful [= having *noos*] or just [*dikaioi*], |$_{134}$ not all of them, and so many of them met up with a bad destiny |$_{135}$ because of the disastrous [*oloē*] anger [*mēnis*] of the daughter of the mighty father—of the goddess with the looks of an owl.

Odyssey iii 130–135†

9§31. In this micro-narrative, we see the outlines of the whole story, but we see no details about the Achaean heroes involved. But a detailed narrative about the immoral behavior of the Achaeans at the end of the Trojan War can be found elsewhere in epic. The most telling example comes from the epic Cycle—in this case, from the *Iliou Persis,* or 'Destruction of Troy', attributed to Arctinus of Miletus. I will now quote the text of the relevant plot summary, where we will see a series of atrocities committed by the Achaean warriors while they are putting an end to the city of Troy. I will concentrate on two parts of the story: first, the anger of Athena, which is highlighted at the end of the narrative, and second, the actions of Odysseus himself, which precede the highlighting of Athena's anger:

HOUR 9 TEXT F

|$_{16}$ After the preceding [= four scrolls of the *Little Iliad*, by Lesches of Lesbos], there follow two scrolls of the *Iliou Persis*, by Arctinus |$_{17}$ of Miletus, containing the following. With regard to the things concerning the Horse, the |$_{18}$ Trojans, suspicious about the horse, stand around wondering what they should |$_{19}$ do. Some think it should be pushed off a cliff, while others |$_{20}$ think it should be burned down, and still others say that it should be dedicated as sacred [*hieros*] to Athena. |$_{21}$ In the end, the opinion of the third group wins out. They turn |$_{22}$ to merriment, feasting as if they had been freed from the war. |$_{23}$ At this point

---

* The use of the epithet *lugros*, 'disastrous', in describing the *nostos*, 'homecoming', of the Achaeans here in iii 132 is reminiscent of the way in which the song of Phemios started in i 326: there too we saw the word *nostos* in the sense of a 'song of homecoming', which is then described by the same epithet *lugros*, 'disastrous', at the beginning of the next verse, i 327.

† |$_{130}$ αὐτὰρ ἐπεὶ Πριάμοιο πόλιν διεπέρσαμεν αἰπήν, |$_{131}$ βῆμεν δ᾽ ἐν νήεσσι, θεὸς δ᾽ ἐκέδασσεν Ἀχαιούς, |$_{132}$ καὶ τότε δὴ Ζεὺς λυγρὸν ἐνὶ φρεσὶ μήδετο νόστον |$_{133}$ Ἀργείοισ᾽, ἐπεὶ οὔ τι νοήμονες οὐδὲ δίκαιοι |$_{134}$ πάντες ἔσαν· τῶ σφεων πολέες κακὸν οἶτον ἐπέσπον |$_{135}$ μήνιος ἐξ ὀλοῆς γλαυκώπιδος ὀβριμοπάτρης.

two serpents appear and |₂₄ destroy Laocoön and one of his sons. At the sight of |₂₅ this marvel, Aeneas and his followers get upset and withdraw |₂₆ to Mount Ida. Sinon lights signal fires for the Achaeans. |₂₇ He had previously entered the city, using a pretext. And they [= the Achaeans], some of them sailing from Tenedos |₂₈ [toward Troy] and others of them emerging from the Wooden Horse, fall upon |₂₉ their enemies. They kill many, and the city |₃₀ is taken by force. Neoptolemos kills |₃₁ Priam, who has taken refuge at the altar of Zeus Herkeios. [p. 108] |₁ Menelaos finds Helen and takes her back down to the ships, after |₂ slaughtering Deiphobos. Ajax son of Oileus takes Kassandra by |₃ force, dragging her away from the wooden statue [*xoanon*] of Athena. At the sight |₄ of this, the Achaeans get angry and decide to stone |₅ Ajax to death, but he takes refuge at the altar of Athena, and so |₆ is preserved from his impending destruction. Then |₇ the Achaeans put the city to the torch. They slaughter Polyxena on the |₈ tomb [*taphos*] of Achilles. Odysseus kills Astyanax, |₉ and Neoptolemos takes Andromache as his prize. The rest |₁₀ of the spoils are distributed. Demophon and Akamas find Aithra |₁₁ and take her with them. Then the Greeks sail off [from Troy], |₁₂ and Athena begins to plan destruction for them at sea.

plot summary by Proclus of the *Iliou Persis* of Arctinus of Miletus pp. 107–108*

9§32. This narrative about the Trojan War as transmitted in the epic Cycle corresponds closely to a narrative we see in *Odyssey* viii. The performer of that

---

* |₁₆ Ἕπεται δὲ τούτοις Ἰλίου πέρσιδος βιβλία δύο Ἀρκτίνου |₁₇ Μιλησίου περιέχοντα τάδε. ὡς τὰ περὶ τὸν ἵππον οἱ |₁₈ Τρῶες ὑπόπτως ἔχοντες περιστάντες βουλεύονται ὅ τι χρὴ |₁₉ ποιεῖν· καὶ τοῖς μὲν δοκεῖ κατακρημνίσαι αὐτόν, τοῖς δὲ |₂₀ καταφλέγειν, οἱ δὲ ἱερὸν αὐτὸν ἔφασαν δεῖν τῇ Ἀθηνᾷ |₂₁ ἀνατεθῆναι· καὶ τέλος νικᾷ ἡ τούτων γνώμη. τραπέντες |₂₂ δὲ εἰς εὐφροσύνην εὐωχοῦνται ὡς ἀπηλλαγμένοι τοῦ πολέ-|₂₃μου. ἐν αὐτῷ δὲ τούτῳ δύο δράκοντες ἐπιφανέντες τόν τε |₂₄ Λαοκόωντα καὶ τὸν ἕτερον τῶν παίδων διαφθείρουσιν. ἐπὶ |₂₅ δὲ τῷ τέρατι δυσφορήσαντες οἱ περὶ τὸν Αἰνείαν ὑπεξῆλθον |₂₆ εἰς τὴν Ἴδην. καὶ Σίνων τοὺς πυρσοὺς ἀνίσχει τοῖς Ἀχαιοῖς, |₂₇ πρότερον εἰσεληλυθὼς προσποίητος. οἱ δὲ ἐκ Τενέδου |₂₈ προσπλεύσαντες καὶ οἱ ἐκ τοῦ δουρείου ἵππου ἐπιπίπτουσι |₂₉ τοῖς πολεμίοις καὶ πολλοὺς ἀνελόντες τὴν πόλιν κατὰ |₃₀ κράτος λαμβάνουσι. καὶ Νεοπτόλεμος μὲν ἀποκτείνει |₃₁ Πρίαμον ἐπὶ τὸν τοῦ Διὸς τοῦ ἑρκείου βωμὸν καταφυγόντα. [p. 108]|₁ Μενέλαος δὲ ἀνευρὼν Ἑλένην ἐπὶ τὰς ναῦς κατάγει, Δηΐ-|₂φοβον φονεύσας. Κασσάνδραν δὲ Αἴας ὁ Ἰλέως πρὸς |₃ βίαν ἀποσπῶν συνεφέλκεται τὸ τῆς Ἀθηνᾶς ξόανον. ἐφ' |₄ ᾧ παροξυνθέντες οἱ Ἕλληνες καταλεῦσαι βουλεύονται τὸν |₅ Αἴαντα. ὁ δὲ ἐπὶ τὸν τῆς Ἀθηνᾶς βωμὸν καταφεύγει καὶ |₆ διασῴζεται ἐκ τοῦ ἐπικειμένου κινδύνου. ἔπειτα ἐμπρή-|₇σαντες τὴν πόλιν Πολυξένην σφαγιάζουσιν ἐπὶ τὸν τοῦ |₈ Ἀχιλλέως τάφον. καὶ Ὀδυσσέως Ἀστυάνακτα ἀνελόντος, |₉ Νεοπτόλεμος Ἀνδρομάχην γέρας λαμβάνει. καὶ τὰ λοιπὰ|₁₀ λάφυρα διανέμονται. Δημοφῶν δὲ καὶ Ἀκάμας Αἴθραν |₁₁ εὑρόντες ἄγουσι μεθ' ἑαυτῶν. ἔπειτα ἀποπλέουσιν οἱ |₁₂ Ἕλληνες, καὶ φθορὰν αὐτοῖς ἡ Ἀθηνᾶ κατὰ τὸ πέλαγος |₁₃ μηχανᾶται.

narrative is the blind singer Demodokos, who is performing an epic in the court of Alkinoos, king of the Phaeacians. In fact, that epic is the third of three songs that he performs in *Odyssey* viii. The audience attending the performance of Demodokos includes Odysseus himself, who has not yet revealed his identity to the Phaeacians:

HOUR 9 TEXT G

$|_{499}$ . . . And he [= Demodokos], setting his point of departure [*hormētheis*], started [*arkhesthai*] from the god. And he made visible [*phainein*] the song, $|_{500}$ taking it *from the point where* they [= the Achaeans], boarding their ships with the strong benches, $|_{501}$ sailed away, setting their tents on fire. $|_{502}$ That is what some of the Argives [= Achaeans] were doing. But others of them were in the company of Odysseus most famed, and they were already $|_{503}$ sitting hidden inside the Horse, which was now in the meeting place of the Trojans. $|_{504}$ The Trojans themselves had pulled the Horse into the acropolis. $|_{505}$ So there it was, standing there, and they talked a great deal about it, in doubt about what to do, $|_{506}$ sitting around it. There were three different plans: $|_{507}$ to split the hollow wood with pitiless bronze, $|_{508}$ or to drag it to the heights and push it down from the rocks, $|_{509}$ or to leave it, great artifact that it was, a charm [*thelktērion*] of the gods $|_{510}$—which, I now see it, was exactly the way it was going to end [*teleutân*], $|_{511}$ because it was fate [*aisa*] that the place would be destroyed, once the city had enfolded in itself $|_{512}$ the great Wooden Horse, when all the best men were sitting inside it, $|_{513}$ the Argives [= Achaeans], that is, bringing slaughter and destruction upon the Trojans. $|_{514}$ He sang how the sons of the Achaeans destroyed the city, $|_{515}$ pouring out of the Horse, leaving behind the hollow place of ambush. $|_{516}$ He sang how the steep citadel was destroyed by different men in different places. $|_{517}$—how Odysseus went to the palace of Deiphobos, $|_{518}$ how he was looking like Arēs, and godlike Menelaos went with him, $|_{519}$ and how in that place, I now see it, he [= Demodokos] said that he [= Odysseus] dared to go through the worst part of the war, $|_{520}$ and how he emerged victorious after that, with the help of Athena, the one with the mighty heart [*thūmos*]. $|_{521}$ So these were the things that the singer [*aoidos*] most famed was singing. As for Odysseus, $|_{522}$ he dissolved [*tēkesthai*] into tears. He made wet his cheeks with the tears flowing from his eyelids, $|_{523}$ just as a woman cries, falling down and embracing her dear husband, |₅₂₄ who fell in front of the city and people he was defending, |₅₂₅ trying to ward off the pitiless day of doom that is hanging over the city and its children. |₅₂₆ She sees him dying, gasping for his last breath, |₅₂₇ and she pours herself all over him as she wails with a piercing cry. But there are men behind her, |₅₂₈ prodding her with their spears, hurting her back and shoulders, |₅₂₉ and they bring for her a life of bondage, which will give her pain and sorrow. |₅₃₀ Her cheeks are wasting away with a sorrow [*akhos*] that is most pitiful [*eleeinon*]. |₅₃₁ So also did Odysseus pour out a piteous tear [*dakruon*] from beneath his brows; |₅₃₂ there he was, escaping the notice of all while he kept pouring out his *tears* [*dakrua*]. |₅₃₃ But Alkinoos was the only one of all of them who was aware, and he *took note* [*noein*].

Odyssey viii 499–533*

9§33. As Odysseus weeps, he is compared here to an unnamed captive woman who is weeping (*klaiein, Odyssey* viii 523) over the dead body of her warrior husband. This woman, within the framework of the plot outline of the *Iliou Persis* that I quoted earlier, would be Andromache.† Within the overall framework of the *Odyssey*, however, this woman is not to be identified. As the unidentified captive woman weeps, she is 'poured all around' her dead husband (*amphi . . . khumenē* 527): in effect, she dissolves into tears. Directly comparable is the primary listener in the audience, Odysseus, who reacts by 'dissolving' (*tēkesthai* 522) into tears.‡

---

* |₄₉₉ ... ὁ δ᾽ ὁρμηθεὶς θεοῦ ἤρχετο, φαῖνε δ᾽ ἀοιδήν, |₅₀₀ ἔνθεν ἑλών, ὡς οἱ μὲν ἐϋσσέλμων ἐπὶ νηῶν |₅₀₁ βάντες ἀπέπλειον, πῦρ ἐν κλισίῃσι βαλόντες, |₅₀₂ Ἀργεῖοι, τοὶ δ᾽ ἤδη ἀγακλυτὸν ἀμφ᾽ Ὀδυσῆα |₅₀₃ εἴατ᾽ ἐνὶ Τρώων ἀγορῇ κεκαλυμμένοι ἵππῳ· |₅₀₄ αὐτοὶ γάρ μιν Τρῶες ἐς ἀκρόπολιν ἐρύσαντο. |₅₀₅ ὡς ὁ μὲν ἑστήκει, τοὶ δ᾽ ἄκριτα πόλλ᾽ ἀγόρευον |₅₀₆ ἥμενοι ἀμφ᾽ αὐτόν· τρίχα δέ σφισιν ἥνδανε βουλή, |₅₀₇ ἠὲ διατμῆξαι κοῖλον δόρυ νηλέϊ χαλκῷ, |₅₀₈ ἢ κατὰ πετράων βαλέειν ἐρύσαντας ἐπ᾽ ἄκρης, |₅₀₉ ἢ ἐάαν μέγ᾽ ἄγαλμα θεῶν θελκτήριον εἶναι, |₅₁₀ τῇ περ δὴ καὶ ἔπειτα τελευτήσεσθαι ἔμελλεν· |₅₁₁ αἶσα γὰρ ἦν ἀπολέσθαι, ἐπὴν πόλις ἀμφικαλύψῃ |₅₁₂ δουράτεον μέγαν ἵππον, ὅθ᾽ εἴατο πάντες ἄριστοι |₅₁₃ Ἀργεῖοι Τρώεσσι φόνον καὶ κῆρα φέροντες. |₅₁₄ ἤειδεν δ᾽ ὡς ἄστυ διέπραθον υἷες Ἀχαιῶν |₅₁₅ ἱππόθεν ἐκχύμενοι, κοῖλον λόχον ἐκπρολιπόντες. |₅₁₆ ἄλλον δ᾽ ἄλλῃ ἄειδε πόλιν κεραϊζέμεν αἰπήν, |₅₁₇ αὐτὰρ Ὀδυσσῆα προτὶ δώματα Δηϊφόβοιο |₅₁₈ βήμεναι, ἠΰτ᾽ Ἄρηα, σὺν ἀντιθέῳ Μενελάῳ. |₅₁₉ κεῖθι δὴ αἰνότατον πόλεμον φάτο τολμήσαντα |₅₂₀ νικῆσαι καὶ ἔπειτα διὰ μεγάθυμον Ἀθήνην. |₅₂₁ ταῦτ᾽ ἄρ᾽ ἀοιδὸς ἄειδε περικλυτός· αὐτὰρ Ὀδυσσεὺς |₅₂₂ τήκετο, δάκρυ δ᾽ ἔδευεν ὑπὸ βλεφάροισι παρειάς. |₅₂₃ ὡς δὲ γυνὴ κλαίῃσι φίλον πόσιν ἀμφιπεσοῦσα, |₅₂₄ ὅς τε ἑῆς πρόσθεν πόλιος λαῶν τε πέσῃσιν, |₅₂₅ ἄστεϊ καὶ τεκέεσσιν ἀμύνων νηλεὲς ἦμαρ. |₅₂₆ ἡ μὲν τὸν θνήσκοντα καὶ ἀσπαίροντα ἰδοῦσα |₅₂₇ ἀμφ᾽ αὐτῷ χυμένη λίγα κωκύει· οἱ δέ τ᾽ ὄπισθε |₅₂₈ κόπτοντες δούρεσσι μετάφρενον ἠδὲ καὶ ὤμους |₅₂₉ εἴρερον εἰσανάγουσι, πόνον τ᾽ ἐχέμεν καὶ ὀϊζύν· |₅₃₀ τῆς δ᾽ ἐλεεινοτάτῳ ἄχεϊ φθινύθουσι παρειαί· |₅₃₁ ὡς Ὀδυσεὺς ἐλεεινὸν ὑπ᾽ ὀφρύσι δάκρυον εἶβεν. |₅₃₂ ἔνθ᾽ ἄλλους μὲν πάντας ἐλάνθανε δάκρυα λείβων, |₅₃₃ Ἀλκίνοος δέ μιν οἶος ἐπεφράσατ᾽ ἠδ᾽ ἐνόησεν.

† *BA* 101 = 6§9.

‡ *HC* 348–349 = 2§344.

9§34. When the scene that shows the double horror of Andromache's capture by the Achaeans and the killing of Astyanax by Odysseus himself is about to be retold in this epic narrative of Demodokos, something happens in the overall narrative of the Homeric *Odyssey*. At the point where the retelling is about to happen, it is blocked. Unlike the *Iliou Persis* of Arctinus, where a climactic moment of the narrative of Troy's destruction is the capture of Andromache and the killing of Astyanax by Odysseus, that moment is missing in the *Odyssey*: instead, the narrator's act of identifying Andromache as a captive woman is screened by a simile about an unidentified captive woman.*

9§35. This sequence of narration in the *Odyssey* achieves an effect of *screen memory*:

> An essential phase in the sequence is being *screened out* by the memory of that narrative. The audience, as foregrounded by Odysseus, is expected to know the sequence, and the sequence is already a reality because the audience already knows where the singer had started. . . . So the audience and the singer, in a combined effort, can now all project the image together, projecting it as a *flashback* on the *screen* of the mind's eye. But the climax of the action, that is, the capturing of the woman who is yet to be identified as Andromache, has been *screened out* by a simile about the capturing of a woman who will never be identified.†
>
> I have used here two distinct metaphors involving the concept of *screen*. The first is the *screening* or projecting of an image on the screen that is the mind's eye. The second is the *screening-out* of that image in the overall narrative of the *Odyssey*. It is pertinent that Odysseus is not only the foregrounded audience of the third song of Demodokos: he is also an agent of the plot that is being narrated by the song, since he is the direct cause of Andromache's sorrows.‡

9§36. The sorrowful scene of Andromache's capture, which is highlighted in the *Iliou Persis* but screened out in the *Odyssey*, is actually foreshadowed in the *Iliad*. I quote here the most telling verses, in which Hector reveals to Andromache his forebodings about his own violent death and about its dire consequences for his wife and child:

---

* *HC* 346 = 2§337.
† *HC* 347 = 2§338.
‡ *HC* = 2§339, with reference to *BA* 101 = 6§9.

HOUR 9 TEXT H

|₄₄₇ For I know well in my thinking, in my heart, that |₄₄₈ there will come a day when, once it comes, the sacred city of Ilios [= Ilion = Troy] will be destroyed |₄₄₉—and Priam, too, and along with him [will be destroyed] the people of that man wielding the good ash spear, that Priam. |₄₅₀ But the pain I have on my mind is not as great for the Trojans and for what will happen to them in the future, |₄₅₁ or for Hecuba or for Priam the king, |₄₅₂ or for my brothers if, many in number and noble as they are, |₄₅₃ they will fall in the dust at the hands of men who are their enemies |₄₅₄—no, [the pain I have on my mind is not as great for them] as it is for you when I think of the moment when some Achaean man, one of those men who wear khitons of bronze, |₄₅₅ takes hold of you as you weep and leads you away as his prize, depriving you of your days of freedom from slavery. |₄₅₆ And you would be going to Argos, where you would be weaving [*huphainein*] at the loom of some other woman [and no longer at your own loom at home] |₄₅₇— and you would be carrying water for her, drawing from the spring called Messēís or the one called Hypereia. |₄₅₈ Again and again you will be forced to do things against your will, and the bondage holding you down will be overpowering. |₄₅₉ And someone some day will look at you as you pour out your tears and will say: |₄₆₀ "Hector is the man whose wife this woman used to be. He used to be the best in battle |₄₆₁—the best of all the Trojans, those tamers of horses, back in those days when they fought to defend Ilion [= Troy]." |₄₆₂ That is what someone some day will say. And just hearing it will give you a new sorrow |₄₆₃ as the widow of this kind of man, the kind that is able to prevent those days of slavery. |₄₆₄ But, once I am dead, may earth be scattered over me and cover me.

Iliad VI 447–464*

---

* |₄₄₇ εὖ γὰρ ἐγὼ τόδε οἶδα κατὰ φρένα καὶ κατὰ θυμόν. |₄₄₈ ἔσσεται ἦμαρ ὅτ᾽ ἄν ποτ᾽ ὀλώλῃ Ἴλιος ἱρὴ |₄₄₉ καὶ Πρίαμος καὶ λαὸς ἐϋμμελίω Πριάμοιο. |₄₅₀ ἀλλ᾽ οὔ μοι Τρώων τόσσον μέλει ἄλγος ὀπίσσω, |₄₅₁ οὔτ᾽ αὐτῆς Ἑκάβης οὔτε Πριάμοιο ἄνακτος |₄₅₂ οὔτε κασιγνήτων, οἵ κεν πολέες τε καὶ ἐσθλοὶ |₄₅₃ ἐν κονίῃσι πέσοιεν ὑπ᾽ ἀνδράσι δυσμενέεσσιν, |₄₅₄ ὅσσον σεῦ, ὅτε κέν τις Ἀχαιῶν χαλκοχιτώνων |₄₅₅ δακρυόεσσαν ἄγηται ἐλεύθερον ἦμαρ ἀπούρας. |₄₅₆ καί κεν ἐν Ἄργει ἐοῦσα πρὸς ἄλλης ἱστὸν ὑφαίνοις, |₄₅₇ καί κεν ὕδωρ φορέοις Μεσσηΐδος ἢ Ὑπερείης |₄₅₈ πόλλ᾽ ἀεκαζομένη, κρατερὴ δ᾽ ἐπικείσετ᾽ ἀνάγκη. |₄₅₉ καί ποτέ τις εἴπῃσιν ἰδὼν κατὰ δάκρυ χέουσαν. |₄₆₀ Ἕκτορος ἥδε γυνὴ ὃς ἀριστεύεσκε μάχεσθαι |₄₆₁ Τρώων ἱπποδάμων ὅτε Ἴλιον ἀμφεμάχοντο. |₄₆₂ ὥς ποτέ τις ἐρέει. σοὶ δ᾽ αὖ νέον ἔσσεται ἄλγος |₄₆₃ χήτεϊ τοιοῦδ᾽ ἀνδρὸς ἀμύνειν δούλιον ἦμαρ. |₄₆₄ ἀλλά με τεθνηῶτα χυτὴ κατὰ γαῖα καλύπτοι.

9§37. With these sad images in mind, I return to the last verse of Text G, *Odyssey* viii 533: we saw there that Alkinoos, the perceptive king of the Phaeacians, is the only one to notice that Odysseus is weeping when he hears the story about the destruction of Troy and about all the sorrows inflicted on those who were part of that pitiful event. In his perceptiveness, Alkinoos infers that his weeping guest, who is at this point still unidentified, must have participated in the Trojan War; and he infers also that the guest must have been on the winning side, not the losing side. So why is Odysseus weeping, then? Alkinoos thinks that it must be because Odysseus had lost someone near and dear who had been fighting on the Achaean side:

HOUR 9 TEXT I

|$_{577}$ Tell us why you are weeping and lamenting in your heart [*thūmos*] |$_{578}$ when you hear the fate of the Argive Danaans [= Achaeans] or the fate of Troy. |$_{579}$ The gods arranged all this, and they wove the fate of doom |$_{580}$ for mortals, so that future generations might have something to sing about. |$_{581}$ Did you lose some kinsman of your wife's when you were at Troy? |$_{582}$ Some such noble person? Or a son-in-law or father-in-law? Such people are most certainly |$_{583}$ the nearest relations a man has outside his own flesh and blood. |$_{584}$ Or was it perhaps a comrade [*hetairos*] who was well aware of the things that were most pleasing to you? |$_{585}$ Some such noble person? For not any less prized than your own brother |$_{586}$ is a comrade [*hetairos*] who is well aware of things you think about.

Odyssey viii 577–586*

9§38. By now we know that there is more to it. Yes, everyone who participated in the Trojan War, whether they were on the losing side or even on the winning side, had reason to feel sorrow, but the fact is that none of the sorrows described by Alkinoos fits the experiences of Odysseus himself. This hero has lost neither a relative nor a best friend at Troy. No, the tears of Odysseus in hearing the sorrows of the Trojan War are more generalized, even universalized.

---

* |$_{577}$ εἰπὲ δ᾽ ὅ τι κλαίεις καὶ ὀδύρεαι ἔνδοθι θυμῷ |$_{578}$ Ἀργείων Δαναῶν ἠδ᾽ Ἰλίου οἶτον ἀκούων. |$_{579}$ τὸν δὲ θεοὶ μὲν τεῦξαν, ἐπεκλώσαντο δ᾽ ὄλεθρον |$_{580}$ ἀνθρώποισ᾽, ἵνα ᾖσι καὶ ἐσσομένοισιν ἀοιδή. |$_{581}$ ἦ τίς τοι καὶ πηὸς ἀπέφθιτο Ἰλιόθι πρό, |$_{582}$ ἐσθλὸς ἐών, γαμβρὸς ἢ πενθερός; οἵ τε μάλιστα |$_{583}$ κήδιστοι τελέθουσι μεθ᾽ αἷμά τε καὶ γένος αὐτῶν. |$_{584}$ ἦ τίς που καὶ ἑταῖρος ἀνὴρ κεχαρισμένα εἰδώς, |$_{585}$ ἐσθλός; ἐπεὶ οὐ μέν τι κασιγνήτοιο χερείων |$_{586}$ γίνεται, ὅς κεν ἑταῖρος ἐὼν πεπνυμένα εἰδῇ.

The sorrow of Odysseus must take part even in the sufferings endured by the other side in the war.

9§39. Such universalizing of sorrow in the tears of Odysseus is a masterstroke of epic empathy, comparable to the words spoken by a weeping Aeneas in Virgil's *Aeneid* (1.462): *sunt lacrimae rerum et mentem mortalia tangunt,* 'there are tears that connect with the universe, and things that happen to mortals touch the mind'.*

9§40. So Penelope was right: the *kleos* of the epic *nostos* sung by Phemios, as signaled in *Odyssey* i 325, conveys a message of sorrow for anyone who feels any personal involvement in the actions that took place in the Trojan War and in its aftermath, as narrated in the epic *nostos*. And the expression of that sorrow, as Penelope says in *Odyssey* i 342, quoted in Text D, is the *penthos alaston* or 'unforgettable grief' of lamentation. Any epic that fails to convey such a sense of sorrow in narrating the actions of war is not a true epic. That is why the narration of Helen in *Odyssey* iv 235–264 about the Trojan War is a false epic, from the standpoint of Homeric poetry.† And the epic narrated by Helen is made false by the fact that any sorrow that could possibly be felt by her listeners is being counteracted by artificial means. Before she narrates her epic, Helen puts into the drinks of her listeners a drug that counteracts all sorrow, all anger, all sense of personal involvement. This drug that goes into the wine of her listeners is described as *nēpenthes,* that is, a substance that negates *penthos*:

HOUR 9 TEXT J

$|_{220}$ She [= Helen] put a drug into the wine from which they drank. $|_{221}$ It [= the drug] was against *penthos* [*nē-penthes*] and against anger [*a-kholon*]. It made one forget all bad things. $|_{222}$ Whoever swallowed it, once it was mixed with the wine into the mixing bowl, $|_{223}$ could not shed a tear from his cheeks for that day, $|_{224}$ even if his mother and father died $|_{225}$ or if he had earlier lost a brother or his own dear son, $|_{226}$ killed by bronze weapons—even if he saw it all happen with his own eyes.

Odyssey iv 220–226‡

---

* I offer a detailed interpretation of this verse in *HC* 168–169 = 1§183.

† I hasten to add that such an epic is not at all false from the standpoint of epic traditions other than Homeric poetry: the epic adventure of Odysseus as narrated by Helen in *Odyssey* iv 235–264 matches closely an episode in the epic Cycle, as we see from the plot summary by Proclus of the *Little Iliad* by Lesches of Lesbos p. 107 lines 4–7.

‡ $|_{220}$ αὐτίκ' ἄρ' εἰς οἶνον βάλε φάρμακον, ἔνθεν ἔπινον, $|_{221}$ νηπενθές τ' ἄχολόν τε, κακῶν ἐπίληθον ἁπάντων. $|_{222}$ ὃς τὸ καταβρόξειεν, ἐπὴν κρητῆρι μιγείη, $|_{223}$ οὔ κεν ἐφημέριός γε βάλοι κατὰ δάκρυ

9§41. The only way that a listener like Telemachus could hear the narrative of Helen about the Trojan War without weeping is to be anesthetized to the sorrows that he too can now understand—now that he has gone after the *nostos* of his father, Odysseus.* Telemachus has started to hear the story of Odysseus, and, in fact, when Menelaos says that he experiences *akhos . . . alaston*, 'unforgettable grief' (iv 508), every time he thinks about the uncertain fate of Odysseus, Telemachus breaks down and weeps (iv 113–116). Directly comparable is the *penthos alaston*, 'unforgettable grief', felt by Penelope (i 342) over the uncertain fate of Odysseus as she hears the *nostos* or 'song of homecoming' (i 326) sung by the singer Phemios.† And yet, Helen says that the false epic she narrates, focusing on the adventures of Odysseus at Troy, will bring pleasure to her listeners (iv 239, 'be pleased with my words').‡

9§42. Such is the nature of Homeric poetry: it is a form of epic that taps into the traditions of lament, as we saw already in Hour 3. Yes, the expressions of sorrow in lament can be anesthetized by the sheer delight experienced in listening to the story for its own sake, but such delight is interwoven with the moral gravity that comes with epic empathy. That is what happens in the Homeric *Odyssey*, in this *nostos* to end all *nostoi*.

παρειῶν, |₂₂₄ οὐδ' εἴ οἱ κατατεθναίη μήτηρ τε πατήρ τε, |₂₂₅ οὐδ' εἴ οἱ προπάροιθεν ἀδελφεὸν ἢ φίλον υἱὸν |₂₂₆ χαλκῷ δηιόῳεν, ὁ δ' ὀφθαλμοῖσιν ὁρῷτο.

* *BA* 99–100 = 6§7.

† In this connection, I note with interest the name of the bastard son of Menelaos, mentioned in passing at *Odyssey* iv 11: he is *Megapenthēs*. For more on such "speaking names," see *BA* 146 = 8§9n2.

‡ μύθοις τέρπεσθε.

The Mind of Odysseus in the Homeric Odyssey

The Meaning of Noos

10§1. The key word for this hour is *noos*. A simple translation could be 'mind' or 'thinking', though these words are too broad in meaning to fit many of the Homeric contexts of *noos*; other translations could be 'perception' or even 'intuition', but these words are in many ways too narrow. In any case, the meaning of *noos* centers on the realm of *rational* as opposed to *emotional* functions. Yet another translation is 'consciousness'. As we will see, this particular translation conveys the mystical meaning of *noos*.

10§2. A most revealing context for this word *noos* occurs in verse 3 of the same text that I quoted to lead off the discussion in Hour 9. Here again is the text:

HOUR 10 TEXT A = HOUR 9 TEXT A

|₁ That man, tell me O Muse the song of that man, who could change in many different ways who he was, that man who in very many ways |₂ veered from his path and wandered off far and wide, after he had destroyed the sacred city of Troy. |₃ Many different cities of many different people did he see, getting to know different ways of thinking [*noos*]. |₄ Many were the pains [*algea*] he suffered in his heart [*thūmos*] while crossing the sea |₅ struggling to merit [*arnusthai*] the saving of his own life [*psūkhē*] and his own homecoming [*nostos*] as well as the homecoming of his comrades [*hetairoi*]. |₆ But do what he might he could not save his comrades [*hetairoi*], even though he very much wanted to. |₇ For they perished through their own deeds of sheer recklessness, |₈ disconnected [*nēpioi*]* as they were, because of what they

---

* On the meaning of *nēpios* as 'disconnected', see the Core Vocabulary.

did to the cattle of the sun-god Hēlios. |₉ They ate them. So the god [Hēlios] deprived them of their day of homecoming [*nostimon*]. |₁₀ Starting from any single point of departure, O goddess, daughter of Zeus, tell me, as you have told those who came before me. |₁₁ So now all those who escaped precipitous death |₁₂ were safely home, having survived the war and the sea voyage. |₁₃ But he [= Odysseus], apart from the others, though he was longing for his homecoming [*nostos*] and for his wife, |₁₄ was detained by the queenly nymph [*numphē*] Calypso, who has her own luminous place among all the goddesses . . .

Odyssey i 1–14

10§3. I focus this time on the contents of verse 3 together with the contents of verse 5:

> In verse 3, we learn that Odysseus saw the cities of many mortals and that he came to know their ways of 'thinking', *noos*. In the original Greek, it is not excluded that Odysseus came to know better his own way of 'thinking', his own *noos*, in the process of getting to know the thinking of others.
>
> In verse 5, we learn that Odysseus was seeking to 'win as a prize' two things: his own life, the word for which is *psūkhē* here, and the homecoming or *nostos* of his comrades—along with his own homecoming.

10§4. The key word for this hour, *noos*, as we see it at verse 3, is actually related to the key word for the previous hour, *nostos*, as we see it at verse 5. As we saw in Hour 9, *nostos* can be interpreted as 'return, homecoming; song about homecoming'. And, as we also saw in that hour, the word *nostos* can also be interpreted as 'return to light and life'. Here in Hour 10, I plan to show how this mystical sense of *nostos*, 'return to light and life', can be explained in terms of the related word *noos* in the mystical sense of 'consciousness'. And we will see a further level of meaning for *noos*: it can be interpreted as 'coming to' in the mystical sense of 'returning to consciousness' after being unconscious—whether in sleep or even in death.

10§5. Before we proceed, I also draw special attention to verse 4 of Text A. This verse, bracketed by verses 3 and 5 containing respectively the words *noos* and *nostos*, contains the word *algea*, 'pains', which refers to the many sufferings of the hero Odysseus in the course of his heroic quest to achieve a safe homecoming. This word has been borrowed into English: *analgesic* means 'negating pain'. Another modern borrowing is the second element of the coined word *nostalgia,* referring to bittersweet yearnings for home.* This word is built from a combination of two elements, *algea,* 'pains' (as in *Odyssey* i 4), and *nostos,* 'homecoming' (as in *Odyssey* i 5).

10§6. I also draw attention to a living derivative of the ancient Greek noun *nostos:* it is the Modern Greek adjective *nostimos,* meaning 'tasty'. This meaning could be described fancifully as reflecting a *nostalgia* for home cooking. Another fanciful association comes to mind: the "episode of the madeleine" in Marcel Proust's *À la recherche du temps perdu* (specifically, at the end of the chapter "Combray 1," in *Du côté de chez Swann,* 1919).

The Interaction of Noos *and* Nostos

10§7. Both words, *noos* and *nostos,* are derived from an Indo-European root **nes-,* the basic meaning of which can be interpreted as 'return to light and life'; when we survey the traditions of Indo-European languages—and Greek is one of these languages—we see that this root **nes-* occurs in myths having to do with the rising of the sun at dawn or with the rising of the morning star.† These myths, as we will now see, are relevant to the meanings of *noos* and *nostos* as these words interact with each other in the overall plot of the Homeric *Odyssey.*

10§8. Such interaction is already signaled at the very beginning of the plot of the *Odyssey.* The hero's *nostos,* 'return', at verse 5 of *Odyssey* i connects with his *noos,* 'thinking', at verse 3 not only in the explicit sense of *thinking about saving his own life* but also in the implicit sense of *being conscious of returning home.*

10§9. This implicit sense is encoded in the telling of the myth about the Land of the Lotus-Eaters in *Odyssey* ix 82–104. When Odysseus visits that land, those of his comrades who eat the lotus lose their consciousness of home and therefore cannot return home. The verb *lēth-,* 'forget', combined with *nostos,* 'return', as its object, conveys the idea of such unconsciousness (ix 97, 102). By contrast, the noun *noos,* 'thinking', conveys the idea of being conscious of *nostos.*‡ So here is the basic teaching to be learned from the myth about the Land of the Lotus-Eaters: if you lose the "implant" of homecoming in your mind, you cannot go home because you no longer know what home is.

10§10. Similar teachings are built into the names of some of the main characters of the *Odyssey.* Two prominent examples are *Antinoos,* leader of the evil

---

* For more on this modern term *nostalgia,* see Boym 2001.
† *GM* 258–259, following Frame 1978; Nagy 2010c:336.
‡ This paragraph is derived from Nagy 2007b:76.

suitors, who tries to sabotage the *nostos* of Odysseus, and *Alkinoos,* the perceptive king of the Phaeacians, who promotes the *nostos* of the hero: their names mean, respectively, 'the one who is opposed to bringing back to light and life' and 'the one who has the power to bring back to light and life.'*

10§11. The very idea of *consciousness* as conveyed by *noos* is derived from the metaphor of *returning to light from darkness,* as encapsulated in the moment of *waking up from sleep,* or of *regaining consciousness after losing consciousness,* that is, of "coming to." This metaphor of *coming to* is at work not only in the meaning of *noos* in the sense of *consciousness* but also in the meaning of *nostos* in the sense of *returning from darkness and death to light and life.* Remarkably, these two meanings converge at one single point in the master myth of the *Odyssey.* It happens when Odysseus finally reaches his homeland of Ithaca:

HOUR 10 TEXT B

$|_{78}$ When they [= the Phaeacian seafarers] began rowing out to sea, $|_{79}$ he [= Odysseus] felt a sweet sleep falling upon his eyelids. $|_{80}$ It was a deep sleep, the sweetest, and most similar to death. $|_{81}$ Meanwhile, the ship was speeding ahead, just as a team of four stallions drawing a chariot over a plain $|_{82}$ speeds ahead in unison as they all feel the stroke of the whip, $|_{83}$ galloping along smoothly, with feet raised high as they make their way forward, $|_{84}$ so also the prow of the ship kept curving upward as if it were the neck of a stallion, and, behind the ship, waves that were $|_{85}$ huge and seething raged in the waters of the roaring sea. $|_{86}$ The ship held steadily on its course, and not even a falcon, $|_{87}$ raptor that he is, swiftest of all winged creatures, could have kept pace with it. $|_{88}$ So did the ship cut its way smoothly through the waves, $|_{89}$ carrying a man who was like the gods in his knowledge of clever ways, $|_{90}$ who had beforehand suffered very many pains [*algea*] in his heart [*thūmos*], $|_{91}$ taking part in wars among men and forging through so many waves that cause pain, $|_{92}$ but now he was sleeping peacefully, forgetful of all he had suffered. $|_{93}$ And when the brightest of all stars began to show, the one that, more than any other star, $|_{94}$ comes to announce the light of the Dawn born in her earliness, $|_{95}$ that is when the ship, famed for its travels over the seas, drew near to the island.

Odyssey xiii 78–95†

---

* On the name of Alkinoos especially, see Frame 2009:54, 245, 266.

† $|_{78}$ εὖθ' οἱ ἀνακλινθέντες ἀνερρίπτουν ἅλα πηδῷ, $|_{79}$ καὶ τῷ νήδυμος ὕπνος ἐπὶ βλεφάροισιν ἔπιπτε, $|_{80}$ νήγρετος ἥδιστος, θανάτῳ ἄγχιστα ἐοικώς. $|_{81}$ ἡ δ', ὥς τ' ἐν πεδίῳ τετράοροι ἄρσενες ἵπποι,

10§12. Odysseus has been sailing home on a ship provided by the Phaeacians, against the will of the god Poseidon, and the hero falls into a deep sleep that most resembles death itself (xiii 79–80). This sleep makes him momentarily unconscious: he 'forgets', as expressed by the verb *lēth-* (xiii 92), all the *algea*, 'pains', of his past journeys through so many different cities of so many different people (xiii 90–91). Then, at the very moment when the ship reaches the shore of Ithaca, the hero's homeland, the morning star appears, heralding the coming of dawn (xiii 93–95). The Phaeacians hurriedly leave Odysseus on the beach where they placed him, still asleep, when they landed (xiii 119), and, once they sail away, he wakes up there (xiii 187). So the moment of the hero's homecoming, which is synchronized with the moment of sunrise, is now further synchronized with a moment of awakening from a sleep that most resembles death.*

The Hero's Return to His Former Social Status

10§13. From this moment on, now that Odysseus has succeeded in making his return from his travels, he must succeed also in making another kind of return. That is, he must now return to his former social status as king at home in Ithaca. In the course of the twenty years that elapsed since his departure for Troy, however, the hero's social status at home has been reduced to nothing. So now, most fittingly, Athena disguises Odysseus as a beggar. Now the hero must work his way up from the bottom of the social scale, starting from nothing. He starts by being a nobody—that is, by being a somebody who has nothing and is therefore a nobody. As a beggar, he hides his social and moral nobility as king. This way, his interaction with the suitors of his wife exposes them as lacking in interior moral nobility despite their exterior social nobility.† In the end, of course, the actions of Odysseus reveal him as the true king. (On the king as the embodiment of the body politic, see Hour 9§6 and Hour 6§13 and §47.)

|₈₂ πάντες ἅμ᾽ ὁρμηθέντες ὑπὸ πληγῇσιν ἱμάσθλης |₈₃ ὑψόσ᾽ ἀειρόμενοι ῥίμφα πρήσσουσι κέλευθον, |₈₄ ὣς ἄρα τῆς πρύμνη μὲν ἀείρετο, κῦμα δ᾽ ὄπισθεν |₈₅ πορφύρεον μέγα θῦε πολυφλοίσβοιο θαλάσσης. |₈₆ ἡ δὲ μάλ᾽ ἀσφαλέως θέεν ἔμπεδον· οὐδέ κεν ἴρηξ |₈₇ κίρκος ὁμαρτήσειεν, ἐλαφρότατος πετεηνῶν· |₈₈ ὣς ἡ ῥίμφα θέουσα θαλάσσης κύματ᾽ ἔταμνεν, |₈₉ ἄνδρα φέρουσα θεοῖσ᾽ ἐναλίγκια μήδε᾽ ἔχοντα, |₉₀ ὃς πρὶν μὲν μάλα πολλὰ πάθ᾽ ἄλγεα ὃν κατὰ θυμόν, |₉₁ ἀνδρῶν τε πτολέμους ἀλεγεινά τε κύματα πείρων· |₉₂ δὴ τότε γ᾽ ἀτρέμας εὗδε, λελασμένος ὅσσ᾽ ἐπεπόνθει. |₉₃ εὖτ᾽ ἀστὴρ ὑπερέσχε φαάντατος, ὅς τε μάλιστα |₉₄ ἔρχεται ἀγγέλλων φάος Ἠοῦς ἠριγενείης, |₉₅ τῆμος δὴ νήσῳ προσεπίλνατο ποντοπόρος νηῦς.

* Nagy 2007b:76–77; see also Frame 2009:54.

† Nagy 2007b:77. For more on the contrast between the suitors, who are noble on the outside and base on the inside, and the hero Odysseus when he is disguised as a beggar, who is base on the outside but noble on the inside, see Nagy 1985:74–76 = §§68–70; PH 426–427 = 14§26.

10§14. The societal return of Odysseus from the status of beggar to the status of king by way of killing the suitors is mythologically parallel to the physical return of the warrior from the dangerous fighting at Troy, and also to the physical return of the seafarer from the dangerous voyaging at sea. But this societal return, along with the two physical returns, is parallel also to the psychic return of Odysseus from the realm of darkness and death, which is Hādēs, to the realm of light and life. This parallelism of the societal and the physical and the psychic returns of Odysseus is made explicit in a poem attributed to Theognis of Megara.* Here is the poem:

HOUR 10 TEXT C

|₁₁₂₃ Do not remind me of my misfortunes! The kinds of things that happened to Odysseus have happened to me too. |₁₁₂₄ He came back, emerging from the great palace of Hādēs, |₁₁₂₅ and then killed the suitors with a pitiless heart [*thūmos*], |₁₁₂₆ while thinking good thoughts about his duly wedded wife Penelope, |₁₁₂₇ who all along waited for him and stood by their dear son |₁₁₂₈ while he [= Odysseus] was experiencing dangers on land and in the gaping chasms of the sea.

Theognis 1123–1128†

The Hero's Return from the Cave

10§15. Odysseus is reduced to nothing not only when he first returns to his homeland of Ithaca and gets transformed into a beggar through the agency of his patroness, the goddess Athena. The hero's social nothingness is preceded by a psychic nothingness that he brings upon himself in the cave of Polyphemus the Cyclops. And that psychic nothingness endangers the *noos* or 'mind' of Odysseus, as we will now see.

10§16. It happens when Odysseus devises the stratagem of calling himself *Outis*, 'no one' (*Odyssey* ix 366), in order to deceive and then blind Polyphemus the Cyclops. The pronoun *ou tis*, 'no one', used by the hero for the crafting of his false name deceives not only the Cyclops but also the monster's fellow Cyclopes

---

* There is no fixed date for Theognis: he is credited with the creation of poems that can be dated as far apart as the late seventh and the early fifth centuries BCE.

† |₁₁₂₃ μή με κακῶν μίμνησκε· πέπονθά τοι οἷά τ' Ὀδυσσεύς, |₁₁₂₄ ὅστ' Ἀίδεω μέγα δῶμ' ἤλυθεν ἐξαναδύς, |₁₁₂₅ ὃς δὴ καὶ μνηστῆρας ἀνείλατο νηλέι θυμῷ, |₁₁₂₆ Πηνελόπης εὔφρων κουριδίης ἀλόχου, |₁₁₂₇ ἥ μιν δήθ' ὑπέμεινε φίλῳ παρὰ παιδὶ μένουσα, |₁₁₂₈ ὄφρα τε γῆς ἐπέβη δειλ' ἁλίους τε μυχούς.

when they use the same pronoun to ask the blinded Polyphemus this question: *Perhaps someone has wronged you?* (ix 405, 406). The syntax of the question, expressing the uncertainty of the questioners, requires the changing of the pronoun *ou tis*, 'no one', into its modal byform *mē tis*, 'perhaps someone', which sounds like the noun *mētis*, which means 'craft'. The modal byform *mē tis* is signaling here, by design, the verbal craft used by Odysseus in devising this stratagem.* And this act of signaling by design is made explicit later on when the narrating hero actually refers to his stratagem as a *mētis* (ix 414). The same can be said about the hero's previous stratagem of blinding the Cyclops with a sharpened stake, an act of craftiness compared to the craft of blacksmiths (ix 390–394). These and all other stratagems used by the hero against the Cyclops qualify as *mētis*, 'craft' (ix 422).†

10§17. This word *mētis*, 'craft', is essential for understanding the epic identity of Odysseus. The rivalry of Odysseus and Achilles in the story of Troy is formalized in a dispute between the two heroes: was the city to be destroyed by *biē*, 'force', as represented by the hero Achilles, or by *mētis*, 'craft', as represented by Odysseus? There are indirect references to this dispute in both the *Iliad* and the *Odyssey*, and some of these references are relevant to the master myths of the two epics (as in *Iliad* IX 423–426 and in *Odyssey* viii 72–82 respectively).‡ Ultimately, *the craft or craftiness of Odysseus in devising the stratagem of the Wooden Horse leads to the destruction of Troy*, as narrated by the disguised hero himself in the *Odyssey* (viii 492–520). This validation of craft at the expense of force does not translate, however, into a validation of Odysseus at the expense of Achilles in the overall story of Troy. As we saw in Hour 9, the story of Troy is the *kleos* of Achilles in the *Iliad*, not the *kleos* of Odysseus in the *Odyssey*.

10§18. Although Odysseus is credited with the epic feat of destroying the city of Troy, as the *Odyssey* proclaims at the very beginning (i 2), his *kleos* in that epic does not and cannot depend on the story of Troy. It depends instead on the story of his homecoming to Ithaca. By contrast, although Achilles is never credited with the destruction of Troy, since he is killed well before that event takes place, his *kleos* nonetheless depends on the story of Troy. More than that, his *kleos* is in fact the story of Troy, as we have already seen in Hour 9. The name of the *Iliad*, which equates itself with the *kleos* of Achilles, means literally 'the tale of Ilion', that is, the story of Troy.§ So for Odysseus to get his own *kleos*, which is

---

BA 321 = 20§4n7.
† Nagy 2007b:71.
‡ *BA* 45–46, 47–48 = 3§§5, 7.
§ EH §49.

the story of his homecoming to Ithaca in the *Odyssey,* he must get over the *kleos* of Achilles, which is the story of Troy in the *Iliad.* He must get over the *Iliad* and get on with the *Odyssey.* In other words, he must get on with his *nostos,* which is not only his *homecoming* to Ithaca but also the *song about this homecoming.* And to get on with his *nostos,* his song about homecoming, the hero needs his *noos,* his special way of 'thinking'. That is the essence of the master myth of the *Odyssey.**

10§19. For Odysseus to get over the *Iliad,* he must sail past it. His ongoing story, which is the *Odyssey,* must be about the seafarer who is making his way back home, not about the warrior who once fought at Troy. The *kleos* of Odysseus at Troy cannot be the master myth of the *Odyssey,* since the *kleos* of Achilles at Troy has already become the master myth of the *Iliad.* As I argued in Hour 9, the *kleos* of Achilles in the *Iliad* has preempted a *kleos* for Odysseus that centers on this rival hero's glorious exploits at Troy. For the hero of the *Odyssey,* the ongoing *kleos* of his adventures in the course of his *nostos* is actually threatened by any past *kleos* of his adventures back at Troy. Such a *kleos* of the past in the *Odyssey* could not rival the *kleos* of the more distant past in the *Iliad.* It would be a false *Iliad.* That is why Odysseus must sail past the Island of the Sirens. The Sirens, as false Muses, tempt the hero by offering to sing for him an endless variety of songs about Troy in particular and about everything else in general:

HOUR 10 TEXT D

|₁₈₄ Come here, Odysseus, famed for your many riddling words [*ainoi*], you great glory to the Achaean name, |₁₈₅ stop your ship so that you may hear our two voices. |₁₈₆ No man has ever yet sailed past us with his dark ship |₁₈₇ without staying to hear the sweet sound of the voices that come from our mouths, |₁₈₈ and he who listens will not only experience great pleasure before he goes back home [*neesthai*]† but will also be far more knowledgeable than before, |₁₈₉ for we know everything that happened at Troy, that expansive place, |₁₉₀—all the sufferings caused by the gods for the Argives [= Achaeans] and Trojans |₁₉₁ and we know everything on earth, that nurturer of so many mortals —everything that happens.

Odyssey xii 184–191‡

* *BA* (1999) xii–xiii = Preface §§16–18, with reference to *BA* 35–41= 2§§10–18; Nagy 2007b:70.

† This verb is cognate with the nouns *nostos* and *noos.*

‡ |₁₈₄ δεῦρ' ἄγ' ἰών, πολύαιν' Ὀδυσεῦ, μέγα κῦδος Ἀχαιῶν, |₁₈₅ νῆα κατάστησον, ἵνα νωϊτέρην ὄπ' ἀκούσῃς. |₁₈₆ οὐ γάρ πώ τις τῇδε παρήλασε νηῒ μελαίνῃ, |₁₈₇ πρίν γ' ἡμέων μελίγηρυν ἀπὸ στομάτων

10§20. The sheer pleasure of listening to the songs of the Sirens threatens not only the *nostos*, 'homecoming', of Odysseus, who is tempted to linger and never stop listening to the endless stories about Troy, but also the soundness of his thinking, his *noos*. And it even threatens the ongoing song about the hero's homecoming, that is, the *Odyssey* itself.*

10§21. Even in situations where the *mētis*, 'craft', of Odysseus helps advance the *nostos*, or 'homecoming', of the hero in the *Odyssey*, as also his sound 'thinking', his *noos*, it does nothing to advance the *kleos*, or poetic 'glory', of his past epic exploits at Troy. A case in point is the decisive moment in the *Odyssey* when Odysseus devises the stratagem of calling himself *Outis*, 'no one' (ix 366), in order to deceive and then blind Polyphemus the Cyclops.

10§22. Granted, the stratagem of crafting the false name *Outis* succeeds in saving the life of Odysseus: when the blinded Cyclops answers the question of his fellow Cyclopes, *perhaps someone has wronged you?* (ix 405, 406), he uses the non-modal form of the pronoun, saying *ou tis*, 'no one' has wronged me (ix 408). Still, though this stratagem succeeds in rescuing Odysseus (and, for the moment, some of his comrades), it fails to rescue the hero's past *kleos* in Troy. In fact, the stratagem of Odysseus in calling himself *Outis*, 'no one', produces just the opposite effect: it erases any previous claim to any *kleos* that the hero would have had before he entered the cave of the Cyclops. Such erasure is signaled by the epithet *outidanos*, 'good-for-nothing', derivative of the pronoun *ou tis*, 'no one': whenever this epithet is applied to a hero in the *Iliad*, it is intended to revile the name of that hero by erasing his epic identity (as in *Iliad* XI 390). Such erasure means that someone who used to have a name will now no longer have a name and has therefore become a *nobody*, a *no one, ou tis*. In the *Odyssey*, the Cyclops reviles the name of the man who blinded him by applying this same epithet *outidanos*, 'good-for-nothing', to the false name *Outis* (ix 460). The effect of applying this epithet completes the erasure of the hero's past identity that was started by Odysseus when he renamed himself as *ou tis*, 'no one'. So Odysseus has suffered a mental erasure. The name that the hero had heretofore achieved for himself has been reduced to nothing and must hereafter be rebuilt from nothing.†

10§23. It is relevant that the annihilation of the hero's identity happens in the

---

ὄπ' ἀκοῦσαι, |₁₈₈ ἀλλ' ὅ γε τερψάμενος νεῖται καὶ πλείονα εἰδώς. |₁₈₉ ἴδμεν γάρ τοι πάνθ', ὅσ' ἐνὶ Τροίῃ εὐρείῃ |₁₉₀ Ἀργεῖοι Τρῶές τε θεῶν ἰότητι μόγησαν, |₁₉₁ ἴδμεν δ' ὅσσα γένηται ἐπὶ χθονὶ πουλυβοτείρῃ.

* *BA* (1999) xii = Preface §17n; EH §50; Nagy 2007b:70.

† Nagy 2007b:72.

darkness of an otherworldly cave, in the context of extinguishing the light of the single eye of the Cyclops, thereby darkening forever the monster's power to perceive the truth—unless he hears it. In the poetics of Greek myth, the identity or non-identity of a hero matches the presence or absence of light: in the words of Pindar (*Pythian* 8.95–97), the difference between being *tis*, 'someone', and being *ou tis*, 'no one', becomes visible when a burst of *light and life* coming from Zeus himself illuminates the void of *darkness and death*.*

10§24. It is just as relevant that the master Narrative of the *Odyssey* situates Odysseus in the darkness of another otherworldly cave at the very beginning of that narrative. At the point chosen for the beginning of the actual storytelling (*entha*, 'there', at *Odyssey* i 11), the first detail to be narrated is that Odysseus is at this moment being deprived of his *nostos* (i 13) by a goddess called Calypso (i 14), who is keeping him concealed in her cave (i 15). The feelings of attraction associated with the beautiful nymph Calypso are matched by feelings of repulsion evoked by her terrifying name, *Kalupsō*, derived from the verb *kaluptein*, 'conceal': this verb is traditionally used in ritual formulas of burial, and it conveys the idea of consigning the dead to concealment in the realm of darkness and death (as in *Iliad* VI 464, XXIII 91).†

10§25. Of all the tales of homecomings experienced by the Achaean heroes after Troy, whether these homecomings succeed or fail, only the tale of Odysseus is still untold at the beginning of the *Odyssey*. His homecoming is the only homecoming still in doubt. This is the point being made at the very start of the tale: that the narrative is being kept in a state of suspension, and the cause of this suspension is said to be the goddess Calypso, who is preventing Odysseus from his *nostos* (i 13) by keeping him concealed in her cave (i 15). For the narrative to start, the *nostos* of Odysseus has to be activated, and so the Olympian gods intervene to ensure the eventual homecoming of Odysseus to Ithaca (i 16–17).‡

10§26. In *Odyssey* v, the Olympians send the god Hermes as their messenger to Calypso, and he tells her that she must allow Odysseus to make his way back home. So she must stop preventing Odysseus from getting started with the master myth of the *Odyssey*. That master myth is the *nostos* of Odysseus, which must be not only the hero's homecoming but also the song about his homecoming.

---

* Nagy 2000:110–111.
† Nagy 2007b:72–73. See also *GM* 254n108; Crane 1988.
‡ Nagy 2007b:73.

10§27. The role of the goddess Calypso in threatening to prevent the *nostos* of the hero Odysseus is reflected in the tales that she herself tells the god Hermes about other heroes who became lovers of other goddesses: the outcome of these tales is death (*Odyssey* v 118–129). For example, the hero Orion is killed off by Artemis because he became the lover of Ēōs, the goddess of the dawn (v 121–124). And the narrative of the *Odyssey* actually foretells a similar death for Odysseus—if he had continued to be the lover of Calypso (v 271–275).*

10§28. The relationship of Odysseus and Calypso shows that the *nostos* of the hero is not only a 'homecoming' but also, more basically, a 'return'. That is, the *nostos* of the hero is not only a *return to Ithaca* but also, in a mystical sense, a *return to light and life.*† To return from the cave of Calypso at the end of *Odyssey* xii is to return from the darkness and death of that cave. The same can be said about the return of Odysseus from the cave of the Cyclops Polyphemus at the end of *Odyssey* ix. Even more basically, the same can also be said about the return of Odysseus from Hādēs at the beginning of *Odyssey* xii. Here too we see the theme of *returning to light and life.*‡

The Return to Light and Life

10§29. This grand theme of *returning to light and life* takes shape at the beginning of *Odyssey* xi, when Odysseus starts to make his descent into Hādēs after a series of wanderings that take him farther and farther westward toward the outer limits of the world. The island of the goddess Circe, situated at these outer limits in the Far West, becomes the point of departure for the hero's planned entry into Hādēs (xi 1–12), but the actual point of entry is situated even farther west than that mystical island, since Odysseus has to cross the river Okeanos before he can cross over into Hādēs (xi 13, 21). The Okeanos must be even farther west than the island of Circe. That is because the Okeanos is the absolute marker of the Far West.§

10§30. The Okeanos is situated at the outermost limits of the world, which is encircled by its stream. The circular stream of the Okeanos flows eternally around the world and eternally recycles the infinite supply of fresh water that

---

* *BA* 202–203 = 10§39.
† Frame 1978.
‡ Nagy 2007b:73.
§ Nagy 2007b:73–74.

feeds upon itself (*Iliad* XIV 246–246a, XVIII 399, XX 65).* This mystical river Okeanos, surrounding not only the earth but even the seas surrounding the earth, defines the limits of the known world. Every evening, as the sun sets at sunset, it literally plunges into the fresh waters of this eternally self-recycling cosmic stream (*Iliad* VIII 485), and it is from these same fresh waters that the sun rises again every morning at sunrise (*Iliad* VII 421–423; *Odyssey* xix 433–434).†

10§31. After his sojourn in Hādēs, which is narrated in *Odyssey* xi, Odysseus finally emerges from this realm of darkness and death at the beginning of *Odyssey* xii. But the island of Circe is no longer in the Far West. When Odysseus returns from Hādēs, crossing again the circular cosmic stream of Okeanos (xii 1–2) and coming back to his point of departure, that is, to the island of the goddess Circe (xii 3), we find that this island is no longer in the Far West: instead, it is now in the Far East, where Hēlios, the god of the sun, has his 'sunrises', *an(a)tolai* (xii 4), and where Ēōs, the goddess of the dawn, has her own palace, featuring a special space for her 'choral dancing and singing', *khoroi* (xii 3–4). Before the hero's descent into the realm of darkness and death, we saw the Okeanos as the absolute marker of the Far West; after his ascent into the realm of light and life, we see it as the absolute marker of the Far East.‡ *In returning to the island of Circe by crossing the circular cosmic river Okeanos for the second time, the hero has come full circle, experiencing sunrise after having experienced sunset.*§ Even the name of Circe may be relevant, since the form *Kirkē* may be cognate with the form *kirkos*, a variant of the noun *krikos*, meaning 'circle, ring'.** As we will now see, this experience of coming full circle is a mental experience—or, to put it another way, it is a psychic experience.

The Journey of a Soul

10§32. This return of the hero from the realm of darkness and death into the realm of light and life is *a journey of a soul.* The word that I translate for the

---

* *HC* 248–276, 282–294 = 2§§123–178, 191–227.

† Nagy 2007b:74.

‡ See also *GM* 237.

§ Nagy 2007b:74.

** Chantraine *DELG* s.v. κρίκος. The variant form *kirkos* (κίρκος) is attested already in the diction of Aeschylus (*Prometheus* 74 κιρκηλάτου, from the denominative verb *kirkoûn*).

moment as 'soul' is *psūkhē*. As we have seen in Hour 8, this word *psūkhē* is used in Homeric poetry to refer to the *spirit* of the dead—or to the *life* of the living.*

10§33. In Hour 7, I used a neutral translation of this word's meaning, as 'spirit', but then, in Hour 8, I concentrated on the more basic meaning of *psūkhē* as 'breath of life', which in the context of hero cults signals the vital force that departs from the body of the hero at the moment of death—only to be reunited with that body after a transition, through Hādēs, into a paradisiacal setting that transcends the temporal and the spatial constraints of mortality.† Such a mystical reunion of the body with the *psūkhē* is the essence of heroic immortalization.‡ In terms of this formulation, as I noted in Hour 8, there is transition of the *psūkhē* through Hādēs: so this realm of Hādēs is transitional, not eschatological. Here in Hour 10, I return to the distinction I was making in Hour 8 between *transitional* and *eschatological* phases in an afterlife.

10§34. As we saw in Hour 8§§40–48, the use of the word *psūkhē* in Homeric poetry indicates that this poetry recognizes and even accepts the idea of heroic immortalization, though this idea is expressed only implicitly.§ Here in Hour 10, I use the translation 'soul' for *psūkhē*, with the understanding that the idea of an immortalized 'soul' is only implicit in Homeric poetry.

10§35. The journey of the soul after death replicates the journey of the sun after sunset, as we see from the wording of a death wish expressed by Penelope in the *Odyssey*: after dying, she pictures herself as journeying to the Far West and, once there, plunging into the waters of the Okeanos (xx 61–65).** As we saw earlier, the sun is imagined as plunging into these waters at sunset and then emerging from these same waters at sunrise. So also the soul of the hero can be imagined as replicating that same cycle.††

10§36. But the return of the hero's *psūkhē* to light and life at sunrise is not made explicit in Homeric poetry. Instead, Odysseus himself personally experiences such a return when he comes back from Hādēs at the beginning of *Odyssey* xii. This experience of Odysseus, by way of replicating the mystical journey

---

* See also *GM* 87–93.

† *GM* 88–93, 115–116.

‡ *GM* 126n30, 142.

§ Detailed arguments in Nagy 2012b.

** *GM* 99n61, following *BA* 194–203 = 10§§25–39; see also Easterling 2006:136.

†† Nagy 2007b:74–75, with reference to *GM* 90–91.

of the sun, is a substitute for the mystical journey of a soul. This way, the *nostos* of Odysseus, as an epic narrative, becomes interwoven with a mystical subnarrative. While the epic narrative tells about the hero's return to Ithaca after all the fighting at Troy and all the travels at sea, the mystical subnarrative tells about the soul's return from darkness and death to light and life.*

10§37. In some poetic traditions, the mystical subnarrative of the hero's *nostos* can even be foregrounded, as we saw in Text C, which I repeat here:

> |₁₁₂₃ Do not remind me of my misfortunes! The kinds of things that happened to Odysseus have happened to me too. |₁₁₂₄ He came back, emerging from the great palace of Hādēs, |₁₁₂₅ and then killed the suitors with a pitiless heart [*thūmos*], |₁₁₂₆ while thinking good thoughts about his duly wedded wife Penelope, |₁₁₂₇ who all along waited for him and stood by their dear son |₁₁₂₈ while he [= Odysseus] was experiencing dangers on land and in the gaping chasms of the sea.
>
> Theognis 1123–1128

10§38. The return of Odysseus from Hādēs leads to a rebuilding of his heroic identity. Earlier in the *Odyssey*, the status of Odysseus as a hero of epic had already been reduced to nothing. As we saw in the tale of his encounter with the Cyclops, the return of Odysseus from the monster's cave deprives him of his past identity at Troy. His epic fame can no longer depend on his power of *mētis*, 'craft', which had led to the invention of the Wooden Horse, which in turn had led to the destruction of Troy. After his encounter with the Cyclops, Odysseus must achieve a new epic identity as the hero of his own epic about homecoming, about his own *nostos*, but, for the moment, his confidence in his power to bring about this *nostos* is reduced to nothing. He has lost his confidence in the power of his own *mētis*, 'craftiness', to devise a stratagem for achieving a *nostos*. When he reaches the island of Circe and learns that this place, though it first seems familiar and reminiscent of his own island, is in fact strange and alien and antithetical to home, he despairs (x 190–202).†

10§39. The Homeric passage in which Odysseus expresses his desperation shows why he despairs. He thinks he has lost his *mētis*:

---

* Nagy 2007b:75.
† Nagy 2007b:77.

HOUR 10 TEXT E

|₁₉₀ My friends, I am speaking this way because I do not know which place is west and which place is east |₁₉₁—which is the place where the sun, bringing light for mortals, goes underneath the earth |₁₉₂ and which is the place where it rises. Still, let us start thinking it through, as quickly as we can, |₁₉₃ whether there is still any craft [*mētis*] left. I must tell you, though, I think there is none.

Odyssey x 190–193*

10§40. The hero feels he has no *mētis*, or 'craft', left in him to devise a stratagem for a successful homecoming, and his despair is expressed as a feeling of disorientation. He is no longer able to distinguish between orient and occident. To restate in terms of two words used elsewhere in the *Odyssey*, the hero is experiencing a loss of orientation in his *noos* or 'thinking', and this loss is presently blocking his *nostos*, 'homecoming'.†

10§41. The hero's despair makes his comrades despair as well: as soon as they hear the news of their leader's disorientation, they break down and cry (x 198–202) as they recall Antiphates the Laestrygonian and Polyphemus the Cyclops (x 199–200). Strangely, when the comrades of Odysseus recall Polyphemus, the monster is described by way of the epithet *megalētōr*, 'great-hearted' (x 200), and this same description applies also to Antiphates in an alternative version of a verse attested in the *Odyssey* (x 106). Beyond these two attestations, this epithet occurs nowhere else in the *Odyssey*, whereas it occurs regularly as a conventional description of generic warriors in the *Iliad*.‡ Why, then, are both Antiphates and Polyphemus described by way of an Iliadic epithet? It is relevant that Antiphates, like Polyphemus, is an eater of raw human flesh in the *Odyssey* (x 116). In the *Iliad*, the urge to eat raw human flesh is experienced by heroes in their darkest moments of bestial fury, as when Achilles says he is sorely tempted to cut up and eat raw his deadliest enemy, Hector (XXII 346–347). So the recalling of the monsters Antiphates and Polyphemus at a moment of disorientation in the *Odyssey* is like a nightmare that conjures up the worst moments of epic

---

* |₁₉₀ ὦ φίλοι, οὐ γὰρ ἴδμεν ὅπῃ ζόφος οὐδ' ὅπῃ ἠώς, |₁₉₁ οὐδ' ὅπῃ ἠέλιος φαεσίμβροτος εἶσ' ὑπὸ γαῖαν |₁₉₂ οὐδ' ὅπῃ ἀννεῖται· ἀλλὰ φραζώμεθα θᾶσσον, |₁₉₃ εἴ τις ἔτ' ἔσται μῆτις· ἐγὼ δ' οὐκ οἴομαι εἶναι.

† Nagy 2007b:78. The next paragraph is also derived from this source.

‡ *BA* 321 = 20§4n8.

heroes. Those moments include not only the cannibalistic feasts of these two monsters, as experienced by Odysseus and his comrades since they left Troy. It evokes also some of the worst moments experienced by all the Achaeans when they were still at Troy. In other words, the heroic disorientation of Odysseus in the *Odyssey* evokes nightmarish memories of heroic dehumanization in the *Iliad.**

10§42. Despite such moments of disorientation for Odysseus, his *noos*, 'thinking', ultimately reorients him, steering him away from his Iliadic past and toward his ultimate Odyssean future. That is, the hero's *noos* makes it possible for him to achieve a *nostos,* which is not only his 'homecoming' but also the 'song about a homecoming' that is the *Odyssey.* For this song to succeed, Odysseus must keep adapting his identity by making his *noos* fit the *noos* of the many different characters he encounters in the course of his *nostos* in progress. In order to adapt, he must master many different forms of discourse, many different kinds of *ainos.* That is why he is addressed as *poluainos,* 'having many different kinds of *ainos*', by the Sirens when he sails past their island (xii 184).†

10§43. Even the transparent meaning of *Polyphemus (Poluphēmos),* the name of the Cyclops blinded by Odysseus, foretells the hero's mastery of the *ainos.* As an adjective, *poluphēmos* means 'having many different kinds of prophetic utterance', derived from the noun *phēmē,* 'prophetic utterance' (as in xx 100, 105);‡ this adjective is applied as an epithet to the singer *Phēmios* (xxii 376), portrayed in the *Odyssey* as a master of the *phēmē,* 'prophetic utterance'.§ In the case of Polyphemus, the very meaning of his name, which conveys the opposite of the meaning conveyed by the false name of Odysseus, *Outis,* 'no one', foretells the verbal mastery of the hero who blinded the monster.**

10§44. After the return of Odysseus from Hādēs, he finds his way to the island of the Phaeacians, where he starts the process of rebuilding his epic identity from nothing by retelling for them all his experiences since he left Troy. This retelling, which extends from the beginning of *Odyssey* ix to the end of *Odyssey* xii, is coterminous with the telling of the *Odyssey* up to the point where Odysseus leaves the cave of Calypso. Then, after Odysseus finishes his narration, he leaves the island of the Phaeacians and finally comes back home to

---

* *BA* 319–321 = 20§4.
† *BA* 240 = 12§19n1; *PH* 236–237 = 8§30.
‡ *HR* 55–59.
§ *BA* 17 = 1§4n1.
** Nagy 2007b:78–79.

Ithaca, where his narration is taken over by the master Narrator of the *Odyssey*. The process of rebuilding the hero's epic identity continues in the master Narration, but now the direct mode of speaking used by Odysseus in telling the Phaeacians about his ongoing *nostos* gives way to an indirect mode, analogous to the indirect mode of speaking that he had used earlier before he made contact with the Phaeacians. Now, after his encounter with the Phaeacians, Odysseus becomes once again the master of the *ainos*.*

10§45. From here on, the tales Odysseus tells are masterpieces of mythmaking as embedded in the master myth of the *Odyssey*. One such tale is a "Cretan lie" told by the disguised Odysseus to the swineherd Eumaios about the Trojan War (xiv 192–359).† At a later point in their verbal exchanges, Eumaios refers to another tale told by Odysseus about the Trojan War (xiv 462–506) by describing it as a faultless *ainos* (xiv 508).‡ As a master of the *ainos*, Odysseus keeps on adapting his identity by making his *noos* fit the *noos* of the many different characters he encounters. And the multiple *ainoi* of Odysseus can thus be adapted to the master myth of the *Odyssey*.

10§46. By the time all is said and done in the master myth of the *Odyssey*, the character of Odysseus has become fully adapted to his ultimate role as the multiform central hero of this epic, a fitting counterpoint to the monolithic central hero of the *Iliad*, Achilles. This ultimate adaptation of Odysseus demonstrates his prodigious adaptability as a character in myth. He is the ultimate multiform. That is why he is called *polutropos* at the very beginning of the *Odyssey*, that is, 'the one who could change in many different ways who he was' (i 1).§

10§47. Odysseus can be all things to all people. His character undergoes the most fantastic imaginable adventures of the mind during his journeys—and the most realistic personal experiences when he finally reaches his home in Ithaca. The psychological realism of this hero's character when we see him at home with himself tempts us to forget about the fantastic journeys of his *psūkhē* in alien realms. Our sense of the familiar blocks our sense of the unfamiliar. Our mentality as modern readers invites us to see Odysseus at home as "reality" and Odysseus abroad as "myth," as if the myth of the hero contradicted the reality of the hero.**

---

* Nagy 2007b:79. The next paragraph is also derived from this source.

† *BA* 138–139, 234–235 = 7§26, 12§14.

‡ *BA* 234–237 = 12§§14–16.

§ Nagy 2007b:79–80.

** Nagy 2007b:80. The next paragraph is also derived from this source.

10§48. Such a split vision is a false dichotomy. The reality of Odysseus is in fact the myth of Odysseus, since that myth derives from the historical reality of Homeric poetry as a medium of myth. The reality of the myth is the reality of the medium that conveys the myth to its listeners over time.

10§49. At the beginning of the *Odyssey*, as we saw at the start of this hour, both the epic narrative about the hero's return to his home and the mystical subnarrative about the soul's return to light and life are recapitulated in the double meaning of *psūkhē* as either 'life' or 'soul'. I repeat here the first five verses of Text A:

|₁ That man, tell me O Muse the song of that man, that versatile [*polu-tropos*] man, who in very many ways |₂ veered from his path and wandered off far and wide, after he had destroyed the sacred city of Troy. |₃ Many different cities of many different people did he see, getting to know different ways of thinking [*noos*]. |₄ Many were the pains [*algea*] he suffered in his heart [*thūmos*] while crossing the sea |₅ struggling to merit [*arnusthai*] the saving of his own life [*psūkhē*] and his own homecoming [*nostos*] as well as the homecoming of his comrades [*hetairos*].

Odyssey i 1–5

10§50. Initially, I had translated *psūkhē* simply as 'life' in this context, where we see Odysseus struggling to save his own life. But by now we see that Odysseus is at the same time struggling to save his 'soul'. That struggle is the journey of his soul, undertaken by the *noos*, 'mind', of Odysseus.

HOUR 11

Blessed Are the Heroes: The Cult Hero in Homeric Poetry and Beyond

The Meaning of Olbios

11§1. They key word for this hour is *olbios,* which as we will see means 'blessed' or even 'blissful' for those who are initiated into the mysteries of hero cult but simply 'prosperous, happy' for the uninitiated. As we will also see, the cult hero is *olbios,* 'blessed', after he or she dies, and the worshipper of a cult hero can become *olbios,* 'blessed', by making mental contact with the hero—which can be achieved by way of physical contact with the earth that contains the corpse of the hero or even with a relic or simulacrum of the hero.

11§2. In the first text to be considered, we find the word *olbios* used with reference to Achilles as a cult hero. The reference is stylized, since Homeric poetry tends to avoid explicit references to hero cult, but the language used in the reference is consistent with the traditional understanding about cult heroes: that they were mortals made immortal after death, and that this immortalization led to the establishment of hero cults in the context of the tombs where the heroes' bodies were buried after a proper funeral.* Later on, in Text G, we will see the same word *olbios* used with reference to Odysseus as a would-be cult hero.

11§3. Here, then, is the text featuring the word *olbios* as applied to Achilles:

Hour 11 Text A

$|_{36}$ O you blessed [*olbios*] son of Peleus, godlike Achilles, $|_{37}$ you who died at Troy far from Argos. And others, those all around you [= your

---

* In Nagy 2012b, I survey the most striking examples of Homeric references to (1) hero cults and (2) the idea of immortalization in the contexts of these cults.

corpse], |₃₈ were being slaughtered, sons of both Trojans and Achae-
ans, the best, |₃₉ as they were fighting over you [= your corpse]. There
you were, lying in a swirl of dust. |₄₀ You lay there so huge in all your
hugeness, no longer thinking about your feats of charioteering. .... |₄₃
Then, when we had taken you [= your corpse] to the ships, out of the
battle, |₄₄ we laid you on your bed and cleansed your beautiful skin |₄₅
with warm water and with oil. And, crying over you, many tears |₄₆ did
the Danaans [= Achaeans] shed, hot tears, and they cut their hair. |₄₇
Your mother came, with her immortal sea nymphs, from out of the sea,
|₄₈ as soon as she heard, and the sound of a great wailing went forth
over the sea, |₄₉ a sound too wondrous for words, and all the Achaeans
were overcome with trembling. .... |₅₈ Standing around you were the
daughters of the Old One of the sea [= Nereus], |₅₉ weeping piteously,
and they [= the Nereids] clothed you [= the corpse of Achilles] in im-
mortalizing [ambrota] clothes. |₆₀ The nine Muses also came, all of
them, and sang antiphonally with a beautiful voice, |₆₁ singing their
song of lament [thrēneîn]; you could not spot a single person who was
not shedding tears, |₆₂ of all the Argives [= Achaeans], so loudly did
the piercing sound of lament rise up. |₆₃ Days and nights seven and ten
|₆₄ we mourned you, we mortals and immortals alike, |₆₅ but on the
eighteenth day we gave you to the flames, and, over the fire, many |₆₆
fat sheep and many horned oxen did we slay in sacrifice. |₆₇ You were
burning while clothed in the clothes of the gods, and with plenty of ol-
ive oil, |₆₈ also sweet honey. And a multitude of Achaean heroes |₆₉
were dancing in their armor around the pyre as you were burning. |₇₀
There were footsoldiers and charioteers, and a great din arose. |₇₁ But
when the flames of Hephaistos had consumed you, |₇₂ we gathered
your white bones at dawn, O Achilles, and laid them |₇₃ in unmixed
wine and in oil. Your mother gave |₇₄ a golden amphora to hold them—
she had received it as a gift from Dionysus, |₇₅ she said, and it was the
work of the famed Hephaistos himself; |₇₆ in this [amphora] were
placed your white bones, O luminous Achilles, |₇₇ mixed together with
the bones of Patroklos who had died before you, |₇₈ and separately
from the bones of Antilokhos, whom you honored most of all |₇₉ your
other comrades [hetairoi] after Patroklos had died. |₈₀ Over these
bones a huge and faultless tomb [tumbos] |₈₁ was built; it was a tumulus
that we the sacred army of spear-fighting Argives [= Achaeans] heaped

up, |₈₂ at a headland jutting out over the open Hellespont, |₈₃ so that it might be visible, shining forth from afar, for men at sea [*pontos*] |₈₄ now living and for those that will be born hereafter. |₈₅ Your mother [Thetis] asked for and received from the gods very beautiful prizes [*āthla*], |₈₆ and she placed them in the middle of the place for competition [*agōn*] among the noblest of the Achaeans. |₈₇ You must have been present at funerals of many men |₈₈ who were heroes, and so you know how, at the death of some great king, |₈₉ the young men gird themselves and make ready to contend for prizes [*āthla*], |₉₀ but even you would have been most amazed in your heart [*thūmos*] to see those things, |₉₁ I mean, those beautiful prizes that were set up by the goddess in your honor [*epi soi*], |₉₂ by Thetis with the silver steps. For you were so very dear to the gods. |₉₃ Thus, even in death, your glorious name, Achilles, has not been lost, and you will have for all eternity, |₉₄ among all humankind, a glory [*kleos*] that is genuine, Achilles. |₉₅ As for me, what solace had I in this, that the days of my fighting in war were over? |₉₆ For, in the course of my homecoming [*nostos*], Zeus masterminded a disastrous [*lugros*] destruction for me, |₉₇ at the hands of Aegisthus and of my disastrous [*oulomenē*] wife.

Odyssey xxiv 36–97*

* |₃₆ ὄλβιε Πηλέος υἱέ, θεοῖσ' ἐπιείκελ' Ἀχιλλεῦ, |₃₇ ὃς θάνες ἐν Τροίῃ ἑκὰς Ἄργεος· ἀμφὶ δέ σ' ἄλλοι |₃₈ κτείνοντο Τρώων καὶ Ἀχαιῶν υἷες ἄριστοι, |₃₉ μαρνάμενοι περὶ σεῖο· σὺ δ' ἐν στροφάλιγγι κονίης |₄₀ κεῖσο μέγας μεγαλωστί, λελασμένος ἱπποσυνάων. . . . |₄₃ αὐτὰρ ἐπεί σ' ἐπὶ νῆας ἐνείκαμεν ἐκ πολέμοιο, |₄₄ κάτθεμεν ἐν λεχέεσσι, καθήραντες χρόα καλὸν |₄₅ ὕδατί τε λιαρῷ καὶ ἀλείφατι· πολλὰ δέ σ' ἀμφὶ |₄₆ δάκρυα θερμὰ χέον Δαναοὶ κείροντό τε χαίτας. |₄₇ μήτηρ δ' ἐξ ἁλὸς ἦλθε σὺν ἀθανάτῃσ' ἁλίῃσιν |₄₈ ἀγγελίης ἀΐουσα· βοὴ δ' ἐπὶ πόντον ὀρώρει |₄₉ θεσπεσίη, ὑπὸ δὲ τρόμος ἤλυθε πάντας Ἀχαιούς. . . . |₅₈ ἀμφὶ δέ σ' ἔστησαν κοῦραι ἁλίοιο γέροντος |₅₉ οἴκτρ' ὀλοφυρόμεναι, περὶ δ' ἄμβροτα εἵματα ἔσσαν. |₆₀ Μοῦσαι δ' ἐννέα πᾶσαι ἀμειβόμεναι ὀπὶ καλῇ |₆₁ θρήνεον· ἔνθα κεν οὔ τιν' ἀδάκρυτόν γ' ἐνόησας |₆₂ Ἀργείων· τοῖον γὰρ ὑπώρορε Μοῦσα λίγεια. |₆₃ ἑπτὰ δὲ καὶ δέκα μέν σε ὁμῶς νύκτας τε καὶ ἦμαρ |₆₄ κλαίομεν ἀθάνατοί τε θεοὶ θνητοί τ' ἄνθρωποι· |₆₅ ὀκτωκαιδεκάτῃ δ' ἔδομεν πυρί· πολλὰ δ' ἐπ' αὐτῷ |₆₆ μῆλα κατεκτάνομεν μάλα πίονα καὶ ἕλικας βοῦς. |₆₇ καίεο δ' ἔν τ' ἐσθῆτι θεῶν καὶ ἀλείφατι πολλῷ |₆₈ καὶ μέλιτι γλυκερῷ· πολλοὶ δ' ἥρωες Ἀχαιοὶ |₆₉ τεύχεσιν ἐρρώσαντο πυρὴν πέρι καιομένοιο, |₇₀ πεζοί θ' ἱππῆές τε· πολὺς δ' ὀρυμαγδὸς ὀρώρει. |₇₁ αὐτὰρ ἐπεὶ δή σε φλὸξ ἤνυσεν Ἡφαίστοιο, |₇₂ ἠῶθεν δή τοι λέγομεν λεύκ' ὀστέ', Ἀχιλλεῦ, |₇₃ οἴνῳ ἐν ἀκρήτῳ καὶ ἀλείφατι. δῶκε δὲ μήτηρ |₇₄ χρύσεον ἀμφιφορῆα· Διωνύσοιο δὲ δῶρον |₇₅ φάσκ' ἔμεναι, ἔργον δὲ περικλυτοῦ Ἡφαίστοιο. |₇₆ ἐν τῷ τοι κεῖται λεύκ' ὀστέα, φαίδιμ' Ἀχιλλεῦ, |₇₇ μίγδα δὲ Πατρόκλοιο Μενοιτιάδαο θανόντος, |₇₈ χωρὶς δ' Ἀντιλόχοιο, τὸν ἔξοχα τῖες ἁπάντων |₇₉ τῶν ἄλλων ἑτάρων μετὰ Πάτροκλόν γε θανόντα. |₈₀ ἀμφ' αὐτοῖσι δ' ἔπειτα μέγαν καὶ ἀμύμονα τύμβον |₈₁ χεύαμεν Ἀργείων ἱερὸς στρατὸς αἰχμητάων |₈₂ ἀκτῇ ἔπι προὐχούσῃ, ἐπὶ πλατεῖ Ἑλλησπόντῳ, |₈₃ ὥς κεν τηλεφανὴς ἐκ ποντόφιν ἀνδράσιν εἴη |₈₄ τοῖσ', οἳ νῦν γεγάασι καὶ οἳ μετόπισθεν ἔσονται. |₈₅ μήτηρ δ' αἰτήσασα θεοὺς περικαλλέ' ἄεθλα |₈₆ θῆκε μέσῳ ἐν ἀγῶνι ἀριστήεσσιν Ἀχαιῶν. |₈₇ ἤδη μὲν πολέων τάφῳ ἀνδρῶν ἀντεβόλησας |₈₈ ἡρώων, ὅτε κέν ποτ' ἀποφθιμένου βασιλῆος |₈₉ ζώννυνταί τε νέοι καὶ ἐπεντύνωνται ἄεθλα· |₉₀ ἀλλά κε κεῖνα μάλιστα ἰδὼν θηήσαο θυμῷ, |₉₁ οἷ' ἐπὶ σοὶ κατέθηκε θεὰ περικαλλέ' ἄεθλα, |₉₂ ἀργυρόπεζα Θέτις· μάλα γὰρ φίλος

11§4. The speaker here is the ghost or, more accurately, the *psūkhē*, 'spirit', of Agamemnon (xxiv 35), who is addressing Achilles, likewise described as a *psūkhē* (xxiv 24). At this moment, both *psūkhai* are in Hādēs. As I argued in Hour 8, Hādēs is a point of transition that can lead from death to immortalization—provided that the ritual prerequisites of hero cult are followed correctly. These prerequisites are in fact being met in the case of Achilles, as we know from the words spoken by Agamemnon in describing the funeral of Achilles and the making of his tomb. As we will see, the funeral and the tomb of a hero are two main prerequisites for hero cult. And, as we will also see, the status of the cult hero as *olbios,* or 'blessed', is a third main prerequisite. So it is significant that the *psūkhē* of Agamemnon addresses the *psūkhē* of Achilles by calling him *olbios* at the beginning of the text I just quoted. Later on, I will argue that both these words, *olbios* and *psūkhē,* convey the promise of heroic immortalization after death.* But first, I propose to delve into other salient details in Text A.

Signs of Hero Cult

11§5. Text A, as I just quoted it, contains some of the clearest references to hero cult in Homeric poetry. In what follows, I will analyze a few of these references.

11§6. I start with the tumulus that will become the tomb shared by Achilles and Patroklos (xxiv 80–84). The reference here in the *Odyssey* to the shared tomb of Achilles and Patroklos complements a set of stylized references to what is understood to be the same tomb in the *Iliad* (especially XIX 368–380; XXIII 125–126, 245–248).† And the Homeric description of the tomb shared by these two heroes matches what we know about the tombs of cult heroes from sources external to Homeric poetry.‡

11§7. After building the tomb, the Achaeans hold funeral games in honor

---

ἦσθα θεοῖσιν. |₉₃ ὡς σὺ μὲν οὐδὲ θανὼν ὄνομ' ὤλεσας, ἀλλά τοι αἰεὶ |₉₄ πάντας ἐπ' ἀνθρώπους κλέος ἔσσεται ἐσθλόν, Ἀχιλλεῦ· |₉₅ αὐτὰρ ἐμοὶ τί τόδ' ἦδος, ἐπεὶ πόλεμον τολύπευσα; |₉₆ ἐν νόστῳ γάρ μοι Ζεὺς μήσατο λυγρὸν ὄλεθρον |₉₇ Αἰγίσθου ὑπὸ χερσὶ καὶ οὐλομένης ἀλόχοιο.

* See also Nagy 2012b:49–50.

† Detailed analysis in *HPC* 149–170 = II §§50–89. As I point out in that analysis, it is made clear in XXIII 245–248 that the tomb to be shared by Achilles and Patroklos should be incomplete while only Patroklos occupies it, and that the final act of making the complete tomb must wait until the death of Achilles. That final act is what we see described in *Odyssey* xxiv 80–84. I should add that the setting of the tomb of Achilles and Patroklos, as primarily indicated by the word *aktē,* 'promontory', in *Odyssey* xxiv 82, is consistent with the setting for the funeral of Patroklos as described in the *Iliad*: here too the primary indicator is the same word *aktē,* as we see in the contexts of XVIII 68, XXIII 125–126, XXIV 97.

‡ *GM* 220; in n52, there is an analysis of the relevant testimony of Pausanias 2.12.5.

of Achilles (xxiv 85–86). The details that we find in the narrative about these games match closely the details we can gather from historical evidence about athletic contests held in honor of cult heroes.*

11§8. The contests at the funeral games of Achilles and the prizes to be won in these contests are instituted for the purpose of compensating for his death, and such an act of compensation is expressed by way of the prepositional phrase *epi soi* (ἐπὶ σοί) at xxiv 91, which can be translated roughly as 'in your honor'. As we can see clearly from a variety of other sources, which I examined already in Hour 8a above, the syntactical construct combining the preposition *epi* with the dative case of any given hero's name refers to the cult of that hero.†

11§9. I find it relevant here to focus on a detail at xxiv 37–39, where we see that the Achaeans and the Trojans are battling over the possession of the corpse of Achilles.‡ The mentality of needing to possess the body of the dead hero, whether he was a friend or an enemy in life, is typical of hero cults, in that *the corpse of the cult hero was viewed as a talisman of fertility and prosperity for the community that gained possession of the hero's body.*§

11§10. There is a related detail at xxiv 39–40: the corpse of Achilles is described here as larger than life.** As we see from lore preserved in the historical period about cult heroes, they were conventionally pictured as far larger in death than they had been in life.††

11§11. The future immortalization of the dead hero in the context of hero cult is indicated by the epithet for the clothes that cover the hero's body: as we see at xxiv 59, the divine mother of Achilles and her sister Nereids clothe the hero's

---

* *BA* 116–117 = 6§30.

† See also *PH* 121 = 4§7. Perhaps the most striking example is this entry in the dictionary attributed to Hesychius: Βαλλητύς· ἑορτὴ Ἀθήνησιν, ἐπὶ Δημοφῶντι τῷ Κελεοῦ ἀγομένη· '*balletus*: a festival event at Athens, held in honor of Demophon son of Keleos' (further references to this athletic event of simulated warfare in *PH* 121 = 4§7n26).

‡ Narratives about this kind of battle are attested also in the visual arts. To cite just one example here, there is a Rhodian Black Figure plate, dated to the second half of the seventh century BCE (London, British Museum 1860,0404.1 A 749), showing the figures of Menelaos and Hector battling over the corpse of Euphorbos (see Bravo 2009:17).

§ *PH* 32, 178 = 1§29, 6§59; *EH* §97.

** I draw special attention to the wording at xxiv 39–40: σὺ δ' ἐν στροφάλιγγι κονίης | κεῖσο μέγας μεγαλωστί, 'There you were, lying in a swirl of dust. | You lay there so huge in all your hugeness'. This same wording applies to Achilles also in *Iliad* XVIII 26–27, where he stages himself as a corpse in mourning the death of Patroklos and where he is mourned by Thetis as if he were already a corpse (*BA* 113 = 6§24, especially with reference to XVIII 71). At XVI 775–776, cognate wording applies to the corpse of the hero Kebriones. The corpse of Achilles is described as nine cubits long in the *Alexandra* of Lycophron (860).

†† Survey by Brelich 1958:233–234. Among the striking examples in this survey is the corpse of Orestes as cult hero, described in Herodotus 1.68.

corpse in 'immortalizing' or *ambrota* clothes.* So there is a special meaning built into the description of the cremation at xxiv 67: 'you were burning while clothed in the clothes of the gods'.

11§12. We see at xxiv 73–77 another indication of the dead hero's future immortalization: after the cremation of the corpse of Achilles, his bones and those of the already cremated corpse of Patroklos are placed into a golden amphora that had been given by the god Dionysus to the goddess Thetis. This amphora, as we know from the comparative evidence of other poetic references (especially Stesichorus *PMG* 234), will mystically bring the hero back to life.†

11§13. We have already seen a variation on the theme of this hero's immortalization in the epic Cycle:

HOUR 11 TEXT B = HOUR 4 TEXT I

$|_{12}$ ... Thetis $|_{13}$ comes with the Muses and her sisters and makes a lament [*thrēnos*] for her son. $|_{14}$ After that, Thetis snatches him off the funeral pyre and carries her $|_{15}$ son over to the White Island [*Leukē*]. Meanwhile the Achaeans $|_{16}$ make [for Achilles] a tomb [*taphos*] and hold funeral games.

Plot summary by Proclus of the *Aithiopis* by Arctinus of Miletus p. 106 lines 12–16

11§14. The question arises: How can a cult hero be visualized as existing in two places at the same time? In the case of Achilles, for example, we see him immortalized in a paradisiacal setting, the White Island *(Leukē),* but we also envision him as the occupant of a tomb that contains his corpse. The answer is, such a bifocal view of the immortalized hero is typical of the mentality of hero cults. Here I review the formulation I gave about this mentality in Hour 8:

The cult hero was considered *dead*—from the standpoint of the place where the hero's *sōma,* or 'body', was situated; at the same time, the hero was considered simultaneously *immortalized*—from the standpoint of the paradisiacal place that awaited all heroes after death. Such a paradisiacal place, which was considered *eschatological,* must be contrasted with Hādēs, which was considered *transitional.* The name and even the visualization of this otherworldly place varied from hero cult to hero

---

*On the vital importance of understanding *ambrotos* as 'immortalizing' as well as 'immortal', I refer to my argumentation in *GM* 141, with reference especially to *Iliad* XVI 670 and 680.

† Nagy 2012b:50–51, following *BA* 209 = 10§50; see also Dué 2001.

cult. Some of these names are: Elysium *(Ēlusion)*, the Islands of the Blessed *(Nēsoi Makarōn)*, the White Island *(Leukē)*, and, exceptionally, even Mount Olympus in the case of Hēraklēs. Many of these names were applied also to the actual site or sacred precinct of the hero cult.*

11§15. Of all these paradisiacal locations that are reserved for immortalized heroes, I highlight here the Islands of the Blessed, since we know a detail about the inhabitants of this mythical place that helps explain why Achilles is addressed as *olbios,* 'blessed', at the beginning of Text A, *Odyssey* xxiv 36. In the Hesiodic *Works and Days,* this same word *olbios* is used to describe cult heroes who are immortalized after death and who enjoy a state of bliss in the Islands of the Blessed, which is a paradisiacal setting that transcends the temporal and the spatial constraints of mortality:†

HOUR 11 TEXT C

|₁₇₀ And they live with a carefree heart [*thūmos*] |₁₇₁ on the Islands of the Blessed [*Nēsoi Makarōn*] on the banks of the deep-swirling river Okeanos, |₁₇₂ blessed [*olbioi*] heroes [*hērōes*] that they are, and for them there is a honey-sweet harvest [*karpos*] |₁₇₃ that comes to fruition three times each year, produced by the life-giving land.

Hesiod *Works and Days* 170–173‡

11§16. As we can see from this text, heroes who are pictured as inhabitants of such paradisiacal settings qualify as *olbioi,* 'blessed' (verse 172). So Achilles, as the once and future inhabitant of the White Island, which is another such paradisacal setting, likewise qualifies as *olbios,* 'blessed'. That is why, I argue, he is addressed as *olbios,* 'blessed', at the beginning of Text A, in *Odyssey* xxiv 36.

Different Meanings of the Word Olbios *for the Initiated and for the Uninitiated*

11§17. Whereas the word *olbios* can be understood as 'blessed' in the sacral context of hero cults, in non-sacral contexts it can be understood neutrally as 'for-

---

* This formulation is derived from EH §98. For an extended discussion, see *BA* ch. 10 ("Poetic Visions of Immortality for the Hero").

† *GM* 126, with further references.

‡ |₁₇₀ καὶ τοὶ μὲν ναίουσιν ἀκηδέα θυμὸν ἔχοντες |₁₇₁ ἐν μακάρων νήσοισι παρ᾽ Ὠκεανὸν βαθυδίνην, |₁₇₂ ὄλβιοι ἥρωες, τοῖσιν μελιηδέα καρπὸν |₁₇₃ τρὶς ἔτεος θάλλοντα φέρει ζείδωρος ἄρουρα.

tunate'. We see both meanings of *olbios* being used in a story of Herodotus (1.29–33) about an encounter of Croesus the king of Lydia with Solon the Athenian lawgiver. Testing Solon, Croesus asks him to name the most *olbios* person on earth (1.30.2), expecting Solon to name Croesus himself (1.30.3). To his great disappointment, Croesus is told by Solon that an Athenian named Tellos is the most *olbios* of all humans (1.30.3–5), and that the second-most *olbioi* are the brothers Kleobis and Biton of Argos (1.31.1–5). As the story progresses, it becomes clear that Croesus understands the word *olbios* only in the non-sacral sense of 'fortunate', while Solon understands it also in the deeper sacral sense of 'blessed', referring to the blissful state of afterlife that is granted by the gods to Tellos of Athens and to the brothers Kleobis and Biton of Argos, since both the Athenian and the two Argive brothers turn out to be cult heroes.* I will have more to say in Hour 13 about these cult heroes, but I would like to highlight here the mentality of mysticism that we see at work in the bifocal meaning of *olbios* in this story of Herodotus. As the story implies, only those who are initiated into the mysteries of hero cult can understand the sacral meaning of *olbios*.† This sacral meaning, I argue, centers on the idea of heroic immortalization after death, which was a traditional teaching to be learned by worshippers of cult heroes in the context of initiation into the mysteries of hero cult. The actual procedures involved in such initiation will be explored in Hour 15, and for now I highlight simply the existence of these mysteries. The evidence comes from traditional wording that refers to initiation.

11§18. The idea of a deeper level of understanding, made available only to initiates, is most evident in contexts where the word *olbios* refers to the bliss of initiation into mysteries of immortalization in general, as we see from the use of this word with reference to the Eleusinian Mysteries:‡

HOUR 11 TEXT D

> Blessed [*olbios*] is he among earthbound mortals who has seen these things.
>
> *Homeric Hymn to Demeter* 480§

Here is another example, found in a song of lament *(thrēnos)* composed by Pindar:**

---

* Nagy 2012b:58–59, following *PH* 243–247 = 8§§45–48.
† Nagy 2012b:59.
‡ *PH* 245 = 8§46n128.
§ ὄλβιος ὃς τάδ' ὄπωπεν ἐπιχθονίων ἀνθρώπων.
** *PH* 245–246 = 8§46.

HOUR 11 TEXT E

Blessed [*olbios*] is he who has already seen those things when he goes below the earth.

Pindar Fragment 137*

11§19. Such contexts show that any initiate is *olbios* in the sense of 'blessed' only to the extent of knowing that one cannot achieve true blessedness before experiencing death, which brings immortalization after death. To illustrate this point, I quote here from an inscription written on gold lamella from Thourioi. This inscribed lamella, dated to the fourth century BCE, was found in a tomb, where it had been buried together with a dead man who is addressed with the following words: *olbie kai makariste*, 'O blessed one, you who are called blessed' (*IG* XIV 641 = *Orphicorum Fragmenta* 488 line 9),† As we can see from the wording in this inscription, only the immortalized dead can truly be addressed as *olbioi*.‡ And there are many other attestations of such inscriptions, which can be seen as initiatory texts that were meant to guide the dead toward some kind of an immortalized existence.§

11§20. By now we can understand more clearly the point of Herodotus' story about Croesus and Solon: only the initiated can understand the deeper meaning of the word *olbios*. And, it is important to add, only the initiated can understand the aphorism uttered by Solon, when he says that one should call no man *olbios* until he is dead. First, Solon lists some examples of good fortune (1.32.5–6), and then, after he finishes these examples, Solon adds:

HOUR 11 TEXT F

If, in addition to all these things [= the examples of good fortune that I have listed], someone reaches the end [*teleutân*] of life in a good way, then this someone is the person for whom you [= Croesus] are searching, that is, the person who deserves to be called *olbios*; but before someone reaches the end [*teleutân*], you should refrain from calling him *olbios*. Rather, just call him fortunate [*eutukhēs*].

Herodotus 1.32.7**

* ὄλβιος ὅστις ἰδὼν κεῖν᾽ εἶσ᾽ ὑπὸ χθόν᾽. . . .

† ὄλβιε καὶ μακαριστέ: we see here the vocatives of *olbios* and *makaristos*, both meaning 'blessed'. The numbering of lines in this fragment from Thourioi follows the edition of Bernabé 2004/2005.

‡ Nagy 2012b:59.

§ For a useful collection of such inscriptions, I cite the work of Tzifopoulos 2010.

** εἰ δὲ πρὸς τούτοισι ἔτι τελευτήσει τὸν βίον εὖ, οὗτος ἐκεῖνος τὸν σὺ ζητέεις, ὁ ὄλβιος κεκλῆσθαι ἄξιός ἐστι· πρὶν δ᾽ ἂν τελευτήσῃ, ἐπισχεῖν μηδὲ καλέειν κω ὄλβιον, ἀλλ᾽ εὐτυχέα.

How a Homeric Hero Can Become Truly Olbios

11§21. By now we have seen that one cannot achieve a state of immortalization until after one is dead: until that time comes, one may be *eutukhēs*, 'fortunate', from one moment to the next, but one cannot be truly *olbios*. This formula holds not only for figures like Croesus, who had fancied himself to be the most *olbios* of all humans in his time, but also for the Homeric heroes themselves: even such figures as Achilles and Odysseus cannot be cult heroes until they are dead, and so they cannot be truly *olbioi* until they reach a blissful state of immortalization after death.

11§22. In testing this formulation, I start with a passage that seems at first to contradict what I just said. When the *psūkhē* of Agamemnon, speaking from Hādēs, apostrophizes the still living Odysseus, here is what he says:

HOUR 11 TEXT G

|₁₉₂ O blessed [*olbios*] son of Laertes, Odysseus of many wiles, |₁₉₃ it is truly with great merit [*aretē*] that you got to have your wife.* |₁₉₄ For the thinking [*phrenes*] of faultless Penelope was sound: |₁₉₅ she, daughter of Ikarios, kept Odysseus well in mind, |₁₉₆ that properly wedded [*kouridios*] husband of hers. Thus the glory [*kleos*] will never perish for him, |₁₉₇ the glory that comes from his merit [*aretē*],† and a song will be created for earth-bound humans |₁₉₈ by the immortals—a song that brings beautiful and pleasurable recompense‡ for sensible Penelope |₁₉₉—unlike the daughter of Tyndareos [= Clytemnestra], who masterminded evil deeds, |₂₀₀ killing her properly wedded [*kouridios*] husband, and a hateful subject of song |₂₀₁ she will be throughout all humankind, and she will give a harsh reputation |₂₀₂ to women, female [*thēluterai*]§ that they are—even for the kind of woman who does noble things.**

Odyssey xxiv 192–202††

* In the original Greek wording, the prepositional phrase meaning 'with great merit' cannot "modify" a noun, and so we cannot translate this wording as 'you got to have a wife with great merit', in the sense of 'you got to have a wife who has great merit'; rather, the phrase modifies the verb 'you got'.

† I translate 'his merit', not 'her merit', interpreting this instance of *aretē* at verse 197 as referring to the previous instance, at verse 193.

‡ The epithet for *aoidē*, 'song', here is *khariessa*, 'having *kharis*', and I interpret the concept of *kharis* as 'beautiful and pleasurable recompense' in this context. On *kharis* as a word that conveys both beauty and pleasure, see HC 203–204 = 2§33.

§ In the original Greek, *thēluterai* means not 'more female' but rather 'female—as opposed to male'.

** I offer an extensive commentary on this text in BA 36–38 = 2§13.

†† |₁₉₂ ὄλβιε Λαέρταο πάϊ, πολυμήχαν' Ὀδυσσεῦ, |₁₉₃ ἦ ἄρα σὺν μεγάλῃ ἀρετῇ ἐκτήσω ἄκοιτιν· |₁₉₄ ὡς ἀγαθαὶ φρένες ἦσαν ἀμύμονι Πηνελοπείῃ, |₁₉₅ κούρῃ Ἰκαρίου, ὡς εὖ μέμνητ' Ὀδυσῆος, |₁₉₆ ἀνδρὸς

11§23. The word *olbios* that we see being used here in the first verse is as yet ambivalent: we cannot be sure whether it means 'fortunate' or 'blessed'. While a hero like Odysseus is still alive, it is dangerous for him to be described as *olbios* in the sense of 'blessed'. A negative example of what can happen is the case of the hero Priam. Most telling are the words that Achilles addresses to him toward the end of the *Iliad*: 'I hear that you, old man, were once upon a time *olbios*' (*Iliad* XXIV 543).* When Achilles is saying this to Priam, the old man is experiencing the worst moments of his life. During those moments, he is neither fortunate nor blessed. Only after death could Priam ever become truly *olbios*.† As we will see in the case of Odysseus, however, the *Odyssey* shows that this Homeric hero is ultimately not only fortunate but also blessed, and so the epithet *olbios* will in fact ultimately apply to him.

11§24. Most telling here is a related context of the same word *olbios*, which I have already quoted in Text A: in the first verse there, we read 'O you *olbios* son of Peleus, godlike Achilles' (xxiv 36).‡ There in Text A, as also here in Text G, the speaker is the *psūkhē* of Agamemnon (xxiv 35), and he is speaking there to the *psūkhē* of Achilles (xxiv 24). In that case, Achilles is by now already dead, already housed in his tomb, already a cult hero. In such a sacral context, the word *olbios* can safely be rendered as 'blessed' or 'blissful'.§

11§25. There is a supreme irony in the fact that the speaker who is calling Achilles *olbios* or 'blessed' in Text A (xxiv 36) is the *psūkhē* of Agamemnon. Since the quarrel of that hero with Achilles was so central to the Trojan War at the beginning of the *Iliad*, it is striking to see what Agamemnon is now saying to Achilles in Text A, which is located at the end of the *Odyssey* and which is showing a retrospective on the entire Trojan War. By now Agamemnon is accepting the status of Achilles as the ultimate winner in the story of the Trojan War. In fact, Agamemnon is even accepting his own status as the ultimate loser.

11§26. Further, in admitting that he is the loser, Agamemnon becomes a foil not only for Achilles but also for Odysseus. And, like Achilles, Odysseus is another ultimate winner—though this hero wins only in the *Odyssey*, not in the

---

κουριδίου. τῷ οἱ κλέος οὔ ποτ' ὀλεῖται |₁₉₇ ἧς ἀρετῆς, τεύξουσι δ' ἐπιχθονίοισιν ἀοιδὴν |₁₉₈ ἀθάνατοι χαρίεσσαν ἐχέφρονι Πηνελοπείῃ, |₁₉₉ οὐχ ὡς Τυνδαρέου κούρη κακὰ μήσατο ἔργα, |₂₀₀ κουρίδιον κτείνασα πόσιν, στυγερὴ δέ τ' ἀοιδὴ |₂₀₁ ἔσσετ' ἐπ' ἀνθρώπους, χαλεπὴν δέ τε φῆμιν ὀπάσσει |₂₀₂ θηλυτέρῃσι γυναιξί, καὶ ἥ κ' εὐεργὸς ἔῃσιν.

* καὶ σὲ γέρον τὸ πρὶν μὲν ἀκούομεν ὄλβιον εἶναι.

† Nagy 2012b:59–60.

‡ ὄλβιε Πηλέος υἱέ, θεοῖσ' ἐπιείκελ' Ἀχιλλεῦ.

§ Nagy 2012b:60.

Iliad. As we saw in Text G, Odysseus owes his own successful homecoming to the faithfulness of his wife, Penelope, who deserves only praise (xxiv 193–198). And it is in this context of success that Agamemnon addresses Odysseus as *olbios*, 'blessed' (xxiv 192). By contrast, as we saw in Text A, Agamemnon blames his own wife, Clytemnestra, for sabotaging his own 'homecoming' or *nostos* (xxiv 96).

11§27. We saw in Text A that Agamemnon contrasts his loss of 'homecoming' or *nostos* (xxiv 96) with the poetic 'glory' or *kleos* (xxiv 94) that Achilles will keep forever. But now, in Text G, we see that Agamemnon makes another basic contrast—between himself and Odysseus. What caused Agamemnon to lose his own *kleos*—and his own *nostos*—was the fact that his wife was Clytemnestra, who was unfaithful to him and who contrived his murder (xxiv 199–202). By contrast, the faithfulness of Penelope to Odysseus helped that hero secure his own *kleos* (xxiv 196, in the context of 196–198). To add to the irony, Agamemnon's words in Text A describe his violent death as *lugros*, 'disastrous' (xxiv 96), and his wife, Clytemnestra, as *oulomenē*, 'disastrous' (xxiv 97). Both of these epithets, as we saw earlier, are words that evoke the poetry of epic: *lugros*, 'disastrous', is the epithet both of the *nostos* or 'song about homecoming' that Phemios sings in *Odyssey* i 327 (Hour 9 Text D) and of the *nostos* that Nestor narrates in *Odyssey* iii 132 (Hour 9 Text E), while *oulomenē*, 'disastrous', is the epithet of the anger of Achilles in *Iliad* I 2 (Hour 9§29).

The Death of Odysseus

11§28. As we have already seen in Text A, Achilles is called *olbios*, 'blessed', in *Odyssey* xxiv 36 precisely because his corpse is already housed in a tomb, as described in xxiv 80–84. So now the question arises: if Odysseus is rightfully to be called *olbios*, 'blessed', in *Odyssey* xxiv 192, where is his tomb? And we have to ask another question even before that: how did Odysseus die?

11§29. We can find an answer to both questions by considering the use of the word *sēma* in both the *Iliad* and the *Odyssey*. In *Odyssey* xxiv 80–84, the tomb that Achilles shares with Patroklos is called a *tumbos* (xxiv 80), but we can see from references in the *Iliad* that the word *sēma* does in fact apply to this tomb. In *Iliad* XXIV 16, the tomb of Patroklos is explicitly called a *sēma*, and, at an earlier point in the narrative of the *Iliad*, this tomb is described as incomplete: it will not be complete until Achilles himself is buried there together with his best friend, Patroklos (XXIII 245–248).

11§30. As I argued at length in Hour 7, quoting Text A there, the word *sēma* is used in *Iliad* XXIII 331 with reference to the same tomb; and, in that same quoted text, we see the same word *sēma* five verses earlier in *Iliad* XXIII 326, where it refers to the riddling 'sign' given by Nestor to Antilokhos—a sign from the father that will instruct the son about how to make a successful left turn around the tomb, used as the turning point of the chariot race in honor of the dead Patroklos. I now concentrate on the riddling use of this word *sēma* as the 'sign' of a cult hero in that text. I quote again the relevant verse:

HOUR 11 TEXT H (PART OF HOUR 7 TEXT A)

And I [= Nestor] will tell you [= Antilokhos] a sign [*sēma*], a very clear one, which will not get lost in your thinking.

Iliad XXIII 326*

11§31. From what we have seen so far in Hours 7 and 8, Nestor's *sēma* for Antilokhos is a 'sign' of death as marked by the 'tomb' of a cult hero who has not yet been identified as Patroklos. But now we will see that this *sēma* is also a 'sign' of life after death, as marked by the same 'tomb'.†

11§32. The words spoken by Nestor to Antilokhos in the verse I just quoted again from *Iliad* XXIII 326 are matched exactly in the *Odyssey,* in a riddling context that refers to the death of Odysseus and, as we will see later, to the tomb that will be built for him:

HOUR 11 TEXT I

I [= Teiresias] will tell you [= Odysseus] a sign [*sēma*], a very clear one, which will not get lost in your thinking.

Odyssey xi 126‡

11§33. This verse in *Odyssey* xi 126 (rephrased later in xxiii 273) comes toward the end of a prophecy spoken by the *psūkhē* or 'spirit' of the seer Teiresias (xi 90, 150; xxiii 251), who appears to Odysseus during that hero's mystical sojourn in Hādēs. Now I quote here the entire text of that prophecy:

---

* σῆμα δέ τοι ἐρέω μάλ' ἀριφραδές, οὐδέ σε λήσει.
† Nagy 2012b:57, following *GM* 219.
‡ σῆμα δέ τοι ἐρέω μάλ' ἀριφραδές, οὐδέ σε λήσει.

HOUR 11 TEXT J (CONTAINING TEXT I)

|₉₀ Then came also the spirit [*psūkhē*] of Theban Teiresias, |₉₁ with a golden scepter in his hand. He recognized me and said, |₉₂ "Odysseus, you who are descended from the gods, noble son of Laertes, |₉₃ why, wretched man, have you left the light of day |₉₄ and come down to see the dead in this place without any delights? |₉₅ Stand back from the trench and draw back your sharp sword |₉₆ so that I may drink of the blood and tell you unmistakably true things." |₉₇ So he spoke, and I [= Odysseus] drew back, and sheathed my silver-studded sword, |₉₈ putting it back into the scabbard, and then he [= Teiresias], after he had drunk the black blood, |₉₉ began to address me with his words, faultless seer [*mantis*] that he was: |₁₀₀ "It's your homecoming [*nostos*] that you seek, a homecoming sweet as honey, O radiant Odysseus. |₁₀₁ But the god will make this painful for you. I say that because I do not think |₁₀₂ that the earth-shaking god [= Poseidon] will not take notice, who has lodged in his heart [*thūmos*] an anger [*kotos*] against you, |₁₀₃ being angry that you blinded his dear son [= Polyphemus]. |₁₀₄ Still, even so, after enduring many bad experiences, you all may get home |₁₀₅ if you are willing to restrain your own heart [*thūmos*] and the heart of your comrades [*hetairoi*] |₁₀₆ when you pilot your well-built ship to |₁₀₇ the island of Thrinacia, seeking refuge from the violet-colored sea, |₁₀₈ and when you find the grazing cattle and the sturdy sheep |₁₀₉ that belong to the god of the sun, Hēlios, who sees everything and hears everything. |₁₁₀ If you leave these herds unharmed and think only about homecoming [*nostos*], |₁₁₁ then you could still make it to Ithaca, arriving there after having endured many bad experiences. |₁₁₂ But if you harm the herds, then I forewarn you of destruction |₁₁₃ both for your ship and for your comrades [*hetairoi*], and, even if you may yourself escape, |₁₁₄ you will return [*neesthai*] in a bad way, losing all your comrades [*hetairoi*], |₁₁₅ in someone else's ship, not your own, and you will find painful things happening in your house, |₁₁₆ I mean, you will find high-handed men there who are devouring your livelihood |₁₁₇ while they are courting your godlike wife and offering wedding-presents to her. |₁₁₈ But you will avenge the outrages committed by those men when you get home. |₁₁₉ But after you kill the suitors in your own house, |₁₂₀

killing them either by trickery or openly, by way of sharp bronze, |₁₂₁ you must go on a journey then, taking with you a well-made oar, |₁₂₂ until you come to a place where men do not know what the sea is |₁₂₃ and do not even eat any food that is mixed with sea salt, |₁₂₄ nor do they know anything about ships, which are painted purple on each side, |₁₂₅ and well-made oars that are like wings for ships. |₁₂₆ And I will tell you a sign [sēma], a very clear one, which will not get lost in your thinking. |₁₂₇ Whenever someone on the road encounters you |₁₂₈ and says that it must be a winnowing shovel that you have on your radiant shoulder, |₁₂₉ at that point you must stick into the ground the well-made oar |₁₃₀ and sacrifice beautiful sacrifices to lord Poseidon |₁₃₁ a ram, a bull, and a boar that mounts sows. |₁₃₂ And then go home and offer sacred hecatombs |₁₃₃ to the immortal gods who possess the vast expanses of the skies. |₁₃₄ Sacrifice to them in proper order, one after the other. As for yourself, death shall come to you from the sea, |₁₃₅ a gentle death, that is how it will come, and this death will kill you |₁₃₆ as you lose your strength in a prosperous old age. And the people all around [your corpse] |₁₃₇ will be blessed [olbioi]. All the things I say are unmistakably true."

Odyssey xi 90–137*

* |₉₀ ἦλθε δ' ἐπὶ ψυχὴ Θηβαίου Τειρεσίαο, |₉₁ χρύσεον σκῆπτρον ἔχων, ἐμὲ δ' ἔγνω καὶ προσέειπε· |₉₂ "διογενὲς Λαερτιάδη, πολυμήχαν' Ὀδυσσεῦ, |₉₃ τίπτ' αὖτ', ὦ δύστηνε, λιπὼν φάος ἠελίοιο |₉₄ ἤλυθες, ὄφρα ἴδῃ νέκυας καὶ ἀτερπέα χῶρον; |₉₅ ἀλλ' ἀποχάζεο βόθρου, ἄπισχε δὲ φάσγανον ὀξύ, |₉₆ αἵματος ὄφρα πίω καί τοι νημερτέα εἴπω." |₉₇ ὣς φάτ', ἐγὼ δ' ἀναχασσάμενος ξίφος ἀργυρόηλον |₉₈ κουλεῷ ἐγκατέπηξ'. ὁ δ' ἐπεὶ πίεν αἷμα κελαινόν, |₉₉ καὶ τότε δή μ' ἐπέεσσι προσηύδα μάντις ἀμύμων· |₁₀₀ "νόστον δίζηαι μελιηδέα, φαίδιμ' Ὀδυσσεῦ· |₁₀₁ τὸν δέ τοι ἀργαλέον θήσει θεός. οὐ γὰρ ὀΐω |₁₀₂ λήσειν ἐννοσίγαιον, ὅ τοι κότον ἔνθετο θυμῷ, |₁₀₃ χωόμενος ὅτι οἱ υἱὸν φίλον ἐξαλάωσας. |₁₀₄ ἀλλ' ἔτι μέν κε καὶ ὥς, κακὰ περ πάσχοντες, ἵκοισθε, |₁₀₅ αἴ κ' ἐθέλῃς σὸν θυμὸν ἐρυκακέειν καὶ ἑταίρων, |₁₀₆ ὁππότε κεν πρῶτον πελάσῃς εὐεργέα νῆα |₁₀₇ Θρινακίῃ νήσῳ, προφυγὼν ἰοειδέα πόντον, |₁₀₈ βοσκομένας δ' εὕρητε βόας καὶ ἴφια μῆλα |₁₀₉ Ἠελίου, ὃς πάντ' ἐφορᾷ καὶ πάντ' ἐπακούει. |₁₁₀ τὰς εἰ μέν κ' ἀσινέας ἐάᾳς νόστου τε μέδηαι, |₁₁₁ καί κεν ἔτ' εἰς Ἰθάκην, κακά περ πάσχοντες, ἵκοισθε· |₁₁₂ εἰ δέ κε σίνηαι, τότε τοι τεκμαίρομ' ὄλεθρον |₁₁₃ νηΐ τε καὶ ἑτάροισ'. αὐτὸς δ' εἴ πέρ κεν ἀλύξῃς, |₁₁₄ ὀψὲ κακῶς νεῖαι, ὀλέσας ἄπο πάντας ἑταίρους, |₁₁₅ νηὸς ἐπ' ἀλλοτρίης· δήεις δ' ἐν πήματα οἴκῳ, |₁₁₆ ἄνδρας ὑπερφιάλους, οἵ τοι βίοτον κατέδουσι |₁₁₇ μνώμενοι ἀντιθέην ἄλοχον καὶ ἕδνα διδόντες. |₁₁₈ ἀλλ' ἦ τοι κείνων γε βίας ἀποτείσεαι ἐλθών· |₁₁₉ αὐτὰρ ἐπὴν μνηστῆρας ἐνὶ μεγάροισι τεοῖσι |₁₂₀ κτείνῃς ἠὲ δόλῳ ἢ ἀμφαδὸν ὀξέϊ χαλκῷ, |₁₂₁ ἔρχεσθαι δὴ ἔπειτα, λαβὼν εὐῆρες ἐρετμόν, |₁₂₂ εἰς ὅ κε τοὺς ἀφίκηαι, οἳ οὐκ ἴσασι θάλασσαν |₁₂₃ ἀνέρες οὐδέ θ' ἅλεσσι μεμιγμένον εἶδαρ ἔδουσιν· |₁₂₄ οὐδ' ἄρα τοὶ ἴσασι νέας φοινικοπαρῄους, |₁₂₅ οὐδ' εὐῆρε' ἐρετμά, τά τε πτερὰ νηυσὶ πέλονται. |₁₂₆ σῆμα δέ τοι ἐρέω μάλ' ἀριφραδές, οὐδέ σε λήσει· |₁₂₇ ὁππότε κεν δή τοι ξυμβλήμενος ἄλλος ὁδίτης |₁₂₈ φήῃ ἀθηρηλοιγὸν ἔχειν ἀνὰ φαιδίμῳ ὤμῳ, |₁₂₉ καὶ τότε δὴ γαίῃ πήξας εὐῆρες ἐρετμόν, |₁₃₀ ἔρξας ἱερὰ καλὰ Ποσειδάωνι ἄνακτι, |₁₃₁ ἀρνειὸν ταῦρόν τε συῶν τ' ἐπιβήτορα κάπρον, |₁₃₂ οἴκαδ' ἀποστείχειν ἔρδειν θ' ἱερὰς ἑκατόμβας |₁₃₃ ἀθανάτοισι θεοῖσι, τοὶ οὐρανὸν εὐρὺν ἔχουσι, |₁₃₄ πᾶσι μάλ' ἑξείης. θάνατος δέ τοι ἐξ ἁλὸς αὐτῷ |₁₃₅ ἀβληχρὸς μάλα τοῖος ἐλεύσεται, ὅς κέ σε πέφνῃ |₁₃₆ γήρᾳ ὕπο λιπαρῷ ἀρημένον· ἀμφὶ δὲ λαοὶ |₁₃₇ ὄλβιοι ἔσσονται. τὰ δέ τοι νημερτέα εἴρω."

11§34. The mysticism of this passage is highlighted by a fact that we can see only when we read the original Greek wording of Text J here: the very first word uttered by the *psūkhē* (xi 90) of Teiresias as a *mantis* or 'seer' (xi 99) after he has drunk the blood of freshly sacrificed sheep (xi 98) is the word *nostos* (xi 100). Here is the Greek wording: *noston dizēai meliēdea ...*, which I translated as 'It's your homecoming [*nostos*] that you seek, a homecoming sweet as honey ...'* The use of this word here is connected with the fact that, earlier in the narrative, the seer Teiresias is described as exceptionally possessing consciousness even in Hādēs, where other *psūkhai* are merely *skiai*, 'shadows' that flit about without any consciousness, and the word used here for the idea of consciousness is *noos*:

HOUR 11 TEXT K

|₄₉₀ But first you [= Odysseus] must bring to fulfillment [*teleîn*] another journey and travel until you enter |₄₉₁ the palace of Hādēs and of the dreaded Persephone, |₄₉₂ and there you all will consult [*khrē-*] the spirit [*psūkhē*] of Teiresias of Thebes, |₄₉₃ the blind seer [*mantis*], whose thinking [*phrenes*] is grounded [*empedoi*]: |₄₉₄ to him, even though he was dead, Persephone gave consciousness [*noos*], |₄₉₅ so as to be the only one there who has the power to think [*pepnusthai*]. But the others [in Hādēs] just flit about, like shadows [*skiai*].

Odyssey x 490–495†

11§35. The speaker here is the goddess Circe, and the words of her own prophecy here in *Odyssey* x about the later prophecy made by the 'spirit' or *psūkhē* of the seer Teiresias in *Odyssey* xi can be viewed as a re-enactment of the etymological link, which I explored already in Hour 10, between *noos* as a mystical form of 'consciousness' and *nostos* as a mystical form of 'homecoming' or 'coming to' from a state of darkness and death to a state of life and light. And it is relevant that the *noos* or 'consciousness' of the 'spirit' or *psūkhē* of the seer Teiresias becomes activated, as it were, only after he drinks the blood of a sacrificial animal that Odysseus has slaughtered in order to make mental contact with the cult hero (xi 96, 98). That animal, as we learn from the explicit instruc-

---

* νόστον δίζηαι μελιηδέα ...

† |₄₉₀ ἀλλ' ἄλλην χρὴ πρῶτον ὁδὸν τελέσαι καὶ ἱκέσθαι |₄₉₁ εἰς Ἀίδαο δόμους καὶ ἐπαινῆς Περσεφονείης |₄₉₂ ψυχῇ χρησομένους Θηβαίου Τειρεσίαο, |₄₉₃ μάντιος ἀλαοῦ, τοῦ τε φρένες ἔμπεδοί εἰσι· |₄₉₄ τῷ καὶ τεθνηῶτι νόον πόρε Περσεφόνεια |₄₉₅ οἴῳ πεπνῦσθαι· τοὶ δὲ σκιαὶ ἀΐσσουσιν.

tions of Circe, is a black ram intended only for Teiresias (x 524–525). And, as we have seen already in the Introduction to Homeric Poetry (0§11), a black ram is the preferred sacrifical animal to slaughter for the purpose of making mental contact with a male cult hero.

11§36. In an essay entitled "*Sēma* and *Noēsis*: The Hero's Tomb and the 'Reading' of Symbols in Homer and Hesiod," I analyzed at some length the mystical prophecy spoken by the *psūkhē* of the seer Teiresias as I have just quoted it in Text J.* As I argued in that essay, the verses of the prophecy point to the future death of Odysseus and to the mystical vision of his own tomb, where he will be worshipped as a cult hero.†

11§37. Most revealing is the description of what will happen to people who live in the proximity of the corpse of Odysseus as a cult hero: 'And the people all around [your corpse] |₁₃₇ will be blessed [*olbioi*]'‡ (xi 136–137; retold at xxiii 283–284). Here I return to an analogous set of verses, already quoted in Text A, which describe the corpse of Achilles: 'And others, those all around you [= your corpse], |₃₈ were being slaughtered, sons of both Trojans and Achaeans, the best, |₃₉ as they were fighting over you [= your corpse]'§ (xxiv 37–39).**

11§38. Having noted this analogy, which touches on the idea of possessing the corpse of the cult hero (I analyzed this idea earlier in this hour, in §9), I can now turn to the meaning of the word *olbioi* describing those who find themselves in the proximity of Odysseus as cult hero (xi 137, xxiii 284). In the Hesiodic *Works and Days* (172), already quoted in Text C, this same word *olbioi* describes cult heroes who are immortalized after death and who enjoy a state of bliss in a paradisiacal setting that transcends the temporal and the spatial constraints of mortality.††

11§39. In such a sacral context, as we have already noted, the word *olbioi* means 'blessed' or 'blissful', and I argue that this same meaning applies also to ordinary humans who come into mental and even physical proximity to cult heroes by way of worshipping them. We will see in Hours 13 and 14 some historical examples of hero cults that express the idea of such mental and physical contact. In the sacral context of such contact, as we will also see, the worship-

* Nagy 1983a, as recast in *GM* 202–222.
† *GM* 212–214.
‡ ἀμφὶ δὲ λαοὶ |₁₃₇ ὄλβιοι ἔσσονται.
§ ἀμφὶ δέ σ᾿ ἄλλοι |₃₈ κτείνοντο Τρώων καὶ Ἀχαιῶν υἷες ἄριστοι |₃₉ μαρνάμενοι περὶ σεῖο.
** Nagy 2012b:58.
†† Nagy 1990b:126, with further references.

pers can be at least momentarily blessed. By contrast, the immortalized cult heroes whom they worship are permanently blessed. The distribution of blessings may be inequitable, but at least the worshippers experience a momentary transfer of bliss from the cult heroes. And there is another side to the picture: whereas the word *olbioi* can be rendered as 'blessed' or 'blissful' in such sacral contexts, in non-sacral contexts it can be rendered neutrally as 'fortunate'. A perfect example is the saying of Solon in the narrative of Herodotus, as quoted already in Text F.

11§40. As I bring this part of my argumentation to a close, I need to emphasize again what I had emphasized already in the Introduction to Homeric Poetry (0§13): references to hero cults tend to be implicit, not explicit, in this poetry. And that is because the religious practice of hero cults is fundamentally a local phenomenon (0§14, 8§39), while the Homeric tradition is non-local or Panhellenic, as I emphasized already in the Introduction to whole book (00§§10–14). We need to keep in mind the non-local orientation of Homeric poetry as we consider the reference in *Odyssey* xi 136–137, as quoted in Text J, to people who are *olbioi*, 'blessed', in the context of the death of Odysseus. Homeric poetry says only implicitly, not explicitly, that these people are made 'blessed' because they worship Odysseus as a cult hero whose corpse is buried in the earth that they cultivate, and that this 'blessing' is realized by way of physical contact with the earth containing the corpse of the hero. This poetry refers only implicitly to existing practices of hero cult, without explicitly revealing the mysteries of the hero cult. As I promised earlier, we will explore some details about these practices when we reach Hour 15.

A Mystical Vision of the Tomb of Odysseus

11§41. I turn to an example of the mysteries of hero cult as implied in Homeric poetry. I have in mind the passage from the *Odyssey* that I have quoted in Text J, xi 90–136, where the *psūkhē* of Teiresias, during his moments of consciousness after drinking the sacrificial ram's blood that is poured for him by Odysseus (xi 95–96, 98), foretells the story of Odysseus beyond the *Odyssey* as we know it. In this meta-narrative, we see that Odysseus confronts his death in a mystical moment where he experiences *a coincidence of opposites*. And what is this mystical moment? It is a point where *the sea and the negation of the sea coincide*. That is, *Odysseus goes as far away as possible from the sea, only to experience death from* *the sea*: 'death shall come to you from the sea, |₁₃₅ a gentle death'* (xi 134–135). And it is at this same point where the oar that he carries on his shoulder, which is an instrument linked exclusively with the sea, is mistaken for a winnowing shovel, which is an instrument linked exclusively with the earth, that is, with the cultivation of the land: 'Whenever someone on the road encounters you |₁₂₈ and says that it must be a winnowing shovel that you have on your radiant shoulder'† (xi 127–128). And here is another coincidence of opposites: Odysseus at this point must sacrifice to Poseidon, god of the sea (xi 130–131)—even though this point is as far away from the sea as possible. And now we come to a mystical vision: in sacrificing to Poseidon, Odysseus must mark the place of sacrifice by sticking into the ground the oar that he was carrying on his shoulder: 'at that point you must stick into the ground the well-made oar'‡ (xi 129). As I will now argue, what we are seeing here is a mystical vision of the tomb of Odysseus himself.

11§42. The key to my argument is what the *psūkhē* of Teiresias says in introducing his prophecy: 'And I [= Teiresias] will tell you [= Odysseus] a sign [*sēma*], a very clear one, which will not get lost in your thinking' (xi 126).§ As I noted earlier, the wording here matches exactly the wording of Nestor addressed to Antilokhos in the *Iliad*: 'And I [= Nestor] will tell you [= Antilokhos] a sign [*sēma*], a very clear one, which will not get lost in your thinking'** (XXIII 326). And, to repeat what we have seen in Hours 7 and 8, the *sēma* of Nestor for Antilokhos is a 'sign' as marked by the 'tomb' of a cult hero who has not yet been identified as Patroklos. In the *Odyssey* as well, I argue, the *sēma* of Teiresias for Odysseus is a 'sign' as marked by the 'tomb' of a cult hero who has not yet been identified as Odysseus himself.

11§43. There is archaeological evidence for the existence of a hero cult of Odysseus on the island of Ithaca, dating back to an early period when the *Odyssey* as we know it was still taking shape.†† And, in the version of the story as we see it in the *Odyssey*, Odysseus dies finally in Ithaca, which figures here as his homeland (xi 132–138). In terms of this version of the story, then, it must be the inhabitants of Ithaca who will be *olbioi*, 'blessed', as a result of the hero's death

* θάνατος δέ τοι ἐξ ἀλὸς αὐτῷ |₁₃₅ ἀβληχρὸς μάλα τοῖος ἐλεύσεται.
† |₁₂₇ ὁππότε κεν δή τοι ξυμβλήμενος ἄλλος ὁδίτης |₁₂₈ φήῃ ἀθηρηλοιγὸν ἔχειν ἀνὰ φαιδίμῳ ὤμῳ.
‡ καὶ τότε δὴ γαίη πήξας εὐῆρες ἐρετμόν.
§ σῆμα δέ τοι ἐρέω μάλ' ἀριφραδές, οὐδέ σε λήσει·
** σῆμα δέ τοι ἐρέω μάλ' ἀριφραδές, οὐδέ σε λήσει.
†† Currie 2005:57, with reference to *Odyssey* xiii 96–112, 345–371.

(xi 136–137; retold at xxiii 283–284). And so we may infer that Ithaca is recognized in the *Odyssey* as a prime location for the hero cult of Odysseus.

11§44. This is not to say, however, that Ithaca was the only place where Odysseus was worshipped as a cult hero. From the testimony of Pausanias, for example, we see traces of a hero cult of Odysseus in landlocked Arcadia, which is located in the Peloponnesus and which is as far away from the sea as you can possibly be in the Peloponnesus:

HOUR 11 TEXT L

There is a path leading uphill from Asea [in Arcadia] to the mountain called the North Mountain [*Boreion*], and on top of that mountain there are traces of a sacred space; it is said that Odysseus had made this sacred space in honor of Athena the Savior [*sōteira*] and in honor of Poseidon, in return for his having arrived back home safely from Ilion [= Troy].

Pausanias 8.44.4*

11§45. Here we see once again the same coincidence of opposites that we saw in Text J, *Odyssey* xi 127–131, where Odysseus must make a sacrifice to Poseidon, god of the sea, at a place that is as far away from the sea as possible. Both Text J and Text L, where we have just read the report of Pausanias (8.44.4) about a sacred space in Arcadia that Odysseus established in honor of Poseidon, point to the existence of hero cults for Odysseus. What both texts have in common is the idea that Odysseus will put an end to the antagonism that exists between him and Poseidon by performing a sacred act in a place that is made sacred by the act itself. And this idea of a sacred space that is somehow shared by a god and a hero whose relationship is mutually antagonistic, as in the case of Poseidon and Odysseus, is typical of hero cults where the body of the hero is venerated within a space that is sacred to the god who is antagonistic to that hero. In the context of hero cults, *god-hero antagonism in myth—including the myths mediated by epic—corresponds to god-hero symbiosis in ritual.*† A classic example is the location of the body of the hero Pyrrhos, son of Achilles, in the sacred precinct of Apollo at Delphi (Pindar *Nemean* 7.44–47; Pausanias 10.24.6); in the myth about

---

* ἔστι δὲ ἄνοδος ἐξ Ἀσέας ἐς τὸ ὄρος τὸ Βόρειον καλούμενον, καὶ ἐπὶ τῇ ἄκρᾳ τοῦ ὄρους σημεῖά ἐστιν ἱεροῦ· ποιῆσαι δὲ τὸ ἱερὸν Ἀθηνᾷ τε Σωτείρᾳ καὶ Ποσειδῶνι Ὀδυσσέα ἐλέγετο ἀνακομισθέντα ἐξ Ἰλίου.

† EH §105, Nagy 2011c §§35–44, 55.

the death of this hero Pyrrhos, it is the god Apollo who causes this death (as we see in Pindar's *Nemean 7* and *Paean 6*).* Similarly, I argue that the god Poseidon ultimately causes the death of the hero Odysseus: death from the sea, in whatever form death may come, would be initiated primarily by Poseidon himself as god of the sea. And I will also argue that the most logical place for Odysseus to have a tomb and a hero cult is precisely at the spot where his oar was mistaken for a winnowing shovel, and that spot would be Arcadia from the standpoint of Arcadian myth.

11§46. In terms of an Arcadian version of the Odysseus myth, as tied to the ritual site of the sacred space described by Pausanias (8.44.4) in Text L, the elemental shape of the hero's tomb could be visualized as an oar stuck into the ground. Such a visualization corresponds to the ritual act of Odysseus in response to the coincidence of opposites that he experienced when his oar was mistaken for a winnowing shovel: as we saw in Text J, he had to make sacrifice to Poseidon at the very point where the coincidence of opposites took place (xi 130–131), and he had to mark the place of sacrifice by sticking into the ground the oar that he was carrying on his shoulder (xi 129). And such an elemental shape—an oar stuck into the ground—is actually pictured as the tomb of a seafarer in the description of the funeral of Elpenor in the *Odyssey* (xii 208–215). Elpenor was the comrade of Odysseus who died of an accidental fall from a roof during the sojourn of Odysseus and his men on the island of Circe, and the funeral of Elpenor is described in detail: Odysseus and his men make for him a tomb by heaping a tumulus of earth over the seafarer's corpse and then, instead of erecting a *stēlē* or vertical 'column' on top, they stick his oar into the heap of earth:

Hour 11 Text M

|₁₄ We heaped up a tomb [*tumbos*] for him, and then, erecting as a column on top, |₁₅ we stuck his well-made oar into the very top of the tomb [*tumbos*].

Odyssey xii 14–15†

11§47. The ritual procedure for making the tomb of Elpenor follows the instructions given to Odysseus during his sojourn in Hādēs (xi 51–80); these in-

---

* *BA* 118–141 = 7§§1–30.
† |₁₄ τύμβον χεύαντες καὶ ἐπὶ στήλην ἐρύσαντες |₁₅ πήξαμεν ἀκροτάτῳ τύμβῳ εὐῆρες ἐρετμόν.

structions were given by Elpenor himself or, more accurately, by his *psūkhē* (xi 51), and the wording makes it explicit that the tomb to be made is a *sēma*:

HOUR 11 TEXT N

|₇₅ Heap up a tomb [*sēma*] for me [= Elpenor] at the shore of the gray sea, |₇₆ wretched man that I am, so that even those who live in the future will learn about it. |₇₇ Make this ritual act [*teleîn*] for me, and stick the oar on top of the tomb [*tumbos*] |₇₈—the oar that I used when I was rowing with my comrades [*hetairoi*].

Odyssey xi 75–78*

11§48. In the light of this description, we can see that the ritual act of Odysseus when he sticks his own well-made oar into the ground (xi 129) and sacrifices to Poseidon (xi 130–131) points to the making of his own *sēma* or 'tomb', corresponding to the *sēma* or 'sign' given to him by Teiresias (xi 126).

Two Meanings of a Sēma

11§49. There are two meanings to be found in this ritual act of Odysseus, since he sticks his oar into the ground at the precise moment when the oar is no longer recognized as an oar (xi 129). In this *coincidence of opposites,* as I have been calling it since §41 in this hour, the oar is now a winnowing shovel (xi 128)—an agricultural implement that is used for separating the grain from the chaff after the harvesting of wheat. You toss the harvested wheat up in the air, and even the slightest breeze will blow the chaff further to the side while the grain falls more or less straight down into a heap in front of you. The winnowing shovel looks exactly like an oar, but it is not an oar for agriculturists. Conversely, the oar looks exactly like the winnowing shovel, but it is not a winnowing shovel for seafarers. For Odysseus, however, this implement could be both an oar and a winnowing shovel, since he could see that the same *sēma* or 'sign' has two distinct meanings in two distinct places: what is an oar for the seafarers is a winnowing shovel for the inlanders. And, in order to recognize that one *sēma* or 'sign' could have two meanings, *Odysseus must travel,* as we see from the key wording he learned from the instructions of Teiresias. Odysseus himself

---

* |₇₅ σῆμά τέ μοι χεῦαι πολιῆς ἐπὶ θινὶ θαλάσσης, |₇₆ ἀνδρὸς δυστήνοιο, καὶ ἐσσομένοισι πυθέσθαι· |₇₇ ταῦτά τέ μοι τελέσαι πῆξαί τ᾽ ἐπὶ τύμβῳ ἐρετμόν, |₇₈ τῷ καὶ ζωὸς ἔρεσσον ἐὼν μετ᾽ ἐμοῖσ᾽ ἑτάροισιν.

uses this key wording when he retells to Penelope a retrospective story of his travels:

HOUR 11 TEXT O

| $_{266}$ Your [= Penelope's] heart [*thūmos*] will not be pleased, nor am I [= Odysseus] | $_{267}$ pleased [by the telling of these adventures], since he [= Teiresias] instructed me to go to very many cities of mortals | $_{268}$ while holding my well-made oar in my hands . . .

Odyssey xxiii 266–268*

As we have seen in Text A of Hour 10 (and in Text A of Hour 9), these travels of Odysseus throughout 'the many cities of mortals' were the key to his achieving his special kind of heroic consciousness, or *noos:*

HOUR 11 TEXT P

| $_3$ Many different cities of many different people did he see, getting to know different ways of thinking [*noos*].

Odyssey i 3†

11§50. Just as the implement carried by Odysseus is one sign with two meanings, so also the picture of this implement that we see stuck into the ground is one sign with two meanings. We have already noted the first of these meanings, namely, that the *sēma* or 'sign' given by Teiresias to Odysseus in *Odyssey* xi 126, Text I, is in fact the tomb of Odysseus, imagined as a heap of earth with an oar stuck into it on top, just as the tomb of the seafarer Elpenor is a heap of earth with his own oar stuck into it on top, as we saw in Text M and Text N (xii 14–15 and xi 75–78 respectively); in fact, as we saw in Text N, this heap of earth is actually called the *sēma* of Elpenor (xi 75), and the word here clearly means 'tomb'. Accordingly, I paraphrase the first of the two meanings as a headline, "the seafarer is dead." As for the second of the two meanings, I propose to paraphrase it as another headline, "the harvest is complete." Here is why: the act of sticking the shaft of a winnowing shovel, with the blade pointing upward, into a heap of harvested wheat after having winnowed away the chaff from the grain is a ritual gesture indicating that the winnower's work is complete (as we see from the

---

* | $_{266}$ οὐ μέν τοι θυμὸς κεχαρήσεται· οὐδὲ γὰρ αὐτὸς | $_{267}$ χαίρω, ἐπεὶ μάλα πολλὰ βροτῶν ἐπὶ ἄστε' ἄνωγεν | $_{268}$ ἐλθεῖν, ἐν χείρεσσιν ἔχοντ' εὐῆρες ἐρετμόν . . .

† πολλῶν δ' ἀνθρώπων ἴδεν ἄστεα καὶ νόον ἔγνω.

wording of Theocritus 7.155–156).* And the act of sticking the shaft of an oar into the ground, again with the blade facing upward, is a ritual gesture indicating that the oarsman's work is likewise complete—as in the case of Odysseus' dead comrade Elpenor, whose tomb is to be a heap of earth with the shaft of his oar stuck into the top (xi 75–78 and xii 13–15, Text N and Text M respectively). So also with Odysseus: he too will never again have to sail the seas.†

An Antagonism between Athena and Odysseus

11§51. The two meanings of the *sēma*, 'sign', (xi 126) communicated by Teiresias to Odysseus can be linked with the concepts of *nostos*, 'homecoming', and *noos*, 'way of thinking', as I have reconstructed them so far. The meaning that I paraphrased as "the seafarer is dead" can be linked with the god-hero antagonism of Poseidon and Odysseus, as also with the *nostos* or 'homecoming' of the hero; as for the meaning that I paraphrased as "the harvest is complete," it can be linked with a more complex god-hero antagonism between Athena and Odysseus, as also with both the *nostos* or 'homecoming' of the hero and his *noos* or 'way of thinking'. We already saw a hint of Athena's involvement in Text L, where Pausanias (8.44.4) says that it was not only Poseidon but also Athena *sōteira*, the 'Savior', who presided over the sacred space established by Odysseus in Arcadia. So not only Poseidon but also Athena participates in a symbiotic relationship with Odysseus as a cult hero. In making this statement, I rely on the formulation I presented a few minutes ago, at §45, where I noted that *god-hero antagonism in myth—including the myths mediated by epic—corresponds to god-hero symbiosis in ritual*.

11§52. Before we consider the negative aspects of the god-hero antagonism of Athena and Odysseus in myth, let us consider the positive aspects of god-hero symbiosis in the ritual context of the sacred space that was founded by Odysseus in honor of Athena as well as Poseidon according to Arcadian myth. In terms of this myth, it was here that Odysseus experienced the coincidence of opposites that signaled his hero cult. So in terms of the meanings that I have reconstructed for *nostos*, 'homecoming', and *noos*, 'way of thinking', it would be in this Arcadian sacred space that Athena, as the *sōteira* or 'Savior', could make it possible for Odysseus to make a mental connection between his *nostos* or

---

* Hansen 1977:38–39; *GM* 214.

† *PH* 232 = 8n25n82. Also *GM* 214; the analysis there shapes the wording of the next paragraph here.

'homecoming' and his future hero cult, and this mental connection would be made possible by the hero's *noos* or 'way of thinking'. There is comparative evidence for such a reconstruction: in some local traditions, Athena is venerated as a goddess who rescues seafarers from mortal dangers at sea by giving their pilot a sense of direction, so that his ways of thinking may focus on a safe homecoming; in this role, Athena has the epithet *aithuia,* which is the name of a diving bird (Pausanias 1.5.4, 1.41.6; Hesychius s.v. ἐν δ' Αἴθυια).*

11§53. There is an indirect reference to this role of Athena in *Odyssey* v, where Ino the White Goddess saves Odysseus from drowning. While saving the hero, the goddess actually assumes the form of the bird called *aithuia* (v 337, 353). And the actions of Ino in saving Odysseus from the mortal dangers of the sea are parallel to the actions of the goddess Athena herself:

> In the Odyssey, Ino as *aithuia* has a parallel in ensuring the salvation of Odysseus from the sea: Athena herself redirects the storm sent against the hero by Poseidon (v 382–387), and then she saves him from immediate drowning by giving him a timely idea for swimming to safety (v 435–439). . . . The submergence and emergence of the hero from the wave that would surely have drowned him had it not been for Athena (v 435, 438) corresponds closely to the preceding emergence and submergence of Ino herself (v 337, 352–353). Such a correspondence suggests that the former 'mortal' [Ino] who is now a 'goddess' (v 334, 335) is indeed a model for a transition from death to life anew—a transition that may be conveyed by the convergence of themes in the words *noos* and *nostos.*†

11§54. The god-hero antagonism between Athena and Odysseus, as I just said a minute ago, is a complex relationship. Unlike the primal god-hero antagonism between Poseidon as god of the sea and Odysseus as the seafaring hero, the negative side of the relationship between Athena and Odysseus is only implied in the Homeric *Odyssey.* By contrast, the positive side is made explicit, as we have seen from the story in *Odyssey* v that tells how Athena together with Ino the White Goddess saved Odysseus from drowning. And the help of Athena becomes even more pronounced toward the end of the epic, starting with Odyssey

---

* I refer to these traditions in Nagy 1985:80 = §77.
† Nagy 1985:80–81 = §78.

xiii 299–310, where the goddess formally declares to Odysseus her support for the hero, which leads ultimately to his success in his final confrontation with the suitors. As I indicated already at the beginning of this book, however, such a positive aspect in a relationship between a divinity and a hero is actually part of the overall scheme of god-hero antagonism. I quote the wording of my formulation in Hour 1§50:

> The hero is antagonistic toward the god who seems to be most like the hero; antagonism does not rule out an element of attraction—often a "fatal attraction"—which is played out in a variety of ways.

We have already seen in Hour 5 a set of texts in the *Iliad* illustrating the "fatal attraction" between the god Apollo and the hero Patroklos as a surrogate of Achilles himself. In the case of the relationship between Athena and Odysseus, the attraction is far less obvious, but we have already seen hints of it in Hour 9§16, where I referred to the moment when Athena herself declares to Odysseus that her *kleos*, 'glory', is due to her own *mētis*, 'intelligence' (*Odyssey* xiii 299).* I also mentioned in Hour 9§16 a primary epithet of Odysseus, *polumētis*, 'intelligent in many ways' (*Iliad* I 311, etc.; *Odyssey* ii 173, and so on), which indicates that the goddess Athena must have a special relationship with this hero; in fact, this same epithet applies to Athena herself (*Homeric Hymn to Athena* 2). We also saw in that same context, in Hour 9§16, that Athena is deeply involved in the *nostos* or 'homecoming' of Odysseus.

11§55. But here is where the negative side of the relationship between Athena and Odysseus becomes more explicit. As we learned from the narrative of Nestor in *Odyssey* iii 130–135 as quoted in Hour 9 Text E, the *nostos* or 'homecoming' of the Achaeans was *lugros*, 'disastrous' (iii 132), because the returning Achaeans had a major lapse in *noos*, that is, in 'being mindful' (iii 133), and this lapse provoked the *mēnis*, 'anger', of the goddess Athena herself (iii 135). Some of the Achaeans, the narrative continues, were *dikaioi*, 'just' (iii 133), but 'not all of them' (iii 134). Unfortunately for Odysseus, he was one of those Achaeans who had a major lapse in being 'just' and 'mindful'. But that lapse is only implied in the *Odyssey* as we have it. The atrocities committed by Odysseus against the enemy during the capture of Troy are shaded over in the *Odyssey*, as we have already seen, but another atrocity that he committed is not even

---

* *BA* 145 = 8§8.

mentioned in that epic: Odysseus desecrated the temple of Athena at Troy by taking away the statue of the goddess. That impious act of taking the statue, known as the Palladium, is mentioned not at all in the *Odyssey* but only in the epic Cycle:

HOUR 11 TEXT Q

And after this [= after Odysseus infiltrates Troy in a previous adventure] he [= Odysseus] along with | Diomedes takes out [*ek-komizein*] the Palladium from Ilion.

Plot summary by Proclus of the *Little Iliad* by Lesches of Lesbos p. 107 lines 7–8*

11§56. Having explored the negative side of the relationship between Athena and Odysseus, I now return to the positive side. Despite the antagonism that Athena would have felt toward Odysseus because of his serious lapses in *noos*, in his 'way of thinking'—lapses that resulted in serious threats to the completion of his ongoing *nostos*, 'homecoming', in the *Odyssey*—this antagonism is in the end resolved in the symbiosis that is achieved in the hero cult of Odysseus, which is a context where Odysseus can finally coexist with both his overt divine antagonist Poseidon and with his latent divine antagonist Athena.

Conclusion: The Seafarer Is Dead and the Harvest Is Complete

11§57. As I have argued, the picturing of Odysseus' own oar stuck into the ground is a stylized image of his own tomb. And, at least from the viewpoint of the Arcadian version of the Odysseus story, such a tomb would be situated as far away from the sea as possible, whereas the hero's death is to come *ex halós*, 'out of the sea', as we can see in *Odyssey* xi 134, quoted in Text J. There is no need to argue on this basis that the phrase *ex halós* somehow means 'away from the sea'.† Rather, the double meaning of the *sēma* or 'sign' for Odysseus in *Odyssey* xi 126, as also quoted in Text J, is formalized in the coincidence of opposites that shapes the whole myth: Odysseus finds the sign for his death from the sea precisely when he is farthest away from the sea. Such a place, where Odysseus is farthest away from the sea and where he sticks his oar into the ground, would

---

* καὶ μετὰ ταῦτα σὺν | Διομήδει τὸ παλλάδιον ἐκκομίζει ἐκ τῆς Ἰλίου.
† Here I disagree with Hansen 1977:42–48. See again *GM* 214.

be of course an agricultural place, not a maritime place. So, from the standpoint of an Arcadian version of the Odysseus myth, the place for the hero cult of Odysseus is oriented toward agriculture, not seafaring. Such an orientation is fundamental for hero cult, when we think of the corpse of the cult hero who is buried in the local earth and who is worshipped there. I recall here the formulation that I gave earlier on, in §9 during this hour: *the corpse of the cult hero was viewed as a talisman of fertility and prosperity for the community that gained possession of the hero's body.** In this light, the two headlines that I formulated as the two meanings of the *sēma*, 'sign', of Teiresias for Odysseus in *Odyssey* xi 126, as quoted in Text J, can be fused into a single headline: "the seafarer is dead and the harvest is complete." Nature and culture are fused in this setting of *agriculture*.

11§58. In other words, the harvest can now become complete because the seafarer has completed his life and died, so that he has now become a cult hero whose corpse gives fertility and prosperity to the people who cultivate the earth that contains that corpse. That is why the prophecy of Teiresias in Text J concludes with these words: 'And the people all around [your corpse] |$_{137}$ will be blessed [*olbioi*]'† (*Odyssey* xi 136–137; retold at xxiii 283–284). As I have argued from the start of this hour, the cult hero is *olbios*, 'blessed', after he or she dies, and the worshipper of a cult hero can become *olbios*, 'blessed', by making mental and even physical contact with the hero.

11§59. So I come back to the invocation of Odysseus as *olbios* at the end of the *Odyssey*, at xxiv 192 as quoted in Text G. By now we have seen that Odysseus becomes eligible for this invocation only after he dies and becomes a cult hero. And we have also seen that the application of this word *olbios* to a cult hero indicates that the hero is immortalized after death.

11§60. But where do we learn of any kind of immortalization in store for Odysseus? The answer is, everywhere in the *Odyssey*—but only in the metaphorical world of *nostos* in the sense of 'return to light and life'. A most striking example is a coincidence of opposites that we observed in Hour 10 (§§29–31): when Odysseus enters Hādēs traveling from the island of Circe, he is in the Far West, but when he emerges from Hādēs and travels back to the island of Circe, he is in the Far East. That is why Circe, after Odysseus and his men arrive back

---

* Again, *PH* 32, 178 = 1§29, 6§59; EH §97.
† ἀμφὶ δὲ λαοὶ |$_{137}$ ὄλβιοι ἔσσονται.

on her island, addresses the whole group as *dis-thanees,* that is, 'those who experience death twice':

HOUR 11 TEXT R

$|_{21}$ Wretched men! You went down to the House of Hādēs while you were still alive. $|_{22}$ You are *dis-thanees* [= you experience death twice], whereas other mortals die only once.

Odyssey xii 21–22*

11§61. So Odysseus dies metaphorically when he goes to Hādēs in *Odyssey* xi and then returns to light and life in *Odyssey* xii. But he will die for real in a future that is beyond the limits of the story told in the *Odyssey* as we have it: just as the seer Teiresias had predicted it when he gave to Odysseus a *sēma* or 'sign' in *Odyssey* xi 126 as quoted in Text J, Odysseus will die after he experiences another coincidence of opposites—while carrying the oar that becomes a winnowing shovel.

11§62. The tradition about this coincidence of opposites as experienced by Odysseus when his oar becomes a winnowing shovel has survived in Modern Greek stories about the Prophet Elias, who figures as a christianized version of the Prophet Elijah of the Hebrew Bible. It is a historical fact that the shrines of Prophet Elias are conventionally situated on tops of hills and mountains in accordance with Greek Orthodox Christian traditions. In Modern Greek folklore, there are stories that account for this convention of situating the shrines of Elias on summits—and thus far away from the sea. According to folktales about Elias, as analyzed by William Hansen, Elias had lived the life of a seafarer, but he eventually tired of seafaring and proceeded to travel inland and upland as far as he could, carrying an oar on his shoulder.† Shrines sacred to the Prophet are built on tops of hills and mountains because, the story goes, it was on top of a mountain that his oar was finally not recognized—and mistaken for 'a stick' or the like. Here are two variants of the story, as paraphrased by Hansen:‡

Variant 1[a]: Saint Elias was a seaman who lived a dissolute life, but he repented of what he had done and thereby detested the sea. (Vari-

---

* $|_{21}$ σχέτλιοι, οἳ ζώοντες ὑπήλθετε δῶμ᾽ Ἀΐδαο, $|_{22}$ δισθανέες, ὅτε τ᾽ ἄλλοι ἅπαξ θνῄσκουσ᾽ ἄνθρωποι.

† Hansen 1977:27–41.

‡ Hansen 1977:29.

ant 1[b]: because he had suffered much at sea and had often nearly drowned, he became disgusted with voyaging.) He resolved to go to a place where people know neither what the sea was nor what ships were. Putting his oar on his shoulder he set out on land, asking everyone he met what he was carrying. So long as they answered that it was an oar, he proceeded to higher and higher ground. Finally, at the top of a mountain he asked his question, and the people answered, 'a stick'. Understanding then that they had never seen an oar, he remained there with them.

Variant 2: The Prophet Elias was a fisherman who, because of terrible weather and terrific storms, became afraid of the sea. So he put an oar on his shoulder and took to the hills. When he met a man, he asked him what it was he was carrying; the man answered that it was an oar, and Elias went on. The same happened when he met a second man. But at the top of a mountain, he asked a third man, who replied, 'why, that's a stick'. Saint Elias resolved to stay there. He planted his oar in the ground, and that is why his chapels are all built on hilltops.

11§63. In yet another version of the Modern Greek story of the sailor who went inland, his oar is actually mistaken for a *phtyari tou phournou*, which refers to a *baker's peel* but which literally means a 'winnowing shovel of the oven'.* As Hansen has shown, winnowing shovels and baker's peels can in fact be virtually isomorphic.† So the Modern Greek stories about the sailor who went inland show clear indications of an agricultural context for an aetiological myth that accounts for an institutional reality, which is, that the shrines of the Prophet Elias are traditionally built on the tops of hills and mountains. And there is a related institutional reality here: the feast day of the Prophet Elias is traditionally celebrated by Greek Orthodox Christians on July 20, which coincides with the season for harvesting and winnowing wheat.‡

11§64. I conclude, then, by observing that the agricultural context of the aetiological myth about the Prophet Elias corresponds to the agricultural context of the myth encoded in the *sēma* or 'sign' given by Teiresias to Odysseus in *Odyssey* xi 126, as also quoted in Text J. Odysseus must stick his oar into the ground in a place where people can think only of agriculture, mistaking his oar for

* Hansen 1977:30.
† Hansen 1977:40.
‡ Hansen 1977:35.

a winnowing shovel. It is in an agricultural world that the cult of the hero must be situated, not in the world of seafarers. And it is in this agricultural world that the hero can become *olbios* or 'blessed', so that the people who cultivate the earth containing his corpse will become *olbioi* or 'blessed' as well—if they worship the hero by maintaining mental and even physical contact with him.

The Cult Hero as an Exponent of Justice in Homeric Poetry and Beyond

The Meaning of Dikē

12§1. The key word for this hour is *dikē*, which means 'justice' long-term and 'judgment' short-term. In ancient Greek poetics, a primary metaphor for *dikē* is a flourishing *field* or *garden* or *orchard* or *grove* or *vineyard* or any other such place where vegetation is cultivated. As I will argue, the typical cult hero is an exponent of *dikē*. And the worshippers of the cult hero can view the presence of his or her corpse in the local earth as the cause of vegetal flourishing or thriving or blooming.

12§2. As we have seen in Hour 11§9 and §57, the corpse of the cult hero, as hidden below in the local earth, is envisioned as a talisman of fertility and prosperity for the worshippers who cultivate that earth. Now we will see that such a vision is a sign of *dikē* in the long-term sense of 'justice'.

An Occurrence of Dikē as 'Justice' in the Odyssey

12§3. We see an example of this vision in a passage quoting the words of the disguised Odysseus, addressed to his wife, Penelope:

HOUR 12 TEXT A

|$_{107}$ My lady, who among mortals throughout the limitless stretches of earth |$_{108}$ would dare to quarrel [*neikeîn*] against you with words? For truly your glory [*kleos*] reaches the wide firmament of the sky itself |$_{109}$—like the glory of some faultless king [*basileus*], who, godlike as he is, |$_{110}$ and ruling over a population that is multitudinous and vigorous,

|₁₁₁ upholds acts of good *dikē* [= *eu-dikiai*], while the dark earth pro-
duces |₁₁₂ wheat and barley, the trees are loaded with fruit, |₁₁₃ the ewes
steadily bring forth lambs, and the sea abounds with fish, |₁₁₄ by reason
of the good directions he gives, and his people are meritorious [*aretân*]
under his rule.

Odyssey xix 107–114*

12§4. The wording of this passage shows the only place in the *Odyssey* where
Penelope is said to have *kleos* or 'glory' herself, but even here the glory emanates
more broadly from the poetic tradition that features primarily Odysseus and
only secondarily those who are close to him, especially Penelope, as we saw in
Hour 9§22 and §23. Moreover, the *kleos* of Penelope depends on the validity of
comparing it with the *kleos* of the unnamed king whose 'acts of good *dikē*' ener-
gize the fertility and prosperity of the land he rules. Since the words about this
just king are spoken by the disguised Odysseus, it is evident that he himself will
take the role of that just king when the time comes. But when exactly will that
time come? Will it be after he kills the suitors? Or will it be after he dies? I ask
the second question because the wording that refers to the inhabitants of the
fertile and prosperous land of the just king is remarkably parallel to the wording
that referred to the inhabitants of the kingdom of Odysseus after he is dead:

HOUR 12 TEXT B (PART OF HOUR 11 TEXT J)

As for yourself [= Odysseus], death shall come to you from the sea, |₁₃₅
a gentle death, that is how it will come, and this death will kill you |₁₃₆
as you lose your strength in a prosperous old age. And the people all
around [your corpse] |₁₃₇ will be blessed [*olbioi*].

Odyssey xi 134–137†

12§5. This wording is taken from the prophecy of Teiresias to Odysseus in
Odyssey xi 90–137, which I quoted in its entirely in Hour 11 Text J. I draw attention once again to the word *olbioi* here, which I continue to translate as 'blessed',
and which describes here the inhabitants of the kingdom of Odysseus. As I ar-

---

* |₁₀₇ ὦ γύναι, οὐκ ἄν τίς σε βροτῶν ἐπ' ἀπείρονα γαῖαν |₁₀₈ νεικέοι· ἦ γάρ σευ κλέος οὐρανὸν εὐρὺν
ἱκάνει, |₁₀₉ ὥς τέ τευ ἢ βασιλῆος ἀμύμονος, ὅς τε θεουδὴς |₁₁₀ ἀνδράσιν ἐν πολλοῖσι καὶ ἰφθίμοισιν
ἀνάσσων |₁₁₁ εὐδικίας ἀνέχῃσι, φέρῃσι δὲ γαῖα μέλαινα |₁₁₂ πυροὺς καὶ κριθάς, βρίθῃσι δὲ δένδρεα
καρπῷ, |₁₁₃ τίκτῃ δ' ἔμπεδα μῆλα, θάλασσα δὲ παρέχῃ ἰχθῦς |₁₁₄ ἐξ εὐηγεσίης, ἀρετῶσι δὲ λαοὶ ὑπ'
αὐτοῦ.
† θάνατος δέ τοι ἐξ ἁλὸς αὐτῷ |₁₃₅ ἀβληχρὸς μάλα τοῖος ἐλεύσεται, ὅς κέ σε πέφνῃ |₁₃₆ γήρᾳ ὕπο
λιπαρῷ ἀρημένον· ἀμφὶ δὲ λαοὶ |₁₃₇ ὄλβιοι ἔσσονται.

gued in Hour 11§§38–39 and §44, this word *olbioi*, 'blessed', refers to the blessings of fertility and prosperity that the inhabitants of Ithaca receive as a result of
the hero's death (xi 136–137; retold at xxiii 283–284). This death, as I argued in
Hour 11§59, leads to the transformation of Odysseus into a cult hero, who is invoked as *olbios*, 'blessed', at the end of the *Odyssey*, at xxiv 192 as quoted in Hour
11 Text G.

12§6. In the Hesiodic *Works and Days*, as we saw in Hour 11§15, this same
word *olbioi*, 'blessed', is used to describe cult heroes who are immortalized after
death and who enjoy a state of bliss in the Islands of the Blessed, which as we
have seen is a paradisiacal setting that transcends the temporal and the spatial
constraints of mortality:

HOUR 12 TEXT C = 11 TEXT C

|₁₇₀ And they live with a carefree heart [*thūmos*] |₁₇₁ on the Islands of
the Blessed [*Nēsoi Makarōn*] on the banks of the deep-swirling river
Okeanos, |₁₇₂ blessed [*olbioi*] heroes [*hērōes*] that they are, and for them
there is a honey-sweet harvest [*karpos*] |₁₇₃ that comes to fruition three
times each year, produced by the life-giving land.

Hesiod *Works and Days* 170–173

12§7. On the basis of these parallel texts, then, I argue that the picture of a
just king who rules over a fertile and prosperous land in Text A, *Odyssey* xix
107–114, refers to the future status of Odysseus as a cult hero. But I still need to
confront a possible objection: why would a cult hero be described as a *basileus*,
'king', at xix 109? And besides, would not the title of 'king' fit Odysseus when he
is alive, right after he kills the suitors and recovers his kingdom—and before he
is dead? True, the title would fit then as well, but I maintain that the context of
the words spoken by the disguised Odysseus to Penelope is more transcendent.
The fact is, the title of 'king' fits the cult hero as well. There is evidence to show
that the generic cult hero is conventionally described as a *basileus*, 'king'.* In
a stylized *thrēnos* or 'lament' composed by Pindar (F 133), for example, *hēroes
hagnoi*, 'holy heroes', are equated with *basilēes*, 'kings'.†

---

* *BA* 170–172 = 9§31. On Odysseus as an ideal king, see Levaniouk 2011:26–28.
† βασιλῆες ἀγαυοί . . . ἥροες ἀγνοί in Pindar F 133, quoted by Plato *Meno* 81b; see *BA* 170–171 = 9§31. Also,
in an inscription grounded in rituals honoring the dead, in a context of promising a blissful life after death, the
dead person is told: καὶ τότ' ἔπειτ' ἄ[λλοισι μεθ'] ἡρώεσσιν ἀνάξει[ς], 'and then you will be king [*anassein*]
among the other heroes [*hērōes*]' (*IG* XIV 638 = *SEG* 40:824[2]); see *BA* 171 = 9§31n3 (where the citation needs
to be corrected).

The Golden Generation of Humankind

12§8. We find another attestation of the idea of cult heroes as *basilēes*, 'kings', in the Hesiodic *Works and Days*, which tells the story of the Golden Generation, a mythological category of humankind that corresponds to the positive aspects of cult heroes:

HOUR 12 TEXT D

|₁₂₂ And they [= the Golden Generation of humankind] are super-humans [*daimones*]. They exist because of the Will of Zeus. |₁₂₃ They are the good, the earthbound [*epi-khthonioi*], the guardians of mortal humans. |₁₂₄ They guard acts of justice [*dikē*] and they guard against wretched acts of evil. |₁₂₅ Enveloped in mist, they roam everywhere throughout the earth. |₁₂₆ They are givers of prosperity. And they had this as a privilege [*geras*], a kingly one [*basilēion*].*

Hesiod *Works and Days* 122–126†

12§9. Elsewhere in the Hesiodic *Works and Days* (248–262), these cult heroes are described as agents of the goddess of justice personified, *Dikē*, who is daughter of Zeus: all these forces of justice are shown as uniting in their mission to punish men who are *adikoi*, 'unjust' (260), especially *basilēes*, 'kings' (261), who make *dikai*, 'judgments', unjustly, that is, 'in a crooked way', *skoliōs* (262).‡

Hesiod as an Exponent of Justice

12§10. By contrast with such unjust men, the persona of Hesiod speaks as an exponent of justice when he admonishes the unnamed kings to speak their words in a way that 'makes them straight', *ithunein* (263). Hesiod has good reason to make this admonition, since he is accusing these unnamed kings of having taken bribes (264) and rendering 'crooked judgments', that is, *skoliai dikai* (264).

12§11. The persona of Hesiod is not only the speaker of the entire *Works and Days*: he is also the main character of the action, from the very start. He and his

---

*Commentary in *BA* 152–154 = 9§4.

†|₁₂₂ τοὶ μὲν δαίμονές εἰσι Διὸς μεγάλου διὰ βουλὰς |₁₂₃ ἐσθλοί, ἐπιχθόνιοι, φύλακες θνητῶν ἀνθρώπων, |₁₂₄ οἵ ῥα φυλάσσουσίν τε δίκας καὶ σχέτλια ἔργα |₁₂₅ ἠέρα ἑσσάμενοι πάντη φοιτῶντες ἐπ' αἶαν, |₁₂₆ πλουτοδόται· καὶ τοῦτο γέρας βασιλήιον ἔσχον. Variant readings in the first two of these verses: |₁₂₂ τοὶ μὲν δαίμονες ἁγνοὶ ἐπιχθόνιοι τελέθουσιν |₁₂₃ ἐσθλοί, ἀλεξίκακοι, φύλακες θνητῶν ἀνθρώπων.

‡ *GM* 68.

brother, named Perses, are engaged in a *neikos*, 'quarrel' (35), over inheritance, and the unnamed kings are supporting the brother against Hesiod, having been bribed (as implied in 264). Whenever Hesiod speaks to Perses or to the kings in the poem, he presents himself as the representative of *dikē*, 'justice' (213, 217, 220, 225, 239, 254, 256, 272, 275, 278, 279, 283), and of whatever is *dikaio-*, 'just' (217, 226, 270, 271, 280), whereas the other side represents the opposite of justice, which is *hubris*, 'outrage' (213, 214, 217, 238), and whatever is *adiko-*, 'unjust' (260, 272). Besides the instances of the word *dikē* in the long-range sense of 'justice', I note the instances of the same word in the short-range sense of 'judgment': in these instances, Hesiod consistently accuses Perses and the unjust kings of making or upholding *dikai*, 'judgments', that are perverted, and a choice adjective for such bad judgments is *skoliai*, 'crooked' (219, 221, 250, 264; adverb *skoliōs*, 'crookedly', at 262), whereas the good judgments of the just are *itheiai*, 'straight' (36, 224, 226).

Metaphors for Dikē *and* Hubris

12§12. We see at work here a metaphor that pervades the Hesiodic *Works and Days*: *dikē* or 'justice' is *straight* and *direct* or *unidirectional*, whereas *hubris* as the opposite of justice is *crooked* and *indirect* or *multidirectional*. The etymology of the noun *dikē*, derived from the verb *deik-nunai*, which means 'to point' or 'to indicate', shows the built-in idea of *direction, directness, directedness*.*

12§13. As for the opposite of *dikē*, which is *hubris*, I have already noted that this word is conventionally translated as 'outrage'. But this translation does not capture adequately the metaphorical world of *hubris* as the opposite of *dikē* in the sense of 'justice'. To understand in more depth the meaning of *hubris* as the opposite of *dikē*, I propose to outline the contexts in which we find the word *hubris*, and I divide these contexts into the realms of (1) humans; (2) animals; and (3) plants. In the human realm, *hubris* refers to acts that provoke a sense of moral outrage, which calls for a response by humans and gods alike, and the response can take the form of social and cosmic sanctions respectively; in the *Odyssey*, for example, *hubris* refers frequently to the behavior of the suitors of Penelope (i 368 and so on). I will have more to say toward the end of this hour about such a human realm of *hubris*. As for the realm of animals, *hubris* refers more simply to any behavior that is violent (Herodotus 1.189) or sexual (as in

* *PH* 260 = 9§15n60.

Pindar *Pythian* 10.36)—though such behavior extends of course from animals to humans. As for the realm of plants, *hubris* refers to excessive productivity in one aspect of the plant, to the detriment of other aspects: for example, in the case of fruit-bearing trees and shrubs, *hubris* would result in the excessive production of wood or of leaves at the expense of the fruit itself.* I turn to a case described by the botanist Theophrastus (fourth / third century BCE). In the passage I am about to quote, Theophrastus is analyzing the behavior of the white lupin plant *(Lupinus albus)*, a kind of shrub that bears a fruit (a kind of "bean") that is even today commonly eaten as a snack in many parts of the Mediterranean world:

Hour 12 Text E

> The white lupin [shrub] becomes *a-karpos* [= stops bearing *karpos*, 'fruit'] when it gets wood-crazy, as it were, and behaves with exuberance [*hubris*].

Theophrastus About the aetiologies of plants (3.1.5)†

Or again, in the case of almond trees, soil that is poor in nutrients is better than rich soil for cultivating these trees if the objective is to produce plenty of almonds:

Hour 12 Text F

> For almond trees, poor soil [is preferable], for if the soil is deep and rich, the trees experience an exuberance [*hubris*] because of all the good nutrition, and they stop bearing fruit [*a-karpeîn*].

Theophrastus About the aetiologies of plants 2.16.8‡

12§14. To counteract the undergrowth of fruit in plants, the cultivator must prevent the overgrowth of wood or leaves in order to restore equilibrium in growth. So the cultivator must *regulate* the plant. Theophrastus, in his trea-

---

* Michelini 1978. She gives a variety of examples, many of which will be cited here as well.

† ὁ δὲ θέρμος ἄκαρπος γίνεται καθάπερ ὑλομανῶν καὶ ἐξυβρίζων. The combination of *hulo-manein*, 'be wood-crazy', and *ex-hubrizein*, 'behave with *hubris*', is also attested in a metaphorical context where it refers to human exuberance: Plutarch *How a youth should hear poetry* 15f. In the usage of Theophrastus, we find another form that shows a close parallelism with *hulo-manein*, 'be wood-crazy': it is *phullo-manein*, 'be leaf-crazy', as attested in *Research about plants* 8.7.4 (twice).

‡ οἷον ταῖς ἀμυγδαλαῖς ἡ λεπτή· βαθείας γὰρ οὔσης καὶ πιείρας ἐξυβρίσασαι διὰ τὴν εὐτροφίαν ἀκαρποῦσι. See also Theophrastus *About the aetiologies of plants* 3.6.8, again about the almond tree.

tise *Research about plants* (2.7.7), mentions a wide variety of ways to *regulate,* including the process of *pruning* (for example, the pruning of grape vines at 3.15.4); and he notes a traditional way for referring to such a process: you can say that the cultivator 'punishes the plant that is committing *hubris*' (*kolazein hōs hubrizon to dendron).** And, giving another example, Theophrastus notes that the native expression in Arcadia for pruning the sorbapple tree is *euthunein,* which means literally 'straighten'. Here is how Theophrastus says it:

HOUR 12 TEXT G

In Arcadia they have an expression 'straightening [*euthunein*] the sorbapple tree [*oa*]'. There are many such trees in their region. And they say that, when this ['straightening'] happens to the trees, those that have not been bearing fruit will now start to bear fruit, and those that bear fruit that will not ripen [on the tree] will now have fruit that ripens, and ripens beautifully.

Theophrastus *Research about plants* 2.7.7†

12§15. As we saw at the beginning of this hour, a primary metaphor for *dikē* in the sense of 'justice' is a flourishing *field* or *garden* or *orchard* or *grove* or *vineyard* or any other such place where vegetation is cultivated. And now we see that *hubris,* which is the opposite of *dikē,* is a negative force that counteracts the flourishing of vegetation: *hubris* results in vegetal overgrowth and undergrowth. From a mythological point of view, the extreme landscapes of *hubris* are a wildland or a desert.

12§16. In the examples of *hubris* as surveyed so far, an excessive production of wood or of leaves prevents a plant from producing fruit. Conversely, as we will now see, excessive production of seed will prevent garden herbs like lettuce from producing leaves, and such herbs will then *go to seed* or *bolt,* as we say. That is why, as Theophrastus notes (*About the aetiologies of plants* 3.9.2), the way to cultivate such herbs is to prevent 'the generating of fruit' (*karpogoneîn*) by promoting 'the production of leaves' (*phullophoreîn*).

12§17. So what are the mythological consequences of *going to seed?* A prime example is a myth that links the *thridax* or 'lettuce' with the hero Adonis, a beautiful mortal boy who became the lover of the goddess Aphrodite herself.

---

* κολάζειν ὡς ὑβρίζον τὸ δένδρον.

† ἐν Ἀρκαδίᾳ δὲ καὶ εὐθύνειν καλοῦσι τὴν ὄαν· πολὺ γὰρ τὸ δένδρον τοῦτο παρ' αὐτοῖς ἐστι. καί φασιν, ὅταν πάθῃ τοῦτο, τὰς μὲν μὴ φερούσας φέρειν τὰς δὲ μὴ πεττούσας ἐκπέττειν καλῶς.

References made by ancient authors to this myth have been collected by an author dated to the early third century CE, Athenaeus of Naucratis (2.69b-d), and from these references we can see a central event of the myth: *Aphrodite hid Adonis inside a head of lettuce*. Since Aphrodite is the goddess of reproduction as well as sex, this action of hers is most counterproductive, since lettuce must be kept from *going to seed* if it is to be good little lettuce. Accordingly, the hiding of Adonis inside a head of lettuce results in sterility for Adonis. And the hero Adonis is in fact associated with sterility. The boy may be a great lover, most appreciated by the goddess of sexuality herself, Aphrodite, but he is still sterile. And there is an ancient traditional proverb that stems from this myth:

HOUR 12 TEXT H

more barren [*a-karpos*] than the Gardens of Adonis

CPG I p. 19.6–11*

12§18. The rituals surrounding the Gardens of Adonis, as Marcel Detienne has shown, are a negative dramatization of fertility.† The so-called Gardens of Adonis *(kēpoi Adōnidos)* are potted herbs that are planted in the most unseasonal of times, the Dog Days of summer: the plants grow with excessive speed and vigor, only to be scorched to death by the sun's excessive heat, and this death is then followed by stylized mourning and lamentations for Adonis, protégé of Aphrodite. In opposition to the normal cycle of seasonal agriculture, which lasts for eight months, the abnormal cycle of the unseasonal Gardens of Adonis lasts but eight days (as we see from Plato *Phaedrus* 276b). Like his suddenly and violently growing plants, Adonis himself dies *prohēbēs*, 'before reaching maturity [*hēbē*]' (CPG I p. 183.3–8, II p. 3.10–13; compare also II p. 93.13).‡

The Silver Generation of Humankind

12§19. The beautiful boy hero Adonis is parallel to the heroes featured in the stylized narrative of the Hesiodic *Works and Days* about a debased second generation of humankind, the Silver Generation, who were created after the first humans, the Golden Generation. Here is the narrative about the Silver Generation:

* ἀκαρπότερος Ἀδώνιδος κήπων.
† Detienne 1972:187–226.
‡ Nagy 1985:62 = §50.

HOUR 12 TEXT I

|₁₂₇ Then a second Generation, a much worse one, a later one, |₁₂₈ the Silver, was made by the gods who abide in their Olympian homes. |₁₂₉ They were like the Golden one neither in their nature nor in their power of perception [*noēma*]. |₁₃₀ As a boy, each one was raised for a hundred years by dear mother; |₁₃₁ each one was playing around, quite inept [*nēpios*], at home. |₁₃₂ But when the time of maturing [*hēbân*] and the full measure of maturity [*hēbē*] arrived, |₁₃₃ they lived only for a very short time, suffering pains [*algea*] |₁₃₄ for their acts of heedlessness [*aphradiai*], since they could not keep overweening *hubris* |₁₃₅ away from each other, and they were not willing to care for [*therapeuein*] the immortal gods, |₁₃₆ not willing at all, nor were they willing to make sacrifice on the sacred altars of the blessed [*makares*] gods, |₁₃₇ the way humans are required by cosmic law [*themis*] to behave, each group according to its own customs. Anyway, they too, when the time came, |₁₃₈ were hidden away by Zeus son of Kronos. He was angry at them because they did not give honors [*tīmai*], |₁₃₉ no they did not, to the blessed [*makares*] gods who possess Olympus. |₁₄₀ But when the earth covered over this generation [*genos*] as well |₁₄₁ (and they are called the blessed [*makares*], abiding below the earth [*hupokhthonioi*],* mortals that they are, |₁₄₂ the Second Ones, though they too [like the First Ones, who are the Golden Generation] get their share of honor [*tīmē*]) ...

Hesiod *Works and Days* 127–142†

---

* This adjective *hupo-khthonioi*, 'abiding below the earth', which is applied to the Silver Generation here at verse 141, seems at first to be perfectly symmetrical with the adjective *epi-khthonioi*, which I translate simply as 'earthbound' and which is applied to the Gold Generation at verse 123. Although the Silver Generation abides below the earth by virtue of being *hupo-khthonioi*, this formation does not imply that the Golden Generation abides above the earth by virtue of being *epi-khthonioi*. True, at verse 125 in Text D, we saw this description: 'enveloped in mist, they roam everywhere throughout the earth'. But at other times they too abide below the earth: see *BA* 153–154 = 9§5.

† |₁₂₇ Δεύτερον αὖτε γένος πολὺ χειρότερον μετόπισθεν |₁₂₈ ἀργύρεον ποίησαν Ὀλύμπια δώματ' ἔχοντες, |₁₂₉ χρυσέῳ οὔτε φυὴν ἐναλίγκιον οὔτε νόημα· |₁₃₀ ἀλλ' ἑκατὸν μὲν παῖς ἔτεα παρὰ μητέρι κεδνῇ |₁₃₁ ἐτρέφετ' ἀτάλλων, μέγα νήπιος, ᾧ ἐνὶ οἴκῳ· |₁₃₂ ἀλλ' ὅτ' ἄρ' ἡβήσαι τε καὶ ἥβης μέτρον ἵκοιτο, |₁₃₃ παυρίδιον ζώεσκον ἐπὶ χρόνον, ἄλγε' ἔχοντες |₁₃₄ ἀφραδίης· ὕβριν γὰρ ἀτάσθαλον οὐκ ἐδύναντο |₁₃₅ ἀλλήλων ἀπέχειν οὐδ' ἀθανάτους θεραπεύειν |₁₃₆ ἤθελον οὐδ' ἔρδειν μακάρων ἱεροῖς ἐπὶ βωμοῖς, |₁₃₇ ᾗ θέμις ἀνθρώποις κατὰ ἤθεα. τοὺς μὲν ἔπειτα |₁₃₈ Ζεὺς Κρονίδης ἔκρυψε χολούμενος, οὕνεκα τιμὰς |₁₃₉ οὐκ ἔδιδον μακάρεσσι θεοῖς οἳ Ὄλυμπον ἔχουσιν. |₁₄₀ αὐτὰρ ἐπεὶ καὶ τοῦτο γένος κατὰ γαῖα κάλυψε, |₁₄₁ τοὶ μὲν ὑποχθόνιοι μάκαρες θνητοὶ καλέονται, |₁₄₂ δεύτεροι, ἀλλ' ἔμπης τιμὴ καὶ τοῖσιν ὀπηδεῖ.

12§20. Like the boy hero Adonis, the heroes of the Silver Generation are unable to achieve a stable maturity or *hēbē*. They are immature and unseasonal. By contrast, in *Works and Days* 115–120 the unspoiled heroes of the Golden Generation live in a Golden Age of stable fertility, as expressed directly by the word *karpos*, 'fruit' (117). They are mature and seasonal. The Golden Age presents an idealized picture of wealth that is won by way of *dikē*: true and lasting, it is antithetical to the sudden and violent wealth that is won by way of *hubris* and that is destined not to last (320–326).

12§21. So, just as the Golden Generation is a positive image of a cult hero, the corresponding Silver Generation is a negative image, as we see from the narrative here in Text I. In this narrative about the Silver Generation, the Hesiodic *Works and Days* shows the dark side of cult heroes: the heroes of the Silver Generation refuse to 'care for' the gods, *therapeuein* (135), as we have just noted here and have already noted in Hour 6§51, and they likewise refuse to perform sacrifices to the gods (136). But despite such impious behavior, which is equated with not giving *tīmē*, 'honor', to the gods (138), these heroes of the Silver Generation are said to receive *tīmē*, 'honor', from humans after they die, just as the heroes of the Golden Generation receive honor (142). And, as we have seen in Hour 8§21 with reference to Text C there, taken from the *Homeric Hymn to Demeter* (259–267), this word *tīmē* can refer to the 'honor' that cult heroes receive in the rituals of hero cult after they die, as in the case of the *tīmē* received by the cult hero Demophon after he dies (261, 263). As we can see in the *Homeric Hymn to Demeter* (268), where the goddess refers to herself as *tīmāokhos*, 'receiver of honor' [*tīmē*], the gods receive *tīmē* just as cult heroes receive *tīmē*, but of course they do not have to die to receive it as heroes have to die. And the heroes of the Silver Generation do have to die, as we have just seen in the text I quoted. So, once again, I apply the formula that I applied in Hour 11§45 and §51: *god-hero antagonism in myth corresponds to god-hero symbiosis in ritual.*

Two Further Generations of Humankind

12§22. In the Hesiodic *Works and Days*, the contrast between *dikē* and *hubris* is re-enacted not only in the contrast between the Golden and the Silver Generations but also in an overall myth of five successive generations of humankind (106–201). As we are about to see, the contrast between the Golden and the Silver Generations is part of an overall system of contrasts between *dikē* and *hu-*

bris, framed within the myth of five generations. This system has been cogently analyzed by Jean-Pierre Vernant, who has shown that the superiority and inferiority of Generations 1 and 2 respectively are marked by their *dikē* and *hubris,* while, inversely, the inferiority and superiority of Generations 3 and 4 respectively are marked by their *hubris* and *dikē.** So we turn next to these Generations 3 and 4.

12§23. I start with Generation 3. Just as the narrative about Generation 2, the Silver Generation, shows the dark side of cult heroes, so also the narrative about Generation 3, the Bronze Generation, shows the dark side of epic heroes. Here is the narrative:

HOUR 12 TEXT J

|₁₄₃ And Zeus the father made another Generation of mortal men, the Third. |₁₄₄ He made it Bronze, not at all like the Silver. |₁₄₅ A Generation born from ash trees, violent and terrible. Their minds were set on the woeful deeds of Arēs |₁₄₆ and on acts of *hubris.* Grain |₁₄₇ they did not eat, but their hard-dispositioned heart [*thūmos*] was made of hard rock. |₁₄₈ They were forbidding: they had great force [*biē*] and overpowering hands |₁₄₉ growing out of their shoulders, with firm foundations for limbs. |₁₅₀ Their implements were bronze, their houses were bronze, |₁₅₁ and they did their work with bronze. There was no black iron. |₁₅₂ And they were wiped out when they killed each other with their own hands, |₁₅₃ and went nameless to the dank house of chill Hādēs, |₁₅₄ yes, nameless [*nōnumnoi*]! Death still took them, terrifying as they were, |₁₅₅ yes, black Death took them, and they left behind them the bright light of the Sun.

Hesiod *Works and Days* 143–155†

12§24. So this negative picture, with its emphasis on *hubris* (146), suits the dark and latent side of the epic hero as we see him in action in Homeric po-

---

* Vernant 1985:100–106.

† |₁₄₃ Ζεὺς δὲ πατὴρ τρίτον ἄλλο γένος μερόπων ἀνθρώπων |₁₄₄ χάλκειον ποίησ᾽, οὐκ ἀργυρέῳ οὐδὲν ὁμοῖον, |₁₄₅ ἐκ μελιᾶν, δεινόν τε καὶ ὄβριμον· οἷσιν Ἄρηος |₁₄₆ ἔργ᾽ ἔμελε στονόεντα καὶ ὕβριες, οὐδέ τι σῖτον |₁₄₇ ἤσθιον, ἀλλ᾽ ἀδάμαντος ἔχον κρατερόφρονα θυμόν. |₁₄₈ ἄπλαστοι· μεγάλη δὲ βίη καὶ χεῖρες ἄαπτοι |₁₄₉ ἐξ ὤμων ἐπέφυκον ἐπὶ στιβαροῖσι μέλεσσι. |₁₅₀ τῶν δ᾽ ἦν χάλκεα μὲν τεύχεα, χάλκεοι δέ τε οἶκοι, |₁₅₁ χαλκῷ δ᾽ εἰργάζοντο· μέλας δ᾽ οὐκ ἔσκε σίδηρος. |₁₅₂ καὶ τοὶ μὲν χείρεσσιν ὑπὸ σφετέρῃσι δαμέντες |₁₅₃ βῆσαν ἐς εὐρώεντα δόμον κρυεροῦ Ἀίδαο, |₁₅₄ νώνυμνοι· θάνατος δὲ καὶ ἐκπάγλους περ ἐόντας |₁₅₅ εἷλε μέλας, λαμπρὸν δ᾽ ἔλιπον φάος ἠελίοιο.

etry.* The negativity extends to the afterlife for such a hero, which is described in a way that seems at first to offer no hope for immortalization after death. The narrative simply says that the dead heroes went to Hādēs. So if Hādēs were a permanent rather than a transitional place of existence for heroes after death, then these heroes of Generation 3 would be forever *nōnumnoi*, 'nameless' (154).

12§25. By contrast, the narrative in the *Works and Days* about Generation 4 features a positive picture of the epic hero, with an emphasis on heroic behavior that is *dikaion*, 'just' (verse 158), and with a promise of immortalization after death:

HOUR 12 TEXT K (INCLUDING TEXT C)

|₁₅₅ But when this Generation too was covered over by the earth, |₁₅₇ Zeus made yet another Generation on earth, which nurtures many, a fourth one. |₁₅₈ This one, by contrast [with the third], was just [*dikaion*].† It was better. |₁₅₉ It was the godlike generation of men who were heroes [*hērōes*], who are called |₁₆₀ demigods [*hēmi-theoi*]; they are the previous generation [= previous to ours] who lived throughout the boundless earth. |₁₆₁ These [demigods] were overcome by evil war and the terrible din of battle. |₁₆₂ Some died at the walls of seven-gated Thebes, the land of Cadmus, |₁₆₃ as they fought over the sheep of Oedipus. |₁₆₄ Others were taken away by war over the great yawning stretches of sea |₁₆₅ to Troy, all on account of Helen with the beautiful hair. |₁₆₆ Then they [= this Generation]‡ were covered over by the finality of death. |₁₆₇ But they received, apart from other humans, a life and a place to live |₁₆₈ from Zeus the son of Kronos, who translated them to the edges of the earth, |₁₆₉ far away from the immortal gods. And Kronos is king over them. |₁₇₀ And they live with a carefree heart [*thūmos*] |₁₇₁ on the Islands of the Blessed [*Nēsoi Makarōn*] on the banks of the deep-swirling river Okeanos, |₁₇₂ blessed [*olbioi*] heroes [*hērōes*] that they

---

* *BA* 158 = 9§11.

† In the original Greek here, the word *dikaioteron* describing the fourth generation means not 'more just' but 'just—as opposed to unjust', where the 'unjust' are the third generation. See also Hour 11§22 for the note on *thēluterai* at *Odyssey* xxiv 202 as meaning not 'more female' but 'female—as opposed to male'.

‡ In the original Greek, the particle *men* here in *Works and Days* 166 is parallel to the *men* as used at verses 122, 137, 141, 161, not to the *men* as used at verse 162. I argue for this interpretation in *GM* 126n17 and *PH* 10§7n16; also in *BA* (1999) xiii = 0§19n2, with bibliography. In terms of this interpretation, the heroes who fought in the Theban War and in the Trojan War were all eligible for immortalization.

are, and for them there is a honey-sweet harvest [*karpos*] |₁₇₃ that comes to fruition three times each year, produced by the life-giving land.

Hesiod Works and Days 155–173*

12§26. I have already quoted the last part of this text, the four verses 170–173, in Hour 11 Text C, where I analyzed the use of the word *olbioi*, 'blessed' (172). This word, as we have seen, occurs typically in contexts in which heroes are pictured as inhabitants of paradisiacal settings in an afterlife. And I quoted these same four verses 170–173 again in Text C of this hour, where I compared the context of the word *olbioi* in Text C with the context of the same word in Text B of this hour, at *Odyssey* xi 137, referring to the blessings brought upon the people of Odysseus after his death as prophesied by Teiresias.

12§27. So in this Hesiodic narrative about Generation 4 we see an alternative visualization of the heroes whom we know from Homeric poetry and from other poetry (especially the Seven against Thebes tradition, which has not survived in any integral text from the ancient world). First of all, the Hesiodic narrative shows the heroes of Generation 4 only in a positive light, and the negative side of the epic hero is reserved for Generation 3; by contrast, Homeric poetry views both the positive and the negative sides of its heroes. Second, the Hesiodic narrative speaks explicitly about the immortalization of the heroes belonging to Generation 4; by contrast, the immortalization of heroes after death is only implied in Homeric poetry, as we have seen in Hour 8§§40–48.

12§28. Another difference that we see here between Homeric and Hesiodic poetry is signaled by the Hesiodic use of the word *hēmi-theoi*, 'demigods', in the *Works and Days* (160) with reference to the epic heroes of Generation 4 who were obliterated in the time of the Theban and the Trojan Wars (161–165)—but who were preserved after death and immortalized by being transported to the Islands of the Blessed (167–173). By contrast, the word *hēmi-theoi* is never used in Homeric poetry—except for one occurrence in *Iliad* XII (23). Matching this

---

* |₁₅₆ αὐτὰρ ἐπεὶ καὶ τοῦτο γένος κατὰ γαῖα κάλυψεν, |₁₅₇ αὖτις ἔτ᾽ ἄλλο τέταρτον ἐπὶ χθονὶ πουλυβοτείρῃ |₁₅₈ Ζεὺς Κρονίδης ποίησε, δικαιότερον καὶ ἄρειον, |₁₅₉ ἀνδρῶν ἡρώων θεῖον γένος, οἳ καλέονται |₁₆₀ ἡμίθεοι, προτέρῃ γενεῇ κατ᾽ ἀπείρονα γαῖαν. |₁₆₁ καὶ τοὺς μὲν πόλεμός τε κακὸς καὶ φύλοπις αἰνὴ |₁₆₂ τοὺς μὲν ὑφ᾽ ἑπταπύλῳ Θήβῃ, Καδμηΐδι γαίῃ, |₁₆₃ ὤλεσε μαρναμένους μήλων ἕνεκ᾽ Οἰδιπόδαο, |₁₆₄ τοὺς δὲ καὶ ἐν νήεσσιν ὑπὲρ μέγα λαῖτμα θαλάσσης |₁₆₅ ἐς Τροίην ἀγαγὼν Ἑλένης ἕνεκ᾽ ἠϋκόμοιο. |₁₆₆ ἔνθ᾽ ἦ τοι τοὺς μὲν θανάτου τέλος ἀμφεκάλυψε |₁₆₇ τοῖς δὲ δίχ᾽ ἀνθρώπων βίοτον καὶ ἤθε᾽ ὀπάσσας |₁₆₈ Ζεὺς Κρονίδης κατένασσε πατὴρ ἐς πείρατα γαίης. |₁₆₉ [see BA 169= 9§29n] |₁₇₀ καὶ τοὶ μὲν ναίουσιν ἀκηδέα θυμὸν ἔχοντες |₁₇₁ ἐν μακάρων νήσοισι παρ᾽ Ὠκεανὸν βαθυδίνην, |₁₇₂ ὄλβιοι ἥρωες, τοῖσιν μελιηδέα καρπὸν |₁₇₃ τρὶς ἔτεος θάλλοντα φέρει ζείδωρος ἄρουρα.

exceptional Homeric occurrence of *hēmi-theoi* is an exceptional shift in the Homeric narrative perspective here: instead of viewing heroes through the lens of the heroic age, seeing them as they were back then, alive and hoping to be remembered, the poetry now views them through the lens of a post-heroic age, seeing them as already dead and about to be forgotten (XII 17–33).* So the scenario of obliteration followed by immortalization for the *hēmi-theoi* in the Hesiodic *Works and Days* (obliteration in 161–165, immortalization in 167–173) must be contrasted with a scenario of obliteration followed by no mention of immortalization for the *hēmi-theoi* mentioned in the Homeric *Iliad* (XII 17–33).†

Hesiod in the Iron Age

12§29. Unlike Homeric poetry, Hesiodic poetry consistently views heroes through the lens of a post-heroic age, as we can see most clearly when Hesiod finally turns to Generation 5 of humankind, which is his own generation:

HOUR 12 TEXT L

|₁₇₄ If only I did not have to be in the company of the Fifth Generation |₁₇₅ of men, and if only I had died before it [= the Fifth Generation] or been born after it, |₁₇₆ since now is the time of the Iron Generation.

Hesiod *Works and Days* 174–176‡

12§30. In this grim Iron Age, which is the here and now for Hesiod, the neat division between *dikē* and *hubris* breaks down. You cannot say that this is a time of either *dikē* or *hubris,* because these two forces are presently engaged in an ongoing struggle, and Hesiod expresses his pessimism in the light of his present *neikos,* 'quarrel' (mentioned in verse 35), with his unjust brother Perses, who is being supported by the unjust kings. Earlier in this hour, at §10, I explored the details of such an ongoing stuggle of *dikē* and *hubris* as viewed through the situation of Hesiod as he describes it. And Hesiod's wording about the Iron Age, as I just quoted it in Text L, reflects his pessimism about the outcome of the struggle. In his anguish, he expresses a riddling wish, as we see it quoted in *Works*

---

* EH §67, following *BA* 159–162 = 9§§13–17.

† Koenen 1994:5n12 calls this Iliadic scenario "the flip side of the same story."

‡ |₁₇₄ Μηκέτ᾽ ἔπειτ᾽ ὤφελλον ἐγὼ πέμπτοισι μετεῖναι |₁₇₅ ἀνδράσιν, ἀλλ᾽ ἢ πρόσθε θανεῖν ἢ ἔπειτα γενέσθαι. |₁₇₆ νῦν γὰρ δὴ γένος ἐστὶ σιδήρεον.

and Days 175–176, which is part of Text L: if only he had died, he says, in the previous generation or been born in the next generation! Well, if Hesiod had died in the previous generation, which is one of his two alterative wishes, he would have found himself in Generation 4, and we have already seen what happened to the epic heroes who died in Generation 4: they became cult heroes by way of becoming immortalized after death in a paradisiacal setting that matches the Golden Age. And if he had been born in the next generation, which is the other one of his two alternative wishes, he would have found himself in the paradisiacal setting of the Golden Age of Generation 1, who are cult heroes to start with, just as Generation 4 are cult heroes to end with, though they had started off as epic heroes. So the two alteratives in the riddling wish of Hesiod are really one and the same thing, which is, to be in the Golden Age.*

12§31. Not only are the end of Generation 4 and the beginning of Generation 1 the same thing. We can also say that Generations 1 and 2 are the same thing, which is, the positive and the negative sides of cult heroes; and that Generations 3 and 4 are the same thing as well, which is, the negative and the positive sides of epic heroes. We can even say that Generations 1 and 2 are the same thing as Generations 3 and 4, since epic heroes do become cult heroes at the end of 4 in the cyclical logic of 1 to 2 to 3 to 4 back to 1 and so on. And this cycle is the same as the present, which is the quintessential here-and-now.† We see this kind of thinking in the mythmaking traditions of other Indo-European languages as well: in Celtic and Indic traditions, for example, the number 5 following the sequence 1, 2, 3, 4 is a symbol of integration and centrality.‡

12§32. Even though Hesiod wishes that he did not live in the Iron Age, he still faces the struggle between *dikē* and *hubris,* which he proceeds to split into two separate worlds, just as he had split the world of heroes into two worlds, occupied by the cult figures on the one hand and the epic heroes on the other hand —and just as he had split those two worlds further into two sub-worlds each, occupied by heroes who are just and heroes who are unjust.

12§33. In a new split between *dikē* and *hubris,* as foreseen by Hesiod in the context of his Iron Age, there is a *polis,* 'city', of *dikē,* and this city abounds in fertility (225–237). By contrast, there is a *polis,* 'city', of *hubris,* and this city is af-

---

* *BA* 168–169 = 9§29.

† *BA* 169 = 9§30.

‡ Rees and Rees 1961:118–204. I highlight these two examples: the 'Five Peoples' in Indic traditions (together with the related idea of five directions—north / south / east / west / 'here') and the notion of Five 'Provinces' in Ireland.

flicted by sterility (238–247): Zeus punishes the people of such a city with famine (243), with the barrenness of their women (244), and with the diminution of their household possessions (244). Moreover, the stylized city of *hubris* is afflicted with shipwrecks in seastorms brought on by Zeus himself (247), whereas the fortunate inhabitants of the stylized city of *dikē* do not have to sail at all (236–237), since the earth bears for them plentiful *karpos* or 'fruit' (237).*

12§34. Hesiod's city of *dikē* is of course very much like the Golden Age of the Golden Generation, and at first sight it fits the heroic world. But the very opposition of *dikē* and *hubris* in this tale of two cities reflects a post-heroic world. By contrast, Homeric poetry, which is mostly situated in the world of heroes, by and large avoids any foregrounding of an opposition of *dikē* and *hubris* in the sense of 'justice' and its opposite. In fact, there are only three attested cases of such a formal opposition in Homeric poetry. In each of these three cases, we see parallel contexts: Odysseus does not yet know where he has just arrived in the course of his travels, and he is asking himself whether the new place he has just reached is populated by people who are *dikaioi*, 'just', or by *hubristai*, that is, by people who commit *hubris* (vi 120, ix 175, xiii 201). In the first case (vi 120), the place is the land of the Phaeacians; in the second, it is the land of the Cyclops (ix 175); and in the third, it is his own homeland, Ithaca. In the course of events, the Phaeacians turn out to be *dikaioi*, while the Cyclops is the ultimate *hubristēs*. But the situation is ambiguous in the case of Ithaca, since the suitors of Penelope fit the desciption *hubristai* while only those who are near and dear to Odysseus would qualify as *dikaioi*. So the political situation in Ithaca at the time of Odysseus' homecoming is the closest Homeric parallel to the political situation in the world of Hesiod. And such a political situation in Homeric poetry is the closest thing to a post-heroic context.

12§35. A related point can be made about the word *dikē* in the absolute sense of 'justice' and about derivative words conveying the same sense. That fact is, Homeric poetry avoids such words. We have already seen two of the most notable exceptions: in Text A of this hour, *Odyssey* xix 107–114, we saw the disguised Odysseus comparing Penelope to a *basileus*, 'king', who 'upholds acts of good, *dikē* [*eu-dikiai*]' (111), and in Text E of Hour 9, *Odyssey* iii 130–135, we saw that Athena punished some of the Achaeans in the course of their travels back home after the capture of Troy, and that the reason for this punishment was their failure to be *dikaioi*, 'just' (133). We can say about both these cases that the

* Nagy 1985:62–63 = §51.

exception proves the rule. In each case, Odysseus is stepping out of his role as epic hero. In the first case, as I argued in §7 near the beginning of this hour, the picture of a just king who rules over a fertile and prosperous land refers to the future status of Odysseus as a cult hero. And in the second case, as I argued in Hour 11§55, Odysseus himself had been one of those offending Achaeans who had failed to be *dikaioi*, but the story of his moral offenses at Troy is screened out by the *Odyssey*. So, technically, neither one of these two examples shows Odysseus as a Homeric hero of the Trojan War.

Back to Hesiod as an Exponent of Dikē

12§36. By contrast with Homeric poetry, Hesiodic poetry explicitly depends on *dikē*. Even the identity of Hesiod as an authoritative poetic voice depends on the justification of *dikē*. Especially in the Hesiodic *Works and Days,* the embedded master narrative starts with the disequilibrium of injustice and moves toward the equilibrium of justice. I offer here an overall summary:

> In response to the injustices committed by the unjust brother Perses
> and by the crooked kings who support Perses, the just brother Hesiod
> literally speaks the *Works and Days,* and his initial poetic speech is
> composed of four parts:
> —First, he retells the myth of Prometheus and Pandora (verses 42–105),
> which is all about a work ethic—an ethic that has to be understood in
> terms of agriculture, which in turn has to be understood as a sacred
> activity that stays in rhythm with the natural life cycle.
> —Second, he tells the myth of the Five Generations of Humankind
> (verses 106–201). As we have seen, the symbolism of the number 5 in
> this myth centers on the idea of a totality that becomes visible only by
> way of understanding how the four parts that lead up to it will in the
> end fit into that totality. And such a totality is the natural life cycle of
> the generic hero as the ultimate representative of humanity. Essentially,
> Generations 1 and 2 stand for the positive and negative images of the
> cult hero; Generations 3 and 4 stand for the negative and positive im-
> ages of the epic hero; Generation 5 is the composite of the generic he-
> ro—as seen in the here-and-now. And the myth of the Five Genera-
> tions of Humankind is also a vision of humanity—and how humanity
> has degenerated from the Golden Age to the Iron Age. The metaphor

of metals correlated with the sequence of Five Generations of Human-kind—Gold / Silver / Bronze / ___ / Iron—is symbolic of this human degeneration. The decreasing of value in this sequence of metals is made possible in the poetics of the *Works and Days* by way of leaving blank the fourth space in the sequence of spaces occupied by Gold / Silver / Bronze / ___ / Iron. The same blank fourth space makes it pos-sible for the poetry to set up the dichotomies of better and worse, worse and better, for Generations 1 and 2, 3 and 4; otherwise, Generation 4 could not be viewed as the 'better' Generation that it is. This is why no metal can occupy the blank fourth space, since the idea of degenera-tion would have required such a metal to be worse, not better, than Bronze. And this is also why the least valuable metal must come last, and that metal is Iron.

—Third, he tells a fable, about the Hawk and the Nightingale (202–212), and he calls this fable an *ainos* (202). The moral of the story is im-plied by what comes after the telling of the fable (275–278), at which point the listeners are told that beasts, unlike humans, habitually de-vour other beasts. By implication, then, the unjust acquisition of wealth through power is like cannibalism. As we have already seen in Hour 10§41, the image of humans devouring other humans is like a night-marish vision that conjures up the worst moments of epic heroes.

—Fourth comes an apocalyptic split vision of absolute *dikē* on one side and absolute *hubris* on the other side. The two sides are seen as a city of *dikē* (225–237) and a city of *hubris* (238–247).

12§37. After these four narratives, the integrating logic of the master narra-tive takes hold. In the Hesiodic *Works and Days,* the man of *dikē* will in the end regain the wealth of the earth that he has justly earned (280–281), while the man of *hubris* will in the end lose all the wealth that he gained unjustly (325–326). And, in fact, the unjust brother Perses does in the end lose all his wealth (396).

A Reconnection of Generations in an Orchard

12§38. By contrast with the myth of the Five Generations of Humankind in the Hesiodic *Works and Days,* where the generic hero is refracted into four different generations, showing split images of cult heroes and epic heroes, of good heroes and bad heroes, the narrative of the Homeric *Odyssey* comes to an end with an integrated vision of heroic generations. This integration is achieved by way of a reconnection that happens between ancestor and descendant, as focused in the relationship of father and son. And this reconnection happens at the moment when Odysseus finds his father, Laertes, in an 'orchard', an *aloē* (*Odyssey* xxiv 226). The son finds the father in the act of cultivating that orchard, which looks just like the paradisiacal garden of a Golden Age. Here is what Odysseus says to Laertes, even before their mutual recognition is complete:

HOUR 12 TEXT M

|₂₄₄ Old sir, it is clear that you are most knowledgeable in tending |₂₄₅ an orchard [*orkhatos*]. It is well tended, with care [*komidē*], and there is nothing, |₂₄₆ no plant at all—no fig tree no grapevine no olive tree |₂₄₇ no pear tree no bed for herbs—no, there is nothing in this whole garden [*kēpos*] that lacks for care [*komidē*].

Odyssey xxiv 244–247*

12§39. Once the father and the son are reconnected, Laertes may start looking like a cult hero from the Golden Age. In the text that we have just seen, however, where Odysseus is addressing Laertes for the first time, the father is not yet ready to connect with the son because he has not yet recognized him. The interior sorrow of Laertes about being disconnected from Odysseus is still reflected in his exterior appearance, and, as the still-unrecognized Odysseus says bluntly but lovingly to his father, Laertes has not taken good 'care' (*komidē* xxiv 249) of himself, even though he has taken very good 'care' of the orchard, as we saw in the wording of Text M (xxiv 245, 247). But beneath the exterior degradation of the father, as Odysseus goes on to note, it is clear that Laertes still has the looks of a *basileus*, 'king' (xxiv 253). So once the son takes proper care of his father, Laertes will once again look like his true self (xxiv 254–255); and, later on in the narrative, this is exactly what happens, with the help of the goddess Athena (xxiv 365–371). But now, so that Laertes may finally recognize Odysseus, the son shows that he knows everything about the orchard that Laertes is tending. Odysseus reveals that his father had actually given that garden to him as a gift when Odysseus was still a boy (xxiv 336–337), and Odysseus shows that he remembers every detail that he learned from his father when he

---

* |₂₄₄ ὦ γέρον, οὐκ ἀδαημονίη σ' ἔχει ἀμφιπολεύειν |₂₄₅ ὄρχατον, ἀλλ' εὖ τοι κομιδὴ ἔχει, οὐδέ τι πάμπαν, |₂₄₆ οὐ φυτόν, οὐ συκῆ, οὐκ ἄμπελος, οὐ μὲν ἐλαίη, |₂₄₇ οὐκ ὄγχνη, οὐ πρασιή τοι ἄνευ κομιδῆς κατὰ κῆπον.

was growing up, about this 'orchard' (*alōē* xxiv 336) or 'garden' (*kēpos* xxiv 338). Odysseus now narrates, in proper order, every beautiful detail that he had learned from his father about this paradisiacal place where they used to take long walks together, and the father would answer every single question asked by the son (xxiv 337–344).

12§40. So once Laertes reclaims his appearance as a king, he can be like a cult hero as he welcomes back to his paradisiacal garden a returning epic hero who has finally achieved a successful homecoming—and who can now reclaim a garden that he has owned all along. Now Odysseus, appearing as a king in his own right, can ultimately become a cult hero in his own right. So the divide between epic hero and cult hero is ultimately repaired, and so too is the divide that separates generations from each other. Now an integrated vision of the generic hero can finally be achieved.

PART TWO

HEROES IN PROSE MEDIA

A Crisis in Reading the World of Heroes

The Meaning of Krinein

13§1. The key word for this hour is *krinein,* the 'middle voice' for which is *krin-esthai,* and the meaning of which is 'judge, distinguish, make distinctions'. Here are words that derive from it:

> *krisis,* 'judgment, crisis'
> *kritērion,* 'criterion' for judging, distinguishing, making distinctions
> *kritikos,* 'critical' in both senses: 'crisis-related' or 'criticism-related'

13§2. Such words are used in prose, not in poetry. And, in fact, the first attestation of *krinein* that we will examine is found in prose. But, as we will see later, this word *krinein* can also be found in poetry.

13§3. A derivative of *krinein* that we will examine later is *hupo-krinesthai,* 'respond'—in the sense that a seer 'responds' to a question about a vision seen by someone else.

13§4. Another derivative of *krinein* that we will examine still later is *dia-krinein,* in the sense of 'settling' a dispute.

13§5. But let me start with my choice attestation of *krinein,* which is found in a work of prose. This attestation exemplifies most clearly what I want to show in this hour, that *krinein* can be used to distinguish a way to understand the world of heroes from the inside, which is separate from the way this world is understood from the outside.

A Story about the Meaning of Olbios *in the* Histories *of Herodotus*

13§6. The story that is told in the passage I quote below is about a cult hero. I have already referred to this story in Hour 11§§17–20, where we saw that both meanings of the word *olbios*, 'blessed' and 'fortunate', are being used by Herodotus (1.29–33) in his overall narrative about an encounter of Croesus the king of Lydia with Solon the Athenian lawgiver. The story I am about to quote comes from the first part of that overall narrative. Testing Solon, Croesus asks him to name the most *olbios* person on earth (1.30.2), expecting Solon to name Croesus himself (1.30.3). To his great disappointment, Croesus is told by Solon that an Athenian named Tellos is the most *olbios* of all humans:

HOUR 13 TEXT A

|_{1.30.2} "Athenian guest [*xenos*], we have heard much about your wisdom [*sophiā*] and your wandering, how you in your love of wise things [*philosopheîn*], have traveled all over the world for the sake of a sacred journey [*theōria*], so now I desire to ask you who is the most *olbios* of all men you have ever seen." |_{1.30.3} Croesus asked this question expecting the answer to be himself, but Solon, instead of flattering him, told it as it was and said, "O King, it is *Tellos* the Athenian." |_{1.30.4} Croesus marveled at what he had said and replied sharply, "In what way do you judge [*krinein*] Tellos to be the most *olbios*?" Solon said, "*Tellos* was from a prosperous city [*polis*] and his children were good and noble [*agathoi*]. He saw them all have children of their own, and all of these survived. His life was well off by our standards, and his death was most distinguished: |_{1.30.5} when the Athenians were fighting their neighbors in Eleusis, he came to help, routed the enemy, and died most beautifully. The Athenians buried him at public expense on the spot where he fell, and they honored [*tīmazein*] him greatly."

Herodotus 1.30.2–5*

13§7. So we see here that *krinein* refers to the act of 'deciding' or 'judging' whether to say one thing or another thing. And, in this case, as we will see, it also refers to the act of saying something on one level of meaning or saying it on

---

* |_{1.30.2} "Ξεῖνε Ἀθηναῖε, παρ' ἡμέας γὰρ περὶ σέο λόγος ἀπῖκται πολλὸς καὶ σοφίης [εἵνεκεν] τῆς σῆς καὶ πλάνης, ὡς φιλοσοφέων γῆν πολλὴν θεωρίης εἵνεκεν ἐπελήλυθας· νῦν ὦν ἐπειρέσθαι σε ἵμερος ἐπῆλθέ μοι εἴ τινα ἤδη πάντων εἶδες ὀλβιώτατον." |_{1.30.3} Ὁ μὲν ἐλπίζων εἶναι ἀνθρώπων ὀλβιώτατος ταῦτα ἐπειρώτα, Σόλων δὲ οὐδὲν ὑποθωπεύσας, ἀλλὰ τῷ ἐόντι χρησάμενος, λέγει· "Ὦ Βασιλεῦ, Τέλλον Ἀθηναῖον." |_{1.30.4} Ἀποθωμάσας δὲ Κροῖσος τὸ λεχθὲν εἴρετο ἐπιστρεφέως· "Κοίῃ δὴ κρίνεις Τέλλον εἶναι ὀλβιώτατον;" Ὁ δὲ εἶπε· "Τέλλῳ τοῦτο μὲν τῆς πόλιος εὖ ἡκούσης παῖδες ἦσαν καλοί τε κἀγαθοί, καί σφι εἶδε ἅπασι τέκνα ἐκγενόμενα καὶ πάντα παραμείναντα, τοῦτο δὲ τοῦ βίου εὖ ἥκοντι, ὡς τὰ παρ' ἡμῖν, τελευτὴ τοῦ βίου λαμπροτάτη ἐπεγένετο· |_{1.30.5} γενομένης γὰρ Ἀθηναίοισι μάχης πρὸς τοὺς ἀστυγείτονας ἐν Ἐλευσῖνι βοηθήσας καὶ τροπὴν ποιήσας τῶν πολεμίων ἀπέθανε κάλλιστα, καί μιν Ἀθηναῖοι δημοσίῃ τε ἔθαψαν αὐτοῦ τῇ περ ἔπεσε καὶ ἐτίμησαν μεγάλως."

another level. First, Solon has to decide whether he will say the truth or not. For him the truth is that the most *olbios* person is Tellos, not Croesus. Second, Solon uses the word *olbios* in one way, to mean 'blessed' like a cult hero, while Croesus uses the same word in another way, to mean 'fortunate'—that is, to be endowed with wealth, power, and prestige. One meaning belongs to the sacred world of cult heroes, while the other meaning belongs to the non-sacred world of ephemeral mortals. As we saw in Hour 11§17, the first meaning applies to Tellos the Athenian, who is honored as a cult hero, while the second meaning applies to Croesus—however temporarily. As the story implies, only those who are initiated into the mysteries of hero cult can understand the sacral meaning of *olbios*. And, as we saw in Hour 11§18, this implication about a deeper level of understanding, made available only to initiates, is most evident in contexts where the word *olbios* refers to the bliss of initiation into mysteries of immortalization in general. I cite once again the use of this word with reference to the Eleusinian Mysteries:*

HOUR 13 TEXT B = HOUR 11 TEXT D

Blessed [*olbios*] is he among earthbound mortals who has seen these things

Homeric Hymn to Demeter 480

I find it significant that the figure of Tellos in the same story as I quoted in Text A is connected with the prehistory of the Eleusis (Herodotus 1.30.5), the site of the Eleusinian Mysteries.

13§8. And there is another revealing word in the same story about Tellos, Text A, that has two levels of meaning: it is the verb *tīmazein*, 'honor' (Herodotus 1.30.5), derived from the noun *tīmē*, 'honor', referring to the honor that Tellos receives after death in Eleusis. As we have already seen, *tīmē* can refer to the honor of hero cult that a cult hero receives after death. I cite again the example of the cult hero Demophon of Eleusis, who receives the honor of seasonally recurring athletic contests that are held at Eleusis and that re-enact a 'war':

HOUR 13 TEXT C = HOUR 8 TEXT C

|259 I [= Demeter] swear by the implacable water of the Styx, the witness of oaths that gods make, as I say this: |260 immortal and ageless for all days |261 would I have made your dear [*philos*] little boy, and I would

* Again, *PH* 245 = 8§46n128.

have given him honor [*tīmē*] that is unwilting [*a-phthi-tos*]. |₂₆₂ But now there is no way for him to avoid death and doom. |₂₆₃ Still, he will have an honor [*tīmē*] that is unwilting [*a-phthi-tos*], for all time, because on my knees |₂₆₄ he had once sat and slept in my arms. |₂₆₅ At the right season [*hōrā*], every year, |₂₆₆ the sons of the Eleusinians will have a war, a terrible battle among each other. |₂₆₇ They will do so for all days to come.

Homeric Hymn to Demeter 259–267

13§9. Once again, as in Hour 8§20, I highlight here at verse 265 the noun *hōrā* (plural *hōrai*), 'season, seasonality, the right time, the perfect time', as I defined it in Hour 1§§26–29 and analyzed it in Hour 1§49 and then again in Hour 8§§20–21. As we see from the context that I just quoted here in the *Homeric Hymn to Demeter,* this noun *hōrā* marks *the seasonal recurrence of rituals honoring cult heroes*. And the Eleusinian Games, which are the rituals in this case, may be related to the prehistory of the 'war' that had led to the death of Tellos in Text A (Herodotus 1.30.5).

13§10. Yet another revealing word in the same story about Tellos that has two levels of meaning is the name *Tellos* itself. It is derived from the word *telos*.* As we will now see, this word *telos* can refer to 'initiation' into the mysteries of hero cult. So far, I have been consistently translating this word as either 'final moment' or 'fulfillment'. In the Core Vocabulary, *telos* is defined as 'end, ending, final moment; goal, completion, fulfillment; coming full circle, rounding out; successfully passing through an ordeal; initiation; ritual, rite'. In terms of these definitions, *telos* has basically two levels of meaning:

1. the end of the line, as in death; or
2. a coming full circle, as in immortalization after death—or as in an initiation from one state of existence into another state of existence.†

As I have argued in Hour 11, the idea of heroic immortalization after death was a traditional teaching that the worshippers of cult heroes learned in the context

---

* The linguistic arguments are presented in *PH* 245 = 8§46n128.

† *HC* 95 =1§49, where I also note that form from which Greek *telos* and related forms derive cannot be reduced to a single Indo-European root. As the discussion proceeds, we will see that there are two roots involved in the formation of *telos* and related forms: *k^wel*- and *tel*-. The first of these two roots conveys the idea of 'come full circle'.

of initiation into the mysteries of hero cult. And, as I noted already there, the actual procedures involved in such initiation will be explored in Hour 15. For now, however, I continue to highlight simply the existence of these mysteries. The evidence, I repeat, comes from traditional wording that refers to initiation into mysteries concerning the immortalization of heroes.

Another Story about the Meaning of Olbios in the Histories of Herodotus

13§11. There is a story that expresses both these levels of meaning of *telos,* and it is linked directly with the story about Tellos in Text A, Herodotus 1.30.2–5. In fact, this story immediately follows the story about Tellos:

HOUR 13 TEXT D

|₁.₃₁.₁ When Solon had provoked him by referring to the things that happened to Tellos, saying that these things were many and blessed [*olbia*], Croesus asked him [= Solon] what person he saw as the next one after him [= Tellos], since he [= Croesus] quite expected to win second prize. Solon answered, "Kleobis and Biton. |₁.₃₁.₂ They were Argive by birth [*genos*], and they made a living that was quite sufficient. And, on top of this, they had such great physical strength! Both were prize-winning athletes [*āthlophoroi*]. Here is the story that is told about them. There was a festival [*heortē*] of Hērā in Argos, and it was absolutely necessary for their mother [= the priestess of Hērā] to be conveyed to the sacred precinct [*hieron*] [of Hērā] by a team of oxen. But their oxen had not come back from the fields in time [*hōrā*], so the youths themselves took the yoke upon their shoulders under constraint of time [*hōrā*] and started pulling the wagon, with their mother riding on top of it, transporting her [their mother] forty-five stadium-lengths until they arrived at the sacred precinct [*hieron*] [of Hērā]. |₁.₃₁.₃ After they [= Kleobis and Biton] had done these things and had been seen [*op-*] doing these things by everyone participating in the festival [*panēguris*],* the very best fulfillment [*teleutē*] of life now happened for them. And in all this the god showed that it is better for a man to be in a state of death than in a state of life [*zōein*].† For the men of Argos,

---

*The visualizing of this scene, as indicated here by *op-*, 'see', is essential to the narrative. Relevant is the insightful analysis by Danielle Arnold Freedman (1998:11–13).

† On the mystical subtext of this formulation, see *PH* 243–247 = 8§§45–48.

standing around the two youths, declared them blessed [*makares*] for having such physical strength, while the women of Argos declared the mother of the youths blessed for having such children as these two. |₁.₃₁.₄ And the mother, overjoyed [*perikharēs*] about what had been accomplished and about what had been said about the things that had been accomplished, stood before the statue [= of Hērā] and prayed on behalf of Kleobis and Biton, her two children, who had so greatly honored [*tīmazein*] her. She prayed that the goddess [= Hērā] should give them [= the two youths] the very best thing that can happen to a mortal. |₁.₃₁.₅ After this prayer, the people sacrificed [*thuein*] and feasted [*eu-ōkheîn*], and the youths went to sleep [*kata-koimâsthai*] right then and there in the sacred precinct [of Hērā]. And they [= the two youths] never got up [*an-histasthai*] again, but were held still [*ekhesthai*] in this fulfillment [*telos*]. And the people of Argos made likenesses [*eikōn* plural] of them and dedicated these at Delphi, saying that these were images of men who had become the very best of men."

Herodotus 1.31.1–5*

13§12. We just saw two key expressions in this text, which both apply not only to the meaning of the story of Kleobis and Biton but also to the meaning of the name Tellos in the preceding story. The first expression was this (1.31.3): 'the very best fulfillment [*teleutē*] of life now happened for them'.† I could have translated *teleutē* as 'final moment', but this word is related to *telos* and shows parallel patterns of double meaning: like *telos*, *teleutē* can be a 'fulfillment' as

---

* |₁.₃₁.₁ Ὡς δὲ τὰ κατὰ τὸν Τέλλον προετρέψατο ὁ Σόλων τὸν Κροῖσον εἴπας πολλά τε καὶ ὄλβια, ἐπειρώτα τίνα δεύτερον μετ᾽ ἐκεῖνον ἴδοι, δοκέων πάγχυ δευτερεῖα γῶν οἴσεσθαι. Ὁ δὲ εἶπε· "Κλέοβίν τε καὶ Βίτωνα. |₁.₃₁.₂ Τούτοισι γὰρ ἐοῦσι γένος Ἀργείοισι βίος τε ἀρκέων ὑπῆν καὶ πρὸς τούτῳ ῥώμη σώματος τοιήδε· ἀεθλοφόροι τε ἀμφότεροι ὁμοίως ἦσαν, καὶ δὴ καὶ λέγεται ὅδε [ὁ] λόγος· ἐούσης ὁρτῆς τῇ Ἥρῃ τοῖσι Ἀργείοισι ἔδεε πάντως τὴν μητέρα αὐτῶν ζεύγεϊ κομισθῆναι ἐς τὸ ἱρόν, οἱ δέ σφι βόες ἐκ τοῦ ἀγροῦ οὐ παρεγίνοντο ἐν ὥρῃ· ἐκκληιόμενοι δὲ τῇ ὥρῃ οἱ νεηνίαι ὑποδύντες αὐτοὶ ὑπὸ τὴν ζεύγλην εἷλκον τὴν ἄμαξαν, ἐπὶ τῆς ἁμάξης δέ σφι ὠχέετο ἡ μήτηρ, σταδίους δὲ πέντε καὶ τεσσεράκοντα διακομίσαντες ἀπίκοντο ἐς τὸ ἱρόν. |₁.₃₁.₃ Ταῦτα δέ σφι ποιήσασι καὶ ὀφθεῖσι ὑπὸ τῆς πανηγύριος τελευτὴ τοῦ βίου ἀρίστη ἐπεγένετο, διέδεξέ τε ἐν τούτοισι ὁ θεὸς ὡς ἄμεινον εἴη ἀνθρώπῳ τεθνάναι μᾶλλον ἢ ζώειν. Ἀργεῖοι μὲν γὰρ περιστάντες ἐμακάριζον τῶν νεηνιέων τὴν ῥώμην, αἱ δὲ Ἀργεῖαι τὴν μητέρα αὐτῶν, οἵων τέκνων ἐκύρησε. |₁.₃₁.₄ Ἡ δὲ μήτηρ περιχαρὴς ἐοῦσα τῷ τε ἔργῳ καὶ τῇ φήμῃ, στᾶσα ἀντίον τοῦ ἀγάλματος εὔχετο Κλεόβι τε καὶ Βίτωνι τοῖσι ἑωυτῆς τέκνοισι, οἵ μιν ἐτίμησαν μεγάλως, τὴν θεὸν δοῦναι τὸ ἀνθρώπῳ τυχεῖν ἄριστόν ἐστι. |₁.₃₁.₅ Μετὰ ταύτην δὲ τὴν εὐχὴν ὡς ἔθυσάν τε καὶ εὐωχήθησαν, κατακοιμηθέντες ἐν αὐτῷ τῷ ἱρῷ οἱ νεηνίαι οὐκέτι ἀνέστησαν, ἀλλ᾽ ἐν τέλεϊ τούτῳ ἔσχοντο. Ἀργεῖοι δέ σφεων εἰκόνας ποιησάμενοι ἀνέθεσαν ἐς Δελφοὺς ὡς ἀνδρῶν ἀρίστων γενομένων.

† τελευτὴ τοῦ βίου ἀρίστη ἐπεγένετο.

well as a 'final moment'. And the second expression was this (1.31.5): 'they [= the two youths] . . . were held still [*ekhesthai*] in this fulfillment [*telos*]'. The moment is like a snapshot, and the person who is taking the picture is saying: "Hold still!" In order to explore the double meanings of *teleutē* and *telos* as 'final moment' and 'fulfillment' here in Text D, I now offer further analysis of the story itself.

13§13. While all the sacrificing and the feasting is going on, the two youths fall asleep inside the sacred precinct of the goddess, and the euphemistic wording that describes this sleep highlights a sacred idea. Here is the idea: these two youths will now be permanently encapsulated in the perfect moment that they had just reached at this climactic point in the story of their lives. As the story says, 'they never got up again'* (1.31.5). That is, the two youths never got up again in this world of mortals. Now they will 'hold still' forever in another world, in exactly the perfect moment that they had just achieved. Let us look back one more time at the expression (1.31.5): 'they [= the two youths] . . . were held still [*ekhesthai*] in this fulfillment [*telos*]'.† The verb *ekhein*, 'hold', in the middle voice, *ekhesthai*, is used here in the sense of capturing a snapshot moment, as I said a minute ago. Another way to say it is this: "Hold it right there!"‡ In other words, the two youths die at the perfect moment in a perfect *pose*.

13§14. My choice of the word *pose* here is based on the meaning of the noun derived from the verb *ekhesthai*, 'hold still', that is, *skhēma*, which can mean the 'pose' of a dancer or even the 'pose' of a statue.§ So we see the two youths settling into a perfect and eternal pose, which becomes a visible sign of their *telos*. And this *telos* in the sense of 'fulfillment' really is the very best *teleutē*—again in the sense of 'fulfillment'. That is what is predicted earlier in the story, as we saw in the expression of Herodotus: 'the very best fulfillment [*teleutē*] of life now happened for them'** (1.31.3).

13§15. So now I am ready to go beyond the translations of *telos* and *teleutē* as either 'final moment' or 'fulfillment'. To these translations I add another: 'coming full circle'. In terms of a straight line, *telos* is the 'end' of that line; in terms of a circle, however, *telos* is a 'coming full circle'.†† In this light, I come back to a

---

* οὐκέτι ἀνέστησαν.
† ἐν τέλεϊ τούτῳ ἔσχοντο.
‡ *HC* 94–95 = 1§47, with reference also to *PH* 38 = 1§39n111. Freedman (1998:13) describes this moment as "photographic."
§ *HC* 95 = 1§47.
** τελευτὴ τοῦ βίου ἀρίστη ἐπεγένετο.
†† Again, *HC* 95 =1§49.

formulation I introduced in Hour 1§49, where I said that the unseasonality of the *hērōs* in mortal life leads to the *telos* or 'fulfillment' of *hōrā*, 'seasonality', in immortal life, which is achieved in the setting of hero cult. Now we have finally seen such a model of achievement in the two parallel stories of Herodotus about cult heroes, and in both stories a key to the meaning is the word *telos* in the sense of 'fulfillment', even 'coming full circle'. In the first story, as quoted in Text A, Tellos achieves the *telos* of a cult hero even by way of his name, which is derived from *telos*. And, in the second story, as quoted in Text D, Kleobis and Biton achieve the best *teleutē* by 'holding still' forever in the *telos* of a perfect moment, which is the *telos* of the cult hero.

13§16. Here I come back to another most telling part of the story of Kleobis and Biton in Text D (Herodotus 1.32.2): 'their oxen had not come back from the fields in time [*hōrā*], so the youths themselves took the yoke upon their shoulders under constraint of time [*hōrā*] and started pulling the wagon'.* In other words, the oxen who were destined to pull the wagon that took the priestess of Hērā all the way to the precinct of Hērā, which was forty-five stadium-lengths away from the city center of Argos, were simply *not on time*. They were untimely, and the timing or *hōrā* was off. But the youths who took their place were perfectly timely: they were on time, since they were constrained by the timing or *hōrā* of the festival. If the oxen had been on time, they would have been slaughtered as the prime sacrificial victims of the sacrifice to the goddess Hērā in her precinct. But they were not on time, and so the youths had to be on time. And the youths died their deaths in place of the prime sacrificial victims.

13§17. This crisis of *hōrā* in the story of Kleobis and Biton is relevant to the goddess who presided over the whole chain of events in the story. That goddess is Hērā. And, as we saw in Hour 1§27, Hērā was the goddess of *hōrā* (plural *hōrai*). And, as we also saw, the two forms *Hērā* and *hōrā* are linguistically related to each other. Hērā was the goddess of seasons, in charge of making everything happen on time, happen in season, and happen in a timely way. But then there is the hero. As we saw in Hour 1§28, the word *hērōs* (plural *hērōes*) meaning 'hero' is related to the words *hōrā* and *Hērā*. But heroes, unlike the goddess Hērā, are not timely. They become timely only when they die. The precise moment when everything comes together for the hero is the moment of death. The

---

* οἱ δέ σφι βόες ἐκ τοῦ ἀγροῦ οὐ παρεγίνοντο ἐν ὥρῃ· ἐκκληιόμενοι δὲ τῇ ὥρῃ οἱ νεηνίαι ὑποδύντες αὐτοὶ ὑπὸ τὴν ζεύγλην εἷλκον τὴν ἅμαξαν.

hero is 'on time' at the *hōrā* or 'time' of death. Before death and in fact during their whole lifetime, however, heroes are *not on time*: rather, they are *unseasonal*, as we saw first and foremost in the case of Hēraklēs in Hour 1§39.

13§18. Being on time for death is precisely what happens to Kleobis and Biton, sons of the priestess of Hērā in the story I quoted in Text D. Their timely death marks them as cult heroes, and the word that expresses this timely death, which will lead to timeless immortalization, is *telos*. And it is most appropriate that Hērā, the goddess of timeliness, presides over the *telos* of heroes: as I noted in Hour 1§49, the connection of Hērā with the idea of *telos* is evident in the adjective *teleia*, derived from *telos*, which is a cult epithet of the goddess Hērā.* Combined with the name of this goddess, *teleia* can mean not only 'bringing fulfillment' but even 'bringing perfection'. If striving to achieve a *telos* is a process, then the achievement itself can be seen as the *perfecting* of that process.† Such an idea of perfection is built into the word *hōrā*: in Hour 1§§26–29, I analyzed the meaning of this word (plural *hōrai*) as 'season, seasonality, the right time, the perfect time'.

13§19. In the case of Herodotus' framing story about Solon's story about Kleobis and Biton, Text D, the framing story reaches its own *telos* or 'fulfillment' in an aetiology (1.31.5). By *aetiology* here, as I repeat from Hour 7A§15, I mean a myth that motivates an institutional reality, especially a ritual. In this case the aetiology has to do with the rituals and the ritual objects connected with the hero cult of Kleobis and Biton at Argos. The ritual objects are the statues of the two young men, and their status as cult heroes is evidently visualized in the form of these statues: 'And the people of Argos made likenesses [*eikōn* plural] of them and dedicated these at Delphi, saying that these were images of men who had become the very best of men'‡ (1.31.5). As we learn from Herodotus, the outcome of the story of these two young men is formalized in these statues. The perfect pose of their perfect moment, rigid to the point of *rigor mortis*, is captured by the creation of their statues. And the two statues have actually survived: you can see them today in the Museum at Delphi:§

13§20. In the context of the Herodotean narrative, a perfect moment of hap-

---

* Again I cite the example in Aristophanes *Women at the Thesmophoria* 973.

† *HC* 95 = 1§49.

‡ Ἀργεῖοι δέ σφεων εἰκόνας ποιησάμενοι ἀνέθεσαν ἐς Δελφοὺς ὡς ἀνδρῶν ἀρίστων γενομένων.

§ *HC* 95 = 1§50. I add there that it does not affect my argument whether or not Kleobis and Biton were the original referents at the time when these statues were made. What matters is that they were truly the referents *as far as the Argives were concerned*, with reference to the time of Herodotus' own narration.

piness was experienced by all who took part in the festival of Hērā, and this moment became concretized in the form of the statues of Kleobis and Biton.* The stylized death of these two youths is a dramatization of the perfect heroic moment—especially since they are sons of the priestess of *Hērā* herself, who is the goddess of that perfect moment.

13§21. Back when we started this hour, I noted the differences in the meaning of *olbios* for those who were initiated into the mysteries of hero cult and for those who were not. These differences are relevant to this riddling statement in Text D: 'and in all this the god showed that it is better for a man to be in a state of death than in a state of life [*zōein*]'† (1.31.3). *For the uninitiated, this wording means that you are better off dead—that you might as well choose to be put out of your misery instead going on with life. For the initiated, this same wording means that a life after death will be better for you than the life you are living now.*

13§22. From my study of such words as *olbios* and *tīmē* and *telos* during this hour, I conclude that the cult hero is literally *defined* in terms of one's ability to *krinein*, 'judge, distinguish', which as we have seen is the power of discerning the true from the untrue.

Variations in Discriminating between the Real and the Unreal

13§23. Now we turn to a derivative of *krinein*, which is *hupo-krinesthai*. I focus on an attestation in the Homeric *Odyssey*, where Penelope is speaking to the disguised Odysseus. She is testing the hero by challenging him to interpret a dream:

HOUR 13 TEXT E

Come, respond [*hupo-krinesthai*] to my dream, and hear my telling of it.

Odyssey xix 535‡

13§24. Here Penelope challenges Odysseus to respond to the omen of her dream about the killing of the geese in her courtyard by an eagle that swoops down on them: the verb *hupo-krinesthai* is used here in the imperative, with the

---

* *HC* 96 = 1§51.

† διέδεξέ τε ἐν τούτοισι ὁ θεὸς ὡς ἄμεινον εἴη ἀνθρώπῳ τεθνάναι μᾶλλον ἢ ζώειν.

‡ ἀλλ' ἄγε μοι τὸν ὄνειρον ὑπόκριναι καὶ ἄκουσον.

word for 'dream' in the accusative.* Within the dream itself, the eagle says to Penelope that he is Odysseus and that the geese are the suitors, who are to be punished for their unjust behavior. The disguised Odysseus responds to the convoluted words of Penelope by saying that her dream has already interpreted itself and that no response is needed from him—except to say what he has said, that the dream has already interpreted itself (xix 555–558). This way, Odysseus postpones identifying himself to Penelope, but at the same time he shows his good judgment in discriminating between what is false and what is true about his own heroic identity as defined by his sense of justice, which is being challenged by the injustices inflicted on him by the suitors.

13§25. In this light, we can see further dimensions in the meaning of *krinein*, from which the compound form *hupo-krinesthai* is derived. This verb *krinein*, in the active voice, can be translated as 'interpret' when combined with the noun *opsis*, 'vision', as its object (Herodotus 7.19.1–2) or with *enupnion*, 'dream', as its object (Herodotus 1.120.1).† It is a question of interpreting-in-performance. In the middle voice, *hupo-krinesthai* suggests that the performer is interpreting for himself as well as for others.‡ The basic idea of *hupo-krinesthai*, then, is to see the real meaning of what others see and to quote back, as it were, what this vision is really telling them.§

Variations in Discriminating between Justice and Injustice

13§26. In discriminating between what is heroic and what is unheroic, derivative forms of *krinein* can refer to moral questions that shape the very foundations of poetry. There is a shining example in the Hesiodic *Theogony*, describing legal actions taken by an ideal king:

HOUR 13 TEXT F

|₈₁ Whosoever among sky-nourished kings is honored [*timân*] by these daughters of great Zeus [= the Muses]** |₈₂ and is beheld by them when he is born, |₈₃ for such a man they pour sweet dew upon his

---

* *HR* 23.
† Koller 1957:101.
‡ Koller 1957:102.
§ *HC* 152 = 1§158, following *HR* 37–38.
** Earlier in the Hesiodic *Theogony* (80), one Muse in particular, Kalliope, is described as the patroness of kings.

tongue, |₈₄ and from his mouth flow sweet words. The people, |₈₅ all of them, look toward him as he sorts out [dia-krinein] the divine laws [themis plural] |₈₆ by way of straight judgments [dikai]. And he, speaking without stumbling |₈₇ and with his powers of understanding, can even put an end to a great quarrel [neikos].* |₈₈ It is for this reason that there are kings, kings with good thinking [phrenes], namely, because when people |₈₉ are wronged in the assembly [agorā], they [= the kings] can turn things right around for them, |₉₀ quite easily, speaking in a deflecting way by using soft words. |₉₁ And when he [= the just king] goes to a gathering [agōn], the people turn to him as if he were a god, |₉₂ because of his gentle command of respect [aidōs], and he stands out among the assembled. |₉₃ Such is the sacred gift of the Muses for humankind. |₉₄ For it is because of the Muses and far-shooting Apollo |₉₅ that there are singers [aoidoi] and players of the lyre [kitharis] on this earth. |₉₆ And it is because of Zeus that there are kings. Blessed [olbios] is he whom the Muses |₉₇ love. And a sweet voice [audē] flows from his mouth.

Hesiod Theogony 81–97†

13§27. As we have just seen at verse 85 here, the ideal king dia-krinei, 'sorts out', what is themis, 'divine law', and what is not. And the king can do this, as we read at verse 86, by way of his dikai, 'judgments'. This way, as we will now see in the Hesiodic Works and Days, the ideal king is the representative of Zeus on earth, since it is Zeus himself who ithunei, 'makes straight', the themistes, 'divine laws':

HOUR 13 TEXT G

|₁ Muses of Pieria, you who make glory [kleos] with your songs, |₂ come and tell of Zeus, making a song about your father, |₃ on account

---

* Compare the context of neikos at Works and Days 35.

† |₈₁ ὅντινα τιμήσουσι Διὸς κοῦραι μεγάλοιο |₈₂ γεινόμενόν τε ἴδωσι διοτρεφέων βασιλήων, |₈₃ τῷ μὲν ἐπὶ γλώσσῃ γλυκερὴν χείουσιν ἐέρσην, |₈₄ τοῦ δ' ἔπε' ἐκ στόματος ῥεῖ μείλιχα· οἱ δέ νυ λαοὶ |₈₅ πάντες ἐς αὐτὸν ὁρῶσι διακρίνοντα θέμιστας |₈₆ ἰθείῃσι δίκῃσιν· ὁ δ' ἀσφαλέως ἀγορεύων |₈₇ αἶψά τι καὶ μέγα νεῖκος ἐπισταμένως κατέπαυσε· |₈₈ τούνεκα γὰρ βασιλῆες ἐχέφρονες, οὕνεκα λαοῖς |₈₉ βλαπτομένοις ἀγορῆφι μετάτροπα ἔργα τελεῦσι |₉₀ ῥηιδίως, μαλακοῖσι παραιφάμενοι ἐπέεσσιν· |₉₁ ἐρχόμενον δ' ἀν' ἀγῶνα θεὸν ὣς ἱλάσκονται |₉₂ αἰδοῖ μειλιχίῃ, μετὰ δὲ πρέπει ἀγρομένοισι. |₉₃ τοίη Μουσάων ἱερὴ δόσις ἀνθρώποισιν. |₉₄ ἐκ γάρ τοι Μουσέων καὶ ἑκηβόλου Ἀπόλλωνος |₉₅ ἄνδρες ἀοιδοὶ ἔασιν ἐπὶ χθόνα καὶ κιθαρισταί, |₉₆ ἐκ δὲ Διὸς βασιλῆες· ὁ δ' ὄλβιος, ὅντινα Μοῦσαι |₉₇ φίλωνται· γλυκερή οἱ ἀπὸ στόματος ῥέει αὐδή.

of whom there are mortals both unworthy of talk and worthy, |₄ both worth speaking of and not—all on account of great Zeus. |₅ Easily he gives power, and just as easily he ruins the powerful. |₆ Easily he diminishes the distinguished and magnifies the undistinguished. |₇ Easily he makes straight the crooked and withers the overweening |₈—Zeus, the one who thunders on high, who lives in the highest abode. |₉ Heed me, seeing and hearing as you do, and with justice [dikē] make straight [ithunein] the divine laws [themis plural]. |₁₀ While you do that, I am ready to tell genuine [etētuma] things to Perses.

Hesiod Works and Days 1–10*

13§28. At verse 9 here, we see also that Zeus is straightening the *themistes*, 'divine laws', by way of his own *dikē*. In this absolutizing context, both the short-term meaning of *dikē* as 'judgment' and its long-term meaning as 'justice' are fused in the absolute figure of Zeus. Only for Zeus is a 'judgment' the same thing as 'justice'. And this absolute model can now absolutely validate the figure of Hesiod himself. As we have just read in *Works and Days* verses 9–10, the *dikē* of Zeus is in action *while Hesiod talks to Perses*. So the action of Zeus is the same thing as the speech of Hesiod. That is how Hesiod becomes the ultimate master of the *speech act*. For background on this term *speech act*, I refer back to Hour 2§§41–43.

13§29. In the *Works and Days*, it is actually Hesiod who becomes the hero of the speech act, since the blessing that the Muses give to the ideal juridical speaker suits him more than any other mortal, even more than any king: as we have just read in the Hesiodic *Theogony* (96–97), 'blessed [olbios] is he whom the Muses |₉₇ love'†. And that blessing, marked by the word *olbios*, signals the making of a cult hero.

13§30. The validation of Hesiod as the ideal juridical speaker is indicated in another way as well. We can see it when we consider what is missing in the picture of an ideal king. And this thing that is missing can be described as a *significant absence*. The one thing that is missing is a *skēptron*, 'scepter', which is tradi-

---

* |₁ Μοῦσαι Πιερίηθεν ἀοιδῆσι κλείουσαι, |₂ δεῦτε Δί᾽ ἐννέπετε, σφέτερον πατέρ᾽ ὑμνείουσαι. |₃ ὅν τε διὰ βροτοὶ ἄνδρες ὁμῶς ἄφατοί τε φατοί τε, |₄ ῥητοί τ᾽ ἄρρητοί τε Διὸς μεγάλοιο ἕκητι. |₅ ῥέα μὲν γὰρ βριάει, ῥέα δὲ βριάοντα χαλέπτει, |₆ ῥεῖα δ᾽ ἀρίζηλον μινύθει καὶ ἄδηλον ἀέξει, |₇ ῥεῖα δέ τ᾽ ἰθύνει σκολιὸν καὶ ἀγήνορα κάρφει |₈ Ζεὺς ὑψιβρεμέτης, ὃς ὑπέρτατα δώματα ναίει. |₉ κλῦθι ἰδὼν ἀίων τε, δίκῃ δ᾽ ἴθυνε θέμιστας |₁₀ τύνη· ἐγὼ δέ κε Πέρσῃ ἐτήτυμα μυθησαίμην.

† ὁ δ᾽ ὄλβιος, ὅντινα Μοῦσαι |₉₇ φίλωνται.

tionally a primary marker of kings who have the authority to make judgments at councils of kings (as in *Iliad* I 279, II 86); when the Achaean kings make *dikai*, 'judgments', at a council of kings, the protocol is for each king to hold the *skēptron*, 'scepter', when it is his turn to speak.* In the *Theogony*, however, someone else already has the scepter. That is, *Hesiod himself receives a scepter from the Muses.* Here is how the persona of Hesiod describes the moment when he receives this gift from the Muses, who offer to teach him how to say the absolute truth:

Hour 13 Text H

|₂₂ [It was the Muses] who taught me, Hesiod, their beautiful song. |₂₃ It happened when I was tending flocks of sheep in a valley of Helikon, that holy mountain. |₂₄ And the very first thing that the goddesses said to me, |₂₅ those Muses of Mount Olympus, those daughters of Zeus who holds the aegis, was this wording [*mūthos*]:† |₂₆ "Shepherds camping in the fields, base objects of reproach, mere bellies!‡ |₂₇ We know how to say many deceptive things looking like genuine [*etuma*] things,§ |₂₈ but we also know how, whenever we wish it, to proclaim things that are true [*alēthea*]."** |₂₉ That is how they spoke, those daughters of great Zeus, who have words [*epea*] that fit perfectly together, |₃₀ and they gave me a scepter [*skēptron*],†† a branch of flourishing laurel, |₃₁ having plucked it. And it was a wonder to behold. Then they breathed into me a voice [*audē*], |₃₂ a godlike one, so that I may make glory [*kleos*] for things that will be and things that have been, |₃₃ and then they told me to sing how the blessed ones [*makares* = the gods] were generated, the ones that are forever, |₃₄ and that I should sing them [= the Muses] first and last.

Hesiod Theogony 22–34‡‡

---

* *GM* 52–53.

† For commentary on *muthos* here in the sense of 'wording meant to be remembered for the record', see *HQ* 119–133, following Martin 1989.

‡ For commentary on these riddling words of insult uttered by the Muses here as a test for Hesiod, see *GM* 44–45, 274–275.

§ For commentary on *homoia*, 'looking like', in this context, see Nagy 2010c.

** For commentary on *alēthea*, 'true things', here in the sense of absolute truth, see *PH* 64–68 = 2§§26–32; also Nagy 2009a:275–277.

†† More on this *skēptron*, 'scepter', in *GM* 49.

‡‡ |₂₂ αἵ νύ ποθ᾽ Ἡσίοδον καλὴν ἐδίδαξαν ἀοιδήν, |₂₃ ἄρνας ποιμαίνονθ᾽ Ἑλικῶνος ὕπο ζαθέοιο. |₂₄ τόνδε δέ με πρώτιστα θεαὶ πρὸς μῦθον ἔειπον, |₂₅ Μοῦσαι Ὀλυμπιάδες, κοῦραι Διὸς αἰγιόχοιο·

13§31. This *skēptron* given to Hesiod by the Muses is a symbol of the authorization inherent in the poetic form of the *Theogony*. From an anthropological point of view, *a theogony is a speech-act of authorization*. But Hesiod's theogony authorizes not kings. Rather, it authorizes Hesiod himself as an overarching representative of authority. *Hesiod is a master of truth, absolute truth:* that is the essence of the word *alēthea*, 'true things', at *Theogony* 28.*

13§32. So both in the *Theogony* and in the *Works and Days*, Hesiod figures as the absolute master of the speech act, as the master of the absolute truth. His status as cult hero is based on this mastery. Hesiod is programmed by the *Theogony* and by the *Works and Days* to become such a cult hero.

13§33. There is historical evidence for the worship of Hesiod as a cult hero, and there is even an allusion to such worship in the *History* of Thucydides (3.96.1).† In this connection, I should also note, historical evidence shows that Homer too was worshipped as a cult hero.‡ Limitations of time and space prevent me, however, from exploring here such external evidence about Homer as well as Hesiod, and I confine myself to highlighting the built-in references that we find in Hesiodic poetry about the status of this poet as a cult hero.§

13§34. I return to the verb *dia-krinein,* as we saw it attested in the description of the ideal king in *Theogony* 85–87. At verses 85–86, we read how an ideal king *dia-krinei*, 'sorts out', what is *themis*, 'divine law', and what is not, and how he accomplishes this 'sorting out' by way of his *dikē*, 'judgment'. By doing so, the ideal king can bring to an end a great *neikos*, 'quarrel', as we read at verse 87.

13§35. In *Works and Days* 9–10, we saw that Zeus straightens *themis*, 'divine law', by way of his *dikē*, 'judgment'—*while Hesiod speaks to Perses*. The speaking of Hesiod, as a speech act, takes place in the context of a *neikos*, 'quarrel', as we read at verse 35, between Hesiod as the just brother and Perses as the unjust brother. And here we come to a most striking attestation of *dia-krinein—*

$|_{26}$ "ποιμένες ἄγραυλοι, κάκ᾽ ἐλέγχεα, γαστέρες οἶον, $|_{27}$ ἴδμεν ψεύδεα πολλὰ λέγειν ἐτύμοισιν ὁμοῖα, $|_{28}$ ἴδμεν δ᾽ εὖτ᾽ ἐθέλωμεν ἀληθέα γηρύσασθαι." $|_{29}$ ὣς ἔφασαν κοῦραι μεγάλου Διὸς ἀρτιέπειαι, $|_{30}$ καί μοι σκῆπτρον ἔδον δάφνης ἐριθηλέος ὄζον $|_{31}$ δρέψασαι, θηητόν· ἐνέπνευσαν δέ μοι αὐδὴν $|_{32}$ θέσπιν, ἵνα κλείοιμι τά τ᾽ ἐσσόμενα πρό τ᾽ ἐόντα, $|_{33}$ καί μ᾽ ἐκέλονθ᾽ ὑμνεῖν μακάρων γένος αἰὲν ἐόντων, $|_{34}$ σφᾶς δ᾽ αὐτὰς πρῶτόν τε καὶ ὕστατον αἰὲν ἀείδειν.

* *PH* 59–61, 68 = 2§§22–23, §31.

† For a survey of the evidence, see Nagy 2009a:304–308. For more on Hesiod as a cult hero, see Bershadsky 2011, especially pp. 19 and 22.

‡ *PP* 113n33; see also *PP* 113n33 about the *Homēridai*, 'sons of Homer', as continuators of a hero cult of Homer, with further analysis in *HPC* = 57–69 = 1§§138–167.

§ For more on such built-in references, see again Bershadsky 2011.

this time, in the middle voice. Hesiod calls on his brother to sort out with him, as expressed by way of *dia-krinesthai,* in the middle voice, a resolution of the quarrel:

HOUR 13 TEXT I

$|_{35}$ . . . But come, let us now sort out [*dia-krinesthai*] for ourselves the quarrel [*neikos*], $|_{36}$ with straight judgments [*dikai*], which are the best when they come from Zeus.

Hesiod Works and Days 35–36*

And such a sorting out actually happens in the course of the *Works and Days,* as I analyzed it in Hour 12, especially in §10 and §36.†

13§36. This kind of *sorting out* does not happen in Homeric poetry. As we saw in Hour 12§34, Homeric poetry does not address the problem of justice, that is, it does not judge what is right and what is wrong. The one place where an opportunity arises, this opportunity is not taken. It is a litigation scene portrayed as a central picture worked into the cosmic artifact known as the Shield of Achilles:

HOUR 13 TEXT J (INCLUDING HOUR 8 TEXT L)

$|_{497}$ Meanwhile the people were gathered in assembly, and there a quarrel [*neikos*] $|_{498}$ had arisen, and two men were quarreling [*neikeîn*] about the blood-price [*poinē*] $|_{499}$ for a man who had died. One of the two claimed [*eukhesthai*] that he had the right to pay off the damages in full, $|_{500}$ declaring this publicly to the population of the district [*dēmos*], and the other of the two was refusing to accept anything. $|_{501}$ Both of them were seeking a limit [*peirar*], in the presence of an arbitrator [*histōr*], $|_{502}$ and the people took sides, each man shouting for the side he was on; $|_{503}$ but the heralds kept them back, and the elders $|_{504}$ sat on benches of polished stone in a sacred [*hieros*] circle, $|_{505}$ taking hold of scepters [*skēptra*] that the heralds, who lift their voices, put into their hands. $|_{506}$ Holding these [scepters] they rose and each in his turn gave judgment [*dikazein*],‡ $|_{507}$ and in their midst there were placed on the

---

* $|_{35}$ . . . ἀλλ' αὖθι διακρινώμεθα νεῖκος $|_{36}$ ἰθείῃσι δίκῃς, αἵ τ' ἐκ Διός εἰσιν ἄρισται.

† Further analysis in Bershadsky 2011:24.

‡ When the Achaean kings make *dikai,* 'judgments', at a council of kings, as I noted earlier, the protocol is for each king to hold the *skēptron,* 'scepter', when it is his turn to speak: see §30.

ground two measures of gold, |₅₀₈ to be given to that one among them who spoke a judgment [*dikē*] in the most straight way [*ithuntata*].*

Iliad XVIII 497–508†

13§37. We see here an unresolved tension between *dikē* as 'justice' in the long term and 'judgment' in the short term. At XVIII 508, we see a contest or debate that centers on the question of the 'straightest' possible formulation of *dikē*—in the context of a *neikos*, 'quarrel', as mentioned in XVIII 497. And we see that the people who have to make up their minds about the big question of justice in the *Iliad* are described as a crowd standing around the central scene of the litigation. That crowd, as I have argued, can be imagined as the timeless audience of Homeric poetry.‡

13§38. By contrast, the narrative of Hesiod is the narrative of a crooked line becoming a straight line. By the time we reach verse 275 of the Hesiodic *Works and Days*, *dikē* has shifted from a relativized concept of 'judgment' to become an absolutized concept of 'justice'.

Heroes as Exponents of Justice in Poetry after Homer and Hesiod

13§39. I bring this hour to a close, but not without leaving open a window into the historical age, that is, into a post-heroic age that we associate with the historical period of Greek civilization, starting around the seventh century BCE.

13§40. By the time we reach the historical period, of course, we find no ultimate city of *dikē*, no ultimate city of *hubris*. Such cities exist only in poetry, as in the apocalyptic vision of the Hesiodic *Works and Days*. But we do find exponents of justice who become cult heroes by way of their poetry. By now this comes as no surprise, since we have already seen in §§32–33 of this hour that

---

*I have produced an extensive commentary on this passage in an essay, the latest version of which can be found in Nagy 2003:72–87.

† |₄₉₇ λαοὶ δ᾽ εἰν ἀγορῇ ἔσαν ἀθρόοι· ἔνθα δὲ νεῖκος |₄₉₈ ὠρώρει, δύο δ᾽ ἄνδρες ἐνείκεον εἵνεκα ποινῆς |₄₉₉ ἀνδρὸς ἀποφθιμένου· ὁ μὲν εὔχετο πάντ᾽ ἀποδοῦναι |₅₀₀ δήμῳ πιφαύσκων, ὁ δ᾽ ἀναίνετο μηδὲν ἑλέσθαι. |₅₀₁ ἄμφω δ᾽ ἱέσθην ἐπὶ ἴστορι πεῖραρ ἑλέσθαι. |₅₀₂ λαοὶ δ᾽ ἀμφοτέροισιν ἐπήπυον ἀμφὶς ἀρωγοί· |₅₀₃ κήρυκες δ᾽ ἄρα λαὸν ἐρήτυον· οἱ δὲ γέροντες |₅₀₄ εἵατ᾽ ἐπὶ ξεστοῖσι λίθοις ἱερῷ ἐνὶ κύκλῳ, |₅₀₅ σκῆπτρα δὲ κηρύκων ἐν χέρσ᾽ ἔχον ἠεροφώνων· |₅₀₆ τοῖσιν ἔπειτ᾽ ἤϊσσον, ἀμοιβηδὶς δὲ δίκαζον. |₅₀₇ κεῖτο δ᾽ ἄρ᾽ ἐν μέσσοισι δύω χρυσοῖο τάλαντα, |₅₀₈ τῷ δόμεν ὃς μετὰ τοῖσι δίκην ἰθύντατα εἴποι.

‡ *HR* 86–87. This argument is designed as the closure for my essay "The Shield of Achilles: Ends of the *Iliad* and Beginnings of the Polis." The most updated version of this essay is embedded in *HR* 72–87.

Homer and Hesiod are both worshipped as cult heroes. And there are exponents of justice who are worshipped as cult heroes in individual city-states. Some of these heroes are viewed as lawgivers or quasi-lawgivers.

13§41. When a hero is viewed by a city-state as its lawmaker, he can also be viewed as the author of that given city's customary laws. In myths about lawmakers, such authorship is traditionally correlated with some kind of fundamental crisis that afflicts the given city.

13§42. Here are three examples of such heroes:

Lycurgus of Sparta

Solon of Athens

Theognis of Megara

13§43. I choose as the final texts for this hour two pieces of poetry attributed to Theognis.* In these two poems, we see variations on ideas that will recur—and recur often—in the remaining hours.

Hour 13 Text K

|$_{39}$ Kyrnos, this city [polis] is pregnant, and I fear that it will give birth to a man |$_{40}$ who will be a straightener [euthuntēr] of our base hubris. |$_{41}$ The citizens [astoi] here [in the city] are still moderate [sōphrones], but the leaders [hēgemones] |$_{42}$ have veered so far as to fall into debasement [kakotēs]. |$_{43}$ Men who are noble [agathoi], Kyrnos, have never yet ruined any city [polis], |$_{44}$ but when people who are base [kakoi] decide to behave with hubris, |$_{45}$ and when they ruin the community [dēmos] and render judgments [dikai] in favor of the unjust [= persons or things without dikē], |$_{46}$ for the sake of private gain [kerdos plural], and for the sake of absolute power [kratos], |$_{47}$ do not expect that city [polis] to be peaceful for long, |$_{48}$ not even if it is now in a state of great serenity [hēsukhiā], |$_{49}$ once the base [kakoi] decide on these things, |$_{50}$ namely, private gains [kerdos plural] entailing public damage. |$_{51}$ From these things result acts of discord [stasis plural], killings [phonoi] within local groups of men, |$_{52}$ and one-man rul-

---

* As I noted already in Hour 10§14, there is no fixed date for Theognis: he is credited with the creation of poems that can be dated as far apart as the late seventh and the early fifth centuries BCE.

ers [*mounarkhoi*]. May this city [*polis*] never decide to accept these things!*

HOUR 13 TEXT L

|₁₀₈₁ Kyrnos, this city [*polis*] is pregnant, and I fear that it will give birth to a man |₁₀₈₂ who will be a *hubristēs* [= perpetrator of *hubris*], a *leader* [*hēgemōn*] of dire discord [*stasis*]. |₁₀₈₂ₐ The citizens [*astoi*] here [in the city] are moderate [*sōphrones*], but the *leaders* [*hēgemones*] |₁₀₈₂ᵦ have veered so far as to fall into debasement [*kakotēs*].‡

Theognis 1081–1082b§

13§44. Although the poetry attributed to Theognis can be traced back primarily to one specific social context, which was the metropolis or 'mother city' of Megara and its daughter cities, most of this poetry is composed in such a generalized way that it can apply to a wide variety of other social contexts in other cities. An example is the set of two poems I just quoted. Both poems apply to historical situations and events that can be localized not only in Megara but elsewhere as well, including the city of Athens in the age of Solon the lawgiver, who was active in the early sixth century BCE. For the moment, though, I will concentrate on those features of the quoted poems that show parallelisms with features we found in the Hesiodic *Works and Days*.

13§45. The speaker in Text K as quoted from Theognis (39–52) is expressing his pessimism about an ongoing struggle between men of *dikē* and men of *hubris* within his city, and he is railing against the elites of that city, accusing them of becoming morally debased by *hubris*. This debasement is pictured as a physi-

---

*Commentary in Nagy 1985:42–45 = §§27–30.

† |₃₉ Κύρνε, κύει πόλις ἥδε, δέδοικα δὲ μὴ τέκῃ ἄνδρα |₄₀ εὐθυντῆρα κακῆς ὕβριος ἡμετέρης. |₄₁ ἀστοὶ μὲν γὰρ ἔθ' οἵδε σαόφρονες, ἡγεμόνες δὲ |₄₂ τετράφαται πολλὴν εἰς κακότητα πεσεῖν. |₄₃ οὐδεμίαν πω Κύρν' ἀγαθοὶ πόλιν ὤλεσαν ἄνδρες· |₄₄ ἀλλ' ὅταν ὑβρίζειν τοῖσι κακοῖσι ἅδῃ |₄₅ δῆμόν τε φθείρωσι δίκας τ' ἀδίκοισι διδῶσιν |₄₆ οἰκείων κερδέων εἵνεκα καὶ κράτεος, |₄₇ ἔλπεο μὴ δηρὸν κείνην πόλιν ἀτρεμίεσθαι, |₄₈ μηδ' εἰ νῦν κεῖται πολλῇ ἐν ἡσυχίῃ, |₄₉ εὖτ' ἂν τοῖσι κακοῖσι φίλ' ἀνδράσι ταῦτα γένηται, |₅₀ κέρδεα δημοσίῳ σὺν κακῷ ἐρχόμενα. |₅₁ ἐκ τῶν γὰρ στάσιές τε καὶ ἔμφυλοι φόνοι ἀνδρῶν |₅₂ μούναρχοί τε· πόλει μήποτε τῇδε ἅδοι.

‡Commentary in Nagy 1985:45–46 = §32.

§ |₁₀₈₁ Κύρνε, κύει πόλις ἥδε, δέδοικα δὲ μὴ τέκῃ ἄνδρα |₁₀₈₂ ὑβριστήν, χαλεπῆς ἡγεμόνα στάσιος· |₁₀₈₂ₐ ἀστοὶ μὲν γὰρ ἔασι σαόφρονες, ἡγεμόνες δὲ |₁₀₈₂ᵦ τετράφαται πολλὴν εἰς κακότητα πεσεῖν.'

cal degeneration from a higher status of humanity to a lower one. It is as if *hubris* had degraded the genes of the elites from nobility to baseness. Such degeneration corresponds to the successive downgrading of humanity from gold to silver to bronze to iron in the Hesiodic *Works and Days,* as we saw in Hour 12. In Text K, this metaphor of genetic debasement is applied to the moral degeneration of the elite. So those who used to be socially *agathoi,* 'noble', have now become morally *kakoi,* 'base'. And even if they are still socially noble, the elite of the city have nevertheless lost their moral claim to be *hēgemones,* 'leaders'.

13§46. Meanwhile, *hubris* brings sterility, as we saw in Hour 12 when we were reading selections from the Hesiodic *Works and Days*—and from the works of prose writers who specialize in botany. So if the city is to flourish like some fruit tree, it will have to be *pruned.* And now the city is pregnant, as we see in Text K (39), and it is about to produce a leader who will become the *euthuntēr,* or 'straightener', of the *hubris* (40). As we saw from the testimony of botanical experts, a traditional metaphor for *pruning* is *euthunein,* 'straightening'. So the future *euthuntēr,* or 'straightener', will *prune* the vegetal overgrowth that is *hubris.* Not only that: this *euthuntēr* or 'straightener' will give the city a sense of *direction, directness, directedness.* He will become the ultimate Director. He will be the exponent of *dikē,* which is seen metaphorically both as a straight line and as a flourishing *field* or *garden* or *orchard* or *grove* or *vineyard* or any other such place where vegetation is cultivated. But why is the speaker afraid of the coming of this Director? It is because he himself is a member of the elite. Although he rails against the elite for becoming moral degenerates, he is still one of them, and so he fears that the future Director will prune 'our' base *hubris.*

13§47. The situation has radically changed for the speaker in Text L as quoted from Theognis (1081–1082b). Here the future Director will be no exponent of *dikē.* Rather, he will be a *hubristēs,* a perpetrator of *hubris.* He will be a dictator, that is, a tyrant. So now the pregnancy of the city becomes a monstrous exercise in sterility. There will be no flourishing at all for this city, since the only thing that sterility can produce is sterility itself, as we will see all too clearly when we read the *Oedipus Tyrannus* of Sophocles in Hour 19.

Longing for a Hero:
A Retrospective

The Meaning of Pothos

14§1. The key words for this hour are the noun *pothos* and its variant *pothē*, which both mean 'longing' or 'yearning' or 'desire', and the verb derived from this noun, which means 'long for' or 'yearn for' or 'desire'. As we will see, such longing can be directed toward the sacred. In fact, as shown in Hour 5 Text M, the longing can be directed toward the gods, with whom worshippers feel a need to establish a physical closeness (Dio of Prusa 12.60–61). And now we will see that this same kind of longing can be directed toward the cult hero.

Testimony from the Hērōikos of Philostratus

14§2. The first relevant text that I will quote in this hour comes from a work composed in prose, known as the *Hērōikos* (sometimes translated as 'On Heroes'). The author is Philostratus, who is dated to the early third century CE. For historical background on the author and on his work, I cite the introduction by Jennifer Berenson Maclean and Aitken to their edition and translation of the *Hērōikos*.* To understand the application of this background to my book about heroes, I cite my Prologue to the text of Berenson Maclean and Aitken.† Here I simply give the bare essentials.

14§3. This work by Philostratus, the *Hērōikos*, is staged as a dialogue between a Phoenician traveler and the groundskeeper of a garden that is sacred to the cult hero Protesilaos, who is mentioned briefly in *Iliad* II—in a part of the epic that is commonly known as the Catalogue of Ships. We will turn to that men-

---

* Berenson Maclean and Aitken 2001. Available online at chs.harvard.edu.
† Nagy 2001a. Also available online at chs.harvard.edu.

tion in a few minutes. But first, I concentrate on the relevance of the work of Philostratus.

14§4. As we learn from the dialogue between the Phoenician and the groundskeeper, these two characters meet outside the garden of Protesilaos. The Phoenician has been sailing from Egypt and Phoenicia toward a destination that he cannot reach, since unfavorable winds have prevented him from sailing on. So he is delayed at the harbor of a city by the sea. This city, by the name of Elaious, which means 'the land of olive trees', is on the coastline of a narrow stretch of sea known as the Hellespont, which separates Europe from Asia. At Elaious, which is situated on the European side of the Hellespont—the side known as the Chersonesus—is the sacred garden of the cult hero Protesilaos, and there is a tumulus in that garden, overlooking the seascape of the Hellespont. This tumulus is the tomb that contains the body of Protesilaos, and, as we will see later, this tumulus containing the body of Protesilaos faces the tumulus containing the body of Achilles—a matching tomb that is situated on the Asiatic side of the Hellespont. The tumulus of Protesilaos, framed in the setting of a fertile garden, is a marvel to behold, and the visiting Phoenician is charmed by the sacred beauty of it all. He found out about this beautiful place after he had disembarked from his ship—and the first person he encountered was the groundskeeper of the garden of Protesilaos (6.5–6). They start talking, and we can track their dialogue from the start at *Hērōikos* 1.1 and following. From the start, they are talking about Protesilaos and his sacred garden. As they keep talking, they are approaching the garden, and the next thing you know, the groundskeeper suggests to the Phoenician that he should come along and enter the garden together with the groundskeeper, so that they may continue the dialogue there. The Phoenican happily accepts. The wording of the offer and the acceptance (*Hērōikos* 3.3) will be quoted later in the larger context of Text E.

14§5. The Phoenician, who is portrayed as a fluent speaker of Greek, is never given a name in the dialogue, nor is the groundskeeper, who is consistently addressed by the Phoenician simply as the *ampelourgos* or 'vineyard-worker'. From here on, I too will refer to this Greek groundskeeper simply as the Ampelourgos.

14§6. In an early phase of their dialogue (*Hērōikos* 6.3), the Phoenician tells the Ampelourgos about a dream he had after he arrived at the seaport of Elaious but before he disembarked: he dreamed that he was reading (*ana-gignōskein*) a part of the *Iliad* that he describes as 'the Catalogue of the Achaeans'—which is

what we know as the Catalogue of Ships, *Iliad* II 484–760. The dream is significant, since it is in this part of the *Iliad* that the story of Protesilaos is told, however briefly, by Homeric poetry. We will get to that story in a few minutes. In his
dream, as the Phoenician is reading (*ana-gignōskein*) the Homeric Catalogue,
he is visited by apparitions: the spirits of the Achaeans come to him, and he invites them all to join him on his ship (again *Hērōikos* 6.3). This dream of apparitions temporarily frightens the Phoenician as he wakes up and proceeds to dis-
embark from the ship.

14§7. It turns out that this dream is relevant to a story that is built into the
dialogue. The Phoenician is passionately interested in Greek heroes—not only
as epic heroes whose stories are told in Homeric poetry but also as cult heroes
who mystically communicate further stories to those who worship them in
places that contain their bodies. And the hero Protesilaos, as the Phoenician
will learn from the Ampelourgos, fits both these categories of hero: Protesilaos
is an epic hero, as we see him in the Homeric *Iliad,* but he is also a cult hero who
is worshipped in the setting of the garden that is sacred to him—a garden
marked by a tumulus that contains his body. As an epic hero who was the first
Achaean to die in the Trojan War, as we will soon see, he is a significant character in the story of that war; and, as a cult hero who communicates with his worshippers, as we will also soon see, he is an independent teller of the story, possessing psychic powers that enable him to know things that 'Homer' could never
know—because, well, Homer had never heard these things. So when the Phoenician expresses his passionate interest in heroes, he is interested not only in the
story about Protesilaos but also in the story by Protesilaos, that is, he is interested in the story as told by Protesilaos himself. And the one person who can
tell the Phoenician that second kind of story is the Ampelourgos, as a true worshipper of the cult hero.

14§8. In the text I am about to quote, the Ampelourgos comments on the
dream of the Phoenician, which I have already summarized (*Hērōikos* 6.3). This
dream must have been sent by the gods, says the Ampelourgos, and the Phoenician must have interpreted it correctly (6.7). According to this intepretation, the
Phoenician's dream about inviting all the Achaeans who had fought in the Trojan War to board his ship is linked with this man's direct engagement with the
story of Protesilaos. And his engagement with that story, just like his engagement with the Catalogue of Achaeans in the *Iliad,* shows a passionate interest in
heroes. I will now quote the wording that expresses the Phoenician's passionate

interest in learning the story as told by Protesilaos himself to the Ampelourgos. In this wording, I highlight the fact that the Phoenican uses the word *potheîn*, showing how he 'longs' or 'yearns' or 'desires' to hear the full story:

HOUR 14 TEXT A

|₆.₇ {Ampelourgos:} "My guest [*xenos*],* you have arrived here truly by the will of a god, and you are interpreting your dream in a sound way. So let us go ahead with the story [*logos*], so that you will not say that I am morally careless by distracting you from it." |₇.₁ {Phoenician:} "So now I see that you understand the things that I am longing [*potheîn*] to learn. For I do need to hear what this relationship [*sunousiā*] is that you have with Protesilaos, and what he is like when he comes to you, and whether he knows anything similar to what the poets know about the events at Troy—or whether he knows anything about them that the poets don't know. |₇.₂ When I say 'about the events at Troy' I mean: about the assembly of the [Achaean] army in Aulis—and about the heroes themselves. I want to know something about each one of them, one by one. Were they beautiful, as they are said to be in song? Were they manly and intelligent? I am talking like this because I'm wondering how he [= Protesilaos] could narrate the story about the war that happened at Troy when he never had a chance to fight in the war to the finish, having been the first of all the Greek forces to die at Troy, as they say, right at the beginning, as soon as he stepped off [his ship]."

Philostratus *Hērōikos* 6.7–7.2†

14§9. The momentary doubt that the Phoenician expresses here about the ability of the cult hero Protesilaos to know things that go well beyond what this hero had experienced in life is instantly corrected by the Ampelourgos, who

---

* Now that the Phoenician has entered the sacred garden of Protesilaos, he is no longer a stranger to the Ampelourgos, who has become his host. That is why, in contexts that come after *Hērōikos* 3.3, quoted in Text E, where the Phoenician first enters the garden, I translate *xenos* no longer as 'stranger' but as 'my guest'; here I follow the principle articulated by Berenson Maclean and Aitken 2001:17n19.

† |₆.₇ {Α.} Κατὰ θεὸν ἥκεις ἀληθῶς, ξένε, καὶ ὑγιῶς ἐξηγῇ τὴν ὄψιν. περαίνωμεν οὖν τὸν λόγον, μὴ καὶ θρύπτεσθαί με φῇς διάγοντά σε ἀπ' αὐτοῦ. |₇.₁ {Φ.} Ἃ ποθῶ μαθεῖν, ξυνίης δή γε· αὐτὴν γὰρ τὴν ξυνουσίαν, ἥτις ἐστί σοι πρὸς τὸν Πρωτεσίλεων, καὶ ὁποῖος ἥκει καὶ εἴ τι παραπλήσιον τοῖς ποιηταῖς ἢ διηγνωημένον αὐτοῖς περὶ τῶν Τρωικῶν οἶδεν, ἀκοῦσαι δέομαι. |₇.₂ Τρωικὰ δὲ λέγω τὰ τοιαῦτα· τήν τε ἐν Αὐλίδι ξυλλογὴν τοῦ στρατοῦ καὶ καθ' ἕνα τοὺς ἥρως εἰ καλοί τε, ὡς ᾄδονται, καὶ ἀνδρεῖοι καὶ σοφοὶ ἦσαν. τὸν γὰρ πόλεμον, ὃς περὶ τῇ Τροίᾳ ἐγένετο, πῶς ἂν διηγοῖτο μήτε διαπολεμήσας αὐτὸν ἀποθανών τε πρῶτος τοῦ Ἑλληνικοῦ παντὸς ἐν αὐτῇ, φασί, τῇ ἀποβάσει;

says that Protesilaos, once he was dead, acquired a consciousness that made connections not only with his own experiences in life but also with the experiences of all the other heroes of his time (*Hērōikos* 7.3). Then the Ampelourgos goes on to explain about this mystical kind of consciousness:

HOUR 14 TEXT B

|$_{7.4}$ At any rate, among those who critically examine Homer's poems, who will you say has read [*ana-gignōskein*] them in such a way as Protesilaos has read them and sees all the way through [*di-horân*] them? |$_{7.5}$ Besides, my guest [*xenos*], before Priam and Troy there wasn't even any epic recitation [*rhapsōidiā*], nor was there any singing about events that had not yet taken place. I say this because the art of composing poetry back then about oracular utterances [*manteîa*] and about, say, Hēraklēs, son of Alkmēnē, was only starting to take shape and had not yet reached a stage of maturity, and there was no Homer yet, so there was no Homer to do any singing. Some say that it was only when Troy was captured, while others say it was eight generations later, that he [= Homer] applied himself to practicing the art of poetry. |$_{7.6}$ But, in spite of all that, Protesilaos knows all the things of Homer and he sings of many Trojan events that took place after the hero's own lifetime, as also of many events that have to do with Greeks and Persians.

Philostratus *Hērōikos* 7.4–6*

14§10. So, metaphorically, the consciousness of the cult hero Protesilaos can *ana-gignōskein*, 'read', all the events of the heroic age, or even events that happened after that age. And, for this hero, the medium for telling stories does not depend on the medium of poetry, which supposedly had not even developed into a full-fledged form of art until later, that is, during the time of the Trojan War, or until even later. This medium of the cult hero can tell these stories because the cult hero is himself the medium.

14§11. The passionate interest of the Phoenician in the cult hero Protesilaos is

---

* |$_{7.4}$ τὰ γοῦν Ὁμήρου ποιήματα τίνα φήσεις οὕτως ἀνεγνωκέναι τῶν σφόδρα βασανιζόντων Ὅμηρον, ὡς ἀνέγνωκέ τε ὁ Πρωτεσίλεως καὶ διορᾷ αὐτά; |$_{7.5}$ καίτοι, ξένε, πρὸ Πριάμου καὶ Τροίας οὐδὲ ῥαψῳδία τις ἦν, οὐδὲ ᾔδετο τὰ μήπω πραχθέντα, ποιητικὴ μὲν γὰρ ἦν περί τε τὰ μαντεῖα περί τε τὸν Ἀλκμήνης Ἡρακλέα, καθισταμένη τε ἄρτι καὶ οὔπω ἡβάσκουσα, Ὅμηρος δὲ οὔπω ᾖδεν, ἀλλ' οἱ μὲν Τροίας ἁλούσης, οἱ δὲ ὀλίγαις, οἱ δ' ὀκτὼ γενεαῖς ὕστερον ἐπιθέσθαι αὐτὸν τῇ ποιήσει λέγουσιν. |$_{7.6}$ ἀλλ' ὅμως οἶδεν ὁ Πρωτεσίλεως τὰ Ὁμήρου πάντα, καὶ πολλὰ μὲν ᾄδει Τρωικὰ μεθ' ἑαυτὸν γενόμενα, πολλὰ δὲ Ἑλληνικά τε καὶ Μηδικά.

symmetrical with another passionate interest of his, and, once again, this interest is expressed by way of the same word *potheîn*: once again, the Phoenician 'longs' or 'yearns' or 'desires' to hear the full story. And, in this other case, the object of his passionate interest is Achilles himself. When the Ampelourgos starts to recount for the Phoenician the stories about Achilles, he says that he will at first confine himself to those stories that are linked to the Trojan War and to the environs of Troy in general (*Hērōikos* 22.1). In this same context, the Ampelourgos also says that only later will he tell those other stories about Achilles that are linked to the cult place called Leuke, the White Island, and in fact those other stories are duly narrated at a later point (54.2–57.17). For the moment, I too will confine myself to the stories that are linked to Troy. In the passage that I am about to quote, the Ampelourgos is about to tell the story of a contest that took place between Protesilaos and Achilles himself over a shield that both heroes claimed as a war prize (23.1, with reference to 13.3–14.1, 14.3–4, 23.24–25). I am about to quote the part of the dialogue where the Ampelourgos is beginning to tell the Phoenician the story about this shield—a story that involves both Achilles and Protesilaos. This story, as originally communicated by the conscious spirit of Protesilaos to the Ampelourgos, is eagerly awaited by the Phoenician:

HOUR 14 TEXT C

|₂₃.₁ {Ampelourgos:} "So now let us take up, my guest [*xenos*], the story of the shield—about which, as Protesilaos says, Homer and all the other poets knew nothing." |₂₃.₂ {Phoenician:} "I am longing [*potheîn*] for the story you are about to recount about it [= the shield], Ampelourgos! I think it will be a rare occasion when I will ever hear it again."

Philostratus *Hērōikos* 23.1–2*

14§12. So the Phoenician is longing to hear about both heroes, Achilles as well as Protesilaos. Both of these heroes are for him objects of longing and desire. And as we will now see, such longing translates into a desire to worship a cult hero.

---

* |₂₃.₁ {Ἀ.} Ἄγε δή, ὦ ξένε, τὴν ἀσπίδα ἤδη ἀναλάβωμεν, ἣν ὁ Πρωτεσίλεως Ὁμήρῳ τε ἠγνοῆσθαί φησι καὶ ποιηταῖς πᾶσιν. |₂₃.₂ {Φ.} Ποθοῦντι ἀποδίδως, ἀμπελουργέ, τὸν περὶ αὐτῆς λόγον, σπάνιον δὲ οἶμαι ἀκούσεσθαι.

Longing for Protesilaos in the Homeric Iliad

14§13. In the Homeric *Iliad,* as we read in the Catalogue of Ships, Protesilaos died an unseasonal death and is sorely missed by his community in his native Thessaly. The natives of this land 'long' for the hero, and this 'longing' is expressed by way of the verb *potheîn:*

HOUR 14 TEXT D

|₆₉₅ And then there were those that held Phylake and Pyrasos, with its flowery meadows, |₆₉₆ precinct of Demeter; and Iton, the mother of sheep; |₆₉₇ Antron upon the sea, and Pteleon that lies upon the grass lands. |₆₉₈ Of these men the Arēs-like Protesilaos had been leader |₆₉₉ while he was still alive, but now he was held down by the black earth that covered him. |₇₀₀ He had left a wife behind him in Phylake to tear both her cheeks in sorrow, |₇₀₁ and his house was only half completed [*hēmi-telēs*]. He was killed by a Dardanian warrior |₇₀₂ while he was leaping out from his ship [on Trojan soil], and he was the very first of the Achaeans to make the leap. |₇₀₃ Still, his people were not without a leader, though they longed [*potheîn*] for their leader. |₇₀₄ But now his people were organized [*kosmeîn*] by Podarkes, attendant [*ozos*] of Arēs. |₇₀₅ He [= Podarkes] was son of Iphiklos, rich in sheep, who was the son of Phylakos, |₇₀₆ and he [= Podarkes] was the blood brother of Protesilaos, the one with the great heart [*thūmos*]. |₇₀₇ But he [= Podarkes] was younger, Protesilaos being both older and more Arēs-like, |₇₀₈ yes, that hero [*hērōs*] Protesilaos, the Arēs-like. Still, his people were not |₇₀₉ without a leader, though they longed [*potheîn*] for him [= Protesilaos], noble [*esthlos*] man that he was.

Iliad II 695–709*

---

* |₆₉₅ Οἳ δ' εἶχον Φυλάκην καὶ Πύρασον ἀνθεμόεντα |₆₉₆ Δήμητρος τέμενος, Ἴτωνά τε μητέρα μήλων, |₆₉₇ ἀγχίαλόν τ' Ἀντρῶνα ἰδὲ Πτελεὸν λεχεποίην, |₆₉₈ τῶν αὖ Πρωτεσίλαος ἀρήιος ἡγεμόνευε |₆₉₉ ζωὸς ἐών· τότε δ' ἤδη ἔχεν κάτα γαῖα μέλαινα. |₇₀₀ τοῦ δὲ καὶ ἀμφιδρυφὴς ἄλοχος Φυλάκῃ ἐλέλειπτο |₇₀₁ καὶ δόμος ἡμιτελής· τὸν δ' ἔκτανε Δάρδανος ἀνὴρ |₇₀₂ νηὸς ἀποθρῴσκοντα πολὺ πρώτιστον Ἀχαιῶν. |₇₀₃ οὐδὲ μὲν οὐδ' οἳ ἄναρχοι ἔσαν, πόθεόν γε μὲν ἀρχόν· |₇₀₄ ἀλλά σφεας κόσμησε Ποδάρκης ὄζος Ἄρηος |₇₀₅ Ἰφίκλου υἱὸς πολυμήλου Φυλακίδαο |₇₀₆ αὐτοκασίγνητος μεγαθύμου Πρωτεσιλάου |₇₀₇ ὁπλότερος γενεῇ· ὁ δ' ἅμα πρότερος καὶ ἀρείων |₇₀₈ ἥρως Πρωτεσίλαος ἀρήιος· οὐδέ τι λαοὶ |₇₀₉ δεύονθ' ἡγεμόνος, πόθεόν γε μὲν ἐσθλὸν ἐόντα.

14§14. As we see from this passage, the people of Protesilaos are said to feel a *pothos* or 'longing' for him (*Iliad* II 703, 709). What we see here, I argue, is an indirect reference by Homeric poetry to the hero cult of Protesilaos.

The Sacred Eroticism of Heroic Beauty

14§15. Why is Protesilaos so dearly missed by his people? As we will now see from Philostratus, this longing is associated with the beauty of the cult hero, who is not only estheticized but also eroticized. And this eroticism, as we will also see, is felt to be sacred. Here is the way this sacred eroticism is introduced at a very early point in the *Hērōikos* of Philostratus:

HOUR 14 TEXT E

|₂.₆ {Phoenician:} "So, Ampelourgos, do you live a reflective way of life?" {Ampelourgos:} "Yes, together with the beautiful [*kalos*] Protesilaos." |₂.₇ {Phoenician:} "What do you have in common with Protesilaos, if you mean the man from Thessaly?" {Ampelourgos:} "I do mean that man, the husband of Laodameia. And I say it that way because he delights in hearing himself described this way." |₂.₈ {Phoenician:} "So, then, what is he doing here?" {Ampelourgos:} "He lives [*zēi*] here, and we work the land [*geōrgoumen*] together." |₂.₉ {Phoenician:} "Has he come back to life [*anabiōnai*], or what?" {Ampelourgos:} "He himself does not speak about his own experiences [*pathos* plural], stranger [*xenos*],* except, of course, that he died at Troy because of Helen, but then came to life [*anabiōnai*] in Phthia because he loved Laodameia." |₂.₁₀ {Phoenician:} "And yet it is said that he died after he came to life [*anabiōnai*] and persuaded his wife to follow him." |₂.₁₁ {Ampelourgos:} "He himself also says these things. But how he returned after this too, he does not tell me even though I've wanted to find out for a long time. He is hiding, he says, some secret [*aporrhēton*] of the Fates [*Moirai*]. And his fellow warriors also, who were there in Troy, still appear [*phainontai*] on the plain, holding the pose [*skhēma*] of fighting men and

---

* Before the Phoenician actually enters the sacred garden of Protesilaos, he is still a 'stranger' to the Ampelourgos; only after he enters, which happens at *Hērōikos* 3.3, quoted in Text E, does the Phoenician become a 'guest' to the Ampelourgos, who then becomes his host. That is why, in contexts that come after *Hērōikos* 3.3, where the Phoenician first enters the garden, I translate *xenos* no longer as 'stranger' but as 'my guest'; here I follow the principle articulated by Berenson Maclean and Aitken 2001:17n19.

shaking the crests of their helmets." |₃.₁ {Phoenician:} "By Athena, Am-
pelourgos, I don't believe [*pisteuein*] it, although I wish these things
were so. But if you are not attending to the plants, nor irrigating them,
tell me now about these things and all that you know about Protesilaos.
After all, you would please the heroes if I would go away believing [*pis-
teuein*]." |₃.₂ {Ampelourgos:} "Stranger [*xenos*],* the plants no longer
need watering at midday, since it is already late autumn and the season
[*hōrā*] itself waters them. So I have leisure to relate everything in detail.
Since these matters are sacred to the gods and so important, may they
not escape the notice of those humans who are cultivated [*kharientes*]!
It is also better for us to sit down in the beauty of this place." {Phoeni-
cian:} "Lead the way; I will follow even beyond the interior of Thrace."
|₃.₃ {Ampelourgos:} "Let us enter the vineyard, Phoenician.† For you
may even discover in it something to give cheer [*euphrosunē*] to you."
{Phoenician:} "Yes, let us enter. I think a sweet scent is being breathed
out [*ana-pnein*] from the plants." |₃.₄ {Ampelourgos:} "What are you
saying, 'sweet'? It is something godlike [*theion*]! The blossoms of the
uncultivated trees are fragrant, as are the fruits of those that are cultivated. If you ever come upon a cultivated plant with fragrant blossoms,
pluck rather the leaves, since the sweet scent comes from them." |₃.₅
{Phoenician:} "How diverse [*poikilē*] is the beauty [*hōrā*] of this place
you have here, and how lush have the clusters of grapes grown! How
well-arranged are all the trees, and how ambrosial [*ambrosiā*] is the
fragrance of the place! And, I think that the walkways [*dromoi*] that
you have left untilled are pleasing, but, Ampelourgos, I think you live
luxuriously [*truphân*] since you use so much uncultivated land." |₃.₆
{Ampelourgos:} "The walkways [*dromoi*] are sacred, my guest [*xenos*],
for the hero strips down and exercises [*gumnazetai*] there."

Philostratus Hērōikos 2.6–3.6‡

---

* On my translation 'stranger' here, see the next note.

† Here is where the Phoenician finally enters the sacred garden of Protesilaos. From now on, he is no longer a
stranger to the Ampelourgos, who has become his host.

‡ |₂.₆ {Φ.} Ἀλλ' ἦ φιλοσοφεῖς, ἀμπελουργέ; {Ἀ.} Καὶ σύν γε τῷ καλῷ Πρωτεσίλεῳ. |₂.₇ {Φ.} Σοὶ δὲ τί καὶ
τῷ Πρωτεσίλεῳ κοινόν, εἰ τὸν ἐκ Θετταλίας λέγεις; {Ἀ.} Ἐκεῖνον λέγω τὸν τῆς Λαοδαμείας, τουτὶ γὰρ
χαίρει ἀκούων. |₂.₈ {Φ.} Τί δὲ δὴ δεῦρο πράττει; {Ἀ.} Ζῇ καὶ γεωργοῦμεν. |₂.₉ {Φ.} Ἀναβεβιωκὼς ἢ τί; {Ἀ.}
Οὐδὲ αὐτὸς λέγει, ὦ ξένε, τὰ ἑαυτοῦ πάθη, πλήν γε δὴ ὅτι ἀποθάνοι μὲν δι' Ἑλένην ἐν Τροίᾳ, ἀναβιώη
δὲ ἐν Φθίᾳ Λαοδαμείας ἐρῶν. |₂.₁₀ {Φ.} Καὶ μὴν ἀποθανεῖν γε μετὰ τὸ ἀναβιῶναι λέγεται, ἀναπεῖσαί τε
τὴν γυναῖκα ἐπισπέσθαι οἱ. |₂.₁₁ {Ἀ.} Λέγει καὶ αὐτὸς ταῦτα, ἀλλ' ὅπως καὶ μετὰ τοῦτο ἀνῆλθε πάλαι μοι
βουλομένῳ μαθεῖν οὐ λέγει, Μοιρῶν τι ἀπόρρητον, ὥς φησι, κρύπτων. καὶ οἱ συστρατιῶται δὲ αὐτοῦ οἱ

14§16. There are many details here that will be relevant to the discussions ahead, and I offer a brief inventory that can be used for the analysis that follows:

- The cult hero Protesilaos is beautiful (2.6).
- Phthia in Thessaly is where he was born, but he is buried in Elaious, the city overlooking the Hellespont (2.7).
- The cult hero helps the worshipper *geōrgein,* 'work the land', and that land is sacred to him (2.8). Working the land or *geōrgiā,* 'agriculture', was considered a sacred activity, as we saw in Hour 12§36.* We may compare the title of Virgil's classic poem on working the land, the *Georgics.*
- Protesilaos experienced a resurrection after death (2.9). Such myths about coming back to life are central to the mysteries of hero cult.
- More than that, Protesilaos experienced two resurrections, though the worshipper has not been initiated into the mysteries of the second of the two experiences of the cult hero (2.10). There can be gradations of initiation into the mysteries. It is implied here that the degree of the initiation of the Ampelourgos is not as high as that of other worshippers.†
- The cult hero manifests himself in epiphanies, signaled by the word *phainesthai,* 'appear' (2.11). I offered a working definition of epiphany in Hour 5§38. When heroes from the heroic past *appear* in the world of the present, what they are doing is *making epiphanies.* As we can see from the behavior of Protesilaos, an epiphany is like a temporary resurrection.

ἐν τῇδε τῇ Τροίᾳ ἔτι ἐν τῷ πεδίῳ φαίνονται μάχιμοι τὸ σχῆμα καὶ σείοντες τοὺς λόφους. |₃,₁ {Φ.} Ἀπιστῶ, νὴ τὴν Ἀθηνᾶν, ἀμπελουργέ, καίτοι οὕτω βουλόμενος ταῦτα ἔχειν. εἰ δὲ μὴ πρὸς τοῖς φυτοῖς εἶ, μηδὲ ὀχετηγεῖς, ἤδη διελθέ μοι ταῦτά τε καὶ ὅσα τοῦ Πρωτεσίλεω γιγνώσκεις· καὶ γὰρ ἂν χαρίζοιο τοῖς ἥρωσιν, εἰ πιστεύων ἀπέλθοιμι. |₃,₂ {Α.} Οὐκέτ᾽, ὦ ξένε, κατὰ μεσημβρίαν τὰ φυτὰ πίνει, μετόπωρον γὰρ ἤδη καὶ ἄρδει αὐτὰ ἡ ὥρα· σχολὴ οὖν μοι διελθεῖν πάντα. μηδὲ γὰρ λανθάνοι τοὺς χαρίεντας τῶν ἀνθρώπων θεῖα οὕτω καὶ μεγάλα ὄντα. βέλτιον δὲ καὶ ἐν καλῷ τοῦ χωρίου ἵζῆσαι. {Φ.} Ἡγοῦ δή, ὡς ἑψομένου καὶ ὑπὲρ τὰ μέσα τῆς Θρᾴκης. |₃,₃ {Α.} Παρέλθωμεν ἐς τὸν ἀμπελῶνα, ὦ Φοῖνιξ, καὶ γὰρ ἂν καὶ εὐφροσύνης τι ἐν αὐτῷ εὕροις. {Φ.} Παρέλθωμεν, ἡδὺ γάρ που ἀναπνεῖ τῶν φυτῶν. |₃,₄ {Α.} Τί λέγεις ἡδύ; θεῖον· τῶν μὲν γὰρ ἀγρίων δένδρων αἱ ἄνθαι εὔοσμοι, τῶν δὲ ἡμέρων οἱ καρποί. εἰ δὲ ἐντύχοις ποτὲ φυτῷ ἡμέρῳ παρὰ τὴν ἄνθην εὐώδει, δρέπου τῶν φύλλων μᾶλλον, ἐκείνων γὰρ τὸ ὀδωδέναι. |₃,₅ {Φ.} Ὡς ποικίλη σοι ἡ ὥρα τοῦ χωρίου, καὶ ὡς ἐκδεδώκασιν ἱλαροὶ οἱ βότρυς, τὰ δένδρα τε ὡς διάκειται πάντα καὶ ὡς ἀμβροσία ἡ ὀσμὴ τοῦ χωρίου. τοὺς δρόμους δέ, οὓς ἀνῆκας, χαρίεντας μὲν ἡγοῦμαι, τρυφᾶν δέ μοι δοκεῖς, ἀμπελουργέ, τοσαύτῃ γῇ ἀργῷ χρώμενος. |₃,₆ {Α.} Ἱεροί, ξένε, οἱ δρόμοι, γυμνάζεται γὰρ ἐν αὐτοῖς ὁ ἥρως.

* See also Bershadsky 2011:23.

† For an attempt at reconstructing the myths about a double resurrection of Protesilaos, see Pelliccia 2010–2011:175–199, especially pp. 178–180 on a relevant passage in Aelius Aristides 3.365 and on the Scholia for that passage.

- The garden of the cult hero is a model of seasonality, the word for which here is *hōrā* (3.2).
- The breeze carrying the aroma of flowering plants is the breath of the hero (3.3).* I note the metonymy here. I use the term *metonymy* here in line with my working definition in Hour 4§32: metonymy is an expression of meaning by way of *connecting* something to something else that is next to that something or at least near to it, thereby establishing *contact*.
- The beauty of the garden in general and of the vineyard in particular is pictured as *hōrā*, 'seasonality'. We may say that the *hōrā* is the beauty. And such beauty is *poikilē*, 'varied' (3.5): that is, the beauty of nature is never the same, always changing from one delightful vision to the next.† So *hōrā*, 'seasonality', is a kind of dynamic perfection.

14§17. I focus on the use of the word *hōrā* in this text (3.2, 3.5). It is the 'perfect time' for the epiphany of Protesilaos (3.5). The beauty of the garden is linked to the presence of the cult hero, who delights in the natural beauty by manifesting himself in epiphanies, showing off his own beauty as an exercising athlete (3.6). I return to my working definition of this word *hōrā*: 'season, seasonality, the right time, the perfect time'. As we saw in Hour 1§§26–29, *hōrā* is a basic concept related to the concept of the goddess *Hērā*, the immortal exponent of seasonality, and to the concept of the human *hērōs*, 'hero' (plural *hērōes*), the mortal exponent of seasonality.

The Beauty of Seasonality in a Modern Greek Poem

14§18. In Modern Greek, the word *oréos* / *oréa* means 'beautiful', directly descended from the ancient Greek *hōraîos* / *hōraíā*, an adjective derived from the noun *hōrā*. This inherited link in meaning between the beauty and the seasonality of *hōrā* is captured in a poem of Giorgos Seferis, where the sensuous experience of marveling at natural beauty is expressed by way of the Modern Greek adverb *oréa*, corresponding to the neuter plural of the ancient Greek adjective, *hōraîa* (ὡραῖα):

---

*On the breath of the hero as a breeze carrying the aroma of the blossoms that flourish in this garden, see also Bershadsky 2011:16.

† On the sense of *poikilos*, 'varied', as 'never the same', see *HC* 306–307 = II§453, with special reference to Plato *Republic* 8.568d.

Hour 14 Text Fa

Στὸ περιγιάλι τὸ κρυφὸ| κι' ἄσπρο σὰν περιστέρι| διψάσαμε τὸ
μεσημέρι·μὰ τὸ νερὸ γλυφό.||Πάνω στὴν ἄμμο τὴν ξανθὴ| γράψαμε τ'
ὄνομά της·| ὡραῖα που φύσηξεν ὁ μπάτης| καὶ σβήστηκε ἡ γραφή.||Μὲ
τί καρδιά, μὲ τί πνοή,| τί πόθους καὶ τί πάθος,| πήραμε τὴ ζωή μας·
λάθος!| κι' ἀλλάξαμε ζωή.*

Giorgos Seferis, ´Arnisi (Ἄρνηση, from the collection Στροφή, 1931)

This poem *Arnisi,* which means 'denial', was made famous in Modern Greek
popular culture after it was set to music by Mikis Theodorakis. His song, known
by the same name, *Arnisi,* was composed in Paris in 1961; it is part of a set of
songs known as *Epiphánia* (Ἐπιφάνεια), and it has remained enormously popular up to the present moment.†

Here is my translation:

Hour 14 Text Fb

At the shoreline the secret one | and white like a dove | we thirsted at
noon. | But the water was salty. || On the sand, golden-blond, | we
wrote down her name. | Beautiful, the way the sea breeze exhaled, |
and the writing was wiped out. || With what heart, with what breath, |
what longings and what passion, | we seized our life—no, wrong! |
—and we changed life.

Here is my translation again, but this time I have inserted some of the original
Modern Greek words, along with their ancient Greek counterparts (each ancient Greek word is transliterated, and preceded by the sign "<" to indicate that
the corresponding Modern Greek word is actually descended from the ancient
counterpart):

---

* There is an accurate transliteration (via International Phonetic Alphabet) for the Modern Greek pronuncia-
tion of the original text, which had been written down in polytonic format by Seferis, at a site that also contains
a wealth of further information about the poem: http://www.webtopos.gr/eng/literature/writers/s/seferis/sef-
eris_denial.htm. The creator of the site is Katerina Sarri (katerina sarri webtopos: www.webtopos.gr—2000,
latest additions in 2010).

† There have been many celebrated recordings of this song, and references can be found at the site of Katerina
Sarri (see the previous note).

Hour 14 Text Fc

At the shoreline the secret one | and white like a dove | we thirsted at
noon. | But the water was salty. || On the sand, golden-blond, | we
wrote down her name. | Beautiful [ὡραῖα < hōraîa], the way the sea
breeze exhaled, | and the writing was wiped out. || With what heart,
with what breath [πνοή < pnoē], | what longings [πόθους < pothous]
and what passion [πάθος < pathos], | we seized our life [ζωή < zōē]
—no, wrong [λάθος]! | and we changed life [ζωή < zōē].*

14§19. The sense of longing for something ineffable in a natural setting is
expressed here by way of the Modern Greek word *pothos,* direct descendant of
the ancient Greek *pothos,* which is the key word for this hour. In the poem of
Seferis, the context is an exclamation: τί πόθους καὶ τί πάθος, 'what longings
[*pothous*] and what passion [*pathos*]!' The Modern Greek πόθους here is a direct descendent of the ancient Greek accusative plural *pothous,* corresponding
to the nominative plural *pothoi,* 'longings'.

14§20. The longing conveyed by 'we thirsted at noon' (διψάσαμε τὸ
μεσημέρι) in stanza 1 is picked up by 'Beautiful [ὡραῖα < hōraîa], the way the
sea breeze exhaled' (ὡραῖα που φύσηξεν ὁ μπάτης) in stanza 2 and by 'we
seized our life—no, wrong!' (πήραμε τὴ ζωή μας· λάθος!) in stanza 3. Then
the longing is intensified: 'With what heart, with what breath [πνοή < pnoē], |
what longings [πόθους < pothous] and what passion [πάθος < pathos]' (Μὲ τί
καρδιά, μὲ τί πνοή, | τί πόθους καὶ τί πάθος).

The Beauty of the Hero in Death

14§21. With this Modern Greek point of comparison in place, I return to Text E,
Philostratus *Hērōikos* 2.6–3.6, where the sensuous and charismatic beauty of the
cult hero is made explicit. Such an idea of beauty is generated, as we saw in that
text, by the idea of the *hōrā,* 'seasonality', of the hero. But the hero becomes seasonal only in death. It is death that makes the hero become a cult hero. Before

---

* The last words of the poem, 'and we changed life', evoke the last words of a poem by Rainer Maria Rilke, *Archaic Torso of Apollo (Archaïscher Torso Apollos):* "Du mußt dein Leben ändern," "You must change your life."
The poem appeared in a collection entitled *Der neuen Gedichte anderer Teil,* published in Leipzig in 1918. The
wording of the dedication in this book reads: *À mon grand ami Auguste Rodin.* This publication is available by
way of the Project Gutenberg: http://www.gutenberg.org/files/33864/33864–8.txt. This ebook was produced by
Marc D'Hooghe at: http://www.freeliterature.org.

death, as we have seen ever since Hour 1, the hero is unseasonal. Only after death can the hero be truly seasonal—and eligible for the description *olbios* in the sense of 'blessed'. That is how the cult hero's worshippers can become *olbioi* in the sense of 'prosperous' by virtue of being connected to the hero's local earth. And that is also how the worshippers can themselves become 'blessed' through the blessings of such prosperity. We saw that sense already in *Odyssey* xi 137, as first quoted in Hour 11 Text J, when we first considered the stylized *sēma* of Odysseus.

14§22. A perfect example of heroic beauty in death is Achilles himself. As we saw in Hour 5§108, Achilles in death is pictured as *le beau mort*, 'the beautiful corpse', by virtue of dying *la belle mort*, 'the beautiful death'. And such a beautiful death, as we can now also see, is basic to the idea of a cult hero.

A Beautiful Setting for the Beautiful Cult Hero

14§23. In the Homeric *Iliad*, the picturing of Achilles as a beautiful corpse highlights the unseasonality of the hero at the moment of his death, as when the goddess Thetis and her fellow Nereids lament the future death of her beloved son in war: in this context, as we have seen in *Iliad* XVIII 54–60, quoted in Hour 4 Text G, the hero Achilles is compared to a beautiful seedling that dies prematurely while it is still in full bloom. This idea of a premature death for a beautiful plant as a model for the premature death of a beautiful hero can be re-enacted in hero cult, as we can see from a most suggestive passage that I am about to quote from the *Hērōikos* of Philostratus. In this passage, I highlight the word that refers to the beautiful natural setting where the cult hero Protesilaos is buried. That word is *kolōnos*:

HOUR 14 TEXT G

|9.1 Listen to such stories now, my guest [*xenos*]. Protesilaos lies buried not at Troy but here on the Chersonesus. This large tumulus [*kolōnos*] over here on the left no doubt contains him. The nymphs generated [*phuein*] these elms [that you see here]* around the tumulus [*kolōnos*], and they wrote, so to speak, the following decree concerning these trees: |9.2 "Those branches that turn toward Ilion [= Troy] will blos-

---

* We may compare *Iliad* VI 419–420, quoted in Hour 3 Text D: there we see that the *sēma*, 'tomb', of Eëtion, father of Andromache, was encircled by elm trees that were generated *(phuteuein)* by forest nymphs.

som early and will then immediately shed their leaves and perish before their season [hōrā]—for this was also the life experience [pathos]
of Protesilaos—but a tree on its other side will live and prosper." |₉.₃ All
the trees that do not stand around the tomb [sēma], such as these trees
[that you see right over here] in the grove, have strength in all their
branches and flourish according to their particular nature.*

Philostratus Hērōikos 9.1–3†

14§24. The word *kolōnos*, which refers two times here in the *Hērōikos* (9.1) to
the tomb of Protesilaos and which I translate as 'tumulus', is a prominent elevation in a local landscape. As we can see, such a *kolōnos* is a landmark that can be
imagined as the *sēma*, 'tomb', of the cult hero. And we see this word *sēma* also
used here in the same text I just quoted (9.3). That said, I concentrate on one
detail about the vegetation surrounding this *kolōnos* or *sēma* of Protesilaos. It is
said that the elm trees planted around this tomb wilt on one side and flourish
on their other side. So the vegetation around the tomb re-enacts here the heroic
oscillation of unseasonality and seasonality as experienced by the hero Protesilaos himself: he was unseasonal in life but now he is seasonal in death. So the
beautiful setting of the *kolōnos*, 'tumulus', of Protesilaos re-enacts the beautiful
death of the hero.

14§25. This *kolōnos* of Protesilaos, situated on the European coast of the Hellespont, is matched by the *kolōnos* of Achilles himself, which is symmetrically
situated on the facing Asiatic coast:

HOUR 14 TEXT H

|₅₁.₁₂ This tumulus [*kolōnos*], my guest [*xenos*], which you see standing at
the brow of the promontory [*aktē*], was heaped up [*ageirein*, 'pile stones
together'] by the Achaeans who came together at the time when he [=
Achilles] was mixed together with Patroklos for their joint burial, having provided for himself [= Achilles] and for that one [= Patroklos]

---

*Translation adapted from Berenson Maclean and Aitken 2001:29–31.

† |₉.₁ Περὶ τῶν τοιούτων ἄκουε, ξένε. κεῖται μὲν οὐκ ἐν Τροίᾳ ὁ Πρωτεσίλεως, ἀλλ᾽ ἐν Χερρονήσῳ
ταύτῃ, κολωνὸς δὲ αὐτὸν ἐπέχει μέγας οὑτοσὶ δήπου ὁ ἐν ἀριστερᾷ, πτελέας δὲ ταύτας αἱ νύμφαι περὶ
τῷ κολωνῷ ἐφύτευσαν καὶ τοιόνδε ἐπὶ τοῖς δένδρεσι τούτοις ἔγραψάν που αὗται νόμον· |₉.₂ τοὺς πρὸς
τὸ Ἴλιον τετραμμένους τῶν ὄζων ἀνθεῖν μὲν πρωί, φυλλορροεῖν δὲ αὐτίκα καὶ προαπόλλυσθαι τῆς
ὥρας—τοῦτο δὴ τὸ τοῦ Πρωτεσίλεω πάθος—τῷ δὲ ἑτέρῳ μέρει ζῆν τὰ δένδρα καὶ εὖ πράττειν. |₉.₃ καὶ
ὁπόσα δὲ τῶν δένδρων μὴ περὶ τὸ σῆμα ἔστηκεν, ὥσπερ καὶ ταυτὶ τὰ ἐν κήπῳ, πᾶσιν ἔρρωται τοῖς ὄζοις
καὶ θαρσεῖ τὸ ἴδιον.

the most beautiful of funeral rites. And this is the origin of the custom of singing his name in praise when people celebrate the bonds of love between friends. |₅₁.₁₃ Of all mortals who ever existed, he [= Achilles] was buried in the most spectacular way, what with all the gifts that Greece [= Hellas] bestowed upon him. *No longer could they [= the Achaeans] consider it a beautiful thing to grow their hair long, once Achilles was gone.* Whatever gold or other possession each of them had brought to Troy or had taken away from the division of spoils [= spoils taken at Troy] was now collected and heaped up on top of the funeral pyre, right then and there. The same thing happened also later when Neoptolemos came to Troy. He [= Achilles] received another round of glorious gifts from his son and from the Achaeans who were trying to show their gratitude [*kharis*] to him. Even as they were getting ready to sail away from Troy, *they would keep throwing themselves on top of the place of burial and believe that they were embracing Achilles.**

Philostratus *Hērōikos* 51.12–13†

14§26. I must note that this tomb of Achilles, which is called *kolōnos*, 'tumulus', here (51.12; also at 53.10, 11), is also called his *sēma* 'tomb' (53.11; also 51.2, 52.3). We see the same pattern in the case of Protesilaos: this hero's *kolōnos*, 'tumulus', as it is called in the *Hērōikos* (9.1, twice), is also called his *sēma*, 'tomb' (9.3). That said, I return to the text I have just quoted concerning the *kolōnos*, 'tumulus', of Achilles, and I highlight the wording that describes two details that I propose to analyze:

14§26A. Commenting on the post-heroic era that follows the death of Achilles, the Ampelourgos says: 'no longer could they [= the Achaeans] consider it a beautiful thing to grow their hair long, once Achilles was gone' (Philostratus *Hērōikos* 51.13).‡ The wording connotes an aetiology, as if the death of Achilles

---

* Translation adapted from Berenson Maclean and Aitken 2001:153.

† |₅₁.₁₂ τὸν μὲν δὴ κολωνὸν τοῦτον, ξένε, ὃν ἐπὶ τοῦ μετώπου τῆς ἀκτῆς ὁρᾷς ἀνεστηκότα, ἤγειραν οἱ Ἀχαιοὶ ξυνελθόντες, ὅτε τῷ Πατρόκλῳ ξυνεμίχθη ἐς τὸν τάφον, κάλλιστον ἐντάφιον ἑαυτῷ τε κἀκείνῳ διδούς, ὅθεν ᾄδουσιν αὐτὸν οἱ τὰ φιλικὰ ἐπαινοῦντες. |₅₁.₁₃ ἐτάφη δὲ ἐκδηλότατα ἀνθρώπων πᾶσιν οἷς ἐπήνεγκεν αὐτῷ ἡ Ἑλλὰς οὐδὲ κομᾶν ἔτι μετὰ τὸν Ἀχιλλέα καλὸν ἡγούμενοι χρυσόν τε καὶ ὅ τι ἕκαστος εἶχεν ἢ ἀπάγων ἐς Τροίαν ἢ ἐκ δασμοῦ λαβών, νήσαντες ἐς τὴν πυρὰν ἀθρόα παραχρῆμά τε καὶ ὅτε ὁ Νεοπτόλεμος ἐς Τροίαν ἦλθε, λαμπρῶν γὰρ δὴ ἔτυχε πάλιν παρά τε τοῦ παιδὸς παρά τε τῶν Ἀχαιῶν ἀντιχαρίζεσθαι αὐτῷ πειρωμένων, οἵ γε καὶ τὸν ἀπὸ τῆς Τροίας ποιούμενοι πλοῦν περιέπιπτον τῷ τάφῳ καὶ τὸν Ἀχιλλέα ᾤοντο περιβάλλειν.

‡ οὐδὲ κομᾶν ἔτι μετὰ τὸν Ἀχιλλέα καλὸν ἡγούμενοι.

were the single reason that explains why adult men of the post-heroic age no longer wore their hair long—except for such notable counterexamples as the Spartans. As we saw in Hour 13§19 when we viewed line drawings of the statues of the Argive youths Kleobis and Biton, the wearing of long hair was a distinctive sign of pre-adult status. Even in the *Iliad*, the long hair of Achilles ostentatiously signals his pre-adult status, as we can see from the scene describing the funeral of Patroklos, where Achilles cuts off his long blond hair as he stands at the funeral pyre of his best friend (XXIII 141). It is at this same place where the tumulus to be shared by Patroklos and Achilles will be built when the time comes for the funeral of Achilles himself (XXIII 126). In this Homeric scene, as Achilles is standing on the heights of the promontory that will become the setting for the tumulus that houses his own body, he wistfully looks out over the seas of the outer Hellespont, fixing his gaze toward the far west, in the direction of his native land of Thessaly, and longing for the river Sperkheios that flows through that distant land: it was to the waters of that river, which he will never live to see again, that he had hoped to sacrifice his long hair after he came of age and was ready to cut it (XXIII 142–153). But now Achilles cuts off his long hair prematurely and unseasonally as he stands there at the Asiatic promontory that will become the setting for the tumulus that houses his body (XXIII 142).* And now the Achaean comrades of Achilles follow his example and likewise cut off their hair (XXIII 135–136). So also in the wording that I have just highlighted from the *Hērōikos* of Philostratus, we see a reference to this ritual of coming of age: now that Achilles is dead, adult males of the future will be wearing their hair short, no longer long. It is as if all the 'sons of the Achaeans' were now ready to shift from pre-adult to adult status—now that Achilles is dead and buried. So now the *huies Akhaiōn*, 'sons of the Achaeans', as the Achaean warriors are regularly called in the *Iliad* (I 162 and so on), have reached a post-heroic maturity that inaugurates a post-heroic age.

14§26B. I have also highlighted in the text I quoted a minute ago from the *Hērōikos* of Philostratus a detail about the reaction of the Achaeans to the death of Achilles: how they embraced the tumulus of Achilles, as if they were embracing the hero himself. The wording of this reaction, as we will now see, provides a telling commentary on an aspect of hero cult that will seem at first to be quite alien to our modern sensibilities.

---

* HPC 166 = II§85.

Paroxysms of Sentimentality in Worshipping Cult Heroes

14§27. The Achaeans, as we saw in Philostratus *Hērōikos* 51.12–13, quoted in Text H, heap up a *kolōnos*, 'tumulus', in order to honor their greatest hero, and then they perform a ritual gesture that centers on this tumulus: 'they would keep throwing themselves on top of the place of burial and believe that they were embracing Achilles'.* We see here a gesture of *ritual metonymy*: touching the tumulus of the cult hero is the next best thing to touching the hero himself. Once again I use here the term *metonymy* in line with the working definition I offered in Hour 4§32: metonymy is an expression of meaning by way of *connecting* something to something else that is next to that something or at least near to it, thereby establishing *contact*. In this case, the contact is expressed by way of an intensely sentimental gesture: the Achaeans embrace the tumulus of Achilles as if to embrace the hero himself. This way, the Achaeans get in touch with Achilles.

14§28. Similarly in the case of the cult hero Protesilaos, his worshippers desire physical contact with him when he appears to them in an epiphany. The Ampelourgos describes such a sensual epiphany:

HOUR 14 TEXT I

|[11.1] {Phoenician:} "So, the passionate love [*erōs*] that he used to have in loving [*erân*] Laodameia—how is it going for him these days?" {Ampelourgos:} "Oh, he is still very much loving [*erân*] her, and he is still being loved [*erâsthai*] right back by her, and they relate to each other just like a couple that has just come out, all hot [*thermoi*], from a honeymoon chamber." |[11.2] {Phoenician:} "And do you embrace him when he comes to you [in the garden]—or does he elude you by going up in a puff of smoke, the same way he eludes the poets?"† {Ampelourgos:} "Actually, he takes pleasure [*khairein*] when I embrace him and lets me kiss [*philein*] him and put my arm around his neck." |[11.3] {Phoenician:} "Does he come to you often or just once in a while?" {Ampelourgos:} "Oh, I guess it's about four or five times a month that I get to have my share of him, whenever he feels like planting one of the plants you see here, or when he harvests one of them, or when he does some cuttings of blossoms [*anthos* plural]. When somebody is a lover of garlands

---

* περιέπιπτον τῷ τάφῳ καὶ τὸν Ἀχιλλέα ᾤοντο περιβάλλειν.

† Some have tried to emend the text, offering the interpretation: 'the way poets say he does' as an alternative to the interpretation given here, 'the same way he eludes the poets'. See Pelliccia 2010–2011:182:97.

[*philo-stephanos*], he will have sweeter-smelling blossoms to show for it [in the garlands he wears] whenever he [= Protesilaos] is all over those blossoms [*anthos* plural]." |₁₁.₄ {Phoenician:} "You're talking about a very convivial hero [*hērōs*]: he must be quite the bridegroom!"

Philostratus *Hērōikos* 11.1–4*

14§29. So, every time Protesilaos makes contact with his worshipper by appearing in an epiphany, it is as if this hero had just finished having sex on his wedding night with his ever-loving bride, Laodameia. With his generative power, Protesilaos makes the garden flourish when he comes to visit, and he can animate the blossoms that are used to plait the garlands worn by brides and grooms when they get married: the hero's presence is 'all over' these blossoms—that is, he is surrounding them, he is 'all around them' *(peri auta)*. Also, the overriding presence of Protesilaos in the blossoms of flowers is signaled by the aroma of these blossoms, which is metonymically the breath of the hero himself:

HOUR 14 TEXT J

|₁₀.₁ {Phoenician:} "Why don't you describe [*dia-graphein*] him to me and share what he looks like." |₁₀.₂ {Ampelourgos:} "With pleasure [*khairein*], my guest, I swear by Athena. He was about twenty years old at most when he sailed to Troy. He teems in his life force [*bruein*] with the luxuriant [*habron*] fuzz on his cheeks, *and he smells sweeter than myrtles in autumn.*† Radiant eyebrows frame the look of his eyes, since whatever is charming [*epi-khari*] is near and dear [*philon*] to him."

Philostratus *Hērōikos* 10.1–2‡

---

* |₁₁.₁ {Φ.} Ὁ δὲ δὴ ἔρως, ὃν τῆς Λαοδαμείας ἦρα, πῶς ἔχει αὐτῷ νῦν; {Ἀ.} Ἐρᾷ, ξένε, καὶ ἐρᾶται καὶ διάκεινται πρὸς ἀλλήλους ὥσπερ οἱ θερμοὶ τῶν νυμφίων. |₁₁.₂ {Φ.} Περιβάλλεις δὲ ἥκοντα ἢ διαφεύγει σε καπνοῦ δίκην, ὥσπερ τοὺς ποιητάς; {Ἀ.} Χαίρει περιβάλλοντι καὶ ξυγχωρεῖ φιλεῖν τε αὐτὸν καὶ τῆς δέρης ἐμφορεῖσθαί γε. |₁₁.₃ {Φ.} Θαμίζει δὲ ἢ διὰ πολλοῦ ἥκει; {Ἀ.} Τετράκις τοῦ μηνὸς ἢ πεντάκις οἶμαι αὐτοῦ μετέχειν, ὁπότ᾽ ἢ φυτεῦσαί ποτε τουτωνὶ τῶν φυτῶν τι βούλοιτο ἢ τρυγῆσαι ἢ ἄνθη κεῖραι. φιλοστέφανος γάρ τις καὶ ἡδίω ἀποφαίνων τὰ ἄνθη, ὁπότε περὶ αὐτὰ εἴη. |₁₁.₄ {Φ.} Ἱλαρόν γε τὸν ἥρω λέγεις καὶ ἀτεχνῶς νυμφίον.

† This detail is linked with an earlier detail, in *Hērōikos* 3.3 as quoted in Text E and as analyzed in §16, where a breeze carrying the aroma of flowering plants is said to be the breath of the hero; see also Bershadsky 2011:16. On the symbolism of myrtles, see *HPC* 294, 295–297 = II§§419–420, 424–428.

‡ |₁₀.₁ {Φ.} Ἦ καὶ διαγράψεις μοι αὐτὸν καὶ κοινωνήσεις τοῦ εἴδους; |₁₀.₂ {Ἀ.} χαίρων γε, νὴ τὴν Ἀθηνᾶν, ὦ ξένε. γέγονε μὲν γὰρ ἀμφὶ τὰ εἴκοσί που μάλιστα ἔτη τηλικόσδε ἐλάσας ἐς Τροίαν, ἁβρῷ δ᾽ ἰούλῳ βρύει καὶ ἀπόζει αὐτοῦ ἥδιον ἢ τοῦ μετοπώρου τῶν μύρτων. φαιδρὰν δὲ ὀφρὺν περὶ τὸ ὄμμα βέβληται, τὸ γὰρ ἐπίχαρι αὐτῷ φίλον.

14§30. Such intense sentimentality gives an erotic as well as an esthetic touch to the practice of worshipping heroes. At first, this erotic touch may seem quite alien to us, but a second look may make things less unfamiliar. The sacral eroticism of Protesilaos reminds me of a parallel in modern popular culture. I am thinking here of the "Krishna phase" in the musical career of George Harrison, culminating in a song he sang to the Indic hero-god Krishna: the title of the song, recorded in 1970, is "My Sweet Lord," and the wording of the song displays the same kind of sentimentality that we just saw in the texts I quoted from the *Hērōikos* of Philostratus. In particular, the singer of "My Sweet Lord" declares that he is longing to see an epiphany of Krishna, so that he may be physically united with the hero-god: "I really want to see you, I really want to be with you": http://www.youtube.com/watch?v=wynYMJwEPH8&feature=related. The melody of Harrison's song was faintly reminiscent of an earlier song, sung by female singers about a male object of desire. Originally recorded in 1963 by the Chiffons, this song is called "He's So Fine": http://www.youtube.com/watch?v=qo-AE0SDCpQ. This is not the time or the place to dwell on the litigation that enveloped George Harrison over perceived similarities between the older and newer songs, but one thing is for sure, to my mind: there is no trace of sacral eroticism in the song of the Chiffons.

Back to the Tumulus of Achilles

14§31. Moving southeast from the *kolōnos*, 'tumulus', of Protesilaos, situated on the European side of the Hellespont, I return to the *kolōnos* of Achilles, situated on the other side, in Asia Minor. In Text H, Philostratus *Hērōikos* 51.12–13, we have already read a description of this tumulus of Achilles. Now we will read a passage that follows that description. In this next passage from the *Hērōikos*, we will learn of a seasonally recurring custom observed by Thessalians who sailed to Troy and performed sacrifices at the tomb of Achilles. In this description, the word *kolōnos* refers, once again, to the tomb of Achilles:

HOUR 14 TEXT K

|$_{53.8}$ The Thessalian sacrificial offerings [*enagismata*] that came regularly to Achilles from Thessaly were decreed for the Thessalians by the oracle at Dodona. You see, the oracle ordered the Thessalians to sail to Troy each year to sacrifice [*thuein*] to Achilles and to slaughter some sacrificial victims as for a god, while slaughtering other victims as for the dead. |$_{53.9}$ From the very beginnings, the following was the proce-

dure: a ship sailed from Thessaly to Troy with black sails raised, bringing twice seven sacred delegates [*theōroi*], one white bull and one black
bull, both tame to the touch, and wood from Mount Pelion, so that
they would need nothing from the city [= New Ilion].* They also
brought fire from Thessaly as well as water drawn from the river
Sperkheios for libations. As a consequence [of these practices], the
Thessalians were the first to institute the custom of using unwilting
garlands [*stephanoi amarantinoi*] for the funerary rituals [*kēdos* plural]
[in honor of Achilles], in order that, even if the wind delayed the ship,
they would not wear garlands [*stephanoi*] that were wilted [*saproi*] or
past their season [*ex-hōroi*]. |₅₃.₁₀ And evidently they found it neces-
sary to put into the harbor at night and, before touching land, to sing
from the ship a hymn [*humnos*] to Thetis, which is composed of these
words:

> Thetis, sea-blue, Thetis consort of Peleus, | you who bore the great
> son | Achilles. The part of him that his mortal | nature brought
> him | was the share of Troy, but the part of him that from your im-
> mortal | lineage was drawn by the child, the sea [*pontos*] has that
> part. | Come, proceed to this steep *tumulus* [*kolōnos*] | in the
> company of Achilles [to receive] the offerings placed over the fire.
> | Come, proceed without tears in the company of Thessaly, | you
> sea-blue Thetis, you consort of Peleus.

|₅₃.₁₁ When they approached the *tomb* [*sēma*] after the hymn [*humnos*],
a shield was banged upon as in battle, and together with rhythmic co-
ordination they cried *alala* while calling upon Achilles. When they had
garlanded [*stephanoûn*] the summit of the tumulus [*kolōnos*] and dug
sacrificial pits on it, they slaughtered the black bull as to one who is
dead. |₅₃.₁₂ They also called upon Patroklos to come to the feast, so as
to gratify [= make *kharis* for] Achilles. |₅₃.₁₃ After they slit the victim's
throat and made this sacrifice [*enagizein*], they evidently proceeded to
go down to the ship, and, after sacrificing [*thuein*] the other bull on the
beach again to Achilles and having begun the offering by taking from

---

* The ritually dramatized hostility between the Thessalians and the city of New Ilion in the region of Troy
seems to be a reflex of political vicissitudes that go back to an era possibly as early as the sixth century BCE. In
that earlier era, the Thessalians would have been *personae non gratae* at the sacred sites of Troy, which were then
controlled by the city of New Ilion. See *HPC* 148–149 = II§§47–49.

the basket and by partaking of the entrails for that sacrifice [*thusia*] (for they sacrificed [*thuein*] that sacrifice [*thusia*] as to a god), they sailed away as dawn approached, taking the sacrificed animal so as not to be feasting in the enemy's territory.*

Philostratus Hērōikos 53.8–13†

14§32. I draw special attention to the ritual offering of *stephanoi*, 'garlands', of blossoms for the dead Achilles in the course of this detailed description of the sacrifices that are being offered to him as a cult hero: it is specified, as we have just read, that the garlands must be *amarantinoi*, 'unwilting'. Technically, the blossoms that form the circles of these garlands come from the flower known as *amaranth* in modern times. The blossoms of the flower *amaranth* that are plaited into garlands mimic eternity, since the blossom of the *amaranth* is observably slow in wilting, unlike the blossoms of most other flowers. This ritual gesture of offering 'unwilting garlands' to the hero is relevant to the *kleos aphthiton* of Achilles in *Iliad* IX 413, which as we have seen in Hour 4§§38–40 is the 'unwilting glory' of epic poetry. Verbs and nouns derived from the verb *phthi-n-ein*, which I had translated up to Hour 4§38 simply as 'perish', convey the idea of *wilting* in contexts referring to the vitality of plants.‡ So Achilles himself 'wilts' like a beautiful plant, if we interpret *phthi-n-ein* as 'wilt' in a passage of Pindar that I had first quoted in Hour 4:

---

* Translation adapted from Berenson Maclean and Aitken 2001:157, 159.

† |₅₃.₈ τὰ δὲ Θετταλικὰ ἐναγίσματα φοιτῶντα τῷ Ἀχιλλεῖ ἐκ Θετταλίας ἐχρήσθη Θετταλοῖς ἐκ Δωδώνης· ἐκέλευσε γὰρ δὴ τὸ μαντεῖον Θετταλοὺς ἐς Τροίαν πλέοντας θύειν ὅσα ἔτη τῷ Ἀχιλλεῖ καὶ σφάττειν τὰ μὲν ὡς θεῷ, τὰ δὲ ὡς ἐν μοίρᾳ τῶν κειμένων. |₅₃.₉ καταρχὰς μὲν δὴ τοιάδε ἐγίγνετο· ναῦς ἐκ Θετταλίας μέλανα ἱστία ἠρμένη ἐς Τροίαν ἔπλει θεωροὺς μὲν δὶς ἑπτὰ ἀπάγουσα, ταύρους δὲ λευκόν τε καὶ μέλανα χειροήθεις ἄμφω καὶ ὕλην ἐκ Πηλίου, ὡς μηδὲν τῆς πόλεως δέοιντο καὶ πῦρ ἐκ Θετταλίας ἦγον καὶ σπονδὰς καὶ ὕδωρ τοῦ Σπερχειοῦ ἀρυσάμενοι, ὅθεν καὶ στεφάνους ἀμαραντίνους ἐς τὰ κήδη πρῶτοι Θετταλοὶ ἐνόμισαν, ἵνα, κἂν ἄνεμοι τὴν ναῦν ἀπολάβωσι, μὴ σαπροὺς ἐπιφέρωσι μηδ' ἐξώρους. |₅₃.₁₀ νυκτὸς μὲν δὴ καθορμίζεσθαι ἔδει καὶ πρὶν ἅψασθαι τῆς γῆς ὕμνον ἀπὸ τῆς νεὼς ᾄδειν ἐς τὴν Θέτιν ὧδε ξυγκείμενον· Θέτι κυανέα, Θέτι Πηλεία, | ἃ τὸν μέγαν τέκες υἱόν, | Ἀχιλλέα, τοῦ θνατὰ μὲν ὅσον | φύσις ἤνεγκεν, | Τροία λάχε, σᾶς δ' ὅσον ἀθανάτου | γενεᾶς παῖς ἔσπασε, πόντος ἔχει. | βαῖνε πρὸς αἰπὺν τόνδε κολωνὸν | μετ' Ἀχιλλέως ἔμπυρα . . . | βαῖν' ἀδάκρυτος μετὰ Θεσσαλίας, | Θέτι κυανέα, Θέτι Πηλεία. |₅₃.₁₁ προσελθόντων δὲ τῷ σήματι μετὰ τὸν ὕμνον ἀσπὶς μὲν ὥσπερ ἐν πολέμῳ ἐδουπεῖτο, δρόμοις δὲ ἐρρυθμισμένοις συνηλάλαζον ἀνακαλοῦντες τὸν Ἀχιλλέα, στεφανώσαντες δὲ τὴν κορυφὴν τοῦ κολωνοῦ καὶ βόθρους ἐπ' αὐτῇ ὀρύξαντες τὸν ταῦρον τὸν μέλανα ὡς τεθνεῶτι ἔσφαττον. |₅₃.₁₂ ἐκάλουν δὲ καὶ τὸν Πάτροκλον ἐπὶ τὴν δαῖτα, ὡς καὶ τοῦτο ἐς χάριν τῷ Ἀχιλλεῖ πράττοντες, |₅₃.₁₃ ἐντεμόντες δὲ καὶ ἐναγίσαντες κατέβαινον ἐπὶ τὴν ναῦν ἤδη καὶ θύσαντες ἐπὶ τοῦ αἰγιαλοῦ τὸν ἕτερον τῶν ταύρων Ἀχιλλεῖ πάλιν κανοῦ τε ἐναρξάμενοι καὶ σπλάγχνων ἐπ' ἐκείνῃ τῇ θυσίᾳ—ἔθυον γὰρ τὴν θυσίαν ταύτην ὡς θεῷ—περὶ ὄρθρον ἀπέπλεον ἀπάγοντες τὸ ἱερεῖον, ὡς μὴ ἐν τῇ πολεμίᾳ εὐωχοῖντο.

‡ I collect some basic attestation in Hour 4§39, the most prominent of which comes from Pindar *Paean* 9.14: καρποῦ φθίσιν, 'wilting of the crops'.

Hour 14 Text L = Hour 4 Text A

$\mid_{56}$ Even when he [= Achilles] died, the songs did not leave him, $\mid_{57}$ but the Maidens of Helicon [= the Muses] stood by his pyre and his funeral mound, $\mid_{58}$ and, as they stood there, they poured forth a song of lamentation [*thrēnos*] that is famed far and wide. $\mid_{59}$ And so it was that the immortal gods decided $\mid_{60}$ to hand over the man, genuine [*esthlos*] as he was even after he had wilted [*phthi-n-ein*] in death, to the songs of the goddesses [= the Muses]. $\mid_{61}$ And this, even now, wins as a prize the words of song, as the chariot-team of the Muses starts moving on its way $\mid_{62}$ to glorify the memory of Nikokles the boxer.

Pindar Isthmian 8.56–62

Whereas Achilles 'wilts', the *kleos* or 'glory' of his song will never 'wilt'. The song is notionally eternal.

14§33. In the ritual of the Thessalians as described in Philostratus *Hērōikos* 53.9 and as quoted in Text K, we saw that the worshippers of Achilles offer him *stephanoi amarantinoi*, 'unwilting garlands'. A *stephanos* or 'garland', as we have already seen, is a circle or 'crown' (as in Latin *corona*) of plaited blossoms to be placed on the wearer's head of hair—and also, in *Hērōikos* 53.11 as also quoted in Text K, on the summit of the *kolōnos*, 'tumulus', that houses the body of Achilles. As I noted earlier, the blossoms of the flower *amaranth* that are plaited into garlands mimic eternity, since the blossom of the *amaranth* is observably slow in wilting, unlike the blossoms of most other flowers. And the ritual function of garlands, as circles of blossoms, is to express the idea of eternity. This idea is made explicit in a song of Bacchylides, who, like his rival Pindar, was active in the first half of the fifth century BCE. In the part of the song that I am about to quote, the ritual garlanding of a victorious athlete is equated with an affirmation of eternity, and this eternity is pictured as the circle of blossoms that adorn the garland of athletic victory:

Hour 14 Text M

[. . .] the blossoms [*anthea*] nurture a *fame* [*doxa*] that is *polu-phantos* (*made visible* [*phainein*] *to many*) in the recircling of time [*aiōn*]—a fame meant for only a few mortals, *lasting forever* [*aiei*].

Bacchylides Ode 13 lines 61–63*

---

* ἄ[ν]θεα [. . .] δόξαν πολύφαντον ἐν αἰ $\mid_{62}$[ῶνι] τρέφει παύροις βροτῶν $\mid_{63}$ [α]ἰεί.

14§34. The ritual tradition of making a garland by linking blossoms together into a circle is relevant to the linking that we see here between the adverb *aiei*, 'forever', and the noun *aiōn* in the sense of a 'life' or a 'life-force' that keeps coming back to life by way of a 'recircling of time'. In fact, the adverb *aiei*, 'forever', is the old locative singular of this noun *aiōn*, and this locative means literally 'in a recircling of time', signaling an eternal return.* As for the *anthea*, 'blossoms', at line 61 here, they are identical with the blossoms that are linked together into the garland mentioned at an earlier point in the song (line 55, not quoted here). As for the *doxa*, 'fame', at line 61, which is 'nurtured' by the blossoms of this garland, it is identical with the *kleos*, 'glory', of song or poetry, as mentioned in the passage that immediately follows this one:

HOUR 14 TEXT N

And when the dark blue cloud of death covers over these few [= the victors], what gets left behind is |₆₅ an undying *glory* [*kleos*] for what they did so well, in accord with a destiny [*aisa*] that cannot be dislodged.

Bacchylides *Ode* 13 lines 63–66†

14§35. Just as the blossoms of the garland nurture the eternal *doxa*, 'fame', of those few mortals whose athletic victories are celebrated at festivals, so also they nurture the eternal *kleos*, 'glory', of those mortals—a glory conferred by song or poetry. The medium of song or poetry is its own message, which is glory. This glory is compared to a garland, a circle of blossoms all linked together, and this circle is eternal.‡

14§36. So also in the ritual of the Thessalians as described in Philostratus *Hērōikos* 53.9–13 and as quoted in Text K, the 'garlanding' (53.12 *stephanoûn*) of the tumulus of Achilles and the wearing of the 'unwilting garlands' (53.9 *stephanoi amarantinoi*) that crown the heads of the participants are both signs of eternity, since the ritual itself is meant to be recycled year after year into eternity.

Longing for Achilles: You're Going to Miss Me

14§37. The people of Protesilaos are not the only ones who feel *pothos* 'longing' for their hero. So too the people of Achilles, who are all the Acheans, will feel

---

* Nagy 2011b:179, following *PH* 195n210 = 6§88.
† καὶ ὅταν θανάτοιο |₆₄ κυάνεον νέφος καλύψηι, λείπεται |₆₅ ἀθάνατον κλέος εὖ ἐρ |₆₆ χθέντος ἀσφαλεῖ σὺν αἴσαι.
‡ Nagy 2011b:179.

pothos, as Achilles himself predicts within his own epic. Here is how he says it, and what he says is framed in a mighty oath:

HOUR 14 TEXT O

|₂₃₂ "This could be the last time, son of Atreus, that you will be hurling insults. |₂₃₃ And here's another thing. I'll tell it to you, and I will swear on top of it a great oath: |₂₃₄ I swear by this scepter [*skēptron*] that I'm holding here, this scepter that will never again have leaves and branches |₂₃₅ growing out of it—and it never has—ever since it left that place in the mountains where it was cut down. |₂₃₆ It will never flourish again, since the bronze implement has stripped it |₂₃₇ of its leaves and its bark. Now the sons of the Achaeans carry it around, |₂₃₈ holding it in their hands whenever they act as makers of judgments [*dikaspoloi*], judging what are and what are not divine laws [*themis* plural], |₂₃₉ which they uphold, taking their authority from Zeus. This is going to be a big oath. |₂₄₀ So here is what I say, and I say it most solemnly: *the day will come when there will be a longing [pothē] for Achilles,* and it will overcome the sons of the Achaeans, |₂₄₁ overcome them all. When that day comes, there is no way you will be able, no matter how much grief you feel [*akh-nusthai*], |₂₄₂ to keep them away from harm. And that is the time when many will be killed at the hands of Hector the man-killer, |₂₄₃ dying as they fall to the ground. And you will have in your insides a heart [*thūmos*] that will be all torn up for you, |₂₄₄ feeling angry about the fact that you have not at all honored the best of the Achaeans." |₂₄₅ Thus spoke [Achilles] the son of Peleus, and he threw the scepter [*skēptron*] to the ground, |₂₄₆ that scepter adorned with golden studs driven into it. Then he sat down.

Iliad I 232–246*

14§38. In the master narrative of the *Iliad,* it is of course the Achaean warriors at Troy who will be longing for Achilles, once he withdraws from the Tro-

---

* |₂₃₂ ἦ γὰρ ἂν Ἀτρεΐδη νῦν ὕστατα λωβήσαιο. |₂₃₃ ἀλλ᾽ ἔκ τοι ἐρέω καὶ ἐπὶ μέγαν ὅρκον ὀμοῦμαι· |₂₃₄ ναὶ μὰ τόδε σκῆπτρον, τὸ μὲν οὔ ποτε φύλλα καὶ ὄζους |₂₃₅ φύσει, ἐπεὶ δὴ πρῶτα τομὴν ἐν ὄρεσσι λέλοιπεν, |₂₃₆ οὐδ᾽ ἀναθηλήσει· περὶ γάρ ῥά ἑ χαλκὸς ἔλεψε |₂₃₇ φύλλά τε καὶ φλοιόν· νῦν αὐτέ μιν υἷες Ἀχαιῶν |₂₃₈ ἐν παλάμῃς φορέουσι δικασπόλοι, οἵ τε θέμιστας |₂₃₉ πρὸς Διὸς εἰρύαται· ὁ δέ τοι μέγας ἔσσεται ὅρκος· |₂₄₀ ἦ ποτ᾽ Ἀχιλλῆος ποθὴ ἵξεται υἷας Ἀχαιῶν |₂₄₁ σύμπαντας· τότε δ᾽ οὔ τι δυνήσεαι ἀχνύμενός περ |₂₄₂ χραισμεῖν, εὖτ᾽ ἂν πολλοὶ ὑφ᾽ Ἕκτορος ἀνδροφόνοιο |₂₄₃ θνήσκοντες πίπτωσι· σὺ δ᾽ ἔνδοθι θυμὸν ἀμύξεις |₂₄₄ χωόμενος ὅ τ᾽ ἄριστον Ἀχαιῶν οὐδὲν ἔτισας. |₂₄₅ Ὣς φάτο Πηλεΐδης, ποτὶ δὲ σκῆπτρον βάλε γαίῃ |₂₄₆ χρυσείοις ἥλοισι πεπαρμένον, ἕζετο δ᾽ αὐτός·

jan War. Beyond the *Iliad*, however, it will be all Greeks throughout all time who will be longing for this hero, once he is dead. The eternity of such longing is fueled by the eternal force of the oath taken by Achilles here at verses 240–243 of *Iliad* I, and this mighty oath is backed up by the *skēptron*, 'scepter', that the hero holds in his hands at verse 233—and that he then throws defiantly to the ground at verse 245.

14§39. When Achaean kings make *dikai*, 'judgments', at a council of kings, as I pointed out in Hour 13§30 and §36, the protocol is for each king to hold the *skēptron*, 'scepter', when it is his turn to speak. That is what Achilles himself is saying here about the scepter in verses 237–239 of *Iliad* I, as quoted in Text O: 'Now the sons of the Achaeans carry it [= the scepter] around, |₂₃₈ holding it in their hands whenever they act as makers of judgments [*dikaspoloi*], judging what are and what are not divine laws [*themis* plural], |₂₃₉ which they uphold, taking their authority from Zeus'. So, the gesture of Achilles when he holds the scepter as he makes his oath has the effect of authorizing this oath. And his added gesture of defiantly throwing down the scepter after he finishes making his oath has the further effect of making the oath permanent, since no one else will now hold the scepter at this council of kings. That is because the oath of Achilles is so powerful that it has made the scepter too powerful for any other speaker to hold at this moment. It is a chicken-and-egg relationship that is typical of mythmaking: the scepter, which authorizes the speaker to speak, is now in turn further authorized by the great oath spoken by the speaker—an oath that confers upon the scepter the same eternal authority that the oath has conferred upon itself by virtue of being performed in the Homeric *Iliad*.

14§40. We can see the results of this further authorization at a later point, when Agamemnon brings the same scepter to an assembly at verses 46–47 of *Iliad* II, and now this *skēptron*, 'scepter', is described as *aphthiton*, 'unwilting', at verse 46. Such an exalted description shows the permanent cosmic power of this mighty object. The *skēptron* is a sacred object that signals eternal ratification, which is expressed in its genealogy as described in *Iliad* II 100–108: there we are told that the *skēptron* as held primarily by Agamemnon as the over-king of the Achaeans had been passed down to him from Zeus himself, who had given it to Hermes to pass on to Pelops and then to Atreus and then to Thyestes and then to Agamemnon.* This *skēptron* is of divine workmanship: originating from something natural, a wooden growth, it has become galvanized into something divinely artificial, an object that is gilded by the divine artisan Hephaistos

---

* On the significance of *Iliad* II 278–282, where Odysseus takes hold of the scepter, see Elmer 2013:97.

himself, as we read in *Iliad* II 101–102. So the fact that this *skēptron* will never again sprout leaves or grow a bark, as the oath of Achilles affirms, validates it as a divine object of eternity. Just as the *kleos* or poetic 'glory' of Achilles is *aphthiton*, 'unwilting', in *Iliad* IX 413, so also the *skēptron* by which he swore his mighty oath in *Iliad* I 233 will be described later in Iliad II 46 as *aphthiton*, 'unwilting', in its own right—because it affirms for all eternity the oath of Achilles, which affirms for all eternity that there will be, as we read in verse 240 of *Iliad* I, a great *pothē*, 'longing', for him as the very best of the Achaeans.

Longing for Patroklos: I'll Miss Him Forever

14§41. The model for the way that Achilles will be sorely missed by all Greeks throughout all time is the way that Patroklos, once he is killed, is missed by Achilles in the *Iliad*. That is why Patroklos as the substitute for Achilles becomes momentarily 'the best of the Achaeans' when he is killed, as one of his Achaean comrades says in announcing the grim news of the hero's death:

HOUR 14 TEXT P

|687 Once you see it with your own eyes |688 you will know that the god is letting roll down from above a pain [*pēma*] upon the Danaans [= Achaeans],* |689 and victory now belongs to the Trojans. He has just been killed, the best of the Achaeans, |690 I mean Patroklos, and the Danaans [= Achaeans] will have a great longing [*pothē*].

Iliad XVII 687–690†

14§42. And this great longing for Patroklos, to be felt by all his Achaean comrades, is felt most deeply and intensely by Achilles himself, who performs his own personal lament for Patroklos by expressing the great longing that he feels for his other self:

HOUR 14 TEXT Q

|319 But now there you are, lying there, all cut up, while my heart |320 is wanting, though I have drink and food [in my shelter], |321 because of my longing [*pothē*] for you. There is nothing I could possibly suffer

---

* We have seen the same metaphor of the breakaway boulder in *Iliad* XVII 98–99, quoted in Hour 5 Text C, where I offer commentary.

† |687 ἤδη μὲν σὲ καὶ αὐτὸν ὀίομαι εἰσορόωντα |688 γιγνώσκειν ὅτι πῆμα θεὸς Δαναοῖσι κυλίνδει, |689 νίκη δὲ Τρώων· πέφαται δ᾽ ὥριστος Ἀχαιῶν |690 Πάτροκλος, μεγάλη δὲ ποθὴ Δαναοῖσι τέτυκται.

that would be worse than this, |₃₂₂ not even if I were to hear news that my father died |₃₂₃—who is now in Phthia weeping gently |₃₂₄ about losing the kind of son that he has, and here I am, this son that I am, in a foreign district [*dēmos*], |₃₂₅ and I am waging war here for the sake of that dreadful Helen |₃₂₆—or if I heard news that my dear son died, the one who is being brought up in Skyros— |₃₂₇ if in fact godlike Neoptolemos is still living.

Iliad XIX 319–327*

* |₃₁₉ νῦν δὲ σὺ μὲν κεῖσαι δεδαϊγμένος, αὐτὰρ ἐμὸν κῆρ |₃₂₀ ἄκμηνον πόσιος καὶ ἐδητύος ἔνδον ἐόντων |₃₂₁ σῇ ποθῇ· οὐ μὲν γάρ τι κακώτερον ἄλλο πάθοιμι, |₃₂₂ οὐδ᾽ εἴ κεν τοῦ πατρὸς ἀποφθιμένοιο πυθοίμην, |₃₂₃ ὅς που νῦν Φθίηφι τέρεν κατὰ δάκρυον εἴβει |₃₂₄ χήτεϊ τοιοῦδ᾽ υἷος· ὃ δ᾽ ἀλλοδαπῷ ἐνὶ δήμῳ |₃₂₅ εἵνεκα ῥιγεδανῆς Ἑλένης Τρωσὶν πολεμίζω. |₃₂₆ ἠὲ τὸν ὃς Σκύρῳ μοι ἔνι τρέφεται φίλος υἱός, |₃₂₇—εἴ που ἔτι ζώει γε Νεοπτόλεμος θεοειδής.

What the Hero 'Means'

The Meaning of Sēmainein

15§1. The key word for this hour is *sēmainein,* which means 'to mean [something], indicate [something] by way of a *sēma*'. In Hour 7, the key word was *sēma* (plural *sēmata*), meaning 'sign, signal, symbol; tomb, tomb of a hero'. The verb *sēmainein* is a derivative of the noun *sēma*. As we will see in this hour, the very idea of 'meaning' in the ancient Greek language is tied to the idea of the hero—in particular, to the idea of the cult hero's death and tomb. It is as if 'meaning' could not be 'meaning' without the hero's death and tomb. And such heroic 'meaning' is tied to the further concept of the hero's consciousness after death—a consciousness that communicates with the living. So the question is, how—or when—is the hero conscious after death? And how—or when—does the hero communicate with the consciousness of the living?

What Protesilaos 'Means'

15§2. We start with a passage about a *teras,* 'portent, miracle', communicated by the cult hero Protesilaos, whose death and whose tomb were the main topic of the previous hour. As we saw in Philostratus *Hērōikos* 9.3, quoted in Hour 14 Text G, the noun *sēma* actually refers to the tomb of Protesilaos. Here in Hour 15, our main source of information about Protesilaos is Herodotus, an author who predates by over 600 years the author of the *Hērōikos*, Philostratus. In the passage I am about to quote from the *Histories* of Herodotus, a source dating from the second half of the fifth century BCE, the word *sēmainein* refers to a communication made by Protesilaos from his tomb. As we will see, this reference fills out the picture we already have of this cult hero.

15§3. The year is 479 BCE, and Athenian forces have just captured Sestos, a strategically vital garrison of the Persian Empire. After the united Hellenic forces had defeated the forces of the Persian Empire in the sea battle of Salamis in 480 BCE and in the land battle of Plataea in 479 BCE, the state of Athens uni-laterally began taking control of Greek-speaking populations previously con-trolled by the Persian Empire. A major prize was the territory of the Chersone-sus, the garrison for which was Sestos. We join the action at a moment when the Athenians have already captured Sestos and taken prisoner the Persian gover-nor, named Artayktes, whom they condemn to death on charges of having vio-lated the hero cult of Protesilaos at Elaious in the Chersonesus. As the Persian man is about to be executed, a *teras,* 'portent, miracle', is seen:

HOUR 15 TEXT A

|$_{9.120.1}$ The people of the Chersonesus say that a portent [*teras*] hap-pened to one of the guards while he was roasting salted fish [*tarīkhoi*]: the salted fish [*tarīkhoi*] on the fire began to jump and writhe just like newly caught fish. |$_{9.120.2}$ A crowd gathered in amazement, but when Artayktes saw the portent [*teras*] he called out to the man roasting the salted fish [*tarīkhoi*] and said, "Athenian stranger [*xenos*], have no fear of this portent [*teras*]; it has not been sent to you. Instead Protesilaos of Elaious indicates [*sēmainein*] to me that even when salted and dead [*tarīkhos*] he holds power from the gods to punish one who treats him without justice [*a-dikeîn*].

Herodotus 9.120.1–2*

15§4. Here the dead Protesilaos sends a 'meaning', as indicated by the verb *sēmainein*. The question is, for whom is the 'meaning' intended? The con-demned Persian, Artayktes, says that the 'meaning' is intended only for him. It can be argued, however, that Herodotus intended the 'meaning' not only for Persians but for Greeks as well.† Moreover, since Herodotus attributes the story to a native of the Chersonesus and since the person addressed by the Persian is an Athenian, the 'meaning' could even be intended especially for Athenians.

15§5. Through a *dunamis,* 'power', given to Protesilaos by the gods, this cult hero can uphold justice by punishing the unjust, just as surely as he can give the

* |$_{9.120.1}$ Καί τεῳ τῶν φυλασσόντων λέγεται ὑπὸ Χερσονησιτέων ταρίχους ὀπτῶντι τέρας γενέσθαι τοιόνδε· οἱ τάριχοι ἐπὶ τῷ πυρὶ κείμενοι ἐπάλλοντό τε καὶ ἤσπαιρον ὅκως περ ἰχθύες νεοάλωτοι. |$_{9.120.2}$ Καὶ οἱ μὲν περιχυθέντες ἐθώμαζον, ὁ δὲ Ἀρταΰκτης, ὡς εἶδε τὸ τέρας, καλέσας τὸν ὀπτῶντα τοὺς ταρίχους ἔφη· «Ξεῖνε Ἀθηναῖε, μηδὲν φοβέο τὸ τέρας τοῦτο· οὐ γὰρ σοὶ πέφηνε, ἀλλ᾽ ἐμοὶ σημαίνει ὁ ἐν Ἐλαιοῦντι Πρωτεσίλεως ὅτι καὶ τεθνεὼς καὶ τάριχος ἐὼν δύναμιν πρὸς θεῶν ἔχει τὸν ἀδικέοντα τίνεσθαι.

† *PH* 268–271 = 9§§26–31.

mystical sign that is narrated by Herdotus: an Athenian is roasting *tarīkhoi*—which I will hereafter translate simply as 'preserved fish'—and the dead fish mysteriously come back to life (9.120.1). So also Protesilaos is now being called a *tarīkhos*: he is as dead as a dead fish, and so he can be seen as a *tarīkhos* by way of metaphor, but he still has the power to intervene in the world of the living (9.120.2). By implication, Protesilaos has mystically come back to life, just like the preserved fish.

15§6. But the metaphor of the preserved fish that come back to life is more complex. The Greek word *tarīkhos*, evidently a borrowing from one of the Indo-European languages of Anatolia, can refer not only to 'preserved' fish but also to human bodies that are artificially 'preserved' in the context of funerary rituals.* The meaning 'preserved' in an everyday sense would apply to the salting or drying of fish in order to keep them from putrefaction (Herodotus 2.77.4; another relevant passage is 4.53.3). In a transcendent sense, however, it could apply to the artificial preservation of a corpse, again in order to keep it from putrefaction. A case in point is the ritual of mummification as practiced in Egypt: we find detailed descriptions in Herodotus (2.85–89), where we see the verb *tarīkheuein,* derivative of the noun *tarīkhos,* in the sense of 'mummify' (2.85.2, 2.86.3, 2.86.5, 2.87.2, 2.88, 2.89.1, 2.90.1). In considering the most expensive and sacred form of mummification, Herodotus says ostentatiously that he does not wish to reveal the name connected to this form (2.86.2). His opaque language here corresponds to other contexts in which he expresses a reluctance to reveal the secrets of mysteries (as at 2.61, 2.86, 2.132, 2.170, 2.171).† In this context, the mystery evidently centers on the Egyptian mythological figure of Osiris, whose resurrection from the dead depends on secret rites of mummification.‡ In the sacred context of the Egyptian mysteries of Osiris, 'preservation' is seen as resurrection after death, and the key to the mystery of resurrection is the ritual of mummification.§

15§7. For Herodotus, I argue, the sacred sense of *tarīkhos* in such contexts was comparable to the mysteries of resurrection in hero cult. In terms of this argument, as we now return to the story told by Herodotus (9.120.1–2) about

---

* Analysis in *PH* 270 = 9§29n102. In that analysis, I consider the possible relationship of *tarīkhos* with other Greek words that are evidently borrowed from one or another of the Indo-European languages of Anatolia. A case in point is *tarkhuein* as attested in the *Iliad* (ταρχύσουσι at VII 85, XVI 456, 674). This form and its Homeric contexts are analyzed in Nagy 2012b:61–69.

† See again Nagy 1987; also *PH* 270–271 = 9§30, with further references.

‡ Lloyd 1976:18.

§ Nagy 2001a:17–18.

the cult hero Protesilaos as quoted in Text A, the 'meaning' of the hero is to be found in the *teras*, 'portent, miracle', of the resurrection of the dead fish and in the riddling use of the word *tarīkhos*.*

The Mystery of a Cult Hero

15§8. The mystification surrounding the Egyptian prototype of resurrection, Osiris, is extended to the Greek hero Protesilaos by the narrative of Herodotus. The mystery inherent in the hero's own cult is signaled by the double meaning of the word *tarīkhos*—either the everyday sense of 'preserved fish' or the hieratic sense of 'preserved corpse'—as in the Egyptian sense of 'mummy':†

> What the two meanings seem to have in common is the idea of 'preservation'. In an everyday sense, rotting is negated by 'preservation' through the drying or salting of fish; in a hieratic sense, rotting *and death itself* are negated by 'preservation' through mummification, which is from the standpoint of Egyptian religion the ritual phase of the mystical process of immortalization.‡ We see further evidence in Alexander Romance (2.39.21).§

15§9. When the dead Protesilaos 'gives a sign', *sēmainei*, to the living, as we saw in Herodotus 9.120.2 as quoted in Text A, the Greek hero's 'meaning' seems at first sight to depend on whether the word *tarīkhos* is to be understood in the everyday Greek sense of 'preserved fish' or in the hieratic non-Greek sense of 'mummy'. But there is a third sense, both hieratic and Greek, and it depends on the meaning of the word *sēmainei*:**

> In the image of a dead fish that mystically comes back to life, we see a convergence of the everyday and the hieratic senses of 'preservation'.

---

* Nagy 2001a:16–17. My formulation here is relevant to two articles about the overall Protesilaos story in Herodotus 9.116–120: Nagy 1987 and Boedeker 1988. Both these articles concern the hero cult of Protesilaos, but they differ in emphasis and in lines of interpretation. Whereas the article of Boedeker (1988) touches on Herodotus' use of the story about Protesilaos as it relates to the narrative ending of the *Histories*, my article (1987) analyzes Herodotus' use of the traditional language inherent in this story (as signaled by such words as *sēmainein*); this language, I argue in that article, conveys not only the mystical agenda of hero cult but also the "subtext" of the entire narration of the *Histories*, ending and all. This argument of mine is elaborated in *PH* 268–273 = 9§§26–35. The commentary of Flower and Marincola 2002:302–311 on the relevant passage of Herodotus (9.116–120) does not cite my analysis of this passage.

† Nagy 2001a:18.

‡ Nagy 1987:210 and *PH* 270 = 9§29.

§ Nagy 2001a:18.

** *PH* 271–272 = 9§32.

This image [in the story of Herodotus], where Protesilaos *sēmainei,* 'indicates' (9.120.2), the power that he has from the gods to exact retribution from the wrongdoer, amounts to a *sēma* or sign of the revenant, the spirit that returns from the dead. The hero Protesilaos himself is represented as giving the *sēma,* the 'sign' of his power as a revenant [from the heroic past].*

15§10. The mystical sense of *sēma,* 'sign, signal, symbol; tomb, tomb of a hero', is a tradition in its own right, well attested already in Homeric poetry.† We have already seen some indications of such mysticism in Hour 7§4, where we considered the mystical power of cult heroes whose restless spirits reside inside the turning points of chariot races. And, as I noted in Hour 7g§4, a *sēma* can be any visual marker for the meaning of the hero: *it is a point of concentration that directs the viewer into the world of heroes.* As we saw in the words of the instructions given by Nestor to his son Antilokhos in *Iliad* XXIII 326–343, quoted in Hour 7 Text A, the *sēma* or 'sign' of the hero, as signaled in verse 326, can be the same thing as the 'tomb' of the hero, as signaled in verse 331. That is the ultimate message conveyed by the words of Nestor: concentrate on the *sēma.* In this Homeric example, the medium of the tomb or *sēma* of the hero *is* the message of the sign or *sēma* of the hero. And, as I already started to argue in Hour 8§10, this word *sēma* in Homeric diction signals not only the *tomb* of a cult hero (as in XXIII 331) but also a *sign* (as in XXIII 326) that indicates the transcendent meaning of that tomb to those who are qualified to understand the mystical language of hero cult. And the essence of that transcendent meaning, as I argued in Hour 11§31, is that the *sēma* or 'tomb' of a hero is a 'sign' not only of death as marked by the tomb but also of life after death, as marked by the same 'tomb'.

---

* Nagy 1987:210 and *PH* 271 = 9§31. See also Nagy 2001a:18. For more on the concept of the cult hero as revenant, see Nagy 1985, especially pp. 76–81 = §§71–79 (a subsection entitled "The Starving Revenant").

† Nagy 2001a:19, with reference to Nagy 1983a, rewritten as ch. 8 of *GM* (pp. 202–222, "*Sēma* and *Noēsis:* The Hero's Tomb and the 'Reading' of Symbols in Homer and Hesiod"). I note here also the mysticism surrounding the funerals of heroes, as discussed in Nagy 1983b, rewritten as part of ch. 5 of *GM* (pp. 122–142, "The Death of Sarpedon and the Question of Homeric Uniqueness"). For a most valuable survey of ancient testimony concerning the tombs of cult heroes, see Brelich 1958:80–90. See also Rusten 1983, who studies a reference to hero cult in the poetry of Pindar. For more on Pindaric references to hero cults, I cite Currie 2005, which I think complements my own work on such references: I have in mind especially *PH* = Nagy 1990a, in which I analyze hero cults in the context of a large-scale comparative study of the relationship between Homeric and Pindaric poetry. I find most relevant to my work the insights of Currie concerning not only the practices of hero cult, which he views in terms of both ritual and myth, but also the genre of the victory ode itself, which he analyzes most effectively in its genuine historical contexts.

What Herodotus 'Means'

15§11. This transcendent mystical meaning of *sēma* as an indication of life after death extends from the noun *sēma* to the verb *sēmainein*, 'give a sign, signal; indicate', as used by Herodotus to indicate the 'meaning' of the cult hero Protesilaos in Herodotus 9.120.2, a passage I quoted in Text A, which comes at the end of the *Histories*. In this passage, we saw that Protesilaos comes back to life as a guardian of *dikē*, 'justice', by virtue of punishing those who are guilty of *a-dikeîn*, that is, of committing unjust deeds against him. But this same 'meaning' is implied already at the beginning of the *Histories*, where it is Herodotus himself who engages in the act of *sēmainein*, 'meaning':

HOUR 15 TEXT B

|₁.₅.₃ Concerning these things, I am not going to say that they were so or otherwise, but I will indicate [*sēmainein*] the one who I myself know [*oida*] first began unjust [*a-dika*] deeds against the Hellenes. I will go on further in my account, treating equally of great and small cities of humankind, |₁.₅.₄ for many of those that were great in the past have become small, and those that were great in my day were formerly small. Knowing that human good fortune [*eudaimoniā*] never remains in the same state, I will mention both equally.

Herodotus 1.5.3–4*

15§12. When Herodotus says 'these things' here, he is referring to charges and counter-charges about wrongs committed by the mythological prototypes of his narration about the world struggle between East and West that culminated in the war of the Persian Empire against the Hellenes of Europe. Such acts of wrongdoing lead to further acts meant to right wrongs, which of course result in still further acts of wrongdoing. This chain of wrongs committed and of rights claimed is expressed by way of the following words: *a-dikēmata*, 'acts of injustice' (1.2.1), *a-dikiē*, 'injustice' (1.2.1), *dikai*, 'acts of compensation for wrongs committed' (1.2.3, two times; 1.3.1; 1.3.2, three times), *a-dikoi*, 'unjust men' (1.4.2).

---

* |₁.₅.₃ Ἐγὼ δὲ περὶ μὲν τούτων οὐκ ἔρχομαι ἐρέων ὡς οὕτως ἢ ἄλλως κως ταῦτα ἐγένετο, τὸν δὲ οἶδα αὐτὸς πρῶτον ὑπάρξαντα ἀδίκων ἔργων ἐς τοὺς Ἕλληνας, τοῦτον σημήνας προβήσομαι ἐς τὸ πρόσω τοῦ λόγου, ὁμοίως μικρὰ καὶ μεγάλα ἄστεα ἀνθρώπων ἐπεξιών. |₁.₅.₄ Τὰ γὰρ τὸ πάλαι μεγάλα ἦν, τὰ πολλὰ αὐτῶν σμικρὰ γέγονε· τὰ δὲ ἐπ' ἐμέο ἦν μεγάλα, πρότερον ἦν σμικρά. Τὴν ἀνθρωπηίην ὦν ἐπιστάμενος εὐδαιμονίην οὐδαμὰ ἐν τὠυτῷ μένουσαν, ἐπιμνήσομαι ἀμφοτέρων ὁμοίως.

So when Herodotus goes on to say in the passage I just quoted in Text B that he will signal, *sēmainein*, the person he knows was the first to commit deeds that are *a-dika*, 'unjust', against the Hellenes (1.5.3), he is referring to the function of his medium, which is history, in the same way as he refers to the function of the cult hero Protesilaos: in the words of the Persian man accused of wronging Protesilaos, as we saw in Text A, the cult hero is signaling, *sēmainein*, that the gods have given him the *dunamis*, 'power', to punish the one who 'treats him without justice', as expressed by the verb *a-dikeîn* (9.120.2).*

15§13. So the medium of history is signaling, *sēmainein*, just as the cult hero himself is signaling, *sēmainein*, within the medium of history. Within the overall narrative framework of the 'inquiry' or *historiē* of Herodotus, the historian says what he 'means' at the very beginning of his *Histories* when he speaks authoritatively about divine retribution, using the word *sēmainein* to signal his meaning in Text B (1.5.3), and this 'meaning' is finally authorized at the very end of his *Histories* when the hero Protesilaos expresses his own meaning, signaled again by the word *sēmainein* in Text A (9.120.2).† Now it is the resurrected hero, not just the historian, who speaks authoritatively about divine retribution, and the semantics of *sēmainein* connect the heroic world of Protesilaos, the first warrior to die in the Trojan War (*Iliad* II 695–710), with the historical world of Herodotus and beyond.‡

15§14. But the hero's meaning is opaque. The condemned Persian man can claim that the meaning of Protesilaos is intended for him, not for the Athenian, let alone the native Greeks of the Chersonesus who worship Protesilaos as their local hero. Who, then, is the intended receiver, the *destinataire*, of the meaning of Protesilaos? The historian does not say, and in this regard his meaning, too, is opaque:§

> When Herodotus 'indicates', *sēmainei*, he is indirectly narrating the actions of the gods by directly narrating the actions of men. And the most powerful 'indication' is the *sēma* of the hero, whose message is also his medium, the tomb. The double meaning of *sēma* as both 'tomb' and 'indication, sign' is itself a monument to the ideology inherent in the

---

* *PH* 233–236 = 8§§27–29.

† *PH* 240–241, 260–261, 329–330 = 8§§37–40, 9§15, 11§27. For a different interpretation of the ending of Herodotus' *Histories*, see Dewald 1997:67 (where she refers to Boedeker 1988).

‡ Nagy 2001a:19.

§ Nagy 2001a:20.

ancient Greek institution of hero cults—an ideology that appropriated the very concept of meaning to the tomb of the hero.*

More on the Mystery of a Cult Hero

15§15. The opaqueness of a cult hero like Protesilaos is a tradition in its own right, grounded in the mystery of his hero cult.† I have been using this term *mystery* in the sense of the ancient Greek noun *mustērion* (attested normally in the plural: *mustēria*). This noun derives ultimately from the verb *muein* (first person *muō*), which means 'have the mouth closed' or 'have the eyes closed' in non-sacred situations—but which implies 'say in a sacred kind of way' or 'see in a sacred kind of way' in sacred situations.‡ The idea of *saying or seeing in a sacred kind of way* is made explicit in the related verb *muein* (first person *mueō*), which means 'initiate into the mysteries'. The idea of *mystery* is embedded in the word *muein* in the sense of 'have the mouth closed' or 'have the eyes closed', as we can see from an observation made by the worshipper of the cult hero Protesilaos: in the *Hērōikos* of Philostratus (11.9), the Ampelourgos observes that you cannot even see the cult hero Protesilaos while he is engaged in the act of consuming the offerings left for him, since it all happens *thatton ē katamusai*, 'quicker than blinking', where *kata-muein*, 'blink', is derived from *muein* in the sense of 'close / open the eyes'.§ When something sacred happens this quickly, how can you open your mouth and say something about it—let alone see anything?

15§16. So what exactly is the 'mystery' of the cult hero Protesilaos? Evidently it has to do with the hero's capacity to come back to life after death—either formally and definitively, as in a resurrection, or personally and episodically, as in an epiphany. In what follows, we will consider first the formal event of a resurrection, and then the more personalized event of an epiphany.

15§17. Near the very beginning of the *Hērōikos* of Philostratus, the reader learns that the cult hero Protesilaos experienced a resurrection—in fact, he experienced not one but two resurrections (2.9–11). *These two resurrections are*

---

* Nagy 1987:213 and *PH* 272–273 = 9§§33–35.

† Nagy 2001a:20–21. On Protesilaos as a mystical cult hero, see Brelich 1958:198; for other heroes, see his pp. 118–123.

‡ *PH* 31–32 = 1§29.

§ Nagy 2001a:20n13.

presented as mysteries that can be understood only if one is initiated into these mysteries. In the *Hērōikos*, the person who is being initiated—let us call him the *initiand*—is the Phoenician. And the person who is initiating him is the Ampelourgos, who has already been initiated. But the Phoenician is not the only initiand of the *Hērōikos*: ultimately, as we will see, the initiands include also the readers of the *Hērōikos*.

15§18. In the *Hērōikos*, the first time the hero Protesilaos came back to life (*anabiōiē* 2.9) was in Phthia in Thessaly after his death at Troy, all because of his love for his bride Laodameia. Then he died a second time—and again it was because he loved his bride—only to come back to life a second time thereafter (*anabiōnai* 2.10). Just exactly how the hero came back for the second time, however, is not revealed even to the initiated Ampelourgos, who says to the Phoenician initiand that Protesilaos chooses not to tell that particular sacred secret or *aporrhēton*, which means literally an 'unsayable thing' (2.11).* So the Ampelourgos is really only half-initiated, since he knows the mystery of only one of the two resurrections of Protesilaos.

15§19. In this context, I highlight the suggestive use of the word *pathos*, 'experience', with regard to the resurrections of Protesilaos: as the Ampelourgos says about the cult hero, 'he himself [Protesilaos] does not speak about his own experiences [*pathē*]' (*Hērōikos* 2.9). The Ampelourgos goes on to say that the *aporrhēton*, 'sacred secret', belongs to the *Moirai*, 'Fates' (2.11). This association of the cult hero Protesilaos with the *Moirai*, 'Fates', is relevant to the etymology of the hero's name *Prōtesi-lāos*, the first part of which is derived from the root of the verb *pe-prō-tai*, 'it is fated' (the form is attested in *Iliad* XVIII 329).† In the master narrative of the Homeric *Iliad*, the name *Prōtesi-lāos* is explicitly associated with the fate of the Achaean *lāos* or 'people': a turning point in the plot of the *Iliad* is the moment when the fire of Hektor reaches the ships of the Achaeans, and here the narrative focuses on the ship of Protesilaos himself (*Iliad* XV 704–705; 716–718; see also XVI 286);‡ this same precise moment is figured as

---

* Signals of initiation, such as ritual silence and ritual whispering, can be formalized as mystical names of cult heroes, as in the case of *Sigēlos* ['The Silent One'] and *Psithuros* ['The Whisperer'] respectively; for documentation, see Brelich 1958:157.

† On the morphology of the name *Prōtesi-lāos*, see *BA* 70 = 5§2n1.

‡ There is also a "folk etymology" at work in the narrative of the *Iliad*: the name *Prōtesi-lāos* is also associated with the word *prōtos*, 'first', in the sense that this hero was the first Achaean to die at Troy (*prōtistos*, 'the very first', at *Iliad* II 702).

a turning point for the very destiny of all Hellenes as descendants of the epic Achaeans, in that the *Iliad* equates the threat of destruction for the Achaeans' ships with the threat of extinction for the Hellenes who are yet to be.*

15§20. So much for the resurrections of Protesilaos in the heroic past. As for the everyday present, by contrast, this cult hero continues to come back again and again as an apparition, in sacred epiphanies, and so too do other heroes of the heroic past keep coming back. As the Ampelourgos says, Protesilaos and the other heroes of the Trojan War have a habit of appearing in epiphanies: they literally 'show up', *phainontai* (*Hērōikos* 2.11).

15§21. The Ampelourgos follows up by proceeding to tell the Phoenician initiand all about the epiphanies of Protesilaos, describing the cult hero's interventions into the world of the everyday. Where is Protesilaos most likely to be sighted? The Ampelourgos reveals an array of places where the hero may 'show up', as it were: sometimes he is in the Chersonesus, sometimes in Phthia, sometimes in Troy—a most notable location for frequent sightings of heroes who died in the Trojan War—and sometimes he is back in Hādēs (*Hērōikos* 11.7). It is in Hādēs that he continues to have sex with his beloved bride Laodameia (11.8).†

15§22. Sometimes the living can even fall in love with the apparitions of such heroes. The Ampelourgos tells this story, for example, about an epiphany that was manifested by the hero Antilokhos, son of Nestor:

HOUR 15 TEXT C

My guest [*xenos*], I will lose my voice if I try to recall all such stories [about heroes who make epiphanies at the Plain of Scamander in the region of Troy]. For example, there is a song about Antilokhos, how a girl from the city of [New] Ilion who was wandering along the banks of the river Scamander had an encounter [*en-tunkhanein*] with the phantom [*eidōlon*] of Antilokhos and embraced his tomb [*sēma*] in a fit of passionate erotic desire [*erôsa*] for the phantom [*eidōlon*].

Philostratus *Hērōikos* 22.3‡

---

* *BA* 335–337 = 20§§16–17.

† Nagy 2001a:2–27.

‡ ἐπιλείψει με ἡ φωνή, ξένε, τῶν τοιούτων μνημονεύοντα· καὶ γάρ τι καὶ περὶ Ἀντιλόχου ᾄδουσιν, ὡς κόρη Ἰλιὰς φοιτῶσα ἐπὶ τὸν Σκάμανδρον εἰδώλῳ τοῦ Ἀντιλόχου ἐνέτυχε καὶ προσέκειτο τῷ σήματι ἐρῶσα τοῦ εἰδώλου.

Back to the 'Meaning' of Protesilaos

15§23. The epiphany of a cult hero can be both *metonymic* and *metaphoric*. That is, a sign connected with the hero can be substituted for the hero. Here again I am using these two words *metonymy* and *metaphor* in terms of my working definitions of Hour 4§32: whereas metaphor has meaning by substituting for something else, metonymy has meaning by connecting something to something else that is next to it or at least near to it, thereby establishing contact. We saw in Hour 11 that the word *sēma* in the sense of 'tomb' indicates that the hero is connected simultaneously to (1) a setting for the hero's body at a given time and place and (2) a setting for the hero's continued existence beyond everyday time and place. And we have seen here in Hour 15 that the same word *sēma* in the sense of 'sign' indicates an epiphany of the hero or of something connected to the hero in the context of his tomb. Further, the meaning of such an epiphany is indicated by the word *sēmainein,* which means literally 'mean' or 'mean in a special way'. An example is the use of this word in the story related by Herodotus (9.120.1–2), as quoted in Text A, concerning the *teras,* 'portent', of the *tarīkhoi,* 'preserved fish', that come back to life while they are being roasted for an everyday meal. As we have seen in this text, the cult hero *sēmainei,* 'indicates' his 'meaning'.

15§24. The 'meaning' in this story as retold by Herodotus is indicated by the corpse of the cult hero Protesilaos, even if the tomb that houses the corpse is not directly mentioned. Still, Herodotus mentions directly the place where the tomb is located: it is the Chersonesus, and the traditional story that is being told about Protesilaos originates from the native Greeks of that region: *kai teōi . . . legetai hupo Khersonēsiteōn . . . tarīkhous optōnti teras genesthai toionde,* 'and *it is said by the people of the Chersonesus* that the following portent [*teras*] happened to a person who was roasting *tarīkhoi*' (9.120.1). Further, in the *Hērōikos* of Philostratus, the portent that is sent as a signal from the hero's corpse is directly linked to the sacred space of Protesilaos at Elaious: *to de ge hieron en hōi, kata tous pateras,* 'the sacred space [*hieron*] in which, in the time of the ancestors . . .' (9.5).

15§25. In other ways, however, the wording of Philostratus is not explicit. For example, in the description of the sacred space where the tomb of Protesilaos is located, we find no direct application of the word *tarīkhos* to the cult hero himself. Here is the relevant wording: *to de ge hieron en hōi, kata tous pateras ho*

Mēdos hubrizen, eph' hōi kai to tarīkhos anabiōnai phāsi, 'the sacred space [*hieron*] in which, in the time of the ancestors, the Persian man committed acts of outrage [*hubrizein*], and in which they say that *even the tarīkhos came back to life* [*anabiōnai*]' (*Hērōikos* 9.5). In this wording, I take it that the word *tarīkhos* applies to the preserved fish directly: even [*kai*] it came back to life from the dead. So the word *tarīkhos* applies to Protesilaos indirectly: the idea that the hero too came back to life from the dead is merely implied. In the narrative of Herodotus, by contrast, the initial mention of the roasting of *tarīkhoi* (9.120.1) is followed up at a later moment with a direct application of the word to Protesilaos himself, when the Persian captive is quoted as interpreting the portent:

HOUR 15 TEXT D (PART OF TEXT A)

But when Artayktes saw the portent [*teras*] he called out to the man roasting the salted fish [*tarīkhoi*] and said, "Athenian stranger [*xenos*], have no fear of this portent [*teras*]; it has not been sent to you. Instead Protesilaos of Elaious indicates [*sēmainein*] to me that even when salted and dead [*tarīkhos*] he holds power from the gods to punish one who treats him without justice [*a-dikeîn*]."

Herodotus 9.120.2*

15§26. These kinds of indirect references to the corpse and to the tomb of Protesilaos in the narratives of both Herodotus and Philostratus are typical of the mystical language that was traditionally used in referring to cult heroes. Among these indirect references are special words that have a general meaning in non-sacral contexts but a specific meaning in the sacred contexts of hero cult. One of these words is *oikos*, which means 'house' in everyday contexts but refers to the sacred space or 'dwelling' that houses the corpse of the hero in the sacred contexts of hero cult.† A striking example of this sacral meaning of *oikos*, as we will see in Hour 18, can be found in a passage in Sophocles' *Oedipus at Colonus* (627).‡ In the narrative of Herodotus about the cult hero Protesilaos, both meanings of *oikos* are activated:

* ὁ δὲ Ἀρταΰκτης, ὡς εἶδε τὸ τέρας, καλέσας τὸν ὀπτῶντα τοὺς ταρίχους ἔφη· "Ξεῖνε Ἀθηναῖε, μηδὲν φοβέο τὸ τέρας τοῦτο· οὐ γὰρ σοὶ πέφηνε, ἀλλ' ἐμοὶ σημαίνει ὁ ἐν Ἐλαιοῦντι Πρωτεσίλεως ὅτι καὶ τεθνεὼς καὶ τάριχος ἐὼν δύναμιν πρὸς θεῶν ἔχει τὸν ἀδικέοντα τίνεσθαι."
† PH 268–269 = 9§29.
‡ PH 269 = 9§29n99, following Edmunds 1981:223n8.

HOUR 15 TEXT E

|₉.₁₁₆.₁ The tyrant [turannos] of this province [= the Chersonesus] was Artayktes, a representative of [the king] Xerxes. He was a Persian, a formidable and impious man. He had deceived the king at the time of the expedition against Athens by robbing from Elaious the possessions [khrēmata] of Protesilaos son of Iphiklos. |₉.₁₁₆.₂ The tomb [taphos] of Protesilaos is at Elaious in the Chersonesus, and there is a sacred precinct [temenos] around it. There was a vast amount of possessions [khrēmata] there: gold and silver bowls, bronze, fabrics, and other dedicated offerings, all of which Artayktes seized and carried off because the king had given them to him. He deceived Xerxes by saying, |₉.₁₁₆.₃ "Master, there is here the house [oikos] of a Hellene who waged war against your land, but he met with justice [dikē] and was killed. Give me his house [oikos] so that all may know not to wage war against your land." This was going to be easy, to persuade Xerxes to give him [= Artayktes] a man's house [oikos] by saying this, since Xerxes had no suspicion of what he [= Artayktes] really thought. When he [= Artayktes] said that Protesilaos waged war against the king's land, he had in mind [noeîn] that the Persians consider all Asia to belong to them and to their successive kings. So the king made him the gift, and he [= Artayktes] carried off the possessions [khrēmata] from Elaious to Sestos. As for the sacred precinct [temenos], he [= Artayktes] used it for planting and farming. And whenever he would come [from Sestos] to Elaious for visits, he would even have sex inside the inner sanctum [aduton] with women.

Herodotus 9.116.1–3*

---

* |₉.₁₁₆.₁ Ἐτυράννευε δὲ τούτου τοῦ νομοῦ Ξέρξεω ὕπαρχος Ἀρταΰκτης, ἀνὴρ μὲν Πέρσης, δεινὸς δὲ καὶ ἀτάσθαλος, ὃς καὶ βασιλέα ἐλαύνοντα ἐπ' Ἀθήνας ἐξηπάτησε, τὰ Πρωτεσίλεω τοῦ Ἰφίκλου χρήματα ἐξ Ἐλαιοῦντος ὑπελόμενος. |₉.₁₁₆.₂ Ἐν γὰρ Ἐλαιοῦντι τῆς Χερσονήσου ἐστὶ Πρωτεσίλεω τάφος τε καὶ τέμενος περὶ αὐτόν, ἔνθα ἦν χρήματα πολλὰ καὶ φιάλαι χρύσεαι καὶ ἀργύρεαι καὶ χαλκὸς καὶ ἐσθὴς καὶ ἄλλα ἀναθήματα, τὰ Ἀρταΰκτης ἐσύλησε βασιλέος δόντος. Λέγων δὲ τοιάδε Ξέρξην διεβάλετο· |₉.₁₁₆.₃ "Δέσποτα, ἔστι οἶκος ἀνδρὸς Ἕλληνος ἐνθαῦτα, ὃς ἐπὶ γῆν τὴν σὴν στρατευσάμενος δίκης κυρήσας ἀπέθανε. Τούτου μοι δός, τὸν οἶκον, ἵνα καί τις μάθῃ ἐπὶ γῆν τὴν σὴν μὴ στρατεύεσθαι." Ταῦτα λέγων εὐπετέως ἔμελλε ἀναπείσειν Ξέρξην δοῦναι ἀνδρὸς οἶκον, οὐδὲν ὑποτοπηθέντα τῶν ἐκεῖνος ἐφρόνεε. Ἐπὶ γῆν δὲ τὴν βασιλέος στρατεύεσθαι Πρωτεσίλεων ἔλεγε νοέων τοιάδε· τὴν Ἀσίην πᾶσαν νομίζουσι ἑωυτῶν εἶναι Πέρσαι καὶ τοῦ αἰεὶ βασιλεύοντος. Ἐπεὶ δὲ ἐδόθη, τὰ χρήματα ἐξ Ἐλαιοῦντος ἐς Σηστὸν ἐξεφόρησε καὶ τὸ τέμενος ἔσπειρε καὶ ἔνεμε, αὐτός τε ὅκως ἀπίκοιτο ἐς Ἐλαιοῦντα, ἐν τῷ ἀδύτῳ γυναιξὶ ἐμίσγετο.

15§27. On the surface of this narrative, a Persian man appropriated the 'house' of a Greek man and farmed the land that surrounded that 'house'. And the pretext for this appropriation was the claim that the Greek man had committed an injustice against the Persians. Earlier in §12, we saw the rationalizations about injustices supposedly committed by Greeks against Persians, starting with the Trojan War: from the standpoint of the Persians, the Greeks started the conflict that led to the Persian Wars by way of invading Asia Minor in the Trojan War. And, as we saw even earlier in Hour 14§8, Protesilaos was the first of the Achaeans to leap from his ship after it was beached on the shores of the Hellespont— and the first hero to die fighting the Trojans.

15§28. Beneath the surface, however, this same narrative shows that the Persian man robbed the sacred dwelling place of a cult hero and violated the sacred precinct that surrounded that dwelling place by turning the precinct into a plantation used for private profit and pleasure. The permanent consequences of this impiety are noted in the *Hērōikos* of Philostratus (9.5–6): what had once been an enormous sacred precinct, with magnificent buildings and wide stretches of cultivated land enveloping it, became a small patch of a garden clustered around the tumulus of the hero. From what we see in the *Hērōikos*, the only thing that really survived the depredations of the Persian occupation was the natural beauty of this place that framed the tumulus of the hero. But this one thing, the natural beauty of the garden of Protesilaos, was really everything from the standpoint of hero cult. As we saw in Hour 14, the beauty of this garden signals the presence of the cult hero and the true justice of the cosmos. The *dikē*, 'justice', signaled by this flourishing garden is what is meant by Protesilaos, this cult hero who died and then came back to life again and again. Whenever he returns from the dead, Protesilaos can either punish the unjust with his grim anger or bless the just with his loving fertility. That is what Protesilaos *sēmainei*, 'means'.

Initiation into the Mysteries of a Cult Hero

15§29. We find a most valuable description of an actual initiation into the mysteries of a cult hero in the writings of Pausanias, an antiquarian who was active in the middle of the second century CE, about a half-century before Philostratus. In previous hours, I relied many times on the testimony of Pausanias, who proves to be a most reliable source about ancient Greek antiquities in general. In the case that we are about to consider, however, he is not only a reliable source: more than that, for all practical purposes, he is our unique source for a detailed description of initiation into the mysteries of a cult hero. The hero in question is Trophōnios, whose hero cult is located in Lebadeia in Boeotia. Pausanias (9.39.5–14) describes an initiation into the mysteries of Trophōnios, and, in the section following this one, I will quote the text of his description in its entirety. Before I can quote this text, however, I need to provide some background.

15§30. At one point in the description given by Pausanias (9.39.12), he will refer to the hero Trophōnios as a *theos,* 'god'. There is a comparable reference to Protesilaos in Herodotus (9.120.3): there the quoted words of Artayktes the Persian express the idea that this non-Greek man has finally recognized the power of the cult hero, and, in this context, Artayktes now refers to Protesilaos as a *theos,* 'god', to whom he hopes to make amends, offering 'to make a deposit of one hundred talents to the god' (*hekaton talanta katatheînai tōi theōi*).

15§31. Such references cannot be interpreted to mean that the hero is some kind of "faded god": what they mean, rather, is that the cult hero becomes a *theos* when he is immortalized after death. And I must stress that such an identification of the cult hero with a *theos,* 'god', can only be understood in the context of initiation into the hero's cult. In terms of the cult, as I have argued, the given cult hero is envisioned as a mortal in the preliminary phase of the ritual program of worship and then as a god in the central phase, at a climactic moment marking the hero's epiphany to his worshippers.*

15§32. I must add that the same kind of mentality is at work in practices of honoring the dead in general, as we can see from inscriptions marking the occasions of organizing funerals for those who have just died. I quote here a verse from one such inscription, written on a gold lamella from Thourioi in Magna Graecia. This inscribed lamella, dated to the fourth century BCE, was found in a tomb, where it had been buried together with a dead man who is addressed with the following words: *olbie kai makariste, theos d' e|sēi anti brotoio,* 'O blessed one, you who are called blessed, you will be a god [*theos*] instead of a mortal [*brotos*]' (*IG* XIV 641 line 9).† I have already quoted a part of this verse in Hour 11§19. As I noted there, we can find many other attestations of such wording in inscriptions that were buried with the dead, and these inscriptions

---

* Nagy 2008b:259, with reference to Nagy 2001a:25n17.

† ὄλβιε καὶ μακαριστέ, θεὸς δ' ἔ|σηι ἀντὶ βροτοῖο. The numbering of lines in this fragment from Thourioi follows the edition of Bernabé 2004/2005 (*Orphicorum Fragmenta* 488).

can be seen as initiatory texts that were meant to guide the dead toward some kind of an immortalized existence.*

15§33. So in the description that I will be quoting from Pausanias concerning an initiation into the hero cult of Trophōnios, the reference to this cult hero as a *theos*, 'god', turns out to be a genuine aspect of initiatory language. Pausanias himself, near the very beginning of his massive work on ancient Greek antiquities, says something that corroborates the formulation I have just offered. In analyzing the myths and rituals connected with the hero cult of Amphiaraos at Oropos in Boeotia, Pausanias (1.34.2) says that the worshippers of this cult hero at Oropos considered him to be a *theos*, 'god', and that all Hellenes eventually accepted such a status for this cult hero; in the same context, Pausanias (1.34.2) goes on to say that the same status of *theos*, 'god', was eventually accepted by all Hellenes in the cases of the cult hero Trophōnios as worshipped at Lebadeia in Boeotia and the cult hero Protesilaos as worshipped in the Chersonesus. Such a formulation is typical of the era of Pausanias, the second century CE, by which time the distinctly localized aura of hero cults was receding and giving way to the far brighter Panhellenic publicity that was being generated by the most famous cult heroes of the time, such as the triad of Amphiaraos, Trophōnios, and Protesilaos. That said, I should emphasize that this triad of cult heroes was already famous in the era of Herodotus, who lived over 600 years earlier than Pausanias. In the case of Protesilaos, we have already read the narrative of Herodotus about this cult hero; in the case of Amphiaraos and Trophōnios, Herodotus (1.46.2) mentions both of them together in the context of narrating oracular consultations made by Croesus, king of the Lydians, at the sites where these two cult heroes were worshipped. Still, my point remains that the mysteries concerning the death and the resurrection of all three of these cult heroes were becoming ever less mysterious in the era of Pausanias. Correspondingly, the eventual status of such heroes as *theoi*, 'gods', became ever more obvious to all.

15§34. The death of Amphiaraos is a most telling example. In the version of the relevant myth as retold by Pausanias (1.34.2), Amphiaraos is riding back home on his war chariot after the defeat of the Seven against Thebes, when suddenly the earth opens up and swallows him—speeding chariot and horses and all. At the spot where this engulfment happened, there is a *hieron*, 'sacred space', where worshippers of the hero come to consult him, though Pausanias reports that there is some disagreement about matching the place of the ritual consulta-

---

* For a useful collection of such inscriptions, I cite again the work of Tzifopoulos 2010.

tions with the actual place of the engulfment. In any case, the engulfment of Amphiaraos by the earth is a sign of his death and of his subsequent return from death as a cult hero. In the *Odyssey* (xv 247 and 253), the death of Amphiaraos after the expedition against Thebes is made explicit, though it is only implicit in the references to the engulfment of this same hero as narrated in the songs of Pindar (*Olympian* 6.14; *Nemean* 9.24–27, 10.8–9). The poetic reticence we see in Pindar's songs about mentioning the actual death of Amphiaraos at the moment of his engulfment by the earth is a sign, I argue, of a keen awareness about the subsequent resurrection of the hero.*

15§35. Like the cult hero Amphiaraos, the cult hero Trophōnios is also engulfed by the earth. As we see in the narrative of Pausanias (9.37.7), the earth opened up and engulfed him, and it happened in an *alsos*, 'grove', marked by the *bothros*, 'pit', of Agamedes, the brother of Trophōnios. So when Pausanias describes an initiation into the mysteries of the cult hero Trophōnios, he is in effect describing a ritual descent that corresponds to the mythological descent of Trophōnios himself into the nether world. And the goal of the initiand is to ascend from this nether world after the descent, just as a cult hero returns to life after death.

The Descent of an Initiand into the Nether World of a Cult Hero

15§36. With this background in place, I am finally ready to quote the narrative of Pausanias about an initiation into the mysteries of the cult hero Trophōnios. In my translation, I attempt to approximate the ritual language as closely as possible, including the numerous repetitions and periphrases:

HOUR 15 TEXT F

|_{9.39.5} At the oracle [*manteîon*], here are the kinds of things that happen. When a man decides to *descend* [*kat-ienai*] to the place of Trophōnios, first of all he undergoes a regimen for a set number of days in a *dwelling* [*oikēma*], and the *dwelling* [*oikēma*] is sacred to Good Superhuman Force [*Agathos Daimōn*] and to Good Fortune [*Agathē Tukhē*]. In undergoing the regimen there, he goes through various procedures of purification, avoiding hot baths; the water for bathing is the river Her-

---

* *BA* 154, 204 = 9§5, 10§41n3. I disagree with the formulation of Currie 2005:42 when he says that Amphiaraos "evades death" when he is engulfed by the earth in the three passages of Pindar (*Olympian* 6.14; *Nemean* 9.24–27, 10.8–9).

cyna. He has unlimited access to meat from the sacrifices, for *he who descends* [*kat-ienai*] makes sacrifices to Trophōnios himself and to the children of Trophōnios; also to Apollo and to Kronos, to Zeus with the epithet King [*Basileus*], to Hera Charioteer [*Hēniokhos* = the one who holds the reins of the chariot], and to Demeter, whom they name with the epithet Europa, saying that she was the wetnurse of Trophōnios. |₉.₃₉.₆ At each of the sacrifices a seer [*mantis*] is present, who inspects the entrails of the sacrificial victim, and after an inspection makes prophecies to *him who descends* [*kat-ienai*], saying whether Trophōnios will be of good intentions [*eu-menēs*] and will be welcoming when he *receives* [verb *dekhesthai*] him. The entrails of the other victims do not make clear all that much the *thinking* [*gnōmē*] of Trophōnios. But the night when each person *descends* [*kat-ienai*], on that night they sacrifice a ram over a pit [*bothros*], invoking Agamedes. Even if the previous sacrifices have appeared propitious, no account is taken of them unless the entrails of this ram mean *the same thing*. If all the sacrifices are in agreement with each other, then each person *descends* [*kat-ienai*], *having good hopes* [*eu-elpis*]. And each person *descends* [*kat-ienai*] in this way: |₉.₃₉.₇ First of all, in the night, they take him to the river Hercyna. Having taken him, they anoint him with olive oil and wash him. They [who do the anointing and the washing] are two boys chosen from among the citizens, about thirteen years old, and they are named Hermae. These are the ones who are washing *the one who descends* [*katabainein*] and who are attending to whatever is needed, in their function as attendant boys. Afterwards he is led by the priests, not immediately to the oracle [*manteîon*], but to fountains of water. These fountains are very near each other. |₉.₃₉.₈ Here it is necessary for him to drink water, called the water of Forgetting [*Lēthē*], so that there may be for him a forgetting [*lēthē*] of all thoughts that he was thinking [*phrontizein*] up to this point. Right after this, it is necessary for him to drink the other water, the water of Memory [*Mnēmosunē*]. From this he remembers [*mnēmoneuei*] the things seen by him as *the one who descended* [*katabainein*]. Having viewed the statue [*agalma*] which they say was made by Daedalus—about this there is no revelation made by the priests except to those who are about to go to Trophōnios—having seen this statue [*agalma*] and having worshipped it and having prayed, he proceeds to the oracle [*manteîon*], wearing a linen khiton and cinching the khiton with ribbons and wearing *the boots of the native locale* [*epikhōriai krēpīdes*]. |₉.₃₉.₉ The oracle [*manteîon*] is beyond the grove [*alsos*], on the mountain. There is a foundation, of white stone, in a circle. The perimeter of the foundation is in the proportion of a very small threshing floor. Its height is just short of two cubits. On the foundation, there are rods standing there. They are of bronze, like the cross-bars holding them together. And through them has been made a double door. Inside the perimeter is a chasm [*khasma*] in the earth, not naturally formed, but artificially constructed as a work of masonry, according to the most exact specifications. |₉.₃₉.₁₀ The form [*skhēma*] of this *constructed dwelling* [*oikodomēma*] is like that of a bread-oven [*kribanos*]. One might estimate its breadth across the middle to be about four cubits. And the depth of the *constructed dwelling* [*oikodomēma*] could be estimated to extend to not more than eight cubits. There has been made by them no constructed *descent* [*kata-basis*] to the bottom level. But when a man comes to Trophōnios, they bring him a ladder—a narrow and light one. There is, for *the one who has descended* [*kata-bainein*], a hole between the bottom level and the *constructed dwelling* [*oikodomēma*]. Its breadth appeared to be two spans, and its height one span. |₉.₃₉.₁₁ So, *the one who descends* [*kat-ienai*] is now lying down in the direction of the bottom level, holding barley-cakes kneaded in honey [*māzai memagmenai meliti*], and he pushes forward with his feet, forward into the hole; he himself pushes forward, eager for his knees to get into the hole. Then, after the knees, the rest of his body is suddenly drawn in, rushing forward, just as the biggest and most rapid river will catch a man in its torrents and carry him under. After this, for those who are now inside the inner sanctum [*aduton*], there is no single or same way [*tropos*] for them to learn the things of the future. One person will see them, another person will hear them. To return and go back for *those who descended* [*kata-bainein*] is through the same mouth, with feet first, pushing forward. |₉.₃₉.₁₂ They say that no one of *those who descended* [*kata-bainein*] has ever been killed, except for one of the bodyguards of Demetrius. They say that this person did not perform any of the customary rituals in the sacred space [*hieron*], and that he *descended* [*kata-bainein*] not in order to consult [*khrēsomenos*] the god but in hopes of stealing gold and silver from the inner sanctum [*aduton*]. It is said that the corpse of this person appeared [*ana-phainesthai*] *in another place,* and was not expelled at the sacred mouth. With reference to this man many other things are said. What has been said by me is what is most worthy of being taken into account. |_{9.39.13} *The one who has ascended* [*ana-bainein*] from Trophōnios is received once again by the priests, who seat him upon what is called the Throne [*thronos*] of Memory [*Mnēmosunē*], which is situated not far from the inner sanctum [*aduton*]. Having seated him, they ask him all he has seen and found out. After learning the answers, they then turn him over to his relatives or friends. These take him to the *dwelling* [*oikēma*] where he had earlier passed through his regimen in the presence of Fortune [*Tukhē*] and Superhuman Force [*Daimōn*], the Good [*agathoi*] ones. They [= relatives or friends] *take* him *back* [verb *komizein*] to this place by lifting him and carrying him off, while he is still possessed [*katokhos*] by terror and still unconscious both of himself and of those who are near him. Afterwards, his mind [*phronēsis*] will again be working not at all less well than before, in all respects, and even laughter *will come back* [*ep-an-ienai*] to him. |_{9.39.14} What I write is not hearsay; I myself have consulted [*khrēsamenos*] Trophōnios and have seen others doing so. And it is a necessity for *those who have descended* [*kat-ienai*] into the sacred space of Trophōnios to dedicate writings on a tablet that record all the things that each person has heard or seen.

Pausanias 9.39.5–14*

* |_{9.39.5} κατὰ δὲ τὸ μαντεῖον τοιάδε γίνεται. ἐπειδὰν ἀνδρὶ ἐς τοῦ Τροφωνίου κατιέναι δόξῃ, πρῶτα μὲν τεταγμένων ἡμερῶν δίαιταν ἐν οἰκήματι ἔχει, τὸ δὲ οἴκημα Δαίμονός τε ἀγαθοῦ καὶ Τύχης ἱερόν ἐστιν ἀγαθῆς· διαιτώμενος δὲ ἐνταῦθα τά τε ἄλλα καθαρεύει καὶ λουτρῶν εἴργεται θερμῶν, τὸ δὲ λουτρὸν ὁ ποταμός ἐστιν ἡ Ἕρκυνα· καί οἱ καὶ κρέα ἄφθονά ἐστιν ἀπὸ τῶν θυσιῶν, θύει γὰρ δὴ ὁ κατιὼν αὐτῷ τε τῷ Τροφωνίῳ καὶ τοῦ Τροφωνίου τοῖς παισί, πρὸς δὲ Ἀπόλλωνί τε καὶ Κρόνῳ καὶ Διὶ ἐπίκλησιν Βασιλεῖ καὶ Ἥρα τε Ἡνιόχῃ καὶ Δήμητρι ἣν ἐπονομάζοντες Εὐρώπην τοῦ Τροφωνίου φασὶν εἶναι τροφόν. |_{9.39.6} καθ᾽ ἑκάστην δὲ τῶν θυσιῶν ἀνὴρ μάντις παρὼν ἐς τοῦ ἱερείου τὰ σπλάγχνα ἐνορᾷ, ἐνιδὼν δὲ προθεσπίζει τῷ κατιόντι εἰ δὴ αὐτὸν εὐμενὴς ὁ Τροφώνιος καὶ ἵλεως δέξεται. τῶν μὲν δὴ ἄλλων ἱερείων τὰ σπλάγχνα οὐχ ὁμοίως δηλοῖ τοῦ Τροφωνίου τὴν γνώμην· ἐν δὲ νυκτὶ ᾗ κάτεισιν ἕκαστος, ἐν ταύτῃ κριὸν θύουσιν ἐς βόθρον, ἐπικαλούμενοι τὸν Ἀγαμήδην. θυμάτων δὲ τῶν πρότερον πεφηνότων αἰσίων λόγος ἐστὶν οὐδείς, εἰ μὴ καὶ τοῦδε τοῦ κριοῦ τὰ σπλάγχνα τὸ αὐτὸ θέλοι λέγειν· ὁμολογούντων δὲ καὶ τούτων, τότε ἕκαστος ἤδη κάτεισιν εὔελπις, κάτεισι δὲ οὕτω. |_{9.39.7} πρῶτα μὲν ἐν τῇ νυκτὶ αὐτὸν ἄγουσιν ἐπὶ τὸν ποταμὸν τὴν Ἕρκυναν, ἀγαγόντες δὲ ἐλαίῳ χρίουσι καὶ λούουσι δύο παῖδες τῶν ἀστῶν ἔτη τρία που καὶ δέκα γεγονότες, οὓς Ἑρμᾶς ἐπονομάζουσιν· οὗτοι τὸν καταβαίνοντά εἰσιν οἱ λούοντες καὶ ὁπόσα χρὴ διακονούμενοι ἅτε παῖδες. τὸ ἐντεῦθεν ὑπὸ τῶν ἱερέων οὐκ αὐτίκα ἐπὶ τὸ μαντεῖον, ἐπὶ δὲ ὕδατος πηγὰς ἄγεται· αἱ δὲ ἐγγύτατά εἰσιν ἀλλήλων. |_{9.39.8} ἐνταῦθα δὴ χρὴ πιεῖν αὐτὸν Λήθης τε ὕδωρ καλούμενον, ἵνα λήθη γένηταί οἱ πάντων ἃ τέως ἐφρόντιζε, καὶ ἐπὶ τῷδε ἄλλο αὖθις ὕδωρ πίνειν Μνημοσύνης· ἀπὸ τούτου τε μνημονεύει τὰ ὀφθέντα οἱ καταβάντι. θεασάμενος δὲ ἄγαλμα ὃ ποιῆσαι Δαίδαλόν> φασιν – ὑπὸ δὲ τῶν ἱερέων οὐκ ἐπιδείκνυται πλὴν ὅσοι παρὰ τὸν Τροφώνιον μέλλουσιν ἔρχεσθαι – τοῦτο τὸ ἄγαλμα ἰδὼν καὶ θεραπεύσας τε καὶ εὐξάμενος ἔρχεται πρὸς τὸ μαντεῖον, χιτῶνα

As we see from the concluding words of Pausanias here, he himself experienced an initiation into the mysteries of the cult hero Trophōnios. This fact makes his testimony all the more important and interesting.

A Brief Commentary on the Text about the Descent

15§37. In the text as I have quoted it, I have italicized my translations of those Greek words that evidently convey a special sacred meaning for the initiated. These words, when translated, seem simplistic when we consider their everyday meaning, but they are intended to be mystical for those who are initiated. Here I list two sets of such words, showing the original Greek forms:

kat-ienai and variant *kata-bainein*, meaning 'descend', and *ana-bainein*, meaning 'ascend': These words correspond to the explicit descent of the hero Trophōnios when he is engulfed by the earth—and to the implicit ascent of the same hero whenever he comes back to life and makes

---

ἐνδεδυκὼς λινοῦν καὶ ταινίαις τὸν χιτῶνα ἐπιζωσθεὶς καὶ ὑποδησάμενος ἐπιχωρίας κρηπῖδας. |₉.₃₉.₉ ἔστι δὲ τὸ μαντεῖον ὑπὲρ τὸ ἄλσος ἐπὶ τοῦ ὄρους. κρηπὶς μὲν ἐν κύκλῳ περιβέβληται λίθου λευκοῦ, περίοδος δὲ τῆς κρηπῖδος κατὰ ἅλων τὴν ἐλαχίστην ἐστίν, ὕψος δὲ ἀποδέουσα δύο εἶναι πήχεις· ἐφεστήκασι δὲ ἐπὶ τῇ κρηπῖδι ὀβελοὶ καὶ αὐτοὶ χαλκοῖ καὶ αἱ συνέχουσαι σφᾶς ζῶναι, διὰ δὲ αὐτῶν θύραι πεποίηνται. τοῦ περιβόλου δὲ ἐντὸς χάσμα γῆς ἐστιν οὐκ αὐτόματον ἀλλὰ σὺν τέχνῃ καὶ ἁρμονίᾳ πρὸς τὸ ἀκριβέστατον ᾠκοδομημένον. |₉.₃₉.₁₀ τοῦ δὲ οἰκοδομήματος τούτου τὸ σχῆμα εἴκασται κριβάνῳ· τὸ δὲ εὖρος ἡ διάμετρος αὐτοῦ τέσσαρας παρέχοιτο ἂν ὡς εἰκάσαι πήχεις· βάθος δὲ τοῦ οἰκοδομήματος, οὐκ ἂν οὐδὲ τοῦτο εἰκάζοι τις ἐς πλέον ὀκτὼ καθήκειν πηχῶν. κατάβασις δὲ οὐκ ἔστι πεποιημένη σφίσιν ἐς τὸ ἔδαφος· ἐπειδὰν δὲ ἀνὴρ ἔρχηται παρὰ τὸν Τροφώνιον, κλίμακα αὐτῷ κομίζουσι στενὴν καὶ ἐλαφράν. καταβάντι δέ ἐστιν ὀπὴ μεταξὺ τοῦ τε ἐδάφους καὶ τοῦ οἰκοδομήματος· σπιθαμῶν τὸ εὖρος δύο, τὸ δὲ ὕψος ἐφαίνετο εἶναι σπιθαμῆς. |₉.₃₉.₁₁ ὁ οὖν κατιὼν κατακλίνας ἑαυτὸν ἐς τὸ ἔδαφος ἔχων μάζας μεμαγμένας μέλιτι προεμβάλλει τε ἐς τὴν ὀπὴν τοὺς πόδας καὶ αὐτὸς ἐπιχωρεῖ, τὰ γόνατά οἱ τῆς ὀπῆς ἐντὸς γενέσθαι προθυμούμενος· τὸ δὲ λοιπὸν σῶμα αὐτίκα ἐφειλκύσθη τε καὶ τοῖς γόνασιν ἐπέδραμεν, ὥσπερ ποταμῶν ὁ μέγιστος καὶ ὠκύτατος συνδεθέντα ὑπὸ δίνης ἀποκρύψειεν ἂν> ἄνθρωπον. τὸ δὲ ἐντεῦθεν τοῖς ἐντὸς τοῦ ἀδύτου γενομένοις οὐχ εἷς οὐδὲ ὁ αὐτὸς τρόπος ἐστὶν ὅτῳ διδάσκονται τὰ μέλλοντα, ἀλλὰ πού τις καὶ εἶδε καὶ ἄλλος ἤκουσεν. ἀναστρέψαι δὲ ὀπίσω τοῖς καταβᾶσι διὰ στομίου τε ἔστι τοῦ αὐτοῦ καὶ προεκθεόντων σφίσι τῶν ποδῶν. |₉.₃₉.₁₂ ἀποθανεῖν δὲ οὐδένα τῶν καταβάντων λέγουσιν ὅτι μὴ μόνον τῶν Δημητρίου τινὰ δορυφόρων· τοῦτον δὲ οὔτε ποιῆσαι περὶ τὸ ἱερὸν φασιν οὐδὲν τῶν νενομισμένων οὔτε χρησόμενον τῷ θεῷ καταβῆναι, χρυσὸν δὲ καὶ ἄργυρον ἐκκομιεῖν ἐλπίσαντα ἐκ τοῦ ἀδύτου. λέγεται δὲ καὶ τούτου τὸν νεκρὸν ἑτέρωθι ἀναφανῆναι καὶ οὐ κατὰ στόμα ἐκβληθῆναι τὸ ἱερόν. ἐς μὲν δὴ τὸν ἄνθρωπον λεγομένων καὶ ἄλλων εἴρηταί μοι τὰ ἀξιολογώτατα. |₉.₃₉.₁₃ τὸν δὲ ἀναβάντα παρὰ τοῦ Τροφωνίου παραλαβόντες αὖθις οἱ ἱερεῖς καθίζουσιν ἐπὶ θρόνον Μνημοσύνης μὲν καλούμενον, κεῖται δὲ οὐ πόρρω τοῦ ἀδύτου, καθεσθέντα δὲ ἐνταῦθα ἀνερωτῶσιν ὁπόσα εἶδέ τε καὶ ἐπύθετο· μαθόντες δὲ ἐπιτρέπουσιν αὐτὸν ἤδη τοῖς προσήκουσιν. οἱ δὲ ἐς τὸ οἴκημα, ἔνθα καὶ πρότερον διῃτᾶτο παρά τε Τύχῃ καὶ Δαίμονι ἀγαθοῖς, ἐς τοῦτο ἀράμενοι κομίζουσι κάτοχόν τε ἔτι τῷ δείματι καὶ ἀγνῶτα ὁμοίως αὐτοῦ τε καὶ τῶν πέλας. ὕστερον μέντοι τά τε ἄλλα οὐδέν τι φρονήσει μεῖον ἢ πρότερον καὶ γέλως ἐπάνεισίν οἱ. |₉.₃₉.₁₄ γράφω δὲ οὐκ ἀκοὴν ἀλλὰ ἑτέρους τε ἰδὼν καὶ αὐτὸς τῷ Τροφωνίῳ χρησάμενος. τοὺς δὲ ἐς τοῦ Τροφωνίου κατελθόντας, ἀνάγκη σφᾶς, ὁπόσα ἤκουσεν ἕκαστος ἢ εἶδεν, ἀναθεῖναι γεγραμμένα ἐν πίνακι.

mental contact with those who worship him; a related form that we see in play here is *ep-an-ienai,* 'come back'.

oikos and *oikēma* and *oikodomēma,* meaning 'house' and 'dwelling' and 'constructed dwelling': These words refer to any built structures within the natural setting of the sacred space of the cult hero; we have seen such wording already in the narrative of Herodotus (9.116.1–3), quoted in Text E, about the dwelling place of the cult hero Protesilaos.

15§38. Besides such everyday words that are re-activated as sacred words in sacral contexts, we find here in the text of Pausanias a number of specialized words that refer directly to sacred contexts. Here I list a set of such specialized words, again showing the original Greek forms:

Agathos Daimōn, which I have translated as 'Good Superhuman Force', in Pausanias 9.39.5 and again in 9.39.13: The word *daimōn,* as we have seen ever since Hour 5, means 'superhuman force', and it is used in situations where the speaker will not or cannot speak the name of a given superhuman force—whether that force be a god or a hero. So the term *daimōn* is already mystical, and here the mysticism inherent in the word is augmented by way of the epithet *agathos,* meaning 'good'. We see here a perfect example of a *euphemism,* where you speak about something that can be either good or bad for you in such a way as to highlight the positive and to shade over the negative (literally, the original Greek word *eu-phēmeîn* means 'say good things'). When the initiand 'descends', he gets a prophecy concerning whether the cult hero will be *eu-menēs,* 'of good intentions', toward him, as we saw in 9.39.6. Whether or not the intentions of the cult hero turn out to be 'good', the descender will descend in the state of being *eu-elpis,* 'having good hopes', as we also saw in 9.39.6.

Theos, 'god', in Pausanias 9.39.12: The hero becomes a *theos* when he is immortalized after death, and Pausanias has already been initiated into that mystery. As we have already seen, Pausanias considers the cult hero Trophōnios to be a *theos,* 'god', in the afterlife. And, as we have also seen, there is a comparable reference in Herodotus (9.120.3) to the cult hero Protesilaos as a *theos,* 'god', in the afterlife.

the *bothros,* 'pit', of Agamedes in Pausanias 9.39.6: The sacrifice of the ram at this *bothros* is typical of hero cult. At Olympia, for example, as we see elsewhere in Pausanias (5.13.1–2), there is a *bothros,* 'pit', of the cult hero Pelops, and over that pit a black ram is sacrificed every year to Pelops, following a prototypical sacrifice made by Hēraklēs himself.* With regard to the *bothros,* 'pit', of Agamedes in Pausanias 9.39.6, we see in an earlier passage of Pausanias (9.37.5–7) that Agamedes is the brother of Trophōnios. When the two brothers are entombed together in a building that they themselves had built, Trophōnios escapes with his life after beheading Agamedes in order to hide their identity; it is only after this escape that Trophōnios experiences a mystical engulfment by the earth (9.37.7).

epikhōriai krēpīdes, 'the boots of the native locale', in Pausanias 9.39.8: By implication, it would be an offense to the local earth if the initiand were to tread upon it while wearing alien footwear, and so the wearing of 'epichoric' boots is a ritual attempt to mask the alien identity of any initiand. Such a taboo shows that the rituals of initiation into the hero cult of Trophōnios were ultimately a local affair, and that the Panhellenization of this cult (as analyzed in §33) needed ritual safeguards to counteract the possibility of alien pollution.

Hermaî, 'Hermae', the plural of 'Hermes', in Pausanias 9.39.7: The god Hermes, as divine patron of all forms of intermediacy, is embodied here in the ritual function of the boy attendants who make it possible for outsiders to be initiated into local mysteries that are controlled by those who are insiders to the locale.

Manteîon, 'oracle', in Pausanias 9.39.5, 9.39.7, 9.39.8, and 9.39.9: The place where the initiand is actually initiated into the mysteries of the cult hero Trophōnios is technically an 'oracle'. As we see from the formation of the word *manteîon,* it is a place where one consults a *mantis,* 'seer', who is in charge of communications from the superhuman force that presides over the sacred space writ large. In the description given by Pauasanias about the *manteîon* of Trophōnios, we see that there is in

---

* *PH* 123 = 4§10, with further references and commentary.

fact a *mantis*, 'seer', present 'at each of the sacrifices' (9.39.6). As for the actual place known as the *manteîon* of Trophōnios, it is a structure or *oikodomēma*, 'constructed dwelling' (9.39.10), that is located not in the *alsos*, 'grove', of the hero but 'on the mountain' (9.39.9).

aduton, 'inner sanctum', in Pausanias 9.39.11, 9.39.12, 9.39.13: Evidently, this location is the holy of holies within the *manteîon*. It is here that the treasures accumulated from offerings to Trophōnios are located, as I infer from the story about the would-be robber of these treasures (9.39.12). In the corresponding story of Herodotus (9.116.1–3) about the robbing of the treasures of the cult hero Protesilaos, as quoted in Text E, we see a reference to the *aduton*, 'inner sanctum', of the hero, where the robber had sex with women (9.116.3). I further infer that the treasures of Protesilaos were likewise stored in this inner sanctum.

māzai memagmenai meliti, 'barley-cakes kneaded in honey', in Pausanias 9.39.11: Elsewhere in Pausanias (6.20.2), we are told of a *hieron*, 'sacred space', of the goddess *Eileithuia* at Olympia in Elis: within that space, a *daimōn* or 'superhuman force' who is described as 'epichoric' or 'local' (*epikhōrios*) is tended by the priestess of the goddess *Eileithuia*, who prepares for the *daimōn* an offering of barley-cakes kneaded in honey (*māzai memagmenai meliti*). The ritual practice of offering honey to *Eileithuia*, who is goddess of childbirth, dates back to the Bronze Age, as we see from the evidence of a Linear B tablet found at Knossos (Gg 705): the inventory of this tablet tells of an offering of honey to a goddess named *Eleuthia*, which is a variant form of *Eileithuia*.* In the context of initiation into the mysteries of the cult hero Trophōnios, we have seen that the initiand experiences a feet-first entry through a hole into the *aduton*, 'inner sanctum', and then a feet-first exit from it through the same hole; and, at the moment of entry, the initiand is holding in both hands *māzai memagmenai meliti*, 'barley-cakes kneaded in honey' (Pausanias 9.39.11). Going through the motions of this double experience, I infer, evokes the idea of birth and rebirth, which is most appropriate to *Eileithuia* as goddess of childbirth.

---

* Nagy 2008a:19; Levaniouk 2011:96n14.

After the description of his initiation, Pausanias (9.40.2) tells a story about the discovery of the site where the oracle is located: a man called *Saōn*, meaning 'Savior', followed a swarm of bees to this mystical place, and there he was taught how to 'do' (*drân*) all the rituals by the cult hero Trophōnios himself.

The Oracular Consultation of Heroes

15§39. In his narrative about his own initiation into the mysteries of the cult hero Trophōnios, Pausanias (9.39.14) sums up his experience by saying that he 'consulted' the cult hero: the form that he uses to express this idea is the aorist participle *khrēsamenos*. Likewise, Pausanias (9.39.12) uses the future participle *khrēsomenos* with reference to the would-be robber who only pretended to 'consult' the same cult hero—and who was mysteriously killed while making an attempt at a false initiation. These forms *khrēsamenos / khrēsomenos* come from a verb-root *khrē-*, which conventionally expresses the idea of consulting oracles: in the middle voice the verb means 'consult an oracle', while in the active and passive voices it means 'speak as an oracle' and 'is spoken by an oracle' respectively. The use of this verb *khrē-* by Pausanias in this context is perfectly in line with the fact that he uses the word *manteîon*, 'oracle', four times with reference to the place where he gets initiated (9.39.5, 9.39.7, 9.39.8, and 9.39.9). And here I highlight a most striking parallel: Herodotus uses the same verb *khrē-* and the same noun *manteîon* in referring to consultations of the oracle of the god Apollo at Delphi. A notable example is his narrative about the consultation of the oracle at Delphi by Croesus, king of the Lydians (χρησόμενοι 1.47.7 and ἐχρήσθη 1.49.1; μαντήιον 1.48.1).

15§40. In this light, I find it most significant that there exists an overt connection between the hero Trophōnios and the god Apollo as oracular figures. According to Pausanias (9.37.5) one version of the myth of Trophōnios says that this hero was the son of a mortal named Ergīnos, but there is another version saying that only Agamedes the brother of Trophōnios was fathered by Ergīnos while Trophōnios himself was fathered by the god Apollo. And Pausanias adds that he believes the second version of the myth precisely because he, Pausanias himself, had been initiated into the mysteries of the cult hero, and he refers to this initiation as an act of consultation. Here is the way Pausanias puts it (9.37.5):

καὶ ἐγώ τε πείθομαι καὶ ὅστις παρὰ Τροφώνιον ἦλθε δὴ μαντευσόμενος,
'I believe it, and so does anyone else who has gone to Trophōnios in order to
consult him [*manteuesthai*]'.

15§41. Pausanias believes because he is initiated. By contrast, the non-
initiated have a hard time believing. A case in point is the exchange between the
Phoenician as initiand and the Ampelourgos as initiator in a lengthy passage
that I quoted earlier from the *Hērōikos* of Philostratus (2.6–3.6), Hour 14 Text E.
In the course of that exchange, when the Phoenician hears from the Ampelourgos about the epiphanies of the hero Protesilaos and of other Achaean heroes of
the Trojan War, he admits that he has a hard time believing it all: 'I do not believe', he says right from the start (*a-pistô* 3.1). In other words, the initiand is not
yet initiated. Still, he wants to be a 'believer' (*pisteuōn* 2.12). So here too, as also
in the case of Trophōnios, the mystery of the hero is for the initiator to know
and for the initiand to find out.* But the more the initiand hears, the more he
believes. After hearing an account of a series of heroic epiphanies as retold by
the Ampelourgos, the Phoenician even exclaims: 'no one can any longer disbe-
lieve [*a-pisteîn*] such stories!' (18.1).

An Initiation for the Reader

15§42. In reading the *Hērōikos* of Philostratus, even the reader of the text can
assume the role of an initiand. The natural beauty of the place sacred to the cult
hero Protesilaos casts a spell not only on the Phoenician as initiand but also, vicariously, on the reader. The spell begins as the Phoenician, accompanied by
the Ampelourgos, enters the sacred garden:

HOUR 15 TEXT G (PART OF HOUR 14 TEXT E)

|₃.₃ {Ampelourgos:} "Let us enter the vineyard, Phoenician. For you
may even discover in it something to give cheer [*euphrosunē*] to you."
{Phoenician:} "Yes, let us enter. I think a sweet scent is being breathed
out [*ana-pneîn*] from the plants." |₃.₄ {Ampelourgos:} "What are you
saying, 'sweet'? It is something godlike [*theion*]! The blossoms of the
uncultivated trees are fragrant, as are the fruits of those that are cultivated. If you ever come upon a cultivated plant with fragrant blossoms,

---

* Nagy 2008a:25–26.

pluck rather the leaves, since the sweet scent comes from them." |₃.₅
{Phoenician:} "How diverse [*poikilē*] is the beauty [*hōrā*] of this place you have here, and how lush have the clusters of grapes grown! How well-arranged are all the trees, and how ambrosial [*ambrosiā*] is the fragrance of the place!"

Philostratus *Hērōikos* 3.3–5

15§43. Now a gentle breeze carries the sweet aroma of flowers in bloom, and the initiand is feeling refreshed. He remarks that the plantlife literally 'breathes out', *ana-pneî*, a sweetness of its own (3.3). It is the right season, the exact time, the perfect moment: it is the *hōrā* (3.5; also at 3.2). The initiand can begin to sense the hero's sacred presence. Through a kind of sacred *metonymy*, as I described it in Hour 14§16, the breath of the hero himself now begins to animate the atmosphere: Protesilaos is now revealing, *apo-phainōn*, the scent of the blossoms at their sweetest (11.3).* The hero's presence smells sweeter than myrtles in autumn (10.2), as we saw in the wording quoted in Hour 14 Text J. The perfect moment or *hōrā*, in all its natural beauty, becomes the ultimate epiphany of the cult hero.

15§44. The concept of *hōrā* as the 'right season' (Philostratus *Hērōikos* 3.2, 3.5) conveys the context of ritual perfection and correctness; in that sense, *hōrā* is conceived as the perfect moment of beauty.† It is relevant to recall here the Modern Greek adjective *oréos*, which means 'beautiful' and which corresponds to ancient Greek *hōraîos*, 'seasonal': as we saw starting at Hour 14§18, the meaning of this word is ultimately derived from *hōrā*. And it is also relevant to recall here once again the formal and semantic connections of *hōrā* and *Hērā* with *hērōs*, 'hero', which I have been tracing ever since Hour 1§27. By now we can see even more clearly that heroes become 'seasonal' after they die and achieve mystical immortalization. That is why, as we saw starting at Hour 5§108, the death of a hero is a beautiful death, *une belle mort*, and that is also why the hero in death can be seen as a beautiful corpse, *un beau mort*. And even the unseasonality of the hero in life can be seen as beautiful, because it will lead to the seasonality of life after death. That is the beauty and the sorrow of an epithet we

---

* Such a traditional metonymy depends on a pre-existing traditional metaphor that pictures an interchangeability between breath and wind, on which see Nagy 1999.

† On the religious mentality of equating ritual perfection with beauty itself, see in general the work of Pache 2004.

find toward the end of the *Iliad* (XXIV 540), where Achilles while he is still alive in his own epic narrative is described as *pan-a-hōrios,* 'the most unseasonal of them all'.*

The Personal Intimacy of Experiencing a Heroic Epiphany

15§45. A sense of personal intimacy is conveyed by the worshipper when he says about the hero (*Hērōikos* 9.7): 'I am with him (*autōi gar xuneimi*), and no cult statue (*agalma*) can be sweeter (*hēdion*) than he, that one (*ekeinos*)'. The worshipper's experience of the hero as a real person, not as a cult statue (*agalma*), is here conveyed by the deictic pronoun *ekeinos,* 'that one', which is conventionally used to refer to a hero who appears in an epiphany.† We have already seen an example of such a use of *ekeinos,* 'that one', in Sappho 31.1, as analyzed in Hour 5§39 (where the dialectal form is *kēnos*).‡ The deixis of *ekeinos,* 'that one', conveys the remoteness ('that' not 'this') of the hero, even in the immediacy of his epiphany. The gap between the superhuman and the human is so great that it sets the superhuman apart from the human even in the process of attempting to bridge that gap in an epiphany.§

15§46. As we have already seen, the human response to the personal experience of such a heroic epiphany can be eroticized. The person who experiences the epiphany can feel the sensual urge to embrace and kiss the cult hero:

HOUR 15 TEXT H (PART OF HOUR 14 TEXT I)

|₁₁.₂ {Phoenician:} "And do you embrace him when he comes to you [in the garden]—or does he elude you by going up in a puff of smoke, the same way he eludes the poets?" {Ampelourgos:} "Actually, he takes pleasure [*khairein*] when I embrace him and lets me kiss [*philein*] him and put my arm around his neck."

Philostratus *Hērōikos* 11.2

15§47. And, as we have also seen, the living can even fall passionately in love with the apparition of a hero who appears in an epiphany. I recall here the song about a girl's experience with the phantom of Antilokhos:

---

* *HQ* 48n79.
† *PH* 200–201 = 7§2, with reference to Mimnermus 14.1.
‡ See also *PH* 201 = 7§2n10, with reference to Sappho 31.1.
§ Nagy 2001a:27n20.

HOUR 15 TEXT I (= TEXT C)

My guest [*xenos*], I will lose my voice if I try to recall all such stories [about heroes who make epiphanies at the Plain of Scamander in the region of Troy]. For example, there is a song about Antilokhos, how a girl from the city of [New] Ilion who was wandering along the banks of the river Scamander had an encounter [*en-tunkhanein*] with the phantom [*eidōlon*] of Antilokhos and embraced his tomb [*sēma*] in a fit of passionate erotic desire [*erôsa*] for the phantom [*eidōlon*].

Philostratus Hērōikos 22.3

15§48. The convention of eroticizing the epiphany of a cult hero is implicit, as I started arguing in Hour 14§14, in the epic usage of *potheîn*, 'long for, yearn for', with reference to Protesilaos in *Iliad* II 703, 709, verses that I quoted in Hour 14 Text D. On one level of meaning, the warriors native to the land of Phthia are longing for the epic hero Protesilaos as their leader, who is also a native of Phthia. On a deeper level, however, the reference implies the emotional response of native worshippers who are longing for their native son, for their local cult hero, in all his immanent beauty.*

Ritual Correctness in Making Mental Contact with the Cult Hero

15§49. In Hour 14 Text E as quoted from the *Hērōikos* of Philostratus (2.6–3.6), we have seen the use of the word *hōrā* in the sense of a 'perfect time' or the 'right time' for making mental contact with the cult hero Protesilaos. And we have seen in general that this 'right time' as expressed by *hōrā* is good and beautiful and pleasurable in situations where the rituals of worshipping the cult hero are conducted correctly. A most striking example in the *Hērōikos* is a detailed description of the local cult heroes who preside over the Plain of Scamander in the region of Troy: in their various epiphanies, they reveal themselves as *megaloi*, 'great'—that is, 'larger than life'—and *theioi*, 'godlike' (18.1–2), and they reward the local herdsmen by keeping their herds healthy and fertile when the *hōrai*, 'times', are right (18.2). At such times, the herdsmen make sacrifices to the heroes by slaughtering sacrificial animals selected from their herds (again, 18.2).

---

* In some Homeric references to heroes as "native sons" of their homelands, a key word is *dēmos* in the sense of 'local district', indicating localized cult practices: see *GM* 132–134, especially with reference to the hero Sarpedon.

15§50. Other times, however, may not be so right, and then the heroes of the Trojan Plain appear in epiphanies that show the ill effects of their changes in mood. If they are dusty in their appearance, then there will be drought; if they are covered with sweat, they portend heavy rains and flooding; if they are stained with blood, then there will be contagious diseases visited upon the herds (again, *Hērōikos* 18.2). Moreover, when a herd animal on the Trojan Plain dies unexpectedly, the herdsmen believe that the cause is surely the angry hero Ajax (18.3), whose anger is linked to the myth about his ritually incorrect slaughtering of herd animals (again, 18.3); this myth, in its classical form, is brought to life in the tragedy *Ajax* by Sophocles.* By implication, the disastrous incorrectness of the hero's slaughtering of the sacred herds in myth must be compensated for all time to come in ritual, and that compensation takes the form of ritually correct sacrificial procedures in the slaughtering of herd animals by herdsmen who tend their herds on the Trojan Plain.

How the Cult Hero Communicates

15§51. The malevolent as well as the benevolent functions of the cult hero are communicated by way of revelations to those who are initiated into the hero cult. In the case of the cult hero Protesilaos, for example, things that are *theia*, 'godlike', and *megala*, 'great'—that is, 'larger than life'—will not escape the notice of those who are 'cultivated', *kharientes* (*Hērōikos* 3.2). For the uninitiated, however, these same secrets are veiled in language that expresses what seems quite ordinary and everyday on the surface. About the cult hero Protesilaos, the initiated Ampelourgos starts the process of initiating the uninitiated Phoenician by saying to him, as we saw in Hour 14 Text E: 'he [= Protesilaos] lives [*zēi*] here, and we work the land [*geōrgoumen*] together' (*Hērōikos* 2.8). What image in life could be more straightforward, more everyday, than life itself? When the Phoenician initiand follows up by asking whether Protesilaos 'lives' in the sense that he is 'resurrected' (*anabebiōkōs*), the initiated Ampelourgos replies: 'He himself does not speak about his own experiences [*pathos* plural]' (2.9). This absolutizing declaration is then followed by a series of qualifications: modifying what he has just said, the initiated Ampelourgos now goes on to say that the hero Protesilaos does in fact speak about his own death at Troy, about his first

* Nagy 2001a:28n21. On the tomb of Ajax, see *HPC* 179 = II§118.

resurrection, and about his second death—though he does not speak about his second resurrection (2.9–11).*

15§52. A vital question remains: how can a cult hero like Protesilaos actually communicate with those who are initiated into his mysteries? According to the traditional mentality of hero cults, the answer is simple: whenever they come back to life, cult heroes are endowed with a superhuman consciousness. And this consciousness of the hero, activated by hero cult, not only informs those who are initiated: it also performs the basic function of ensuring the seasonality of nature, and it manifests itself in such positive functions as the maintaining of health and fertility for humans—or for animals and plants. For example, Protesilaos is described as the *iatros*, 'healer' of sheep, beehives, and trees (*Hērōikos* 4.10).† Cult heroes, when they feel benevolent, will cure illnesses afflicting humans, animals, and plants—just as they will inflict these same illnesses when they feel malevolent. And the presence of the hero in such situations is signaled by feelings of a certain kind of sacred "frisson," conveyed by the evocative word *phrikē*, 'shudder'—as when the angry phantom of Ajax makes an epiphany by shouting at shepherds who have been foolishly taunting his restless spirit (18.4).

More on the Oracular Consultation of Heroes

15§53. When the superhuman consciousness of cult heroes is activated, they can be *consulted*, as we saw in Text F, where Pausanias describes his own consulting of Trophōnios at the oracle of that hero. Similarly in *Hērōikos* of Philostratus, we see that a cult hero like Protesilaos has to be actively consulted by his worshippers: from the start, in fact, the Ampelourgos says that Protesilaos is his own personal 'advisor', *xumboulos* (Ionic for *sumboulos; 4.7). And if the ritual of consultation were ever to fail, the Ampelourgos says that he would know for sure, since Protesilaos would then be silent, *esiōpā* (4.8). By contrast, the success of any consultation is manifested whenever the cult hero speaks. Of special interest are some special kinds of consultants. For example, among those who consult Protesilaos are athletes: as the Ampelourgos says, Protesilaos is generally a *sumboulos*, 'advisor', to athletes who cultivate him (14.4); in one specific

---

* Nagy 2001a:28–29.
† On the "iatric" function of cult heroes, see in general Brelich 1958:113–118.

case, Protesilaos is said to 'give oracular consultations', *khrēsai*, to an athlete who consults him on how to win a given athletic event (15.5).*

15§54. Such consulting of oracular cult heroes concerns not only the fundamentals of nature as defined metonymically by these heroes. It concerns also the fundamental nature of the heroes themselves. Their heroic essence has two aspects, one of which is defined by epic narrative traditions, while the other is defined by hero cult. In the *Hērōikos* of Philostratus, these two aspects of the hero are treated holistically as integral parts of a single concept. Thus the process of consulting oracular heroes leads to the initiand's knowledge about their epic aspects, not only about their ritual aspects as oracles. As the Ampelourgos declares, cult heroes have their own knowledge of epic narrative because they are endowed with *mantikē sophia*, 'the skill of a seer [*mantis*]', and there is an 'oracular' principle, *khrēsmōdes*, operating within them (7.3–4). That is why, as we saw in Hour 14 Text B, a hero like Protesilaos 'sees all the way through', *di-horâi*, the poems of Homer (7.5), knowing things that go beyond his own experiences when he, Protesilaos, had lived in the past of heroes (7.5–6); the hero even knows things about which Homer himself did not sing (7.5).†

15§55. So the *Hērōikos* of Philostratus provides a model of poetic inspiration that centers on the superhuman consciousness of the oracular hero, which has a totalizing control of epic narrative. As we shall now see, this model is not an innovation but an archaism, stemming from oral poetic traditions that predate even the Homeric traditions of the *Iliad* and the *Odyssey*.‡

15§56. When we are confronted with the idea that an oracular cult hero possesses total mastery of epic narrative, our first impression is that this idea cannot be reconciled with what we find in Homeric poetry. According to the poetics of the Homeric *Iliad* and *Odyssey*, as we saw in Hour 2, it is of course the Muses who 'inspire' epic narrative. At first glance, then, these goddesses of memory seem to be the sole source for the superhuman consciousness that informs the content of Homeric poetry and gives it the authority to tell about the gods and heroes of heroic times. This authority, however, is actually shared with the heroes who are quoted by Homeric performance, as a closer look at the *Iliad* and the *Odyssey* reveals clearly.

15§57. In his book about the "quotations" of heroes in Homeric poetry, Rich-

* Nagy 2001a:29n23.
† Nagy 2001a:29–30.
‡ The argumentation that follows is based on Nagy 2001a:30–35.

ard Martin has demonstrated that the "voice" of the poet becomes traditionally identified with the "voices" of the heroes quoted by the poetic performance:

> My central conclusion is that the *Iliad* takes shape as a poetic composition in precisely the same "speaking culture" that we see foregrounded in the stylized words of the poem's heroic speakers, especially those speeches designated as *mūthos,* a word I redefine as "authoritative speech act." The poet and the hero are both "performers" in a traditional medium. The genre of *mūthos* composing requires that its practitioners improve on previous performances and surpass them, by artfully manipulating traditional material in new combinations. In other words, within the speeches of the poem, we see that it is traditional to be spontaneous: no hero ever merely repeats; each recomposes the traditional text he performs, be it a boast, threat, command, or story, in order to project his individual personality in the most convincing manner. I suggest that the "voice" of the poet is the product of the same traditional performance technique.*

15§58. Recent ethnographic work on oral poetic performance traditions has provided typological parallels in support of Martin's demonstration. In the *Sīrat Banī Hilāl* epic singing tradition of the poets of al-Bakātūsh in contemporary Egypt, for example, Dwight Reynolds has sought—and found—an analogy for Martin's model of the interchangeable "voice" of poet and hero in epic performance:

> [T]he social reality of the al-Bakātūsh poets involves a distinctly negative position for the epic singer within the greater social hierarchy; in marked contrast to the poet's marginalized status in village society, however, are the moments of centrality, power, and "voice" he achieves in epic performance. This disjunctive persona has produced not only a fascinating process of deep self-identification with the epic tradition on the part of the poets, but has clearly, over generations, shaped and indeed constituted many aspects of the content of the epic itself—an epic tradition, as I have termed it, of heroic poets and poetic heroes.†

---

* Martin 1989:xiv.

† Reynolds 1995:208; at p. 207, Reynolds quotes the formulation of 1989:xiv as a heuristic paradigm for his own ethnographic fieldwork.

15§59. A plethora of ethnographic work also documents the widespread mentality of heroic "possession," where the consciousness of the poet is "possessed" by the consciousness of the hero as soon as the poet, in performance, starts "quoting" the hero.* As one ethnographer puts it, there can be "a transition from a story *about* a spirit, to one told *to* a spirit, to one told *by* a spirit."† In this comparative context, it is relevant to reconsider Philostratus *Hērōikos* 12.3, where Protesilaos *epaineî*, 'confirms', the words spoken by Homer 'to' (*es*) himself, not 'about' himself. The implication of *epaineî* is that Protesilaos 'confirms' the epic verses in the *Iliad* about his epic deeds at Troy, and he performs this 'confirmation' by way of *re-performing* these Homeric verses.‡ We have already seen these verses, *Iliad* II 695–709, which I quoted in Hour 14 Text D.

15§60. All this is not to say that the *Hērōikos* of Philostratus has preserved for us a direct continuation of living oral epic traditions in which heroes are being "quoted" through the supernatural consciousness of the heroes themselves. I have little doubt that the oral traditions of composition-in-performance, as still reflected in the hexameter poetry of the *Iliad* and the *Odyssey* and of the epic Cycle in general, had been dead for well over half a millennium by the time Philostratus composed his *Hērōikos*. Still, it is essential to stress that the traditions of hero cults were evidently still alive in the era of Philostratus. Moreover, the archaic mentality of seeking communion with the consciousness of cult heroes was likewise still alive. Even though the Homeric poems and the epic Cycle were now literary rather than oral traditions, they still preserved, as traditions per se, a vital link with the rituals of hero cult. The *Hērōikos* bridges the chasm between the mythical world of epic heroes and the ritual world of cult heroes. In this masterpiece of the era known nowadays as the Second Sophistic, a continuum is still felt to exist between these two diverging worlds. The spirit of this age is captured by this formulation of the Phoenician initiand in the *Hērōikos*

---

* For a particularly valuable collection of examples, see Blackburn et al. 1989; see especially p. 60, where Claus notes: "In his performance the possessed priest must not only recite Kordabbu's story, but also assume his character and dramatically portray his exploits for several hours on end."

† P. J. Claus, in Blackburn et al. 1989:74; he adds: "Accompanying these transitions are shifts in verbal style: from the third person pronominal referent, to the second, to the first. There are also changes in the behavior of the performers and the audience."

‡ On the poetics of authentication-by-reperformance, as implied by the verb *epaineîn*, which I have translated here as 'confirm', see the comments on the use of this word by Lycurgus *Against Leokrates* 102, in *PR* 11n7, 27–28, 33, 44. For a wealth of information about and insights into the poetics of the verb *epaineîn* as used in Homeric poetry, see Elmer 2013.

(6.3): 'I dreamed I was reading aloud [*ana-ginōskein*] the epic verses [*epos* plural] of Homer'.*

15§61. As in the *Hērōikos* of Philostratus, we can see in other literatures as well the stylized efforts of literati to maintain a continuum between myths and rituals associated with heroes. A notable example comes from an anecdote, dated to the ninth century CE,† concerning the rediscovery of a supposedly lost book, the *Táin Bó Cuailnge* ("The Cattle Raid of Cooley"), which is a collection of "epic" narratives about Ireland's greatest heroes.‡ This anecdote is in effect a "charter myth,"§ explaining the raison d'être of the *Táin*.** In terms of the myth, this book of narratives, the *Táin*, is equivalent to an integral epic performance. The myth narrates how this book was once lost and how the assembled poets of Ireland 'could not recall it in its entirety,' since they knew only *bloga*, 'fragments'.†† In a quest to find the lost integral book, the poet Muirgen happens to travel past the tomb of Fergus mac Roich, one of the chief heroes featured in the narrative of the *Táin*. It is nighttime. Muirgen sits down at the gravestone of the tomb, and he sings an incantation to this gravestone 'as though it were Fergus himself'.‡‡ Responding to the incantation, Fergus himself appears in all his heroic glory, and he 'recited him [= to Muirgen] the whole *Táin*, how everything had happened, from start to finish'.§§ As in the *Hērōikos* of Philostratus, we see that the superhuman consciousness of the hero can take over or even possess the narration of epic.***

15§62. In sum, the *Hērōikos* of Philostratus makes it clear that heroes cannot be defined exclusively in terms of their epic dimensions, though this aspect becomes vitally important in the history of ideas about heroism, especially in view

---

* Nagy 2001a:32–33.

† For a brief summary of the manuscript sources, see J. F. Nagy 1986:292.

‡ There are two main surviving recensions of the *Táin*, as attested in (1) the *Book of the Dun Cow* (*Lebor na Huidre,* eleventh century CE) and (2) the *Book of Leinster* (twelfth century). For editions of these respective recensions, see (1) O'Rahilly 1976 and (2) O'Rahilly 1967. For background, see J. F. Nagy 1986:278. For a synthetic translation, see Kinsella 1969.

§ On the concept of "charter myth," see Leach 1982:5.

** There is a translation provided by Kinsella 1969:1–2.

†† Kinsella 1969:1. The concept of a *blog*, 'fragment', of a corpus that has disintegrated is a traditional theme found in the charter myths of many cultures; for a brief survey, see *HQ* 70–74.

‡‡ Kinsella 1969:1.

§§ Kinsella 1969:1–2. The point of this charter myth, then, is that the corpus of the *Táin* is reintegrated in performance, and thus the "lost book" is finally recovered, even resurrected. See *HQ* 70, following especially J. F. Nagy 1986:284, 289, 292–294. On traditional metaphors about a book (or a library of books) as a corpus destined for resurrection, see Nagy 1998:196–198.

*** Nagy 2001a:33–34.

of the ultimate cultural prestige surrounding the prime medium that conveys these ideas, Homeric poetry. For Philostratus, the prestige of Homer and the Homeric hero is a given. In his *Hērōikos,* however, he goes further, much further, by reconnecting that epic prestige with the sacred charisma possessed by the cult hero.*

Coming Back Once Again to What the Hero 'Means'

15§63. I round out my analysis of the word *sēmainein* by coming back to the message of the cult hero Protesilaos, as indicated by this word *sēmainein* in Herodotus 9.120.2, quoted in Text A. By now we have seen that Protesilaos 'means' something that goes far deeper than any everyday meaning could ever go, and that this deeper meaning taps into the cosmic order of *dikē* as 'justice', which is seen as an absolute value that is safeguarded not only by the gods but also by cult heroes as natural forces that express the power of the gods.

15§64. And this deepest of meanings is also the highest of meanings. This is clear from the fact that the word *sēmainein* can be used to indicate an act of communication by someone whose perspective originates from the highest of all imaginable points of view. That someone who commands the highest vantage point of them all is Apollo, god of intelligence: as a sun-god, he has an intellect that soars above the whole universe. That is why Heraclitus of Ephesus, that towering intellectual of the Ionian world whose life spanned the late sixth and early fifth centuries BCE, can say of Apollo:

HOUR 15 TEXT J

The Lord [= Apollo], whose oracle [*manteîon*] is in Delphi, neither says [*legei*] nor conceals [*kruptei*]: he indicates [*sēmainei*].

Heraclitus 22 B 93 DK, as quoted by Plutarch
On the Oracular Pronouncements of the Pythia 404d†

15§65. So Apollo *sēmainei,* 'means', what he means by way of communicating from the vantage point of the sun: he is all-seeing.‡ That is why, when Herodo-

---

* Nagy 2001a:34–35.
† ὁ ἄναξ, οὗ τὸ μαντεῖόν ἐστι τὸ ἐν Δελφοῖς, οὔτε λέγει οὔτε κρύπτει ἀλλὰ σημαίνει.
‡ *PH* 164–165 = 6§37.

tus first quotes the oracle of Apollo, the god is quoted as saying in his divine poetic language:*

HOUR 15 TEXT K

I know [*oida*] the number of the grains of sand and the measure of the sea. | I understand the mute and I hear the one who does not speak. | The smell has come to my senses of a hard-shelled tortoise, | boiling with meat of lamb,† | where bronze is spread below, bronze set above.

Herodotus 1.47.3‡

15§66. The verb *oida*, 'I know', here, which is the first word of the first quotation of poetry in the *Histories* of Herodotus, is the perfect form of the verb-root *id-*, which in its non-perfect forms means 'to see': so *oida* means, more literally, 'I have just seen, therefore I know'.§ What is known, however, can be expressed in a mystical way, and only those who are mentally and morally and emotionally qualified can understand it.

15§67. When Herodotus himself chooses a moment to speak from the highest possible vantage point of authority, he too says *oida*, 'I know':

HOUR 15 TEXT L = TEXT B

|₁.₅.₃ Concerning these things, I am not going to say that they were so or otherwise, but I will indicate [*sēmainein*] the one who I myself know [*oida*] first began unjust [*a-dika*] deeds against the Hellenes. I will go on further in my account, treating equally of great and small cities of humankind, |₁.₅.₄ for many of those that were great in the past have become small, and those that were great in my day were formerly small. Knowing that human good fortune [*eudaimoniā*] never remains in the same state, I will mention both equally.

Herodotus 1.5.3–4

---

* *PH* 165 = 6§38.

† Boiled lamb is a typical offering to cult heroes; boiled tortoise is meant to be a strange additional ingredient.

‡ Οἶδα δ' ἐγὼ ψάμμου τ' ἀριθμὸν καὶ μέτρα θαλάσσης, | καὶ κωφοῦ συνίημι καὶ οὐ φωνεῦντος ἀκούω. | Ὀδμή μ' ἐς φρένας ἦλθε κραταιρίνοιο χελώνης | ἑψομένης ἐν χαλκῷ ἅμ' ἀρνείοισι κρέεσσιν, ᾗ χαλκὸς μὲν ὑπέστρωται, χαλκὸν δ' ἐπίεσται.

§ *PH* 231–233 = 8§25.

15§68. It is essential to note here that the use of the word *oida*, 'I know', by Herodotus in this context is both formally and functionally related to his use of the word *historiē*, which refers to his activity as a historian—and which also refers at the very start of his *Histories* (in the first sentence of the prooemium) to his *Histories* as a whole: this word *historiē*, which for Herodotus indicates the 'inquiry' that he undertook in making all the observations that add up to his *Histories*, is derived from the verb *oida*, 'I know', by way of the intermediate derivative forms *histōr*, 'witness, inquirer, arbitrator', and *historeîn*, 'bear witness, arbitrate, make inquiries'.* And the model for the superior vantage point claimed by Herodotus when he says *oida*, 'I know', is the supreme vantage point of the god Apollo at his oracle in Delphi when he says *oida*, 'I know', in declaring absolute knowledge of everything—even the exact number of grains of sand.

15§69. Similarly, the model for Herodotus when he uses the word *sēmainein*, 'indicate', in this same context (1.5.3) is the authority of Apollo himself, who has a special way of communicating from his *manteîon*, 'oracle', at Delphi: to repeat the wording of Heraclitus (22 B 93 DK), as quoted in Text J, the god *sēmainei*, 'indicates'. And the modeling extends even further: this same word *sēmainein* is conventionally used to designate communication by someone whose perspective originates from a vantage point that is superior to someone else's. For example, in situations where scouts ascend to elevated places in missions of reconnaissance and then descend in order to report what they have seen to those who have stayed at ground level, so to speak, this word *sēmainein* is used to show what these scouts 'indicate' from their superior vantage point (Herodotus 7.192.1, 7.219.1).† But sometimes there is no way to get above ground level, and then the only way to achieve the superior perspective of a scout is to make the effort of traveling the distance that is covered by the superior view from above. Such an effort will take a far longer time, and it may be hard, very hard, to make the effort. That is the essence of the metaphor brought to life by Herodotus (1.5.3) when he speaks of the many *astea*, 'cities', through which he will figuratively travel in his ongoing quest for a superior perspective; by way of this metaphor the historian evokes the heroic experiences of Odysseus, who saw so many *astea*, 'cities', of men in the course of so many laborious travels in the *Odyssey*

* *PH* 250–251 = 9§1.
† *PH* 165 = 6§38.

(i 3, xxiii 267).* So the historian is emulating not only the solar vantage point of the god Apollo but also the ground-level vantage point of the hero who travels the distance.

15§70. In the case of heroes, their vantage point can in some cases re-enact the supreme vantage point of the god Apollo. That is the mentality we have seen in the report of Pausanias (9.39.5–14), as quoted in Text F, where we have read that the worshipper of the cult hero Trophōnios 'consults' him, as expressed by the verb-root *khrē-* (9.39.14), and that this consultation happens in the cult hero's 'oracle', the word for which is *manteîon* (9.39.5, 9.39.7, 9.39.8, and 9.39.9). Similarly in the case of Apollo himself, as we saw in §39, Herodotus uses the same verb-root *khrē-* and the same noun *manteîon* in his narrative about the consultation by Croesus of the god's oracle at Delphi ($\chi\rho\eta\sigma\acute{o}\mu\epsilon\nu o\iota$ 1.47.7 and $\acute{\epsilon}\chi\rho\acute{\eta}\sigma\theta\eta$ 1.49.1; $\mu\alpha\nu\tau\acute{\eta}\iota o\nu$ 1.48.1). It is this particular consultation, I should add, that leads to the oracular pronouncement of Apollo that starts with the words: 'I know [*oida*] the number of the grains of sand' (1.47.3, quoted in Text K).

15§71. In the case of the cult hero Trophōnios, the parallelism between him and the god Apollo as authoritative sources of oracular revelations is indicated in other ways as well. As we saw earlier in this hour, at §40, Pausanias reveals that Trophōnios, unlike the hero's brother Agamedes, was actually fathered by Apollo. And Pausanias adds that this revelation originates from the fact that he had actually been initiated into the mysteries of Trophōnios (9.37.5).

15§72. As for the cult hero Protesilaos, the parallelism between him and the god Apollo as authoritative sources of oracular revelations is indicated primarily by the use of the word *sēmainein*, 'indicate', in the narrative of Herodotus (9.120.1–2) about the cult hero's revenge against wrongdoers, as quoted in Text A. As we saw there, the narrative of Herodotus is concerned with human events, at least on the surface. Underneath the surface, however, it is concerned with the workings of the cosmic order as encoded in the world of nature. On the surface, the historical events are conveyed by the main framing narrative. Underneath the surface, however, the workings of the cosmic order are conveyed by the framed narrative of 'meanings' emanating from Apollo and from cult heroes. The agents of this cosmic order are cult heroes, who in death are completely in synchronization with the cosmos. That is why Protesilaos in death

---

* *PH* 232 = 8§25.

can be an agent of the cosmic order, which comes from the gods. He rewards the just and punishes the unjust. He is thus the agent of *dikē*. In Hour 14, we saw how this cult hero rewards those who worship him and who are thereby models of just behavior. Here in Hour 15, we saw how this same cult hero punishes the unjust.

The Cult Hero as a Medium

15§73. In making physical contact with a cult hero by way of worshipping that hero, the worshipper hopes to get in touch with a mind that knows everything. That is what we saw in this hour, as we looked at narratives concerning cult heroes like Protesilaos and Trophōnios. These heroes are "psychic" about the heroic past: in other words, when worshippers in the present make contact with the consciousness of the heroes of the past, those heroes will know everything about the world of heroes, not only about their own world in the past. They thus surpass the power of poets in knowing about the world of heroes:

HOUR 15 TEXT M = HOUR 14 TEXT B

|_{7.4} At any rate, among those who critically examine Homer's poems, who will you say has read [*ana-gignōskein*] them in such a way as Protesilaos has read them and sees all the way through [*di-horân*] them? |_{7.5} Besides, my guest [*xenos*], before Priam and Troy there wasn't even any epic recitation [*rhapsōidiā*], nor was there any singing about events that had not yet taken place. I say this because the art of composing poetry back then about oracular utterances [*manteîa*] and about, say, Hēraklēs, son of Alkmēnē, was only starting to take shape and had not yet reached a stage of maturity, and there was no Homer yet, so there was no Homer to do any singing. Some say that it was only when Troy was captured, while others say it was eight generations later, that he [= Homer] applied himself to practicing the art of poetry. |_{7.6} But, in spite of all that, Protesilaos knows all the things of Homer and he sings of many Trojan events that took place after the hero's own lifetime, as also of many events that have to do with Greeks and Persians.

Philostratus *Hērōikos* 7.4–6

PART THREE

HEROES IN TRAGEDY

Introduction to Tragedy

III§1. In considering the traditions of tragedy, we must keep in mind that the medium of tragedy in particular and of drama in general was the central context for the evolution of traditions in poetry, song, and dance in Athens during the classical period of the fifth century BCE and thereafter. The primary setting was a synthetic festival in honor of the god Dionysus. This festival was known as the City Dionysia (or Great Dionysia), and its significance is captured in the following brief description:

> The importance of the festival was derived not only from the performances of dramatic and lyric poetry but from the fact that it was open to the whole Hellenic world and was an effective advertisement of the wealth and power and public spirit of Athens, no less than of the artistic and literary leadership of her sons. By the end of March the winter was over, the seas were navigable, and strangers came to Athens from all parts for business or pleasure.*

III§2. From the text of Aristophanes *Birds* 786-789, we witness the central program of the City Dionysia in a given year, 414 BC: three days, each taken up with three tragedies, one satyric drama, and one comedy.

III§3. In the highly complex institution of the Athenian dramatic festivals in the fifth century BCE, those who perform are the *khoros,* 'chorus', the song-and-dance ensemble, and the so-called first, second, and third actors. The *khoros,* 'chorus', in Athenian drama during that period performed by singing and dancing to the musical accompaniment of an *aulos,* 'reed', while the actors performed by reciting their parts, ordinarily without musical accompaniment. In Athens, the *khorēgos,* 'chorus-leader', was no longer a performer: he had become differentiated as a contemporary non-performer, who organized and subsidized both

---

* Pickard-Cambridge 1989:58.

the composition and the performance.* Meanwhile, the differentiated function of a *performing* chorus leader was further differentiated by another split in functions, with a specialized "first actor" on one hand and an unspecialized chorus leader on the other. This further differentiation is represented in the story that tells of the primordial dramaturge Thespis and his putative invention of the *first actor* (Aristotle via Themistius *Orations* 26.316d; Charon of Lampsacus *FGH* 262 F 15).† The dialogue between the Thespian *first actor* and the *chorus leader* would be a specialization of a more basic dialogue between an undifferentiated *khorēgos,* 'chorus-leader', and the chorus. There are yet further stages of differentiation with the putative invention of the *second actor,* sometimes attributed to Aeschylus, and of a *third actor,* sometimes attributed to Sophocles.‡ In terms of such formulations, the first actor was once the same person as the composer. Ostensibly, that was the situation with Aeschylus, whereas with Sophocles there was further differentiation between composer and actor, in that Sophocles, tradition has it, ceased to act.§

III§4. The chorus represents a "go-between" or "twilight zone" between the heroes of the there-and-then and the audience of the here-and-now, which happens to be, in the case of the dramas, Athens in the fifth century.** The chorus reacts *both* as if it were the audience itself *and* as if its members were contemporaries of the heroes. The members of the chorus, who sang and danced the roles of groups such as old men or young girls who are "on the scene" in the mythical world of heroes, were non-professionals, whereas the actors (the first, second, and third actor), who spoke the parts of the main characters, were professionals. For Athenian society, the ritual emphasis is on the experience of the pre-adult chorus and, through them, of the adult audience (many of whom had once been members of the chorus themselves): there is a high value placed on the experience of the chorus members, which is regarded as simultaneously civic and deeply personal, in undergoing the educational process of performing in the chorus of a tragedy.

III§5. In the classical period, the chorus members in the seasonally recurring

---

* *PH* 378–379 = 12§76.

† *PH* 378 = 12§76, following Pickard-Cambridge 1968:130–131.

‡ *PH* 378–379 = 12§76.

§ *PH* 378 = 12§76. In earlier stages of his career, Sophocles reportedly accompanied himself on the lyre when he played the role of Thamyras in the play *Thamyras,* and he played the ball with great skill when he played the role of Nausikaa in the *Nausikaa* (Athenaeus 1.20ef).

** In Athenian tragedy, as in the *Hippolytus* of Euripides, all main characters are heroes. That includes Phaedra, of course.

dramatic festivals of Athens like the City Dionysia were normally the young elite, citizens-in-the-making, but they were at the moment of their performance still marginal to society: they were selected from an age-class of pre-adult males, not yet of civic age. (As for ancient Greek society in general, however, choruses were not exclusively male. In various ritual events of various city-states, members of female choruses could be selected from age-classes of pre-adult females.)

III§6. The members of the male choruses in Athenian tragedy *acted out* various members of society in the world of heroes, such as old men, young girls, prisoners of war, and the like. Their acting out such roles conformed to the function of the chorus as an educational collectivization of experience. Their educational experience in the chorus was like a stylized rite of passage, which led from the marginality of their current status into the eventual centrality of their future status as citizens. In tragedy, the focus of attention was on the heroes, played by the actors. The hero, and his or her suffering, which is called *pathos,* was central. The witnesses to this suffering, as played by the chorus, could be marginal. They got involved in the experience of the hero, but they also had an element of distance from the hero, in their links to the here-and-now of the audience.*

III§7. Passive *pathos* or *action experienced* by the hero within the world of tragedy is active *drāma,* that is, *sacrifice and the performance of ritual,* from the standpoint of the outer world that frames this world of tragedy. Such an outer world is constituted by the audience of the theater, visualized as a community that becomes engaged in the *drāma* and that thereby participates in the inner world that is the *pathos* or 'suffering' of the hero.

III§8. The audience, through the chorus, reacts to the experience of the hero, and this reaction translates into the personal experience of an individual in synchronizing the world of heroes with the world of the individual's present-day society. These worlds share the stages of life through which an individual passes, such as birth, youth, adulthood, marriage, parenthood, divorce, aging, death, and a hoped-for rebirth. They also share the various ordeals in passing from one stage to another, such as the primal pain of being born, the intensity of playing games, the thrill of sexuality, the pangs of falling in love, the toils of hunting, the labor of giving birth, the exertion of athletics, the shock of combat,

---

*In some tragedies, the role of the chorus can be central to the action. Such roles are examined by Dhuga 2011.

the tedium of aging, the throes of dying, and so on. The chorus reacts to such ordeals on the part of the hero. In this way, a chorus member can be made to experience, to feel personally, the painful process of "growing up" by performing in the chorus, which is acting on behalf of the adult audience in reacting, through the ritual experience of song and dance, to a given mythical action experienced by a given hero of drama.*

III§9. The Greek word *mīmēsis*, as I already indicated in Hour 8e, designates the reenactment, through ritual, of the events of myth. In the case of a highly stylized ritual complex like Athenian tragedy, the reenactment is equivalent to acting out the roles of mythical figures. The acting out can take place on the level of speech alone, or else on the level of speech combined with bodily movement, that is, dance: it is in this broader sense of *acting* that we can understand the force of *pros*, 'corresponding to', in the expression *pros ta pathea autou*, 'corresponding to his sufferings [*pathea*, plural of *pathos*]', in Herodotus 5.67.5, describing the singing and dancing by *tragikoi khoroi*, 'tragic choruses', at the city-state of Sikyon in the time of the tyrant Kleisthenes, in reenactment of the *pathea*, 'sufferings', of the hero Adrastos.† The fundamental meaning of *mīmēsis*, to repeat, is that of reenacting the events of myth. By extension, however, *mīmēsis* can designate not only the reenacting of the myth but also the present reenacting of previous reenactments. So *mīmēsis* is a current 'imitation' of earlier reenactments.‡ That is because the newest instance of reenacting has as its model, cumulatively, all the older instances of performing the myth and not just the oldest and supposedly original instance of the myth itself.

III§10. This line of thought corresponds to the celebrated description of *mīmēsis* in the *Poetics* of Aristotle as the mental process of identifying the representing 'this' in the ritual of acting the drama with the represented 'that' in the myth that is being acted out by the drama. In Greek this mental process is expressed thus: *houtos ekeinos*, 'this is that!' (Aristotle *Poetics* 1448b17). Such a mental process, Aristotle goes on to say, is itself a source of pleasure (1448b11, 13, 18). This pleasure is not incompatible with an anthropological understanding of ritual:

> Fixed rhythm, fixed pitch are conducive to the performance of joint
> social activity. Indeed, those who resist yielding to this constraining in-

---

* Nagy 1994/95:50–51.
† *PH* 43, 387 = 1§47, 13§12.
‡ *PH* 373 = 12§68; also 349 = 12§24n58.

fluence are likely to suffer from a marked unpleasant restlessness. In comparison, the experience of constraint of a peculiar kind acting upon a collaborator induces in him, when he yields himself to it, the pleasure of self-surrender.*

This anthropological formulation corresponds to Aristotle's idea of *catharsis,* as I quoted it in Hour 8e§3.

* Tambiah 1985:123.

HOUR 16

Heroic Aberration in the
Agamemnon of Aeschylus

The Meaning of Atē

16§1. The key word for this hour is *atē*, the meaning of which can be interpreted as 'aberration, derangement, veering off-course; disaster; punishment for disaster'. In Homeric poetry, as we saw in *Iliad* XIX 91 as quoted in Hour 1 Text C, *atē* is perceived as a noun derived from the verb *aâsthai*, 'veer off-course'. A basic metaphor conveyed by the word *atē* is this: *being blown off-course*, as when sailing a ship.* I draw special attention to the ambivalence of this word with regard to *cause* and *effect*: *atē* can be the *result* of damage as well as its *cause*; it can be 'punishment for disaster' as well as 'disaster'.† As we will see from here on, *atē* is a key concept not only in the *Agamemnon,* a tragedy of Aeschylus, but also in the *Oresteia* trilogy writ large.

The Oresteia *Trilogy of Aeschylus in the Larger Context of His Other Tragedies*

16§2. Aeschylus is best known for the trilogy *Oresteia,* produced in the year 458 BCE, and consisting of three tragedies: *Agamemnon, Libation Bearers, Eumenides;* at the same event, there was a fourth drama presented, the *Proteus,* which has not survived. An earlier tragedy of Aeschylus was the *Seven against Thebes,* produced in the year 467 BCE. All four of the tragedies I have just mentioned center on heroes who are well known in epic traditions. This kind of epic centering is typical of the tragedies of Aeschylus.‡ And, as we are about to see, the use of the key word for this hour, *atē,* in the *Oresteia* trilogy is a striking

---

* *PH* 242–243 = 9§42n120.
† *PH* 241–249, 254–255, 282–264, 310–311 = 8§41–50, 9§5, 9§18, 10§52.
‡ Nagy 2000:98–101.

example of the convergence of epic and tragic elements in the tragedies of Aeschylus.

16§3. A still earlier tragedy of Aeschylus was the *Persians*, produced in 472 BCE; the official 'producer' of this drama was Pericles (*IG* II2 2318.10). (In this era of Athens, the 'producer' was called the *khorēgos*, which means literally 'leader of the chorus [*khoros*].') Unlike the other tragedies of Aeschylus, this drama centered on an event that happened in the post-heroic age: the naval victory of Athens and its allies over the fleet of the Persian Empire at Salamis in 480 BCE.* The sponsorship of this drama by Pericles is most significant, since this Athenian statesman is remembered in hindsight as the chief exponent of democracy in the Classical period of the fifth century. So the sponsorship of Aeschylus by Pericles is a telling sign of the status of Aeschylus himself as a state poet, as it were.†

The Atē *of Agamemnon in Epic and Tragedy*

16§4. A special point of interest in this hour is the hero Agamemnon. In Hour 1, we took a close look at his status as a hero in the epic *Iliad*, where he becomes a foil for the superior hero Achilles. The inferiority of Agamemnon as a hero in the *Iliad* stands in sharp contrast to his social superiority as over-king. Although the epic recognizes Agamemnon's social superiority, it also highlights his heroic inferiority by showing the disastrous outcome of the quarrel he provoked when he insulted Achilles. That outcome is *atē*. As for the tragedy named after him, the *Agamemnon* of Aeschylus, this drama does not directly link the status of Agamemnon as a hero to his rivalry with Achilles, but the outcome of Agamemnon's actions in the tragedy is *atē* all the same.

16§5. As we saw in *Iliad* XIX 76–138, Hour 1 Text C, Agamemnon evades personal responsibility by blaming *atē* for his behavior during the quarrel. He says at verses 86–87 of that text that he is not personally *aitios*, 'responsible', for the disaster that resulted from his quarreling; that disaster happened, he claims at verse 88, because the gods inflicted on him an *atē*, 'aberration, derangement'. So, as I pointed out in my commentary for Hour 1 Text C, the word *atē*, 'derangement', is both a passive experience, as described by Agamemnon at verse 88, and an active force that becomes personified as the goddess *Atē*, as we see later at

---

* In the *Persians* of Aeschylus, this near-contemporary event is articulated in heroic forms of discourse. On the principles of such discourse, I recommend the study of Ebbott 2000.

† *PH* 310–313 = 10§§52–54.

verse 91 and following. As we will now see, the dual function of *atē* as both the cause and the effect of aberration is explored further in the tragedy *Agamemnon*—and in the two other tragedies of the *Oresteia* trilogy.

16§6. In studying the deployment of the word *atē* in the *Oresteia* trilogy, we need to keep track of the sequence of old wrongs committed—and of new wrongs meant to avenge the old wrongs, leading to ever newer wrongs—in the overall myth about the House of Atreus. This sequence can be viewed as the chain of evil that links the causes and effects of *atē* in the trilogy. We can piece together the past events of this myth, leading up to the present events that actually take place in the trilogy itself, by studying the multiple references to this gruesome past as we read through the *Oresteia*. The sequence of these past events can be summarized roughly as follows:

> Atreus and Thyestes, sons of Pelops, are twin brothers who compete with each other in a quest to become the king of Mycenae. Thyestes seduces the wife of Atreus, who has his revenge by engaging in a corrupted sacrifice: he slaughters the sons of Thyestes and then tricks his brother into eating the cooked flesh of these children.* Thyestes impregnates his surviving daughter, who bears for him a new son named Aegisthus. Thyestes is eventually avenged by this Aegisthus, who is welcomed into the home of Atreus as a child and then grows up to slaughter Atreus. (The events as I have summarized them up to this point can be found in the retellings of Apollodorus *Epitome* 2.10–14 and Hyginus *Fabulae* 86–88.) After the death of Atreus, Agamemnon becomes king of Mycenae and over-king of the Achaeans. He launches the war against Troy in order to avenge the abduction of Helen from Sparta by Paris, son of Priam. The Trojan dynasty of Priam, who welcomed Helen to his home, must be punished. In order to have his revenge, however, Agamemnon must first engage in a corrupted sacrifice: before his fleet can sail off to Troy from its launching point at Aulis, Agamemnon must slaughter his own daughter, Iphigeneia. This corrupted sacrifice is meant to stop the adverse winds that prevent the fleet of the Achaeans from sailing to Troy—and to activate the favorable winds that will propel them to their destination. In the words of Agamemnon himself, the *thusiā*, 'sacrifice', of Iphigeneia will be *pausanemos*, an act that 'stops the winds' (παυσανέμου . . . θυσίας Ag-

---

* On the motif of the corrupted sacrifice in the *Oresteia* of Aeschylus, see in general Zeitlin 1965.

amemnon 214–215). These adverse winds had been activated by the goddess Artemis, who controls the winds. This goddess also controls wild animals, and she regulates the hunting of these animals by virtue of being the best of all hunters. So Artemis was angry when Agamemnon at Aulis had boasted to be a better hunter than the goddess herself after he shot down a deer. The story is retold in the epic Cycle (plot summary by Proclus of the *Cypria* by Stasinus p. 104 lines 12–30), where the word for the 'anger' of Artemis is *mēnis* (lines 14, 16). After Troy is finally destroyed by the Achaeans, Agamemnon compels the captured Trojan princess Cassandra to become his bedmate; meanwhile, back in Argos, Clytemnestra willingly accepts Aegisthus as her own bedmate. So, just as Thyestes had seduced the wife of Atreus, Aegisthus the son of Thyestes has now seduced the wife of Agamemnon the son of Atreus. When Agamemnon comes back home to Argos, Clytemnestra helps Aegisthus kill her husband. This way, Clytemnestra avenges the death of her daughter Iphigeneia. Vengeance for the slaughtering of Agamemnon will in turn be exacted by Orestes and Electra, who are the children of Agamemnon. Orestes, with the help of his sister Electra, slaughters not only Aegisthus but also Clytemnestra. The problem is, Clytemnestra is the mother of Orestes and Electra. It would have been simple if these two children of Agamemnon had only their father to avenge. Now who will avenge the mother, for whose murder they are responsible?

An Ainos *about a Lion Cub*

16§7. Near the middle of Aeschylus' *Agamemnon*, the ongoing story of this chain of evil is retold indirectly in a song sung and danced by the chorus of the drama. The form of this retelling is a special kind of speaking known as the *ainos*, which is conventionally signaled by way of a special word *houtōs*.* We have already seen this word in *Iliad* IX 524, quoted in Hour 2 Text B, and I had translated *houtōs* there as 'this is how'. In that context, the word was introducing an *ainos* about the hero Meleagros and his wife Kleopatra. Comparable to the signaling of an *ainos* by this word *houtōs* is the expression *once upon a time*, which signals the start of a fairy tale in English. But the *ainos* is more than just a story. As I explained in Hour 2§60, an *ainos* is *a performance of ambivalent wording that*

---

* Fraenkel 1950 II 338–339; *PH* 310 = 10§52n164.

becomes clarified once it is correctly understood and then applied in moments of making moral decisions affecting those who are near and dear. In the story as we see it being retold in the *Agamemnon*, the word *houtōs* in the sense of 'this is how (it was when)' is used at lines 718–719, signaling that an *ainos* has just been activated:

HOUR 16 TEXT A

> This is how [*houtōs*] it was when a man brought back home a lion cub and raised him. He [= the lion cub] was deprived of his mother's milk, yet still desiring the breast. Gentle he was, |₇₂₀ in the preliminaries [*pro-teleia*] of his life, friendly to children, and a delight to the old. He was often cradled in the arms, like some nursing child, with his |₇₂₅ bright eye turned toward the hand that held him. He was fawning, forced by the needs of his stomach to fawn. But then, brought to full growth in the course of time, he demonstrated the nature [*ēthos*] he had from his parents. Without being invited to do so, doing it as a compensation [*kharis*] to those who fostered him, |₇₃₀ he prepared a feast [*dais*], bringing disasters [*atai*], with sheep being slaughtered. And the house was defiled with blood. Those who lived there could not fight back their pain [*algos*], and great was the destruction, with much slaughter. |₇₃₅ He was something that comes from a god [*theos*]—some kind of a priest [*hiereus*] of disaster [*Atē*], as if he had been nurtured for that purpose, right inside the house.
>
> Aeschylus *Agamemnon* 717–735*

16§8. On the surface, then, this story is about a lion cub, welcomed as a pet in the home of the family that adopts it, but it grows up to become a vicious carnivorous lion in the grim *telos* or 'fulfillment' of its true nature as it reaches adulthood. When it is still a lion cub, it is in the *pro-teleia*, 'preliminaries', of its destiny as a ruthless killer. But when the lion finally reaches the *telos* or 'fulfillment' of its maturation and goes on to slaughter not only the sheep of the family but evidently the family itself, we see that the word referring to the gruesome consequences is *atē*, 'disaster', which is *atai* in the plural. The deployment of *atai*

---

* |₇₁₇ ἔθρεψεν δὲ λέοντος ἶ |₇₁₈ νιν δόμοις ἀγάλακτον οὕ |₇₁₉ τως ἀνὴρ φιλόμαστον, |₇₂₀ ἐν βιότου προτελείοις |₇₂₁ ἄμερον, εὐφιλόπαιδα |₇₂₂ καὶ γεραροῖς ἐπίχαρτον. |₇₂₃ πολέα δ' ἔσκ' ἐν ἀγκάλαις |₇₂₄ νεοτρόφου τέκνου δίκαν, |₇₂₅ φαιδρωπὸς ποτὶ χεῖρα σαίνων τε γαστρὸς ἀνάγκαις. |₇₂₆ χρονισθεὶς δ' ἀπέδειξεν ἦ |₇₂₇ θος τὸ πρὸς τοκέων· χάριν |₇₂₈ γὰρ τροφεῦσιν ἀμείβων |₇₃₀ μηλοφόνοισιν ἄταις |₇₃₁ δαῖτ' ἀκέλευστος ἔτευξεν, |₇₃₂ αἵματι δ' οἶκος ἐφύρθη, |₇₃₃ ἄμαχον ἄλγος οἰκέταις, |₇₃₄ μέγα σίνος πολυκτόνον. |₇₃₅ ἐκ θεοῦ δ' ἱερεύς τις ἄτας δόμοις προσεθρέφθη.

in the dative plural here expresses subjectively the attendant circumstances of the beast's vicious behavior. But then the same word *atē* is re-deployed in the singular, and this time it becomes personified as a malevolent goddess named *Atē*. This time, we can see *atē* as the actual cause of the carnage, since the ravenous lion has evidently been sent by a divinity, a *theos*. And now the agent sent by the divinity is revealed as the *hiereus*, 'priest', of this goddess *Atē*. So once again we see *atē* as both the cause and the effect of the 'disaster' that the word means. In the translation, it would have been easier at first to use the pronoun 'it' with reference to the lion, thus highlighting the non-human agency of the animal, but 'he' is closer to the Greek original. And this 'he' is also closer to the personification of the lion, as when this animal starts to be treated as a human infant: 'he was often cradled in the arms, like some nursing child'. From the start, in fact, the lion is described as 'still desiring the breast'. And, as the description of the vicious animal proceeds, the human agency of the 'he' becomes ever more evident. By the end of the story, in the last line, the lion is fully personified as a terrifying *hiereus*, 'priest', of *Atē*.

16§9. In the lines that precede this story at lines 717–735 as also in the lines that follow the story, the narration by the chorus centers on the ominous moment when Helen was welcomed to Troy after her abduction by Paris from Sparta—an abduction that will cause all the slaughter that ultimately takes place in the Trojan War. So underneath the surface of the story about the lion cub, is it really Helen to whom this *ainos* refers? Helen too, like the lion cub, was unquestioningly welcomed by a family to their home, and she too ingratiated herself, only to become the cause of disaster. But there is another possible referent. After all, Paris too was unquestioningly welcomed by a family to their home when he visited the household of Menelaos as his guest, and Paris too became the cause of disaster when he abducted Helen. But there are still other possible referents: the story of the lion cub, it has been argued, refers also to the stories of Agamemnon, Clytemnestra, even Orestes.*

16§10. Herodotus himself deploys such an *ainos* about a lion cub in his *Histories*. In this case, the referent is none other than the Athenian statesman Pericles, who as we saw in §3 was a prominent political sponsor of Aeschylus.† Herodotus (6.131.2) tells the story of a woman named Agariste, granddaughter of the statesman Kleisthenes of Athens, who dreamed that she became the mother of a lion; a few days later, she gave birth to a son, Pericles.‡ In another

---

* Nagy 2011c §125, with reference to *PH* 310 = 10§52n164, citing Knox 1952 and Goldhill 1984:63.

† *PH* 310 = 10§52.

‡ Relevant commentaries are mentioned in *PH* 310 = 10§52n163.

context, Herodotus (3.108.4) presents as a scientific observation the claim that lionesses give birth only once in their lifetime: supposedly, an embryonic lion club claws away at the insides of its mother—so that the womb is destroyed by the time of the cub's birth. Then the historian goes on to argue that such a savage limitation on the fertility of female lions is a form of cosmic compensation paid by predatory animals for their viciously predatory nature (3.108.1–3).*

Predators as Agents of Dikē

16§11. In the example we have just considered in the *Histories* of Herodotus, cosmic justice punishes predatory animals for their viciousness by limiting their fertility. But now we come to an example in the *Agamemnon* of Aeschylus, where predatory animals are pictured as agents of punishment emanating from the same sense of cosmic justice. Soon after the chorus of the drama starts singing and dancing, the subject of its choral song and dance turns to the abduction of Helen by Paris, which happened while Paris was a guest at the home of Helen's husband, Menelaos, in Sparta. This act of abduction, which violates the rules of behavior for *xenoi* in the dual sense of 'guests' and 'hosts', is seen as an outrage against *dikē*, 'justice'—an outrage that must be avenged by way of launching the Trojan War. As the leaders of the forces marshalled for the destruction of Troy, the heroes Agamemnon and Menelaos are compared to two eagles screaming for vengeance after their nest has been robbed of its nestlings:

HOUR 16 TEXT B

$|_{40}$ This is now the tenth year since the mighty plaintiff [*anti-dikos*] against Priam, King Menelaos, and with him King Agamemnon, the both of them linked by Zeus in honor [*tīmē*] of throne and scepter, that steady pair of Atreus' sons, launched from this land [of Argos] $|_{45}$ an armada of a thousand ships, with a mass of Argive warriors coming to their aid. Loud rang the battle-cry that the two of them shouted from the heart [*thūmos*]. Just as eagles scream, $|_{50}$ in lonely grief for their children, as they circle over their nest, high up above, rowing with the oars of their wings, screaming because they have lost their nestlings—having now wasted all the pain [*ponos*] of watching over their nest. $|_{55}$ But high up above there is someone who hears—Apollo perhaps or

---

* PH 311 = 10§52.

Pan, or Zeus—hearing the shrill wailing scream of the clamorous birds, those sojourners in the air space of these gods. And against the transgressors the god sends a Fury [Erinys] at last, though it was late in coming. |₆₀ This is how [*houtōs*] it was when the sons of Atreus were sent by Zeus, whose power is over all, Zeus *xenios* [= god of *xenoi*, 'guests and hosts'], against Alexander [= Paris]. Zeus was about to cause, for the sake of a woman with many a husband, a multitude of struggles most wearying, with many a knee buckling in the dust |₆₅ and many a spear splintering in the preliminaries [*pro-teleia*] [of close combat]—Zeus was about to cause all this for Danaans [= Achaeans] and Trojans alike. So things are where they are right now. And it all moves to fulfillment [*teleîsthai*], toward what is destined [*pe-prōmenon*]. Not by setting fires underneath a sacrifice, not by pouring libations on top of it, |₇₀ not by tears, can anyone charm away [*parathelgein*] the implacable feelings of anger coming out of a ritual performed without fire.

Aeschylus Agamemnon 40–71*

16§12. Who is the nestling here? In the immediate context, the metaphor points to Helen, who has been robbed from her nest just as the nestlings of the eagles have been robbed from theirs. And the avenging eagles are clearly identified with Agamemnon and Menelaos.

Predators as Agents of Deeds Contrary to Dikē

16§13. This metaphor featuring Agamemnon and Menelaos as eagles is two-sided, however. At a later point in the drama of Aeschylus, the singing and dancing of the chorus concentrates on the negative side of this same metaphor:

---

* |₄₀ δέκατον μὲν ἔτος τόδ᾽ ἐπεὶ Πριάμῳ |₄₁ μέγας ἀντίδικος |₄₂ Μενέλαος ἄναξ ἠδ᾽ Ἀγαμέμνων, |₄₃ διθρόνου Διόθεν καὶ δισκήπτρου |₄₄ τιμῆς ὀχυρὸν ζεῦγος Ἀτρειδᾶν, |₄₅ στόλον Ἀργείων χιλιοναύταν |₄₆ τῆσδ᾽ ἀπὸ χώρας |₄₇ ἦραν, στρατιῶτιν ἀρωγάν, |₄₈ μέγαν ἐκ θυμοῦ κλάζοντες Ἄρη |₄₉ τρόπον αἰγυπιῶν, οἵτ᾽ ἐκπατίοις |₅₀ ἄλγεσι παίδων ὕπατοι λεχέων |₅₁ στροφοδινοῦνται |₅₂ πτερύγων ἐρετμοῖσιν ἐρεσσόμενοι, |₅₃ δεμνιοτήρη |₅₄ πόνον ὀρταλίχων ὀλέσαντες· |₅₅ ὕπατος δ᾽ ἀΐων ἤ τις Ἀπόλλων |₅₆ ἢ Πὰν ἢ Ζεὺς οἰωνόθροον |₅₇ γόον ὀξυβόαν τῶνδε μετοίκων |₅₈ ὑστερόποινον |₅₉ πέμπει παραβᾶσιν Ἐρινύν. |₆₀ οὕτω δ᾽ Ἀτρέως παῖδας ὁ κρείσσων |₆₁ ἐπ᾽ Ἀλεξάνδρῳ πέμπει ξένιος |₆₂ Ζεὺς πολυάνορος ἀμφὶ γυναικός, |₆₃ πολλὰ παλαίσματα καὶ γυιοβαρῆ, |₆₄ γόνατος κονίαισιν ἐρειδομένου |₆₅ διακναιομένης τ᾽ ἐν προτελείοις |₆₆ κάμακος, θήσων Δαναοῖσιν |₆₇ Τρωσί θ᾽ ὁμοίως. ἔστι δ᾽ ὅπη νῦν |₆₈ ἔστι· τελεῖται δ᾽ ἐς τὸ πεπρωμένον· |₆₉ οὔθ᾽ ὑποκαίων οὔτ᾽ ἐπιλείβων |₇₀ οὔτε δακρύων ἀπύρων ἱερῶν |₇₁ ὀργὰς ἀτενεῖς παραθέλξει.

HOUR 16 TEXT C

|₁₀₄ I am authorized [kurios] to narrate the power [kratos] of men to set in motion an expedition. It is a predestined power, belonging to men |₁₀₅ who are granted control [telos]. This [authority of mine to narrate] is because the life force, still vital within me, is taking its breath from the inspiration of the gods to give me the ability to make people believe, which is the strength of singing and dancing. It is all about the twin-throned power [kratos] of the Achaeans, |₁₁₀ how this single-minded pair, in charge of all the young men of Hellas, was sent off, with spear and with avenging hand holding the spear. They were sent off against the land of the Teukroi, [Troy,] by an onrushing bird omen, and the omen was the king of birds—[two] birds appearing to the [two] kings of the ships. |₁₁₅ One of them was black all over, while the other one was black, too, but it was white at the other end. They appeared [phainesthai] [in an epiphany] near the palace, on the right hand—the hand that holds the spear. They [had come down from the air and] were roosting in a most visible space, for all to see. And they were devouring a rabbit that was bursting with the vitality of offspring ready to be born. |₁₂₀ She was caught in the moment of her very last effort to run away.

Sing the song of lament for Linus, for Linus sing it, but let the victory belong to whatever is genuinely good.

Then the wise seer [mantis] of the army, seeing that the two warlike sons of Atreus were twins in character, recognized the devourers of the rabbit and |₁₂₅ the leaders of the expedition already under way, [that they were the same,] and this is the way [houtō] he spoke, speaking the language of omens [terazein]: "In due time this expedition, set in motion, will capture the city of Priam as its prey, and, at the ground level of that city's towered walls, all the plentiful herds of the community |₁₃₀ will be ravaged most violently by fate [Moira]. The only thing to guard against is this: may it not happen that some resentment [agā] sent by the gods may cloud over and ruin the mighty bit forged for Troy's mouth by the army. I say this because she, in her pity, is angry. I mean, holy [hagnā] Artemis. She is angry |₁₃₅ at the winged hunting dogs of her father [Zeus], for they are sacrificing [thuein] a miserable frightened thing, together with her offspring that were ready to be born, before she has brought them forth. She [Artemis] has a loathing for the feast of the eagles."

Sing the song of lament for Linus, for Linus sing it, but let victory belong to whatever is genuinely good.

|$_{140}$ "Though she [= the goddess Artemis] is full of good intentions [*euphrōn*], the beautiful [*kalā*] one, toward the tender cubs of vicious lions, and though she takes delight in the breast-loving young of all wild animals that roam the fields, she now demands that the symbols [*sumbola*] of these things be brought to fulfillment [*krainein*], I mean, the epiphanies [*phasmata*], |$_{145}$ which are auspicious in a right-handed kind of way even if they are reprehensible. And I call upon Paean, the healer, praying that she [Artemis] will not stop the sailing of ships, holding them back for a long time |$_{150}$ by causing the winds to blow in the opposite direction for the Danaans [Achaeans]. She [Artemis] is urging a sacrifice of another kind, [a sinister one,] the kind that knows no law [*nomos*], the kind that is unsuited for feasting [*dais*] [on meat], the kind that naturally creates quarrel after quarrel, resulting in vengeance, and the kind that shows no fear of any man [who is a husband]. I say this because there is something that has stayed behind here at home: it is something terrifying, which keeps coming back again and again. |$_{155}$ It is a treacherous keeper of the household. It is an anger [*mēnis*] that remembers, and it comes with punishment for whatever happened to a child." Such dire things did Kalkhas proclaim, speaking the language of omens. But the omens, signaled by the birds seen during the expedition, came also with big benefits for the palaces of the kings. I connect what is sounded out in these omens with what I say:

Sing the song of lament for Linus, for Linus sing it, but let victory belong to whatever is genuinely good.

Aeschylus Agamemnon 104–159*

---

* |$_{104}$ κύριός εἰμι θροεῖν ὅδιον κράτος αἴσιον ἀνδρῶν |$_{105-106}$ ἐκτελέων· ἔτι γὰρ θεόθεν καταπνεύει |$_{107}$ πειθώ, μολπᾶν ἀλκάν, σύμφυτος αἰών· |$_{108-109}$ ὅπως Ἀχαιῶν δίθρονον κράτος, Ἑλλάδος ἥβας |$_{110}$ ξύμφρονα ταγάν, |$_{111}$ πέμπει σὺν δορὶ καὶ χερὶ πράκτορι |$_{112}$ θούριος ὄρνις Τευκρίδ᾽ ἐπ᾽ αἶαν, |$_{114-115}$ οἰωνῶν βασιλεὺς βασιλεῦσι νεῶν ὁ κελαινός, ὅ τ᾽ ἐξόπιν ἀργᾶς, |$_{116}$ φανέντες ἴκταρ μελάθρων χερὸς ἐκ δοριπάλτου |$_{118}$ παμπρέποις ἐν ἕδραισι, |$_{119}$ βοσκόμενοι λαγίναν ἐρικύμονα φέρματι γένναν, |$_{120}$ βλαβέντα λοισθίων δρόμων. |$_{121}$ αἴλινον αἴλινον εἰπέ, τὸ δ᾽ εὖ νικάτω. |$_{122}$ κεδνὸς δὲ στρατόμαντις ἰδὼν δύο λήμασι δισσοὺς |$_{123-124}$ Ἀτρείδας μαχίμους ἐδάη λαγοδαίτας |$_{125}$ πομπούς τ᾽ ἀρχὰς· οὕτω δ᾽ εἶπε τεράζων· |$_{126-127}$ "χρόνῳ μὲν ἀγρεῖ Πριάμου πόλιν ἅδε κέλευθος, |$_{128}$ πάντα δὲ πύργων |$_{129}$ κτήνη πρόσθε τὰ δημιοπληθῆ |$_{130}$ Μοῖρα λαπάξει πρὸς τὸ βίαιον· |$_{131-133}$ οἶον μή τις ἄγα θεόθεν κνεφάσῃ προτυπὲν

16§14. The first line of this choral passage is composed most tellingly in a rhythm that matches the rhythm of epic, which is the dactylic hexameter. The medium of tragedy is here re-enacting the medium of epic, and the 'I' of the chorus presents himself as divinely inspired to tell the true story, just as the 'I' of Homeric poetry is inspired by the Muse, goddess of total recall, to sing the epics of the *Iliad* and the *Odyssey*. So the song and dance of the chorus here in the *Agamemnon* of Aeschylus is telling the epic story of what happened in the Trojan War.

16§15. But there is something in the story here that goes wrong for Agamemnon and Menelaos, and it goes wrong already at the very beginning of the Trojan War. What causes things to go wrong is the same metaphor that applies to Agamemnon and Menelaos when they are pictured as eagles robbed of the nestlings in their nest. In seeking vengeance for the wrongs committed against them, this pair of leaders are agents of *dikē*—just like the eagles who seek vengeance for the wrong committed against them. But then the eagles, predatory animals that they are, go on to commit a deed most typical of their nature: they are seen devouring a pregnant rabbit, embryos and all. This time, the vision is not a metaphor. It is an omen made visible by the gods. Still, the metaphor and the omen are parallel, as visions, if we may consider the metaphor itself to be an omen in its own right.

16§16. So what is so wrong with the vision of the two eagles devouring a pregnant rabbit? Because of their viciously predatory nature, the eagles are behaving in a way that is antithetical to the forces of fertility and prosperity. Thus if Agamemnon and Menelaos are like eagles—and they do in fact resemble eagles in the course of their lifetime—then their inborn nature is likewise predatory and antithetical to the forces of fertility and prosperity. In the realm of humans, however, as we saw in Hours 12 and 13, *dikē* as 'justice' is the clear sign of fertility and prosperity, as defended and guarded by heroes after their unseasonal lifetime is ended—and after they begin their renewed life of eternal sea-

---

στόμιον μέγα Τροίας |₁₃₄ στρατωθέν. οἴκτῳ γὰρ ἐπίφθονος Ἄρτεμις ἀγνὰ |₁₃₅ πτανοῖσιν κυσὶ πατρὸς |₁₃₆₋₁₃₇ αὐτότοκον πρὸ λόχου μογερὰν πτάκα θυομένοισι· |₁₃₈ στυγεῖ δὲ δεῖπνον αἰετῶν." |₁₃₉ αἴλινον αἴλινον εἰπέ, τὸ δ' εὖ νικάτω. |₁₄₀ "τόσον περ εὔφρων ἁ καλά, |₁₄₁ δρόσοις ἀέπτοις μαλερῶν λεόντων |₁₄₂ πάντων τ' ἀγρονόμων φιλομάστοις |₁₄₃ θηρῶν ὀβρικάλοισι τερπνά, |₁₄₄ τούτων αἰτεῖ ξύμβολα κρᾶναι, |₁₄₅ δεξιὰ μὲν κατάμομφα δὲ φάσματα. |₁₄₆ ἰήιον δὲ καλέω Παιᾶνα, |₁₄₇₋₁₄₉ μή τινας ἀντιπνόους Δαναοῖς χρονίας ἐχενῇδας ἀπλοίας |₁₅₀₋₁₅₂ τεύξῃ σπευδομένα θυσίαν ἑτέραν, ἄνομόν τιν', ἄδαιτον, |₁₅₃₋₁₅₄ νεικέων τέκτονα σύμφυτον, οὐ δεισήνορα. μίμνει γὰρ φοβερὰ παλίνορτος |₁₅₅ οἰκονόμος δολία μνάμων μῆνις τεκνόποινος." |₁₅₆ τοιάδε Κάλχας ξὺν μεγάλοις ἀγαθοῖς ἀπέκλαγξεν |₁₅₇ μόρσιμ' ἀπ' ὀρνίθων ὁδίων οἴκοις βασιλείοις· |₁₅₈ τοῖς δ' ὁμόφωνον |₁₅₉ αἴλινον αἴλινον εἰπέ, τὸ δ' εὖ νικάτω.

sonality as cult heroes. So in their actions during the Trojan War, it is not at all clear whether Agamemnon and Menelaos are or are not agents of *dikē*—and the goddess Artemis knows it.

16§17. Artemis is angry. But the question is, angry at whom? And for what? On the surface, the goddess is angry at the eagles for what they have done in killing and devouring the pregnant rabbit, and that is what is said by the seer named Kalkhas: 'for they [= the eagles] are sacrificing a miserable frightened thing, together with her offspring that were ready to be born, before she has brought them forth'. The seer goes on to say about Artemis: 'she has a loathing for the feast of the eagles'.

16§18. There is a problem here: Agamemnon and Menelaos have not done anything against *dikē*—at least, not yet. Only the eagles are being vicious, but that is their inborn nature. Artemis is the protector of the young and the gentle and the innocent, as we hear in the description of the goddess: but this same description means that she is also the protector of the young and gentle and innocent offspring of predatory animals such as lions. Artemis dearly loves the young of animals that prey upon other animals, not only the young of animals that are preyed upon, like rabbits. We have just read, in the passage I quoted, this description of Artemis: 'you are full of good intentions [*euphrōn*], you, the beautiful [*kalā*] one, toward the tender cubs of vicious lions'. So the lion cub of the *ainos* at verses 717–735 of the *Agamemnon,* as I quoted it in Text A, is just as dear to Artemis as is the embryo of a pregnant rabbit—even though that lion cub is destined to become the predatory beast that will viciously ruin the family that adopted it.

16§19. But the vicious eagles that devour the pregnant rabbit together with her embryos are not just eagles. They are not just killing and devouring the rabbit. They are also sacrificing her. I quote again the words that tell what the eagles are doing: 'they are sacrificing [*thuein*] a miserable frightened thing, together with her offspring that were ready to be born, before she has brought them forth'. And who are the real sacrificers? They are Agamemnon and Menelaos. That is the point of the story, operating underneath the surface. While the eagles simply kill and devour the pregnant rabbit, Agamemnon and Menelaos perform a sacrifice. They do so by slaughtering the daughter of Agamemnon, Iphigeneia. And it is of course a corrupted sacrifice, a feast where the slaughtered victim cannot be cut up and cooked and eaten, as in the case of ritually correct sacrifices of sacrificial animals, since the victim of this corrupted sacrifice is not an animal. The intended victim is human. She is Iphigeneia. She is a human sacrifice. And such a sacrifice will surely corrupt the sacrificer. But who is insisting on such a corrupted sacrifice? It is the goddess Artemis herself, as the seer Kalkhas says most clairvoyantly about the goddess: 'she is urging a sacrifice of another kind, [a sinister one,] the kind that knows no law [*nomos*], the kind that is unsuited for feasting [*dais*] [on meat]'.

16§20. So Artemis, as the divine force that demands the human sacrifice of Iphigeneia, is the same divine force that must surely be loathing this sacrifice—just as she loathes the feasting of the predatory eagles on their defenseless victim. We see here once again both the cause and the effect of *atē* in the sense of 'disaster'.

16§21. But how can *atē* be so two-sided for a goddess like Artemis, who can feel angry at the evil committed by Agamemnon and Menelaos while at the same time making it necessary for these two predatory leaders to commit the evil of slaughtering Iphigeneia in the first place? The problem cannot be solved by claiming that this corrupted sacrifice was not evil after all, on the grounds that the goddess Artemis had required it. Nor can it be solved by claiming that Artemis herself was somehow evil for insisting on such a requirement. And it cannot even be solved by claiming that the inborn predatory nature of Agamemnon and Menelaos was the original evil, since it is already most clearly understood that there was in fact an evil that preceded their evil, namely, the abduction of Helen by Paris.

16§22. Still, Agamemnon and Menelaos can be blamed for committing an act of evil, a corrupted sacrifice. On the other hand, the goddess Artemis cannot be blamed for ordaining that Iphigeneia the daughter of Agamemnon needs to be sacrificed in compensation for her changing the direction of the winds that were preventing the Achaeans from sailing to Troy. In the end, the goddess allows the changing of the winds, so that Agamemnon and Menelaos may go ahead and sail off to Troy in order to exact their vengeance. But the goddess does not allow the killing of Iphigeneia. If we return to the story as retold in the epic Cycle (plot summary by Proclus of the *Cypria* by Stasinus p. 104 lines 12–30), we see that Artemis miraculously substitutes a deer for the girl at the sacrificial altar, and this substitution takes place at the exact moment when Iphigeneia is about to be killed (lines 19–20). So a deer is killed instead of Iphigeneia, and, in the meantime, Artemis transports the girl to a remote place named Tauroi, where Iphigeneia is immortalized as a *theos*, 'goddess', in her own right (lines 18–19). In the *Agamemnon* of Aeschylus, however, this salvation of Iphigeneia is not made explicit, since the trilogy of the *Oresteia* is highlighting the anger of Artemis against Agamemnon and Menelaos for desiring a change of winds. In the epic Cycle as well, the anger of Artemis is being highlighted, and the word for this anger is *mēnis* (*Cypria* p. 104 lines 14, 16), but there the word refers to the anger of the goddess at Agamemnon for boasting that he is a better hunter after he shoots down a deer, as I noted in an earlier paragraph (§6). It is no coincidence that the sacrificial substitute for Iphigeneia is likewise a deer, as we just saw (*Cypria* p. 104 lines 19–20).

16§23. The anger of the goddess Artemis is a timeless anger. The timelessness is indicated by the word *mēnis,* which as we have just seen refers to the anger of this goddess at Agamemnon in the epic Cycle. This word traditionally signals a kind of anger that is generated by the divinely controlled cosmos itself in reaction to a human violation of the comsic order. As I noted already in the Introduction (0§20), *mēnis* is a *cosmic sanction.** That is why such an anger can apply timelessly. I quote again here from the words of Kalkhas the seer in the *Agamemnon* (155): 'It is an anger [*mēnis*] that remembers, and it comes with punishment for whatever happened to a child' *(mnāmōn mēnis teknopoinos).*

16§24. I find it most significant that Agamemnon reacts in a most self-incriminating way to what is said here by Kalkhas the seer: in effect, Agamemnon accepts what is for him the necessity of killing his own daugher, and he is described as 'blaming no seer' (186). So Agamemnon does not revile Kalkhas for the formula that requires him to give up his own daughter, though he reviles the same seer at the beginning of the *Iliad* for another formula that requires him to give up his intended concubine. When Agamemnon is told that he must give up his own daughter, he fails to resist the same way as he had resisted the giving up of his concubine. As we might say in modern terms, Agamemnon shows signs of a bad character both in the *Iliad* and in the *Agamemnon* of Aeschylus.

16§25. Before I leave my analysis of the extended passage I just quoted from Aeschylus, I return one more time to the detail about the winds that were blowing in the opposite direction before the corrupted sacrifice was conducted by Agamemnon. If these winds, controlled by the goddess Artemis, had continued to blow the opposite way, against the direction of a sea voyage to Troy, then there would have been no need to sacrifice Iphigeneia in the first place. But Agamemnon wanted the winds to blow in the direction of Troy. And so Artemis, as the goddess who controls the winds, made it happen. But she was angry about it, and that anger was all part of the cosmic sanction. And, as we will see before

---

* Muellner 1996:8, 39, 129, 145.

the drama of the *Agamemnon* is complete, Artemis will make the winds blow again when the time comes for Cassandra the prophetess to be slaughtered by Clytemnestra.

A Sequence of Symbols

16§26. As we have seen, the omen of the two eagles feasting on a pregnant rabbit is a sight that is 'loathed' by the goddess Artemis (*Agamemnon* 137). But this omen is part of a sequence of symbols that stand for a sequence of events demanded by Artemis: 'she now demands that the symbols [*sumbola*] of these things be brought to fulfillment [*krainein*], I mean, the epiphanies [*phasmata*], $|_{145}$ which are auspicious in a right-handed kind of way even if they are reprehensible' (*Agamemnon* lines 144–145). For the moment, I translate *sumbola* (*xumbola*) here as 'symbols', which is the modern derivative of the ancient word, though this translation does not quite capture the ancient meaning. As we will now see, a *sumbolon* is not so much a symbol. It is more like a piece of a puzzle—if we may imagine this puzzle as a sequence of pieces that achieve a meaning only after all the pieces are in place. Whatever sign is indicated by this word *sumbolon* can have a meaning only by way of linking each sign to each following sign, one by one, from start to finish. The reading of *sumbola* from start to finish, from A to Z, is what I mean when I say that we are reading here *a sequence of symbols*.

16§27. Such a sequence of symbols can be visualized as a relay, and in fact the beginning of the drama named after Agamemnon shows an actual relay of signals, as described by Clytemnestra in the *Agamemnon* (lines 281–316).* It is a sequence of pre-arranged signal fires that indicate the fall of Troy, starting with the destructive fire, most visible from afar, that consumes the citadel of Troy. This initial fire is then seen at a signal station posted at the next pre-arranged elevation, which is Mount Ida (*Agamemnon* line 281), then at the next, then at the next, and so on, all the way from Troy to Argos. At the top of each of these consecutive elevations, a signal fire is lit in a chain reaction to the initial fire that was seen destroying the citadel of Troy. And what starts as a *sumbolon* of destruction in Troy at point A becomes at point Z a *sumbolon* of salvation in Argos. It is that kind of a two-way *sumbolon* that we find in the words of an anony-

---

* On the relevance of the relay torch races held at Athens in the era of Aeschylus, an indispensable guide is Ferrari 1997.

mous watchman whom we see posted on top of the terminal elevation, at point Z, which is the signal station of the citadel of Argos. I quote here what the watchman says, which marks the very beginning of the *Oresteia* trilogy of Aeschylus:

HOUR 16 TEXT D

|₁ I ask the gods for release from these ordeals [*ponoi*] of mine here. I have by now been a watchman here for the length of a whole year, during which time I have been spending my nights here on the palace roof of the sons of Atreus, as I rest on my elbows, like a dog. I have learned to know well the gathering of the night's stars, |₅ bringers of winter and summer to humankind, those radiant potentates shining in the firmament, and I know when they set and when they rise. Even now I am still watching for the signal [*sumbolon*] of the flame, the gleam of fire bringing news from Troy |₁₀ and shouts announcing its capture. . . . |₂₀ But now may there be a fortunate release from these ordeals [*ponoi*] of mine! May the fire bringing good news flash through the gloom! [Now, right at this moment, the watchman sees a flash of light.] Oh welcome, you flashing light, you who make the darkness of the night as bright as day, you who signal the arranging [*kata-stasis*] of many choruses [*khoroi*] in Argos in thanksgiving for this fortunate event! |₂₅ Iou! Iou! This is the way I signal [*sēmainein*] clearly to Agamemnon's Queen to rise from her bed and, as quickly as possible, to shout out in the halls of the palace a cry of *ololu*, which says in a proper way [*eu-phēmeîn*] that she welcomes with her cry this flash of light—that is, if the city of Ilion |₃₀ truly is taken, as this signal fire announces in all its shining eminence. And I will join the chorus [*khoros*] in singing and dancing a prelude [*pro-oimion*] of my own. . . . |₃₆ As for all other things I stay silent. A great ox has stepped on my tongue. But the house itself, if it had a voice, would tell it all most clearly: I speak to those who know, and to those who do not know, I am without memory.

Aeschylus Agamemnon 1–36*

---

* |₁ θεοὺς μὲν αἰτῶ τῶνδ' ἀπαλλαγὴν πόνων, | φρουρᾶς ἐτείας μῆκος, ἣν κοιμώμενος | στέγαις Ἀτρειδῶν ἄγκαθεν, κυνὸς δίκην, | ἄστρων κάτοιδα νυκτέρων ὁμήγυριν, |₅ καὶ τοὺς φέροντας χεῖμα καὶ θέρος βροτοῖς | λαμπροὺς δυνάστας, ἐμπρέποντας αἰθέρι | ἀστέρας, ὅταν φθίνωσιν, ἀντολάς τε τῶν. | καὶ νῦν φυλάσσω λαμπάδος τὸ σύμβολον, | αὐγὴν πυρὸς φέρουσαν ἐκ Τροίας φάτιν |₁₀ ἁλώσιμόν τε βάξιν· . . . |₂₀ νῦν δ' εὐτυχὴς γένοιτ' ἀπαλλαγὴ πόνων | εὐαγγέλου φανέντος ὀρφναίου πυρός. | ὦ χαῖρε

The Symbolic Wording of the Watchman

16§28. At line 8 here in the *Agamemnon*, the watchman is watching out for a *sumbolon*, which is a 'sign' or 'signal' transmitted by the fire signals. Or let us say that the *sumbolon* is a 'symbol'. After all, the English word *symbol* is derived from *sumbolon*. This *sumbolon* here is symbolic of destruction at the initial point A of the relay of symbols, in Troy, and of salvation at the terminal point Z, in Argos. The watchman is speaking in an initiatory mode, saying that some will already understand what he says while others cannot yet understand (lines 36–39). As we will see in Hour 22, the word *ponoi* (lines 1 and 20), referring to the 'ordeals' endured by the watchman, conventionally refers to the ordeals of initiation.

16§29. The watchman speaks in a special mode reserved for those who have a privileged perspective. He is doubtless the first person in Argos to see the *sumbolon*, since he is posted on top of the highest elevation in Argos, on the roof of the palace situated on top of the citadel, where he can see something that others cannot yet see. That something is a signal fire that is blazing at the top of the nearest elevation, which as we learn later in the drama is 'the place of the spider', Arakhnaion (*Agamemnon* line 309)—an elevation located thirteen miles away from the citadel at Argos. So from his privileged vantage point, once he can see the *sumbolon*, the watchman can 'signal', *sēmainein* (line 26), to the queen down below. And the watchman refers ostentatiously to his privileged perspective, as I convey at the beginning of the translation by using the word 'here' three times in a row. In the original Greek, the idea of 'here' is conveyed by the deictic pronoun τῶνδ' used by the speaker from the start (line 1). This pronoun *hode* (as it is listed in dictionaries) means 'this, relating to me here', as opposed to *houtos,* meaning 'this, relating to you there', or to *ekeinos,* meaning 'that', not necessarily relating to you there or to me here.

16§30. Once the watchman on the roof conveys the *sumbolon* to the queen in her chambers down below, she is expected to respond by uttering 'a cry of *ololu,* which says in a proper way [*eu-phēmeîn*] that she welcomes with her cry this flash of light' (*Agamemnon* lines 28–29). The choice of the word *eu-phēmeîn*

λαμπτήρ, νυκτὸς ἡμερήσιον | φάος πιφαύσκων καὶ χορῶν κατάστασιν | πολλῶν ἐν Ἄργει, τῆσδε συμφορᾶς χάριν. |₂₅ ἰοὺ ἰού. | Ἀγαμέμνονος γυναικὶ σημαίνω τορῶς | εὐνῆς ἐπαντείλασαν ὡς τάχος δόμοις | ὀλολυγμὸν εὐφημοῦντα τῇδε λαμπάδι | ἐπορθιάζειν, εἴπερ Ἰλίου πόλις |₃₀ ἑάλωκεν, ὡς ὁ φρυκτὸς ἀγγέλλων πρέπει· | αὐτός τ' ἔγωγε φροίμιον χορεύσομαι. . . . |₃₆ τὰ δ' ἄλλα σιγῶ· βοῦς ἐπὶ γλώσσῃ μέγας | βέβηκεν· οἶκος δ' αὐτός, εἰ φθογγὴν λάβοι, | σαφέστατ' ἂν λέξειεν· ὡς ἑκὼν ἐγὼ | μαθοῦσιν αὐδῶ κοὐ μαθοῦσι λήθομαι.

here is most significant: although I translate it as 'utter in a proper way', this same word can also mean 'be silent'.* In Hour 15§15, we saw a comparable split in meaning when we considered the word *muein* (first person *muō*), which means 'have the mouth closed' (or 'have the eyes closed') for non-initiates but 'say in a sacred kind of way' (or 'see in a sacred kind of way') for initiates.† The idea of *saying (or seeing) in a sacred kind of way* is made explicit in the related verb *muein* (first person *mueō*), which means 'to initiate into the mysteries'. So also in the case of *eu-phēmeîn,* there is a mystical meaning at work here.

16§31. For Clytemnestra to cry out *ololu* at line 28 of the *Agamemnon* seems ritually appropriate, since the *ololugmos* or 'ululation' of women is a proper re-action to the defeat of an enemy, as we see later in *Libation Bearers* lines 386–387, where the singing and dancing chorus of Argive women declare their readiness to ululate as soon as Aegisthus and Clytemnestra are slaughtered by Orestes. And, back in *Agamemnon* lines 587–589, Clytemnestra herself refers to her own ululation, seemingly in reaction to the defeat of the Trojans, which is parallel to the reaction of the Argive women and of Argives in general, who are all de-scribed in lines 594–597 as ululating in response to the defeat of the Trojans; in line 596, this ululation is described once again as an act of *eu-phēmeîn* in the sense of 'make proper utterances'.

16§32. The ritual act of *ololugmos* or 'ululation' is a choral activity.‡ That is why the cue for performing this act is said to lead to the *kata-stasis,* 'arranging', of *khoroi,* 'choruses', in the watchman's words (*Agamemnon* line 23), and to the joining of the *khoros,* 'chorus', by the watchman himself as the choral perfor-mance gets started (line 31). So the solo performance of the watchman's words can now merge with the group performance of the words sung and danced by the chorus that actually starts performing at line 40. It is as if the entire drama of the *Agamemnon* had originated from 'the arranging of choruses', prompted by a vision of a signal fire.

16§33. But the ululation of Clytemnestra is not in response to the defeat of the Trojans: rather, it anticipates the impending slaughter of Agamemnon, now that this over-king is returning to Argos after the destruction of Troy. And so the *sumbolon* at line 8 of the drama, which signals the salvation of Argos to-gether with the destruction of Troy, signals also the destruction of Agamemnon

---

* For two clear examples of *eu-phēmeîn* in the sense of 'be ritually silent', I cite Aristophanes *Clouds* 263 and 297.

† *PH* 31–32 = 1§29.

‡ *HPC* 237 = II§§289–290.

himself. It all comes together at line 315 of the drama, where we see the word *sumbolon* used once again. This time it is Clytemnestra who says the word, claiming that the sequence of signal fires extending from Troy all the way to Argos add up to a message sent to her by her husband all the way from Troy, and the message is explained at lines 312–316 in the mystical form of a riddle about a relay torch race. Here is the precise wording of the riddle at line 314: νικᾷ δ' ὁ πρῶτος καὶ τελευταῖος δραμών, 'the first and the last runner will both be winners'. That is the *sumbolon*, Clytemnestra goes on to say at line 315. At line 8, we saw that the *sumbolon* of the relay of fire signals means that there is destruction at the initial point A, at Troy, and salvation at the terminal point Z, at Argos. But now at line 315 we see that this same *sumbolon* of the relay of fire signals also means something else: though there was victory in Troy for Agamemnon, there will be victory in Argos for Clytemnestra—and defeat for Agamemnon.

Three Further Examples of Symbolic Wording

16§34. I bring this hour to a close with three passages spoken by women. Each one of these passages is suffused with symbolic wording that connects with the main themes of the *Oresteia*. In the first passage, Clytemnestra speaks words of welcome to her hated husband, Agamemnon, just before he enters his palace. She rejoices that the king has returned home safely to Argos—not because she loves him but because, quite the opposite, she desires to be personally responsible for killing him in a perverted form of ritual slaughter that she herself will perform with the help of her lover Aegisthus. In the second and the third passages, the prophetess Cassandra speaks after Agamemnon has already entered the palace and just before she too enters. A perverted form of ritual slaughter awaits her as well, and she can foresee it with her prophetic mental powers.

16§35. The first passage is a riddling challenge directed by Clytemnestra at Agamemnon as the homecoming conqueror of Troy. She tempts her hated husband to perform a perverted form of ritual triumph, inviting him to step on an intricately woven fabric (*Agamemnon* lines 905–913) suffused with purple dye (line 910). The fabric is visualized as a masterpiece of the intricate art of pattern-weaving (lines 923, 926, 936).* To trample on it is thus to ruin a most expensive work of art. And, like the fabric, the dye would have been exorbitantly expen-

---

* In all three of these lines, the word indicating the art of pattern-weaving is *poikilo-*, the literal meaning of which is 'variegated'; see *PR* 93, citing Wace 1948, where I stress that *pattern-weaving* is not the same thing as *embroidery*.

sive. In the ancient world, such dye was extracted from a gland in the mantle cavity in the shell of a living murex, a tiny mollusk harvested from the sea. It has been estimated that only .0001 gram of purple dye could be extracted from each living murex shell, and that it would take as many as 12,000 of these tiny mollusks to supply enough purple for dyeing merely the trim of a single garment.[*] It is staggering, then, to contemplate the scale of human effort required to harvest so many murex shells—let alone the labor of the dye-workers who actually extracted the purple dye. And the fabric that Clytemnestra spreads on the ground for Agamemnon to step on is dyed purple not only around its trim: the whole fabric is suffused in purple dye. So the number of murex shells required to dye this massive fabric must surely be multiplied exponentially. To trample on such a purple garment is a gesture of ostentatious waste. And it is not only an arrogant act of wasting all the work that went into the weaving and the dyeing of the fabric. It is also a massive waste of the natural resources provided by the sea. Even the arrogant Agamemnon hesitates to step on the fabric. But Clytemnestra eggs him on, telling him that the sea is inexhaustible—that it will never run out of its natural resources:

Hour 16 Text E

> There is the sea—and who shall drain it dry? | It produces the oozing stain of abundant purple, equal in value to silver |₉₆₀ —an ooze that forever renews itself, with which to dye garments; | and the palace, O king, with the help of the gods, is sustainable—with its supply of these [purple garments]. | The palace doesn't know what it is to be in poverty of these things. | And I would have vowed in my prayers to arrange for the trampling of not one but many garments, if it had been so ordered by the oracles for the palace, |₉₆₅ back when I was planning to arrange a payback for your life [*psūkhē*].

Aeschylus Agamemnon 958–965†

16§36. These riddling words spoken by the queen carry a wrong message for the king, who is urged to feel a sense of entitlement to waste away the seemingly boundless resources of the natural world. But these same words are poetically

---

* Rees 1986:183.

† ἔστιν θάλασσα—τίς δέ νιν κατασβέσει; | —τρέφουσα πολλῆς πορφύρας ἰσάργυρον |₉₆₀ κηκῖδα παγκαίνιστον, εἱμάτων βαφάς. | οἶκος δ' ὑπάρχει τῶνδε σὺν θεοῖς, ἄναξ, ἔχειν· | πένεσθαι δ' οὐκ ἐπίσταται δόμος. | πολλῶν πατησμὸν δ' εἱμάτων ἂν ηὐξάμην, | δόμοισι προυνεχθέντος ἐν χρηστηρίοις, |₉₆₅ ψυχῆς κόμιστρα τῆσδε μηχανωμένη.

meant to carry a right message for the citizens of Athens who congregate at the State Theater of Dionysus. The ostentatious wastefulness of dysfunctional hero-kings in the heroic age can become for these citizens a foil for appreciating the civic ideals of moderation in the post-heroic age of their city-state.

16§37. In the second passage, which is a prophecy spoken by the prophetess Cassandra, her words conjure the image of a wind that starts to blow when the time comes for her to enter the palace, where she will be slaughtered by Clytemnestra and Aegisthus:

HOUR 16 TEXT F

And now, no more shall my prophecy peer forth from behind a veil like a newlywed bride; |₁₁₈₀ but it appears to be rushing toward me, breathing, blowing, toward the sun's rising, so as to dash against its rays, like a wave. It is something far mightier than this pain of mine here. No more by riddles [ainigma plural] will I put knowledge into your thinking [phrenes].

Aeschylus *Agamemnon* 1178–1183*

16§38. As Cassandra prepares to die, a wind starts blowing—in her vision. And this wind is for her a signal that the clarity of her prophetic vision has returned. What was once veiled like some demure bride is now unveiled by a gust of wind. And just as the power of prophetic vision, if it ever lapses, is imagined as something that must return to the prophetess, so also the wind that signals this power is something that must return whenever she sees a prophetic vision. So the wind itself is seen as a repeated experience, just as the experience of prophetic vision is something that keeps on returning to the prophetess. Conversely, the cessation of winds would be the same thing as a cessation of vision—of prophetic vision.

16§39. The returning wind in the prophetic vision of Cassandra is a repeated experience not only for her but also for the audience that sees and hears the drama, since they will remember an earlier wind. It was the malignant wind that started blowing eastward, in the direction of Troy, prompting the corrupted sacrifice of Iphigeneia. Now another malignant wind will blow eastward, toward the rays of the rising sun, prompting the corrupted sacrifice of Cassandra.

---

* καὶ μὴν ὁ χρησμὸς οὐκέτ᾽ ἐκ καλυμμάτων | ἔσται δεδορκὼς νεογάμου νύμφης δίκην· |₁₁₈₀ λαμπρὸς δ᾽ ἔοικεν ἡλίου πρὸς ἀντολὰς | πνέων ἐσάξειν, ὥστε κύματος δίκην | κλύζειν πρὸς αὐγάς, τοῦδε πήματος πολὺ | μεῖζον· φρενώσω δ᾽ οὐκέτ᾽ ἐξ αἰνιγμάτων.

16§40. In the third passage, we see another prophecy uttered by Cassandra. Here she predicts the chain of violence that will follow her own slaughter:

HOUR 16 TEXT G

|₁₃₀₉ This house stinks of blood-dripping slaughter. . . . |₁₃₁₁ It is like a breath from a grave. . . . |₁₃₂₂ I still want to have the chance, just for one moment, to make a speech—or a lament [*thrēnos*] that I perform for my own self. I pray to the sun, as I face its light for the last time, that the enemies may pay a bloody penalty to compensate for my death as well, |₁₃₂₅ which is the murder of a slave, an easy defeat. Ah, I cry out about the things that happen to humans! Even when things go well, one can still compare it all to a shadow [*skiā*]; but when things go badly, the dabbing of a wet sponge blots out the drawing. |₁₃₃₀ And this I think is far more pitiable than that.

Aeschylus Agamemnon 1309, 1311, 1322–1330*

16§41. The words of Cassandra lament her own misfortune, but the lament turns into a curse on those who are about to murder her. And the blotting out of Cassandra, as if she were a two-dimensional sketch rather than a three-dimensional person, is an act that will call for further vengeance in what seems to be an endless chain of evil.

---

* |₁₃₀₉ φόνον δόμοι πνέουσιν αἱματοσταγῆ. . . . |₁₃₁₁ ὅμοιος ἀτμὸς ὥσπερ ἐκ τάφου πρέπει. . . . |₁₃₂₂ ἅπαξ ἔτ᾽ εἰπεῖν ῥῆσιν, ἢ θρῆνον θέλω | ἐμὸν τὸν αὐτῆς. ἡλίου δ᾽ ἐπεύχομαι | πρὸς ὕστατον φῶς τοῖς ἐμοῖς τιμαόροις |₁₃₂₅ ἐχθροὺς φόνευσιν τὴν ἐμὴν τίνειν ὁμοῦ, | δούλης θανούσης, εὐμαροῦς χειρώματος. | ἰὼ βρότεια πράγματ᾽· εὐτυχοῦντα μὲν | σκιᾷ τις ἂν πρέψειεν· εἰ δὲ δυστυχοῖ, | βολαῖς ὑγρώσσων σπόγγος ὤλεσεν γραφήν. |₁₃₃₀ καὶ ταῦτ᾽ ἐκείνων μᾶλλον οἰκτίρω πολύ.

HOUR 17

Looking beyond the Cult Hero in the Libation Bearers *and the* Eumenides *of Aeschylus*

The Meaning of Tīmē

17§1. The key word for this hour is *tīmē*, plural *tīmai*, 'honor; honor paid to a superhuman force by way of cult'. So far, we have seen situations in which cult heroes as well as gods can receive *tīmē*. But now, as we will see in this hour, *tīmē* is also demanded by the Furies. The name 'Furies' here is a translation of the original Greek *Erīnues* or Erinyes, the singular form of which is *Erīnus* or Erinys. We already saw this word *Erīnus* in a most revealing context when we were reading *Iliad* IX 571, quoted in Hour 2 Text E. There the mother of Meleagros curses her son for having accidentally killed his maternal uncle, that is, her brother (IX 566–567). In uttering her curse, she beats the ground with down-turned hand, and the thumping sound is eerily heard from down below by an Erinys *(Erīnus)* or 'Fury' (IX 568–572). Such an Erinys is a superhuman personification of the vengeful anger stored up in those who have died—and whose death requires vengeance. When someone dies angry, there is unfinished business to be processed after death. The Erinyes or Furies represent that unfinished business. They are the angry spirits of the dead, including dead heroes.*

The Agenda of Athena

17§2. The program, as it were, of the *Oresteia* trilogy is to transform the unfinished business of angry dead heroes into the social agenda of the living citizens of Athens. Such a transformation can happen only if the Erinyes or Furies them-

---

* Henrichs 1994:44–45.

selves are transformed into *Eu-menides,* which means 'they of good intentions'.*
As we saw in Hour 15§38, the adjective *eu-menēs* applies to a cult hero who is 'of
good intentions' toward the worshipper.

17§3. In the *Eumenides* of Aeschylus, it is the goddess Athena who presides
over the transformation of the Erinyes into the Eumenides. And she takes this
action as the goddess who represents Athens, a city idealized as the best of all
cities in the *Eumenides* of Aeschylus. Further, in speaking to the Erinyes about
their transformation into the Eumenides, Athena promises them that they will
receive the kind of honors that heroes receive in hero cult:†

HOUR 17 TEXT A

And you [= the Erinyes], if you have a place of honor [*tīmē*] |₈₅₅ at the
house of Erekhtheus, you will be honored by the processions of men
and women and you will have more honor than you would ever have
from other mortals. So do not place on my land whetstones that hone
my peoples' desire for bloodshed, harmful to the insides |₈₆₀ of young
men, making them lose their minds with passionate feelings caused
not by wine;‡ and do not turn my people into fighting-cocks, making
reckless internecine war [Ares] for them, so that they kill each other. If
there is war [Ares], let it be with outsiders, and let it keep on happen-
ing, |₈₆₅ since war brings a terrific passion for genuine glory [*kleos*]; but
I say there will be no bird-fights in my dwelling place [*oikos*]. I make it
possible for you to choose to do [*drân*] good and to be treated [*paskhein*] well and with genuine honor [*tīmē*] to share in this land that is
most dear [*philē*] to the gods.

Aeschylus *Eumenides* 854–869§

* The clearest attestation of this term *Eumenides,* 'they of good intentions', is in Pausanias 2.11.4, as analyzed by
Henrichs 1994:42.

† By implication, the Erinyes cannot receive such honors if they continue to be Erinyes, that is, if they are not
transformed, becoming the *Eumenides,* that is, 'they of good intentions': see Henrichs 1994:38.

‡ Here the passionate feelings are caused by blood, not by wine. In the case of the Eumenides, as we will see in
Hour 18, passionate feelings would be caused by libations of wine.

§ καὶ σὺ τιμίαν |₈₅₅ ἕδραν ἔχουσα πρὸς δόμοις Ἐρεχθέως | τεύξῃ παρ' ἀνδρῶν καὶ γυναικείων στόλων
| ὅσ' ἂν παρ' ἄλλων οὔποτ' ἂν σχέθοις βροτῶν. | σὺ δ' ἐν τόποισι τοῖς ἐμοῖσι μὴ βάλῃς |
αἱματηρὰς θηγάνας, σπλάγχνων βλάβας |₈₆₀ νέων, ἀοίνοις ἐμμανεῖς θυμώμασιν, | μήτ', ἐξελοῦσ' ὡς
καρδίαν ἀλεκτόρων, | ἐν τοῖς ἐμοῖς ἀστοῖσιν ἱδρύσῃς Ἄρη | ἐμφύλιόν τε καὶ πρὸς ἀλλήλους θρασύν. |
θυραῖος ἔστω πόλεμος, οὐ μόλις παρών, |₈₆₅ ἐν ᾧ τις ἔσται δεινὸς εὐκλείας ἔρως· | ἐνοικίου δ' ὄρνιθος οὐ
λέγω μάχην. | τοιαῦθ' ἑλέσθαι σοι πάρεστιν ἐξ ἐμοῦ, | εὖ δρῶσαν, εὖ πάσχουσαν, εὖ τιμωμένην |
χώρας μετασχεῖν τῆσδε θεοφιλεστάτης.

17§4. In this passage, the Erinyes or Furies are being promised a *tīmē*, 'honor', that is analogous to the *tīmē*, 'honor', received by the cult hero Erekhtheus (line 855). This Erekhtheus is mentioned prominently in *Iliad* II 547–551 as the primary cult hero of Athens: he is said to be worshipped by the Athenians in a festive setting of seasonally recurring sacrifices. In this same Homeric context, Erekhtheus is described as a prototypical human: he is born of the goddess Earth, and then the goddess Athena literally 'nurses' him (II 548 *threpse*). In his role as son of the Earth and nursling of Athena, Erekhtheus is venerated as a notional prototype of all Athenians.* The intimate connection between Athena and Erekhtheus is highlighted also in another Homeric reference, in *Odyssey* vii 80–81: in that context, this cult hero is described as sharing a dwelling with the goddess Athena herself on the acropolis in Athens.†

Pouring Libations for Cult Heroes or for Ancestors

17§5. In Text A, we have seen a connection being made between the worshipping of a cult hero like Erekhtheus and the worshipping of the Furies or Erinyes, once they are transformed into the benign Eumenides. More basically, however, the worshipping of heroes in hero cults is connected with the *cult of the dead*, that is, with *ancestor worship*. It can even be said that the rituals of hero cult derive, in the long run, from rituals of ancestor worship.‡ A case in point is the practice of making a *libation*, which is a ritual pouring.§ I have already referred to such a practice in Hour **8§2**, where we considered the vessel known as the hydria, used for the ritual pouring of water to honor cult heroes or ancestors. There existed many different forms of libation in the ancient Greek world, but I focus now on libations offered to cult heroes or to ancestors. When I say *ancestors* here, I include the *immediate dead,* by which I mean blood relatives who died within one's own lifetime.

17§6. Libations offered to heroes or to the dead in general involved the ritual pouring of water or wine or oil or milk or honey or some combination of these ingredients.** Another ingredient was the blood of animal sacrifices, though

---

* *HC* 1§138.

† *HTL* 159–160. For an overall analysis of *Iliad* II 547–551 and *Odyssey* vii 81, see Frame 2009:395 and 445–446.

‡ *BA* 115–116 = 6§28. *PH* 144, 153–156 = 5§15, 6§§16–20.

§ For an overall introduction to the practice of making libations, see Patton 2009:27–56; also Henrichs 1983:95–97.

** Ekroth 2002:67–68, 254–268; see also Henrichs 1983:99.

the recipients of blood-libations were mostly cult heroes, not the "ordinary" dead.* Conversely, as we will see in Hour 18, some cult heroes were considered to be incompatible with wine-libations.

17§7. What we see happening in the *Libation Bearers* of Aeschylus is an example of a libation performed both for an ancestor and for a cult hero. In the passage I am about to quote, Electra is preparing to perform such a libation in honor of her dead father and immediate ancestor, Agamemnon, who as we know from external evidence was worshipped as a cult hero at Mycenae and elsewhere.† Electra asks the chorus, who represent the handmaidens working for the rulers of the palace, to teach her the correct way to perform the libation:

HOUR 17 TEXT B

| $_{84}$ {Electra:} You handmaidens who set our house in order, | $_{85}$ since you are here at this ritual of supplication as my | $_{86}$ attendants, become my partners by giving advice about these things here: | $_{87}$ what should I say while I pour [*kheîn*] these libations [*khoai*] of sorrowful caring? | $_{88}$ How shall I say words that show good thinking [*eu-phrona*], how shall I make a prayer [*kat-eukhesthai*] to my father? | $_{89}$ Shall I say that I bring these offerings from a woman who is near and dear [*philē*] to a man who is near and dear [*philos*], | $_{90}$ from wife to husband—from my own mother?

Aeschylus *Libation Bearers* 84–90‡

17§8. Here Electra, daughter of Agamemnon and Clytemnestra, is attempting to perform a ritual of libation as an act of ancestor worship—which can be equated, as I have argued, with the cult of the dead. In performing this ritual of libation, Electra intends to give worshipful honor to her father, Agamemnon, but she is not yet sure about the rules of the ritual. In expressing her desire to perform the libation, she is morally correct, but she does not know how to be

---

*The historical evidence is summarized thus by Ekroth 2002:268: "The ordinary dead do not seem to have been called, contracted or invited by means of blood and there is little evidence that there was any desire for that kind of closeness with the departed."

† On the hero cults of Agamemnon, see Salapata 2011.

‡ | $_{84}$ δμωαὶ γυναῖκες, δωμάτων εὐθήμονες, | $_{85}$ ἐπεὶ πάρεστε τῆσδε προστροπῆς ἐμοὶ | $_{86}$ πομποί, γένεσθε τῶνδε σύμβουλοι πέρι· | $_{87}$ τί φῶ χέουσα τάσδε κηδείους χοάς; | $_{88}$ πῶς εὔφρον' εἴπω, πῶς κατεύξωμαι πατρί; | $_{89}$ πότερα λέγουσα παρὰ φίλης φίλῳ φέρειν | $_{90}$ γυναικὸς ἀνδρί, τῆς ἐμῆς μητρὸς πάρα;

ritually correct.* All she knows is that her mother is not morally correct, since Clytemnestra had actually killed her own husband, Electra's father.

What Stands in the Way of a Ritually Correct Libation by Electra

17§9. The libation intended by Electra for Agamemnon could be considered a standard procedure for those engaging in the cult of the dead, that is, in ancestor worship. But Agamemnon is not only an ancestor for Electra. He is also a cult hero in the making. And the destiny of Agamemnon as a cult hero stands in the way of successfully performing a libation in his honor. That is because cult heroes require libations that are different from the kinds of libations offered by ordinary persons to their immediate ancestors. The difference emerges as the handmaidens begin to instruct Electra about the performance of her libation:

HOUR 17 TEXT C

|₁₁₈ {Electra:} What should I say? Instruct me, inexperienced as I am, and lead me in my thinking.

|₁₁₉ {Chorus:}—Pray that some superhuman force [daimōn] or some mortal may come to them [= Clytemnestra and Aegisthus]

|₁₂₀ {Electra:} As judge [dikastēs] or as bringer of vindication [dikē], do you mean?

|₁₂₁ {Chorus:} Very simply, just signal that you are acting as one who will kill in repayment for a killing.

|₁₂₂ {Electra:} And is it ritually correct [eu-sebê] for me, from the standpoint of the gods?

|₁₂₃ {Chorus:}—Why not? It is an act of repaying bad things with bad things.

|₁₂₄ {Electra:} ... O Hermes of the nether world, summon for me |₁₂₅ the superhuman forces [daimones] beneath the earth to hear my |₁₂₆ prayers—forces that watch over my father's house, |₁₂₇ and [summon] Earth herself, who gives birth to all things, |₁₂₈ and, having nurtured them, receives from them the flow that they produce. |₁₂₉ And, mean-

---

*On the general relationship of moral and ritual correctness, I offer a brief comparative analysis in Nagy 1985:57 = §§21–22; see also GM 70, 110–111.

while, as I pour [*kheîn*] these liquids of libation [*khernibes*] to the dead, |₁₃₀ I say these things as I call on my father.

Aeschylus *Libation Bearers* 118–130*

17§10. As we see from this passage as also from other related passages in the *Libation Bearers*, the ritual actions of Electra are interwoven with her own emotional need to exact vengeance from Clytemnestra and Aegisthus for their murder of her father.† And this emotional need for vengeance is a channeling, as it were, of the anger or fury emanating from the restless spirit of her dead father, the hero Agamemnon.

17§11. Such a fury can be pictured as an Erinys that calls for a libation of blood:

HOUR 17 TEXT D

|₃₉₉ {Electra:} Hear, O Earth, and you forces of the earth below [*khthonioi*] who have your own honors [*tīmai*]!

|₄₀₀ {Chorus:} And it is the customary law [*nomos*] that drops of blood |₄₀₁ spilled [*kheîn*] on the ground demand yet more |₄₀₂ blood. The devastation [*loigos*] cries out for the Fury [Erinys], |₄₀₃ which from those who died [*phthinesthai*] before brings one disaster [*atē*] |₄₀₄ after another disaster [*atē*].

Aeschylus *Libation Bearers* 399–404‡

17§12. Again we see a 'Fury' or Erinys as the personification of the anger stored up inside someone who died angry. The anger is unfinished business that has to get finished off somehow. But the finishing off never seems to happen: it is a seemingly endless chain of evil: what keeps happening is 'one disaster [*atē*]

---

* |₁₁₈ {Ηλ.} τί φῶ; δίδασκ' ἄπειρον ἐξηγουμένη. |₁₁₉ {Χο.} ἐλθεῖν τιν' αὐτοῖς δαίμον- ἢ βροτῶν τινα— |₁₂₀ {Ηλ.} πότερα δικαστὴν ἢ δικηφόρον λέγεις; |₁₂₁ {Χο.} ἁπλωστὶ φράζουσ', ὅστις ἀνταποκτενεῖ. |₁₂₂ {Ηλ.} καὶ ταῦτά μούστὶν εὐσεβῆ θεῶν πάρα; |₁₂₃ {Χο.} πῶς δ' οὔ, τὸν ἐχθρὸν ἀνταμείβεσθαι κακοῖς; |₁₂₄ ...Ἑρμῆ χθόνιε, κηρύξας ἐμοὶ |₁₂₅ τοὺς γῆς ἔνερθε δαίμονας κλύειν ἐμὰς |₁₂₆ εὐχάς, πατρῴων δωμάτων ἐπισκόπους, |₁₂₇ καὶ γαῖαν αὐτήν, ἣ τὰ πάντα τίκτεται |₁₂₈ θρέψασά τ' αὖθις τῶνδε κῦμα λαμβάνει· |₁₂₉ κἀγὼ χέουσα τάσδε χέρνιβας νεκροῖς |₁₃₀ λέγω καλοῦσα πατέρ(α).

† Here I am guided by a formulation developed by Seaford 1994:91 in his overall analysis of the *Libation Bearers* of Aeschylus.

‡ |₃₉₉ κλῦτε δὲ Γᾶ χθονίων τε τιμαί. |₄₀₀ {Χο.} ἀλλὰ νόμος μὲν φονίας σταγόνας |₄₀₁ χυμένας ἐς πέδον ἄλλο προσαιτεῖν |₄₀₂ αἷμα· βοᾷ γὰρ λοιγὸς Ἐρινὺν |₄₀₃ παρὰ τῶν πρότερον φθιμένων ἄτην |₄₀₄ ἑτέραν ἐπάγουσαν ἐπ' ἄτῃ.

after another disaster [*atē*]'. From here on, the expression I will use in referring to this chain of evil, fueled by an insatiable desire for vengeance, is the spirit of an ongoing *vendetta*. I will even go so far as to add that such a spirit is the essence of the word 'Fury' that I have been using to convey the idea of an Erinys.

17§13. So the libation that needs to be performed at the tomb of Agamemnon cannot follow the ordinary rules of libation as performed by participants in cults of the dead. In the words of the chorus, as we have just read them, the spirit of the *vendetta* requires that the spilling of Agamemnon's blood must lead to the further spilling of blood. In the cult of heroes, such further spilling could be fulfilled by way of blood-libations, where the blood originated from sacrificial animals that were slaughtered in honor of the heroes. By contrast, as we have already seen, the use of animal blood is rare in the case of libations performed in honor of the "ordinary" dead.*

17§14. But the libation poured for Agamemnon in the *Libation Bearers* of Aeschylus is no ordinary ritual performed for a cult hero. In this case, the spirit of the ongoing *vendetta* requires that the spilling of Agamemnon's blood must lead to further spilling of blood that originates not from sacrificial animals but from human victims:

HOUR 17 TEXT E

|₅₇₅ {Orestes is speaking:} Before he [= Aegisthus] can even say "Who is the stranger [*xenos*] and where is he from?" he will become a corpse. |₅₇₆ That is what I will do to him, skewering him with my swift sword. |₅₇₇ The Fury [Erinys] that has no fill of slaughter |₅₇₈ will have unmixed blood to drink as her third and crowning drink!

Aeschylus *Libation Bearers* 575–578†

17§15. The killing of Aegisthus by Orestes, brother of Electra, is visualized here as a libation of human blood, to be drunk by an Erinys. So the blood here originates not from some animal slaughtered at a sacrifice, which would be ritu-

---

* I recall the formulation of Ekroth 2002:268: "The ordinary dead do not seem to have been called, contracted or invited by means of blood and there is little evidence that there was any desire for that kind of closeness with the departed."

† |₅₇₅ πρὶν αὐτὸν εἰπεῖν 'ποδαπὸς ὁ ξένος;' νεκρὸν |₅₇₆ θήσω, ποδώκει περιβαλὼν χαλκεύματι. |₅₇₇ φόνου δ' Ἐρινὺς οὐχ ὑπεσπανισμένη |₅₇₈ ἄκρατον αἷμα πίεται τρίτην πόσιν.

ally correct in the case of pouring a libation to honor a cult hero. Rather, the blood originates from Aegisthus himself, slaughtered in a corrupted sacrifice that is viewed as a killing fueled by the spirit of the ongoing *vendetta*.

Transcending the Spirit of Vendetta

17§16. In the myth that we see unfolding in the *Oresteia* trilogy of Aeschylus, what needs to happen is a solution for stopping a chain of evil originating from the heroic age and perpetuated by an insatiable desire for vengeance. What I have been calling the spirit of an ongoing *vendetta* can be stopped only by a new world order, which is what we see emerging in the *Eumenides* of Aeschylus. And this new world order, which is represented by the city of Athens, is made possible by the intervention of the goddess of that city, Athena, who becomes the embodiment of the ideals of Athens as these ideals take shape in the *Oresteia* trilogy.

17§17. Athena's intervention achieves a transformation of the malevolent Erinyes into the benevolent Eumenides. Whereas the Erinyes represent the spirit of an ongoing *vendetta* originating from angry ghosts of heroes, the Eumenides represent the positive mentality of those same heroes. And the transformation of the Erinyes into the Eumenides represents their acculturation within the framework of Athenian society, where they are also known as the *Semnai* or 'Revered Ones' (there is a most revealing report about them in Pausanias 1.28.6–7). Conversely, such acculturation represents the transformation of the dead heroes of the past into the cult heroes of the immediate present. These cult heroes could now be worshipped by the pouring of libations of blood originating from animal sacrifice, and they would no longer have to call for the spilling of human blood.* Further, just as cult heroes received libations as well as sacrifices in general from their worshippers, so also the Eumenides could receive corresponding honors.† By contrast, the Erinyes would receive no libations, no sacrifices—at least, not in Athens.‡

---

* For a survey of practices involving blood-libations offered to cult heroes, see Ekroth 2002:68–72, 257–268.

† For a survey of the kinds of libations and sacrifices that worshippers offered to the Eumenides, see Henrichs 1994:40–43.

‡ The absence or near-absence of attestations showing any libation or sacrifice offered to the Erinyes is noted by Henrichs 1994:37–38, 44.

A New World Order for Athens

17§18. Once the Eumenides are differentiated from the Erinyes, the city of Athens can become an idealized society according to the mythology of the *Oresteia* trilogy. In this society, the positive mentality of cult heroes is acculturated into a social as well as a cosmic force of fertility and prosperity for the entire community. And that force is *dike* in the sense of absolutized 'justice'. For this justice to emerge out of the dysfunctional old world of kings who were heroes and heroes who were kings, a judgment has to be made, and this judgment will be the first verdict ever pronounced in what we call a court of law. Here is how the goddess Athena herself says it:

HOUR 17 TEXT F

|₆₉₆ Neither anarchy nor tyranny |₆₉₇ —I advise the citizens of my city not to hold either of these things in honor as they go on managing their affairs, |₆₉₈ but I also advise them not to drive fear out of the city altogether. |₆₉₉ For who among mortal men, if he fears nothing, behaves with justice [*dike*]? |₇₀₀ If you [Athenians], acting with justice [*dike*], would treat reverence [*sebas*] for the divine as a thing to be feared, |₇₀₁ then there would be for you a protection that brings salvation [*sōtērios*] for your land and for your city [*polis*] |₇₀₂ —that is what you would have, the kind of protection that no other human could have anywhere else, |₇₀₃ either among the Scythians or in the territories of Pelops. |₇₀₄ I establish this lawcourt, which is untouched by desire for profit [*kerdos*]. |₇₀₅ It is fully deserving of reverence and is quick to anger. Watching over those who sleep, |₇₀₆ it is a wakeful guardian of the land. Yes, this is what I establish. |₇₀₇ I have given to you at some length this set of instructions [*par-ainesis*] |₇₀₈ to be heeded for all time by you as the citizens of my city. So now you must stand up, |₇₀₉ take a ballot, and make a decision [*diagnōsis*] about the case [*dike*], |₇₁₀ showing respect for your oath. The word has been spoken.

Aeschylus *Eumenides* 696–710*

---

* |₆₉₆ τὸ μήτ᾽ ἄναρχον μήτε δεσποτούμενον |₆₉₇ ἀστοῖς περιστέλλουσι βουλεύω σέβειν, |₆₉₈ καὶ μὴ τὸ δεινὸν πᾶν πόλεως ἔξω βαλεῖν. |₆₉₉ τίς γὰρ δεδοικὼς μηδὲν ἔνδικος βροτῶν; |₇₀₀ τοιόνδε τοι ταρβοῦντες ἐνδίκως σέβας |₇₀₁ ἔρυμά τε χώρας καὶ πόλεως σωτήριον |₇₀₂ ἔχοιτ᾽ ἄν, οἷον οὔτις ἀνθρώπων ἔχει, |₇₀₃ οὔτ᾽ ἐν Σκύθῃσιν οὔτε Πέλοπος ἐν τόποις. |₇₀₄ κερδῶν ἄθικτον τοῦτο βουλευτήριον, |₇₀₅ αἰδοῖον, ὀξύθυμον, εὑδόντων ὕπερ |₇₀₆ ἐγρηγορὸς φρούρημα γῆς καθίσταμαι. |₇₀₇ ταύτην μὲν ἐξέτειν᾽ ἐμοῖς

17§19. Athena, goddess of the new world order, has just made possible the first vote of the first jury in the first trial by jury. This moment inaugurates, in terms of the myth created by the *Oresteia* trilogy, the beginnings of the institution known as the city-state or *polis*. The institution of trial by jury, as an alternative to the institution of the *vendetta*, is imagined here as the first step leading toward an ideal civilization as defined by the *polis*. I recall the formulation of Aristotle, which we had read at the very beginning (00§8): humans reach their full potential as organisms of the *polis*.

17§20. In the *Eumenides*, the first vote of the first jury in the first trial by jury leads to a suspended verdict for Orestes, avenger of his father on the one hand and killer of his mother on the other. As we are about to see, this suspended verdict is seen as an 'equal vote' prompted by the two mutually contradictory actions taken by Orestes, the avenging of his father and the killing of his mother. The 'equal vote' of the jury will not really absolve Orestes of his guilt for killing his mother: it will only make it possible for the guilt itself to be processed by a new rule of law. And that processing, that process, is the rule of law itself. In this chicken-and-egg relationship, as articulated in the myth, the processing of the guilt leads to the rule of law that processes the guilt. Such a rule is at first resisted by the Erinyes as embodiments of the spirit of the ongoing *vendetta,* but it is ultimately accepted by them, once they are persuaded by Athena, and this persuasion can now transform them into the Eumenides. And once the Erinyes are transformed into the Eumenides, the ongoing *vendetta* comes to an end. The very institution of the hot-blooded *vendetta,* as traced back in time to a retrospectively dysfunctional heroic age, is now stopped cold. Here is how the goddess Athena herself says it:

HOUR 17 TEXT G

|₇₉₄ You [Erinyes] must be persuaded by me not to bear the decision with heavy grief. |₇₉₅ For you are not defeated; the trial [*dikē*] resulted in an equal vote, |₇₉₆ that is truly [*alēthōs*] how it came out, and so you are not deprived of your honor [*tīmē*], |₇₉₇ since there were clear pieces of testimony from Zeus. |₇₉₈ And the one who spoke the oracle himself, he [= Apollo] was also the same one who came to give evidence himself, |₇₉₉ with the result that Orestes could not suffer harm, even though

---

παραίνεσιν |₇₀₈ ἀστοῖσιν ἐς τὸ λοιπόν· ὀρθοῦσθαι δὲ χρὴ |₇₀₉ καὶ ψῆφον αἴρειν καὶ διαγνῶναι δίκην |₇₁₀ αἰδουμένους τὸν ὅρκον. εἴρηται λόγος.

he did [*drân*] these things that he did. |₈₀₀ But here you are, vomiting your heavy anger [*kotos*] on this land. |₈₀₁ Do reconsider. Do not get passionately angry. Do not cause deprivation of fruit [*a-karpiā*], |₈₀₂ making the land sterile by releasing toxic drops dripping from super-human powers [*daimones*], |₈₀₃ drops becoming savage piercing pains that eat away the seeds. |₈₀₄ For I do promise you, in all justness [*dikē*], |₈₀₅ that you will have sanctuaries and sacred hollows in this land of justice [*dikē*], |₈₀₆ where you will sit on bright thrones at places of fire-sacrifice, |₈₀₇ that is what you will have, earning honor [*tīmē*] from the citizens here. [. . .] |₈₂₄ You are not without honor [*tīmē*], so do not be moved by your excessive feeling [*thūmos*], |₈₂₅ O goddesses, by making the land cursed in the worst way for mortals. |₈₂₆ I also rely on Zeus—what need is there to say that?— |₈₂₇ and I alone of the gods know where the keys are to the house |₈₂₈ where his thunderbolt is kept safe, under a seal [*sphrāgīs*]. |₈₂₉ But there is no need for it. So be obedient to me in the best possible way, |₈₃₀ and do not hurl words against the land from a tongue uttering threats that cannot be fulfilled, |₈₃₁ threatening that all things bearing fruit [*karpos*] will not prosper. |₈₃₂ Put to sleep the bitter power [*menos*] of your dark flow, |₈₃₃ since you will receive an honor [*tīmē*] that is revered [*semnē*], and you will share your dwelling [*sun-oikeîn*] with me. |₈₃₄ You will have the first-fruits of this plentiful land, |₈₃₅ and fire-sacrifices before childbirth—as also before matrimo-nial initiation [*telos*] |₈₃₆ —that is what you will have. And, once you have these things, you will keep on transmitting forever these words of mine here, giving your approval [*ep-aineîn*].

Aeschylus Eumenides 794–807, 824–836*

---

* |₇₉₄ ἐμοὶ πίθεσθε μὴ βαρυστόνως φέρειν. |₇₉₅ οὐ γὰρ νενίκησθ᾽, ἀλλ᾽ ἰσόψηφος δίκη |₇₉₆ ἐξῆλθ᾽ ἀληθῶς, οὐκ ἀτιμίᾳ σέθεν· |₇₉₇ ἀλλ᾽ ἐκ Διὸς γὰρ λαμπρὰ μαρτύρια παρῆν, |₇₉₈ αὐτός θ᾽ ὁ χρήσας αὐτὸς ἦν ὁ μαρτυρῶν, |₇₉₉ ὡς ταῦτ᾽ Ὀρέστην δρῶντα μὴ βλάβας ἔχειν. |₈₀₀ ὑμεῖς δ᾽ ἐμεῖτε τῇδε γῇ βαρὺν κότον; |₈₀₁ σκέψασθε, μὴ θυμοῦσθε, μηδ᾽ ἀκαρπίαν |₈₀₂ τεύξητ᾽, ἀφεῖσαι δαιμόνων σταλάγματα, |₈₀₃ βρωτῆρας αἰχμὰς σπερμάτων ἀνημέρους. |₈₀₄ ἐγὼ γὰρ ὑμῖν πανδίκως ὑπίσχομαι |₈₀₅ ἕδρας τε καὶ κευθμῶνας ἐνδίκου χθονὸς |₈₀₆ λιπαροθρόνοισιν ἡμένας ἐπ᾽ ἐσχάραις |₈₀₇ ἕξειν, ὑπ᾽ ἀστῶν τῶνδε τιμαλφουμένας. . . . |₈₂₄ οὐκ ἔστ᾽ ἄτιμοι, μηδ᾽ ὑπερθύμως ἄγαν |₈₂₅ θεαὶ βροτῶν κτίσητε δύσκηλον χθόνα. |₈₂₆ κἀγὼ πέποιθα Ζηνὶ καί—τί δεῖ λέγειν;— |₈₂₇ καὶ κλῇδας οἶδα δώματος μόνη θεῶν |₈₂₈ ἐν ᾧ κεραυνός ἐστιν ἐσφραγισμένος· |₈₂₉ ἀλλ᾽ οὐδὲν αὐτοῦ δεῖ· σὺ δ᾽ εὐπιθὴς ἐμοὶ |₈₃₀ γλώσσης ματαίας μὴ ᾽κβάλῃς ἔπη χθονί |₈₃₁ καρπὸν φέροντα πάντα μὴ πράσσειν καλῶς. |₈₃₂ κοίμα κελαινοῦ κύματος πικρὸν μένος |₈₃₃ ὡς σεμνότιμος καὶ ξυνοικήτωρ ἐμοί· |₈₃₄ πολλῆς δὲ χώρας τῆσδε τἀκροθίνια |₈₃₅ θύη πρὸ παίδων καὶ γαμηλίου τέλους |₈₃₆ ἔχουσ᾽ ἐς αἰεὶ τόνδ᾽ ἐπαινέσεις λόγον.

17§21. Athena has now transformed the anger of the Furies or Erinyes into the social force that makes it possible to achieve justice under the rule of law. The angry spirits of the Erinyes, analogous to the spirits of cult heroes when they get angry at the unjust, are being acculturated by the overarching idea of *dikē* or 'justice' as established in the city-state, the *polis*. The poetic words of fertility and prosperity, as conferred by the cult hero upon the just, have now been re-applied to the social institution of trial by jury, which replaces the "tribal" system of the *vendetta*, an institution that notionally predates the era of civilization inaugurated by the invention, as it were, of the *polis*.

17§22. So the idea of the hero as a champion of absolute justice, *dikē*, is validated by the civilization of the *polis* of Athens. And the goddess Athena is pictured as the idealized representative of this idealized Athens. In the words of the goddess herself, Athens is a beautiful garden, and Athena is the caring gardener who makes everything fertile and prosperous. Here is how she says it, calling on the Eumenides to celebrate their transformation into the benevolent spirits that protect the heroic ideal of absolute justice:

HOUR 17 TEXT H

|$_{902}$ {Chorus of Eumenides:} So, what kind of hymn [*humnos*] are you telling me to sing for this land?

|$_{903}$ {Athena:} Sing the kinds of songs that are not about evil victory, |$_{904}$ but songs of the land and of the currents of the sea, [*pontos*] |$_{905}$ and of the sky; and sing that the gusts of wind |$_{906}$ will come with good sunlight and blow over this land, |$_{907}$ and that the fruit of the earth and the offspring of the animals of the field |$_{908}$ will flourish abundantly for my citizens and will not wear out in the course of time, |$_{909}$ and that there will be the salvation [*sōtēriā*] of human seed. |$_{910}$ May you be ready to promote the fertility of those who worship well [*eu-sebeîn*]; |$_{911}$ for I cherish, like a gardener, |$_{912}$ the progeny [*genos*] of these people here, who are so just [*dikaioi*]—and who must be protected from sorrow [*penthos*]. |$_{913}$ Such things are for you to do. As for me, when it comes to deeds of war, |$_{914}$ ordeals [*agōnes*] that bring distinction, I will not stand for it if |$_{915}$ this citadel [*polis*], this victorious city [*astu*], is not honored [*tīmân*] among mortals.

Aeschylus *Eumenides* 902–915*

* |$_{902}$ {Χο.} τί οὖν μ' ἄνωγας τῇδ' ἐφυμνῆσαι χθονί; |$_{903}$ {Αθ.} ὁποῖα νίκης μὴ κακῆς ἐπίσκοπα, |$_{904}$ καὶ ταῦτα γῆθεν ἔκ τε ποντίας δρόσου, |$_{905}$ ἐξ οὐρανοῦ τε, κἀνέμων ἀήματα |$_{906}$ εὐηλίως πνέοντ' ἐπιστείχειν

17§23. In the *Agamemnon,* we had seen malevolent winds signaling evil deeds, like the corrupt sacrifices that were staged for shedding the blood of victims like Iphigeneia and Cassandra. Now in the *Eumenides* we see benevolent winds signaling the good deeds promoted by the rule of law in the city of Athens. And this city is idealized in the image of the goddess Athena as its 'gardener'. Now the idea of Athens as a perfect society can be made complete.

17§24. Looking back at the poetry that glorified the benevolent aspects of heroes as cult heroes, we can see that the imagery of the paradisiacal garden tended by the goddess Athena as its gardener is derived ultimately from the symbolic world of hero cult. In the passage we have just read, Athena as the goddess of her city teaches the Eumenides how to celebrate their new status as the protectors of this symbolic world. The celebration takes the form of a hymn, and the hymn that this goddess teaches the Eumenides to perform becomes a hymn to be performed for Athena herself, recurrently for all eternity, as the embodiment of this new world order.

χθόνα· |907 καρπόν τε γαίας καὶ βοτῶν ἐπίρρυτον |908 ἀστοῖσιν εὐθενοῦντα μὴ κάμνειν χρόνῳ, |909 καὶ τῶν βροτείων σπερμάτων σωτηρίαν. |910 τῶν δ' εὐσεβούντων ἐκφορωτέρα πέλοις. |911 στέργω γάρ, ἀνδρὸς φιτυποίμενος δίκην, |912 τὸ τῶν δικαίων τῶνδ' ἀπένθητον γένος. |913 τοιαῦτα σοῦστι. τῶν ἀρειφάτων δ' ἐγὼ |914 πρεπτῶν ἀγώνων οὐκ ἀνέξομαι τὸ μὴ οὐ |915 τήνδ' ἀστύνικον ἐν βροτοῖς τιμᾶν πόλιν.

Sophocles' Oedipus at Colonus and the Power of the Cult Hero in Death

The Meaning of Kolōnos

18§1. The key word for this hour is *kolōnos,* which means a 'tumulus' or 'elevation' in a local landscape. As we will see, *kolōnos* means also the whole landscape itself, which is a garden or grove that is entered by Oedipus. Further, Colonus / *Kolōnos* is the name of a district or *dēmos,* 'deme', of Attica, which was named after this prominent landmark. When I say *Attica* here, I mean the name of the overall region controlled by the metropolis of Athens.

18§2. And there is also another meaning of *kolōnos* at work here in the context of Colonus / *Kolōnos* as a name for a deme of Attica: Colonus / *Kolōnos* is the name of a local cult hero who resides in the deme of Colonus / *Kolōnos.*

18§3. All these meanings are activated in a dialogue between Oedipus and a representative of the local population of Colonus, whom the old hero addresses as *xenos,* 'stranger':

HOUR 18 TEXT A

|₄₉ {Oedipus:} I implore you by the gods, stranger [*xenos*], do not deprive me of honor [*a-tīmân*], |₅₀ wanderer that I am, and do point out to me the things I ask you to tell me.

|₅₁ {Xenos:} Indicate [*sēmainein*] to me, and it will be clear that you will not be without honor [*a-tīmos*] from me.

|₅₂ {Oedipus:} What, then, is the place [*khōros*] that I [we] have entered?

|₅₃ {Xenos:} All that I myself know, you will hear and learn. |₅₄ This whole place [*khōros*] is sacred [*hieros*]; it is possessed |₅₅ by the revered

[*semnos*] Poseidon, and inside it is the fire-bringing god, |₅₆ the Titan Prometheus. As for the place [*topos*] where you have set foot, |₅₇ it is called the Bronze-Step Threshold of this land here. |₅₈ It is the Protection of Athens. And the neighboring fields |₅₉ claim as their own this person here, Colonus [*Kolōnos*], who is the rider of chariots [*hippotēs*], |₆₀ as their ancient ruler; and all the population bear the name of |₆₁ this person here [= Colonus] as their shared [*koinon*] possession. |₆₂ Such, you see, stranger [*xenos*], are these things, which are what they are not because what we say |₆₃ gives them honor [*tīmân*], but rather because we live in communion [*sun-ousiā*] with them.

|₆₄ {Oedipus:} So there are in fact some dwellers in these places [*topoi*] here?

|₆₅ {Xenos:} Oh, yes, very much so, and they are the namesakes of this god [*theos* = Colonus] here.

Sophocles *Oedipus at Colonus* 49–65*

18§4. For the moment, I highlight only three details in this remarkable passage. First, the language describing the sacred place that Oedipus has entered uses the deictic pronoun *hode,* which can be translated as 'this person here', in referring to the local cult hero of this place, whose name is Colonus/*Kolōnos*. The reference is most ostentatious, since it happens three times in a row, at lines 59 (τόνδ'), 61 (τοῦδε), and 65 (τοῦδε). So the immediate presence of this hero named Colonus / *Kolōnos* is deeply felt by the local population of a district that is likewise named Colonus / *Kolōnos*. Second, this hero is described by the epithet *hippotēs* at line 59, which I interpret as 'the rider of a horse-drawn chariot'. I will have more to say later about the significance of associating both the hero and the place named Colonus/*Kolōnos* with horses. Third, in the last line of what I just quoted, we see the word *theos,* 'god', applied to this local cult hero. As we already saw in Hour 15§30, local cult heroes may be called *theoi,* 'gods', at climactic moments in the course of rituals that venerate them.

---

* |₄₉ {ΟΙ.} Πρός νυν θεῶν, ὦ ξεῖνε, μή μ' ἀτιμάσῃς |₅₀ τοιόνδ' ἀλήτην ὧν σε προστρέπω φράσαι. |₅₁ {ΞΕ.} Σήμαινε, κοὐκ ἄτιμος ἔκ γ' ἐμοῦ φανῇ. |₅₂ {ΟΙ.} Τίς δ' ἔσθ' ὁ χῶρος δῆτ' ἐν ᾧ βεβήκαμεν; |₅₃{ΞΕ.} Ὅσ' οἶδα κἀγὼ πάντ' ἐπιστήσῃ κλύων. |₅₄ Χῶρος μὲν ἱρὸς πᾶς ὅδ' ἔστ'· ἔχει δέ νιν |₅₅ σεμνὸς Ποσειδῶν· ἐν δ' ὁ πυρφόρος θεὸς |₅₆ Τιτὰν Προμηθεύς· ὃν δ' ἐπιστείβεις τόπον |₅₇ χθονὸς καλεῖται τῆσδε χαλκόπους ὁδός, |₅₈ ἔρεισμ' Ἀθηνῶν· οἱ δὲ πλησίοι γύαι |₅₉ τόνδ' ἱππότην Κολωνὸν εὔχονται σφίσιν |₆₀ ἀρχηγὸν εἶναι, καὶ φέρουσι τοὔνομα |₆₁ τὸ τοῦδε κοινὸν πάντες ὠνομασμένοι. |₆₂ Τοιαῦτά σοι ταῦτ' ἐστίν, ὦ ξέν', οὐ λόγοις |₆₃ τιμώμεν', ἀλλὰ τῇ ξυνουσίᾳ πλέον. |₆₄ {ΟΙ.} Ἦ γάρ τινες ναίουσι τούσδε τοὺς τόπους; |₆₅ {ΞΕ.} Καὶ κάρτα, τοῦδε τοῦ θεοῦ γ' ἐπώνυμοι.

More on the Meaning of Colonus

18§5. I started this hour by observing that the cult hero Colonus / *Kolōnos* is named after a landmark that distinguishes the district in which he resides, and that this landmark is a *kolōnos* or 'tumulus' of a hero. To pick up on this observation, I find it most relevant to recall the use of the word *kolōnos* in the *Hērōikos* of Philostratus:

HOUR 18 TEXT B = HOUR 14 TEXT G

|₉.₁ Listen to such stories now, my guest [*xenos*]. Protesilaos lies buried not at Troy but here on the Chersonesus. This large tumulus [*kolōnos*] over here on the left no doubt contains him. The nymphs generated [*phuein*] these elms [that you see here] around the tumulus [*kolōnos*], and they wrote, so to speak, the following decree concerning these trees: |₉.₂ "Those branches that turn toward Ilion [= Troy] will blossom early and will then immediately shed their leaves and perish before their season [*hōrā*]—for this was also the life experience [*pathos*] of Protesilaos—but a tree on its other side will live and prosper." |₉.₃ All the trees that do not stand around the tomb [*sēma*], such as these trees [that you see right over here] in the grove, have strength in all their branches and flourish according to their particular nature.

Philostratus Hērōikos 9.1–3

18§6. In this passage, I translated *kolōnos* as 'tumulus', but the word can also be rendered more generally as 'landmark'; it marks the mound, surrounded by elm trees, that 'extends over' *(epekhei)* the body of the cult hero Protesilaos at Elaious in the Chersonesus. We may compare the expression *kolōnos lithōn*, in Herodotus 4.92, which can be translated as 'mound of stones'. In *Hērōikos* 51.12–13, which I quoted in Hour 14 Text H, this same word *kolōnos* designates the mound that the Achaeans had built to extend over the bodies of Achilles and Patroklos; the verb there, *ageirein,* suggests a piling of stones. This mound or tumulus, as we saw in Hour 14 Text H, was situated on a headland overlooking the Asiatic side of the Hellespont, facing the tumulus of Protesilaos situated on a corresponding headland overlooking the European side of the strait. Also, in *Hērōikos* 53.10–11, *kolōnos* refers, again, to the tomb of Achilles, and there the word is used synonymously with *sēma* in the sense of 'tomb' (53.11).

18§7. So how are all these contexts of the word *kolōnos* relevant to the meaning of the place-name Colonus / *Kolōnos* in the *Oedipus at Colonus* of Sophocles? In the wording of the drama, this place-name *Kolōnos* is used as a general reference, at lines 670 and 889, to the sacred space that Oedipus the wanderer has entered in a quest to find a permanent resting place for his wretched body, polluted by all the deeds he had committed in a chronologically earlier phase of the story of Oedipus. That earlier phase is retold in another drama of Sophocles, the *Oedipus Tyrannus*. As for the *Oedipus at Colonus,* produced in 401 BCE after the death of Sophocles (as we read in *Hypothesis* 2 for the drama), it focuses on the final phase of the story, retold in a distinctly Athenian way. In the Athenian version of the story as retold in the *Oedipus at Colonus,* the sacred space of Colonus will receive the body of Oedipus, after he is purified of his pollutions, and it will offer him an *oikos,* that is, a 'dwelling place' or 'abode' befitting a cult hero. I have already noted in Hour 15§26 the meaning of *oikos* as a cult hero's 'dwelling place'. And, as Oedipus himself says at line 627 of the *Oedipus at Colonus,* he desires to be an *oikētēr* or 'dweller' within the sacred space of Colonus.* In other words, he desires to be a cult hero at Colonus.

18§8. In what follows, I intend to argue that the idea of Oedipus as a cult hero who is worshipped by the people of Athens in the days of Sophocles is essential for understanding the idea of Oedipus as a polluted abomination who was once upon a time rejected by the people of Thebes, where he had ruled as their king. That is why I chose to analyze first the *Oedipus at Colonus,* which tells how Oedipus was accepted by the Athenians as their cult hero, before I go on to analyze the *Oedipus Tyrannus,* which tells how Oedipus was rejected by the Thebans as their king.†

How to Imagine Colonus

18§9. From the perspective of ritual, Colonus is a *temenos,* a sacred space or 'precinct', as we see it described at line 136 of the *Oedipus at Colonus.* And, as I have already noted, this same space is described at line 54 as a place that is *hieros* or 'sacred'. Further, from the perspective of myth, this place is a paradisiacal space, a stylized garden or grove inhabited by the most potent superhuman

---

*On this context of *oikos,* see *PH* 268–269 = 9§27, following Edmunds 1981:223n8. See also Calame 1998:336n11, with reference to Nagy 1993 on the use of the verb *oikeîn,* 'occupy a dwelling', in Alcaeus F 130b 10 and 16.

† For an overall study of Oedipus as a cult hero worshipped by the Athenians, see Calame 1998, with a vast array of references to other studies; also Edmunds 1996.

powers. I quote here a lyrical description that is sung and danced by the chorus in the role of a speaker addressing Oedipus after he has just arrived in the sacred space of Colonus, seeking to be purified of the unholy pollution he has already experienced in his most wretched life. Here are the words of the speaker, addressing Oedipus as a *xenos,* 'stranger' (since both Oedipus and the speaker are still strangers to each other):

HOUR 18 TEXT C

This place [*khōrā*] here, having good power from horses [*eu-hippos*], O stranger [*xenos*], is the most potent inhabitation on earth—that is where you have just arrived. |₆₇₀ It is Colonus [*Kolōnos*], shining white [*argēs*]. Here the nightingale, a constant visitor, trills her clear note under the trees of green glades, dwelling in the midst of the wine-colored ivy |₆₇₅ and the god's inviolate foliage, rich in berries and fruit, unvisited by sun, unvexed by the wind of any storm. Here the Bacchic reveler Dionysus ever walks the ground, |₆₈₀ companion of the nymphs that nursed him. And, feeding on heavenly dew, the narcissus blooms day by day with its fair clusters, over and over again; it is the ancient garland [*stephanōma*] of the two Great Goddesses. |₆₈₅ And the crocus blooms with a golden gleam. Nor do the ever-flowing springs diminish, from which the waters of Cephisus wander off, and each day this river, swift in making things fertile, |₆₉₀ moves with its pure current over the broad plains of Earth with her swelling breasts. Nor have the singing and dancing choruses [*khoroi*] of the Muses shunned this place, nor Aphrodite of the golden rein. |₆₉₅ And there is a thing such as I have not heard of on Asian ground, nor as ever yet originating in the great Dorian island of Pelops: it is a plant unconquered, self-renewing, causing terror for enemies armed with spears. |₇₀₀ It greatly flourishes in this land—the gray-leafed olive, nurturer of children. No young man may harm it by the ravages of his hand, nor may anyone who lives with old age. For the sleepless circular eye |₇₀₅ of Zeus Morios [guard of the sacred olive trees] watches over it, and so too does gray-eyed Athena. And I have another word of praise [*ainos*] to say for this city, our mother [*mātro-polis*], and it is a most potent word: |₇₁₀ [I praise] the gift of the great superhuman force [*daimōn*]. It is the greatest thing worthy of praise. It has the good power of horses [*eu-hippon*], the good power of colts [*eu-pōlon*], the good power of the sea [*eu-thalasson*]. I say this because you, son of Kronos, lord Poseidon, have set the city on the throne of these words of praise $|_{715}$ by inventing, first of all on our own roadways, the bit that cures the rage of horses. Meanwhile the oar, well shaped for rowing on the sea, is gliding past the land as it leaps [*thrōiskein*] to keep time with the singing and dancing of the hundred-footed Nereids.

Sophocles *Oedipus at Colonus* 668–719*

Colonus, Land of Running Horses

18§10. As we can see from this lyrical description of Colonus, it is a place that is specially linked with horses and with Poseidon as the god of horses. Further, Colonus as a personified hero is imagined at line 59 as a *hippotēs,* and I have already argued that this epithet refers to a rider on a chariot drawn by horses. Even further, as we are about to see, Poseidon can be imagined as begetting the First Horse at Colonus.

18§11. In the *Oedipus at Colonus,* we find a mystical reference to a myth, evidently local to Colonus, about a prototypical stallion fathered by Poseidon. The myth is connected to the last moments of Oedipus as a living mortal. In the drama, a messenger narrates these last moments:

HOUR 18 TEXT D

$|_{1586}$ This [= the death of Oedipus] has already happened, and it was something that was outstandingly wondrous. $|_{1587}$ As for how he started

---

* Εὐίππου, ξένε, τᾶσδε χώρας ἵκου τὰ κράτιστα γᾶς ἔπαυλα, $|_{670}$ τὸν ἀργῆτα Κολωνόν, ἔνθ' ἁ λίγεια μινύρεται θαμίζουσα μάλιστ' ἀηδὼν χλωραῖς ὑπὸ βάσσαις, τὸν οἰνῶπα νέμουσα κισ- $|_{675}$ σὸν καὶ τὰν ἄβατον θεοῦ φυλλάδα μυριόκαρπον ἀνήλιον ἀνήνεμόν τε πάντων χειμώνων· ἵν' ὁ Βακχιώτας ἀεὶ Διόνυσος ἐμβατεύει $|_{680}$ θείαις ἀμφιπολῶν τιθήναις. Θάλλει δ' οὐρανίας ὑπ' ἄχνας ὁ καλλίβοτρυς κατ' ἦμαρ αἰεὶ νάρκισσος, μεγάλαιν θεαῖν ἀρχαῖον στεφάνωμ', ὅ τε χρυσαυγὴς κρόκος· οὐδ' ἄυπνοι κρῆναι μινύθουσιν Κηφισοῦ νομάδες ῥεέθρων, ἀλλ' αἰὲν ἐπ' ἤματι ὠκυτόκος πεδίων ἐπινίσεται $|_{690}$ ἀκηράτῳ σὺν ὄμβρῳ στερνούχου χθονός· οὐδὲ Μουσᾶν χοροί νιν ἀπεστύγησαν, οὐδ' αὖ ἁ χρυσάνιος Ἀφροδίτα. $|_{695}$ Ἔστιν δ' οἷον ἐγὼ γᾶς Ἀσίας οὐκ ἐπακούω, οὐδ' ἐν τᾷ μεγάλᾳ Δωρίδι νάσῳ Πέλοπος πώποτε βλαστὸν φύτευμ' ἀχείρωτον αὐτοποιόν, ἐγχέων φόβημα δαΐων, $|_{700}$ ὃ τᾷδε θάλλει μέγιστα χώρᾳ, γλαυκᾶς παιδοτρόφου φύλλον ἐλαίας· τὸ μέν τις οὐ νεαρὸς οὔτε γήρᾳ σημαίνων ἁλιώσει χερὶ πέρσας· ὁ γὰρ αἰὲν ὁρῶν κύκλος $|_{705}$ λεύσσει νιν Μορίου Διὸς χἀ γλαυκῶπις Ἀθάνα. Ἄλλον δ' αἶνον ἔχω ματροπόλει τᾷδε κράτιστον, $|_{710}$ δῶρον τοῦ μεγάλου δαίμονος, εἰπεῖν, <ἐμὸν> αὔχημα μέγιστον, εὔιππον, εὔπωλον, εὐθάλασσον. Ὦ παῖ Κρόνου, σὺ γάρ νιν εἰς τόδ' εἷσας αὔχημ', ἄναξ Ποσειδάν, ἵπποισιν τὸν ἀκεστῆρα χαλινὸν $|_{715}$ πρώταισι ταῖσδε κτίσας ἀγυιαῖς· ἁ δ' εὐήρετμος ἔκπαγλ' ἁλία χερσὶ παραπτομένα πλάτα θρῴσκει, τῶν ἑκατομπόδων Νηρῇδων ἀκόλουθος.

to depart from this world, you yourself know that full well, since you were here: |₁₅₈₈ he did not have any of his dear ones [*philoi*] as guide, |₁₅₈₉ but rather he himself was leading the way for us all. |₁₅₉₀ Then, when he arrived at the Threshold for Descending, |₁₅₉₁ with its bronze foundations rooted in the earth deep below |₁₅₉₂ he stopped still at one place where paths were leading in many directions, |₁₅₉₃ near the Hollow Crater, which was where Theseus |₁₅₉₄ and Peirithoos had made their faithful covenant lasting forever—it is marked there. |₁₅₉₅ Midway he [= Oedipus] stood there between that place [= the Hollow Crater] and the *Thorikios Petros*, |₁₅₉₆ between the Hollow Pear Tree and the *Stone Tomb* [*lāinos taphos*]. |₁₅₉₇ Next, he sat down and loosened his filthy clothing. |₁₅₉₈ And then he called out to his daughters, ordering them to bring from flowing streams |₁₅₉₉ water for ritual washing [*loutra*] and for *libations* [*khoai*]—to bring him the water from wherever [*pothen*] they brought it. |₁₆₀₀ And the two daughters went to the place of Demeter, the one who has the beautiful greenness [*khloē*]. |₁₆₀₁ The place was a Hill, and they went to it. |₁₆₀₂ In a short time they brought back what their father had ordered them to bring, and then they gave him ritual washing [*loutra*] |₁₆₀₃ and dressed him, as is the custom [*nomos*]. |₁₆₀₄ But when all his desire was fulfilled, |₁₆₀₅ and nothing that he required was still undone, |₁₆₀₆ then Zeus, He of the Earth Below [*khthonios*], *made a thunderclap.*

Sophocles *Oedipus at Colonus* 1586–1606*

18§12. Among the many landmarks of the mystical topography of Colonus that we see described in this most remarkable passage, I highlight a rock that is called by the name of Thorikios Petros at line 1595. The meaning of this place-name is complex. The noun *petros* means 'rock' or 'stone', while the adjective

* |₁₅₈₆ {ΑΓ.} Τοῦτ' ἐστὶν ἤδη κἀποθαυμάσαι πρέπον. |₁₅₈₇ Ὡς μὲν γὰρ ἐνθένδ' εἷρπε, καὶ σύ που παρὼν |₁₅₈₈ ἔξοισθ', ὑφηγητῆρος οὐδενὸς φίλων, |₁₅₈₉ ἀλλ' αὐτὸς ἡμῖν πᾶσιν ἐξηγούμενος· |₁₅₉₀ ἐπεὶ δ' ἀφῖκτο τὸν καταρράκτην ὁδὸν |₁₅₉₁ χαλκοῖς βάθροισι γῆθεν ἐρριζωμένον, |₁₅₉₂ ἔστη κελεύθων ἐν πολυσχίστων μιᾷ, |₁₅₉₃ κοίλου πέλας κρατῆρος, οὗ τὰ Θησέως |₁₅₉₄ Περίθου τε κεῖται πίστ' ἀεὶ ξυνθήματα· |₁₅₉₅ ἀφ' οὗ μέσος [emended from ἐφ' οὗ μέσου] στὰς τοῦ τε Θορικίου πέτρου |₁₅₉₆ κοίλης τ' ἀχέρδου κἀπὸ λαΐνου τάφου, |₁₅₉₇ καθέζετ'· εἶτ' ἔλυσε δυσπινεῖς στολάς, |₁₅₉₈ κἄπειτ' ἀΰσας παῖδας ἠνώγει ῥυτῶν |₁₅₉₉ ὑδάτων ἐνεγκεῖν λουτρὰ καὶ χοάς ποθεν. |₁₆₀₀ Τὼ δ', εὐχλόου Δήμητρος εἰς προσόψιον |₁₆₀₁ πάγον μολοῦσαι, τάσδ' ἐπιστολὰς πατρὶ |₁₆₀₂ ταχεῖ 'πόρευσαν σὺν χρόνῳ λουτροῖς τέ νιν |₁₆₀₃ ἐσθῆτί τ' ἐξήσκησαν ᾗ νομίζεται. |₁₆₀₄ Ἐπεὶ δὲ παντὸς εἶχε δρῶντος ἡδονὴν |₁₆₀₅ κοὐκ ἦν ἔτ' ἀργὸν οὐδὲν ὧν ἐφίετο, |₁₆₀₆ κτύπησε μὲν Ζεὺς Χθόνιος.

thorikios is derived from the verb *thrōiskein,* which means both 'leap' and 'emit semen'.* I quote here an antiquarian report about the relevant myth:

HOUR 18 TEXT E

Others say that, in the vicinity of the rocks at Athenian Colonus [*Kolōnos*], he [Poseidon], falling asleep, had an emission of semen, and a horse named *Skuphios* came out, who is also named *Skīrōnitēs.*

Scholia for Lycophron 766†

18§13. There are other versions of the myth that are tied to places other than Colonus. Here is an example:

HOUR 18 TEXT F

Poseidon *Petraios* ['of the rocks'] has a cult among the Thessalians . . . because he, having fallen asleep at some rock, had an emission of semen; and the earth, receiving the semen, produced the first horse, whom they called *Skuphios.* . . . And they say that there was a festival established in worship of Poseidon *Petraios* at the spot where the first horse leapt forth.

Scholia for Pindar *Pythian* 4.246‡

18§14. As we consider further the antiquarian report, just quoted, about the myth originating from Colonus, I draw attention to the name *Skīrōnitēs* for the prototypical horse. This name means 'the one who originates from a white rock [*skīros*/*skirros*]', and such a meaning can be connected with a variety of other myths about leaping and about the emission of semen.§ For the moment, however, I concentrate simply on the connection between the Thorikios Petros at Colonus and the idea of a white rock. I find it most significant that Colonus itself, as a place, is pictured as a white rock shining from afar: as we saw in Text C, the epithet describing Colonus at line 670 is *argēs*, which means 'shining white'.**

---

* *GM* 231.
† ἄλλοι δέ φασιν ὅτι καὶ περὶ τοὺς πέτρους τοῦ ἐν Ἀθήναις Κολωνοῦ καθευδήσας ἀπεσπέρμηνε καὶ ἵππος Σκύφιος ἐξῆλθεν ὁ καὶ Σκιρωνίτης λεγόμενος.
‡ Πετραῖος τιμᾶται Ποσειδῶν παρὰ Θεσσαλοῖς . . . ὅτι ἐπί τινος πέτρας κοιμηθεὶς ἀπεσπερμάτισε, καὶ τὸν θορὸν δεξαμένη ἡ γῆ ἀνέδωκεν ἵππον πρῶτον, ὃν ἐπεκάλεσαν Σκύφιον. . . . φασὶ δὲ καὶ ἀγῶνα διατίθεσθαι τῷ Πετραίῳ Ποσειδῶνι, ὅπου ἀπὸ τῆς πέτρας ἐξεπήδησεν ὁ πρῶτος ἵππος.
§ *GM* 231–233.
** See also *GM* 231.

And this shining white rock Colonus becomes personified as a cult hero who bears the same name: as we saw in Text A, this hero is the mysterious *Kolōnos,* described as *hippotēs* at line 59, which I have interpreted as 'the rider of a chariot drawn by horses'.

Further Perspectives on the Meanings Connected to the Word Kolōnos and to the Name Kolōnos

18§15. These connections of the Thorikios Petros at Colonus with the idea of Colonus itself as a white rock lead me to consider some further perspectives on the meanings connected to the word *kolōnos* and to the name *Kolōnos.* In developing these perspectives, I find it most useful to return to the definition I offered in Hour 4§32 for the concept of *metonymy.* As I defined it there, metonymy is an expression of meaning by way of *connecting* something to something else that is next to that something or at least near to it, thereby establishing contact. Applying that definition, I now argue that there is a metonymy built into the word *kolōnos* and the name *Kolōnos.*

18§16. Let us start again with *kolōnos* as a word for a landmark, a shining white rock. As we have seen, this rock is personified as a cult hero, and the word becomes the name of that hero. By extension, the word also becomes the name of an entire sacred space, *Kolōnos.* And, by further extension, *Kolōnos* becomes the name of the entire deme of Attica in which the sacred space is situated. Throughout the *Oedipus at Colonus,* the wording of Sophocles explores the politics as well as the poetics of the dynamic tension between Colonus as a deme of Attica and Athens as the centralized *polis* or 'city'. Especially suggestive are the distinctions between the word *khōros* or 'place', referring to the sacred space of Colonus (as at line 54), and a more general word for 'place', *khōrā,* which can refer to the entire deme of Colonus (as at line 89).*

18§17. The metonymic personification of a rock or a stone as a hero, as we see it at work in the mythological landscape of Colonus, can be compared to what we saw in the medieval Irish saga of the *Táin.* As I noted in Hour 15§61, the singing of an incantation to the gravestone of the hero Fergus, long dead, becomes the equivalent of singing this incantation to the hero himself, who is thus temporarily brought back to life. So here too we see a metonymy, and this time

---

* For an analysis of all the contexts of *khōros* and *khōrā* in the *Oedipus at Colonus,* see Edmunds 1996:101–103; also Calame 1998:334n10.

the metonymy is achieved by way of incantation: a man sings to the gravestone 'as though it were Fergus himself', and then the hero Fergus materializes from the dead.

Oedipus as Cult Hero at Colonus

18§18. So how does Oedipus fit into the complex of myths and rituals connected with the sacred space of Colonus? The answer is simple, even if the details are complicated: in the myth that takes shape in the drama *Oedipus at Colonus* by Sophocles, Oedipus becomes a cult hero of Colonus. In terms of my argumentation, to put it more precisely, Oedipus develops into a cult hero of Colonus in the course of the developing story as told in the Oedipus at Colonus. And a key to understanding the idea of Oedipus as a cult hero is the messenger's narrative about his mysterious death in a locale that is marked by a set of six mysterious landmarks, which are mentioned in the following order at lines 1590–1601 of the passage I just quoted, Text D: the Threshold for Descending (1590–1592), the Hollow Crater (1593), the Thorikios Petros (1595), the Hollow Pear Tree (1596), the Stone Tomb or *lāïnos taphos* (1596), and the Hill of Demeter (1600–1601). According to the narrative, as I interpret it, Oedipus comes to a stop at the first landmark, the Threshold for Descending, which is pictured as a sheer drop downward into the depths of the earth below.* This landmark is a centerpoint that is equidistant from the next four of the six landmarks, which are the Hollow Crater, the Thorikios Petros, the Hollow Pear Tree, and the Stone Tomb. In terms of my interpretation, the Threshold for Descending is the crossroads that Oedipus reaches when he comes to a full stop (1592).† Farther away, but within view, is the sixth landmark, the Hill of Demeter. In my analysis so far, I have focused on the Thorikios Petros. In what follows, I will focus on the Hill of Demeter. As I will argue, this sacred place of Demeter is connected with the Thorikios Petros, which as we have seen is a sacred place of Poseidon. And this connection, I will also argue, is relevant to the status of Oedipus as cult hero at Colonus.

18§19. The myth of the Thorikios Petros, as we have seen so far, is about a shining white rock that marks the place where Mother Earth produced a prototypical horse when Poseidon, falling asleep at this rock and having a dream

---

* Here I follow, at least in part, the wording of Easterling 2006:147.

† This interpretation resembles, but does not exactly converge with, the one given by Easterling 2006:1941.

there, emitted semen that dropped on the ground, fertilizing it. As we have also seen, this prototypical horse that leapt out of the fertilized ground was named *Skīrōnitēs* according to one version of the myth. That is, this mythical First Horse was named after the shining white rock.

18§20. Here I draw attention to a parallel myth studied by Pausanias (8.25). According to this myth, originating from the Arcadian community of Thelpousa, the god Poseidon and the goddess Demeter were the father and mother of a divine horse named Areion (8.25.7); according to another version of this myth, also reported by Pausanias, the parents of Areion were Poseidon and Mother Earth (8.25.8–10). I also draw attention to two details in the Arcadian version of the myth as studied by Pausanias:

(1) Both Demeter and Poseidon assumed the form of horses when they actually mated with each other (8.25.5).

(2) The epithet that applies to Demeter when she mated with Poseidon and produced the divine horse Areion is *erīnūs* or Erinys (8.25.4–7), and this noun is reported to be derived from a verb used in the Arcadian dialect to mean 'be angry', *erīnuein* (Pausanias 8.25.6).

18§21. In the myth about the begetting of the divine horse Areion by Poseidon, we have just seen from the two different attested versions that the mother is either the goddess Demeter Erinys or the goddess Earth; by contrast, in the myth about the begetting of the prototypical horse *Skīrōnitēs* by the same god Poseidon, we can find only one version, featuring Earth instead of Demeter as the divine mother. And yet, even if Demeter Erinys is not overtly featured as the divine mother of the prototypical horse of Colonus, we see in the *Oedipus at Colonus* that the goddess Demeter is explicitly named as a resident of this sacred space. The naming is tied to the moment when Oedipus sits down in preparation for receiving fresh water to be used for performing the rituals of *loutra* or 'washings' and of *khoai* or 'libations', mentioned at line 1599. This fresh water, as we see at lines 1600–1601, is brought from a hill named after the goddess Demeter. After the performing of these rituals, as we will see later on, Oedipus will be lovingly engulfed by Mother Earth, never to be seen again by mortals.

18§22. Just as Demeter is a resident of Colonus, so too are the Eumenides, who are mentioned by that name at lines 42 and 486 of the *Oedipus at Colonus*. These Eumenides, according to the myth we considered in Hour 17, were formerly the Erinyes before they were transformed into their benevolent aspect—

and before they were renamed, as it were, as the Eumenides or the *Semnai*, the 'Revered Ones'. There are significant parallels to be noted in the wording of the *Oedipus at Colonus*. At line 41, for example, it is made explicit that the Eumenides are called the Eumenides because the local population of Colonus wishes to call them by a name that is *semnon* or 'revered'. And these Eumenides as goddesses of Colonus are actually called the *Semnai* or the 'Revered Ones' at lines 90 and 458.*

18§23. Given that the Eumenides were divine occupants of the sacred space of Colonus in the *Oedipus at Colonus*, I find it essential to compare another sacred space that these goddesses occupied: it was located at a cleft in the rocks at the foot of the northeast side of the Areopagos, to the west of the Acropolis of Athens.† It was here at the Areopagos, according to the local myth reported by Pausanias (1.28.5), that Orestes was tried for killing his mother.‡ It was this local myth that shaped the retelling in the *Eumenides* of Aeschylus, a drama that becomes an aetiology for the cult of the Eumenides or the *Semnai* in their sacred place at the Areopagos.§ And, as we learn from Pausanias (1.28.6–7) in his description of the sacred space of the Eumenides at the Areopagos, there was a tomb of the hero Oedipus inside this space (1.28.7).** So Oedipus was evidently worshipped as a cult hero within this sacred space of the Eumenides at the Areopagos. Similarly, Oedipus was worshipped as a cult hero within the sacred space of Colonus. According to Pausanias (1.30.4), the first place in Attica where Oedipus came as an exile from Thebes was *Kolōnos Hippios,* or 'Colonus of the Horses', where he shares with Theseus, Peirithoos, and Adrastos a *hērōion,* that is, a sacred precinct for worshipping heroes.

18§24. Whereas Oedipus as a cult hero of the sacred space at the Areopagos shares that space only with the Eumenides, he shares the corresponding sacred space of Colonus not only with the Eumenides but also with other divinities, including Demeter and Poseidon, as we saw earlier, and with other heroes, as we have just seen from the report of Pausanias. Still, even at Colonus, the Eumenides are the primary divinities that define Oedipus as a cult hero. Already at lines 84–110 of the *Oedipus at Colonus,* he prays to the Eumenides to allow him to 'dwell', *oikeîn* (92), in the sacred space that he describes as the *alsos* or 'grove'

---

* Henrichs 1994:48–49.
† Henrichs 1994:39.
‡ Henrichs 1994:39–40, with an analysis of Pausanias 1.28.5 and of additional ancient sources.
§ Henrichs 1994:40.
** Besides Pausanias 1.28.7, there is also the testimony of Valerius Maximus 5.3.3; see Henrichs 1994:41.

of these goddesses (98). Then, at lines 466–492, Oedipus receives instructions from the inhabitants of Colonus, as represented by the chorus, about the ritually correct procedures that will be needed for the hero to worship the Eumenides—and thereby to purify himself of his pollution. And the primary form of this worship is the pouring of 'libations', *khoai,* of clear spring water, for the Eumenides (469–470). This 'pouring of libations', *khoas kheâsthai* (477), must be performed in a standing position, while facing the first light of dawn (477), and the water of libation must be mixed with honey and not with wine (481). Further, while pouring the libations, Oedipus must address the Eumenides exactly that way, as *Eumenides* (486), since the hearts of these goddesses will now be *eumenê,* 'of good intentions' (486–487). Once Oedipus properly worships the Eumenides, he will be purified of his pollution, and he can then become a cult hero for the people of Colonus in particular and for Athens in general. In the words of the prayer that Oedipus is instructed to utter while pouring his libations, this polluted suppliant will become transformed into a 'bringer of salvation', a *sōtērios,* for the whole community (487).* But this transformation can happen only if Oedipus properly invokes the Eumenides as Eumenides while pouring his libations.

18§25. At this moment in the *Oedipus at Colonus,* the transformation of Oedipus into a cult hero is actually postponed. The old man says that he is in no state of mind to perform the ritual of libations himself, blind as he is (495–496), and so it should be one of his two accompanying daughters who will do it for him (497) while the other one of the two will stay behind to look after him (498–502); the daughter Ismene volunteers to go, asking the chorus to reveal to her the place where she will find the source for the waters of libation (503–504). But the wording of the chorus is ostentatiously secretive: the source of the waters is 'on that side of this grove [*also*] here' (505 τοὐκεῖθεν ἄλσους, ὦ ξένη, τοῦδ'), and, if Ismene needs further instructions along the way to that source, some *ep-oikos* or 'dweller in the locale' will indicate the place to her (505–506). But Ismene is prevented from reaching the source: she is kidnapped, after her exit, by the men of Creon (818–821). Only toward the end of the drama, as we already saw in Text D (1598–1603), does Oedipus get to perform the libations himself, and only then is he finally purified by way of a ritual washing. As we also already saw in Text D, Oedipus has by now reached a different state of

---

* Like Calame 1998:336, I retain the manuscript reading σωτήριον at line 487 of the *Oedipus at Colonus.* As we see at line 480, Oedipus declares that he, as a cult hero, will become a *sōtēr* or 'savior' for the Athenians.

mind, since his blindness no longer holds him back, and some mysterious force is now enabling him to lead the way, instead of blindly following along, as he proceeds toward the place where he will die (1587–1589). Once Oedipus reaches that place, he himself will perform his own libations: so now he calls for his daughters to bring him clear spring water for ritual washing, *loutra*, and for libations, *khoai* (1599). After he is purified by the washing (1602–1603), the ritual of libation can take place, though the procedures for the ritual pouring as prescribed earlier by the chorus (469–470, 477–484) are this time not specified by the messenger. Instead, what does get specified now, and ostentatiously so, is a revelation of the source for the clear spring water that will be used for the washings and for the libations, and that source is the Hill of Demeter (1600–1601). What makes the revelation ostentatious is the ritualistic hesitation in specifying the source even in this context. I repeat here my translation of the wording: 'And then he called out to his daughters, ordering them to bring from flowing streams | water for ritual washing [*loutra*] and for *libations* [*khoai*]—to bring him the water from wherever [*pothen*] they brought it' (1598–1599). Having made his libation, Oedipus will be eligible to receive libations in his own right— once he becomes a cult hero. He has predicted this eligibility already at the beginning of the drama when he first prayed to the Eumenides (84–110): there he described himself as *nēphōn* or 'sober' while praying to these divinities, whom he described in turn as *a-oinoi* or 'wineless' (100).* This initial description of the Eumenides as abstaining from wine, *aoinoi*, suits the offering that Oedipus is instructed to make to these goddesses: as we saw, the water of libation for the Eumenides must be mixed with honey and not with wine (481).

18§26. I return here to the revelation, toward the end of the *Oedipus at Colonus*, that the source for the waters of libation for the Eumenides comes from the Hill of Demeter (1600–1601). This revelation signals what it is that Demeter has in common with the Eumenides: this goddess too, like the Eumenides, is connected with the libations that will transform Oedipus into a cult hero who will reside in Colonus. And the Hill of Demeter, along with the Thorikios Petros, is one of the six mystical landmarks that marks the actual locale where Oedipus died and where his tomb hides his body. That body, once Oedipus is purified, will become a talisman of fertility and prosperity not only for the local community that worships this new cult hero of Colonus but also, by sacred metonymy,

---

*For an incisive analysis of this ritual correlation between Oedipus as a cult hero and the Eumenides, see Henrichs 1983 and 1984.

for the overall community of Athens.* The words of Oedipus himself predict his new status as the cult hero of Colonus when he expresses his intention to donate his body to Theseus in that hero's capacity as king and virtual high priest of Athens:

HOUR 18 TEXT G

|$_{576}$ I [= Oedipus] come to donate this wretched body of mine |$_{577}$ as a gift to you [= Theseus]—a gift that seems not to be important when you look at it. But it has |$_{578}$ benefits coming out from it that have more power than any form of beauty.

Sophocles *Oedipus at Colonus* 576–578†

18§27. The exact location of the death and entombment of Oedipus will be shown only to Theseus as king and virtual high priest of Athens—and to his successors. That is what Oedipus himself promises to Theseus in the *Oedipus at Colonus* (1518–1539): driven by a mysterious divine force (1540), the blind man will now take the lead, needing no human guide, he says, as he heads toward that mysterious location (1521, 1540–1545), where he will find what he describes as his own *hieros tumbos*, 'sacred tomb' (1545). This landmark seems to match the mystical Stone Tomb or *lāïnos taphos* (1596), listed as one of the six mystical landmarks marking the place where Oedipus died.

18§28. Here I return to another one of those six mystical landmarks in the *Oedipus at Colonus,* the Hill of Demeter (1600–1601). The association of this place as the source for the libation of Oedipus to the Eumenides shows that the goddess Demeter herself, like the Eumenides, is somehow involved in the death and entombment of Oedipus.

18§29. In another version of the Oedipus myth as retold in an antiquarian source dated to the fourth century BCE (Androtion *FGH* 334 F 62), we see relevant details about the relationship of Demeter with Oedipus, which I paraphrase here:

- Oedipus comes to a place in Attica called *Kolōnos Hippeus,* where he 'occupies a dwelling', as expressed by the verb *oikeîn.*
- Just before he dies, Oedipus persuades Theseus to promise him that the loca-

---

* *PH* 178 = 6§59; see also Edmunds 1981:223n8 and Brelich 1958:40, 69–73.

† |$_{576}$ Δώσων ἱκάνω τοὐμὸν ἄθλιον δέμας |$_{577}$ σοὶ δῶρον, οὐ σπουδαῖον εἰς ὄψιν· τὰ δὲ |$_{578}$ κέρδη παρ' αὐτοῦ κρείσσον' ἢ μορφὴ καλή.

tion of his *taphos* or 'tomb' will be kept a secret, so that the people of Thebes may not come to Colonus, find his body, and abuse it.

· Oedipus had been received as a suppliant at Colonus in the *hieron* or 'sacred precinct' of Demeter, which this goddess shares with Athena *Polioukhos,* or 'guardian of the city [of Athens]', and with Zeus himself.

18§30. In yet another version of the Oedipus myth, transmitted by a source dated around 200 BCE (Lysimachus of Alexandria *FGH* 382 F 2), we see further relevant details, which I again paraphrase here:

· When Oedipus died, the Thebans refused him a proper burial. Then his body was taken by his near-and-dear ones to a place called Keos in Boeotia, where it was buried. But the people of this place blamed their misfortunes on the presence of the body, and so his near-and-dear were forced to remove it.

· Then the near-and-dear of Oedipus took his body to another place in Boeotia, called Eteonos. There they buried it secretly in the *hieron* or 'sacred space' of the goddess Demeter. When the people of Eteonos found out, they consulted an oracle, and the god ordained that they must not disturb *(kineîn)* the body of Oedipus, since he is 'the suppliant [*hiketēs*] of the goddess'. Accordingly, the *hieron* or 'sacred space' is named the *Oidipodeion.*

18§31. So also in the *Oedipus at Colonus* (44) Oedipus is a *hiketēs* or 'suppliant'—this time, not of Demeter but of the Eumenides (42). And once again there is an oracular pronouncement (84–110), given by Apollo himself (86, 102).* The oracle ordains that the local population should receive Oedipus and assign to him a *hedrā* or 'station' in the *gē* or 'earth' that is Colonus (84–85; also already 45), where he will 'occupy a dwelling', *oikeîn* (92); thus Oedipus will become a cult hero of Colonus.† And the key to the new status of Oedipus as a cult hero is that he will be buried in territory belonging to Athens (582). As a new cult hero, Oedipus will now benefit the native population who have received him (*dekhesthai* 92)—but he will become a source of *atē* or 'disaster' for those who have expelled him, namely, his former countrymen in Thebes (93).

---

*For an incisive analysis of Apollo's oracular pronouncement and its integration with the plot of the *Oedipus at Colonus,* see Easterling 2012.

†In the *Oedipus at Colonus,* there are many other instances where the word *oikein* in the sense of 'occupy a dwelling' refers to the status of Oedipus as a cult hero: besides line 92 here and line 627 as mentioned in §7, I highlight lines 27 and 28.

Later on in the *Oedipus at Colonus,* where the native population of Colonus as represented by the chorus is giving instructions to Oedipus about the proper way to pray while performing the rituals of libation (486–489), it is said that the words of his prayer must describe him as a *hiketēs* or 'suppliant' who will be a 'bringer of salvation', a *sōtērios* (487), for the Athenians. And I note, once again, that Oedipus here is a suppliant of the Eumenides, not of Demeter. And it is to the Eumenides, not to Demeter, that he pours libations while praying.

18§32. Having analyzed these parallelisms between Demeter and the Eumenides, let us consider the thinking of Oedipus as an agent of the Eumenides —which is how he describes himself (457–459) when he declares that he, as a cult hero, will become a *sōtēr* or 'savior' for the Athenians (460; see also 463). While the thinking of Oedipus here shows his benevolence toward his new countrymen, it shows also his malevolence toward the Thebans as the enemies of the Athenians (460). Even in this negative frame of mind, Oedipus is thinking as an agent of the Eumenides. We see this negativity elsewhere as well. A striking example is the passage where Oedipus expresses the malevolence that he as a cult hero of the Athenians will direct against his former countrymen, the Thebans, if they ever dare to attack Athens. Here is that passage:

HOUR 18 TEXT H

|$_{621}$ [there in my tomb under the Earth,] where my sleeping and hidden corpse, |$_{622}$ cold as it is, will at some moment in the future drink their hot blood.

Sophocles Oedipus at Colonus 621–622*

18§33. Oedipus here is thinking the thoughts of a cult hero as he thinks about his enemies, and these thoughts correspond to the malevolent thinking of the Erinyes before they became the Eumenides. Only after their transformation from Erinyes to Eumenides can these goddesses show a positive frame of mind that leads them to think benevolent thoughts. As we saw in Hour 17, the Erinyes in their thirst for vengeance had craved human blood, not the blood of animal sacrifice. And, in the passage we have just read, Oedipus as a cult hero can still show the malevolence of the Erinyes. This malevolence, however, will be directed not at the Athenians but at the Thebans as the enemies of Athens.

18§34. Signs of such malevolence tend to be suppressed in the case of the

---

* |$_{621}$ ἵν' οὑμὸς εὕδων καὶ κεκρυμμένος νέκυς |$_{622}$ ψυχρός ποτ' αὐτῶν θερμὸν αἷμα πίεται.

Eumenides, who are implicitly the Erinyes of the heroic past, but these negative signs do come to the surface in the case of Demeter, since she can even bear explicitly the epithet Erinys, as we saw in the Arcadian myth about the divine horse Areion, conceived when Poseidon impregnated the goddess Demeter Erinys: as we already saw, Demeter's epithet Erinys is understood to convey the idea of 'feeling angry', *erīnuein* (Pausanias 8.25.4–7). Further, as we saw in §30, Demeter would have 'felt angry' at the people of Eteonos in Boeotia if they had disturbed the body of Oedipus, who shared with this goddess a *hieron* or 'sacred space' that was named after him as the *Oidipodeion*. I highlight here, however, not the differences between Demeter Erinys and the Eumenides but rather the parallelisms, as indicated by their shared inheritance of the name Erinys or Erinyes in the plural.

18§35. Now I extend the comparison further by highlighting also a parallelism between Demeter Erinys and Mother Earth: in §§19–20, we have already seen myths where either one or the other of these two goddesses was impregnated by the god Poseidon and gave birth to a prototypical horse. But now I come to the most striking parallelism of them all, involving the Eumenides and Demeter and Mother Earth—all three together. We have just seen a separate parallelism involving Demeter and the Eumenides, where these goddesses receive Oedipus into their respective sacred spaces, thus transforming him into a cult hero. But now we will see, in the *Oedipus at Colonus,* the picturing of Mother Earth herself in the act of receiving Oedipus, literally engulfing him. And just as Demeter and the Eumenides have the power to transform Oedipus into a cult hero, so also the goddess Earth has that power. Moreover, in the case of the Eumenides, Mother Earth is even the genetic source of their power to transform Oedipus into a cult hero: that is because these goddesses, as Oedipus is told by the native inhabitants of Colonus in the *Oedipus at Colonus* (40), are pictured as the children of feminine *Gē* or 'Earth' and of masculine *Skotos* or 'Darkness'.

The Mysterious Death of Oedipus

18§36. As we have seen in the *Oedipus at Colonus,* the references made to the death and entombment of Oedipus, as also to his transformation into a cult hero, are ostentatiously secretive. Only Theseus and his successors may have full access to the mysteries of the hero cult of Oedipus. Still, there are many hints in the drama.

18§37. Among these hints are six mystical landmarks that are located near the place where Oedipus was seen by mortals for the very last time. These landmarks, as we have seen, are recounted in the part of the messenger's narration that I quoted in Text D, and I have already reviewed all six of them in §18. Further, I have already highlighted two of these landmarks:

· The Thorikios Petros (1595). This landmark is imagined as a shining white rock that marks the place where the First Horse leapt forth, begotten of the goddess Earth by the god Poseidon.
· The Hill of Demeter (1600–1601). Here is the source of the fresh waters used by Oedipus in pouring his libations to the Eumenides while praying to them.

18§38. Along the way, I have also highlighted the Stone Tomb or *lāïnos taphos* (1596), which may be identical with the Thorikios Petros. And now I highlight also the last three of the mystical landmarks, following the wording of the messenger's narration as quoted in Text D:

· The Hollow Pear Tree (1596). Oedipus is standing between this landmark and the Stone Tomb (1596), just as he is standing between the Hollow Crater (1593) and the white rock named the Thorikios Petros (1595). Whatever myth was connected with the Pear Tree is left untold in the messenger's narration. For now, all I can add is the observation that this tree is *koilē*, 'hollow' (1596), just as the crater is *koilos*, 'hollow' (1593). And we do know from Pherecydes (*FGH* 3 F 33, by way of scholia for *Odyssey* xi 289) of a myth about a wild pear tree— called an *akherdos*, just like the Hollow Pear Tree—which contained a dagger embedded within its trunk: the rust from this dagger, after it was found and removed from inside the tree, proved to be a cure, when mixed with wine, for the impotence of the hero Iphiklos, who became the father of Protesilaos.
· The Hollow Crater (1593). This landmark was evidently a depression in the earth, shaped like a *krātēr*, that is, a 'mixing bowl' used for the mixing of wine and water. We might have thought that such a shape, which I interpret as a natural rock formation imprinted into the earth, would be an ideal place for Oedipus to pour a libation—except that this hero, as we know, will be pouring not wine mixed with water but only water mixed with honey (481). So the Crater is *koilos*, 'hollow' (1593), empty of libations, just as the Pear Tree is *koilē*, 'hollow' (1596), empty of any elixirs that may be concocted for the cure of impotence. In any case, it was near this Hollow Crater, the messenger says,

that the heroes Theseus and Peirithoos had started their own Descent into Hādēs (1593–1594)—though such a version of the myth is not developed further in the messenger's narration.

· The Threshold for Descending (1590–1592), with its bronze foundations rooted in the world below the earth. This centerpoint, since the Hollow Crater is 'near' it, is evidently the place where Theseus and Peirithoos started their Descent. There is a reference to this same place already at the beginning of the drama, as quoted in Text A, where the speaker who receives Oedipus tells him that he is stepping on a *topos* or 'place' (56) that is known by the local inhabitants as 'the Bronze-Step Threshold of this land here' (57). In the guarded wording of that description, the Threshold seems to be a metonymic reference to the entire sacred space of Colonus.

18§39. Before we proceed, I take this opportunity to note in passing a similar catalogue of mystical landmarks that separate the world of the living from the world of the dead: we find it in *Odyssey* xxiv 11–13, where the *psūkhai* or 'spirits' of the suitors enter Hādēs. Those landmarks are, in the order in which they are listed, the Streams of Okeanos (11), the White Rock (11), the Gates of the Sun (12), the District of Dreams (12), and the Meadow of Asphodel (13).*

18§40. Besides the hints about the mysterious death and entombment of Oedipus, as signaled by the landmarks that I have surveyed, we can also get a glimpse—just a glimpse—of the actual moment of his death. It happens in the middle of a final narration performed by the messenger who is reporting to all assembled:

HOUR 18 TEXT I

|₁₆₃₈ Then, right away, Oedipus |₁₆₃₉ felt for his children with blind hands, and said: |₁₆₄₀ "Children, you must endure in a noble way in your hearts [*phrenes*] |₁₆₄₁ and depart from these places [*topoi*]; and, as for things forbidden by divine law [*themis*], do not |₁₆₄₂ consider it just [*dikaion*] to *look upon* those things, or to *hear* things you must not hear. |₁₆₄₃ So go away, go, as fast as you can—except for the one who is authorized, |₁₆₄₄ Theseus, who must be present and must learn the things that are being done [*drân*]." |₁₆₄₅ Such things he spoke, and we listened, |₁₆₄₆ each and every one of us. With streaming tears we

---

* Commentary in *GM* 223–227.

mourned as we accompanied the maidens |$_{1647}$ and went off. But after we had departed, |$_{1648}$ in a short time, we turned around and looked back and saw |$_{1649}$ that the man was nowhere present any more |$_{1650}$ and that our king [= Theseus] was alone, screening his eyes |$_{1651}$ by holding his hand in front of his head, as if some terrifying |$_{1652}$ thing to fear had appeared before him, something unbearable to look at. |$_{1653}$ And then, after a short time, |$_{1654}$ we saw him adore the Earth |$_{1655}$ and also the Olympus that belongs to the gods, using the same wording for both. |$_{1656}$ But by what fate Oedipus perished, no one |$_{1657}$ among mortals can indicate, except the head of Theseus alone. |$_{1658}$ You see, what happened to him [= Oedipus] was not that the god's fiery |$_{1659}$ thunderbolt did him in, nor was he done in by anything that comes from the sea [*pontos*], |$_{1660}$ by some stirring of a gust of wind [*thuella*], coming for him in the fullness of time. |$_{1661}$ No, it was either some escort sent by the gods, or else it was that thing from the nether world, |$_{1662}$ that thing that has good intentions [*noos*], that gaping unlit foundation of the earth. |$_{1663}$ You see, the man did not need lamentations, and there were no diseases |$_{1664}$ that gave him any pain at the moment when he was escorted away. No, if there was ever any mortal |$_{1665}$ who was wondrous [*thaumastos*], it was he.

Sophocles *Oedipus at Colonus* 1638–1665*

18§41. There seem to be four possible alternatives for imagining the mysterious death of Oedipus here. The first and the second alternatives are, respectively, death by being struck by the thunderbolt of Zeus (1658–1659) or death by being spirited away by a violent gust of wind (1659–1660). These two alternatives are dismissed, however, and it seems as if there are now only two remain-

---

* |$_{1638}$ ... εὐθὺς Οἰδίπους |$_{1639}$ ψαύσας ἀμαυραῖς χερσὶν ὧν παίδων λέγει· |$_{1640}$ "Ὦ παῖδε, τλάσας χρὴ τὸ γενναῖον φρενὶ |$_{1641}$ χωρεῖν τόπων ἐκ τῶνδε, μηδ' ἃ μὴ θέμις |$_{1642}$ λεύσσειν δικαιοῦν, μηδὲ φωνούντων κλύειν. |$_{1643}$ Ἀλλ' ἕρπεθ' ὡς τάχιστα· πλὴν ὁ κύριος |$_{1644}$ Θησεὺς παρέστω μανθάνων τὰ δρώμενα." |$_{1645}$ Τοσαῦτα φωνήσαντος εἰσηκούσαμεν |$_{1646}$ ξύμπαντες· ἀστακτὶ δὲ σὺν ταῖς παρθένοις |$_{1647}$ στένοντες ὡμαρτοῦμεν· ὡς δ' ἀπήλθομεν, |$_{1648}$ χρόνῳ βραχεῖ στραφέντες, ἐξαπείδομεν |$_{1649}$ τὸν ἄνδρα τὸν μὲν οὐδαμοῦ παρόντ' ἔτι, |$_{1650}$ ἄνακτα δ' αὐτὸν ὀμμάτων ἐπίσκιον |$_{1651}$ χεῖρ' ἀντέχοντα κρατός, ὡς δεινοῦ τινος |$_{1652}$ φόβου φανέντος οὐδ' ἀνασχετοῦ βλέπειν. |$_{1653}$ Ἔπειτα μέντοι βαιὸν οὐδὲ σὺν χρόνῳ |$_{1654}$ ὁρῶμεν αὐτὸν Γῆν τε προσκυνοῦνθ' ἅμα |$_{1655}$ καὶ τὸν θεῶν Ὄλυμπον ἐν ταὐτῷ λόγῳ. |$_{1656}$ Μόρῳ δ' ὁποίῳ κεῖνος ὤλετ' οὐδ' ἂν εἷς |$_{1657}$ θνητῶν φράσειε, πλὴν τὸ Θησέως κάρα· |$_{1658}$ οὐ γάρ τις αὐτὸν οὔτε πυρφόρος θεοῦ |$_{1659}$ κεραυνὸς ἐξέπραξεν οὔτε ποντία |$_{1660}$ θύελλα κινηθεῖσα τῷ τότ' ἐν χρόνῳ, |$_{1661}$ ἀλλ' ἤ τις ἐκ θεῶν πομπός, ἢ τὸ νερτέρων |$_{1662}$ εὔνουν διαστὰν γῆς ἀλάμπετον βάθρον. |$_{1663}$ Ἀνὴρ γὰρ οὐ στενακτὸς οὐδὲ σὺν νόσοις |$_{1664}$ ἀλγεινὸς ἐξεπέμπετ', ἀλλ' εἴ τις βροτῶν |$_{1665}$ θαυμαστός.

ing alternatives for explaining what it was that brought about the death of Oedipus: so it was either an escort sent by the gods who took away Oedipus so that he might join their divine company, presumably in Olympus (1661), or else the goddess Earth lovingly engulfed him (1661–1662). Here is the way these two alternatives were translated by Robert Fitzgerald:

> But it was either a messenger from the gods, or else the underworld
> opened in love the unlit door of earth.*

18§42. These two alternatives for explaining the death of Oedipus are mirrored by the ritualized response of Theseus to whatever it was that he saw: he reacts to the death of Oedipus by adoring both Olympus and Earth, using for both divinities the same words of prayer (1653–1655). The double response of Theseus indicates a double outcome: first, Oedipus descends into the depths of Earth, and then he will somehow ascend to Olympus. We can see comparable double outcomes in myths about other cult heroes as well. And there are many different ways of picturing such a double outcome, but it all comes down to the basic sequence of death followed by some kind of return to life.

Scenarios for Dying and Then Coming Back to Life

18§43. In the course of many years of research on the ancient Greek hero, I have collected a vast variety of traditional narratives, stemming ultimately from hero cults, about mortals who die and then come back to life again. I offer here a small selection of five such traditional narratives, summarizing them in the form of scenarios:†

- Scenario 1: to die from a thunderstroke—and then to come back to life. An example is the ultimate hero Hēraklēs, who is vaporized by the thunderbolt of Zeus on top of Mount Oeta, only to be brought back to life thereafter on Mount Olympus, where he joins the company of the immortal gods. I summarized this myth in Hour 1§46 and analyzed it briefly in 1§47.

---

*Fitzgerald 1941. I had the chance to read these lines, as he had translated them, at an event held at Harvard University and entitled "An Evening for Robert Fitzgerald," May 6, 1993, chaired by William Alfred. There is a recording of that event, archived by the Woodberry Poetry Room, in Harvard College Library, PS3511.I922 Z62 1993x.

†I have more to say about these five scenarios in BA 189–210 = 10§§20–50.

- Scenario 2: to die after being spirited away by a gust of wind—and then to come back to life. An example is the hero Phaethon, whose story is told in Hesiod *Theogony* 986–991.* A conventional word for such a gust of wind is *thuella,* as we can see from the wording of a death wish uttered by Penelope in *Odyssey* xx 83.†

- Scenario 3: to die after leaping from the top of a shining white rock—and then to come back to life. An example is the female hero Ino, as we see from the testimony of Pausanias 1.44.7–9: according to one version of the myth about Ino, she makes such a leap from the rocky heights of Megara, plunging into the dark watery depths below and drowning in the sea—only to come back to life thereafter as the *Leukotheā* or 'White Goddess' (there is a reference to this myth in *Odyssey* v 333–335).‡ Up on the heights of Megara, according to Pausanias (1.44.7–8), there was a rock formation named Molouris, frequented by a monstrous brigand named *Skīrōn,* meaning 'he of the white rock'. According to other reports (Strabo 9.1.4 C391, Plutarch *Theseus* 10), Theseus threw *Skīrōn* down into the sea from the top of a rock formation named *Skīrōnides Petrai,* or 'the shining white rocks', thus killing him. Pausanias (1.44.7–8) goes on to say that the rocky heights of Molouris were sacred to the *Leukotheā* or 'White Goddess', and that it was from the top of Molouris that Ino had taken her fatal leap.§ In the poetry of Pindar (*Olympian* 2.29), the immortal afterlife of Ino is described as a *biotos,* 'life', that is *aphthitos,* 'unwilting'.**

- Scenario 4: to die after being engulfed by the earth from down below—and then to come back to life. An example we have already seen is the hero Amphiaraos, who is engulfed—chariot and horses and all—as he is riding across a plain after the defeat of the Seven against Thebes. I summarized this myth and analyzed it briefly in Hour 15§34. In the course of that analysis, I argued that the references in the odes of Pindar (*Olympian* 6.14; *Nemean* 9.24–27, 10.8–9) to the engulfment of Amphiaraos show a keen awareness that this hero comes back to life after death. Another example of a hero who experiences such an engulfment is Trophōnios, as we saw in Hour 15§35.

- Scenario 5: to die in whatever way—and then to come back to life *simply by returning home.* An example is Memnon, king of the *Aithiopes* or 'Ethiopians'.

* *BA* 190–194 = 10§§22–24.
† *GM* 99n61, following *BA* 194–203; see also Easterling 2006:136.
‡ *BA* 175 = 10§1n4; Nagy 1985:79–81 = §§76–79.
§ *GM* 231, where Pausanias "1.33.8" should be corrected to 1.44.8 (also at n8).
** *GM* 126, following *BA* 175, 203 = 10§1n4 and 10§41n2.

This hero is the son of Ēōs, the goddess of the dawn. The home of both Memnon and Ēōs is the mystical land of the Ethiopians, which is located at the extremities of the world. After Memnon is killed by Achilles, Ēōs immortalizes her son (plot summary by Proclus of the *Aithiopis* by Arctinus p. 106 lines 4–7).* This immortalization of the mortal hero is achieved by way of escorting the body of Memnon back to the realm of light and life.† For Memnon, then, immortalization is a kind of individualized *nostos* or 'homecoming'.‡

18§44. Each one of these five scenarios is in some way relevant to the messenger's narrative about the death of Oedipus in Text I as quoted from the *Oedipus at Colonus:*

(1) A death caused by a thunderstroke is ostentatiously denied for Oedipus (1658–1659). But the possibility of such a death for Oedipus is still brought to mind by the very ostentatiousness of the denial. After all, the messenger's speech goes on to leave the door open to the possibility that the hero ascended to Olympus after his death. As we have seen, Theseus reacts to the death of Oedipus by adoring both Olympus and Earth, using for both divinities the same words of prayer (1653–1655), and this double response of Theseus indicates a double outcome: first, Oedipus descends into the depths of Earth, and then he will somehow ascend to Olympus. So the experience of Oedipus may in the end resemble the experience of Hēraklēs, who is immortalized in Olympus after his death by thunderstroke.

(2) A death caused by being spirited away by a *thuella* or a violent 'gust of wind' is likewise ostentatiously denied for Oedipus (1659–1660). But the possibility of such a death, which leads to immortalization, is once again brought to mind by the very ostentatiousness of the denial.

(3) A death caused by leaping from the top of a shining white rock is not even considered an alternative for Oedipus. But the place where this hero dies is marked by a shining white rock, the Thorikios Petros, and this rock conveys the idea of immortalization after death for Oedipus. Similarly, such an idea is conveyed by the name of the grove that features the Thorikios Petros as its landmark. That name is Colonus, which likewise refers to the shining white rock: as we saw in Text C, the epithet describing Colonus at line 670 is *argēs,*

---

* *BA* 164 = 9§23
† *BA* 205–208 = 10§§43–47.
‡ *BA* 213 = 11§1.

which means 'shining white'. Further, the adjective *thorikios* that forms the first part of the place name Thorikios Petros is derived from the verb *thrōiskein,* which means both 'leap' and 'emit semen'.* As we saw in Text E, the myth about the origin of the First Horse that leapt forth from the Earth of Colonus is shaped by the idea of a shining white stallion named *Skīrōnitēs,* begotten by the semen emitted by Poseidon when he lost consciousness and slept on the ground at the shining white rock that marks the place where the horse was conceived by Mother Earth. The idea of a shining white rock as a landmark for Oedipus brings me back to the myth about Ino and her leap from a shining white rock. As I have noted already, the immortal afterlife of Ino is described as a *biotos,* 'life', that is *aphthitos,* 'unwilting', in the poetry of Pindar (*Olympian* 2.29). And here I find it relevant to quote the words of the messenger in the *Oedipus at Colonus* when he has just been asked whether Oedipus is dead. The messenger replies (1583–1584): Ὡς λελογχότα | κεῖνον τὸν αἰεὶ βίοτον ἐξεπίστασο, 'that one, I want you to understand, has received as his fate a life [*biotos*] that is forever [*aiei*]'. This reading, I must warn, is not certain, since it depends on an emendation of λελοιπότα, 'has left behind', which is what we find in the manuscript tradition, to λελογχότα, 'has received as his fate'.† Still, I am inclined to accept the emendation, not only because I find the Pindaric analogy most compelling but also because the adverb *aiei,* which I translate as 'forever' and which we see here in collocation with *biotos,* is attested in analogous contexts centering on the idea of immortalization after death. As we saw in Hour 14§34, the adverb *aiei,* 'forever', is the old locative singular of the noun *aiōn* in the sense of a 'life' or a 'life-force' that keeps coming back to life by way of a 'recircling of time', and this locative *aiei* means literally 'in a recircling of time', signaling an eternal return.‡

(4) A death caused by being engulfed by the Earth from down below is in fact considered one of two possible alternative explanations for the mysterious disappearance of Oedipus. Here again I return to the double response of Theseus (1653–1655), indicating a double outcome: first, Oedipus descends into the depths of Earth, and then he will somehow ascend to Olympus. That ascent is the second of the two possible explanations for the mysterious disappearance of Oedipus.

---

* *GM* 231.
† Easterling 2006:39–40 gives an evenhanded evaluation of the arguments for and against this emendation.
‡ Nagy 2011b:179, following *PH* 195n210 = 6§88.

(5) A death, whatever its cause, that leads to a mystical return to light and life fits the myth of Oedipus as it takes shape in the *Oedipus at Colonus*. In what follows, I will develop further the formulation I have just offered.

The Mystification of the Hero's Tomb in the Oedipus at Colonus

18§45. By now we have seen a number of variations on the basic theme of death followed by some kind of return to life for the hero. What must remain an invariable, however, is the institutional requirement of establishing a hero cult that is tied to correct procedures of worshipping a cult hero in the setting of a tomb. In the case of Oedipus, as in other cases, these correct procedures are dutifully observed—but they are clouded in mysteries, just as the outcome of life after death is clouded for this hero. There is, then, a veritable poetics of mystification in representing the tomb of Oedipus in the *Oedipus at Colonus*.

18§46. Here I focus again on the mysterious disappearance of Oedipus, pictured either as an ascent to divine Olympus or as a descent into the depths of the goddess Earth. As we can see in the *Oedipus at Colonus,* the picturing of the hero's tomb is correspondingly mysterious. I note especially the vagueness of the reference made by Oedipus himself to his own *hieros tumbos*, 'sacred tomb' (1545): when he finds the place where this tomb will be, wherever it is, he will be 'hidden' by the earth there (*kruptesthai* 1546). And, as Theseus says to Antigone, it is forbidden to see the tomb or to approach it—let alone to address it (1754–1765). What we find here is an analogue in ritual to the mystical engulfment of Oedipus in myth: the secrets of establishing and maintaining the tomb of this hero in ritual correspond to the secrets about the way he died.*

18§47. As we have already seen in the *Oedipus at Colonus,* the essence of the idea of Oedipus as a cult hero is that he will be buried in the territory of Athens (582). But how and where he will be buried is a sacred secret, just as the story of how and where he died is left untold. It should be enough for his worshippers to know that Oedipus will dwell inside a Mother Earth that belongs to the *polis* or 'city' of Athens. I say it this way because we have already seen at line 707 of a choral lyric song, as quoted in Text C, that Colonus is an integral part of Athens, which is called in this song the Mother City or *mētropolis* (in the Doric dialect of choral lyric, this word is pronounced *mātropolis*). For the grove as for

---

* More on the engulfment of Oedipus by Earth in Easterling 2006:137.

the deme of Colonus, where Oedipus is secretly buried, Athens is truly a metropolis.

18§48. For the metropolis of Athens, Theseus is the ideal prototype for maintaining the mysteries of the tomb and the hero cult of Oedipus. After all, Theseus is also the ideal prototype for maintaining the Eleusinian Mysteries for the Athenians, as Claude Calame has shown; in fact, there are telling references to the Eleusinian Mysteries in the *Oedipus at Colonus* (as at 1049–1058).* Even the language used by Oedipus in formulating his heroic legacy for Theseus evokes the secret language of the Eleusinian Mysteries:†

HOUR 18 TEXT J (PART OF TEXT I)

Children, you must endure in a noble way in your hearts [*phrenes*] |$_{1641}$ and depart from these places [*topoi*]; and, as for things forbidden by divine law [*themis*], do not |$_{1642}$ consider it just [*dikaion*] to *look upon* those things, or to *hear* things you must not hear. |$_{1643}$ So go away, go, as fast as you can—except for the one who is authorized, |$_{1644}$ Theseus, who must be present and must learn the things that are being done [*drân*].

Sophocles *Oedipus at Colonus* 1640–1644

18§49. The *drōmena* here at line 1644, referring to 'the things that are being done [*drân*]', are the secret agenda of mysteries that can be visualized and verbalized only in special sacred circumstances.‡ Otherwise, as we learn at line 1642, these *drōmena* must not be seen and must not be heard. Such, then, are the mysteries of the cult hero. And we have already noted in Hour 15§15 the basic words for visualizing and verbalizing such mysteries.

Personalizing the Death of Oedipus

18§50. Whenever I return to reading the final words of the messenger who reports the mysterious death of Oedipus, I am struck by a sense of *wonder*—the Greek word for which is *thauma*—as I contemplate the wording:

---

* Calame 1998:349–351; see also Easterling 2006:139, 143.

† Calame 1998:349–351.

‡ Easterling 2006:135 and 145n14, citing *PH* 32 = 1§29n82. See also Calame 1998:349n34, citing *PH* 31-33 = 1§§29-30.

HOUR 18 TEXT K (PART OF TEXT I)

$|_{1661}$ No, it was either some escort sent by the gods, or else it was that thing from the nether world, $|_{1662}$ that thing that has good intentions [*noos*], that gaping unlit foundation of the earth. $|_{1663}$ You see, the man did not need lamentations, and there were no diseases $|_{1664}$ that gave him any pain at the moment when he was escorted away. No, if there was ever any mortal $|_{1665}$ who was wondrous [*thaumastos*], it was he.

Sophocles *Oedipus at Colonus* 1661–1665

18§51. The words describing this wondrous man fit not only Oedipus as a cult hero but also the tragedy of the *Oedipus at Colonus*—and even Sophocles himself, who was in his own time perhaps the most admired citizen of Athens.* And the emotions surrounding the mystical death of Oedipus may match the emotions of Sophocles, who was surely contemplating the prospect of his own death as he was composing the *Oedipus at Colonus* toward the end of his long life. So I find it most relevant to note that this wondrous man was not only a proud citizen of Athens but also a native son of Colonus.† For Sophocles, the idea of being engulfed and embraced by the loving goddess Earth of Colonus is a death that becomes a true 'homecoming', a *nostos*. And this *nostos* may reveal, after death, a true return to light and life.

---

*I am guided here by the incisive essay of Slatkin 1987 especially pp. 219–221. See also Easterling 2006:147n50.

† On the political implications of the fact that Sophocles was a native of the deme of Colonus, see Edmunds 1996:163–168.

Sophocles' Oedipus Tyrannus
and Heroic Pollution

The Meaning of Miasma

19§1. The key word for this hour is *miasma,* meaning 'pollution, miasma', a noun derived from the verb *miainein,* meaning 'pollute'. In the last hour, we saw that Oedipus in the *Oedipus at Colonus* of Sophocles needed to perform libations to the Eumenides in order to free himself of pollution, which was preventing him from becoming the cult hero of Colonus in particular and of Athens in general. In this hour, as we consider the *Oedipus Tyrannus* of Sophocles, we will see how Oedipus became polluted in the first place. (I should note here that many experts have been tempted to link the historical context of this drama with the great plague that devastated Athens in 430 BCE and that flared up intermittently in the years that followed. But the fact remains that the date for the production of the *Oedipus Tyrannus* is unknown.)

19§2. The essentials of the story as told in the *Oedipus Tyrannus* are well known: Oedipus unintentionally killed his own father and unintentionally had sex with his own mother. The action that started the pollution was the actual killing, even though Oedipus did not know that Laios, the man he killed in a fit of rage at a crossroads, was his real father—and that Iocasta, the woman he married after he immigrated to Thebes, was his real mother. The fact that the actions of Oedipus were unintended did not mitigate the fact that these actions —killing the father and having sex with the mother—caused him to become polluted.

19§3. These negative actions committed by Oedipus, along with the pollution they caused, are typical of the heroic age. As we saw already in Hour 16§6, where I went through the grim exercise of summarizing the central myths concerning the men and women who belonged to the dynastic family known as the House of Atreus, some of the actions committed by those male and female heroes in the heroic age were likewise shockingly negative. In this hour, we will see that the pollution caused by such negative actions of heroes in the heroic age needed to be purified by way of ritual re-enactment in the drama of Athenian State Theater, featuring tragedies composed by such eminent state poets as Aeschylus and Sophocles. For the moment, however, I concentrate on the negative actions themselves, and on the pollution that they caused. And I continue to highlight the parallelisms we can find in the negative actions committed by Oedipus and by the heroes stemming from the dynastic family of Atreus. As in the case of Oedipus, the heroes of the House of Atreus were guilty of committing such negative actions as the slaughter of blood relatives and incest. We already saw this in the summary of events presented in Hour 16§6. And, as we also saw, there was even cannibalism in that family.

19§4. So when we consider patterns of behavior that are typical of the heroic age, the actions of Oedipus in killing his father and having sex with his mother are hardly exceptional. Shocking, yes, but not exceptional. Granted, heroes of the heroic age perform mostly positive actions, and these actions are extraordinary. A hero like Oedipus performs extraordinarily positive actions: after all, as we will see, he becomes the savior of the city of Thebes by way of solving the Riddle of the Sphinx and thus saving his new community from destruction. This action of Oedipus is properly glorified in the *Oedipus Tyrannus* of Sophocles (35–39). But the point is, the heroes of the heroic age are also capable of performing negative actions, and these actions too are extraordinary. In fact, they are not only extraordinary: they also cause pollution. And, as we will now see, such polluting actions as performed in heroic times are considered to be analogous to polluted thoughts and feelings that may be afflicting citizens in the historical times of Athenian State Theater.

19§5. So how do the citizens of Athens experience polluted thoughts and feelings? My answer is, they do so by channeling, as it were, the polluted thoughts and feelings of tyrants.

The Pollution of Tyrants

19§6. In this book, the last time I used the word *tyrant* for purposes of my own argumentation was in Hour 13§47, which was the last paragraph of that hour. Back then, I was interpreting a passage in Theognis (1081–1082b), Hour 13 Text L, where the speaker was referring to a hypothetical dictator of a hypothetical city-state. In that context, I said that such a dictator was the equivalent of a *tyrant*. This word *tyrant* comes from the Greek noun *turannos,* which has a long and complicated history that I studied in great detail in other work.* I will now attempt a formulation that summarizes all that work, focusing here on what the word *turannos* meant in the political context of Athens in the second half of the fifth century BCE, the era of Sophocles:

> A *turannos,* translated as 'tyrant', is a ruler who has seized power in a state by resorting to actions that turn out to be tainted, that is, polluted. The tyrant may seem to be a very accomplished and even charismatic king, modeling himself on the hero-kings of the heroic age, but he is really a dictator, polluted by his actions just as the hero-kings of the heroic age were polluted by their own actions. The pollution is a sign of *hubris* or moral 'outrage'—which is the opposite of *dikē* or 'justice'. In moralizing stories about tyrants, such *hubris* is destined to be punished by divine sanction. And the two most common metaphors for expressing such a sanction against a tyrant's *hubris* are shipwreck and sterility.

19§7. A model for such a *turannos* is the hero-king Oedipus, and that is why the tragedy we are now considering has the title *Oedipus Tyrannus,* written here in its latinized form, and not *Oedipus Rex,* since Latin *rēx* is the word for a legitimate 'king', not for a 'tyrant'.†

19§8. In Athens, the form of government that came to power in 508 BCE and that eventually became known as a *dēmokratiā* or 'democracy' was shaped by political leaders who tended to demonize as *turannoi* the leaders of the dynasty that preceded them, namely, the powerful family of the Peisistratidai, who had dominated the city both politically and culturally for most of the second half of the sixth century BCE.‡ By the time we reach the second half of the fifth century BCE, which is the era of Sophocles, the dangers posed by the very concept of a *tyrant* are still a preoccupation for the State, as we can see from the deeply probing explorations of such dangers in the poetry of Athenian State Theater.

19§9. As we will see from the wording of the *Oedipus Tyrannus* of Sophocles, the dangers of tyranny threaten the citizens of Athens not from the outside but rather from inside their own city. And that is because such dangers can emanate from the thoughts and feelings of the city's own citizens.

19§10. That said, I return to the formulation I offered already in §5: *the citi-*

---

* *PH* 174–175, 181–188; 229–231; 264–269; 274–313 = 6§§54, 64–76; 8§§22–23; 9§§21–29; 10§§1–54.

† *PH* 309 = 10§50n158, following Knox 1952.

‡ In *PH* 382–413 = 13§§1–65, I explore at length and in detail the cultural domination of Athens by the Peisistratidai.

zens of Athens in the time of Sophocles will experience polluted thoughts and feelings if they channel the polluted thoughts and feelings of tyrants. And, in terms of this formulation, *the polluted thoughts and feelings of tyrants are modeled on the polluting actions of heroes in the heroic age.*

19§11. In the *Republic* of Plato, such polluted thoughts and feelings are analyzed in terms of a psychology of the unconscious. The pollution of a citizen's thoughts and feelings is something that can happen, as we will soon see, when he is dreaming. Here is how it works: when the citizen is awake, he has civic thoughts and feelings, but when the citizen is asleep, he can dream the kinds of dreams that translate into the polluting actions of dysfunctional heroes. I will now quote the relevant text, where Plato's Socrates speaks about various kinds of pollution caused by various *epithumiai* or 'desires' and *hēdonai* or 'pleasures' experienced in sleep:

HOUR 19 TEXT A

I am talking, I [= Socrates] said, about those [desires and pleasures] that are awakened when one part of the soul [*psūkhē*] sleeps—I mean the part that is rational [*logistikon*] and domesticated [*hēmeron*] and in control [*arkhon*] of the other part, which is beast-like [*thēriōdes*] and savage [*agrion*]. Then, [when the rational part is asleep,] this other part, which is glutted with grain [*sīta*] or intoxicants [*methē*], starts bolting [*skirtāi*] and seeks to push aside sleep and to satiate its own ways of behaving [*ēthos* plural]. When it is like this, it dares to do everything, released as it is from all sense of shame [*aiskhunē*] and thinking [*phronēsis*]. It does not at all recoil from attempting to |$_{571d}$ lay hands on his own mother in order to have sex with her—or to lay hands on any other human or god or beast—and to commit whatever polluting [*miasma*-making] murder, or to eat whatever food. In a word, there is nothing in the realm of consciousness [*noos*, pronounced as *nous* in Plato's time] and shame that it will not do.

Plato *Republic* 9.571c–d*

* Τὰς περὶ τὸν ὕπνον, ἦν δ᾽ ἐγώ, ἐγειρομένας, ὅταν τὸ μὲν ἄλλο τῆς ψυχῆς εὕδῃ, ὅσον λογιστικὸν καὶ ἥμερον καὶ ἄρχον ἐκείνου, τὸ δὲ θηριῶδές τε καὶ ἄγριον, ἢ σίτων ἢ μέθης πλησθέν, σκιρτᾷ τε καὶ ἀπωσάμενον τὸν ὕπνον ζητῇ ἰέναι καὶ ἀποπιμπλάναι τὰ αὑτοῦ ἤθη· οἶσθ᾽ ὅτι πάντα ἐν τῷ τοιούτῳ τολμᾷ ποιεῖν, ὡς ἀπὸ πάσης λελυμένον τε καὶ ἀπηλλαγμένον αἰσχύνης καὶ φρονήσεως. μητρί τε γὰρ ἐπι |$_{571d}$ χειρεῖν μείγνυσθαι, ὡς οἴεται, οὐδὲν ὀκνεῖ, ἄλλῳ τε ὁτῳοῦν ἀνθρώπων καὶ θεῶν καὶ θηρίων, μιαιφονεῖν τε ὁτιοῦν, βρώματός τε ἀπέχεσθαι μηδενός· καὶ ἑνὶ λόγῳ οὔτε ἀνοίας οὐδὲν ἐλλείπει οὔτ᾽ ἀναισχυντίας. This text of Plato is most deftly applied by Clay 1978:17 to the *Oedipus Tyrannus* of Sophocles.

19§12. Up to now I have nowhere translated *psūkhē* simply as 'soul', except for the stretch of paragraphs in Hour 10 (§§32–50) where I spoke about *a journey of a soul* in the Homeric *Odyssey*. And now I make another exception as I once again make use of that translation 'soul' in the general context of Plato's overall theorizing about a *psychology of the soul*. Granted, in the specific context of the text I have just quoted, I could just as easily have translated *psūkhē* as 'mind', since Socrates here speaks of a division between the conscious and the unconscious parts of the mind. Still, I chose 'soul' because, as we will soon see, Sophocles uses this same word *psūkhē* in contexts where the hero Oedipus himself is speaking about his own mind. And that usage is relevant to what Plato's Socrates is saying in the passage I have just quoted, which is, that there are polluting actions just waiting to be released from inside the *psūkhē* whenever its unconscious part starts to wake up, as it were, in the dreams that are dreamed during sleep—while the conscious part continues to sleep. And such a release leads to thoughts and feelings about polluting actions. The word *miaiphonein* in the text I have just quoted means 'to commit polluting [= *miasma*-making] murder', and it implies the taboo topic of killing one's own blood-relatives. As for the wording that I translate 'to eat whatever food', it implies the taboo topic of cannibalism. And as for the taboo topic of having sex with one's own mother, it is not even made implicit in this text. It is quite explicit, and even the 'it' that refers to the unconscious part of the *psūkhē* now becomes a 'he' that seeks to have sex with 'his' mother.

A Look inside the Psūkhē of Oedipus

19§13. Of the three taboo topics mentioned by Plato's Socrates in analyzing the desires and the pleasures of the mind or, to say it his way, of the *psūkhē,* all three of them apply to a wide variety of heroes in the heroic age, and two of them apply directly to Oedipus in the *Oedipus Tyrannus*. So the *psūkhē* of this hero must surely have an unconscious part, which is the part that drove him to kill his father and to have sex with his mother. But it also has a conscious part, which can be described as 'rational [*logistikon*] and domesticated [*hēmeron*] and in control [*arkhon*] of the other part, which is beast-like [*thēriōdes*] and savage [*agrion*]'— if I may borrow the words used by Socrates. We see this rational side of Oedipus most clearly when he reacts to the news brought to him by Creon about the response of the oracle of Apollo at Delphi:

HOUR 19 TEXT B

|₉₁ {Creon:} If you want to hear in the presence of these people here, |₉₂ I am ready to speak: otherwise we can go inside.

|₉₃ {Oedipus:} Speak to all. I say this because the load I am carrying for the sake of these people here, |₉₄ that sorrow [*penthos*], is more than the load I carry for my own soul [*psūkhē*].

|₉₅ {Creon:} I should tell you what I heard from the god: |₉₆ we have been given clear orders by Phoebus [Apollo] the lord |₉₇ to take the *pollution* [*miasma*] that he said has been nurtured in the land, |₉₈ in this one, and to expel it, not continuing to nurture it till it cannot be healed.

|₉₉ {Oedipus:} To expel it [= the pollution] by using what kind of *purification* [*katharmos*]? What is the kind of misfortune that has happened?

|₁₀₀ {Creon:} To expel it [= the pollution] by expelling the man, or by paying back bloodshed with bloodshed. |₁₀₁ That is the solution, since it is the blood that brings the *tempest* to our city [*polis*].

|₁₀₂ {Oedipus:} And who is the man whose fate [*tukhē*] he [= Apollo] thus reveals?

|₁₀₃ {Creon:} We once had, my king, Laios as the leader |₁₀₄ of this land here before you started being the director [= *euthunein*, 'to direct', literally means 'to make straight'] of this city [*polis*] here.

|₁₀₅ {Oedipus:} I know it well—by hearsay, for I never saw him.

|₁₀₆ {Creon:} The man is dead, and now the god gives clear orders |₁₀₇ to take vengeance against those, whoever they are, who caused his death with their own hands.

|₁₀₈ {Oedipus:} Where on earth are they? Where will this thing be found, |₁₀₉ this dim trail of an ancient guilt [*aitiā*]?

Sophocles *Oedipus Tyrannus* 91–109*

* |₉₁ {ΚΡ.} Εἰ τῶνδε χρῄζεις πλησιαζόντων κλύειν, |₉₂ ἕτοιμος εἰπεῖν, εἴτε καὶ στείχειν ἔσω. |₉₃ {ΟΙ.} Ἐς πάντας αὔδα· τῶνδε γὰρ πλέον φέρω |₉₄ τὸ πένθος ἢ καὶ τῆς ἐμῆς ψυχῆς πέρι. |₉₅ {ΚΡ.} Λέγοιμ᾽ ἂν οἷ᾽ ἤκουσα τοῦ θεοῦ πάρα. |₉₆ Ἄνωγεν ἡμᾶς Φοῖβος ἐμφανῶς ἄναξ |₉₇ μίασμα χώρας ὡς τεθραμμένον χθονὶ |₉₈ ἐν τῇδ᾽ ἐλαύνειν μηδ᾽ ἀνήκεστον τρέφειν. |₉₉ {ΟΙ.} Ποίῳ καθαρμῷ; τίς ὁ τρόπος τῆς ξυμφορᾶς; |₁₀₀ {ΚΡ.} Ἀνδρηλατοῦντας, ἢ φόνῳ φόνον πάλιν |₁₀₁ λύοντας, ὡς τόδ᾽ αἷμα χειμάζον πόλιν. |₁₀₂ {ΟΙ.} Ποίου γὰρ ἀνδρὸς τήνδε μηνύει τύχην; |₁₀₃ {ΚΡ.} Ἦν ἡμίν, ὦναξ, Λάϊός ποθ᾽ ἡγεμὼν |₁₀₄ γῆς τῆσδε, πρὶν σὲ τήνδ᾽ ἀπευθύνειν πόλιν. |₁₀₅ {ΟΙ.} Ἔξοιδ᾽ ἀκούων· οὐ γὰρ εἰσεῖδόν γέ πω. |₁₀₆ {ΚΡ.} Τούτου

19§14. In the words of Oedipus, the collective burden of lamentable 'sorrow' or *penthos* that is carried by his suffering people is added to the individual burden carried by his own larger-than-life *psūkhē*, which thus suffers beyond all suffering (93–94).

The Pollution Caused by Oedipus

19§15. In the Hesiodic *Works and Days*, as I analyzed it in Hour **12§33**, we saw a prophetic vision of two cities: one was the city of *dikē* or 'justice', while the other was the city of the opposite of justice, *hubris*, which is moral 'outrage'. Whereas the city of *dikē* abounds in fertility (225–237), the city of *hubris* is afflicted by sterility (238–247). Zeus punishes the city of *hubris* with famine (243), with the barrenness of its women (244), and with the diminution of household possessions (244). Moreover, the city of *hubris* is afflicted with shipwrecks in sea-storms brought on by Zeus himself (247), whereas the fortunate inhabitants of the city of *dikē* do not have to sail at all (236–237), since the earth bears for them plentiful *karpos* or 'fruit' (237). In this catalogue of multiple calamities that afflict the city of *hubris*, I focus on two: *shipwreck* and *sterility*. As I already noted at the beginning of this hour, **§6**, *shipwreck* and *sterility* are likewise the two most common metaphors for expressing the idea of divine punishment for the *hubris* of a tyrant. And now we will see the same two metaphors as symptoms of the pollution unknowingly caused by Oedipus. Here is how it is said, by the priest of Zeus:

HOUR 19 TEXT C

|14 Oedipus, ruler of my land, |15 you see the ages of those who are seated |15 at your altars: some, nestlings that cannot yet get very far |17 by flying, they don't have the strength, while others are weighted down with age. |18 The priest of Zeus, that is who I am, while these others are from the ranks of young men, |19 specially selected. The rest of the people, wearing garlands, |20 are seated at the place of assembly [*agorai*], at the twin buildings of Athena, |21 temples, where Ismenos gives prophetic answers with his fiery ashes. |22 This is all because the city [*po-*

θανόντος νῦν ἐπιστέλλει σαφῶς |107 τοὺς αὐτοέντας χειρὶ τιμωρεῖν τινας. |108 {ΟΙ.} Οἱ δ' εἰσὶ ποῦ γῆς; ποῦ τόδ' εὑρεθήσεται |109 ἴχνος παλαιᾶς δυστέκμαρτον αἰτίας;

lis], as you yourself see, is very much |₂₃ afflicted with a seastorm now, and it cannot lift its head |₂₄ any longer out of the depths of the murderous churning of the sea. |₂₅ Something that makes things wilt [*phthinein*] has descended on the buds containing the fruit [*karpos*] of the land. |₂₆ Yes, making things wilt [*phthinein*], it has also descended on the herds of cattle grazing in the pastures. And on whatever is produced |₂₇ from women, which has become lifeless. And the flaming god |₂₈ has swooped down. He is a most hateful plague, afflicting the city [*polis*]; because of him the house of Cadmus is emptied, while black |₃₀ Hādēs is enriched with sobs and laments [*gooi*].

Sophocles *Oedipus Tyrannus* 14–30*

Oedipus as Savior

19§16. In the *Oedipus Tyrannus*, the story of the pollution as signaled by the priest of Zeus is preceded by another story. In this preceding story, also signaled by the priest, Oedipus was the *sōtēr* or 'savior' of the people of Thebes:

HOUR 19 TEXT D

|₃₁ It is not because we rank you [= Oedipus] equal [*isos*] to the gods |₃₂ that I and these children are suppliants at your hearth, |₃₃ but because we think of you as the first among men in life's shared fortunes, |₃₄ judging [*krinein*] you that way, and first also in dealings with superhuman forces [*daimones*]. |₃₅ You freed us when you came to the city of the Cadmeans [= Thebans], |₃₆ ridding us of the tribute we had to keep on giving to the harsh female singer of songs, |₃₇ and though you knew no more than anyone else, |₃₈ nor had you been taught, but rather by the assistance of a god [*theos*], |₃₉ it is said and it is thought that you resurrected [*orthoûn*, 'make straight'] our life. |₄₀ Now, as we all address your most powerful head, the head of Oedipus, as we touch it, |₄₁ we, your suppliants, implore you as we turn to you |₄₂ to find some

* |₁₄ Ἀλλ', ὦ κρατύνων Οἰδίπους χώρας ἐμῆς, |₁₅ ὁρᾷς μὲν ἡμᾶς ἡλίκοι προσήμεθα |₁₆ βωμοῖσι τοῖς σοῖς, οἱ μὲν οὐδέπω μακρὰν |₁₇ πτέσθαι σθένοντες, οἱ δὲ σὺν γήρᾳ βαρεῖς, |₁₈ ἱερεύς, ἐγὼ μὲν Ζηνός, οἵδε τ' ἠθέων |₁₉ λεκτοί· τὸ δ' ἄλλο φῦλον ἐξεστεμμένον |₂₀ ἀγοραῖσι θακεῖ, πρός τε Παλλάδος διπλοῖς |₂₁ ναοῖς, ἐπ' Ἰσμηνοῦ τε μαντείᾳ σποδῷ. |₂₂ Πόλις γάρ, ὥσπερ καὐτὸς εἰσορᾷς, ἄγαν |₂₃ ἤδη σαλεύει, κἀνακουφίσαι κάρα |₂₄ βυθῶν ἔτ' οὐχ οἵα τε φοινίου σάλου, |₂₅ φθίνουσα μὲν κάλυξιν ἐγκάρποις χθονός, |₂₆ φθίνουσα δ' ἀγέλαις βουνόμοις τόκοισί τε |₂₇ ἀγόνοις γυναικῶν· ἐν δ' ὁ πυρφόρος θεὸς |₂₈

protection [*alkē*] for us, whether from one of the gods |₄₃ you hear some prophetic wording [*phēmē*], or learn of it perhaps from some man. |₄₄ I say this because those who are experienced, |₄₅ thanks to the advice they give, can make—I see it—even accidental things have the power of life. |₄₆ Come, best [*aristos*] among mortals, resurrect [*an-orthoûn*, 'make straight'] our city [*polis*]! |₄₇ Come! And do be careful, since now this land here |₄₈ calls you a savior [*sōtēr*], thanks to your willingness to help in the past. |₄₉ And, concerning your rule [*arkhē*], do not let it happen that our memory of it will be |₅₀ that we were first set up straight [*es orthon*] and then let down, falling again. |₅₁ So give us safety and resurrect [*an-orthoûn*, 'make straight'] this city [*polis*]! |₅₂ With a favorable omen of birds was the past good fortune |₅₃ provided by you for us, and so become now the same person, equal [*isos*] to who you were, |₅₄ since, if in fact you are to rule this land just as you have power over it now, |₅₅ it is better to have power over men than over a wasteland. |₅₆ Neither tower nor ship is anything, |₅₇ if it is empty and no men dwell [*sun-oikeîn*] inside.

Sophocles *Oedipus Tyrannus* 31–57*

19§17. The word *sōtēr* or 'savior', as used here at line 48, applies to Oedipus in the context of the greatest and most glorious action performed by this hero for the people of Thebes: by using his superior intelligence, the hero solved the riddle of the Sphinx and thus freed those people (35) from the harsh afflictions caused by that 'female singer of songs' (36). By freeing those people, Oedipus had set them up 'in standing position', *es orthon* (50), by contrast with their dejected prone position, when they had abjectly fallen down because of the

---

σκήψας ἐλαύνει, λοιμὸς ἔχθιστος, πόλιν, |₂₉ ὑφ' οὗ κενοῦται δῶμα Καδμεῖον, μέλας δ' |₃₀ Ἅιδης στεναγμοῖς καὶ γόοις πλουτίζεται.

* |₃₁ Θεοῖσι μέν νυν οὐκ ἰσούμενός σ' ἐγὼ |₃₂ οὐδ' οἵδε παῖδες ἑζόμεσθ' ἐφέστιοι, |₃₃ ἀνδρῶν δὲ πρῶτον ἔν τε συμφοραῖς βίου |₃₄ κρίνοντες ἔν τε δαιμόνων ξυναλλαγαῖς, |₃₅ ὅς γ' ἐξέλυσας ἄστυ Καδμεῖον μολὼν |₃₆ σκληρᾶς ἀοιδοῦ δασμὸν ὃν παρείχομεν, |₃₇ καὶ ταῦθ' ὑφ' ἡμῶν οὐδὲν ἐξειδὼς πλέον |₃₈ οὐδ' ἐκδιδαχθείς, ἀλλὰ προσθήκῃ θεοῦ |₃₉ λέγῃ νομίζῃ θ' ἡμῖν ὀρθῶσαι βίον. |₄₀ Νῦν τ', ὦ κράτιστον πᾶσιν Οἰδίπου κάρα, |₄₁ ἱκετεύομέν σε πάντες οἵδε πρόστροποι |₄₂ ἀλκήν τιν' εὑρεῖν ἡμίν, εἴτε του θεῶν |₄₃ φήμην ἀκούσας εἴτ' ἀπ' ἀνδρὸς οἶσθά του· |₄₄ ὡς τοῖσιν ἐμπείροισι καὶ τὰς ξυμφορὰς |₄₅ ζώσας ὁρῶ μάλιστα τῶν βουλευμάτων. |₄₆ Ἴθ', ὦ βροτῶν ἄριστ', ἀνόρθωσον πόλιν· |₄₇ ἴθ', εὐλαβήθηθ'· ὡς σὲ νῦν μὲν ἥδε γῆ |₄₈ σωτῆρα κλῄζει τῆς πάρος προθυμίας· |₄₉ ἀρχῆς δὲ τῆς σῆς μηδαμῶς μεμνώμεθα |₅₀ στάντες τ' ἐς ὀρθὸν καὶ πεσόντες ὕστερον, |₅₁ ἀλλ' ἀσφαλείᾳ τήνδ' ἀνόρθωσον πόλιν. |₅₂ Ὄρνιθι γὰρ καὶ τὴν τότ' αἰσίῳ τύχην |₅₃ παρέσχες ἡμῖν, καὶ τανῦν ἴσος γενοῦ· |₅₄ ὡς, εἴπερ ἄρξεις τῆσδε γῆς ὥσπερ κρατεῖς, |₅₅ ξὺν ἀνδράσιν κάλλιον ἢ κενῆς κρατεῖν· |₅₆ ὡς οὐδέν ἐστιν οὔτε πύργος οὔτε ναῦς |₅₇ ἔρημος ἀνδρῶν μὴ ξυνοικούντων ἔσω.

Sphinx—and now they do not want to be 'falling down again' (50)—because of the pollution. Nor do the people of Thebes want their own city to 'fall down again' because of the pollution, and that is why they implore Oedipus, now that the city has in fact 'fallen down again', to 'raise it up again', *an-orthoûn* (51). I must add that this word *an-orthoûn* can also mean 'make straight', and that this idea conjures the metaphor of straightness as applied to *dikē* or 'justice', as opposed to the metaphor of crookedness as applied to *hubris* or 'outrage'. We have already seen in Hour **12§12** some striking examples of these two antithetical metaphors. Moreover, the verb *an-orthoûn* can mean, in a mystical sense, the 'resurrecting' of the dead through some superhuman agency, as we see in the case of Theocritus 1.139, where the goddess Aphrodite wants to *an-orthoûn* or 'resurrect' the beautiful dead hero Daphnis;* in that same context, in a concurrently mystical sense, Aphrodite wants not only the hero's 'resurrection' but also his 'erection'.† Similarly in line 39 of the *Oedipus Tyrannus*, as I have just quoted it, Oedipus is both said to have and thought to have 'resurrected', *orthoûn*, the very life of the people of Thebes when he had saved them from the Sphinx. So now he is implored at lines 46 and 51 to *an-orthoûn* or 'resurrect' once again the city of the Thebans. And, to complete the circle, it is only by way of 'resurrecting' that city once again that Oedipus will become once again the *sōtēr* or 'savior'—which is what he had been when he had saved Thebes from the Sphinx.

19§18. But the fact is, Oedipus will not become the savior of the Thebans once again. He will not be able to save them from the pollution in an active way—which is how he had saved them from the Sphinx. The only way for Oedipus to remove the pollution from Thebes will be a distinctly passive way—to be removed, expelled. But then he will go on to purify his own pollution, as we already saw in the *Oedipus at Colonus,* not in Thebes but in Athens. This way, as we have seen in Hour **18§24,** Oedipus will become an active 'bringer of salvation', a *sōtērios,* for the whole community of Athens (487), and this will happen because he will actively purify himself of his pollution by pouring a libation to the Eumenides. Further, as we have seen in Hour **18§32,** Oedipus will thus become a cult hero of the Athenians, and he will even be called their own *sōtēr* or 'savior' (460; see also 463).

19§19. So the application of the word *sōtēr* or 'savior' to Oedipus at line 48 of

---

* *HC* 303 = 2§250n248.
† *HC* 304–305 = 2§253.

the *Oedipus Tyrannus* is misplaced in this context. The people of Thebes are treating him as a cult hero in return for the action of Oedipus in saving them from the Sphinx, but he cannot be a cult hero for them in the context of the pollution that he himself unknowingly caused for himself and also for his whole community. Moreover, there is something very wrong in the application of this epithet in the larger context of the pollution, since the god Apollo himself is called a *sōtēr* or 'savior' by the priest at line 150, who utters here a short prayer to the god, asking him to free the people from the pollution caused by the plague. Similarly at line 304, Oedipus himself says that he is relying on Teiresias the seer, devotee of Apollo, to be a *sōtēr* or 'savior' of the city by freeing Thebes from the plague. So the application of this same word *sōtēr* to Oedipus himself at line 48 indicates the beginning of an antagonistic relationship between this hero and the god Apollo. And here I return to my general formulation in Hour 1§50 about god-hero antagonism: The hero is antagonistic toward the god who seems to be most like the hero; antagonism does not rule out an element of attraction—often a "fatal attraction"—which is played out in a variety of ways.

A Second Look inside the Psūkhē of Oedipus

19§20. The pollution that afflicts both Oedipus and the whole community of Thebes takes the form of a plague, and this plague is pictured as a sickness that afflicts the body. So the need for purification can be pictured correspondingly as a need for a medical cure—not only for the body but also for the body politic. The metaphor that we see at work in this English expression *body politic* is most apt here, since Oedipus in the *Oedipus Tyrannus* is the king of the whole community that is Thebes. And here I return to the anthropological formulation of the very idea of a *king*, as I presented it in Hour 6§13: *the king is an incarnation of the body politic, of society itself, which needs to be renewed periodically by being purified of pollution.* This formulation can be applied to what is being said by Oedipus at lines 93–94 of the *Oedipus Tyrannus*, quoted in Text B: as he contemplates the burden of lamentable 'sorrow' or *penthos* that is carried by his suffering people, the hero says that this collective burden is added to the individual burden carried by his own larger-than-life *psūkhē*, which thus suffers beyond all suffering. I now show an earlier passage in the *Oedipus Tyrannus* where Oedipus is already describing this burden of his *psūkhē*—and already prescribing a remedy for the suffering caused by the pollution:

HOUR 19 TEXT E

|₅₈ My piteous children, I know—they are not unknown to me— |₅₉ the desires you have as you come to me. You see, I know well that |₆₀ you are all sick, and that, sick as you are, when it comes to me, |₆₁ there is not a single one of you who is as sick as I am. |₆₂ You see, your pain [*algos*] goes into each one of you |₆₃ alone, all by yourself, and into no other person, but my |₆₄ soul [*psūkhē*] mourns for the city [*polis*], for myself, and for you—it does it all together. |₆₅ So you are not awakening me from sleep; |₆₆ no, I want you to know that I have by now wept many tears, |₆₇ gone many ways in the wanderings of my thinking. |₆₈ After giving it some good thought, I came up with one and only one remedy [*iasis*], |₆₉ and I acted on it. You see, the son of Menoikeus, |₇₀ Creon, my wife's brother, was sent to the Pythian place, |₇₁ sent by me to the dwellings of Phoebus [Apollo], so that he could find out what |₇₂ I should do [*drân*] or say to save this city [*polis*] here. |₇₃ And now, when the lapse of days is reckoned, |₇₄ it bothers me what he might be doing, because it is beyond my expectation, |₇₅ how much longer he is gone past the fitting length of time. |₇₆ But when he does arrive, I will be worthless [*kakos*] |₇₇ if I do not do [*drân*] all the things indicated by the god.

Sophocles *Oedipus Tyrannus* 58–77*

Purifying the Pollution in Tragedy

19§21. The *iasis* or 'remedy' (68) found by Oedipus for *noseîn*, 'being sick' (60–61: the word *noseîn* occurs three times within this stretch of two lines), is pictured here as a medical solution. But this remedy is not only for *being sick*. It must also be a remedy for *being polluted*. Pollution is the basic problem, and

---

* |₅₈ ὦ παῖδες οἰκτροί, γνωτὰ κοὐκ ἄγνωτά μοι |₅₉ προσῆλθεθ' ἱμείροντες· εὖ γὰρ οἶδ' ὅτι |₆₀ νοσεῖτε πάντες, καὶ νοσοῦντες ὡς ἐγὼ |₆₁ οὐκ ἔστιν ὑμῶν ὅστις ἐξ ἴσου νοσεῖ. |₆₂ Τὸ μὲν γὰρ ὑμῶν ἄλγος εἰς ἕν' ἔρχεται |₆₃ μόνον καθ' αὑτόν, κοὐδέν' ἄλλον, ἡ δ' ἐμὴ |₆₄ ψυχὴ πόλιν τε κἀμὲ καὶ σ' ὁμοῦ στένει. |₆₅ Ὥστ' οὐχ ὕπνῳ γ' εὕδοντά μ' ἐξεγείρετε· |₆₆ ἀλλ' ἴστε πολλὰ μέν με δακρύσαντα δή, |₆₇ πολλὰς δ' ὁδοὺς ἐλθόντα φροντίδος πλάνοις· |₆₈ ἣν δ' εὖ σκοπῶν εὕρισκον ἴασιν μόνην, |₆₉ ταύτην ἔπραξα· παῖδα γὰρ Μενοικέως |₇₀ Κρέοντ', ἐμαυτοῦ γαμβρόν, ἐς τὰ Πυθικὰ |₇₁ ἔπεμψα Φοίβου δώμαθ', ὡς πύθοιθ' ὅ τι |₇₂ δρῶν ἢ τί φωνῶν τήνδε ῥυσαίμην πόλιν. |₇₃ Καί μ' ἦμαρ ἤδη ξυμμετρούμενον χρόνῳ |₇₄ λυπεῖ τί πράσσει· τοῦ γὰρ εἰκότος πέρα |₇₅ ἄπεστι πλείω τοῦ καθήκοντος χρόνου. |₇₆ Ὅταν δ' ἵκηται, τηνικαῦτ' ἐγὼ κακὸς |₇₇ μὴ δρῶν ἂν εἴην πάνθ' ὅσ' ἂν δηλοῖ θεός.

this pollution is clearly indicated by the word *miasma,* as we saw it used at line 97 of the *Oedipus Tyrannus,* quoted in Text B. And, as we also saw at line 99 of the same text, the basic remedy in tragedy for this problem of pollution is purification, as expressed by the word *katharmos.*

19§22. As the oracle of Apollo ordains at line 100, quoted in Text B, the purification of the city of Thebes must take the form of expelling the man who was guilty of killing the king Laios and whose guilt had caused the pollution; alternatively, as we see in the same line, the blood-guilt for the killing of Laios must be paid back with the shedding of the killer's blood.

19§23. Such a purification, even though it is hardly a medical remedy for an individual body, is seen nevertheless as a collective cure for the body politic of the people of Thebes. And such a mentality of a collective cure can extend from the body politic of the Thebans in myth all the way to the audience of tragedy in the ritual complex of State Theater in Athens. In such an Athenian context, what I have been describing up to now as the *audience* represents in its own way the *body politic.*

19§24. In the myth of Oedipus as retold in the *Oedipus Tyrannus,* we have seen from the wording of Text B that the antidote to *miasma* or 'pollution' (97) is *katharmos* or 'purification' (99). In the ritual complex of drama as brought to life in Athenian State Theater, on the other hand, we see another word for 'purification', and that is *katharsis,* conventionally latinized as *catharsis.* I have already highlighted this word in Hour 8e§3: there I quoted a celebrated formulation of Aristotle, who links *katharsis* with *mīmēsis*—a word that I defined there as 're-enactment'. I now quote this formulation again, in the context of analyzing tragedy as a ritual process:

HOUR 19 TEXT F = HOUR 8 TEXT N

> Tragedy, then, is the re-enactment [*mīmēsis*] of a serious and complete action. It has magnitude, with language embellished individually for each of its forms and in each of its parts. It is done by performers [*drôntes*] and not by way of narrative, bringing about through pity [*eleos*] and fear [*phobos*] the purification [*katharsis*] of such emotions [*pathēmata*].

Aristotle Poetics 1449b24–28

19§25. From the standpoint of the myth of Oedipus, as retold in the drama *Oedipus Tyrannus,* purification takes the form of eliminating pollution by expelling the one who is guilty, or even by shedding his blood. From the standpoint of the ritual of drama, the corresponding purification takes the form of eliminating the same pollution. But what exactly is the pollution that gets eliminated? In terms of Aristotle's formulation, tragedy works at eliminating the pollution that resides in one's own world of emotions. By engaging with the larger-than-life emotions of a larger-than-life hero like Oedipus, the audience in the role of the body politic can purge its own emotions, especially the emotions of fear and pity.

19§26. As I noted in the Introduction to Part III (§9), a choice word for such heroic emotions is *pathos,* which can be seen as an all-encompassing Passion in comparison with any emotions experienced by any ordinary person—even though the same word *pathos* applies here as well.

19§27. If the Passion of a larger-than-life hero like Oedipus dwarfs the emotions of ordinary persons, then a vitally important question arises about the *miasma* or 'pollution' that causes all the suffering, as highlighted in the wording I quoted in Text B from the *Oedipus Tyrannus* (97). The question is, can we say that this pollution is likewise larger-than-life? And the answer is, yes: the pollution caused by a hero's actions is so enormous that it can only be remedied by a purification performed by the entire population. In the myth of Oedipus as it plays out in the *Oedipus Tyrannus,* the purification ultimately takes the ritual form of a public expulsion, to be performed by the people of Thebes. Such a Greek ritual of expulsion is analogous to the Hittite ritual of elimination as I analyzed it in Hour 6§18. On the other hand, in the myth of Oedipus as it plays out in the *Oedipus at Colonus,* we saw in Hour 18 that the purification of the pollution takes the ritual form of a libation, first performed by the hero himself for the Eumenides before he dies and then performed thereafter, at the right recurring time, notionally for all eternity, by the people of Athens, who have by now become the hero's worshippers. And these worshippers will perform the libation not only for the Eumenides but also for Oedipus himself, who has by now become a new cult hero in Athens by way of demonstrating to his new countrymen how to perform the libation. The mentality of the actual demonstration is straightforward: *do as I do.*

The Reaction of Oedipus to His Own Pollution in the Oedipus Tyrannus

19§28. By contrast with the *Oedipus at Colonus,* the *Oedipus Tyrannus* of Sophocles dramatizes the immediate reaction of Oedipus to the reality of his own pollution, once he finally recognizes it. And, once this recognition happens, the world that had been illuminated for Oedipus by his own intellectual brightness, rivaling the solar supremacy of the god Apollo himself, tragically comes to an end. The same man who could confidently speak as a solar agent, declaring at line 132 of the *Oedipus Tyrannus*, 'I will shed light' on the matter, *ego phanô* (ἐγὼ φανῶ), will in the end put out the light of his own eyes, which had failed to shed light—as the sun would have shed light—on the dark pollution that had already enveloped the hero. When he sees the lifeless body of his mother and wife, who has just committed suicide, Oedipus reacts to this sight, marked by fear and pity, by taking out his own eyesight:

HOUR 19 TEXT G

And when, on the ground, $|_{1267}$ that wretched person was lying there, terrifying were the things to be seen from that point onward. $|_{1268}$ For he [= Oedipus] tore from her clothing those gold-worked $|_{1269}$ brooches of hers, with which she had ornamented herself, $|_{1270}$ and, holding them high with raised hand, he struck his own eyeballs, $|_{1271}$ uttering words like these: that they should not see him $|_{1272}$ either experience such things as he was experiencing [*paskhein*] or doing [*drân*] such things— $|_{1273}$ but, from now on, in total darkness, those persons whom he ought never $|_{1274}$ to have seen, they could see them now, and, as for those persons whom he needed to know, they would fail to know them now. $|_{1275}$ Uttering such incantations, many times and not just one time $|_{1276}$ did he strike with raised hand the spaces where the eyes open and close. And, at each blow the bloody $|_{1277}$ eyeballs made wet his bearded cheeks, and did not send forth $|_{1278}$ sluggish drops of gore, but all at once $|_{1279}$ a dark shower of blood poured down, like hail. $|_{1280}$ These evil happenings burst forth, coming out of the two of them together, not from only one of them. $|_{1281}$ No, they were mixed together, for both the man and the woman, these evil happenings. $|_{1282}$ Their old prosperity [*olbos*] was once $|_{1283}$ true blessedness [*olbos*], and justly [*dikaiôs*] so. But now on this day here $|_{1284}$ there is the groaning of lamentation, there is aberration [*atê*], there is death, there is shame; of all the evil things $|_{1285}$ that can be named, all of them, not one is missing.

Sophocles *Oedipus Tyrannus* 1266–1285*

---

* $|_{1266}$ ... ἐπεὶ δὲ γῇ $|_{1267}$ ἔκειθ᾽ ὁ τλήμων, δεινὰ δ᾽ ἦν τἀνθένδ᾽ ὁρᾶν. $|_{1268}$ Ἀποσπάσας γὰρ εἱμάτων χρυσηλάτους $|_{1269}$ περόνας ἀπ᾽ αὐτῆς, αἷσιν ἐξεστέλλετο, $|_{1270}$ ἄρας ἔπαισεν ἄρθρα τῶν αὑτοῦ κύκλων, $|_{1271}$ αὐδῶν τοιαῦθ᾽, ὁθούνεκ᾽ οὐκ ὄψοιντό νιν $|_{1272}$ οὔθ᾽ οἷ᾽ ἔπασχεν οὔθ᾽ ὁποῖ᾽ ἔδρα κακά, $|_{1273}$ ἀλλ᾽ ἐν σκότῳ τὸ λοιπὸν οὓς μὲν οὐκ ἔδει $|_{1274}$ ὀψοίαθ᾽, οὓς δ᾽ ἔχρῃζεν οὐ γνωσοίατο. $|_{1275}$ Τοιαῦτ᾽ ἐφυμνῶν

19§29. By depriving himself of his own eyesight, Oedipus puts out the light that illuminated his world of intellect. It is as if the inner fires that fueled this light have been extinguished:

HOUR 19 TEXT H

|₁₃₂₇ {Chorus:} You who have done [*drân*] such terrible things, how could you bring yourself |₁₃₂₈ to extinguish [*marainein*] your eyesight? Who among the superhuman powers [*daimones*] urged you on? |₁₃₂₉ {Oedipus:} It was Apollo, dear ones [*philoi*], Apollo |₁₃₃₀ who brought to fulfillment [*teleîn*] these evil, evil experiences [*pathos* plural] of mine. |_{1331–1334} But no one with his own hand did the striking. I myself did that, wretch that I am! Why was I to see, |₁₃₃₅ when eyesight showed me nothing sweet?

Sophocles *Oedipus Tyrannus* 1327–1335*

19§30. The verb that is used here to express the idea of 'extinguishing' the eyesight of Oedipus is *marainein,* in the active voice. Aristotle (*On the Heavens* 305a11) notes that the middle voice of this verb, *marainesthai,* is used with reference to situations in which a fire goes out by itself; by contrast, in situations in which a fire is put out by human agency, another word is used, *sbennusthai* in the passive voice, as opposed to *sbennunai* in the active voice, which refers to situations in which someone puts out a fire. This distinction, as noted by Aristotle, helps us understand the peculiarity of using the active voice, *marainein,* with reference to the agency of Oedipus when he puts out the fires, as it were, that fuel the light of his eyesight. Ordinarily, the active form *sbennunai* would be used with reference to situations in which someone puts out a fire, just as the passive form *sbennusthai* refers to situations in which the fire is put out by someone. So how could the middle form *marainesthai,* which refers to situations in which a fire goes out by itself, be converted to an active form with reference to an extraordinary situation in which Oedipus puts out his own eyesight?

πολλάκις τε κοὐχ ἅπαξ |₁₂₇₆ ἤρασσ' ἐπαίρων βλέφαρα· φοίνιαι δ' ὁμοῦ |₁₂₇₇ γλῆναι γένει' ἔτεγγον, οὐδ' ἀνίεσαν |₁₂₇₈ φόνου μυδώσας σταγόνας, ἀλλ' ὁμοῦ μέλας |₁₂₇₉ ὄμβρος χαλάζης αἵματός τ' ἐτέγγετο. |₁₂₈₀ Τάδ' ἐκ δυοῖν ἔρρωγεν, οὐ μόνου, κακά, |₁₂₈₁ ἀλλ' ἀνδρὶ καὶ γυναικὶ συμμιγῆ κακά. |₁₂₈₂ Ὁ πρὶν παλαιὸς δ' ὄλβος ἦν πάροιθε μὲν |₁₂₈₃ ὄλβος δικαίως· νῦν δὲ τῇδε θἡμέρᾳ |₁₂₈₄ στεναγμός, ἄτη, θάνατος, αἰσχύνη, κακῶν |₁₂₈₅ ὅσ' ἐστὶ πάντων ὀνόματ', οὐδέν ἐστ' ἀπόν.

* |₁₃₂₇ {ΧΟ.} Ὦ δεινὰ δράσας, πῶς ἔτλης τοιαῦτα σὰς |₁₃₂₈ ὄψεις μαρᾶναι; τίς σ' ἐπῆρε δαιμόνων; |₁₃₂₉ {ΟΙ.} Ἀπόλλων τάδ' ἦν, Ἀπόλλων, φίλοι, |₁₃₃₀ ὁ κακὰ κακὰ τελῶν ἐμὰ τάδ' ἐμὰ πάθεα. |_{1331–1334} Ἔπαισε δ' αὐτόχειρ νιν οὔτις, ἀλλ' ἐγὼ τλάμων. |₁₃₃₅ Τί γὰρ ἔδει μ' ὁρᾶν, ὅτῳ γ' ὁρῶντι μηδὲν ἦν ἰδεῖν γλυκύ;

It is as if the agency of Oedipus here were no agency at all. I find a similarly extraordinary situation in the *Homeric Hymn to Hermes,* where the god Hermes makes the first fire and then puts out that first fire at line 140: when he puts the fire out, the active form *marainein* is used. Again, it is as if the agency of Hermes were no agency at all. But that is not so: although there is no human agency at work here, there is divine agency. The fire goes out by itself because it was started by divine agency, which means that the fire, to human eyes, had also started by itself, animated by the divine force of the god Hermes. I think there is something similarly extraordinary in the use of the active voice of *marainein* when Oedipus puts out his eyes at line 1328 of the *Oedipus Tyrannus.* The agency is not human. It is beyond the human. The self-blinding of Oedipus will lead this hero into an existence that transcends the human.

The Hero as Mirror of Men's and Women's Experiences in the Hippolytus *of Euripides*

The Meaning of Telos

20§1. The key word for this hour is *telos*, 'end, ending, final moment; goal, completion, fulfillment; coming full circle, rounding out; successfully passing through an ordeal; initiation; ritual, rite'. We have already seen this word in many of the contexts that fit the translations that I give here (1§49, 5§119, 9§29, 13§§10–22, 16§8). A verb derived from this noun *telos* is *teleîn*, which I have been translating as 'carry out the fulfillment' (2§44) or 'bring to fulfillment' (11§34, 19§29) or 'make a ritual act' (11§47). As we will see in the course of this hour, the many different ways of translating the word *telos* have one thing in common: each translation conveys, in its own way, the idea of a transition from one phase of human experience into another. And, toward the end of this hour, we will see that the world of ancient Greek myth and ritual tends to differentiate, like it or not, the experiences of men and women from each other.

Two Contexts of Telos *for Hippolytus*

20§2. In the *Hippolytus* of Euripides, we find two occurrences of this word *telos*. As we will see, the contexts of both these occurrences are relevant to the myths and the rituals concerning Hippolytus.

20§3. I start with the second of the two contexts, at line 87 of the drama. The word *telos* in this context—and I am about to quote the text—can be understood in two different ways. In terms of what the speaker intends—and this speaker is none other than Hippolytus—we may translate *telos* as 'the end'. In terms of what is really meant by the myths and the rituals concerning Hippolytus, however, such a translation is overly restrictive. I say that because the myths concerning Hippolytus, as we will see later, are directly linked with rituals of female initiation. And, in terms of such a link between myth and ritual, the subtext of the word *telos* here is 'initiation'.

20§4. So now I proceed to a close reading of the text where we find this occurrence of the word *telos* in the *Hippolytus*. As we join the action, near the beginning of the drama, we find the young hero Hippolytus in the act of praying to the goddess Artemis while offering her the gift of a garland of flowers that he consecrates for her blond hair:

Hour 20 Text A

|₇₃ For you this plaited garland [*stephanos*] culled from an unspoiled |₇₄ meadow [*leimōn*], O my lady [= Artemis], do I [= Hippolytus] bring, arranging [*kosmeîn*] it properly. |₇₅ It is from a place where it is not fit for the shepherd to pasture his flocks, |₇₆ nor has iron yet come there, but it is unspoiled, |₇₇ this meadow [*leimōn*], and the bee in springtime goes through and through. |₇₈ The goddess named Modesty [*Aidōs*] tends this place with pure river water, |₇₉ and those who do not have to be taught but by their own nature [*phusis*] |₈₀ are endowed with moderation [*sōphrosunē*] always in all things, |₈₁ they are allowed by divine sanction to pick flowers there, but it is not sanctioned by divine law [*themis*] for those who are bad. So, my lady near and dear [*philē*], for your golden locks of hair |₈₃ accept this headband from my properly worshipful hand. |₈₄ For I alone among mortals have this privilege [*geras*]: |₈₅ I keep company with you and I exchange words with you, |₈₆ hearing your voice though not looking you in the eye. |₈₇ That is the same way I should go round the turning post, heading toward the end [*telos*] of life just as I began it.

Euripides *Hippolytus* 73–87*

20§5. In expressing his desire to be a devotee of the virgin goddess Artemis from the beginning of his life all the way to the end, the militantly virginal hero Hippolytus speaks the language of metaphor: accomplished charioteer that he

---

* |₇₃ σοὶ τόνδε πλεκτὸν στέφανον ἐξ ἀκηράτου |₇₄ λειμῶνος, ὦ δέσποινα, κοσμήσας φέρω, |₇₅ ἔνθ' οὔτε ποιμὴν ἀξιοῖ φέρβειν βοτὰ |₇₆ οὔτ' ἦλθέ πω σίδηρος, ἀλλ' ἀκήρατον |₇₇ μέλισσα λειμῶν' ἠρινὴ διέρχεται, |₇₈ Αἰδὼς δὲ ποταμίαισι κηπεύει δρόσοις, |₇₉ ὅσοις διδακτὸν μηδὲν ἀλλ' ἐν τῆι φύσει |₈₀ τὸ σωφρονεῖν εἴληχεν ἐς τὰ πάντ' ἀεί, |₈₁ τούτοις δρέπεσθαι, τοῖς κακοῖσι δ' οὐ θέμις. |₈₂ ἀλλ', ὦ φίλη δέσποινα, χρυσέας κόμης |₈₃ ἀνάδημα δέξαι χειρὸς εὐσεβοῦς ἄπο. |₈₄ μόνωι γάρ ἐστι τοῦτ' ἐμοὶ γέρας βροτῶν· |₈₅ σοὶ καὶ ξύνειμι καὶ λόγοις ἀμείβομαι, |₈₆ κλύων μὲν αὐδῆς, ὄμμα δ' οὐχ ὁρῶν τὸ σόν. |₈₇ τέλος δὲ κάμψαιμ' ὥσπερ ἠρξάμην βίου.

is, he thinks of his life as the course of a chariot race, and he thinks of the finish line of the race as the end of his life. After Hippolytus rounds the turning post for the last time in the course of his life, the finish line will be waiting for him. But this metaphor can lead to other meanings of the word *telos*. After all, the rounding of a turning post in a chariot race takes the charioteer back to the starting point, where the rounding continues back to the turning post and then back to the starting point and then back to the turning post, over and over again—until the charioteer rounds the turning post for the last time. Then, after the last rounding of the turning post, he will be heading down the home stretch, eagerly rushing toward the finish line. But the finish line becomes a finish line only after the last turn around the turning post.

20§6. For Hippolytus, the end of life is the finish line of a chariot race. That is all there is to it. He does not see, in terms of his own metaphor, that the finish line can also be a coming full circle. After all, as I have just pointed out, the finish line is truly the finish line only when the turning post has been rounded for the very last time. Otherwise, the finish line can still become a re-starting, that is, the starting point of a new round.

20§7. So we find here an unintended meaning in the words spoken just now by Hippolytus. Still, the intent of the young athlete is clear: he wants to go through life, from beginning to end, as a devotee of the virgin goddess Artemis. And, by implication, he desires to reach the end of his life the same way he had begun it, as a virgin. The thinking of Hippolytus is linear here: for him, *telos* is the end of a line.

20§8. But there is also the idea of *telos* as a coming full circle, and this alternative idea cannot be evaded in the *Hippolytus* of Euripides. Such an idea, which is most compatible with the metaphorical world of ritual, leads to a further idea—initiation. A telling sign of this further idea can be found in the context of the second of the two attestations of the word *telos* in the *Hippolytus* of Euripides. In this other context, the idea of initiation is overtly expressed. It happens in a story told by Aphrodite, goddess of sexuality and love, at the very beginning of the drama. As we are about to see, there is a moment in the story when the beautiful young queen Phaedra, married to an older man, the king-hero Theseus, first lays eyes on the beautiful young bastard son of the king, Hippolytus. At that moment, as we see from the narration of Aphrodite, this goddess of erotic desire arranges for Phaedra to fall instantly in love with Hippolytus. In the version of the story that is told here by Aphrodite, Phaedra first falls in love with Hippolytus in Athens, not in Trozen, which is the native city of the hero.* Hippolytus has traveled from Trozen and has just arrived in the territory of Athens, described as the land of Pandion, who was a primeval ruler of the territory. The young hero has come to Athens because he desires to be initiated into the Eleusinian Mysteries, described at line 25 as *telē*, the plural of *telos*, which I will translate for the moment as 'rituals'. So we are about to see an overt reference to initiation, as expressed by the word *telos*:

HOUR 20 TEXT B

|$_{24}$ When he [= Hippolytus] went, once upon a time, from the palace of Pittheus [in Trozen] |$_{25}$ [to the territory of Athens] for the vision and rituals [*telos* plural] of the revered Mysteries [*mustērion* plural], |$_{26}$ to the land of Pandion [= to the territory of Athens], then it was that the noble wife of the father [of Hippolytus] |$_{27}$ saw him, yes, Phaedra saw him, and she was possessed in her heart |$_{28}$ by a passionate love [*erōs*] that was terrifying—all because of the plans I planned.

Euripides *Hippolytus* 24–28†

Hippolytus as a Cult Hero in Athens

20§9. As we have just seen, the onset of the passionate love experienced by Phaedra when she first catches sight of Hippolytus happens in the territory of Athens, where the young hero is visiting in his quest to be initiated into the Eleusinian Mysteries. As we will now see, this mention of Athens indicates that the story of Hippolytus as it plays out in the tragedy of Euripides stems from a complex of myths and rituals that are grounded in two locales, one of which is Trozen but the other one of which is Athens. And, as we will also see, these myths and rituals concern Hippolytus as a cult hero who was worshipped both in Trozen and in Athens. I will concentrate first on Athens.

20§10. I start by observing that Athens is the dramatic setting of another tragedy of Euripides about Hippolytus, which has not survived except for a few fragments.‡ Here I turn to relevant information provided by external evidence. Surviving along with our text of the *Hippolytus* is the text of an accompanying

---

* Here and everywhere, I spell the name of this city *Trozen*, not *Troizen*, following Barrett 1964:157.

† |$_{24}$ ἐλθόντα γάρ νιν Πιτθέως ποτ' ἐκ δόμων |$_{25}$ σεμνῶν ἐς ὄψιν καὶ τέλη μυστηρίων |$_{26}$ Πανδίονος γῆν πατρὸς εὐγενὴς δάμαρ |$_{27}$ ἰδοῦσα Φαίδρα καρδίαν κατέσχετο |$_{28}$ ἔρωτι δεινῷ τοῖς ἐμοῖς βουλεύμασιν.

‡ Barrett 1964:159.

Hypothesis that stems from Aristophanes of Byzantium, Director of the Library of Alexandria in the early second century BCE. From the external evidence of this *Hypothesis,* we learn that the surviving *Hippolytus* of Euripides was produced in 428 BCE, winning first prize in the competitions at the dramatic festival of the City Dionysia in Athens. And we learn also from the same *Hypothesis* that the lost *Hippolytus* was an earlier production.

20§11. That said, I come back to the reference in Text B, lines 24–28 of the surviving *Hippolytus*—back to the moment when Phaedra falls passionately in love with the virgin hero during his pilgrimage in Athens. I will now consider these lines in combination with lines 29–33, which immediately follow and which I now quote here:

HOUR 20 TEXT C

|₂₉ And before she [= Phaedra] came to this land of Trozen, |₃₀ she established—on a side of the Rock of Pallas [= Athena], from where one could see a view |₃₁ of this land [of Trozen] here—[she established] a shrine [*nāos*] of Kypris [= Aphrodite], |₃₂ since she loved [*erân*] a love [*erōs*], a passionate love, a love alien to the population [*ek-dēmos*]. In compensation for [*epi*] Hippolytus |₃₃—she gave that name, which will last for all time to come—that is why, she said, the goddess has been installed there.

Euripides *Hippolytus* 29–33*

20§12. Viewing these lines in Text C together with the immediately preceding lines 24–28 in Text B, we can see that the reference to Phaedra's falling in love with Hippolytus in Athens is really a cross-reference to the lost *Hippolytus*. In the complex wording of Text C as I just quoted it, the persona of Aphrodite herself narrates how the lovesick young queen Phaedra established a *nāos* or 'shrine' (31) in honor of the goddess before departing from Athens and journeying to Trozen, never again returning to Athens. The details about the establishment of the shrine of Aphrodite in Athens must have derived from the lost *Hippolytus*, since, as I already noted, Athens was the dramatic setting for Phaedra's

---

* |₂₉ καὶ πρὶν μὲν ἐλθεῖν τήνδε γῆν Τροζηνίαν, |₃₀ πέτραν παρ᾽ αὐτὴν Παλλάδος, κατόψιον |₃₁ γῆς τῆσδε, ναὸν Κύπριδος ἐγκαθείσατο, |₃₂ ἐρῶσ᾽ ἔρωτ᾽ ἔκδημον, Ἱππολύτῳ δ᾽ ἔπι |₃₃ τὸ λοιπὸν ὠνόμαζεν ἱδρῦσθαι θεάν. At line 33, I retain the reading ὠνόμαζεν as transmitted by the medieval manuscripts. So I do not follow the emendation ὀνομάσουσιν, which is accepted by most editors, including Barrett 1964:161–162. While I disagree with Barrett about the emendation, I agree with him about his interpretation of *onomazein* in the sense of 'give X the name Y, saying that . . . '.

death in that other tragedy. Only the detail about the departure of Phaedra from Athens belongs to the present tragedy, which relocates her suicide from Athens to Trozen.

20§13. I will now start to examine more closely the details we find in Text C about the story of Hippolytus in Athens—and about the myths and rituals that are linked to it. The *nāos* or 'shrine' (31) of Aphrodite in Athens, as the goddess says, is located 'on the side of the Rock of Pallas' (30). The 'Rock' is the Athenian Acropolis, which was sacred primarily to Pallas Athena. Where the wording describes the establishment of this shrine of Aphrodite at the initiative of Phaedra, the goddess refers to herself ostentatiously in the third person as the divinity who has been 'installed' there (33).

20§14. In this same Text C, the wording of Aphrodite quotes the expression *epi Hippolutōi,* or 'in compensation for Hippolytus' (32). I say that Aphrodite is engaging in an act of *quotation* here because this expression *epi Hippolutōi* is actually part of the traditional nomenclature for a historically attested *nāos* or 'shrine', sacred to Aphrodite, which was located on the south slope of the Athenian Acropolis. According to the Athenian version of the myth of Hippolytus, it was this shrine that Phaedra established *epi Hippolutōi,* that is, 'in compensation for Hippolytus'. And the same expression *epi Hippolutōi* is actually attested in an Athenian inscription dated to 429/8 BCE or thereabouts, where we read ... αφροδ]ιτες ε | [πι ιπ]πολυτο, '. . . of Aphrodite, [in the place] for [*epi*] Hippolytus' (*IG* I3 310.233–234). In another Athenian inscription, dated to 426/5 BCE, we read αφροδιτες εν hιππολυ[τειοι . . ., 'of Aphrodite, in the precinct of Hippolytus [= the *Hippoluteion*] . . .' (*IG* I3 369.66). Both of these inscriptions are referring to Aphrodite as she was actually worshipped in her shrine located on the south slope of the Acropolis. Further, as we see from the contexts of these and other inscriptions, there was a hero cult of Hippolytus within the precinct or sacred space that contained the shrine of Aphrodite, and the name of this precinct, as we see in the second of the two inscriptions I just cited, was the *Hippoluteion.** So the cult of the hero Hippolytus was the sacred framework for the cult of the goddess Aphrodite in her shrine, which was located inside the hero's precinct. In the course of his tour of important sights to be seen in Athens, Pausanias (1.22.1) took note of this precinct of Hippolytus, observing that he saw there a *mnēma* or 'memorial marker' that had been built for the hero.

* Barrett 1964:5.

20§15. I have saved for this moment what I think is the most important fact about the expression *epi Hippolutōi*, 'in compensation for Hippolytus', as we have seen it attested in the *Hippolytus* of Euripides and in one of the two Athenian inscriptions I have just mentioned. The fact is, even the syntax of this expression shows that Hippolytus was a cult hero in Athens. We have already seen other contexts in which the syntactical combination of the preposition *epi* with a hero's name in the dative case indicates the historical existence of a hero cult that was meant to be an eternally recycled compensation for a given hero's death (8§19, 8a§10, 11§8).

Hippolytus as a Cult Hero in Trozen

20§16. In the same context in which Pausanias (1.22.1) remarks that he saw a *mnēma* or 'memorial marker' of the hero Hippolytus in Athens, he goes on to say (1.22.2) that there is 'also' a *taphos* or 'tomb' of this hero in Trozen. Pausanias goes out of his way to emphasize that this relatively small city, located at the southeast corner of the Peloponnese and about thirty miles across the sea from Peiraieus, the main harbor of Athens, is known for a different set of myths and rituals concerning Hippolytus. According to the traditions that are local to Trozen, the first time that Phaedra laid eyes on Hippolytus was in Trozen, not in Athens. Pausanias makes this detail quite explicit: καὶ Φαίδρα πρώτη ἐνταῦθα εἶδεν Ἱππόλυτον, 'it was first here that Phaedra saw Hippolytus' (1.22.2).

20§17. In the same context, Pausanias (1.22.2) reports another detail that is local to Trozen. This detail comes from an aetiological myth explaining why one particular myrtle bush that Pausanias saw in Trozen showed holes evenly distributed all over all its leaves: as our traveler retells the local traditional story, these leaves originally did not have holes in them, but then, once upon a time, Phaedra experienced such a 'saturation of passion' or *asē* in her irrational love for Hippolytus that she took out a *peronē* or 'pin' that was holding up her hair and started to prick holes into every single leaf of that myrtle bush. Only at a later point in the reportage of Pausanias, however, do we see the fuller significance of this aetiology explaining why the holes in the leaves of the myrtle bush are really pinpricks originating from the heroic age, and now, in my own eagerness, I will immediately shift ahead to that later point. The context is most suggestive. Pausanias is in the middle of describing a place in central Trozen that features a *nāos* or 'shrine' of Aphrodite:

HOUR 20 TEXT D

|₂.₃₂.₃ Along the other part of the enclosure [*peribolos*] is a racecourse [*stadion*] that is named after Hippolytus. And there is also a shrine [*nāos*] situated on a slope overlooking it [= the racecourse], and this shrine is sacred to Aphrodite *kataskopiā*, 'the one who is looking down from on high'. She is called that because it was from this place, when Hippolytus was once upon a time exercising naked, that Phaedra took just one look at him, looking down from where she was, and right away she became afflicted with passionate love [*erân*]. It was also at this same place where the myrtle tree was, I mean, the one I wrote about earlier [= 1.22.2]—the one with leaves that had holes pricked into them. It happened when Phaedra, at a total loss about what to do, and not finding any remedy that could alleviate her passionate love [*erōs*], mutilated the leaves of the myrtle bush. |₂.₃₂.₄ And there is also a tomb [*taphos*] of Phaedra there, and it is not far away from the memorial marker [*mnēma*] of Hippolytus. That marker in turn has been built not far away from the myrtle bush.

Pausanias 2.32.3–4*

20§18. So this myrtle bush is a most visible marker of local Trozenian traditions about both Hippolytus and Phaedra. We have already seen in Hour 14§29 the erotic symbolism of myrtle flowers, and we now see that such symbolism is localized in Trozen by way of associating the myrtle bush of Phaedra with her tomb—as also with the tomb of Hippolytus. These two tombs were contained within an overall *peribolos* or 'enclosure', as we have just seen from the description given by Pausanias, who at an earlier point of his description actually equates this enclosure with the overall *temenos* or 'sacred space' of Hippolytus:

HOUR 20 TEXT E

|₂.₃₂.₁ Hippolytus son of Theseus has a most prominent sacred space [*temenos*] set aside for him [in Trozen]. And there is a shrine [*nāos*]

---

* |₂.₃₂.₃ κατὰ δὲ τὸ ἕτερον τοῦ περιβόλου μέρος στάδιόν ἐστιν Ἱππολύτου καλούμενον καὶ ναὸς ὑπὲρ αὐτοῦ Ἀφροδίτης Κατασκοπίας· αὐτόθεν γάρ, ὁπότε γυμνάζοιτο ὁ Ἱππόλυτος, ἀπέβλεπεν ἐς αὐτὸν ἐρῶσα ἡ Φαίδρα. ἐνταῦθα ἔτι πεφύκει ἡ μυρσίνη, τὰ φύλλα ὡς καὶ πρότερον ἔγραψα ἔχουσα τετρυπημένα· καὶ ἡνίκα ἠπορεῖτο ἡ Φαίδρα καὶ ῥᾳστώνην τῷ ἔρωτι οὐδεμίαν εὕρισκεν, ἐς ταύτης τὰ φύλλα ἐσιναμώρει τῆς μυρσίνης. |₂.₃₂.₄ ἔστι δὲ καὶ τάφος Φαίδρας, ἀπέχει δὲ οὐ πολὺ τοῦ Ἱππολύτου μνήματος· τὸ δὲ οὐ πόρρω κέχωσται τῆς μυρσίνης.

inside this space, with an archaic statue [inside it]. They say that Diomedes made these things and, on top of that, that he was the first person to make sacrifice [*thuein*] to Hippolytus. The people of Trozen have a priest of Hippolytus, and this priest is consecrated [*hieroûsthai*] as a priest for the entire duration of his life. There are sacrifices [*thusiai*] that take place at a yearly festival, and among the ritual actions that the people do [*drân*], I describe this event that takes place [at the festival]: each and every virgin girl [*parthenos*] in the community cuts off a lock of her hair [*plokamos*] for him [= Hippolytus] before she gets married, and, having cut it off, each girl ceremonially carries the lock to the shrine [*nāos*] and deposits it there as a dedicatory offering. The people [of Trozen] wish that he [= Hippolytus] had not died when he was dragged by the horses drawing his chariot, and they do not show his tomb [*taphos*], even though they know where it is. As for the constellation in the heavens that is called the Charioteer [*hēniokhos*], they [= the people of Trozen] have a customary way of thinking [*nomizein*] that this one [*houtos* = the Charioteer] is that one [*ekeinos*], Hippolytus, who has this [*hautē*] honor [*tīmē*] from the gods. |₂.₃₂.₂ Inside this [*houtos*] enclosure [*peribolos*] is also the shrine [*nāos*] of Apollo the *Epibatērios* ['the one who steps on'—either on the platform of a chariot or on board a ship], established by Diomedes as a votive offering because he had escaped the seastorm inflicted on the Hellenes while they were trying to get back home safely after Ilion [= Troy].

Pausanias 2.32.1–2*

20§19. As we see from the wording of this description by Pausanias, the *temenos* or 'sacred precinct' of Hippolytus that is mentioned at the beginning of Text E here (2.32.1) is the same thing as the overall *peribolos* or 'enclosure' mentioned at the end of this same Text E (2.32.2). We can also see from this wording

* |₂.₃₂.₁ Ἱππολύτῳ δὲ τῷ Θησέως τέμενός τε ἐπιφανέστατον ἀνεῖται καὶ ναὸς ἐν αὐτῷ καὶ ἄγαλμά ἐστιν ἀρχαῖον. ταῦτα μὲν Διομήδην λέγουσι ποιῆσαι καὶ προσέτι θῦσαι τῷ Ἱππολύτῳ πρῶτον· Τροιζηνίοις δὲ ἱερεὺς μέν ἐστιν Ἱππολύτου τὸν χρόνον τοῦ βίου πάντα ἱερώμενος καὶ θυσίαι καθεστήκασιν ἐπέτειοι, δρῶσι δὲ καὶ ἄλλο τοιόνδε· ἑκάστη παρθένος πλόκαμον ἀποκείρεταί οἱ πρὸ γάμου, κειραμένη δὲ ἀνέθηκεν ἐς τὸν ναὸν φέρουσα. ἀποθανεῖν δὲ αὐτὸν οὐκ ἐθέλουσι συρέντα ὑπὸ τῶν ἵππων οὐδὲ τὸν τάφον ἀποφαίνουσιν εἰδότες· τὸν δὲ ἐν οὐρανῷ καλούμενον ἡνίοχον, τοῦτον εἶναι νομίζουσιν ἐκεῖνον Ἱππόλυτον τιμὴν παρὰ θεῶν ταύτην ἔχοντα. |₂.₃₂.₂ τούτου δὲ ἐντὸς τοῦ περιβόλου ναός ἐστιν Ἀπόλλωνος Ἐπιβατηρίου, Διομήδους ἀνάθημα ἐκφυγόντος τὸν χειμῶνα ὃς τοῖς Ἕλλησιν ἐπεγένετο ἀπὸ Ἰλίου κομιζομένοις.

of Pausanias that the *peribolos* he mentions here at the end of Text E (2.32.2) is the same thing as the *peribolos* he mentions at the beginning of Text D (2.32.3), so that the entire enclosure is the same thing as the *temenos* or 'sacred space' of Hippolytus mentioned at the beginning of Text E (2.32.1). So, practically, all the sacred sites that are inventoried by Pausanias in both Texts D and E belong to the overall *temenos* or 'sacred space' of Hippolytus.

20§20. Among the sites contained by the *temenos* or 'sacred space' of Hippolytus is a *nāos* or 'shrine' that belongs to Aphrodite *kataskopiā*, 'the one who is looking down from on high', as we saw in Text D, Pausanias 2.32.3. This stance of the goddess of love and sexuality is duplicated by the stance of the beautiful mortal Phaedra when she herself was 'looking down' from her vantage point on high, next to the myrtle bush, and saw Hippolytus exercising naked.

20§21. This same *nāos* or 'shrine' in Trozen belongs not only to Aphrodite but also to Hippolytus himself, as we saw not once but twice in Text E. Similarly in the myth-ritual complex of Hippolytus in Athens, as we saw in Text C when we were reading lines 31–32 of the *Hippolytus* of Euripides, there is a *nāos* or 'shrine' of Aphrodite, and the goddess herself says that this *nāos* was established *epi Hippolutōi* or 'in compensation for Hippolytus'. Retrospectively, what is being compensated here is the death of the hero, caused by his antagonism with Aphrodite. And, as I already argued in §§14–15, this expression *epi Hippolutōi* or 'in compensation for Hippolytus' indicates the existence of a hero cult of Hippolytus, anchored in the same place where the *nāos* or 'shrine' of Aphrodite is located. So in both the Athenian and the Trozenian evidence, we see a pattern of coexistence or symbiosis between Aphrodite and Hippolytus inside a ritual space that corresponds to the myth about their mutual antagonism. For other examples of such a symbiosis linking a divinity and a hero in ritual, correlated with a pattern of antagonism that links them in myth, I refer back to Hour 11§§45, 51–52, 56, and Hour 12§21.

Comparing the Trozenian and the Athenian Versions of the Hippolytus Tradition

20§22. The striking parallelism we have just seen between the Trozenian and the Athenian versions of the Hippolytus tradition does not mean that the Athenian version, which is less rich in detail, was merely a borrowing from the Trozenian version. In making this point, I am following a general methodology that I have developed over the years while analyzing the comparative evidence of myths and rituals.* Applying this methodology, I now argue that the points of comparison we see in the Hippolytus traditions of Trozen and Athens are primarily a matter of common inheritance. Granted, we can find examples where the Athenian version of the Hippolytus tradition involves borrowings from the Trozenian version, but I argue that such examples are secondary. In other words, the parallelisms we see in the Trozenian and Athenian traditions concerning Hippolytus are for the most part cognate features that survive independent of each other. Even if the surviving features of Hippolytus in Athens may at first seem less compelling than what we see in Trozen, they are still important pieces of evidence for reconstructing the myths and rituals concerning this hero.

20§23. Pursuing this argument, I now take a second look at the relationship between the shrine of Aphrodite and the precinct of Hippolytus in Athens. The wording that expresses this relationship, *epi Hippolutōi*, or 'in compensation for Hippolytus', is surely independent of what we see in the Trozenian tradition, where the relationship between the shrine of Aphrodite and the precinct of Hippolytus is expressed differently—by way of the epithet *kataskopiā*, 'the one who is looking down from on high'.

20§24. This line of argumentation cannot be blunted even if we concede that the overall myth of Hippolytus was to some degree appropriated by the state of Athens, which had reshaped the figure of Theseus, father of Hippolytus, as an idealized hero-king of Athens. Such an idealization is clearly at work in the *Oedipus at Colonus* of Sophocles, for example. In that drama, as we saw in Hour 18§26, Theseus is pictured as a prototype of the Athenian democracy of the fifth century BCE. We may also concede that such a prominent status for Theseus in Athens cannot be reconstructed much farther back in time than the sixth century BCE.† And we may even concede that Theseus too, like Hippolytus, was a figure deeply rooted in the myths and rituals of Trozen: for example, it is universally acknowledged that Theseus was born in Trozen, and that his mother was Aithra, daughter of the king of Trozen, Pittheus (as we see, for example, in lines 207–209 of the *Herakleidai* of Euripides). But I maintain that the rootedness of Theseus in the local mythmaking traditions of Trozen cannot justify the inference that this hero was simply appropriated from there into Athenian mythmaking. And my point remains that the parallelisms we find in the Troze-

---

* I offer an introduction to this methodology, giving many examples, in Nagy 2011a.

† On this chronology, see Barrett 1964:2.

nian and Athenian versions of myths concerning both Hippolytus and Theseus indicate mostly cognate rather than borrowed features.

Two Conventional Patterns of Thinking about Hippolytus as a Cult Hero in Trozen

20§25. That said, I return to the testimony of Pausanias concerning the hero cult of Hippolytus in Trozen. In Text E, which I have already quoted, Pausanias accentuates two conventional patterns of thinking about this cult hero:

- First, Pausanias notes the mysticism surrounding the actual location of the tomb where Hippolytus is buried in Trozen. As we saw in Text E, Pausanias 2.32.1, the people of Trozen 'do not show his tomb [taphos], even though they know where it is'. We have already seen in Hour 18§§36–38 and 45–49 a comparable mentality of mysticism with regard to the tomb of Oedipus at Colonus. It can be said in general that cult heroes attract a variety of ritualized gestures indicating that a reverential silence is required of those who are initiated into the mysteries of worshipping them.*
- Second, Pausanias notes the ideological denial of the death of Hippolytus. I have already quoted the relevant wording in text E, Pausanias 2.32.1, where it is said that 'the people [of Trozen] wish that he [= Hippolytus] had not died when he was dragged by the horses drawing his chariot'. The sanctioned wish-fulfillment, as we will now see, is the immortalization of Hippolytus as a cult hero. And, as we will also see, the idea of this cult hero's immortalization is expressed in mystical terms.

20§26. For the people of Trozen, one way to formulate the mystical immortalization of Hippolytus after his death was to picture the *tīmē* or 'honor' that he gets as a cult hero in the form of a *catasterism,* which is *the transformation of a mortal human into an immortal star or constellation that dwells in the heavens.* Such a catasterism of Hippolytus is evident in the wording I already quoted from Pausanias 2.32.1 in Text E: 'As for the constellation in the heavens that is called the Charioteer [hēniokhos], they, [= the people of Trozen] have a customary way of thinking [nomizein] that this one [houtos = the Charioteer] is that one [ekeinos], Hippolytus, who has this [hautē] honor [tīmē] from the gods'.

---

* HPC 184 = II§134. See also Brelich 1958:156–157.

The *houtos* or 'this one' who appears as the constellation of the *Hēniokhos* or 'Charioteer' in the starry skies at night (the Latin word for this constellation is *Auriga*, which likewise means 'Charioteer') is identical to the *ekeinos* or 'that one' who is Hippolytus, receiving 'this' (*hautē*) *tīmē* or 'honor' of hero cult in Trozen.

20§27. In my brief introduction to Greek tragedy, Part III (§10), I cited a most revealing observation made by Aristotle (*Poetics* 1448b17): he says that the formula *houtos ekeinos,* meaning 'this one is that one', is the essence of *mīmēsis* or 'representation', which is the mental process of identifying the representing *houtos* or 'this'—in the ritual of acting the drama—with the represented 'that' or *ekeinos* in the myth that is being acted out by the drama. And now we see the same formula in the case of Hippolytus, cult hero of Trozen: every time the constellation known as the *hēniokhos* or *Auriga* or Charioteer appears in the starry skies at night, this constellation re-enacts or even acts out the hero Hippolytus himself. So the *houtos* or 'this one', who is the Charioteer in the night sky, becomes identical to *ekeinos* or 'that one', who is the hero Hippolytus, prototypical charioteer of the Trozenians.

20§28. A comparable example is the hero Orion, a prototypical hunter, whose constellation in the heavens is mentioned in *Odyssey* v 121–124, a mystical passage referring to the antagonism between Orion and Artemis, the goddess who presides over the ritualized activity of hunting.* And I should add that Hippolytus himself is a prototypical hunter as well as a prototypical charioteer, as we will see presently. Moreover, not only is Hippolytus connected with a *nāos* or 'shrine' of Aphrodite in his own precinct, as we saw in Pausanias 2.32.1, quoted in Text E, but he is also said to have established a *nāos* or 'shrine' of Artemis elsewhere in Trozen:

HOUR 20 TEXT F

> Near the theater is a shrine [*nāos*] of Artemis of the Wolves [*Lukeia*], which was made for her by Hippolytus. With regard to the epithet 'of the Wolves', I received no information from the local guides [*ex-hēgētai*]. It seemed to me at the time that it might have to do with wolves that had been devastating the territory of the Trozenians and that had been killed by Hippolytus. Or the epithet 'of the Wolves' might

---

* For more on this passage in *Odyssey* v 121–124, see *GM* 207, 242–248, 251–253.

have applied to Artemis among the Amazons, since Hippolytus was related to them on his mother's side. Or again there might be some other explanation that I do not know.

Pausanias 2.31.4*

Hippolytus in Epidaurus

20§29. Another way to formulate the mystical immortalization of Hippolytus as a local cult hero was to picture a resurrection of his body through the agency of the hero Asklepios, son of Apollo. We see a retelling of such a myth at an earlier stage in the travels of Pausanias, when he visits the *peribolos* or 'precinct' of Asklepios on the outskirts of the city of Epidaurus:

HOUR 20 TEXT G

Inside the enclosure [*peribolos*] are slabs [*stēlai*]. There used to be many more of these in ancient times, but in my time there were only six surviving. On these slabs are inscriptions recording the names of men and women who were healed by Asklepios, including details about the kinds of illness experienced by each one of them—and about how each one of them was healed. And they are all written in the Dorian dialect. |_{2.27.4} Standing apart from these slabs is one particularly ancient one, which says that Hippolytus dedicated to the god [*theos*] forty horses. What the inscription on this slab says is in conformity with what is said by the people of Aricia: according to them, after Hippolytus died as a result of the curses [*ārai*] hurled at him by Theseus, Asklepios resurrected [*an-histanai*] him. And, after he [= Hippolytus] came back to life [*authis biōnai*], he decided not to grant forgiveness to his father [= Theseus]. Instead, showing contempt for the father's entreaties, he [= Hippolytus] went to Italy to dwell among the people of Aricia. He became king there, and he established a sacred space [*temenos*] for Artemis, where to this day, even in my time, there are athletic contests

---

* πλησίον δὲ τοῦ θεάτρου Λυκείας ναὸν Ἀρτέμιδος ἐποίησεν Ἱππόλυτος· ἐς δὲ τὴν ἐπίκλησιν οὐδὲν εἶχον πυθέσθαι παρὰ τῶν ἐξηγητῶν, ἀλλὰ ἢ λύκους ἐφαίνετό μοι τὴν Τροιζηνίαν λυμαινομένους ἐξελεῖν ὁ Ἱππόλυτος ἢ Ἀμαζόσι, παρ' ὧν τὰ πρὸς μητρὸς ἦν, ἐπίκλησις τῆς Ἀρτέμιδός ἐστιν αὕτη· εἴη δ' ἂν ἔτι καὶ ἄλλο οὐ γινωσκόμενον ὑπ' ἐμοῦ.

[āthla] featuring one-on-one combat [monomakhiā], and the winner is considered to be consecrated [hierâsthai] to the goddess [= Artemis].

Pausanias 2.27.3–4*

20§30. In this retelling of the Hippolytus myth, Asklepios as the son of Apollo possesses extraordinary skills as a physician, and he uses these skills to bring Hippolytus back to life after that hero dies in a chariot crash caused by the *ārai* or 'curses' hurled at him by Theseus. From another retelling of the myth, however, we learn that the resurrection of Hippolytus, engineered by the skills of Asklepios, was not only the result of his death: it was also the cause of another death. And the one whose death was caused by the resurrection of Hippolytus was Asklepios himself. As the story goes, Zeus incinerated Asklepios with his divine thunderbolt, and he did so precisely because this hero had used his extraordinary skills as a physician to resurrect Hippolytus after that hero's death (scholia for Pindar *Pythian* 3.54). This version of the myth seems to be quite ancient, datable at least as far back as the sixth century BCE.†

20§31. In the wording of Pausanias 2.27.4, as I quoted it in Text G, we see that Hippolytus had expressed his gratitude for his resurrection by making an offering of forty horses to Asklepios, who is described in this context as a *theos* or 'god'. In terms of traditional language used in referring to cult heroes, the title of 'god' is appropriate here because Asklepios too, like Hippolytus, is destined to be immortalized after his own death. As we last saw in Hour 18§43, heroes who die by the thunderbolt of Zeus are made eligible for immortalization after death.

20§32. The earliest attested phases of the cult of Asklepios, localized in Epidaurus, can be dated as far back as the sixth century BCE, and the cult then spread to places like Trozen and Athens in the fifth century.‡ By the time of Pausanias, in the second century CE, the cult had spread even farther, including

---

* στῆλαι δὲ εἱστήκεσαν ἐντὸς τοῦ περιβόλου τὸ μὲν ἀρχαῖον καὶ πλέονες, ἐπ' ἐμοῦ δὲ ἓξ λοιπαί· ταύταις ἐγγεγραμμένα καὶ ἀνδρῶν καὶ γυναικῶν ἐστιν ὀνόματα ἀκεσθέντων ὑπὸ τοῦ Ἀσκληπιοῦ, προσέτι δὲ καὶ νόσημα ὅ τι ἕκαστος ἐνόσησε καὶ ὅπως ἰάθη· γέγραπται δὲ φωνῇ τῇ Δωρίδι. |2.27.4 χωρὶς δὲ ἀπὸ τῶν ἄλλων ἐστὶν ἀρχαία στήλη· ἵππους δὲ Ἱππόλυτον ἀναθεῖναι τῷ θεῷ φησιν εἴκοσι. ταύτης τῆς στήλης τῷ ἐπιγράμματι ὁμολογοῦντα λέγουσιν Ἀρικιεῖς, ὡς τεθνεῶτα Ἱππόλυτον ἐκ τῶν Θησέως ἀρῶν ἀνέστησεν Ἀσκληπιός· ὁ δὲ ὡς αὖθις ἐβίω, οὐκ ἠξίου νέμειν τῷ πατρὶ συγγνώμην, ἀλλὰ ὑπεριδὼν τὰς δεήσεις ἐς Ἰταλίαν ἔρχεται παρὰ τοὺς Ἀρικιεῖς, καὶ ἐβασίλευσέ τε αὐτόθι καὶ ἀνῆκε τῇ Ἀρτέμιδι τέμενος, ἔνθα ἄχρι ἐμοῦ μονομαχίας ἆθλα ἦν καὶ ἱερᾶσθαι τῇ θεῷ τὸν νικῶντα.

† Barrett 1964:8 and n1. See also the MW collection of Hesiodic fragments: 50, 51, 53; also Philodemus *On Piety* 4901–4904 ed. Obbink 1996.

‡ Barrett 1964:5n4.

places like Pergamon, Smyrna, and Cyrene (2.26.8–9). Moreover, as time went by, "Asklepios seems to have made a habit of supplanting local heroes [who also had] healing powers."* And, in the process, Asklepios became less and less of a hero and more and more of a god. We have already seen this kind of historical process in Hour 15§33, where we considered the widespread worship of cult heroes like Amphiaraos, Trophōnios, and Protesilaos in the second century CE—which was the era of Pausanias himself. Similarly, by the time we reach this era, the cult of this Asklepios had become so widespread—and commensurately elevated—that people could think of him as a god who had always been a god. And that is precisely how Pausanias thought of Asklepios (2.26.10).

20§33. Although the myths and rituals that we have just examined concerning the special relationship of Hippolytus to Asklepios are localized not in Trozen but in nearby Epidaurus, there is reason to think that these myths and rituals apply to Trozen as well, since the cult of Asklepios is strongly attested in Trozen as well as in Epidaurus. In fact, archaeologists have found that the precinct of Asklepios was actually embedded within the precinct of Hippolytus in Trozen.† Moreover, the myths and rituals concerning Asklepios in Trozen had become so tightly integrated with the myths and rituals of Hippolytus that it became a challenge for Pausanias even to distinguish between some of the visual representations of Asklepios and Hippolytus that he saw on display in that city—even though he claims to have the expertise to make such distinctions (2.32.4).

Euripides Recapitulates a Trozenian Ritual

20§34. I return here to the description of a ritual that we have already read in Pausanias 2.32.1, as quoted in Text E. This ritual, which was performed on the occasion of a seasonally recurring festival at Trozen, was linked with the *nāos* or 'shrine' that was sacred to both the hero Hippolytus and the goddess Aphrodite. Here I quote again the relevant wording:

HOUR 20 TEXT H (PART OF TEXT E)

There are sacrifices [*thusiai*] that take place at a yearly festival, and among the ritual actions that the people do [*drân*], I describe this event

---

* Barrett 1964:5.
† Barrett 1964:5n4.

that takes place [at the festival]: each and every virgin girl [*parthenos*] in the community cuts of a lock of her hair [*plokamos*] for him [= Hippolytus] before she gets married, and, having cut it off, each girl ceremonially carries the lock to the shrine [*nāos*] and deposits it there as a dedicatory offering.

Pausanias 2.32.1

20§35. Toward the end of the *Hippolytus* of Euripides, we find a passage that makes an explicit reference to the same ritual—as it already existed well over half a millennium earlier. As we are about to see, the speaker in this passage is the goddess Artemis, and she is addressing Hippolytus, who is going through his final agonizing moments of dying as a result of the horrific injuries he suffered when his chariot crashed—a fatal crash caused by the curses unjustly hurled at him by his father, Theseus. The goddess tells Hippolytus that he will have, after death, the *tīmai* or 'honors' of a cult hero, and that these honors will take the form of seasonally recurring choral lyric performances of unmarried girls who will cut their hair and then present severed locks of that hair to the hero as a compensation for his sufferings. And the wording of the prediction makes it clear that the ritual acts of cutting the hair and then presenting the severed locks of that hair to the hero in his shrine are part of an overall ritual activity of choral performance. Here, then, are the relevant words spoken by the goddess:

HOUR 20 TEXT I

|₁₄₂₃ To you, poor sufferer, in compensation for these bad things that have happened to you here, |₁₄₂₄ the greatest honors [*tīmai*] in the city [*polis*] of Trozen |₁₄₂₅ I will give to you: unwed girls before they get married |₁₄₂₆ will cut off their hair for you, and throughout the length of time [*aiōn*] |₁₄₂₇ you will harvest the very great sorrows [*penthos* plural] of their tears. |₁₄₂₈ And for all time there will be a thought that comes along with the songmaking directed at you by virgin girls, |₁₄₂₉ and it will be a troubled thought. The story and the names will not fall aside unremembered |₁₄₃₀—the story of the passionate love [*erōs*] of Phaedra for you. No, it will never be passed over in silence.

Euripides Hippolytus 1423–1430*

---

* |₁₄₂₃ σοὶ δ', ὦ ταλαίπωρ', ἀντὶ τῶνδε τῶν κακῶν |₁₄₂₄ τιμὰς μεγίστας ἐν πόλει Τροζηνίᾳ |₁₄₂₅ δώσω· κόραι γὰρ ἄζυγες γάμων πάρος |₁₄₂₆ κόμας κεροῦνταί σοι, δι' αἰῶνος μακροῦ |₁₄₂₇ πένθη μέγιστα

20§36. With these words, the entire myth concerning Hippolytus and Phaedra as dramatized in the *Hippolytus* of Euripides is transformed into an aetiology of the seasonally recurring ritual event that is being described. Euripides is well known for making the literary gesture of equating the myths that he dramatizes with local myths that function as aetiologies for rituals that are actually attested in the traditions of various locales.* In using the term *aetiology* here, I return to my original working definition in Hour 7a§15: *an aetiology is a myth that motivates an institutional reality, especially a ritual.*

20§37. As I have argued in my earlier work on this passage in Euripides *Hippolytus* 1423–1430, as quoted here in Text I, the performing of the song about Hippolytus and Phaedra by unmarried girls is a ritual of female initiation, formalized as choral singing and dancing that takes place at a seasonally recurring festival in the city of Trozen. And, in synchronization with this choral singing and dancing, local girls cut their hair and then present severed locks of that hair to Hippolytus, lamenting the death of this beautiful hero as a formal sign of their own coming of age.†

Love Song and Song of Laments

20§38. The myth about the death of Hippolytus and about the unrequited love of Phaedra will be perpetuated in choral singing and dancing, as we have just seen in Euripides *Hippolytus* 1423–1430, Text I. And the seasonally recurring performance by choruses of Trozenian girls is described here as a sad love song, 'a troubled thought that comes along with songmaking' (*mousopoios . . . merimna* 1428–1429).‡ But this love song is also a song of laments (*penthē* 1427). As I already noted in Hour 3§13, love songs can modulate into laments, just as laments can modulate into love songs. And I return to the question I asked back then in Hour 3: why should a traditional love song be sad the same way as a lament is sad? We can see the answer more clearly now, in the light of the myth about Hippolytus and Phaedra. And the answer is this: most traditional love songs are preoccupied with the themes of *unrequited love*. Also, in most song cultures, love songs about unrequited love are felt to be deeply erotic.

δακρύων καρπουμένῳ· |₁₄₂₈ ἀεὶ δὲ μουσοποιὸς ἐς σὲ παρθένων |₁₄₂₉ ἔσται μέριμνα, κοὐκ ἀνώνυμος πεσὼν |₁₄₃₀ ἔρως ὁ Φαίδρας ἐς σὲ σιγηθήσεται.

† Barrett 1964:158–159, with a set of examples from other dramas of Euripides.

‡ PP 95.

§ In Bacchylides 19.11, the same noun *merimna*, which I translate here as 'a troubling thought', refers to the thought-processes of the poet himself as he is pictured composing his song. On *merimna* as a song that is 'on one's mind' see PH 284 and 287 = 10§16n42 and 10§20n63.

20§39. For purposes of comparison, I cite here some empirical observations made by the folklorist Vladimir Propp about love-songs in Russian folk traditions.* He notes that "the songs are about unhappy love more often than about happy love."† He goes on to note that traditional Russian women's songs at weddings, including the bride's songs, include instances of formal lamentation;‡ in fact, "the wailing of the bride is one of the richest and artistically complete forms of ancient peasant poetry."§ Given that weddings are elaborate rites of passage in Russian folk traditions and that "many wedding songs were never performed outside the wedding ritual,"** we stand to gain a wealth of comparative insights from detailed descriptions of women's songmaking in the context of weddings, especially in view of Propp's conclusion that traditional Russian wedding songs "are so closely related to love and family lyrics that they cannot be studied outside the framework of women's folk lyrics in general."†† Of special interest for the study of archaic Greek choral traditions is the Russian tradition of the ritual unplaiting of the maiden's braid as a preparation for the wedding, where the unplaiting is accompanied by songmaking, and where the bride's girlfriends sing *in the name of the bride*.‡‡

20§40. There are further points of comparison to be found in modern Russian folk lyric, and some of these points prove to be most valuable for understanding what exactly is "choral" about ancient Greek choral lyric.§§ For example, we may note in Russian folk lyric a performative distinction between singing combined with dance and singing without dancing.*** And here is another example: in certain forms of song-and-dance in Russian folk lyric, it is presupposed that one girl in a given performance will be selected, in the dynamic context of the actual performance, as better in beauty or skill than the other girls, so that the song becomes in effect *her* praise song by virtue of formally making an admission or acknowledgment of her poeticized superiority.††† We saw a comparable mentality in ancient Greek choral lyric poetry when we were reading the Maiden Song of Alcman in Hour 5§59.

* What follows in this paragraph is extracted from *PP* 94–95.
† See Propp 1961 [1975:13].
‡ Propp 1961 [1975:17–23].
§ Propp 1961 [1975:19–20].
** Propp 1961 [1975:18].
†† Propp 1961 [1975:18].
‡‡ Propp 1961 [1975:23].
§§ The rest of this paragraph follows closely what I wrote in *PP* 94–95n23. For more on Russian wedding songs, I cite the important new work of Levaniouk 2011.
*** Propp 1961 [1975:14].
††† Propp 1961 [1975:15].

The Trouble with Hippolytus

20§41. Here I return to the basic idea in Euripides' *Hippolytus* 1423–1430, Text I. The choral singing and dancing of unmarried girls, together with the gesture of offering locks of shorn hair to Hippolytus in his shrine, is an act of ritual that matches the myth about the death of this hero—and about the unrequited love of Phaedra. This myth, I have argued, is an aetiology of a ritual, and the ritual is in turn a re-enactment of the myth. And this ritual, I now argue further, is an initiation from one phase of life into another. The girls who are initiated by way of participating in the ritual are transformed into women who are now ready to get married. So now these girls can make a transition from a phase of virginity, as represented by the goddess Artemis, into a phase of heterosexuality, as represented by the goddess Aphrodite. In terms of the ritual, there should be no trouble for the female initiands in making a transition from Artemis to Aphrodite. In terms of the myth of Hippolytus and Phaedra, on the other hand, the transition is most troubled. And this troubled transition will cause troubled thinking even for the female initiands. As Artemis says to the dying Hippolytus, 'for all time there will be a thought [*merimna*] that comes along with the songmaking directed at you by virgin girls, | and it will be a troubled thought' (1428–1429). So what is the trouble with Hippolytus? The answer is, Hippolytus himself simply cannot make the transition from the phase of virginity into the phase of heterosexuality.

20§42. Whereas the transition from virginity into heterosexuality is facilitated in the ritual of initiation, leading to social equilibrium, this same transition is blocked in myth, leading to personal disequilibrium for the hero and, ultimately, to catastrophe. In the light of these observations, I now offer this formulation: *equilibrium in ritual is matched by disequilibrium in myth, and this disequilibrium leads to catastrophe for the hero.**

The Complementarity of Artemis and Aphrodite

20§43. Because Hippolytus cannot make a transition from the phase of virginity to the phase of heterosexuality, he must remain a devotee of Artemis while avoiding any devotion to Aphrodite. And he must remain an antagonist of Aphrodite in myth, while Aphrodite follows up on her own antagonism toward Hippolytus by becoming the ultimate cause of his violent death in a chariot crash—

---

* For an earlier attempt at such a formulation, see *GM* 4; see also Bershadsky 2013:27n97.

even if the immediate cause is a horrific bull that emerges from the sea, sent by the curses of Theseus to panic the speeding horses that draw the chariot of the hero. Nevertheless, the antagonism of Aphrodite toward Hippolytus in myth translates into a symbiosis of the goddess and hero inside the ritual complex of the precinct sacred to Hippolytus, which as we have seen actually encloses the shrine of Aphrodite herself. And this symbiosis, as we will now see, indicates a basic pattern of complementarity between Aphrodite and Artemis.

20§44. As I have already argued, the ritual that is described in *Hippolytus* 1423–1430 as quoted in Text I is an initiation from one phase of life into another. The girls who are initiated by way of participating in the ritual are transformed into women who are now ready to get married. And, as I also argued, these female initiands are making a transition from a phase of virginity, as represented by the goddess Artemis, into a phase of heterosexuality, as represented by the goddess Aphrodite. Moreover, as I argued already in Hour 5§111, the nuptial goddess Aphrodite and the prenuptial as well as postnuptial goddess Artemis reveal, as a pair, different phases of erotic engagement in the life cycle of a woman, determining when she is attainable—and when she is unattainable. The two goddesses are complementary in human life as controlled by ritual, even if they are at odds in the superhuman life of a hero like Hippolytus—a life that is controlled by myth.

From Native Trozenian Ritual to the Drama of Athenian State Theater

20§45. In my earlier work on the *Hippolytus* of Euripides, I argued that the choral lyric performances of real-life girls in the real-life community of Trozen were appropriated by this master poet and director in the creation of his own drama.* What these girls experienced as their real-life initiation by way of singing and dancing the death of Hippolytus and the unrequited love of Phaedra was thus translated into the stylized ritual experience of Athenian State Theater. In other words, the songs of initiation as performed at a seasonally recurring festival in Trozen were dramatically replayed as songs performed by a chorus of young men in the tragedy of Euripides.† And this chorus of young men, as they sang and danced the choral lyric songs of the *Hippolytus* in Athenian State Theater, would be re-enacting a chorus of young women in Trozen as they sang and danced their native songs of initiation.‡

* PP 95–96.
† PP 95.
‡ PP 96.

20§46. Such re-enactment is evident in the *parodos* or introductory choral performance of the *Hippolytus*. I quote here some of the wording, which shows that the content of what the chorus of singers and dancers is performing here could match the content of a corresponding chorus performing in Trozen:

HOUR 20 TEXT J

|₁₂₁₋₁₂₄ There is a rock that is said to drip fresh water from the stream of Okeanos, sending forth from the crags above a steady flow for us to scoop up in our jars. |₁₂₅ It was there that my friend [*philē*] was washing |₁₂₆ purple robes |₁₂₇ in the flowing stream, |₁₂₈ washing them, and then, on the face of a rock warmed |₁₂₉ by the kindly sunlight did she throw them. From there |₁₃₀ the rumor first came to me about the lady of the house, |₁₃₁₋₁₃₄ how she is wasting away on her sickbed, keeping herself indoors, and a thin veil shadows her blond head. . . . |₁₆₁ Often, in women's badly modulated [*dus-tropos*] |₁₆₂ tuning [*harmoniā*], a bad and |₁₆₃ wretched sort of helplessness [*amēkhaniā*] dwells, |₁₆₄ arising both from the pains of labor and from lack of sensibility [*aphrosunē*]. |₁₆₅ Right through my womb I once felt a rush of this |₁₆₆ burst of wind [*aurā*] here, and, calling upon the one who helps in the labor of childbirth, the one who is the sky-dweller, |₁₆₇ the one who has power over the arrows, I shouted out her name, |₁₆₈ Artemis, and she, very much sought after, always |₁₆₉ comes to me, if the gods are willing. |₁₇₀ But look, the aged Nurse before the palace doors |₁₇₁ is bringing this one [Phaedra] from the palace, |₁₇₂ and on her [= Phaedra's] brow a gloomy cloud gathers. |₁₇₃ To know what on earth is happening—my soul [*psūkhē*] passionately desires [*erâsthai*] to know this. |₁₇₄ Why has she become completely undone? |₁₇₅ Why has the complexion of the queen turned so strangely pale?

Euripides *Hippolytus* 121–134, 161–175*

---

* |₁₂₁₋₁₂₄ Ὠκεανοῦ τις ὕδωρ στάζουσα πέτρα λέγεται, βαπτὰν κάλπισι παγὰν ῥυτὰν προιεῖσα κρημνῶν. |₁₂₅ τόθι μοί τις ἦν φίλα |₁₂₆ πορφύρεα φάρεα |₁₂₇ ποταμίᾳ δρόσῳ |₁₂₈ τέγγουσα, θερμᾶς δ᾽ ἐπὶ νῶτα πέτρας |₁₂₉ εὐαλίου κατέβαλλ᾽· ὅθεν μοι |₁₃₀ πρῶτα φάτις ἦλθε δεσποίνας, |₁₃₁₋₁₃₄ τειρομέναν νοσερᾷ κοίτᾳ δέμας ἐντὸς ἔχειν οἴκων, λεπτὰ δὲ φάρη ξανθὰν κεφαλὰν σκιάζειν. . . . |₁₆₁ φιλεῖ δὲ τᾷ δυστρόπῳ γυναικῶν |₁₆₂ ἁρμονίᾳ κακὰ δύ|₁₆₃στανος ἀμηχανία συνοικεῖν |₁₆₄ ὠδίνων τε καὶ ἀφροσύνας. |₁₆₅ δι᾽ ἐμᾶς ᾖξέν ποτε νηδύος ἅ|₁₆₆δ᾽ αὔρα· τὰν δ᾽ εὔλοχον οὐρανίαν |₁₆₇ τόξων μεδέουσαν ἀύτευν |₁₆₈ Ἄρτεμιν, καί μοι πολυζήλωτος αἰεὶ |₁₆₉ σὺν θεοῖσι φοιτᾷ. |₁₇₀ ἀλλ᾽ ἥδε τροφὸς γεραιὰ πρὸ θυρῶν |₁₇₁ τήνδε κομίζουσ᾽ ἔξω μελάθρων. |₁₇₂ στυγνὸν δ᾽ ὀφρύων νέφος αὐξάνεται· |₁₇₃ τί ποτ᾽ ἐστὶ μαθεῖν ἔραται ψυχή, |₁₇₄ τί δεδήληται |₁₇₅ δέμας ἀλλόχροον βασιλείας.

20§47. It remains to be seen whether the choral performances at Trozen in the days of Euripides featured a full-scale dramatic re-enactment of the myth of Hippolytus and Phaedra, including actors as well as a chorus. If there were no actors, then the wording that starts at line 170 in the passage I just quoted would not be compatible with the singing and dancing performed by the female initiands of Trozen, since the wording here in the *Hippolytus* introduces a speaking actor, namely, the Nurse. But the wording that precedes line 170 could in any case be suitable for a choral performance featuring no actors.

20§48. A distinctly choral aspect of the wording I just quoted from the *Hippolytus* is the variability of references to women's experiences of the most intimate kind. Between lines 161 and 170, the collective voice of the chorus refers to the pains suffered by women at the moment of childbirth, and there may be an added reference to the pains of menstruation in the wording that I translate this way: 'right through my womb I once felt a rush of this | burst of wind [*aurā*] here'.* Whether or not the referent of the added reference is the experience of menstruation, the basic idea here is that the goddess Artemis controls all the functions of the uterus, and that the metaphor telling of an *aurā* or 'burst of wind' applies to these functions. I find it relevant to mention here the passages we have already seen in Hour 16 where the goddess Artemis is said to control the winds, as in Aeschylus *Agamemnon* 214–215 (**16§6**), 150 (**16§13**), and 1178–1182 (**16§37**).

20§49. Mention of the pains of labor in the choral passage of the *parodos* in the *Hippolytus* has led some interpreters to think that the chorus of this tragedy must be imagined as an ensemble of "young married women."† I disagree. In choral performances by women, as we have seen before, the experiences of life can vary from woman to woman. A striking example is the lament of Briseis for the death of Patroklos in the *Iliad* (XIX 287–300), along with the framing narrative concerning the antiphonal responses of the stylized chorus of women attending Briseis (XIX 301–302). As I noted in Hour **5§105**, this example re-enacts most accurately the morphology of a genuine choral lyric lament, indicating a wide variety of personal experiences that merge into the collective choral voice. In the *Hippolytus* of Euripides, we see a comparably wide variety of personal experiences expressed in another choral lyric song (third *stasimon*, 1102–1150),

---

* At a working session in Paris, dating back to January 1994 (noted in *PP* Preface p. x), the late Nicole Loraux and I discussed this choral wording of Euripides, and she mentioned to me the possibility that the expression I have highlighted here refers to menstruation.

† That is the wording of Barrett 1964:182.

and in that case the expressions seem typical of unmarried girls, not of ma-trons.*

Empathy for Female and Male Experiences

20§50. In the choral lyric passage we have just read, Text J, we saw at line 173 a most profound declaration of empathy: 'To know what on earth is happen-ing—my soul [*psūkhē*] passionately desires [*erâsthai*] to know this'. Once again I translate *psūkhē* as 'soul', as I did in Hour 19 Text B, where Oedipus at line 94 of the *Oedipus Tyrannus* speaks of the collective pain that he feels in his own *psūkhē* for the whole community of Thebes; likewise in Hour 19 Text E, Oedi-pus at line 64 says that his *psūkhē* mourns for the collective pain felt by every single person in the city. And now, in the passage I quoted from the *Hippolytus* of Euripides, Text J, we see that the collective *psūkhē* of the chorus desires pas-sionately to know the troubled thinking of one single person, Phaedra.

20§51. The empathy that is felt by the chorus for the experiences of Phaedra in Text J is an empathy for female experiences. Without knowing what is wrong with Phaedra, the chorus projects its own female experiences, focusing on pains in the uterus. Presiding over these pains is the goddess Artemis.

20§52. By contrast, as I will now show, Phaedra feels an empathy for the ex-periences of Hippolytus, which are male experiences. Her wandering mind fo-cuses on the hero's two primary activities—now on one and then on the other:

1. Hippolytus is hunting in the mountainous region of Trozen.
2. Hippolytus is performing athletic exercises in the seacoast region of Trozen. In particular, Hippolytus is racing his chariot on the sands of a long beach that extends along a lagoon next to the seacoast of Trozen.

Presiding over both these activities, as we will see, is the goddess Artemis. Her role, as we will also see, is essential. Here, then, is the relevant passage, where we join an ongoing dialogue between Phaedra and her Nurse:

HOUR 20 TEXT K

|198 {Phaedra:} Lift my body, keep my head up. |199 The fastenings [*sun-desma*] of my dear [*phila*] limbs [*melea*] have come apart [*le-lū-tai*].

---

* Barrett 1964:375 resorts to special pleading with reference to lines 1142–1150 of the *Hippolytus*: "The language is as suitable on the lips of young matrons as of girls."

|₂₀₀ Hold on to my shapely arms, attendants. |₂₀₁ My hair all done up on top of my head is a heavy load to bear. |₂₀₂ Take out my hair pinnings, let the curls of my hair cascade over my shoulders. . . . |₂₀₈ I only wish I could, from a dewy spring, |₂₀₉ scoop up a drink of pure water, |₂₁₀ and, lying down beneath the poplars in a grassy |₂₁₁ meadow [leimōn], I could find relief. . . . |₂₁₅ Take me to the mountains—I will go to the woods, |₂₁₆ to the pine trees, where the beast-killing |₂₁₇ hounds track their prey, |₂₁₈ getting closer and closer to the dappled deer. |₂₁₉ I swear by the gods, I have a passionate desire [erâsthai] to give a hunter's shout to the hounds, |₂₂₀ and, with my blond hair and all, to throw |₂₂₁ a Thessalian javelin, holding the barbed |₂₂₂ dart in my hand.

|₂₂₃ {Nurse:} Why on earth, my child, are you sick at heart about these things? |₂₂₄ Why is the hunt your concern [meletē]? |₂₂₅ And why do you feel a passionate desire [erâsthai] for streams flowing from craggy heights |₂₂₆ when nearby, next to these towers, there is a moist |₂₂₇ hillside with a fountain? You could get your drink from here.

|₂₂₈ {Phaedra:} My lady Artemis! You who preside over the lagoon by the sea! |₂₂₉ You are where the place is for exercising, and it thunders with horses' hooves! |₂₃₀ Oh, if only I could be there, on your grounds, |₂₃₁ masterfully driving Venetian horses!

|₂₃₂ {Nurse:} Why in your madness have you hurled out of your mouth this wording here? |₂₃₃ One moment you were going up the mountain to hunt |₂₃₄—you were getting all set, in your longing [pothos], to do that, and then, the next moment, you were heading for the beach |₂₃₅ sheltered from the splashing waves, in your passionate desire [erâsthai] for the horses. |₂₃₆ These things are worth a lot of consultation with seers: |₂₃₇ which one of the gods is steering you off course |₂₃₈ and deflects your thinking [phrenes], child?

Euripides Hippolytus 198–202, 208–211, 215–238*

* |₁₉₈ {Φα.} αἴρετέ μου δέμας, ὀρθοῦτε κάρα· |₁₉₉ λέλυμαι μελέων σύνδεσμα φίλων. |₂₀₀ λάβετ᾽ εὐπήχεις χεῖρας, πρόπολοι. |₂₀₁ βαρύ μοι κεφαλῆς ἐπίκρανον ἔχειν· |₂₀₂ ἄφελ᾽, ἀμπέτασον βόστρυχον ὤμοις. . . . |₂₀₈ πῶς ἂν δροσερᾶς ἀπὸ κρηνῖδος |₂₀₉ καθαρῶν ὑδάτων πῶμ᾽ ἀρυσαίμαν, |₂₁₀ ὑπό τ᾽ αἰγείροις ἔν τε κομήτῃ |₂₁₁ λειμῶνι κλιθεῖσ᾽ ἀναπαυσαίμαν; . . . |₂₁₅ πέμπετέ μ᾽ εἰς ὄρος· εἶμι πρὸς ὕλαν |₂₁₆ καὶ παρὰ πεύκας, ἵνα θηροφόνοι |₂₁₇ στείβουσι κύνες |₂₁₈ βαλιαῖς ἐλάφοις ἐγχριμπτόμεναι. |₂₁₉ πρὸς θεῶν· ἔραμαι κυσὶ θωΰξαι |₂₂₀ καὶ παρὰ χαίταν ξανθὰν ῥῖψαι |₂₂₁ Θεσσαλὸν ὅρπακ᾽, ἐπίλογχον ἔχουσ᾽ |₂₂₂ ἐν χειρὶ βέλος. |₂₂₃ {Τρ.} τί ποτ᾽, ὦ τέκνον, τάδε κηραίνεις; |₂₂₄ τί κυνηγεσίων καὶ σοὶ μελέτη; |₂₂₅ τί δὲ κρηναίων νασμῶν ἔρασαι; |₂₂₆ πάρα γὰρ δροσερὰ πύργοις συνεχὴς |₂₂₇ κλειτύς, ὅθεν σοι πῶμα γένοιτ᾽ ἄν. |₂₂₈ {Φα.} δέσποιν᾽ ἁλίας Ἄρτεμι Λίμνας |₂₂₉ καὶ γυμνασίων τῶν ἱπποκρότων, |₂₃₀ εἴθε γενοίμαν ἐν σοῖς δαπέδοις |₂₃₁ πώλους Ἐνετὰς δαμαλιζομένα. |₂₃₂ {Τρ.} τί τόδ᾽ αὖ παράφρων ἔρριψας ἔπος; |₂₃₃ νῦν δὴ μὲν

20§53. From the wording of this exchange between Phaedra and her Nurse in Text K, it is revealed that the female experiences that we saw being projected through the feelings of the female chorus in Text J have come true in the feelings of Phaedra herself. In lines 161–168 of Text J, we saw a metaphor that connects a woman whose uterus is in pain and a stringed instrument that is out of tune—as when the *harmoniā* (162) or 'accordatura' or 'tuning' of a lyre is *dus-tropos* (161), 'having bad modulations [*tropoi*]'.* So also in line 199 of Text K, the words of Phaedra herself declare: 'the fastenings [*sun-desma*] of my dear [*phila*] limbs [*melea*] have come apart'. The form *melea* here is the plural of the word *melos*, which is in fact not one word but two. One of these two words means 'limb' but the other means 'tune'. So there is another possible meaning that comes out of Phaedra's wording, and it is this: 'the fastenings [*sun-desma*] of my dear [*phila*] tunes [*melea*] are unstrung'—as if the woman were a stringed instrument that had lost its *harmoniā* or 'tuning' (162). Phaedra is now like a lyre that is out of tune, since the tuning is *dus-tropos* or 'badly modulated' (161). So Phaedra herself is out of tune. A more literal translation of her wording would be: 'I have come apart [*le-lū-mai*] in all the places where the tunes [*melea*] dear [*phila*] to me are connected with each together'—or '. . . where my dear [*phila*] limbs [*melea*] are connected with each together'. These two meanings can even come together in Text J when the members of the chorus are dancing with their own 'dear' limbs while singing their feelings of disconnectedness. And just as the collectivized female voice of the chorus of women in Text J feels an *amēkhaniā* or 'helplessness' (163), shouting out the name of Artemis in hopes of relief (167–168), so also Phaedra in Text K shouts out the name of the goddess (228–230) in her own moment of utter helplessness.

20§54. The troubled thinking that a woman experiences is blamed on her uterus in the choral song of Text J (165), but there is no such direct blaming in the words uttered by Phaedra herself in Text K. She does not understand the cause of her troubled thinking—why her mind wanders. But her own wording, without her intending it, does show the cause. She is 'out of tune', and that is a metaphorical way of blaming the uterus after all. In the words of the chorus, as quoted in Text J, a woman's bad tuning is caused by an inner *amēkhaniā* or 'helplessness' (163), which is in turn caused simultaneously by *ōdīnes* or 'pains of labor' and by *aphrosunē* or 'lack of sensibility' (164). So a 'lack of sensibility' is

---

ὅρος βᾶσ' ἐπὶ θήρας |₂₃₄ πόθον ἐστέλλου, νῦν δ' αὖ ψαμάθοις |₂₃₅ ἐπ' ἀκυμάντοις πώλων ἔρασαι. |₂₃₆ τάδε μαντείας ἄξια πολλῆς, |₂₃₇ ὅστις σε θεῶν ἀνασειράζει |₂₃₈ καὶ παρακόπτει φρένας, ὦ παῖ.

* I analyze in *PP* 57–58 the Greek word *tropos* in the musical sense of 'modulation'.

supposedly just like a pain in the uterus, which a woman can feel rushing through her insides like a sudden burst of wind (165–166).

20§55. Such disturbingly troubled thinking, which is surely troubling even for modern readers, emerges from the empathy felt by the chorus for the female experiences of Phaedra. But then Phaedra herself shows the empathy she feels for the male experiences of the one with whom she is madly in love. As we have seen in Text K, the wandering mind of Phaedra conceives a passionate desire to be a hunter just like Hippolytus (215–222, 233–234) and, the next moment, to be an athlete just like Hippolytus (228–230, 234–235).

20§56. Artemis presides over these male experiences of Hippolytus just as surely as she presides over the female experiences of Phaedra. After all, Artemis is the goddess of the hunt, and she is also the goddess who presides over the athletic exercises of Hippolytus. So Phaedra is really at one with Artemis when this troubled woman lets her mind wander off—first to the mountains where Hippolytus would do his hunting (215–222, 233–234) and then to the sheltered long beach where Hippolytus would speed around in his racing chariot (228–230, 234–235).

20§57. I focus for a minute here on a most telling detail, already quoted in Text J, about the passionate desire of Phaedra for the hunt. Here is how she puts it: 'I swear by the gods, I have a passionate desire [erâsthai] to give a hunter's shout to the hounds, | and, with my blond hair and all (in the background), to throw |₂₂₁ a Thessalian javelin, holding (in the foreground) the barbed |₂₂₂ dart in my hand' (219–222). In repeating my translation here, I have now added within parentheses the cues "in the background" and "in the foreground." That is because, in her painterly imagination, Phaedra even poses here in the act of hurling a hunting javelin that is foregrounded against the golden background of her blond hair flowing in the wind. Holding this pose, Phaedra can become the very image of Artemis.

20§58. The tragedy in all this is that Artemis, who presides over both the male experiences of Hippolytus and the female experiences of Phaedra, makes it impossible for a woman like Phaedra to share in the male experiences that Artemis reserves for Hippolytus. Only Aphrodite allows female and male experiences to merge, but that merger can happen only in the adult world of heterosexuality, not in the pre-adult world represented by Hippolytus. In the pre-adult world, activities like hunting and athletics can already become part of male experiences, but the experience of heterosexual relationships must wait until adulthood is reached.

20§59. Earlier in §44 and even earlier in Hour 5§111, I described Artemis as a prenuptial as well as a postnuptial goddess in comparison to Aphrodite as a nuptial goddess. My purpose was to highlight the complementarity of these goddesses in the lives of women. And by now we have seen the most obvious example of complementarity in the case of Artemis: she presides over a woman's uterus both before and after marriage, but the heterosexual experience of intercourse and becoming impregnated is reserved for Aphrodite. As for the lives of men, the complementarity of these two goddesses is less clearly defined. For example, although Artemis presides over the activities of hunting and athletics as ritualized preliminaries to adulthood, these activities are clearly not restricted to pre-adults. It is only in the case of mythological figures like Hippolytus that the linking of these activities with pre-adulthood is accentuated.

20§60. I began this hour by noting that the world of ancient Greek myth and ritual tends to differentiate, like it or not, the experiences of men and women from each other. Now we see the cost of such differentiation, as expressed in myth: Phaedra must die because the experiences of men and women must be kept distinct.

The Death of Phaedra

20§61. In another choral lyric passage of the *Hippolytus* (second *stasimon*), which I will now quote in its entirety, Phaedra is committing suicide offstage while the chorus sings and dances, showing once again the empathy of collective female experiences:

HOUR 20 TEXT L

|$_{732}$ Oh if only I could be down under the steep heights in deep cavernous spaces, |$_{733}$ where I could become a winged bird |$_{734}$—a god would make me into that, and I would become one of a whole flock of birds in flight, yes, a god would make me that. |$_{735}$ And if only I could then lift off in flight and fly away, soaring over the waves of the sea [*pontos*] |$_{736}$ marked by the Adriatic |$_{737}$ headland, and then over the waters of the river Eridanos |$_{738}$ where into the purple swirl comes |$_{739}$ a cascade from unhappy |$_{740}$ girls in their grief for Phaethon—a cascade of tears that pour down |$_{741}$ their amber radiance. |$_{742}$ Then to the apple-bearing headland of the Hesperides |$_{743}$ would I finally arrive, to the land of those singers of songs |$_{744}$ where the ruler of the sea [*pontos*],

with its seething purple stretches of water, |₇₄₅ no longer gives a path for sailors to proceed any further, |₇₄₆ and there I would find the revered limit |₇₄₇ of the sky, which Atlas holds, |₇₄₈ and there the immortalizing [*ambrosiai*] spring waters flow |₇₄₉ right next to the place where Zeus goes to lie down, |₇₅₀ and where she who gives blessedness [*olbos*] makes things grow. She is the most fertile one. |₇₅₁ She is the Earth, the one who makes the good blessing of superhuman powers [*eudaimoniā*] keep growing for the gods.

Euripides Hippolytus 732–751*

20§62. As I argued in the Introduction to Part III (§9), the larger-than-life *pathos* or primal 'suffering' experienced by a hero like Phaedra becomes identified with the *pathos* or 'emotion' experienced by the audience of Athenian State Theater, and such identification is achieved through the empathy activated by the performance of the chorus.†

Epilogue: The Death of Phaethon

20§63. In the choral song that I have just quoted, Text L, there is a fleeting reference to the hero Phaethon (737–741), whose sisters mourn his death every sunset by shedding amber tears from their celestial dwellings. I have spent much time and energy studying this figure, and I have already published elsewhere the main results of my study.‡ Here I propose to undergo the mental exercise of retelling, in the briefest possible way, the relevant part of the Phaethon myth—without even citing any primary sources. Here, then, is my own retelling:

The sun-god Helios had sex with a mortal woman and fathered the hero Phaethon. To prove to himself that Helios was really his father, Phaethon requested permission to drive the chariot of the sun-god

---

* |₇₃₂ ἠλιβάτοις ὑπὸ κευθμῶσι γενοίμαν, |₇₃₃ ἵνα με πτεροῦσσαν ὄρνιν |₇₃₄ θεὸς ἐν ποταναῖς ἀγέλαις θείη· |₇₃₅ ἀρθείην δ᾽ ἐπὶ πόντιον |₇₃₆ κῦμα τᾶς Ἀδριηνᾶς |₇₃₇ ἀκτᾶς Ἠριδανοῦ θ᾽ ὕδωρ, |₇₃₈ ἔνθα πορφύρεον σταλάσσ|₇₃₉ουσ᾽ ἐς οἶδμα τάλαιναι |₇₄₀ κόραι Φαέθοντος οἴκτῳ δακρύων |₇₄₁ τὰς ἠλεκτροφαεῖς αὐγάς· |₇₄₂ Ἑσπερίδων δ᾽ ἐπὶ μηλόσπορον ἀκτὰν |₇₄₃ ἀνύσαιμι τᾶν ἀοιδῶν, |₇₄₄ ἵν᾽ ὁ πορφυρέας ποντομέδων λίμνας |₇₄₅ ναύταις οὐκέθ᾽ ὁδὸν νέμει, |₇₄₆ σεμνὸν τέρμονα κυρῶν |₇₄₇ οὐρανοῦ, τὸν Ἄτλας ἔχει, |₇₄₈ κρῆναί τ᾽ ἀμβρόσιαι χέον|₇₄₉ται Ζηνὸς παρὰ κοίταις, |₇₅₀ ἵν᾽ ὀλβιόδωρος αὔξει ζαθέα |₇₅₁ χθὼν εὐδαιμονίαν θεοῖς.

† See also *PP* 95–96.

‡ The latest synthesis of my work on the hero Phaethon can be found in *GM* 223–265.

across the sky for just one day. The request was granted, and he got to drive the chariot, but he lost control while driving and nearly set the world on fire. Just in time, Zeus stopped it all, killing Phaethon with his thunderbolt.

This myth, at its core, recapitulates virtually everything that is essential to know about the ancient Greek hero. We have by now seen a vast array of variations, but it all comes down to this: heroes keep trying to prove to themselves that they belong somehow to a world of immortals, but, after all is said and done, heroes only end up proving that they deserve to die for trying.

20§64. There is a lesson here for Phaedra, whose wandering mind desired passionately to go to forbidden places where only Hippolytus could go. What was she trying to do? She desired to be like the goddess Artemis. And she conceived this desire because she loved Hippolytus, who loved Artemis and who therefore angered Aphrodite. So why did Phaedra love Hippolytus? It was only because Aphrodite made her love him in order to punish him with death.

20§65. So there is an even bigger lesson here for Hippolytus, who tried to love Artemis in a way that could never be reciprocated. What he got for his pains was death, caused by the love of Phaedra, which in turn was caused by the anger of Aphrodite. And this death of Hippolytus took the form of a spectacular chariot crash that had not yet happened when Phaedra was killing herself—and when the chorus was singing a song that evoked the ultimately spectacular chariot crash of Phaethon.

HOUR 21

The Hero's Agony in the
Bacchae *of Euripides*

The Meaning of Agōn

21§1. The key word for this hour is *agōn,* plural *agōnes.* In the Core Vocabulary, I give three basic definitions: (1) 'coming together', (2) 'competition' or *antagonism,* and (3) 'ordeal' or *agony.* Here I follow up on an earlier formulation I gave in Hour **8b§4,** which I now divide into three parts:

1. The noun *agōn* is derived from the root *ag-* of the verb *agō* as it is used in the compound formation *sun-agein,* which means 'bring together, assemble, gather'. Basically, an *agōn* is a 'bringing together' of people.
2. The occasion of such a 'bringing together' is a 'competition'. This meaning, 'competition', is still evident in the English borrowing of a compound formation involving the word *agōn,* that is, *antagonism.* Similarly, the basic meaning of Latin *com-petere* is 'to come together', and to come together is to *compete.**
3. The activity of 'competition' as expressed by the Greek word *agōn* was understood to be a ritual 'ordeal', just as the Greek word *āthlos* meant 'ordeal' as well as 'contest', that is, 'competition'. The concept of 'ordeal' as embedded in the Greek word *agōn* is still evident in the English word borrowed from the Greek, *agony.*

21§2. As I noted in Hour **8b§5,** both words *āthlos* and *agōn* can refer to the experience of competition in athletics, and both words can also refer to the most extreme form of competition imaginable, which is war. But other kinds of ritualized competition also qualify as an *agōn,* though not as an *āthlos.* As I

* *PH* 136–137 = 5§2.

noted in Hour 7 (E§2), *agōn* can refer to competition in the verbal arts, and I highlighted the example of the grand *agōn* or 'competition' in *mousikē tekhnē*, 'the art of the Muses', at the festival of the Great Panathenaia in Athens. And now in Hour 21, we will see that this word *agōn* can also refer to competition in the verbal art of tragedy, especially as it evolved at the festival of the City Dionysia in Athens.*

21§3. But there is more to it. As we will see, this word *agōn* is not only a word for tragedy as a ritual of competition: it is also the word used for expressing a primal experience in myth—an experience that aetiologizes tragedy as a coming together, a competition, and an ordeal.

The Agōn *of Pentheus*

21§4. In the *Bacchae* of Euripides, produced in Athens some time after the author's death (he died probably in Macedonia, in 407/406 BCE), we see the dramatization of a myth concerning such a primal experience. At its core, the story is this: the hero Pentheus, king of the venerable ancient Greek city of Thebes, is dismembered by the women of this city. As we will see, this dismemberment of Pentheus is the hero's *agōn*.

21§5. In the myth of Pentheus, the women of Thebes who dismember the hero have become *bakkhai* or 'Bacchants', that is, female worshippers of the god *Bakkhos* or Bacchus. The other name of Bacchus is Dionysus. The god has come to Thebes from Asia Minor, accompanied by Asiatic Bacchants who are represented by the chorus of the tragedy. That is where we get the name of this tragedy, *Bacchae*, which is a latinized spelling of *bakkhai*, or 'Bacchants'. Although the god seems alien to the people of Thebes, he is really their native son, since Dionysus was conceived in the city of Thebes when Zeus impregnated Semele, one of the daughters of Cadmus, who was the founder of Thebes.† The persona of Dionysus himself tells the essentials of the myth at the beginning of the *Bacchae*, lines 1–63.

21§6. The catastrophic behavior of the Thebans in not recognizing Dionysus as one of their own leads to their collective punishment, which comes to a head at the climactic moment when Pentheus suffers dismemberment at the hands of

---

* For an introduction to tragedy as it evolved in the historical context of the festival of the City Dionysia in Athens, I cite my detailed analysis in *PH* 384–391 = 13§§6–20.

† On this essential characteristic of the god Dionysus in myth, that he is a native son who is not recognized by his own people because of his alien appearances, I offer an overall formulation in *PH* 296–297 = 10§27.

the Theban Bacchants. This moment is narrated by a messenger at lines 1043–1147 of the drama. By the time Dionysus is recognized as *oikeios* or 'native' to Thebes at line 1250, it is too late. By contrast, the behavior of the Asiatic Bacchants who are the chorus is not at all catastrophic. Rather, they exhibit ritually correct behavior, since they not only represent Bacchants but also function as the chorus of the drama. And, as the chorus, these Asiatic Bacchants are an integral part of the ritual aspect of theater. The chorus must be ritually correct, since Dionysus is after all the god of theater.*

21§7. Tragically, the leader of the Theban Bacchants who tore the hero limb from limb was the mother of Pentheus himself, Agaue, who claimed as her prize the best portion of the dismembered body, the head (*Bacchae* 1168–1329). In terms of the myth, to repeat the point of my argument, this dismemberment of the hero Pentheus is his *agōn*.

The Meaning of Pathos

21§8. Before I can proceed with my argumentation about the *agōn* of Pentheus, I need to explain what I mean when I speak of the *primal experience* of any hero. Here I elaborate on my Introduction to Part III (§§6–7), where I dealt with the meaning of the word *pathos* as 'experience' or 'emotion' or 'suffering'.

· The translation 'experience' for the noun *pathos* conveys its general meaning, since this noun is derived from the verb *paskhein,* which can be translated as 'to experience'—in the sense that the person who is the subject of the verb is experiencing an action that is being done to this subject. Such an experiencing is the essence of the passive function of any verb, to be contrasted with the active function, where the subject of the verb is doing something to the object of the verb. In the case of *paskhein,* 'to experience', this verb is active in form but passive in function, and, in this passive function, it is opposed to the active function of the verbs *poieîn* and *drân,* which both mean 'to do'. In the medium of tragedy, there is a working opposition between the active function of *drân,* which indicates that someone is 'doing' something to someone, and the passive function of *paskhein,* which indicates that someone is 'experiencing' something that is being done to that someone.

· The translation 'emotion' conveys a secondary aspect of the general meaning

---

* *PH* 397 = 13§36. For Dionysus in Greek tragedy, see in general Bierl 1991.

of *pathos*. This word *pathos* can refer to any given emotion, in the sense that an emotion is something that is *experienced*.

- The translation 'suffering' conveys the specialized meaning of *pathos*. Such specialization suits the medium of tragedy, since the primary kind of experience that happens to heroes in this medium is *suffering*.

21§9. Just as the verb *paskhein* indicates the 'experiencing' of something and functions as the antithesis of the poetic verb *drân*, which indicates the 'doing' of something to someone, so also the noun *pathos*, derived from *paskhein*, indicates an 'experience'. And so this noun *pathos* is the antithesis of the noun *drâma*, derived from *drân*. But the meanings of *pathos* and *drâma* are complicated by the fact that the corresponding verbs from which they are derived, *paskhein* and *drân*, have specialized meanings. In the case of *paskhein*, as we have just seen, it can mean 'suffering' as well as 'experiencing'. And, in the case of *drân*, as we saw earlier in the usage of Pausanias (9.40.2 in Hour 15§38; also 2.32.1 in Hour 20§18), it can mean 'performing ritual' as well as simply 'doing'; further, as we saw in the usage of Sophocles (*Oedipus at Colonus* 1644 in Hour 18§49), the participial form *drômena* of *drân* refers to ritual acts that are 'done' in mysteries connected with the cults of heroes.

21§10. Such specialized meanings of the nouns *pathos* and *drâma* are the basis for the compressed formulation I offered in the Introduction to Part III (§7), which I repeat here:

> What is passive *pathos* or *action experienced* by the hero within the world of tragedy is active *drâma*, that is, *sacrifice and the performance of ritual*, from the standpoint of the outer world that frames this world of tragedy. Such an outer world is constituted by the audience of the theater, visualized as a community that becomes engaged in the *drâma* and that thereby participates in the inner world that is the *pathos* or 'suffering' of the hero.*

Staging the Dismemberment of Pentheus

21§11. Now that I have explained what I mean when I speak of the *primal experience* of a hero, I am ready to take a closer look at the experience of Pentheus in

---

* A more detailed argumentation is offered in *PH* 387–388 = 13§13.

the *Bacchae* of Euripides. In the specific case of this hero, as I already noted, his experience of suffering takes the form of being dismembered by the women of Thebes. So my question is this: how can we relate this primal experience of Pentheus to the three-way meaning of the word *agōn* as a *coming together,* a *competition,* and an *ordeal?* To formulate an answer, which will take the rest of this hour to shape, I begin by analyzing a passage in the *Bacchae* where the god Dionysus himself refers indirectly to the dismemberment of Pentheus. As we will see, this reference is expressed in terms of the hero's *agōn* or 'ordeal'—and also in terms of the *pathos* or 'suffering' that awaits him.

21§12. The context of the passage we are about to read is this: the young king Pentheus has conceived an obsessive desire to spy on the women of Thebes, who have all become Bacchants and have headed off to the mountains, led by his own mother, Agaue, together with his aunts Ino and Autonoe. As the scene begins, Pentheus is offstage, still inside the palace, but he has already been costumed to look like a Bacchant. Intending to head for the mountains himself in order to join the Theban Bacchants there, Pentheus is ready to act as if he were really one of them, hoping to discover the truth about them. And the one who arranges the costuming for this intended piece of acting by Pentheus is the god of theater himself, Dionysus, who is acting as the god Dionysus. For reasons that will be explained shortly, I use the word *acting* here in two senses: the god here is both an *actor* and an *agent* of his own self. And Dionysus is most effective as both agent and actor, since Pentheus does not recognize him as the god that he is. Nor is Pentheus even meant to recognize Dionysus—for now. As we join the action, Dionysus is already on stage, and he calls out to Pentheus, who is still offstage and inside the palace, ordering the hero to come out and make his grand entrance:

HOUR 21 TEXT A

$|_{912}$ {Dionysus:} You there! Yes, I'm talking to you, to the one who is so eager to see the things that should not be seen $|_{913}$ and who rushes to accomplish things that cannot be rushed. It is you I am talking to, Pentheus. $|_{914}$ Come out from inside the palace. Let me have a good look at you $|_{915}$ wearing the costume of a woman who is a *maenad* [*mainas*], a *Bacchant* [*bakkhē*], $|_{916}$ ready to spy on your mother and her company. $|_{917}$ The way you are shaped, you look just like one of the daughters of Cadmus.

|₉₁₈ {Pentheus:} What is this? I think I see two suns, |₉₁₉ and not one seven-gated city [*polisma*] of Thebes but two. |₉₂₀ And, as you are leading me, you look like a bull |₉₂₁ and horns seem to have sprouted on your head. |₉₂₂ Were you ever before a beast? You have certainly now become a bull.

|₉₂₃ {Dionysus:} The god accompanies us, though formerly he was not of good intentions [*eu-menēs*]. |₉₂₄ He has a truce with us, and now you see what you should be seeing.

|₉₂₅ {Pentheus:} So what do I appear [*phainesthai*] to be? Do I not have the dancing pose [*stasis*] of Ino |₉₂₆ or of Agaue, my mother?

|₉₂₇ {Dionysus:} Looking at you I think I see them right now. |₉₂₈ Oh, but watch out: this lock of hair [*plokamos*] here is out of place. It stands out, |₉₂₉ not the way I had secured it, to be held down by the headband [*mitra*].

|₉₃₀ {Pentheus:} While I was inside, I was shaking it [= the lock of hair] forward and backward, |₉₃₁ and, in a Bacchic state of mind [*bakkhiazōn*], I displaced it, moving it out of place.

|₉₃₂ {Dionysus:} Then I, whose concern it is to care [*therapeuein*] for you, will |₉₃₃ arrange it [= the lock of hair] all over again. Come on, hold your head straight.

|₉₃₄ {Pentheus:} You see it [= the lock of hair]? There it is! You arrange [*kosmeîn*] it for me. I can see I am really depending on you.

|₉₃₅ {Dionysus:} And your waistband has come loose. And those things are not in the right order, |₉₃₆ I mean, the pleats of your robe [*peplos*], the way they extend down around your ankles.

|₉₃₇ {Pentheus:} That's the way I see it from my angle as well. At least, that is the way it is down around my right foot, |₉₃₈ but, on this other side, the robe [*peplos*] does extend in a straight line down around the calf.

|₉₃₉ {Dionysus:} I really do think you will consider me the foremost among those who are near and dear [*philoi*] to you |₉₄₀ when, contrary to your expectations, you see that *Bacchants* [*bakkhai*] are moderate [= *sōphrones*].

|₉₄₁ {Pentheus:} So which one will it be? I mean, shall I hold the wand [*thursos*] with my right hand |₉₄₂ or with this other one here? Which is the way I will look more like a *Bacchant* [*bakkhē*]?

|$_{943}$ {Dionysus:} You must hold it in your right hand and, at the same time, with your right foot |$_{944}$ you must make an upward motion. I approve [*aineîn*] of the way you have shifted in your thinking [*phrenes*].

|$_{945}$ {Pentheus:} Could I not carry on my shoulders the ridges of Mount Kithairon, |$_{946}$ Bacchants and all?

|$_{947}$ {Dionysus:} You could if you wanted to. Your earlier thoughts [*phrenes*] |$_{948}$ were not sound, but now they are the way they should be.

|$_{949}$ {Pentheus:} Shall we bring levers, or shall I use my hands for lifting, |$_{950}$ throwing a shoulder or arm under the mountains as I raise them up?

|$_{951}$ {Dionysus:} But you must not destroy the dwelling places of the Nymphs |$_{952}$ and the places where Pan stays, playing on his pipe.

|$_{953}$ {Pentheus:} You said it well. It is not by force that my victory over |$_{954}$ the women should happen. I will hide my body under the shelter of the fir trees.

|$_{955}$ {Dionysus:} You will hide yourself by hiding as you should be hidden, |$_{956}$ coming as a crafty spy on the maenads [*mainades*].

|$_{957}$ {Pentheus:} You know, I have this vision of them: there they are in the bushes, like birds in their most beloved [*phila*] hiding places, held in the tight grip of making love.

|$_{959}$ {Dionysus:} Yes, and are you not like a guardian who has been sent out to counter exactly this kind of thing? |$_{960}$ Perhaps you will catch them, unless they beat you to it and you yourself get caught.

|$_{961}$ {Pentheus:} Bring me there, let us go there, passing right through the middle of Thebes on our way. |$_{962}$ I am the only one of those [Thebans] who dares to do this.

|$_{963}$ {Dionysus:} You alone [*monos*] enter the struggle for the sake of this city [*polis*], you alone [*monos*]. |$_{964}$ And so the ordeals [*agōnes*] that must happen are awaiting you. |$_{965}$ Follow me. I am your guide, giving salvation [*sōtērios*]. |$_{966}$ But then, on the way back, someone else will lead you down from up there.—{Pentheus:} Yes, it will be my mother.

|$_{967}$ {Dionysus:} And you will be a distinctive sign [*epi-sēmon*] to all. {Pentheus:}—I am going with that objective in mind.

|$_{968}$ {Dionysus:} You will return here being carried—{Pentheus:} You are talking about my desire for luxury [*habrotēs*].

|₉₆₉ {Dionysus:}—in the arms of your mother. {Pentheus:} So you will make me revel in luxury [*truphân*].

|₉₇₀ {Dionysus:} Yes indeed, in such luxury [*truphē*]. {Pentheus:} I am reaching for things I deserve.

|₉₇₁ {Dionysus:} A man of terror [*deinos*] you are, a man of terror [*deinos*], and you are going after experiences [*pathos* plural] that are things of terror [*deina*]. |₉₇₂ The result will be that you will find a glory [*kleos*] reaching all the way up to the sky. |₉₇₃ Hold out your hands, Agaue, and you too, her sisters, |₉₇₄ daughters of Cadmus. The young man is being led by me |₉₇₅ to this great ordeal [*agōn*] here. |₉₇₆ And the one who will win the victory—that will be I myself. *Bromios* [= Dionysus the Thunderer] and I myself will be the victors. What signals [*sēmainein*] it are other things that are yet to happen.

Euripides *Bacchae* 912–976*

---

* |₉₁₂ {Δι.} σὲ τὸν πρόθυμον ὄνθ᾿ ἃ μὴ χρεὼν ὁρᾶν |₉₁₃ σπεύδοντά τ᾿ ἀσπούδαστα, Πενθέα λέγω, |₉₁₄ ἔξιθι πάροιθε δωμάτων, ὄφθητί μοι, |₉₁₅ σκευὴν γυναικὸς μαινάδος βάκχης ἔχων, |₉₁₆ μητρός τε τῆς σῆς καὶ λόχου κατάσκοπος· |₉₁₇ πρέπεις δὲ Κάδμου θυγατέρων μορφὴν μιᾷ. |₉₁₈ {Πε.} καὶ μὴν ὁρᾶν μοι δύο μὲν ἡλίους δοκῶ, |₉₁₉ δισσὰς δὲ Θήβας καὶ πόλισμ᾿ ἑπτάστομον· |₉₂₀ καὶ ταῦρος ἡμῖν πρόσθεν ἡγεῖσθαι δοκεῖς |₉₂₁ καὶ σῷ κέρατα κρατὶ προσπεφυκέναι. |₉₂₂ ἀλλ᾿ ἦ ποτ᾿ ἦσθα θήρ; τεταύρωσαι γὰρ οὖν. |₉₂₃ {Δι.} ὁ θεὸς ὁμαρτεῖ, πρόσθεν ὢν οὐκ εὐμενής, |₉₂₄ ἔνσπονδος ἡμῖν· νῦν δ᾿ ὁρᾷς ἃ χρή σ᾿ ὁρᾶν. |₉₂₅ {Πε.} τί φαίνομαι δῆτ᾿; οὐχὶ τὴν Ἰνοῦς στάσιν |₉₂₆ ἢ τὴν Ἀγαυῆς ἑστάναι, μητρός γ᾿ ἐμῆς; |₉₂₇ {Δι.} αὐτὰς ἐκείνας εἰσορᾶν δοκῶ σ᾿ ὁρῶν. |₉₂₈ ἀλλ᾿ ἐξ ἕδρας σοι πλόκαμος ἐξέστηχ᾿ ὅδε, |₉₂₉ οὐχ ὡς ἐγώ νιν ὑπὸ μίτρᾳ καθήρμοσα. |₉₃₀ {Πε.} ἔνδον προσείων αὐτὸν ἀνασείων τ᾿ ἐγὼ |₉₃₁ καὶ βακχιάζων ἐξ ἕδρας μεθώρμισα. |₉₃₂ {Δι.} ἀλλ᾿ αὐτὸν ἡμεῖς, οἷς σε θεραπεύειν μέλει, |₉₃₃ πάλιν καταστελοῦμεν· ἀλλ᾿ ὄρθου κάρα. |₉₃₄ {Πε.} ἰδού, σὺ κόσμει· σοὶ γὰρ ἀνακείμεθα δή. |₉₃₅ {Δι.} ζῶναί τέ σοι χαλῶσι κοὐχ ἑξῆς πέπλων |₉₃₆ στολίδες ὑπὸ σφυροῖσι τείνουσιν σέθεν. |₉₃₇ {Πε.} κἀμοὶ δοκοῦσι παρά γε δεξιὸν πόδα· |₉₃₈ τἀνθένδε δ᾿ ὀρθῶς παρὰ τένοντ᾿ ἔχει πέπλος. |₉₃₉ {Δι.} ἦ πού με τῶν σῶν πρῶτον ἡγήσῃ φίλων, |₉₄₀ ὅταν παρὰ λόγον σώφρονας βάκχας ἴδῃς. |₉₄₁ {Πε.} πότερα δὲ θύρσον δεξιᾷ λαβὼν χερὶ |₉₄₂ ἢ τῇδε βάκχῃ μᾶλλον εἰκασθήσομαι; |₉₄₃ {Δι.} ἐν δεξιᾷ χρὴ χἄμα δεξιῷ ποδὶ |₉₄₄ αἴρειν νιν· αἰνῶ δ᾿ ὅτι μεθέστηκας φρενῶν. |₉₄₅ {Πε.} ἆρ᾿ ἂν δυναίμην τὰς Κιθαιρῶνος πτυχὰς |₉₄₆ αὐταῖσι βάκχαις τοῖς ἐμοῖς ὤμοις φέρειν; |₉₄₇ {Δι.} δύναι᾿ ἄν, εἰ βούλοιο· τὰς δὲ πρὶν φρένας |₉₄₈ οὐκ εἶχες ὑγιεῖς, νῦν δ᾿ ἔχεις οἵας σε δεῖ. |₉₄₉ {Πε.} μοχλοὺς φέρωμεν ἢ χεροῖν ἀνασπάσω |₉₅₀ κορυφαῖς ὑποβαλὼν ὦμον ἢ βραχίονα; |₉₅₁ {Δι.} μὴ σύ γε τὰ Νυμφῶν διολέσῃς ἱδρύματα |₉₅₂ καὶ Πανὸς ἕδρας ἔνθ᾿ ἔχει συρίγματα. |₉₅₃ {Πε.} καλῶς ἔλεξας· οὐ σθένει νικητέον |₉₅₄ γυναῖκας· ἐλάταισι δ᾿ ἐμὸν κρύψω δέμας. |₉₅₅ {Δι.} κρύψῃ σὺ κρύψιν ἥν σε κρυφθῆναι χρεών, |₉₅₆ ἐλθόντα δόλιον μαινάδων κατάσκοπον. |₉₅₇ {Πε.} καὶ μὴν δοκῶ σφας ἐν λόχμαις ὄρνιθας ὡς |₉₅₈ λέκτρων ἔχεσθαι φιλτάτοις ἐν ἕρκεσιν. |₉₅₉ {Δι.} οὔκουν ἐπ᾿ αὐτὸ τοῦτ᾿ ἀποστέλλῃ φύλαξ; |₉₆₀ λήψῃ δ᾿ ἴσως σφας, ἢν σὺ μὴ ληφθῇς πάρος. |₉₆₁ {Πε.} κόμιζε διὰ μέσης με Θηβαίας χθονός· |₉₆₂ μόνος γὰρ αὐτῶν εἰμ᾿ ἀνὴρ τολμῶν τόδε. |₉₆₃ {Δι.} μόνος σὺ πόλεως τῆσδ᾿ ὑπερκάμνεις, μόνος· |₉₆₄ τοιγάρ σ᾿ ἀγῶνες ἀναμένουσιν οὓς ἐχρῆν. |₉₆₅ ἕπου δέ· πομπὸς εἰμ᾿ ἐγὼ σωτήριος, |₉₆₆ κεῖθεν δ᾿ ἀπάξει σ᾿ ἄλλος {Πε.} ἡ τεκοῦσά γε. |₉₆₇ {Δι.} ἐπίσημον ὄντα πᾶσιν. {Πε.} ἐπὶ τόδ᾿ ἔρχομαι. |₉₆₈ {Δι.} φερόμενος ἥξεις {Πε.} ἁβρότητ᾿ ἐμὴν λέγεις. |₉₆₉ {Δι.} ἐν χερσὶ μητρός. {Πε.} καὶ τρυφᾶν μ᾿ ἀναγκάσεις. |₉₇₀ {Δι.} τρυφάς γε τοιάσδ᾿. {Πε.} ἀξίων μὲν ἅπτομαι. |₉₇₁ {Δι.} δεινὸς σὺ δεινὸς κἀπὶ δείν᾿ ἔρχῃ πάθη, |₉₇₂ ὥστ᾿ οὐρανῷ στηρίζον εὑρήσεις κλέος. |₉₇₃ ἔκτειν᾿, Ἀγαυή, χεῖρας αἵ θ᾿ ὁμόσποροι |₉₇₄ Κάδμου θυγατέρες· τὸν νεανίαν ἄγω |₉₇₅ τόνδ᾿ εἰς ἀγῶνα μέγαν, ὁ νικήσων δ᾿ ἐγὼ |₉₇₆ καὶ Βρόμιος ἔσται. τἄλλα δ᾿ αὐτὸ σημανεῖ.

21§13. I propose to analyze this passage by starting near the end of the text and then, later on, restarting at the beginning, working my way back down to the end. So, looking ahead to the end of the text, I will now focus on the word *agōn* at lines 964 and 975, after which I will focus on the word *pathos* at line 971.

21§14. In the case of *agōn,* this word is used twice by Dionysus—each time in a riddling way. The first time, at line 964, the god says to the hero: 'The ordeals [*agōnes*] that must happen are awaiting you'. From the perspective of Pentheus, *agōn* here means the hero's 'ordeal' in fighting a personal war against the Bacchants of Thebes. From the perspective of Dionysus, however, this same word means the hero's 'ordeal' of dismemberment. As for the second time when Dionysus uses this word *agōn,* at line 975, the god is addressing the absent mother and aunts of Pentheus in the hero's presence, saying to them: 'the young man is being led by me |₉₇₅ to this great ordeal [*agōn*] here'. From the perspective of Pentheus, *agōn* here means once again the hero's 'ordeal' in fighting his personal war against the Bacchants. From the perspective of Dionysus, however, this same word means the hero's 'competition' with the god. When Dionysus at lines 975–976 goes on to say about himself that he will win in this competition, Pentheus does not understand that the mysterious stranger who has costumed him is really his divine competitor or antagonist, Dionysus himself. Not suspecting that this stranger is his own divine antagonist, Pentheus does not understand that the winner is not on his side but on the other side.

21§15. In the case of *pathos,* this word too is used in a riddling way by Dionysus. At line 971, the god says to Pentheus: 'A man of terror [*deinos*] you are, a man of terror [*deinos*], and you are going after experiences [*pathos* plural] that are things of terror [*deina*]'. From the perspective of Pentheus, he is actively pursuing *pathē*—which is the plural form of *pathos*—in the general sense of 'experiences' that are *deina* in the sense of 'terrific'. We may compare the meaning of the English word *terrific,* derived from a Latin word that means 'terrifying'. In English too as in Latin, this word once had the generally negative meaning of 'terrifying', but it eventually took on the specifically positive meaning of 'terrific'. So also the ancient Greek adjective *deinos* once had the generally negative meaning of 'terrifying' but then eventually took on the specifically positive meaning of 'terrific'. From the perspective of Pentheus, then, the mysterious stranger is telling him: 'A terrific man you are, terrific, and you are going to face experiences or *pathē* that are terrific'. So Pentheus can think that the stranger is saying to him: *You and your future experiences are so terrific that I fear you.* From the perspective of Dionysus, however, he is telling Pentheus: 'A terrible man you are, terrible, and you are going to face sufferings or *pathē* that are terrible'. So Dionysus is in effect saying to Pentheus: *You and your future experiences are so terrible that I pity you.* For the god Dionysus, the idea of fear as conveyed by the word *deinos* needs to be seen in terms of the basic meaning of this word. That is why I translate *deinos* in Text A here as 'of terror' where it applies to Pentheus. In other words, 'a man of terror' may be either someone who actively makes others feel terror or who is passively made to feel terror himself. It all depends on how you look at the *pathē* that 'await' Pentheus. Pentheus may think that these *pathē* will be 'experiences' that are 'terrific' for him, in the positive sense of 'terrific'. But these *pathē* will really be the 'sufferings' of Pentheus, who will be dismembered by the Bacchants of Thebes and who will in the end experience personally the holy terror of his own grisly death.

21§16. This death of Pentheus is evidently different from heroic death in war, but it still earns the hero a *kleos* or poetic 'glory' that will reach all the way up to the sky, as the words of the god Dionysus himself predict at line 972 of the *Bacchae,* quoted in Text A. This one part of the god's prediction has no double meaning. Just as death in war leads to *kleos,* as we saw in the case of Achilles already at the very beginning of this book, so also death by dismemberment leads to the *kleos* of Pentheus as the victim of his own antagonism with a god. Earlier, in Hour 8b§5, we saw that the expression *arēios agōn,* 'the *agōn* of Arēs' (as used by Herodotus 9.33.3), refers to the ritualized experience of combat in war. Later on, in Hour 17 Text H, we saw the goddess Athena herself referring to 'deeds of war, | ordeals [*agōnes*] that bring distinction' (Aeschylus *Eumenides* 914–915). And now we see that the experience of war is not the only kind of *agōn* that can bring poetic *kleos* or 'glory'.

The Staging of Dionysus

21§17. As we can see from the exchange between Pentheus and Dionysus in Text A, the hero fails to understand that the mysterious character who has costumed him as a Bacchant is the god Dionysus. The hero is deluded into thinking that the god on stage is merely a male worshipper of the god. As I pointed out already, the word for such a male worshipper is *bakkhos*. And, since this word is also the other name of Dionysus, which as I also pointed out is *Bakkhos* or Bacchus, the god on stage has staged himself to possess a double identity. He is both the god and the worshipper of the god. But this double identity is double only for those who do not understand that the worshipper or *bakkhos* who re-enacts *Bakkhos* or Dionysus becomes one with the god during the act of worship. I have already analyzed in Hour 5 such a pattern of merged identities, where the participant in a ritual becomes one with the god who is worshipped in the ritual. Clearly, Pentheus does not understand such oneness, and that is why he sees double when he comes on stage, at lines 918–919 of Text A. The diplopia experienced by the hero indicates that he has not been initiated into the mysteries of the rituals that celebrate the god Dionysus.

21§18. Dionysus is a double signifier. He has the power to stage himself and his other self simultaneously. He has that power because he is not only a god on the stage: he is the god of the stage. As I have already noted, Dionysus is the god of theater. So, unlike other characters who are re-enacted by actors wearing masks over their faces, the character of Dionysus can in principle be re-enacted by Dionysus himself. In other words, Dionysus can act Dionysus. And that is because there is no face under the mask of Dionysus: the god's mask is his face.

The Subjectivity of Dionysus

21§19. To elaborate on what I just said, that the mask of Dionysus is his face, I need to consider the idea of *subjectivity* and how it applies to Dionysus as a god. I start with three basic observations:*

—In the usage of everyday people, *subjectivity* is simply the opposite of *objectivity.*

—In the usage of philosophers, *subjectivity* is a key word for debating questions about the nature of the human *self* and about the ways in which that self operates in the context of historical contingencies. Even in this kind of usage, the word *subjectivity* is normally treated as the opposite of *objectivity.*

—In the usage of linguists, *subjectivity* can be analyzed *grammatically* in terms of *person.* When I say *person* here, I mean the first, second, and third persons of personal pronouns and verbs. The classic study of grammatical persons is by Émile Benveniste, and it is his approach that will shape the argumentation that follows.†

21§20. As Benveniste shows, the grammatical first-person singular or the 'I' is the basis of subjectivity in its distinctness from the second person or the 'you'

---

* What follows here in §§19–29 is derived from an essay, Nagy 2010e:34–39.
† Benveniste 1958.

with whom the 'I' engages in what can best be described as a *dialogue*. Further, the 'I and you' dialogue of the first and the second persons is subjective in its distinctness from the third person, which can be a 'he' or a 'she' or an 'it' or a 'they' as well as a zero person who is neither a first nor a second person, as when we use the pronoun 'it' in making a statement like 'it is raining'.

21§21. To what extent, though, is the third person objective? In terms of linguistics, we can say that even the objectivity of the third person depends on the subjectivity of the first and the second persons. When I speak with you and I say 'he' or she' or 'it' or 'they', the identity that is marked by these pronouns in the third person depends on whom or what we mean when we use these third-person pronouns 'he' or she' or 'it' or 'they'. In our dialogue, we may also use nouns for identifying the various persons that mark what we are speaking about. For example, 'he' may be the king of Thebes and 'she' may be his mother, while 'it' may be the sun that shines and 'they' may be the mother and the aunts of the king. But the objectivity of these identifications of personal pronouns in the third person with corresponding nouns still depends on the subjectivity of the dialogue between the first and the second persons.

21§22. In the use of personal pronouns, we can say that all three persons are subjective, in that the making of references by way of all three persons can *shift,* depending on the subjectivity of the speaker who owns the personal pronoun 'I' at the moment of speaking. When I say 'I' or 'you' to you, the 'I' is I and the 'you' is you, but when *you* say 'I' or 'you' to *me,* then the 'I' is *you* and the 'you' is *I,* and these usages of 'I' and 'you' will shift depending on who is speaking to whom. Likewise in the third person, 'he' and 'she' and 'it' and 'they' will shift identities depending on who is speaking about whom or what.* There can even be shifts in inclusiveness and exclusiveness in what we say in an 'I and you' dialogue. For example, when I say 'we' in English I can *include you* if I mean 'I and you' or *exclude you* if I mean 'I and he' or 'I and she' or 'I and they'.

21§23. What makes it possible to study the subjective uses of shifting personal pronouns objectively is the fact that every occasion of speech where a speaker uses the pronoun 'I' is a historical contingency that is located in the context of the time and the place when the speaker spoke. When I or you study such a historical contingency, our own speaking about it may be ultimately subjective, but we can be objective about the contingency to the extent that we can keep ourselves aware of our own historical contingencies.

21§24. Just as *subjectivity* can be analyzed in terms of the *person* in *grammar,*

---

* On the linguistic concept of the *shifter,* I refer to the pioneering work of Jakobson 1957.

it can also be analyzed in terms of the *persona* in *theater*. When I say *persona*, I mean not only a dramatic *character* like, say, the young hero Pentheus who is king of Thebes in the *Bacchae* composed by Euripides. I mean also the *mask* worn by the actor who represented Pentheus at the premiere of the drama in the late fifth century—as also the corresponding masks worn by countless later actors who represented Pentheus in countless 're-runs' of the drama in later times. In Latin the noun *persona* actually means 'theatrical mask'. And in Greek, the noun *prosōpon* (πρόσωπον) likewise means 'theatrical mask'. More than that, Greek *prosōpon* refers not only to the *persona* in *theater* but also to the *person* in *grammar*, whether it be the first or the second or the third person. *And the Greek theatrical mask, as indicated by the word prosōpon, is a subjective agent, an 'I' who is looking for a dialogue with a 'you'.*

21§25. The subjectivity of the *prosōpon* as a mask used in theater is evident in the components of the word, which are *pros-*, 'toward', and *ōp-*, 'look'. These components derive from the syntax of expressing the mutuality of looking straight into the eyes of another person who is looking straight back at you. But the mutuality of this act of looking at each other is uneven in the ritualized setting of ancient Greek theater. That is because the ultimate model for this mutuality of looking at each other in theater is the god of ancient Greek theater himself, Dionysus, who is seen as the ultimate subjective agent. As the god of *theātron*, which means literally 'the instrument for looking' (this noun combines the root of the verb *theâsthai*, which means 'look', with the suffix of instrumentality, *-tron*), Dionysus is the god of the instrumentality of looking, and the actual instrument for looking is the *prosōpon* or 'mask'.

21§26. In the interaction of ancient Greek myth and ritual, the god in the myth is the model for the ritual in which his human worshippers engage—and that is how Dionysus becomes the role model for the ritualized use of masks in Greek theater. The god shows how. As the role model, he is the absolute model for all the roles, all the personae, all the persons of ancient Greek theater. And he is also the absolute model for every *pathos* or 'emotion' experienced by every person. As we have seen, all emotions can be enacted through the *mīmēsis* or 're-enactment' achieved by way of theater (Hour 8e§3). So the god shows the way, and he can do so *by wearing a mask himself.*

21§27. By wearing a mask, Dionysus becomes the ultimate agent of subjectivity, the ultimate model for all other agents of subjectivity. That is why Dionysus can be represented in the ancient Greek visual arts as wearing a mask that must be recognized as the ultimate mask, the mask that ends all masks, which is the face of the god himself.

21§28. I cite as an example a terracotta representation of the god Dionysus wearing a mask; it was found in Myrina (Turkey) and is dated to the second or first century BCE.*

What we see is the god Dionysus wearing a mask, or, better, wearing a face that is his mask, and this mask is the ultimate mask because it shows the looks of his own face. That is the point of such a representation of the god of masks, who is the god of theater.

21§29. I see here a fusion of emotions: there is fear, and there is also sorrow (or pity) and anger and hate and love and happiness. Dionysus fuses all emotions into one single primal emotion. What happens, then, when 'you' look at such a mask? In other words, what happens when the 'I' who is looking for a dialogue with you is the ultimate agent of subjectivity, even the god of subjectivity? My answer is that *'you' experience the emotion of primal fear, because 'you' are looking at the god of absolute subjectivity,* looking him in the face, looking back at him while he is looking at 'you'.†

Staging the Bacchants

21§30. We saw in §17 that Pentheus experiences diplopia in viewing Dionysus. The hero, seeing double, cannot understand that the god is one with those who participate in the god's rituals, and so Pentheus mistakenly views Dionysus merely as a male worshipper of Dionysus, not as Dionysus himself. From this mistaken point of view, Pentheus sees the male worshipper negatively. Likewise, Pentheus sees negatively the female worshippers of Dionysus, the Bacchants of Thebes. Again he shows a mistaken point of view, since he cannot understand that the Bacchants of Thebes are staged by the god Dionysus himself.

21§31. I need to elaborate by making two points. The first point is that the Bacchants of Thebes are women who have lost control of themselves. But that does not mean that they are "out of control"—to use a modern expression. They are still under control, but the controller is now the god. So the women of Thebes are now *mainades* or 'maenads', and that is what the god calls them at line 956 of the *Bacchae*, as we saw in Text A. This word means that the minds of these women are possessed by the god. We saw this meaning already in *Iliad* XXII 460, quoted in Hour 3 Text C, where Andromache is described as *mainadi*

---

* Terracotta, 2nd-1st centuries BCE. Paris. Musée du Louvre. Department of Greek, Etruscan and Roman Antiquities (Myr. 347).

† I added at this point in my essay (Nagy 2010e:39), "This kind of primal fear is an emotion that transcends all other human emotions." My views have shifted, and I now back away from that statement.

īsē, 'same as a maenad' or 'just like a maenad', when she faces the terrifying vision of her husband's corpse being dragged by Achilles. As I noted in Hour 3§20, the context of this expression indicates that Andromache has lost control of herself. So, to recap my first point, a *mainas* or 'maenad' loses control of her own mind because she is possessed by the mind of Dionysus. But my second point is that the possession of a woman's mind by Dionysus is not necessarily a negative thing. In the case of Andromache, for example, her experience of a maenadic seizure in *Iliad* XXII leads to her performance of a lament for Hector at lines 477–514, introduced at line 476. From my analysis in Hour 3§§20–21, it is evident that the performance of this lament by Andromache is pictured as a genuine ritual and, as such, it is viewed as a positive experience. But I must add that this experience is positive only because it is ritualized. Without the ritualization, the disheveled appearance of Andromache could turn negative:

> Only the ritual of lament protects her modesty. Without such ritual protection, this modesty would be destroyed. But the cover of ritual allows her to appear in public with her hair completely undone.*

21§32. So the possession of a woman's mind by Dionysus is a positive experience when the woman possessed is performing a ritual. And that is also what we see when we consider the chorus of Asiatic Bacchants in the *Bacchae* of Euripides. By singing and dancing, the chorus is performing the ritual of Dionysus, god of State Theater. As participants in the ritual of drama, the members of the chorus are undergoing a positive experience as they re-enact the myth of Dionysus by singing and dancing the myth.

21§33. So Dionysus is saying a fundamental truth when he tells Pentheus at lines 939–940 of the *Bacchae,* as quoted in Text A: 'I really do think you will consider me the foremost among those who are near and dear [*philoi*] to you | when, contrary to your expectations, you see that Bacchants [*bakkhai*] are moderate [= *sōphrones*].' What Dionysus means is that his own true worshippers, who are the chorus representing the Bacchants from Asia Minor, are in a mental state of equilibrium or balance when they participate in the rituals of Dionysiac theater by performing the myth that motivates these rituals. As a chorus, they perform the myth by singing and dancing it. By contrast, the mental state exhibited by the Bacchants of Thebes when they dismember Pentheus shows a

---

* Nagy 2007c:256.

violent departure from moderation, which can happen because they are participating not in the rituals of Dionysus but in the primal myth that motivates these
rituals. And this myth is a catastrophic experience for the women of Thebes as
Bacchants—as also for the hero Pentheus whom these Bacchants dismember.
The formulation that I developed in Hour 20§42 in the case of the hero Hippolytus applies here again in the case of the hero Pentheus and the Bacchants of
Thebes: *equilibrium in ritual is matched by disequilibrium in myth, and this disequilibrium leads to catastrophe.*

21§34. The disequilibrium of Pentheus and the Bacchants of Thebes is most
clearly dramatized in Text A, where Pentheus is given the opportunity of being
initiated as a member of a chorus of Bacchants. Dionysus has costumed Pentheus as a Bacchant, and the hero is being taught by the god how to perform in
a chorus of Bacchants. But this would-be chorus is not the chorus of the *Bacchae*. It is not the chorus of Asiatic women who have followed Dionysus to
Thebes—and who are the ritually correct chorus of the drama. Rather, this
would-be chorus consists of all the women of Thebes. They have left the urban
civilization of Thebes and have relocated themselves in the wilderness of the
mountains, where Dionysus has trained them to perform as a chorus. Already
at the beginning of the drama, at lines 32–38, the god himself announces his intention to relocate the women of Thebes to the mountains, saying that he will
train them there to become his chorus. But the trouble is, the choral training of
the Theban women—and of Pentheus—happens in myth, and they all fail to
become integral members of a true chorus, which is a ritually correct chorus. So
instead of integration, there is disintegration—and dismemberment. After all,
the thinking of the Thebans was polluted from the start, since they failed to receive Dionysus as one of their own.

21§35. So if characters in myth fail to become true worshippers of Dionysus
in his role as *Bakkhos*, then they cannot become *bakkhoi* or embodiments of the
god in ritual. The words of Socrates as quoted by Plato apply here:

HOUR 21 TEXT B

As those who are involved in the mysteries [*teletai*] say, "Many are the
carriers of the Bacchic wand [*narthēx*], |₆₉d but few are the *bakkhoi* [=
the true worshippers of Bacchus]."

Plato *Phaedo* 69c–d*

---

* εἰσὶν γὰρ δή, ὥς φασιν οἱ περὶ τὰς τελετάς, "ναρθηκοφόροι μὲν πολλοί, βάκχοι δέ τε παῦροι."

As we will see, the Bacchic wand used in rituals sacred to Dionysus is ordinarily called a *thursos* or 'thyrsus', which is a fennel stalk or *narthēx* that is stuffed with ivy.

21§36. Comparable is the aphorism of Jesus in the *New Testament*:

HOUR 21 TEXT C

"Many are called but few are chosen."

Matthew 22:14*

21§37. Keeping in mind the catastrophic failure of Pentheus and the Theban women in their choral experience, let us take a second look at what Dionysus is saying to Pentheus at lines 939–940 of the *Bacchae*, as I quoted it from Text A: 'I really do think you will consider me the foremost among those who are near and dear [*philoi*] to you | when, contrary to your expectations, you see that Bacchants [*bakkhai*] are moderate [= *sōphrones*]'. The god here is giving a primal lesson about his own divine essence. Dionysus is in effect saying to Pentheus: *you would know that the Bacchants are moderate and balanced if you were a true member of my chorus, and then I would be near and dear to you.* But the trouble with Pentheus is that he does not truly become a member of a Dionysiac chorus, and so the god cannot be near and dear to him. Pentheus only pretends to be a true member, asking whether his 'appearance', signaled by the epiphanic word *phainesthai* at line 925, is successful. If his 'appearance' really were successful, then there could be a real 'epiphany', and Pentheus could even become the god himself at the climax of the ritual. We saw this word *phainesthai* used in such a way in Song 31 of Sappho, as I explained in Hour 5§38. In other words, Pentheus as a true worshipper of Dionysus or Bacchus could 'appear' as the god Bacchus. Then he would not just 'appear' to be the god: he would instead, to repeat, 'appear' as the god in a true epiphany.

Staging Pentheus

21§38. From what we have seen so far, the *Bacchae* of Euripides is dramatizing a missed opportunity of major proportions—or, I may say, of heroic proportions. At line 915, the god Dionysus says that he himself has prepared the hero Pentheus to be costumed as someone who is a *mainas* or 'maenad'. Such a someone

---

* πολλοὶ γάρ εἰσιν κλητοὶ ὀλίγοι δὲ ἐκλεκτοί.

is further described here in the god's own words as a *bakkhē* or 'Bacchant'. But the opportunity for Pentheus is an illusion. The hero cannot really become a *mainas* or 'maenad', that is, a *bakkhē* or 'Bacchant'. To put it another way, Pentheus cannot really participate in Dionysiac ritual. And that is because he is not really a part of a ritual: rather, he has a major part in the Dionysiac myth that motivates the Dionysiac ritual. That is what I mean when I speak of the staging of Pentheus.

21§39. As someone whose mind is possessed negatively by the god in myth, Pentheus will behave catastrophically, while someone whose mind is possessed positively by the god in the ritual of drama will behave moderately, with decorum. The collective mind of the chorus in the drama of the *Bacchae* experiences such a positive possession. For this chorus, engaged as it is in the ritual of choral performance, the costuming will not come apart and the hairdo will not come undone. The arrangement of *kosmos* or 'order' will be maintained.

21§40. What I just said about *kosmos* can be illustrated negatively by considering what happens to Pentheus and the women of Thebes. First we consider Pentheus. By contrast with the chorus of the *Bacchae*, everything keeps coming apart and coming undone for him. At line 934, Pentheus actually asks the god to maintain the *kosmos* or 'order' that is needed for participating in a chorus: the verb used in this line is *kosmeîn,* derived from the noun *kosmos,* in the sense of 'arranging' the hairdo that keeps coming undone for Pentheus. As the hero keeps on shaking his unruly locks of hair at lines 930–931, he is 'in a Bacchic state of mind', *bakkhiazōn* (931). At a later point, we will consider the women of Thebes as described in a messenger's speech at lines 693–713, which I will be quoting. As we will see, these Bacchants of myth seem at first to be in a calm state of mind: reposing 'in a moderate way', *sōphronōs* (686). But then, once they roused up, they will shift from an appearance of 'proper arrangement' or *eukosmiā* (693) to a mental state that shows their full Bacchic frenzy. And the first sign of this frenzy, as we will also see, is that they let their hair down to their shoulders, reveling in their sacred dishevelment (695).* Bacchic possession in myth is like that: the action is disorderly and wild. By contrast, Bacchic possession in the ritual of singing and dancing by the chorus is orderly and moderated.

21§41. Just as the hairdo of Pentheus becomes disorderly, so too does his costuming. He says he depends on Dionysus to rearrange properly the waistband

---

* Nagy 2007c:255; see also Seaford 1996:206.

of his choral costume, which has come loose (935), as well as the pleats of his robe, which have lost their alignment (936–938).

21§42. The wording of Text A shows that Pentheus does not even know how to hold the *thursos* or 'thyrsus', that is, the Bacchic wand, which as we have seen is a fennel stalk or *narthēx* that is stuffed with ivy. He hesitates whether to wield this ritual object with his right or his left hand—as he tries to coordinate his gestures with the movement of his feet in choral dance (941–944).

21§43. The trouble is, Pentheus wants to look like a *bakkhē* or 'Bacchant', and he himself says so at line 941, but he does not want to become a Bacchant. Or, to put it more precisely, Pentheus never says that he wants to become a Bacchant in ritual. He only wants to look like a Bacchant in the myth. So he persists in his frenzied quest to defeat the Bacchants of Thebes, as he declares at line 945, and this unrelenting hostility is expressed in a delusional language of cosmic grandeur: I will lift with my own hands the mountains that harbor the Bacchants (949–950). In his deluded imagination, Pentheus thinks that he will defeat the women of Thebes and that he will celebrate his victory by allowing the defeated Bacchants to carry him back to the city as their champion—while his mother is cradling his head in her arms (966–970).

21§44. The outcome of all this delusional thinking is catastrophic. Once the mind of Pentheus is possessed negatively by the god in Dionysiac myth, the hero will be led to experience the catastrophe of dismemberment. By contrast, every time the mind of the chorus is possessed by Dionysus in Dionysiac ritual, it will be a positive possession, and each member of the chorus will experience the emotional equilibrium of membership. Such is the ritual experience of the chorus in Athenian State Theater. And such is the theology of Dionysus as the god of Athenian State Theater.

21§45. I have come to the end of my lengthy analysis of Text A. I had started by focusing on the word *agōn* at lines 964 and 975, and then on the word *pathos* at line 971. And, now that I have finished my close reading of the whole text, I can conclude that the *agōn* of Pentheus is in fact his 'ordeal' in undergoing the *pathos* or 'experience' of dismemberment, which is a larger-than-life 'suffering' or Passion that fits the larger-than-life dimensions of the hero in the *drāma* or ritual action of tragedy. This Passion of Pentheus is worthy of much lamentation, and it earns him the name *Pentheus,* which means 'the man of sorrow', derived from the noun *penthos.** As we saw in Hour 3§1, *penthos* is a formal ex-

---

* *PH* 387 = 13§12.

pression of sorrow or grief by way of performing songs of lament. Most fittingly, this word *penthos* is intoned at line 1244 of the *Bacchae* by the grieving Cadmus, aged founder of Thebes, as he speaks of the collective grief experienced by the Thebans over the catastrophic death of his grandson and their king, Pentheus.

A Divine Prototype for the Passion of Pentheus

21§46. The Passion of Pentheus, pictured as a dismemberment, is a form of death that is shaped by his heroic antagonism with the god Dionysus, who is traditionally worshipped in rituals of animal sacrifice that feature the ideas of *sparagmos* or 'dismemberment' and even *ōmophagia* or 'eating of raw flesh'.* Both these specific ideas are correlated with the general idea of disintegration followed by reintegration, in the sense that the body of an animal victim is dismembered and then eaten by the body politic: this way, the body politic can be reintegrated as a community through the communion of dividing and consuming the body of the victim.† As I will now argue, the general idea of disintegration followed by reintegration can be viewed as a Dionysiac model or prototype for the Passion of Pentheus.

21§47. I start by highlighting the existence of myths that tell how the god Dionysus himself was dismembered by the Titans, only to be reassembled later by divine intervention (for example, in Cornutus *On the Nature of the Gods* p. 62 lines 10–11 ed. Lang 1881, the divinity that reassembles Dionysus is Rhea, mother of Zeus).

21§48. There are references to such myths in the *Bacchae* of Euripides. I focus here on a choral song that links such myths with Dionysiac ritual themes of dismemberment and eating raw flesh:‡

HOUR 21 TEXT D

|$_{135}$ Sweet [*hēdus*] he is in the mountains, when, |$_{136}$ after running in the sacred band [*thiasos*] |$_{137-138}$ he drops to the ground, wearing the sacred [*hieron*] garment of fawn-skin, hunting |$_{139}$ the blood of the goat killed, tracking the beauty and the pleasure [*kharis*] of raw flesh de-

---

*On these ritual terms *sparagmos* or 'dismemberment' and *ōmophagia* or 'eating of raw flesh', see Henrichs 1978 and 1981.

† Henrichs 1978:148.

‡ There are many controversies surrounding this choral song in *Bacchae* 135–169; for a balanced analysis, I recommend Seaford 1996:165–166.

voured, |₁₄₀ rushing to the Phrygian, the Lydian mountains, |₁₄₁ and the chorus leader [ex-arkhos] is Bromios [= Dionysus the Thunderer]. Cry "Euhoi!" |₁₄₂ The plain flows with milk, it flows with wine, |₁₄₃ it flows with the nectar of bees. |₁₄₄ Like the smoke of Syrian incense, |₁₄₅ the Bacchic one [Bakkheus], raising high |₁₄₆ the fiery flame from the pine torch, |₁₄₇ bursts forth from the stalk [narthēx], |₁₄₈ arousing the stragglers with his running and with his dance-steps [khoroi], |₁₄₉ agitating them with his cries [iakkhai], |₁₅₀ tossing his luxuriant [trupheros] locks into the upper air. |₁₅₁ And amidst cries of "Euhoi!" his voice thunders words like this: |₁₅₂ "Come on [and join the chorus], Bacchants [bakkhai], |₁₅₃ come on [and join it], Bacchants, |₁₅₄ surrounded by the luxuriant beauty of Mount Tmolos, watered by streams flowing with gold. |₁₅₅ You all must sing and dance [melpein] Dionysus, |₁₅₆ in tune with the thundering beat of kettle-drums, |₁₅₇₋₁₅₈ glorifying with cries of 'Euhoi!' the god of the cry 'Euhoi!' |₁₅₉ with Phrygian shouts and clamor, |₁₆₀ when with its sweet song the pipe, |₁₆₁₋₁₆₃ sacred [hieros] it is, thunders its pulsating sacred [hiera] tunes |₁₆₄ for those who wander off to the mountain, to the mountain!" |₁₆₅ And she, taking sweet pleasure [hēdesthai], |₁₆₆₋₁₆₉ like a foal next to its grazing mother, rouses her swift-stepping legs to take one leap after the next, she the Bacchant [bakkhē].

Euripides Bacchae 135–169*

21§49. At first the communal thinking of the chorus here centers on a male *ex-arkhos* or 'leader' of a primordial chorus (141). He is 'in the mountains', and he is 'sweet', *hēdus* (135). Later the thinking shifts to a female member of this chorus. She is a Bacchant who is 'taking sweet pleasure', *hēdesthai* (165). Why is the male leader of the chorus 'sweet', and why does the female member 'take sweet pleasure'? I argue it is because he is 'sweet' *to the taste*, 'sweet' *to devour*.

---

* |₁₃₅ ἡδὺς ἐν ὄρεσσιν ὅταν |₁₃₆ ἐκ θιάσων δρομαίων |₁₃₇ πέσῃ πεδόσε, νεβρίδος ἔχων |₁₃₈ ἱερὸν ἐνδυτόν, ἀγρεύων |₁₃₉ αἷμα τραγοκτόνον, ὠμοφάγον χάριν, |₁₄₀ ἱέμενος εἰς ὄρεα Φρύγια Λύδι' |₁₄₁ ὁ δ' ἔξαρχος Βρόμιος· εὐοῖ. |₁₄₂ ῥεῖ δὲ γάλακτι πέδον, ῥεῖ δ' οἴνῳ, |₁₄₃ ῥεῖ δὲ μελισσᾶν νέκταρι. |₁₄₄ Συρίας δ' ὡς λιβάνου κα|₁₄₅πνὸς ὁ Βακχεὺς ἀνέχων |₁₄₆ πυρσώδη φλόγα πεύκας |₁₄₇ ἐκ νάρθηκος ἀίσσει |₁₄₈ δρόμῳ καὶ χοροῖσιν ἐρεθίζων πλανάτας |₁₄₉ ἰαχαῖς τ' ἀναπάλλων |₁₅₀ τρυφερὸν πλόκαμον εἰς αἰθέρα ῥίπτων. |₁₅₁ ἅμα δ' ἐπ' εὐάσμασιν ἐπιβρέμει τοιάδ'· |₁₅₂ ὦ ἴτε βάκχαι, |₁₅₃ ὦ ἴτε βάκχαι, |₁₅₄ Τμώλου χρυσορόου χλιδᾷ, |₁₅₅ μέλπετε τὸν Διόνυσον |₁₅₆ βαρυβρόμων ὑπὸ τυμπάνων, |₁₅₇₋₁₅₈ εὔια τὸν εὔιον ἀγαλλόμεναι θεὸν |₁₅₉ ἐν Φρυγίαισι βοαῖς ἐνοπαῖσί τε, |₁₆₀ λωτὸς ὅταν εὐκέλαδος |₁₆₁₋₁₆₃ ἱερὸς ἱερὰ παίγματα βρέμῃ σύνοχα |₁₆₄ φοιτάσιν εἰς ὄρος εἰς ὄρος· ἡδομέ|₁₆₅να δ' ἄρα πῶλος ὅπως ἅμα ματέρι |₁₆₆₋₁₆₉ φορβάδι κῶλον ἄγει ταχύπουν σκιρτήμασι βάκχα.

The communal thinking of this chorus centers on the communion of devouring raw flesh. The thought comes alive when the male leader drops to the ground (137–138). He has fallen into a trance, or even into a state of rapture. He is possessed by the god, and now he has become *Bromios,* Dionysus the 'Thunderer' (141). The moment of *kharis* has arrived, and I translate this eucharistic word as 'beauty and pleasure' (139)*. It is the *kharis* of 'raw flesh devoured' (139). But is it really Dionysus who will be dismembered and devoured? Or is it a goat? The full wording of the text here points to the goat, since the male leader of the chorus was 'hunting | the blood of the goat killed, tracking the beauty and the pleasure [*kharis*] of raw flesh devoured' (138–139). He had in his thoughts the blood of a goat at the very moment when he dropped to the ground in an altered mental state. So the thought of raw flesh devoured is transferred from Dionysus as the object of desire. Now the new object of desire is the blood of a sacrificial goat that is slaughtered. Relevant is the meaning of the word *tragōidiā* or 'tragedy', derived from the more basic word *tragōidoi* or 'performers of tragedy', who are 'goat singers' in the sense of *performers of choral song and dance who compete to win the prize of a sacrificial goat.*†

21§50. The prototypical chorus that is pictured here is literally singing and dancing Dionysus, and such a choral performance is signaled by the word *melpein* (155). As we saw in Hour 5§33, this word refers to both the singing and the dancing performed by a chorus. But the god is not only the object of this singing and dancing. He is also the subject. In other words, he is also the power that activates the choral performance. To say it grammatically, Dionysus behaves like the subject of the active verbs that express the activation of choral performance. Another aspect of the active involvement of the god Dionysus in the choral performance is the interjection *ite . . . ite* at lines 152–153, which I have translated as 'come on [and join the chorus], Bacchants [*bakkhai*], | come on [and join it]'.‡ As a divine activator, Dionysus literally ignites the singing and the dancing as he leaps out, in an elemental burst of flame, from inside the fennel stalk or *narthēx* of the sacred wand used for Bacchic worship.§ The picturing of such a flaming emergence from inside a stalk or a reed is a traditional idea that can be traced back, I argue, to Indo-European mythology, since there

---

* On *kharis* as a word that conveys both beauty and pleasure, see *HC* 203-204 = 2§33.

† *PH* 389–390 = 13§18, following Burkert 1966.

‡ Comparable is the interjection *itō* as an impersonal way of saying 'come on, let's go' in choral performance: I offer some preliminary remarks in *PP* 41n7.

§ In my translation of lines 144–145 of the *Bacchae,* I follow the reading καπνός (in the nominative case) as transmitted in the medieval manuscripts.

is a corresponding idea attested in Indo-Iranian traditions and assimilated into Armenian heroic narratives (by way of Iranian models). I have in mind here a song preserved in the *History of the Armenians* by Moses of Khoren (1.31): this song pictures the cosmic moment when the dragon-slayer Vahagn is born from a reed that is said to be in labor as it expels first a burst of smoke, then a burst of flame, and then, out of the flame, a youth with his hair on fire and with eyes that are two suns.*

21§51. In sum, the chorus that is pictured in Text D as quoted from the *Bacchae* of Euripides does not belong to the here and now of Dionysiac ritual in the choral performances of Athenian State Theater. Rather, this chorus of Text D is rooted in the primordial past of Dionysiac myth. The choral action in the myth is disorderly and wild. By contrast the choral action that re-enacts the myth in the ritualized drama of Athenian State Theater is orderly and moderated. As a most striking point of contrast, the wild disorder of the chorus in the myth is signaled by the sacred dishevelment of the male chorus leader as he tosses the unruly locks of his loose hair to the winds stirred up by the dance fever of his own mad rush toward the mountains up ahead. In the end, that chorus leader is the god Dionysus.

21§52. I use the expression 'in the end' here because it suits the wording spoken by Dionysus himself when he goes offstage to outfit Pentheus with the costume that will kill the hero:

HOUR 21 TEXT E

|₈₅₇ I am going now. The costume [*kosmos*] that he will take with him to the house of Hādēs |₈₅₈ when he goes off to that place, slaughtered by the two hands of his own mother |₈₅₉—that costume will I attach to Pentheus. And he will come to know the son of Zeus, |₈₆₀ Dionysus, the one who is by his own nature a god in the end [*telos*], |₈₆₁ the one who is most terrifying [*deinos*], but, for humans, also most gentle [*ēpios*].

Euripides *Bacchae* 857–861†

---

*More on this song in Dumézil 1970:127–129. Watkins 1995:167 suggests some modifications for Dumézil's translation of the Armenian text, but those suggestions are not relevant to the meaning of the text as I paraphrase it here.

† |₈₅₇ ἀλλ᾽ εἶμι κόσμον ὅνπερ εἰς Ἅιδου λαβὼν |₈₅₈ ἄπεισι μητρὸς ἐκ χεροῖν κατασφαγεὶς |₈₅₉ Πενθεῖ προσάψων· γνώσεται δὲ τὸν Διὸς |₈₆₀ Διόνυσον, ὃς πέφυκεν ἐν τέλει θεὸς |₈₆₁ δεινότατος, ἀνθρώποισι δ᾽ ἠπιώτατος.

21§53. Dionysus speaks of himself in the third person here as he foretells his divine intervention. Similarly in Hour 20§13, we have seen Aphrodite speaking of herself in the third person in another case of divine intervention. As for the wording of Dionysus in the text I just quoted, the use of the third person here highlights the mystical meaning of *telos*: as the one 'who is by his own nature a god in the end [*telos*]', the god indicates not only the 'end' or 'fulfillment' of the myth of Pentheus but also the ultimate lesson of 'initiation' into the mysteries of Dionysus.* We have already seen such mystical uses of the word *telos* in Hour 20.

Tracking Down the Origins of Tragedy

21§54. I bring this hour to an end by considering an aetiological myth that we find embedded in the *Bacchae* of Euripides. This myth is about the origins of tragedy as a ritual, viewed in terms of the *agōn* or 'ordeal' to be experienced by Pentheus in myth. The telling of the myth takes place before the primal experience actually happens. A herdsman has seen the behavior of the Theban women who had taken to the mountains, and he becomes a messenger who now tells his eyewitness story to Pentheus:

HOUR 21 TEXT F

|677 I was just driving the herd up the slope, |678 a herd of cattle, driving them uphill from further downhill, at the time when the sun |679 sends forth its rays, warming the earth. |680 And I see three companies [*thiasoi*] of women's choruses [*khoroi*], |681 one of which Autonoe was leading, the second, |682 your mother, Agaue, and the third chorus [*khoros*], Ino. |683 All were sleeping, their bodies relaxed, |684 some resting their backs on the leaves of fir trees, |685 while others were laying their heads on oak leaves strewn on the ground, |686 lying here and there in a moderate way [*sōphronōs*] and not, as you say, |687 filled with wine in a scene of wine-cups and tunes played on the pipe, |688 and not at all hunting to find Kypris [= Aphrodite] while roaming through the woods on their own. |689 Then your mother raised the cry of *ololu* as she was |690 standing in the midst of the Bacchants. She was signaling them to rouse

---

* Resisting the attempts of some editors to emend the wording here, I retain the reading found in the manuscript tradition of the *Bacchae*.

their bodies and awaken from sleep |₆₉₁ as soon as she heard the lowing of the horned cattle. |₆₉₂ So they threw potent sleep from their eyes |₆₉₃ and sprang upright—a marvel [*thauma*] of proper arrangement [*eukosmiā*] to behold |₆₉₄—young, old, and still unmarried virgins. |₆₉₅ First they let their hair loose over their shoulders, |₆₉₆ and then they re-arranged their fawn-skins, which already had |₆₉₇ the fastenings of their knots come loose. |₆₉₈ So they girded these spotted hides with serpents that licked their cheeks, |₆₉₉ and some women were cradling in their arms a gazelle—or the cubs of wolves— |₇₀₀ and, holding these wild things, they gave them white milk |₇₀₁—I mean, those women who had recently given birth and had their breasts still swollen, |₇₀₂ having left behind at home their own babies. And they placed on their heads ivy |₇₀₃ as garlands, and oak, and flowering yew. |₇₀₄ One took her wand [*thursos*] and struck it against a rock, |₇₀₅ and out of it a dewy stream of water sprang forth. |₇₀₆ Another let her wand [*narthēx*] strike the ground of the earth, |₇₀₇ and there the god sent forth a stream of wine. |₇₀₈ All who had a desire [*pothos*] for the white drink |₇₀₉ patted the earth with the tips of their fingers |₇₁₀ and obtained jets of milk. And from the wands stuffed with ivy, |₇₁₁ from those wands [*thursoi*] sweet streams of honey were dripping. |₇₁₂ So, if you [= Pentheus] had been present, then the god whom you now blame— |₇₁₃ you would have approached him with prayers, yes, if you had seen these things. |₇₁₄ And we herdsmen and shepherds came together [*sun-ēlthomen*] |₇₁₅ so that we could give each other a competition [*eris*] of words that we had in common, |₇₁₆ concerning what kinds of terrifying things they do [*drân*], yes, terrifying and worthy of wonder [*thauma*].

Euripides *Bacchae* 677–716*

* |₆₇₇ ἀγελαῖα μὲν βοσκήματ’ ἄρτι πρὸς λέπας |₆₇₈ μόσχων ὑπεξήκριζον, ἡνίχ’ ἥλιος |₆₇₉ ἀκτῖνας ἐξίησι θερμαίνων χθόνα. |₆₈₀ ὁρῶ δὲ θιάσους τρεῖς γυναικείων χορῶν, |₆₈₁ ὧν ἦρχ’ ἑνὸς μὲν Αὐτονόη, τοῦ δευτέρου |₆₈₂ μήτηρ Ἀγαυὴ σή, τρίτου δ’ Ἰνὼ χοροῦ. |₆₈₃ ηὗδον δὲ πᾶσαι σώμασιν παρειμέναι, |₆₈₄ αἱ μὲν πρὸς ἐλάτης νῶτ’ ἐρείσασαι φόβην, |₆₈₅ αἱ δ’ ἐν δρυὸς φύλλοισι πρὸς πέδῳ κάρα |₆₈₆ εἰκῇ βαλοῦσαι σωφρόνως, οὐχ ὡς σὺ φὴς |₆₈₇ ᾠνωμένας κρατῆρι καὶ λωτοῦ ψόφῳ |₆₈₈ θηρᾶν καθ’ ὕλην Κύπριν ἠρημωμένας. |₆₈₉ ἡ σὴ δὲ μήτηρ ὠλόλυξεν ἐν μέσαις |₆₉₀ σταθεῖσα βάκχαις ἐξ ὕπνου κινεῖν δέμας, |₆₉₁ μυκήμαθ’ ὡς ἤκουσε κεροφόρων βοῶν. |₆₉₂ αἱ δ’ ἀποβαλοῦσαι θαλερὸν ὀμμάτων ὕπνον |₆₉₃ ἀνῇξαν ὀρθαί, θαῦμ’ ἰδεῖν εὐκοσμίας, |₆₉₄ νέαι παλαιαὶ παρθένοι τ’ ἔτ’ ἄζυγες. |₆₉₅ καὶ πρῶτα μὲν καθεῖσαν εἰς ὤμους κόμας |₆₉₆ νεβρίδας τ’ ἀνεστείλανθ’ ὅσαισιν ἁμμάτων |₆₉₇ σύνδεσμ’ ἐλέλυτο, καὶ καταστίκτους δορὰς |₆₉₈ ὄφεσι κατεζώσαντο λιχμῶσιν γένυν. |₆₉₉ αἱ δ’ ἀγκάλαισι δορκάδ’ ἢ σκύμνους λύκων |₇₀₀ ἀγρίους ἔχουσαι λευκὸν ἐδίδοσαν γάλα, |₇₀₁ ὅσαις νεοτόκοις μαστὸς ἦν σπαργῶν ἔτι |₇₀₂ βρέφη λιπούσαις· ἐπὶ δ’ ἔθεντο κισσίνους |₇₀₃ στεφάνους δρυός τε μίλακός τ’ ἀνθεσφόρου. |₇₀₄ θύρσον

21§55. As I noted earlier, these Bacchants of myth seem at first to be in a calm state of mind—but that is only because they are now in a state of repose. When they are in such a state, they are behaving 'in a moderate way', *sōphronōs* (686). But then, once they are roused up, they will shift from an appearance of 'proper arrangement' or *eukosmiā* (693) to a mental state that shows their full Bacchic frenzy. The herdsman who is telling his eyewitness story to Pentheus the king is trying here to attenuate what he reports about the Theban Bacchants, since his own experience with them has already made him fear the god Dionysus even more than he fears the king, but the story nevertheless develops its own momentum, contradicting the herdsman's claims about the 'moderation' and the 'proper arrangement' of the prototypical choruses of Theban women. The decisive moment that leads to the frenzy of these women is clearly highlighted in the herdsman's story.

21§56. This moment arrives when Agaue, the mother of Pentheus, hears the lowing of the cattle that are being driven up the mountain by the herdsman, and now she calls out to her fellow Bacchants, alerting them (689–691). Once the Theban Bacchants are alerted, the stage is set for these frenzied women to dismember the herded cattle and to devour them raw—in a scene described in a later part of the herdsman's story, not quoted here (735–747). But the dismemberment and the eating of raw flesh cannot happen until the god Dionysus himself makes it all possible. As we can see from yet another part of the herdsman's story, likewise not quoted here (717–721), Dionysus succeeds in inducing all the herdsmen to attack the Theban Bacchants. The god succeeds because, as the wording of the story reveals, he has not been recognized by the herdsmen, who are deluded into thinking that Dionysus is merely 'a wanderer who is clever with words' (717). So, in another passage that is not quoted here (721–733), the deluded herdsmen are induced to attack the Theban Bacchants, and they are defeated. More than that, these herdsmen barely escape with their lives, almost suffering the fate of *sparagmos* or 'dismemberment' (734). And that is when the Theban Bacchants finally turn their attention to the cattle that are being herded uphill by the herdsmen, among whom is the teller of the story. The frenzied women now dismember all these cattle, tearing them apart with their own

δέ τις λαβοῦσ' ἔπαισεν ἐς πέτραν, |₇₀₅ ὅθεν δροσώδης ὕδατος ἐκπηδᾷ νοτίς· |₇₀₆ ἄλλη δὲ νάρθηκ' ἐς πέδον καθῆκε γῆς |₇₀₇ καὶ τῇδε κρήνην ἐξανῆκ' οἴνου θεός· |₇₀₈ ὅσαις δὲ λευκοῦ πώματος πόθος παρῆν, |₇₀₉ ἄκροισι δακτύλοισι διαμῶσαι χθόνα |₇₁₀ γάλακτος ἑσμοὺς εἶχον· ἐκ δὲ κισσίνων |₇₁₁ θύρσων γλυκεῖαι μέλιτος ἔσταζον ῥοαί. |₇₁₂ ὥστ', εἰ παρῆσθα, τὸν θεὸν τὸν νῦν ψέγεις |₇₁₃ εὐχαῖσιν ἂν μετῆλθες εἰσιδὼν τάδε. |₇₁₄ ξυνήλθομεν δὲ βουκόλοι καὶ ποιμένες |₇₁₅ κοινῶν λόγων δώσοντες ἀλλήλοις ἔριν |₇₁₆ ὡς δεινὰ δρῶσι θαυμάτων τ' ἐπάξια.

hands, limb from limb (735–747). Then the orgy of dismemberment spreads beyond the immediate vicinity of Thebes (748–758), and all the menfolk of the entire region take up arms against the Bacchants—only to be soundly defeated by them (758–768).

21§57. The delusion of the herdsmen, who were induced by Dionysus to attack the Theban Bacchants, sets the stage for the delusion of Pentheus himself. We have already seen in Text A how Dionysus induces the young king to attack the Theban Bacchants. And it is in this context that I can now focus on the aetiological myth that we find embedded in Text F. So I now highlight the key wording of the herdsman's story, at lines 714–716 of Text F, where the storyteller says: 'we herdsmen and shepherds came together [*sun-ēlthomen*] | so that we could give each other a competition [*eris*] of words that we had in common, | concerning what kinds of terrifying things they do [*drân*], yes, terrifying and worthy of wonder [*thauma*]'. Here at last we see the three meanings of *agōn*, as I outlined them at the beginning of this hour:

1. the *coming together* of the herdsmen and
2. their *competition* with each other by way of
3. their re-enacting, in words they have in common, the experiences they also have in common, which are the terrifying things that the Bacchants do (*drân*)—and which will lead ultimately to the *ordeal* of Pentheus, that is, the supreme *agony* of his dismemberment.

21§58. So we see here the three meanings of the word *agōn* as I had defined them in §1 of this hour. And these three meanings add up to an aetiological myth that tells the origin of tragedy as a primal moment initiated by the god Dionysus. People come together for a competition in words about terrifying experiences. They come together at a festival featuring competitions in the verbal art of choral singing and dancing, and, ultimately, the song is all about the larger-than-life agony of a hero. Dionysus makes it all happen.

Hope for a Reassembly of the Body after Its Dismemberment

21§59. While Pentheus is being costumed offstage by Dionysus for the hero's impending ordeal in the mountains, where he will be torn limb from limb by the Bacchants of myth, there is a choral song being sung and danced by the Bacchants of the ritual that is the drama of the *Bacchae*. The words of this choral song, lines 862–912, celebrate the impending liberation of the devotees of Dionysus from the persecution of Pentheus, and these words can be seen as self-references to the exuberant but at the same time measured choral behavior of the Bacchants who are represented as singing and dancing this choral song. As I will argue, this celebration is relevant to the dismemberment of Pentheus as king of Thebes, and it holds out hope for the ultimate reassembly of his kingly body—or, better, of the body politic that is Thebes.

21§60. Here is how the choral song of celebration begins:

HOUR 21 TEXT G

|₈₆₂ Shall I ever, in choruses that last all night long, |₈₆₃ set in motion my gleaming white |₈₆₄ foot in a Bacchic revel as I thrust my throat |₈₆₅ toward the upper air wet with dew, yes, thrusting it forward |₈₆₆—just like a fawn playfully |₈₆₇ skipping around in the green delights of a meadow |₈₆₈ after she has escaped from the terrifying |₈₆₉ hunt. Now she is out of reach, |₈₇₀ having leapt beyond their hunting nets, |₈₇₁ even while the hunter keeps shouting |₈₇₂ his hunting cry to his hounds, urging them to run faster and faster. |₈₇₃ But the fawn, like a gust of wind with the vigor of her swift running, is now bounding past the meadow |₈₇₄ that has the river next to it, and she can take sweet delight |₈₇₅ in the absence of mortal men |₈₇₆ amidst the tender shoots growing in the forest with its shady leaves.

Euripides Bacchae 862–876*

21§61. This choral song, expressing the beauty and the pleasure of Dionysiac liberation, is marked by a most striking refrain:

HOUR 21 TEXT H

Whatever is beautiful [*kalon*] is near and dear [*philon*] forever.

Euripides Bacchae 881 and 901†

---

* |₈₆₂ ἆρ᾽ ἐν παννυχίοις χοροῖς |₈₆₃ θήσω ποτὲ λευκὸν |₈₆₄ πόδ᾽ ἀναβακχεύουσα, δέραν |₈₆₅ αἰθέρ᾽ ἐς δροσερὸν ῥίπτουσ᾽, |₈₆₆ ὡς νεβρὸς χλοεραῖς ἐμπαί|₈₆₇ζουσα λείμακος ἡδοναῖς, |₈₆₈ ἁνίκ᾽ ἂν φοβερὰν φύγῃ |₈₆₉ θήραν ἔξω φυλακᾶς |₈₇₀ εὐπλέκτων ὑπὲρ ἀρκύων, |₈₇₁ θωύσσων δὲ κυναγέτας |₈₇₂ συντείνῃ δράμημα κυνῶν, |₈₇₃ μόχθοις δ᾽ ὠκυδρόμοις ἀελλὰς θρῴσκῃ πεδίον |₈₇₄ παραποτάμιον, ἡδομένα |₈₇₅ βροτῶν ἐρημίαις σκιαρο|₈₇₆κόμοιό τ᾽ ἔρνεσιν ὕλας;

† ὅτι καλὸν φίλον αἰεί.

21§62. This refrain, which equates the beauty of the song with the pleasure of nearness and dearness, is an echo of a song sung at a most auspicious occasion. We know it from the poetry of Theognis:*

HOUR 21 TEXT I

|₁₅ Muses and Graces [Kharites], daughters of Zeus! You were the ones who once came |₁₆ to the wedding of Cadmus, and you sang this beautiful set of words [epos]: |₁₇ "Whatever is beautiful [kalon] is near and dear [philon], and whatever is not beautiful [kalon] is not near and dear [philon]." |₁₈ That is the set of words [epos] that came through their immortal mouths.

Theognis 15–18†

21§63. In another project, I studied closely the myriad implications of this most compressed passage.‡ Here I focus on its relevance to the refrain of the *Bacchae,* which as we have seen equates the beauty of song with the pleasure of nearness and dearness. The wedding of Cadmus is most relevant to such an equation, since he is the founder of the city of Thebes, and his wedding marks the actual moment of this city's foundation. So the nearness and the dearness expressed by the beauty of the song is also an expression of the institutional and emotional bonds that integrate society, thus creating the body politic. Performing along with the Muses at the wedding of Cadmus are the *Kharites* or 'Graces', who are the embodiment of *kharis,* which expresses the beauty and the pleasure of the ties that bind men and women together, thus integrating the body politic.§ And we know from the poetry of Hesiod (*Theogony* 937, 975) that the name of the bride of Cadmus is *Harmoniā,* which is a word that expresses the idea of integration for both song and society. The word is borrowed into English as *harmony,* which expresses the same idea—even if the modern musical concept of harmony is different from the ancient concept of *harmoniā* as the tuning or accordatura of a seven-stringed lyre (as we saw in Hour 20§53).**

21§64. So there is an irony in the echoing of this song of beauty and social

---

* Nagy 1982.

† |₁₅ Μοῦσαι καὶ Χάριτες, κοῦραι Διός, αἵ ποτε Κάδμου |₁₆ ἐς γάμον ἐλθοῦσαι καλὸν ἀείσατ' ἔπος, |₁₇ "ὅττι καλόν, φίλον ἐστί· τὸ δ' οὐ καλὸν οὐ φίλον ἐστί." |₁₈ τοῦτ' ἔπος ἀθανάτων ἦλθε διὰ στομάτων.

‡ Nagy 1985:27–28 = §§6–7.

§ On *kharis* as a word that conveys both beauty and pleasure, see *HC* 203–204 = 2§33.

** On other metaphors expressing the idea of the body politic in myths about the "harmonious" foundation of Thebes, see *PH* 145 = 5§16n45.

integration in the refrain of the *Bacchae*, which marks the ultimate disintegration of the king Pentheus, the grandson of Cadmus the founder of Thebes. But there is also an implied hope expressed in this echoing, since the integration of the body politic can be seen as a correlate of the disintegration suffered by the body of the king. I say this because, as we have already seen in earlier hours, the generic king can be pictured as the body politic (6§13 and §47; 9§6; 10§13; 19§20). Plutarch in his *Life of Romulus* (27.5) reports a myth about Romulus that I find most relevant: according to the myth, this prototypical king of Rome is killed and dismembered by the members of the prototypical senate, each one of whom takes home with him a portion of the body. My reading of this myth is that it aetiologizes the recurrent convenings of the Roman senate: every time the senate comes together to represent the body politic in the political present, it reintegrates the body of the prototypical king whom the prototypical senators had dismembered in the mythical past. So there may be hope for Pentheus as well: every time a chorus sings and dances the refrain 'whatever is beautiful is near and dear', the body of the primordial king may once again get to be reassembled as the body politic.

PART FOUR

HEROES IN TWO
DIALOGUES OF PLATO

The Living Word I: Socrates in Plato's Apology of Socrates

The Meaning of Daimonion

22§1. The key word for this hour is *daimonion,* which is a neuter adjective derived from the noun *daimōn.* In Hour 5§1, we saw that this word *daimōn* (plural *daimones*) is used to refer to an unspecified god or hero intervening in human life. By contrast, *theos,* 'god', is used to refer to a specified god. Accordingly, I have been translating the noun *daimōn* as 'superhuman force'. And now I will apply this translation to the derivative form *daimonion.*

22§2. In the usage of Plato's Socrates, as in Plato's *Republic* (6.496c), *daimonion* functions as the adjective of the neuter noun *sēmeion,* which is derived from another neuter noun, *sēma.* As we saw in Hour 7§1, *sēma* means 'sign, signal, symbol; tomb, tomb of a hero'. Since *sēmeion* can be translated as 'signal', I propose to translate the expression *to daimonion sēmeion,* as we find it in the *Republic,* as 'the superhuman signal'. Elsewhere in the usage of Plato's Socrates, however, as in Plato's *Apology of Socrates,* the expressions *to daimonion* and *to sēmeion* are used separately as synonyms; in these cases, I will translate *to daimonion* as 'the superhuman thing' and *to sēmeion* as 'the signal'.

The Subversive Threat of 'the Superhuman Signal'

22§3. In Plato's *Apology of Socrates* (31d), in a passage I will not be quoting here, Plato's Socrates says that 'the superhuman thing', *to daimonion,* had prevented him from participating in the public life of the Athenian state, restricting him to a private way of interacting with his fellow citizens. He describes this superhuman thing as an inner *phōnē,* 'voice', that never tells him what to do but only what not to do. One of the things that this inner voice tells Socrates not to do is to participate in the public life of the Athenian State. As Plato's Socrates says in the *Apology* (32a), in another passage I will not be quoting, he must not 'lead the public life of a citizen', *politeuein*, and so, by default, he will 'lead the private life', *idiōteuein*. That is how he gets into trouble with the Athenian State: as we learn in Plato's *Euthyphro* (3b), in yet another passage I will not be quoting, Socrates was accused of subversion, on the grounds that he was corrupting the young men of Athens by speaking to them about *to daimonion*, 'the superhuman thing', which did not fit the traditional concept of *theoi*, 'gods'.

22§4. I will now quote from the *Apology* another passage in which this expression *to daimonion*, 'the superhuman thing', occurs. In this passage, as we will see, the synonymous expression *to sēmeion*, 'the signal', is also used:

HOUR 22 TEXT A1

In the past, the oracular [*mantikē*] art of the superhuman thing [*to daimonion*] within me was in the habit of opposing me, each and every time, even about minor things, if I was going to do anything not correctly [*orthōs*]. But now that these things, as you can see, have happened to me—things that anyone would consider, by general consensus, to be the worst possible things to happen to someone— |₄₀b the signal [*to sēmeion*] of the god [*theos*] has not opposed me, either as I was leaving my house and going out in the morning, or when I was coming up to this place of judgment, or as I was speaking. No, it has not opposed me about anything I was going to say, though on other occasions when I was speaking, it [= the signal] has often stopped me, even when I was in the middle of saying something. But now in nothing I either said or did concerning this matter has it opposed me. So what do I take to be the explanation of this? I will tell you. Perhaps this is a proof that what has happened to me is something good [*agathon*], |₄₀c and it cannot be that we are thinking straight [*orthōs*] if we think that death is something bad [*kakon*]. This is a great proof to me of what I am saying, since the signal [*to sēmeion*] that I am used to would surely have opposed me if I had been heading toward something not good [*agathon*].

Plato *Apology of Socrates* 40a-c*

---

*ἡ γὰρ εἰωθυῖά μοι μαντικὴ ἡ τοῦ δαιμονίου ἐν μὲν τῷ πρόσθεν χρόνῳ παντὶ πάνυ πυκνὴ ἀεὶ ἦν καὶ πάνυ ἐπὶ σμικροῖς ἐναντιουμένη, εἴ τι μέλλοιμι μὴ ὀρθῶς πράξειν. νυνὶ δὲ συμβέβηκέ μοι ἅπερ ὁρᾶτε καὶ αὐτοί, ταυτὶ ἅ γε δὴ οἰηθείη ἄν τις καὶ νομίζεται ἔσχατα κακῶν εἶναι· ἐμοὶ δὲ |₄₀b οὔτε ἐξιόντι ἕωθεν οἴκοθεν ἠναντιώθη τὸ τοῦ θεοῦ σημεῖον, οὔτε ἡνίκα ἀνέβαινον ἐνταυθοῖ ἐπὶ τὸ δικαστήριον, οὔτε ἐν τῷ

22§5. So what does 'the superhuman signal' tell Socrates *not* to experience? The answer to that question will be clear when we reach Text A5. As we will see in that text, this 'signal' does not tell Socrates not to choose death. And that is because, as we will also see in that text, dying 'now' is not wrong—it is right. The present time will be for Socrates the 'right time', the *hōrā*, to die.

What Happens to Socrates after Death

22§6. As Plato's Socrates argues, one of two things is most likely to happen after he or anyone else dies, and neither one of them is bad:

HOUR 22 TEXT A2

> Let us think about it this way: there is plenty of reason to hope that death is something good [*agathon*]. I say this because death is one of two things: either it is a state of nothingness and utter unconsciousness for the person who has died, or, according to the sayings [*legomena*], there is some kind of change [*meta-bolē*] that happens—a relocation [*met-oikēsis*] for the soul [*psūkhē*] from this place [*topos*] to another place [*topos*].

> Plato *Apology of Socrates* 40c*

22§7. The *legomena* or 'sayings' here are the revelations of a mystical hero named Orpheus, which are mediated in Athenian traditions by another mystical hero named Musaeus. Both of these figures will be mentioned by name later, in Text A4. In the dialogues composed by Plato, Socrates frequently expresses interest in the mystical teachings attributed to Orpheus and Musaeus, who are associated with the elitist predemocratic agenda of the Peisistratidai, a dynasty of tyrants who ruled Athens before the advent of the democratic regime.† In

---

λόγῳ οὐδαμοῦ μέλλοντί τι ἐρεῖν. καίτοι ἐν ἄλλοις λόγοις πολλαχοῦ δή με ἐπέσχε λέγοντα μεταξύ· νῦν δὲ οὐδαμοῦ περὶ ταύτην τὴν πρᾶξιν οὔτ᾽ ἐν ἔργῳ οὐδενὶ οὔτ᾽ ἐν λόγῳ ἠναντίωταί μοι. τί οὖν αἴτιον εἶναι ὑπολαμβάνω; ἐγὼ ὑμῖν ἐρῶ· κινδυνεύει γάρ μοι τὸ συμβεβηκὸς τοῦτο ἀγαθὸν γεγονέναι, καὶ οὐκ ἔσθ᾽ ὅπως ἡμεῖς ὀρθῶς ὑπολαμβάνομεν, |₄₀c ὅσοι οἰόμεθα κακὸν εἶναι τὸ τεθνάναι. μέγα μοι τεκμήριον τούτου γέγονεν· οὐ γὰρ ἔσθ᾽ ὅπως οὐκ ἠναντιώθη ἄν μοι τὸ εἰωθὸς σημεῖον, εἰ μή τι ἔμελλον ἐγὼ ἀγαθὸν πράξειν.

*'Ἐννοήσωμεν δὲ καὶ τῇδε ὡς πολλὴ ἐλπίς ἐστιν ἀγαθὸν αὐτὸ εἶναι. δυοῖν γὰρ θάτερόν ἐστιν τὸ τεθνάναι· ἢ γὰρ οἷον μηδὲν εἶναι μηδὲ αἴσθησιν μηδεμίαν μηδενὸς ἔχειν τὸν τεθνεῶτα, ἢ κατὰ τὰ λεγόμενα μεταβολή τις τυγχάνει οὖσα καὶ μετοίκησις τῇ ψυχῇ τοῦ τόπου τοῦ ἐνθένδε εἰς ἄλλον τόπον.

† *HPC* 340–352 = E§§95–128.

19§8, I already noted the ideological antipathy of the Athenian democracy toward the Peisistratidai.

22§8. The interest expressed by Socrates in the *legomena* or 'sayings' of figures like Orpheus and Musaeus does not make him dependent on their teachings, however. Plato's Socrates is equally interested in another scenario for an afterlife, which is no afterlife at all:

HOUR 22 TEXT A3

> Now if you suppose that there is no consciousness, |₄₀d but a sleep like the sleep of someone who sees nothing even in a dream, death will be a wondrous gain [kerdos]. For if a person were to select the night in which he slept without seeing anything even in a dream, and if he were to compare this with the other days and nights of his life, and then were to tell us how many days and nights he had passed in the course of his life in a better and more pleasant way than this one, I think that any person—I will not say a private individual [idiōtēs], but even the great king—|₄₀e will not find many such days or nights, when compared with the others. Now if death is like this, I say that to die is a gain [kerdos]; for the sum total of time is then only a single night.
>
> Plato *Apology of Socrates* 40c-e*

22§9. That said, Plato's Socrates proceeds to consider in some detail the alternative scenario, giving a precious glimpse into the mystical *legomena* or 'sayings' about an afterlife:†

HOUR 22 TEXT A4

> But if death is the journey [apo-dēmiā] to another place [topos], and, if the sayings [legomena] are true [alēthē], that all the dead are over there [ekeî], then what good [agathon], O jurors, [dikastai], can be greater

---

* καὶ εἴτε δὴ μηδεμία αἴσθησίς ἐστιν ἀλλ' |₄₀d οἷον ὕπνος ἐπειδάν τις καθεύδων μηδ' ὄναρ μηδὲν ὁρᾷ, θαυμάσιον κέρδος ἂν εἴη ὁ θάνατος—ἐγὼ γὰρ ἂν οἶμαι, εἴ τινα ἐκλεξάμενον δέοι ταύτην τὴν νύκτα ἐν ᾗ οὕτω κατέδαρθεν ὥστε μηδὲ ὄναρ ἰδεῖν, καὶ τὰς ἄλλας νύκτας τε καὶ ἡμέρας τὰς τοῦ βίου τοῦ ἑαυτοῦ ἀντιπαραθέντα ταύτῃ τῇ νυκτὶ δέοι σκεψάμενον εἰπεῖν πόσας ἄμεινον καὶ ἥδιον ἡμέρας καὶ νύκτας ταύτης τῆς νυκτὸς βεβίωκεν ἐν τῷ ἑαυτοῦ βίῳ, οἶμαι ἂν μὴ ὅτι ἰδιώτην τινά, ἀλλὰ τὸν μέγαν βασιλέα εὐαριθμήτους |₄₀e ἂν εὑρεῖν αὐτὸν ταύτας πρὸς τὰς ἄλλας ἡμέρας καὶ νύκτας—εἰ οὖν τοιοῦτον ὁ θάνατός ἐστιν, κέρδος ἔγωγε λέγω· καὶ γὰρ οὐδὲν πλείων ὁ πᾶς χρόνος φαίνεται οὕτω δὴ εἶναι ἢ μία νύξ.

† Herodotus 2.8.2 speaks of *hieros logos* or 'sacred discourse' attributed to the followers of Orpheus, among others; I offer comments in *HPC* 343–344 = E§§104–105.

than this? | ₄₁ₐ If, when someone arrives in the world of Hādēs, he is freed from those who call themselves jurors [*dikastai*] here, and finds the true [*alētheîs*] judges [*dikastai*] who are said to give judgment [*dikazein*] over there [*ekeî*]—Minos and Rhadamanthus and Aiakos and Triptolemos, and other demigods [*hēmi-theoi*] who were righteous [*dikaioi*] in their own life—that would not be a bad journey [*apo-dēmiā*], now would it? To make contact with Orpheus and Musaeus and Hesiod and Homer—who of you would not welcome such a great opportunity? Why, if these things are true [*alēthē*], let me die again and again. | ₄₁ᵦ I, too, would have a wondrous activity [*diatribē*] there, once I make contact with Palamedes, and with Ajax the son of Telamon, and with other ancient men who have suffered death through an unjust [*a-dikos*] judgment [*krisis*]. And there will be no small pleasure, I think, in comparing my own experiences [*pathos* plural] with theirs. Further— and this is the greatest thing of all—I will be able to continue questioning those who are over there [*ekeî*], just as I question those who are over here [*entautha*], and investigating who among them is wise [*sophos*] and who among them thinks he is wise [*sophos*] but is not. Who would not welcome the great opportunity, O jurors [*dikastai*], of being able to question the leader of the great Trojan expedition; | ₄₁c or Odysseus or Sisyphus, or one could mention countless other men— and women too! What unmitigated happiness [*eudaimoniā*] would there be in having dialogues [*dialegesthai*] with them over there [*ekeî*] and just being in their company and asking them questions! And I say it absolutely: those who are over there [*ekeî*] do not put someone to death for this; certainly not. I say that because those who are over there [*ekeî*] are happier [*eu-daimonesteroi*] than those who are over here [*en-tautha*]. And they are already immortal [*athanatoi*] for the rest of time, if in fact the sayings [*legomena*] are true [*alēthē*].

Plato *Apology of Socrates* 40e-41c*

---

* εἰ δ᾽ αὖ οἷον ἀποδημῆσαί ἐστιν ὁ θάνατος ἐνθένδε εἰς ἄλλον τόπον, καὶ ἀληθῆ ἐστιν τὰ λεγόμενα, ὡς ἄρα ἐκεῖ εἰσι πάντες οἱ τεθνεῶτες, τί μεῖζον ἀγαθὸν τούτου εἴη ἄν, ὦ ἄνδρες δικασταί; εἰ γάρ τις | ₄₁ₐ ἀφικόμενος εἰς Ἅιδου, ἀπαλλαγεὶς τουτωνὶ τῶν φασκόντων δικαστῶν εἶναι, εὑρήσει τοὺς ὡς ἀληθῶς δικαστάς, οἵπερ καὶ λέγονται ἐκεῖ δικάζειν, Μίνως τε καὶ Ῥαδάμανθυς καὶ Αἰακὸς καὶ Τριπτόλεμος καὶ ἄλλοι ὅσοι τῶν ἡμιθέων δίκαιοι ἐγένοντο ἐν τῷ ἑαυτῶν βίῳ, ἆρα φαύλη ἂν εἴη ἡ ἀποδημία; ἢ αὖ Ὀρφεῖ συγγενέσθαι καὶ Μουσαίῳ καὶ Ἡσιόδῳ καὶ Ὁμήρῳ ἐπὶ πόσῳ ἄν τις δέξαιτ᾽ ἂν ὑμῶν; ἐγὼ μὲν γὰρ πολλάκις ἐθέλω τεθνάναι εἰ ταῦτ᾽ ἔστιν ἀληθῆ. ἐπεὶ | ₄₁ᵦ ἔμοιγε καὶ αὐτῷ θαυμαστὴ ἂν εἴη ἡ διατριβὴ αὐτόθι, ὁπότε ἐντύχοιμι Παλαμήδει καὶ Αἴαντι τῷ Τελαμῶνος καὶ εἴ τις ἄλλος τῶν παλαιῶν διὰ κρίσιν

22§10. The world of such an afterlife, which is indicated mystically as *ekeî*, 'over there' in the sense of *in that life*, in opposition to *entautha*, 'over here' in the sense of *in this life*, is evidently a world in which heroes themselves achieve an afterlife. And such an afterlife, as I have been arguing in this book, is the third of three experiences: (1) death itself, (2) arrival in Hādēs, and (3) passing through Hādēs into a mystical otherworldly life. In the process of passing through Hādēs what is just and what is unjust will clearly be seen. Plato's Socrates has a keen interest in such a prospect: he shows it by highlighting the heroes Palamedes and Ajax, both of whom died unjust deaths and both of whom could blame their deaths not only on the unjust treatment they received from their fellow Achaeans but also, more importantly, on the machinations of an unjust Odysseus.

22§11. Plato's Socrates is saying here that Odysseus was unjust—and recognized as unjust—in the myths about the deaths of Palamedes and Ajax. From these myths, we learn that Odysseus was instrumental in causing the deaths of both these heroes. In the case of Ajax, the relevant myth is well known from sources such as Pindar's *Nemean* 8. In the case of Palamedes, the myth is retold briefly by the figure of Socrates himself in the *Memorabilia* of Xenophon (4.2.33)—and in Xenophon's version of the *Apology of Socrates* (26).

22§12. In Text A4, which I just quoted from Plato's own version of the *Apology of Socrates* (41c), we saw the figure of Odysseus associated with the figure of Sisyphus, who is a prototypical trickster. In *Odyssey* xi 593–600, this trickster is actually punished in the afterlife for his trickery. This is not to say, however, that the world 'over there' is a place of eternal punishment even for tricksters like Sisyphus. More simply, it is a place where unjust as well as just deeds are sorted out and judged for all to see. In the case of Sisyphus, his negative side is highlighted in the *Odyssey* while his positive side is shaded over. But we have already seen a glimpse of this hero's positive side in Hour **8a§13**, where we read the report of Pausanias (2.1.3) concerning Sisyphus as the founder of the Isthmian Games. Conversely, in the case of Odysseus, the Homeric *Odyssey* consistently highlights this hero's positive side and shades over his negative side. Still, the

---

ἄδικον τέθνηκεν, ἀντιπαραβάλλοντι τὰ ἐμαυτοῦ πάθη πρὸς τὰ ἐκείνων – ὡς ἐγὼ οἶμαι, οὐκ ἂν ἀηδὲς εἴη – καὶ δὴ τὸ μέγιστον, τοὺς ἐκεῖ ἐξετάζοντα καὶ ἐρευνῶντα ὥσπερ τοὺς ἐνταῦθα διάγειν, τίς αὐτῶν σοφός ἐστιν καὶ τίς οἴεται μέν, ἔστιν δ' οὔ. ἐπὶ πόσῳ δ' ἄν τις, ὦ ἄνδρες δικασταί, δέξαιτο ἐξετάσαι τὸν ἐπὶ Τροίαν ἀγαγόντα |₄₁c τὴν πολλὴν στρατιὰν ἢ Ὀδυσσέα ἢ Σίσυφον ἢ ἄλλους μυρίους ἄν τις εἴποι καὶ ἄνδρας καὶ γυναῖκας, οἷς ἐκεῖ διαλέγεσθαι καὶ συνεῖναι καὶ ἐξετάζειν ἀμήχανον ἂν εἴη εὐδαιμονίας; πάντως οὐ δήπου τούτου γε ἕνεκα οἱ ἐκεῖ ἀποκτείνουσι· τά τε γὰρ ἄλλα εὐδαιμονέστεροί εἰσιν οἱ ἐκεῖ τῶν ἐνθάδε, καὶ ἤδη τὸν λοιπὸν χρόνον ἀθάνατοί εἰσιν, εἴπερ γε τὰ λεγόμενα ἀληθῆ.

myths that involve him in the deaths of Palamedes and Ajax show that Odysseus too, like Sisyphus, had his negative side—as a trickster.

22§13. It comes as no surprise, then, that Socrates in Text A4 from Plato's *Apology of Socrates* (41c) seeks to cross-examine Odysseus as an exponent of injustice—if, that is, there is really an afterlife, and if Socrates will really get a chance to make contact with that hero in such an afterlife. As we can also see in Text A4 from Plato's *Apology of Socrates* (41c), another exponent of injustice whom Socrates would hope to cross-examine in such an afterlife is the hero Agamemnon himself as the leader of the expedition against Troy. That hero too can be considered an exponent of injustice, as we have seen more than once in this book. And such a negative view is highlighted by the fact that Plato's Socrates does not even mention that hero by name in this context.

22§14. After speaking about men who lived in the heroic past, Socrates now turns his attention to men of his own time, especially to the *dikastai,* or 'jurors', who condemn him to death. He speaks to them ironically and even sarcastically:

Hour 22 Text A5

But even you, O jurors [*dikastai*], should have good hopes when you face death, and you should have in mind [*dia-noeîsthai*] this one thing as true [*alēthes*]: |₄₁d that nothing bad [*kakon*] can happen to a good [*agathos*] person, either in life or when he comes to its completion [*teleutân*]. The events involving this person are not neglected by the gods [*theoi*]. Nor is it by chance that the events involving me have happened. Rather, this one thing is clear to me, that to be already dead and to be in a state where I am already released from events involving me was better for me. And it is for this reason that the signal [*sēmeion*] in no way diverted me from my path. Further, it is for this reason that I am not at all angry with those who accused me or with those who condemned me. Granted, it was not with this in mind that they accused me and condemned me, since they thought they were doing me harm, |₄₁e and for this they deserve to be blamed. In any case, I ask them for only one thing. When my sons are grown up, I would ask you men to punish them [= my sons] and give them pain, as I have given you pain—if they seem to care about material things or the like, instead of striving for merit [*aretē*]. Or, if they seem to be something but are not at all that thing—then go ahead and insult them, as I am now insulting you, for not caring about things they ought to care about, and for thinking they are something when they are really worth nothing. And if | ₄₂ₐ you do this, then the things I have experienced because of what you have done to me will be just [*dikaia*]—and the same goes for my sons.

Plato *Apology of Socrates* 41c-42a*

22§15. These jurors who condemn Socrates to death are supposedly the upholders of justice, but for Socrates they are exactly the opposite, despite the term *dikastai* that they apply to themselves. Socrates has in mind here the literal meaning of *dikastai*. This word means not only 'jurors' in the political context of Athens in the world of the historical present time of Socrates in 399 BCE. In the world of the distant heroic past, this same word means, literally, 'judges' in the sense of 'men of justice'. Those *dikastai* are the 'men of justice' who once upon a time lived in the heroic age and who now judge each and every person who dies and passes through Hādēs. According to the relevant myth cited by Socrates in Plato's *Apology of Socrates* (41a), as I quoted it in Text A4, these otherworldly 'judges' include Minos, Rhadamanthus, Aiakos, and Triptolemos. Further, as we saw in the quoted text, all four of these heroes qualify as *hēmi-theoi* or 'demigods'. We have already seen in Hour 12§28 the use of this word *hēmi-theoi* with reference to the great heroes of the heroic age—as viewed from the perspective of the present.

22§16. So now we can finally see why the mysterious *superhuman signal* or *sēmeion* of Socrates never did divert him from doing or saying what he did or said in his own life. It is because he deserves to be judged as a man of justice, while the jurors who condemned him fail to merit such a judgment. And, as a man of justice, Socrates even deserves to become a hero.

---

*Ἀλλὰ καὶ ὑμᾶς χρή, ὦ ἄνδρες δικασταί, εὐέλπιδας εἶναι πρὸς τὸν θάνατον, καὶ ἕν τι τοῦτο διανοεῖσθαι ἀληθές, ὅτι |₄₁ₐ οὐκ ἔστιν ἀνδρὶ ἀγαθῷ κακὸν οὐδὲν οὔτε ζῶντι οὔτε τελευτήσαντι, οὐδὲ ἀμελεῖται ὑπὸ θεῶν τὰ τούτου πράγματα· οὐδὲ τὰ ἐμὰ νῦν ἀπὸ τοῦ αὐτομάτου γέγονεν, ἀλλά μοι δῆλόν ἐστι τοῦτο, ὅτι ἤδη τεθνάναι καὶ ἀπηλλάχθαι πραγμάτων βέλτιον ἦν μοι. διὰ τοῦτο καὶ ἐμὲ οὐδαμοῦ ἀπέτρεψεν τὸ σημεῖον, καὶ ἔγωγε τοῖς καταψηφισαμένοις μου καὶ τοῖς κατηγόροις οὐ πάνυ χαλεπαίνω. καίτοι οὐ ταύτῃ τῇ διανοίᾳ κατεψηφίζοντό μου καὶ κατηγόρουν, ἀλλ' οἰόμενοι βλάπτειν· |₄₁ₑ τοῦτο αὐτοῖς ἄξιον μέμφεσθαι. τοσόνδε μέντοι αὐτῶν δέομαι· τοὺς ὑεῖς μου, ἐπειδὰν ἡβήσωσι, τιμωρήσασθε, ὦ ἄνδρες, ταὐτὰ ταῦτα λυποῦντες ἅπερ ἐγὼ ὑμᾶς ἐλύπουν, ἐὰν ὑμῖν δοκῶσιν ἢ χρημάτων ἢ ἄλλου του πρότερον ἐπιμελεῖσθαι ἢ ἀρετῆς, καὶ ἐὰν δοκῶσί τι εἶναι μηδὲν ὄντες, ὀνειδίζετε αὐτοῖς ὥσπερ ἐγὼ ὑμῖν, ὅτι οὐκ ἐπιμελοῦνται ὧν δεῖ, καὶ οἴονταί τι εἶναι ὄντες οὐδενὸς ἄξιοι. καὶ ἐὰν |₄₂ₐ ταῦτα ποιῆτε, δίκαια πεπονθὼς ἐγὼ ἔσομαι ὑφ' ὑμῶν αὐτός τε καὶ οἱ ὑεῖς.

A Heroic Timing for the Death of Socrates

22§17. This idea that Socrates deserves to become a hero starts to take shape in the context of the passage I quoted in Text A4 from Plato's *Apology of Socrates* (40e-41c). This passage centered on the possibility of an afterlife as predicted in the mystical *legomena* or 'sayings' attributed to figures like Orpheus and Musaeus. If there is to be such an afterlife, then Socrates after death will be judged to be a just man by otherworldly judges like the heroes Minos, Rhadamanthus, Aiakos, and Triptolemos, and then, once judged, he will be allowed to pass through Hādēs into a mystical place of afterlife. This mystical place, as we see from the context of Text A4, is populated not only by the four heroes who judge the incoming dead and who are described as *hēmi-theoi* or 'demigods' but also by heroes in general, who likewise qualify as *hēmi-theoi* or 'demigods'. Among these heroes are the poets Orpheus, Musaeus, Hesiod, and Homer, listed in order of seniority, from the supposedly earliest to the latest.* As we have already seen in Hour 13§33, both Hesiod and Homer were actually worshipped as cult heroes. After the four poets, mentioned as heroes here in the *Apology of Socrates* (41a), Plato's Socrates goes on to mention the heroes Palamedes and Ajax (41b), whom we have already considered, and then, as he nears the end of his speech, he makes this general statement about all the heroes whom he hopes to join in the afterlife: 'And they [= all these heroes] are already immortal [*athanatoi*] for the rest of time, if in fact the sayings [*legomena*] are true [*alēthē*]' (41c). Finally, in the last sentence of his speech, Plato's Socrates says that the time has come for him to die. I will now quote this sentence and then argue that it signals the idea that Socrates will be dying the death of a hero:

HOUR 22 TEXT A6

> But let me interrupt. You see, the hour [*hōrā*] of departure has already arrived. So now we all go our ways—I to die, and you to live. And the question is, which one of us on either side is going toward something that is better? It is not clear, except to the god.
>
> Plato *Apology of Socrates* 42a†

---

* On this canonical sequence of listing the four poets Orpheus, Musaeus, Hesiod, and Homer, see *HC* 394–398 = 3§§99–102.

† ἀλλὰ γὰρ ἤδη ὥρα ἀπιέναι, ἐμοὶ μὲν ἀποθανουμένῳ, ὑμῖν δὲ βιωσομένοις· ὁπότεροι δὲ ἡμῶν ἔρχονται ἐπὶ ἄμεινον πρᾶγμα, ἄδηλον παντὶ πλὴν ἢ τῷ θεῷ.

22§18. So the death of Socrates will take place at exactly the right 'time', which is the *hōrā*. And we come back full circle to Hour 1 of this book, where we saw that the very idea of the ancient Greek hero is defined by *hōrā* as the right 'time' of death.

Socrates and Achilles

22§19. As we have seen, those whom Socrates will meet in an afterlife—if there is to be an afterlife—include heroes like Odysseus, who committed acts of injustice against other heroes. They also include Agamemnon, who as we know from our readings can likewise be considered guilty of having committed acts of injustice. These examples of inclusion make it clear that membership in a heroic afterlife as pictured in the sayings of mystical poets like Orpheus and Musaeus is not restricted to paragons of justice like Minos, Rhadamanthus, Aiakos, and Triptolemos. Even heroes who are known to have committed catastrophically unjust deeds are still eligible for immortalization in an afterlife. The wording of Socrates in Plato's *Apology of Socrates* (41c) takes for granted such eligibility when he says that all the heroes whom he will meet and with whom he will engage in dialogue 'are already immortal [*athanatoi*] for the rest of time, if in fact the sayings [*legomena*] are true [*alēthē*]'. So the assumption here is that Homeric heroes like Odysseus and Agamemnon are already immortalized by the time Plato's Socrates initiates his dialogues with them. But something seems to be missing in this picture. Socrates does not mention another most prominent Homeric hero here. I mean Achilles. But Socrates does not need to mention Achilles in this context—because Socrates has already been having a dialogue with Achilles in a previous context.

22§20. Even before Socrates dies, he is already interrogating Achilles—however indirectly—about that hero's motives as they play out in the *Iliad*:

HOUR 22 TEXT B

Perhaps someone might say: And are you not ashamed, Socrates, of pursuing such a goal in life, which is likely to cause you to die right now? To him I would reply—and I would be replying justly [*dikaiōs*]: You, my good man, are not saying it well, if you think it is necessary for a man to calculate the risks of living or dying; there is little use in doing that. Rather, he should only consider whether in doing anything he is doing things that are just [*dikaia*] or unjust [*adika*], acting the part of a good [*agathos*] man or of a bad [*kakos*] one. Worthless men, |₂₈c according to your view, would be the demigods [*hēmi-theoi*] who fulfilled their lives by dying at Troy, especially the son of Thetis [= Achilles], who so despised the danger of risk, preferring it to waiting for disgrace. His mother, goddess that she was, had said to him, when he was showing his eagerness to slay Hector, something like this, I think: My child, if you avenge the slaying of your comrade [*hetairos*] Patroklos and kill Hector, you will die yourself. "Right away your fate [*potmos*]"— she says—"is ready for you after Hector." And he [= Achilles], hearing this, utterly despised danger and death, |₂₈d and instead of fearing them, feared rather to live like a worthless [*kakos*] man, and not to avenge his friend. "Right away may I die next," he says, "and impose justice [*dikē*] on the one who committed injustice [*adikeîn*], rather than stay behind here by the curved ships, a laughing stock and a heavy load for Earth to bear." Do you think that he had any thought of death and danger?

Plato *Apology of Socrates* 28b–d*

22§21. Now I will elaborate on what I already said about this passage in Hour 2§77. Socrates here is paraphrasing the relevant verses of *Iliad* XVIII 90–104, but he weaves into his paraphrases some actual quotations of the original Homeric wording. Likewise in Plato's *Symposium* (179e-180a), we see a second paraphrase of the same verses. In the case of that second paraphrase, however, the choice made by Achilles to forfeit his life in order to avenge the death of Patroklos appears to be conflated with another choice that faces the hero. At an earlier point in the *Iliad,* in the context of the so-called Embassy Scene where Achilles is speaking to Phoenix and the other delegates (IX 410–416), he says

---

*Ἴσως ἂν οὖν εἴποι τις· Εἶτ' οὐκ αἰσχύνῃ, ὦ Σώκρατες, τοιοῦτον ἐπιτήδευμα ἐπιτηδεύσας ἐξ οὗ κινδυνεύεις νυνὶ ἀποθανεῖν; ἐγὼ δὲ τούτῳ ἂν δίκαιον λόγον ἀντείποιμι, ὅτι Οὐ καλῶς λέγεις, ὦ ἄνθρωπε, εἰ οἴει δεῖν κίνδυνον ὑπολογίζεσθαι τοῦ ζῆν ἢ τεθνάναι ἄνδρα ὅτου τι καὶ σμικρὸν ὄφελός ἐστιν, ἀλλ' οὐκ ἐκεῖνο μόνον σκοπεῖν ὅταν πράττῃ, πότερον δίκαια ἢ ἄδικα πράττει, καὶ ἀνδρὸς ἀγαθοῦ ἔργα ἢ κακοῦ. φαῦλοι |₂₈c γὰρ ἂν τῷ γε σῷ λόγῳ εἶεν τῶν ἡμιθέων ὅσοι ἐν Τροίᾳ τετελευτήκασιν οἵ τε ἄλλοι καὶ ὁ τῆς Θέτιδος ὑός, ὃς τοσοῦτον τοῦ κινδύνου κατεφρόνησεν παρὰ τὸ αἰσχρόν τι ὑπομεῖναι ὥστε, ἐπειδὴ εἶπεν ἡ μήτηρ αὐτῷ προθυμουμένῳ Ἕκτορα ἀποκτεῖναι, θεὸς οὖσα, οὑτωσί πως, ὡς ἐγὼ οἶμαι· Ὦ παῖ, εἰ τιμωρήσεις Πατρόκλῳ τῷ ἑταίρῳ τὸν φόνον καὶ Ἕκτορα ἀποκτενεῖς, αὐτὸς ἀποθανῇ – "αὐτίκα γάρ τοι," φησί, "μεθ' Ἕκτορα πότμος ἑτοῖμος" – ὁ δὲ τοῦτο ἀκούσας τοῦ μὲν θανάτου καὶ τοῦ κινδύνου ὠλιγώρησε, πολὺ δὲ μᾶλλον |₂₈d δείσας τὸ ζῆν κακὸς ὢν καὶ τοῖς φίλοις μὴ τιμωρεῖν, "αὐτίκα," φησί, "τεθναίην, δίκην ἐπιθεὶς τῷ ἀδικοῦντι, ἵνα μὴ ἐνθάδε μένω καταγέλαστος παρὰ νηυσὶ κορωνίσιν ἄχθος ἀρούρης." μὴ αὐτὸν οἴει φροντίσαι θανάτου καὶ κινδύνου;

that he must decide between two *kēres* or 'fated ways' (IX 411): either he dies at a ripe old age after a safe *nostos*, 'homecoming', to his homeland Phthia or he dies young on the battlefield in Troy—and thereby wins for himself a *kleos*, 'glory', that will last forever (IX 413). This is the passage I first quoted in Hour 0 Text F and in Hour 1 Text A.

22§22. And now I will elaborate on what I said in Hour 2§78. I noted there that Plato's apparent conflation of two choices facing Achilles turns out to be justified: the two choices are in fact one choice. In the Embassy Scene of the *Iliad*, when Achilles says he must choose between two *kēres* or 'fated ways' (IX 411), either a *nostos*, 'homecoming', or a *kleos*, 'glory', that will last forever (IX 413), he is actually not yet ready to make his choice: the two alternative fates have simply been foretold for him by his mother, the goddess Thetis (IX 410–411). Later on, after Patroklos has been killed, Achilles is facing the same choice, but by now he has made his decision. He says that there cannot be a homecoming for him (*nosteîn* XVIII 90) because he must kill Hector in order to avenge the death of Patroklos, and, once he kills Hector, his own death in battle will become a certainty (XVIII 90–93), just as his mother had foretold—and as she now foretells again (XVIII 96–97).

22§23. In the passage from Plato that I quoted in Text B, *Apology of Socrates* 28b-d, we saw that Thetis is first being paraphrased. Since it is easy to overlook the distinction that Plato's verbal art is making here between *paraphrasing* and *quoting*, I will repeat here the wording of the paraphrase: 'His mother, goddess that she was, had said to him, when he was showing his eagerness to slay Hector, something like this, I think: My child, if you avenge the slaying of your comrade [*hetairos*] Patroklos and kill Hector, you will die yourself' (28c). So the paraphrase is signaled ostentatiously as a paraphrase. Then, immediately after we hear this paraphrase, we hear Thetis being quoted directly (28c again), and the wording that I will translate as 'she says' (φησί) signals just as ostentatiously that we are now hearing a quotation: '"Right away your fate [*potmos*]"—she says —"is ready for you after Hector".* The quotation corresponds exactly to what we find in *Iliad* XVIII 96, where Thetis says: 'Right away your fate [*potmos*] is next, ready for you after Hector'.† And then, immediately after the quotation from Thetis, Achilles himself seems to be quoted directly as he responds to Thetis (28d). The wording that I will translate as 'he says' (φησί) indicates—

---

* "αὐτίκα γάρ τοι," φησί, "μεθ' ῞Εκτορα πότμος ἑτοῖμος."
† αὐτίκα γάρ τοι ἔπειτα μεθ' ῞Εκτορα πότμος ἑτοῖμος.

again, ostentatiously—that we are once again hearing a quotation: "'Right away may I die next,' he says, "and impose justice [*dikē*] on the one who committed injustice [*adikeîn*], rather than stay behind here by the curved ships, a laughing stock and a heavy load for Earth to bear'".* So Achilles wants to punish Hector for having 'committed injustice', and this punishment is viewed as the imposing of 'justice'. But in this case the words of Achilles as quoted by Plato's Socrates do not at all correspond to the words we find in *Iliad* XVIII 98–104, where Achilles says something different—and something that takes much longer to say. What the hero does say here in the *Iliad* is a spectacular masterpiece of virtuosity in verbal pyrotechnics, full of the most intensely emotive outbursts. Here is my translation of these lines in *Iliad* XVIII 98–104: 'Right away may I die next, since it turns out that I did not help my comrade [*hetairos*] |₉₉ by protecting him when he was about to be killed. And there he was, far away from his fatherland, |₁₀₀ and he died. He missed having me as his protector from harm. |₁₀₁ And now, since I will not have a homecoming [*neesthai*] to my dear fatherland, |₁₀₂ and I did not become the light [of salvation] for Patroklos or for my other companions, |₁₀₃ those others, many of them, who were also dispatched by radiant Hector |₁₀₄—and here I am by the ships, just sitting here, a heavy load for Earth to bear—...'.†

22§24. At this juncture, exactly at the point where Achilles has just spoken of himself as 'a heavy load for Earth to bear', the wording of the hero as quoted by Plato's Socrates in the *Apology* (28d) breaks off, as we saw. I repeat the wording: "'Right away may I die next,' he says, "and impose justice [*dikē*] on the one who committed injustice [*adikeîn*], rather than stay behind here by the curved ships, a laughing stock and a heavy load for Earth to bear'".‡ In the *Iliad*, however, we see that the wording of Achilles does not break off but continues for several more lines, moving past the parenthetical expression at line 104 where the hero had said: 'and here I am by the ships, just sitting here, a heavy load for Earth to bear'.§ Not only does the wording of Achilles continue. It must continue. And

---

* "αὐτίκα," φησί, "τεθναίην, δίκην ἐπιθεὶς τῷ ἀδικοῦντι, ἵνα μὴ ἐνθάδε μένω καταγέλαστος παρὰ νηυσὶ κορωνίσιν ἄχθος ἀρούρης."

† αὐτίκα τεθναίην, ἐπεὶ οὐκ ἄρ' ἔμελλον ἑταίρῳ |₉₉ κτεινομένῳ ἐπαμῦναι· ὃ μὲν μάλα τηλόθι πάτρης |₁₀₀ ἔφθιτ', ἐμεῖο δὲ δῆσεν ἀρῆς ἀλκτῆρα γενέσθαι. |₁₀₁ νῦν δ' ἐπεὶ οὐ νέομαί γε φίλην ἐς πατρίδα γαῖαν, |₁₀₂ οὐδέ τι Πατρόκλῳ γενόμην φάος οὐδ' ἑτάροισι |₁₀₃ τοῖς ἄλλοις, οἳ δὴ πολέες δάμεν Ἕκτορι δίῳ, |₁₀₄ ἀλλ' ἧμαι παρὰ νηυσὶν ἐτώσιον ἄχθος ἀρούρης.

‡ (Plato *Apology* 28d:) "αὐτίκα," φησί, "τεθναίην, δίκην ἐπιθεὶς τῷ ἀδικοῦντι, ἵνα μὴ ἐνθάδε μένω καταγέλαστος παρὰ νηυσὶ κορωνίσιν ἄχθος ἀρούρης."

§ (*Iliad* XVIII 104): ἀλλ' ἧμαι παρὰ νηυσὶν ἐτώσιον ἄχθος ἀρούρης.

that is because this wording is, so far, still incomplete in syntax, as also in meaning. At this point, there is no syntactical follow-up for the clause indicated by the second 'since' in my translation, which I will now highlight as I repeat what Achilles is saying so passionately: 'Right away may I die next, since it turns out that I did not help my comrade [*hetairos*] |₉₉ by protecting him when he was about to be killed. And there he was, far away from his fatherland, |₁₀₀ and he died. He missed having me as his protector from harm. |₁₀₁ And now, *since* I will not have a homecoming [*neesthai*] to my dear fatherland, |₁₀₂ and I did not become the light [of salvation] for Patroklos or for my other companions, |₁₀₃ those others, many of them, who were also dispatched by radiant Hector |₁₀₄— and here I am by the ships, just sitting here, a heavy load for Earth to bear—. . .'. Picking up from this point onward, both the syntax and the meaning of Achilles will keep moving on, from line 105 all the way to line 121, where the hero will finally have the chance to say what his motive is. Leading up to line 121, Achilles had said that his determination to kill Hector shows that he chooses to die young on the battlefield, and he refers to this death as his inevitable *kēr* or 'fated way' at line 115. And now, highlighting what he will get for himself as his compensation, he declares at line 121 that he will win *kleos*, that is, the 'glory' of epic song. For Achilles, to die this way is the right thing to do.

22§25. For Socrates as well, to die as he chooses to die is the right thing to do. And he expresses this idea by using the words *dikē* or 'justice' and *dikaios* or 'just'. It is true of course that the Homeric wording used by Achilles in the *Iliad* to motivate his own choice is not replicated by the Platonic wording used by Plato's Socrates when the hero is quoted as saying that he chooses to die for a just cause, but I still find the Platonic wording to be true to Homeric poetry—in the sense that it conveys with psychological insight and accuracy the larger-than-life feelings expressed by Achilles. So even before he dies and goes off to a heroic afterlife—if there is such a thing—Socrates is already having a dialogue with Achilles by quoting him in this special way, using words that Achilles himself does not use in his own *Iliad*. Moreover, since the readers of Plato's *Apology of Socrates* are reading the words of Socrates at a time when the man they are reading is already dead, we may say that Socrates is having his dialogue with Achilles every time we read him quoting the hero of the *Iliad*.

22§26. Plato's Socrates is meeting Achilles half way by using the diction of Homeric poetry in speaking about 'a heavy load for Earth to bear', but Achilles in turn is meeting Socrates half way by letting himself be quoted in the act of speaking about dying for a just cause. And this special way of letting Achilles speak about the just cause of dying for his comrade Patroklos, even if it is too late now to save him, matches the special way of speaking that is chosen by Socrates when he says that he fights for justice as a philosopher the same way he fights in war as a citizen soldier. In the *Apology* (28a), Socrates goes out of his way to remind his listeners that he was a distinguished combat veteran of three famous battles in the Peloponnesian War—Potidaea, Amphipolis, and Delium. Each one of these three battles was a military disaster for Athens, the homeland of Socrates, and in each one of these battles, as Socrates is proud to remind his fellow Athenians, he showed to all his bravery in the face of death. This bravery is portrayed also in Plato's *Symposium* (220d–221c), where we find a vivid retelling of the admirable comportment of Socrates at a critical moment in the battle of Delium. Summing up the stories of his reputation for bravery on the battlefield, Socrates says in the *Apology* (28e): 'I stood my ground [*e-men-on*] and put my life at risk', following the orders of military commanders. Socrates is saying here that he was always ready to die for his fellow citizens in war—not only to die with them—just as Achilles is saying that he is ready to die for his comrade, since that is the right thing to do. In the same way, as we read in the *Apology* (29a), Socrates will not break rank and flee when he follows the dictates of his own moral responsibilities as a philosopher: that is, he will not abandon the *taxis* or 'military formation' of the just cause that he pursues.

An Odyssean Way for the Journey of Socrates

22§27. We have already seen that Socrates in Plato's *Apology of Socrates* views Odysseus in an unfavorable light when he refers to injustices committed by this hero against other heroes such as Ajax and Palamedes. But Socrates shows a different attitude when it comes to the overall story of Odysseus as narrated in the Homeric *Odyssey*. As we will now see, Socrates views this story in a favorable light, modeling his own evolution as a philosopher on the idea of an Odyssean journey of a soul. I used this expression *journey of a soul* when I analyzed the overall narrative of the Homeric *Odyssey* in Hour 10§§32–50. In the context of that analysis, I was emphasizing not the specific idea of the *soul,* which is the English word I used there as a working translation of *psūkhē,* but rather the more general idea of a mystical *journey* experienced by the *psūkhē*—however we may translate that Greek word. As the *psūkhē* travels on its journey, it passes through a transitional phase visualized as Hādēs and eventually reaches an eschatological phase or afterlife visualized as the Island of the Blessed—or as various other such kinds of mystical places where heroes are immortalized. Socrates in the *Apology of Socrates* hopes to reach such a place after his death, and, in such an afterlife, he hopes to have dialogues with a variety of heroes, including Odysseus. In Text A4, I have already quoted the passage where Socrates refers to such hoped-for dialogues in the afterlife (41c). But now the question is, how will Socrates reach such an afterlife? As I will argue, the way for Socrates to journey to such an afterlife is an Odyssean way.

22§28. The impetus for this spiritual journey of Socrates is a visit to the Oracle of Apollo at Delphi by a man named Chaerephon. The story of this visit is retold by Plato's Socrates in the *Apology*: he describes Chaerephon as someone who has been a *hetairos* or 'comrade' of his ever since the two of them were young men (20e-21a). As we see from the retelling of the story by Plato's Socrates, Chaerephon went to Delphi and formally asked the Oracle whether there existed anyone more *sophos* or 'wise' than Socrates, and the priestess of Apollo, the Pythia, responded that there was no such man; when Socrates finds out about this oracular pronouncement, he interprets it as an *ainigma* or 'riddle' sent to him by the god Apollo himself (21a).* In this retelling by Plato's Socrates, it is made clear that Chaerephon had consulted the Oracle on his own. Clearly he was not some kind of official emissary—the kind that would have been delegated to consult the Oracle on behalf of the Athenian State. In other words, Chaerephon was not an official *theōros* or 'sacred delegate'. I will wait until Hour 23 to analyze the relevance of this word *theōros;* for now I simply emphasize that Chaerephon consulted the Oracle on his own. And, given the nature of the question that was asked of the Oracle, we can understand how such a consultation could be viewed by the State as an act of provocation—even of subversion. The wording of Socrates is actually implying such a view when he says that Chaerephon 'dared to do it' (ἐτόλμησε 21a). Then, in Plato's dramatization of the speech by Socrates, the hostile listeners to his speech react by shouting their sense of outrage at the very thought of such a consultation, and Socrates needs to quiet them down, saying to them: 'stop your shouting' (μὴ θορυβεῖτε, again 21a). Continuing his story, Socrates now describes what happened after he learned of the Oracle's response: ever since, he says, he has been wandering around and testing what the god said by engaging in dialogue with any and all persons who may be more *sophos* or 'wise' than he is (21b-22a). And the word that Plato's Socrates uses for 'engaging in dialogue', *dialegesthai* (21c), is the key to understanding the entire spiritual journey of Socrates. The never-ending

---

* In play here is a distinction between transcendent and everyday understandings of the word *sophos* as 'wise' and 'skilled' respectively. I analyze the distinction in *HC* 398 = 3§303; 533–536 = 4§§161–162.

quest of Socrates to engage in dialogue extends even into his hoped-for afterlife: he says he intends to continue doing in this afterlife what he has been doing throughout his life ever since he heard what the Oracle said. So Socrates will continue testing the truth of Apollo by seeking to discover whether those whom he encounters in the afterlife are 'wise', *sophoi,* or whether they merely think they are 'wise' but are not (41b).* And, once again, the discovery procedure for Plato's Socrates is expressed by way of the word *dialegesthai,* which means 'engaging in dialogue' (41c). I have already quoted the context of this passage in Text A4.

22§29. So now we come at last to the wording used by Plato's Socrates to describe his spiritual journey. He taps into the language of initiation in telling about his wanderings through life, describing these wanderings as an ordeal of initiation, 'laboring [*poneîn*] to achieve labors [*ponoi*]':

HOUR 22 TEXT C

I must perform for you the tale of my wandering [*planē*], just as if I had been laboring [*poneîn*] to achieve labors [*ponoi*] that I endured for this purpose: that the [god's] oracular wording [*manteiā*] should become impossible to refute.

Plato *Apology of Socrates* 22a†

22§30. Words like *ponos* and *kamatos,* both of which mean 'ordeal, labor, pain', can apply to the life-and-death struggles of heroes in stories about their larger-than-life struggles. A classic example is the *ponos* or 'labor' of Hēraklēs himself in the act of literally wrestling with Thanatos or Death incarnate in the *Alcestis* of Euripides (1027). In that context as also elsewhere, especially in related contexts that we find in the songs of Pindar, such mythical experiences of heroes are presented as models for the ritual experiences of humans who engage in ritual activities such as athletic competitions,‡ and this kind of engagement can be seen in anthropological terms as a shining example of what we know as initiation.§

---

* Again in play here is the distinction between transcendent and everyday understandings of this word *sophos.*

† δεῖ δὴ ὑμῖν τὴν ἐμὴν πλάνην ἐπιδεῖξαι ὥσπερ πόνους τινὰς πονοῦντος ἵνα μοι καὶ ἀνέλεγκτος ἡ μαντεία γένοιτο.

‡ *PH* 138–139 = 5§4.

§ *PH* 139–144 = 5§§5–15.

22§31. I highlight again the *ponoi* or 'labors' of Socrates, which he equates with his *planē* or 'wandering' all over the world, as it were, in the course of his unending spiritual journey. The wording that Socrates uses here evokes the experiences of heroes like Hēraklēs himself. For example, the canonical Labors of Hēraklēs are described this way in a *Homeric Hymn*:

HOUR 22 TEXT D

|₄ He [= Hēraklēs] used to travel all over the boundless earth and all over the sea, |₅ veering from his path and wandering off, all because of the missions assigned to him by Eurystheus the king. |₆ He [= Hēraklēs] performed many reckless things on his own, and he suffered many such things in return.

Homeric Hymn to Herakles 4–6*

22§32. The words used here in telling about the ordeals of Hēraklēs match closely the words used at the very beginning of the *Odyssey* to tell about the ordeals of Odysseus:†

HOUR 22 TEXT E (PART OF HOUR 9 TEXT A AND HOUR 10 TEXT A)

|₁ That man, tell me O Muse the song of that man, that versatile [*polutropos*] man, who in very many ways |₂ veered from his path and wandered off far and wide, after he had destroyed the sacred citadel of Troy. |₃ Many different cities of many different people did he see, getting to know different ways of thinking [*noos*]. |₄ Many were the pains [*algea*] he suffered in his heart [*thūmos*] while crossing the sea |₅ struggling to merit [*arnusthai*] the saving of his own life [*psūkhē*] and his own homecoming [*nostos*] as well as the homecoming of his comrades [*hetairoi*]. *Odyssey* i 1–5‡

22§33. The philosophical wandering of Socrates in the course of his spiritual journey matches in wording the heroic wandering of Odysseus as we described

---

* |₄ ὃς πρὶν μὲν κατὰ γαῖαν ἀθέσφατον ἠδὲ θάλασσαν |₅ πλαζόμενος πομπῇσιν ὑπ' Εὐρυσθῆος ἄνακτος |₆ πολλὰ μὲν αὐτὸς ἔρεξεν ἀτάσθαλα, πολλὰ δ' ἀνέτλη.
† I offer commentary in *GM* 14–15 about the striking correspondences in the wording.
‡ |₁ ἄνδρα μοι ἔννεπε, Μοῦσα, πολύτροπον, ὃς μάλα πολλὰ |₂ πλάγχθη, ἐπεὶ Τροίης ἱερὸν πτολίεθρον ἔπερσε· |₃ πολλῶν δ' ἀνθρώπων ἴδεν ἄστεα καὶ νόον ἔγνω, |₄ πολλὰ δ' ὅ γ' ἐν πόντῳ πάθεν ἄλγεα ὃν κατὰ θυμόν, |₅ ἀρνύμενος ἥν τε ψυχὴν καὶ νόστον ἑταίρων.

it here at the very beginning of the *Odyssey* (i 1–5), where it is said that the hero kept on wandering off (i 2) as he kept on learning all kinds of things (i 3) in the course of his painful struggle to save his own *psūkhē* (i 5). I had translated this word *psūkhē* simply as 'life' when I first quoted the beginning of the *Odyssey* in Hour 9 Text A and in Hour 10 Text A. Now I am ready to interpret *psūkhē* in the present context as 'soul'—in the transcendent sense that Odysseus experiences a journey of a soul. And this *psūkhē* or 'soul' is destined for immortalization after death. In the *Phaedo* of Plato, to which we will turn in Hour 23, the very idea of such a destiny for the *psūkhē* will be most passionately debated.

The Swan Song of Socrates

22§34. Before I bring this hour about Plato's *Apology of Socrates* to a close, I will show a preview from his *Phaedo*. In the passage I am about to quote, Plato's Socrates is speaking about this final dialogue of his, comparing the words in this dialogue to the song sung by a swan before death:

HOUR 22 TEXT F

When he heard [what Simmias said] Socrates laughed in a measured way and said: |₈₄ₑ "Well, well, Simmias, so I guess I am not very likely to persuade other people that I do not regard my present situation as a misfortune, if I am unable to persuade even you, and if you keep worrying whether I am at all more troubled now than I was in my earlier phase of life—and whether I am inferior to swans [*kuknoi*] in my prophetic [*mantikē*] capacity. It seems that swans, when they get the feeling that they must die, even though they were singing throughout their earlier phase of life, |₈₅ₐ will now sing more and better than ever, rejoicing in the thought that they are about to go away to the god whose attendants [*therapōn* plural] they are. But humans, because of their fear of death, tell lies about the swans [*kuknoi*], claiming that swans are lamenting [*thrēnein*] their own death when they sing their hearts out in sorrow. So humans are not taking into account the fact that no bird sings when it is hungry or cold or experiences some other such pain— not even the nightingale herself or the swallow or the hoopoe. All these birds are said to be singing in their sorrow because they have something to lament. But I do not believe that these birds sing because of some sorrow—and I do not believe it about the swans [*kuknoi*], either.

|₈₅ᵦ Rather, as I believe, it is because swans are sacred to Apollo and have a prophetic [*mantikē*] capacity and foresee the good things that will happen in the house of Hādēs—that is why they sing and rejoice in that [last] day of theirs more than they ever did in the previous time of their life. And I, too, think of myself as the consecrated [*hieros*] agent of the same god, and a fellow temple-servant [*homo-doulos*] with the swans [*kuknoi*], and, thinking that I have received from my master [*despotēs*] a prophetic [*mantikē*] capacity that is not inferior to theirs, I would not part from life in a less happy state of mind [*thūmos*] than the swans. And it is for this reason *that you must speak and ask whatever questions you want,* so long as the Athenian people's Board of Eleven allows it."

Plato *Phaedo* 84d-85b*

22§35. The swan song of Socrates is not the last word. In other words, it is not the same thing as the last dialogue—as staged by Plato—in which Socrates engages while he is still alive. Rather, the swan song of Socrates is the living word that he perpetuates by way of his eternal quest for the truth. That is why I give the title "The Living Word" to this present hour—as also to the hour that will now follow.

Καὶ ὃς ἀκούσας ἐγέλασέν τε ἠρέμα καί φησιν· Βαβαῖ, ὦ Σιμμία· ἦ που χαλεπῶς ἂν τοὺς ἄλλους ἀνθρώπους πείσαιμι |₈₄ₑ ὡς οὐ συμφορὰν ἡγοῦμαι τὴν παροῦσαν τύχην, ὅτε γε μηδ' ὑμᾶς δύναμαι πείθειν, ἀλλὰ φοβεῖσθε μὴ δυσκολώτερόν τι νῦν διάκειμαι ἢ ἐν τῷ πρόσθεν βίῳ· καί, ὡς ἔοικε, τῶν κύκνων δοκῶ φαυλότερος ὑμῖν εἶναι τὴν μαντικήν, οἳ ἐπειδὰν αἴσθωνται ὅτι δεῖ αὐτοὺς ἀποθανεῖν, ᾄδοντες καὶ ἐν |₈₅ₐ τῷ πρόσθεν χρόνῳ, τότε δὴ πλεῖστα καὶ κάλλιστα ᾄδουσι, γεγηθότες ὅτι μέλλουσι παρὰ τὸν θεὸν ἀπιέναι οὗπέρ εἰσι θεράποντες. οἱ δ' ἄνθρωποι διὰ τὸ αὑτῶν δέος τοῦ θανάτου καὶ τῶν κύκνων καταψεύδονται, καί φασιν αὐτοὺς θρηνοῦντας τὸν θάνατον ὑπὸ λύπης ἐξᾴδειν, καὶ οὐ λογίζονται ὅτι οὐδὲν ὄρνεον ᾄδει ὅταν πεινῇ ἢ ῥιγῷ ἤ τινα ἄλλην λύπην λυπῆται, οὐδὲ αὐτὴ ἥ τε ἀηδὼν καὶ χελιδὼν καὶ ὁ ἔποψ, ἃ δή φασι διὰ λύπην θρηνοῦντα ᾄδειν. ἀλλ' οὔτε ταῦτά μοι φαίνεται |₈₅ᵦ λυπούμενα ᾄδειν οὔτε οἱ κύκνοι, ἀλλ' ἅτε οἶμαι τοῦ Ἀπόλλωνος ὄντες, μαντικοί τέ εἰσι καὶ προειδότες τὰ ἐν Ἅιδου ἀγαθὰ ᾄδουσι καὶ τέρπονται ἐκείνην τὴν ἡμέραν διαφερόντως ἢ ἐν τῷ ἔμπροσθεν χρόνῳ. ἐγὼ δὲ καὶ αὐτὸς ἡγοῦμαι ὁμόδουλός τε εἶναι τῶν κύκνων καὶ ἱερὸς τοῦ αὐτοῦ θεοῦ, καὶ οὐ χεῖρον ἐκείνων τὴν μαντικὴν ἔχειν παρὰ τοῦ δεσπότου, οὐδὲ δυσθυμότερον αὐτῶν τοῦ βίου ἀπαλλάττεσθαι. ἀλλὰ τούτου γ' ἕνεκα λέγειν τε χρὴ καὶ ἐρωτᾶν ὅτι ἂν βούλησθε, ἕως ἂν Ἀθηναίων ἐῶσιν ἄνδρες ἕνδεκα.

The Living Word II: More on Plato's Socrates in the Phaedo

The Meaning of Theōriā

23§1. My abbreviated translation of the noun *theōriā* is 'sacred journey'. This noun is related to the noun *theōros,* referring to a person who is officially delegated to embark on such a sacred journey. I will translate this noun as 'sacred delegate'. And I will translate the corresponding verb *theōreîn* this way: 'to journey as a sacred delegate'. Etymologically, *theōros* means 'one who sees [root *hor-*] a vision [*theā*]'. So the basic meaning of *theōriā* can be reconstructed as *a ritualized journey undertaken for the purpose of achieving a sacralized vision.* This basic meaning is most evident in the context of athletics as a ritual activity. In the wording of Herodotus (1.59.1, 8.26), for example, a *theōros* is a 'sacred delegate' of a given community who is sent out to observe a given athletic competition and who then returns to his community with news of what he has seen.* Similarly, this same word *theōros* can refer to a 'sacred delegate' of a given community who is sent out to consult an oracle and who then returns with news of what the oracle said: we see a famous example in the *Oedipus Tyrannus* of Sophocles (114), where Creon is sent out as a *theōros* to consult the Oracle of Apollo at Delphi.† When a *theōros* reports to his community what the Oracle has said, the content of his report is considered to be visual as well as verbal, since the god of the Oracle communicates not so much by saying or by not saying but rather by 'indicating', *sēmainein,* as we saw in an aphorism of Heraclitus (22 B 93 DK) that I quoted in Hour 15 Text J and analyzed in §§64–72 of the same hour (especially in §69). When the god Apollo of the Oracle at Delphi engages in the act of *sēmainein,* 'indicating', he is conferring an inner vision

---

* *PH* 164 = 6§35.
† *PH* 164 = 6§36.

upon the *theōros*, who thus becomes worthy of the meaning of this word as 'the one who sees [root *hor-*] a vision [*theā*]'; so both the encoder and the decoder of the oracular message are operating on the basis of the same inner vision.* This relationship between the words *sēmainein* and *theōros* is pertinent to the usage of the modern lexical creations *semantics* or *semiotics* and *theory* respectively.†

23§2. In the case of the modern word *theory*, I must add, the lengthy history of its eventual meaning is mediated by philosophical reinterpretations of the words *theōriā*, *theōros*, and *theōreîn* already in ancient times. The most familiar interpretation is Aristotle's concept of *theōriā* as a 'contemplation' of the divine, especially by the divine (*Nicomachean Ethics* 10.1174b). From the standpoint of Plato's philosophical agenda, to go back to a broader understanding, *theōriā* is the inner vision of the mind, and that is how it can come to mean 'theory' or 'theorizing', as best represented by the theoretical thinking of Socrates himself when he engages in dialogue (as in Plato *Philebus* 38b). It is this kind of theoretical thinking, brought to life in dialogue, that Socrates says he adopted as his mission in life after he heard the response of the Oracle of Apollo to the question posed by Chaerephon—whether there existed anyone more *sophos* or 'wise' than Socrates. In Hour 22, we already read about this moment, retold in Plato's *Apology of Socrates* (21a). But now there is more to be said about the mission that was launched because of Apollo's response to this question. That mission, which is the perpetual engagement of Socrates in dialogue with anyone he encountered after he had heard about the response, is the essence of *theōriā*.

23§3. But such a *theōriā* of Socrates, in the sense of a dialogic mission, was obviously not sanctioned by the Athenian State. Likewise, Chaerephon had not been given any authorization to become a *theōros* or 'sacred delegate' of the State. It should come as no surprise, then, that the word *theōros* is not applied to Chaerephon in Plato's *Apology of Socrates*. Nor is the word applied to Chaerephon in Xenophon's *Apology of Socrates* (14), where we find a parallel version of the story about his consultation of the Oracle. I note also an interesting additional detail in Xenophon's version: that there were many witnesses to this particular consultation of the Oracle at Delphi (again, *Apology of Socrates* 14).

23§4. So the word *theōros*, in the sense of a 'sacred delegate', would not be an appropriate term for a private agent who consults the Oracle at Delphi—at least, not from the standpoint of the Athenian State. In terms of this reasoning, the

---

* *PH* 164 = 6§37. On the linguistic relationship between *sēmainein* and *theōros*, see Rutherford 2000:137.
† *PH* 164–165 = 6§37.

word *theōros* should apply only to public agents, especially as exemplified by great figures in the past.* A case in point is the lawgiver Lycurgus of Sparta, who, according to Herodotus (1.65.4), received from the Oracle of Apollo at Delphi the law code that he gave to the people of Sparta.† In Xenophon's *Apology of Socrates* (15), Socrates himself makes a reference to the visit of Lycurgus to the Oracle at Delphi, and the philosopher goes out of his way to contrast what the lawgiver was told and what Chaerephon himself was told by the Oracle. In the case of Lycurgus, according to Socrates as mediated in Xenophon's *Apology of Socrates* (15), the Oracle addressed Lycurgus by professing ambivalence about whether the lawgiver is a human or a god; an earlier source, Herodotus (1.65.2–5), also mentions this detail about the consultation of the Oracle by Lycurgus. In the case of Socrates, by contrast, Xenophon's version of the *Apology of Socrates* (again, 15) reports a contrast that was highlighted by Socrates himself in his speech: here the philosopher is emphasizing a major difference between himself and the famed lawgiver from Sparta's glorious past—whereas Apollo's Oracle compared Lycurgus to a god, Socrates was compared only to other mortals.

23§5. Parallel to such an idealization of Lycurgus, lawgiver of Sparta, is the idealization of Solon, lawgiver of Athens. According to a traditional story attested in Herodotus (1.29.1), Solon left Athens for ten years after he gave the Athenians their laws, so that he would not be forced to change any of these laws. Herodotus adds that Solon had made the Athenians swear that they would make no changes in his absence (1.29.2). Herodotus also adds that Solon gave the Athenians a *prophasis* or 'pretext' for his departure and for his subsequent wanderings all over the world, saying that he was embarking on a *theōriā* or 'sacred journey' (θεωρίης πρόφασιν 1.29.2, θεωρίης . . . εἵνεκεν 1.30.1).‡ The subtext of this pretext, as I have already noted, was that the Athenians were thus bound by oath not to change anything in the laws that Solon had given them—so long as he was away on his *theōriā*. Solon's sacred journey or *theōriā* obligated the Athenians.

23§6. In the course of his wandering all over the world on his sacred journey, Solon comes to the court of Croesus, king of the Lydians, who addresses the Athenian lawgiver with these words:

---

*On the connection of the words *theōros* and *theōreîn* with the idea of "state-delegation," see Rutherford 2000:136–138.

† Commentary in *PH* 165–167 = 6§§39–42.

‡ Commentary in *PH* 167 = 6§42n93.

HOUR 23 TEXT A (PART OF HOUR 13 TEXT A)

|₁.₃₀.₂ Athenian guest [*xenos*], we have heard much about your wisdom [*sophiā*] and your wandering [*planē*], how you in your love of wise things [*philosopheîn*] have traveled all over the world for the sake of a sacred journey [*theōriā*], so now I desire to ask you who is the most fortunate [*olbios*] of all men you have ever seen.

Herodotus 1.30.2*

23§7. The wording that describes the philosophical mission of Solon here is most revealing. It helps us understand the wording used by Plato's Socrates in describing his own philosophical mission:

HOUR 23 TEXT B = HOUR 22 TEXT C

I must perform for you the tale of my wandering [*planē*], just as if I had been laboring [*poneîn*] to achieve labors [*ponoi*] that I endured for this purpose: that the [god's] oracular wording [*manteiā*] should become impossible to refute.

Plato *Apology of Socrates* 22a†

23§8. As I argued in Hour 22, Hēraklēs and even Odysseus can be seen as heroic models for the metaphor that pictures the *planē* or 'wandering' of Socrates all over the world in the course of his unending spiritual journey. Now we see that Solon too is a comparable model, especially since this idealized lawgiver's own spiritual journey is described as a philosophical quest: in the wording of Herodotus (1.30.2), Solon is said to love wise things, *philosopheîn*. The one big difference, however, in describing the spiritual journeys of the lawgiver who acts as a philosopher and of the philosopher who acts as a lawgiver is that the *theōriā* or 'sacred journey' of Solon the lawgiver is explicitly linked with his love of wise things, *philosopheîn*, whereas the same word *theōriā* is only implied in the description given by Plato's Socrates of his own mission as a philosopher. For Socrates, *theōriā* cannot be made explicit because he is acting as a private

---

* |₁.₃₀.₂ "Ξεῖνε Ἀθηναῖε, παρ' ἡμέας γὰρ περὶ σέο λόγος ἀπῖκται πολλὸς καὶ σοφίης εἵνεκεν τῆς σῆς καὶ πλάνης, ὡς φιλοσοφέων γῆν πολλὴν θεωρίης εἵνεκεν ἐπελήλυθας· νῦν ὦν ἐπειρέσθαι σε ἵμερος ἐπῆλθέ μοι εἴ τινα ἤδη πάντων εἶδες ὀλβιώτατον."

† δεῖ δὴ ὑμῖν τὴν ἐμὴν πλάνην ἐπιδεῖξαι ὥσπερ πόνους τινὰς πονοῦντος ἵνα μοι καὶ ἀνέλεγκτος ἡ μαντεία γένοιτο.

agent while he wanders around the world, as it were, on his sacred journey. So the word *theōriā* is politically inappropriate for someone who does not represent the Athenian State.

The Symbolism of Theōriā in Plato's Phaedo

23§9. For Socrates in his own lifetime, as we have just seen, the word *theōriā* was politically off limits. In the fullness of time, however, Plato's Socrates will have the last word. Ultimately, the philosophical meaning of *theōriā* as 'theory' will be victorious over the political meaning of *theōriā* as a 'sacred journey' undertaken for the good of the Athenian State. Even the meaning of the modern word *theory* symbolizes the ultimate victory of philosophy, as brought to life in Socratic dialogue, over the politics that brought about the philosopher's death. In Plato's *Phaedo,* as we will now see, the symbolism of this word *theōriā* as a 'sacred journey' vindicates the philosophical mission of Socrates.

23§10. I start by examining the use of this word *theōriā* in the context of a passage we find at the very beginning of Plato's *Phaedo.* The dramatic setting of this dialogue is Phleious, a city in the North Peloponnesus, far away from Athens. The speaker Echecrates is from Phleious, and he is having his own dialogue with another speaker, Phaedo, who is from Athens and who had been a student of Socrates:

HOUR 23 TEXT C

|$_{57a}$ {Echecrates:} Were you yourself, Phaedo, in the prison with Socrates on the day when he drank the poison [*pharmakon*]? Or did you hear about it from some other person?

{Phaedo:} I myself was there, Echecrates.

{Echecrates:} So what were the things the man said before his death? And how did he reach the fulfillment [*teleutân*] of his life? I would be very glad to hear about it. For neither does any one of us Phliasians nowadays visit Athens, and it has been a long time since any guest from there [= Athens] |$_{57b}$ has visited here [= Phleious], who would be able to report to us clearly about these things—except for the detail that he took poison [*pharmakon*] and died. As for the other related matters, no one had anything to indicate.

{Phaedo:} |$_{58a}$ So then you have not been informed about the trial [*dikē*] and about how it went?

{Echecrates:} Well, someone did tell us about those things, but we were wondering why, after the trial [*dikē*] had already taken place some time earlier, he was put to death not right then and there, it seems, but much later. So why did it happen that way, Phaedo?

{Phaedo:} It was a matter of chance [*tukhē*], Echecrates, that things happened that way for him. The reason was that the stern of the ship that the Athenians send to Delos happened to be garlanded [*stephein*] on the day before the trial [*dikē*].

{Echecrates:} What is this ship?

{Phaedo:} This is the ship in which, as the Athenians say, Theseus went to Crete when he took with him those famous two-times-seven young people. |₅₈ᵦ He saved [*sōzein*] them and he too was saved [*sōzein*]. And they were said to have vowed to Apollo at that time, that if they were saved [*sōzein*] they would make an annual sacred journey [*theōriā*] to Delos. And even now, ever since that time, year after year, they send the ship to the god. So every time they begin the sacred journey [*theōriā*], they have a custom [*nomos*] at this time of the year to purify [*kathareuein*] the city and to refrain from publicly executing anybody before the ship goes to Delos and then comes back from there. And sometimes this takes a long time, whenever the winds |₅₈ᵧ happen to detain them. And the beginning of the sacred journey [*theōriā*] is when the priest of Apollo garlands [*stephein*] the stern of the ship. This happened, as I say, on the day before the trial [*dikē*]. And this was the reason Socrates spent a long time in prison between the time of his trial [*dikē*] and the time of his death.

Plato Phaedo 57a–58c*

---

* |₅₇ₐ {ΕΧ.} Αὐτός, ὦ Φαίδων, παρεγένου Σωκράτει ἐκείνῃ τῇ ἡμέρᾳ ᾗ τὸ φάρμακον ἔπιεν ἐν τῷ δεσμωτηρίῳ, ἢ ἄλλου του ἤκουσας; {ΦΑΙΔ.} Αὐτός, ὦ Ἐχέκρατες. {ΕΧ.} Τί οὖν δή ἐστιν ἅττα εἶπεν ὁ ἀνὴρ πρὸ τοῦ θανάτου; καὶ πῶς ἐτελεύτα; ἡδέως γὰρ ἂν ἐγὼ ἀκούσαιμι. καὶ γὰρ οὔτε Φλειασίων οὐδεὶς πάνυ τι ἐπιχωριάζει τὰ νῦν Ἀθήναζε, οὔτε τις ξένος ἀφῖκται χρόνου συχνοῦ |₅₇ᵦ ἐκεῖθεν ὅστις ἂν ἡμῖν σαφές τι ἀγγεῖλαι οἷός τ' ἦν περὶ τούτων, πλήν γε δὴ ὅτι φάρμακον πιὼν ἀποθάνοι· τῶν δὲ ἄλλων οὐδὲν εἶχεν φράζειν. |₅₈ₐ {ΦΑΙΔ.} Οὐδὲ τὰ περὶ τῆς δίκης ἄρα ἐπύθεσθε ὃν τρόπον ἐγένετο; {ΕΧ.} Ναί, ταῦτα μὲν ἡμῖν ἤγγειλέ τις, καὶ ἐθαυμάζομέν γε ὅτι πάλαι γενομένης αὐτῆς πολλῷ ὕστερον φαίνεται ἀποθανών. τί οὖν ἦν τοῦτο, ὦ Φαίδων; {ΦΑΙΔ.} Τύχη τις αὐτῷ, ὦ Ἐχέκρατες, συνέβη· ἔτυχεν γὰρ τῇ προτεραίᾳ τῆς δίκης ἡ πρύμνα ἐστεμμένη τοῦ πλοίου ὃ εἰς Δῆλον Ἀθηναῖοι πέμπουσιν. {ΕΧ.} Τοῦτο δὲ δὴ τί ἐστιν; {ΦΑΙΔ.} Τοῦτ' ἔστι τὸ πλοῖον, ὥς φασιν Ἀθηναῖοι, ἐν ᾧ Θησεύς ποτε εἰς Κρήτην τοὺς "δὶς ἑπτὰ" ἐκείνους ᾤχετο |₅₈ᵦ ἄγων καὶ ἔσωσέ τε καὶ αὐτὸς ἐσώθη. τῷ οὖν Ἀπόλλωνι ηὔξαντο ὡς λέγεται τότε, εἰ σωθεῖεν, ἑκάστου ἔτους θεωρίαν ἀπάξειν εἰς Δῆλον· ἣν δὴ ἀεὶ καὶ νῦν ἔτι ἐξ ἐκείνου κατ' ἐνιαυτὸν τῷ θεῷ πέμπουσιν. ἐπειδὰν οὖν ἄρξωνται τῆς θεωρίας, νόμος ἐστὶν αὐτοῖς ἐν τῷ χρόνῳ τούτῳ καθαρεύειν τὴν πόλιν καὶ δημοσίᾳ μηδένα ἀποκτεινύναι, πρὶν ἂν εἰς Δῆλόν τε ἀφίκηται τὸ πλοῖον καὶ

23§11. In this passage, we see that Theseus the Athenian hero saves the people of Athens by freeing them from being dominated by the naval empire of Minos, king of the city of Knossos on the island of Crete. In the Athenian myth, as we see it retold briefly by Plutarch in his *Life of Theseus* (15.1–2), this domination took the form of a seasonally recurring human sacrifice of fourteen young Athenians, seven boys and seven girls, offered to the monster son of Minos, called the Minotaur, who was half man and half bull and who dwelled in Knossos inside a maze known as the *laburinthos* or 'Labyrinth' (15.2). Joining the original ensemble of seven boys and seven girls who are destined for human sacrifice, Theseus sails with them to Knossos in Crete. There Ariadne the daughter of Minos falls in love with Theseus. She helps him penetrate the Labyrinth, where Theseus finds the Minotaur and kills him. Then, retracing his steps by following the thread that Ariadne gave him, Theseus escapes from the Labyrinth and thus 'saves' both himself and the other young Athenians. This act of 'saving' the Athenians is expressed by the verb *sōzein* in the passage we have just read in Plato's *Phaedo*, where we learn also that Theseus celebrated his salvation and the salvation of the other young Athenians by sailing together with them to Delos, sacred island of Apollo, on a prototypical *theōriā* or 'sacred journey'. In Plutarch's *Life of Theseus* (21.1–3), we can read further details about that prototypical celebration in Delos. There Theseus and the other young Athenians are transformed into a choral ensemble that sings and dances the story of the hero's victory over the Minotaur inside the Labyrinth of Crete, and the Labyrinth itself is re-enacted by way of the singing and dancing, which is traditionally called the *geranos* or 'crane'. This song and dance of the crane, as traditionally performed at the festival of Apollo at Delos, literally re-enacts the Cretan Labyrinth, since the dance steps danced by cranes in the course of these birds' courtship rituals during mating season seem to be re-tracing the patterns of a maze or Labyrinth, as Plutarch says explicitly in his *Life of Theseus* (21.2), following the report of the antiquarian Dicaearchus (F 85 ed. Wehrli), who lived in the fourth/third century BCE.*

23§12. As we see from the *Phaedo* of Plato, this prototypical *theōriā* or 'sacred journey' of Theseus is re-enacted in an Athenian state festival held in honor of

---

πάλιν δεῦρο· τοῦτο δ' ἐνίοτε ἐν πολλῷ χρόνῳ γίγνεται, ὅταν τύχωσιν ἄνεμοι | ₅₈c ἀπολαβόντες αὐτούς. ἀρχὴ δ' ἐστὶ τῆς θεωρίας ἐπειδὰν ὁ ἱερεὺς τοῦ Ἀπόλλωνος στέψῃ τὴν πρύμναν τοῦ πλοίου· τοῦτο δ' ἔτυχεν, ὥσπερ λέγω, τῇ προτεραίᾳ τῆς δίκης γεγονός. διὰ ταῦτα καὶ πολὺς χρόνος ἐγένετο τῷ Σωκράτει ἐν τῷ δεσμωτηρίῳ ὁ μεταξὺ τῆς δίκης τε καὶ τοῦ θανάτου.

* Calame 1990:239–242.

Apollo at Delos, marked by a ritualized *theōriā* or 'sacred journey' of the ship of Theseus from Athens to Delos and back. As we learn from Plutarch's *Life of Theseus* (23.1) the *triākontoros* or thirty-oar ship that sailed every year on this ritualized journey to Delos and back was believed to be the same ship on which Theseus had sailed to Delos together with the rest of the young Athenians who had been saved from being sacrificed to the Minotaur. Plutarch in the *Life of Theseus* (again, 23.1) says that the ancient traditions about this ship could be traced forward in time from the mythical era of Theseus all the way to the historical era of Demetrius of Phaleron, a philosopher who dominated Athens both politically and culturally in the late fourth century BCE: according to these ancient traditions, Plutarch reports, the ship of Theseus had always remained the same ship, except that each and every piece of it had been replaced, one by one, in the course of time. Thus the ship as it existed in the ritual present time of Demetrius in the late fourth century BCE—or, as it existed less than a century earlier, in the year 399 BCE, when Socrates died—consisted of parts that included not a single piece that could be dated all the way back to the mythical past when Theseus had sailed to the island of Delos on this same ship. Plutarch in the *Life of Theseus* (again, 23.1) also says that it had become a philosophical game to debate whether the ship that sailed annually in the ritual was really the same thing as the ship that sailed prototypically in the myth.

23§13. A far more sophisticated form of such a philosophical game is being played out in Plato's *Phaedo,* since the *theōriā* or 'sacred journey' of the Athenian Ship of State that sails to Delos and back is an occasion for testing Plato's Theory of Forms as it plays out in the dramatized dialogue of Socrates with his students in the *Phaedo.* The Athenian Ship of State that is sailing to Delos and back while Socrates is having the last dialogue of his life is materially the exact replica of the supposedly original ship. The ship of the *theōriā* or 'sacred journey' in myth is the absolute ship, the ideal ship, comparable to an ideal ship in Plato's Theory of Forms, whereas the ship of the real world is not absolute, not ideal, just as the things of this world are not real in terms of Plato's Theory of Forms. The word in Greek that we translate as 'Form' is *ideā*, and it is from this Greek word that such English words as *idea, ideal,* and *idealism* are borrowed. Of these borrowings, the adjective and noun *ideal* and *the ideal* come closest to the philosophical concept that we translate in English as *Form*.

23§14. So far, we have seen an ideal of salvation that is mythologically launched, as it were, when the ship of Theseus starts sailing on its sacred voyage or *theōriā*. For Plato's Socrates, however, there is also a parallel ideal of salvation that will be philosophically continued by the theory or *theōriā* that will forever be fueled by the living word of Socratic dialogue. In what follows, I will start to explore the shaping of such an ideal.

The Garlanding of the Theoric Ship

23§15. As we can see from the wording of Plato's *Phaedo* (58a and 58c), quoted in Text C, the priest of Apollo attaches garlands to the stern of the Athenian Ship of State as the formal ritual act of launching this ship on its sacred voyage or *theōriā* to Delos and back. I now focus on the word used in the text of Plato here, *stephein,* which means 'to garland, to make garlands for' (again, 58a and 58c). But what does it really mean, to 'garland' a theoric ship? In ancient Greek, the noun that derives from this verb *stephein* is *stephanos,* meaning 'garland'. Both the noun and the verb refer to blossoms or leaves that are strung together and then ritually attached to an object or to a person. In Modern Greek, the noun corresponding to ancient *stephanos* is *stephánē* (*stepháni*), likewise meaning 'garland'. There is also a neuter plural form of the noun in Modern Greek, *stéphana,* which can mean 'wedding garlands': I note with special interest the metonymy embedded in the phrase used to offer best wishes to newlywed couples: *kalá stéphana,* meaning literally '[may you have] good garlands!' In one Modern Greek phrasebook for English speakers, this expression is translated 'may you have a quick and happy wedding'.

23§16. The mind set that corresponds to such a usage in Modern Greek throws light on the fact that the garlanding of objects or of persons is a way of delineating a ritual framework. The attaching of a garland marks the beginning of engagement in a ritual—and a ritual must always have a notionally perfect beginning. So the attaching of a garland to the stern of the theoric ship is meant to be a perfect *send-off* for the sacred voyage ahead, which must also be notionally perfect and therefore unpolluted. For the Athenian State to execute Socrates while the sacred voyage is in progress would be to pollute the ritual—and to pollute the State. I should add that the ritual practice of garlanding a ship before a sea voyage survives to this day in the Greek-speaking world, and such rituals of garlanding are linked with important festive occasions—including Easter.

23§17. As we take an overall view of the many diverse civilizations that have taken shape in the course of the last four or five thousand years in the islands as well as the mainland coastlines mediated by the Aegean Sea, we can see that the ritual of garlanding the stern of a theoric ship is a custom of the greatest antiquity. The primary attestation comes from the evidence of pictures painted on the plastered surface of inner walls at the site of Akrotiri on the Aegean island of Santorini, the ancient name of which was Thera. This evidence can be dated back to the time when the prehistoric volcano that once occupied most of this island exploded, some time around the middle of the second millennium BCE, leaving behind a gigantic caldera that now occupies the space where the mountain once stood. The wall paintings to which I refer were preserved by the volcanic ash that buried the site of Akrotiri in the wake of the explosion. I concentrate here on a band of paintings that line the inner walls of "Room 5" in a building known to archaeologists as the West House—although there is currently no agreement about what exactly is meant by the term "house" in this instance.* This band of paintings, known as the Miniature Frieze, has been described as "one of the most important monuments in Aegean art."†

23§18. The Miniature Frieze occupies the upper third of the inner walls of Room 5, where the doors and the windows would not interrupt the flow of the narrative that was painted on all four of the inner walls. The narrative of the Frieze moves clockwise, beginning and ending at the same point. The point of beginning, situated at the southernmost end of the west wall, shows part of a harbor city or "Town I," while the point of ending, situated at the westernmost end of the south wall, shows the other part of the same harbor city, "Town I." So the narrative comes full circle back to "Town I."‡ The north wall shows, again, a coastal city, which is "Town II"; as for "Town III," which overlaps the north and the east walls, this site is yet another coastal city, and, in this case, it is situated at the mouth of a river; the same can be said for "Town IV," at the eastern side of the south wall, which is once again a coastal city situated at the mouth of a river; actually, "Town IV" may be another way of looking at one and the same city, "Town III."§ Then there is the south wall, showing a fleet of ships sailing from the harbor of "Town IV" toward the "home port," that is, toward the same place that had also served as a point of departure, which was "Town V."** The fleet consists of seven large ships, only one of which is under sail;†† the other six ships are being rowed by multitudes of oarsmen; further back to our left, in

---

* Doumas 1999:44–97.
† Doumas 1999:47.
‡ Doumas 1999:47–49.
§ Doumas 1999:48.
** Doumas 1999:47–48.
†† Morris 1989:517.

front of "Town IV," there is also a small boat, equipped with no mast, which is rowed by only five oarsmen.* All seven of the large ships are heading from left to right in the direction of the harbor of "Town V." Located at the stern of each one of these seven large ships is a structure that looks like a cabin, and there is a male figure seated inside each one of these "cabins."

23§19. The middle zone of wall paintings in Room 4, situated to the south of Room 5 in the same "West House," shows a variety of close-up pictures featuring enlarged views of the same kinds of decorations that are attached to the "cabins" located at the sterns of the seven large ships. Of particular interest are two semi-circular garlands of flowers that decorate the "cabin" of the first ship: this detail matches most closely the two semi-circular garlands of flowers that decorate the wall of the adjacent Room 4.†

23§20. Painted on the wall of Room 4 is the same garlanded frame of vision painted in the Miniature Frieze decorating the south wall of Room 5. But there is a big difference. Whereas the man who is seated in the "cabin" positioned at the stern of the ship in the picture painted on the plaster wall of Room 5 can look through the garlanded frame of vision and see the sights to be seen as he sails ahead on his sea voyage, a viewer who looks at the plaster wall of Room 4 and sees a picture of the same garlanded frame of vision could merely imagine the sights to be seen in the course of such a sea voyage. Having noted this difference, however, I must return to what the two painted details have in common: whether the sights to be seen are really seen or only imagined, these sights could be interpreted as a *theōriā* or the 'seeing of a vision'. What is being represented in both paintings, I argue, is a prototype of a *theōriā* in the sense of a 'sacred journey' that leads to the achievement of a mystical vision. And that view of that vision is framed by the two semi-circular garlands through which the viewer views what is seen. To borrow from a modern idiom, the vision is viewed through rose-colored glasses.

Revisiting another Theōriā

23§21. At an earlier point in this book, we had a chance to observe another example of *theōriā* in the sense of a 'sacred journey'. In this example as well, the *theōriā* is signaled by the ritual gesture of garlanding. The example I have in

---

* Doumas 1999:47.
† Doumas 1999:95.

mind is a seasonally recurring ritual of the Thessalians as described in the wording of Philostratus (*Hērōikos* 53.9–13) and as quoted in Hour 14 Text K: these Thessalians, representing the Aeolians of Europe who are separated by the Aegean Sea from the Aeolians of Asia Minor, send across the sea to the Asiatic region of Troy an ensemble of 'twice seven' *theōroi* or 'sacred delegates' (53.9), who perform the ritual gesture of 'garlanding' (53.12 *stephanoûn*) the tumulus of Achilles while wearing 'garlands of amaranth' on their own heads (53.9 *stephanoi amarantinoi*). In this example, the ideal of ritual perfection is expressed by way of symbolizing the ideal of eternity, since the ritual itself is meant to be recycled year after year into eternity. The ideal of eternity is symbolized by the Greek expression for 'garlands of amaranth' (again 53.9, *stephanoi amarantinoi*), since *amaranton* or 'amaranth' literally means 'unwilting', as we saw in Hour 14§§32 and 36.

Theorizing about Theōriā

23§22. So the ritual act of garlanding, which marks *theōriā* as a sacred voyage or even as a "vision quest," is a sign of immortality. For Plato's Socrates, *theōriā* is not only a journey of a ship or a journey of a soul: it is also a metaphor for philosophical inquiry through *dialogue*. That, as we have seen, is the way we get the word *theory* from *theōriā*. Such *theory* is a journey of a soul that is meant to be ongoing forever, through dialogue.

23§23. In arriving at such a formulation, I have all along had in mind the title I gave to this hour and to the hour before, "the living word," Parts I and II. For Plato's Socrates, the living word of dialogue can live only if it avoids getting killed by the written word. There are moments in Plato's *Phaedo* when Socrates catches himself in the act of talking in a way that makes him imagine that some reader is already reading him as a piece of writing—as what we would call a book. But the very idea of Socrates as the author of a book is something to be resisted. It makes him smile knowingly and say:

HOUR 23 TEXT D

Then he smiled and said, "It seems just now that I am speaking as an author of some piece of writing [*sungraphikōs ereîn*]. Still, what I am saying does hold, I think."

Plato *Phaedo* 102d*

---

* Καὶ ἅμα μειδιάσας, Ἔοικα, ἔφη, καὶ συγγραφικῶς ἐρεῖν, ἀλλ᾽ οὖν ἔχει γέ που ὡς λέγω.

23§24. But of course Socrates is in fact mediated here and everywhere by an author, who is none other than his old student Plato. Whatever Socrates says is being written down for him by Plato, who seems to be saying it for him. So the dialogues that Socrates is having with his students in Plato's *Phaedo,* for example, are really mediated by the writings of Plato. That is why Plato has to suppress himself as a writer—if the living word of the dialogues is to come alive and stay alive. That is why it would be best for Plato to stay out of any of these dialogues, avoiding his own presence especially in the last of all the dialogues that Socrates will have with his students while he is still alive. That is why, as Phaedo implies in Plato's *Phaedo*—I stress that this speaker only implies it—Plato himself was not there in the course of that last dialogue. He could not be there because he could not be there as an author. Plato would not be up to it. Here is the way Plato's Phaedo speaks of Plato's absence, notional or otherwise, while Phaedo is telling about those Athenians who were present when Socrates died:

HOUR 23 TEXT E

Of native Athenians who were present, there were, besides the Apollodorus I just mentioned, Critobulus and his father, Crito; Hermogenes; Epigenes; Aeschines; and Antisthenes; also present was Ctesippus of the deme of Paiania; Menexenus; and some other native Athenians. As for Plato, I think he was not feeling up to it [= he was feeling weak, *a-stheneîn*].

Plato *Phaedo* 59b*

23§25. This riddling reference to the absence of Plato raises more questions than it answers. Here is the only mention of Plato in the dialogues attributed to Plato's authorship—other than the reference made by Plato's Socrates in Plato's *Apology of Socrates* to the presence of his supporters on the occasion of his trial (34a, 38b). So if Plato was really not there to transcribe, as it were, the things that Socrates said in his last days and hours while alive, how can we trust what he says Socrates said? But this question is misleading: except for the letters that are ascribed to Plato, this man does not say anywhere that he is saying anything. Socrates is saying everything, and even Socrates leaves open-ended what Socrates says. The students of Socrates are not getting the last word from their teacher when he engages them in dialogue for the last time. Rather, the students are get-

---

*Οὗτός τε δὴ ὁ Ἀπολλόδωρος τῶν ἐπιχωρίων παρῆν καὶ Κριτόβουλος καὶ ὁ πατὴρ αὐτοῦ καὶ ἔτι Ἑρμογένης καὶ Ἐπιγένης καὶ Αἰσχίνης καὶ Ἀντισθένης· ἦν δὲ καὶ Κτήσιππος ὁ Παιανιεὺς καὶ Μενέξενος καὶ ἄλλοι τινὲς τῶν ἐπιχωρίων. Πλάτων δὲ οἶμαι ἠσθένει.

ting the latest word, which can ever be renewed whenever the dialogue is restarted.

23§26. Yes, our first impression may be that Socrates speaks to us as if he were a book, and yet, it is the live speech of dialogue that makes the word come alive. What matters is not the wording of Socrates but the words that he is starting in the process of engaging in dialogue, to be continued by his interlocutors and by succeeding interlocutors in generations to come, generation after generation, notionally forever. That is why the dialogues as framed by Plato are not authorial. That is why Socrates is not an author.

Socrates, Master of Poetry as well as Dialogue

23§27. The time frame of the ritual *theōriā* or sacred voyage of the Athenian Ship of State makes room for three phases: (1) the ship sails from Athens to Delos, bringing celebrants; (2) these Athenian celebrants participate in celebrating the festival of the god Apollo at Delos; and (3) the ship sails back to Athens from Delos, taking back the celebrants. Within this time frame, as we have seen, Socrates will engage in dialogues with his followers, and these dialogues are figured as a philosophical form of *theōriā*. But Socrates will be engaging not only in philosophy within this time frame but also in poetry, spending some of his remaining time composing a hymn to Apollo and turning the prose fables of Aesop into poetry:

HOUR 23 TEXT F

In the course of my life I have often had the same recurrent dream, which appeared in different forms in different versions of my envisaging the dream, but which always said the same thing: "Socrates," it said, "go and practice the craft of the Muses [*mousikē*] and keep on working at it." Previously, I had imagined that this was only intended to urge | 61a and encourage me to keep on doing what has always been the pursuit of my life, in the same way that competitors in a footrace are called on by the spectators to run when they are already running. So I thought that the dream was calling on me to keep on doing what I was already doing, which is, to practice philosophy as the craft of the Muses [*mousikē*], since philosophy is the greatest form of this craft and since I practiced philosophy. But now that the trial [*dikē*] has taken place and the festival of the god [Apollo] has been causing the postponement of my execution, I got the idea that I should do something different, just in case the dream was ordering me to practice the craft of the Muses [*mousikē*] in the popular [*dēmōdēs*] sense of the word—so I got the idea that I should not disobey it [= the dream] and that I should go ahead and practice this craft. I was thinking that it would be a safer thing not to depart [this world] before performing a sacred rite by making poetry [*poiēmata*] and thus |₆₁ᵦ obeying the dream. So the first thing I did was to make a poem [*poieîn*] in honor of the god who is the recipient of the current festival, and then, after [*meta*] having finished with the god, here is what I [= Socrates] did: keeping in mind that a poet must, if he is really going to be a poet, make [*poieîn*] myths [*mûthoi*] and not just words [*logoi*] in general, and that I was no expert in the discourse of myth [*mûtho-logikos*], I took some myths [*mûthoi*] of Aesop that I knew and had on hand, and I made poetry [*poieîn*] out of the first few of these that I happened upon.

Plato *Phaedo* 60e-61b*

23§28. In two other projects, I have analyzed this passage in some detail, and I offer here only an abridged version of that analysis:†

In this passage from the *Phaedo*, Plato's Socrates is extolling the supremacy of philosophy as *mousikē*. This word *mousikē,* meaning 'the art of the Muses', conventionally refers to high poetry and song, especially to Homeric poetry, but Plato's Socrates refers to philosophy itself as an even higher form of *mousikē,* unlike any given poetic form of *mousikē,* which is by contrast provincial because it is 'local' or 'popular', that is, *dēmōdēs*. As Socrates says here in the *Phaedo,* he had a dream in

---

* πολλάκις μοι φοιτῶν τὸ αὐτὸ ἐνύπνιον ἐν τῷ παρελθόντι βίῳ, ἄλλοτ᾽ ἐν ἄλλῃ ὄψει φαινόμενον, τὰ αὐτὰ δὲ λέγον, "Ὦ Σώκρατες," ἔφη, "μουσικὴν ποίει καὶ ἐργάζου." καὶ ἐγὼ ἔν γε τῷ πρόσθεν χρόνῳ ὅπερ ἔπραττον τοῦτο ὑπελάμβανον αὐτό μοι παρακελεύεσθαί τε |₆₁ₐ καὶ ἐπικελεύειν, ὥσπερ οἱ τοῖς θέουσι διακελευόμενοι, καὶ ἐμοὶ οὕτω τὸ ἐνύπνιον ὅπερ ἔπραττον τοῦτο ἐπικελεύειν, μουσικὴν ποιεῖν, ὡς φιλοσοφίας μὲν οὔσης μεγίστης μουσικῆς, ἐμοῦ δὲ τοῦτο πράττοντος. νῦν δ᾽ ἐπειδὴ ἥ τε δίκη ἐγένετο καὶ ἡ τοῦ θεοῦ ἑορτὴ διεκώλυέ με ἀποθνῄσκειν, ἔδοξε χρῆναι, εἰ ἄρα πολλάκις μοι προστάττοι τὸ ἐνύπνιον ταύτην τὴν δημώδη μουσικὴν ποιεῖν, μὴ ἀπειθῆσαι αὐτῷ ἀλλὰ ποιεῖν· ἀσφαλέστερον γὰρ εἶναι μὴ ἀπιέναι πρὶν ἀφοσιώσασθαι |₆₁ᵦ ποιήσαντα ποιήματα πιθόμενον τῷ ἐνυπνίῳ. οὕτω δὴ πρῶτον μὲν εἰς τὸν θεὸν ἐποίησα οὗ ἦν ἡ παροῦσα θυσία· μετὰ δὲ τὸν θεόν, ἐννοήσας ὅτι τὸν ποιητὴν δέοι, εἴπερ μέλλοι ποιητὴς εἶναι, ποιεῖν μύθους ἀλλ᾽ οὐ λόγους, καὶ αὐτὸς οὐκ ἦ μυθολογικός, διὰ ταῦτα δὴ οὓς προχείρους εἶχον μύθους καὶ ἠπιστάμην τοὺς Αἰσώπου, τούτων ἐποίησα οἷς πρώτοις ἐνέτυχον.

† *HC* 387–388 = 3§81, Nagy 2011c §§92–93 (also §§96, 168).

which an oracular voice kept telling him to make such a poetic kind of *mousikē*, and he then decided that such *mousikē* would in fact be quite appropriate for marking the occasion of Apollo's *heortē* or 'festival'. So Socrates proceeded to compose two kinds of poetry as his swan song. One kind was a *Hymn to Apollo,* a form of poetry identified with Homer himself in the era of Plato. After all, the part of the Homeric *Hymn to Apollo* that celebrates Apollo at Delos was most suited for performance at the festival of the god at Delos. And the other kind of poetry was a set of *mūthoi* or 'myths' by Aesop that Socrates turned into verse. This terminal gesture that Plato's Socrates makes toward the *mousikē* of poetry puts Homer in his place. The most exalted representative of poetry, Homer the Poet par excellence, is implicitly paired here in the *Phaedo* with his lowly counterpart Aesop: both are exponents of *mūthos,* which Socrates links with the discourse of poetry, contrasting it with *logos,* which he links with the discourse of philosophy. The pairing of the lofty Homer with the lowly Aesop in this context not only lowers the status of Homeric poetry, though only from the standpoint of the philosopher: it also at the same time raises the status of the Aesopic fable, which is represented here as potential poetry by virtue of being *mūthos* in the sense of 'myth'.

23§29. In the analysis that I have just summarized, I used the term *swan song* in referring to the two kinds of poetry that Socrates composed before his death. But Socrates himself reserves the concept of a *swan song* for a higher form of expression. As we have just seen in Plato's *Phaedo,* as quoted in Text F, the 'art of the Muses' or *mousikē* applies not only to song and poetry but also to philosophy, which for Socrates is the highest form of *mousikē.* And, as we saw in a passage I quoted earlier, in Hour 22 Text F, the real swan song of Socrates is not poetry. Rather, it is a continued dialogue with his students:

Hour 23 Text G (Part of Hour 22 Text F)

It is because they [= swans] are sacred to Apollo and have a prophetic [*mantikē*] capacity and foresee the good things that will happen in the house of Hādēs—that is why they sing and rejoice in that [last] day of theirs more than they ever did in the previous time of their life. And I, too, think of myself as the consecrated [*hieros*] agent of the same god, and a fellow temple-servant [*homo-doulos*] with the swans [*kuknoi*],

and, thinking that I have received from my master [*despotēs*] a prophetic [*mantikē*] capacity that is not inferior to theirs, I would not part
from life in a less happy state of mind [*thūmos*] than the swans. And it
is for this reason *that you must speak and ask whatever questions you
want,* so long as the Athenian people's Board of Eleven allows it.

Plato Phaedo 85b

23§30. Just as the ritual journey or *theōriā* that is undertaken by celebrants
who sail to Delos culminates in the hymning of Apollo on his sacred island,
so also the philosophical journey or *theōriā* that is undertaken by Socrates in
prison culminates in the hymning of the same god by way of a dialogue that
must never end.

23§31. The hymning of Apollo at the cult center of his sacred island of Delos
is idealized, as I have argued, in the first part of the *Homeric Hymn to Apollo*
(the second part honors the god as worshipped at the rival cult center of Delphi). But the actual hymning of the god takes on other forms in the historical
present. Whereas Apollo is hymned by an idealized chorus of Delian Maidens
in the *Homeric Hymn to Apollo* (156–178), there is evidence for real choruses
that hymned the god at his Delian festival in the historical period of the fifth
century BCE and thereafter.

23§32. As we see from the testimony of the fifth-century historian Thucydides (3.104.6), the chorus of the Delian Maidens who are described in the *Homeric Hymn to Apollo* are to be viewed as prototypes for the choruses that
actually performed at the Delia, that is, at the festival of Apollo at Delos in historical times.* At the Delia, as Thucydides (3.104.6) observes, city-states participated in the ritual of 'sending' (*anagein*) their local choruses to perform there
as part of a 'sacrifice', conveyed by the word *hiera*, 'sacrificial offerings'. In fact, a
traditional word for a festival like the Delia was *thusiā*, which literally means
'sacrifice'.† There is a most relevant attestation of both these words, *hiera* or 'sacrificial offerings' and *thusiā* or 'sacrifice, festival', in an account concerning the
celebration of the Delia at Delos in the glory days of the Athenian empire. This
account, as we will now see, gives a full-blown description of the magnificent
spectacle of choral performances at the Delia:‡

---

* Nagy 2011d:308.
† I have studied this word extensively in *PR* 40–41, 48–49, 52–53, 83.
‡ Nagy 2011d:308–309.

HOUR 23 TEXT H

Nikias is remembered for his ambitious accomplishments with regard to Delos—accomplishments most spectacular in all their splendor and most worthy of the gods in all their magnificence. Here is an example. The choral groups [khoroi] that cities used to send [to Delos] for the performances of songs sacred to the god (Apollo) used to sail in [to the harbor of Delos] in a haphazard fashion, and the crowds that would gather to greet the ship used to start right away to call on the performers to start singing their song. There was no coordination, since the performers were still in the process of disembarking in a rushed and disorganized way, and they were still putting on their garlands and changing into their costumes. But when he [= Nikias] was in charge of the sacred voyage [theōriā] [to Delos], he first took a side trip to the island of Rheneia, bringing with him the choral group [khoros] and the sacrificial offerings [hiereia] and all the rest of the equipment. And he brought with him a bridge that had been made in advance, back in Athens, to fit the present occasion, and this bridge was most splendidly adorned with golden fixtures, with dyed colors, with garlands, with tapestries. Overnight, he took this bridge and spanned with it the strait between Rheneia and Delos—not a very great distance. |₃.₆ Then, come daylight, he led the procession in honor of the god and brought across the bridge to their destination the performers of the choral group [khoros], who were outfitted most magnificently and were all along performing their song. |₃.₇ Then, after the sacrifice [thusiā] and after the competition [agōn] and after the feasting, he set up as a dedication to the god the [famous] bronze palm tree.

Plutarch *Life of Nikias* 3.5–7*

---

* μνημονεύεται δ' αὐτοῦ καὶ τὰ περὶ Δῆλον ὡς λαμπρὰ καὶ θεοπρεπῆ φιλοτιμήματα. τῶν γὰρ χορῶν, οὓς αἱ πόλεις ἔπεμπον ᾀσομένους τῷ θεῷ, προσπλεόντων μὲν ὡς ἔτυχεν, εὐθὺς δ' ὄχλου πρὸς τὴν ναῦν ἀπαντῶντος ᾄδειν κελευομένων κατ' οὐδένα κόσμον, ἀλλ' ὑπὸ σπουδῆς ἀσυντάκτως ἀποβαινόντων ἅμα καὶ στεφανουμένων καὶ μεταμφιεννυμένων, ἐκεῖνος ὅτε τὴν θεωρίαν ἦγεν, αὐτὸς μὲν εἰς Ῥήνειαν ἀπέβη, τὸν χορὸν ἔχων καὶ τὰ ἱερεῖα καὶ τὴν ἄλλην παρασκευήν, ζεῦγμα δὲ πεποιημένον Ἀθήνησι πρὸς τὰ μέτρα καὶ κεκοσμημένον ἐκπρεπῶς χρυσώσεσι καὶ βαφαῖς καὶ στεφάνοις καὶ αὐλαίαις κομίζων, διὰ νυκτὸς ἐγεφύρωσε τὸν μεταξὺ Ῥηνείας καὶ Δήλου πόρον, οὐκ ὄντα μέγαν· |₃.₆ εἶθ' ἅμ' ἡμέρᾳ τήν τε πομπὴν τῷ θεῷ καὶ τὸν χορὸν ἄγων κεκοσμημένον πολυτελῶς καὶ ᾄδοντα διὰ τῆς γεφύρας ἀπεβίβαζε. |₃.₇ μετὰ δὲ τὴν θυσίαν καὶ τὸν ἀγῶνα καὶ τὰς ἑστιάσεις τόν τε φοίνικα τὸν χαλκοῦν ἔστησεν ἀνάθημα τῷ θεῷ.

23§33. This description by Plutarch, composed half a millennium after the events described, which took place in 426 BCE, still features the essential ritual concepts of *hier(ei)a*, 'sacrificial offerings', and *thusiā*, 'sacrifice, festival'.* And we know that the practice of sending choral groups to perform at Delos, as attested in this narrative about events taking place in the second half of the fifth century, was in full bloom already in the first half of the fifth century BCE, when choruses sang and danced choral songs composed by such master poets as Simonides and Pindar. The primary evidence comes from surviving fragments of their choral songs,† and the majority of these songs performed in honor of Apollo can be identified as *paianes* or 'paeans'.‡ We have already noted this kind of choral song in Hour 5§113. And there is an explicit reference to such a paean as chorally performed by the prototypical Delian Maidens themselves at Delos:

HOUR 23 TEXT I

|₆₈₇ A paean do the Delian Maidens |₆₈₈ sing as a hymn [*humnos*] around the temple gates, |₆₈₉ singing [Apollo] the true child of Leto |₆₉₀ as they swirl, and they have such a beautiful chorus [*khoros*] [of singers and dancers]. |₆₉₁ I too, singing paeans at your palace, |₆₉₂ aged singer that I am, like a swan [*kuknos*], |₆₉₃ from my graybearded throat, |₆₉₄ will send forth a cry. For whatever is real |₆₉₅ has a place to stay in my hymns [*humnoi*].

Euripides *Herakles* 687–695§

23§34. As we can see from this wording, sung and danced in a choral song composed by Euripides, the prototypical Delian Maidens are pictured in the act of performing the kind of choral song that is known as the *paian*, 'paean', which is equated here with the performing of a *humnos*.** The equation is made clear in the syntax of the wording, which can be analyzed in two steps. First, the verb *humnein*, 'sing a *humnos*', takes as its inner object the song that is sung as a *humnos*, and this song is in fact a *paian* or 'paean'. Second, the same verb *humnein* takes as its outer object the name of the god Apollo, who is both the object of

* Nagy 2011d:285.
† Nagy 2011d:309–310.
‡ Nagy 2011d:310; Kowalzig 2007:57.
§ |₆₈₇ παιᾶνα μὲν Δηλιάδες |₆₈₈ ναῶν ὑμνοῦσ᾽ ἀμφὶ πύλας |₆₈₉ τὸν Λατοῦς εὔπαιδα γόνον, |₆₉₀ εἱλίσσουσαι καλλίχοροι· |₆₉₁ παιᾶνας δ᾽ ἐπὶ σοῖς μελάθροις |₆₉₂ κύκνος ὡς γέρων ἀοιδὸς |₆₉₃ πολιᾶν ἐκ γενύων |₆₉₄ κελαδήσω· τὸ γὰρ εὖ |₆₉₅ τοῖς ὕμνοισιν ὑπάρχει.
** Nagy 2011d:310; Kowalzig 2007:66; on Euripides *Herakles* 687–695, see also in general Henrichs 1996.

praise and the subject of the song that is the *humnos.* When I use the expression *subject of the song* here, I mean the *subject matter,* not the *grammatical subject.* In the grammar of a *humnos* as a song, the divinity that figures as the subject of the song is in fact the grammatical object of the verb of singing the song.*

23§35. In the passage I have just quoted from the *Herakles* of Euripides (687–695), Text I, we have seen once again the idea of a *swan song* with reference to the hymning of the god Apollo. That idea fits the context of the drama here, since the chorus represents a group of elderly men who are on the threshold of death in their old age and who rejoice at the prospect—a sadly false prospect, as it turns out—of happy events awaiting Hēraklēs. So we see here once again an old man's song of joy at the prospect of good things to come—in this case, for someone other than the self.

23§36. I find it apt here to return to the swan song of Socrates, who rejoices at the prospect of good things to come—both for himself after his own death and for others, whoever may be listening to the dialogue:

HOUR 23 TEXT J (= TEXT G)

It is because they [= swans] are sacred to Apollo and have a prophetic [*mantikē*] capacity and foresee the good things that will happen in the house of Hādēs—that is why they sing and rejoice in that [last] day of theirs more than they ever did in the previous time of their life. And I, too, think of myself as the consecrated [*hieros*] agent of the same god, and a fellow temple-servant [*homo-doulos*] with the swans [*kuknoi*], and, thinking that I have received from my master [*despotēs*] a prophetic [*mantikē*] capacity that is not inferior to theirs, I would not part from life in a less happy state of mind [*thūmos*] than the swans. And it is for this reason *that you must speak and ask whatever questions you want,* so long as the Athenian people's Board of Eleven allows it.

Plato *Phaedo* 85b

23§37. The devotional tone of the words that Socrates reserves here for his very own 'art of the Muses' reminds me of a *Lied* composed by Schubert as his own personal hymn to Music:

*Nagy 2011d:310–311.

Hour 23 Text K

Du holde Kunst, in wieviel
  grauen Stunden,
	You, O sacred art, how often, in
	  hours that were gray,

Wo mich des Lebens wilder
  Kreis umstrickt,
	while I was caught up in the savage
	  cycle of life,

Hast du mein Herz zu
  warmer Lieb entzünden,
	you brought back my heart to warm
	  love, reigniting it,

Hast mich in eine beßre Welt entrückt!	and spirited me off to a better world.

Oft hat ein Seufzer, deiner
  Harf' entflossen,
	Often has a sigh drifted from your
	  harp—

Ein süßer, heiliger Akkord
  von dir
	a sweet and holy chord coming from
	  you,

Den Himmel beßrer Zeiten
  mir erschlossen,
	revealing from the heavens a
	  glimpse of better times

Du holde Kunst, ich danke
  dir dafür!
	You, O sacred art, I thank you for
	  this.

"An die Musik" ("To Music") by Franz Schubert (D. 547 Op. 88 No. 4),

text by Franz von Schober

23§38. But of course Socrates reserves the concept of a *swan song* not for "music" as we know it but for an even higher form of human expression. As we have seen in Plato's *Phaedo,* quoted in Text F, the 'art of the Muses' or *mousikē* applies not only to song and poetry but also to philosophy, which for Socrates is the highest form of *mousikē*. And, as we see once again in the passage I quoted in Text J, the real swan song of Socrates is not poetry but continued dialogue with his students.

A New Way to Imagine Immortalization after Death

23§39. For Plato's Socrates, philosophy is not only the highest art of the Muses. It is also the highest form of all communication, surpassing even the exalted language that reveals the mysteries of immortalization after death. The practice of philosophy can thus become a new way to imagine the mystical experience of being initiated into these mysteries:

HOUR 23 TEXT L (INCLUDING HOUR 21 TEXT B)

> And perhaps even those who established for us the mysteries [teletai]
> were not unworthy but had a real meaning when they said long ago in
> a riddling way [ainittesthai = verb of ainigma] that he who arrives
> without initiation [amuētos] and without ritual induction [a-teles-tos,
> from verb of telos] into the realm of Hādēs will lie in mud, but that he
> who arrives at that place [ekeîse] after purification [= verb of katharsis]
> and induction [from verb of telos] will dwell [oikeîn] with the gods. As
> those who are involved in the mysteries [teletai] say, "Many are the car-
> riers of the Bacchic wand [narthēx], |₆₉d but few are the bakkhoi [= the
> true worshippers of Bacchus]." And these [true worshippers] are, in my
> opinion, none other than those who have practiced philosophy [phi-
> losopheîn] correctly.

Plato Phaedo 69c-d*

23§40. A question remains: what kind of immortalization after death can we
hope for if we do in fact 'practice philosophy correctly'? As we will now see,
what is at stake here for Plato's Socrates is not the resurrection of the sōma, the
'body', or even the preservation of the psūkhē, the 'soul', but simply the idea that
the living word of philosophical dialogue must stay alive.†

23§41. So the only thing that should make us mourn or lament is not death
pure and simple but the death of dialogue. The prospect of such a death is the
thing that is really being lamented by the wife of Socrates in the final moments
of his life:

HOUR 23 TEXT M

> |₅₉d On previous days, the usual way that I [Phaedo] and the others
> visited Socrates was by congregating in the morning at the place where
> trials are held and where his own trial had taken place. That was be-
> cause this place was near the prison. So every day, we used to wait until
> the entrance to the prison was opened, having conversations with each

---

* καὶ κινδυνεύουσι καὶ οἱ τὰς τελετὰς ἡμῖν οὗτοι καταστήσαντες οὐ φαῦλοί τινες εἶναι, ἀλλὰ τῷ ὄντι
πάλαι αἰνίττεσθαι ὅτι ὃς ἂν ἀμύητος καὶ ἀτέλεστος εἰς Ἅιδου ἀφίκηται ἐν βορβόρῳ κείσεται, ὁ δὲ
κεκαθαρμένος τε καὶ τετελεσμένος ἐκεῖσε ἀφικόμενος μετὰ θεῶν οἰκήσει. εἰσὶν γὰρ δή, ὥς φασιν οἱ
περὶ τὰς τελετάς, "ναρθηκοφόροι |₆₉d μὲν πολλοί, βάκχοι δέ τε παῦροι." οὗτοι δ᾽ εἰσὶν κατὰ τὴν ἐμὴν
δόξαν οὐκ ἄλλοι ἢ οἱ πεφιλοσοφηκότες ὀρθῶς.

† These Socratic priorities are examined with uncanny acuity by Loraux 1982.

other while waiting, since the prison usually did not open all that early. And, once it opened, we used to go in and visit with Socrates, usually spending the whole day with him. On the last day, we met earlier than usual. That was because we had found out on the previous day, |₅₉ₑ as we were leaving the prison in the evening, that the [sacred] ship had arrived from Delos. So we agreed to meet very early at the usual place. We went to the prison, and the guard who used to let us in came up to us and told us to wait and not to go further until he called us. "That is because the Board of Eleven," he said, "are now with Socrates, and they are taking off his chains. They are giving him the order that he is to end it all on this very day." Not too long after that, the guard came back and told us that we may come in. When we entered, |₆₀ₐ we found Socrates just released from chains, and Xanthippe—you know her, right?—was sitting next to him and holding his child. When Xanthippe saw us, she said some ritualized words [*an-eu-phēmeîn*], the kind that women are accustomed to say, and the wording went something like this: "Socrates, now is the last time when your dear ones will be talking to you and you to them." Socrates glanced at Crito and said to him: "Crito, will someone please take her home?" Then a few of Crito's people led her away; she was crying |₆₀ᵦ and hitting herself.

Plato *Phaedo* 59d-60b*

23§42. From a philosophical perspective, the focus has shifted away from the lamenting wife and the helpless child. The poetic perspective had been so different, we may recall, in the Homeric scene in *Iliad* VI when Hector experiences

---

* |₅₉ᵈ ἀεὶ γὰρ δὴ καὶ τὰς πρόσθεν ἡμέρας εἰώθεμεν φοιτᾶν καὶ ἐγὼ καὶ οἱ ἄλλοι παρὰ τὸν Σωκράτη, συλλεγόμενοι ἕωθεν εἰς τὸ δικαστήριον ἐν ᾧ καὶ ἡ δίκη ἐγένετο· πλησίον γὰρ ἦν τοῦ δεσμωτηρίου. περιεμένομεν οὖν ἑκάστοτε ἕως ἀνοιχθείη τὸ δεσμωτήριον, διατρίβοντες μετ᾽ ἀλλήλων, ἀνεῴγετο γὰρ οὐ πρῴ· ἐπειδὴ δὲ ἀνοιχθείη, εἰσῇμεν παρὰ τὸν Σωκράτη καὶ τὰ πολλὰ διημερεύομεν μετ᾽ αὐτοῦ. καὶ δὴ καὶ τότε πρῳαίτερον συνελέγημεν· τῇ γὰρ προτεραίᾳ ἡμέρᾳ |₅₉ₑ ἐπειδὴ ἐξήλθομεν ἐκ τοῦ δεσμωτηρίου ἑσπέρας, ἐπυθόμεθα ὅτι τὸ πλοῖον ἐκ Δήλου ἀφιγμένον εἴη. παρηγγείλαμεν οὖν ἀλλήλοις ἥκειν ὡς πρῳαίτατα εἰς τὸ εἰωθός. καὶ ἥκομεν καὶ ἡμῖν ἐξελθὼν ὁ θυρωρός, ὅσπερ εἰώθει ὑπακούειν, εἶπεν περιμένειν καὶ μὴ πρότερον παριέναι ἕως ἂν αὐτὸς κελεύσῃ· "Λύουσι γάρ," ἔφη, "οἱ ἕνδεκα Σωκράτη καὶ παραγγέλλουσιν ὅπως ἂν τῇδε τῇ ἡμέρᾳ τελευτᾷ." οὐ πολὺν δ᾽ οὖν χρόνον ἐπισχὼν ἧκεν καὶ ἐκέλευεν ἡμᾶς εἰσιέναι. εἰσιόντες οὖν |₆₀ₐ κατελαμβάνομεν τὸν μὲν Σωκράτη ἄρτι λελυμένον, τὴν δὲ Ξανθίππην – γιγνώσκεις γάρ – ἔχουσάν τε τὸ παιδίον αὐτοῦ καὶ παρακαθημένην. ὡς οὖν εἶδεν ἡμᾶς ἡ Ξανθίππη, ἀνηυφήμησέ τε καὶ τοιαῦτ᾽ ἄττα εἶπεν, οἷα δὴ εἰώθασιν αἱ γυναῖκες, ὅτι "Ὦ Σώκρατες, ὕστατον δή σε προσεροῦσι νῦν οἱ ἐπιτήδειοι καὶ σὺ τούτους." καὶ ὁ Σωκράτης βλέψας εἰς τὸν Κρίτωνα, "Ὦ Κρίτων," ἔφη, "ἀπαγέτω τις αὐτὴν οἴκαδε." Καὶ ἐκείνην μὲν ἀπῆγόν τινες τῶν τοῦ Κρίτωνος βοῶσάν |₆₀ᵦ τε καὶ κοπτομένην.

his final moments together with his wife, Andromache, and his infant son, Astyanax. By the time the philosophical contingent reaches the scene of Socrates' final moments together with his wife and his child, there is no longer any room for hearing and seeing whatever tender words and gestures may or may not have been exchanged.

23§43. From a philosophical perspective, the main thing to lament is *the termination of opportunities to have dialogues with Socrates in person*. It is this termination that Xanthippe laments in her own way, both for the followers of Socrates and even for herself.

23§44. But the perception of such a termination turns out to be erroneous, as we see from the final passage that I will quote in this hour. At the beginning of this quoted passage, we find something extraordinary going on in the dialogue of Plato's *Phaedo*. Starting at section 88c, Echecrates interrupts the narrative of Phaedo containing the dialogue of Socrates with Phaedo and others. The interruption of the narrative is like a derailing of the dialogue contained by the narrative. Then the speaker Phaedo in section 88e responds to the interruption by the speaker Echecrates, and the recontinued dialogue contained by the now recontinued narrative gets the argument back on track. And this argument, as we will see, corrects the erroneous impression that Socratic dialogue will be terminated by the death of Socrates:

HOUR 23 TEXT N

{Echecrates:} I swear by the gods, Phaedo, I myself now feel totally the same way as you people felt back then. I mean, as I am now listening to you saying the kinds of things you are saying, this is the thought that comes to me: |₈₈d "What argument [*logos*] can we ever trust again? For what could be more trustworthy than the argument [*logos*] of Socrates, which has now fallen into the status of untrustworthiness?" You see, the argument [*logos*] that the soul [*psūkhē*] is some kind of a tuning [*harmoniā*] has always been wonderfully attractive to me, and, when this argument was put into words, it was as if it connected me in my thinking with the fact that these things had been figured out earlier by me as well. And now I am in need of finding some other argument [*logos*], starting all the way back from the beginning—some argument that will make me believe that, when someone dies, the soul [*psūkhē*] does not die along with that someone. Tell me, for Zeus' sake, tell me! How did Socrates follow up on the argument [*logos*] [of Simmias and

Cebes]? |₈₈ₑ Did he too get visibly upset, the same way you say that you all got upset? Or was he not upset and instead responded calmly to the cry for help and ran to the rescue [*boētheîn*] of the argument [*logos*]? And did he respond and run to the rescue [*boētheîn*] in a way that was sufficient or defective? Go through for us everything that happened, as accurately as you can.

[Here the narrative of Phaedo containing the dialogue of Socrates with Phaedo and others is resumed after the interruption, after the derailment.]

{Phaedo:} I tell you, Echecrates: as often as I have admired Socrates, I have never been so awed by him as I was when I was there at that moment. |₈₉ₐ The fact that he had something to say in response was perhaps nothing all that unusual, but the thing that really astounded me was, first, how gently and pleasantly and respectfully he received the argument [*logos*] of the young men [Simmias and Cebes], and, second, how acutely he sensed that we all had suffered injury from the arguments [*logoi*] [of Simmias and Cebes], and then, how well he healed us of our sufferings. It was as if he were calling out to us, fleeing and defeated as we were, urging us to follow him and to take another good look at our argument [*logos*].

{Echecrates:} And how did he do that?

{Phaedo:} I will tell you. You see, I happened to be seated close to him, at his right hand. I was sitting on a kind of stool, |₈₉ᵦ while he was lying on a couch that was quite a bit higher than where I was. So then he stroked my head and fondled the locks of hair along my neck—he had this way of playing with my hair whenever he had a chance. And then he said: "Tomorrow, Phaedo, you will perhaps be cutting off these beautiful locks of yours?" "Yes, Socrates," I replied, "I guess I will." He shot back: "no you will not, if you listen to me." "So what will I do?" I said. He replied: "Not tomorrow but today I will cut off my own hair and you too will cut off these locks of yours—if our argument [*logos*] comes to an end [*teleutân*] for us and we cannot bring it back to life again [*ana-biōsasthai*]. |₈₉ᵧ Moreover, if I were you and the argument [*logos*] eluded me, I would make an oath and bind myself to it, as the men of Argos had done once upon a time, that I would not wear my hair long until I won in renewed battle against the argument [*logos*] of

Simmias and Cebes." "Yes," I said, "but even Hēraklēs is said not to be a match for two opponents." "Then summon me," he said, "as your Iolaos, so long as there is still sunlight before the sun sets." "Then I summon you," I said, "not as Hēraklēs: rather, I summon you the same way as Iolaos summons Hēraklēs."

Plato Phaedo 88c-89c*

23§45. As David Elmer has shown, what we see here is a moment in the inset narrative performed by Phaedo where "the frame narrative breaks into the inset narrative."† This moment happens when Echecrates interrupts, as we have just seen, the narrative of the speaker Phaedo, who is reporting the dialogue that took place during the last days and hours of Socrates. As Elmer has also shown, "this moment is just exactly after Socrates has asked someone else to respond to the objections of Simmia; in the inset narrative, Socrates then turns to Phaedo himself, who is the frame narrator to Echecrates."‡ And it is at this moment that Echecrates interrupts, in exasperation and even despair, the inset narrative containing the inset dialogue. After the two young philosophers Simmias and Cebes complete their *logos* or 'argument' against the *logos* or 'argument' for the

---

* {ΕΧ.} Νὴ τοὺς θεούς, ὦ Φαίδων, συγγνώμην γε ἔχω ὑμῖν. καὶ γὰρ αὐτόν με νῦν ἀκούσαντά σου τοιοῦτόν τι λέγειν |₈₈d πρὸς ἐμαυτὸν ἐπέρχεται· "Τίνι οὖν ἔτι πιστεύσομεν λόγῳ; ὡς γὰρ σφόδρα πιθανὸς ὤν, ὃν ὁ Σωκράτης ἔλεγε λόγον, νῦν εἰς ἀπιστίαν καταπέπτωκεν." θαυμαστῶς γάρ μου ὁ λόγος οὗτος ἀντιλαμβάνεται καὶ νῦν καὶ ἀεί, τὸ ἁρμονίαν τινὰ ἡμῶν εἶναι τὴν ψυχήν, καὶ ὥσπερ ὑπέμνησέν με ῥηθεὶς ὅτι καὶ αὐτῷ μοι ταῦτα προυδέδοκτο. καὶ πάνυ δέομαι πάλιν ὥσπερ ἐξ ἀρχῆς ἄλλου τινὸς λόγου ὅς με πείσει ὡς τοῦ ἀποθανόντος οὐ συναποθνῄσκει ἡ ψυχή. λέγε οὖν πρὸς Διὸς πῇ ὁ Σωκράτης μετῆλθε τὸν λόγον· καὶ πότερον |₈₈e κἀκεῖνος, ὥσπερ ὑμᾶς φῄς, ἐνδηλός τι ἐγένετο ἀχθόμενος ἢ οὔ, ἀλλὰ πρᾴως ἐβοήθει τῷ λόγῳ· ἦ καὶ ἱκανῶς ἐβοήθησεν ἢ ἐνδεῶς; πάντα ἡμῖν δίελθε ὡς δύνασαι ἀκριβέστατα. {ΦΑΙΔ.} Καὶ μήν, ὦ Ἐχέκρατες, πολλάκις θαυμάσας Σωκράτη οὐ πώποτε μᾶλλον ἠγάσθην ἢ τότε παραγενόμενος. |₈₉a τὸ μὲν οὖν ἔχειν ὅτι λέγοι ἐκεῖνος ἴσως οὐδὲν ἄτοπον· ἀλλ᾿ ἔγωγε μάλιστα ἐθαύμασα αὐτοῦ πρῶτον μὲν τοῦτο, ὡς ἡδέως καὶ εὐμενῶς καὶ ἀγαμένως τῶν νεανίσκων τὸν λόγον ἀπεδέξατο, ἔπειτα ἡμῶν ὡς ὀξέως ᾔσθετο ὃ 'πεπόνθεμεν ὑπὸ τῶν λόγων, ἔπειτα ὡς εὖ ἡμᾶς ἰάσατο καὶ ὥσπερ πεφευγότας καὶ ἡττημένους ἀνεκαλέσατο καὶ προύτρεψεν πρὸς τὸ παρέπεσθαί τε καὶ συσκοπεῖν τὸν λόγον. {ΕΧ.} Πῶς δή; {ΦΑΙΔ.} Ἐγώ ἐρῶ. ἔτυχον γὰρ ἐν δεξιᾷ αὐτοῦ καθήμενος |₈₉b παρὰ τὴν κλίνην ἐπὶ χαμαιζήλου τινός, ὁ δὲ ἐπὶ πολὺ ὑψηλοτέρου ἢ ἐγώ. καταψήσας οὖν μου τὴν κεφαλὴν καὶ συμπιέσας τὰς ἐπὶ τῷ αὐχένι τρίχας – εἰώθει γάρ, ὁπότε τύχοι, παίζειν μου εἰς τὰς τρίχας – Αὔριον δή, ἔφη, ἴσως, ὦ Φαίδων, τὰς καλὰς ταύτας κόμας ἀποκερῇ. Ἔοικεν, ἦν δ᾿ ἐγώ, ὦ Σώκρατες. Οὔκ, ἄν γε ἐμοὶ πείθῃ. Ἀλλὰ τί; ἦν δ᾿ ἐγώ. Τήμερον, ἔφη, κἀγὼ τὰς ἐμὰς καὶ σὺ ταύτας, ἐάνπερ γε ἡμῖν ὁ λόγος τελευτήσῃ καὶ μὴ δυνώμεθα αὐτὸν ἀναβιώσασθαι. |₈₉c καὶ ἔγωγ᾿ ἄν, εἰ σὺ εἴην καί με διαφεύγοι ὁ λόγος, ἔνορκον ἂν ποιησαίμην ὥσπερ Ἀργεῖοι, μὴ πρότερον κομήσειν, πρὶν ἂν νικήσω ἀναμαχόμενος τὸν Σιμμίου τε καὶ Κέβητος λόγον. Ἀλλ᾿, ἦν δ᾿ ἐγώ, πρὸς δύο λέγεται οὐδ᾿ ὁ Ἡρακλῆς οἷός τε εἶναι. Ἀλλὰ καὶ ἐμέ, ἔφη, τὸν Ἰόλεων παρακάλει, ἕως ἔτι φῶς ἐστιν. Παρακαλῶ τοίνυν, ἔφην, οὐχ ὡς Ἡρακλῆς, ἀλλ᾿ ὡς Ἰόλεως τὸν Ἡρακλῆ.

† Elmer 2010.
‡ Elmer 2010.

immortality of the *psūkhē* or 'soul', the other dialogic partners of Socrates are all at a loss, clearly. So the interruption by Echecrates happens at a moment when the flow of argumentation has in any case been interrupted by the inability of the original dialogic partners to come up with a good response to the argument of Simmias and Cebes. The *logos* or 'argument' for the immortality of the *psūkhē* or 'soul', pictured as the perfect *harmoniā* or 'tuning' of Apollo's seven-stringed lyre, has been shattered in the course of the dialogue reported by Phaedo.* And the same argument is now being shattered for Echecrates, who is just hearing for the first time the content of this dialogue that took place while Socrates was still alive. But Socrates is now dead. So how can the argument for the immortality of the *psūkhē* or 'soul' have any chance to live on?

23§46. This is where the continuation of the argument comes into the picture. After the interruption of the argument, the argument will begin again, as Phaedo recontinues the inset narrative, and, in this recontinued narrative, the dialogue of Socrates gets a new life. The dialogue is brought back to life again. The dialogue, as Socrates himself implies, is resurrected. His use of the expression *ana-biōnai*, 'bring back to life again', in the text I just quoted conveys the idea of resurrecting the *logos*, 'argument', the literal meaning of which can also be translated, more simply, as 'word'. The followers of Socrates should lament not for the death of Socrates but for the death of the word. And if the living word stays alive, then there is no need to mourn for Socrates—even if his *psūkhē* or 'soul' were to die along with him. Plato's Socrates refers in this context to a celebrated story about the men of Argos who refused to wear their hair long until they got a rematch with the long-haired men of Sparta who had defeated them (Herodotus 1.82.7). So also, says Socrates, the followers of Socrates should cut their hair in mourning for his death only if they are ready to fight once again for the argument that the *psūkhē* or 'soul' is immortal. So maybe Socrates himself has been immortalized after all. It is in such a context that I can understand the argument of those who see traces of a hero cult of Socrates as instituted by Plato and his followers within the space of Plato's Academy.†

23§47. In the passage I have just quoted in Text N from Plato's *Phaedo* (88e), we find a most striking metaphor applied to Socrates in the act of defending the *logos* or 'argument': he is said to *boētheîn*, which means literally that he is re-

---

* In a separate project, Nagy 2009c, I have studied other examples of this metaphor of the shattering of the perfect *harmoniā* or 'tuning' of a seven-stringed lyre. Of particular interest is the tragedy *Thamyras* by Sophocles, where the lyre of Thamyras the lyre singer disintegrates while he is playing it.

† White 2000.

sponding to a 'cry for help', a *boē*, by running, *theîn*, to the rescue.* This metaphor is not only military: it is also heroic, as we see in Homeric contexts (*Iliad*
XIII 477). And, in historical times, when heroes are called upon to help their
worshippers in their hour of need, the appropriate word for a positive response
is *boētheîn*, as we see for example in Plutarch's *Life of Nikias* (1.3), where the hero
Hēraklēs is said to have intervened on behalf of the Syracusans by saving them
in their military victory against the Athenians. Moreover, when Socrates is
asked to respond to a cry for help from his beleaguered fellow debaters as the
argumentation proceeds in Plato's *Phaedo*, he is compared to the ultimate hero
Hēraklēs. Phaedo wants to 'summon' or *para-kaleîn* Socrates, just as the worshippers of Hēraklēs 'summon' that hero. This way, the argument for immortality will be saved.

23§48. Socrates, however, prefers to be 'summoned' not as Hēraklēs but
as Iolaos, the young nephew and junior partner of Hēraklēs. Socrates wants
Phaedo to be his Hēraklēs after Socrates is dead. No, Phaedo will not be able to
fight against the likes of Simmias and Cebes if the two of them fight against him
as a pair. That would be a one-against-two fight. When Hēraklēs is fighting solo
against two, even he needs the help of his nephew Iolaos. But the dialogic partner of Socrates, Phaedo, wants to summon Socrates as if Socrates were Hēraklēs.
Phaedo can be Iolaos to Socrates while Socrates is Hēraklēs, although Socrates
thinks that he should be Iolaos and should let Phaedo be Hēraklēs in a debate
with Simmias and Cebes. Either way, Socrates would be dead, and the living
dialogic partner would have to team up with the dead words of Socrates, who is
shown engaging in dialogue inside the book that is Plato's *Phaedo*. These dead
words embedded inside the book can be made to come alive only when the
word comes back to life again in a live dialogue.

* Chantraine *DELG* s.v. βοή.

PART FIVE

HEROES TRANSCENDED

The Hero as Savior

The Meaning of Sōzein and Sōtēr

24§1. The key word for this hour is the verb *sōzein,* meaning 'save (someone)'. Derived from this verb is the noun *sōtēr,* which means 'savior' in the sense of 'one who brings (someone) back to safety' or, mystically, 'one who brings (someone) back to life'. We have already seen in Pausanias 8.44.4 (Hour 11 Text L) the feminine form of *sōtēr, sōteira,* with reference to the goddess Athena as the 'savior' of the hero Odysseus. Derived from this noun *sōtēr* is the adjective *sōtērios* and the noun *sōtēriā,* which mean 'saving' and 'salvation'. We have already seen these words in Aeschylus *Eumenides* 701 and 909 respectively (Hour 17 Text F and Text H), with reference to the goddess Athena as the promoter of eternal well-being for the Athenians. But this word applies not only to salvation promoted by gods. Heroes, too, can promote salvation. For example, in Sophocles *Oedipus at Colonus* 487, we saw Oedipus described as a 'bringer of salvation', a *sōtērios,* for the whole community of Athens, once he achieves the status of cult hero (Hour 18§§24, 31); he is also described as a *sōtēr* or 'savior' of the Athenians at lines 460 and 463 (18§32). In Sophocles *Oedipus Tyrannus* 48, Oedipus is invoked as a *sōtēr* or 'savior' because he saved the people of Thebes from the monstrous Sphinx (Hour 19 Text D; commentary in 19§19).

24§2. As we think through the list of examples I just offered, we need to keep reminding ourselves that such concepts of *savior* and *salvation* are not borrowings from Christian discourse. The fact is, Christian discourse inherited the words *sōzein,* 'save', and *sōtēr,* 'savior', from pre-Christian phases of the Greek language. And we also need to keep in mind that some uses of these words are metaphorical. In the course of this last hour, Hour 24, we will see salient examples of metaphorical uses in the works of Plato and Aristotle. I will begin, however, with an example that highlights the non-metaphorical uses of these words.

Theseus as a Savior for the Athenians

24§3. For my first example of the hero as savior, I return to Hour 23 Text C, focusing on the part of that passage where Theseus the hero is featured as savior of the Athenians:

HOUR 24 TEXT A (PART OF HOUR 23 TEXT C)

{Phaedo:} This is the ship in which, as the Athenians say, Theseus went to Crete when he took with him those famous two-times-seven young people. |₅₈ᵦ He saved [*sōzein*] them and he too was saved [*sōzein*]. And they were said to have vowed to Apollo at that time, that if they were saved [*sōzein*] they would make an annual sacred journey [*theōriā*] to Delos. And even now, ever since that time, year after year, they send the ship to the god. So every time they begin the sacred journey [*theōriā*], they have a custom [*nomos*] at this time of the year to purify [*kathareuein*] the city and to refrain from publicly executing anybody before the ship goes to Delos and then comes back from there. And sometimes this takes a long time, whenever the winds |₅₈c happen to detain them. And the beginning of the sacred journey [*theōriā*] is when the priest of Apollo garlands [*stephein*] the stern of the ship. This happened, as I say, on the day before the trial [*dikē*]. And this was the reason why Socrates spent a long time in prison between the time of his trial [*dikē*] and the time of his death.

Plato *Phaedo* 58a-c*

24§4. As we saw in Hour 23, the Athenian myth of Theseus tells how this hero saved the Athenians by killing the Minotaur inside the Labyrinth—and then by escaping from this monster's pernicious maze. And we saw how Theseus in myth became the founder of a famous Athenian ritual when he cele-

---

* Τοῦτ᾽ ἔστι τὸ πλοῖον, ὥς φασιν Ἀθηναῖοι, ἐν ᾧ Θησεύς ποτε εἰς Κρήτην τοὺς "δὶς ἑπτὰ" ἐκείνους ᾤχετο |₅₈ᵦ ἄγων καὶ ἔσωσέ τε καὶ αὐτὸς ἐσώθη. τῷ οὖν Ἀπόλλωνι ηὔξαντο ὡς λέγεται τότε, εἰ σωθεῖεν, ἑκάστου ἔτους θεωρίαν ἀπάξειν εἰς Δῆλον· ἣν δὴ ἀεὶ καὶ νῦν ἔτι ἐξ ἐκείνου κατ᾽ ἐνιαυτὸν τῷ θεῷ πέμπουσιν. ἐπειδὰν οὖν ἄρξωνται τῆς θεωρίας, νόμος ἐστὶν αὐτοῖς ἐν τῷ χρόνῳ τούτῳ καθαρεύειν τὴν πόλιν καὶ δημοσίᾳ μηδένα ἀποκτεινύναι, πρὶν ἂν εἰς Δῆλόν τε ἀφίκηται τὸ πλοῖον καὶ πάλιν δεῦρο· τοῦτο δ᾽ ἐνίοτε ἐν πολλῷ χρόνῳ γίγνεται, ὅταν τύχωσιν ἄνεμοι |₅₈c ἀπολαβόντες αὐτούς. ἀρχὴ δ᾽ ἐστὶ τῆς θεωρίας ἐπειδὰν ὁ ἱερεὺς τοῦ Ἀπόλλωνος στέψῃ τὴν πρύμναν τοῦ πλοίου· τοῦτο δ᾽ ἔτυχεν, ὥσπερ λέγω, τῇ προτεραίᾳ τῆς δίκης γεγονός. διὰ ταῦτα καὶ πολὺς χρόνος ἐγένετο τῷ Σωκράτει ἐν τῷ δεσμωτηρίῳ ὁ μεταξὺ τῆς δίκης τε καὶ τοῦ θανάτου.

brated his own salvation and the salvation of the other young Athenians whom he saved: according to Athenian myth, this celebration took the form of a sea voyage to the sacred island of Delos, where the hero re-enacted his experience in the Labyrinth by way of a prototypical song and dance performed by a chorus consisting of the young Athenians who were saved and by Theseus himself as their choral leader. Still further, we saw how this re-enactment in myth was continued—notionally forever—by way of the famous Athenian ritual of sending the Ship of State to sail to and from Delos on a seasonally recurring sacred voyage or *theōriā*, which was seen as a seasonally recurring achievement of a mystical inner vision of salvation from death.

24§5. In Hour 23§14, I launched a related argument that I will now continue here. As I said then, the ritualized idea of *theōriā* as a re-enactment of salvation for the Athenian State was transformed by Plato's Socrates into a philosophical idea of *theōriā*—to be understood not only as the sacred voyage of the Athenian Ship of State to and from Delos but also as the philosophical theorizing that will be going on within the confines of the prison where Socrates is awaiting the moment of his execution by the State. The time frame of the ritual *theōriā* as a sacred journey to Delos and back coincides with the time frame of the philosophical *theōriā* as a set of dialogues centering on the immortality of the living word that is forever being brought back to life in the very act of having a dialogue. And just as the *theōriā* of a sacred voyage to and from Delos could be seen as the achievement of a mystical inner vision of salvation from death—an inner vision that was meant to recur year after year forever—so also the synchronized *theōriā* of the dialogue that is dramatized in Plato's *Phaedo* could be seen as a parallel achievement of a different kind of vision that was meant to recur every time the original dialogue of the *Phaedo* is continued by way of further dialogue.

A Metaphorical Use of the Word Sōzein by Plato's Socrates

24§6. By now we have seen that the word *theōriā*, meaning 'sacred voyage', was used metaphorically to express the idea of philosophical contemplation. And we have also seen that the ritual of *theōriā* as a 'sacred voyage' was linked with the myth that told about the salvation of the hero Theseus—how he saved both himself and the other young Athenians who were traveling with him. So the idea of philosophical contemplation is linked not only with the ritual of the sacred voyage but also with this myth of salvation. Moreover, as we are about to see, Plato's Socrates can even bring himself to say that myth itself is worthy of salvation. And, in saying such a thing, Socrates is making a metaphorical use of the word *sōzein,* meaning 'save'.

24§7. Before we consider this metaphorical use, however, I must first reconsider the meaning of 'myth', expressed by the Greek word *mūthos.* As I noted already in Hour 1§36, the most ancient meaning of *mūthos* is 'something said for the record': in terms of such a meaning, then, any story that is called a *mūthos* is considered to be genuine and true, precisely because it is said for the record.* By contrast, the modern word *myth,* derived from *mūthos,* has obviously veered from this meaning: in popular usage, *myth* is a story that is not genuine, not true. Already in the works of Plato, as we can see most glaringly from an overall reading of Scroll 10 of his *Republic, mūthos* is destabilized as a truth value. And we can see why it is that Plato's Socrates has a problem with *mūthos* if we take another look at a passage in the *Phaedo* (60e-61b) that I quoted in Hour 23 Text F: there Socrates is making a distinction between poetry and prose, saying that poetry is the natural medium of *mūthos* while the prose of *logos* is the logical medium of philosophy.

24§8. Nevertheless, despite his preference for the *logos* of philosophy over the poetry of *mūthos,* Plato's Socrates declares that *mūthos* can ultimately be saved. And his declaration, as we will now see, features a most striking example of the word *sōzein,* 'save', used in a metaphorical sense.

24§9. Although *mūthos* or 'myth' is not only discredited but even banned from the ideal state of Plato's *Republic,* we find in the end that it gets re-admitted. What happens in the end is that Plato's Socrates allows myth to stage a stealthy re-entry—through the back door, as it were. But this re-entry is subject to a condition: myth must prove itself useful in serving what is truly ideal. Such proof comes with the telling of the Myth of Er, which is Plato's own creation of a myth at the conclusion of the *Republic.* And this myth, which is about a philosophical kind of salvation, is in the end linked with the salvation of myth itself. Plato has Socrates himself saying at the end of the *Republic,* with reference to this Myth of Er:†

---

* *HQ* 119–125, 127–133, 152.
† Nagy 2002b.

HOUR 24 TEXT B

And so, Glaukon, myth [*mūthos*] was saved [*e-sō-thē*, from *sōzein*], |₆₂₁c
and it could save [*sōzein*] us in turn, if we trust it.

Plato *Republic* 10.621b-c*

A Metaphorical Use of the Word Sōphrōn *in an Archaic Hymn*

24§10. To make a metaphor out of the idea of salvation is not only a philosophical project, as we have seen it take shape in the case of the word *theōriā* in Plato's *Phaedo*. We can see such metaphors at work already in the earliest forms of Greek poetry, as for example in the *Homeric Hymn* (7) *to Dionysus*. In this archaic hymn, the metaphor of salvation applies to a *kubernētēs* or 'pilot' of a ship who is saved by the god Dionysus himself from being transformed into a dolphin. The key to salvation here is to be found in a metaphor built into the word describing this pilot, *sōphrōn,* which means 'moderate' or 'balanced'. Literally, this word is a compound adjective consisting of the elements *sō-* and *-phrōn,* meaning 'the one whose thinking [*phrēn*] is safe', and the element *sō-* actually derives from the verb *sōzein.*† As we saw in Hour 21§33, this adjective *sōphrōn* in the sense of 'moderate' or 'balanced' applies to worshippers of the god Dionysus who find themselves in a mental state of equilibrium or balance when they participate in the rituals of Dionysus.

24§11. As we are about to see, the application of this adjective *sōphrōn* to the pilot in the *Homeric Hymn to Dionysus* is the signal of this man's salvation, since he behaves in a morally moderate way—unlike the captain of the ship and the sailors commanded by the captain. Another signal of the pilot's salvation is his actual role as pilot. As we saw in Hour 9§6, the word that I have been translating as 'pilot' is *kubernētēs:* so the pilot is literally the 'steersman' who directs not only the ship but also, metaphorically, the community that is the ship. This Greek word *kubernētēs,* as we also saw, was eventually borrowed into Latin as *gubernātor,* which in turn has been borrowed into English as *governor.* Thus the *governor,* the one who *governs* a *government*, is metaphorically the 'steersman' who directs the 'ship of state'.

---

* Καὶ οὕτως, ὦ Γλαύκων, μῦθος ἐσώθη καὶ οὐκ ἀπώλετο, |₆₂₁c καὶ ἡμᾶς ἂν σώσειεν, ἂν πειθώμεθα αὐτῷ.

† Chantraine *DELG* s.v. σώζω.

24§12. As we now proceed to read the *Homeric Hymn* (7) *to Dionysus,* we may observe the metaphorical interplay of the word *sōphrōn,* meaning 'moderate, balanced' (line 49), with the role of the *kubernētēs* (lines 15, 43, 49, 53), which I will hereafter translate simply as 'steersman':

HOUR 24 TEXT C

|₁ About Dionysus son of most glorious Semele |₂ my mind will connect, how it was that he made an appearance [*phainesthai*] by the shore of the barren sea |₃ on a prominent headland, looking like a young man |₄ at the beginning of adolescence. Beautiful were the locks of hair as they waved in the breeze surrounding him. |₅ They were the color of deep blue. And a cloak he wore over his strong shoulders, |₆ color of purple. Then, all of a sudden, men seen from a ship with fine benches |₇—men who were pirates—came into view, as they were sailing over the wine-colored [*oinops*] sea [*pontos*]. |₈ They were Etruscans. And they were being driven along by a destiny that was bad for them. The moment they saw him [= Dionysus], |₉ they gave each other a knowing nod, and the very next thing, they were ashore, jumping out of the ship. Quickly they seized him and |₁₀ sat him down inside their ship, happy in their hearts |₁₁ because they thought that he was the son of a line of kings nurtured by the sky god. |₁₂ That is what they thought he was. And they wanted to tie him up in harsh bondage, |₁₃ but the ties of the bonds could not hold him, and the cords made of willow fell off him, all over the place, |₁₄ falling right off his hands and feet. And he just sat there, smiling, |₁₅ looking on with his deep blue eyes. Meanwhile the steersman [*kubernētēs*] took note [*noeîn*], |₁₆ right away, and he called out to his comrades [*hetairoi*] and said to them: |₁₇ "What kind of superhuman force [*daimōn*] has possessed you all! What kind of god [*theos*] is this that you have seized and tried to tie up, |₁₈ powerful as he is? Why, he is too much for the well-built ship to make room for. |₁₉ You see, he must be either Zeus or Apollo, the one with the silver quiver, |₂₀ or Poseidon. I tell you, he is not like mortal humans, |₂₁ he is not like [*eikelos*] them at all. Rather, he is like the gods who have their dwellings in Olympus. |₂₂ So come on, we should let him go, leaving him on the dark earth of the mainland. |₂₃ Let us do it right away. Do not manhandle him. What if he gets angry |₂₄ and stirs up winds that will make hardship, and a huge whirlwind?" |₂₅ That is how he [=

the steersman] spoke. But the leader of the men reviled him [= the steersman], speaking with hateful words [*mūthos*]: |₂₆ "No, [not we but] you are the one who is possessed by some kind of superhuman force [*daimōn*]. Just [do your work and] watch for the wind [to start blowing from behind, and, once it starts blowing], you start hoisting the sail of the ship |₂₇ and hold on to all the ropes. As for this one [= the unrecognized Dionysus], he will be the concern [*melein*] of my men. |₂₈ I expect he will arrive [with us] in Egypt or maybe in Cyprus |₂₉ or maybe even in the land of the Hyperboreans or beyond. Wherever. In the end, |₃₀ he will tell all: he will come around to saying who are his near and dear ones [*philoi*] and what are all the possessions he has |₃₁ and he will tell about his siblings. And that is because a superhuman force [*daimōn*] has put him in our pathway." |₃₂ Having said this, he [= the leader himself] started hoisting the sail of the ship. |₃₃ Now a wind came and blew right into the middle of the sail, and the ropes that held it at both ends |₃₄ got all stretched to the limit. Then, right away, there appeared [*phainesthai*] to them things that would make anyone marvel. |₃₅ Wine. That is what happened first of all. It was all alongside the swift black ship. |₃₆ Sweet to drink, it was splashing around [the ship as if it were inside a cup], smelling good, and the fragrance that rose up |₃₇ was something immortalizing [*ambrosiā*]. The sailors were seized with amazement, all of them, at the sight. |₃₈ And then, all of a sudden, next to the top of the sail on both sides, there reached out |₃₉ a vine—here, and here too—and hanging from it were many |₄₀ clusters of grapes. Around the mast, dark ivy was winding around, |₄₁ teeming with blossoms. And—a thing of beauty and pleasure [*kharieis*]—the berry sprang forth [from the ivy]. |₄₂ The benches for rowing now had garlands [*stephanoi*] all over them. Once they [= the sailors] saw all this, |₄₃ they started shouting at the steersman [*kubernētēs*], urging him |₄₄ to sail the ship back to land. Meanwhile, he [= Dionysus] turned into a lion for them, right there in the ship, |₄₅ looking horrific [*deinos*], at the prow. It roared a mighty roar. Then, in the middle of the ship, |₄₆ he [= Dionysus] made a bear, with a shaggy neck. Thus he [= Dionysus] made his signals [*sēmata*] appear [*phainein*]. |₄₇ It [= the bear] reared up, raging, while the lion, at the top of the deck, |₄₈ glared at them with its horrific looks. The men, terrified, were fleeing toward the stern of the ship, |₄₉ crowding around the steersman [*kubernētēs*], the one who had a heart [*thūmos*] that is moderate [*sōphrōn*]. |₅₀ They just stood there, astounded [*ek-plag-entes*]. Then it [= the lion] all of a sudden leapt up |₅₁ and took hold of the leader of the men, while they were trying to get out, rushing away from the bad destiny that was theirs. |₅₂ They all together at the same time leapt out, once they saw what they saw, into the gleaming salt sea. |₅₃ They became dolphins. As for the steersman [*kubernētēs*]—he [= Dionysus] took pity on him, |₅₄ holding him back [from leaping overboard]. He [= Dionysus] caused it to happen that he [= the steersman] became the most blessed [*olbios*] of all men, and he [= Dionysus] spoke for the record this set of words [*mūthos*]: |₅₅ "Have courage, you radiant man, reached by a force that works from far away.* You have achieved beauty and pleasure [*kharizesthai*] for my heart [*thūmos*]. |₅₆ I am Dionysus, the one with the great thundering sound. The mother who bore me |₅₇ was Semele, daughter of Cadmus, and Zeus made love to her." |₅₈ Hail and take pleasure [*khaire*], [O Dionysus,] child of Semele with the beautiful looks. There is no way |₅₉ I could have my mind disconnect from you as I put together the beautiful cosmic order [*kosmeîn*] of my song.

Homeric Hymn (7) *to Dionysus* 1–59†

* My interpretation of this uniquely attested word *hekatōr* as 'reached by a force that works from far away' is based on attestations of *hekatos* and related forms as studied by Chantraine *DELG* s.v. ἑκατηβόλος.

† |₁ Ἀμφὶ Διώνυσον Σεμέλης ἐρικυδέος υἱὸν |₂ μνήσομαι, ὡς ἐφάνη παρὰ θῖν᾽ ἁλὸς ἀτρυγέτοιο |₃ ἀκτῇ ἐπὶ προβλῆτι νεηνίῃ ἀνδρὶ ἐοικώς· |₄ πρωθήβῃ· καλαὶ δὲ περισσείοντο ἔθειραι |₅ κυάνεαι, φᾶρος δὲ περὶ στιβαροῖς ἔχεν ὤμοις |₆ πορφύρεον· τάχα δ᾽ ἄνδρες ἐϋσσέλμου ἀπὸ νηὸς |₇ ληϊσταὶ προγένοντο θοῶς ἐπὶ οἴνοπα πόντον· |₈ Τυρσηνοί· τοὺς δ᾽ ἦγε κακὸς μόρος· οἱ δὲ ἰδόντες |₉ νεῦσαν ἐς ἀλλήλους, τάχα δ᾽ ἔκθορον, αἶψα δ᾽ ἑλόντες |₁₀ εἷσαν ἐπὶ σφετέρης νηὸς κεχαρημένοι ἦτορ. |₁₁ υἱὸν γάρ μιν ἔφαντο διοτρεφέων βασιλήων |₁₂ εἶναι, καὶ δεσμοῖς ἔθελον δεῖν ἀργαλέοισι. |₁₃ τὸν δ᾽ οὐκ ἴσχανε δεσμά, λύγοι δ᾽ ἀπὸ τηλόσ᾽ ἔπιπτον |₁₄ χειρῶν ἠδὲ ποδῶν· ὁ δὲ μειδιάων ἐκάθητο |₁₅ ὄμμασι κυανέοισι, κυβερνήτης δὲ νοήσας |₁₆ αὐτίκα οἷς ἑτάροισιν ἐκέκλετο φώνησέν τε· |₁₇ Δαιμόνιοι τίνα τόνδε θεὸν δεσμεύεθ᾽ ἑλόντες |₁₈ καρτερόν; οὐδὲ φέρειν δύναταί μιν νηῦς εὐεργής. |₁₉ ἢ γὰρ Ζεὺς ὅδε γ᾽ ἐστὶν ἢ ἀργυρότοξος Ἀπόλλων |₂₀ ἠὲ Ποσειδάων· ἐπεὶ οὐ θνητοῖσι βροτοῖσιν |₂₁ εἴκελος, ἀλλὰ θεοῖς οἳ Ὀλύμπια δώματ᾽ ἔχουσιν. |₂₂ ἀλλ᾽ ἄγετ᾽ αὐτὸν ἀφῶμεν ἐπ᾽ ἠπείροιο μελαίνης |₂₃ αὐτίκα, μηδ᾽ ἐπὶ χεῖρας ἰάλλετε μή τι χολωθεὶς |₂₄ ὄρσῃ ἀργαλέους τ᾽ ἀνέμους καὶ λαίλαπα πολλήν. |₂₅ Ὣς φάτο· τὸν δ᾽ ἀρχὸς στυγερῷ ἠνίπαπε μύθῳ· |₂₆ δαιμόνι᾽ οὖρον ὅρα, ἅμα δ᾽ ἱστίον ἕλκεο νηὸς |₂₇ σύμπανθ᾽ ὅπλα λαβών· ὅδε δ᾽ αὖτ᾽ ἄνδρεσσι μελήσει. |₂₈ ἔλπομαι ἢ Αἴγυπτον ἀφίξεται ἢ ὅ γε Κύπρον |₂₉ ἢ ἐς Ὑπερβορέους ἢ ἑκαστέρω· ἐς δὲ τελευτὴν |₃₀ ἔκ ποτ᾽ ἐρεῖ αὐτοῦ τε φίλους καὶ κτήματα πάντα |₃₁ οὕς τε κασιγνήτους, ἐπεὶ ἡμῖν ἔμβαλε δαίμων. |₃₂ Ὣς εἰπὼν ἱστόν τε καὶ ἱστίον ἕλκετο νηός. |₃₃ ἔμπνευσεν δ᾽ ἄνεμος μέσον ἱστίον, ἀμφὶ δ᾽ ἄρ᾽ ὅπλα |₃₄ καττάνυσαν· τάχα δέ σφιν ἐφαίνετο θαυματὰ ἔργα. |₃₅ οἶνος μὲν πρώτιστα θοὴν ἀνὰ νῆα μέλαιναν |₃₆ ἡδύποτος κελάρυζ᾽ εὐώδης, ὤρνυτο δ᾽ ὀδμὴ |₃₇ ἀμβροσίη· ναύτας δὲ τάφος λάβε πάντας ἰδόντας. |₃₈ αὐτίκα δ᾽ ἀκρότατον παρὰ ἱστίον ἐξετανύσθη |₃₉ ἄμπελος ἔνθα καὶ ἔνθα, κατεκρημνῶντο δὲ πολλοὶ |₄₀ βότρυες· ἀμφ᾽ ἱστὸν δὲ μέλας εἱλίσσετο κισσός |₄₁ ἄνθεσι τηλεθάων, χαρίεις δ᾽ ἐπὶ καρπὸς ὀρώρει· |₄₂ πάντες δὲ σκαλμοὶ στεφάνους ἔχον· οἱ δὲ ἰδόντες |₄₃ νῆ᾽ ἤδη τότ᾽ ἔπειτα κυβερνήτην ἐκέλευον |₄₄ γῇ πελάαν· ὁ δ᾽ ἄρα σφι λέων γένετ᾽ ἔνδοθι νηὸς |₄₅ δεινὸς ἐπ᾽ ἀκροτάτης,

24§13. Following the narration up through line 58, we come to a point where the narrator appears to break off: he now turns to the god Dionysus and addresses him directly, asking the god to stay mentally connected with the performance. In addressing the god, the performer is calling out to him with the salutation *khaire* (again, line 58), which is the imperative of the verb *khairein*, meaning 'to take pleasure'. So I translate the salutation *khaire* as 'hail and take pleasure!' (again, line 58), adding the word 'hail!' because the imperative *khaire* (plural *khairete*) is used in contexts of marking the beginning or ending of a personal encounter. In the *Homeric Hymns*, this salutation *khaire* (plural *khairete*) marks a transition from focusing on a god or on an aspect of a god to focusing on the rest of the song.* This verb *khairein*, 'to take pleasure', is related to the noun *kharis*, which is analogous to the Latin noun *gratia* in combining the ideas of pleasure ('gratification') and beauty ('gracefulness') by way of reciprocity ('graciousness').† In Hour 21 (§§49, 63), we have already seen contexts where this word *kharis* combines the ideas of beauty and pleasure. And such a combination is implied also in the salutation *khaire* as we see it used in the *Homeric Hymns*. Accordingly, in the case of *khaire* at line 58 of this *Homeric Hymn to Dionysus*, we can interpret this salutation even more precisely as 'hail and take pleasure in the beauty'.

24§14. Such a salutation, as we will now see, implies salvation. At lines 55–57 of the *Hymn*, we can read how the steersman who is saved at sea is addressed by the god who granted him his salvation. But then, as we have already seen at line 58, the narrator who performs the narration turns right around and addresses this saving god, Dionysus, asking him to stay mentally connected with the performance. It is as if the saving words of the saving god can now extend their saving grace or *kharis* to the performer as well, who prays for the god's grace or *kharis* by calling out: 'Hail and take pleasure in the beauty'. And such pleasure is already being experienced by Dionysus in the words that he addresses at lines 55–57 to the steersman whom he has just saved: as the god says to the steersman

μέγα δ' ἔβραχεν, ἐν δ' ἄρα μέσσῃ |₄₆ ἄρκτον ἐποίησεν λασιαύχενα σήματα φαίνων· |₄₇ ἂν δ' ἔστη μεμαυῖα, λέων δ' ἐπὶ σέλματος ἄκρου |₄₈ δεινὸν ὑπόδρα ἰδών· οἱ δ' εἰς πρύμνην ἐφήθεν, |₄₉ ἀμφὶ κυβερνήτην δὲ σαόφρονα θυμὸν ἔχοντα |₅₀ ἔσταν ἄρ' ἐκπληγέντες· ὁ δ' ἐξαπίνης ἐπορούσας |₅₁ ἀρχὸν ἕλ', οἱ δὲ θύραζε κακὸν μόρον ἐξαλύοντες |₅₂ πάντες ὁμῶς πήδησαν ἐπεὶ ἴδον εἰς ἅλα δῖαν, |₅₃ δελφῖνες δ' ἐγένοντο· κυβερνήτην δ' ἐλεήσας |₅₄ ἔσχεθε καί μιν ἔθηκε πανόλβιον εἶπέ τε μῦθον· |₅₅ Θάρσει δῖ' ἑκάτωρ τῷ ἐμῷ κεχαρισμένε θυμῷ· |₅₆ εἰμὶ δ' ἐγὼ Διόνυσος ἐρίβρομος ὃν τέκε μήτηρ |₅₇ Καδμηῒς Σεμέλη Διὸς ἐν φιλότητι μιγεῖσα. |₅₈ Χαῖρε τέκος Σεμέλης εὐώπιδος· οὐδέ πῃ ἔστι |₅₉ σεῖό γε ληθόμενον γλυκερὴν κοσμῆσαι ἀοιδήν.

* HC 200 = 2§27.
† HC 11, 203–204 = P§35, 2§33.

at line 55, 'You have achieved beauty and pleasure [*kharizesthai*] for my heart [*thūmos*]'. It is as if the steersman and the performer were one and the same persona.

24§15. The beauty and the pleasure of this *Homeric Hymn*, as evoked at lines 58–59, radiate from 'cosmic ordering' of the song, as expressed by *kosmeîn* at line 59. Such cosmic order is made visible in the myriad details shown in the picturing of the miracles performed by Dionysus in the ship at sea: one such detail stands out, and here is how I translated it at line 41: 'And—a thing of beauty and pleasure [*kharieis*]—the berry sprang forth [from the ivy]'. Earlier, at lines 35–37, the cosmic beauty of it all fuses the macrocosm of the sea and the microcosm of wine as it splashes around inside the cup of a reveler, since Dionysus at this moment has changed the entire sea into wine. So now the wine is splashing around the outside of the ship, as if it were still the wine that is splashing inside of the cup. The 'wine-colored' sea, as conveyed by the epithet *oinops* at line 7, has a good reason for looking like wine.

24§16. The salvation of the steersman by the grace of Dionysus earns him the epithet *olbios* at line 54 of this *Hymn*. We have already seen in Hours 11 and 13 that this word *olbios* means 'blessed' in the context of describing cult heroes who are granted the salvation of immortalization through the graciousness of the gods—and who can then show their own graciousness by saving the ordinary mortals who worship them. Since Dionysus, as we read at line 54 of the *Hymn*, 'caused it to happen' that the steersman 'became the most blessed [*olbios*] of all men', I interpret this divine action as the transforming of a man into a cult hero. The narrative does not say how this transformation happened, but I think that the saving of the steersman by Dionysus was imagined as the initial phase.

Achilles as Saved Hero and as Savior Hero

24§17. In the case of Achilles, there is a visible sign that shows how the god Dionysus is involved in this particular hero's immortalization. That sign is a golden amphora, given by the god to Thetis, the mother of Achilles, which contains the bones of the hero and which will save him by bringing him back to life after death. It is this salvation, I will argue, that empowers Achilles to become in turn the savior of his own people. To make my argument, I start by reviewing the story about the golden amphora given by the god Dionysus. We have already seen a direct reference to this talismanic object in the Homeric *Odyssey*. I quote again the relevant text, where we see the spirit of Agamemnon in Hādēs in the act of addressing the spirit of Achilles:

Hour 24 Text D (Part of Hour 11 Text A)

|₃₆ O you blessed [*olbios*] son of Peleus, godlike Achilles, |₃₇ you who died at Troy far from Argos. And others, those all around you [= your corpse], |₃₈ were being slaughtered, sons of both Trojans and Achaeans, the best, |₃₉ as they were fighting over you [= your corpse]. There you were, lying in a swirl of dust. |₄₀ You lay there so huge in all your hugeness, no longer thinking about your feats of charioteering. . . . |₄₃ Then, when we had taken you [= your corpse] to the ships, out of the battlezone, |₄₄ we laid you on your bed and cleansed your beautiful skin |₄₅ with warm water and with oil. And, crying over you, many tears |₄₆ did the Danaans [= Achaeans] shed, hot tears, and they cut their hair. |₄₇ Your mother came, with her immortal sea nymphs, from out of the sea, |₄₈ as soon as she heard, and the sound of a great wailing went forth over the sea, |₄₉ a sound too wondrous for words, and all the Achaeans were overcome with trembling. . . . |₅₈ Standing around you were the daughters of the Old One of the sea [= Nereus], |₅₉ weeping piteously, and they [= the Nereids] clothed you [= the corpse of Achilles] in immortalizing [*ambrota*] clothes. |₆₀ The nine Muses also came, all of them, and sang antiphonally with a beautiful voice, |₆₁ singing their song of lament [*thrēnein*]; you could not spot a single person who was not shedding tears, |₆₂ of all the Argives [= Achaeans], so loudly did the piercing sound of lament rise up. |₆₃ Days and nights seven and ten |₆₄ we mourned you, we mortals and immortals alike, |₆₅ but on the eighteenth day we gave you to the flames, and, over the fire, many |₆₆ fat sheep and many horned oxen did we slay in sacrifice. |₆₇ You were burning while clothed in the clothes of the gods, and with plenty of olive oil, |₆₈ also sweet honey. And a multitude of Achaean heroes |₆₉ were dancing in their armor around the pyre as you were burning. |₇₀ There were footsoldiers and charioteers, and a great din arose. |₇₁ But when the flames of Hephaistos had consumed you, |₇₂ we gathered your white bones at dawn, O Achilles, and laid them |₇₃ in unmixed wine and in oil. Your mother gave |₇₄ a golden amphora to

hold them—she had received it as a gift from Dionysus, |$_{75}$ she said, and it was the work of the famed Hephaistos himself; |$_{76}$ in this [amphora] were placed your white bones, O luminous Achilles, |$_{77}$ mixed together with the bones of Patroklos who had died before you, |$_{78}$ and separately from the bones of Antilokhos, whom you honored most of all |$_{79}$ your other comrades [*hetairoi*] after Patroklos had died. |$_{80}$ Over these bones a huge and faultless tomb [*tumbos*] |$_{81}$ was built; it was a tumulus that we the sacred army of spear-fighting Argives [= Achaeans] heaped up, |$_{82}$ at a headland jutting out over the open Hellespont, |$_{83}$ so that it might be visible, shining forth from afar, for men at sea [*pontos*] |$_{84}$ now living and for those that will be born hereafter.

Odyssey xxiv 36–84*

24§18. At lines 73–78 here, as I noted already in Hour 11 (§12), the reference to a golden amphora containing the bones of Achilles and Patroklos is an implicit sign of the immortalization that awaits Achilles after his bones stored inside this golden vessel are regenerated into a living body by the power of the god Dionysus, who had originally given the amphora to Thetis, the mother of Achilles (there is a reference to this myth in Stesichorus *PMG* 234). And this reference at lines 73–78 of *Odyssey* xxiv here is matched by another reference at lines 91–92 in *Iliad* XXIII, as quoted in Hour 8 Text A. In those two lines from

---

* |$_{36}$ ὄλβιε Πηλέος υἱέ, θεοῖσ᾽ ἐπιείκελ᾽ Ἀχιλλεῦ, |$_{37}$ ὃς θάνες ἐν Τροίῃ ἑκὰς Ἄργεος· ἀμφὶ δέ σ᾽ ἄλλοι |$_{38}$ κτείνοντο Τρώων καὶ Ἀχαιῶν υἷες ἄριστοι, |$_{39}$ μαρνάμενοι περὶ σεῖο· σὺ δ᾽ ἐν στροφάλιγγι κονίης |$_{40}$ κεῖσο μέγας μεγαλωστί, λελασμένος ἱπποσυνάων. . . . |$_{43}$ αὐτὰρ ἐπεί σ᾽ ἐπὶ νῆας ἐνείκαμεν ἐκ πολέμοιο, |$_{44}$ κάτθεμεν ἐν λεχέεσσι, καθήραντες χρόα καλὸν |$_{45}$ ὕδατί τε λιαρῷ καὶ ἀλείφατι· πολλὰ δέ σ᾽ ἀμφὶ |$_{46}$ δάκρυα θερμὰ χέον Δαναοὶ κείροντό τε χαίτας. |$_{47}$ μήτηρ δ᾽ ἐξ ἁλὸς ἦλθε σὺν ἀθανάτῃσ᾽ ἁλίῃσιν |$_{48}$ ἀγγελίης ἀίουσα· βοὴ δ᾽ ἐπὶ πόντον ὀρώρει |$_{49}$ θεσπεσίη, ὑπὸ δὲ τρόμος ἤλυθε πάντας Ἀχαιούσᾶ. . . . |$_{58}$ ἀμφὶ δέ σ᾽ ἔστησαν κοῦραι ἁλίοιο γέροντος |$_{59}$ οἴκτρ᾽ ὀλοφυρόμεναι, περὶ δ᾽ ἄμβροτα εἵματα ἔσσαν. |$_{60}$ Μοῦσαι δ᾽ ἐννέα πᾶσαι ἀμειβόμεναι ὀπὶ καλῇ |$_{61}$ θρήνεον· ἔνθα κεν οὔ τιν᾽ ἀδάκρυτόν γ᾽ ἐνόησας |$_{62}$ Ἀργείων· τοῖον γὰρ ὑπώρορε Μοῦσα λίγεια. |$_{63}$ ἑπτὰ δὲ καὶ δέκα μέν σε ὁμῶς νύκτας τε καὶ ἦμαρ |$_{64}$ κλαίομεν ἀθάνατοί τε θεοὶ θνητοί τ᾽ ἄνθρωποι· |$_{65}$ ὀκτωκαιδεκάτῃ δ᾽ ἔδομεν πυρί· πολλὰ δ᾽ ἐπ᾽ αὐτῷ |$_{66}$ μῆλα κατεκτάνομεν μάλα πίονα καὶ ἕλικας βοῦς. |$_{67}$ καίεο δ᾽ ἔν τ᾽ ἐσθῆτι θεῶν καὶ ἀλείφατι πολλῷ |$_{68}$ καὶ μέλιτι γλυκερῷ· πολλοὶ δ᾽ ἥρωες Ἀχαιοὶ |$_{69}$ τεύχεσιν ἐρρώσαντο πυρὴν πέρι καιομένοιο, |$_{70}$ πεζοί θ᾽ ἱππῆές τε· πολὺς δ᾽ ὀρυμαγδὸς ὀρώρει. |$_{71}$ αὐτὰρ ἐπεὶ δή σε φλὸξ ἤνυσεν Ἡφαίστοιο, |$_{72}$ ἠῶθεν δή τοι λέγομεν λεύκ᾽ ὀστέ᾽, Ἀχιλλεῦ, |$_{73}$ οἴνῳ ἐν ἀκρήτῳ καὶ ἀλείφατι. δῶκε δὲ μήτηρ |$_{74}$ χρύσεον ἀμφιφορῆα· Διωνύσοιο δὲ δῶρον |$_{75}$ φάσκ᾽ ἔμεναι, ἔργον δὲ περικλυτοῦ Ἡφαίστοιο. |$_{76}$ ἐν τῷ τοι κεῖται λεύκ᾽ ὀστέα, φαίδιμ᾽ Ἀχιλλεῦ, |$_{77}$ μίγδα δὲ Πατρόκλοιο Μενοιτιάδαο θανόντος, |$_{78}$ χωρὶς δ᾽ Ἀντιλόχοιο, τὸν ἔξοχα τῖες ἁπάντων |$_{79}$ τῶν ἄλλων ἑτάρων μετὰ Πάτροκλόν γε θανόντα. |$_{80}$ ἀμφ᾽ αὐτοῖσι δ᾽ ἔπειτα μέγαν καὶ ἀμύμονα τύμβον |$_{81}$ χεύαμεν Ἀργείων ἱερὸς στρατὸς αἰχμητάων |$_{82}$ ἀκτῇ ἔπι προὐχούσῃ, ἐπὶ πλατεῖ Ἑλλησπόντῳ, |$_{83}$ ὥς κεν τηλεφανὴς ἐκ ποντόφιν ἀνδράσιν εἴη |$_{84}$ τοῖσ᾽, οἳ νῦν γεγάασι καὶ οἱ μετόπισθεν ἔσονται.

the *Iliad,* the *psūkhē* or 'spirit' of Patroklos speaks about a golden amphora that will contain his own bones mixed together with the bones of Achilles. As I noted in Hour 8 (§38), this reference in the *Iliad* to the same golden amphora is likewise an implicit sign of the immortalization that awaits Achilles.

24§19. In the text I just quoted from *Odyssey* xxiv, Achilles is not only saved by being brought back to life after death. He is also a savior, as we see at lines 80–84, where the tumulus that contains his bones is pictured as a kind of lighthouse overlooking the sea and flashing a beacon light of salvation for sailors whose lives are threatened by the dangerous waters of the sea.

Achilles, Hero of the Hellespont

24§20. A key to this role of Achilles as savior of sailors is the location of the tumulus that once contained the golden amphora that in turn contained his bones together with the bones of Patroklos. At line 82 in the passage I just quoted a minute ago from *Odyssey* xxiv in Text D, that location is described as a mountainous headland overlooking the sea of the Hellespont. As we saw in Hour 14§4, the Hellespont is a narrow stretch of sea that separates Europe from Asia Minor. And, as we saw in Hour 14§25, the tumulus of the hero Protesilaos is situated on the European coast of the Hellespont, to the northwest, while the tumulus of Achilles himself is symmetrically situated on the facing Asiatic coast, to the southeast. The 'Hellespont', or *Hellēspontos* in Greek, is mentioned by name at line 82 of *Odyssey* xxiv as I quoted it in Text D. In that same passage, we saw that the tumulus of Achilles is flashing a beacon light of salvation for sailors whose lives are threatened by the dangerous waters of the sea—and the word for 'sea' is *pontos* at line 84. As I have shown in an earlier project, the link between the name *Hellēs-pontos* for 'Hellespont' at line 82 and the word *pontos* for 'sea' at line 84 is most significant in the light of the etymology of *pontos,* which shows the following cognates in Indo-European languages other than Greek:

Indic *pánthāḥ,* 'crossing', from one given point to another: such a 'crossing' is both dangerous and sacralizing.

Latin *pōns* (genitive *pontis*), 'bridge'. Most relevant is the report of Varro (*On the Latin Language* 5.83) about a famous bridge, the *Pōns Sublicius,* which spans the river Tiber in Rome: the prototype of this bridge was built and ritually maintained by a prototype of the chief priest of Rome, the *pontifex maximus*. The Latin word *ponti-fex* means, etymologically, 'the one who makes the crossing'.

Armenian *hun*, 'fording'.*

24§21. The idea of a 'crossing' that is both dangerous and sacralizing is built into the name *Hellēs-pontos,* which means literally 'the crossing of Hellē', and this meaning is embedded in a myth that we see summarized in most of its major details in the *Library* attributed to Apollodorus (1.9.1). According to this myth, there was once a boy named Phrixos and a girl named Hellē who were children of the hero Athamas and of a goddess called Nephelē, meaning 'Cloud'; the divine mother of these children saved them from being murdered by their stepmother, named Ino, by sending to them as their helper the Ram with the Golden Fleece, who took the children on his back and flew away with them; as the ram was flying across the Hellespont, Hellē lost her grip and slipped off, plunging into the Hellespont and drowning there; and that is why the name of this dangerous body of water that Hellē was crossing is *Hellēs-pontos* or 'crossing of Hellē'.† But Phrixos succeeds in crossing the Hellespont safely, and he escapes to the Far East, where he sacrifices the Ram with the Golden Fleece in thanksgiving for his salvation (again, Apollodorus *Library* 1.9.1). This salvation of Phrixos is explicitly marked by the words *pontos,* 'crossing', and *sōzein,* 'save', in a song of Pindar (*Pythian* 4.161): τῷ ποτ᾽ ἐκ πόντου σαώθη, 'by way of this [= the Golden Fleece] he [= Phrixos] was saved [*saō-thē,* from *sōzein*], getting away from the sea [*pontos*]'.‡

24§22. The meaning of this name *Hellēs-pontos* is relevant to the role of Achilles as hero of the Hellespont. As we saw in Text D, where I quoted lines 80–84 of *Odyssey* xxiv, the tumulus that contains the bones of Achilles and Patroklos is pictured as a kind of lighthouse overlooking the Hellespont and flashing a beacon light of salvation for sailors whose lives are threatened by the dangerous waters of this stretch of sea. But how are we to imagine this beacon light of salvation? It would be misleading for us to think of it as the kind of modern lighthouse that New Englanders, for example, might expect to visualize. In the original Greek context, as we will now see, the beacon light is pictured as coming from a blazing fire that is lit at a herdsman's station situated in the solitary

---

* Benveniste 1966 [1954] 296–298; *BA* 339 = 20§21. For more on the *Pōns Sublicius* and the *pontifex maximus,* see Hallett 1970.

† Benveniste 1966 [1954] 298; *BA* 339 = 20§21.

‡ *BA* 339–340 = 20§21.

heights of a headland overlooking the sea. Such a visualization comes to life in a vivid description of a gleam of light emanating from the Shield of Achilles as he arms himself to rejoin, at long last, the war against the Trojans:

Hour 24 Text E

|₃₆₈ He [= Achilles] put it [= his armor] on, the gifts of the god, which Hephaistos had made for him with much labor. |₃₆₉ First he put around his legs the shin guards, |₃₇₀ beautiful ones, with silver fastenings at the ankles. |₃₇₁ Next he put around his chest the breastplate, |₃₇₂ and around his shoulders he slung the sword with the nails of silver, |₃₇₃ a sword made of bronze. Next, the Shield [*sakos*], great and mighty, |₃₇₄ he took on, and from it there was a gleam [*selas*] from afar, as from the moon, |₃₇₅ or as when, from the sea [*pontos*], a gleam [*selas*] to sailors appears [*phainesthai*] |₃₇₆ from a blazing fire, the kind that blazes high in the mountains |₃₇₇ at a solitary [*oiopolos*] station [*stathmos*], as the sailors are carried unwilling by gusts of wind |₃₇₈ over the fish-swarming sea [*pontos*], far away from their loved ones [*philoi*] |₃₇₉—so also did the gleam [*selas*] emanating from the Shield [*sakos*] of Achilles reach all the way up to the aether.

Iliad XIX 368–379*

24§23. The gleam of light that flashes from the smooth bronze surface of the Shield of Achilles at line 374 emanates from a source that is not indicated. But this gleam is first compared to the light of the moon, at line 374, and so the initial impression is that the source of light here could be the moon at night. In other words, the initial comparison sets up a nighttime scene, even though the epic event that is being pictured is really a daytime scene. But the nighttime vision fits the poetic design here, since the next comparison maintains a picture of darkness at night. In the original Greek, at line 375, the gleam of light that flashes from the Shield is now being compared not to the light of the moon but to a light that flashes from a blazing fire that is lit at a solitary *stathmos*, that is, at a herdsman's 'station', situated on the mountainous heights overlooking the

* |₃₆₈ δύσετο δῶρα θεοῦ, τά οἱ Ἥφαιστος κάμε τεύχων. |₃₆₉ κνημῖδας μὲν πρῶτα περὶ κνήμῃσιν ἔθηκε |₃₇₀ καλὰς ἀργυρέοισιν ἐπισφυρίοις ἀραρυίας· |₃₇₁ δεύτερον αὖ θώρηκα περὶ στήθεσσιν ἔδυνεν. |₃₇₂ ἀμφὶ δ' ἄρ' ὤμοισιν βάλετο ξίφος ἀργυρόηλον |₃₇₃ χάλκεον· αὐτὰρ ἔπειτα σάκος μέγα τε στιβαρόν τε |₃₇₄ εἵλετο, τοῦ δ' ἀπάνευθε σέλας γένετ' ἠΰτε μήνης. |₃₇₅ ὡς δ' ὅτ' ἂν ἐκ πόντοιο σέλας ναύτῃσι φανήῃ |₃₇₆ καιομένοιο πυρός, τό τε καίεται ὑψόθ' ὄρεσφι |₃₇₇ σταθμῷ ἐν οἰοπόλῳ· τοὺς δ' οὐκ ἐθέλοντας ἄελλαι |₃₇₈ πόντον ἐπ' ἰχθυόεντα φίλων ἀπάνευθε φέρουσιν· |₃₇₉ ὣς ἀπ' Ἀχιλλῆος σάκεος σέλας αἰθέρ' ἵκανε.

sea. Here again the comparison sets up a nighttime scene.* And the light that flashes from the herdsman's station at line 375 is pictured as visible 'from' the *pontos* or 'sea', that is, from the perspective of the sailors who are sailing over the dangerous waters of this sea. Similarly in *Odyssey* xxiv 82–84, as I quoted it in Text D, we saw that the tumulus of Achilles is situated 'at a headland jutting out over the open Hellespont, $|_{83}$ so that it might be visible, shining forth from afar, for men at sea [*pontos*] $|_{84}$ now living and for those that will be born hereafter'. In the original Greek, what I have translated as 'so that it [= the tumulus] might be visible, shining forth from afar for men at sea [*pontos*]' can be rendered more literally as 'so that it might be appearing radiantly from afar [*tēle-phanēs*] for men looking at it [= the tumulus] from the sea [*pontos*]'.† The parallelism with the wording of *Iliad* XIX 375–377 is most striking: 'or as when, from the sea [*pontos*], a gleam [*selas*] to sailors appears [*phainesthai*] $|_{376}$ from a blazing fire, the kind that blazes high in the mountains $|_{377}$ at a solitary [*oiopolos*] station [*stathmos*]'.‡ So, both in *Iliad* XIX and in *Odyssey* xxiv, the poetry is picturing what is seen 'from' the sea, that is, from the perspective of those who are at sea.§

24§24. A question remains: how is a herdsman's solitary *stathmos* or 'station' as described in *Iliad* XIX 377 connected to the tumulus of Achilles as described in Odyssey xxiv 80–84? There is an answer to be found in the wording that describes a picture made by the divine artisan Hephaistos on the Shield of Achilles, where we see a revealing attestation of this same word *stathmos* in collocation with two related words:

Hour 24 Text F

$|_{587}$ Next, the one with the two great arms [= Hephaistos], whose fame is supreme, made [an image of] a space for pasturing $|_{588}$ in a beautiful mountainous place. It was a vast space, full of sheep with shining fleeces. $|_{589}$ It [= this space for pasturing] had *stathmoi, klisiai* with covering on top, and *sēkoi*.

Iliad XVIII 587–589**

---

* There is a fuller analysis of these poetic images in *BA* 338–339 = 20§20. As I say already there at the end of the paragraph, "Achilles is emerging as savior of the Achaeans."

† ὥς κεν τηλεφανὴς ἐκ ποντόφιν ἀνδράσιν εἴη.

‡ ὡς δ' ὅτ' ἂν ἐκ πόντοιο σέλας ναύτῃσι φανήῃ $|_{376}$ καιομένοιο πυρός, τό τε καίεται ὑψόθ' ὄρεσφι $|_{377}$ σταθμῷ ἐν οἰοπόλῳ.

§ *HPC* 150–151 = II§50n11 and II§54n14.

** $|_{587}$ ἐν δὲ νομὸν ποίησε περικλυτὸς ἀμφιγυήεις $|_{588}$ ἐν καλῇ βήσσῃ μέγαν οἰῶν ἀργεννάων, $|_{589}$ σταθμούς τε κλισίας τε κατηρεφέας ἰδὲ σηκούς.

24§25. In this picture of a space for pasturing, which is also the space for picturing what is in the pasture, we see three words that relate to the pastoral activities of herdsmen: *stathmos, klisiā,* and *sēkos.* In another project, I compared the etymologies of these three words with the contexts of their usage in other pastoral settings, and I found that their reconstructed meanings are interrelated:*

> The *stathmos* (derived from the root **sta-* meaning 'stand up') is a makeshift post of a herdsman's shelter or tent.
> The *klisiā* (derived from the root **kli-* meaning 'lie down' or 'lean') is a space in the shelter where the herdsman reclines—or, alternatively, it is a 'lean-to' covering, which affords a makeshift shelter.
> The *sēkos* (derived from the root **sak-* meaning 'fill [an empty space]') is an enclosure where the herdsman's herd is penned in.

There are further implications. By way of metonymy, the *klisiā* is not only an aspect of the shelter but also the entire shelter. Likewise, the *stathmos* is not only the post of the shelter but also the entire shelter and everything contiguous with the shelter, including the *sēkos.* That is how I understand that definition of the *stathmos* as a herdsman's 'station'.†

24§26. The pastoral word *sēkos* refers not only to the enclosure where a herd is penned in but also to the enclosure where a cult hero is buried and worshipped.‡ And, I argue, such sacral connotations are attached to the pastoral words *klisiā* and *stathmos* as well. All three words connote traditional images typical of cult heroes.§

24§27. In the *Iliad*, the word *klisiā* refers to the abode that a hero like Achilles frequents in life: his *klisiā* is his shelter, which marks the place where his ship is beached on the shores of the Hellespont during the Trojan War (VIII 224, XI 7, and so on). In later poetry we see a related use of *stathmos* (plural *stathma*) with reference to the places where the ships of Achaean heroes are beached on the shores of the Hellespont ("Euripides" *Rhesus* 43); these places are also called *naustathma,* 'ship stations' (*Rhesus* 136, 244, 448, 582, 591, 602, 673). Among these *stathma,* 'stations', lining the coast of the Hellespont is the heroic space occupied by Achilles.

---

* *HPC* 152 = II§56.
† Again, *HPC* 152 = II§56.
‡ There is a short survey of epigraphical and literary contexts by Chantraine *DELG* s.v. σηκός.
§ This paragraph and the two paragraphs that follow are derived from *HPC* 153 = II§§57–59.

24§28. According to the *Iliad* (VIII 220–226 and XI 5–9), the ship of Achilles is beached farthest to the west on the coastline of the Hellespont, and the station of Achilles on the coast of the Hellespont is marked by the space where his *klisiā* or 'shelter' stands at the beach (again, VIII 220–226 and XI 5–9). In the narrative topography of the *Iliad,* the hero's *stathmos* or 'station' is imagined as the abode he frequents in the heroic time of the Trojan War. But it is also imagined as the abode that the hero frequents after death, in the future time of audiences listening to the story of the Trojan War. So I am arguing that the *stathmos oiopolos* or 'solitary station' of Achilles in *Iliad* XIX 377 can be viewed, by way of metonymy, as his tomb, situated on the heights overlooking the space where his ship had once been beached. The wording σταθμῷ ἐν οἰοπόλῳ here in *Iliad* XIX 377, which I translate 'at a solitary [*oiopolos*] station [*stathmos*]', is analogous to an expression we see in *Odyssey* xi 574, ἐν οἰοπόλοισιν ὄρεσσιν, 'in the solitary [*oiopola*] heights of the mountains'.*

24§29. The *stathmos* or 'station' of Achilles can be pictured bilocally: either as a herdsman's shelter on the beach where the ship of Achilles is beached or as a herdsman's shelter in the heights of the headland that overlooks the beach. In the *Hērōikos* of Philostratus (53.8–13), as quoted in Hour 14 Text K, we saw a sacrificial symmetry that corresponds to such bilocation: whereas a black bull is sacrificed to Achilles on the heights of the headland where the hero's tumulus is situated, a white bull is sacrificed to him on the beach. I see this bilocalism as a kind of sacral metonymy, since the very idea of a sacred space reserved for Achilles is expandable, accommodating the full range of his roles as epic hero and as cult hero. Examples can be found in the contexts that I studied in Hour 14 (§§25, 26A, 31).

24§30. By now we have seen how the Hellespont has a special meaning as a scenic setting for the solitary tomb of Achilles. This tomb, mystically inhabited by the restless spirit of that alienated hero, is a source of salvation for sailors who brave the dangerous waters of the Hellespont not only in the heroic time of epic and but also in the present time extending from that glorious past. Paradoxically, this brooding and alienated hero of the Hellespont becomes a kindly and saving helper of all Greeks in their historical present, and Homeric poetry pictures these once and future Greeks collectively as sailors lost at sea and yearning to be reunited at long last with their loved ones. Showing the way to salvation is the light that emanates from the hero's tomb, situated in the heights

---

* *HPC* 151 = II§54n15.

overlooking the Hellespont. It is a light fueled by beacon fires burning at the tumulus of Achilles, looming over the Hellespontine shoreline where the hero's 'station' gave him shelter in the glory days of the Trojan War.*

24§31. Not only at the Hellespont but also in other parts of the Greek-speaking world, the power of Achilles can manifest itself in the form of a wind called 'the one from the Hellespont', the *Hellēspontiēs*. There is a stirring narrative about a moment in history when Achilles is thought to have intervened and saved the Greeks by unleashing the power of this wind. It happened in 480 BCE, at Cape Sepias in Magnesia, on the European coast of the Aegean Sea, when part of the fleet sent by the Persian Empire to destroy the Athenians and their allies was wrecked by a windstorm:

HOUR 24 TEXT G

|$_{7.188.1}$ The armada [of the Persians] got started and sailed on until they arrived at the beach of the land mass of Magnesia, between the *polis* of Kasthanaia and the headland of Sepias. The first ships to arrive were moored to the land, while the others after them were anchored off-shore; since the beach was not large, they were anchored in rows that were eight ships deep, extending out into the sea [*pontos*]. This was what was going on in the evening. At dawn, out of a clear and wind-less sky, a storm descended upon them and the sea began to boil. A strong east wind blew, which the people dwelling around there call the *Hellēspontiēs*. Those who felt the wind gaining strength and were moored to the land dragged their ships up on shore ahead of the storm and so survived along with their ships. But the wind carried the ships that were stuck in the open and smashed them against the rocks called the Ovens at Pelion—or straight to the beach. Some ships were wrecked at the headland called Sēpias, while others were cast ashore at the city of Meliboia or at Kasthanaia. The power of the storm was beyond en-durance. |$_{7.189.1}$ ... |$_{7.191.2}$ The storm lasted three days. Finally the Magi made sacrificial offerings and sang incantations to the wind. In addi-tion, they sacrificed [*thuein*] to Thetis and the Nereids. Doing so, they made the wind stop on the fourth day. Or, alternatively, it stopped somehow all by itself. They [= the Persians] sacrificed to Thetis after finding out from [their allies] the Ionians the story [*logos*] that it was

---

* This paragraph can be supplemented by a fuller analysis in *BA* 338–339 = 20§20.

from this place that she had been abducted by Peleus, and that all the headland of Sepias belonged to her and to the other Nereids.

Herodotus 7.188.1–7.189.1, 7.191.2*

24§32. The place where Peleus abducted Thetis, Cape Sepias, is named after a polymorphous invertebrate animal called the *sēpiā*. The Greek word is ordinarily translated into English as 'cuttlefish'. The Greek name is most significant in the mythology surrounding Cape Sepias, since it was here that the hero Achilles was conceived by the goddess Thetis at the time of her abduction by Peleus. And, according to the myth as reported in the scholia for the *Alexandra* of Lycophron (175), the polymorphous goddess Thetis had just turned into a *sēpiā* at the very moment when she conceived Achilles. In the symbolism of the myth, this polymorphous conception is of cosmic importance, and I have spent much time and effort studying the implications in another project.† Here I confine myself to one detail of the myth, as we find it narrated in the exquisitely compressed lyrical wording of Pindar (*Isthmian* 8.31.35): if Peleus had not fathered Achilles, then Zeus himself or Poseidon would have mated with Thetis, and this divine son would have overthrown the regime of the Olympian gods.‡ Thus the demigod Achilles, if we think of the father he never had, is a hero of infinite cosmic potential.§

---

* |₇.₁₈₈.₁ Ὁ δὲ δὴ ναυτικὸς στρατὸς ἐπείτε ὁρμηθεὶς ἔπλεε καὶ κατέσχε τῆς Μαγνησίης χώρης ἐς τὸν αἰγιαλὸν τὸν μεταξὺ Κασθαναίης τε πόλιος ἐόντα καὶ Σηπιάδος ἀκτῆς, αἱ μὲν δὴ πρῶται τῶν νεῶν ὅρμεον πρὸς γῇ, ἄλλαι δ᾽ ἐπ᾽ ἐκείνῃσι ἐπ᾽ ἀγκυρέων· ἅτε γὰρ τοῦ αἰγιαλοῦ ἐόντος οὐ μεγάλου πρόκροσσαι ὅρμεον τὸ ἐς πόντον καὶ ἐπὶ ὀκτὼ νέας. |₇.₁₈₈.₂ Ταύτην μὲν τὴν εὐφρόνην οὕτω. Ἅμα δὲ ὄρθρῳ ἐξ αἰθρίης τε καὶ νηνεμίης, τῆς θαλάσσης ζεσάσης, ἐπέπεσέ σφι χειμών τε μέγας καὶ πολλὸς ἄνεμος ἀπηλιώτης, τὸν δὴ Ἑλλησποντίην καλέουσι οἱ περὶ ταῦτα τὰ χωρία οἰκημένοι. |₇.₁₈₈.₃ Ὅσοι μὲν νυν αὐτῶν αὐξόμενον ἔμαθον τὸν ἄνεμον καὶ τοῖσι οὕτω εἶχε ὅρμου, οἱ δ᾽ ἔφθησαν τὸν χειμῶνα ἀνασπάσαντες τὰς νέας· καὶ αὐτοί τε περιῆσαν καὶ αἱ νέες αὐτῶν. Ὅσας δὲ τῶν νεῶν μεταρσίας ἔλαβε, τὰς μὲν ἐξέφερε πρὸς Ἴπνους καλεομένους τοὺς ἐν Πηλίῳ, τὰς δὲ ἐς τὸν αἰγιαλόν· αἱ δὲ περὶ αὐτὴν τὴν Σηπιάδα περιέπιπτον, αἱ δὲ ἐς Μελίβοιαν πόλιν, αἱ δὲ ἐς Κασθαναίην ἐξεβράσσοντο. Ἦν τε τοῦ χειμῶνος χρῆμα ἀφόρητον. |₇.₁₈₉.₁ … |₇.₁₉₁.₂ Ἡμέρας γὰρ δὴ ἐχείμαζε τρεῖς· τέλος δὲ ἔντομά τε ποιεῦντες καὶ καταείδοντες βοῇσι οἱ μάγοι τῷ ἀνέμῳ, πρὸς δὲ τούτοισι καὶ τῇ Θέτι καὶ τῇσι Νηρηίσι θύοντες ἔπαυσαν τετάρτῃ ἡμέρῃ, ἢ ἄλλως κως αὐτὸς ἐθέλων ἐκόπασε. Τῇ δὲ Θέτι ἔθυον πυθόμενοι παρὰ τῶν Ἰώνων τὸν λόγον ὡς ἐκ τοῦ χώρου τούτου ἁρπασθείη ὑπὸ Πηλέος, εἴη τε ἅπασα ἡ ἀκτὴ ἡ Σηπιὰς ἐκείνης τε καὶ τῶν ἀλλέων Νηρηίδων.

† The essentials of the symbolism surrounding the polymorphous conception of the hero Achilles are presented in *BA* 345–347 = 20§§27–29.

‡ *BA* 346 = 20§28. See also Slatkin 2011, who gives a luminously comprehensive reading of the poetic traditions centering on the goddess Thetis.

§ *BA* 345–347 = 20§§27–29.

Three More Glimpses of Heroic Salvation

24§33. In what follows, I offer a triptych of poetic images focusing on salvation either granted or received by a hero. In the first two of the three images, the hero is once again Achilles, and he is seen in the act of bringing salvation. Then, in the third image, we will see Odysseus at a moment of receiving salvation—from the White Goddess herself. What all three images have in common, as we will see, is the generalized idea of Greeks as a seafaring people.

24§34. The first image comes from a moment in the *Iliad* when Achilles has not yet received the armor that he will wear for his renewed war with the Trojans. But the divine messenger Iris tells him to signal to his Achaean comrades that he will be rejoining them. As Achilles now stands up, he experiences a burst of fire emanating from his head:

HOUR 24 TEXT H

|₂₀₃ As for Achilles, dear to Zeus, he stood up, and Athena |₂₀₄ flung over his mighty shoulders her tasseled aegis. |₂₀₅ And around his head a cloud was garlanded by this goddess of goddesses whose radiance comes from the sky. |₂₀₆ The cloud was golden, and from it she ignited a blazing burst of fire. |₂₀₇ Just as the smoke that goes up into the aether from some city |₂₀₈ on some island—and the smoke is visible from afar—as the enemy are surrounding the city and fighting to capture it, |₂₀₉ while the people [inside the city] are engaged in a life-and-death struggle all day long in the hateful war of Arēs, |₂₁₀ and they are fighting back, bursting out from inside their city, but then, as the sun is going down, |₂₁₁ beacon fires blaze forth, one after the other, and the light that comes from the fires shoots high up into the sky |₂₁₂ for those to see who dwell [in other places] near the island, |₂₁₃ in hopes that somehow they will come with their ships and become saviors [*alk-tēres*], saving the people from destruction |₂₁₄—so also did the gleam [*selas*] emanating from the head of Achilles reach all the way up to the aether.

Iliad XVIII 203–214*

* |₂₀₃ αὐτὰρ Ἀχιλλεὺς ὦρτο Διΐ φίλος· ἀμφὶ δ᾽ Ἀθήνη |₂₀₄ ὤμοις ἰφθίμοισι βάλ᾽ αἰγίδα θυσσανόεσσαν, |₂₀₅ ἀμφὶ δέ οἱ κεφαλῇ νέφος ἔστεφε δῖα θεάων |₂₀₆ χρύσεον, ἐκ δ᾽ αὐτοῦ δαῖε φλόγα παμφανόωσαν. |₂₀₇ ὡς δ᾽ ὅτε καπνὸς ἰὼν ἐξ ἄστεος αἰθέρ᾽ ἵκηται |₂₀₈ τηλόθεν ἐκ νήσου, τὴν δήιοι ἀμφιμάχωνται, |₂₀₉ οἵ τε πανημέριοι στυγερῷ κρίνονται Ἄρηϊ |₂₁₀ ἄστεος ἐκ σφετέρου· ἅμα δ᾽ ἠελίῳ

24§35. The people in the unnamed city of this unnamed island are hoping that the burst of light emanating from their burning beacon fires will be a signal to their allies across the sea, who will then sail over on their ships and become *alk-tēres* or 'saviors' (*alk-tēr* is a synonym of *sō-tēr*, 'savior'). Compared to these fires signaling the hope of salvation for the anonymous islanders is the fire that bursts forth from the hero's head at line 206, producing an explosion of light or *selas*, 'gleam', which reaches all the way up to the aether. This gleam anticipates the gleam that will emanate from the Shield of Achilles, signaling salvation for his people. I review here the wording:

HOUR 24 TEXT I (PART OF TEXT E)

Next, the Shield [*sakos*], great and mighty, |₃₇₄ he [= Achilles] took on, and from it there was a gleam [*selas*] from afar, as from the moon, |₃₇₅ or as when, from the sea [*pontos*], a gleam [*selas*] to sailors appears [*phainesthai*] |₃₇₆ from a blazing fire, the kind that blazes high in the mountains |₃₇₇ at a solitary [*oiopolos*] station [*stathmos*], as the sailors are carried unwilling by gusts of wind |₃₇₈ over the fish-swarming sea [*pontos*], far away from their loved ones [*philoi*] |₃₇₉—so also did the gleam [*selas*] emanating from the Shield [*sakos*] of Achilles reach all the way up to the aether.

Iliad XIX 373–379*

24§36. The second image in my triptych of three glimpses of heroic salvation comes from a song of Pindar, dated to 446 BCE, which celebrates the glorious past of the people who inhabited the island state of Aegina. The song expresses a fond hope of salvation for these islanders, who are dramatized as singing and dancing their hope in the form of a choral prayer:

HOUR 24 TEXT J

|₉₅ Creatures of a day. What is a someone, what is a no one? A dream of a shade |₉₆ is man. But when the radiance [*aiglē*] that is given by Zeus

---

καταδύντι |₂₁₁ πυρσοί τε φλεγέθουσιν ἐπήτριμοι, ὑψόσε δ' αὐγὴ |₂₁₂ γίγνεται ἀΐσσουσα περικτιόνεσσιν ἰδέσθαι, |₂₁₃ αἴ κέν πως σὺν νηυσὶν ἄρεω ἀλκτῆρες ἴκωνται· |₂₁₄ ὡς ἀπ' Ἀχιλλῆος κεφαλῆς σέλας αἰθέρ' ἵκανε.

* αὐτὰρ ἔπειτα σάκος μέγα τε στιβαρόν τε |₃₇₄ εἵλετο, τοῦ δ' ἀπάνευθε σέλας γένετ' ἠΰτε μήνης. |₃₇₅ ὡς δ' ὅτ' ἂν ἐκ πόντοιο σέλας ναύτῃσι φανήῃ |₃₇₆ καιομένοιο πυρός, τό τε καίεται ὑψόθ' ὄρεσφι |₃₇₇ σταθμῷ ἐν οἰοπόλῳ· τοὺς δ' οὐκ ἐθέλοντας ἄελλαι |₃₇₈ πόντον ἐπ' ἰχθυόεντα φίλων ἀπάνευθε φέρουσιν· |₃₇₉ ὡς ἀπ' Ἀχιλλῆος σάκεος σέλας αἰθέρ' ἵκανε.

comes, |₉₇ then there is a light shining over men, and the recircling of time [aiōn] is sweet to the taste. |₉₈ Aegina! Mother near and dear [philē]! Make a [naval] mission [stolos] of freedom |₉₉ for this polis [= the island state of Aegina] as you bring it back to safety [komizein], back to Zeus! May it happen with the help of Aiakos the Ruler. |₁₀₀ And of Peleus. And of noble Telamon. And especially of Achilles.

Pindar Pythian 8.95–100*

24§37. The land of this island, named after the local goddess Aegina, is invoked here as the Mother Earth of the island's population. As I have argued at length in another project, this reverent invocation of Mother Aegina is a pointed reference to the glorious past of the island state, likewise called Aegina, as a major maritime power in the Mediterranean world.† In a gesture of sacred nostalgia, the people of Aegina are represented here as praying to their mother goddess to send for them 'a [naval] mission of freedom', an eleutheros stolos (line 98), which is to be activated by the superhuman help of the prototypical native son of Aegina, the hero Aiakos (line 99), and of his heroic descendants, namely Peleus, Telamon, and 'especially' Achilles (line 100).

24§38. The aiglē or 'radiance' of Zeus in line 96 of this song is imagined as the power of song to visualize this radiance. And the light that comes from Zeus is envisioned as a clear sky that follows a spell of fearsome darkness for sailors beset by a storm at sea.‡ Such a salvation from darkness and death is expressed by the use of the word aiglē, 'radiance', in line 140 of Ode 13 of Bacchylides, which signals the cessation of violent winds and the ultimate salvation of the Achaeans.§

24§39. As I already argued in Hour 10§23, the identity or non-identity of a hero matches the presence or absence of light: in the words of Pindar at lines 95–97 of this song, the difference between being tis, 'someone', and being ou tis, 'no one', becomes visible when a burst of light and life coming from Zeus himself illuminates the void of darkness and death.**

---

* |₉₅ ἐπάμεροι· τί δέ τις; τί δ' οὔ τις; σκιᾶς ὄναρ |₉₆ ἄνθρωπος. ἀλλ' ὅταν αἴγλα διόσδοτος ἔλθῃ, |₉₇ λαμπρὸν φέγγος ἔπεστιν ἀνδρῶν καὶ μείλιχος αἰών. |₉₈ Αἴγινα φίλα μᾶτερ, ἐλευθέρῳ στόλῳ |₉₉ πόλιν τάνδε κόμιζε Δὶ καὶ κρέοντι σὺν Αἰακῷ |₁₀₀ Πηλεῖ τε κἀγαθῷ Τελαμῶνι σύν τ' Ἀχιλλεῖ.

† Nagy 2011a:47–49.

‡ Nagy 2011b:191–192

§ Nagy 2011b:192.

** Nagy 2000:110–111. Here I also analyze the relevance of the riddling expression 'a dream of a shade is man' at lines 95–96 of Pythian 8.

24§40. The word *komizein* at line 99 of this song, which I translate as 'bring back to safety', can be interpreted in the mystical sense of 'bring back to light and life', parallel to the mystical sense of the noun *nostos,* 'return to light and life'.* This meaning connects with the meaning of *aiōn* at line 97 in the sense of an eternally recycling and luminous 'life-force'. As we saw in Hour 14§34 (also in Hour 18§44), the adverb *aiei,* 'forever', is the old locative singular of the noun *aiōn* in the sense of a 'life' or a 'life-force' that keeps coming back to life by way of a 'recircling of time', and this locative *aiei* means literally 'in a recircling of time', signaling an eternal return.†

24§41. I come now to the third image in my triptych of heroic salvation. In this image, the hero is Odysseus, and we see him being saved by the White Goddess, known as Ino before her death and immortalization. I have already referred in Hour 11§53 to this moment of salvation. We join the action just as Odysseus is about to drown, but the White Goddess sees him:

HOUR 24 TEXT K

|₃₃₃ He [= Odysseus] was seen by the daughter of Cadmus. She is Ino, with the beautiful ankles, |₃₃₄ and she is also called the White Goddess [*Leukotheā*], but she had been a mortal before that, endowed with a special voice [*audē*]. |₃₃₅ But now, in the depths, she had a share in the honor [*tīmē*] that belongs to gods. |₃₃₆ She took pity on Odysseus, lost at sea and suffering pains [*algea*]. |₃₃₇ Appearing as a winged diving bird [*aithuia*], she emerged from the waters |₃₃₈ and perched on the raft, addressing him with this set of words [*mūthos*]: |₃₃₉ "Unfortunate man, why on earth is Poseidon the earth-shaker |₃₄₀ so terribly hateful toward you, creating so many bad experiences for you? |₃₄₁ But I now see that he will not destroy you, much as he wants to. |₃₄₂ Do as I tell you, and I think you will not miss in your mind what I tell you: |₃₄₃ get out of these clothes of yours and let your raft be carried off by the winds. |₃₄₄ Just let it go. Then start paddling with your hands and strive for your homecoming [*nostos*] |₃₄₅ by heading for the land of the Phaeacians, where your destiny [*moira*] for escape awaits you. |₃₄₆ Here, take my veil [*krēdemnon*] and wrap it around your chest. |₃₄₇ It is a veil that is immortalizing [*ambroton*], and there is nothing to be afraid of:

---

* Nagy 2011a:47n15; also Nagy 2001c:152–155 (with notes 13 and 22).
† Nagy 2011b:179, following *PH* 195n210 = 6§88.

you will not suffer anything or be destroyed. |₃₄₈ But as soon as you touch land with your hands, |₃₄₉ at that moment take off the veil and throw it into the wine-colored sea [*pontos*]. |₃₅₀ Throw it as far back as you can into the sea, while you turn in the other direction." |₃₅₁ Speaking these words, the goddess took off her veil [*krēdemnon*] and gave it him. |₃₅₂ Then she plunged down again into the seething sea [*pontos*], |₃₅₃ looking like the diving bird [*aithuia*], |₃₅₃ and vanished beneath the dark waves.

Odyssey v 333–353*

24§42. As we saw in Hour 18§43, the female hero named Ino leapt to her death by diving into the sea from the top of a shining white rock—and then came back to life. According to one of the local versions of this myth, recorded by Pausanias (1.44.7–9), Ino made her leap from the rocky heights of Megara, plunging into the dark watery depths below and drowning in the sea—only to come back to life thereafter as the *Leukotheā* or 'White Goddess'. The Homeric version of the myth, as reflected in the passage I just quoted, corresponds in most details to this local myth.† Also, in the poetry of Pindar (*Olympian* 2.29), the immortal afterlife of Ino is described as a *biotos*, 'life', that is *aphthitos*, 'unwilting'.‡

24§43. As the White Goddess tells Odysseus at line 344 of the text I just quoted from *Odyssey* v, she is helping the hero achieve his ultimate *nostos*, which is not only *a safe homecoming* but also, as we have seen many times in this book, *a return to light and life*. Just as Ino drowned, Odysseus was about to drown, and so the White Goddess appears to the hero as a model of salvation. But the hero must achieve this salvation in his own way, and that way is his own personalized *nostos*, achieved by living through the entire plot of the Homeric *Odyssey*.

---

* |₃₃₃ τὸν δὲ ἴδεν Κάδμου θυγάτηρ, καλλίσφυρος Ἰνώ, |₃₃₄ Λευκοθέη, ἣ πρὶν μὲν ἔην βροτὸς αὐδήεσσα, |₃₃₅ νῦν δ' ἁλὸς ἐν πελάγεσσι θεῶν ἐξέμμορε τιμῆς. |₃₃₆ ἥ ῥ' Ὀδυσῆ' ἐλέησεν ἀλώμενον, ἄλγε' ἔχοντα· |₃₃₇ αἰθυίῃ δ' εἰκυῖα ποτῇ ἀνεδύσετο λίμνης, |₃₃₈ ἷζε δ' ἐπὶ σχεδίης καί μιν πρὸς μῦθον ἔειπε· |₃₃₉ "κάμμορε, τίπτε τοι ὧδε Ποσειδάων ἐνοσίχθων |₃₄₀ ὠδύσατ' ἐκπάγλως, ὅτι τοι κακὰ πολλὰ φυτεύει; |₃₄₁ οὐ μὲν δή σε καταφθείσει, μάλα περ μενεαίνων. |₃₄₂ ἀλλὰ μάλ' ὧδ' ἔρξαι, δοκέεις δέ μοι οὐκ ἀπινύσσειν· |₃₄₃ εἵματα ταῦτ' ἀποδὺς σχεδίην ἀνέμοισι φέρεσθαι |₃₄₄ κάλλιπ', ἀτὰρ χείρεσσι νέων ἐπιμαίεο νόστου |₃₄₅ γαίης Φαιήκων, ὅθι τοι μοῖρ' ἐστὶν ἀλύξαι. |₃₄₆ τῇ δέ, τόδε κρήδεμνον ὑπὸ στέρνοιο τανύσσαι |₃₄₇ ἄμβροτον· οὐδέ τί τοι παθέειν δέος οὐδ' ἀπολέσθαι. |₃₄₈ αὐτὰρ ἐπὴν χείρεσσιν ἐφάψεαι ἠπείροιο, |₃₄₉ ἂψ ἀπολυσάμενος βαλέειν εἰς οἴνοπα πόντον |₃₅₀ πολλὸν ἀπ' ἠπείρου, αὐτὸς δ' ἀπονόσφι τραπέσθαι." |₃₅₁ ὣς ἄρα φωνήσασα θεὰ κρήδεμνον ἔδωκεν, |₃₅₂ αὐτὴ δ' ἂψ ἐς πόντον ἐδύσετο κυμαίνοντα |₃₅₃ αἰθυίῃ εἰκυῖα· μέλαν δέ ἑ κῦμ' ἐκάλυψεν.

† *BA* 175 = 10§1n4; Nagy 1985:79–81 = §§76–79.

‡ *GM* 126, following *BA* 175, 203 = 10§1n4 and 10§41n2.

The Living Word of Plato's Socrates

24§44. In all three examples of heroic salvation that I have just analyzed, the experience of being saved has been connected in one way or another with the sea.* Here I return once again to the metaphor of salvation that pervades Plato's *Phaedo,* noting that there is a connection here again with the sea. As we saw in Hour 23, the idea of *theōriā* as a sacred voyage of the Ship of State is synchronized with the idea of *theōriā* as philosophical contemplation, which is meant to continue as the living word of the dialogue that is dramatized in the *Phaedo.* And there is hope that such dialogue will continue and thus be saved even after the death of Socrates, just as the Myth of Er is saved at the end of Plato's *Republic.*

24§45. But this hope seems to be in doubt as the death of Socrates draws near. His followers show their doubt by weeping uncontrollably before he dies:

HOUR 24 TEXT L

"Go," said he [= Socrates], "and do as I say." Crito, when he heard this, signaled with a nod to the boy servant who was standing nearby, and the servant went in, remaining for some time, and then came out with the man who was going to administer the poison [*pharmakon*]. He was carrying a cup that contained it, ground into the drink. When Socrates saw the man he said: "You, my good man, since you are experienced in these matters, should tell me what needs to be done." The man answered: "You need to drink it, that's all. Then walk around until you feel a heaviness |₁₁₇ᵦ in your legs. Then lie down. This way, the poison will do its thing." While the man was saying this, he handed the cup to Socrates. And Socrates took it in a cheerful way, not flinching or getting pale or grimacing. Then looking at the man from beneath his brows, like a bull—that was the way he used to look at people—he said: "What do you say about my pouring a libation out of this cup to someone? Is it allowed or not?" The man answered: "What we grind is measured out, Socrates, as the right dose for drinking." "I understand," he said, |₁₁₇ᵪ "but surely it is allowed and even proper to pray to the gods so that my transfer of dwelling [*met-oikēsis*] from this world [*enthende*] to that world [*ekeîse*] should be fortunate. So that is what I too am now praying for. Let it be this way." And, while he was saying this, he took

---

* For Modern Greek myths about salvation at sea, see Payne 1991:176–181.

the cup to his lips and, quite readily and cheerfully, he drank down the whole dose. Up to this point, most of us had been able to control fairly well our urge to let our tears flow; but now when we saw him drinking the poison, and then saw him finish the drink, we could no longer hold back, and, in my case, quite against my own will, my own tears were now pouring out in a flood. So, I covered my face and had a good cry. You see, I was not crying for him, |₁₁₇d but at the thought of my own bad fortune in having lost such a comrade [*hetairos*]. Crito, even before me, found himself unable to hold back his tears: so he got up and moved away. And Apollodorus, who had been weeping all along, now started to cry in a loud voice, expressing his frustration. So he made everyone else break down and cry—except for Socrates himself. And he said: "What are you all doing? I am so surprised at you. I had sent away the women mainly because I did not want them |₁₁₇e to lose control in this way. You see, I have heard that a man should come to his end [*teleutân*] in a way that calls for measured speaking [*euphēmeîn*]. So you must have composure [*hēsukhiā*], and you must endure." When we heard that, we were ashamed, and held back our tears. He meanwhile was walking around until, as he said, his legs began to get heavy, and then he lay on his back—that is what the man had told him to do. Then that same man who had given him the poison [*pharmakon*] took hold of him, now and then checking on his feet and legs; and after a while he pressed his foot hard and asked him if he could feel it; and he said that he couldn't; and then he pressed his shins, |₁₁₈a and so on, moving further up, thus demonstrating for us that he was cold and stiff. Then he [= Socrates] took hold of his own feet and legs, saying that when the poison reaches his heart, then he will be gone. He was beginning to get cold around the abdomen. Then he uncovered his face, for he had covered himself up, and said—this was the last thing he uttered—"Crito, I owe the sacrifice of a rooster to Asklepios; will you pay that debt and not neglect to do so?" "I will make it so," said Crito, "and, tell me, is there anything else?" When Crito asked this question, no answer came back any more from Socrates. In a short while, he stirred. Then the man uncovered his face. His eyes were set in a dead stare. Seeing this, Crito closed his mouth and his eyes. Such was the end [*teleutē*], Echecrates, of our comrade [*hetairos*]. And we may say about him that he was in his time the best [*aristos*] of all men we ever encountered—and the most intelligent [*phronimos*] and most just [*dikaios*].

Plato *Phaedo* 117a-118a*

24§46. Here at the end of the *Phaedo*, Socrates says: sacrifice a rooster to Asklepios. As we saw in Hour 20 (§§29–33), this hero was the son of Apollo, and he had special powers of healing. Asklepios also had the power of bringing the dead back to life. Some interpret the final instruction of Socrates to mean simply that death is a cure for life. I disagree. After sacrificing a rooster at day's end, sacrificers will sleep the sleep of incubation and then, the morning after the sacrifice, they will wake up to hear other roosters crowing.† So Asklepios is the model for keeping the voice of the rooster alive. And, for Socrates, Asklepios can become the model for keeping the word alive.

24§47. That living word is dialogue. We saw it when Socrates says that the

---

* ἀλλ' ἴθι, ἔφη, πείθου καὶ μὴ ἄλλως ποίει. Καὶ ὁ Κρίτων ἀκούσας ἔνευσε τῷ παιδὶ πλησίον ἑστῶτι. καὶ ὁ παῖς ἐξελθὼν καὶ συχνὸν χρόνον διατρίψας ἧκεν ἄγων τὸν μέλλοντα δώσειν τὸ φάρμακον, ἐν κύλικι φέροντα τετριμμένον. ἰδὼν δὲ ὁ Σωκράτης τὸν ἄνθρωπον, Εἶεν, ἔφη, ὦ βέλτιστε, σὺ γὰρ τούτων ἐπιστήμων, τί χρὴ ποιεῖν; Οὐδὲν ἄλλο, ἔφη, ἢ πιόντα περιιέναι, ἕως ἄν σου βάρος |₁₁₇b ἐν τοῖς σκέλεσι γένηται, ἔπειτα κατακεῖσθαι· καὶ οὕτως αὐτὸ ποιήσει. Καὶ ἅμα ὤρεξε τὴν κύλικα τῷ Σωκράτει. Καὶ ὃς λαβὼν καὶ μάλα ἵλεως, ὦ Ἐχέκρατες, οὐδὲν τρέσας οὐδὲ διαφθείρας οὔτε τοῦ χρώματος οὔτε τοῦ προσώπου, ἀλλ' ὥσπερ εἰώθει ταυρηδὸν ὑποβλέψας πρὸς τὸν ἄνθρωπον, Τί λέγεις, ἔφη, περὶ τοῦδε τοῦ πώματος πρὸς τὸ ἀποσπεῖσαί τινι; ἔξεστιν ἢ οὔ; Τοσοῦτον, ἔφη, ὦ Σώκρατες, τρίβομεν ὅσον οἰόμεθα μέτριον εἶναι πιεῖν. |₁₁₇c Μανθάνω, ἦ δ' ὅς· ἀλλ' εὔχεσθαί γέ που τοῖς θεοῖς ἔξεστί τε καὶ χρή, τὴν μετοίκησιν τὴν ἐνθένδε ἐκεῖσε εὐτυχῆ γενέσθαι· ἃ δὴ καὶ ἐγὼ εὔχομαί τε καὶ γένοιτο ταύτῃ. Καὶ ἅμ' εἰπὼν ταῦτα ἐπισχόμενος καὶ μάλα εὐχερῶς καὶ εὐκόλως ἐξέπιεν. καὶ ἡμῶν οἱ πολλοὶ τέως μὲν ἐπιεικῶς οἷοί τε ἦσαν κατέχειν τὸ μὴ δακρύειν, ὡς δὲ εἴδομεν πίνοντά τε καὶ πεπωκότα, οὐκέτι, ἀλλ' ἐμοῦ γε βίᾳ καὶ αὐτοῦ ἀστακτὶ ἐχώρει τὰ δάκρυα, ὥστε ἐγκαλυψάμενος ἀπέκλαον ἐμαυτόν—οὐ γὰρ δὴ ἐκεῖνόν γε, ἀλλὰ τὴν ἐμαυτοῦ τύχην, οἵου ἀνδρὸς |₁₁₇d ἑταίρου ἐστερημένος εἴην. ὁ δὲ Κρίτων ἔτι πρότερος ἐμοῦ, ἐπειδὴ οὐχ οἷός τ' ἦν κατέχειν τὰ δάκρυα, ἐξανέστη. Ἀπολλόδωρος δὲ καὶ ἐν τῷ ἔμπροσθεν χρόνῳ οὐδὲν ἐπαύετο δακρύων, καὶ δὴ καὶ τότε ἀναβρυχησάμενος κλάων καὶ ἀγανακτῶν οὐδένα ὅντινα οὐ κατέκλασε τῶν παρόντων πλήν γε αὐτοῦ Σωκράτους. Ἐκεῖνος δέ, Οἶα, ἔφη, ποιεῖτε, ὦ θαυμάσιοι. ἐγὼ μέντοι οὐχ ἥκιστα τούτου ἕνεκα τὰς γυναῖκας ἀπέπεμψα, ἵνα μὴ |₁₁₇e τοιαῦτα πλημμελοῖεν· καὶ γὰρ ἀκήκοα ὅτι ἐν εὐφημίᾳ χρὴ τελευτᾶν. ἀλλ' ἡσυχίαν τε ἄγετε καὶ καρτερεῖτε. Καὶ ἡμεῖς ἀκούσαντες ᾐσχύνθημέν τε καὶ ἐπέσχομεν τοῦ δακρύειν. ὁ δὲ περιελθών, ἐπειδή οἱ βαρύνεσθαι ἔφη τὰ σκέλη, κατεκλίνη ὕπτιος—οὕτω γὰρ ἐκέλευεν ὁ ἄνθρωπος—καὶ ἅμα ἐφαπτόμενος αὐτοῦ οὗτος ὁ δοὺς τὸ φάρμακον, διαλιπὼν χρόνον ἐπεσκόπει τοὺς πόδας καὶ τὰ σκέλη, κἄπειτα σφόδρα πιέσας αὐτοῦ τὸν πόδα ἤρετο εἰ αἰσθάνοιτο, |₁₁₈a ὁ δ' οὐκ ἔφη. καὶ μετὰ τοῦτο αὖθις τὰς κνήμας· καὶ ἐπανιὼν οὕτως ἡμῖν ἐπεδείκνυτο ὅτι ψύχοιτό τε καὶ πήγνυτο. καὶ αὐτὸς ἥπτετο καὶ εἶπεν ὅτι, ἐπειδὰν πρὸς τῇ καρδίᾳ γένηται αὐτῷ, τότε οἰχήσεται. Ἤδη οὖν σχεδόν τι αὐτοῦ ἦν τὰ περὶ τὸ ἦτρον ψυχόμενα, καὶ ἐκκαλυψάμενος—ἐνεκεκάλυπτο γάρ—εἶπεν—ὃ δὴ τελευταῖον ἐφθέγξατο—Ὦ Κρίτων, ἔφη, τῷ Ἀσκληπιῷ ὀφείλομεν ἀλεκτρυόνα· ἀλλὰ ἀπόδοτε καὶ μὴ ἀμελήσητε. Ἀλλὰ ταῦτα, ἔφη, ἔσται, ὁ Κρίτων· ἀλλ' ὅρα εἴ τι ἄλλο λέγεις. Ταῦτα ἐρομένου αὐτοῦ οὐδὲν ἔτι ἀπεκρίνατο, ἀλλ' ὀλίγον χρόνον διαλιπὼν ἐκινήθη τε καὶ ὁ ἄνθρωπος ἐξεκάλυψεν αὐτόν, καὶ ὃς τὰ ὄμματα ἔστησεν· ἰδὼν δὲ ὁ Κρίτων συνέλαβε τὸ στόμα καὶ τοὺς ὀφθαλμούς. Ἥδε ἡ τελευτή, ὦ Ἐχέκρατες, τοῦ ἑταίρου ἡμῖν ἐγένετο, ἀνδρός, ὡς ἡμεῖς φαῖμεν ἄν, τῶν τότε ὧν ἐπειράθημεν ἀρίστου καὶ ἄλλως φρονιμωτάτου καὶ δικαιοτάτου.

† On rituals of overnight incubation in the hero cults of Asklepios, see Brelich 1958:113–118.

only thing worth crying about is the death of the word. Calling out to Phaedo, Socrates tells him:

HOUR 24 TEXT M (PART OF HOUR 23 TEXT N)

"Tomorrow, Phaedo, you will perhaps be cutting off these beautiful locks of yours?" "Yes, Socrates," I [= Phaedo] replied, "I guess I will." He shot back: "No you will not, if you listen to me." "So, what will I do?" I said. He replied: "Not tomorrow but today I will cut off my own hair and you too will cut off these locks of yours—if our argument [logos] comes to an end [teleutân] for us and we cannot bring it back to life again [ana-biōsasthai]."

Plato *Phaedo* 89b*

24§48. What matters for Socrates is the resurrection of the word, even if death may be the necessary *pharmakon* or 'poison' for leaving the everyday life and for entering the everlasting cycle of resurrecting the word.

24§49. Something comparable can be said about the ancient Greek hero. So long as the idea of the hero is alive, the word about the hero will be a living word. And if the word is alive, the hero will live on.

---

* Αὔριον δή, ἔφη, ἴσως, ὦ Φαίδων, τὰς καλὰς ταύτας κόμας ἀποκερῇ. Ἔοικεν, ἦν δ' ἐγώ, ὦ Σώκρατες. Οὔκ, ἄν γε ἐμοὶ πείθῃ. Ἀλλὰ τί; ἦν δ' ἐγώ. Τήμερον, ἔφη, κἀγὼ τὰς ἐμὰς καὶ σὺ ταύτας, ἐάνπερ γε ἡμῖν ὁ λόγος τελευτήσῃ καὶ μὴ δυνώμεθα αὐτὸν ἀναβιώσασθαι.

CORE VOCABULARY OF KEY GREEK WORDS

ABBREVIATIONS

REFERENCES

INDEX

Core Vocabulary of Key Greek Words

Depending on context, adjectives in *-os* (masculine) may be given with other endings: *-ē* (feminine), *-on* (neuter), *-oi* (masculine plural), *-ai* (feminine plural), *-a* (neuter plural).

agathos 'good, noble'

agōn, plural *agōnes* 'coming together, bringing together, gathering, assembly; competition (antagonism); ordeal (agony)'

agorā, plural *agorai* 'public assembly, place of public assembly'

aidōs 'shame, sense of shame; sense of respect for others; modesty; honorableness'

ainos 'authoritative utterance for and by a social group [see Hour 2§§60, 72; Hour 7§7; Hour 16§7]; praise; fable'; *ainigma:* 'riddle, enigma'

aitios 'responsible, guilty'; *aitiā:* 'responsibility, guilt; cause, case'

akhos 'grief, sorrow; public expression of grief, sorrow, by way of lamentation or keening'; synonym of *penthos*

alēthēs (adjective) 'true'; *alētheia* (noun): 'truth'

aphthito- 'imperishable, unfailing, unwilting'

aretē 'striving for a noble goal, for high ideals; noble goal, high ideals; merit'

aristos 'best', superlative of *agathos*; *aristeiā:* designates the hero's great epic moments that demonstrate his being *aristos*

atē, plural *atai* 'aberration, derangement, veering off-course; disaster; punishment for disaster'

āthlos (aethlos) 'ordeal, contest; labor; competition'; *āthlētēs:* 'athlete'

biā (*biē* in the language of Homeric poetry) 'force, violence' *daimōn,* plural *daimones* 'superhuman force (= unspecified god or hero) intervening in human life'; *eudaimoniā:* 'good blessing of superhuman powers; good fortune'

daimonion 'a superhuman thing' (see Hour 22§§1–2)

dēmos, plural *dēmoi* 'district, locale; population of a district, locale; community'

dikē, plural *dikai* 'judgment (short-range); justice (long-range)'; *dikaios:* 'just'

ekhthros 'enemy [within the community], non-*philos*'

epos, plural *epea* 'word(s) said, utterance, poetic utterance'

eris 'strife, conflict, competition'

esthlos 'genuine, good, noble'; synonym of *agathos genos:* 'stock ("breeding"); generating [of something or someone]; progeny; generation'

hērōs, plural *hērōes* 'hero'

hēsukhos 'serene'; *hēsukhiā:* 'state of being *hēsukhos*; composure'

hieros 'sacred, consecrated, holy'

hōrā, plural *hōrai* 'season, seasonality, the right time, the perfect time; beauty'

hubris 'outrage'; the opposite of *dikē*

kakos 'bad, evil, base, worthless, ignoble'; *kakotēs:* 'state of being *kakos*; debasement'

kamatos 'ordeal, labor, pain'

kerdos, plural *kerdea* 'gain, profit; desire for gain; craft employed for gain; craftiness; craft'

kharis, plural *kharites* 'reciprocity, give-and-take, compensation, reciprocal relationship; initiation of reciprocal relationship; the beauty (as in the word "gracefulness") and the pleasure (as in the word "gratification") that result from reciprocity, from a reciprocal relationship (as in the word "graciousness"); grace, gracefulness, charm; gratification; graciousness; favor, favorableness; gratitude'

khoros 'chorus', 'group of singers/dancers'

kleos, plural *klea* 'glory, fame (especially as conferred by poetry or song); that which is heard'

kolōnos 'tumulus' (see Hour 18§§1–8)

koros 'being satiated; being insatiable'

kosmos 'arrangement, order, organization; law and order, the social order; the cosmic order; the orderliness of a person's costume, hairdo; the orderliness of a group, of society, of the cosmos, of a song'

krinein 'judge, distinguish, make distinctions; decide; interpret; sort out'

lyssa [or, more accurately, *lussa*] 'rage, fury, frenzy'. This word is related to *lykos*, 'wolf' [or, more accurately, *lukos*]; so the image is one of 'wolfish rage'

mantis 'seer, prophet'

memnēmai 'I have total recall' (see Hour 2§1)

mēnis 'superhuman anger; cosmic sanction'

menos 'power, power source, strength, life-force, activation' (divinely infused into cosmic forces, like fire and wind, or into heroes); a partial synonym of *thūmos*; a partial synonym of *mēnis*

mētis 'artifice, stratagem, craft, craftiness, intelligence, cunning intelligence'

miasma 'pollution, miasma'

moira, plural *moirai* 'portion; portion of meat divided at a sacrifice; lot in life, fate, destiny'

mūthos 'wording, words; special speech; special wording; something said for the record [see Hour 1§36, in the commentary for Hour 1 Text C]; authoritative speech-act [see Hour 15§57]; myth [see Hour 24§§7–9]'

nemesis indicates the process whereby everyone gets what he or she deserves

nēpios, plural *nēpioi* 'disconnected' (the disconnection can be mental, moral, or emotional); on this meaning, see Edmunds 1990

nomos, plural *nomoi* 'local custom; customary law; law'

noos 'mind, thinking; perception; intuition; consciousness'; also, this word stands for the principle that reintegrates *thūmos* (or *menos*) and *psūkhē* after death

nostos 'return, homecoming; song about homecoming; safe homecoming; return to light and life'

oikos 'house, dwelling, abode; resting place of cult hero; family line'; verb *oikeîn*: 'have a dwelling'

olbios 'blessed, blissful; fortunate, prosperous, happy'; *olbos*: 'bliss' (ordinarily pictured as material security)

paskhein 'suffer, experience, be treated [badly or well]'; *pathos*: 'suffering, experience; emotion' (see Hour 21§§8–10) *penthos* 'grief, sorrow; public expression of grief, sorrow, by way of lamentation or keening'; synonym of *akhos*

philos 'friend' (noun); 'dear, near-and-dear, belonging to self' (adjective); *philotēs* or *philiā*: 'the state of being *philos*'

phrēn, plural *phrenes* physical localization of the *thūmos*; depending on the context, can be translated as either 'mind' ('thinking') or 'heart' ('feeling')

polis 'city, city-state; citadel, acropolis'

ponos 'ordeal, labor, pain'

pontos 'sea; crossing' (see Hour 24§§20–32)

pothos 'longing, yearning, desire'; a variant form is *pothē*, with the same meaning; the verb derived from this noun is *potheîn*: 'long for, yearn for, desire'

psūkhē, plural *psūkhai* 'life, life's breath; spirit; soul; mind'; synonym of *thūmos* (or *menos*) at the moment of death; in Homeric Greek, this word refers to the essence of life when one is alive and to the disembodied conveyor of identity when one is dead

sēma, plural *sēmata* 'sign, signal, symbol; tomb'; *sēmainein* (verb): 'mean something, indicate something by way of a *sēma*'

sophos 'skilled, skilled in understanding special language'; *sophiā*: 'being *sophos*'

sōphrōn 'moderate, balanced, with equilibrium'; *sōphrosunē*: 'being *sōphrōn*'

sōtēr 'savior' (either 'bringing to safety' or, mystically, 'bringing back to life'); *sōtēriā*: 'safety, salvation'

sōzein 'save; be a *sōtēr* (for someone)'

stasis 'division in a group; discord, strife; division [= part of an organization, like a chorus]; dancing pose'

telos 'end, ending, final moment; goal, completion, fulfillment; coming full circle, rounding out; successfully passing through an ordeal; initiation; ritual, rite'

themis, plural *themistes* 'something divinely or cosmically ordained; divine law; cosmic law'

theōriā 'sacred journey, pilgrimage; contemplation of the divine' (see Hour 23§§1–8)

therapōn, plural *therapontes* 'attendant; ritual substitute'

thūmos 'mind, thinking; heart, spirit' (designates realm of consciousness, of rational and emotional functions); depending on the context, can be translated as either 'mind' ('thinking') or 'heart' ('feeling')

tīmē, plural *tīmai* 'honor; honor paid to a superhuman force by way of cult'

turannos, plural *turannoi* (Lydian word for 'king') 'king' (from the viewpoint of most Greek dynasties); 'unconstitutional ruler' (from the viewpoint of Greek democracy: see Hour 19§6)

xenos, plural *xenoi* 'stranger who should be treated like a guest by a host, or like a host by a guest'; *xeniā:* 'reciprocal relationship between *xenoi*'; when the rules of *xeniā* do not work, a *xenos* risks defaulting to the status of simply a stranger

Abbreviations

ABV   Beazley, J. 1956. *Attic Black-Figure Vase Painters.* Oxford.

BA   Nagy, G. 1999. *The Best of the Achaeans: Concepts of the Hero in Archaic Greek Poetry.* Rev. ed. with new intro. Baltimore. (Available online.)

CPG   Leutsch, E. L. von, and F. G. Schneidewin, eds. 1839–1851. *Corpus Paroemiographorum Graecorum.* Göttingen.

DELG   Chantraine, P. 2009. *Dictionnaire étymologique de la langue grecque: histoire des mots.* Ed. J. Taillardat, O. Masson, and J.-L. Perpillou. With a supplement *Chroniques d'étymologie grecque* 1–10. Ed. A. Blanc, Ch. de Lamberterie, and Jean-Louis Perpillou. Paris.

EH   Nagy, G. 2006. "The Epic Hero." Expanded version of "The Epic Hero." 2005. *A Companion to Ancient Epic.* 71–89. Ed. J. M. Foley. Oxford. (Available online.)

FGH   Jacoby, F. 1923–58. *Die Fragmente der griechischen Historiker.* 3 vols. Berlin.

GM   Nagy, G. 1990b. *Greek Mythology and Poetics.* Ithaca NY. (Available online.)

HC   Nagy, G. 2009. *Homer the Classic.* Hellenic Studies 36. Cambridge MA and Washington DC. (Available online.)

HPC   Nagy, G. 2010. *Homer the Preclassic.* Berkeley and Los Angeles CA. (Available online.)

HQ   Nagy, G. 1996b. *Homeric Questions.* Austin TX. (Available online.)

HR   Nagy, G. 2003. *Homeric Responses.* Austin TX.

HTL   Nagy, G. 2004a. *Homer's Text and Language.* Urbana and Chicago.

IG   Deutsche Akademie der Wissenschaften. 1873–. *Inscriptiones Graecae.* Berlin.

LSJ   Liddell, H. G., R. Scott, and H. S. Jones. 1940. *A Greek-English Lexicon.* 9th ed. Oxford.

MW   *Fragmenta Hesiodea.* Ed. R. Merkelbach and M. West. 1967. Oxford.

PH   Nagy, G. 1990a. *Pindar's Homer: The Lyric Possession of an Epic Past.* Baltimore. (Available online.)

PMG   Page, D. L. 1962. *Poetae Melici Graeci.* Oxford.

PP   Nagy, G. 1996a. *Poetry as Performance: Homer and Beyond.*
        Cambridge. (Available online.)

PR   Nagy, G. 2002. *Plato's Rhapsody and Homer's Music: The Poetics of the*
        Panathenaic Festival in Classical Athens. Cambridge MA and Athens.
        (Available online.)

SEG   Gieben, J. C., et al. 1923–. *Supplementum Epigraphicum Graecum.*
        Amsterdam.

References

Albersmeier, S., ed. 2009. *Heroes: Mortals and Myths in Ancient Greece*. Baltimore.

Alexiou, M. 1974. *The Ritual Lament in Greek Tradition*. Cambridge. 2nd ed. 2002. Revised and with introduction by P. Roilos and D. Yatromanolakis. Lanham MD.

Allen, N. J. 1993. "Arjuna and Odysseus: A Comparative Approach." *South Asia Library Group Newsletter* 40:39–43.

Allen, T. W., ed. 1912. *Homeri Opera* V (Hymns, Cycle, fragments). Oxford.

Antonaccio, C. M. 1995. *An Archaeology of Ancestors: Tomb Cult and Hero Cult in Early Greece*. Lanham MD.

Bakker, E. 2005. *Pointing at the Past: From Formula to Performance in Homeric Poetics*. Hellenic Studies 12. Cambridge MA and Washington DC.

Baldick, J. 1994. *Homer and the Indo-Europeans: Comparing Mythologies*. London and New York.

Barrett, W. S., ed. 1964. *Euripides: Hippolytus*. Oxford.

Beazley, J. 1956. *Attic Black-Figure Vase Painters*. Oxford.

Beissinger, M., J. Tylus, and S. Wofford, eds. 1999. *Epic Traditions in the Contemporary World: The Poetics of Community*. Berkeley and Los Angeles.

Bell, M. 1995. "The Motya Charioteer and Pindar's *Isthmian* 2." *Memoirs of the American Academy in Rome* 40:1–42.

Benveniste, E. 1954. "Fonctions sémantiques de la reconstruction." *Word* 10:251–264. Reprinted in Benveniste 1966, 289–307.

Benveniste, E. 1958. "De la subjectivité dans le langage." *Journal de Psychologie normale et pathologique* 1958:257–265. Reprinted in Benveniste 1966, 258–266.

Benveniste, E. 1966–1974. *Problèmes de linguistique générale*. 2 vols. Paris.

Benveniste, E. 1971. *Problems in General Linguistics*. Translated by M. E. Meek. Miami OH. (I recommend especially the formulation about *intersubjectivity*, p. 266.)

Berenson Maclean, J. K., and E. B. Aitken, trans. and eds. 2001. Flavius Philostratus, *Heroikos*. Atlanta. Available at http://chs.harvard.edu/wa/pageR?tn=ArticleWrapper&bdc=12&mn=3565.

Bernabé, A., ed. 1987. *Poetae Epici Graeci* I. Leipzig.

Bernabé, A., ed. 2004/2005. *Poetae epici graeci* II. Fascicles 1/2. Munich and Leipzig.

Bers, V., D. Elmer, D. Frame, and L. Muellner, eds. 2012. *Donum Natalicium Digitaliter*

Confectum Gregorio Nagy Septuagenario a Discipulis Collegis Familiaribus Oblatum. A Virtual Birthday Gift Presented to Gregory Nagy on Turning Seventy by His Students, Colleagues, and Friends. Available at http://nrs.harvard.edu/urn-3:hul.ebook:CHS_Bers_etal_eds.Donum_Natalicium_Gregorio_Nagy.2012.

Bershadsky, N. 2013. "A Picnic, a Tomb, and a Crow." *Harvard Studies in Classical Philology* 106:1–45.

Bierl, A. 1991. *Dionysos und die griechische Tragödie: Politische und "metatheatralische" Aspekte im Text.* Tübingen.

Blackburn, S. H. 1989. "Patterns of Development for Indian Oral Epics." Blackburn, Claus, Flueckiger, and Wadley 1989:15–32.

Blackburn, S. H., P. J. Claus, J. B. Flueckiger, and S. S. Wadley, eds. 1989. *Oral Epics in India.* Berkeley and Los Angeles.

Blackburn, S. H., and J. B. Flueckiger, 1989. "Introduction." Blackburn, Claus, Flueckiger, and Wadley 1989:1–11.

Boedeker, D. 1988. "Protesilaos and the End of Herodotus' *Histories.*" *Classical Antiquity* 7:30–48.

Boyd, T. W. 1995. "A Poet on the Achaean Wall." *Oral Tradition* 10:181–206.

Boym, S. 2001. *The Future of Nostalgia.* New York.

Bravo, J. J. 2009. "Recovering the Past: The Origins of Greek Heroes and Hero Cults." Albersmeier 2009:10–29.

Brelich, A. 1958. *Gli eroi greci: Un problema storico-religioso.* Rome.

Burgess, J. S. 2001. *The Tradition of the Trojan War in Homer and the Epic Cycle.* Baltimore.

Burkert, W. 1966. "Greek Tragedy and Sacrificial Ritual." *Greek, Roman, and Byzantine Studies* 7:87–121.

Burkert, W. 1983. *Homo Necans: The Anthropology of Ancient Greek Sacrificial Ritual and Myth.* Translated by P. Bing. Berkeley and Los Angeles. (Originally published 1972 as *Homo Necans,* Berlin.)

Burkert, W. 1984. *Die Orientalisierende Epoche in der griechischen Religion und Literatur.* Heidelberg.

Burkert, W. 1985. *Greek Religion.* Translated by J. Raffan. Cambridge MA. (Originally published 1977 as *Griechische Religion der archaischen und klassischen Epoche,* Stuttgart.)

Burkert, W. 1992. *The Orientalizing Revolution: Near Eastern Influence on Greek Culture in the Early Archaic Age.* Translated by M. Pinder and W. Burkert. Cambridge MA. (Translation of Burkert 1984.)

Burkert, W. 1995. "Lydia between East and West." Carter and Morris 1995:139–148.

Calame, C. 1990. *Thésée et l'imaginaire athénien: Légende et culte en Grèce antique.* Lausanne.

Calame, C. 1998. "Mort héroïque et culte à mystère dans l'*Œdipe à Colone* de Sophocle." *Ansichten griechischer Rituale: Geburtstags-Symposium für Walter Burkert.* Edited by F. Graf. 326–356. Stuttgart and Leipzig.

Carter, J. B., and S. P. Morris, eds. 1995. *The Ages of Homer: A Tribute to Emily Townsend Vermeule.* Austin TX.

Cassio, A. C. 1999. "Epica greca e scrittura tra VIII e VII a.C.: madrepatria e colonie d'occidente." *Atti del Convegno "Scritture mediterranee tra il IX e il VII secolo a.C."* Edited by G. Bagnasco Gianni and F. Cordano. 67–84. Milan.

Cassio, A. C. 2002. "Early Editions of the Greek Epics and Homeric Textual Criticism in the Sixth and Fifth Centuries BC." *Omero tremila anni dopo.* Edited by F. Montanari. 105–136. Rome.

Cerri, G. 2010. "Théorie de l'oralité et analyse stratigraphique du texte homérique: le concept de 'poème traditionnel.'" *Gaia: Revue interdisciplinaire sur la Grèce archaïque* 13:81–106.

Chantraine, P. 2009. *Dictionnaire étymologique de la langue grecque: histoire des mots.* Edited by J. Taillardat, O. Masson, and J.-L. Perpillou. With a supplement *Chroniques d'étymologie grecque* 1–10. Edited by A. Blanc, Ch. de Lamberterie, and Jean-Louis Perpillou. Paris.

Clay, D. 1978. "Introduction." *Sophocles: Oedipus the King.* Translated by S. Berg and D. Clay. 3–20. New York.

Colarusso, J., ed. 2002. *Nart Sagas from the Caucasus: Myths and Legends from the Circassians, Abazas, Abkhaz, and Ubykhs.* Princeton.

Conway, J. K., K. Keniston, and L. Marx, eds. 1999. *Earth, Air, Fire, Water: Humanistic Studies of the Environment.* Amherst MA.

Cook, E. 2004. "Near Eastern Sources for the Palace of Alkinoos." *American Journal of Archaeology* 108:43–77.

Crane, G. 1988. *Calypso: Backgrounds and Conventions of the Odyssey.* Frankfurt.

Cross, F. M. 1973. *Canaanite Myth and Hebrew Epic.* Cambridge MA.

Crowther, N. B. 1991. "The Apobates Reconsidered (Demosthenes lxi 23–9)." *Journal of Hellenic Studies* 111:174–176.

Currie, B. G. F. 2003. Review of Ekroth 2002. *Journal of Hellenic Studies* 123:238–241.

Currie, B. G. F. 2005. *Pindar and the Cult of Heroes.* Oxford.

Dale, A. 2011. "Sapphica." *Harvard Studies in Classical Philology* 106:47–74.

Davidson, O. M. 1980. "Indo-European Dimensions of Herakles in *Iliad* 19.95–133." *Arethusa* 13:197–202.

Davidson, O. M. 1994. *Poet and Hero in the Persian Book of Kings.* Ithaca NY. 2nd ed. 2006. Costa Mesa CA.

Davidson, O. M. 2000. *Comparative Literature and Classical Persian Poetics: Seven Essays.* Bibliotheca Iranica: Intellectual Traditions Series no. 4. Costa Mesa CA.

Davidson, O. M. 2001. "Some Iranian Poetic Tropes as Reflected in the 'Life of Ferdowsi' Traditions." *Philologica et Linguistica: Festschrift für Helmut Humbach.* Edited by M. G. Schmidt and W. Bisang. Supplement 1–12. Trier.

Davidson, O. M. 2013a. *Poet and Hero in the Persian Book of Kings.* 3rd ed. Cambridge MA.

Davidson, O. M. 2013b. *Comparative Literature and Classical Persian Poetics.* 2nd ed. Cambridge MA.

de Jong, J. W. 1985. "The Over-Burdened Earth in India and Greece." *Journal of the American Oriental Society* 105:397–400.

Detienne, M. 1972. *Les jardins d'Adonis: La mythologie des aromates en Grèce.* Paris.

Detienne, M. 1977. *The Gardens of Adonis.* Translated by J. Lloyd. Sussex. (Translation of Detienne 1972.)

Deutsche Akademie der Wissenschaften. 1873–. *Inscriptiones Graecae.* Berlin.

Dewald, C. 1997. "Wanton Kings, Pickled Heroes, and Gnomic Founding Fathers: Strategies of Meaning at the End of Herodotus' *Histories.*" *Classical Closure: Reading the End in Greek and Latin Literature.* Edited by D. H. Roberts, F. M. Dunn, and D. Fowler. 62–82. Princeton.

Dhuga, U. S. 2011. *Choral Identity and the Chorus of Elders in Greek Tragedy.* Lanham MD.

Doumas, C. G. 1999. *The Wall Paintings of Thera.* 2nd ed. Athens.

Dova, S. 2000. "Who Is *makartatos* in the Odyssey?" *Harvard Studies in Classical Philology* 100:53–65.

Dova, S. 2012. *Greek Heroes In and Out of Hades.* Lanham MD.

Ducrot, O., and Tz. Todorov. 1979. *Encyclopedic Dictionary of the Sciences of Language.* Translated by C. Porter. Baltimore.

Dué, C. 2000. "Poetry and the Dēmos: State Regulation of a Civic Possession." Stoa Consortium. Edited by R. Scaife. Available at http://www.stoa.org/projects/demos/poetry_and_demos.pdf.

Dué, C. 2001. "Achilles' Golden Amphora in Aeschines' *Against Timarchus* and the Afterlife of Oral Tradition." *Classical Philology* 96:33–47.

Dué, C. 2002. *Homeric Variations on a Lament by Briseis.* Lanham MD. Available at http://nrs.harvard.edu/urn-3:hul.ebook:CHS_Due.Homeric_Variations_on_a_Lament_by_Briseis.2002.

Dué, C. 2006. *The Captive Woman's Lament in Greek Tragedy.* Austin TX. Available at http://nrs.harvard.edu/urn-3:hul.ebook:CHS_Due.The_Captive_Womans_Lament_in_Greek_Tragedy.2006.

Dumézil, G. 1968. *Mythe et épopée.* Vol. 1, *L'idéologie des trois fonctions dans les épopées des peuples indo-européennes.* Paris. (2nd ed. 1986.)

Dumézil, G. 1969. *Heur et malheur du guerrier: Aspects mythiques de la fonction guerrière ches les Indo-Européens.* Paris.

Dumézil, G. 1970. *The Destiny of the Warrior.* Translated by A. Hiltebeitel. Chicago. (Translation of Dumézil 1969.)

Dumézil, G. 1971. *Mythe et épopée.* Vol. 2, *Types épiques indo-européens: un héros, un sorcier, un roi.* Paris. (2nd ed. 1986.)

Dumézil, G. 1973a. *Mythe et épopée.* Vol. 3, *Histoires romaines.* Paris. (2nd ed. 1978. 3rd ed. 1981.)

Dumézil, G. 1973b. *The Destiny of a King.* Translated by A. Hiltebeitel. Chicago. (Translation of *Mythe et épopée*, vol. 2, pt. 3.)

Dumézil, G. 1975. *Fêtes romaines d'été et d'automne, suivi de dix questions romaines.* Paris.

Dumézil, G. 1980. *Camillus: A Study of Indo-European Religion as Roman History.* Translated by A. Aranowicz and J. Bryson. Edited and with introduction by U. Strutynski. Berkeley and Los Angeles. (Translation of *Mythe et épopée*, vol. 3, pt. 2, plus Dumézil 1973a, app. 1 and 2, and Dumézil 1975, app. 3 and 4.)

Dumézil, G. 1983. *The Stakes of the Warrior.* Translated by D. Weeks. Edited and with introduction by J. Puhvel. Berkeley and Los Angeles. (Translation of *Mythe et épopée* vol. 2, pt. 1.)

Dumézil, G. 1986. *The Plight of the Sorcerer.* Translated by D. Weeks and others. Edited by J. Puhvel and D. Weeks. Introduction by D. Weeks. (Translation of *Mythe et épopée*, vol. 2, pt. 2.)

Dumézil, G. 1995. *Mythe et épopée* I, II, III. New combined and corrected edition of the original three volumes, with original paginations retained in the inner margins. Preface by J. Grisward, pp. 7–30. Paris.

Easterling, P. E. 2006. "The Death of Oedipus and What Happened Next." *Dionysalexandros: Essays on Aeschylus and His Fellow Tragedians in Honour of Alexander F. Garvie.* Edited by D. Cairns and V. Liapis. 133–150. Swansea.

Easterling, P. E. 2012. "Getting to Grips with the Oracles: *Oedipus at Colonus.*" Bers et al. 2012. Available at http://nrs.harvard.edu/urn-3:hlnc.essay:EasterlingPE.Getting_to_ Grips_with_the_Oracles.2012.

Ebbott, M. 2000. "The List of the War Dead in Aeschylus' *Persians.*" *Harvard Studies in Classical Philology* 100:83–96.

Ebbott, M. 2003. *Imagining Illegitimacy in Classical Greek Literature.* Lanham MD. Available at http://nrs.harvard.edu/urn-3:hul.ebook:CHS_Ebbott.Imagining_Illegitimacy_in_ Classical_Greek_Literature.2003.

Edmunds, L. 1981. "The Cults and the Legend of Oedipus." *Harvard Studies in Classical Philology* 85:221–238.

Edmunds, L. 1996. *Theatrical Space and Historical Place in Sophocles' Oedipus at Colonus.* Lanham MD.

Edmunds, S. T. 1990. *Homeric Nēpios.* New York.

Ekroth, G. 2002. *The Sacrificial Rituals of Greek Hero-Cults in the Archaic to the Early Hellenistic Periods.* Liège.

Ekroth, G. 2009. "The Cult of Heroes." Albersmeier 2009:121–143.

Elmer, D. F. 2008. "*Epikoinos*: The Ball Game *Episkyros* and *Iliad* 12.421–3." *Classical Philology* 103:414–422.

Elmer, D. F. 2010. "'It's Not Me, It's You, Socrates': The Problem of the Charismatic Teacher in Plato's *Symposium.*" Martin Weiner Lecture, Brandeis University, November 10, 2010.

Elmer, D. F. 2013. *The Poetics of Consent: Collective Decision Making and the Iliad.* Baltimore.

Ferrari, G. 1997. "Figures in the Text: Metaphors and Riddles in the *Agamemnon.*" *Classical Philology* 92:1–45.

Ferrari, G. 2000. "The *Ilioupersis* in Athens." *Harvard Studies in Classical Philology* 100:119–150.

Fitzgerald, R. 1941. *Sophocles, The Oedipus at Colonus: An English Version.* New York.

Flower, M. A., and J. Marincola, eds. 2002. *Herodotus: Histories Book IX.* Cambridge.

Flueckiger, J. B. 1989. "Caste and Regional Variants in an Oral Epic Tradition." Blackburn, Claus, Flueckiger, and Wadley 1989:33–54.

Flueckiger, J. B. 1996. *Gender and Genre in the Folklore of Middle India.* Ithaca NY.

Foley, J. M. 1990. *Traditional Oral Epic.* Berkeley and Los Angeles.

Foley, J. M. 1991. *Immanent Art.* Bloomington IN.

Foley, J. M. 1995. *The Singer of Tales in Performance.* Bloomington IN.

Foley, J. M. 1996. "*Guslar* and *Aoidos*: Traditional Register in South Slavic and Homeric Epic." *Transactions of the American Philological Association* 126:11–41.

Foley, J. M., ed. 1998. *Teaching Oral Traditions.* New York.

Foley, J. M. 1999. *Homer's Traditional Art.* University Park PA.

Foley, J. M. 2002. *How to Read an Oral Poem.* Champaign IL.

Foster, B. R., ed., trans., and introd. 2001. *The Epic of Gilgamesh.* New York.

Fraenkel, E., ed. 1950. *Aeschylus: Agamemnon.* 3 vols. Oxford.

Frame, D. 1978. *The Myth of Return in Early Greek Epic.* New Haven. Available at http://nrs.harvard.edu/urn-3:hul.ebook:CHS_Frame.The_Myth_of_Return_in_Early_Greek_Epic.1978.

Frame, D. 2009. *Hippota Nestor.* Hellenic Studies 34. Cambridge MA and Washington DC. Available at http://nrs.harvard.edu/urn-3:hul.ebook:CHS_Frame.Hippota_Nestor.2009.

Freedman, D. G. 1998. "Sokrates: The Athenian Oracle of Plato's Imagination." Ph.D. diss., Harvard University.

Friis Johansen, K. 1967. *The Iliad in Early Greek Art.* Copenhagen.

Gieben, J. C., et al. 1923–. *Supplementum Epigraphicum Graecum.* Amsterdam.

Gill, D. 1974. "Trapezomata: A Neglected Aspect of Greek Sacrifice." *Harvard Theological Review* 67:117–137.

Goldhill, S. 1984. *Language, Sexuality, Narrative: The Oresteia.* Cambridge.

Gresseth, G. K. 1975. "The Gilgamesh Epic and Homer." *Classical Journal* 70:1–18.

Gresseth, G. K. 1979. "The Odyssey and the Nalopākhyāna." *Transactions of the American Philological Association* 109:63–85.

Griffiths, A. 1985. "Patroklos the Ram." *Bulletin of the Institute for Classical Studies* 32:49–50.

Griffiths, A. 1989. "Patroklos the Ram (Again)." *Bulletin of the Institute for Classical Studies* 36:139.

Grossardt, P. 2006. *Einführung, Übersetzung und Kommentar zum* Heroikos *von Flavius Philostrat* I/II. Schweizerische Beiträge zur Altertumswissenschaft 33. Basel.

Hadzisteliou-Price, T. 1973. "Hero-Cult and Homer." *Historia* 22:129–144.

Hallett, J. P. 1970. "'Over Troubled Waters': The Meaning of the Title *Pontifex.*" *Transactions of the American Philological Association* 101:219–227.

Hansen, W. F. 1977. "Odysseus' Last Journey." *Quaderni Urbinati di Cultura Classica* 24:27–48.

Harlan, L. 2003. *The Goddesses' Henchmen: Gender in Indian Hero Worship.* New York.

Hatto, A. T., ed. 1980. *Traditions of Heroic and Epic Poetry*. London.

Häusle, H. 1979. *Einfache und frühe Formen des griechischen Epigramms*. Commentationes Aenipontanae 25. Innsbruck.

Hendel, R. S. 1987a. *The Epic of the Patriarch: The Jacob Cycle and the Narrative Traditions of Canaan and Israel*. Harvard Semitic Monographs 42. Atlanta.

Hendel, R. S. 1987b. "Of Demigods and the Deluge: Toward an Interpretation of *Genesis* 6:1–4." *Journal of Biblical Literature* 106:13–26.

Henrichs, A. 1978. "Greek Maenadism from Olympias to Messalina." *Harvard Studies in Classical Philology* 82:121–169.

Henrichs, A. 1981. "Human Sacrifice in Greek Religion: Three Case Studies." *Le sacrifice dans l'antiquité*. Edited by J. Rudhardt and O. Reverdin. 195–235. Entretiens sur l'antiquité classique 27. Vandoevres–Genève.

Henrichs, A. 1983. "The 'Sobriety' of Oedipus: Sophocles *OC* 100 Misunderstood." *Harvard Studies in Classical Philology* 87:87–100.

Henrichs, A. 1984. "The Eumenides and Wineless Libations in the Derveni Papyrus." *Atti del XVII Congresso Internazionale di Papirologia* (Napoli, 19–26 maggio 1983). 2:255–268. Naples.

Henrichs, A. 1994. "Anonymity and Polarity: Unknown Gods and Nameless Altars at the Areopagos." *Illinois Classical Studies* 19 (Studies in Honor of Miroslav Marcovich):27–58.

Henrichs, A. 1996. "Dancing in Athens, Dancing in Delos: Some Patterns of Choral Projection in Euripides." *Philologus* 140:48–62.

Henry, P. L. 1982. "Furor Heroicus." *Zeitschrift für celtische Philologie* 39:235–242.

Hiltebeitel, A. 1976. *The Ritual of Battle: Krishna in the Mahābhārata*. Ithaca NY. (Reprinted 1990, Albany NY.)

Irigoin, J. 1952. *Histoire du texte de Pindare*. Paris.

Jacoby, F. 1923–58. *Die Fragmente der griechischen Historiker*. 3 vols. Berlin.

Jacopin, P.-Y. 1988. "Anthropological Dialectics: Yukuna Ritual as Defensive Strategy." *Schweizerische Amerikanisten-Gesellschaft, Bulletin* 52:35–46.

Jakobson, R. 1931. "Über die phonologischen Sprachbünde." Jakobson 1971:137–143.

Jakobson, R. 1949. "On the Theory of Phonological Affinities between Languages." Jakobson 1990:202–213. (For the date of the original article, see 1990:544 under Jakobson 1949b.)

Jakobson, R. 1952. "Studies in Comparative Slavic Metrics." *Oxford Slavonic Papers* 3:21–66. (Reprinted in Jakobson 1966:414–463.)

Jakobson, R. 1957. *Shifters, Verbal Categories, and the Russian Verb*. Cambridge MA. (Reprinted in Jakobson 1971:130–147.)

Jakobson, R. 1966. *Selected Writings* IV. The Hague.

Jakobson, R. 1971. *Selected Writings* I. 2nd ed. Berlin, New York, and Amsterdam.

Jakobson, R. 1990. *On Language*. Edited by L. R. Waugh and M. Monville-Burston. Cambridge MA.

Jameson, M. H., D. R. Jordon, and R. D. Kotansky. 1993. *A lex sacra from Selinous.* Greek, Roman, and Byzantine Studies Monographs 11. Durham NC.

Janko, R. 1982. *Homer, Hesiod and the Hymns: Diachronic Development in Epic Diction.* Cambridge.

Janko, R. 1992. *The Iliad: A Commentary.* Vol. 4, *Books 13–16.* Cambridge.

Janko, R. 1998. "The Homeric Poems as Oral Dictated Texts." *Classical Quarterly* n.s. 48:1–13.

Jasanoff, J., H. C. Melchert, and L. Oliver, eds. 1998. *Mír Curad: Studies in Honor of Calvert Watkins.* Innsbruck.

Jeffreys, E., and M. Jeffreys. 1986. "The Oral Background of Byzantine Popular Poetry." *Oral Tradition* 1:504–547.

Jones, B. 2010. "Relative Chronology within (an) Oral Tradition." *Classical Journal* 105:289–318.

Kearns, E. 1989. *The Heroes of Attica.* London.

Kierkegaard, S. 1843 [1983]. *Fear and Trembling. Repetition.* Translated, with introduction and notes, by H. V. Hong and E. H. Hong. Princeton.

Kinsella, T., trans. 1969. *The Táin.* Dublin.

Kirk, G. S. 1962. *The Songs of Homer.* Cambridge.

Knox, B. M. W. 1952. "The Lion in the House." *Classical Philology* 47:17–25. (Reprinted in Knox 1979:27–38.)

Knox, B. M. W. 1954. "Why is Oedipus called *Tyrannos?*" *Classical Journal* 50:97–102. (Reprinted in Knox 1979:87–95.)

Knox, B. M. W. 1979. *Word and Action: Essays on the Ancient Theater.* Baltimore.

Koenen, L. 1994. "Cyclic Destruction in Hesiod and the Catalogue of Women." *Transactions of the American Philological Association* 124:1–34.

Koller, H. 1957. "Hypokrisis und Hypokrites." *Museum Helveticum* 14:100–107.

Kowalzig, B. 2007. *Singing for the Gods: Performances of Myth and Ritual in Archaic and Classical Greece.* Oxford.

Kümmel, H. M. 1967. *Ersatzrituale für den hethitischen König.* Wiesbaden.

Kurke, L. 1991. *The Traffic in Praise: Pindar and the Poetics of Social Economy.* Ithaca NY.

Lamberterie, C. de. 1997. "Milman Parry et Antoine Meillet." Létoublon 1997:9–22. (Translated as "Milman Parry and Antoine Meillet" in Loraux, Nagy, and Slatkin 2001:409–421.)

Lang, C., ed. 1881. *Cornuti theologiae Graecae compendium.* Leipzig.

Larson, J. 1995. *Greek Heroine Cults.* Madison WI.

Larson, J. 2009. "The Singularity of Herakles." Albersmeier 2009:32–38.

Leach, E. R. 1982. "Critical Introduction" to M. I. Steblin-Kamenskij, *Myth.* Translated by M. P. Coote. 1–20. Ann Arbor.

Lessing, G. E. 1766. *Laokoon, oder Über die Grenzen der Mahlerey und Poesie.* (Translated by E. A. McCormick as *Laocoön: An Essay on the Limits of Painting and Poetry.* 1962. Rev. ed. 1984. Baltimore.)

Létoublon, F., ed. 1997. *Hommage à Milman Parry: le style formulaire de l'épopée et la théorie de l'oralité poétique.* Amsterdam.

Leutsch, E. L. von, and F. G. Schneidewin, eds. 1839–1851. *Corpus Paroemiographorum Graecorum.* Göttingen.

Levaniouk, O. 2011. *Eve of the Festival: Making Myth in Odyssey 19.* Hellenic Studies 46. Cambridge MA and Washington DC. Available at http://nrs.harvard.edu/urn-3:hul. ebook:CHS_Levaniouk.Eve_of_the_Festival.2011.

Levaniouk, O. 2012. "Sky-Blue Flower: Songs of the Bride in Modern Russia and Ancient Greece." Bers et al. 2012.

Liddell, H. G., R. Scott, and H. S. Jones. 1940. *A Greek-English Lexicon.* 9th ed. Oxford.

Lincoln, B. 1975. "Homeric Lyssa: Wolfish Rage." *Indogermanische Forschungen* 80:98–105.

Lincoln, B. 1981. "On the Imagery of Paradise." *Indogermanische Forschungen* 85:151–164.

Lloyd, A. B. 1976. *Herodotus, Book II,* vol. 2. Leiden.

Lloyd-Jones, H. 1983. *The Justice of Zeus.* 2nd ed. Berkeley.

Loraux, N. 1982. "Donc Socrate est immortel." *Le Temps de la Réflexion* 3:19–46. (Recast as "Therefore Socrates Is Immortal" in Loraux 1995:145–167.)

Loraux, N. 1995. *The Experiences of Tiresias: The Feminine and the Greek Man.* Translated by P. Wissing. Princeton.

Loraux, N., G. Nagy, and L. Slatkin, eds. 2001. *Antiquities.* Translated by Arthur Goldhammer and others. Postwar French Thought vol. 3, ed. R. Naddaff. New York.

Lord, A. B. 1960. *The Singer of Tales.* Harvard Studies in Comparative Literature 24. Cambridge MA. (See also Lord 2000.)

Lord, A. B. 1991. *Epic Singers and Oral Tradition.* Ithaca NY.

Lord, A. B. 1995. *The Singer Resumes the Tale.* Edited by M. L. Lord. Ithaca NY.

Lord, A. B. 2000. *The Singer of Tales.* 2nd ed. Edited, with new introduction, by S. Mitchell and G. Nagy. Cambridge MA.

Lowenstam, S. 1981. *The Death of Patroklos: A Study in Typology.* Beiträge zur Klassischen Philologie 133. Königstein/Ts.

Lowenstam, S. 1997. "Talking Vases: The Relationship between the Homeric Poems and Archaic Representations of Epic Myth." *Transactions of the American Philological Association* 127:21–76.

Lowenstam, S. 2008. *As Witnessed by Images: The Trojan War Tradition in Greek and Etruscan Art.* Baltimore.

Martin, R. P. 1989. *The Language of Heroes: Speech and Performance in the Iliad.* Ithaca NY. Available at http://nrs.harvard.edu/urn-3:hul.ebook:CHS_Martin.The_Language_of_ Heroes.1989.

Martin, R. P. 1993. "Telemachus and the Last Hero Song." *Colby Quarterly* 29:222–240.

Martin, R. P. 2000. "Synchronic Aspects of Homeric Performance: The Evidence of the *Hymn to Apollo.*" *Una nueva visión de la cultura griega antigua hacia el fin del milenio.* Edited by A. M. González de Tobia. 403–432. La Plata.

Mason, H. J. 2004. "Sappho's Apples." *Metamorphic Reflections: Essays Presented to Ben*

Hijmans at His 75th Birthday. Edited by M. Zimmerman and R. Van Der Paardt. 243–253. Leuven.

Mayer, K. 1996. "Helen and the *Dios Boulē.*" *American Journal of Philology* 117:1–15.

McGrath, K. 2004. *The Sanskrit Hero: Karna in Epic Mahābhārata.* Leiden.

McLuhan, M. 1964. *Understanding Media: The Extensions of Man.* New York.

Meillet, A. 1921–1936. *Linguistique historique et linguistique générale.* 2 vols. Paris.

Meillet, A. 1925. *La méthode comparative en linguistique historique.* Paris.

Mellink, M. J., ed. 1986. *Troy and the Trojan War.* Bryn Mawr PA.

Mellink, M. J. 1995. "Homer, Lycia, and Lukka." Carter and Morris 1995:33–43.

Merkelbach, R., and M. L. West, eds. 1967. *Fragmenta Hesiodea.* Oxford.

Michelini, A. 1978. ""ΥΒΡΙΣ and Plants." *Harvard Studies in Classical Philology* 82:85–44.

Mitchell, S. 1991. *Heroic Sagas and Ballads.* Ithaca NY.

Mitchell, S., and G. Nagy, eds. 2000. New introduction to Lord, *Singer of Tales.* Lord 2000:vii–xxix.

Moon, W. G., ed. 1983. *Ancient Greek Art and Iconography.* Madison WI.

Muellner, L. 1996. *The Anger of Achilles: Mēnis in Greek Epic.* Ithaca NY.

Nagy, G. 1972. Introduction, Parts I and II, and Conclusions. *Greek: A Survey of Recent Work.* F. W. Householder and G. Nagy. 15–72. Janua Linguarum Series Practica 211. The Hague.

Nagy, G. 1974. *Comparative Studies in Greek and Indic Meter.* Harvard Studies in Comparative Literature 33. Cambridge MA.

Nagy, G. 1979. *The Best of the Achaeans: Concepts of the Hero in Archaic Greek Poetry.* Baltimore. (See Nagy 1999.)

Nagy, G. 1982. "Translation beyond Betrayal: Some Observations on the *Bacchae.*" *Harvard Advocate* 115(4):84–86.

Nagy, G. 1983a. "*Sēma* and *Noēsis:* Some Illustrations." *Arethusa* 16:35–55. (Recast as *GM* = Nagy 1990b, ch. 8.)

Nagy, G. 1983b. "On the Death of Sarpedon." *Approaches to Homer.* Edited by C. A. Rubino and C. W. Shelmerdine. 189–217. Austin TX. (Recast as *GM* = Nagy 1990b, ch. 5.)

Nagy, G. 1985. "Theognis and Megara: A Poet's Vision of His City." *Theognis of Megara: Poetry and the Polis.* Edited by T. J. Figueira and G. Nagy. 22–81. Baltimore. Available at http://nrs.harvard.edu/urn-3:hlnc.essay:Nagy.Theognis_and_Megara.1985. (Corrigenda: at §77, "Pausanias 1.5.3" should be "Pausanias 1.5.4.")

Nagy, G. 1987. "The Sign of Protesilaos." *METIS: Revue d'anthropologie du monde grec ancien* 2:207–213.

Nagy, G. 1990a. *Pindar's Homer: The Lyric Possession of an Epic Past.* Baltimore. Available at http://www.press.jhu.edu/books/nagy/PHTL/toc.html.

Nagy, G. 1990b. *Greek Mythology and Poetics.* Ithaca NY. (Revised ed. 1992.) Available at http://nrs.harvard.edu/urn-3:hul.ebook:CHS_Nagy.Greek_Mythology_and_ Poetics.1990. (Corrigenda: on p. 203 between "same line)" and "specified," insert "of the marital bed; similarly, she 'recognizes' (ἀναγνούσῃ xix 250) as *sēmata* (same line) the clothes . . ." (in the present printed version, the reference to the marital bed as *sēmata* at *Odyssey* xxiii 206 is distorted by a mistaken omission of the wording that needs to be restored here: by haplography, the mention of the marital bed is omitted, and this omission distorts the point being made about the clothes and brooch of Odysseus as *sēmata* in their own right at xix 250). On p. 214n42, "Pausanias 9.44.44" should be 8.44.4. GN.)

Nagy, G. 1992. Introduction. Homer. *The Iliad*. v–xxi. Translated by R. Fitzgerald. Everyman's Library no. 60. New York.

Nagy, G. 1993. "Alcaeus in Sacred Space." *Tradizione e innovazione nella cultura greca da Omero all' età ellenistica: Scritti in onore di Bruno Gentili*. Edited by R. Pretagostini. 221–225. Rome.

Nagy, G. 1994. "The Name of Apollo: Etymology and Essence." Solomon 1994:3–7. (Rewritten as Nagy 2004a, ch. 7.)

Nagy, G. 1994/95. "Transformations of Choral Lyric Traditions in the Context of Athenian State Theater." *Arion* 3:41–55. Available at http://nrs.harvard.edu/urn-3:hlnc.essay:Nagy. Transformations_of_Choral_Lyric_Traditions.1995.

Nagy, G. 1996a. *Poetry as Performance: Homer and Beyond*. Cambridge. Available at http://nrs.harvard.edu/urn-3:hul.ebook:CHS_Nagy.Poetry_as_Performance.1996.

Nagy, G. 1996b. *Homeric Questions*. Austin TX. Available at http://nrs.harvard.edu/urn-3:hul.ebook:CHS_Nagy.Homeric_Questions.1996.

Nagy, G. 1998. "The Library of Pergamon as a Classical Model." *Pergamon: Citadel of the Gods*. Edited by H. Koester. 185–232. Harvard Theological Studies 46. Philadelphia. Available at http://nrs.harvard.edu/urn-3:hlnc.essay:Nagy.The_Library_of_Pergamon_as_a_Classical_Model.1998.

Nagy, G. 1999. *The Best of the Achaeans: Concepts of the Hero in Archaic Greek Poetry*. Rev. ed. with new intro. Baltimore. Available at http://www.press.jhu.edu/books/nagy/BofATL/toc.html.

Nagy, G. 1999a. "Epic as Genre." Beissinger, Tylus, and Wofford 1999:21–32.

Nagy, G. 1999b. "As the World Runs Out of Breath: Metaphorical Perspectives on the Heavens and the Atmosphere in the Ancient World." Conway, Keniston, and Marx 1999:37–50.

Nagy, G. 1999c. Review of Vielle 1996. *Classical Review* 49:279–280.

Nagy, G. 1999d. Preface to 2nd ed. of Nagy 1979.

Nagy, G. 2000. "'Dream of a Shade': Refractions of Epic Vision in Pindar's *Pythian* 8 and Aeschylus' *Seven against Thebes*." *Harvard Studies in Classical Philology* 100:97–118. Available at http://nrs.harvard.edu/urn-3:hlnc.essay:Nagy.Dream_of_a_Shade_Refractions_of_Epic_Vision.2000.

Nagy, G. 2001a. "The Sign of the Hero: A Prologue." Berenson Maclean and Aitken 2001:xv–xxxv. Available at http://nrs.harvard.edu/urn-3:hlnc.essay:Nagy.The_Sign_of_the_Hero.2001.

Nagy, G. 2001b. "Reading Bakhtin Reading the Classics: An Epic Fate for Conveyors of the Heroic Past." *Bakhtin and the Classics.* Edited by R. B. Branham. 71–96. Evanston IL. Available at http://nrs.harvard.edu/urn-3:hlnc.essay:Nagy.Reading_Bakhtin_Reading_the_Classics.2002.

Nagy, G. 2001c. "Homère comme modèle classique pour la bibliothèque antique: les métaphores du corpus et du cosmos." *Des Alexandries.* Vol. 1: *Du livre au texte.* Edited by L. Giard and Ch. Jacob. 149–161. Paris.

Nagy, G. 2001d. "Éléments orphiques chez Homère." *Kernos* 14:1–9.

Nagy, G. 2002a. *Plato's Rhapsody and Homer's Music: The Poetics of the Panathenaic Festival in Classical Athens.* Cambridge MA and Athens. Available at http://nrs.harvard.edu/urn-3:hul.ebook:CHS_Nagy.Platos_Rhapsody_and_Homers_Music.2002.

Nagy, G. 2002b. "Can Myth Be Saved?" *Myth: A New Symposium.* Edited by G. Schrempp and W. Hansen. 240–248. Bloomington IN.

Nagy, G. 2003. *Homeric Responses.* Austin TX. Available at http://nrs.harvard.edu/urn-3:hul.ebook:CHS_Nagy.Homeric_Responses.2003.

Nagy, G. 2004a. *Homer's Text and Language.* Urbana and Chicago. Available at http://nrs.harvard.edu/urn-3:hul.ebook:CHS_Nagy.Homers_Text_and_Language.2004.

Nagy, G. 2004b. "L'aède épique en auteur: la tradition des Vies d'Homère." *Identités d'auteur dans l'Antiquité et la tradition européenne.* Edited by C. Calame and R. Chartier. 41–67. Grenoble.

Nagy, G. 2005a. "The Epic Hero." *A Companion to Ancient Epic.* Edited by J. M. Foley. 71–89. Oxford.

Nagy, G. 2005b. "An Apobatic Moment for Achilles as Athlete at the Festival of the Panathenaia." *Imeros* 5:311–317. (See Nagy 2009b.)

Nagy, G. 2006. "The Epic Hero." Available at http://nrs.harvard.edu/urn-3:hlnc.essay:Nagy.The_Epic_Hero.2005. (Fuller version, with notes, of Nagy 2005a.)

Nagy, G. 2007a. "Lyric and Greek Myth." *The Cambridge Companion to Greek Mythology.* Edited by R. D. Woodard. 19–51. Cambridge. Available at http://nrs.harvard.edu/urn-3:hlnc.essay:Nagy.Lyric_and_Greek_Myth.2007.

Nagy, G. 2007b. "Homer and Greek Myth." *The Cambridge Companion to Greek Mythology.* Edited by R. D. Woodard. 52–82. Cambridge. Updated version available at http://nrs.harvard.edu/urn-3:hlnc.essay:Nagy.Homer_and_Greek_Myth.2007.

Nagy, G. 2007c. "Did Sappho and Alcaeus Ever Meet?" *Literatur und Religion: Wege zu einer mythisch–rituellen Poetik bei den Griechen.* Edited by A. Bierl, R. Lämmle, and K. Wesselmann. 1:211–269. MythosEikonPoiesis 1.1. Berlin and New York. Available at http://nrs.harvard.edu/urn-3:hlnc.essay:Nagy.Did_Sappho_and_Alcaeus_Ever_Meet.2007.

Nagy, G. 2008a. *Greek: An Updating of a Survey of Recent Work.* Cambridge MA and Washington DC. Available at http://nrs.harvard.edu/urn-3:hul.ebook:CHS_Nagy.Greek_an_Updating.2008. (Updating of Nagy 1972, using original page numbering.)

Nagy, G. 2008b. "Convergences and Divergences between God and Hero in the Mnesiepes

Inscription of Paros." *Archilochus and His Age.* Edited by D. Katsonopoulou, I. Petropoulos, and S. Katsarou. 2:259–265. Athens.

Nagy, G. 2009. *Homer the Classic.* Hellenic Studies 36. Cambridge MA and Washington DC. Available at http://nrs.harvard.edu/urn-3:hul.ebook:CHS_Nagy.Homer_the_Classic.2008.

Nagy, G. 2009a. "Hesiod and the Ancient Biographical Traditions." *The Brill Companion to Hesiod.* Edited by F. Montanari, A. Rengakos, and Ch. Tsagalis. 271–311. Leiden. Available at http://nrs.harvard.edu/urn-3:hlnc.essay:Nagy.Hesiod_and_the_Ancient_Biographical_Traditions.2005.

Nagy, G. 2009b. "An Apobatic Moment for Achilles as Athlete at the Festival of the Panathenaia." Available at http://nrs.harvard.edu/urn-3:hlnc.essay:Nagy.An_Apobatic_Moment_for_Achilles.2005. (Fuller version of Nagy 2005b.)

Nagy, G. 2009c. "The Fragmentary Muse and the Poetics of Refraction in Sappho, Sophocles, Offenbach." *Theater des Fragments: Performative Strategien im Theater zwischen Antike und Postmoderne.* Edited by A. Bierl, G. Siegmund, Ch. Meneghetti, C. Schuster. 69–102. Bielefeld. Online and fuller version: http://nrs.harvard.edu/urn-3:hlnc.essay:Nagy.The_Fragmentary_Muse_and_the_Poetics_of_Refraction.2009.

Nagy, G. 2010. *Homer the Preclassic.* Berkeley and Los Angeles. Available at http://nrs.harvard.edu/urn-3:hul.ebook:CHS_Nagy.Homer_the_Preclassic.2009.

Nagy, G. 2010a. "The 'New Sappho' Reconsidered in the Light of the Athenian Reception of Sappho." *The New Sappho on Old Age: Textual and Philosophical Issues.* Edited by E. Greene and M. Skinner. 176–199. Cambridge MA and Washington DC. Available at http://nrs.harvard.edu/urn-3:hlnc.essay:Nagy.The_New_Sappho_Reconsidered.2011.

Nagy, G. 2010b. "Ancient Greek Elegy." *The Oxford Handbook of the Elegy.* Edited by K. Weisman. 13–45. Oxford. Available at http://nrs.harvard.edu/urn-3:hlnc.essay:Nagy.Ancient_Greek_Elegy.2010.

Nagy, G. 2010c. "The Meaning of *homoios* (ὁμοῖος) in Verse 27 of the Hesiodic *Theogony* and Elsewhere." *Allusion, Authority, and Truth: Critical Perspectives on Greek Poetic and Rhetorical Praxis.* Edited by P. Mitsis and Ch. Tsagalis. 153–167. Trends in Classics 7. Berlin and New York.

Nagy, G. 2010d. Review of West 2007. *Classical Review* 60:333–338. (See Nagy 2012a for a revised and expanded edition.)

Nagy, G. 2010e. "The Subjectivity of Fear as Reflected in Ancient Greek Wording." *Dialogues* 5:29–45. Available at http://nrs.harvard.edu/urn-3:hlnc.essay:Nagy.The_Subjectivity_of_Fear.2010. (Online and fuller version in Nagy 2012a. *Short Writings* I.)

Nagy, G. 2011a. "Asopos and His Multiple Daughters: Traces of Preclassical Epic in the Aeginetan Odes of Pindar." *Aegina: Contexts for Choral Lyric Poetry: Myth, History, and Identity in the Fifth Century BC.* Edited by D. Fearn. 41–78. Oxford.

Nagy, G. 2011b. "A Second Look at the Poetics of Reenactment in *Ode* 13 of Bacchylides." *Archaic and Classical Choral Song: Performance, Politics and Dissemination.* Edited by L. Athanassaki and E. L. Bowie. 173–206. Berlin.

Nagy, G. 2011c. "Diachrony and the Case of Aesop." Classics@ Issue 9: Defense Mechanisms in Interdisciplinary Approaches to Classical Studies and Beyond. Available at http://nrs.harvard.edu/urn-3:hlnc.essay:Nagy.Diachrony_and_the_Case_of_Aesop.2011.

Nagy, G. 2011d. "The Earliest Phases in the Reception of the Homeric Hymns." *The Homeric Hymns: Interpretative Essays*. Edited by A. Faulkner. 280–333. Oxford. Available at http://nrs.harvard.edu/urn-3:hlnc.essay:Nagy.The_Earliest_Phases_in_the_Reception_of_the_Homeric_Hymns.2011.

Nagy, G. 2012a. *Short Writings*. 2 vols. Available at http://nrs.harvard.edu/urn-3:hul.ebook:CHS_Nagy.Short_Writings_v1.2012 and http://nrs.harvard.edu/urn-3:hul.ebook:CHS_Nagy.Short_Writings_v2.2012.

Nagy, G. 2012b. "Signs of Hero Cult in Homeric Poetry." *Homeric Contexts: Neoanalysis and the Interpretation of Homeric Poetry*. Edited by F. Montanari, A. Rengakos, and Ch. Tsagalis. 27–71. Trends in Classics Supplementary Vol. 12. Berlin and Boston.

Nagy, J. F. 1985. *The Wisdom of the Outlaw: The Boyhood Deeds of Finn in Gaelic Narrative Tradition*. Los Angeles and Berkeley.

Nagy, J. F. 1986. "Orality in Medieval Irish Literature: An Overview." *Oral Tradition* 1:272–301.

Nagy, J. F. 1997a. *Conversing with Angels and Ancients: Literary Myths of Medieval Ireland*. Ithaca NY.

Nagy, J. F. 1997b. "How the Táin Was Lost." *Zeitschrift für Celtische Philologie* 49/50:603–609.

Nietzsche, F. 1885. *Werke: Kritische Gesamtausgabe* (Nachgelassene Fragmente, Herbst 1884–Herbst 1885), vol. 7, part 3, p. 412, 41(4). Edited by G. Colli and M. Montinari. Berlin.

Nilsson, M. P. 1906. *Griechische Feste*. Leipzig.

Obbink, D., ed. 1996. *Philodemus: On Piety*. Pt. 1. Oxford.

Ó Cathasaigh, T. 1977. *The Heroic Biography of Cormac mac Airt*. Dublin.

Okpewho, I. 1979. *The Epic in Africa: Toward a Poetics of the Oral Performance*. New York.

O'Rahilly, C., ed. and trans. 1967. *Táin Bó Cúailnge from the Book of Leinster*. Dublin.

O'Rahilly, C., ed. and trans. 1976. *Táin Bó Cúailnge: Recension I*. Dublin.

Pache, C. O. 2004. *Baby and Child Heroes in Ancient Greece*. Urbana and Chicago.

Pache, C. O. 2009. "The Hero beyond Himself: Heroic Death in Ancient Greek Poetry and Art." Albersmeier 2009:88–107.

Page, D. L. 1962. *Poetae Melici Graeci*. Oxford.

Parpola, S. 1970–1983. *Letters from Assyrian Scholars to the Kings Esarhaddon and Assurbanipal*. 2 vols. Neukirchen-Vluyn.

Parry, A., ed. 1971. *The Making of Homeric Verse: The Collected Papers of Milman Parry*. Oxford.

Patton, K. C. 2009. *Religion of the Gods: Ritual, Paradox, and Reflexivity*. Oxford.

Payne, M. 1991. "Alexander the Great: Myth, the Polis, and Afterward." *Myth and the Polis*. Edited by D. C. Pozzi and J. M. Wickersham. 164–181. Ithaca NY.

Pelliccia, H. 2010–2011. "Unlocking *Aeneid* 6.460: Plautus' *Amphitryon*,

Euripides' *Protesilaus* and the Referents of Callimachus' *Coma*." *Classical Journal* 106:149–221.

Pfister, F. 1909–1912. *Der Reliquienkult im Altertum*. 2 vols. Giessen.

Pickard-Cambridge, A. W. 1989. *Dramatic Festivals of Athens*. 2nd ed. Revised by D. M. Lewis and J. Gould. Oxford

Pinney, G. F. 1983. "Achilles Lord of Scythia." *Moon* 1983:127–146.

Power, T. 2010. *The Culture of Kitharōidia*. Hellenic Studies 15. Cambridge MA and Washington DC. Available at http://nrs.harvard.edu/urn-3:hul.ebook:CHS_Power. The_Culture_of_Kitharoidia.2010.

Propp, V. Ja. 1975. "The Russian Folk Lyric." *Down along the Mother Volga: An Anthology of Russian Folk Lyrics*. Translated and edited by R. Reeder. 1–73. Philadelphia. (Introductory essay originally published in Russian in 1961.)

Puhvel, J. 1987. *Comparative Mythology*. Baltimore.

Radloff, W. 1885. *Proben der Volksliteratur der nördlichen türkischen Stämme V: Der Dialekt der Kara-Kirgisen*. St. Petersburg.

Radloff, W. 1990. Preface of Radloff 1885. Translated by G. B. Sherman and A. B. Davis. *Oral Tradition* 5:73–90.

Rees, A., and B. Rees. 1961. *Celtic Heritage: Ancient Tradition in Ireland and Wales*. London.

Rees, D. S. 1986. "The Mediterranean Shell Purple-Dye Industry." *American Journal of Archaeology* 90:183.

Reichl, K. 1992. *Turkic Oral Epic Poetry: Traditions, Forms, Poetic Structure*. New York.

Reichl, K. 2000. *Singing the Past: Turkic and Medieval Poetry*. Ithaca NY.

Reynolds, D. F. 1995. *Heroic Poets, Poetic Heroes: An Ethnography of Performance in an Arabic Oral Epic Tradition*. Ithaca NY.

Rodin, B. P. 2009. "Pindaric Epinikion and the Evolution of Poetic Genres in Archaic Greece." Ph.D. diss., University of California, Berkeley.

Roller, L. E. 1981a. "Funeral Games in Greek Art." *American Journal of Archaeology* 85:107–119.

Roller, L. E. 1981b. "Funeral Games for Historical Persons." *Stadion* 7:1–17.

Rousseau, P. 1992. "Fragments d'un commentaire antique du récit de la course des chars dans le XXIIIe Chant de l'*Iliade*." *Philologus* 136:158–180.

Rousseau, P. 1996. "Dios d' eteleieto boulē: Destin des héros et dessein de Zeus dans l'intrigue de l'*Iliade*." Doctorat d'Etat thesis, Université Charles de Gaulle—Lille III.

Rusten, J. 1983. "*Geitōn Hērōs*: Pindar's Prayer to Heracles (*N*. 7.86–101) and Popular Religion." *Harvard Studies in Classical Philology* 87:289–297.

Rutherford, I. 2000. "Theoria and Darśan: Pilgrimage and Vision in Greece and India." *Classical Quarterly* 50:133–146.

Salapata, G. 2011. "The Heroic Cult of Agamemnon." *Electra* 1. Available at http://electra.lis. upatras.gr/index.php/electra/article/view/29/35.

Saussure, F. de. 1916. *Cours de linguistique générale*. Critical ed. prepared by T. de Mauro. 1972. Paris.

Saussure, F. de. 1966. *Course in General Linguistics*. Translated and with introduction by W. Baskin. New York.

Sax, W. S. 1999. "Worshipping Epic Villains: A Kaurava Cult in the Central Himalayas." Beissinger, Tylus, and Wofford 1999:169–186.

Sax, W. S. 2002. *Dancing the Self: Personhood and Performance in the Pāndav Līlā of Garhwal*. New York.

Scanlon, T. F. 2004. "Homer, the Olympics, and the Heroic Ethos." *The Olympic Games in Antiquity: 'Bring Forth Rain and Bear Fruit.'* Edited by M. Kaila et al. 61–91. Athens.

Schmitt, R. 1967. *Dichtung und Dichtersprache in indogermanischer Zeit*. Wiesbaden.

Schultz, P. 2007. "The Iconography of the Athenian *apobates* Race: Origins, Meanings, Transformations." *The Panathenaic Games*. Edited by A. Choremi and O. Palagia. 59–72. Oxford.

Schwartz, M. 2003. "Encryptions in the Gathas: Zarathustra's Variations on the Theme of Bliss." *Religious Themes and Texts of Pre-Islamic Iran and Central Asia: Studies in Honour of Gherardo Gnoli on the Occasion of His 65th Birthday*. Edited by C. Cereti, M. Maggi, and E. Provasi. 375–390. Wiesbaden.

Scodel, R. 1982. "The Achaean Wall and the Myth of Destruction." *Harvard Studies in Classical Philology* 86:33–50.

Seaford, R. 1994. *Reciprocity and Ritual: Homer and Tragedy in the Developing City-State*. Oxford.

Seaford, R., trans. 1996. Euripides, *Bacchae*. With introduction and commentary by R. Seaford. Warminster.

Shapiro, H. A. 1984. "Herakles and Kyknos." *American Journal of Archaeology* 88:523–529.

Shear, J. L. 2001. "Polis and Panathenaia: The History and Development of Athena's Festival." Ph.D. diss., University of Pennsylvania.

Sinos, D. S. 1980. *Achilles, Patroklos, and the Meaning of Philos*. Innsbrucker Beiträge zur Sprachwissenschaft 29. Innsbruck.

Sjoestedt, M.-L. 1940. *Dieux et héros des Celtes*. Paris.

Skjærvø, P. O. 1998a. "Eastern Iranian Epic Traditions I: Siyāvash and Kunāla." Jasanoff, Melchert, and Oliver 1998:645–658.

Skjærvø, P. O. 1998b. "Eastern Iranian Epic Traditions II: Rostam and Bhīṣma." *Acta Orientalia Academiae Scientiarum Hungaricae* 51:159–170.

Slatkin, L. 1986. "Oedipus at Colonus: Exile and Integration." *Greek Tragedy and Political Theory*. Edited by J. P. Euben. 210–221. Berkeley and Los Angeles.

Slatkin, L. 1987. "Genre and Generation in the *Odyssey*." *METIS: Revue d'anthropologie du monde grec ancien* 2:259–268.

Slatkin, L. 1991. *The Power of Thetis: Allusion and Interpretation in the Iliad*. Berkeley and Los Angeles.

Slatkin, L. 2011. *The Power of Thetis and Selected Essays*. Hellenic Studies 16. Cambridge MA and Washington DC. Available at http://nrs.harvard.edu/urn-3:hul.ebook:CHS_Slatkin. The_Power_of_Thetis_and_Selected_Essays.2011.

Smith, J. D. 1980. "Old Indian: The Two Sanskrit Epics." Hatto 1980:48–78.

Smith, J. D. 1989. "Scapegoats of the Gods: The Ideology of the Indian Epics." Blackburn, Claus, Flueckiger, and Wadley 1989:176–194.

Smith, J. D. 1990. "Worlds Apart: Orality, Literacy, and the Rajasthani Folk-*Mahābhārata*." *Oral Tradition* 5:3–19.

Solomon, J., ed. 1994. *Apollo: Origins and Influences*. Tucson AZ.

Stähler, K. P. 1967. *Grab und Psyche des Patroklos: Ein schwarzfiguriges Vasenbild*. Münster.

Szegedy-Maszák, A. 1981. *The Nomoi of Theophrastus*. New York.

Tambiah, S. J. 1985. *Culture, Thought, and Social Action*. Cambridge MA.

Tarenzi, V. 2005. "Patroclo ΘΕΡΑΠΩΝ." *Quaderni Urbinati di Cultura Classica* 80:25–38.

Theiler, W. 1962. "*Ilias* und *Odyssee* in der Verflechtung ihres Entstehens." *Museum Helveticum* 19:1–27.

Tischler, J. 1993. *Hethitisches Etymologisches Glossar*, Teil III, Lieferung 9. Innsbruck. (Pp. 207–212 deal with the words *tarpašša-* and *tarpalli-/tarpanalli-*.)

Tsagalis, C. 2004. *Epic Grief: Personal Laments in Homer's Iliad*. Berlin.

Tzifopoulos, Y. 2010. *Paradise Earned: The Bacchic-Orphic Gold Lamellae of Crete*. Hellenic Studies 23. Cambridge MA and Washington DC.

Van Brock, N. 1959. "Substitution rituelle." *Revue Hittite et Asianique* 65:117–146.

Van Brock, N. 1961. *Recherches sur le vocabulaire médical du grec ancien*. Paris.

Van Nortwick, T. 1992. *Somewhere I Have Never Travelled: The Second Self and the Hero's Journey in Ancient Epic*. New York.

Vendryes, J. 1937. "Antoine Meillet." *Bulletin de la Société de Linguistique de Paris* 38:1–42.

Vermeule, E. 1965. "The Vengeance of Achilles: The Dragging of Hektor at Troy." *Bulletin of the Museum of Fine Arts, Boston* 63:34–52.

Vermeule, E. 1986. "Priam's Castle Blazing." *Troy and the Trojan War*. Edited by M. Mellink. 77–92. Bryn Mawr PA.

Vernant, J.-P. 1985. *Mythe et pensée chez les Grecs. Études de psychologie historique*. 2nd ed., rev. and expanded. Paris. (The English-language version, *Myth and Thought among the Greeks*, London, 1983, is based on the first ed., Paris 1965, and needs to be updated. See pp. 86–106 of this 1985 2nd ed., especially pp. 100–106, on the Hesiodic myth of the five generations of humankind.)

Vielle, Ch. 1996. *Le mytho-cycle héroïque dans l'aire indo-européenne: Correspondances et transformations helléno-aryennes*. Louvain.

Wace, A. 1948. "Weaving or Embroidery?" *American Journal of Archaeology* 52:51–55.

Walsh, T. R. 2005. *Fighting Words and Feuding Words: Anger and the Homeric Poems*. Lanham MD.

Watkins, C. 1967. "Latin *sōns*." *Studies in Historical Linguistics in Honor of George Sherman Lane*. Edited by W. W. Arndt et al. 186–194. Chapel Hill NC. (Reprinted in C. Watkins. 1994. *Selected Writings*. 2:405–413. Edited by L. Oliver. Innsbruck.)

Watkins, C. 1995. *How to Kill a Dragon: Aspects of Indo-European Poetics*. New York and Oxford.

West, M. L. 1999. "The Invention of Homer." *Classical Quarterly* 49:364–382.

West, M. L. 2000. *The East Face of Helicon: West Asiatic Elements in Greek Poetry and Myth.* Oxford.

West, M. L. 2007. *Indo-European Poetry and Myth.* Oxford.

White, S. A. 2000. "Socrates at Colonus: A Hero for the Academy." *Reason and Religion in Socratic Philosophy.* Edited by N. D. Smith and P. Woodruff. 151–175. Oxford.

Whitman, C. H. 1958. *Homer and the Heroic Tradition.* Cambridge MA.

Yatromanolakis, D. 2003. "Ritual Poetics in Archaic Lesbos: Contextualizing Genre in Sappho." *Towards a Ritual Poetics.* D. Yatromanolakis and P. Roilos. 43–59. Athens.

Zeitlin, F. 1965. "The Motif of the Corrupted Sacrifice in Aeschylus' *Oresteia.*" *Transactions of the American Philological Association* 96:463–508.

Index Locorum

Ancient Texts

"Achilles," *Astronomica* 24, 1§53

Aelius Aristides 1.362 (scholia), 7c§1p217

Aeschylus

    Agamemnon: 1, 16§28, 16§29; 1–39, 16§27 (Hour 16 Text D), 16§27p477n1; 8, 16§28, 16§33; 20, 16§28; 23, 16§32; 26, 16§29; 28, 16§31; 28–29, 16§30; 31, 16§32; 36–39, 16§28; 40, 16§32; 40–71, 16§11 (Hour 16 Text B), 16§11p469n1; 104–159, 16§13 (Hour 16 Text C), 16§13p471n1; 137, 16§26; 144–145, 16§26; 150, 20§48; 155, 16§23; 186, 16§24; 214–215, 16§6, 20§48; 281–316, 16§27; 309, 16§29; 312–316, 16§33; 587–589, 16§31; 594–597, 16§31; 717–735, 16§7 (Hour 16 Text A), 16§7p466n1, 16§9, 16§18; 718–719, 16§7; 905–913, 16§35; 923, 16§35; 926, 16§35; 936, 16§35; 958–965, 16§35 (Hour 16 Text E), 16§35p481n2; 1178–1182, 20§48; 1178–1183, 16§37 (Hour 16 Text F), 16§37p482n1; 1309, 16§40 (Hour 16 Text G), 16§40p483n1; 1311, 16§40 (Hour 16 Text G), 16§40p483n1; 1322–1330, 16§40 (Hour 16 Text G), 16§40p483n1; 1444–1445, 1§31

    Eumenides: 292–296, 7e§7p225n4; 696–710, 17§18 (Hour 17 Text F), 17§18p492n1; 701, 24§1; 794–807,

17§20 (Hour 17 Text G), 17§20p494n1; 824–836, 17§20 (Hour 17 Text G), 17§20p494n1; 854–869, 17§3 (Hour 17 Text A), 17§3p485n4; 855, 17§4; 902–915, 17§22 (Hour 17 Text H), 17§22p495n1; 909, 24§1; 914–915, 21§16

    Libation Bearers: 84–90, 17§7 (Hour 17 Text B), 17§7p487n3; 118–130, 17§9 (Hour 17 Text C), 17§9p489n1; 386–387, 16§31; 399–404, 17§11 (Hour 17 Text D), 17§11p489n3; 575–578, 17§14 (Hour 17 Text E), 17§14p490n2

    Prometheus 74, 10§31p307n5

Alcaeus

    49.12, 5§26; 130b, 5§30; 130b.10, 18§7p500n1; 130b.16, 18§7p500n1

    Source 1, 5§26

Alcman

    Partheneion 'Maiden Song': 39–49, 5§59 (Hour 5 Text G), 5§59p126n3, 5§61, 5§64; 58–59, 5§68

Alexander Romance, the, 2.39.12, 15§9p418n5

Apollodorus

    Epitome: 2.7, 7a§17, 8§15, 8a§11; 2.10–14, 16§6

    Library: 1.9.1, 24§21; 2.4.8, 1§53; 3.14.6, 7c§1p217n3

Archilochus 121, 5§113